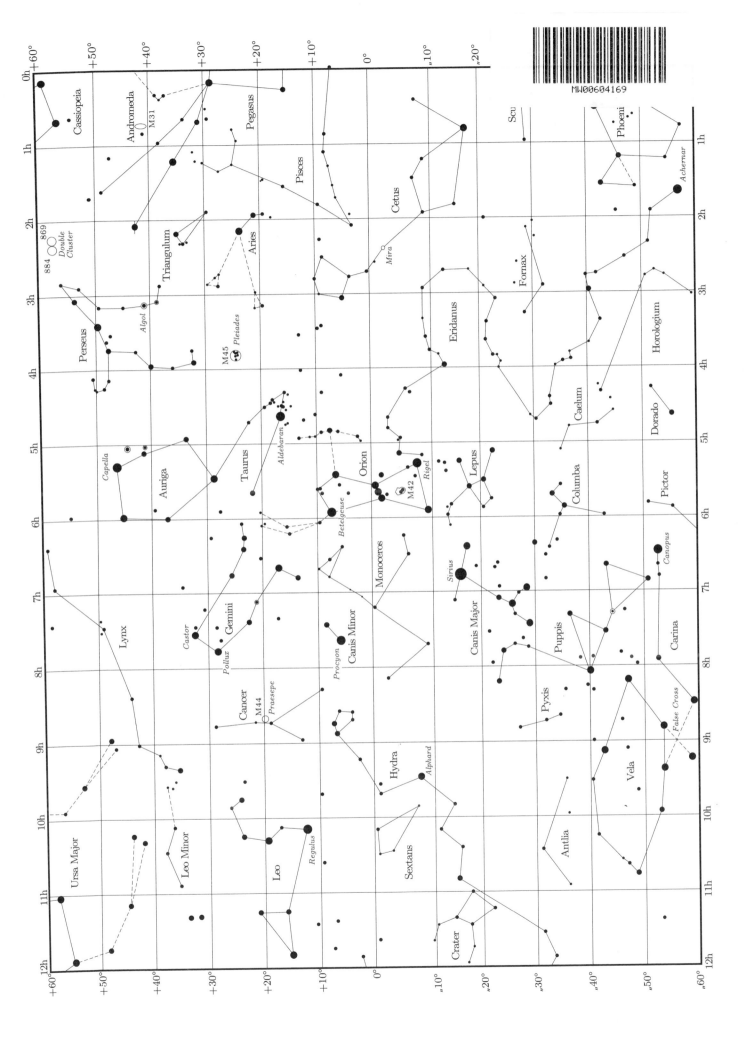

MW00604169

The Night Sky Observer's Guide

Volume 2
Spring & Summer

George Robert Kepple • Glen W. Sanner

Published by

T.M.

Willmann-Bell, Inc.

Publishers and Booksellers Serving Astronomers Worldwide Since 1973

P.O. Box 35025 • Richmond, Virginia 23235 • USA • ☎ (804) 320-7016 • Fax (804) 272-5920
www.willbell.com

Eight Printing 2020
Printed in the United States of America

Library of Congress Cataloging-in-Publication Data.

Kepple, George Robert.
   The night sky observer's guide / George Robert Kepple, Glen W.
Sanner.
      p. cm.
   Includes bibliographical references and index.
   Contents: v. 1. Autumn and winter -- v. 2. Spring and summer.
   ISBN 0-943396-58-1 (v. 1). -- ISBN 0-943396-60-3 (v. 2)
   1. Astronomy--Observers' manuals. I. Sanner, Glen W. II. Title.
QB64.K46 1998   98-31044
523.8'02'16--dc21   CIP

Preface

This is the second volume to The Night Sky Observers Guide. Volume 1 covers Autumn and Winter while this volume is devoted to Spring and Fall. Volume 1 contains introductory and background information for both volumes. Both volumes have a cumulative Index with the volume number followed by the page number.

Appendix C of Volume 1 is dedicated to the observers who have participated in creating the descriptions, sketches and photographs for the Night Sky Observers Guide. We again thank all of these individuals for their participation. A special thanks must be extended to Martin Germano who has provided nearly 75 percent of the photographs and to Steve Gottlieb and Steve Coe who sent us thousands of observations.

Where possible we have obtained photographs of these individuals with their telescopes to drive home the point that most of the instruments used are just like yours.

We were also fortunate to be able to provide bound reading copies of both volumes to Brian Skiff, Richard Berry, and Harold Suiter. Their comments helped us improve these books.

Finally, we wish to express our appreciation to our wives, Barbara Kepple and Deanna Sanner to whom we dedicate this work.

George R. Kepple
Glen W. Sanner
September 1998

Table of Contents

Chapter 31

Antlia, the Air Pump

31.1 Overview

Antlia was invented by the French astronomer Nicolas Louis de Lacaille (1713–1762) in honor of physicist Robert Boyle's pneumatic air pump used in experiments with gases. Lacaille's original name for the constellation was Antlia Pneumatica, but it has been shortened for convenience. It is little more than an area of the sky, for it has no stars brighter than magnitude 4.25. Though it lies on the fringes of the southern Milky Way, it contains no real Milky Way objects (diffuse nebula, open clusters), just a scattering of faint galaxies and a handful of double stars.

Antlia: ANT-lee-ah
Genitive: Antliae, ANT-lee-e
Abbreviation: Ant
Culmination: 9pm–Apr. 10, midnight–Feb. 24
Area: 239 square degrees
Best Deep-Sky Objects: ζ Ant, δ Ant, NGC 2997, NGC 3175
Binocular Objects: S Ant, NGC 2997

31.2 Interesting Stars

S Antliae Variable Star Type EW Spec. A9
m6.4 to 6.92 in 0.64 days $09^h32.3^m -28° 38'$
Constellation Chart 31-1 ★★★

S Antliae, discovered in 1888, is an eclipsing binary star with a range of 0.5 magnitude in a period of just 7 hours and 47 minutes. At the time of its discovery S Antliae boasted the shortest known variable star period. It is a W Ursae Majoris type eclipsing binary, a system in which two dwarf stars orbit each other nearly in contact, and thus have a very short period. The observed luminosity of W UMa systems continuously change as the two ovoid components present continuously changing surface areas in our line of sight.

Zeta-one (ζ^1) Antliae Double Star Spec. A0
m6.2, 7.1, Sep. 8.0″, P.A. 212° $09^h29.9^m -26° 35'$
Constellation Chart 31-1 ★★★★
4/6″ Scopes–75x: Zeta-one Antliae is a bright pair of yellowish stars well suited to small telescopes.

Delta (δ) Antliae Double Star Spec. A0
m5.6, 9.6, Sep. 11.0″, P.A. 226° $10^h29.6^m -30° 36'$
Finder Chart 31-3 ★★★★
4/6″ Scopes–75x: Delta Antliae is an unequally bright pair of pale yellow and grayish-white stars.

31.3 Deep-Sky Objects

NGC 2997 H50^5 Galaxy Type SA(s)c I–II
ϕ 10.0′ × 6.3′, m9.3v, SB13.6 $09^h45.6^m -31° 11'$
Finder Chart 31-3, Figure 31-1 ★★★★
8/10″ Scopes–100x: NGC 2997 has a moderately faint 4′ × 3′ E–W halo with a faint core. A 12th magnitude star lies on the SW edge of the galaxy.
12/14″ Scopes–125x: NGC 2997 has a fairly bright 6′ × 4′ E–W halo with a bright extended core. A dark ring surrounds the core; but the surface brightness increases near the outer edge of the galaxy.
16/18″ Scopes–150x: Large telescopes show a moderately bright 7′ × 5′ ENE–WSW oval halo around a 1′ × 0.5′ core. With averted vision and 200x, a very faint spiral structure coiled counterclockwise can be discerned. The southern spiral arm arcs from the core to a 12th magnitude field star embedded on the halo's SW edge.

NGC 3001 A183 Galaxy Type SAB(rs)bc IC
ϕ 3.1′ × 2.1′, m11.4v, SB13.3 $09^h46.3^m -30° 26'$
Finder Chart 31-3, Figure 31-2 ★★★
8/10″ Scopes–100x: NGC 3001, located 45′ north of NGC 2997 and 15′ SE of a 6th magnitude star, is a very faint amorphous glow about 1.5′ across with a slight brightening at its center. A 12th magnitude star touches the galaxy's NNW edge.

Antlia, the Air Pump

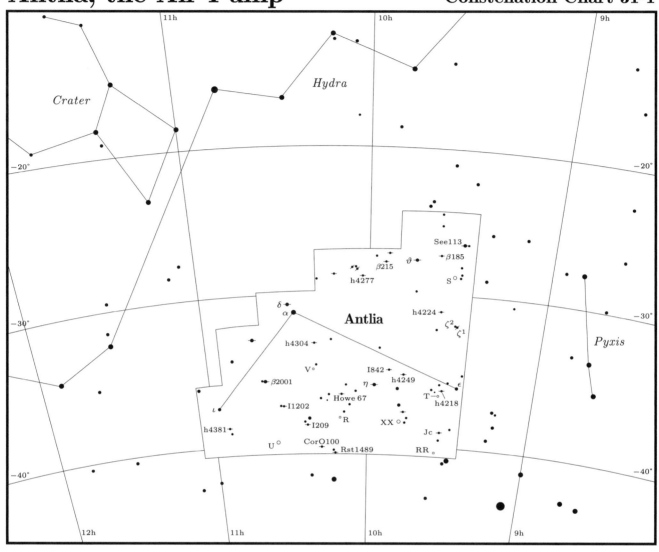

Chart Symbols

Constellation Chart

Stellar Magnitudes   0 1 2 3 4 5 6

Finder Charts   0/1 2 3 4 5 6 7 8 9

Master Finder Chart   0 1 2 3 4 5

→ Guide Star Pointer   ⊙ ○ Variable Stars   Planetary Nebulae

●—● Double Stars   ○ Open Clusters   □ Small Bright Nebulae

Finder Chart Scale   ⊕ Globular Clusters   Large Bright Nebulae

(One degree tick marks)   ⬭ Galaxies   Dark Nebulae

Table 31-1: Selected Variable Stars in Antlia

Name	HD No.	Type	Max.	Min.	Period (Days)	F*	Spec. Type	R.A. (2000)	Dec.	Finder Chart No.	Notes
S Ant	82610	EW	6.4	6.92	0.64		A9	09ʰ32.3ᵐ	−28° 38′	31-1	
T Ant		Cδ	8.89	9.76	5.89	0.22	F6	33.8	−36 37	31-1	
RR Ant	83199	Lb	9.4	10.9			M5–M5.5	35.7	−39 54	31-1	
XX Ant	85207	EB/DM	8.7	9.2	8.11		F2	49.4	−38 20	31-1	
V Ant		M	9.2	>12.5	302		M7	10ʰ21.2ᵐ	−34 48	31-3	
U Ant	91793	Lb	8.1	9.7			C5,3	35.2	−39 34	31-4	

F* = The fraction of period taken up by the star's rise from min. to max. brightness, or the period spent in eclipse.

Table 31-2: Selected Double Stars in Antlia

Name	ADS No.	Pair	M1	M2	Sep.″	P.A.°	Spec	R.A. (2000)	Dec.	Finder Chart No.	Notes
See 113	7405		5.5	14.1	11.6	135	K3	09ʰ29.9ᵐ	−26° 35′	31-1	
ζ¹ Ant			6.2	7.1	8.0	212	A0	30.8	−31 53	31-1	Pale yellowish pair
Jc			6.4	9.9	55.2	204	F2 G0	33.1	−39 08	31-1	
h4218			7.6	10.5	5.9	30	A0	33.2	−36 24	31-1	
β185	7452		7.6	10.6	3.6	205	A0	36.0	−27 31	31-3	
h4224			8.3	8.8	7.5	117	G A3	36.1	−31 14	31-3	
h4249			8.0	8.1	4.3	123	A3	48.8	−35 01	31-3	
β215	7570		7.0	9.0	1.7	343	B9		−28 00	31-3	
I842			7.5	11.3	3.9	31	A2	54.5	−34 54	31-3	
η Ant			5.2	11.2	31.0	318	F0	58.9	−35 53	31-1	
h4277	7614		8.5	8.9	21.9	32	A0 A0	10ʰ01.9ᵐ	−28 41	31-3	
Howe 67			8.6	9.0	3.9	129	A2	10.6	−36 36	31-4	
Rst 1489			6.3	13.3	12.7	215	K0	13.8	−40 21	31-4	
Cor O 100			8.3	9.4	6.0	323	A0	18.1	−40 14	31-4	
h4304			7.6	10.1	9.5	286	A2	20.2	−33 08	31-4	
I209			8.4	8.6	1.2	131	F0	24.4	−38 35	31-4	
δ Ant			5.6	9.6	11.0	226	A0	29.6	−30 36	31-3	Pale yellow and grayish-white
I1202			7.2	11.0	3.7	131	B9	34.3	−37 23	31-4	
β2001			6.4	8.9	0.7	63	G5	40.9	−35 44	31-4	
h4381			7.0	8.4	25.8	42	B9 A	54.6	−38 45	31-4	

Footnotes: *= Year 2000, a = Near apogee, c = Closing, w = Widening. Finder Chart No: All stars listed in the tables are plotted in the large Constellation Chart, but when a star appears in a Finder Chart, this number is listed. Notes: When colors are subtle, the suffix *-ish* is used, e.g. *bluish*.

16/18″Scopes–150x: NGC 3001 has a faint 2′×1.25′ NNE–SSW halo with a small, inconspicuous core. The 12th magnitude star is clearly inside the halo's NNW edge. A 1.5′×1′ triangle of 12th magnitude stars is centered 5′ WSW. The field is well sprinkled with faint stars, including a 12th magnitude star 2.5′ NE of the galaxy.

NGC 3038 Galaxy Type SA(rs)b: II
φ 3.0′×1.6′, m11.7v, SB13.3   09h51.3m −32° 45′
Finder Chart 31-3, Figure 31-3   ★★★
12/14″Scopes–125x: NGC 3038, located 13′ NNW of a 7th magnitude star and 10′ NE of a 10th magnitude star, is situated within a 7′×4′ NE–SW kite-shaped asterism of 12th magnitude stars. It has a moderately bright core containing a stellar nucleus embedded in a faint 2′×1′ NW–SE halo. A 13th magnitude star lies 1′ SW.

NGC 3056 Galaxy Type SAB(rs)0+:
φ 2.1′×1.3′, m11.6v, SB12.5   09h54.5m −28° 18′
Finder Chart 31-3, Figure 31-4   ★★★
12/14″Scopes–125x: NGC 3056 is in a rather well populated field that includes five 8th magnitude stars within half a degree, and half a dozen 12th magnitude stars within 5′, of the galaxy. It has a bright 20″ diameter core surrounded by a 1.5′×0.75′ NNE–SSW oval halo. A 12.5 magnitude star is embedded on the galaxy's NNE edge, and a 12th magnitude star lies 1.5′ NE.

IC 2522 Galaxy Type SB(s)c I–II
φ 2.2′×1.7′, m11.9v, SB13.2   09h55.2m −33° 13′

IC 2523 Galaxy Type SB(s)bc pec? II-III
φ 1.3′×0.5′, m12.8v, SB12.2   09h55.2m−33° 08′
Finder Chart 31-3, Figure 31-5   ★★★/★★★
16/18″Scopes–150x: IC 2522, lying 1.75′ south of a 9th magnitude star, has a faint, diffuse 1.5′×1.25′ N–S halo that is slightly brighter at its center. Companion galaxy IC2523, only 4′ south, has a faint lens-shaped halo elongated 1′×0.25′ NNE–SSW.

NGC 3087 Galaxy Type SA(rs)0−:
φ 2.2′×1.9′, m11.7v, SB13.1   09h59.2m −34° 13′
Finder Chart 31-3   ★★★
8/10″Scopes–100x: This galaxy is visible as a faint, small, round glow in a group of 12th and 13th magnitude stars. The closest star in the field lies to the ENE and the next closest is WSW.
16/18″Scopes–150x: NGC 3087 has a moderately bright, 1′ diameter halo with a well concentrated core containing a faint stellar nucleus.

NGC 3089 Galaxy Type SAB(rs)bc pec:
φ 1.9′×1.3′, m12.5v, SB13.3   09h59.6m −28° 20′
Finder Chart 31-3   ★★★
8/10″Scopes–100x: NGC 3089, located 2.25′ west of an 8th magnitude star, is a very faint, small, round smudge.

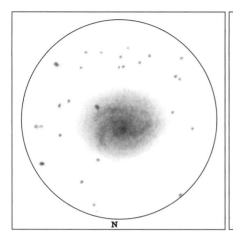

Figure 31-1. NGC 2997
20″, f4.5-175x, by Richard W. Jakiel

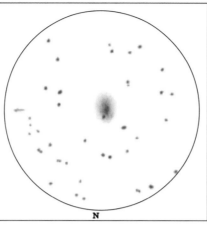

Figure 31-2. NGC 3001
16″, f5-250x, by G. R. Kepple

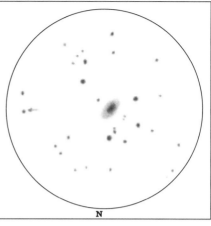

Figure 31-3. NGC 3038
16″, f5-250x, by G. R. Kepple

16/18″ Scopes–150x: NGC 3089 has a faint, diffuse, 1.25′ diameter halo without central brightening. A 13th magnitude star lying near the east edge of the galaxy has a 14th magnitude companion to its north. Another 14th magnitude star lies on the galaxy's south edge, and a 13th magnitude star lies 50″ south of the galaxy's center. 5.5′ north of NGC 3089 is a conspicuous 25″ wide NE–SW pair of magnitude 9.5 stars, and 6′ NNW is a 6th magnitude star.

NGC 3095 Galaxy Type SAB(rs)c pec II-III
φ 3.7″ × 1.8′, m11.8v, SB 13.7   10ʰ00.1ᵐ −31° 33′
Finder Chart 31-3, Figure 31-6   ★★★
12/14″ Scopes–125x: NGC 3095, located 10′ south of a 7th magnitude star, is a very faint 2.5′ × 1.5′ NW–SE oval with a small, dim core. A 12th magnitude star is on the halo's west edge and a 13th magnitude

star is within its NNW periphery. A threshold star lies at the SE tip. NGC 3095 is the faintest of three galaxies in the same field of view: NGC 3100 lies 8′ SE and NGC 3108 is 30′ ESE.

NGC 3100 Galaxy Type SAB0° pec:
φ 3.5′ × 2.1′, m11.2v, SB 13.2   10ʰ00.7ᵐ −31° 40′
Finder Chart 31-3, Figure 31-6   ★★★
8/10″ Scopes–100x: NGC 3100 is the brightest of three galaxies in the same low power field of view: NGC 3095 is 8′ to its NW and NGC 3108 about 25′ east. NGC 3100 has a very faint 1.5′ × 1′ N–S halo with a bright center. A 1′ triangle of stars lies just ESE, the star at the north vertex at magnitude 9.5 and the other two at magnitude 10.5.
16/18″ Scopes–150x: NGC 3100 displays a bright core surrounded by a 2′ × 1′ NNW–SSE halo. A 30″ triangle of magnitude 10.5, 12, and 13 stars lies on the ESE edge, the magnitude 10.5 star also forming the eastern vertex of a 1′ triangle with magnitude 9.5 and 10.5 stars that lie outside the galaxy to its east. Another 13th magnitude star is on the SSW edge.

NGC 3108 Galaxy Type SA(s)0+
φ 2.3′ × 2.0′, m11.5v, SB 13.0   10ʰ02.6ᵐ −31° 41′
Finder Chart 31-3   ★★★
8/10″ Scopes–100x: This is the faintest of three galaxies visible in the same field, the other two being NGC 3100 lying 25′ west and NGC 3095 located 30′ WNW. NGC 3108 is merely a small, very faint glow. It is contained within a rectangle of one 10th magnitude and three 12th magnitude stars.
16/18″ Scopes–150x: NGC 3108 has a faint 1′ diameter

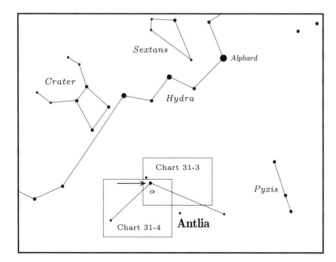

Master Finder Chart 31-2. Antlia Chart Areas
Guide stars indicated by arrows.

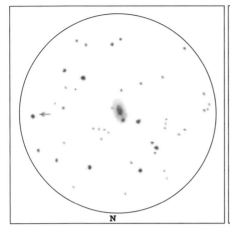

Figure 31-4. NGC 3056
16″, f5–250x, by G. R. Kepple

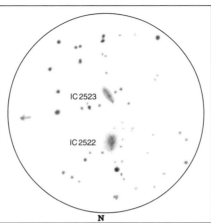

Figure 31-5. IC 2522 & IC 2523
13″, f4.5–165x, by Tom Polakis

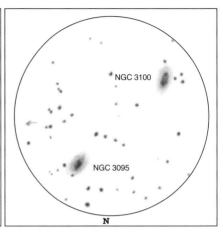

Figure 31-6. NGC 3095 & NGC 3100
16″, f5–250x, by G. R. Kepple

halo around a moderately concentrated center that contains a dim stellar nucleus.

IC 2537 A197 Galaxy Type SB(rs)c I–II
ϕ 2.5′ × 1.8′, m12.2v, SB13.7   10^{h}03.9^m −27° 34′
Finder Chart 31-3, Figure 31-7   ★★
12/14″ Scopes–125x: IC 2537 is between 8th magnitude stars 12′ to its NNW and SSE. The halo is a faint, diffuse 2.5′ × 1.25′ NNE–SSW oval of uniform surface brightness except for a dim stellar nucleus. A 14.5 magnitude star lies near the SSW tip.

NGC 3125 Galaxy Type I0?
ϕ 1.2′ × 0.7′, m12.5v, SB12.2   10^{h}06.6^m −29° 56′
Finder Chart 31-3   ★★
12/14″ Scopes–125x: NGC 3125 lies 4′ NW of an 8th magnitude star that is at the northern vertex of an 18′ × 10′ triangle of 8th magnitude stars. The galaxy has a small core containing a faint stellar nucleus embedded in a faint 45″ diameter halo slightly elongated NW–SE. A 13.5 magnitude star lies on the halo's SW edge 15″ from the galaxy's center. A 10th magnitude star lies 2.5′ NW.

NGC 3175 A207 Galaxy Type SA(s)ab:
ϕ 5.0′ × 1.3′, m11.3v, SB13.2   10^{h}14.7^m −28° 52′
Finder Chart 31-3, Figure 31-8   ★★★★
8/10″ Scopes–100x: NGC 3175 is located in a fairly well populated field of faint and moderately bright stars. It is a fairly faint lenticular galaxy with a much-elongated 2.5′ × 0.75′ NE–SW halo that is a little brighter along its center. A 9th magnitude star 3.5′ to the NNE forms one corner of an irregular pentagon of stars that partially contains the galaxy,

its SW tip just protruding beyond the pentagon's southern side.
16/18″ Scopes–150x: NGC 3175 is a nice but moderately faint edge-on galaxy elongated 4′ × 1′ NE–SW. The central area has an extended, poorly concentrated core and displays some mottling. A faint knot is just west of the core. A 13.5 magnitude star touches the galaxy's SW tip.

NGC 3223 Galaxy Type SA(r)bc I–II
ϕ 4.0′ × 2.6′, m11.0v, SB13.4   10^{h}21.6^m −34° 16′
Finder Charts 31-3 and 31-4, Figure 31-9   ★★★
8/10″ Scopes–100x: This galaxy has a faint 2′ × 1.5′ NW–SE halo with some brightening at its center. Two stars of magnitude 9.5 lie 4′ SW of the galaxy and near its eastern edge.
16/18″ Scopes–150x: NGC 3223 has a moderately faint 3′ × 1.75′ NW–SE halo around a 1′ × 0.5′ core. The

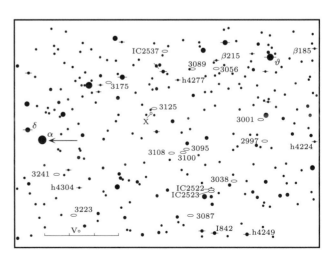

Finder Chart 31-3. α Ant: 10^{h}27.2^m −31° 04′

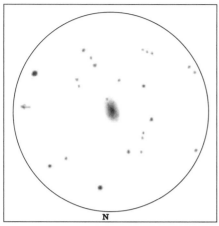

Figure 31-7. IC 2537
20″, f4.5–175x, by Richard W. Jakiel

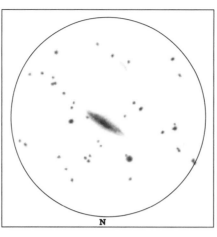

Figure 31-8. NGC 3175
13″, f4.5–165x, by Tom Polakis

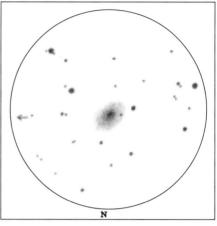

Figure 31-9. NGC 3223
13″, f4.5–165x, by Tom Polakis

core is poorly concentrated but displays a slight mottling and a few faint spots.

NGC 3241 Galaxy Type SAB(r)b II–III
φ 2.2′ × 1.4′, m12.1v, SB13.2   10ʰ24.3ᵐ −32° 29′
Finder Charts 31-3 and 31-4   ★★
12/14″ Scopes–125x: NGC 3241, located 1.5′ SE of a 10th magnitude star, has a bright stellar nucleus within a faint, diffuse 1.5′ × 1′ NW–SE halo. 13th magnitude stars are 35″ NE and 50″ west of the galaxy's center. A 9.5 magnitude star lies 6.5′ NW.

NGC 3244 Galaxy Type SA(rs)c II
φ 2.2′ × 1.7′, m12.4v, SB13.7   10ʰ25.5ᵐ −39° 50′
Finder Chart 31-4, Figure 31-10   ★★
16/18″ Scopes–150x: NGC 3244 is 5′ WNW of a 9th

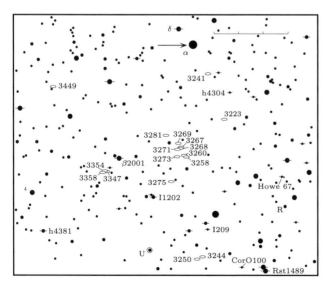

Finder Chart 31-4. α Ant: 10ʰ27.2ᵐ −31° 04′

magnitude star and 1.75′ south of an 11th magnitude star. It has a faint 1.5′ diameter halo around a poorly concentrated central region. Three threshold stars are on the halo's SSE edge.

NGC 3250 Galaxy Type E3-4
φ 2.8′ × 2.1′, m11.3v, SB13.1   10ʰ26.5ᵐ −39° 57′
Finder Chart 31-4, Figure 31-10   ★★★
8/10″ Scopes–100x: NGC 3250 is 3.75′ SW of a 9.5 magnitude star and 8.5′ SE of a 9th magnitude star. It has a moderately faint 1.5′ diameter halo which smoothly brightens toward the center and a faint stellar nucleus.
16/18″ Scopes–150x: In large telescopes NGC 3250 has a small, fairly bright core containing a stellar nucleus and surrounded by a faint 2′ × 1.5′ NW–SE halo. The halo gradually fades to diffuse edges. A pair of threshold stars is embedded in the halo ENE of the galaxy's core.

NGC 3258 Galaxy Type SA0−
φ 2.6′ × 2.3′, m11.5v, SB13.3   10ʰ28.9ᵐ −35° 36′
Finder Chart 31-4   ★★★
16/18″ Scopes–150x: NGC 3258 has a stellar nucleus embedded in a fairly bright 1.5′ diameter halo. A 10.5 magnitude star 1.75′ to the SE and a 9th magnitude star 2.5′ to the WSW form an obtuse triangle with the galaxy. It is larger and more conspicuous than its companion NGC 3260, just 2.5′ to its east. 3.5′ SSW is NGC 3257, which has a very faint, diffuse 30″ wide halo elongated slightly N–S and closely surrounded by four threshold stars. Galaxy A1026–35, located 7.5′ SW of NGC 3258, is very faint and elongated 30″ × 15″ NNE–SSW.

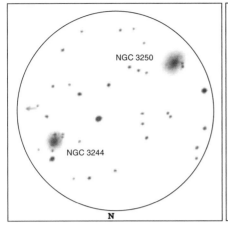

Figure 31-10. NGC 3244 & NGC 3250
16″, f5–250x, by G. R. Kepple

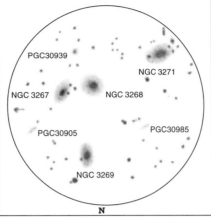

Figure 31-11. NGC 3267-81 Group
16″, f5–250x, by G. R. Kepple

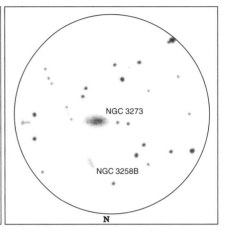

Figure 31-12. NGC 3273 & NGC 3258B
16″, f5–250x, by G. R. Kepple

NGC 3260 Galaxy Type SA(r)0–? pec
ϕ **1.5′ × 1.0′, m12.7, SB13.0**   **10^{h}29.1^m −35° 36′**
Finder Chart 31-4   ★★
16/18″Scopes–150x: NGC 3260 is fainter and smaller than NGC 3258, only 2.5′ to its west. The moderately well concentrated halo is oval-shaped 1′ × 0.5′ nearly N–S and is of uniform surface brightness. A 12.5 magnitude star is embedded in the halo 25″ south of center and a slightly fainter star is 50″ SSW.

NGC 3267 Galaxy Type SAB(rs)0°
ϕ **1.9′ × 0.9′, m12.5v, SB12.9**   **10^{h}29.8^m −35° 19′**
Finder Chart 31-4, Figure 31-11   ★★
12/14″Scopes–125x: NGC 3267, situated near the center of the NGC 3267–81 galaxy group, is nearly the same size as its companion NGC 3268, which lies 2.5′ east. NGC 3267 has a diffuse 1.5′ × 0.5′ NNW–SSE halo with a small, faint core. A tiny triangle of 14th magnitude stars lies between it and NGC 3268.

NGC 3268 Galaxy Type SA(rs)0–
ϕ **3.2′ × 2.4′, m11.6v, SB13.7**   **10^{h}30.0^m −35° 20′**
Finder Chart 31-4, Figure 31-11   ★★★
12/14″Scopes–125x: NGC 3268 is the brightest member of the 3267-81 galaxy group, of which at least a dozen members are visible in medium-size telescopes. It has a fairly bright stellar nucleus in a faint core embedded in a diffuse 1.50′ × 1′ ENE–WSW oval halo. Its companion NGC 3267 lies just 2.5′ to its west.

NGC 3269 Galaxy Type (R)SAB(r)0+?
ϕ **2.5′ × 1.1′, m12.2v, SB13.1**   **10^{h}30.0^m −35° 13′**
Finder Chart 31-4, Figure 31-11   ★★★
12/14″Scopes–125x: NGC 3269, located 2.5′ SSE of a 9.5 magnitude star in the NGC 3267-81 galaxy group, has a fairly faint 1.5′ × 1′ N–S oval halo with a nonstellar nucleus. A 13th magnitude star lies just beyond the SE edge, and a 14th magnitude star touches the NNW edge. Galaxies NGC 3267 and NGC 3268 are 6′ south.

NGC 3271 Galaxy Type (R′)SAB(rs)0°
ϕ **2.8′ × 1.5′, m11.7v, SB13.1**   **10^{h}30.5^m −35° 22′**
Finder Chart 31-4, Figure 31-11   ★★★
12/14″Scopes–125x: A member of the NGC 3267-81 galaxy group, NGC 3271 appears slightly fainter but larger than companion NGC 3268 lying 5.5′ to its WNW. NGC 3271 has an oval core with a faint stellar nucleus surrounded by a diffuse 2′ × 1′ ESE–WNW halo. A jagged row of 14th magnitude stars runs along the galaxy's southern edge.

NGC 3273 Galaxy Type SAB(rs)0°
ϕ **1.7′ × 0.8′, m12.5v, SB12.7**   **10^{h}30.5^m −35° 37′**
Finder Chart 31-4, Figure 31-12   ★★
12/14″Scopes–125x: NGC 3273, located 15′ south of NGC 3271 in the NGC 3267-81 galaxy group, has a fairly faint 1.25′ × 0.5′ E–W halo that moderately brightens at the galaxy's center. 13th magnitude stars lie 1.5′ and 3′ from the galaxy's center beyond its east tip. NGC 3258B, 3′ NNW of NGC 3273, is an extremely faint 30″ × 10″ NE–SW smudge.

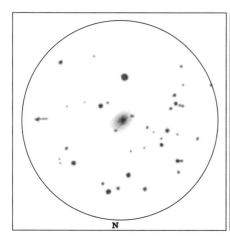

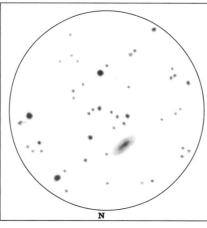

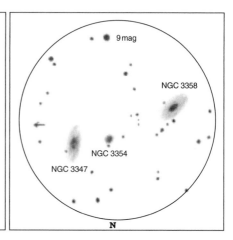

Figure 31-13. NGC 3275
16", f5-275x, by G. R. Kepple

Figure 31-14. NGC 3281
16", f5-250x, by G. R. Kepple

Figure 31-15. NGC 3347-54-58
16", f5-250x, by G. R. Kepple

NGC 3275 Galaxy Type SAB(rs)a pec
ϕ **2.8′ × 1.9′, m11.6v, SB 13.3**   **10^{h}30.9^m −36° 44′**
Finder Chart 31-4, Figure 31-13   ★★★
12/14″Scopes–125x: NGC 3275 is 7′ ESE of an 8th
   magnitude star and 4′ north of a 9th magnitude
   star. It has a fairly faint 1.75′ × 1.5′ NW–SE halo
   that brightens slightly in toward the center, at
   which is a faint stellar nucleus. 13.5 magnitude stars
   lie on the galaxy's NNW and ESE edges.

NGC 3281 Galaxy Type SA(s)ab? pec
ϕ **3.1′ × 1.3′, m11.7v, SB 13.1**   **10^{h}31.9^m −34° 51′**
Finder Chart 31-4, Figure 31-14   ★★★
12/14″Scopes–125x: NGC 3281 is the northernmost
   member of the NGC 3267-81 galaxy group, of which
   at least a dozen members are visible in medium-
   size telescopes. NGC 3281 has a faint halo elongated
   2′ × 0.75′ NW–SE with a poorly concentrated core
   extending along the major axis. 175x shows some
   mottling in and around the core. NGC 3281 lies 15′
   north of a 7th magnitude star: most of the other
   galaxies of the group are spread up to a degree SW
   of the star. The field to the west has many bright
   stars, including 9th magnitude stars 7′ WNW, 7′
   SSW, and 9′ WSW of the galaxy which form a rough
   square with it at the NE corner.

NGC 3347 Galaxy Type SB(r)bc I-II
ϕ **3.7′ × 1.9′, m11.4v, SB 13.4**   **10^{h}42.8^m −36° 22′**
Finder Chart 31-4, Figure 31-15   ★★★
8/10″Scopes–100x: NGC 3347 forms the eastern vertex
   of a 10′ triangle with two 8th magnitude stars. It
   has a faint 1′ × 0.5′ N–S halo with a prominent stellar
   nucleus.

16/18″Scopes–150x: Larger instruments reveal a bright
   stellar nucleus in an oval 1′ × 0.5′ core surrounded
   by a tenuous 3′ × 1′ N–S halo. NGC 3354 lies 3′ east
   and NGC 3358 is 10′ ESE.

NGC 3354 Galaxy Type S: pec
ϕ **0.9′ × 0.8′, m13.0v, SB 12.5**   **10^{h}43.1^m −36° 22′**
Finder Chart 31-4, Figure 31-15   ★★
16/18″Scopes–150x: NGC 3354 is a small companion
   galaxy of NGC 3347 located 3′ to its west. It has a
   well concentrated 30″ × 20″ N–S oval halo. A 13th
   magnitude star touches its northern edge.

NGC 3358 Galaxy Type (R′)SB(rs)ab:
ϕ **3.8′ × 1.7′, m11.5v, SB 13.4**   **10^{h}43.6^m −36° 23′**
Finder Chart 31-4, Figure 31-15   ★★★
12/14″Scopes–125x: NGC 3358, located 9′ NE of a 9th
   magnitude star, appears rather faint, is elongated
   2.5′ × 1.5′ NW–SE, and has a prominent stellar
   nucleus. A wide pair of 12th and 13th magnitude
   stars lies 2.5′ north of the galaxy's center. NGC
   3358 is 6.5′ ESE of NGC 3354 and 10′ ESE of NGC
   3347.

NGC 3449 Galaxy Type SA(s)b II
ϕ **3.5′ × 1.1′, m12.1v, SB 13.4**   **10^{h}52.9^m −32° 56′**
Finder Chart 31-4   ★★★
16/18″Scopes–150x: NGC 3449, located 4.5′ NW of an
   8th magnitude star, appears fairly faint and
   elongated 2.5′ × 0.75′ NNW–SSE with a poorly
   concentrated oval core containing a very faint
   stellar nucleus. A 13.5 magnitude star touches the
   SW edge. A 30″ equilateral triangle of 12th
   magnitude stars is centered 2′ NE.

Chapter 32

Aquila, the Eagle

32.1 Overview

Aquila, the Eagle, is probably one of the oldest constellations in the sky. It was inherited by the ancient Greeks from the older cultures of Mesopotamia, the Babylonians and the Sumerians. The celestial Eagle had been sacred to the Sumerian god of war, Ninurta, who was figured in the stars of the classical Sagittarius. Ninurta's war-bird, shown as a lion-headed spread-eagle, was one of the most common motifs in Sumerian art around 2600 B.C., by which time the constellation was almost certainly in the sky.

Aquila is on the celestial equator and cut through by the Milky Way, which here runs NE–SW and is divided by the dark dust clouds of the Great Rift. The scan across the Great Rift from the star-strewn western branch of the Milky Way into the bright billowy star clouds of the eastern branch of the Milky Way around Altair is a stunning sight in binoculars and RFTs. Altair, at magnitude 0.77, is the brightest star in the constellation, and, at a distance of 16.5 light years, is one of the nearest naked eye stars to the Solar System. It is a blue-tinted white A7 IV–V star with a luminosity of 11 suns. Altair is at the southern angle of the "Summer Triangle" of 1st magnitude stars, its associates being Deneb in Cygnus and Vega in Lyra. The name "Altair" is from the Arabic for "The Eagle." The names of the stars which conspicuously flank Altair, "Alshain" for Beta Aquilae to the ESE and "Tarazed" for Gamma to the WNW, together mean "The Plundering Falcon."

Though Aquila is squarely on the heart of the Milky Way, it is peculiarly poor in open clusters. Part of the fault for this is the obscuring clouds of the Great Rift, which are between 500 and 1,000 light years away and block the light of distant open clusters. Aquila is, however, exceptionally rich in planetary nebulae, though none are among the brightest in the sky. Because of the Great Rift, Aquila is one of the best areas along the Milky Way in which to look for peculiarly-shaped dark dust clouds.

Aquila: AK-will-ah
Genitive: Aquilae, AK-will-ee
Abbreviation: Aql
Culmination: 9pm–Aug. 30, midnight–Jul. 16
Area: 652 square degrees
Best Deep-Sky Objects: Σ 2404, 11 Aql, 15 Aql, 23 Aql, NGC 6709, NGC 6755, NGC 6781
Binocular Objects: 15 Aql, B132, B133, B135-6, B142-3, NGC 6709, NGC 6738, NGC 6755

32.2 Interesting Stars

11 Aquilae = Σ2424 Double Star   **Spec. F5**
AB: m5.2, 8.7, Sep. 17.5″, P.A. 286° $18^h59.1^m$ +13° 37′
Constellation Chart 32-1   ★★★★
2/3″ Scopes–75x: 11 Aquilae is a color contrast pair with a yellowish primary and a blue secondary.

15 Aquilae = S,h286 Double Star   **Spec. K0, K0**
m5.5, 7.2, Sep. 38.4″, P.A. 209° $19^h05.0^m$ +04° 02′
Finder Chart 32-4   ★★★★
2/3″ Scopes–50x: 15 Aquilae is a nice pair of pale yellow and deep yellow stars.

R Aquilae Variable Star Type M   **Spec. M5–M9**
m5.5 to 12.0 in 284 days $19^h06.4^m$ +08° 14′
Finder Chart 32-3   ★★★★
R Aquilae is the brightest Mira-type pulsating red giant long-period variable in Aquila. It lies in the Milky Way's Great Rift about 5.5° south of Zeta (ζ) = 17 Aquilae. Its range of 6.5 magnitudes and period of about 284 days (both of which are average values since LPVs are not really regular in either period or range) are typical for stars of its class. The star's color is redder

9

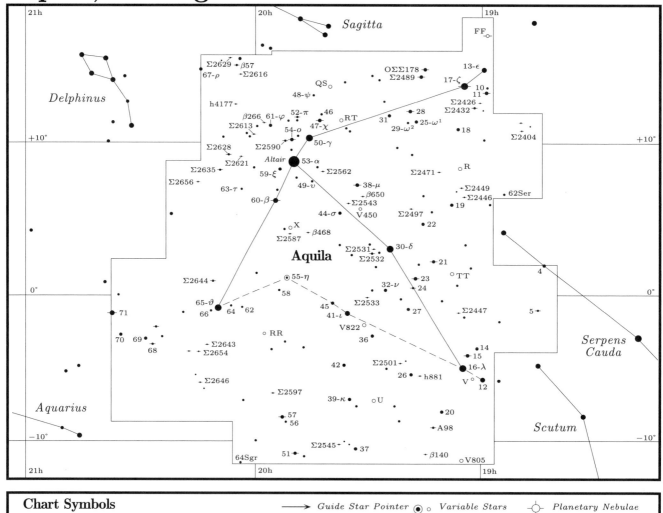

Chart Symbols

Constellation Chart   0 1 2 3 4 5 6
Stellar Magnitudes
Finder Charts   0/1 2 3 4 5 6 7 8 9
Master Finder Chart   0 1 2 3 4 5

→ Guide Star Pointer
●—• Double Stars
Finder Chart Scale
(One degree tick marks)

⊙ ○ Variable Stars
◯ Open Clusters
⊕ Globular Clusters
⬭ Galaxies

◇ Planetary Nebulae
☐ Small Bright Nebulae
Large Bright Nebulae
Dark Nebulae

Table 32-1: Selected Variable Stars in Aquila

Name	HD No.	Type	Max.	Min.	Period (Days)	F*	Spec. Type	R.A. (2000)	Dec.	Finder Chart No.	Notes
FF Aql	176155	Cds	5.1	5.6	4.47	0.48	F5-F8	18^{h}58.2^m	+17° 22′	32-1	
V Aql	177336	SRb	6.6	8.4	353		C5-C6	19^{h}04.4^m	−05 41	32-5	
V805 Aql	177708	EA/DM	7.5	8.2	2.40	0.11	A2-A7	06.3	−11 39	32-5	
R Aql	177940	M	5.5	12.0	284	0.42	M5-M9	06.4	+08 14	32-3	
TT Aql	178359	Cd	6.4	7.7	13.75	0.34	F6-G5	08.2	+01 18	32-4	
U Aql	183344	Cd	6.0	6.8	7.02	0.30	F5-G1	29.4	−07 03	32-5	
V822 Aql	183794	EB/DM	6.8	7.4	5.29		B5-B8	31.3	−02 07	32-4	
V450 Aql	184313	SRb	6.3	6.6	64	0.52	M5-M8	33.8	+05 28	32-3	
RT Aql	185293	M	7.6	14.5	327	0.42	M6-M8	38.0	+11 43	32-6	
55-η Aql	187929	Cd	3.4	4.3	7.17	0.32	F6-G4	52.5	+01 00	32-7	
RR Aql	188915	M	7.8	14.5	394	0.30	M6-M9	57.6	−01 53	32-7	

F* = The fraction of period taken up by the star's rise from min. to max. brightness, or the period spent in eclipse.

Table 32-2: Selected Double Stars in Aquila

Name	ADS No.	Pair	M1	M2	Sep.′	P.A.°	Spec	R.A. (2000)	Dec	Finder Chart No.	Notes
5 Aql	11667	AB	6.0	7.8	13.0	121	A0 A0	18ʰ46.6ᵐ	−00° 58′	32-1	
	11667	AC		11.2	26.3	146					
Σ2404	11750		6.9	8.1	3.6	183	K2	50.8	+10 59	32-3	Close orange pair
11 Aql	11902	AB	5.2	8.7	17.5	286	F5	59.1	+13 37	32-1	Yellowish-white and blue
Σ2426	11916	AB	7.4	8.8	16.9	260	K5 F	19ʰ00.0ᵐ	+12 53	32-1	Reddish-orange and yellowish
Σ2432	11952	AB	6.7	9.2	14.8	93	B9	01.8	+12 32	32-1	
15 Aql	12007		5.5	7.2	38.4	209	K0 K0	05.0	−04 02	32-4	Pale and deep yellow pair
Σ2446	12029	AB	7.1	9.1	9.6	153	F5	05.8	+06 33	32-3	
	12029	AC		10.2	34.5	341					
Σ2449	12037		7.2	7.9	8.0	291	F2	06.4	+07 09	32-3	Yellowish-white and bluish
Σ2447	12038	AB	6.8	9.2	13.9	344	B8	06.6	−01 21	32-4	
Σ2471	12129		7.5	10.3	8.3	124	A5	10.9	+08 07	32-3	
A98	12188	AB	6.5	11.0	26.0	128	K0	14.3	−08 43	32-5	
		BC		11.1	1.2	54					
OΣΣ178			5.7	7.8	89.6	268	G5 A0	15.3	+15 05	32-1	Beautiful gold and blue
Σ2489	12248		5.6	8.6	8.2	348	A0	16.4	+14 33	32-6	
β 140	12244	AB	7.0	10.4	39.4	321	G0	16.9	−10 58	32-5	
	12244	BC		10.6	7.5	209					
h881	12283	AB	7.9	10.1	33.2	*341	K0	18.1	−05 25	32-5	AB: Orange and blue
Ho574	12283	Aa		11.5	15.7	62					
h881	12283	BC		10.1	7.0	307					C: bluish
23 Aql	12289	AB	5.3	9.3	3.1	5	K0	18.5	+01 05	32-4	Yellow and greenish
	12289	AC		13.5	11.3	66					
24 Aql		AB	6.4	6.6	423.4	316	K0 F0	18.8	+00 20	32-4	Binocular double
28 Aql		AB	5.5	9.0	60.2	175	F0	19.7	+12 22	32-6	
Σ2497			8.0	9.1	30.0	357	G5	20.0	+05 35	32-3	
Σ2501	12347	AB	7.7	10.2	19.8	22	F5	22.1	−04 44	32-4	
A2197	12508	AB	8.0	13.0	2.5	242	B5	29.5	+03 05		
Σ2531	12508	AC		9.9	31.4	30				32-3	AC: White and blue
Σ2533	12518		7.4	9.2	22.8	212	A3	30.1	−00 27	32-4	
Σ2532	12520	AB	6.1	10.3	33.7	5	K5	30.2	+02 54	32-3	Fine orange and blue pair
	12520	BC		13.6	34.0	135					
β 650	12569	AB	7.6	11.1	6.5	146	A0	32.2	+06 30	32-6	
	12569	AC		12.5	11.5	330					
	12569	AD		9.7	26.7	254					
Σ2543	12661		6.8	9.7	12.6	155	K0	36.2	+06 00	32-3	
Σ2545	12715	AB	6.8	8.7	3.7	324	A5	38.7	−10 09	32-5	
	12715	AC		11.4	26.1	16.5					
47–χ Aql	12808	AB	5.6	6.8	0.5	77	F5	42.6	+11 50	32-6	
Σ2562	12813	AB	6.9	8.6	27.1	252	F5	42.8	+08 23	32-3	
β 468	12882		7.0	11.3	9.7	183	G0	46.0	+04 15	32-1	
52–π Aql	12962	AB	6.1	6.9	1.4	110	F2	48.7	+11 49	32-6	
Σ2587	13019		6.7	9.4	4.1	100	K0	51.4	+04 05	32-1	
Σ2590	13041		6.6	9.5	13.5	309	B5	52.3	+10 21	32-6	
57 Aql	13087		5.8	6.5	35.7	170	B3 B	54.6	−08 14	32-7	White duo
60–β Aql	13110	AB	3.7	11.6	12.9	5	K0	55.3	+06 24	32-6	
Σ2597	13104		6.8	7.9	0.6	82	F2	55.3	−06 44	32-7	Yellow and light blue
β 266	13168		7.4	11.5	15.8	167	A3	57.9	+11 25	32-6	
Σ2613	13256		7.6	7.8	3.9	353	F2	20ʰ01.4ᵐ	+10 45	32-6	
Σ2616	13290		6.8	9.7	3.3	265	K0	02.8	+14 35	32-6	
Σ2621	13330		8.6	8.8	5.7	223	B9	04.6	+09 04	32-6	
β 57	13344		6.3	10.7	2.3	120	M	05.4	+15 30	32-6	
h1477	13377		7.6	10.2	20.0	271	K5	06.6	+12 41	32-6	
Σ2629	13394		7.6	10.7	9.2	188	B9	07.3	+16 05	32-6	
Σ2628	13403		6.5	8.6	3.4	341	F5	07.8	+09 24	32-6	Unique yellow and purple
Σ2635	13443	AB	6.6	10.1	7.4	79	F8	10.1	+08 27	32-6	
Σ2644	13506		6.9	7.2	3.0	208	A0	12.6	+00 52	32-7	Equal while pair
Σ2643	13511		7.0	9.5	3.0	76	A0	12.8	−03 00	32-7	
Σ2646	13552	AB	7.3	9.3	20.0	44	F0	14.4	−06 03	32-7	
Σ2654	13574		6.9	9.3	14.2	233	F0	15.2	−03 30	32-7	
Σ2656	13590		7.2	11.9	9.5	234	A2	15.6	+07 49	32-1	
71 Aql	14081		4.3	10.8	32.0	282	K0	38.3	−01 06	32-7	

Footnotes: *= Year 2000, a = Near apogee, c = Closing, w = Widening. Finder Chart No: All stars listed in the tables are plotted in the large Constellation Chart, but when a star appears in a Finder Chart, this number is listed. Notes: When colors are subtle, the suffix -ish is used, e.g. *bluish*.

Figure 32-1. *NGC 6709 is a bright, fairly rich, triangular cluster of about 60 stars. Image courtesy Lee C. Coombs.*

Figure 32-2. *The dark nebulous complex of Barnard 130, 127, and 129 (top to bottom) lies just north of 12 Aquilae (upper left). Martin C. Germano took this 45 minute exposure on hypered 2415 film with an 8″, f5 Newtonian.*

near minimum – which again is typical for an LPV. Its temperature range is from 2350° K just after maximum light to only 1890° K around minimum. The star's luminosity change of 6.5 magnitudes (400 times) is something of an optical illusion: in reality most of its light output shifts from visible to infrared wavelengths as it cools; hence its total energy output drops only 0.9 magnitude (2.3 times) as it approaches minimum. R Aquilae's absolute magnitude at maximum is −1.5, a luminosity of 330 suns and apparently typical for LPVs. Its distance is around 1,100 light years.

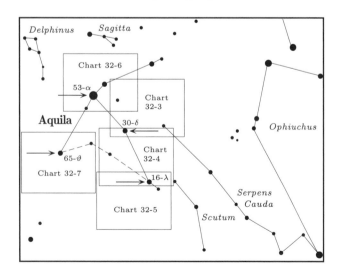

Master Finder Chart 32-2. Aquila Chart Areas
Guide stars indicated by arrows.

23 Aquilae = Σ2492 Double Star   Spec. K0
m5.3, 9.3, Sep. 3.1″, P.A. 5°   19ʰ18.5ᵐ +01° 05′
Finder Chart 32-4   ★★★★
4/6″ Scopes–100x: 23 Aquilae is a beautiful deep yellow
and greenish star pair.

Pi (π) = 52 (Σ2583) Aquilae Double Star   Spec. F2
m6.1, 6.9, Sep. 1.4″, P.A. 110°   19ʰ48.7ᵐ +11° 49′
Finder Chart 32-6   ★★★★
4/6″ Scopes–150x: At medium power, Pi Aquilae shows
a pair of pretty yellow stars in contact.

32.3 Deep-Sky Objects

NGC 6709 Cr 392 Open Cluster 40★ Tr Type III 2 m
φ 13.0′, m6.7v, Br★ 9.07v   18ʰ51.5ᵐ +10° 21′
Finder Chart 32-3, Figure 32-1   ★★★★
4/6″ Scopes–50x: NGC 6709 is quite rich and well
resolved in small telescopes. It contains forty stars
in an irregularly triangular area, its brighter members toward the west and north of the cluster. An
8×50 finder shows NGC 6709 as a bright, hazy glow
in the rich Milky Way star field.
8/10″ Scopes–100x: This fine cluster has sixty 10th to
11.5 magnitude stars in an 18′ × 12′ E–W triangular
area. The cluster's two brightest members are a
wide pair of blue and gold 9th magnitude stars on
its western edge. A couple more wide pairs are on the

Figure 32-3. *LDN 582 is an obvious dark streak extending nearly a degree E–W through the Milky Way. Martin C. Germano took this 65 minute exposure on hypered 2415 Kodak Tech Pan film with an 8″, f5 Newtonian.*

cluster's eastern edge. The center is packed with a few small starless voids, the cluster's richest concentration being near its WSW edge. Several star chains stand out in the cluster, one of which is in the shape of a wishbone with its stem pointing north.

LDN 582 Dark Nebula
ϕ 50′ × 10′, Opacity 5   18^{h}52.6^m −01° 56′
Finder Chart 32-4, Figure 32-3   ★★★
12/14″ Scopes–50x: LDN 582 is a thin, irregular dark patch extending 45′ due west from a 6th magnitude field star. It is more opaque on its far west, where the Milky Way star background thins noticeably.

NGC 6738 Open Cluster Tr Type IV 2 p
ϕ 15′, m8.3p   19^{h}01.4^m +11° 36′
Finder Chart 32-3   ★★★
12/14″ Scopes–75x: NGC 6738, centered 10′ NNW of an 8th magnitude star, is a loose and irregular open cluster of 50 stars spread over a 30′ area. A N–S chain of its brighter members runs through its center. A fainter star chain is on the east side of the cluster. It has seven 9.5 magnitude stars near its center, the remaining stars being fainter. 100x reveals 75 stars.

Barnard 127 Dark Nebula
ϕ 4.5′, Opacity 5   19^{h}01.6^m −05° 28′

Barnard 130 Dark Nebula
ϕ 7′, Opacity 5   19^{h}01.9^m −05° 34′

Barnard 129 Dark Nebula
ϕ 5′, Opacity 5   19^{h}02.1^m −05° 19′
Finder Chart 32-5, Figure 32-2   ★★★/★★★/★★★
12/14″ Scopes–50x: NNE of 12 Aquilae (m4.0) the three

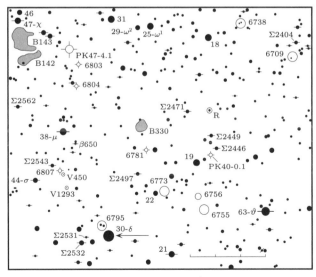

Finder Chart 32-3. 30–δ Aql: 19^{h}25.5^m +03° 07′

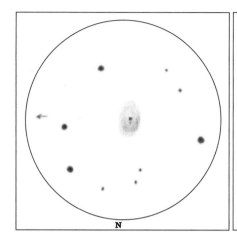

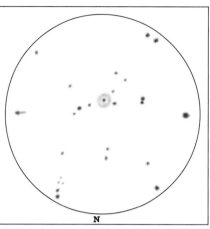

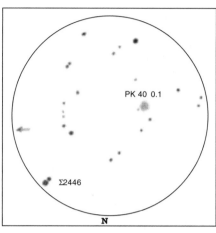

Figure 32-4. PK36–1.1
12.5″, f5–200x, by G.R. Kepple

Figure 32-5. NGC 6751
12.5″, f5–330x, by Chris Schur

Figure 32-6. PK40–0.1
17.5″, f4.5–150x, by Dr. Jack Marling

dark nebulae B127, B129, and B130, connect to form a distinct, C-shaped starless patch convex to the west. On the NE end of the "C," standing out sharply against the rich Milky Way field, is B129, a very dark, sharply defined, irregular 4′ patch with two projections to the east and a faint star in its west end. The southernmost dust cloud, B130, is an irregular 5′ patch elongated NW–SE but less defined than its companions. B129, west of the line adjoining B129 and B130 in the middle of the "C," is a very opaque 4′ long patch shaped like a "V" pointing south.

PK36–1.1 Sh2-71 Planetary Nebula Type 3b+3
ϕ >107″, m13.2v, CS13.8v   19^{h}02.0^m +02° 09′
Finder Chart 32-4, Figure 32-4   ★★
12/14″Scopes–125x: As seen with a UHC filter, this planetary is a faint, large 2′ × 1.25′ N–S oval disk with a 13.8 magnitude central star. The NE side

appears slightly more concentrated and distinct than the SW. At 175x a threshold star is visible 30″ north of the central star.

NGC 6741 PK33–2.1 Planetary Nebula Type 4
ϕ 6″, m11.4v, CS17.6:v   19^{h}02.6^m −00° 27′
Finder Chart 32-4   ★★★
8/10″Scopes–250x: NGC 6741 has a tiny greenish-blue disk with an 11th magnitude star touching it on its west edge.
12/14″Scopes–300x: NGC 6741 has a bright 10″ disk with a nice greenish-blue color. An 11th magnitude star is on the west edge. A faint star lies just beyond the NW edge.

Barnard 132 LDN567 Dark Nebula
ϕ 16′ × 8′, Opacity 6   19^{h}04.0^m −04° 30′
Finder Chart 32-4   ★★★
12/14″Scopes–50x: Barnard 132, conspicuous in a profuse Milky Way star field, lies 40′ NW of magnitude 3.4 Lambda (λ) = 16 Aquilae. It is elongated 16′ × 8′ NE–SW, the SW end being wider and more diffuse than the NE end, which tapers to a point.

NGC 6749 Globular Cluster Class?
ϕ 6.3, m12.4v   19^{h}05.1^m +01° 47′
Finder Chart 32-4   ★
12/14″Scopes–125x: NGC 6749, located in a well populated Milky Way field, is a faint, unresolved object with a 3′ diameter halo. A 12th magnitude star nearly touches its eastern edge, and a couple 14th magnitude stars are visible on its southern edge.

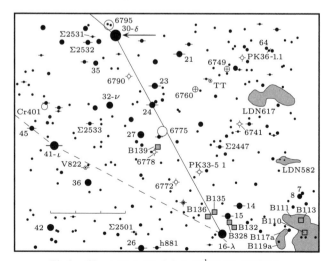

Finder Chart 32-4. 30–δ Aql: 19^{h}25.5^m +03° 07′

Figure 32-7. *Barnard 133 (left) and Barnard 134 (right), 2° south of Lambda (λ) = 16 Aquilae, are two conspicuous dark patches in the rich star field of the southern Aquila Milky Way. Martin C. Germano made this 45 minute exposure on hypered Kodak 2415 Tech Pan film with an 8″, f5 Newtonian reflector at prime focus.*

NGC 6751 PK29–5.1 Planetary Nebula Type 3
φ 20″, m11.9v, CS15.44v   19ʰ05.9ᵐ −06° 00′
Finder Chart 32-5, Figure 32-5   ★★★★

8/10″Scopes–200x: This planetary nebula is one degree ESE of magnitude 4.0 star 12 Aquilae in a Milky Way field rich with 10th to 13th magnitude stars. The disk is faint, moderately small, and round. The central star is very faint.

12/14″Scopes–125x: NGC 6751 has a fairly bright 20″ diameter disk with a greenish hue and hints of ring structure on good nights. The central star is easily visible. A 13th magnitude star is on the NE edge. Two more stars lie off the west edge, the one closer to the planetary being fainter.

Barnard 133 LDN531 Dark Nebula
φ 10′ × 3′, Opacity 6   19ʰ06.1ᵐ −06° 50′
Finder Chart 32-5, Figure 32-7   ★★★

12/14″Scopes–75x: Barnard 133 is 2° south of Lambda (λ) = 16 Aquilae on the NE fringes of the Scutum Star Cloud. It appears as a kidney-bean-shaped dust cloud elongated 10′ × 3′ NW–SE, its SE lobe being darker. A 9th magnitude star is on its east edge. Barnard 134 is in the same rich star field 1/2° to the NNE.

PK40–0.1 Abell 53 Planetary Nebula Type 4
φ 31″, m15.5v, CS20.3v   19ʰ06.7ᵐ +06° 24′
Finder Chart 32-3, Figure 32-6   ★

16/18″Scopes–150x: PK40–0.1 is 16′ SE of the double star Σ2446 (7.1, 9.1; 9.6″; 153°) and 18′ NW of a second 7th magnitude star. Even with a large telescope and an O-III filter it is a challenging object, for it is an extremely faint glow only 30″ in diameter. A 9th magnitude star lies 7.5′ SSW, and a 10th magnitude star 10′ WNW, of the planetary.

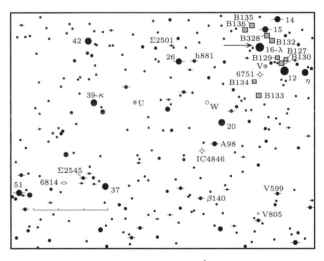

Finder Chart 32-5. 16–λ Aql: 19ʰ06.2ᵐ −04° 53′

Figure 32-8. *Barnard 135 and 136 (center and right) are two starless patches east of magnitude 5.4 star 15 Aquilae. Martin C. Germano took this 60 minute exposure on hypered 2415 film with an 8″, f5 Newtonian.*

Figure 32-9. *The open clusters NGC6755 (upper left) and NGC6756 (lower right) are only 0.5° apart and therefore in the same low power field of view. Lee C. Coombs made this 10 minute exposure on 103a-O film with a 10″, f5 Newtonian.*

Barnard 134 LDN 543 Dark Nebula
φ 6′, Opacity 6   19ʰ06.9ᵐ −06° 14′
Finder Chart 32-5, Figure 32-7   ★★★
12/14″ Scopes–75x: The dark cloud Barnard 134,
   located 1.5° south of Lambda (λ) = 16 Aquilae, is
   smaller and more circular than Barnard 133 half a
   degree to its SSW. Faint stars lie on its north and
   south edges. Planetary nebula NGC 6751 is 20′ NW.

Barnard 135 Dark Nebula
φ 13′, Opacity 6   19ʰ07.4ᵐ −03° 56′
Barnard 136 Dark Nebula
φ 8′, Opacity 6   19ʰ08.8ᵐ −04° 05′
Finder Chart 32-4, Figure 32-8   ★★★/★★★
12/14″ Scopes–50x: Barnard 135, located 55′ NNE of
   Lambda (λ) = 16 Aquilae and 35′ due east of 15
   Aquilae, is a circular 13′ wide dark nebula centered
   on, but extending SW and NE beyond, a thin NNW-
   pointing triangle of one 10th and two 9.5 magnitude
   stars. 20′ to its ESE is Barnard 135, a smaller and
   less distinct dark patch 8′ across and with a 10th
   magnitude star at its center.

NGC 6755 Open Cluster 100★ Tr Type II 2 r
φ 14′, m7.5v, Br★ 10.23v   19ʰ07.8ᵐ +04° 14′
Finder Chart 32-3, Figure 32-9   ★★★★
4/6″ Scopes–50x: NGC 6755, half a degree east of a 7th

magnitude star, is a fairly conspicuous, irregular
concentration of several dozen stars. It stands out
well from the surrounding Milky Way field
8/10″ Scopes–75x: This is a fine, moderately rich cluster
   of sixty 10th magnitude and fainter stars spread
   irregularly over a 15′ area. Near its center is a short
   NE–SW row of four 14th magnitude stars that
   appears nebulous at low power. A dark lane running
   ENE–WSW divides the cluster into two unequal
   sections, the southern section being larger and
   brighter.
12/14″ Scopes–100x: NGC 6755 is a bright, attractive
   cluster of eighty 10th to 14th magnitude stars in a
   20′ area. The stars are irregularly distributed
   around several starless gaps, but lay in three more
   or less distinctive concentrations: the southern
   group of 35 stars is the densest and has the brightest
   stars; the northern group is smallest in size but has
   25 stars and therefore is fairly well concentrated;
   and the eastern group, with only 20 stars, is loose
   and irregular but contains a very attractive N–S
   star chain. A couple more star chains extend south
   from the southern group. Half a dozen doubles are
   scattered around the cluster. Open cluster NGC
   6756 is a half degree NNE in the same low power
   field.

Figure 32-10. *NGC 6772 is a large planetary nebula which in larger telescopes appears as an irregular, annular disk. Image courtesy of Bill McLaughlin.*

Figure 32-11. *NGC 6781 is a beautiful planetary nebula with an irregularly bright disk around a dark center. Image courtesy of Chris Schur.*

NGC 6756 Open Cluster 40★ Tr Type I 1 m
φ 4′, m10.6p, Br★ 13.0p   19ʰ08.7ᵐ +04° 41′
Finder Chart 32-3, Figure 32-9   ★★

8/10″ Scopes-100x: This cluster is much smaller and fainter than NGC 6755 half a degree to the SSW. A dozen stars in a 3′ area stand out against a faint, unresolved background.

12/14″ Scopes-125x: NGC 6756 is a fairly faint, tight cluster of twenty 12th to 15th magnitude stars concentrated in a 4′ area. It is most concentrated toward the NNE, but the cluster's two brightest stars, magnitude 11.5 and 12 objects, are on its southern edge. Two short extensions protrude from the cluster to the south and west.

PK33–5.1 Abell 55 Planetary Nebula Type 3
φ 41′, m15.4p, CS19.2v   19ʰ10.5ᵐ −02° 21′
Finder Chart 32-4, Figure 32-12   ★

16/18″ Scopes-150x: PK33–5.1 lies 6.5′ north of a wide double with a 9th magnitude primary and a 10th magnitude secondary to its NE. This is another of Aquila's many challenging planetary nebulae, for it is only an extremely faint 40″ × 30″ E–W oval disk slightly brighter in its center. A 10.5 magnitude star lies 2.5′ north.

NGC 6760 Globular Cluster Class IX
φ 6.6′, m9.1v   19ʰ11.2ᵐ +01° 02′
Finder Chart 32-4, Figure 32-13   ★★

8/10″ Scopes-100x: This globular cluster is a faint, round, unresolved glow about 2.5′ in diameter with a slightly brighter core. A 10.5 magnitude star lies just to the NE.

12/14″ Scopes-125x: NGC 6760 has a fairly bright, circular 4′ diameter halo with some granularity and a few resolved stars around its periphery. The core is broadly concentrated but not significantly brighter.

NGC 6772 H14⁴ Planetary Neb. Type 3b+2
φ >62″, m12.7v, CS18.2v   19ʰ14.6ᵐ −02° 42′
Finder Chart 32-4, Figure 32-10   ★★★

8/10″ Scopes-125x: NGC 6772, situated 4.5′ SW of a 10th magnitude star, is a faint, large, round, diffuse glow without a visible central star.

12/14″ Scopes-150x: In a UHC filter, NGC 6772 is a 1′ diameter, slightly N–S elongated, vaguely annular, disk.

16/18″ Scopes-175x: An O-III filter shows a moderately bright, fairly well-defined annular disk elongated 1.25′×1′ N–S.

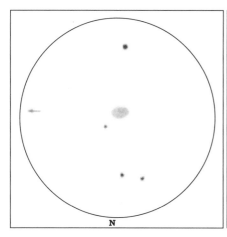

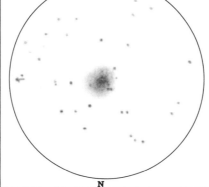

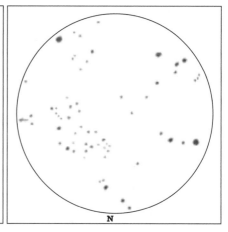

Figure 32-12. PK33–5.1 Abell 55
17.5″, f4.5–150x, by Dr. Jack Marling

Figure 32-13. NGC 6760
13″, f5.6–275x, by Steve Coe

Figure 32-14. NGC 6773
12.5″, f5–100x, by G. R. Kepple

NGC 6773 Open Cluster [30★]
[φ 12′ × 7′]   19ʰ15.0ᵐ +04° 53′
Finder Chart 32-3, Figure 32-14   ★★★

12/14″Scopes–100x: NGC 6773, though catalogued as "nonexistent," stands out fairly well from the surrounding Milky Way field at medium power. It is located 20′ west of magnitude 5.6 22 Aquilae and 12′ NNE of an 8th magnitude star. It contains thirty 12th to 14th magnitude members in a 12′ × 7′ NNE–SSW area, but is not compressed. The cluster is shaped rather like an irregular peanut, its outline

being pinched just south of the cluster center. The larger northern lobe has a starless gap west of its center.

IC 4846 PK27–9.1 Planetary Neb. Type 2
φ 5′, m11.9v, CS15.45v   19ʰ16.5ᵐ −09° 03′
Finder Chart 32-5   ★★★

12/14″Scopes–250x: IC 4846 is 20′ south of a 7.5 magnitude star and 28′ SE of a 6th magnitude star. It is fairly faint and nearly stellar, but high power shows a tiny, smooth disk. A wide pair of 11th and 13th magnitude stars lies to the east.

NGC 6775 Open Cluster [15★]
[φ 15′]   19ʰ16.8ᵐ −00° 55′
Finder Chart 32-4   ★★★

12/14″Scopes–100x: NGC 6775 was classified as "nonexistent" in the *RNGC* and with some justice, for it is not easily distinguished from the surrounding star field. It is a large, loose, irregular collection of 15 stars spread over a 15′ × 8′ E–W area. It has half a dozen 10th and 11th magnitude stars, the rest being fainter.

Barnard 139 LDN 619 Dark Nebula
φ 10′ × 2′, Opacity 5   19ʰ18.1ᵐ −01° 28′
Finder Chart 32-4, Figure 32-15   ★★★

12/14″Scopes–125x: Barnard 139 is a distinct dark patch elongated 10′ × 2′ NW–SE lying 12′ NW of an 8th magnitude star. It is more sharply defined on its SE edge near a 10th magnitude star, but toward the NW its perimeter is more ambiguous. A magnitude 10.5 star touches its SE edge.

Figure 32-15. *NGC 6778 is an oval-shaped planetary nebula (top right center) 5′ west of an 8th magnitude star. Barnard 139 is a distinct oblong dark patch (below center) located 12′ NW of the 8th magnitude star. Martin C. Germano made this 60 minute exposure on hypered 2415 film with a 14.5″, f5 Newtonian reflector.*

Figure 32-16. *LDN 684 is a highly extended dark streak half a degree east of 28 Aquilae (not visible in photo). Martin C. Germano made this 90 minute exposure on hypered 2415 film with an 8″, f5 Newtonian at prime focus.*

NGC 6778 PK34–6.1 Planetary Neb. Type 3+3
φ 16″, m12.3v, CS14.8   19ʰ18.4ᵐ −01° 36′
Finder Chart 32-4, Figure 32-15   ★★★
8/10″Scopes–200x: NGC 6778, located 5′ west of an 8.5 magnitude star, appears considerably faint, small, and indistinctly round.
12/14″Scopes–250x: NGC 6778 has a fairly bright oval disk elongated 25″ × 20″ E–W. The central star requires averted vision, and even then reveals only an occasional twinkle.

NGC 6781 H743³ Planetary Nebula Type 3b+3
φ 109″, m11.4v, CS16.2   19ʰ18.4ᵐ +06° 33′
Finder Chart 32-3, Figure 32-11   ★★★★
8/10″Scopes–125x: NGC 6781 is situated in a rich Milky Way field between a 6th magnitude star half a degree to its west and a 7th magnitude star half a degree to its east. It is large and round and quite conspicuous. Its northern edge is noticeably fainter, and a darkening at its center is just discernible with averted vision. A faint star nearly touches its NE edge.
12/14″Scopes–150x: NGC 6781 has a fairly bright 1.5′ diameter disk with a slightly darker center. The southern periphery is brighter and better defined than the northern periphery. A 12.5 magnitude star nearly touches the disk at the NE edge.

16/18″Scopes–175x: NGC 6781 is a beautiful object at this aperture! It has a bright, circular 2′ diameter disk with a darker center. At 250x, five 13.5 to 14th magnitude stars are visible embedded in the halo, three north of center and the other two south of center. A UHC filter significantly enhances the annularity. The periphery is noticeably fainter and more diffuse at the northern edge.

LDN 684 Dark Nebula
φ 50′ × 10′, Opacity 5   19ʰ21.8ᵐ +12° 26′
Finder Chart 32-6, Figure 32-16   ★★★
12/14″Scopes–50x: The dark dust cloud LDN 684 is located half a degree east of the wide double star 28 Aquilae (5.5, 9.0; 60.2″, 175°). It is an irregular, 50′ × 10′ N–S, starless streak. A 9th magnitude star lies on its south edge.

NGC 6790 Planetary Nebula Type 2
φ 7.0″, m10.5v, CS15.5:v   19ʰ23.2ᵐ +01° 31′
Finder Chart 32-4   ★★★
8/10″Scopes–200x: NGC 6790 is stellar at low power: at least 200x is necessary to discern its tiny disk. It is at the southern vertex of an 8′ × 5′ triangle with a magnitude 9.5 star at its NNW vertex and a magnitude 10.5 star at its NE vertex.
12/14″Scopes–250x: At low power NGC 6790 appears

Figure 32-17. *NGC 6804 is a planetary nebula with a cometary-like disk. Image courtesy of Bill McLaughlin.*

merely as a magnitude 10.5 point. But 250x shows it as a tiny disk in a field sprinkled with faint 12th to 14th magnitude stars.

NGC 6795 Open Cluster [60★]
[φ 30′ × 15′]   19^{h}26.0^m +03° 31′
Finder Charts 32-3, 32-4   ★★★
12/14″ Scopes–100x: Though listed as "nonexistent" in the *Revised NGC*, this open cluster is a large 30′ × 15′ NNE–SSW triangular group of some sixty stars. Delta (δ) Aquilae is at the SSW vertex of the triangle, and two 9th magnitude stars define its

NNE side. Around each of the 9th magnitude stars is a concentration of faint stars. The cluster has some twenty magnitude 10 to 11 members, the rest being fainter. Some of its stars form a semicircle open to the west; and along the NNE side, between the 9th magnitude corners of the cluster, is a loose, jagged star chain.

NGC 6803 H743^3 Planetary Nebula Type 2
φ 6.0″, m11.4v, CS14.0v   19^{h}31.3^m +10° 03′
Finder Chart 32-6   ★★★
8/10″ Scopes–200x: This planetary is stellar even at medium power. It can be revealed by passing an O-III filter in front of the eyepiece, thereby causing it to "blink" against the stars surrounding it. The planetary is brighter than the primary of the close, unequally bright double to its north.
12/14″ Scopes–250x: At low power, NGC 6803 is bright but stellar, appearing as an 11.5 magnitude dot just south of an 11th magnitude star. 250x shows a tiny, bluish 6″ disk with a bright center.

NGC 6804 H38^6 Planetary Nebula Type 4+2
φ 31/66″, m12.0v, CS14.4v   19^{h}31.6^m +09° 13′
Finder Chart 32-6, Figure 32-17   ★★★
8/10″ Scopes–125x: This planetary nebula has a faint, large, diffuse disk elongated NE–SW with a faint central star. Another faint star lies on its NE edge.
12/14″ Scopes–150x: NGC 6804 is a fairly bright planetary nebula with a 60″ × 45″ NE–SW disk shaped rather like a comet, its "head" to the NE and its short "tail" streaming SW. In the "head" is the planetary's 14th magnitude central star. Another 14th magnitude star is 1′ west of the planetary's nucleus, and a magnitude 12.5 star on the nebula's NE edge. Further NE is an E–W row of three magnitude 12.5 to 13 stars. Two more magnitude 12.5 stars lie 45″ south and 1.25′ SW of the nebula's center.

PK47–4.1 Abell 62 Planetary Nebula Type 2c
φ 156″, m14.8p, CS18.2v   19^{h}33.4^m +10° 38′
Finder Chart 32-6   ★
16/18″ Scopes–100x: PK47–4.1, a challenge even for large telescopes, is a very large and extremely faint glow in a rich star field.

NGC 6807 PK42–6.1 Planetary Nebula Type 2
φ 2″, m12.0v, CS?   19^{h}34.6^m +05° 41′
Finder Chart 32-3   ★
12/14″ Scopes–200x: Even at 200x, NGC 6807 is only a stellar dot in a fairly rich star field. It can be

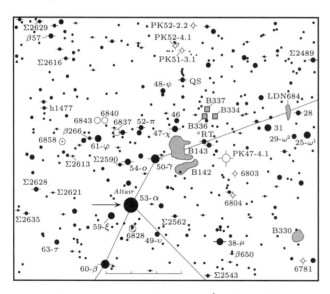

Finder Chart 32-6. 53-α Aql: 19^{h}46.3^m +10° 37′

Figure 32-18. *Barnard 143 (left) and 142 (right), 1.5 degrees west of Gamma (γ) = 50 Aquilae (left), are the "E nebula" or "double dark nebula." Chris Schur made this 15 minute exposure on 2415 film with an 8", f1.5 Schmidt Camera.*

identified by "blinking" with an O-III filter. It is 1' SE of a 10th magnitude star and 8' WSW of a 9th magnitude star.

Collinder 401 Open Cluster Tr Type IV 2 m
ϕ 1', m7.0p   19^{h}38.4^{m} −00° 20'
Finder Chart 32-4, Figure 32-19   ★★
12/14"Scopes–150x: Collinder 401 is a small 1.5' diameter patch of a dozen faint stars sprinkled around a 7th magnitude lucida. A small NE–SW knot of six stars is 35" SW of the lucida. Two 13th magnitude stars are just east and 35" NE of the bright star, and magnitude 12.5 stars are 2.75' to its west and 3.25' to its SW. A few threshold stars are also scattered about.

PK52–2.2 Merrill 1-1 Planetary Nebula Type 4
ϕ <10", m11.8v, CS?   19^{h}39.2^{m} +15° 57'
Finder Chart 32-6   ★★★
16/18"Scopes–250x: PK52–2.2, in far northern Aquila near the Sagitta border, has a fairly bright, round 10" disk without a visible central star.

Barnard 142 Dark Nebula
ϕ 40', Opacity 6   19^{h}41.0^{m} +10° 31'

Barnard 143 Dark Nebula
[ϕ 60' × 40'], Opacity 6   19^{h}41.4^{m} +11° 01'
Finder Chart 32-6, Figure 32-18   ★★★★/★★★★
12/14"Scopes–60x: Barnard 142 and Barnard 143 are a N–S pair of extremely dark dust clouds located 1.25° west of magnitude 2.7 Gamma (γ) = 50 Aquilae in a Milky Way field rich with faint stars embedded in a soft background glow. B143, the northern component, is a very distinct dark mass with two conspicuous prongs facing west. The contrast with the Milky Way background is so good that with averted vision the prongs can be seen even in 10×50 binoculars. B142 to the south is elongated E–W, the east end being wider but more ambiguous than the west. B143 and B142 are two of the few dark nebulae that, particularly in wide field oculars, actually appear suspended in front of their Milky Way background.

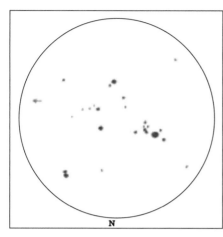

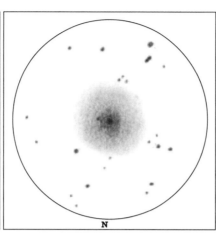

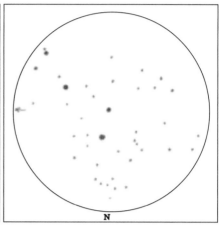

Figure 32-19. Collinder 401
12.5″, f5–250x, by G. R. Kepple

Figure 32-20. NGC 6814
12.5″, f5–250x, by G. R. Kepple

Figure 32-21. NGC 6828
12.5″, f5–250x, by G. R. Kepple

PK51–3.1 Minkowski 1-73 Planetary Nebula Type 2
ϕ **5″, m13.7v, CS?**   **19ʰ41.2ᵐ +14° 57′**
Finder Chart 32-6   ★

16/18″Scopes–300x: This tiny planetary nebula is stellar at nearly all powers, and requires "blinking"
with an O-III filter to be certainly identified. 300x
reveals a faint, smooth, tiny 5″ disk without a central
star.

PK52–4.1 Minkowski 1-74 Planetary Nebula Type 1
ϕ **<10″, m12.9v, CS18.1:v**   **19ʰ42.3ᵐ +15° 09′**
Finder Chart 32-6   ★★

16/18″Scopes–250x: PK52–4.1, located 7′ south of an
8th magnitude star, has a fairly bright 8″ diameter
disk without a visible central star. It is stellar at
low power.

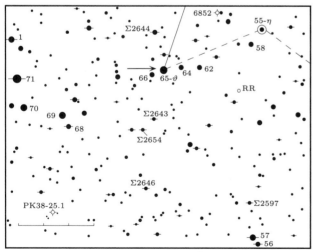

Finder Chart 32-7. 65–ϑ Aql: 20ʰ11.3ᵐ +00° 49′

NGC 6814 H744³ Galaxy Type SAB(s)bc I–II
ϕ **3.0′ × 3.0′, m11.2v, SB13.5**   **19ʰ42.7ᵐ −10° 19′**
Finder Chart 32-5, Figure 32-20   ★★★

12/14″Scopes–125x: NGC 6814 has a fairly bright,
circular halo slightly elongated 2.25′ × 2′ ENE–
WSW with a broad, weakly concentrated core
containing a stellar nucleus. A 12.5 magnitude star
lies 1′ NW, and a 25″ wide E–W pair of 13.5
magnitude stars is 1.5′ ENE. A tighter, fainter
double is 2.5′ SSE of the galaxy just NW of a
magnitude 12.5 star.

NGC 6828 H73⁸ Open Cluster 20★ Tr Type IV 1 p
[ϕ 3′, m11.5v]   **19ʰ50.4ᵐ +07° 55′**
Finder Chart 32-6, Figure 32-21   ★★★

12/14″Scopes–175x: NGC 6828, a degree south of
Altair, is another of the *RNGC*'s "nonexistent"
open clusters. And indeed it is rather poor, with
just 40 stars spread over a 30′ area. An 8th
magnitude star near the group's center forms an
obtuse triangle with 9th magnitude stars to its south
and WSW. Beyond (that is, SW) of the WSW star
is a NW–SE pair of 10th and 11th magnitude stars
which turn the triangle into a lopsided bow tie. The
group's three dozen 12th to 14th magnitude stars
are scattered mostly north and east of the 8th
magnitude central star.

NGC 6837 H18⁸ Open Cluster 20★ Tr Type IV 1 p
[ϕ 3′, m11.5v]   **19ʰ53.5ᵐ +11° 41′**
Finder Chart 32-6, Figure 32-22   ★★

12/14″Scopes–175x: NGC 6837 is listed as "nonexistent" in the *RNGC* probably because it does not
stand out well on the Palomar Observatory Sky
Survey plates. Nevertheless, it is visible 15′ ENE of

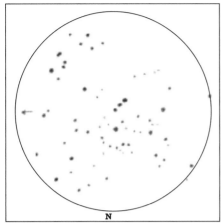

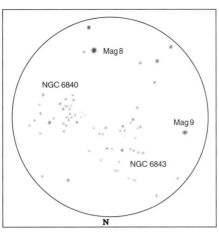

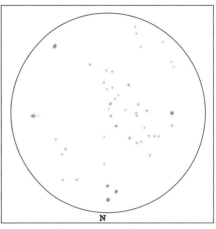

Figure 32-22. NGC 6837
12.5″, f5–200x, by G. R. Kepple

Figure 32-23. NGC 6840 and NGC 6843
12.5″, f5–150x, by G. R. Kepple

Figure 32-24. NGC 6858
12.5″, f5–200x, by G. R. Kepple

a 6th magnitude star as a small clump of half a dozen stars on the suggestion of a hazy background.

16/18″ Scopes–150x: Larger telescopes show two dozen mostly 13th magnitude and fainter stars in a somewhat NE–SW elongated 8′ area. The stars are irregularly distributed in at least three coarse clumps. The 8th magnitude star near the group's center is surrounded by a hazy background of unresolved and threshold stars. To its north is an E–W row of four 14th magnitude stars, and to its south a 1′ long NW–SE row of three 13th magnitude stars. To the central star's west is a 1′ almost equilateral triangle of faint stars. On the group's NW, SW, and ESE edges lie a few slightly brighter stars.

NGC 6840 H19[8] Open Cluster
[φ 7′, m10.0v]   19^{h}55.3^m +12° 06′
Finder Chart 32-6, Figure 32-23   ★★
12/14″ Scopes–175x: NGC 6840, though listed as a "nonexistent" open cluster, is quite visible at low power 10′ SW of NGC 6843. NGC 6840 is richer and rounder than its companion cluster, with some thirty faint stars scattered over a 7′ area. An E–W line of seven or eight stars is on the cluster's northern side. An 8th magnitude star lies 10′ south.

NGC 6843 Open Cluster
[φ 5′, m10.0v]   19^{h}56.1^m +12° 09′
Finder Chart 32-6, Figure 32-23   ★★★
12/14″ Scopes–175x: NGC 6843 is another "nonexistent" *RNGC* cluster that does not show on the POSS plates but in the eyepiece. It has twenty faint stars in a 5′ diameter area, six of the brighter stars forming a crooked E–W line at the cluster's north-

ern edge. The fainter stars give the cluster a horseshoe-shape with a gap at center.

NGC 6852 PK42–14.1 Planetary Nebula Type 4
φ 28″, m12.6:v, CS 17.90v   20^{h}00.6^m +01° 43′
Finder Chart 32-7, Figure 32-25   ★★★
12/14″ Scopes–250x: NGC 6852, located 4.5′ ENE of a 7th magnitude star, has a fairly bright, round 25″ diameter disk. The halo seems brighter on the northern side and there is a hint of ring structure. Two very faint stars lie to the SE of the nebula, the

Figure 32-25. *NGC 6852, located 4.5′ ENE of a 7th magnitude star, has an irregularly bright disk with a hint of ring structure. Martin C. Germano made this 30 minute exposure on hypered 2415 film with a 14.5″, f5 Newtonian reflector. The scale is 4.9mm per arc second.*

Figure 32-26. *PK38–25.1, located 5′ west of a 10th magnitude star, has an irregularly illuminated disk with a subtle ring structure. A background galaxy can be seen in this photo touching the northern edge of the planetary. Martin C. Germano made this 65 minute exposure on hypered 2415 film with a 14.5″, f5 Newtonian reflector. The scale is 4.9mm per arc second. South is up in this 23x enlargement.*

fainter of which touches its edge. An extremely faint star is in the disk 15″ NW of its center. A 13th magnitude star lies 1′ west, and a faint pair is 1′ WNW of the nebula.

NGC 6858 Open Cluster [30★]
[φ 15′ × 5′]   20ʰ03.1ᵐ +11° 16′
Finder Chart 32-6, Figure 32-24   ★★★
12/14″Scopes–100x: NGC 6858 is another star cluster that the *RNGC* catalogues as "nonexistent" but which stands out quite well from the surrounding star field. It is contained by a triangle formed by a 9th magnitude star at the north and 11th magnitude stars at the east and SW vertices. The cluster has thirty 13th and 14th magnitude stars in a 10′ × 5′, somewhat triangular, area, the southwestern end tapering to a point. The NW side is outlined by a NE–SW star chain. A starless gap is in the NW part of the cluster. The bright star east of it is part of the cluster.

PK38–25.1 Abell 70 Planetary Nebula Type 4
φ 43″, m14.5v, CS18.4v   20ʰ31.6ᵐ −07° 06′
Finder Chart 32-7, Figure 32-26   ★★
16/18″Scopes–250x: PK38–25.1, located 5′ west of a 10th magnitude star, has a circular 40″ diameter disk which seems brighter than the catalogue magnitude. Averted vision gives the impression of subtle ring structure with a more concentrated cusp on the northern edge of the ring. The cusp is a background galaxy (MAC 2031-0705). A 13th magnitude star lies 1′ SE, and a 14th magnitude star is 30″ SSW. 7′ to the planetary's SW is a wide NW–SE double of 11th magnitude stars which are the base of a thin stellar triangle pointing SSE.

Chapter 33

Boötes, the Herdsman

33.1 Overview

In classical mythology, Boötes was the son of Jupiter and Callisto. He was imagined to be chasing the Great Bear around the sky; indeed, the meaning of the Greek name for the brightest star in the constellation, Arcturus, is "Bear-Guard." The name Boötes, however, means "Ox-driver," and alludes to the early Greek conception of the seven stars of the Big Dipper as an ox-drawn Wagon. The ancient Babylonians apparently also had thought of Arcturus as the driver of the celestial Wagon, for their title for the star was Shupa, "Hand-Staff" and referred particularly to the sacred staff of the weather god Enlil, to whom the celestial Wagon was sacred. Boötes' staff was considered such an important attribute of the constellation that he is shown holding it on the Farnese Globe, a celestial sphere carved in the 1st century B.C. and extremely sparse in its embellishments of the basic constellation figures. 16th Century A.D. European uranographers followed the ancient authorities and faithfully depicted Boötes with his Staff; but they broke from tradition by also giving him two dogs, later named Canes Venatici.

Boötes is far off the Milky Way and therefore lacks open clusters and diffuse nebulae. Like most off-Milky Way constellations it is well populated with faint external galaxies. None of its galaxies are exceptionally bright, but many are in interesting galaxy pairs or galaxy groups. Its one globular cluster is of interest for being an extremely loose, low-star-density, Class XII globular.

The Quadrantids, a rich meteor shower which peaks every January 3 and 4, radiate from northern Boötes, an area once part of the now obsolete constellation Quadrans Muralis, the Mural Quadrant.

33.2 Interesting Stars

Kappa (κ) **= 17 Boötis (Σ1821) Double Star Spec. A5**
m4.6, 6.6; Sep.13.4″; P.A.236°   14ʰ13.5ᵐ +51° 47′
Finder Chart 33-7   ★★★★
4/6″Scopes–75x: Kappa is a beautiful double for small

> **Boötes:** Bo-OH-teez
> **Genitive:** Boötis, Bo-OH-tis
> **Abbreviation:** Boö
> **Culmination:** 9pm–Jun. 16, midnight–May 2
> **Area:** 907 square degrees
> **Showpieces:** 17–κ Boö, 21–ι Boö, 29–π Boö, 36–ϵ Boö, 37–ξ Boö, 51–μ Boö
> **Best Deep-Sky Objects:** IC 1029, NGC 5529, NGC 5248, NGC 5676, NGC 5689
> **Binocular Objects:** NGC 5466, NGC 5529, NGC 5676, NGC 5689

telescopes with a bright, white primary and a bluish secondary.

Iota (ι) **= 21 Boötis (ΣI26) Triple Star   Spec. A5**
AB:m4.9, 7.5; Sep.38.5″; P.A.33°   14ʰ16.2ᵐ +51° 22′
Finder Chart 33-7   ★★★★
4/6″Scopes–75x: Iota Boötis is a wide double well suited to small telescopes or binoculars. Its two bright components are yellowish and bluish stars. A faint magnitude 12.6 companion lies 85.9″ distant in P.A. 197°.

Pi (π) **= 29 Boötis (Σ1864) Double Star   Spec. A0**
m4.9, 5.8; Sep.5.6″; P.A.108°   14ʰ40.7ᵐ +16° 25′
Finder Chart 33-8   ★★★★
4/6″Scopes–100x: Pi Boötis is a fine, bright pair of white stars.

Epsilon(ϵ)**=36 Boötis (Σ1877) Triple Star Spec. K0, A0**
AB:m2.9, 4.9; Sep.2.8″; P.A.339°   14ʰ45.0ᵐ +27° 04′
Finder Chart 33-5   ★★★★
2/3″Scopes–175x: The AB pair is a marvelous color contrast double of golden yellow and greenish stars.

Boötes, the Herdsman

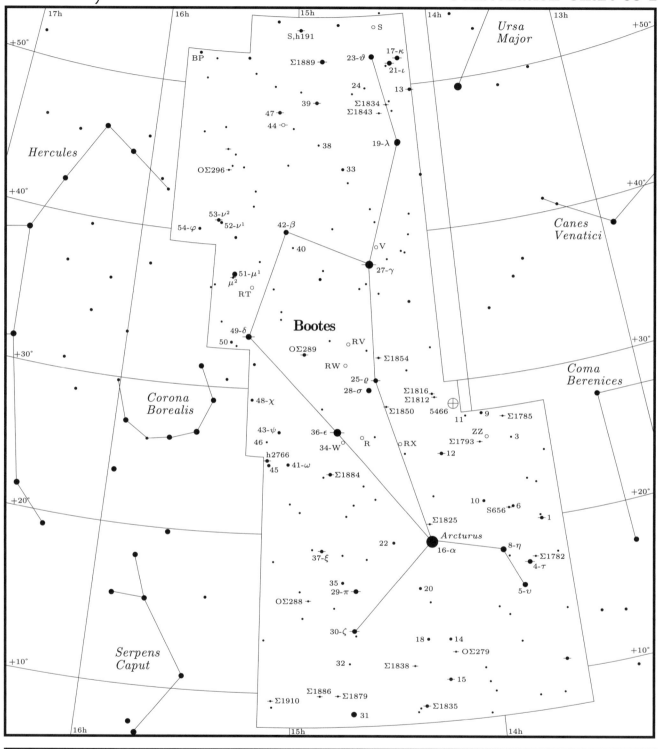

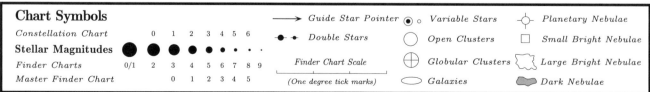

Chart Symbols

Constellation Chart   0   1   2   3   4   5   6
Stellar Magnitudes

Finder Charts   0/1   2   3   4   5   6   7   8   9

Master Finder Chart   0   1   2   3   4   5

→ *Guide Star Pointer*   *Variable Stars*   *Planetary Nebulae*

○ *Double Stars*   ○ *Open Clusters*   □ *Small Bright Nebulae*

Finder Chart Scale   ⊕ *Globular Clusters*   *Large Bright Nebulae*

(One degree tick marks)   *Galaxies*   *Dark Nebulae*

Table 33-1: Selected Variable Stars in Boötes

Name	HD No.	Type	Max.	Min.	Period (Days)	F*	Spec. Type	R.A. (2000) Dec.		Finder Chart No.s	Note
S Boö	126289	M	7.8	13.8	270	0.44	M3–M6	14^{h}22.9^m	+53° 49′	33-7	
V Boö	127335	SRa	7.0	12.0	258	0.49	M6	29.8	+38 52	33-6	
R Boö	128609	M	6.2	13.1	223	0.46	M3–M8	37.2	+26 44	33-4	
RV Boö	129004	SRb	7.9	9.88	137	0.50	M5–M7	39.3	+32 32	33-5	
W Boö	129712	SRb?	4.73	5.4	450	.	M2–M4	43.4	+26 32	33-1	
44 Boö	133640	EW	6.5	7.1	0.267	.	G2+G2	15^{h}03.8^m	+47 39	33-7	

F* = The fraction of period taken up by the star's rise from min. to max. brightness, or the period spent in eclipse.

Table 33-2: Selected Double Stars in Boötes

Name	ADS No.	Pair	M1	M2	Sep.″	P.A.°	Spec	R.A. (2000) Dec.		Finder Chart No.	Notes
1 Boö	8991	AB	5.8	8.7	4.6	136	A2	13^{h}40.7^m	+19° 57′	33-1	White and light blue
Σ1782			7.8	9.3	29.8	186	F5	45.1	+18 22	33-4	
4–τ Boö	9025		4.5	11.1	4.8	11	F5	47.3	+17 27	33-4	
Σ1785	9031		7.6	8.0	3.3	*174	N2	49.1	+26 59	33-4	
S 656			6.8	7.3	85.8	208	G0 G0	50.4	+21 17	33-4	Binocular pair
Σ1793	9076		7.5	8.5	4.6	242	A5	59.1	+25 49	33-4	
13 Boö			5.3	9.8	79.7	274	M	14^{h}08.3^m	+49 27	33-7	and
OΣ277	9158	AB	8.3	8.5	0.4	19	F2	12.4	+28 43	33-5	
Σ1812	9158	AC		9.3	14.2	108					AC: White and bluish
	9158	AD		11.8	72.6	153					
17–κ Boö	9173		4.6	6.6	13.4	236	A5	13.5	+51 47	33-7	White and bluish
OΣ279	9168		6.7	8.9	2.2	253	K0	13.8	+12 00	33-3	Yellowish and orange
Σ1816	9174		7.5	7.6	1.1	88	F0	13.9	+29 06	33-5	
21–ι Boö	9198	AB	4.9	7.5	38.5	33	A5	16.2	+51 22	33-7	Yellowish and bluish
Σ1825	9192		6.5	8.2	4.4	163	F5	16.5	+20 07	33-4	Fine yellow and orange
Σ1834	9229		8.0	8.3	1.4	105	F8	20.3	+48 30	33-7	
Σ1835	9247	AxBC	5.1	7.6	6.2	192	A0	23.4	+08 27	33-3	White and deep yellow
β 1111	9247	BC	7.6	7.7	0.2	123					
Σ1838	9251		7.4	7.5	9.1	334	F5	24.1	+11 15	33-8	
Σ1843	9259		7.6	9.1	20.1	188	F5	24.6	+47 50	33-7	
Σ1850	9277		7.0	7.4	25.6	262	A0 A0	28.6	+28 17	33-5	
25–ϱ Boö	9296		3.6	11.3	42.2	339	K0	31.8	+30 22	33-5	
Σ1854	9288		6.1	9.6	25.8	256	B9	29.8	+31 47	33-5	
27–γ Boö	9300		3.0	12.7	33.4	111	F0	32.1	+38 19	33-5	
29–π Boö	9338	AB	4.9	5.8	5.6	108	A0	40.7	+16 25	33-8	White pair
30–ζ Boö	9343	AB	4.5	4.6	c0.8	*300	A2	41.1	+13 44	33-8	
HIV 104	9343	AC		10.9	99.3	259					
36–ε Boö	9372	AB	2.5	4.9	2.8	339	K0 A0	45.0	+27 04	33-5	Golden and greenish-blue
Σ1879	9380	AB	7.8	8.4	1.5	85	F8	46.3	+09 39	33-8	Close yellowish pair
Σ1884	9389		6.1	7.7	1.7	55	F5	48.4	+24 22	33-1	
Σ1889	9405		6.5	9.8	15.7	88	F2	49.5	+51 22	33-7	Yellowish and blue
39 Boö	9406		6.2	6.9	2.9	45	F5	49.6	+48 43	33-7	Close yellow suns
Σ1886	9410		7.6	9.6	7.7	227	K0	51.0	+09 43	33-8	Orange and bluish
37–ξ Boö	9413	AB	4.7	7.0	c6.6	*318	G5	51.4	+19 06	33-1	Yellow and reddish-orange
OΣ288	9425		6.8	7.5	c0.8	*159	G0	53.4	+15 42	33-8	
OΣ289	9442		6.1	9.6	4.8	112	A0	56.0	+32 18	33-5	
S, h191	9474		6.8	7.4	40.5	342	F0 F0	59.6	+53 52	33-7	Pale yellow pair
44 Boö	9494		5.3	6.2	a2.2	53	G0	15^{h}03.8^m	+47 39	33-7	Close yellow pair
Σ1910	9507		7.5	7.5	4.3	211	G5	07.5	+09 14	33-8	Fine yellowish pair
h2766			5.8	9.9	57.5	331	K0	08.6	+25 07	33-1	
49–δ Boö			3.5	8.7	104.7	79	K0	15.5	+33 19	33-1	Wide yellow and blue stars
51–μ Boö	9626	AxBC	4.3		108.3	171	F0	24.5	+37 23	33-1	Primary yellowish
Σ1938	9626	BC	7.0	7.6	a2.3	8	K0				BC: Yellowish and orange
OΣ296	9639	AB	7.6	9.2	1.8	286	G5	26.4	+44 00	33-9	

Footnotes: *= Year 2000, a = Near apogee, c = Closing, w = Widening. Finder Chart No: All stars listed in the tables are plotted in the large Constellation Chart, but when a star appears in a Finder Chart, this number is listed. Notes: When colors are subtle, the suffix *-ish* is used, e.g. *bluish*.

Figure 33-1. *NGC 5248 has a bright core and a stellar nucleus surrounded by a spiral structure. Image courtesy of Jim Burnell.*

12/14″ Scopes–200x: Medium-size telescopes show a yellow primary with a white or slightly bluish companion.

Xi (ξ) = 37 Boötis (Σ1888) Quadruple Star Spec. G5
AB:m4.7, 7.0; Sep.6.6″; P.A.318°   14ʰ51.4ᵐ +19° 06′
Constellation Chart 33-1   ★★★★★
4/6″ Scopes–100x: The AB pair is a beautiful yellow and reddish-orange double. A 12.6 magnitude companion lies 66.7″ away in P.A. 348°, and a 9.6 magnitude star is 148.9″ distant in P.A. 286°.

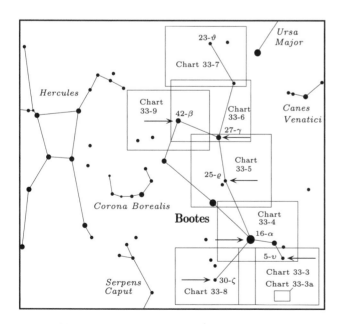

Master Finder Chart 33-2. Boötes Chart Areas
Guide stars indicated by arrows.

Mu (μ) = 51 Boötis (ΣI28) Triple Star   Spec. F0
AxBC: m4.3, 7.0; Sep.108.3″; P.A.171°
BC: m7.0. 7.6; Sep. 2.3″; P.A. 8°   15ʰ24.5ᵐ +37° 23′
Constellation Chart 33-1   ★★★★★
4/6″ Scopes–100x: Mu Boötis is a fine triple of a yellowish primary almost 2′ from a close 2.3″ BC pair of yellowish and orange stars.

33.3 Deep-Sky Objects

NGC 5248 H34[1] Galaxy Type SAB(rs)bc I-II
φ 6.2′ × 4.6′, m10.3v, SB13.8   13ʰ37.5ᵐ +08° 53′
Finder Chart 33-3, Figure 33-1   ★★★★
8/10″ Scopes–100x: NGC 5248 is on the east side of an isosceles triangle of stars which points south. It contains a bright stellar nucleus surrounded by a fairly bright 2.5′×1.5′ NW–SE oval halo.
16/18″ Scopes–150x: Larger instruments show a bright 4′×2′ NW–SE oval halo around a well concentrated 30″×20″ core with a stellar nucleus. A dark patch is south of the core, and the outer regions of the halo are mottled with a hint of spiral structure. A few bright spots stand to the east and west of the core, one of the spots on the east being especially conspicuous. A 13th magnitude star lies 1.75′ SSW.

NGC 5409 Galaxy Type (R′)SAB(s)b
φ 1.6′×1.0′, m13.3v, SB13.6   14ʰ01.7ᵐ +09° 30′
Finder Chart 33-3a, Figure 33-2   ★★
16/18″ Scopes–150x: NGC 5409, the westernmost member of the NGC 5416 galaxy group, is 16′ SW of a 6.2 magnitude star and 12′ NNE of a 6.8 magnitude star. The galaxy is a faint but conspicuous 1.5′×1′ NE–SW oval with a small, faint core extended 30″×15″. 13th magnitude stars are 4.5′ SSW, 3.5′ ENE, and 3.5′ NNW of the galaxy.

NGC 5411 Galaxy Type S0–:
φ 1.4′×0.5′, m13.3v, SB12.8   14ʰ01.9ᵐ +08° 57′
Finder Chart 33-3   ★★
16/18″ Scopes–150x: NGC 5411, located 9′ ENE of a 6.0 magnitude star, is the southernmost galaxy in the NGC 5416 galaxy group, though somewhat isolated from the other members. It has a very faint 45″×30″ NW–SE halo containing a faint core. A 13th magnitude star lies 45″ NE of the galaxy's center.

NGC 5416 H56[3] Galaxy Type Scd:
φ 1.4′×0.7′, m13.3v, SB13.1   14ʰ02.1ᵐ +09° 27′
Finder Chart 33-3a, Figure 33-2   ★★
16/18″ Scopes–150x: NGC 5416, the titulary object of

the NGC 5416 galaxy group, is almost exactly midway between a magnitude 6.2 star 14.5′ to its NNE and a magnitude 6.8 star 13.5′ to its SW. It has a faint but well concentrated 45″×30″ ESE–WNW halo brightening toward the center. A magnitude 12.5 star is 3′ south.

NGC 5423 Galaxy Type S0−:
φ 1.5′×0.9′, m12.8v, SB13.0   **14ʰ02.7ᵐ +09° 21′**
Finder Chart 33-3a   ★★
16/18″Scopes–150x: NGC 5423, the brightest member of the NGC 5416 galaxy group, has a 45″ diameter halo slightly elongated ENE–WSW and gradually brighter toward a faint stellar nucleus. It appears smaller than NGC 5424 located 5′ to its NNE. 1.5′ WNW is the nearly stellar 15″ wide smudge of galaxy CGCG 74-58; and 1.75′ ENE is galaxy CGCG 74-62, an extremely faint pip.

NGC 5424 Galaxy Type S0
φ 1.6′×1.3′, m13.1v, SB13.7   **14ʰ02.7ᵐ +09° 26′**
Finder Chart 33-3a, Figure 33-2   ★★
16/18″Scopes–150x: NGC 5424, a member of the NGC 5416 galaxy group, is 7′ WNW of a 9.5 magnitude star and 9′ SW of a 9th magnitude star. It has a faint but well concentrated 1′ diameter halo that is slightly elongated NW–SE and gradually brightens toward the very faint stellar nucleus at its center. A 13th magnitude star lies 1′ south. 45″ SE of NGC 5424 is galaxy NGC 5431, a very faint 30″×20″ NE–SW oval with a faint stellar nucleus.

NGC 5434 Galaxy Type SAc
φ 1.6′×1.6′, m13.2v, SB14.1   **14ʰ03.4ᵐ +09° 27′**

NGC 5434B Galaxy Type Sbc
φ 1.8′×0.4′, m13.9v, SB13.4   **14ʰ03.5ᵐ +09° 29′**
Finder Chart 33-3a, Figure 33-3   ★/★
16/18″Scopes–150x: NGC 5434 and NGC 5434B, interacting members of the NGC 5416 galaxy group, are between a 9th magnitude star 6′ north and a 9.5 magnitude star 4′ south. They appear virtually in contact. NGC 5434, the SW galaxy of the pair, has a faint, round 1.25′ diameter halo slightly brighter in its center. NGC 5434B, centered 1.5′ NE, is faint, quite elongated 1.5′×0.25′ ENE–WSW, and has a faint extended core. A 13th magnitude star is 2.5′ SE of the galaxy pair.

NGC 5436 Galaxy Type S0/a
φ 1.0′×0.5′, m13.8v, SB12.9   **14ʰ03.6ᵐ +09° 35′**
Finder Chart 33-3a, Figure 33-3   ★
16/18″Scopes–150x: NGC 5436, an NGC 5416 group

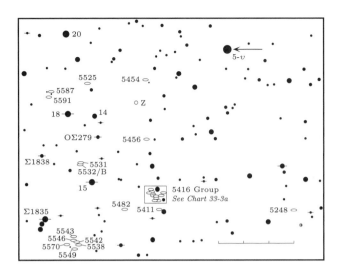

Finder Chart 33-3. 5–υ Boö: 14ʰ15.7ᵐ +19° 11′

galaxy, is 5.25′ ENE of a 9th magnitude star. It has a faint 45″×25″ NE–SW oval halo with a well concentrated center. 3′ to its NE is a 12th magnitude star. NGC 5436 forms a triangle with NGC 5437, located 3.5′ to its SSW, and NGC 5438, just 2.75′ to its NNE.

NGC 5437 Galaxy Type?
φ 0.9′×0.5′, m14.1v, SB13.1   **14ʰ03.7ᵐ +09° 31′**
Finder Chart 33-3a, Figure 33-3   ★
16/18″Scopes–150x: NGC 5437, an NGC 5416 galaxy group member 7′ ESE of a 9th magnitude star, has a very faint 30″×15″ N–S halo that is slightly brighter in the center. An 11.5 magnitude star lies 3.25′ south. NGC 5437 is at the southern corner of a galaxy triangle, NGC 5436 lying 2.75′ NNE, and NGC 5438 lying 5.25′ north.

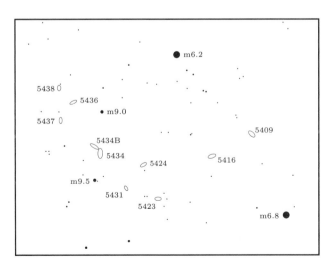

Finder Chart 33-3a. NGC 5416 Group
See Finder Chart 33-3 (Faintest stars 13th magnitude)

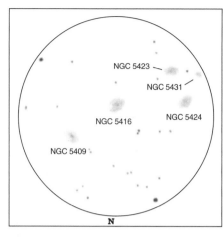

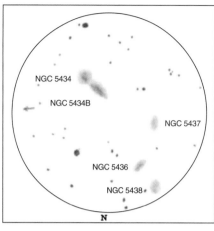

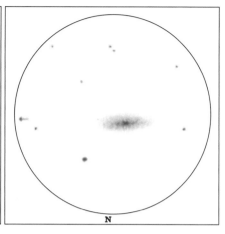

Figure 33-2. NGC 5416 Group West
17.5″, f4.5–150x, by G. R. Kepple

Fig. 33-3. NGC 5492 Area (5416 Group East)
17.5″, f4.5–250x, by G. R. Kepple

Figure 33-4. NGC 5523
17.5″, f4.5–250x, by G. R. Kepple

NGC 5438 Galaxy Type E/S0
φ **0.3′×0.3′, m.12.7v**   **14ʰ03.7ᵐ +09° 37′**
Finder Chart 33-3a, Figure 33-3   ★
16/18″Scopes–150x: NGC 5438, is a member of the NGC
   5416 galaxy group 7.5′ ESE of a 9th magnitude star.
   NGC 5438 has a very faint, circular 30″ diameter
   halo with a slightly brighter center. It is the
   northernmost and faintest member of a triangle
   with NGC 5436 lying 2.75′ SSW and NGC 5437
   lying 5.25′ south. A 14th magnitude star is 30″ NW,
   and a 12th magnitude star lies 2′ NW.

NGC 5454 Galaxy Type S0
φ **1.6′×1.0′, m12.7v, SB13.1**   **14ʰ04.7ᵐ +14° 23′**
Finder Chart 33-3   ★★
16/18″Scopes–150x: NGC 5454, located 9′ NE of a 9th

magnitude star, is at the eastern vertex of a triangle
with a 10th magnitude star 2.25′ west and a 10.5
magnitude star 2.5′ WSW. It has a faint 1′ diameter
halo slightly elongated NW–SE and moderately
brighter in its center. One 13th magnitude star
touches the galaxy's NNE edge and a second lies
1′ WNW. 6′ south is an unidentified galaxy that
can be seen with averted vision as an extremely
faint, thin ESE–WNW streak.

NGC 5456 Galaxy Type S0
φ **1.2′×1.0′, m12.9v, SB12.9**   **14ʰ04.9ᵐ +11° 53′**
Finder Chart 33-3   ★★
16/18″Scopes–150x: NGC 5456, located 7′ south of a
   10.5 magnitude star, has a faint, diffuse 1′ diameter
   halo slightly elongated N–S with a moderately
   concentrated core. 13th magnitude stars are 1′ NE
   and 1.75′ east. A small, conspicuous 1′ triangle of
   one magnitude 9.5 and two magnitude 10 stars lies
   10′ south.

NGC 5466 H9⁶ Globular Cluster Class XII
φ **11′, m9.0v**   **14ʰ05.5ᵐ +28° 32′**
Finder Chart 33-5   ★★
8/10″Scopes–125x: NGC 5466, located 19′ WNW of a
   7th magnitude star, is a fairly faint 6′ diameter
   patch of loosely concentrated stars slightly elongated E–W. The core is unevenly mottled, and a
   few 11th magnitude stars can be resolved in it. The
   periphery shows many faint outlying stars.
12/14″Scopes–150x: NGC 5466 is fairly faint, its broad,
   mottled 5′ diameter core lies within an 8′ diameter
   halo of faint outlying stars. Three dozen cluster
   members can be resolved in the outer regions, and
   half a dozen in the core.

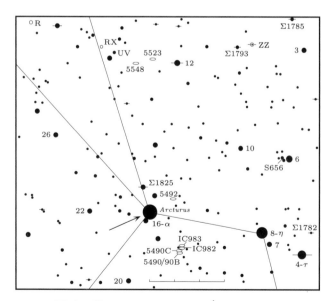

Finder Chart 33-4. 16–α Boö: 14ʰ31.8ᵐ +30° 22′

NGC 5481   H693[2]   Galaxy Type E+
ϕ **1.8′×1.3′, m12.2v, SB13.0   14^{h}06.7^m+50° 43′**
Finder Chart 33-7   ★★
12/14″Scopes–125x: NGC 5481 is 3′ east of the
galaxy NGC 5480 in Ursa Major. It has a
fairly faint, 1.25′ diameter halo containing a
faint stellar nucleus. NGC 5480 appears similar but is a little brighter, elongated 1.5′×1′
N–S, and contains a more distinct stellar
nucleus.

NGC 5482   H59[3]   Galaxy Type S0
ϕ **1.2′×0.9′, m12.9v, SB12.9   14^{h}08.4^m +08° 56′**
Finder Chart 33-3   ★★
16/18″Scopes–150x: NGC 5482 has a faint 1′
diameter halo slightly elongated E–W with
a slightly brighter center. A 13th magnitude
star touches the galaxy's western edge, and
a 12th magnitude star lies 4′ west.

NGC 5490   H32[3]   Galaxy Type E
ϕ **2.3′×1.8′, m12.1v, SB13.5   14^{h}10.0^m +17° 33′**

NGC 5490B   Galaxy Type?
ϕ **0.7′×0.4′, m14.6v, SB13.1   14^{h}10.1^m +17° 33′**

NGC 5490C   Galaxy Type SB(s)bc
ϕ **1.1′×0.8′, m13.9v, SB13.6   14^{h}10.1^m +17° 37′**
Finder Chart 33-4, Figure 33-5   ★★★/★/★
16/18″Scopes–125x: NGC 5490 is 8′ south of an
8th magnitude star which is at the NE vertex
of a 25′×18′ triangle of 8th magnitude stars. The
galaxy's 1.5′ diameter halo appears fairly faint and
is circular, or just slightly elongated N–S, and is
considerably brighter at its center. A dozen faint
stars are scattered within 5′ of the galaxy. 1.25′
ENE of NGC 5490 is NGC 5490B, a faint stellar
object. NGC 5490C, located 4′ NNE of NGC 5490,
is a faint 30″ diameter haze with a stellar nucleus.

IC 982   Galaxy Type SA0+
ϕ **1.1′×1.1′, m13.0v, SB13.1   14^{h}10.4^m +17° 42′**

IC 983   Galaxy Type SB(r)bc
ϕ **5.5′×5.0′, m11.7v, SB15.1   14^{h}10.5^m +17° 44′**
Finder Chart 33-4, Figure 33-5   ★★/★★
16/18″Scopes–125x: IC983, located 11′ north of NGC
5490 and just NW of an 8th magnitude star, has a
bright ESE–WNW oval core embedded in a very
faint 1.75′ diameter halo. IC982, located 2′ SSW of
IC 983, is a fairly bright, but nearly stellar, object.

Figure 33-5. *IC 983 (bottom) has a bright core and a faint circular halo
made difficult to observe by an 8th magnitude star touching its SE edge.
IC982 is a stellar object to its SW. NGC 5490 is a fairly faint elliptical
(top), and NGC5490C (at center) is a small glow. Martin C. Germano made
this two hour exposure on hypered 2415 film with a 14.5″, f5 Newtonian.*

NGC 5492   H876[2]   Galaxy Type Sb pec?
ϕ **1.6′×0.4′, m12.8v, SB12.2   14^{h}10.5^m +19° 37′**
Finder Chart 33-4   ★★
12/14″Scopes–125x: NGC 5492 lies 1.25° WNW of
Arcturus and just east of a 20′ equilateral triangle
of three 8th magnitude stars. It is a faint but distinct
1.5′×0.5′ NNW–SSE streak with a slight brightening along its center.

NGC 5523   H134[3]   Galaxy Type SA(s)cd: II-III
ϕ **4.3′×1.3′, m12.1v, SB13.8   14^{h}14.8^m +25° 19′**
Finder Chart 33-4, Figure 33-4   ★★
12/14″Scopes–125x: This faint galaxy is a degree east
and a little north of 12 Boötis. It has a diffuse halo
elongated 2.5′×1.25′ E–W and slightly brighter at
its center.
16/18″Scopes–150x: NGC 5523 has a low surface brightness 3.5′×1.5′ E–W halo containing an inconspicuous core extended along its major axis. An 11th
magnitude star lies 2.75′ NW, and a 14th magnitude
star is 3.25′ east.

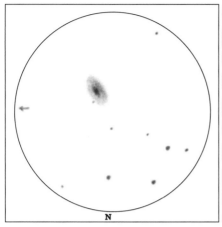
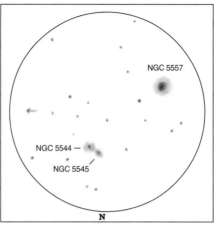
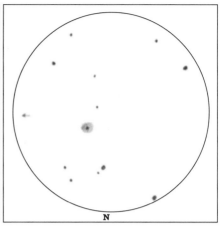

Figure 33-6. NGC 5533
12.5″, f5–100x, by G. R. Kepple

Figure 33-7. NGC 5544, 5545 and 5557
13″, f5.6–100x, by Steve Coe

Figure 33-8. NGC 5548
12.5″, f5–100x, by G. R. Kepple

NGC 5525 Galaxy Type S0
φ **1.2′×0.7′, m12.8v, SB12.5**   **14ʰ15.6ᵐ +14° 17′**
Finder Chart 33-3   ★★
16/18″ Scopes–150x: NGC 5525 is 20′ NE of a 7th
    magnitude star and 7′ SW of a 10.5 magnitude
    star that forms a wide pair with another 10.5 magnitude
    star 2.5′ NNE. The galaxy has a faint 45″×30″ NNE–
    SSW oval halo with a moderate central brightening.
    A threshold star is visible 30″ SSW of the galaxy's
    center, and a 14th magnitude star lies 1.5′ SW.

NGC 5529 H414³ Galaxy Type
φ **5.7′×0.7′, m11.9v, SB13.3**   **14ʰ15.6ᵐ +36° 13′**
Finder Chart 33-5   ★★★
12/14″ Scopes–125x: NGC 5529 appears fairly faint,

elongated 4′×1′ ESE–WNW, and moderately
brighter at its center. A 12th magnitude star lies
1.5′ south of the galaxy's center, and a 12.5
magnitude star is beyond the ESE tip 1.75′ from
the center. Companion galaxy NGC 5527, located
4′ SW, is very faint, small and circular.

NGC 5533 H418² Galaxy Type SA(rs)ab I-II
φ **3.4′×1.9′, m11.8v, SB13.7**   **14ʰ16.1ᵐ +35° 21′**
Finder Chart 33-5, Figure 33-6   ★★★
8/10″ Scopes–100x: NGC 5533, located 25′ SW of a 5th
    magnitude star, appears faint, diffuse, and elon-
    gated 1.5′×0.75′ NNE–SSW with a moderately
    brighter center.
12/14″ Scopes–125x: NGC 5533 has a 2′×1′ NNE–SSW
    halo with a poorly concentrated core containing a
    stellar nucleus. A threshold star lies 1′ south of the
    nucleus.

NGC 5532 H47³ Galaxy Type S0
φ **1.6′×1.6′, m12.9v, SB12.7**   **14ʰ16.9ᵐ +10° 49′**
Finder Chart 33-3   ★★
16/18″ Scopes–150x: NGC 5532, located 10′ SE of a 10th
    magnitude star, has a circular 1.25′ diameter halo
    with a broadly concentrated center. NGC 5532B is
    a faint, nearly stellar knot on the SSE edge of NGC
    5532. A 13th magnitude star is visible 1.75′ NNE
    of the galaxy pair. NGC 5531, located 5.5′ NNE of
    NGC 5532 and 5′ SE of the 10th magnitude star,
    is a very faint double galaxy appearing as one diffuse
    object elongated 30″×20″ NNW–SSE. A 12th mag-
    nitude star lies 4′ NE of NGC 5531.

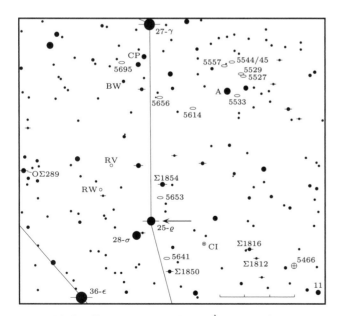

Finder Chart 33-5. 25–ρ Boö: 14ʰ32.1ᵐ +30° 19′

NGC 5544 Galaxy Type (R)SB(rs)0/a
ϕ 0.9′×0.9′, m13.4v, SB13.0   14^{h}17.0^m +36° 34′

NGC 5545 Galaxy Type SA(s)bc:
ϕ 1.0′×0.3′, m15.2, SB13.7   14^{h}17.1^m +36° 35′
Finder Chart 33-5, Figure 33-7   ⋆/⋆
12/14″Scopes–125x: These galaxies are two faint, diffuse knots in contact. NGC 5544, the western component, appears smaller but more concentrated. A third galaxy, NGC 5557, lies 16′ ESE in the same field.
16/18″Scopes–150x: This faint galaxy pair can be just separated at 150x in larger telescopes. NGC 5544 has a diffuse 1′ diameter halo of uniform surface brightness, and NGC 5545 is elongated 1′×0.25′ ENE–WSW and angles toward its companion. Both galaxies show faint cores.

NGC 5548 H194^2 Galaxy Type (R′)SA(s)0/a
ϕ 1.6′×1.4′, m12.6v, SB13.3   14^{h}18.0^m +25° 08′
Finder Chart 33-4, Figure 33-8   ⋆⋆
12/14″Scopes–125x: NGC 5548 has a prominent stellar nucleus embedded in a diffuse, circular 1′ diameter halo. The field includes two 9th magnitude stars to the NE and NNE, and two 10th magnitude stars to the SE and SSW, of the galaxy.

NGC 5546 H551^3 Galaxy Type E
ϕ 1.3′×1.1′, m12.3v, SB12.5   14^{h}18.1^m +07° 34′
Finder Chart 33-3   ⋆⋆
16/18″Scopes–150x: NGC 5546, the most conspicuous member in the Abell 1890 galaxy group, has a faint 45″×30″ NNE–SSW halo with a broadly concentrated center. A 1.5′ right triangle of 13th magnitude stars is centered 2′ south. The field includes the following faint galaxies, each measured from NGC 5546 itself: 4′ west is NGC 5542, a faint 30″×15″ N–S oval halo. 5.5′ NNW is NGC 5543, a faint 20″×10″ NNW–SSE halo with a 13th magnitude star 1.25′ to its north. 8.5′ SW is NGC 5538, a faint pip elongated 30″×10″ NE–SW. 12′ SSE is NGC 5549, a faint 1′×0.5′ ESE–WNW halo with a broadly concentrated center. 8′ east of NGC 5549 is a 9th magnitude star, 5.5′ NE of which is NGC 5570, a smudge requiring averted vision.

NGC 5557 H948^3 Galaxy Type E1
ϕ 2.2′×2.0′, m11.0v, SB12.5   14^{h}18.4^m +36° 30′
Finder Chart 33-5, Figure 33-7   ⋆⋆⋆
8/10″Scopes–100x: This galaxy has a fairly bright 1′ diameter halo containing a broad, prominent core spanning half the halo's width.

12/14″Scopes–125x: NGC 5557 displays a bright stellar nucleus in a broad core surrounded by a 1.5′ diameter halo. A very faint star is on the SE side. Galaxies NGC 5544 and NGC 5545 lie 16′ WNW.

NGC 5582 H754^2 Galaxy E
ϕ 2.8′×1.8′, m11.6v, SB13.2   14^{h}20.7^m +39° 42′
Finder Chart 33-6   ⋆⋆⋆
12/14″Scopes–125x: NGC 5582, located 12′ NW of an 8th magnitude star, has a fairly bright 1.5′×1′ NNE–SSW halo considerably brighter at its center. 175x shows a faint stellar nucleus in the center.

NGC 5587 H110^3 Galaxy Type S0/a
ϕ 2.5′×0.8′, m12.5v, SB13.1   14^{h}22.2^m +13° 55′
Finder Chart 33-3   ⋆⋆
16/18″Scopes–150x: NGC 5587 forms a right triangle with 9th magnitude stars 5′ to its south and 7′ to its east. This fairly conspicuous edge-on galaxy has a much elongated 1.75′×0.5′ NNW–SSE halo with a well concentrated center. A 14th magnitude star is just visible 45″ ENE of the galaxy's center.

NGC 5608 H673^3 Galaxy Type Im:
ϕ 2.7′×1.6′, m13.4v, SB14.8   14^{h}23.3^m +41° 46′
Finder Chart 33-6   ⋆
12/14″Scopes–125x: NGC 5608 has a very faint, diffuse halo elongated 1.75′×1′ E–W and slightly brighter in its center. 9th magnitude stars lie 8′ north, 10′ ESE, and 12′ NNE of the galaxy.

NGC 5600 H177^2 Galaxy Type Sc pec
ϕ 1.3′×1.3′, m12.1v, SB12.6   14^{h}23.8^m +14° 38′
Finder Chart 33-8, Figure 33-9   ⋆⋆⋆
12/14″Scopes–125x: NGC 5600 has a fairly bright, round 1.25′ diameter halo with a broad, well concentrated core. An 11th magnitude star 8′ NE of the galaxy, and two magnitude 12.5 stars to its north and SE, form a diamond with it, the galaxy being at the figure's SW corner.

NGC 5614 H420^2 Galaxy Type SA(r)ab pec
ϕ 2.6′×2.0′, m11.7v, SB13.3   14^{h}24.1^m +34° 52′
Finder Chart 33-5, Figure 33-10   ⋆⋆⋆
12/14″Scopes–125x: This galaxy is a fairly faint, circular glow considerably brighter at its center. 2′ to its NNW is its interacting companion, NGC 5613, a very faint, small round smudge.
16/18″Scopes–150x: NGC 5614 has a well concentrated 1.5′ diameter halo slightly elongated NE–SW con-

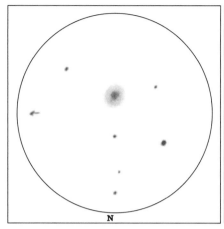

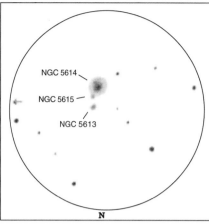

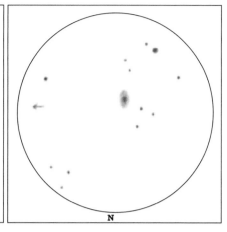

Figure 33-9. NGC 5600
12.5″, f5–100x, by G. R. Kepple

Figure 33-10. NGC 5614
12.5″, f5–100x, by G. R. Kepple

Figure 33-11. NGC 5633
12.5″, f5–100x, by G. R. Kepple

taining a broad core with a stellar nucleus. Interacting companion galaxy NGC 5615 is a faint spot on its NW edge. A 13th magnitude star lies 2.5′ SE of the big galaxy.

NGC 5633 H185[1] Galaxy Type (R)SA(rs)b II-III
ϕ **2.3′×1.0′, m12.4v, SB13.2**   **14^{h}27.5^m +46° 09′**
Finder Chart 33-6, Figure 33-11   ★★
12/14″Scopes–125x: NGC 5633, located 6′ south of an 11th magnitude star, is a faint, diffuse 1′×0.75′ N–S oval slightly brighter at its center. A triangle of 12th magnitude stars lies 2′ NE.
16/18″Scopes–150x: NGC 5633 shows a well concentrated core surrounded by a diffuse, 1.5′ diameter halo slightly elongated NNE–SSW.

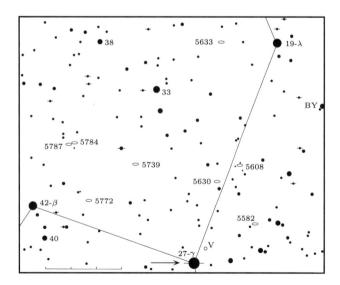

Finder Chart 33-6. 27–γ Boö: 14^{h}32.1^m +38° 19′

NGC 5630 H674[2] Galaxy Type Sdm:
ϕ **2.3′×0.7′, m13.1v, SB13.4**   **14^{h}27.6^m +41° 16′**
Finder Chart 33-6   ★★
16/18″Scopes–150x: NGC 5630, located 14′ north of a 6.5 magnitude star, is a faint silvery 2′×0.5′ E–W streak with a nonstellar nucleus.

IC 1014 U9275 Galaxy Type Sdm
ϕ **2.6′×1.7′, m12.5v, SB14.0**   **14^{h}28.3^m +13° 47′**
Finder Chart 33-8   ★★
16/18″Scopes–150x: IC1014 has a faint halo elongated 2′×1.5′ E–W and slightly brighter at the center. The galaxy lies in a sparse field of faint stars.

NGC 5627 Galaxy Type S0
ϕ **1.6′×0.9′, m12.9v, SB13.2**   **14^{h}28.5^m +11° 22′**
Finder Chart 33-8   ★★
16/18″Scopes–150x: NGC 5627 is 20′ NNW of an 8.5 magnitude star and 3′ ENE of a 10th magnitude star. Its faint halo is elongated 1.25′×0.75′ ESE–WNW and contains a well concentrated center. A threshold star is discernible with averted vision just 50″ NW of the galaxy's center. NGC 5627 is the most conspicuous member of a group of otherwise very faint galaxies. 3.75′ to its NW is MCG+2-37-11, a diffuse smudge in a triangle with 12th magnitude stars 1′ to its north and 1.5′ to its NE. 12′ SSE of NGC 5627 and 9′ north of the magnitude 8.5 star is UGC 9286, which has a very faint 1.5′×0.5′ NNW–SSE halo.

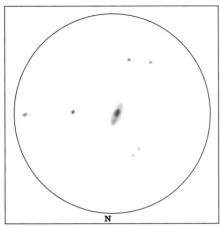

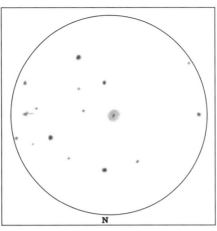

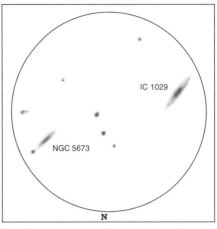

Figure 33-12. NGC 5641
12.5″, f5–175x, by G. R. Kepple

Figure 33-13. NGC 5653
12.5″, f5–100x, by G. R. Kepple

Figure 33-14. NGC 5673 and IC 1029
12.5″, f5–100x, by G. R. Kepple

NGC 5641 Galaxy Type (R′)SAB(r)ab I
ϕ **2.4′×1.3′, m12.2v, SB13.3**   **14ʰ29.3ᵐ +28° 49′**
Finder Chart 33-5, Figure 33-12   ★★★
12/14″Scopes–125x: NGC 5641 is fairly faint and elongates 2′×0.5′ NNW–SSE to tapered ends. The oval core contains a very faint stellar nucleus. A 13th magnitude star lies 2.5′ west.

NGC 5660 H695² Galaxy Type SAB(rs)c II
ϕ **2.9′×2.6′, m11.9, SB14.0**   **14ʰ29.8ᵐ +49° 37′**
Finder Chart 33-7   ★★
8/10″Scopes–100x: NGC 5660, located 20′ SE of a 5.5 magnitude star, has a faint, round 1.25′ diameter halo that gradually brightens toward its center.
12/14″Scopes–125x: NGC 5660 is fairly faint, its circular 2′ diameter halo containing a broad, moderately well concentrated core with a very faint nonstellar nucleus. Galaxy NGC 5676 lies 28′ ESE.

NGC 5653 H330² Galaxy Type (R′)SA(rs)b III-IV
ϕ **1.6′×1.4′, m12.2v, SB12.9**   **14ʰ30.2ᵐ +31° 13′**
Finder Chart 33-5, Figure 33-13   ★★★
8/10″Scopes–100x: This galaxy is considerably faint with a round, diffuse 1′ diameter halo. Averted vision is needed.
12/14″Scopes–125x: NGC 5653 has a fairly faint, diffuse 1.25′ diameter halo surrounding a moderately brighter core with a stellar nucleus.

NGC 5644 Galaxy Type S0
ϕ **1.2′×1.2′, m12.5v, SB12.8**   **14ʰ30.4ᵐ +11° 55′**
Finder Chart 33-8   ★★
16/18″Scopes–150x: NGC 5644 is within an 8′×4′ N–S

triangle of three 10th magnitude stars, the star at the western corner of the triangle located 1.5′ SW of the galaxy. NGC 5644 has a faint 45″ diameter halo with a broadly concentrated center. A 13th magnitude star lies 50″ NNW of the galaxy. 4′ SE of NGC 5644 and 1′ NW of the 10th magnitude star at the triangle's southern corner is NGC 5647, which has a very faint, much elongated 45″×15″ N–S halo. A 13th magnitude star is visible 1.25′ east.

NGC 5656 H421² Galaxy Type Sab
ϕ **1.6′×1.3′, m11.8v, SB12.5**   **14ʰ30.4ᵐ +35° 19′**
Finder Chart 33-5   ★★★
12/14″Scopes–125x: NGC 5656, located 5′ west of a 9.5 magnitude star, is fairly faint, slightly elongated 1.5′×0.75′ NE–SW, and has a considerably brighter center. A 13th magnitude star lies 1′ south of the galaxy's center.

NGC 5673 H696² Galaxy Type SBc? sp
ϕ **2.4′×0.5′, m12.1v, SB12.1**   **14ʰ31.5ᵐ +49° 58′**
Finder Chart 33-7, Figure 33-14   ★★★
12/14″Scopes–125x: NGC 5673, located 25′ ENE of 24 Boötis, is a fairly faint 2.5′×0.5′ NW–SE streak with considerable brightening along its major axis. A 13th magnitude star lies on the NW tip 1.25′ from the galaxy's center. 175x shows a very faint stellar nucleus. Galaxy IC 1029 is 10′ ESE.

NGC 5665 H27² Galaxy Type SAB(rs)c pec IV-V
ϕ **2.1′×1.3′, m12.0v, SB12.9**   **14ʰ32.4ᵐ +08° 05′**
Finder Chart 33-8   ★★★
8/10″Scopes–100x: NGC 5665 is 5.5′ west of a 10.5 magnitude star. It appears diffuse and slightly

elongated 1.25′×1′ N–S.

12/14″Scopes–125x: NGC 5665 has a fairly faint halo elongated 1.75′×0.75′ NNW–SSE and broadly brighter toward a faint stellar nucleus.

IC 1029 Galaxy Type SAb:sp II-III
ϕ 2.6′×0.5′, m11.3v, SB11.4   14^{h}32.5^m +49° 54′
Finder Chart 33-7, Figure 33-14   ★★★

8/10″Scopes–100x: IC 1029, located 3′ west of an 11th magnitude star, has a fairly faint 1′×0.5′ NNW–SSE halo with a slightly brighter center.

16/18″Scopes–150x: IC 1029 shows a fairly bright 30″×20″ core embedded within a faint, highly elongated 3′×0.5′ NNW–SSE halo. Galaxy NGC 5673 lies 10′ WNW.

NGC 5669 H79² Galaxy Type SAB(rs)cd IV
ϕ 4.1′×3.0′, m11.3v, SB13.9   14^{h}32.7^m +09° 53′
Finder Chart 33-8   ★★

12/14″Scopes–125x: NGC 5669 forms a triangle with 11th magnitude stars 6′ to its NNW and 6′ to its WNW. It has a faint 3′×2′ NNE–SSW halo with a broad but faint core containing a stellar nucleus. A 14th magnitude star is immersed in the outer halo 1′ north of the galaxy's center.

NGC 5676 H189¹ Galaxy Type SA(rs)bc II
ϕ 3.7′×1.6′, m11.2v, SB13.0   14^{h}32.8^m +49° 28′
Finder Chart 33-7, Figure 33-15   ★★★★

8/10″Scopes–100x: NGC 5676, located 15′ WNW of a 6.5 magnitude star, is fairly bright, elongated 2′×1.5′ NE–SW, and has a slightly brighter center. Galaxy NGC 5660 lies 28′ WNW.

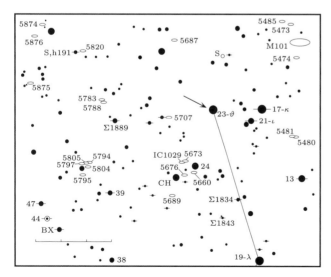

Finder Chart 33-7. 23–ϑ Boö: 14^{h}25.2^m +51° 51′

12/14″Scopes–125x: NGC 5676 has a bright 4′×2′ NE–SW halo containing a broad oval core. 14th magnitude stars are 1′ west, 2.25′ ESE, and 2′ north of the galaxy.

NGC 5666 Galaxy Type S?
ϕ 0.8′×0.6′, m12.8v, SB11.9   14^{h}33.1^m +10° 29′
Finder Chart 33-8   ★★

16/18″Scopes–150x: NGC 5666 is 13.5′ west of a 7th magnitude star and 5′ south of a 10.5 magnitude star. The galaxy appears nearly stellar at low power. However, 150x reveals a fairly faint 30″ diameter halo that smoothly brightens to a well concentrated center. A threshold star lies 50″ SSE, and a 13th magnitude star is 2.25′ ESE, of the galaxy's center.

NGC 5687 H808² Galaxy Type S0–?
ϕ 2.3′×1.7′, m11.8v, SB13.1   14^{h}34.9^m +54° 29′
Finder Chart 33-7, Figure 33-16   ★★★

8/10″Scopes–100x: NGC 5687 is an interesting galaxy 2′ north of a 9th magnitude star. The halo is moderately faint, elongated 1′×0.25′ ESE–WNW, and slightly brighter at its center.

12/14″Scopes–125x: In medium-size instruments, NGC 5687 appears a little more elongated, about 1.5′×0.5′ ESE–WNW, than it does in smaller instruments. Three 13th magnitude stars are embedded in the halo 30″ east, 30″ west, and 35″ SW of the galaxy's center. A 12th magnitude star lies 1.25′ SW. A nearly N–S row of three stars extends south from the west end of the galaxy.

NGC 5689 H188¹ Galaxy Type SB(s)0/a:
ϕ 3.7′×1.0′, m11.9v, SB13.1   14^{h}35.5^m +48° 45′
Finder Chart 33-7, Figure 33-17   ★★★★

8/10″Scopes–100x: NGC 5689 is a glowing streak elongated 1.75′×0.5′ E–W containing a prominent oval core with a faint stellar nucleus.

12/14″Scopes–125x: NGC 5689 is a fine spindle-shaped galaxy with a bright, much elongated 3′×0.75′ E–W halo containing an extended, mottled core with a stellar nucleus. Two 14th magnitude stars are 2.75′ and 3.25′ ENE of the galaxy. The close galaxy pair NGC 5682-83 lies 8′ SW, and galaxy NGC 5693 is 12′ SSE, of the galaxy.

NGC 5695 H423² Galaxy Type S?
ϕ 1.5′×1.0′, m12.8v, SB13.1   14^{h}37.3^m +36° 34′
Finder Chart 33-5   ★★

12/14″Scopes–125x: NGC 5695, located half a degree east of a 6th magnitude star, has a fairly bright

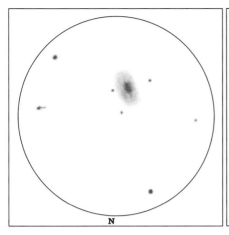

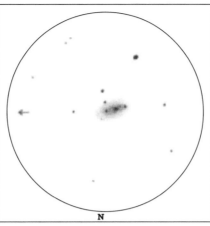

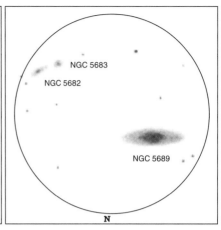

Figure 33-15. NGC 5676
8″, f4.5–90x, by Dennis E. Hoverter

Figure 33-16. NGC 5687
13″, f5.6–165x, by Steve Coe

Figure 33-17. NGC 5689
17.5″, f4.5–250x, by G. R. Kepple

1.5′×1′ NNW–SSE halo containing a well concentrated center.

NGC 5707 Galaxy Type Sab: sp
φ 2.4′×0.4′, m12.5v, SB12.3   14ʰ37.5ᵐ +51° 34′
Finder Chart 33-7   ★★
12/14″ Scopes–125x: NGC 5707, located 5′ west of a 7th magnitude star, is a faint 2′×0.5′ NNE–SSW streak considerably brighter along its major axis.

NGC 5739 H171¹ Galaxy Type SAB(r)0+:
φ 1.8′×1.8′, m12.1v, SB13.2   14ʰ42.5ᵐ +41° 50′
Finder Chart 33-6, Figure 33-18   ★★★
8/10″ Scopes–100x: NGC 5739 appears faint, small, and round with a bright core.
12/14″ Scopes–125x: This galaxy has a well concentrated core with a stellar nucleus embedded in a moderately faint 1.5′ diameter halo slightly elongated NNE–SSW. Several faint stars are to the east of the galaxy, and a 14th magnitude star is on its NE edge.

NGC 5762 Galaxy Type S?
φ 1.8′×1.4′, m12.7v, SB13.6   14ʰ48.7ᵐ +12° 28′
Finder Chart 33-8   ★★
16/18″ Scopes–150x: NGC 5762, located 20′ NW of a 7th magnitude star, has a faint but conspicuous circular 30″ diameter halo with a diffuse periphery. A 14th magnitude star is 1.75′ SW, and a 13th magnitude star 3.5′ NW of the galaxy. 4.5′ NE of NGC 5762 is the galaxy NGC 5763, a very faint, nearly stellar object with a faint stellar nucleus. A 13th magnitude star lies 1.5′ SSW, and two 14th magnitude stars are 1′ and 1.75′ NW, of NGC 5763.

NGC 5772 = NGC 5770 Galaxy Type SA(r)b: II-III
φ 2.1′×1.3′, m12.8v, SB13.8   14ʰ51.7ᵐ +40° 36′
Finder Chart 33-6   ★★
12/14″ Scopes–125x: NGC 5772, located 2.5′ north of a 12th magnitude star, displays a prominent stellar nucleus embedded in a fairly faint halo elongated 2′×1′ in P.A. 35°. An 11th magnitude star lies 5′ south.

NGC 5783 Galaxy Type SAB(s)c
φ 2.6′×1.5′, m12.8v, SB14.1   14ʰ53.5ᵐ +52° 05′
Finder Chart 33-7   ★★
16/18″ Scopes–150x: NGC 5783 touches the SSW base of a 3.25′×2.5′ right triangle of magnitude 10.5 stars. The star at the NE vertex of the triangle has a 12th magnitude companion 17″ away in P.A. 20°. The galaxy has a faint, diffuse 2′×1′ N–S halo slightly brighter in its center. A very faint star is embedded 20″ NNE of the galaxy's center. 2.5′ SSW

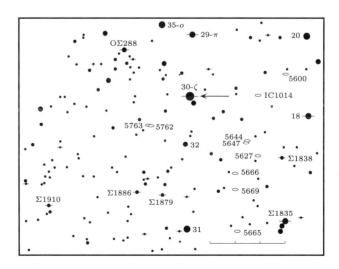

Finder Chart 33-8. 30–ζ Boö: 14ʰ41.1ᵐ +13° 44′

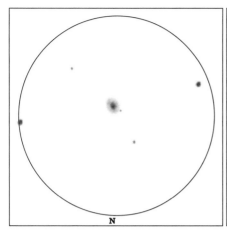
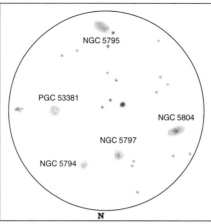
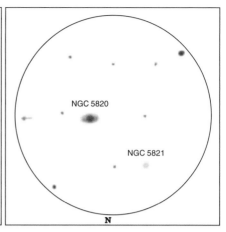

Figure 33-18. NGC 5739
12.5″, f5–100x, by G. R. Kepple

Figure 33-19. NGC 5795 Group
13″, f5.6–135x, by Steve Coe

Figure 33-20. NGC 5820
17.5″, f4.5–250x, by G. R. Kepple

of NGC 5783 is NGC 5788, which has a very faint 20″×15″ NE–SW halo slightly brighter at its center. A 14th magnitude star lies between the two galaxies 1′ NE of NGC 5788.

NGC 5784 H676² Galaxy Type S0
ϕ 1.9′×1.8′, m12.4v, SB13.6   14^{h}54.2^m +42° 33′

NGC 5787 H677² Galaxy Type S?
ϕ 1.0′×0.9′, m13.1v, SB12.9   14^{h}55.3^m +42° 30′
Finder Chart 33-6   ★★/★
16/18″Scopes–150x: These two galaxies form a large triangle with a 9th magnitude star to their south. NGC 5784 is 9′ NNW of this bright star and has a faint, diffuse, circular 1′ diameter halo broadly brighter toward its center. A 10.5 magnitude star lies 5′ of the galaxy. 13′ ENE of NGC 5784, and 10′ NE of the 9th magnitude star, is NGC 5787, similar in size to NGC 5784 but slightly fainter, with a small, poorly concentrated core and a diffuse periphery. A threshold star nearly touches its south edge.

NGC 5794 U9610 Galaxy Type S?
ϕ 1.0′×1.0′, m13.4v, SB13.2   14^{h}55.7^m +49° 44′
Finder Chart 33-7, Figure 33-19   ★
12/14″Scopes–125x: NGC 5794 is the northernmost member in a group of galaxies that includes PGC 53381, NGCs 5795, 5797, and 5804 in a field clustered around a bright 6th magnitude field star. NGC 5794 is similar in appearance to PGC 53381, having a very faint 45″ diameter halo slightly brighter toward the center.

NGC 5804 H679³ Galaxy Type SB(s)b
ϕ 1.2′×1.0′, m13.1v, SB13.2   14^{h}57.1^m +49° 40′
Finder Chart 33-7, Figure 33-19   ★★
12/14″Scopes–125x: NGC 5804, nearly the twin of NGC 5797 to its NW, is a faint, round 1′ diameter glow with some central brightening. Galaxies NGC 5795-97 and PGC 53381 are also part of this group of faint galaxies.

PGC 53381 Galaxy Type Sc
ϕ 0.7′×0.5′, m14.3v   14^{h}55.9^m +49° 39′
Finder Chart 33-7, Figure 33-19   ★
12/14″Scopes–125x: PGC 53381 appears much fainter than, NGC 5794 and NGC 5804. Its 1′ diameter halo is very faint and round.

NGC 5795 Galaxy Type S?
ϕ 1.6′×0.3′, m13.8v, SB12.8   14^{h}56.3^m +49° 23′
Finder Chart 33-7, Figure 33-19   ★★
12/14″Scopes–125x: NGC 5795, located 14′ south of a 6th magnitude star, has a faint 1.25′×0.5′ ENE–WSW halo slightly brighter toward its center. In the same low power field of view with NGC 5795 is a chain of four galaxies, NGCs 5804, 5797, 5794, and PGC 53381, which arc in a semicircle from east, through north, to west of a 6th magnitude star.

NGC 5797 H678³ Galaxy Type S0/a
ϕ 1.0′×0.6′, m12.8v, SB12.1   14^{h}56.3^m +49° 42′
Finder Chart 33-7, Figure 33-19   ★★
12/14″Scopes–125x: NGC 5797 is the middle and brightest galaxy in a group that includes NGC 5794 to its west, and NGC 5804 to its east. NGC 5797 has

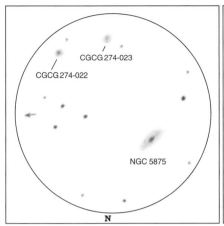

Figure 33-21. NGC 5875
17.5″, f4.5–250x, by G. R. Kepple

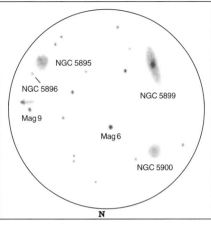

Figure 33-22. NGC 5899 Group
13″, f5.6–100x, by Steve Coe

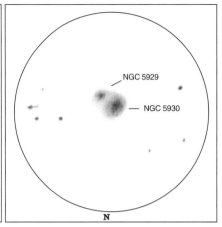

Figure 33-23. NGC 5929 and NGC 5930
20″, f4.5–175x, by Richard W. Jakiel

a fairly faint 1′×0.5′ ESE–WNW halo with some brightening at its center.

NGC 5820 H756² Galaxy Type S0
φ 2.2′×2.0′, m12.4v, SB13.9   14ʰ58.7ᵐ +53° 53′
Finder Chart 33-7, Figure 33-20   ★★
8/10″Scopes–100x: This galaxy lies 8′ west of a wide, bright double of yellowish stars (S,h191: 6.6, 7.4; 40.5″; 342°). Its small, well concentrated halo is elongated 45″×30″ E–W and has a stellar nucleus at its center.
12/14″Scopes–125x: NGC 5820 has a stellar nucleus embedded in a tiny, bright core surrounded by a 1′×0.5′ E–W oval halo. A 14th magnitude star lies 1.5′ WSW. 4′ NE of NGC 5820 is NGC 5821A-B, with averted vision seen as one object elongated 1′×0.5′ NNW-SSE.

NGC 5874 Galaxy Type SAB(rs)c I-II
φ 2.4′×1.6′, m12.4v, SB13.8   15ʰ07.9ᵐ +54° 45′
Finder Chart 33-7   ★★
12/14″Scopes–125x: NGC 5874, located 17′ NE of a 5th magnitude star, is a very faint, diffuse 1′ diameter smudge somewhat elongated NE–SW. Two 9th magnitude stars are 5′ SW and 8′ NNW of the galaxy.
16/18″Scopes–150x: NGC 5874 has a faint 2′×1.25′ NE–SW halo with a broad central brightening. Galaxy NGC 7876 lies 20′ SE.

NGC 5875 H755² Galaxy Type SAb: II
φ 2.4′×1.2′, m12.4v, SB13.4   15ʰ09.2ᵐ +52° 32′
Finder Chart 33-7, Figure 33-21   ★★
12/14″Scopes–125x: NGC 5875 is 8′ NW of a 2′ wide pair of 7.5 and 8th magnitude stars that point

toward it. The galaxy's halo is elongated 1.5′×0.75′ NW–SE and slightly brighter in its center.
16/18″Scopes–150x: NGC 5875 is fairly faint, elongated 2′×1′ NW–SE, and has a moderately well concentrated core. A 13th magnitude star is beyond the galaxy's SE tip 2.75′ from its center. A threshold star nearly touches the east edge. Two very faint, 15th magnitude CGCG galaxies are 5.5′ SSW and 6.75′ SW.

NGC 5876 Galaxy Type SB(r)ab:
φ 2.6′×1.2′, m12.7v, SB13.8   15ʰ09.5ᵐ +54° 30′
Finder Chart 33-7   ★★★
12/14″Scopes–125x: NGC 5876, located 25′ east of a 5th magnitude star, appears fairly faint, elongated 1′×0.5′ NE–SW, and has a prominent stellar nucleus.

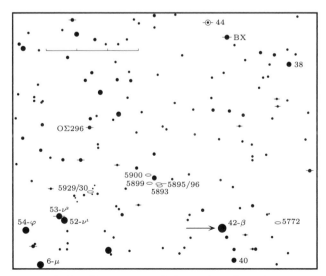

Finder Chart 33-9. 42–β Boö: 15ʰ01.9ᵐ +40° 23′

16/18″ Scopes–150x: NGC 5876 is nearly the same size as its companion galaxy NGC 5874, located 20′ to the NW, but appears somewhat brighter. Because its catalogued magnitude is in fact 0.3 fainter than that of NGC 5874, its seeming greater brightness probably is an optical illusion caused by its conspicuous stellar nucleus. Its halo is elongated 2′×1′ NE–SW.

NGC 5895 Galaxy Type Sc
φ 0.9′×0.2′, m15.5v, SB13.5   15ʰ13.8ᵐ +41° 59′

NGC 5896 Galaxy Type S?
φ 0.2′×0.2′, m15.3v, SB11.7   15ʰ13.8ᵐ +41° 59′
Finder Chart 33-9, Figure 33-22   ★/★

16/18″ Scopes–150x: NGC 5895 is 10′ SSW of a 6th magnitude star and 4.25′ south of a 9th magnitude star. It is a faint, diffuse object elongated 30″×15″ NNE–SSW. 1′ to its NNW is its companion, NGC 5896, a faint, stellar spot. Galaxies NGC 5899 and NGC 5900 are 13′ east and 18′ NE, respectively, and NGC 5893 is 5′ SW.

NGC 5899 H650² Galaxy Type SAB(rs)c II
φ 2.6′×1.1′, m11.7v, SB12.7   15ʰ15.0ᵐ +42° 03′
Finder Chart 33-9, Figure 33-22   ★★★

12/14″ Scopes–125x: NGC 5699, located 10′ SE of a 6th magnitude star, is an edge-on galaxy and the brightest in a small galaxy group of five members, the other four being extremely faint. Its companions are NGC 5893 located 17′ to its WSW, the NGC 5895-96 pair 13′ to its west, and NGC 5900 some

9′ to its north. NGC 5899 has a bright 3′×1′ NNE–SSW halo that smoothly brightens to a large circular core.

NGC 5900 H660³ Galaxy Type Sb: sp III
φ 1.4′×0.4′, m14.0v, SB13.2   15ʰ15.1ᵐ +42° 13′
Finder Chart 33-9, Figure 33-22   ★

12/14″ Scopes–125x: NGC 5900 is one of three faint companions of NGC 5899 and is located 9′ to the bright galaxy's north. It is a very faint, small NW–SE streak with no central brightening.

NGC 5929 U9851 Galaxy Type Sab: pec
φ 1.0′×0.9′, m13.6v, SB13.3   15ʰ26.1ᵐ +41° 40′

NGC 5930 H651² Galaxy Type SAB(rs)b pec HII
φ 1.8′×0.7′, m12.2v, SB12.3   15ʰ26.1ᵐ +41° 41′
Finder Chart 33-9, Figure 33-23   ★/★★

12/14″ Scopes–125x: NGC 5929 and NGC 5930 are a NE–SW contact pair which appear as a hazy figure 8. Both galaxies are fairly faint, small, and round with little central brightening. NGC 5930, the northwestern nodule, is the larger of the two.

20/22″ Scopes–175x: This is a classic example of interacting galaxies connected by a thin nebulous bridge. NGC 5930 is the larger and brighter of the pair, appearing elongated 1′×0.5′ NNW–SSE with an oval core that contains a stellar nucleus. NGC 5929, only half the size of its companion, is an amorphous glow about 30″ diameter with a very faint stellar nucleus.

Chapter 34

Canes Venatici, the Hunting Dogs

34.1 Overview

Canes Venatici, the Hunting Dogs, occupies the rather blank area of the sky between the tail of Ursa Major to the north, the back legs of Ursa Major to the east, Coma Berenices to the south, and the kite-shape of Boötes to the east. Its invention is commonly attributed to Hevelius in the late 17th century, but this is a mistake: the two Hunting Dogs, unlabeled but held on leashes by Boötes in the traditional manner, first appear on star maps drawn in the early 16th century. Hevelius in any case can be credited with the individual names of the two dogs: Asterion, "Starry" (18, 19, 20, and 23 Canum Venaticorum), and Chara, "Dear" (Alpha and Beta CVn). The brightest star in the constellation, the magnitude 2.9 Alpha, was named Cor Caroli, "Heart of Charles" by Halley in honor of King Charles I of England, beheaded under the rule of Oliver Cromwell in the mid-17th century.

Although star-poor, the area of Canes Venatici is part of a "Stream" of galaxies that begins to its north and NW in Ursa Major and extends south from it through Coma Berenices and Virgo to northern Centaurus. Virtually all of the galaxies visible in small telescopes in this band are members of the huge Local Supercluster, centered some 60 million light years away toward southern Coma Berenices and NW Virgo. Our Local Galaxy Group seems to be near an outer edge of the Local Supercluster. Toward Canes Venatici we seem to look through three layers of galaxy groups. The closest group, perhaps 20 million light years distant on the average, is called the Canes Venatici I Cloud and includes M94, M106, and NGCs 4214, 4244, 4395, and 4449. The next group, the Canes Venatici II Cloud, might be centered 35–40 million light years away and includes the M101 group, M51, M63, and NGCs 4111, 4242, 4490, 4618, 4631, and 4800. The third layer are Canes Venatici galaxies that are members of the extensive, and 70–80 million light year distant, Ursa Major I Cloud, including NGCs 4145, 4151, 4217, 4369, and possibly 5005 and 5033.

Canes Venatici: KAY-neez Ve-NAT-i-sy **Genitive:** Canum Venaticorum, KAY-num, Ve-NAT-i-kor-um **Abbreviation:** CVn **Culmination:** 9pm–May 22, midnight–April 7 **Area:** 465 square degrees **Showpieces:** 2 CVn, 12–α CVn, M3 (NGC 5272), M51(NGC 5194), M63 (NGC 5055), M94 (NGC 4736), M106 (NGC 4258), NGC 4244, NGC 4449, NGC 4631, NGC 5005 **Binocular Objects:** 7 CVn, 15 & 17 CVn, 25 CVn, S654, M3 (NGC 5272), M51(NGC 5194), M63 (NGC 5055), M94 (NGC 4736), M106 (NGC 4258), NGC 4244, NGC 4449, NGC 4631, NGC 5005

34.2 Interesting Stars

2 CVn = Σ1622 Double Star   **Spec. K5**
m5.8, 8.1; Sep. 11.4″; P.A. 260° $12^h16.1^m +40°\,40'$
Finder Chart 34-3   ★★★★
2/3″ Scopes–75x: 2 Canum Venaticorum has a beautiful color contrast of golden yellow and pale blue.

Y CVn Variable Star Type SRb   **Spec. N3**
m4.8 to 6.4 in 157 days $12^h45.1^m +45°\,26'$
Finder Chart 34-3   La Superba   ★★★★
4/6″ Scopes–75x: Y Canum Venaticorum, called "La Superba" by the 19th century Italian astronomer Father Angelo Secchi, is one of the deeply red-toned "carbon stars." Y Canum's range is magnitudes 4.8 to 6.4 in a period that roughly averages 157 days. Its beautiful poppy-red tone is easy to see in 50mm binoculars or 60mm telescopes. Carbon stars are highly evolved cool red giants with atmospheres rich in Carbon molecules. The unusually deep red color of these stars is the consequence of the efficiency of these carbon molecules in absorbing the star's blue light.

Canes Venatici, the Hunting Dogs Constellation Chart 34-1

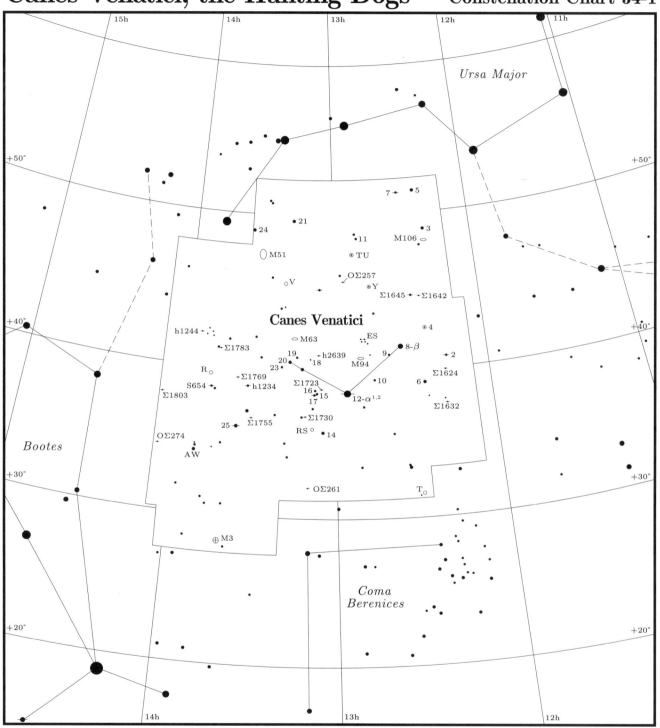

Ursa Major

+50°   +50°

7 ●— ● 5

24   21   11   ● 3
                                     M106 ○

◯ M51   ⊙ TU

○V   ○ Σ257
                    ⊙ Y
                    Σ1645 ←—● Σ1642

Canes Venatici   ⊙ 4

h1244 ←— ○ M63   ∴ ES
          Σ1783   19   ←— h2639   9   ● 8-β
                    20   18   M94 ○   ←— 2
          R ○   23   Σ1624
          S654 ←—   ← Σ1769   10   6
          Σ1803   ← h1234   Σ1723
                              16 ● 15   12-α^{1,2}   Σ1632
                              17
                    25 ●— Σ1755   ← Σ1730
          O Σ274   RS ○ ● 14
          AW

Bootes   ← O Σ261   T ○

+30°   +30°

⊕ M3

*Coma
Berenices*

+20°   +20°

14h   13h   12h

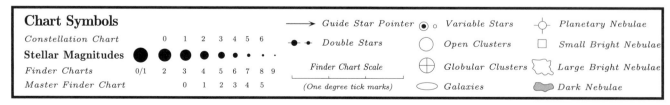

Table 34-1: Selected Variable Stars in Canes Venatici

Name	HD No	Type	Max.	Min.	Period (Days)	F*	Spec. Type	R.A. (2000) Dec.		Finder Chart No.	Notes
T CVn	108833	M?	7.6	12.6	290	0.42	M6.5	$12^h30.2^m$ +31° 30'		34-4	
Y CVn	110914	SRb	7.4	10.0	157		C5, 4J	45.1	+45 26	34-3	La Superba; deep red
TU CVn	112264	SRb	5.55	6.6	50		M5	54.9	+47 12	34-3	
RS CVn	114519	EA/AR/RS	7.93	9.14	4.79	0.11	F4+K0	$13^h10.6^m$ +35 56		34-7	
V CVn	115898	SRa	6.52	8.56	191	0.50	M4+M6	19.5	+45 32	34-5	
R CVn	120499	M	6.5	12.9	328	0.46	M5.5–M9	49.0	+39 33	34-7	Deep orange

F* = The fraction of period taken up by the star's rise from min. to max. brightness, or the period spent in eclipse.

Table 34-2: Selected Double Stars in Canes Venatici

Name	ADS No.	Pair	M1	M2	Sep."	P.A.°	Spec	R.A. (2000) Dec.		Finder Chart No.	Notes
2 CVn	8489		5.8	8.1	11.4	260	K5	$12^h16.1^m$ +40° 40		34-3	Gold and blue
Σ1624	8495		7.2	10.1	6.1	150	A2	16.7	+39 36	34-4	
Σ1632	8516		6.8	10.0	10.2	193	K0	20.2	+37 54	34-4	
Σ1642	8546		8.4	9.2	2.6	180	F5	25.0	+44 44	34-3	
Σ1645	8561		7.4	8.0	9.9	158	F5	28.1	+44 48	34-3	
7 CVn		AB	6.2	10.4	109.2	172	F8	30.0	+51 32	34-1	Binocular triple
		AC		9.0	229.0	327	A5				
Es			7.7	8.1	47.4	50	G5	49.1	+42 13	34-3	
12–α CVn	8706		2.9	5.5	19.4	229	A0	56.0	+39 19	34-4	Bluish and greenish
OΣ257	8714		8.5	9.2	13.0	353	F2	56.8	+45 36	34-1	
h2639		AB	7.5	10.5	31.4	160	K5	$13^h06.2^m$ +40 55		34-1	
		AC		9.5	57.2	137					
Σ1723	8795		7.3	8.6	6.6	8	K0	08.2	+38 44	34-7	
17 CVn	8805	AB	6.0	6.2	84.4	297	F0 B9	10.1	+38 30	34-7	
15 and 17			6.3	6.0	284.0	277	B9 F0	09.6	+38 32	34-7	
OΣ261	8814		7.2	7.7	2.2	342	F8	12.0	+32 05	34-6	
Σ1730	8815		8.2	9.9	1.8	338	F0	12.1	+36 54	34-7	
Σ1755	8934		7.2	8.1	4.4	131	G5	32.4	+36 49	34-7	
h1234	8956		6.4	11.2	30.6	14	A3	34.4	+38 47	34-7	
25 CVn	8974	AB	5.0	6.9	1.8	99	F0	37.5	+36 18	34-7	Pale yellow binary
	8974	AC		8.6	217.7	141					
Σ1769	8981	AB	7.8	10.2	2.1	35	G5	38.0	+39 10	34-7	
	8981	AC		9.6	56.1	259					
	8981	AD		11.7	167.6	194					
Σ1783	9020		8.1	10.3	2.2	49	K0	46.1	+41 02	34-7	
S 654			5.6	8.8	71.3	23.8	K0	47.0	+38 33	34-7	
h1244	9044		6.9	11.4	6.8	131	A0	53.3	+42 11	34-5	
Σ1803	9111		8.1	9.9	17.8	43	K0	$14^h06.4^m$ +38 25		34-1	
OΣ274	9112		7.2	10.2	13.1	59	K0	06.7	+34 47	34-1	

Footnotes: *= Year 2000, a = Near apogee, c = Closing, w = Widening. Finder Chart No: All stars listed in the tables are plotted in the large Constellation Chart, but when a star appears in a Finder Chart, this number is listed. Notes: When colors are subtle, the suffix *-ish* is used, e.g. *bluish*.

Alpha (α) = 12 CVn (Σ1692) Double Star Spec. A0
m2.9,5.5; Sep.19.4"; P.A.229° $12^h56.0^m$ +38° 19'
Finder Chart 34-4   ★★★★★

Cor Caroli

Cor Caroli, 120 light years distant, is a long period binary of two stars separated by at least 770 A.U., the width of five Solar Systems. The A0 primary is 80 times, and the F0 secondary 7 times, as luminous as the Sun.
2/3" Scopes–75x: A fine double for small telescopes, Cor Caroli is a pair of unequally bright yellowish stars.
8/10" Scopes–100x: At first glance the two stars of this binary appear merely white, but close attention, and racking them slightly out of focus, reveals that the stars have subtle bluish and greenish shades.

25 CVn = Σ1768 Triple Star   Spec. F0
AB: m5.0,6.9; Sep.1.8"; P.A.99° $13^h37.5^m$ +36° 18'
Finder Chart 34-7   ★★★★
6/8" Scopes–200x: 25 Canum Venaticorum appears as two pale yellow disks in contact. A magnitude 8.6 C component lies 217" distant in P.A.141°.

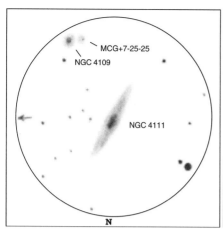

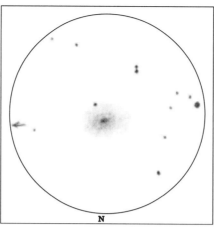

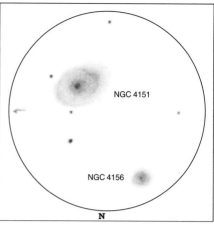

Figure 34-1. NGC 4111
18.5″, f5–200x, by Glen W. Sanner

Figure 34-2. NGC 4145
18.5″, f5–250x, by Glen W. Sanner

Figure 34-3. NGC 4151 & NGC 4156
20″, f4.5–175x, by Richard Jakiel

34.3 Deep-Sky Objects

NGC 4111 H195[1] Galaxy Type SA(r)0+: sp
ϕ **4.4′ × 0.9′, m10.7v, SB 12.1   12^{h}07.1^m +43° 04′**
Finder Chart 34-3, Figure 34-1   ★★★★
8/10″ Scopes–100x: This galaxy lies 4′ SW of a double consisting of an 8th magnitude primary with a magnitude 10.5 secondary 34″ from it toward the SW. NGC 4111 has a bright stellar nucleus embedded in a large, bright extended core surrounded by a fainter halo elongated 3′ × 0.5′ NNW–SSE.
12/14″ Scopes–125x: NGC 4111 is a bright galaxy elongated 3′ × 0.75′ NNW–SSE with a 1′ long core and a brilliant stellar nucleus.
16/18″ Scopes–150x: In larger telescopes NGC 4111 has a well concentrated, much elongated 4′ × 0.75′ NNW–SSE halo containing a highly extended core and an intense nucleus. The halo is mottled, and several faint knots are along the major axis. Averted

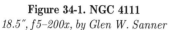

Master Finder Chart 34-2. Canes Venatici Chart Areas
Guide stars indicated by arrows.

vision reveals a dark dust lane. 4.75′ to the SSW of NGC 4111 is its companion galaxy NGC 4109, a faint spot with a stellar nucleus. 9′ NE of NGC 4111 is NGC 4117, a faint, diffuse glow elongated 1′ × 0.5′ NE–SW.

NGC 4138 H196[1] Galaxy Type SA(r)0+
ϕ **2.9′ × 1.8′, m11.3v, SB 13.0   12^{h}09.5^m +43° 41′**
Finder Chart 34-3   ★★★
8/10″ Scopes–100x: NGC 4138, located just south of a triangle of fairly bright stars, is a moderately faint galaxy with a 2′ × 1′ NNW–SSE halo containing a broad oval core with a faint stellar nucleus.
16/18″ Scopes–150x: NGC 4138 has a fairly faint 2.5′ × 1.5′ NNW–SSE halo around a large, moderately well concentrated oval core. The core covers nearly 70% of the halo, and at its center is a faint stellar nucleus and a bright mottled streak.

NGC 4143 H54[4] Galaxy Type SAB(s)0°
ϕ **2.9′ × 1.9′, m10.7v, SB 12.4   12^{h}09.6^m +42° 32′**
Finder Chart 34-3   ★★★
12/14″ Scopes–125x: NGC 4143 has a faint 3′ × 1.25′ NW–SE halo elongated to tapered ends containing a brighter, broad, 1.5′ × 0.75′ nearly N–S core. The bright nonstellar nucleus is somewhat extended ESE–WNW.

NGC 4145 H169[1] Galaxy Type SAB(rs)d II
ϕ **6.0′ × 4.0′, m11.3v, SB 14.6   12^{h}10.0^m +39° 53′**
Finder Chart 34-4, Figure 34-2   Holmberg 342a ★★★
8/10″ Scopes–100x: NGC 4145, located 9′ west of a 7th magnitude star, is a faint, diffuse, uniform glow elongated 3′ × 2′ E–W.

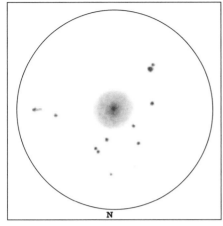

Figure 34-4. NGC 4214
13″, f5.6–165x, by Steve Coe

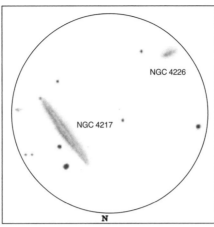

Figure 34-5. NGC 4217 & NGC 4226
17.5″, f4.5–225x, by G. R. Kepple

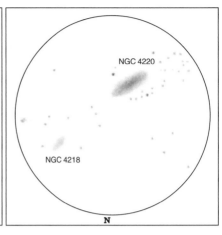

Figure 34-6. NGC 4218 & NGC 4220
20″, f4.5–175x, by Richard Jakiel

16/18″Scopes–150x: NGC 4145 has a low surface brightness 4′ × 2.5′ E–W halo within which is a slight, broad central brightening with some mottling. A 13th magnitude star lies 1.5′ SSW.

NGC 4151 H165[1] Galaxy Type (R′)SAB(rs)ab:
φ **6.4′ × 5.5′, m10.8v, SB14.5**   **12h10.5m +39° 24′**

NGC 4156 H642[2] Galaxy Type SB(rs)b I
φ **1.3′ × 1.2′, m13.2v, SB13.5**   **12h10.8m +39° 28′**
Finder Chart 34-4, Figure 34-3   ★★★/★

8/10″Scopes–100x: NGC 4151 is a Type I Seyfert galaxy with a nucleus that varies in brightness by about one magnitude, at maximum reaching about magnitude 12.4. The nucleus appears bright, but the surrounding halo is faint, diffuse, and elongated 2.5′ × 1′ NW–SE.

16/18″Scopes–150x: NGC 4151 has a 3′ × 1.75′ NW–SE halo that smoothly brightens toward its center. A 12th magnitude star 2.5′ north is just slightly brighter than the galaxy's nucleus. A 13th magnitude star between the 12th magnitude star and the galaxy's center just touches the halo. Another magnitude 14 star is 1.5′ WSW. 5.5′ to the NE is galaxy NGC 4156, faint but quite obvious, with a diffuse 1′ diameter halo slightly elongated E–W.

NGC 4183 H697[3] Galaxy Type SA(s)cd? sp III-IV
φ **5.0′ × 0.6′, m12.3v, SB13.4**   **12h13.3m +43° 42′**
Finder Chart 34-3   ★★

16/18″Scopes–150x: NGC 4183 is a faint ghostly streak elongated 3.5′ × 0.5′ NNW–SSE and only slightly brighter at its center. A 14th magnitude star touches the eastern edge of the galaxy 50″ SSE of its center. A magnitude 13.5 star is 3′ south.

NGC 4190 H409[2] Galaxy Type Im pec IV-V
φ **1.6′ × 1.6′, m13.3v, SB14.2**   **12h13.7m +36° 38′**
Finder Chart 34-4   ★

16/18″Scopes–150x: NGC 4190, located 6′ south of an 8.5 magnitude star, is a very faint, diffuse, uniform glow 1.5′ in diameter.

NGC 4214 H95[1] Galaxy Type IAB(s)m III-IV
φ **10.0′ × 8.3′, m9.8v, SB14.4**   **12h15.6m +36° 20′**
Finder Chart 34-4, Figure 34-4   ★★★

8/10″Scopes–100x: NGC 4214 lies 4.5′ NW of a double consisting of an 11th magnitude primary with a magnitude 12.5 companion 8″ to its SE. The galaxy has a bright halo that grows smoothly brighter toward its center. It is elongated 2.5′ × 2′ NW–SE in the direction of its companion, NGC 4190, located nearly half a degree to the NW.

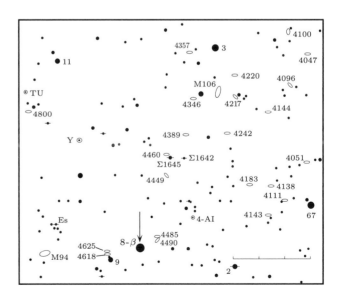

Finder Chart 34-3. 8–β CVn: 12h33.7m +41° 21′

Figure 34-7. *NGC 4244 is a huge, beautiful spindle. Image courtesy of Tim Hunter and James McGaha.*

16/18″ Scopes–150x: NGC 4217 is highly extended 4.5′ × 1′ NE–SW with a weakly concentrated central area. 250x and averted vision reveal a faint dust lane along the SE edge. A 13.5 magnitude star is at the galaxy's SW tip, and a 12.5 magnitude star is 2′ south. 7.5 to the SE of NGC 4217 is its companion galaxy NGC 4226, a very faint NW–SE oval elongated in the direction of the larger galaxy. A 13th magnitude star lies 1.5′ to its west.

NGC 4220 H209[1] Galaxy Type SA(r)0+
φ 3.5′ × 1.3′, m11.4v, SB12.9   12ʰ16.2ᵐ +47° 53′
Finder Chart 34-3, Figure 34-6   ★★★
12/14″ Scopes–125x: NGC 4220, a faint lenticular galaxy, is elongated 3.5′ × 1′ NW–SE with a stellar nucleus. Its poorly concentrated core has a slightly brighter streak along its major axis. A 13th magnitude star lies 1.25′ WSW. 15′ north of NGC 4220 is NGC 4218, a faint 1.5′ × 0.5′ NW–SE streak with a tiny core. It is just WNW of a 10th magnitude star and 1.25′ ENE of a magnitude 13.5 star.

12/14″ Scopes–125x: NGC 4214 has a large unevenly illuminated core covering half the 3′ × 2′ NW–SE halo. An irregular NW–SE chain of 13th magnitude stars passes along the NE edge of the galaxy.
16/18″ Scopes–150x: In larger telescopes the halo can be traced with averted vision out to 4′ × 3′. The core is quite elongated, measuring about 1.5′ × 0.5′, and has tapered ends. It lacks a nucleus, but its texture is mottled and several bright knots are SE of its center. An elegant double of a 13th magnitude primary with a magnitude 14.5 companion 10″ to its NE is 3.5′ NW of the galaxy.

NGC 4217 H748[2] Galaxy Type Sb
φ 5.0′ × 1.5′, m11.2v, SB13.2   12ʰ15.8ᵐ +47° 06′
Finder Chart 34-3, Figure 34-5   ★★★
8/10″ Scopes–100x: NGC 4217 is nestled among three stars, the glare of which makes this faint galaxy that much more difficult to see. Just north are a 9th and an 11th magnitude star, the latter nearly touching the galaxy's halo; and 2′ south of the galaxy's center is a 12th magnitude star. The halo is elongated 3′ × 1′ NE–SW and slightly brighter along its center. To the galaxy's west and SW is a field of relatively bright stars.

NGC 4242 H725[3] Galaxy Type SAB(s)dm III-IV
φ 5.2′ × 3.5′, m10.8v, SB13.8   12ʰ17.5ᵐ +45° 37′
Finder Chart 34-3, Figure 34-18   ★★★
8/10″ Scopes–100x: NGC 4242, located 2′ west of a 12th magnitude star, is a faint, amorphous glow about 2.5′ across.
12/14″ Scopes–125x: NGC 4242 has a fairly faint 3.5′ diameter halo with poor central concentration. A 14th magnitude star nearly touches the south edge.

NGC 4244 H41[5] Galaxy Type SA(s)cd: sp IV
φ 17.0′ × 2.2′, m10.4v, SB14.2   12ʰ17.5ᵐ +37° 49′
Finder Chart 34-4, Figure 34-7   ★★★★
8/10″ Scopes–75x: NGC 4244 is an extraordinarily long, thin, bright 15′ × 1.25′ NE–SW spindle with a slightly brighter, extended core. Its SW tip touches an 11th magnitude star. The NE tip extends slightly past a 12th magnitude star.
12/14″ Scopes–100x: Magnificent! This bright shaft of light is elongated 15′ × 1.5′ NE–SW and has a highly extended 5′ long core which is noticeably bulged at its center and of a mottled texture throughout. A faint irregular knot is near each tip of the core. A NE–SW double of 14th magnitude stars is 3′ NNE of the galaxy's center just off the NW edge of its halo.

Figure 34-8. *Messier 106 (NGC 4258) has a bright core in a mottled inner region surrounded by a large, faint halo. NGC 4248 lies 13′ NW (lower left of center) while NGC 4231-32 are visible near the left side of the image. Image courtesy of Martin C. Germano.*

NGC 4258 Messier 106 Galaxy Type SAB(s)bc II-III
ϕ **20.0′ × 8.4′, m8.4v, SB 13.8**   **12^{h}19.0^m +47° 18′**
Finder Chart 34-3, Figure 34-8   ★★★★★

Messier 106, some 35 million light years distant, is a large, massive system with a tightly wound spiral structure tilted 25° to our line of sight. It is a source of radio emission. Messier 106 was discovered by Mechain in 1781.

4/6″ Scopes–60x: A fine sight in small telescopes, NGC 4258 is bright, elongated 10′ × 7′ NNW–SSE, and has a large, bright core with a prominent nucleus.

8/10″ Scopes–75x: Impressive! A bright core containing a nonstellar nucleus is embedded in a well concentrated 5′ × 2′ inner region which in turn is surrounded by a much fainter halo elongated 12′ × 4′ NNW–SSE. At it northern end the halo extends to a magnitude 12.5 star and at its southern end to a magnitude 13 star. A 10th magnitude star lies 3′ further south of the southern end.

12/14″ Scopes–100x: Messier 106 is a fine, bright galaxy with a mottled, well concentrated 5′ × 3′ central region containing a 1′ diameter core with a bright nonstellar nucleus. The outer halo is much fainter and more diffuse, extending to 16′ × 5′ in P.A. 150°. With averted vision hints of spiral structure can be glimpsed in the form of two broadly brighter exten-

sions from the central region out into the halo, the northern extension being more prominent. Both extensions have an indistinct dark streak. Several stars are embedded in the outer arms on both sides. Companion galaxy NGC 4248, lying 13′ NW, has a faint halo elongated 1.25′ × 0.5′ ESE–WNW.

NGC 4346 H210[1] Galaxy Type S0
ϕ **3.2′ × 1.4′, m11.1v, SB 12.6**   **12^{h}23.5^m +47° 00′**
Finder Chart 34-3, Figure 34-19   ★★★

8/10″ Scopes–100x: This lens-shaped galaxy has a faint halo elongated 1.5′ × 0.5′ E–W and slightly brighter at its center.

16/18″ Scopes–150x: NGC 4346 shows a well concentrated, circular core containing a bright stellar nucleus and embedded in a much fainter 2.5′ × 1′ E–W halo. The outer halo fades abruptly 1′ from the galaxy's center.

NGC 4357 Galaxy Type SAbc II
ϕ **3.6′ × 1.4′, m12.4v, SB 14.0**   **12^{h}24.0^m +48″46′**
Finder Chart 34-3   ★★

16/18″ Scopes–150x: NGC 4357 lies 40′ ESE of magnitude 5.3 star 3 Canum Venaticorum and 10′ ESE of an 8th magnitude star. It has a very faint 2′ × 0.75′

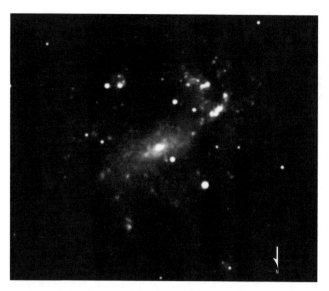

Figure 34-9. *NGC 4395 has a very low surface brightness, but large aperture telescopes show several knots within it. Image courtesy of Chris Schur.*

Figure 34-10. *NGC 4449 is an interesting galaxy with a rough rectangular halo showing considerable detail. Image courtesy of Tim Hunter and James McGaha.*

ENE–WSW halo containing a faint stellar nucleus. The immediate field is barren of stars.

NGC 4369 H166[1] Galaxy Type (R)SA(rs)a
φ **2.2′ × 2.2′, m11.7v, SB 13.2**   12^{h}24.6^m +39° 23′
Finder Chart 34-4   ★★★
8/10″Scopes–100x: NGC 4369, located 2.5′ north of a 12th magnitude star, has a faint, circular 1′ diameter halo with a prominent stellar nucleus.

12/14″Scopes–125x: NGC 4369 shows a bright, tiny core containing a stellar nucleus surrounded by a faint, diffuse 2′ diameter halo. 5′ south of the galaxy is a 23″ wide ENE–WSW pair of 12th magnitude stars.

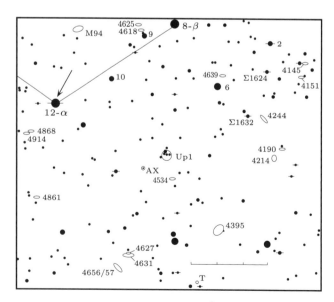

Finder Chart 34-4. 12–α CVn: 12^{h}56.0^m +38° 19′

NGC 4389 H749[2] Galaxy Type SB(rs)bc pec: IV
φ **2.4′ × 1.7′, m11.7v, SB 13.1**   12^{h}25.6^m +45° 41′
Finder Chart 34-3, Figure 34-20   ★★★
12/14″Scopes–125x: NGC 4389 has a faint halo elongated 1.75′ × 1.0′ ESE–WNW within which is a thin, poorly concentrated core extended 0.75′×0.15′. A 12th magnitude star lies 2.25′ NNW; and a 13.5 magnitude star is 1′ SE of the galaxy's center.

NGC 4395 H29[5] Galaxy Type SA(s)m: IV
φ **14.5′×12.0′, m10.2v, SB 15.6**   12^{h}25.8^m +33° 33′
Finder Chart 34-4, Figure 34-9   ★★
16/18″Scopes–150x: NGC 4395 has a diffuse, very low surface brightness halo about 8′across. 200x reveals several broad, slightly brighter areas aligned NW–SE, the extreme SE patch being the most prominent. Three of these patches have their own NGC numbers: from west to east 4399, 4400, and 4401.

NGC 4449 H213[1] Galaxy Type IBm IV
φ **5.5′×4.1′, m9.6v, SB 12.8**   12^{h}28.2^m +44° 06′
Finder Chart 34-3, Figure 34-10   ★★★★
8/10″Scopes–100x: This galaxy has a stellar nucleus embedded in a fairly well concentrated 3′×2′ NE–SW halo of uniform surface brightness.

12/14″Scopes–125x: NGC 4449 is an interesting galaxy with an unusual rectangular halo measuring 5′×3′ NE–SW. The core is elongated and has several bright spots near its center, the most prominent just SW of the nucleus. The outer halo is mottled throughout.

16/18″Scopes–150x: A fine sight! This galaxy is quite

Figure 34-11. *NGC 4490 has a bright teardrop-shaped halo while its interacting companion galaxy NGC 4485 is a small, unconcentrated patch. Image courtesy of Jim Burnell.*

Figure 34-12. *Upgren 1, the lone star cluster in Canes Venatici, is a coarse group of ten stars. Martin C. Germano made this 15 minute exposure on hypered 2415 film with an 8″, f5 Newtonian reflector.*

bright with an irregular rectangular 6′×3′ NE–SW halo. The 1.5′×0.75′ core is bright and contains several knots, the brightest just SW of the nucleus. Averted vision reveals a dark spot SE of the nucleus and very faint spiral pattern. A very faint star is embedded 1′ ENE of the core's center, and a 13th magnitude star is 2.5′ to the galaxy's ESE.

NGC 4460 H212[1] Galaxy Type SB(s)0+? sp
ϕ **4.3′×1.3′, m11.3v, SB13.0   12ʰ28.8ᵐ +44° 52′**
Finder Chart 34-3, Figure 34-21   ★★★
12/14″Scopes–125x: NGC 4460 is situated 5′ NE of the attractive double star Σ1645 (7.5, 8.0; 9.9″; 158°). It has a faint 3′×0.75′ NE–SW halo with a long central concentration containing several faint, diffuse knots but no bright nucleus. A threshold star is just visible 20″ SSE of the galaxy's center. 4′ to its NNE is an elegant little double of a magnitude 13.5 primary with a magnitude 14.5 secondary 10″ distant in P.A. 30°.

NGC 4485 H197[1] Galaxy Type IB(s)m pec III-IV
ϕ **2.7′×2.3′, m11.9v, SB13.8   12ʰ30.5ᵐ +41° 42′**

NGC 4490 H198[1] Galaxy Type SB(s)d pec III
ϕ **6.4′×3.3′, m9.8v, SB13.0   12ʰ30.6ᵐ +41° 38′**
Finder Chart 34-3, Figure 34-11   ★★★/★★★★
NGC *4490: Cocoon Galaxy*
8/10″Scopes–100x: NGC 4490 and NGC 4485 are interacting galaxies located 42′ NW of Beta (β) = 8 Canum Venaticorum. They are separated 3.5′ N–S. The southern component, NGC 4490, is the larger and brighter of the two: it is highly elongated 5′×2′

NW–SE with a moderately brighter center. NGC 4485, the northern galaxy, is a fairly bright, but small, circular patch.
12/14″Scopes–125x: NGC 4490 has a bright teardrop-shaped halo elongated 6′×3.5′ NW–SE, the long, thin "stem" pointing NW. A well concentrated, mottled core is embedded in an irregularly bright inner halo which has bright spots along its major axis. The inner halo's NE edge is flattened, and a dim dark lane runs nearly its entire length. The central area is noticeably bulged SW. A 13th magnitude star is superimposed 2′ SE of the galaxy's center. NGC 4490's interacting companion NGC 4485 is a circular 1.5′ diameter unconcentrated patch lying 3.5′ to the NNW.

NGC 4534 H410[2] Galaxy Type SA(s)dm:
ϕ **4.1′×3.0′, m12.3v, SB14.9   12ʰ34.1ᵐ +35° 31′**
Finder Chart 34-4   ★
16/18″Scopes–150x: NGC 4534, located 48′ SSW of star cluster Upgren 1, is a very faint, diffuse haze slightly elongated 1.25′×1′ ESE–WNW without central brightening. A threshold star lies 1′ NW, and a 14th magnitude star 1.5′ SW, of the galaxy's center.

Upgren 1 Open Cluster 10★ Tr Type IV 2 p
ϕ **14′, m ?   12ʰ35.0ᵐ +36° 18′**
Finder Chart 34-4, Figure 34-12   ★★★
8/10″Scopes–100x: Yes, Canes Venatici does have an open star cluster. Though known to few amateur astronomers, Upgren 1 is a bright, coarse group of

Figure 34-13. *NGC 4656 and NGC 4657 (upper right) form a "Hockey Stick" while NGC 4631 and NGC 4627 (lower left) are popularly known in more recent times as the "Whale and Pup." Image courtesy of Josef Pöpsel and Stefan Binnewies.*

ten stars spread over a 14′ area. Its brightest star, a 7th magnitude object on the cluster's northern edge, forms a wide double with a 9th magnitude star to its west. Three magnitude 7.5 stars lie in an E–W row across the group's center. Upgren 1 is only 390 light years distant, and its true size is a mere 1.6 light years.

NGC 4618 H178[1] Galaxy Type SB(rs)m II-III
ϕ 4.1′×3.2′, m10.8v, SB13.4   12^{h}41.5^m +41° 09′
Finder Chart 34-3, Figure 34-22   ★★★★
8/10″Scopes–100x: NGC 4618, located 6′ north of a
   magnitude 10.5 star, appears fairly bright, its 3′×2′
   NNE–SSW halo containing a stellar nucleus.
16/18″Scopes–150x: NGC 4618 has a circular 4′ diameter halo with a fairly bright stellar nucleus. The
   halo has a mottled texture, a few bright knots are
   visible in the southern portion, and with averted
   vision a faint spiral structure can be just discerned.
   A 12th magnitude star lies 3.5′ south and the galaxy
   NGC 4625 is 8′ NNE.

NGC 4625 H660[2] Galaxy Type SAB(rs)m pec
ϕ 1.4′×1.3′, m12.3v, SB12.9   12^{h}41.9^m +41° 16′
Finder Charts 34-3, 34-4   ★★
12/14″Scopes–125x: NGC 4625 is a faint 2′ diameter

glow with a well concentrated center but no stellar nucleus. A 12th magnitude star lies 1.75′ WSW.

NGC 4627 H659[2] Galaxy Type E4 pec, "The Pup"
ϕ 2.1′×1.6′, m12.4v, SB13.6   12^{h}42.0^m +32° 34′

NGC 4631 H42[5] Galaxy Type SB(s)d III "The Whale"
ϕ 15.5′×3.3′, m9.2v, SB13.3   12^{h}42.1^m +32° 32′
Finder Chart 34-4, Figure 34-13   ★★/★★★★★
8/10″Scopes–75x: NGC 4631 is a striking edge-on spiral
   galaxy. It appears as a bright glowing streak highly
   elongated 14′×1.5′ E–W with tapered ends and a
   mottled texture. The western end is longer and more
   pointed than the fainter, broader and blunted
   eastern end. The central bulge is offset to the east
   and more protruded on the north.
16/18″Scopes–125x: Awesome! NGC 4631 is an
   extremely long, very thin 15′×2′ E–W spindle with
   an irregularly bright, mottled halo and highly
   tapered ends. A well concentrated knot is on the
   western tip, and numerous bright and dark
   splotches are along the length of the major axis. A
   12th magnitude star touches the northern edge of
   the halo near the spindle's center, and a 13th
   magnitude star is just north of the galaxy's western
   tip. 2′ NW of the 12th magnitude star is companion
   galaxy NGC 4627, a faint 1′×0.5′ N–S smudge.

Figure 34-14. *Messier 94 (NGC 4736) is an impressive galaxy with a brilliant core surrounded by a tenuous halo. Image courtesy of Jim Burnell.*

Figure 34-15. *NGC 5005 has a tenuous elongated halo around a bright core. Image courtesy of Jim Burnell.*

NGC 4656-57 H176[1] Galaxy Type SB(s)m pec IV
φ **15.0′×3.0′, m10.5v, SB14.8**   **12ʰ44.0ᵐ +32° 10′**
Finder Chart 34-4, Figure 43-13 "Hockey Stick" ★★★★
8/10″Scopes–75x: NGC 4656 is a fairly faint 8′×1′ NE–SW streak with a slightly brighter core. A 10th magnitude star lies 10′ NE.
12/14″ Scopes–100x: NGC 4656 is, like NGC 4631 a half degree to its NW, an exceptionally long edge-on galaxy. The 10′×1.5′ NE–SW halo has a mottled texture. Its core is irregular, with several bright concentrations but no central stellar nucleus. The halo's SW extension is very faint but has a knot near its tip. Interacting companion NGC 4657 extends 2′ east forming the base of a "hockey stick". Careful scrutiny reveals a few very faint knots along the short length of NGC 4657.

NGC 4736 Messier 94 Galaxy Type (R)SA(r)ab II
φ **13.0′×11.0′, m8.2v, SB13.5**   **12ʰ50.9ᵐ +41° 07′**
Finder Charts 34-3, 34-4, Figure 34-14 ★★★★
  Messier 94, discovered by Pierre Mechain in 1781, is about 21 million light years distant in the Canes Venatici I Galaxy Cloud.
8/10″Scopes–100x: M94 has a bright, circular core surrounded by a fainter outer oval halo. It rather resembles an unresolved globular cluster. A 12th magnitude star lies 5.5′ west, and a 13th magnitude star is 4′ south.
16/18″Scopes–125x: Messier 94 is an impressive object with a brilliant core brightening to a nonstellar

nucleus and surrounded by a diffuse halo elongated 4′×3′ ESE–WNW. 125x shows a mottled texture in the halo, especially near the core. A series of knots on the east and SE sides suggest a spiral pattern.

NGC 4800 H211[1] Galaxy Type SA(rs)b III
φ **1.6′×1.1′, m11.5v, SB12.0**   **12ʰ54.6ᵐ +46° 32′**
Finder Chart 34-3 ★★★
12/14″Scopes–125x: NGC 4800, located 13′ SE of a 7th magnitude star, is a fairly faint, 1.5′×1′ NNE–SSW oval glow. Its halo has broad central brightening and a faint nonstellar nucleus. A 13th magnitude star lies 1′ WNW.

NGC 4861 H30[4] Galaxy Type SB(s)m:
φ **4.1′×1.6′, m12.3v, SB14.2**   **12ʰ59.0ᵐ +34° 52′**
Finder Chart 34-4 ★★★
12/14″Scopes–125x: NGC 4861 is 12′ WSW of a wide N–S pair of 7.5 magnitude stars. It is a very faint, diffuse patch elongated 2.5′×1′ NNE–SSW with a 12.5 magnitude star touching each of its tips.

NGC 4868 H644[2] Galaxy Type SAab? II
φ **1.5′×1.4′, m12.2v, SB12.8**   **12ʰ59.1ᵐ +37° 19′**
Finder Chart 34-4 ★★★
12/14″Scopes–125x: NGC 4868 has a circular 1.5′ diameter halo with broad central concentration. An 11th magnitude star lies near the north edge, and a 14th magnitude star is at the SW edge. Galaxy NGC

Figure 34-16. *In large telescopes M63 (NGC 5055) reveals the bright mottled halo which has given it the name of "The Sunflower Galaxy." Image courtesy of Tim Hunter and James McGaha.*

4914 lies 18′ east.

NGC 4914 H645[2] Galaxy Type E+
ϕ **3.5′×2.1′, m11.6v, SB13.6**   **13ʰ00.7ᵐ +37° 19′**
Finder Chart 34-4   ★★★
12/14″ Scopes–125x: NGC 4914, located 7′ SW of a 9th magnitude star, has a faint 2′×1′ NNW–SSE halo around a small extended core. Several spots in the core are nearly as bright as the core's stellar nucleus. Galaxy NGC 4868 lies 18′ west.

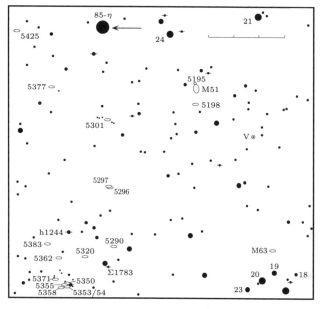

Finder Chart 34-5. 85–η UMa: 13ʰ47.5ᵐ +49° 19′

NGC 5005 H96[1] Galaxy Type SAB(rs)bc II
ϕ **5.8′×2.8′, m9.8v, SB12.7**   **13ʰ10.9ᵐ +37° 03′**
Finder Chart 34-7, Figure 34-15   ★★★★
8/10″ Scopes–100x: This galaxy is easily found on the line joining two magnitude 7.5 stars, one 10′ to its NW and the other 15′ to its SE. NGC 5005 has a nice bright 4′×1.5′ ENE–WSW halo with tapered ends. The bright oval core contains a stellar nucleus.
12/14″ Scopes–125x: NGC 5005 has a highly lustrous core with a bright nonstellar nucleus surrounded by a well concentrated oval halo elongated 5′×2′ ENE–WSW. A bright spot NE of the core is separated from the nucleus by a dark area.

NGC 5033 H97[1] Galaxy Type SA(s)c I-II
ϕ **10.5′×5.1′, m10.2v, SB14.4**   **13ʰ13.4ᵐ +36° 36′**
Finder Chart 34-7, Figure 34-15   ★★★★
8/10″ Scopes–100x: NGC 5033, located 15′ south of a 6th magnitude star, has a well concentrated 2.5′×0.5′ N–S halo with tapered ends. The core is small and extended and contains a stellar nucleus.
12/14″ Scopes–125x: NGC 5033 has a bright halo elongated 3.5′×1′ NNW–SSE and brightening to a stellar nucleus. A 14th magnitude star lies 1.5′ NNW.
16/18″ Scopes–150x: A faint, tenuous 8′×4′ halo with at least four faint stars superimposed on it surrounds a bright central region elongated 4′×1.5′ N–S.

NGC 5055 Messier 63 Galaxy Type SA(rs)bc II-III
ϕ **13.5′×8.3′, m8.6v, SB13.6**   **13ʰ15.8ᵐ +42° 02′**
Finder Chart 34-5, Figure 34-16   ★★★★
                    Sunflower Galaxy

Discovered by Pierre Mechain in 1779, Messier 63 has a spiral pattern which resembles a giant celestial flower: hence its name, the Sunflower Galaxy. M63 has a large central hub surrounded by tightly wound spiral arms. It is one of the classic examples of a "flocculent" spiral galaxy: that is, one in which the spiral features are in a multitude of short arcs rather than along two or three well-defined and easily-traced arms. The distance to M63 is about 35 million light years.
8/10″ Scopes–100x: M63, located just east of an 8.5 magnitude star, has a large, bright core containing a stellar nucleus embedded in a 3′×1.5′ ESE–WNW halo.
12/14″ Scopes–125x: M63 has a stellar nucleus in a broad, highly lustrous oval core with granular texture. The 5′×3′ ESE–WNW halo is mottled in its central region but fades abruptly outward. There is an abrupt difference between the inner and outer halo.

Figure 34-17. *Messier 51 is a beautiful face-on "grand design" spiral galaxy. Its arms are slightly distorted from perfect grand design form by its close companion NGC 5195. The satellite appears to be connected, but, as the above photograph shows, dust lanes of the big spiral are silhouetted in front of the small galaxy, implying it to be somewhat farther. Image courtesy of Chris Schur.*

NGC 5074 H309³ Galaxy Type SAb pec?
φ 0.7'×0.6', m14.0v, SB12.9   13ʰ18.4ᵐ +31° 28'
Finder Chart 34-6   ★
16/18"Scopes–150x: NGC 5074, located 8.5' SSE of an
    8th magnitude star, is a very faint, circular 30"
    diameter glow. Two 13th magnitude stars lie 4'
    ENE of the galaxy, and three more stars are 5' NNE.

NGC 5112 H646² Galaxy Type SB(rs)cd II
φ 3.7'×2.6', m12.1v, SB14.4   13ʰ21.9ᵐ +38° 44'
Finder Chart 34-7, Figure 34-23   ★★
16/18"Scopes–150x: NGC 5112, located 9' SSW of a
    7th magnitude star, has a fairly faint 2.5'×1.5' NW–
    SE halo. The center is just slightly brighter and
    contains a very faint stellar nucleus. A 12.5 magni-
    tude star lies outside the halo 2' SSE of the galaxy's
    center. Galaxy NGC 5107 is 14' SSW.

NGC 5194 Messier 51 Galaxy Type SA(s)bc pec I-II
φ 8.2'×6.9', m8.4v, SB12.6   13ʰ29.9ᵐ +47° 12'

NGC 5195 H186¹ Galaxy Type I0 pec
φ 6.4'×4.6', m9.6v, SB13.1   13ʰ30.0ᵐ +47° 16'
Finder Chart 34-5,Figures 34-17, 34-24   ★★★★★/★★★
M51: Whirlpool Galaxy

    Messier 51 was discovered by Messier in October,
1773. However, its remarkable "whirlpool" spiral pattern was not seen until 1845 when Lord Rosse discerned
it in his 6-foot reflector at Parsonstown, Ireland. At
first its spiral pattern was thought to confirm Laplace's
Nebular Hypothesis of solar system formation. This
misconception was not dispelled until 1923 when it was
finally recognized that "spiral nebulae" are in fact
external galaxies and much more remote than previously
suspected. Messier 51 is comparable to the Andromeda
Galaxy (M31) and our own Milky Way Galaxy in size,
mass, and luminosity. And, like M31 and the Milky

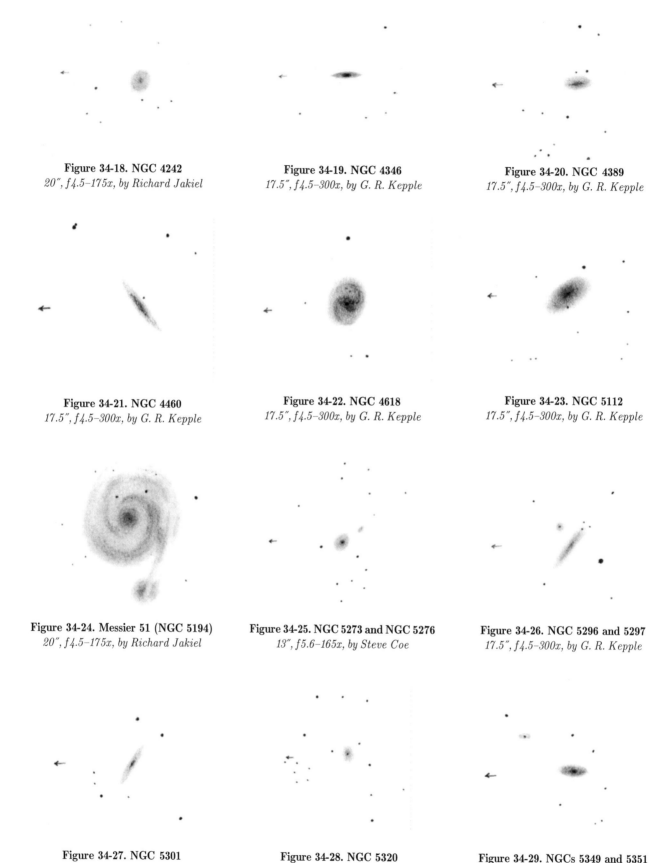

Figure 34-18. NGC 4242
20″, ƒ4.5–175x, by Richard Jakiel

Figure 34-19. NGC 4346
17.5″, ƒ4.5–300x, by G. R. Kepple

Figure 34-20. NGC 4389
17.5″, ƒ4.5–300x, by G. R. Kepple

Figure 34-21. NGC 4460
17.5″, ƒ4.5–300x, by G. R. Kepple

Figure 34-22. NGC 4618
17.5″, ƒ4.5–300x, by G. R. Kepple

Figure 34-23. NGC 5112
17.5″, ƒ4.5–300x, by G. R. Kepple

Figure 34-24. Messier 51 (NGC 5194)
20″, ƒ4.5–175x, by Richard Jakiel

Figure 34-25. NGC 5273 and NGC 5276
13″, ƒ5.6–165x, by Steve Coe

Figure 34-26. NGC 5296 and 5297
17.5″, ƒ4.5–300x, by G. R. Kepple

Figure 34-27. NGC 5301
17.5″, ƒ4.5–300x, by G. R. Kepple

Figure 34-28. NGC 5320
17.5″, ƒ4.5–150x, by G. R. Kepple

Figure 34-29. NGCs 5349 and 5351
17.5″, ƒ4.5–300x, by G. R. Kepple

Way, M51 has a major satellite galaxy, NGC 5195 to its north. Presently it is thought by some professional astronomers that 5195 crossed the south area of 5194 several hundred million years ago and that it is at a distance of between 65,000 and 150,000 light years behind 5194. Other professionals believe several crossings have occurred.

8/10″Scopes–100x: NGC 5194 has a well concentrated, mottled halo that suddenly brightens through the core to a stellar nucleus. The bridge to NGC 5195 is undetectable.

12/14″Scopes–125x: These two objects make an impressive sight! Messier 51 has a large, diffuse $10' \times 7'$ N–S halo containing a well concentrated core. With averted vision, the spiral arms are quite visible, separated by dark swirls north and SW of the core. The spiral arm east and NE of the core is the most prominent. Averted vision is also necessary to see the bridge between M51 and NGC 5195. The latter has a core nearly as bright as, but smaller than, the large spiral's. The halo of the satellite is elongated $5' \times 4'$ N–S and highly variegated. A dark notch is on its SE edge.

16/18″Scopes–150x: Messier 51 is a stunning object. Its $10' \times 7.5'$ NE–SW halo contains a clockwise spiral structure of two arms arcing almost completely around the large, bright core. The brighter arm springs from the south side of the core and curves east, north, west, and finally SW, where it is separated from the core by a fainter arm. The bridge that appears to link the spiral to its NGC 5195 satellite extends to the north tangentially from the bright spiral arm. The two spiral arms are mottled with bright areas and laced through with dark dust lanes. NGC 5195 is 4′ in diameter, as bright as the core of the spiral, and contains a stellar nucleus off-center to the SE. At least ten stars are superimposed upon the halo of M51, the brighter of them on the SW.

NGC 5198 H689[2] Galaxy Type E1-2:
ϕ **2.0′×1.7′, m11.8v, SB12.9**   **13^{h}30.2^m +46° 40′**
Finder Chart 34-5   ★★★

8/10″Scopes–100x: NGC 5198, located 3/4° south of Messier 51, has a faint, circular 1.5′ diameter halo with a faint stellar nucleus.

12/14″Scopes–125x: NGC 5198 appears moderately bright with a circular 2′ diameter halo and a well concentrated core. A 14.5 magnitude star is in the halo west of the core, and a 14th magnitude star lies just outside the halo to the north.

Figure 34-30. *Messier 3 (NGC 5272), a beautiful glittering sphere of stars, is one of the finer globular clusters in the northern hemisphere. Image courtesy of Martin C. Germano.*

NGC 5272 Messier 3 Globular Cluster Class VI
ϕ **16.2′, m5.9v, Br★ 12.7**   **13^{h}42.2^m +28° 23′**
Finder Chart 34-6, Figure 34-30   ★★★★★

Messier 3, discovered in 1764 by Charles Messier, is one of the three brightest globular clusters in the northern hemisphere. This splendid object which has an estimated 45,000 members is a sphere about 130 light years in diameter. Its distance is perhaps 27,000 light years. M3 has an absolute magnitude of −8.7, a luminosity of 260,000 suns.

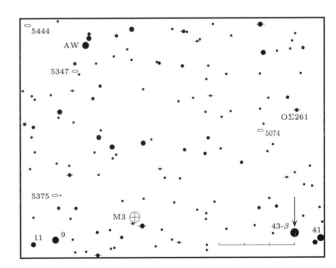

Finder Chart 34-6. 43–β Com: 13^{h}11.8^m +27° 53′

4/6″ Scopes–100x: This globular is a fine sight in small
  telescopes! It is bright, large, and round with a rich
  granular halo growing smoothly brighter to a small
  brilliant core.

8/10″ Scopes–100x: Messier 3 is a beautiful globular
  cluster that rivals Messier 13 in Hercules. It has a
  very bright, large core spanning half of the 10′
  diameter halo which thins gradually to a loose
  periphery of outlying stars. The halo is well resolved
  nearly to the cluster's center.

12/14″ Scopes–125x: Superb! Messier 3 is a glittering
  ball of stars with an extremely bright, rich, oval
  core elongated 5′×4′ NW–SE and surrounded by a
  16′ diameter halo of pinpoint stars. The stars are
  well resolved even across the core, and radiate
  outward from it in curved chains.

NGC 5273 H98[1] Galaxy Type SA(s)0°
ϕ **2.8′×2.4′, m11.6v, SB13.5**   **13^{h}42.1^m +35° 39′**
Finder Chart 34-7, Figure 34-25   ★★★
8/10″ Scopes–100x: NGC 5273, located 18′ WSW of an
  8th magnitude star, is a faint but not inconspicuous
  circular 1′ diameter glow. It grows smoothly
  brighter to a well concentrated core.

12/14″ Scopes–125x: NGC 5273 has a faint stellar
  nucleus in a bright core surrounded by a fainter
  circular 2′ diameter halo. Only 3.5′ SE of NGC 5273
  is NGC 5276, an amorphous smudge requiring
  averted vision.

NGC 5290 H170[1] Galaxy Type Sbc: sp
ϕ **3.3′×0.8′, m12.5v, SB13.4**   **13^{h}45.3^m +41° 43′**
Finder Chart 34-5   ★★
16/18″ Scopes–150x: NGC 5290 has a fairly faint
  2.5′×0.5′ E–W halo containing a poorly concentrated, extended core with a conspicuous stellar

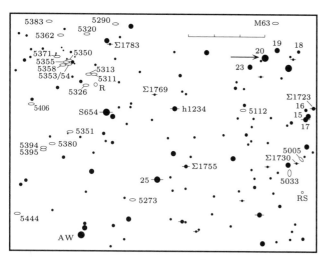

Finder Chart 34-7. 20 CVn: 13^{h}17.5^m +40° 34′

nucleus. 12.5 magnitude stars lie 1.75′ NW and 3′
NNW of the galaxy.

NGC 5297 H180[1] Galaxy Type SAB(s)c: sp I-II
ϕ **5.3′×0.9′, m11.8v, SB13.4**   **13^{h}46.4^m +43° 52′**
Finder Chart 34-5, Figure 34-26   ★★★★
12/14″ Scopes–125x: NGC 5297, located 2′ SW of a 9th
  magnitude star, is a faint 4.5′×0.75′ NW–SE streak
  with a large, smooth core that extends for nearly
  half the length of the halo. A magnitude 11.5 star
  lies 2.5′ NNW of the galaxy's center.

16/18″ Scopes–150x: NGC 5297 is a fine edge-on galaxy
  with an extremely thin 5.5′×1.0′ NNW–SSE halo.
  The well concentrated core is likewise extremely
  thin, being extended 2′×0.75′. Several bright knots
  are near the center. Galaxy NGC 5296 is a very
  faint hazy spot lying 1.5′ SW.

NGC 5301 H688[2] Galaxy Type SA(s)bc: sp II-III
ϕ **3.8′×0.8′, m12.7v, SB13.8**   **13^{h}46.4^m +46° 06′**
Finder Chart 34-5, Figure 34-27   ★★★
12/14″ Scopes–125x: NGC 5301 is a faint galaxy NE of
  a NE–SW pair of 9th magnitude stars 8′ and 12′
  away. To the galaxy's NE, about 10′ distant, are
  three more 9th magnitude stars. NGC 5301 is highly
  elongated 3.25′×1′ NNW–SSE, its diffuse, low surface brightness halo containing a faint nonstellar
  nucleus. 2.5′ SE and 2.75′ SW of the southern tip
  of the axis are two 12th magnitude stars aligned
  perpendicularly to the orientation of the axis.

NGC 5311 H710[2] Galaxy Type S0/a
ϕ **2.0′×1.6′, m12.3v, SB13.4**   **13^{h}49.0^m +40° 00′**

NGC 5313 H711[2] Galaxy Type Sb? II
ϕ **1.5′×0.8′, m12.0v, SB12.1**   **13^{h}49.7^m +39° 59′**
Finder Chart 34-7   ★/★★
12/14″ Scopes–125x: NGC 5311 and NGC 5313 are an
  E–W pair of faint galaxies. The easternmost of the
  two, NGC 5313, is the more conspicuous. It has a
  faint 1.5′×0.75′ NE–SW halo within which a diffuse
  core extended along the halo's major axis contains
  a very faint stellar nucleus. NGC 5311 to its west
  is much fainter and smaller, though its circular 30″
  diameter halo also contains a stellar nucleus. A 10th
  magnitude star lies between the two galaxies 3′ east
  of NGC 5311. 8′ SSE is a wide pair of 12th magnitude
  stars.

NGC 5320 H669[2] Galaxy Type SAB(rs)c:
ϕ **3.3′×1.7′, m12.1v, SB13.8**   **13^{h}50.3^m +41° 22′**
Finder Chart 34-7, Figure 34-28   ★★
16/18″ Scopes–150x: NGC 5320 has a faint 2′×1′

Figure 34-31. *NGC 5350 is the largest object in a nice group of five galaxies including the close interacting pair of NGC 5353 and NGC 5354. Image courtesy of Jim Burnell.*

NNE–SSW halo that gradually brightens to its center and a very faint stellar nucleus discernible only with averted vision. 11.5 magnitude stars are 3′ ESE and 3.75′ NE of the galaxy.

NGC 5326 H712² Galaxy Type SAa:
ϕ **2.0′×0.9′, m11.9v, SB12.4**   **13^{h}50.8^m +39° 34′**
Finder Chart 34-7   ★★★
12/14″ Scopes–125x: NGC 5326 lies 7′ SW of an E–W row of three stars of the 7th, 10th, and 9th magnitudes. The galaxy has a very faint 2′×0.75′ NW–SE envelope containing a well concentrated, extended core with a stellar nucleus. Another 10th magnitude star lies 3′ SSW.

NGC 5347 H424² Galaxy Type (R′)SB(rs)ab II
ϕ **1.6′×1.3′, m12.6v, SB13.3**   **13^{h}53.3^m +33° 29′**
Finder Chart 34-6   ★★★
12/14″ Scopes–125x: NGC 5347 is a faint target situated 21′ south of a 7th magnitude and 12′ NE of an 8th magnitude star. It is a faint haze elongated 1.25′×0.75′ NW–SE with a slightly brighter center. A 10th magnitude star lies 3.5′ NE.

NGC 5351 H697² Galaxy Type SA(r)b: I-II
ϕ **2.7′×1.5′, m12.1v, SB13.4**   **13^{h}53.5^m +37° 55′**
Finder Chart 34-7, Figure 34-29   ★★
12/14″ Scopes–125x: NGC 5351 has a very faint, diffuse, oval halo elongated 1.5′×1′ ESE-WNW containing an extended core with a faint stellar nucleus. A 9th magnitude star lies 5′ SE, and a 13th magnitude star is 2′ south. Only 3.5′ SW of NGC 5351 is NGC 5349, a faint 30″×15″ E–W oval with a stellar nucleus.

NGC 5350 H713² Galaxy Type SB(r)b I-II
ϕ **3.1′×2.5′, m11.3v, SB13.4**   **13^{h}53.4^m +40° 22′**
Finder Chart 34-7, Figure 34-31   ★★★
8/10″ Scopes–100x: NGC 5350 is the northernmost and largest in a galaxy group with NGC 5353-54, NGC 5355, and NGC 5358. It is located just 3′ NE of an orange 6.5 magnitude star, and has a fairly faint, diffuse 1.5′×1.25′ NNE–SSW halo that becomes slightly brighter toward its center. A 10th magnitude star lies 3.5′ to its NE.
12/14″ Scopes–125x: NGC 5350 shows a very faint bar-like core elongated ESE–WNW surrounded by a

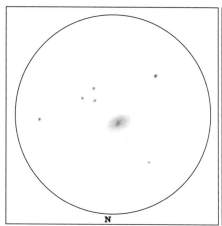

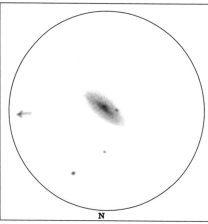

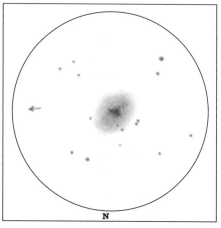

Figure 34-32. NGC 5375
17.5″, f4.5–250x, by G. R. Kepple

Figure 34-33. NGC 5377
17.5″, f4.5–250x, by G. R. Kepple

Figure 34-34. NGC 5383
17.5″, f4.5–250x, by G. R. Kepple

faint, diffuse 2.5′ × 1.5′ NNE–SSW halo. NGC 5353-54 make a fine pair 3′ to 5′ SSE.

NGC 5353 H714[2] Galaxy Type S0
φ 2.8′ × 1.9′, m11.0v, SB 12.7   13ʰ53.5ᵐ +40° 17′

NGC 5354 H715[2] Galaxy Type SA(r)b: I-II
φ 2.2′ × 2.0′, m11.4v, SB 12.8   13ʰ53.5ᵐ +40° 18′
Finder Chart 34-7, Figure 34-31   ★★★/★★★
8/10″Scopes–125x: NGC 5353 and NGC 5354 are an interacting close galaxy pair centered 4.5′ SE of a magnitude 6.5 star on the southern edge of the compact NGC 5350 galaxy group. NGC 5350 itself is only 3′ to the north, and two faint members of the group, NGC 5355 and NGC 5358, are 5′ NE and 6.5′ east, respectively. NGC 5353 and NGC 5354 are aligned N–S, their halos nearly in contact. The brighter of the two is the southern galaxy, NGC 5353, which has a fairly bright, strongly elongated 1.5′ × 0.75′ NNW–SSE lens-shaped halo slightly brighter in its center. NGC 5354 to its north is a little fainter and slightly smaller: its circular 1.25′ diameter halo has a stellar nucleus.
12/14″Scopes–150x: NGC 5353 and NGC 5354 are a galaxy pair with contrasting shapes. The southern galaxy, NGC 5353, is a bright lens-shaped lenticular S0 galaxy: its halo is highly elongated 2′ × 1′ NNW–SSE and contains an extended oval core with a stellar nucleus. NGC 5354, which touches the northern tip of the halo of NGC 5353, is, by contrast, a spiral galaxy, viewed face-on: consequently its halo, which contains a stellar nucleus, is circular, a fairly bright 1.5′ diameter disc.

NGC 5355 H699[3] Galaxy Type S0?
φ 1.2′ × 0.7′, m13.1v, SB 12.8   13ʰ53.8ᵐ +40° 21′
Finder Chart 34-7, Figure 34-31   ★★
8/10″Scopes–100x: NGC 5355 is a very faint, round glow no larger than 30″ containing a very faint stellar nucleus. It is 7.5′ east of a 6.5 magnitude orange star in a group of galaxies with NGC 5350, NGC 5353-54, and NGC 5358.
12/14″Scopes–125x: In medium-size telescopes NGC 5355 has a faint 1.5′ × 1′ NNE–SSW halo with a faint stellar nucleus. A wide N–S pair of 13th and 14th magnitude stars is halfway between this galaxy and NGC 5354 to its west.

NGC 5358 Galaxy Type S0/a
φ 1.2′ × 0.3′, m13.6v, SB 12.3   13ʰ54.1ᵐ +40° 17′
Finder Chart 34-7, Figure 34-31   ★
12/14″Scopes–150x: NGC 5358 lies at the SE edge of a small galaxy group that includes NGC 5350, NGC 5353-54, and NGC 5355. It is visible as a very faint 45″ × 30″ NW–SE smudge with a stellar nucleus. A NE–SW pair of 12.5 magnitude stars lies 1.25′ SW of the galaxy's center.

NGC 5362 H671[2] Galaxy Type Sb? pec
φ 2.2′ × 0.9′, m12.3v, SB 12.9   13ʰ54.9ᵐ +41° 19′
Finder Chart 34-7   ★★
12/14″Scopes–125x: NGC 5362, located 19′ SSE of an 8th magnitude star, has a very faint, diffuse halo elongated 1.5′ × 0.5′ E–W. 150x reveals a very faint stellar nucleus and a faint star 1.5′ ESE.

Figure 34-35. *In medium-size telescopes NGC 5371 shows a faint core with a stellar nucleus surrounded by a faint halo. Image courtesy of Bill McLaughlin.*

Figure 34-36. *NGC 5395 has a fairly bright core and halo. Faint interacting companion NGC 5394 is on its NNW edge. Alexander Brownlee made this 60 minute exposure on 2415 film with a 16", f5 Newtonian reflector.*

NGC 5371 H716[2] Galaxy Type SAB(rs)bc I
ϕ 4.1′×3.2′, m10.6v, SB13.3   13^{h}55.7^m +40° 28′
Finder Chart 34-7, Figure 34-35   ★★★
8/10″Scopes–100x: NGC 5371 is at the SSW vertex of an obtuse triangle with two 9th magnitude stars 2.5′ NE and 5′ NNE from its center. Its halo is faint, diffuse, elongated 3.5′×2′ N–S, and slightly brighter in its center.
12/14″Scopes–125x: NGC 5371 has a fairly faint halo elongated 4′×2.5′ NNE–SSW. 150x reveals within the halo a faint, tiny core containing a stellar nucleus. The core has a slightly granular texture.

NGC 5377 H187[1] Galaxy Type (R)SB(s)a
ϕ 4.1′×2.3′, m11.3v, SB13.6   13^{h}56.3^m +47° 14′
Finder Chart 34-5, Figure 34-33   ★★★
8/10″Scopes–100x: This galaxy has a fairly faint 2.5′×0.5′ NNE–SSW halo containing a bright oval core with a stellar nucleus.
12/14″Scopes–125x: NGC 5377 displays a bright nonstellar nucleus in an extended core surrounded by a much fainter halo elongated 3′×0.75′ NNE–SSW. A 13th magnitude star lies 40″ NE of the galaxy's center.

NGC 5375 Galaxy Type SB(r)ab
ϕ 3.2′×2.5′, m11.5v, SB13.6   13^{h}56.8^m +29° 10′
Finder Chart 34-6, Figure 34-32   ★★
16/18″Scopes–150x: NGC 5375, located 9′ east of a 9.5 magnitude star, has a faint 30″ diameter core containing a very faint stellar nucleus, the core embedded in a very faint, diffuse 2.5′×2′ N–S halo. The immediate star field is rather barren except for a 2′ wide triangle of 11.5 magnitude stars centered 5′ WSW.

NGC 5380 H698[2] Galaxy Type SA0–
ϕ 1.8′×1.8′, m12.3v, SB13.4   13^{h}56.9^m +37° 37′
Finder Chart 34-7   ★★
12/14″Scopes–125x: NGC 5380 is 10′ south of an 8th magnitude star. It has a nonstellar nucleus embedded in a round, faint 1′ diameter halo. A 13th magnitude star is 1.75′ NE, and a 12th magnitude star 4.5′ NE, of the galaxy.

NGC 5383 H181[1] Galaxy Type (R′)SB(rs)b: pec II
ϕ 3.2′×2.2′, m11.4v, SB13.4   13^{h}57.1^m +41° 51′
Finder Chart 34-7, Figure 34-34   ★★★
8/10″Scopes–100x: NGC 5383 is a rather faint object with a diffuse envelope elongated about 2′×1′ NW–SE. 3′ to its SE is a wide NW–SE pair of 12th and 13th magnitude stars. Two more 13th magnitude stars are 3′ NNW and 4′ ENE of the galaxy. A close NW–SE pair of 14th magnitude stars parallels the NE periphery of the galaxy's halo just 1′ from its edge.
12/14″Scopes–125x: NGC 5383 has a fairly faint halo elongated 3′×2′ NW–SE containing a variegated, highly irregular core with a stellar nucleus. Two threshold stars are embedded on the northern edge of the galaxy.

NGC 5394 H191[1] Galaxy Type SB(s)b pec I-II
ϕ 1.7′×0.7′, m13.0v, SB13.0   13^{h}58.6^m +37° 27′

NGC 5395 H190[1] Galaxy Type SA(s)b pec I-II
ϕ 2.7′×1.2′, m11.4v, SB12.5   13^{h}58.6^m +37° 25′
Finder Chart 34-7, Figure 34-36   ★/★★★
8/10″Scopes–100x: NGC 5395 and NGC 5394 are a

NNW–SSE pair of physically interacting galaxies. NGC 5395, the SSE component, is the larger and brighter, its 1.5′×1′ N–S halo slightly brighter in the center. A 13th magnitude star is 1.5′ to its south, and two 14th magnitude stars are the same distance to its north and NW. NGC 5394, centered 2′ NNW of the main galaxy, is a faint, nearly stellar object flanked by the two 14th magnitude stars.

12/14″ Scopes–125x: NGC 5395 has a fairly bright 2′×1′ NNW–SSE halo with a well concentrated core. NGC 5394 is a faint, 30″ diameter spot.

NGC 5406 H699^2 Galaxy Type SAB(rs)bc I-II
ϕ **1.7′×1.3′, m12.3v, SB 13.0   14^{h}00.3^m +38° 55′**
Finder Chart 34-7   ★★
12/14″ Scopes–125x: NGC 5406, located 7′ due south of a 7th magnitude star, is a faint, 1.5′ diameter glow

slightly elongated ESE–WNW containing a faint stellar nucleus. The immediately surrounding star field is nearly blank.

NGC 5444 H417^2 Galaxy Type E+:
ϕ **2.5′×2.1′, m11.8v, SB 13.5   14^{h}03.4^m +35° 08′**
Finder Chart 34-7   ★★★
12/14″ Scopes–125x: NGC 5444 is located in a field barren of background stars. It has a moderately bright, tiny core embedded in a faint 1.5′×1′ NE–SW halo. Galaxy 5445, located 7′ south of NGC 5444, has a fairly conspicuous 1.5′×0.5′ NNE–SSW halo. A magnitude 11.5 star is just west of the latter galaxy's SSW tip.

Chapter 35

Capricornus, the Horned Sea Goat

35.1 Overview

Capricornus, the Horned Goat, is the tenth constellation of the Zodiac. Despite its name, the Greeks and Romans always figured it as a composite monster with the head and front legs of a goat and the hindquarters of a fish. In Greek mythology, Capricornus represents the goat-footed god Pan, who, when chased by the wind monster Typhon, leapt into the Nile to escape and in mid-leap was changed into a goat-headed fish. But this story was just the Greek mythographers's effort to explain a figure that was already in their heavens; for the Greeks had inherited the celestial goat-fish from Babylonia, where it had been sacred to the god of fresh waters, Enki. The constellation seems to have made a rather late appearance in the ancient Mesopotamian sky, however, for the figure of the goat-fish does not appear in Babylonian art until after 2100 B.C.

Though Capricornus is immediately east of the rich Milky Way constellation of Sagittarius, and though it occupies a respectable 414 square degrees of sky, it is surprisingly sparse in deep sky objects, even in galaxies. The Alpha-Beta Capricorni region has several splendid double and multiple stars for binoculars and small telescopes, and in wide-field eyepieces almost looks like a loose open cluster. But otherwise Capricornus boasts only the globular cluster M30.

35.2 Interesting Stars

Alpha ($\alpha^1 = 5 / \alpha^2 = 6$) Capricorni   Spec. G9, G3
m3.6,4.2; Sep.378″; P.A.291°   20^{h}18.1^m −12° 33′
Constellation Chart 35-1 Al Giedi, "The Goat" ★★★★

Alpha-1 (α^1) and Alpha-2 (α^2) Capricorni are an extremely wide naked eye double at the NW corner of Capricornus' rather conspicuous boat-shaped outline. The two stars are in fact only an optical pair, the magnitude 3.56 Alpha-1 being only 100 light years distant and the magnitude 4.24 Alpha-2 500 light years away. However, both stars have a rich yellowish-orange

color, and both are true binaries with faint companions that can be resolved in small telescopes (See Table 35-2). The absolute magnitudes of Alpha-1 and Alpha-2 Capricorni are respectively +1.1 and −1.7, luminosities of about 30 and 400 suns.

4/6″ Scopes–75x: Very nice! Alpha Capricorni is a wide double-double, though the secondaries are rather fainter than the primaries. Both primaries have an attractive yellow color. The companion of Alpha-1 is a reddish star.

Sigma (σ) = 7 Capricorni (H V 87) Double Star Spec. K4
m5.5,9.0; Sep.55.9″; P.A.179°   20^{h}19.4^m −19° 07′
Finder Chart 35-3 ★★★★

4/6″ Scopes–75x: Sigma Capricorni has a deep yellow primary with a pale blue companion.

Beta (β) = 9 Capricorni (ΣI 52) Triple Star Spec. K0 B9
AB: m3.4,6.2; Sep.205.3″; P.A.267° 20^{h}21.0^m −14° 47′
Constellation Chart 35-1   Dabih ★★★★

4/6″ Scopes–75x: Beta Capricorni is a wide triple for binoculars and small telescopes. The yellow primary contrasts nicely with the bluish secondary. The 9th magnitude third component also appears yellowish. A faint 13th magnitude pair with a separation of 6″ is nestled between the wide components.

Capricornus: KAP-ri-kor-nus
Genitive: Capricorni, KAP-ri-kor-ni
Abbreviation: Cap
Culmination: 9pm–Sept. 22, midnight–Aug. 8
Area: 414 square degrees
Showpieces: M30 (NGC 7099)
Binocular Objects: $\alpha^{1,2}$ Cap, $\beta^{1,2}$ Cap, 11–ϱ Cap, 39–ϵ Cap, M30, (NGC 7099)

Capricornus, the Horned Sea Goat Constellation Chart 35-1

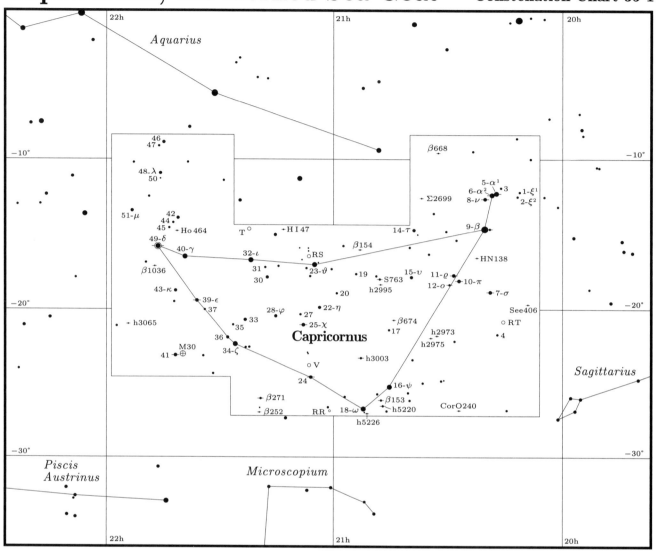

Chart Symbols

Constellation Chart

Stellar Magnitudes   ● ● ● ● ● ● · ·   0 1 2 3 4 5 6

Finder Charts   0/1 2 3 4 5 6 7 8 9

Master Finder Chart   0 1 2 3 4 5

→ Guide Star Pointer

●—● Double Stars

Finder Chart Scale
(One degree tick marks)

◉ ○ Variable Stars

◯ Open Clusters

⊕ Globular Clusters

⬭ Galaxies

⊕ Planetary Nebulae

☐ Small Bright Nebulae

Large Bright Nebulae

Dark Nebulae

Table 35-1: Selected Variable Stars in Capricornus

Name	HD No.	Type	Max.	Min.	Period (Days)	F*	Spec. Type	R.A. (2000) Dec.		Finder Chart No. Notes
RR Cap	200128	M	7.8	15.5	277	0.40	M5-M8	21h02.3m	−27° 05′	35-3
RS Cap	200994	SRb	8.3	10.3	340		M4	07.2	−16 25	35-4
V Cap	201015	M	8.2	14.4	275	0.42	M5-M8	07.6	−23 55	35-4
T Cap	203349	M	8.4	14.3	269	0.44	M2-M8	22.0	−15 10	35-1
49-δ Cap	207098	EA	2.81	3.05	1.02	0.08	A7	47.0	−16 08	35-4

F* = The fraction of period taken up by the star's rise from min. to max. brightness, or the period spent in eclipse.

Table 35-2: Selected Double Stars in Capricornus

Name	ADS No.	Pair	M1	M2	Sep.*	P.A.°	Spec	R.A. (2000)	Dec.	Finder Chart No.	Notes
See 406			7.9	10.8	2.7	1		20h07.3m	−19° 35′	35-1	
5–α¹ Cap	13632	AB	4.2	13.7	44.3	182	G3	17.6	−12 30	35-1	
	13632	AC	4.2	9.2	45.4	221					
	13632	AD		13.9	29.3	290					
6–α² Cap	13645	AB	3.6	11.0	6.6	172	G3	18.1	−12 33	35-1	Yellow and reddish
	13645	AD		9.3	154.6	156					
	13645	BC		11.3	1.2	240					
α², α¹ Cap	13645		3.6	4.2	377.7	291	G9 G3	18.1	−12 33	35-1	Bright golden stars
7–σ Cap	13675		5.5	9.0	55.9	179	K4	19.4	−19 07	35-3	
8–ν Cap	13714		4.8	11.8	54.1	211	A0	20.7	−12 46	35-1	
9–β¹,²		AB	3.4	6.2	205.3	267	K0 B9	21.0	−14 47	35-1	Brilliant yellow and white
		AC		9.0	226.6	134	F8				
HN138	13751		8.5	9.0	3.0	330	G5	22.2	−16 47	35-1	
10–π Cap	13860	AB	5.3	8.9	3.2	v148	B8	27.3	−18 13	35-3	Fine white pair
11–ϱ Cap	13887	AD	5.0	6.7	247.6	150	F0 K0	28.9	−17 49	35-3	Bright yellow and orange
CorO240	13896		8.2	10.0	6.9	21	F0	29.6	−27 19	35-3	
12–o Cap	13902		6.1	6.6	21.9	239	A2 A3	29.9	−18 35	35-3	Pale yellowish pair
h2973			7.8	8.4	39.3	129	F0 F0	32.2	−22 09	35-3	
β 668	13960	AB	5.7	11.2	2.9	29	G5	32.4	−09 51	35-1	
	13960	AC		9.9	103.2	200					
h2975	13988		7.4	12.0	9.8	23	F8	33.5	−22 14	35-3	
Σ 2699	14054	AB	8.1	9.1	9.5	195	F0	36.9	−12 44	35-1	
β 674	14218		7.7	10.0	1.6	99	K0	44.8	−20 54	35-3	
h5220	14258		7.0	9.2	18.0	354	F2	46.5	−26 52	35-3	
β 153	14280		7.3	9.1	1.6	265	A2	47.3	−26 25	35-3	
h2995			8.1	11.1	20.0	284	G0	47.4	−18 37	35-3	
S763	14299	AB	6.7	8.6	15.8	294	G5	48.4	−18 12	35-3	
		CD	10.3	10.5	9.4	159					
h5226	14335		7.0	9.0	18.6	68	K0 K	50.1	−27 22	35-3	
β 154	14377		8.3	9.6	2.8	61	G5	52.8	−16 09	35-1	
h3003	14380		6.3	8.5	1.7	206	G5	53.0	−23 47	35-3	
24 Cap	14632		4.6	11.7	26.2	186	M1	21h07.1m	−25 00	35-3	
25–χ Cap		AB	5.3	11.0	67.0	66	A0	08.6	−21 12	35-4	
		Bb		12.2	18.2	89					
HI47	14736		8.0	8.0	3.7	313	G5	12.3	−15 00	35-1	
β 271	14847		6.6	9.5	3.2	255	G4	19.8	−26 21	35-1	Yellow and white
β 252	14852		8.0	8.1	2.4	94	G5	20.1	−27 19	35-1	
39–ε Cap			4.7	9.5	68.1	47	B5	37.1	−19 28	35-4	
Ho 464	15216		7.1	11.4	17.5	104	F0	41.5	−14 50	35-1	
41 Cap	15223		5.3	11.5	5.5	205	G9	42.0	−23 16	35-4	
β 1036	15325		7.3	10.3	4.7	206	B9	47.6	−17 18	35-4	
h3065		AB	7.2	11.5	39.6	133	M3	55.6	−21 08	35-4	
		AC		10.0	57.6	149					

Footnotes: *= Year 2000, a = Near apogee, c = Closing, w = Widening. Finder Chart No: All stars listed in the tables are plotted in the large Constellation Chart, but when a star appears in a Finder Chart, this number is listed. Notes: When colors are subtle, the suffix *-ish* is used, e.g. *bluish*.

Pi (π) = 10 Capricorni (β 60) Triple Star   Spec. B8
AB: m5.3, 8.9; Sep. 3.2″; P.A. 148°   20h27.3m −18° 13′
Finder Chart 35-3   ★★★★
8/10″ Scopes–200x: Pi Capricorni is a close pair of white and blue stars.

Rho (ϱ) = 11 Capricorni Quadruple Star Spec. F0 K0
AD: m5.0, 6.7; Sep. 247.6″; P.A. 150° 20h28.9m −17° 49′
Finder Chart 35-3   ★★★★
4/6″ Scopes–75x: Quite nice in binoculars and small

telescopes, Rho Capricorni is a very wide, colorful pair of yellow and purplish stars.

Omicron (o) = 12 Capricorni Double Star Spec. A2, A3
m6.1, 6.6; Sep. 21.9″; P.A. 239°   20h29.9m −18° 35′
Finder Chart 35-3   ★★★★
4/6″ Scopes–75x: Omicron Capricorni is a beautiful double of bright bluish-white and blue stars easily separated in small telescopes.

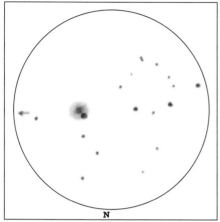

Figure 35-1. NGC 6903
16″, f5–200x, by G. R. Kepple

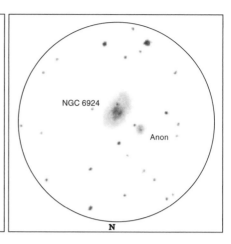

Figure 35-2. NGC 6907
13″, f4.5–165x, by Tom Polakis

Figure 35-3. NGC 6924
16″, f5–200x, by G. R. Kepple

β 271 Double Star   **Spec. G4**
m6.6,9.5; Sep.3.2″; P.A.255°   **21ʰ19.8ᵐ −26° 21′**
Constellation Chart 35-1   ★★★★
4/6″Scopes–150x: Burnham 271 is a close color-contrast pair with a deep yellow primary and a white secondary. The duo dominates a rather rich field of faint stars.

35.3 Deep-Sky Objects

NGC 6903 Galaxy Type S0? pec
φ 2.1′ × 1.9′, m11.9v, SB13.3   **20ʰ23.6ᵐ −19° 19′**
Finder Chart 35-3, Figure 35-1   ★★★
16/18″Scopes–150x: NGC 6903 has a faint, circular 1.5′

diameter halo with a bright core. The glare of a magnitude 10.5 star superimposed on the galaxy 35″ NE of its center interferes with the view. A 13th magnitude star is 1′ north of the galaxy. To the ESE the field is well sprinkled with faint stars, including a chain of 12th magnitude stars spaced 1.75′ to 2′ apart.

NGC 6907 H141³ Galaxy Type SB(rs)bc pec II
φ 3.2′×2.3′, m11.1v, SB13.1   **20ʰ25.1ᵐ −24° 49′**
Finder Chart 35-3, Figure 35-2   ★★★
8/10″Scopes–100x: NGC 6907 is a very faint, diffuse, circular 1′ diameter glow.
12/14″Scopes–125x: The halo appears fairly faint, elongated 1.75′×1.25′ E–W, and moderately concentrated toward the core, in which is a stellar

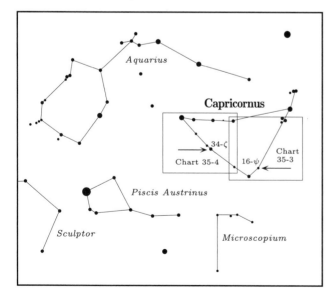

Master Finder Chart 35-2. Capricornus Chart Areas
Guide stars indicated by arrows

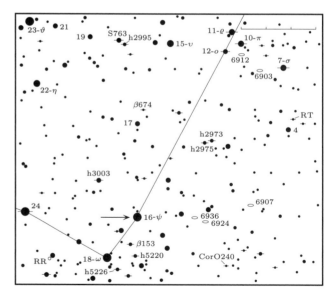

Finder Chart 35-3. 16–ψ Cap: 20ʰ46.1ᵐ +25° 16′

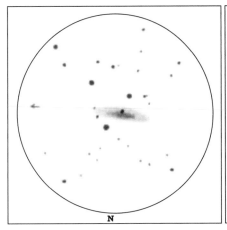

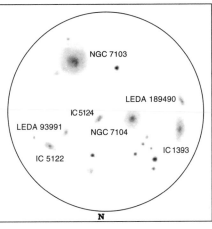

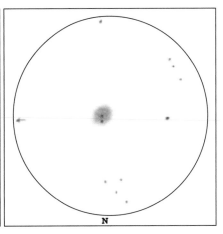

Figure 35-4. IC 5078
16″, f5–200x, by G. R. Kepple

Figure 35-5. NGC 7103 Area
16″, f5–200x, by G. R. Kepple

Figure 35-6. Palomar 12
16″, f5–150x, by Glen W. Sanner

nucleus. An 11th magnitude star is 3.25′ south. Between the star and the galaxy is an ENE–WSW pair of 13th magnitude stars. 2′ west of the 11th magnitude star is a NW–SE 12th magnitude pair. An 11.5 magnitude star is 2.75′ due east of the galaxy.

16/18″Scopes–150x: In larger instruments NGC 6907 appears fairly bright. It has a 3′ diameter halo containing an ENE–WSW bar-like inner region. A spiral arm extending from the east end of the bar curves northward and has a knot near its end. The northern area of the inner halo is more diffuse and does not display an arm. A 14.5 magnitude star nearly touches the bar's west edge.

NGC 6912 Galaxy Type SB(s)c I
ϕ **1.2′×0.9′, m13.6v, SB13.5**   **20ʰ26.9ᵐ −18° 38′**
Finder Chart 35-3   ★★

12/14″Scopes–125x: NGC 6912 is 24′ SSW of the double star Pi (π) = 10 Capricorni (5.3, 8.9; 3.2″; 148°). It is a faint, diffuse, circular 1′ diameter glow. Two faint stars are 2′, and two magnitude 9.5 stars 7′, NE of the galaxy.

NGC 6924 Galaxy Type SA(s)0−:
ϕ **1.7′×1.4′, m12.4v, SB13.2**   **20ʰ33.2ᵐ −25° 30′**
Finder Chart 35-3, Figure 35-3   ★★

16/18″Scopes–150x: NGC 6924, located 2′ NNW of a 9th magnitude star, has a fairly faint, slightly oval, 1.5′×1.25′ NW–SE halo with a bright center. A 13th magnitude star is embedded 20″ south of the galaxy's center. Just 1′ NE of NGC 6924 is an extremely faint anonymous companion galaxy: it appears stellar, and is just 15″ NE of a 13th magnitude star which is in a 7.5′ long NW–SE line of four magnitude 12.5 to 13 stars.

NGC 6936 Galaxy Type SA0− sp:
ϕ **1.6′×1.0′, m12.8v, SB13.2**   **20ʰ35.9ᵐ −25° 17′**
Finder Chart 35-3   ★★

16/18″Scopes–150x: NGC 6936 is 4′ NNW of a 10th magnitude star, the southernmost object in a 3.5′ NNE–SSW arc of three stars, the other two of the 11th and 12th magnitudes. The galaxy has a fairly faint 1′×0.5′ N–S oval halo containing a small, bright core. A 13th magnitude star lies 1.25′ SW.

IC 5078 Galaxy Type?
ϕ **4.1′×1.1′, m12.7v**   **21ʰ02.6ᵐ −16° 49′**
Finder Chart 35-4, Figure 35-4   ★★

16/18″Scopes–150x: IC 5078, located 50′ NW of the magnitude 4.1 Theta (ϑ) = 23 Capricorni, is on the NE side of a 2.5′×1.75′ triangle of four 10th and 11th magnitude stars. The star at the midpoint of

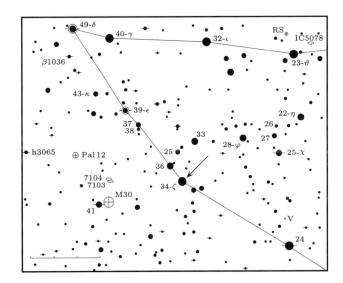

Finder Chart 35-4. 34–ζ Cap: 21ʰ26.7ᵐ −22° 25′

Figure 35-7. *Messier 30 (NGC 7099) is an incredible swarm displaying a myriad of stellar points twinkling in and out of resolution. Image courtesy of Martin C. Germano.*

the NE side of the triangle is superimposed upon the galaxy's halo just south of its center and makes observation difficult. The halo is very faint, elongated 3′×0.5′ E–W, and contains a faint, extended core. 40% of the galaxy is within the triangle, 60% of it extending outside the triangle to the east. This galaxy is not plotted in *Sky Atlas 2000*.

NGC 7103 Galaxy Type E+1
φ 1.4′×1.2′, m12.6v, SB13.0   21ʰ39.9ᵐ −22° 28′

NGC 7104 Galaxy Type E0 pec:
φ 0.6′×0.5′, m14.4v, SB12.9   21ʰ40.1ᵐ −22° 25′
Finder Chart 35-4, Figure 35-5   ★★/★
16/18″Scopes–150x: NGC 7103 is the most conspicuous member in a cluster of faint galaxies. Its faint, circular 1′ diameter halo is slightly elongated ENE–WSW and has a faint core. A 14th magnitude star or stellar companion galaxy is 50″ WNW and a threshold star is 1′ south. A 12th magnitude star lies 2′ ENE. Most of the other members of the NGC 7103 group lie along an E–W arc, concave to the north, that extends from the NE to the north of the main galaxy. NGC 7104, located 4′ NE of NGC 7103, has a circular 30′ diameter halo with a small faint core. 2.5′ ENE of NGC 7104, at the east end of the galaxy-arc, is IC 1393, merely a very faint 20″×15″ N–S smudge. Just beyond the southern tip

of IC 1393 is LEDA 189490, an extremely faint galaxy. 4′ WNW of NGC 7104, at the galaxy-arc's west end, is IC 5122, a very faint 20″×10″ ENE–WSW glow. Between IC 5122 and NGC 7104 two galaxies can be seen with averted vision as extremely faint, stellar spots, they are LEDA 93991 and IC 5124.

NGC 7099 Messier 30 Globular Cluster Class V
φ 11′, m7.3v, Br★ 12.1v   21ʰ40.4ᵐ −23° 11′
Finder Chart 35-4, Figure 35-7   ★★★★★
Discovered by Charles Messier in August 1764, this globular lies 26,700 light years away.
8/10″Scopes–100x: Messier 30, located 6′ east of an 8th magnitude star, is a bright, 4′ diameter globular cluster with a broad central blaze of unresolved stars. The periphery is irregular and very loose, outlying stars being visible to 2.5′ from the cluster center.
12/14″Scopes–125x: Messier 30 is a swarm of stellar points twinkling in and out of resolution. The core is broad and bright and surrounded by an irregular outer area of glittering stars in numerous star chains, the most prominent of which extend north and NW from the cluster core.
16/18″Scopes–150x: This fine globular cluster is a bright, well resolved 6′ diameter disk of minute stellar points. It is distinctly elongated E–W, implying that the globular may be flattened by rotation. The star density increases dramatically as the center is approached, culminated in a congested 3.5′ diameter core of star-specks. The outer halo extends to a radius of at least 5′ from the cluster center, reaching on the west almost to an 8th magnitude field star 6′ from the center. The halo is filled with numerous star chains.

Palomar 12 Globular Cluster Class XII
φ 2.9′, m11.7v, Br★ 14.6v   21ʰ46.5ᵐ −21° 14′
Finder Chart 35-4, Figure 35-6   ★
8/10″Scopes–125x: Palomar 12 is situated just NNW of a compact triangle of 10th magnitude stars and 6′ SW of a fourth 10th magnitude star. It is visible only under exceptionally good skies, and appears merely as an extremely faint, small, round and unresolved haze.
16/18″Scopes–175x: Even in larger telescopes Palomar 12 remains faint, diffuse, and elusive. With averted vision it can be seen as a 2′ diameter object with a few faint stars resolved against a background glow.

Chapter 36

Centaurus, the Centaur

36.1 Overview

In classical mythology the Centaurs were composite creatures with the bodies of horses but the upper torsos, arms, and heads of men. Their dispositions were as monstrous as their construction. Two or three ancient legends narrate their origin. One story relates that the god Cronos, father and predecessor of Zeus as paramount deity in the pantheon, attempted to conceal an illicit affair with the sea nymph Phylira from his jealous and suspicious wife Rhea by changing himself into a horse whenever he visited his paramour: hence the issue of their clandestine passion were creatures that were in form partly horse and partly human. According to another ancient myth, Ixion, the deity symbolizing the scorching midday Sun, conceived a great lust for Juno, Jupiter's wife. To protect his spouse from Ixion, Jupiter formed a cloud in her image; the result of Ixion's sexual liaison with this cloud were the Centaurs.

The constellation Centaurus represents the one mild-mannered Centaur, Chiron, famed for his abilities in music, poetry, mathematics, and medicine. Chiron was said to have invented the constellations to assist his pupil, Jason, and the Argonauts in their voyage after the Golden Fleece. He also was the tutor of Hercules: after one of the latter's poisoned arrows accidently wounded him Chiron renounced his earthly immortality in favor of Prometheus, creator of fire, and was rewarded by Jupiter instead with immortality in the heavens as the constellation of the Centaur.

The constellation Centaurus seems to be an early Greek invention. But the image of the Centaur was not, for Centaurs had been common in Babylonian and Assyrian art before about 1200 B.C. The Greek myths about the Centaurs were therefore the mythographers' efforts to explain the origins of a strange composite monster figure which they found already current in the general culture of the eastern Mediterranean.

Centaurus is a large and rich constellation. The creature's hooves are in the Milky Way, and between its fore hooves and back hooves is the brilliant Crux,

---

Centaurus: Sen-TORE-us
Genitive: Centauri, Sen-TORE-i
Abbreviation: Cen
Culmination: 9pm–May 14, midnight–Mar. 30
Area: 1,060 square degrees
Showpieces: NGC 5128 (Centaurus A), NGC 5139 (Omega Centauri)
Binocular Objects: NGC 5128 (Centaurus A), NGC 5139 (Omega Centauri)

---

the Southern Cross. Unfortunately all this, and the bright star-pair Alpha (α) and Beta (β) Centauri, are too far south for observers in Europe and the United States. Nevertheless northern Centaurus, accessible from the southern U.S., is rich in galaxies, including the large, bright, rifted NGC 5128, one of the strangest radio sources in the sky. NGC 5128 is the largest and brightest member of a galaxy group that extends north from Centaurus into eastern Hydra and southern Virgo. Centaurus has two globular clusters, including the great Omega Centauri, finest in the entire heavens.

36.2 Interesting Stars

Herschel 4423 Double Star Spec. F2
m6.9, 7.2; Sep. 2.4″, P.A. 276° $11^h16.5^m$ $-45°\,53'$
Constellation Chart 36-1 ★★★★
4/6″ Scopes–150x: Herschel 4423 is an attractive pair of yellowish stars dominating a rather sparse star field.

Rumker 14 Double Star Spec. M0
m5.6, 6.8; Sep. 2.9″, P.A. 244° $12^h14.0^m$ $-45°\,43'$
Constellation Chart 36-1 ★★★★
4/6″ Scopes–150x: Rumker 14 is a close but pretty pair of orange and yellow stars.

Centaurus, the Centaur

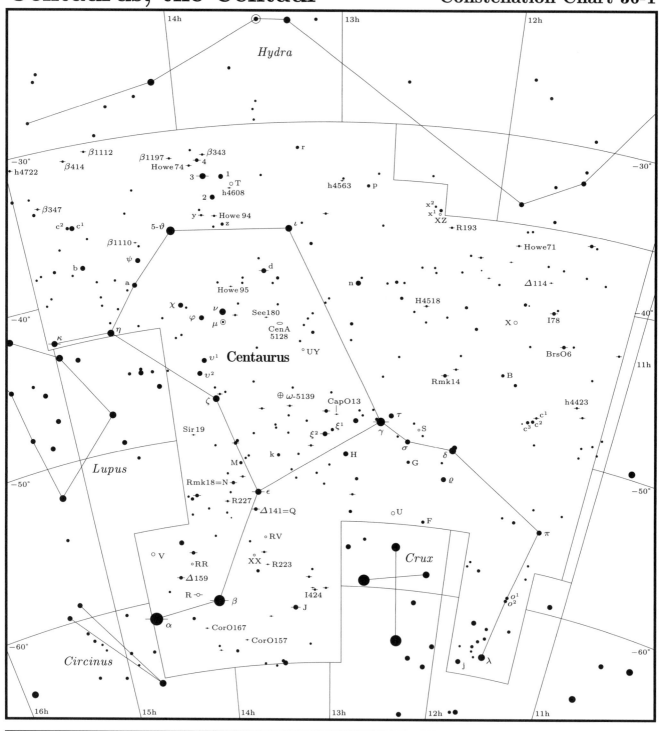

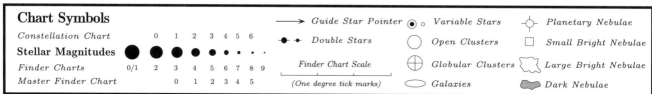

Chart Symbols

Constellation Chart
Stellar Magnitudes

| | 0 | 1 | 2 | 3 | 4 | 5 | 6 |

Finder Charts 0/1 2 3 4 5 6 7 8 9

Master Finder Chart 0 1 2 3 4 5

⟶ *Guide Star Pointer*

•—• *Double Stars*

Finder Chart Scale

(One degree tick marks)

⊙ ∘ *Variable Stars*

◯ *Open Clusters*

⊕ *Globular Clusters*

⬭ *Galaxies*

⊖ *Planetary Nebulae*

▢ *Small Bright Nebulae*

Large Bright Nebulae

Dark Nebulae

Table 36-1: Selected Variable Stars in Centaurus

Name	HD No.	Type	Max.	Min.	Period (Days)	F*	Spec. Type	R.A. (2000)	Dec.	Finder Chart No.	Notes
X Cen	102681	M	7.0	13.8	315	0.41	M5-M6	$11^h49.2^m$	$-41°45'$	36-1	
XZ Cen	107913	M	7.8	10.7	290		M5	$12^h24.2^m$	$-35\ 28$	36-3	
S Cen	107957	SR	9.2	10.7	65		C4,5	24.6	$-49\ 26$	36-1	
U Cen	109231	M	7.0	14.0	220	0.47	M3-M5	33.5	$-54\ 40$	36-1	
UY Cen	115236	SR	9.22	11.2	114		SC	$13^h16.5^m$	$-44\ 42$	36-4	
RV Cen	118322	M	7.0	10.3	446	0.56	N3	37.5	$-56\ 29$	36-1	
XX Cen	118769	Cδ	7.3	8.31	10.95	0.49	F6-G4	40.3	$-57\ 37$	36-1	
T Cen	119090	SRa	5.5	9.0	90	0.47	K0:-M4	41.8	$-33\ 36$	36-5	
R Cen	124601	M	5.3	11.8	546		M4-M8	$14^h16.6^m$	$-59\ 55$	36-1	
V Cen	127297	Cδ	6.43	7.21	5.49	0.26	F5-G0	32.5	$-56\ 53$	36-1	

F* = The fraction of period taken up by the star's rise from min. to max. brightness, or the period spent in eclipse.

Table 36-2: Selected Double Stars in Centaurus

Name	ADS No.	Pair	M1	M2	Sep."	P.A.°	Spec	R.A. (2000)	Dec.	Finder Chart No.	Notes
h4423			6.9	7.2	2.4	276	F2	$11^h16.5^m$	$-45°53'$	36-1	Fine yellow pair
BrsO6			5.2	7.9	13.1	16.7	B9	28.6	$-42\ 40$	36-1	
I78			6.2	6.2	1.0	97	A2	33.6	$-40\ 35$	36-1	Pale yellow pair
Δ114			6.7	9.5	17.0	95	G5	40.0	$-38\ 07$	36-1	
Howe 71			6.8	8.1	1.3	275	F8	54.4	$-37\ 45$	36-1	and
Rmk 14			5.6	6.8	2.9	244	M0	$12^h14.0^m$	$-45\ 43$	36-1	Orange and white
R193			6.8	7.1	0.6	164	A0	17.8	$-36\ 06$	36-1	
H4518			6.3	9.6	10.0	208	K0	24.7	$-41\ 23$	36-3	
γ Cen		AB	2.9	2.9	c1.0	*347	A0	41.5	$-48\ 58$	36-1	
CapO13			7.1	9.2	5.1	67	K0	$13^h00.3^m$	$-48\ 36$	36-1	
h4563			7.0	8.4	6.4	237	G5	01.1	$-33\ 37$	36-1	
ξ² Cen			4.3	9.4	25.1	100	B3	06.9	$-49\ 54$	36-4	
I424		ABxC	5.0	8.4	1.7	2	B8	12.3	$-59\ 55$	36-1	
See 180			6.7	9.2	3.7	231	K0	31.4	$-42\ 28$	36-4	Orange and white
R223			6.4	11.0	2.5	23	K0	38.1	$-58\ 25$	36-1	
Δ141			5.3	6.7	5.3	163	B9	41.7	$-54\ 34$	36-1	Fine white pair
h4608			7.4	7.5	4.2	185	F5	42.3	$-33\ 59$	36-5	
Howe95			7.6	7.9	1.6	187	A5	43.8	$-40\ 11$	36-1	
CorO157			6.5	10.5	9.4	318	G5	47.2	$-62\ 35$	36-1	Yellow and gray
Howe94			6.6	9.6	11.6	355	F8	48.9	$-35\ 42$	36-5	
3 Cen			4.5	6.0	7.9	10.8	B5 B8	51.8	$-33\ 00$	36-5	Unequal white pair
β 343			6.5	7.5	0.7	66	F8	52.0	$-31\ 37$	36-5	Tight yellow double
Rmk18			5.4	7.6	18.0	289	B8 A3	52.0	$-52\ 49$	36-1	White pair
4 Cen			4.7	8.4	14.9	185	B7	53.2	$-31\ 56$	36-5	Bluish and gray-white
Howe 74			7.1	9.6	6.2	117	G5	55.3	$-32\ 06$	36-5	
R227			6.5	7.5	1.8	4	A2	56.3	$-54\ 08$	36-1	
β 1197			6.5	7.6	1.9	211	F5	$14^h03.0^m$	$-31\ 41$	36-5	Yellow and white
β Cen			0.7	3.9	1.3	251	B1	03.8	$-60\ 22$	36-1	
Sir 19			7.2	7.4	1.4	295	G0	07.7	$-49\ 52$	36-4	Deep yellow pair
CorO167			6.6	8.4	2.8	159	O5	15.0	$-61\ 42$	36-1	
β 1110			6.9	11.5	3.9	132	M	19.7	$-36\ 52$	36-1	Red and white stars
Δ 159			5.0	7.1	9.3	160	G0	22.6	$-58\ 28$	36-1	Yellow and white
β 1112			6.2	9.5	2.5	12	K0	33.2	$-30\ 43$	36-1	
α Cen		AB	0.0	1.3	c14.1	*222	G2 K1	39.6	$-60\ 50$	36-1	Golden yellow binary
		AC		11.0	131.0	sp	M5				C: Proxima
β 414			6.9	7.8	1.0	347	B9	41.9	$-30\ 56$	36-1	Close white pair
β 347		AB	6.0	10.8	13.3	319	K0	54.6	$-33\ 18$	36-1	
		AC		10.0	58.1	243					
κ Cen			3.1	11.2	3.9	82	B2	59.2	$-42\ 06$	36-1	
h4722			7.2	9.3	8.6	337	F0	59.5	$-30\ 43$	36-1	

Footnotes: *= Year 2000, a = Near apogee, c = Closing, w = Widening. Finder Chart No: All stars listed in the tables are plotted in the large Constellation Chart, but when a star appears in a Finder Chart, this number is listed. Notes: When colors are subtle, the suffix *-ish* is used, e.g. *bluish*.

3 Centauri = HIII101 Double Star   Spec. B5, B8
m4.5, 6.0; Sep.7.9″, P.A.108°   13ʰ51.8ᵐ −33° 00′
Finder Chart 36-5   ★★★★
4/6″Scopes–75x: 3 Centauri is a striking pair of
    unequally bright bluish-white stars.

4 Centauri = HN51 Double Star   Spec. B7
m4.7, 8.4; Sep.14.9″, P.A.185°   13ʰ53.2ᵐ −31° 56′
Finder Chart 36-5   ★★★★
4/6″Scopes–75x: 4 Centauri is an attractive double
    with a bluish-white primary and a grayish-white
    secondary.

Burnham 1110 Double Star   Spec. M
m6.9, 11.5; Sep.3.9″, P.A.132°   14ʰ19.7ᵐ −36° 52′
Constellation Chart 36-1   ★★★★
4/6″Scopes–75x: Burnham 1110 has a ruddy primary
    with a tiny white companion.

Alpha (α) Centauri Triple Star   Spec. G2, K1, M5e
AB: m0.0,1.3; Sep. 14.1″, P.A. 222°
AC: 11.0   131.0′   14ʰ39.6ᵐ −60° 50′
Constellation Chart 36-1   ★★★★★

Rigel Kentaurus

Alpha Centauri, the third brightest star in the sky,
is well-known as the closest star to our Solar System.
It is only 4.3 light years distant. Alpha Centauri is in
fact a triple star consisting of two rather close, comparably bright stars that orbit each other in a period of
only about 80 years accompanied by a very distant,
very faint red dwarf that orbits the bright pair in a
period of perhaps several hundred thousand years. The
red dwarf is called Proxima Centauri because it seems

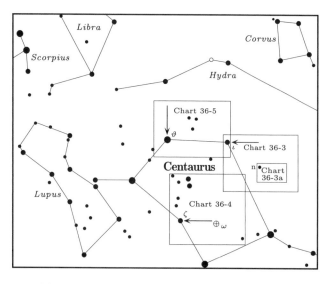

Master Finder Chart 36-2. Centaurus Chart Areas
Guide stars indicated by arrows

to be about 0.1 light year nearer to us than the two
bright stars and therefore is the nearest individual star
to the Solar System. Alpha Centauri A is very similar
to the Sun; it has a G2 V spectrum, an absolute
magnitude of +4.4, and is about 1.5 times as luminous
and 1.1 times as massive as the Sun. Alpha Centauri B
is a K1 V star with an absolute magnitude of +5.7 and
a luminosity and a mass of 40% and 85% the Sun's.
Proxima Centauri, however, is extremely small, its mass
only one-tenth the Sun's, and extremely faint, its
luminosity a mere 0.0008 that of the Sun. It is two
degrees away from the bright star pair and therefore
not even in the same telescopic field of view.
4/6″Scopes–75x: The bright stars form a fine, easily
    separated pair of golden yellow suns.

36.3 Deep-Sky Objects

NGC 4373 Galaxy Type SAB(s)0−:
ϕ **4.6′×2.0′, m10.6v, SB12.9   12ʰ25.3ᵐ −39° 45′**
Finder Chart 36-3, Figure 36-1   ★★★★
12/14″Scopes–125x: NGC 4373 has a stellar nucleus
    embedded within a large bright core which is
    surrounded by a much fainter halo elongated
    2.5′×1.5′ NNE–SSW. A 13th magnitude star is on
    the halo's north edge. 2′ SW of NGC 4273 is its
    companion galaxy IC 3290, a faint glow elongated
    1′×0.5′ NE–SW.

NGC 4373A Galaxy Type SA0°: sp
ϕ **2.7′×1.1′, m12.1v, SB13.1   12ʰ25.6ᵐ −39° 18′**
Finder Chart 36-3   ★★
12/14″Scopes–125x: NGC 4373A, located 2′ NNW of a
    9th magnitude star, is a fairly faint smudge of
    uniform surface brightness with a very faint stellar
    nucleus. Its halo seems elongated 1.5′×1′ N–S.

IC 3370 Galaxy Type SC0° ?
ϕ **3.0′×2.5′, n11.0v, SB13.0   12ʰ27.6ᵐ −39° 20′**
Finder Chart 36-3   ★★★
12/14″Scopes–125x: IC 3370, located 3′ east of a 9th
    magnitude star, has a fairly bright 3.5′×3.0′ NE–
    SW oval halo with a faint stellar nucleus. A 13th
    magnitude star is 1′ east.

NGC 4507 Galaxy Type Sb pec II
ϕ **1.6′×1.3′, m12.1v, SB12.7   12ʰ35.6ᵐ −39° 55′**
Finder Chart 36-3a   ★★
12/14″Scopes–125x: NGC 4507 is only 5.25′ SW of a
    magnitude 5.8 star, the glare of which makes this
    faint object that much more difficult to see. The
    galaxy has a small, fairly bright core surrounded by

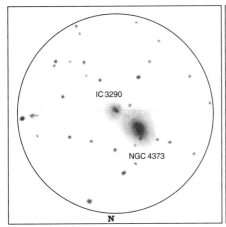

Figure 36-1. NGC 4373 & IC 3290
16″, f5–175x, by G. R. Kepple

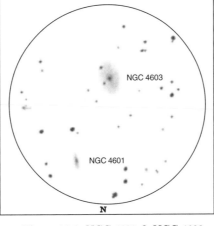

Figure 36-2. NGC 4601 & NGC 4603
16″, f5–175x, by G. R. Kepple

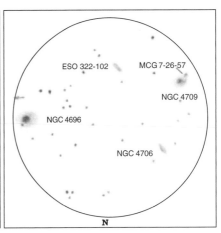

Figure 36-3. NGC 4696 Area
16″, f5–175x, by G. R. Kepple

a faint, diffuse 45″ diameter halo. 9th magnitude stars lie 4′ to its WSW and 5′ to its WNW. The surrounding field is well sprinkled with 12th and 13th magnitude stars.

NGC 4603 Galaxy Type SAB(rs)c IC
ϕ **3.2′×2.1′, m11.7v, SB13.6**   **12ʰ40.9ᵐ −40° 59′**
Finder Chart 36-3a, Figure 36-2   ★★
12/14″ Scopes–125x: NGC 4603 has a fairly bright stellar nucleus surrounded by a faint 2.5′×1.5′ NNE–SSW halo. 13th magnitude stars are superimposed upon the halo 20″ WNW and 50″ SW of the nucleus. 5′ to the NNW of NGC 4603, is NGC 4601, which has a very faint 1′×0.25′ NNE–SSW halo. A 12th magnitude star lies 1.75′ from its center beyond its southern tip.

NGC 4616 Galaxy Type SA(s)0–:
ϕ **1.1′×1.0′, m13.1v, SB13.1**   **12ʰ42.3ᵐ −40° 39′**
Finder Chart 36-3a   ★★
16/18″ Scopes–150x: NGC 4616, located only 40″ SW of a 10th magnitude star, has a faint core embedded in a diffuse 45″ diameter halo. A very faint, nearly stellar companion galaxy lies just 1′ ESE. 9th magnitude stars are 6.5′ ENE and 8′ WSW. NGC 4616 forms a pair with the brighter galaxy NGC 4622 lying 8.5′ SSE.

NGC 4622 Galaxy Type SA(r)a pec
ϕ **1.8′×1.7′, m12.4v, SB13.5**   **12ʰ42.6ᵐ −40° 45′**
Finder Chart 36-3a   ★★
16/18″ Scopes–150x: NGC 4622 is 4.5′ NE of a double consisting of a 10.5 magnitude star with a 13th magnitude companion 20″ distant in P.A. 190°. This galaxy has a small, fairly bright 15″ diameter core

surrounded by a faint, diffuse 1.5′ diameter halo. Several threshold stars lie near the halo's SW edge, and another is 1′ from its SE edge. 8.5′ SW of NGC 4622 and 4′ WSW of the 10.5 magnitude star is the very faint, 1′×0.5′ ENE–WSW galaxy NGC 4603D. It lies within a 2.5′×1.5′ isosceles triangle of 13th magnitude stars.

NGC 4645 Galaxy Type SA0–
ϕ **2.2′×1.5′, m11.8v, SB12.9**   **12ʰ44.2ᵐ −41° 45′**
Finder Chart 36-3a   ★★★
12/14″ Scopes–125x: NGC 4645, located 9′ SE of a 9th magnitude star, has a bright, nonstellar nucleus in an oval core elongated 45″×30″ NE–SW. The galaxy's halo is diffuse and fades suddenly, reaching only to 1′×0.75′ NE–SW. An irregular, 3′ long V of 12th and 13th magnitude stars is centered 3′ north of the galaxy.

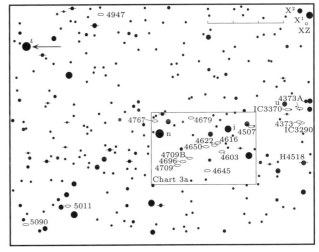

Finder Chart 36-3. *ι* Cen: 13ʰ20.6ᵐ −36° 42′

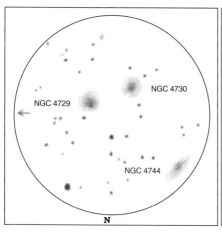

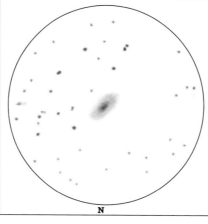

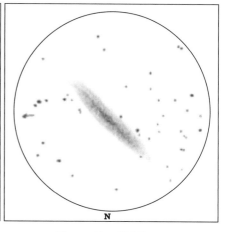

Figure 36-4. NGC 4729-30 & NGC 4744
16″, f5–175x, by G. R. Kepple

Figure 36-5. NGC 4767
16″, f5–175x, by G. R. Kepple

Figure 36-6. NGC 4945
16″, f5–175x, by G. R. Kepple

NGC 4672 Galaxy Type S0/a: pec sp
φ **2.5′×0.8′, m13.1v, SB13.7**   12ʰ46.3ᵐ −41° 43′
Finder Chart 36-3a   ★★
16/18″Scopes–150x: NGC 4672 is 6′ ESE of a 9th
    magnitude star. An 11th magnitude star is 2.25′ to
    the SE and a 10th magnitude star 2.75′ SSW. The
    galaxy has a faint, diffuse halo elongated 1.5′×0.5′
    NE–SW. Although poorly concentrated, the central
    portion of the galaxy is conspicuously bulged.

NGC 4677 Galaxy Type SB(s)+:
φ **1.8′×0.9′, m12.7v, SB13.1**   12ʰ47.0ᵐ −41° 35′
Finder Chart 36-3a   ★★
16/18″Scopes–150x: NGC 4677 has a faint halo elon-
    gated 1.5′×0.5′ NNE–SSW with a very faint non-
    stellar nucleus. A threshold star touches the halo's
    edge 30″ SSW of the galaxy's center. Two wide

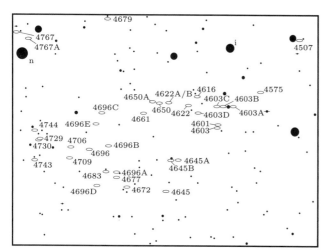

Finder Chart 36-3a. Centaurus Galaxy Cluster.
n Cen: 12ʰ53.5ᵐ −40° 11′
See Finder Chart 36-3 (Faintest stars 10th magnitude)

doubles of 12.5 and 13th magnitude stars are visible
1.5′ south and 2′ SW. NGC 4696A, located 5.5′
north of NGC 4677, is a fainter and slightly smaller
version of the latter. 1.75′ to the WSW of NGC
4696A is an 11th magnitude star, and 1.25′ to its
ESE is a 12th magnitude star.

NGC 4679 Galaxy Type SB(s)c II
φ **2.3′×0.9′, m12.6v, SB13.2**   12ʰ47.5ᵐ −39° 34′
Finder Chart 36-3a   ★★
16/18″Scopes–150x: NGC 4679, located 5.5′ SSE of an
    8.5 magnitude star, has a faint 2.5′×0.75′ N–S halo
    with a poorly concentrated 40″×20″ core. A 13.5
    magnitude star lies 40″ SE of the galaxy's center;
    and 2.5′ south is a wide NW–SE pair of 13th
    magnitude stars. Galaxy ESO 322-84, situated 7′
    ESE of NGC 4679, is a fairly conspicuous 1′×0.25′
    NE–SW patch.

NGC 4696B Galaxy Type SA0°:
φ **1.3′×0.8′, m12.8v, SB12.7**   12ʰ47.5ᵐ −41° 14′
Finder Chart 36-3a   ★★
12/14″Scopes–125x: NGC 4696B, located 3′ west of a
    12th magnitude star, has a fairly faint, diffuse halo
    elongated 1.25′×0.75′ NE–SW. Superimposed upon
    the SW edge of the halo is a tiny triangle of 13th
    and 14th magnitude stars.

NGC 4696 Galaxy Type E+2
φ **5.4′×3.9′, m10.2v, SB13.4**   12ʰ48.8ᵐ −41° 19′
Finder Chart 36-3a, Figure 36-3   ★★★★
12/14″Scopes–125x: NGC 4696 has a fairly bright,
    circular 3′ diameter halo with a faint stellar nucleus.
    13th magnitude stars are 1′ NW, 1′ SW, and 1′ SE
    of the nucleus on the edge of the galaxy's halo.
    NGC 4706 is 12′ ENE, and NGC 4709 is 15′ ESE
    of NGC 4696.

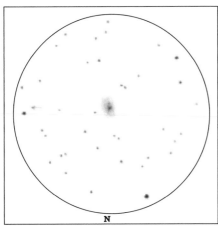

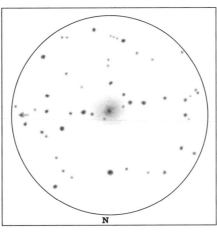

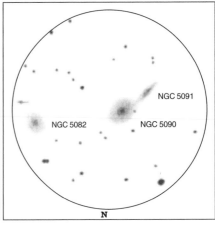

NGC 5091 · NGC 5082 · NGC 5090

Figure 36-7. NGC 4947
16″, f5–175x, by G. R. Kepple

Figure 36-8. NGC 5011
16″, f5–175x, by G. R. Kepple

Figure 36-9. NGC 5082 & NGC 5090-91
16″, f5–175x, by G. R. Kepple

NGC 4706 Galaxy Type SB(s)0°
ϕ 1.3′×0.8′, m13.0v, SB12.9   12^{h}49.9^m −41° 17′

NGC 4709 Galaxy Type E+1
ϕ 2.8′×2.4′, m11.5v, SB13.4   12^{h}50.1^m −41° 23′
Finder Chart 36-3a, Figure 36-3   ★/★★★
12/14″ Scopes–125x: NGC 4709 has a fairly bright,
   circular 2′ diameter halo with a stellar nucleus. The
   galaxy is 10′ west of a diamond-shaped asterism of
   12th magnitude stars and framed by a circlet of
   13th magnitude stars, two of which lie 1.5′ south
   and 2′ west of the galaxy. Just 1′ SE of NGC 4709
   is its small but fairly bright companion, MCG–7-
   26-57. NGC 4706, located 6.25′ NNW of NGC 4709,
   is a faint 1′×0.5′ NNE–SSW oval with a moderately
   concentrated core. NGC 4696 is 15′ WNW.

NGC 4729 Galaxy Type SA0−:
ϕ 1.7′×1.6′, m12.5v, SB13.4   12^{h}51.8^m −41° 08′

NGC 4730 Galaxy Type SA(r)0−
ϕ 1.2′×1.0′, m12.9v, SB12.9   12^{h}52.0^m −41° 09′
Finder Chart 36-3a, Figure 36-4   ★★/★★
16/18″ Scopes–150x: These two galaxies form a triangle
   with a 10th magnitude star to their north. NGC
   4729, located 3′ SSW of the star, has a well
   concentrated 30″ core within a very faint, diffuse 1′
   diameter halo. A 12th magnitude star lies 1′ to its
   NNW. 3′ ESE of NGC 4729 and 4′ SSE of the 10th
   magnitude star is NGC 4730, nearly a twin of NGC
   NGC 4729 but just a little fainter. A 12.5 magnitude
   star lies 40″ south and a 13th magnitude star 35″
   SE of the center of NGC 4730. Galaxy NGC 4744
   is 5′ NE of the 10th magnitude star.

NGC 4744 Galaxy Type SB(s)0+
ϕ 2.1′×1.0′, m12.4v, SB13.1   12^{h}52.4^m −41° 04′
Finder Chart 36-3a, Figure 36-4   ★★
16/18″ Scopes–150x: NGC 4744, located 6′ SSW of an
   8th magnitude star, has a faint, diffuse 2.5′×0.75′
   NNW–SSE halo with a bar-shaped core and a fairly
   bright nucleus. Only 1.25′ NE of the galaxy is a
   double of 12th and 13th magnitude stars 10″ apart
   in P.A. 315°. A second 12th magnitude star is 1.75′
   WSW. The 3′ wide galaxy pair NGC 4729+30 is 7′
   to the SW.

NGC 4767 Galaxy Type SA0−
ϕ 2.7′×1.4′, m11.6v, SB12.9   12^{h}53.9^m −39° 43′
Finder Chart 36-3a, Figure 36-5   ★★★
12/14″ Scopes–125x: NGC 4767 is 5.5′ east of one 9th
   magnitude star, 6′ WSW of another 9th magnitude
   star, and 6.5′ SSE of a 7″ N–S double of 10th
   magnitude stars. The galaxy has a fairly bright
   2′×1′ NW–SE halo with a broad, well concentrated
   center. A 13th magnitude star lies 1.25′ to its NW.

NGC 4945 Galaxy Type SA(s)d: III-IV
ϕ 23.0′×5.9′, m8.8v, SB14.0   13^{h}05.4^m −49° 28′
Finder Chart 36-4, Figure 36-6   ★★★
12/14″ Scopes–125x: NGC 4945, located 10′ east of Xi-
   1 (ξ^1) Centauri (m4.85), is a prominent member of
   the NGC 5128 Galaxy Group. This cluster, located
   perhaps 22 million light years away, includes NGCs
   5128, 4945, 5102, and 5253 in Centaurus, M83 and
   NGC 5624 in Hydra, and NGC 5068 in Virgo. NGC
   4945 is a faint, diffuse, nearly edge-on galaxy
   elongated 14′×2′ NE–SW with moderate central
   brightening along its major axis. At 175x, the
   galaxy has a highly mottled texture with a faint

irregular core. A 13th magnitude star lies on the halo's edge 1.5′ east of the galaxy's center and a slightly brighter star lies on the edge 4′ from the center. A small companion galaxy lies 6.5′ NW, and the star Xi-2 (ξ^2) Centauri (m4.27) is 26′ SE. NGC 4945 has an absolute magnitude of −20.9, a luminosity of 19 billion suns, and a true diameter of at least 150,000 light years.

NGC 4947   Galaxy Type SAB(r)bc II
ϕ **2.5′×1.3′, m11.9v, SB13.0**   13^{h}05.4^m −35° 20′
Finder Chart 36-3, Figure 36-7   ★★★
12/14″Scopes–125x: NGC 4947, located 9.5′ SSW of a 9th magnitude star, has a faint, diffuse 2.5′×1.25′ N–S halo with a broad but poorly concentrated center. A 13th magnitude star lies 1.5′ WNW. A 25″ wide NNE–SSW double of 13th magnitude stars is 2′ SSE.

NGC 4976   Galaxy Type SAB(s)0–:
ϕ **5.4′×3.3′, m10.1v, SB13.1**   13^{h}08.6^m −49° 30′
Finder Chart 36-4   ★★★★
12/14″Scopes–125x: NGC 4976, located just west of an 8th magnitude star, has a fairly bright 3.5′×2′ halo that slightly brightens toward its center. Galaxy NGC 4945 is half a degree west, and 4.3 magnitude Xi-2 (ξ^2) Centauri lies half a degree SW.

NGC 5011   Galaxy Type E1
ϕ **2.9′×2.3′, m11.1v, SB13.0**   13^{h}12.9^m −43° 06′
Finder Chart 36-4, Figure 36-8   ★★★
12/14″Scopes–125x: NGC 5011 lies within the bowl of

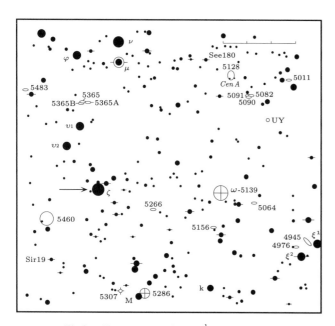

Finder Chart 36-4. ζ Cen: 13^{h}55.5^m −47° 17′

a one degree long, dipper-shaped asterism of one 5th, one 7th, and three 6th magnitude stars. The dipper opens toward the west. The galaxy is a faint, circular 1.5′ diameter glow with a stellar nucleus. Two 12th magnitude stars lie to the west of the galaxy, and two 12.5 magnitude stars lie to its ESE, the nearest of each pair touching the halo's edge.

NGC 5064   Galaxy Type SAb: II-III
ϕ **2.6′×1.3′, m12.0v, SB13.2**   13^{h}19.0^m −47° 55′
Finder Chart 36-4   ★★★
16/18″Scopes–150x: NGC 5064, located 6.5′ NE of a 9th magnitude star, has a faint, diffuse 2′×0.75′ NNE–SSW halo around a well concentrated 45″×30″ inner region containing a fairly bright nucleus. 13th magnitude stars are 1′ NNW, 1′ WNW, and 1.5′ SSE of the galaxy.

NGC 5082   Galaxy Type SB(s)0+
ϕ **1.5′×1.0′, m12.8v, SB13.1**   13^{h}20.9^m −43° 42′

NGC 5090   Galaxy Type E2
ϕ **2.7′×2.2′, m11.6v, SB13.4**   13^{h}21.1^m −43° 44′

NGC 5091   Galaxy Type Sb: sp
ϕ **2.0′×0.8′, m13.1v, SB13.5**   13^{h}21.2^m −43° 44′
Finder Chart 36-4, Figure 36-9   ★★/★★★/★
16/18″Scopes–150x: These three galaxies are near a 6th magnitude star nearly a degree SW of Centaurus A (NGC 5128). NGC 5090, the brightest of the trio, is 4.25′ SSW of the 6th magnitude star and has a small, bright core within a faint 1′ diameter halo. A threshold star touches the halo's ESE edge. Attached to the galaxy's SSE edge is its companion, NGC 5091, which has a very faint 1.5′×0.25′ NW-SE halo with a faint, extended core. 5.75′ west of NGC 5090 and 9′ WSW of the 6th magnitude star is the galaxy NGC 5082, the faint, slightly elongated 45″×30″ NE–SW halo which contains a poorly concentrated center. A threshold star touches the galaxy's east edge.

NGC 5102   Galaxy Type SA(s)0− pec:
ϕ **9.8′×4.0′, m8.8v, SB12.6**   13^{h}22.0^m −36° 38′
Finder Chart 36-5, Figure 36-12   ★★★★
12/14″Scopes–125x: NGC 5102, located 14′ NE of Iota (ι) Centauri, is an attractive galaxy with a bright 8′×3′ NE–SW halo containing an extended, well concentrated core. An 8th magnitude star 6′ NW, a 9.5 magnitude star 4.5′ NNE, and a 9th magnitude star 8′ west form a parallelogram with the galaxy. NGC 5102 is a member of the NGC 5128 Galaxy Group. Its absolute magnitude is −18.8, a luminosity of 2.7 billion suns, and its true diameter 63,000 light years.

Figure 36-10. *NGC5128, the famous radio galaxy known as Centaurus A, displays the broadest and most obvious dark band of any galaxy visible in amateur telescopes. Image courtesy Steven Juchnowski.*

Figure 36-11. *NGC5139, the magnificent Omega Centauri, is the brightest and largest of all globular clusters. Low power is required for the best view. Image courtesy of Jim Burnell.*

NGC 5128 Galaxy Type S0 pec
ϕ **31.0′×23.0′, m6.7v, SB13.7**   **13ʰ25.5ᵐ −43° 01′**
Finder Chart 36-4, Figure 36-10   ★★★★★
Centaurus A

12/14″Scopes–125x: One of the strongest emitters of radio signals in the sky, Centaurus A is a bright and interesting galaxy with a conspicuous broad dark band crossing the halo in position angle 120°. The galaxy has a bright, circular 15′ diameter halo. The halo is larger and brighter south of the dark band, which is broader on each end than it is in the middle. One star is superimposed upon the dark band near its center and another is near its west edge.

NGC 5139 Globular Cluster Class VIII
ϕ **36.3′, m3.5:v, Br★ 11.5v**   **13ʰ26.8ᵐ −47° 29′**
Finder Chart 36-4, Figure 36-11   ★★★★★
Omega Centauri

Omega (ω) Centauri has been known since antiquity, for the Greek astronomer Ptolemy included it in a star catalogue he compiled in the mid-2nd century A.D. When Johannes Bayer assigned Greek letters to the brighter stars he also mistook this cluster for a star and designated it Omega Centauri. The first recorded observation of the object as a cluster was made by Halley in 1677.

Omega Centauri, 15,600 light years distant, is one of the nearest globular clusters to the earth. It is the brightest known globular in our Galaxy's family of 150+ globulars, its absolute magnitude of −10.3 implying a true luminosity of 1.1 million suns. Its stellar population probably also exceeds one million. It is also a very large globular: its visual size of about 36′ corresponds to a true diameter of 174 light years, but its photographic size is 65′, implying a diameter of over 300 light years. As in all globular clusters, its stellar density increases rapidly toward its interior. The average distance between stars at its center is only about 0.1 light year.

Omega Centauri is visible to the naked eye, impressive in binoculars, and simply awesome when viewed through any size telescope. It is the brightest and largest globular cluster in the entire sky. It is a rather loose Class VIII globular and its stars are rather bright compared to those in other globular clusters, some of its members are as bright as magnitude 11.5 making it fairly easy to resolve in small telescopes.

4/6″Scopes–50x: Omega Centauri is a 35′ diameter swarm of a myriad of twinkling points massing to a broadly concentrated 8′ diameter core.

8/10″Scopes–100x: Incredible! This huge star sphere spans a diameter of 36′ with outlying members found as far as 22′ from the cluster center. Hundreds of resolved stars scintillate in the granular background glow. The star density rapidly increases inward, massing to a grand core ablaze with countless tiny star-sparks. The core is about 9′ across, somewhat elongated E–W, and lacks a sharp nucleus. Half a dozen magnitude 9.5–10 foreground stars, outlying

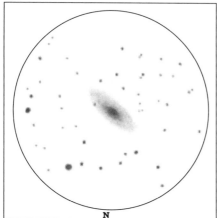

Figure 36-12. NGC 5102
16″, f5–175x, by G. R. Kepple

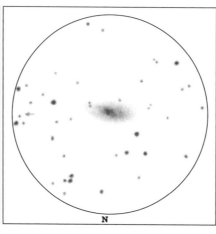

Figure 36-13. NGC 5161
16″, f5–175x, by G. R. Kepple

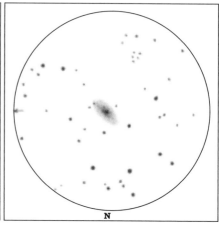

Figure 36-14. NGC 5253
16″, f5–175x, by G. R. Kepple

members of the Centaurus Milky Way, are peppered across the cluster; but its brightest true members are magnitude 12–13 objects.

NGC 5156 Galaxy Type SB(r)bc II
φ 2.6′×1.9′, m11.7v, SB13.3   13ʰ28.7ᵐ −48° 55′
Finder Chart 36-4   ★★★
12/14″Scopes–125x: NGC 5156 is 1.5° SSE of Omega Centauri (NGC 5139) and 4.5′ to the NNE of an 8th magnitude star. The galaxy has a fairly bright nonstellar nucleus surrounded by a 45″ core embedded in a much fainter 2′ diameter halo slightly elongated ESE–WNW. A 13th magnitude star is superimposed upon the galaxy's halo 30″ SE of its center. A concentration of faint stars is 1.5′ SW of the galaxy. A 10th magnitude star lies 7′ ENE and a 10.5 magnitude star 7′ NE.

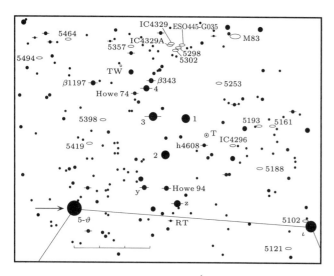

Finder Chart 36-5. 3 Cen: 13ʰ51.8ᵐ −33° 00′

NGC 5161 Galaxy Type SA(s)cd IC
φ 4.3′×1.9′, m11.4v, SB13.5   13ʰ29.2ᵐ −33° 10′
Finder Chart 36-5, Figure 36-13   ★★★
12/14″Scopes–125x: NGC 5161 lies between a 9th magnitude star 3.5′ to the west and an 11th magnitude star 2.5′ to the NE. It has a broad but irregularly concentrated core with a small, bright nucleus. The outer halo is highly elongated 4′×1.5′ ENE–WSW. At 200x, vague hints of spiral structure can be glimpsed. A 15″ N–S double of very faint stars is in the halo 1.75′ WSW of center.

NGC 5188 Galaxy Type SAB(s)ab? I-II
φ 3.4′×1.4′, m11.8v, SB13.3   13ʰ31.3ᵐ −34° 47′
Finder Chart 36-5   ★★★
12/14″Scopes–125x: NGC 5188, located 1.75′ ESE of a 10.5 magnitude star, has a fairly bright nucleus within a 1′×0.75′ concentrated central region surrounded by a much fainter halo elongated 3′×1′ ESE–WNW. A clump of four faint stars lies 3′ WSW.

NGC 5193 Galaxy Type E0 pec:
φ 2.3′×2.0′, m11.7v, SB13.2   13ʰ31.9ᵐ −33° 14′
Finder Chart 36-5   ★★★
12/14″Scopes–125x: NGC 5193 is 4.5′ east and slightly north of an 8th magnitude star and 6′ SE of a 9th magnitude star. It has a bright 45″ core embedded in a faint, diffuse 1.5′ diameter halo. An 11.5 magnitude star is 1.25′ to its NNW, a 12th magnitude star 1.75′ to its SE, and a 13th magnitude star 1.25′ to its ENE. NGC 5193A, which may be an interacting companion, touches the WSW edge of NGC 5193 and is elongated 1′×0.25′ NE–SW with tapered ends. Another companion galaxy is 3′ WSW of NGC

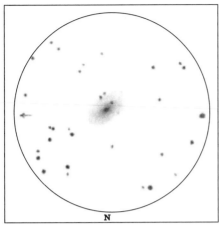

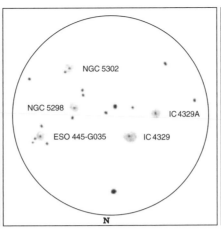

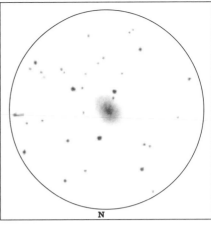

Figure 36-15. NGC 5266
16", f5–175x, by G. R. Kepple

Figure 36-16. NGC 5291-98 Area
16", f5–175x, by G. R. Kepple

Figure 36-17. NGC 5357
16", f5–175x, by G. R. Kepple

5193 but visible even with averted vision only as a very faint 30″ diameter smudge.

IC 4296 Galaxy Type E0
φ 4.0′×3.7′, m10.5v, SB13.3   13ʰ36.6ᵐ −33° 58′
Finder Chart 36-5   ★★★
12/14″Scopes–125x: IC 4296, located 14′ ENE of an 8th magnitude star, appears fairly faint. Its diffuse, circular 3′ diameter halo has a slight NE–SW elongation, gradually brightens toward the galaxy's center, and seems larger with averted vision. The galaxy forms a triangle with two stars of 11th and 12th magnitudes lying to its west.

NGC 5253 Galaxy Type Im: pec
φ 5.1′×2.3′, m10.2v, SB12.7   13ʰ39.9ᵐ −31° 39′
Finder Chart 36-5, Figure 36-14   ★★★
12/14″Scopes–125x: NGC 5253, another member of the 22 million light year distant NGC 5128 Galaxy Group, is a bright system elongated 3.5′×1.5′ NE–SW with an extended, well concentrated core. A 14.5 magnitude star is just within its SW tip. A second magnitude 14.5 star lies 30″ NW of the first. A few minutes of arc north and northwest of the galaxy is a 6′ long line of three 13th magnitude stars. The absolute magnitude of NGC 5253 is −18.5, a luminosity of 2.1 billion suns, and its true diameter is at least 33,000 light years.

NGC 5266 Galaxy Type S0° pec
φ 3.9′×2.6′, m10.9v, SB13.3   13ʰ43.0ᵐ −48° 11′
Finder Chart 36-4, Figure 36-15   ★★★
12/14″Scopes–125x: NGC 5266 is located 2.25′ SW of the magnitude 2.5 Zeta (ζ) Centauri and 18′ ENE of an 8th magnitude star. It has a small, bright core containing a stellar nucleus embedded in a very

tenuous outer halo elongated 2′×1.5′ ESE–WNW. A 13th magnitude star is superimposed upon the halo just 30″ SE of the galaxy's nucleus. A 20″ wide NW–SE pair of 13th magnitude stars lies just outside the halo 50″ from the galaxy's center.

NGC 5286 Globular Cluster Class V
φ 9.1′, m7.2v, Br★ 13.5   13ʰ46.4ᵐ −51° 22′
Finder Chart 36-4   ★★★
12/14″Scopes–125x: NGC 5286 is a moderately concentrated 5′ diameter glow located 6′ NNW of the 4.6 magnitude reddish-orange star M Centauri. It appears as a hazy ball with a bright core. Several dozen stars can be resolved around its periphery, including a slightly brighter one on the cluster's NE edge.

ESO 445-G035 Galaxy Type SB(rs)b
φ 0.9′×0.6′, m14.1v, SB13.3   13ʰ48.1ᵐ −30° 27′
Finder Chart 36-5, Figure 36-16   ★
12/14″Scopes–125x: NGC 5291, circumscribed by an isosceles triangle of 12th magnitude stars, has a very faint, circular 1′ diameter halo containing a very faint stellar nucleus. Galaxy NGC 5298 lies 6′ ENE.

NGC 5298 Galaxy Type SB(r)ab
φ 1.6′×0.8′, m12.9v, SB13.0   13ʰ48.2ᵐ −30° 27′
Finder Chart 36-5, Figure 36-16   ★★
12/14″Scopes–125x: NGC 5298 is situated between 12th magnitude stars 2′ east and 4′ to its west. The galaxy's 1′ diameter halo is very faint, diffuse, and circular, and contains a faint stellar nucleus. Galaxy ESO 445-G035 lies 6′ WNW.

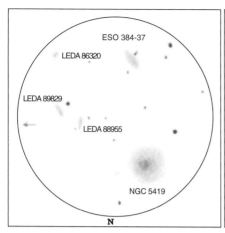

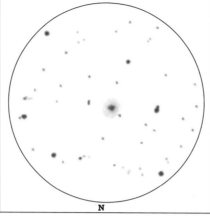

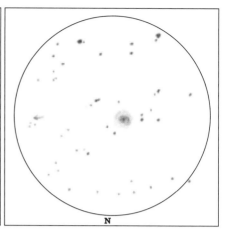

Figure 36-18. NGC 5419
16″, f5–175x, by G. R. Kepple

Figure 36-19. NGC 5483
16″, f5–175x, by G. R. Kepple

Figure 36-20. NGC 5494
16″, f5–175x, by G. R. Kepple

NGC 5302 Galaxy Type SA(s)0/a
ϕ 2.1′×1.2′, m12.2v, SB13.1   13ʰ48.8ᵐ −30° 31′
Finder Chart 36-5, Figure 36-16   ★★
12/14″Scopes–125x: NGC 5302 is a very faint 2′×1′
  NNW–SSE oval with a stellar nucleus. A 13th
  magnitude star lies 3′ west.

IC 4329 Galaxy Type SAB(s)0–
ϕ 4.1′×2.3′, m11.0v, SB13.3   13ʰ49.1ᵐ −30° 18′

IC 4329A Galaxy Type S0+
ϕ 1.5′×0.7′, m12.8v, SB12.7   13ʰ49.3ᵐ −30° 19′
Finder Chart 36-5, Figure 36-16   ★★★/★★
12/14″Scopes–125x: IC4329 appears fairly faint with a
  diffuse 2′×1.5′ ENE–WSW halo containing a stellar
  nucleus. IC4329A, located 3′ east of IC 4329, has
  a very faint 1′ diameter halo with a stellar nucleus.

NGC 5307 PK312+10.1 Planetary Nebula Type 3
ϕ 13″, m11.2v, CS14.58   13ʰ51.1ᵐ −51° 12′
Finder Chart 36-4   ★★★
12/14″Scopes–250x: NGC 5307 is 10′ west of an 8th
  magnitude star and 8′ WSW of a magnitude 9.5
  star. Its 15″ diameter disk is fairly bright and evenly
  illuminated. The 15th magnitude central star is not
  visible. A 1′ long NW–SE row of three 12.5 to 13th
  magnitude stars begins 1′ SE of the planetary.

NGC 5357 Galaxy Type E2
ϕ 1.8′×1.5′, m12.1v, SB13.0   13ʰ56.0ᵐ −30° 20′
Finder Chart 36-5, Figure 36-17   ★★★
12/14″Scopes–125x: NGC 5357 lies on the eastern side
  of a 3.25′×2′ triangle of 10th magnitude stars. Its

halo is faint, slightly elongated 1.5′×1.25′ NNE–
SSW, and surrounds a broad, moderately concentrated 45″ diameter inner region.

NGC 5365 Galaxy Type (R)SB(rs)0/a
ϕ 3.7′×2.7′, m11.2v, SB13.5   13ʰ57.9ᵐ −43° 57′
Finder Chart 36-4   ★★★
12/14″Scopes–125x: NGC 5365, located 50′ north of
  magnitude 3.9 Nu-1 (ν^1) Centauri, is surrounded
  by a faint, irregular circlet of 13th and 14th magnitude stars. It has a fairly bright stellar nucleus in
  a 20″ diameter core embedded in a very faint 3′×1.5′
  N–S halo. The galaxy's northern extension protrudes beyond the circlet. A 12th magnitude star
  is 3′ NW of the galaxy. 15′ WSW of NGC 5365 is
  NGC 5365A, a fairly conspicuous 2′×0.25′ E–W
  streak touched on the northern edge of its eastern
  tip by a 12th magnitude star. NGC 5365B, located
  7′ ESE of NGC 5365, is a slightly fainter and shorter
  streak than NGC 5365A.

NGC 5398 Galaxy Type SB(s)dm IV
ϕ 2.8′×1.8′, m12.4v, SB14.0   14ʰ01.4ᵐ −33° 04′
Finder Chart 36-5   ★★
16/18″Scopes–150x: NGC 5398 lies 4′ east of a 10th
  magnitude star with an 11th magnitude companion
  1′ to the star's SE. The galaxy has a very faint,
  irregularly concentrated 3′×1.5′ N–S halo that
  slightly brightens toward its center and a faint
  stellar nucleus. A second 11th magnitude star lies
  3′ NNW of the galaxy, and a 12th magnitude star
  is 2′ SW. A very faint companion galaxy to NGC
  5398 is visible as a small streak 3′ to its east.

NGC 5419 Galaxy Type E+1
φ **3.9′×3.2′, m10.8v, SB 13.4**   14^{h}03.7^m −33° 59′
Finder Chart 36-5, Figure 36-18   ★★★
12/14″Scopes–125x: NGC 5419, located 8.5′ SE of a 9th magnitude star, has a bright 1′ diameter central area but a very tenuous outer halo that with averted vision can be just discerned out to a diameter of 3′. A threshold star is superimposed on the inner halo 45″ north of its center. A magnitude 10.5 star is 3′ NE. Galaxy ESO 384-37 is 6′ due south of NGC 5419. Three even fainter and smaller galaxies can be glimpsed 5′ WSW, 7′ WSW, and 9.5′ SW of the big galaxy.

NGC 5460 Open Cluster 40★ Tr Type I 3 m
φ **64′, m5.6v, Br★ 8.01**   14^{h}07.6^m −48° 19′
Finder Chart 36-4   ★★★
12/14″Scopes–50x: NGC 5460 is a huge, irregularly scattered cluster of fifty 9th magnitude and fainter stars that requires low power to retain any semblance of "clusterness." It is segmented into three subgroups, each appearing almost as a separate cluster unto itself. The central subgroup has a 4′ long arc of seven 9th and 10th magnitude stars concave to the SW, two stars at the arc's center forming an equally bright double. In the southern subgroup five stars lie along a NNW–SSE arc, the second star from the north being a close double. Just south of this star pair is an extremely faint galaxy. The third subgroup is in the western part of the cluster. An 8th magnitude star is detached from the cluster to its east. A 6th magnitude star lies 9′ south of the cluster's southernmost concentration.

NGC 5483 Galaxy Type SAB(s)c? II
φ **3.3′×3.0′, m11.2v, SB 13.5**   14^{h}10.4^m −43° 19′
Finder Chart 36-4, Figure 36-19   ★★★
12/14″Scopes–125x: NGC 5483, located 18′ ENE of a 6th magnitude star, has a fairly faint, circular 2′ diameter halo that gradually brightens to a faint 45″×30″ NE–SW oval core. A 14th magnitude star touches the NE edge of the halo. A pair of 12th and 13th magnitude stars lies 4′ east of the galaxy, and a fainter N–S double is 2′ WSW.

NGC 5494 Galaxy Type SA(s)bc? I-II
φ **2.3′×1.9′, m11.8v, SB 13.3**   14^{h}12.4^m −30° 39′
Finder Chart 36-5, Figure 36-20   ★★★
12/14″Scopes–125x: NGC 5494, located 7′ NNE of a 9.5 magnitude star, appears fairly bright, its circular 2′ diameter halo broadly brighter toward its center. At 175x a faint spiral arm can be seen curling northward from the east or SE edge of the faint E–W core. A few faint knots are near the northern and southern rim of the halo. Just outside the edge of the halo to the east, NW, WNW, and south are several 13th and 14th magnitude stars.

Chapter 37

Coma Berenices, Berenice's Hair

37.1 Overview

Coma Berenices, specifically, the fine naked eye star cluster in the NW part of the modern constellation area, represents the hair of Queen Berenice of Egypt, who cut off her flowing locks and placed them in a shrine as an offering to the gods for the safe return from battle of her husband Ptolemy II (Euergetes). When the hair disappeared the next night, the royal astronomer Conon saved the priests from execution by claiming the offering had met with such favor that the gods placed it in the sky for all to see.

This legend has the ring of truth about it. In any event Coma Berenices must be a late addition to the classical constellations, because Ptolemy II (Euergetes) reigned from 246 to 221 B.C. Chances are that before this the Greeks thought of the Coma star cluster as the tuft at the end of the tail of the celestial Lion, though we have no documentary evidence proving this. In previous millennia the ancient Babylonians had known the Coma Star Cluster as a Date cluster sacred to the goddess of love and fertility, Ishtar.

Toward Coma Berenices, in the vicinity of Beta (β) Comae, is the north galactic pole, the direction of the axis of rotation of our Galaxy. Thus when we look toward Coma Berenices we look perpendicular to the dust-rich spiral plane of our Galaxy out into intergalactic space. We would therefore expect to see a lot of galaxies in Coma, but the constellation is exceptionally rich in galaxies even for an off-Milky Way area of the sky. The reason is that toward southwest Coma is the dense Coma-Virgo Galaxy Cluster, which is the very heart of the Local Supercluster. Thus what Sagittarius is to our Galaxy (that is, the direction toward the star-dense central bulge of our Galaxy), Coma Berenices and adjacent NW Virgo are to our galactic neighborhood. Many of the galaxies in Coma Berenices are excellent even in modest-size telescopes: the constellation has not less than seven Messier-numbered galaxies.

Coma Berenices: KO-ma Be-ren-EYE-Seez
Genitive: Comae Berenices, KO-me Be-ren-EYE-seez
Abbreviation: Com
Culmination: 9pm–May 17, midnight–Apr. 2
Area: 386 square degrees
Showpieces: 24 Com, 35 Com, β 800, Mel 111, M53 (NGC 5024), M64 (NGC 4826), M85 (NGC 4382), M88 (NGC 4501), M98 (NGC 4192), M99 (NGC 4254), M100 (NGC 4321), NGC 4274, NGC 4559, NGC 4565, NGC 4725
Binocular Objects: 32 and 33 Com, Mel 111, M53 (NGC 5024), M64 (NGC 4826), M85 (NGC 4382), M88 (NGC 4501), M98 (NGC 4192), M99 (NGC 4254), M100 (NGC 4321), NGC 4559, NGC 4565, NGC 4725

37.2 Interesting Stars

2 Comae Berenices = Σ1596 Double Star   Spec. F0
m5.9, 7.4; Sep. 3.7″; P.A. 237°   12^{h}04.3^m +21° 28′
Finder Chart 37-4   ★★★★
4/6″ Scopes–150x: 2 Comae Berenices is a fine pair of pale and deep yellow stars requiring moderately high power to separate.

Σ1615 Triple Star   Spec. K0
AB: m6.9, 9.7; Sep. 26.7″; P.A. 88°   12^{h}14.1^m +32° 47′
Finder Chart 37-3   ★★★★
4/6″ Scopes–150x: Struve 1615 AB is a double of bright yellowish and pale blue stars. The 14th magnitude C component lies 2.7″ from the B component in P.A. 276°.

24 Comae Berenices = Σ1657 Double Star Spec. K0, A3
m5.2, 6.7; Sep. 20.3″; P.A. 271°   12^{h}35.1^m +18° 23′
Finder Chart 37-4   ★★★★★
4/6″ Scopes–150x: 24 Comae Berenices is a beautiful color contrast double star of a bright yellowish-

Coma Berenices, Berenice's Hair Constellation Chart 37-1

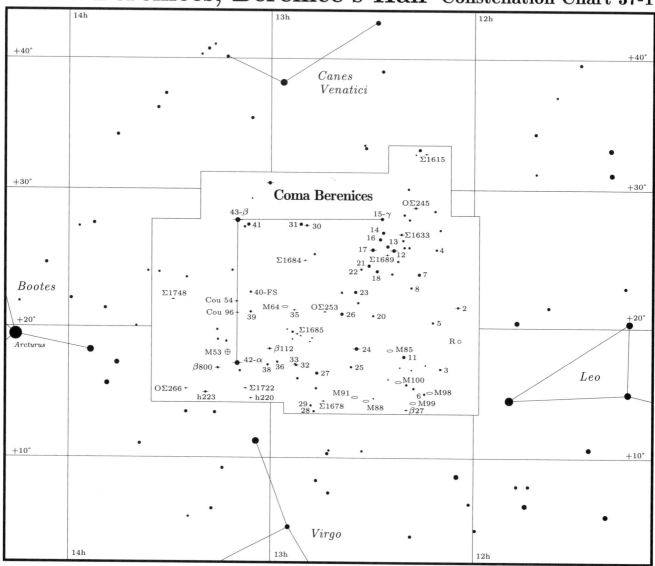

Chart Symbols

Constellation Chart	0 1 2 3 4 5 6
Stellar Magnitudes	● ● ● ● ● ● · ·
Finder Charts	0/1 2 3 4 5 6 7 8 9
Master Finder Chart	0 1 2 3 4 5

→ *Guide Star Pointer*   ⊙ ○ *Variable Stars*   ⟡ *Planetary Nebulae*

●—● *Double Stars*   ○ *Open Clusters*   □ *Small Bright Nebulae*

Finder Chart Scale   ⊕ *Globular Clusters*   *Large Bright Nebulae*

(One degree tick marks)   ⬭ *Galaxies*   *Dark Nebulae*

Table 37-1: Selected Variable Stars in Coma Berenices

Name	HD No.	Type	Max.	Min.	Period (Days)	F*	Spec. Type	R.A. (2000) Dec.		Finder Chart No. & Notes
R Com	104785	M	7.1	14.6	362	0.38	M5-M8	$12^h04.0^m$	$+18°49'$	37-4
40–FS Com	113866	SRb	5.3	6.1	58		M5	$13^h06.4^m$	$+22\ 37$	37-5

F* = The fraction of period taken up by the star's rise from min. to max. brightness, or the period spent in eclipse.

Table 37-2: Selected Double Stars in Coma Berenices

Name	ADS No.	Pair	M1	M2	Sep."	P.A. °	Spec	R.A. (2000) Dec		Finder Chart No.	Notes
2 Com	8406		5.9	7.4	3.7	237	F0	12ʰ04.3ᵐ	+21° 28′	37-4	Pale and deep yellow pair
Σ1615	8470	AB	6.9	9.7	26.7	*88	K0	14.1	+32 47	37-3	Yellowish and pale blue
OΣ 245	8501		5.7	9.8	8.6	280	A0	17.5	+28 56	37-3	
β 27	8514		6.9	10.8	3.5	106	K0	20.1	+13 51	37-4	
Σ1633	8519		7.0	7.1	9.0	245	F2	20.7	+27 03	37-3	Equal yellowish pair
12 Com	8530	AB	4.8	11.8	35.0	54	F5	22.5	+25 51	37-3	
	8530	AC		8.3	65.2	167	A3				
Σ1639	8539	AB	6.8	7.8	w1.7	*323	A5	24.4	+25 35	37-3	
17 Com	8568	AB	5.3	6.6	145.4	251	A0 A3	28.9	+25 55	37-3	
24 Com	8600		5.2	6.7	20.3	271	K0 A3	35.1	+18 23	37-4	Yellowish-orange and blue
OΣ253	8649		8.0	11.2	6.6	237	F0	44.0	+21 10	37-4	
Σ1678	8659		6.8	8.5	34.1	181	A0	45.4	+14 22	37-4	
30 Com	8674		5.8	11.5	42.5	13	A0	49.3	+27 33	37-3	
Σ1684			7.7	10.7	29.2	268	K5	51.9	+25 40	37-5	
Σ1685	8690	AB	7.3	7.9	16.0	202	F2	51.9	+19 10	37-4	
S, h123	8690	AC		8.3	247.4	327					
32 and 33 Com		AB	6.3	6.7	95.2	49	K5 F8	52.2	+17 04	37-6	
		AC		8.7	897.3	262					
35 Com	8695	AB	5.1	7.2	1.2	182	K0	53.3	+21 14	37-6	Orangish and yellowish
	8695	AC		9.1	28.7	126					C: purple or bluish
β 112	8735	AB	6.1	9.5	149.9	350	F5	13ʰ00.6ᵐ	+18 22	37-6	
	8735	BC		9.9	2.0	293					
42–α Com	8804	AB	5.1	5.1	0.4	11	F5	10.0	+17 32	37-6	25.9 year binary
h220	8766		7.8	12.1	17.6	42	F8	05.5	+14 44	37-6	
Σ 1722	8796		8.3	9.3	2.9	339	K0	08.4	+15 29	37-6	
Cou 96			7.0	10.8	10.7	312	F2	10.9	+21 14	37-5	
Cou 54			6.8	10.4	10.3	291	G5	11.5	+21 55	37-5	
43–β Com			4.3	10.1	90.8	251	G0	11.9	+27 53	37-5	
β 800	8841	AB	6.6	9.7	6.8	106	K0	16.9	+17 01	37-6	Orange and reddish pair
	8841	AC		10.4	92.5	3					
h223			7.4	9.9	36.4	348	G5	20.2	+15 34	37-6	
OΣ266	8914		8.4	8.9	2.0	351	F5	28.6	+15 43	37-6	
Σ1748	8918	AB	8.1	11.1	5.7	182	F8	29.2	+22 11	37-5	
	8918	AC		10.8	105.1	353					

Footnotes: *= Year 2000, a = Near apogee, c = Closing, w = Widening. Finder Chart No: All stars listed in the tables are plotted in the large Constellation Chart, but when a star appears in a Finder Chart, this number is listed. Notes: When colors are subtle, the suffix *-ish* is used, e.g. *bluish*.

orange primary with a blue secondary –a springtime version of Albireo (Beta Cygni).

35 Comae Berenices Triple Star   Spec. K0
AB: m5.1, 7.2; Sep.1.2″; P.A.182°   12ʰ53.3ᵐ+21° 14′
Finder Chart 37-6   ★★★★★
4/6″ Scopes–150x: 35 Comae Berenices is a color contrast double of yellow and purple stars. It is one of the few binaries with what appears to be a purple member.
8/10″ Scopes–100x: Light orange and dull blue.

β 800 Triple Star   Spec. K0
AB: m6.6, 9.7; Sep.6.8″; P.A.106°   13ʰ16.9ᵐ+17° 01′
Finder Chart 37-7   ★★★★★
4/6″ Scopes–150x: Burnham 800 is a beautiful, though unequally bright, double of orange and reddish stars. The magnitude 10.4 C component is 92.5″ north of the primary.

37.3 Deep-Sky Objects

NGC 4032 Galaxy Type Im: III
φ 1.7′×1.7′, m12.2v, SB13.3   12ʰ00.6ᵐ +20° 04′
Finder Chart 37-4, Figure 37-1   ★★
12/14″ Scopes–125x: This galaxy has a very faint, circular 2.5′ diameter halo surrounding an elongated core. A 12.5 magnitude star lies 3′ north. NGC 4032 is 3/4° WSW of a group of very faint galaxies.

NGC 4064 Galaxy Type SB(s)a: pec
φ 3.8′×1.7′, m11.4v, SB13.3   12ʰ04.2ᵐ +18° 27′
Finder Chart 37-4, Figure 37-2   ★★★
8/10″ Scopes–100x: NGC 4064 has a fairly faint 2.25′×1′ NNW–SSE halo with tapered ends. The halo grows brighter to a broad central core lacking a nucleus.
12/14″ Scopes–125x: NGC 4064, a nice object for medium size telescopes, has a bright 3.5′×1.25′ NNW–SSE halo containing a bulging oval core. The

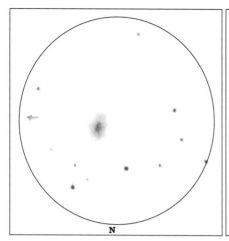

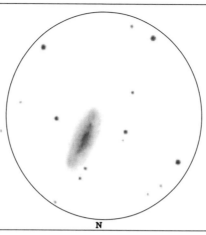

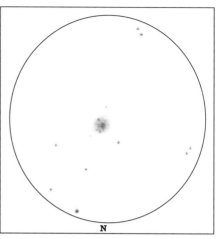

Figure 37-1. NGC 4032 Area
18.5″, f5–255x, by Glen W. Sanner

Figure 37-2. NGC 4064
17.5″, f4.5–225x, by G. R. Kepple

Figure 37-3. NGC 4147
8″, f6–100x, by A. J. Crayon

halo's extension SSE of the core is noticeably shorter than its NNW extension. Along the major axis of the galaxy on either side of the core is a bright streak peppered with tiny bright spots. A knot or a very faint star is in the halo just ENE of the core. A 13th magnitude star is 1.5′ SSW of the galaxy, and two 14th magnitude stars are 1.25′ and 1.75′ to its north.

NGC 4136 H321[2] Galaxy Type SAB(r)c II
ϕ **3.8′×3.8′, m11.0v, SB13.7**   **12ʰ09.3ᵐ +29° 56′**
Finder Chart 37-3   ★★★
12/14″ Scopes–125x: NGC 4136 has a fairly faint, diffuse, circular 3′ diameter halo with a faint stellar nucleus. A 14.4 magnitude star touches the halo's SE edge.

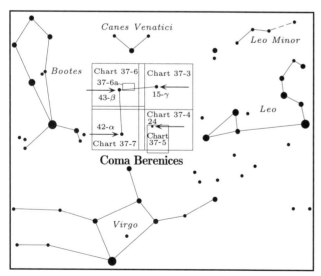

Master Finder Chart 37-2. Coma Berenices Chart Areas
Guide stars indicated by arrows.

NGC 4147 H19[1] Globular Cluster Class VI
ϕ **4′, m10.2v, Br★ 14.5**   **12ʰ10.1ᵐ +18° 33′**
Finder Chart 37-4, Figure 37-3   ★★
8/10″ Scopes–100x: NGC 4147, located 12′ SW of an 8th magnitude star, is a moderately faint, diffuse, unresolved glow containing a stellar nucleus.
12/14″ Scopes–125x: This globular cluster is a fairly bright, unresolved 2.5′ diameter sphere with a bright but tiny core. A few field stars stand out around an irregular periphery that seems slightly elongated NE–SW.

NGC 4150 H73[1] Galaxy Type SA(r)0° ?
ϕ **2.1′×1.5′, m11.6v, SB12.7**   **12ʰ10.6ᵐ +30° 24′**
Finder Chart 37-3   ★★★
8/10″ Scopes–100x: NGC 4150, located 5′ east of a 9th magnitude star, has a bright stellar nucleus surrounded by a faint 1.5′×1′ NW–SE halo. The halo fades smoothly to a diffuse periphery.
12/14″ Scopes–125x: NGC 4150 has a fairly bright 2.5′×1.5′ NNW–SSE halo. The core is weakly concentrated, but the stellar nucleus is quite prominent.

NGC 4152 H83[2] Galaxy Type SAB(rs)c II
ϕ **2.0′×1.7′, m12.2v, SB13.4**   **12ʰ10.6ᵐ +16° 02′**
Finder Chart 37-4   ★★
12/14″ Scopes–125x: NGC 4152 is 20′ south of a wide pair of 7th and 8th magnitude stars. The halo is faint, elongated 1′×0.75′ ESE–WNW, and slightly brightens to a broad, diffuse core with a faint stellar nucleus. The surrounding star field is sparse.

NGC 4158 H405² Galaxy Type SA(r)b:
φ 1.6′×1.5′, m12.1v, SB12.9 12ʰ11.2ᵐ+20° 11′
Finder Chart 37-4 ★★

12/14″Scopes–125x: NGC 4158, located 1.5′
NW of a 10.5 magnitude star, has a faint
1′ diameter halo with diffuse edges and a
slight E–W elongation. The well concentrated core displays some mottling.

NGC 4162 H353² Galaxy Type (R)SA(rs)bc II
φ 2.3′×1.3′, m12.2v, SB13.3 12ʰ11.9ᵐ +24° 07′
Finder Chart 37-3 ★★

12/14″Scopes–125x: NGC 4162 is situated
between a 10.5 magnitude star 2.5′ to its
WSW and a 12.5 magnitude star 2′ to its
ENE. The halo is fairly faint, elongated
2′×1′ nearly N–S, and is slightly brighter
toward its core. A very faint star is just
north of the galaxy's center and a 14th
magnitude star is 1′ WNW. A wide 12.5
magnitude pair lies 7′ south.

NGC 4189 Galaxy Type SAB(rs)cd? II-III
φ 2.5′×2.0′, m11.7v, SB13.1 12ʰ13.8ᵐ +13° 26′
Finder Chart 37-4 ★★★

12/14″Scopes–125x: NGC 4189, located near the Virgo
border, is 2′ WSW of a 12.5 magnitude star. The
halo is a faint, slightly mottled 2′×1.5′ E–W oval
with a small round core. A 14th magnitude star is
just within the halo near its NE edge.

NGC 4192 Messier 98 Galaxy Type SAB(s)ab-II
φ 9.1′×2.1′, m10.1v, SB13.2   12ʰ13.8ᵐ +14° 54′
Finder Chart 37-4, Figure 37-4 ★★★★★

Messier 98 was discovered in 1781 by Mechain and
confirmed later in the same year by Messier. It is one
of the brighter members of the Coma-Virgo Galaxy
Cluster, which is estimated to be 65 or 70 million light
years away. M98 is one of the handful of Coma-Virgo
galaxies with a *blue* shift rather than a red shift, for it
is approaching us with a velocity of 243 kilometers per
second. The galaxy's absolute magnitude is −21.8, a
luminosity of 85 billion suns, and its true diameter is
at least 185,000 light years.

4/6″Scopes–75x: Messier 98 is a bright galaxy located
half a degree west of 5th magnitude star 6 Comae
Berenices. The halo appears large, diffuse and very
elongated NNW–SSE, and has a bright, irregularly
concentrated central region.

8/10″Scopes–100x: This fine galaxy has a large, bright,
mottled halo elongated 6′×2′ NNW–SSE and containing an irregularly bright central region with a
stellar nucleus.

Figure 37-4. *Messier 98 (NGC4192)is an interesting galaxy with a bright,
mottled core and an irregular halo. Image courtesy of Jim Burnell.*

12/14″Scopes–125x: Messier 98 is an interesting galaxy
with a bright irregularly concentrated halo elongated 7′×2′ NNW–SSE and containing a mottled
central area with a 1′ diameter core and a stellar
nucleus. A faint star is 2′ NNE of the galaxy. NGC
4168, 10′ south of M98, is a very faint spot with a
stellar nucleus.

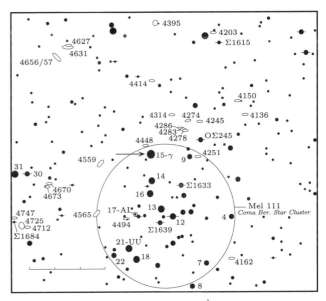

Finder Chart 37-3. 15-γ Com: 12ʰ26.9ᵐ +28° 16′

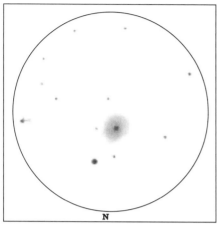

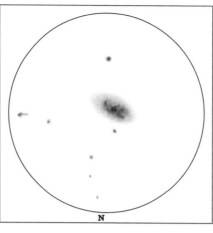

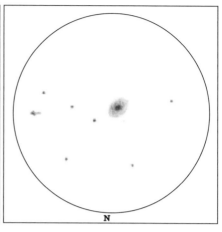

Figure 37-5. NGC 4203
13", f4.5–165x, by Tom Polakis

Figure 37-6. NGC 4212
12.5", f5–175x, by G. R. Kepple

Figure 37-7. NGC 4245
8", f6–100x, by A. J. Crayon

NGC 4203 H175¹ Galaxy Type SAB0–:
ϕ **3.5'×3.4', m10.9v, SB 13.4**   **12ʰ15.1ᵐ +33° 12'**
Finder Chart 37-3, Figure 37-5   ★★★
8/10" Scopes–100x: This galaxy forms a nearly equilateral triangle with an 8th magnitude star 3' to its NNW and a 10th magnitude star 3' to its ENE. It has a bright stellar nucleus embedded in a faint, round 1.25' diameter halo.
12/14" Scopes–125x: NGC 4203 displays a small, very bright core in a 1.5' diameter halo that fades rapidly to a diffuse periphery.

Figure 37-8. *Messier 99 (NGC 4254) has a bright core with spiral arms that can be seen even in medium-size telescopes. Image courtesy of Tim Hunter and James McGaha.*

NGC 4212 H108² Galaxy Type SAc: III
ϕ **2.7'×1.8', m11.2v, SB 12.7**   **12ʰ15.7ᵐ +13° 54'**
Finder Chart 37-4, Figure 37-6   ★★★
8/10" Scopes–100x: This galaxy has a fairly bright 2'×1' E–W oval halo with a slightly brighter core. A row of three magnitude 11.5 stars begins 2.5' south of the galaxy and arcs SE.
12/14" Scopes–125x: NGC 4212 has a bright, mottled 2.5'×1.5' ENE–WSW oval halo. The galaxy's inner region is variegated, and its indistinct core has at least three tiny knots. A 14th magnitude star lies 1.25' north of the galaxy's center. 13' to the NW of NGC 4212 is its companion galaxy IC 3061, a very faint glow elongated 1'×0.25' WNW–ESE.

NGC 4237 H11² Galaxy Type SAB(rs)bc III
ϕ **2.0'×1.3', m11.6v, SB 12.5**   **12ʰ17.2ᵐ +15° 19'**
Finder Chart 37-4   ★★★
8/10" Scopes–100x: NGC 4237, located 12' NNW of a 5th magnitude star, is a fairly faint, circular 1' glow.
12/14" Scopes–125x: NGC 4237 has a 1.25'×0.75' ESE–WNW oval halo around a faint, irregularly bright core. An occasional twinkle glitters from the very faint stellar nucleus.

NGC 4245 H74¹ Galaxy Type SB(r)0/a:
ϕ **3.2'×3.0', m11.4v, SB 13.7**   **12ʰ17.6ᵐ +29° 36'**
Finder Chart 37-3, Figure 37-7   ★★★
8/10" Scopes–100x: This galaxy is just ESE of the NE end of a chain of four 11th magnitude stars. It has a fairly faint 1.5'×1' NW–SE halo that gradually brightens to the tiny core.
12/14" Scopes–125x: Medium size instruments show a fairly bright, mottled halo elongated 2'×1.5' NW–SE with a small, bright core.

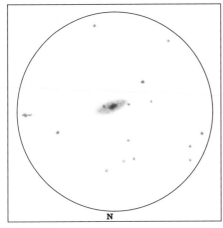

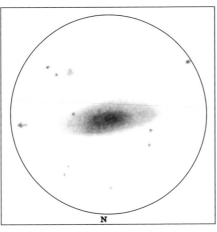

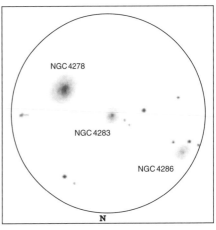

Figure 37-9. NGC 4251
13″, f4.5-115x, by Tom Polakis

Figure 37-10. NGC 4274
12.5″, f5-175x, by G. R. Kepple

Figure 37-11. NGC 4278 Area
12.5″, f5-175x, by G. R. Kepple

NGC 4251 H89[1] Galaxy Type SB0? sp
ϕ 3.7′×2.1′, m10.7v, SB 12.8   12^{h}18.1^m +28° 10′
Finder Chart 37-3, Figure 37-9   ★★★
12/14″ Scopes–125x: NGC 4251, located 18′ west of 6th magnitude 9 Comae Berenices, has a bright 1.5′×1′ ESE–WNW oval halo containing a bright core with a stellar nucleus. A very faint star lies on the WSW edge, and a 13th magnitude star is 3′ ESE of the galaxy.

NGC 4254 Messier 99 Galaxy Type SA(s)c I-II
ϕ 4.6′×4.3′, m9.9v, SB 13.0   12^{h}18.8^m +14° 25′
Finder Chart 37-4, Figure 37-8   ★★★★★
Messier 99 is another of Mechain's 1781 discoveries confirmed later in the same year by Messier. It is also another Coma-Virgo Cluster galaxy and therefore 65–70 million light years distant. It has one of the largest red shifts in the cluster, its recessional velocity being 2380 kilometers per second. M99 has an absolute magnitude around −22, a luminosity of 53 billion suns, and its true diameter is at least 95,000 light years.
4/6″ Scopes–75x: M99, located 9′ SW of a 7th magnitude star, has a fairly bright, large, circular halo with a bright core about 1/6 as large. The halo is granular and its inner region irregularly concentrated. A NW–SE chain of 12th magnitude stars passes along the galaxy's eastern edge, one of the stars touching the halo's SE periphery.
8/10″ Scopes–100x: M99 is a bright galaxy elongated 4′×3′ E–W with a broad, bright core. With averted vision a vague spiral pattern may just be discerned.
12/14″ Scopes–125x: The halo extends 5′×4′ E–W, and within it is a bright core. From the north and south sides of the core the spiral arms curve counterclockwise. The more prominent southern arm arcs toward the west, the fainter, shorter northern arm toward the NE. A conspicuous dark gap separates the

galaxy's core from the western curve of the southern arm. A magnitude 12.5 star is on the halo's SE edge, and a magnitude 13.5 star on its NNE edge.

NGC 4262 H110[2] Galaxy Type SB(s)0–?
ϕ 1.9′×1.8′, m11.6v, SB 12.7   12^{h}19.5^m +14° 53′
Finder Chart 37-4   ★★★
12/14″ Scopes–125x: NGC 4262 is 28′ NNE of M99 and 20′ from a 7th magnitude star that is situated between the two galaxies. Its very bright, tiny core is surrounded by a faint, diffuse, circular 1′ diameter halo.

NGC 4274 H75[1] Galaxy Type (R)SB(r)ab II-III
ϕ 6.7′×2.5′, m10.4v, SB 13.3   12^{h}19.8^m +29° 37′
Finder Chart 37-3, Figure 37-10   ★★★★
8/10″ Scopes–100x: This galaxy is a conspicuous 5′×1.25′ E–W streak that gradually brightens to its center.
12/14″ Scopes–125x: NGC 4274 is a highly elongated 6′×2.5′ ESE–WNW galaxy with a broad, oval core containing a stellar nucleus. 14th magnitude stars are on the halo's ENE and WSW edges. 22′ to the SSE of NGC 4274 is the galaxy trio NGC 4278, NGC 4283, and NGC 4286.

NGC 4278 H90[1] Galaxy Type E1-2
ϕ 3.5′×3.5′, m10.2v, SB 12.7   12^{h}20.1^m +29° 17′

NGC 4283 H323[2] Galaxy Type E0
ϕ 1.1′×1.1′, m12.1v, SB 12.1   12^{h}20.3^m +29° 19′
Finder Chart 37-3, Figure 37-11   ★★★/★★
8/10″ Scopes–100x: NGC 4278 and NGC 4283 form a 3′ wide NE–SW galaxy pair. NGC 4278, the southwestern system, is the larger and brighter of the two: its fairly bright, 1′ diameter halo considerably brightens toward the center. NGC 4283 to the NE appears only half the size of NGC 4278. It is merely a faint,

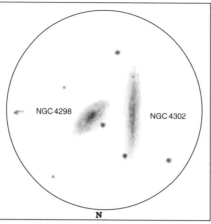

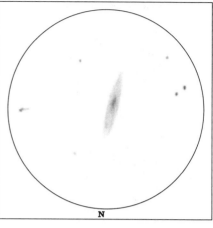

Figure 37-12. NGC 4293
13″, f5.6–135x, by Steve Coe

Figure 37-13. NGC 4298 and NGC 4302
10″, f7–115x, by Dr. Leonard Scarr

Figure 37-14. NGC 4312
12.5″, f5–175x, by G. R. Kepple

round glow.

12/14″ Scopes–125x: NGC 4278 has a bright, circular 1.5′ diameter halo with a small faint core and a stellar nucleus. The halo of NGC 4783 is faint, less than 1′ in diameter, and contains a very faint stellar nucleus. 8′ NE of NGC 4278 is the galaxy NGC 4286, a very faint smudge about the same size as NGC 4283.

NGC 4293 H5⁵ Galaxy Type (R)SB(s)0/a
φ 5.3′×3.1′, m10.4v, SB13.2   12ʰ21.2ᵐ +18° 23′
Finder Chart 37-4, Figure 37-12   ★★★★

8/10″ Scopes–100x: NGC 4293, located half a degree NNE of 5th magnitude star 11 Comae Berenices, has a faint, large, diffuse 4′×1′ ENE–WSW halo.

12/14″ Scopes–125x: NGC 4293 is a fairly bright, thin oval elongated 5′×1.25′ ENE–WSW containing a

small core with a very faint stellar nucleus. East of the core is a dark patch. A magnitude 13.5 star touches the halo's ENE tip, and a second magnitude 13.5 star is on its SSW edge. 3′ NE of the galaxy's center is a 1.5′×1′ triangle of one 13th and two 12th magnitude stars.

NGC 4298 H111² Galaxy Type SA(rs)c III-IV
φ 2.7′×1.6′, m11.3v, SB12.8   12ʰ21.5ᵐ +14° 36′

NGC 4302 H112² Galaxy Type Sc: sp
φ 4.7′×0.9′, m11.6v, SB13.0   12ʰ21.7ᵐ +14° 36′
Finder Chart 37-5, Figure 37-13   ★★★/★★★

8/10″ Scopes–100x: NGC 4298 and NGC 4302 are a visually contrasting galaxy pair 17′ NE of a 25″ wide double of 11th magnitude stars. Their halos are separated by only 1′. NGC 4298 is a fairly faint, diffuse 1.5′×1′ NW–SE oval with little or no central brightening. By contrast NGC 4302 is a narrow streak elongated 3.5′×0.5′ N–S.

12/14″ Scopes–125x: NGC 4298 has a fairly bright 2′×1.5′ NW–SE halo containing a broad, slightly brighter core with a very faint stellar nucleus. A 13th magnitude star touches the NE edge of the halo. NGC 4302 is a fairly bright, thin spindle much elongated 5′×0.75′ with a narrow, slightly brighter core. A 13.5 magnitude star lies just west of the halo's northern tip.

NGC 4312 Galaxy Type SA(rs)ab: sp III
φ 3.8′×0.9′, m11.7v, SB12.9   12ʰ22.5ᵐ +15° 32′
Finder Chart 37-5, Figures 37-14, 37-15   ★★★

12/14″ Scopes–125x: NGC 4312, located 18′ SSW of Messier 100, is a fairly faint, lens-shaped object elongated 3′×0.5′ NNW–SSE and slightly brighter through its center. 2.5′ ESE of the galaxy is a 25″ wide NW–SE pair of 13th magnitude stars.

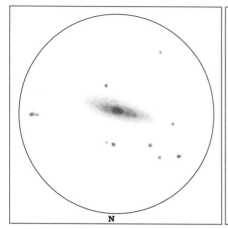

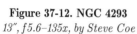

Finder Chart 37-4. 24 Com: 12ʰ35.1ᵐ +18° 23′

Figure 37-15. *Messier 100(NGC4321), a large spiral galaxy in the Coma-Virgo Galaxy Cluster, is a bright object with spiral arms that are visible in larger amateur instruments. Its companions are labeled in the photo above. Image courtesy Jim Burnell.*

NGC 4314 H76[1]   Galaxy Type SB(rs)a
φ 4.2′×4.1′, m10.6v, SB13.5   12^{h}22.6^m +29° 53′
Finder Chart 37-3, Figure 37-18   ★★★★

8/10″Scopes–100x: This galaxy has a fairly bright
  2.5′×1′ NNW–SSE halo around a bright oval core.

16/18″Scopes–150x: NGC 4314 displays a bright 3.5′×1′
  NNW–SSE halo around a bright, circular core with
  a stellar nucleus. A 14th magnitude star is superimposed upon the halo 45″ SE of the core. 13th
  magnitude stars lie on the halo's edge 1.25′ NE and
  2′ NW of the galaxy's center. With averted vision
  a very tenuous outer shell may be glimpsed encir-
  cling the brighter inner regions.

NGC 4321 Messier 100 Galaxy Type SAB(s)bc I
φ 6.2′×5.3′, m9.3v, SB13.0   12^{h}22.9^m +15° 47′
Finder Chart 37-5, Figure 37-15   ★★★★★

   Messier 100 is another of the large spiral galaxies
in the 65–70 million light year distant Coma-Virgo
Cluster. It seems to be exceptionally luminous, its
apparent magnitude implying (if the distance is correct)
an absolute magnitude of −22.5, a brilliance of 83 billion
suns. The galaxy's diameter is also a very respectable
130,000 light years. Like M98 and M99, M100 was first

seen by Mechain and only later in 1781 confirmed by
Messier. Its spiral structure was detected by Lord Rosse
in 1850 with his six-foot reflector.

4/6″Scopes–75x: Messier 100 is considerably bright in
  small telescopes, its elliptical halo elongated 4′×3′
  ESE–WNW, and its core quite luminous, small, and
  round.

8/10″Scopes–100x: Messier 100 has a bright, small core
  embedded in a 5′×4′ ESE–WNW oval halo. The
  halo is generally smooth and its edges diffuse, but
  some variation in brightness can be seen near the
  center around the core.

12/14″Scopes–125x: This is a fine, face-on galaxy with
  a bright 6′×5′ ESE–WNW halo surrounding a
  bright core. 150x shows a vague spiral pattern in
  the halo and a mottled texture immediately around
  the core. A few faint stars are superimposed upon
  the halo NW of the galaxy's center. Three magnitude 13.5 stars are near the halo's NNW, WSW,
  and SE periphery. Two faint companions of M100,
  NGC 4322 located 5′ to the NNE and NGC 4328
  located 6′ east, are visible only as diffuse circular
  spots.

Figure 37-16. *The Coma Berenices Star Cluster, catalogued as Melotte 111, is so large, about 5 degrees across, that it is at its best in binoculars. G. R. Kepple made this three minute exposure on Tri-X film with a 200mm telephoto lens.*

Figure 37-17. *Messier 85 (NGC4382), at left, has a bright core surrounded by a diffuse halo, while NGC4394, at right, appears small and faint. Image courtesy of Martin C. Germano.*

NGC 4340   H85² Galaxy Type SB(r)0+
ϕ **3.7′×3.1′, m11.2v, SB13.7**   **12ʰ23.6ᵐ +16° 43′**

NGC 4350   H86² Galaxy Type SA0
ϕ **2.5′×1.0′, m11.0v, SB11.8**   **12ʰ24.0ᵐ +16° 42′**
Finder Chart 37-5, Figure 37-19   ★★★/★★★
12/14″Scopes–125x: NGC 4340 and NGC 4350 are nearly half a degree east of a 6.5 magnitude star. NGC 4350, located 5.5′ east and slightly south of NGC 4340, is smaller but brighter than its companion: its much elongated 2′×0.75′ NNE–SSW halo contains a bright core with a stellar nucleus. NGC 4340, the western galaxy of the pair, has a broad, faint 1.5′×1.25′ E–W halo with a small bright core around an inconspicuous stellar nucleus.

Melotte 111   Open Cluster 80★ Tr Type II 3 p
ϕ **275′, m1.8v, Br★ 4.35v**   **12ʰ25:ᵐ +26°:**
Finder Chart 37-3, Figure37-16   ★★★★★
Coma Berenices Cluster

The Coma Berenices Star Cluster is a large, rather conspicuous but unconcentrated gathering of 5th and 6th magnitude stars. Its enormous 5° diameter makes it ideal for binoculars; but even the lowest power eyepieces in telescopes spread it out of all resemblance to a cluster. The Coma Cluster is 260 light years distant, the third nearest star cluster, after the Ursa Major Moving Group and the Hyades, to the Solar System. As its visual appearance suggests, it is a loose, poor cluster: it has only 38 confirmed members down to magnitude 9.3 in an area 12° across. The total mass of the whole cluster is only about 100 times that of the Sun, and the mass density even in the core of the group, the 3.3° from 14 to 22 Comae, is only three times the mass density of the star field in the Sun's vicinity. The internal gravitational field of the Coma Cluster must be so weak that the group is probably on the verge of complete disruption. Already most of its low-mass red dwarf members have escaped from it into the Galaxy's general disk population. The total luminosity of the cluster is as pathetic as its total mass: it has an absolute magnitude of only −2.0, corresponding to a mere 525 suns.

The Coma Star Cluster is estimated to be about 500 million years old. It is intermediate in age between the 70 million year old Pleiades and the 660 million year old Hyades. It has evolved to the point where it no longer has any late-B or even early-A blue or blue-white stars. Its two G-type yellow giants are representative of the brightest stars of the clusters around its age. The seven brightest Coma Star Cluster members, with their apparent magnitudes and spectral types, are 12 Comae (4.8, G0 III + A3 V), 31 Comae (4.9, G0 III), 14 Comae (5.0, F0), 16 Comae (5.0, A4 V), 13 Comae (5.2, A3 V), 17 Comae (5.3, A0), and 21 Comae (5.5, A2). The cluster lucida, 12 Comae, not only is a spectroscopic binary, it has two visual companions, a magnitude 11 star 35″ away and a magnitude 8.3 star 65″ distant. 17 Comae is a binocular double with a magnitude 6.7 cluster member 2.5′ to its west. The Coma Star Cluster was not included in either Messier's catalogue or in the NGC.

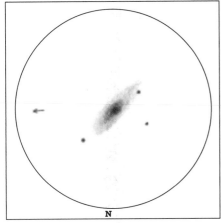
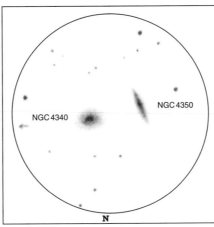
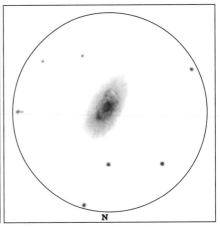

Figure 37-18. NGC 4314
17.5″, ƒ4.5–175x, by G. R. Kepple

Figure 37-19. NGC 4340 and NGC 4350
13″, ƒ5.6–135x, by Steve Coe

Figure 37-20. NGC 4414 Group
13″, ƒ4.5–185x, by George de Lange

NGC 4377 H12¹ Galaxy Type SA0–
φ 1.5′×1.2′, m11.9v, SB12.4   12ʰ25.2ᵐ +14° 46′
Finder Chart 37-5   ★★★
8/10″Scopes–100x: NGC 4377, located 4.75′ SSW of a
   10th magnitude star, is a relatively faint, small,
   round object with a stellar nucleus.
12/14″Scopes–125x: NGC 4377 has a fairly bright,
   circular 1′ diameter halo without central brightening except for a stellar nucleus.

NGC 4379 H87² Galaxy Type S0– pec:
φ 1.5′×1.3′, m11.7v, SB12.3   12ʰ25.2ᵐ +15° 36′
Finder Chart 37-5   ★★★
8/10″Scopes–100x: NGC 4379 is a faint, small, circular
   1′ diameter glow surrounding a bright core. It lies
   in a barren star field.
12/14″Scopes–125x: NGC 4379 has a small, bright core
   containing a stellar nucleus surrounded by a fairly
   faint 1′×0.75′ ESE–WNW halo.

NGC 4382 Messier 85 Galaxy Type SA(s)0+ pec
φ 7.5′×5.7′, m9.1v, SB13.0   12ʰ25.4ᵐ +18° 11′
Finder Chart 37-5, Figure 37-17   ★★★★★
   Messier 85 was discovered in 1781 by Mechain and
confirmed later that same year by Messier. It is one of
the brighter members of the 65-70 million light year
distant Coma-Virgo Cluster. M85 is one of the brightest
and largest of the Coma-Virgo galaxies. Its absolute
magnitude is −22.5, a luminosity of 83 billion suns, and
its true diameter is greater than 150,000 light years.
4/6″Scopes–75x: Messier 85, located 5′ NW of a 10th
   magnitude star, has a bright, small elliptical halo
   elongated 2′×1.75′ N–S. The core is very bright,
   and the halo fades smoothly to its periphery. A

magnitude 12.5 star is on the halo's north edge.
M85 forms an attractive galaxy-pair with NGC 4394
located 8′ to its east.
8/10″Scopes–100x: M85's large, bright oval core is
   embedded in a much fainter halo extending 6′×4′
   nearly N–S. A magnitude 12.5 star is superimposed
   upon the halo just north of the core. A magnitude
   10.5 star is 2.75′ NE of the galaxy.
12/14″Scopes–125x: Larger instruments show that M85
   has a brilliant nonstellar nucleus within a 2′×1.75′
   NNE–SSW core embedded in a faint halo which
   with averted vision can be seen extended to 7′×5′.
   Besides its bright companion NGC 4394, located 8′
   to its east, M85 also has a very faint companion,
   IC3292, a tiny spot lying 8.5′ to its west.

NGC 4383 Galaxy Type Sa? pec
φ 1.6′×0.8′, m12.1v, SB12.2   12ʰ25.4ᵐ +16° 28′
Finder Chart 37-5   ★★
12/14″Scopes–125x: NGC 4383, located 1.5′ SW of a
   12th magnitude star, has a fairly bright nucleus
   embedded in a tiny core surrounded by a much
   fainter 1′×0.5′ NNE–SSW halo. The halo fades
   rapidly to a diffuse periphery.

NGC 4394 H55² Galaxy Type (R)SB(r)b II
φ 3.3′×3.1′, m10.9v, SB13.3   12ʰ25.9ᵐ +18° 13′
Finder Chart 37-5, Figure 37-17   ★★★
8/10″Scopes–100x: NGC 4394, located 8.5′ east of
   Messier 85, has a NW–SE lens-shaped halo with a
   bright stellar nucleus. A 12.5 magnitude star 3′
   south of NGC 4394 is due east of a 10.5 magnitude
   star SE of Messier 85.
12/14″Scopes–125x: NGC 4394 has a small, circular

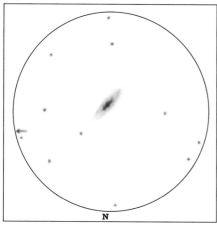

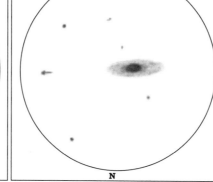

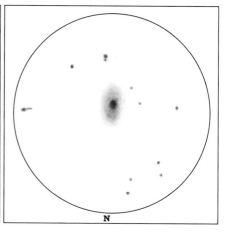

Figure 37-21. NGC 4419
10″, f7–115x, by Dr. Leonard Scarr

Figure 37-22. NGC 4448
12.5″, f5–200x, by G. R. Kepple

Figure 37-23. NGC 4450
10″, f7–115x, by Dr. Leonard Scarr

core with a faint stellar nucleus centered in a 2′×0.75′ NW–SE bar. The tenuous outer halo can be glimpsed only with averted vision.

NGC 4414 H77[1] Galaxy Type SA(rs)c? II-III
ϕ **4.4′×3.0′, m10.1v, SB12.8** $12^{h}26.4^{m}$ +31° 13′
Finder Chart 37-3, Figure 37-20   ★★★★
8/10″Scopes–100x: This galaxy displays a prominent, compact core immersed in a moderately bright 2′×1′ NNW–SSE glow.
12/14″Scopes–125x: NGC 4414 is a bright object with a kidney bean-shaped halo elongated 3′×1.5′ NNW–SSE and containing an oval core with a stellar nucleus. At 150x the halo shows subtle variations in brightness, and in the core can be seen an indistinct dark streak SE, and a bright spot NW, of the nucleus. A 13th magnitude star lies 3′ north.

NGC 4419 H113[2] Galaxy Type SB(s)a
ϕ **2.8′×0.9′, m11.2v, SB12.0** $12^{h}26.9^{m}$ +15° 03′
Finder Chart 37-5, Figure 37-21   ★★★
12/14″Scopes–125x: NGC 4419, located 2′ north of a magnitude 12 star, has a bright, smooth 2.5′×0.5′ NW–SE lens-shaped halo that tapers to sharply pointed tips. The core is highly extended, and a faint star or tiny knot is on its NW edge.

NGC 4421 H89[2] Galaxy Type SB(s)0/a
ϕ **2.3′×1.7′, m11.6v, SB12.9** $12^{h}27.0^{m}$ +15° 28′
Finder Chart 37-5   ★★★
12/14″Scopes–125x: NGC 4421, located 2.5′ ESE of a 9th magnitude star, shows a fairly bright, tiny core with a stellar nucleus surrounded by a moderately faint 1.5′×0.75′ NNW–SSE halo.

NGC 4448 H91[1] Galaxy Type SB(r)ab II
ϕ **3.7′×1.4′, m11.1v, SB12.7** $12^{h}28.2^{m}$ +28° 37′
Finder Chart 37-3, Figure 37-22   ★★★
12/14″Scopes–125x: NGC 4448, located 24′ NE of 4.3 magnitude Gamma (γ) = 15 Comae Berenices, has a fairly bright 2.5′×1′ E–W halo containing an oval core with a stellar nucleus. The eastern extension of the halo is longer and thinner than the western. 14th magnitude stars lie 1.5′ NNE and 1.25′ SSW.

NGC 4450 H56[2] Galaxy Type SA(s)ab I-II
ϕ **5.0′×3.4′, m10.1v, SB13.0** $12^{h}28.5^{m}$ +17° 05′
Finder Chart 37-5, Figure 37-23   ★★★★
8/10″Scopes–100x: This galaxy forms a triangle with a 9th magnitude star 4′ to its SW and a 12.5 magnitude star slightly closer to its south. It displays a conspicuous stellar nucleus surrounded by a diffuse 2.5′×1.25′ N–S halo fading smoothly to the edges.
12/14″Scopes–125x: NGC 4450 has a bright 4′×2.5′ N–S oval halo containing a mottled core with a stellar nucleus noticeably off center to the east. A 13.5 magnitude star lies on the halo's SE edge. A wide N–S double of magnitude 12.5 and 15 stars lies 3.5 SSW.

NGC 4455 H355[2] Galaxy Type SB(s)d? sp IV
ϕ **2.5′×0.9′, m12.3v, SB13.1** $12^{h}28.7^{m}$ +22° 49′
Finder Chart 37-4   ★★
12/14″Scopes–125x: NGC 4455, located 4′ south of a wide N–S pair of 12th magnitude stars, has a faint, diffuse 2.5′×1′ NNE–SSW halo with little central brightening.

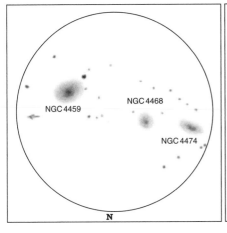

Figure 37-24. NGC 4459-4474 Area
13″, f5.6–135x, by Steve Coe

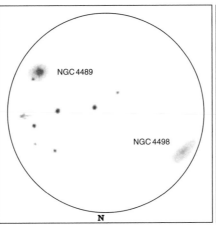

Figure 37-25. NGC 4489 and NGC 4498
12.5″, f5–150x, by G. R. Kepple

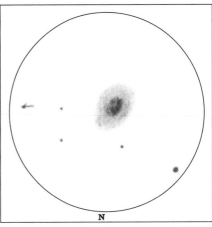

Figure 37-26. NGC 4494
13″, f4.5–185x, by George de Lange

NGC 4459 H161¹ Galaxy Type SA(r)0+
φ **3.5′×2.8′, m10.4v, SB12.7**   12ʰ29.0ᵐ +13° 59′

NGC 4468 H639² Galaxy Type SA0–?
φ **1.2′×0.9′, m12.8v, SB12.7**   12ʰ29.5ᵐ +14° 03′
Finder Chart 37-5, Figure 37-24   ★★★/★★
12/14″Scopes–125x: NGC 4459, located 2′ NW of an 8.5 magnitude star, displays a prominent stellar nucleus embedded in a fairly bright, circular 1.5′ diameter halo with a diffuse periphery. The surrounding field contains numerous faint galaxies including NGC 4468 which lies 10′ ENE of NGC 4459, NGC 4468, a faint, small, circular spot with a stellar nucleus.

NGC 4473 H114² Galaxy Type E5
φ **3.7′×2.4′, m10.2v, SB12.4**   12ʰ29.8ᵐ +13° 26′
Finder Chart 37-5   ★★★
12/14″Scopes–125x: NGC 4473 is a bright lenticular galaxy elongated 2.25′×1.25′ E–W. It has a brighter, irregular core containing a stellar nucleus.

NGC 4474 H117² Galaxy Type S0 pec:
φ **1.9′×1.1′, m11.5v, SB12.2**   12ʰ29.9ᵐ +14° 04′
Finder Chart 37-5, Figure 37-24   ★★★
12/14″Scopes–125x: NGC 4474 is fairly bright, elongated 1′×0.5′ ENE–WSW, and has an elongated core containing a faint stellar nucleus. A double (11.5, 12.5; 20″; 285°) 25′ NNE of the galaxy is in a NW–SE line of stars. NGC 4468 lies 6′ west and NGC 4459 is 16′ WSW.

NGC 4477 H115² Galaxy Type SB(s)0:?
φ **3.9′×3.6′, m10.4v, SB13.1**   12ʰ30.0ᵐ +13° 38′
Finder Chart 37-5   ★★★
12/14″Scopes–125x: NGC 4477 is a moderately bright

galaxy with a diffuse 2′×1.75′ NNE–SSW halo containing a stellar nucleus. 13th magnitude stars are 2′ to its NNE and 1.5′ to its south. Galaxy NGC 4479 lies 6′ SE.

NGC 4479 H116² Galaxy Type SB(s)0° :?
φ **1.5′×1.4′, m12.4v, SB13.1**   12ʰ30.3ᵐ +13° 35′
Finder Chart 37-5   ★★
12/14″Scopes–125x: NGC 4479 is a small companion of the bright NGC 4477 located 6′ to its SE. It has a sharp stellar nucleus immersed in a diffuse, moderately faint, circular 1′ diameter halo.

NGC 4489 H91² Galaxy Type E
φ **1.8′×1.7′, m12.0v, SB13.1**   12ʰ30.8ᵐ +16° 45′
Finder Chart 37-5, Figure 37-25   ★★
12/14″Scopes–125x: NGC 4489, located 8′ NNW of a 7th magnitude star, is a diffuse, circular glow less than 1′ across containing a stellar nucleus. A 14th magnitude star is on the NW edge of the halo. Galaxy NGC 4498 lies 13′ to its NE.

NGC 4494 H83¹ Galaxy Type E1-2
φ **4.6′×4.4′, m9.8v, SB12.9**   12ʰ31.4ᵐ +25° 47′
Finder Chart 37-3, Figure 37-26   ★★★★
8/10″Scopes–100x: NGC 4494, located 5′ SSW of an 8th magnitude star, is a fairly bright 1.5′×1′ N–S oval.
12/14″Scopes–125x: NGC 4494 is a broad oval elongated 4′×3′ slightly NNE–SSW containing a large, but inconspicuous oval core. The core is noticeably brighter on its western side; but the halo is somewhat fainter and more diffuse along its western periphery.

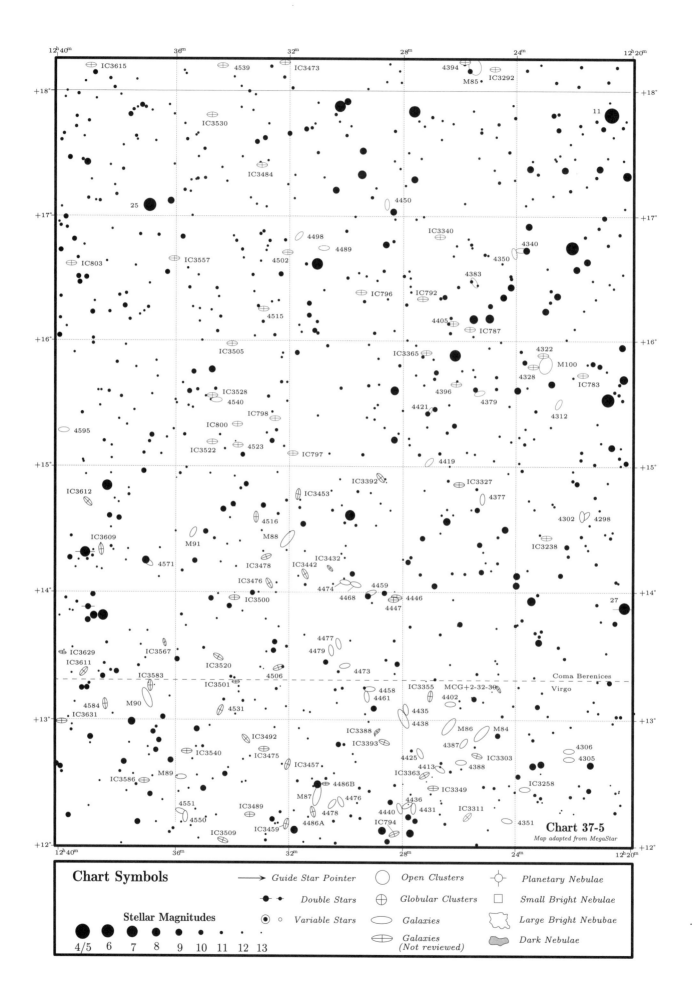

Chart 37-5

Map adapted from MegaStar

Chart Symbols

→ Guide Star Pointer

•—•—• Double Stars

◉ ○ Variable Stars

Stellar Magnitudes

● ● ● ● ● ● · ·
4/5 6 7 8 9 10 11 12 13

◯ Open Clusters

⊕ Globular Clusters

⬭ Galaxies

⊖ Galaxies (Not reviewed)

✦ Planetary Nebulae

□ Small Bright Nebulae

⬭ Large Bright Nebubae

▨ Dark Nebulae

Table 37-3: Data for galaxies not reviewed in Chart 37-5

Name	Hershel No.	Type	Size(')	Mag.(v)	SB	P.A.°	R.A. (2000.0)	Dec.
IC 783		SAB(rs)0/a?	1.1×1.0	13.8	13.6	141	12h21.6m	+15° 45′
NGC 4322		SB(r)0°	0.9×0.6	13.9	13.7	140	23.0	+15 54
IC 3228			0.6×0.4	14.1	12.4		23.1	+14 25
NGC 4328	H84²	SA0⁻:	1.5×1.5	13.0	13.8		23.3	+15 48
IC 3292		L	0.8×0.4	14.5	12.6	135	24.8	+18 11
IC 787		S?	1.0×0.5	14.2	13.4	178	25.5	+16 06
NGC 4394	H55²	(R)SB(r)b II	3.3×3.1	10.9	13.3	145	25.9	+18 13
IC 3327		SB	0.4×0.4	15.4			26.0	+14 52
NGC 4396		SAd:sp	3.2×1.1	12.6	13.7	125	26.0	+15 40
NGC 4405	H88²	SA(rs)0/a:	1.8×1.1	12.0	12.6	20	26.1	+16 11
IC 3340		SB	0.7×0.4	15.5		28	26.5	+16 50
IC 3365		Im	1.7×0.7	13.8	13.8	72	27.1	+15 54
IC 792		Sb III	1.6×0.5	14.0	13.6	59	27.1	+16 20
NGC 4446		Scd:	1.0×0.8	13.9	13.6	106	28.2	+13 55
NGC 4447		SB0?	0.9×0.7	14.0	13.3	105	28.3	+13 54
IC 3392		SAb:	2.3×0.9	12.2	12.8	40	28.7	+15 00
IC 796		S0/a	1.3×0.6	13.1	12.7	145	29.4	+16 24
IC 3432		S?	0.7×0.6	14.6	13.0	54	30.4	+14 10
IC 3442		E0:	1.2×0.8	13.5	13.1	33	31.3	+14 07
IC 3453		Irr	1.7×0.5	15.5		160	31.5	+14 51
IC 797		SBcd?	1.3×0.9	12.9	12.9	108	31.9	+15 07
NGC 4502	H92²	Scd:	1.1×0.6	13.9	13.3	40	32.1	+16 42
NGC 4506	H631²	Sa pec?	1.6×1.1	12.7	13.2	110	32.2	+13 25
IC 3473		Sd:	1.1×0.8	15.0		45	32.3	+18 14
IC 798		C	0.5×0.5	15.3			32.5	+15 24
IC 3476		IB(s)m:	2.2×1.4	12.7	13.7	30	32.7	+14 03
IC 3478		SAB0:	1.1×0.9	13.3	13.1	105	32.7	+14 12
NGC 4515	H93²	S0⁻:	1.3×1.1	12.3	12.3	9	33.0	+16 15
IC 3484		S	0.6×0.5	15.2		57	33.1	+17 24
NGC 4516	H78²	SB(rs)ab?	1.7×1.0	12.8	13.2	0	33.1	+14 34
NGC 4523		SAB(s)m V	2.0×1.9	14.1	15.4	45	33.8	+15 10
IC 3500		SB?	0.6×0.3	15.4		89	33.8	+13 58
IC 800		SB(rs)c pec?	1.5×1.1	13.4	13.8	157	33.9	+15 21
IC 3505		SB	0.9×0.4	15.2	12.9	160	34.1	+15 57
IC 3520		S?	0.8×0.5	14.0	13.5	55	34.5	+13 30
NGC 4539		SB(s)a: sp	2.7×1.0	12.0	12.9	95	34.6	+18 12
IC 3522		IBm: sp V	1.4×0.6	14.7	14.4	95	34.8	+15 13
IC 3530		S0	1.2×0.9	14.0	13.9	162	34.8	+17 48
IC 3528		SAB(r)b	0.5×0.4	14.5			34.9	+15 34
IC 3557		S	0.8×0.6	14.6		115	36.1	+16 38
IC 3567		S	0.8×0.7	13.9	13.1	10	36.4	+13 36
IC 3609		S	0.4×0.3	15.3		1	38.5	+14 22
IC 3615		Sc	1.0×0.2	15.3		11	39.0	+18 11
IC 3611		S?	1.4×0.8	13.3	13.3	137	39.1	+13 22
IC 3612		S	1.8×0.5	15.0		50	39.1	+14 43
IC 803		S	0.5×0.2	15.9		130	39.6	+16 36
IC 3629		S	0.8×0.3	14.3	12.5	72	39.8	+13 31

NGC 4498 H69³ Galaxy Type SAB(s)d
φ 3.2′×1.6′, m12.2v, SB13.8   12ʰ31.7ᵐ +16° 51′
Finder Chart 37-5, Figure 37-25   ★★
12/14″Scopes–125x: NGC 4498, located 20′ NE of a 7th magnitude star, is a diffuse glow elongated 1.5′×0.75′ NW–SE. Galaxy NGC 4489 lies 13′ SE.

NGC 4501 Messier 88 Galaxy Type SA(rs)b I-II
φ 6.1′×2.8′, m9.6v, SB12.6   12ʰ32.0ᵐ +14° 25′
Finder Chart 37-5, Figure 37-27   ★★★★★
Messier discovered this galaxy on March 18, 1781.

Messier 88 is one of the giant spiral members of the 65-70 million light year distant Coma-Virgo Galaxy Cluster. It lies near the northern end of a three degree long arc of galaxies that begins to the SW in Virgo with the M84+M86 galaxy pair and curves east and NE to M88. This galaxy has the very respectable absolute magnitude of −22, a luminosity of 52 billion suns, and its true diameter probably is in excess of 125,000 light years.
4/6″Scopes–75x: Messier 88, located 5′ north of a 30″ pair of 11.5 and 12.5 magnitude stars, has a bright, broad oval core embedded in a diffuse halo elongated 5′×2′ NW–SE.

Figure 37-27. *Messier 88 (NGC 4501) has an irregularly bright, mottled halo with a faint spiral structure. Image courtesy of Jim Burnell.*

Figure 37-28. *NGC 4548, possibly M91, one of the missing objects in Messier's catalogue, has a bright core but a very diffuse halo. Image courtesy of Tim Hunter and James McGaha.*

8/10″Scopes–100x: This interesting galaxy has an irregular 6′×2.5′ halo somewhat pointed on the SE but rounded on the NW. The oval core is quite bright. A 15″ wide NNE–SSW double of 14th magnitude stars is superimposed upon the halo near its SE end.

12/14″Scopes–125x: Messier 88 is a bright galaxy with an irregularly bright halo elongated 6.5′×3′ NW–SE. The core is bright and elongated 2.5′×2′. The halo has a mottled texture immediately around the core; and with averted vision spiral structure is suspected, especially along the SW flank and SE of the core. Knots can be seen NW and SE of the core and in the NNW portion of the halo.

NGC 4540 H94² Galaxy Type SAB(rs)cd IV
φ 1.9′×1.6′, m11.7v, SB 12.8   12ʰ34.8ᵐ +15° 33′
Finder Chart 37-5   ★★★
12/14″Scopes–125x: This fairly faint galaxy lies at the SSW vertex of the 15′×10′ triangle it forms with two 7.5 magnitude stars. It has a diffuse, circular 1.5′ diameter halo brightening toward the center. Four faint stars superimposed upon the halo give the galaxy the appearance of a partially resolved globular cluster.

NGC 4548 Messier 91 Galaxy Type SB(rs)b I-II
φ 5.0′×4.1′, m10.2v, SB 13.3   12ʰ35.4ᵐ +14° 30′
Finder Chart 37-5, Figure 37-28   ★★★★
M91 is one of the "missing" Messier objects, the true identity of which is still in dispute. However it seems likely that M91 is a duplicate observation of one

of the other Messier objects in the region given an erroneous position – Owen Gingerich suggests M58. Of the possible non-Messier galaxies in southern Coma and NW Virgo that might have been the original M91, NGC 4548 and NGC 4571 are the best candidates, though the latter is rather faint. Or M91 may have actually been a comet that Messier did not recognize as such!

Whether or not NGC 4548 is the original M91, it is in the 65–70 million light year distant Coma-Virgo Galaxy Cluster. Though neither one of the brighter nor one of the larger spirals in the cluster, it nevertheless has the very healthy absolute magnitude of −21.3, a luminosity of 28 billion suns. Its true diameter is over 100,000 light years.

4/6″Scopes–75x: This galaxy has a small, bright core immersed in a smooth, circular glow.

8/10″Scopes–100x: Messier 91 has a fairly bright, diffuse halo that is elongated 2.5′×1.5′ NNW–SSE and brightens smoothly to a small, circular core.

12/14″Scopes–125x: In moderate-aperture telescopes NGC 4548 enlarges to a 4′×2′ NNW–SSE oval, but is still diffuse and featureless. The halo fades rapidly from the central region. The galaxy's small, round, bright core has an inconspicuous stellar nucleus.

NGC 4559 H92¹ Galaxy Type SAB(rs)cd II-III
φ 12.0′×4.9′, m10.0v, SB 14.3   12ʰ36.0ᵐ +27° 58′
Finder Chart 37-3, Figure 37-30   ★★★★
8/10″Scopes–100x: This galaxy is a faint but interesting object. Its variegated, much elongated 8′×2′

Figure 37-29. *NGC 4565, a beautifully detailed streak with a prominent dark lane, is perhaps the finest of all edge-on galaxies. Image courtesy Bill McLaughlin.*

NW–SE halo brightens only moderately to an irregular, extended core. Three 12th to 13th magnitude stars cap the SE tip.

12/14″ Scopes–125x: NGC 4559, a pleasing sight, has a highly irregular 10′×4′ NNW–SSE halo with subtle dark streaks and a moderately brighter, highly extended core. The core seems off center to the SE, and the halo is not as extensive in that direction. With averted vision a dark patch can be seen just SE of the core. Three stars surround the SE tip: a 13th magnitude star at its end, and magnitude 12 and 12.5 stars east and south of the galaxy's center.

NGC 4565 H24⁵ Galaxy Type SA(s)b? sp I
ϕ 14.0′×1.8′, m9.6v, SB 12.9   12ʰ36.3ᵐ +25° 59′
Finder Chart 37-3, Figure 37-29   ★★★★★

NGC 4565 is one of the brightest members of the 31 million light year distant Coma I Galaxy Cloud. Its edge-on absolute magnitude is −20.3, a luminosity of 11 billion suns; but if we saw it face-on, these values would be much higher. Its true length is in excess of 125,000 light years.

8/10″ Scopes–100x: This edge-on galaxy is absolutely phenomenal! The halo is moderately faint, but extremely large and highly elongated 12′×1.5′ NW–SE with a bulging core at its center. A 13.5 magnitude star lies 1.5′ NE of the center. A faint dust lane is just visible without averted vision passing off-center on the NE side of the core.

12/14″ Scopes–125x: NGC 4565 is "the showpiece" of all edge-on galaxies! It is a beautiful streak elongated 14′×1.5′ NW–SE with a bright 3′×2′ central bulge flanked by 13.5 magnitude stars 1.5′ to its NE and 7′ to its SSW. The dust lane is quite obvious, passing NE of the core and extending for 60% of the halo's length. Some faint mottling can be seen along

Figure 37-30. *NGC 4559 has a highly extended core surrounded by subtle dark streaks. Image courtesy of Jim Burnell.*

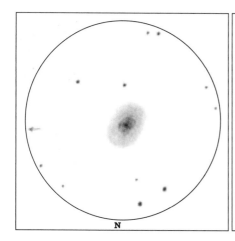

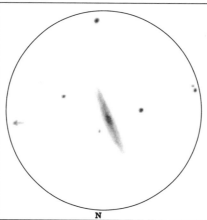

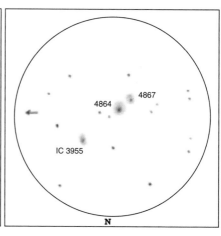

Figure 37-31. NGC 4689
17.5″, f4.5–250x, by G. R. Kepple

Figure 37-32. NGC 4710
17.5″, f4.5–250x, by G. R. Kepple

Figure 37-33. NGC 4864 Area
17.5″, f4.5–300x, by G. R. Kepple

the lane, and a few knots are visible SE of the core.
16/18″ Scopes–150x: At this magnification, NGC 4565
is awesome, filling the entire field of view. The halo
is elongated 16′×2′ NW–SE, and the dust lane extending for nearly all this length, fading near the edges.
The core is a bright 4′×3′ oval with the dark lane off-
center to the NE. A prominent bright streak is NW
of the core, and some mottling is visible along the
central stretch of the dark lane. Smaller bright streaks
are along the SE extension of the dark lane. A very
faint threshold star touches the core's SW edge.

NGC 4571 H602³ Galaxy Type SA(r)d III
φ **4.1′×3.4′, m11.3v, SB14.0**   **12ʰ36.9ᵐ +14° 13′**
Finder Chart 37-5   ★★★
12/14″ Scopes–125x: NGC 4571, located 1.5′ SW of a
9th magnitude star, has a faint, circular 1.5′ diameter halo surrounding a very faint stellar nucleus.
A 14.5 magnitude star lies on the halo's west edge.
Because NGC 4571 probably could not be seen in
Messier's telescope, it is an unlikely candidate for
the missing M91.

NGC 4595 H632² Galaxy Type SAB(rs)b? III
φ **1.6′×1.0′, m12.1v, SB12.5**   **12ʰ39.9ᵐ +15° 18′**
Finder Chart 37-5   ★★
12/14″ Scopes–125x: NGC 4595, located 17′ WSW of an
8th magnitude star, is a faint 1.25′ glow slightly
elongated ESE–WNW and slightly brighter in the
center.

NGC 4651 H12² Galaxy Type SA(rs)c II
φ **3.5′×2.3′, m10.8v, SB12.9**   **12ʰ43.7ᵐ +16° 24′**
Finder Chart 37-4   ★★★
12/14″ Scopes–125x: NGC 4651 shows a fairly bright

3′×2′ WSW–ENE halo that gradually brightens to
a faint core containing a stellar nucleus. At 175x
the galaxy appears slightly mottled near the center,
but its edges remain diffuse. A very faint star lies
near the halo's ENE tip.

NGC 4670 H328³ Galaxy Type SB(s)0/a pec
φ **1.5′×1.3′, m12.7v, SB13.3**   **12ʰ45.3ᵐ +27° 08′**

NGC 4673 H329³ Galaxy Type E1-2
φ **1.0′×0.8′, m12.9v, SB12.5**   **12ʰ45.6ᵐ +27° 04′**
Finder Chart 37-3   ★★/★★
12/14″ Scopes–125x: NGC 4670 displays a bright stellar
nucleus embedded in a faint, diffuse 1.25′×1′ E–W
halo. 5.5′ SE of NGC 4670 is NGC 4673, half its
size and noticeably fainter but also with a stellar
nucleus. The two galaxies form a triangle with a
9th magnitude star.

NGC 4689 H128² Galaxy Type SA(rs)bc II-III
φ **3.7′×3.2′, m10.9v, SB13.5**   **12ʰ47.8ᵐ +13° 46′**
Finder Chart 37-4, Figure 37-31   ★★★★
12/14″ Scopes–125x: NGC 4689 forms a 15′ equilateral
triangle with a 7th magnitude star to its SE and
an 8th magnitude star to its SW. This galaxy has
a fairly bright 3.5′×3′ NNW–SSE halo that brightens slightly to a large mottled core containing a
faint stellar nucleus. 3.5′ NNE is a very wide ESE–
WNW pair of 12th magnitude stars.

NGC 4710 H95² Galaxy Type SA(r)0+ sp
φ **3.9′×1.2′, m11.0v, SB12.5**   **12ʰ49.6ᵐ +15° 10′**
Finder Chart 37-4, Figure 37-32   ★★★★
12/14″ Scopes–125x: NGC 4710 is a bright edge-on
galaxy much-elongated 3.5′×0.5′ NNE–SSW. Its

Figure 37-34. *NGC 4725 has a bright core and spiral arms which may be glimpsed under good observing conditions. Image courtesy Chris Schur.*

Figure 37-35. *Messier 64 (NGC 4826) has a dark dust lane arcing along the NE edge of its core, the feature from which it has gotten the name "Black-Eye Galaxy." Image courtesy Jim Burnell.*

halo is mottled and irregularly concentrated along its major axis. A 13th magnitude star lies 1.5′ east and slightly south of the galaxy's center.

NGC 4712 Galaxy Type SA(s)bc III
ϕ 2.2′×0.8′, m12.8v, SB 13.2   12^{h}49.6^m +25° 28′
Finder Chart 37-3   ★★
8/14″ Scopes–125x: NGC 4712 is a faint galaxy 12′ west of the very large and bright galaxy NGC 4725. Its halo is elongated 2′×0.75′ NNW–SSE, is of uniform surface brightness, and lacks discernible details. A 12.5 magnitude star lies 4′ south.

NGC 4725 H84[1] Galaxy Type SAB(r)ab pec II
ϕ 11.0′×8.3′, m9.4v, SB 14.1   12^{h}50.4^m +25° 30′
Finder Chart 37-3, Figure 37-34   ★★★★★
8/10″ Scopes–100x: This galaxy has a bright 5′×3′ NE–SW halo that gradually brightens even more toward its center.
12/14″ Scopes–125x: NGC 4725 is quite large and bright, appears elongated 10′×7′ NE–SW, and has a bright, sharp nucleus in a bright but small core. Its broad spiral arms form a ring around the interior of the galaxy, the ring brightest along its NE and SW arcs. A very faint central bar may be glimpsed in the core of the galaxy elongated, like the halo, NE–SW. A magnitude 12.5 star lies 2.5′ NNW, and magnitude 14.5 stars are superimposed upon the halo 1.5′ east and 2′ NE of the galaxy's center.

NGC 4747 H344[2] Galaxy Type SBcd? pec sp
ϕ 3.2′×1.4′, m12.3v, SB 13.8   12^{h}51.8^m +25° 47′
Finder Chart 37-3   ★★
12/14″ Scopes–125x: NGC 4747 lies 7′ north of a wide double consisting of an orange 7.5 magnitude primary with a 12th magnitude companion. It has a faint 3′×1′ NNE–SSW halo that is only slightly brighter in its center. The large, bright galaxy NGC 4725 is 24′ SW.

NGC 4793 H93[1] Galaxy Type SAB(rs)c III
ϕ 3.1′×1.7′, m11.6v, SB 13.3   12^{h}54.6^m +28° 56′
Finder Chart 37-6   ★★★
12/14″ Scopes–125x: NGC 4793, located 2′ south of an 8th magnitude star, has a fairly bright 2′×1′ NE–SW halo that is slightly brighter at its center.
16/18″ Scopes–150x: NGC 4793 shows a bright 2.5′×1.25′ NE–SW halo which slightly brightens to a faint stellar nucleus. The central area has a mottled texture. A 14th magnitude star lies 1.75′ SW.

NGC 4826 Messier 64 Galaxy Type (R)SA(rs)ab II-III
ϕ 9.2′×4.6′, m8.5v, SB 12.4   12^{h}56.7^m +21° 41′
Finder Chart 37-7, Figures 37-35, 37-36   ★★★★★
The Black-Eye Galaxy
J. E. Bode discovered Messier 64 in 1779, though he recorded it only as a "small nebulous star." M64 is part of a 24 million light year distant galaxy group with M94 in Canes Venatici. Its absolute magnitude is −21,

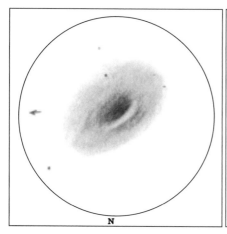

Figure 37-36. Messier 64
13″, f4.5–150x, by George de Lange

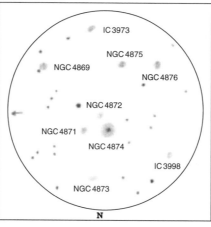

Figure 37-37. NGC 4874 Area
17.5″, f4.5–300x, by G. R. Kepple

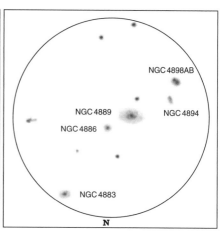

Figure 37-38. NGC 4889 Area
17.5″, f4.5–300x, by G. R. Kepple

a luminosity of 21 billion suns, and its true size at least 65,000 light years.

4/6″ Scopes–75x: Messier 64 is a bright 5′×3′ ESE–WNW oval containing a large, bright core.

8/10″ Scopes–100x: This bright galaxy is elongated 6′×3′ ESE–WNW and has a prominent core. An 11th magnitude star lies 4′ NE.

12/14″ Scopes–125x: The Black-Eye Galaxy is a bright, beautiful object elongated 7′×4′ ESE–WNW containing a bright core that is conspicuously off center to the SSW. The dark patch arcing along the NE periphery of the core requires averted vision at low power, but at 150x may be viewed directly. A bright, diffuse rim lies outside the dark lane.

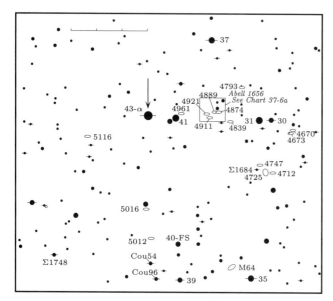

Finder Chart 37-6 43–β Com: 13ʰ11.8ᵐ +27° 53′

NGC 4839 H386² Galaxy Type E+
φ 4.1′×1.9′, m12.1v, SB14.1   12ʰ57.4ᵐ +27° 30′
Finder Chart 37-6   ★★
16/18″ Scopes–150x: NGC 4839 is between a 12th magnitude star 2.5′ to its NE and a 13th magnitude star 2′ to its SW. It has a stellar nucleus embedded in a prominent core enveloped by a much fainter diffuse halo elongated 1.5′×0.75′ ENE–WSW. NGC 4839 is a member of the 400 million light year distant Coma Galaxy Cluster.

NGC 4860 Galaxy Type E2:
φ 0.8′×0.7′, m13.5v, SB12.7   12ʰ59.1ᵐ +28° 07′
Finder Chart 37-6a   ★
16/18″ Scopes–150x: NGC 4860, a member of the Coma Galaxy Cluster, has a faint stellar nucleus embedded in a diffuse 45″ diameter halo.

NGC 4864 Galaxy Type E2
φ 0.5′×0.3′, m13.6v, SB11.4   12ʰ59.2ᵐ +27° 59′

NGC 4867 Galaxy Type E-3
φ 0.6′×0.6′, m14.5v, SB13.2   12ʰ59.3ᵐ +27° 58′
Finder Chart 37-6a, Figure 37-33   ★★/★
16/18″ Scopes–150x: NGC 4864 and NGC 4867, located 5′ west and slightly north of the relatively bright NGC 4874 in the Coma Galaxy Cluster, are a close 30″ NW–SE pair of tiny galaxies. NGC 4864, the NW object, is the brighter and larger of the two, measuring 45″×30″ NW–SE with a stellar nucleus. NGC 4867 on the SE is merely a faint, tiny spot. 2′ NW of NGC 4864 is the Coma Cluster galaxy IC 3955, a very faint 20″ diameter smudge slightly elongated NNE–SSW.

NGC 4865 Galaxy Type E6
ϕ 1.3′×0.7′, m13.7v, SB13.4   12^{h}59.3^m +28° 05′
Finder Chart 37-6a   ★★★
16/18″Scopes–150x: NGC 4865, a Coma Cluster galaxy, is 3′ NW of a 7th magnitude star. It is moderately faint but not difficult to spot. Its halo is of even surface brightness and elongated 45″×30″ ESE–WNW. A small, faint, diffuse companion galaxy, M+05-31-63, is 1.5′ to the WSW.

NGC 4871 Galaxy Type SA0
ϕ 0.5′×0.3′, m14.1v, SB11.9   12^{h}59.5^m +27° 57′

NGC 4872 H389^2 Galaxy Type SB0
ϕ 1.5′×1.5′, m14.4v, SB15.1   12^{h}59.6^m +27° 57′

NGC 4873 Galaxy Type SA0
ϕ 0.7′×0.5′, m14.1v, SB12.8   12^{h}59.6^m +27° 59′

IC 3998 Galaxy Type
ϕ 0.6′×0.4′, m14.7v, SB13.1:   12^{h}59.8^m +27° 58′
Finder Chart 37-6a, Figure 37-37   ★/★/★/★
16/18″Scopes–150x: These four galaxies are all close companions of NGC 4874, the second brightest member of the Coma Galaxy Cluster. NGC 4871, located 1.5′ west of the bright galaxy, is a small, faint, 15″ diameter smudge. NGC 4872, less than 1′ SSW of NGC 4874, is a slightly brighter version of NGC 4871. Next, NGC 4873, only 1.5′ NNW of NGC 4874, is about the same size, but fainter than, NGCs 4871 and 4872. Finally, IC 3998, located 2.5′ from NGC 4874 in the direction of the other bright Coma Cluster galaxy NGC 4889, is merely a fairly faint spot smaller than the other companions.

NGC 4874 Galaxy Type E+0
ϕ 2.4′×2.4′, m11.7v, SB13.4   12^{h}59.6^m +27° 58′
Finder Chart 37-6a, Figure 37-37   ★★★
16/18″Scopes–150x: NGC 4874, the second brightest galaxy in the 400 million light year distant Coma Galaxy Cluster, is 6′ south of a 7th magnitude star. Its rather faint, circular 1.5′ diameter halo brightens slightly to a small core. A magnitude 12.5 star lies 2′ SW. Photographs reveal several faint satellite galaxies around this supergiant elliptical system, the best visual observing being NGC 4871 located 1.5′ west, and NGC 4872, only 1′ SSW, and NGC 4873, just 1.5′ NNW. NGC 4874 has an absolute magnitude of at least −23.8, a luminosity of 275 million suns, and a diameter in excess of 260,000 light years.

NGC 4886 (=NGC 4882) Galaxy Type E0
ϕ 0.7′×0.7′, m13.9v, SB12.9   13^{h}00.0^m +27° 59′

NGC 4889 H321^2 Galaxy Type E+4
ϕ 2.8′×2.1′, m11.5v, SB13.3   13^{h}00.1^m +27° 58′
Finder Chart 37-6a, Figure 37-38   ★/★★★
16/18″Scopes–150x: NGC 4889 is the brightest member of the Coma Galaxy Cluster. It and NGC 4874 located 7.5′ to its west mark the core of this huge aggregation of 400 million light year distant galaxies, some of which lie 100 million light years from the NGC 4874/4889 center. NGC 4889 has a 1.5′ diameter, slightly E–W elongated, halo that brightens into a broad oval core containing a faint stellar nucleus. A magnitude 13.5 star is 1′ SE. Only 1′ north is satellite galaxy NGC 4886, a faint, tiny spot. NGC 4889 has an absolute magnitude of around −24, a luminosity of about 330 billion suns, and a major axis at least 330,000 light years long. Supergiant ellipticals like NGC 4889 and NGC 4874 are thought to have gotten so big by absorbing satellite galaxies.

NGC 4898AB Galaxy Type E pec
ϕ ?, m13.5v, SB?   13^{h}00.3^m +27° 57′
Finder Chart 37-6a, Figure 37-38   ★★
16/18″Scopes–150x: NGC 4898AB, located 2.5′ SE of NGC 4889 in the Coma Galaxy Cluster, is composed of two systems in contact. They appear, however, as a single, fairly conspicuous object elongated 30″×15″ ENE–WSW.

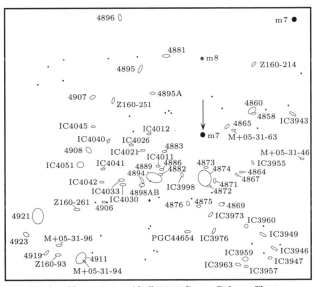

Finder Chart 37-6a. Abell 1656 Coma Galaxy Cluster
See Finder Chart 35-5 (Faintest stars 13th magnitude)

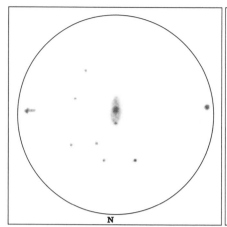
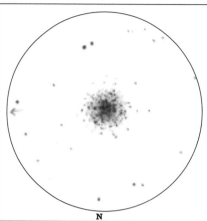
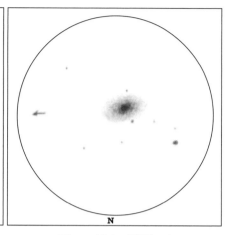

Figure 37-39. NGC 5012
17.5″, f4.5–250x, by G. R. Kepple

Figure 37-40. Messier 53
17.5″, f4.5–250x, by G. R. Kepple

Figure 37-41. NGC 5172
17.5″, f4.5–250x, by G. R. Kepple

NGC 4911 H392² Galaxy Type SAB(r)bc
φ **1.2′×1.0′, m12.8v, SB 12.8**   **13ʰ00.9ᵐ +27° 47′**
Finder Chart 37-6a   ★★
16/18″Scopes–150x: NGC 4911, a Coma Galaxy Cluster
member, is a fairly obvious 1.25′ diameter glow with
a broad, slightly brighter center. A 14th magnitude
star lies just outside its SE edge. With averted vision
a companion galaxy, M+05-31-94, can be seen as a
knot just outside the SW edge of NGC 4911. Two
12.5 magnitude stars lie 1.5′ WNW and 4′ NW of
the galaxy pair.

NGC 4919 Galaxy Type (R′)SA(r)0°:
φ **1.1′×0.6′, m14.1v, SB 13.5**   **13ʰ01.3ᵐ +27° 48′**
Finder Chart 37-6a   ★
16/18″Scopes–150x: NGC 4919 is located SE of a line

between NGC 4911 and NGC 4921 and equidistant
from each. Its faint stellar nucleus is immersed in
a well concentrated 15″ halo.

NGC 4921 H393² Galaxy Type SB(rs)ab
φ **2.3′×1.8′, m12.2v, SB 13.6**   **13ʰ01.4ᵐ +27° 53′**
Finder Chart 37-6a   ★★
16/18″Scopes–150x: NGC 4921, a member of the Coma
Galaxy Cluster, is a faint object elongated 1.25′×1′
NNW–SSE. The core is slightly brighter and con-
tains a stellar nucleus. Galaxy NGC 4911 lies 10′
SW.

NGC 4923 H394² Galaxy Type (R′)SA(r)0-?
φ **0.9′×0.9′, m13.7v, SB 13.3**   **13ʰ01.5ᵐ +27° 51′**
Finder Chart 37-6a   ★★
16/18″Scopes–150x: Located 2.5′ SE of NGC 4921 in
the Coma Galaxy Cluster, NGC 4923 has a bright
stellar nucleus embedded in a faint, diffuse, round
30″ diameter halo.

NGC 4961 H398² Galaxy Type SB(s)cd III-IV
φ **1.5′×1.0′, m13.6v, SB 13.8**   **13ʰ05.8ᵐ +27° 44′**
Finder Chart 37-6   ★
16/18″Scopes–150x: NGC 4961, located 18′ WNW of 41
Comae Berenices, appears very faint, elongated
1.25′×0.75′ ESE–WNW, and has a faint stellar nucleus.

NGC 5012 H85¹ Galaxy Type SAB(rs)c II
φ **2.7′×1.6′, m12.2v, SB 13.6**   **13ʰ11.6ᵐ +22° 55′**
Finder Chart 37-6, Figure 37-39   ★★
12/14″Scopes–125x: NGC 5012, located 5′ west of a 9th
magnitude star, has a faint, diffuse 2′×1′ N–S oval
halo containing a faint core. A 13th magnitude star
lies at the galaxy's north tip.

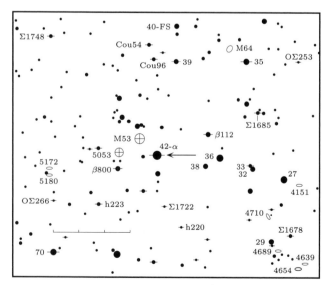

Finder Chart 37-7. 42–α Com: 13ʰ10.0ᵐ +17° 32′

Figure 37-42. *Messier 53 (NGC 2024) displays a halo of star chains radiating outward from a bright core. Image courtesy of Martin C. Germano.*

Figure 37-43. *NGC 5053 lying one degree SE of Messier 53 is a much fainter and less concentrated globular cluster than its neighbor. Image courtesy of Martin C. Germano.*

NGC 5016 H356² Galaxy Type SAB(rs)c II-III
ϕ **1.7′×1.3′, m12.8v, SB13.5**   **13ʰ12.1ᵐ +24° 06′**
Finder Chart 37-6   ★★
12/14″Scopes–125x: NGC 5016, located only 8′ south of a 6th magnitude star the glare of which makes it even more difficult to see, is a faint, circular 1′ diameter smudge.

NGC 5024 Messier 53 Globular Cluster Class V
ϕ **12.6′, m7.5v, Br?13.8v**   **13ʰ12.9ᵐ +18° 10′**
Finder Chart 37-7, Figures 37-40, 37-42   ★★★★★
   This globular cluster was discovered by J. E. Bode in February 1775, and independently observed two years later by Messier, who made the globular the 53rd entry in his catalogue of comet-like objects. The cluster is 65,000 light years distant and blazes with a total luminosity of 330,000 times that of the Sun. The extremely loose globular NGC 5053 lies just one degree SE.
4/6″Scopes–75x: Messier 53 is a bright 3′ diameter glowing sphere with a broad, well concentrated core. Except for two small concentrations in the northern part, the cluster's surface brightness fades evenly out toward its periphery.
8/10″Scopes–100x: This globular has a well resolved 5′ diameter halo containing a bright core with a granular texture. One star stands out in the core, but at least fifty are visible around the halo's periphery. An 11th magnitude star is visible in the globular's NE quadrant. A wide ENE–WSW pair of 9th and 10th magnitude stars lies 9′ SSE of the cluster.

12/14″Scopes–125x: Messier 53 is a an exquisite globular with a bright, moderately concentrated, rather well resolved, 1.5′ diameter core. The 6′ diameter halo sparkles with a myriad of tiny stars and is surrounded by a much thinner, irregular periphery, many of the minute stars of which fall along chains radiating from the denser interior. Outlying stars increase the overall diameter to 12′.

NGC 5053 H7⁶ Globular Cluster Class XI
ϕ **10.5′, m9.9v, Br★ 14.0**   **13ʰ16.4ᵐ+17° 42′**
Finder Chart 37-7, Figure 37-43   ★★
   NGC 5053 is located one degree SW of Messier 53. Both objects may be viewed with a low power ocular and offer instructive as well as visually interesting structural contrast. M53 is a "normal" globular of concentration class V, with a dense, distinctive core embedded in a gradually out-thinning halo. NGC 5053, on the other hand, is a class XI globular with no dense core or nucleus, and a much smaller total stellar population than M53. It might even be mistaken for a rich M11-type open cluster but for its RR Lyrae variable stars and the shape of its color-magnitude diagram. NGC 5053 contains only about 3,400 stars, sparse for a globular. It lies 49,500 light years away and has a diameter of about 150 light years. The total luminosity is about 21,000 suns, one of the lowest for any globular: Omega Centauri, by contrast, has a luminosity of a million suns. The object was discovered in 1784 by Sir

William Herschel.

8/10"Scopes–100x: NGC 5053, located 6′ WNW of a 9.5 magnitude star, is a very faint, round, unresolved, 6′ diameter glow. An 11th magnitude star lies on its ESE edge.

12/14"Scopes–125x: Though NGC 5053 resembles a rich open cluster, it is in fact an underpopulated, poorly concentrated globular cluster. Three dozen 14th and 15th magnitude stars can be resolved in an 8′ diameter area.

NGC 5116 H368³ Galaxy Type SB(s)c: II
φ 2.1′×0.7′, m12.7v, SB13.0   **13ʰ22.9ᵐ +26° 59′**
Finder Chart 37-6   ★★

12/14"Scopes–125x: NGC 5116, located 2′ ESE of a magnitude 12.5 star, has a faint, diffuse 1.25′×0.5′ NE–SW halo that slightly brightens through its center.

NGC 5172 Galaxy Type SAB(rs)bc: I-II
φ 3.0′×1.8′, m11.9v, SB13.6   **13ʰ29.3ᵐ +17° 03′**
Finder Chart 37-7, Figure 37-41   ★★★

12/14"Scopes–125x: NGC 5172 is 11′ NW of a 7th magnitude star and 3.5′ SW of a 12th magnitude star. The halo is fairly faint, elongated 2.5′×1.5′ ESE–WNW, and has a broad, well concentrated core. A 14th magnitude star is superimposed upon the halo near its NNE edge. 14′ south, beyond the 7th magnitude star, is galaxy NGC 5180.

NGC 5180 H71³ Galaxy Type S0?
φ 1.5′×1.0′, m13.0v, SB13.3   **13ʰ29.4ᵐ +16° 49′**
Finder Chart 37-7   ★★

12/14"Scopes–125x: NGC 5180 is 14′ south of NGC 5172 and 6′ SSW of a 7th magnitude star. In spite of its proximity to the star, the galaxy can be seen to have a fairly conspicuous 45″×25″ NNE–SSW halo that is slightly brighter through its center. A threshold star is superimposed upon the halo NW of its center.

Chapter 38

Corona Australis, the Southern Crown

38.1 Overview

Corona Australis, the Southern Crown, is the counterpart of the Northern Crown, Corona Borealis. However, it was a latecomer to the ancient heavens, for it is first mentioned in the constellation-list of the Greek writer Geminos of the early 1st century B.C. Later classical writers associated it with both Sagittarius and Centaurus, for in ancient art Centaurs were frequently represented wearing the laurel wreath figured in Corona Australis. It also was said to have been placed in the sky by Bacchus in honor of his mother Semele. The Bedouin of the Arabian Desert, in the centuries before medieval Arabian astronomers adopted the Greco-Roman constellations *en masse*, called this distinctive circlet of stars Al Kubbah, The Tortoise; Al Hiba, The Tent; Al Fakkah, The Dish; and Al Udha al Na' am, The Ostrich Nest.

Corona Australis lies on the SE edge of the Milky Way due south of the Teapot asterism of Sagittarius. Though it has no bright stars, its shape makes it fairly conspicuous. It occupies only 128 square degrees; only eight constellations are smaller. However, it contains a number of good objects, including two doubles with beautiful blue-white, comparably bright, components, a large bright globular cluster, and an interesting complex of dark dust clouds and bright reflection nebulae.

38.2 Interesting Stars

h5014 Double Star   **Spec. A5**
m5.7, 5.7; Sep.0.9″; P.A.345° $18^h06.8^m -43° 25'$
Finder Chart 38-2   ★★★★
12/14″Scopes–250x: Herschel 5014, located in a rich Milky Way field, is a very close pair of stars visible at high power as two whitish disks in contact.

Kappa (κ) Coronae Australis Dbl Star   **Spec. B8, B9**
m5.9, 6.6; Sep.21.4″; P.A.359° $18^h33.4^m -38° 44'$
Finder Chart 38-2   ★★★★
4/6″Scopes–75x: Kappa Coronae Australis, which like

h5014 lies in a rich Milky Way star field, is a fine, wide pair of bright bluish-white stars easily separated in small telescopes.

BrsO 14 Double Star   **Spec. B8, B8**
m6.6, 6.8; Sep.12.7″; P.A.281° $19^h01.1^m -37° 04'$
Finder Chart 38-2   ★★★★
4/6″Scopes–75x: Brisbane 14, located 12′ WSW of reflection nebulae NGC 6726-27, is an equally matched pair of bluish-white stars easily split in small instruments.

38.3 Deep-Sky Objects

NGC 6496 Globular Cluster Class XII
φ 6.9′, m8.5: $17^h59.0^m -44° 16'$
Constellation Chart 38-1, Figure 38-1   ★★★
12/14″Scopes–125x: NGC 6946 is 22′ ENE of a 5th magnitude star just across Corona Australis' western border in extreme SE Scorpius. NGC 6496 lies in Scorpius, but we have included it in Corona Australis for your observing convenience. It appears as a faint, diffuse, 3′ diameter patch peppered with threshold stars. On the east side of the cluster a magnitude 11.5 star with two companions begins an E-W star-chain that transits the center of the cluster. A few slightly brighter stars are on the cluster's NE and SW edges.

Corona Australis, the Southern Crown Constellation Chart 38-1

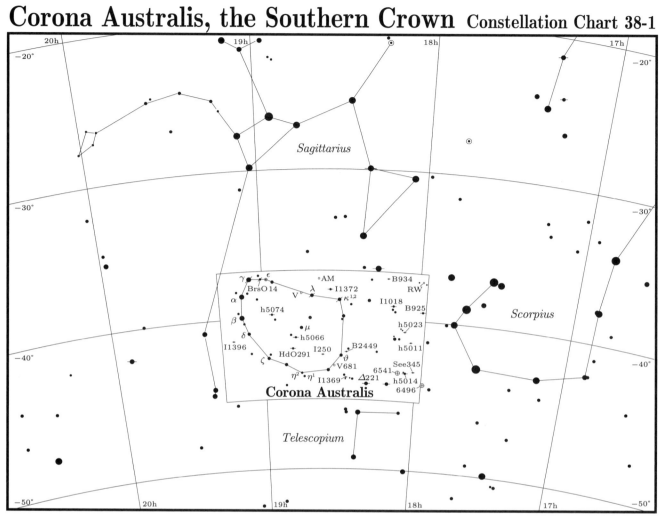

Table 38-1: Selected Variable Stars in Corona Australis

Name	HD No.	Type	Max.	Min.	Period (Days)	F*	Spec. Type	R.A. (2000) Dec.		Finder Chart No.	Notes
RW CrA	163726	EA/SD	9.3	10.3	1.68	0.18	A0	$17^h59.3^m$	$-37°53'$	38-1	
V681		EA/DM	7.6	98.1	2.16		B9.5	$18^h37.7^m$	-42 57	38-2	
AM CrA	172321	SR	8.6	12.7	187		M3	41.2	-37 29	38-2	
V CrA	173539	RCB	8.3	>16.5			C(R0)	47.5	-38 09	38-2	
ε CrA	175813	EW	4.74	5.0	0.59		F2	58.7	-37 06	38-2	

F* = The fraction of period taken up by the star's rise from min. to max. brightness, or the period spent in eclipse.

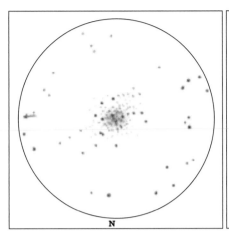

Figure 38-1. NGC 6496
16″, f5–100x, by G. R. Kepple

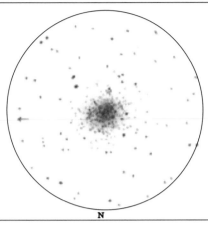

Figure 38-2. NGC 6541
16″, f5–100x, by G. R. Kepple

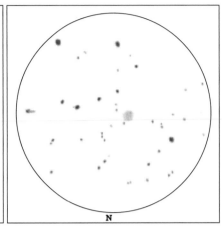

Figure 38-3. IC 1297
16″, f5–275x, by Glen W. Sanner

NGC 6541 Globular Cluster Class III
φ 13.1′, m6.1, Br★ 12.1   18ʰ08.0ᵐ −43° 42′
Finder Chart 38-2, Figure 38-2   ★★★

12/14″ Scopes–125x: NGC 6541, located 18′ SSE of a 4.5 magnitude star, is a well resolved globular cluster with a bright, broadly concentrated core embedded in a 6′ diameter halo which thins rapidly out to an irregular, star-poor periphery. An 11th magnitude star is prominent on the east edge of the periphery, and between this star and the globular's core is a dark patch. A thin triangle of faint stars lies to the SSW of the cluster.

NGC 6726-27 Reflection Nebula
φ 9′ × 7′, Photo Br 1-5, Color ?   19ʰ01.7ᵐ −36° 53′

NGC 6729 Emission and Reflection Nebula
φ Var., Photo Br 2-5, Color ?   19ʰ01.9ᵐ −36° 57′
Finder Chart 38-2, Figure 38-4   ★★★/★★

12/14″ Scopes–125x: NGC 6726-27 is 50′ west of Gamma (γ) Coronae Australis and 12′ ENE of the double star Brisbane 14 (6.6, 6.8; 12.7″; 281°). It is a fairly bright, several minute long, nebulosity with a diffuse, irregular periphery. It has two lobes, the SW reflecting the light of a magnitude 7.2 A2 star and the NE reflecting the erratic nebular variable

Table 38-2: Selected Double Stars in Corona Australis

Name	ADS No.	Pair	M1	M2	Sep.″	P.A.°	Spec	R.A. (2000) Dec.		Finder Chart No.	Notes
B925			7.2	10.8	4.8	269	K0	18ʰ00.0ᵐ	−39° 04′	38-1	
See 345			7.5	12.0	16.0	141	K0	03.0	−43 28	38-1	
h5011			7.7	9.1	29.6	350	A0	06.4	−41 45	38-2	
h5014			5.7	5.7	c0.9	*345	A5	06.8	−43 25	38-2	Close whitish pair
h5023			8.1	8.4	8.7	276	A2	10.8	−40 26	38-2	
I1018			7.3	10.8	1.4	283	G0	13.0	−39 10	38-2	
B934		AB	7.7	11.5	14.7	30	A0	14.2	−37 37	38-2	
		BC		12.0	2.4	185					
Δ 221			5.3	9.9	75.3	164	B5	24.3	−44 07	38-2	
B2449			8.0	12.0	8.0	p	K0	29.3	−41 57	38-2	
I1369			7.9	12.2	4.2	238	B3	31.2	−43 44	38-2	
κ CrA			5.9	6.6	21.4	359	B8 B9	33.4	−38 44	38-2	Bluish-white pair
I1372			7.3	11.5	8.2	18	M	36.3	−38 09	38-2	
I250			7.6	8.7	1.0	120	A0	41.2	−42 10	38-2	
λ CrA			5.1	9.7	29.2	214	A0 K0	43.8	−38 19	38-2	
h5066			6.5	9.5	10.1	85	B5	51.0	−41 04	38-2	
HdO 291		AxBC	6.5		36.0	342	K2	52.2	−41 43	38-2	
		BC	10.2	12.2	0.6	292					
h5074			6.5	11.8	15.9	246	A0	59.2	−39 32	38-2	
BrsO 14			6.6	6.8	12.7	281	B8 B8	19ʰ01.1ᵐ	−37 04	38-2	Bluish-white stars
γ CrA			4.8	5.1	w1.3	*55	F8 F8	06.4	−37 04	38-2	
I1396			7.6	11.0	5.2	91	K0	13.2	−40 45	38-2	

Footnotes: *= Year 2000, a = Near apogee, c = Closing, w = Widening. Finder Chart No: All stars listed in the tables are plotted in the large Constellation Chart, but when a star appears in a Finder Chart, this number is listed. Notes: When colors are subtle, the suffix *-ish* is used, e.g. *bluish*.

Figure 38-4. *The dark nebula Bernes 157 (at center), extends nearly a degree NW–SE. Embedded on its NW end are the reflection nebulae NGC 6726-27 and the reflection+emission variable nebulae NGC 6729 (left center). IC 4812 surrounds the double star Brisbane 14. Globular cluster NGC 6723 (upper left) lies just across the border in Sagittarius. Image courtesy of Dean Salman.*

star TY Coronae Australis, which has a light range between magnitudes 8.8 and 12.6. 5′ SE of NGC 6726-27 is the tiny comet-shaped emission reflection nebulae NGC 6729, an object which, like the more famous Hubble's Variable Nebula (NGC 2261) in Monoceros, changes unpredictably in brightness, size, and shape. In the "head" of NGC 6729 is the nebular variable R CrA, which varies erratically

between magnitudes 9.5 and 13. The faint nebular variable T CrA (magnitude range 11.7–13.5) is in the "tail" of NGC 6729. Globular cluster NGC 6723 lies 30′ NE of NGC 6726-7/6729 complex in Sagittarius.

Bernes 157 Dark Nebula
ϕ 55′, Opacity 6   19ʰ02.9ᵐ −37° 08′
Finder Chart 38-2, Figure 38-4   ★★★
12/14″ Scopes–125x: Bernes 157 is a conspicuous dark dust cloud extending 50′ × 15′ NW–SE from half a degree west to half a degree SW of Gamma (*γ*) Coronae Australis. It is visible as a large curved starless area, its outline shaped rather like a cashew nut concave to the SW. At its NW end are the small nebulous patches NGC 6726-27 and NGC 6729. Another faint nebulous patch, catalogued IC 4812, is 10′ SW of NGC 6726-27 around the bright 6th magnitude double Brisbane 14 (6.6, 6.8; 12.7″; 281°), a beautiful binary of blue-white, B-type stars. IC 4812 is misplotted on both the *Sky Atlas 2000* and *Uranometria 2000.0*. The distance to Bernes 7157 and its embedded nebulae NGCs 6726-27 and NGC 6729 and IC 4812 is only 420 light years. The

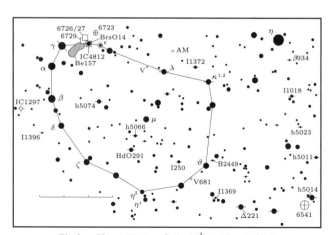

Finder Chart 38-2. *α* CrA: 19ʰ09.5ᵐ −37° 54′

dust cloud is therefore only about 7 light years long and NGC 6726-27 a mere 1 light year in width.

IC 1297 PK358–21.1 Planetary Nebula Type?
φ 7″, m10.7v, CS14.22v   19ʰ17.4ᵐ −39° 37′
Finder Chart 38-2, Figure 38-3   ★★★
12/14″Scopes–300x: IC1297 is just outside the thin triangle of stars formed by a 9.5 magnitude star 3.75′ to its ENE, a 10th magnitude star 5′ to its south, and a 9th magnitude star 7′ to its SW. Although bright the planetary nebula requires high power for a good view. At 300x the disk seems to be nearly half again as large as the 7″ catalog size. A 14th magnitude star is superimposed upon the disk just within its SE edge, and a 13th magnitude star lies 30″ NNW of the planetary's center.

Chapter 39

Corona Borealis, the Northern Crown

39.1 Overview

Corona Borealis, the Northern Crown, is a conspicuous semicircle of seven stars (eight if Pi Coronae is included) between the kite-shaped body of Boötes and the broad shoulders of the kneeling Hercules. It represents a wreath of laurel, the prize which the early Greeks awarded the victors of athletic contests and poetry competitions. The laurel later was worn by Roman generals who were voted a Triumph by the Roman Senate. In mythology the celestial Wreath was the crown of Ariadne, given to her at their wedding by the hero Theseus, who had killed the Minotaur which lurked in the Labyrinth built by her father, King Minos of Crete.

The brightest star in the Northern Crown is the 2.3 magnitude Alpha Coronae Borealis, named Gemma or Alpheca, the later from the Arabic for "The Plate." It is an attractive blue-white object with the same space motion as the Ursa Major Moving Group, centered upon the middle five stars of the Big Dipper. Corona Borealis is far away from the Milky Way, and, like most other off-Milky Way constellations, has lots of galaxies and little else. Few of its galaxies are even moderately bright. Astronomically the most interesting object in the constellation is the extremely rich but billion light year distant Abell 2065 galaxy cluster. Unfortunately the brightest Abell 2065 members are only 16th magnitude objects and therefore accessible only to large telescopes.

39.2 Interesting Stars

Σ1932 Double Star   **Spec. F8**
m7.3, 7.4; Sep. 1.6″; P.A. 259°   **15^{h}18.3^m +26° 50′**
Constellation Chart 39-2   ★★★★
8/10″ Scopes–200x: Moderately high power shows Struve 1932 as a contact binary of equally bright yellow stars.

Corona Borealis: Kor-OH-na Bor-ee-AL-is
Genitive: Coronae Borealis, Kor-OH-ne Bor-ee-AL-is
Abbreviation: CrB
Culmination: 9pm–July 3, midnight–May 19
Area: 179 square degrees
Showpieces: None
Binocular Objects: 1 CrB, 2–η CrB, 11–κ CrB, 12–λ CrB, 15–ϱ CrB, 18–υ CrB, 20–ν^1 and 21–ν^2 CrB

Zeta (ζ) = 7 Coronae Borealis Double Star Spec. B8
m5.1, 6.0; Sep. 6.3″; P.A. 305°   **15^{h}39.4^m +36° 38′**
Constellation Chart 39-2   ★★★★★
4/6″ Scopes–100x: Zeta Coronae Borealis consists of comparably bright stars delicately but definitely bluish and greenish in color.

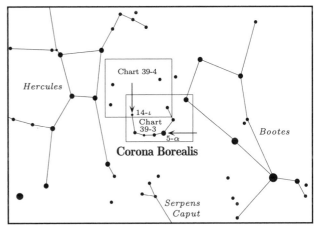

Master Finder Chart 39-1. Corona Borealis Chart Areas
Guide stars indicated by arrows.

Corona Borealis, the Northern Crown Constellation Chart 39-2

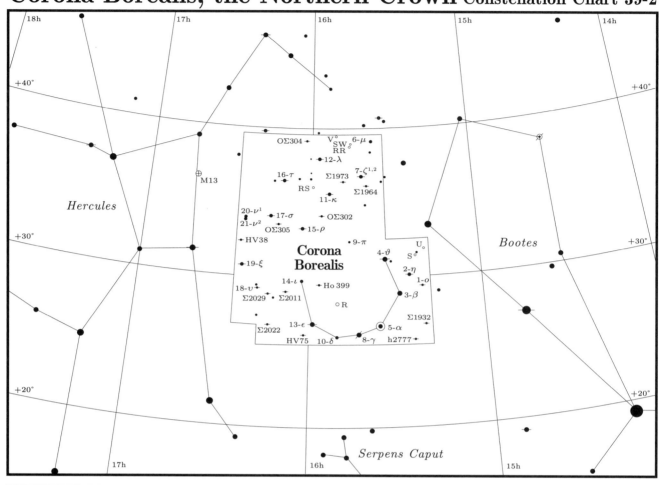

Chart Symbols

Constellation Chart

Stellar Magnitudes   0 1 2 3 4 5 6

Finder Charts   0/1 2 3 4 5 6 7 8 9

Master Finder Chart   0 1 2 3 4 5

→ *Guide Star Pointer*   ◉ ○ *Variable Stars*   ⊕ *Planetary Nebulae*

•—• *Double Stars*   ○ *Open Clusters*   □ *Small Bright Nebulae*

Finder Chart Scale   ⊕ *Globular Clusters*   *Large Bright Nebulae*

(One degree tick marks)   ⬭ *Galaxies*   *Dark Nebulae*

Table 39-1: Selected Variable Stars in Corona Borealis

Name	HD No.	Type	Max.	Min.	Period (Days)	F*	Spec. Type	R.A. (2000) Dec.		Finder Chart No.	Notes
U CrB	136175	EA/SD	7.66	8.79	3.45	0.14	B6+F8	$15^h18.2^m$	$+31°\ 39'$	39-3	
S CrB	136753	M	5.8	14.1	360	0.35	M6-M8	21.4	+31 22	39-3	
SW CrB	140155	SRb	7.8	8.5	100		M0	40.8	+38 43	39-4	
RR CrB	140297	SRb	8.4	10.1	60	0.50	M5	41.4	+38 33	39-4	
R CrB	141527	RCB	5.71	14.8			C0	48.6	+28 09	39-3	
V CrB	141826	M	6.9	12.6	357	0.41	C6,2	49.5	+39 34	39-4	

F* = The fraction of period taken up by the star's rise from min. to max. brightness, or the period spent in eclipse.

Table 39-2: Selected Double Stars in Corona Borealis

Name	ADS No.	Pair	M1	M2	Sep."	P.A.°	Spec	R.A. (2000) Dec		Finder Chart No.	Notes
Σ1932	9578	AB	7.3	7.4	1.6	*259	F8	15^{h}18.3^m	+26° 50'	39-3	Nice close yellow pair
1–o CrB			5.5	9.4	147.3	337	K0	20.1	+29 37	39-3	
h2777			7.3	10.2	40.8	345	K0	22.4	+25 37	39-3	
2–η CrB	9617	AB	5.6	5.9	1.0	*36	G0	23.2	+30 17	39-3	Yellowish pair in contact
	9617	ABxD		10.9	215.0	47					
	9617	AC		12.5	57.7	12					
Σ1964	9731	AC	7.0	7.6	15.2	86	F5	38.2	+36 15	39-4	All yellow quadruple
	9713	CD		8.7	1.6						
7–ζ CrB	9737		5.1	6.0	6.3	305	B8	39.4	+36 38	39-4	Blue and greenish pair
8–γ CrB	9757		4.1	5.5	c0.8	*114	A0	42.7	+26 18	39-3	Difficult yellowish pair
Σ1973			8.0	9.2	30.6	322	F5	46.5	+36 26	39-4	Yellowish and bluish
11–κ CrB			4.8	11.5	136.6	202	K0	51.2	+35 39	39-4	
OΣ302	9838		7.2	9.2	28.6	52	A2	54.9	+34 22	39-4	Whitish and bluish
Ho399	9844		7.8	10.3	3.2	119	A0	55.4	+29 32	39-3	
12–λ CrB			5.5	10.0	94.3	66	F2	55.8	+37 57	39-4	
OΣ304	9887		6.7	10.8	10.7	175	A0	16^{h}00.9^m	+39 11	39-4	
15–ρ CrB			5.5	8.7	89.6	71	F8	01.0	+33 18	39-3	
HV75			8.0	11.0	49.3	11	F2	01.1	+26 10	39-3	
Σ2011	9930		7.8	10.4	2.4	67	A3	07.6	+29 00	39-4	
OΣ305	9958		6.3	10.3	5.4	263	K0	11.7	+33 21	39-4	Fine orange and blue duo
Σ2022	9966		6.4	10.0	2.5	146	F2	12.8	+26 40	39-1	
Σ2029	9973		7.7	9.5	6.3	187	F2	13.8	+28 44	39-4	
17–σ CrB	9979	AB	5.6	6.6	w7.1	*236	G0	14.7	+33 52	39-4	
	9979	AC		13.1	8.7	148					
	9979	AD		10.6	71.0	85					
18–υ CrB	9990	AB	5.8	11.8	54.5	29	A0	16.7	+29 09	39-4	
	9990	AC		12.8	86.8	22					
	9990	AD		11.8	123.6	52					
20–υ¹, 21–υ²		AB	5.4	5.3	364.4	165	M K5	22.4	+33 48	39-4	Orange binocular pair
		Aa		11.1	68.8	238					
		Ab		12.7	180.0	152					
HV38			6.3	8.8	34.7	19	A2	22.9	+32 20	39-4	White pair

Footnotes: *= Year 2000, a = Near apogee, c = Closing, w = Widening. Finder Chart No: All stars listed in the tables are plotted in the large Constellation Chart, but when a star appears in a Finder Chart, this number is listed. Notes: When colors are subtle, the suffix -*ish* is used, e.g. *bluish*.

Sigma (σ) = 17 Coronae Borealis Quadruple Star Spec. G0
AB: m5.6,6.6; Sep.7.1″; P.A.236°   16^{h}14.7^m+33°52′
Constellation Chart 39-2   ★★★★
4/6″ Scopes–100x: Sigma Coronae is an easily separated double of pale yellow and deep yellow stars.

39.3 Deep-Sky Objects

Abell 2065 Galaxy Cluster   15^{h}22.7^m +27° 43′
Finder Chart 39-3, Figure 39-1   ★
16/18″ Scopes–150x: Owners of large aperture instruments will find the billion light year distant Abell 2065 galaxy cluster a challenging group of 16th magnitude and fainter galaxies. Under clear, dark skies at the Texas Star Party, ten extremely faint smudges could be glimpsed with averted vision. Eight galaxies are concentrated in a 3′ area. Two more galaxies were visible SE of this area, and a few more suspected within it.

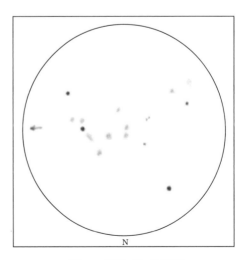

Figure 39-1. Abell 2065
16″, ƒ5–300x, by G. R. Kepple

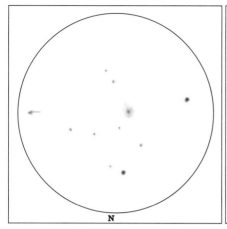
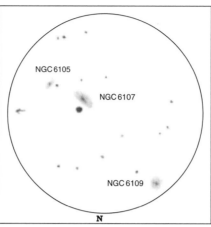
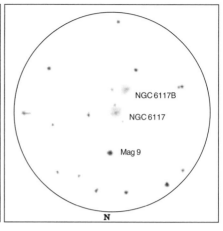

Figure 39-2. NGC 5958
17.5″, ƒ4.5–225x, by Glen W. Sanner

Figure 39-3. NGC 6107-09 Area
17.5″, ƒ4.5–225x, by G. R. Kepple

Figure 39-4. NGC 6117-17B
17.5″, ƒ4.5–250x, by Glen W. Sanner

NGC 5958 H399² Galaxy Type S?
φ 1.0′ × 0.9′, m12.6v, SB12.3 15ʰ34.7ᵐ +28° 40′
Finder Chart 39-3, Figure 39-2 ★★
16/18″ Scopes–150x: NGC 5958, located 10′ WSW of a
9th magnitude star, appears fairly faint and small,
its halo a 1′ × 0.75′ N–S oval that gradually brightens to a core containing a faint stellar nucleus. A
13th magnitude star lies 1′ NW, a 12.5 magnitude
star 2′ south, and 12th magnitude stars 3.5′ NW
and 4′ east.

NGC 5961 Galaxy Type S?
φ 0.8′ × 0.3′, m14.1, SB12.4 15ʰ35.2ᵐ +30° 51′
Finder Chart 39-3 ★
16/18″ Scopes–150x: NGC 5961, located 45′ SE of magnitude 4.1 Theta (ϑ) = 4 Coronae Borealis, appears
fairly faint, elongated 45″ × 25″ ESE–WNW, and
slightly brighter at its center. It lies within, and

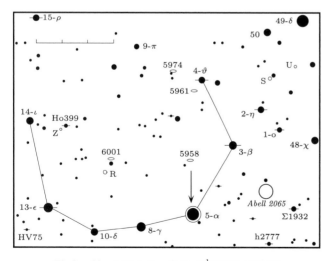

Finder Chart 39-3. 5–α CrB: 15ʰ34.7ᵐ +26° 43′

just north of the center of, a 3.5′ × 2′ diameter
triangle of magnitude 12.5 stars. 4′ south is the
galaxy UGC 9920, a very faint 1′ × 0.15′ NE–SW
streak. A 14th magnitude star lies 30″ north, and
a 12th magnitude star 1′ WNW, of the center of
UGC 9920.

NGC 6001 H371³ Galaxy Type Sc
φ 1.0′ × 1.0′, m13.6v, SB13.4 15ʰ47.7ᵐ +28° 38′
Finder Chart 39-3 ★
16/18″ Scopes–150x: NGC 6001, located 10′ north of a
7.5 magnitude star, has a fairly faint, circular 45″
diameter halo that is slightly brighter at its center.
A 14th magnitude star lies 1.5′ east.

NGC 6104 H688³ Galaxy Type S?
φ 0.8′ × 0.6′, m13.2v, SB12.3 16ʰ16.5ᵐ +35° 42′
Finder Chart 39-4 ★
16/18″ Scopes–150x: NGC 6104 is near the center of a
25′ × 12′ triangle of one 7.5 and two 8th magnitude
stars, the magnitude 7.5 star at the eastern vertex.
The galaxy is a faint, circular 30″ diameter glow
with a slight concentration at its core. 3′ east of
NGC 6104 is the galaxy MCG+6-36-12, a very faint
20″ haze.

NGC 6107 U10311 Galaxy Type E:
φ 1.5′ × 1.1′, m13.8v, SB14.2 16ʰ17.2ᵐ +34° 53′
Finder Chart 39-4, Figure 39-3 ★
16/18″ Scopes–150x: NGC 6107, located only 50″ SSE
of a 10th magnitude star, appears faint and small,
its tiny 30″ halo slightly elongated NNE–SSW and
containing a small prominent core. NGC 6107 is
the most conspicuous member of a small group of
galaxies that includes NGC 6105 lying 3′ SW and
NGC 6109 located 8.5′ NE.

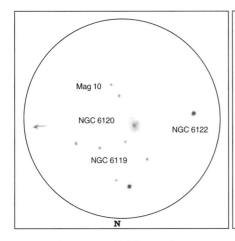
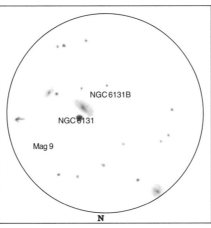
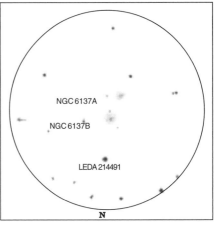

Figure 39-5. NGC 6120 Area
18.5″, f5–250x, by Glen W. Sanner

Figure 39-6. NGC 6131-31B
17.5″, f4.5–300x, by G. R. Kepple

Figure 39-7. NGC 6137A-B
18.5″, f5–250x, by Glen W. Sanner

NGC 6109 U10316 Galaxy Type S?
φ 0.9′ × 0.9′, m12.7v, SB12.4   **16ʰ17.7ᵐ +35° 00′**
Finder Chart 39-4, Figure 39-3   ★
16/18″ Scopes–150x: NGC 6104, located 8.5′ NNE of NGC 6107 in a small group of galaxies, has a very faint 30″ diameter halo with a small, faint core. A 13th magnitude star lies 1.25′ SW.

NGC 6117 U10338 Galaxy Type SA(s)bc
φ 1.2′ × 1.2′, m13.6, SB13.8   **16ʰ19.3ᵐ +37° 06′**
Finder Chart 39-4, Figure 39-4   ★
16/18″ Scopes–150x: NGC 6117, located 3′ south of a 9.5 magnitude star, has a faint nonstellar nucleus embedded in a very faint 30″ diameter halo. A 14th magnitude star is 45″ south of the galaxy's center. A 13.5 magnitude star lies 1.75′ to the galaxy's west, and a 12th magnitude 3′ to its SSE. 1.75′ SSE is the galaxy NGC 6117B, a very faint patch with a faint stellar nucleus.

NGC 6120 H623³ Galaxy Type Pec
φ 0.5′ × 0.4′, m13.8v, SB13.3   **16ʰ19.8ᵐ +37° 46′**
Finder Chart 39-4, Figure 39-5   ★
16/18″ Scopes–150x: NGC 6120, located 8′ east of a 7th magnitude star, is the most conspicuous of a trio of very faint galaxies. It is a faint, circular 25″ diameter glow of uniform surface brightness. A threshold star lies 25″ SW of the galaxy's center. A wide unequally bright double (10, 12; 45″; 45°) lies 2′ SSW. 2.5′ NNW of NGC 6120 is the galaxy NGC 6119, a very faint 15″ diameter spot 20″ NNE of a 14th magnitude star. 4.5′ NE of NGC 6120 is NGC 6122, a very faint 45″ × 10″ NNW–SSE streak.

NGC 6129 H891³ Galaxy Type
φ 0.7′ × 0.7′, m13.7v, SB12.8   **16ʰ21.8ᵐ +37° 59′**
Finder Chart 39-4   ★
16/18″ Scopes–150x: NGC 6129 is a very faint 30″ diameter glow with a poorly concentrated core. A 12th magnitude star lies 5′ to its WSW and a 10″ wide N–S pair of 13th magnitude stars is 5′ to its WNW.

NGC 6131 U10356 Galaxy Type SABcd:
φ 1.0′ × 1.0′, m13.3v, SB13.1   **16ʰ21.9ᵐ +38° 57′**
Finder Chart 39-4, Figure 39-6   ★
16/18″ Scopes–150x: NGC 6131, located 4′ east of a 9th magnitude star, is a very faint 1′ × 0.75′ NNW–SSE glow with a mottled texture and a poorly concentrated core. A 13th magnitude star is 1′ NW of the

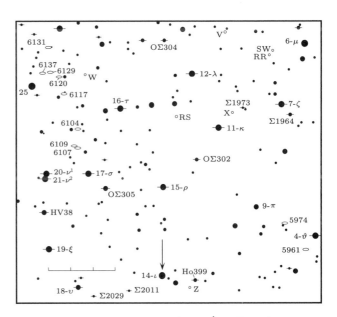

Finder Chart 39-4. 14–ι CrB: 16ʰ01.5ᵐ +29° 51′

galaxy. 2′ to its SE is its companion NGC 6131B, a very faint pip elongated NE–SW.

NGC 6137 H624³ Galaxy Type E
φ **1.9′ × 1.2′, m12.4v, SB13.2**   16ʰ23.0ᵐ +37° 56′
Finder Chart 39-4, Figure 39-7   ★
16/18″ Scopes–150x: NGC 6137A, located 7′ south of a

10th magnitude star, shows a faint stellar core embedded in a very faint, diffuse 1.5′ × 1′ N–S oval halo. The galaxy is flanked by 14th magnitude stars 1′ to its ESE and NW. 1.75′ to the NNW of NGC 6137A is NGC 6137B, a very faint, nebulous 15″ diameter spot. Two minutes NNW of 6137B you find LEDA 214491, a very faint 15″ spot.

Chapter 40

Corvus, the Crow

40.1 Overview

Corvus is Latin for "Crow," but the early Greeks had called this constellation *Corax*, "Raven." It originated in ancient Mesopotamia, where the Babylonians and Assyrians had also known it as a Raven. Even the manner in which the Romans and Greeks pictured the Crow/Raven – as pecking at the tail of the Serpent Hydra – was inherited from the Mesopotamians. Even as early as 2700 B.C. one of the most common motifs in Mesopotamian art was a lion-headed bird perched upon the back of a bull or some other ruminant vigorously biting its hindquarters in the exact manner the Roman Corvus was to perch upon the back and peck the tail of Hydra.

However, the Greco-Roman stories about the celestial Crow are legends in their own concoction, created to explain the juxtaposition of Corvus with Hydra to its south and Crater the Cup to its west. Apollo, so the myth-makers tell us, sent Corvus with the Cup to obtain pure water for a sacrifice to Jupiter. However, the bird came upon a fig tree and dallied in its branches until its fruit had ripened. When the Crow finally returned with the water-filled Cup, it also came carrying a Water-Serpent in its claws, claiming that the Snake was the cause for the delay. Apollo was not deceived and punished the Crow by placing him in the heavens with the Cup and the Water-Serpent, forbidding him ever to dip his beak into the cooling waters of the Cup – hence, the harsh, parched croaking which crows make.

Corvus is a distinctive trapezoid of 3rd magnitude stars in a rather star-sparse area 10° SW of Spica. The constellation occupies only 184 square degrees of sky, making Corvus the 70th largest of the 88 constellations. Nevertheless it contains quite a few interesting objects for an off-Milky Way area, including a couple attractive double stars, a bright planetary nebula, and several rather bright galaxies. Its most notable object is NGC 4038-39, a pair of interacting galaxies called the Ring-Tail.

Corvus: KOR-vus
Genitive: Corvi, KOR-vi
Abbreviation: Crv
Culmination: 9pm–May 12, midnight–Mar. 28
Area: 184 square degrees
Best Deep-Sky Objects: 7–δ Crv, Σ1669, NGC 4027, NGC 4038-39, NGC 4361, NGC 4782-83.

40.2 Interesting Stars

β 920   Double Star   **Spec. F5**
m6.8, 7.9; Sep.1.2″; P.A.293° $12^h15.8^m -23° 21'$
Finder Chart 40-3   ★★★★
8/10″ Scopes–200x: Burnham 920 is a close pair of yellow and white stars appearing as two disks in contact.

R Corvi   Variable Star   **Spec. M4.5–9**
m6.7 to 14.4; Per.317 days $12^h19.6^m -19° 35'$
Finder Chart 40-3   ★★★★
8/10″ Scopes–100x: R Corvi is at the western vertex of the triangle it forms with two 7.5 magnitude stars. At maximum this orange-red variable outshines the two magnitude 7.5 stars; but at minimum it can barely be detected.

Delta (δ) = 7 Corvi (S,h1435)   Double Star   Spec. A0
m3.0, 9.2; Sep.24.2″; P.A.214° $12^h29.9^m -16° 31'$
Finder Chart 40-3   ★★★★★
4/6″ Scopes–75x: Delta Corvi has a brilliant white primary and a faint pale blue secondary.
8/10″ Scopes–100x: This is a fine double of white and reddish-purple stars.

Corvus, the Crow

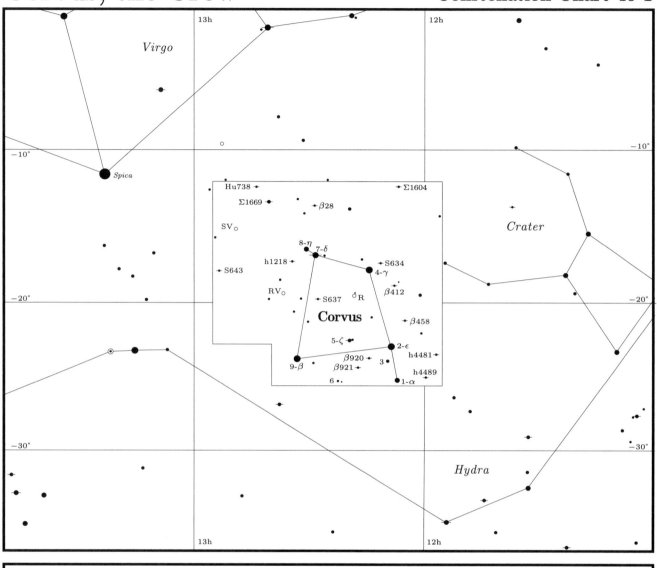

Virgo

13h

12h

−10°

Spica

−10°

Hu738

Σ1604

Σ1669

β28

SV

Crater

8-η

7-δ

h1218

S634

S643

4-γ

β412

RV

δ R

S637

Corvus

β458

5-ζ

2-ε

h4481

β920

3

9-β

β921

h4489

6

1-α

−20°

−20°

−30°

Hydra

−30°

13h

12h

Chart Symbols

Constellation Chart	0 1 2 3 4 5 6	⟶ Guide Star Pointer ⊙ ∘ *Variable Stars*
Stellar Magnitudes	● ● ● ● • • • ·	•—• *Double Stars* ○ *Open Clusters*
Finder Charts	0/1 2 3 4 5 6 7 8 9	*Finder Chart Scale* ⊕ *Globular Clusters*
Master Finder Chart	0 1 2 3 4 5	*(One degree tick marks)* ⬭ *Galaxies*

⊘ *Planetary Nebulae*
□ *Small Bright Nebulae*
⬭ *Large Bright Nebulae*
▨ *Dark Nebulae*

Table 40-1: Selected Variable Stars in Corvus

Name	HD No.	Type	Max.	Min.	Period (Days)	F*	Spec. Type	R.A. (2000) Dec.		Finder Chart No.	Notes
R Crv	107199	M	6.7	14.4	317	0.41	M4.5-9	12^{h}19.6^m	−19° 35′	40-3	
RV Crv	109796	EB	8.6	9.16	0.74		F0+G0	37.7	−19 35	40-1	
SV Crv	111499	SRb	6.78	7.6	70		M5	49.8	−15 05	40-4	

F* = The fraction of period taken up by the star's rise from min. to max. brightness, or the period spent in eclipse.

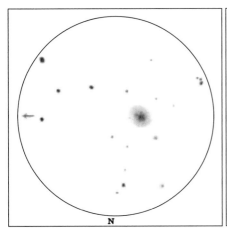

Figure 40-1. NGC 4024
12.5″, f5–200x, by G. R. Kepple

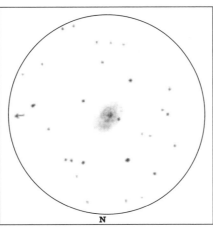

Figure 40-2. NGC 4027
13″, f5.6–165x, by Steve Coe

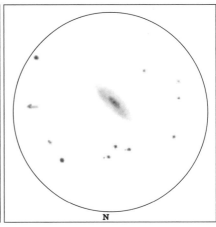

Figure 40-3. NGC 4033
12.5″, f5–200x, by G. R. Kepple

β 28 Double Star   **Spec. G0**
AB: m6.5, 8.6; Sep. 2.2″; P.A. 329°   12ʰ30.1ᵐ −13° 24′
Finder Chart 40-4   ★★★★
8/10″ Scopes–200x: Burnham 28 is a pair of yellow and white disks in contact. Two more widely separated stars are also involved (see Table 40-2).

Σ1669 Double Star   **Spec. F5**
m6.0, 6.1; Sep. 5.4″; P.A. 311°   12ʰ41.3ᵐ −13° 01′
Finder Chart 40-4   ★★★★★
4/6″ Scopes–75x: Struve 1669 is an elegant, equally bright, pair of yellow stars in a sparsely scattered star field. The secondary has a somewhat deeper hue than the primary.

40.3 Deep-Sky Objects

NGC 4024 H295² Galaxy Type SB(sr)0°
φ 1.7′ × 1.4′, m11.9v, SB 12.7   11ʰ58.5ᵐ −18° 21′
Finder Chart 40-3, Figure 40-1   ★★★
12/14″ Scopes–125x: This galaxy has a faint but conspicuous 1′ × 0.75′ NE–SW oval halo with a stellar nucleus. Centered 6′ SW of the galaxy is an equilateral triangle with 5′ long sides composed of one 10th and two 11th magnitude stars. A magnitude 11.5 star is at the center of the triangle.
16/18″ Scopes–150x: NGC 4024 has a bright stellar nucleus embedded in a tiny core surrounded by a fainter 1.5′ × 1.25′ NE–SW halo. A 13th magnitude star lies 2′ SW of the galaxy, and a fainter star is 2′ NW.

Table 40-2: Selected Double Stars in Corvus

Name	ADS No.	Pair	M1	M2	Sep.″	P.A.°	Spec	R.A. (2000) Dec.		Finder Chart No.	Notes
h4481	8361		8.0	8.1	3.6	194	F5	11ʰ57.3ᵐ	−22° 32′	40-3	
h4489	8385		8.5	9.0	9.9	153	A2	12ʰ00.5ᵐ	−24 27	40-1	
β 458			7.9	10.0	30.5	233	A2	04.3	−21 02	40-3	
β 412	8436		8.4	8.9	2.0	160	F2	08.3	−18 34	40-3	
Σ1604	8440	AB	6.8	9.3	9.9	89	G0	09.5	−11 51	40-1	
	8440	AC		9.2	19.1	25					
S 634	8444		7.2	8.4	5.5	291	G5	11.4	−16 47	40-3	
β 920	8481		6.8	7.9	1.2	293	F5	15.8	−23 21	40-3	Close yellow and white pair
β 921	8503	AxBC	7.0	11.2	3.4	219	B9	17.9	−24 01	40-3	
S 637			8.6	9.0	60.6	203	F5 G0	27.2	−19 58	40-3	
7-δ Crv	8572		3.0	9.2	24.2	214	A0	29.9	−16 31	40-3	White and reddish-purple
β 28	8573	AB	6.5	8.6	w2.2	*329	G0	30.1	−13 24	40-4	Yellow and white
	8573	AC		11.1	91.0	294					
	8573	AD		12.1	79.2	183					
h1218	8603	AB	6.6	11.0	11.8	259	F2	35.7	−16 50	40-4	
Σ1669	8627	AB	6.0	6.1	5.4	311	F5	41.3	−13 01	40-4	Matched pale yellow pair
	8627	AC		10.5	59.0						
Hu738	8645		6.8	11.8	9.1	259	K0	43.8	−12 01	40-4	
S 643	8699		6.8	9.3	23.4	294	A0 A2	54.0	−18 02	40-4	

Footnotes: *= Year 2000, a = Near apogee, c = Closing, w = Widening. Finder Chart No: All stars listed in the tables are plotted in the large Constellation Chart, but when a star appears in a Finder Chart, this number is listed. Notes: When colors are subtle, the suffix *-ish* is used, e.g. *bluish*.

Figure 40-4. *The Ring-Tail Galaxy (NGC 4038-39) is a visually interesting pair of colliding galaxies. Image courtesy of Daniel Verschatse.*

NGC 4027 H296² Galaxy Type SB(s)dm II-III
φ 3.8′ × 2.3′, m11.2v, SB13.4   11ʰ59.5ᵐ −19° 16′
Finder Chart 40-3, Figure 40-2   ★★★
8/10″Scopes-100x: This galaxy is 41′ SW of the Ring-
   Tail Galaxy (NGC 4038–39) and 27′ NW of a 5th
   magnitude star. It has a fairly faint 2′ × 1′ NNW–

SSE halo containing a faint core. Two 11th
magnitude stars about 3′ to its NE and NW form
an equilateral triangle with the galaxy.
16/18″Scopes-150x: NGC 4027 is fairly bright,
   elongated 2.5′ × 1.5′ NNW–SSE, and has a core
   extended E–W rather than along the major axis of
   the halo. 150x shows an irregular periphery and
   some mottling in the inner regions. A 14th
   magnitude star lies near the NE edge.

NGC 4033 H508² Galaxy Type SA:0−
φ 2.2′ × 1.1′, m11.8v, SB12.6   12ʰ00.6ᵐ −17° 51′
Finder Chart 40-3, Figure 40-3   ★★★
8/10″Scopes-100x: This galaxy has a stellar nucleus
   within a bright core surrounded by faint extensions
   elongated 1.5′ × 0.5′ NE–SW. 10th magnitude stars
   are 5.25′ NW and 6.5′ SW of the galaxy.
16/18″Scopes-150x: NGC 4033 has a fairly bright,
   highly elongated 2′ × 0.75′ NE–SW halo that tapers
   to pointed ends. The core is also extended and
   contains a stellar nucleus. Three faint stars form a
   small triangle 3′ north of the galaxy.

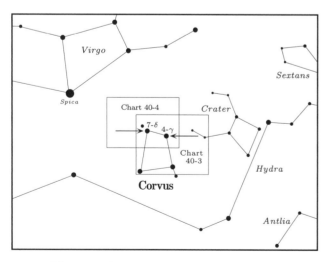

Master Finder Chart 40-2. Corvus Chart Areas
Guide stars indicated by arrows.

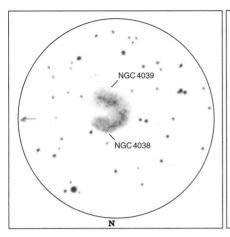

Figure 40-5. NGC 4038-39
13″, f5.6–165x, by Steve Coe

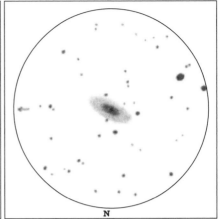

Figure 40-6. NGC 4050
13″, f5.6–165x, by Steve Coe

Figure 40-7. NGC 4094
12.5″, f5–225x, by G. R. Kepple

NGC 4038 H28.1[4] Galaxy Type SB?(s:)m pec II-III:
ϕ 5.4′ × 3.9′, m10.5v, SB13.7 $12^h01.9^m$ −18° 52′

NGC 4039 H28.2[4] Galaxy Type IB:(s)m pec III:
ϕ 5.4′ × 2.5′, m10.3v, SB13.0 $12^h01.9^m$ −18° 53′

Finder Chart 40-3, Figures 40-4, 40-5   ★★★★/★★★★
Ring-Tail Galaxy

8/10″Scopes–100x: NGC 4038 and NGC 4039, located
6′ SSE of a 9th magnitude star is an interacting
galaxy pair that appears as one fairly bright,
irregularly round, 2.5′ diameter glow with a dark
notch in its SW flank.

12/14″Scopes–125x: NGC 4038–39 is a bright, bizarre
object shaped like a comma or a shrimp concave to
the WSW. Close inspection reveals that the brighter
and larger northern segment has a mottled texture
and some dark patches in its NW area. The shrimp's
"tail" curls first SE, then south, and finally SW.
The combined size of NGC 4038 and NGC 4039 is
3.5′ × 2.5′ N–S.

16/18″Scopes–150x: In larger telescopes the Ring-Tail
Galaxy is particularly visually interesting. The two
components can be individually discerned. NGC
4038, the northern galaxy, is the larger and brighter
and is shaped like a 3′ × 1.5′ E–W crescent concave
to the south. On its NW it is wider, irregularly
illuminated, and contains a dark patch. Several
bright knots can be seen near its NW and southern
edges. The SE edge of NGC 4038 connects with the
NE edge of the southern galaxy of this colliding
pair, NGC 4039, which is elongated 3′ × 1.5′ NE–
SW. A 14th magnitude star is 1.5′ NW of the center
of NGC 4038, and a magnitude 11.5 star is 4′ SSE
of NGC 4039.

NGC 4050 H509[2] Galaxy Type SB(r)ab pec
ϕ 3.4′ × 2.1′, m12.2v, SB14.2 $12^h02.9^m$ −16° 22′

Finder Chart 40-3, Figure 40-6   ★★★

8/10″Scopes–100x: NGC 4050, located 6′ NNW of an
8th magnitude star, is a very faint, small, diffuse
glow of uniform surface brightness.

16/18″Scopes–150x: NGC 4050 has a faint, diffuse
2.5′ × 1.5′ ENE–WSW halo containing a weakly
concentrated core. A 13th magnitude star is on the
galaxy's north edge.

NGC 4094 A269 Galaxy Type SB:(rs)cd II-III
ϕ 3.5′ × 1.1′, m11.8v, SB13.2 $12^h05.9^m$ −14° 32′

Finder Chart 40-3, Figure 40-7   ★★★

12/14″Scopes–125x: NGC 4094 is a very faint galaxy

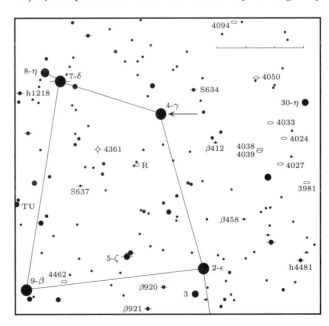

Finder Chart 40-3. 4–γ Crv: $12^h15.5^m$ −17° 32′

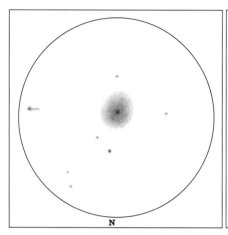

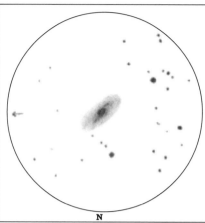

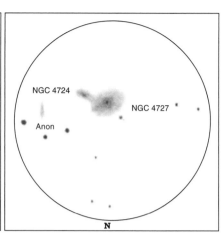

Figure 40-8. NGC 4361
13″, ƒ5.6–300x, by Steve Coe

Figure 40-9. NGC 4462
17.5″, ƒ4.5–250x, by Glen W. Sanner

Figure 40-10. NGC 4724 and NGC 4727
17.5″, ƒ4.5–225x, by G. R. Kepple

with an ill-defined 3′ × 1.5′ ENE–WSW halo that only very slightly brightens in toward its center. The galaxy forms a triangle with two 11th magnitude stars 1.5′ ESE and 2′ ENE of its center.

NGC 4361 PK294+43.1 Planetary Neb. Type 3a+2
φ >45″, m10.9v, CS13.18v   12ʰ24.5ᵐ −18° 48′
Finder Chart 40-3, Figure 40-8   ★★★★
8/10″Scopes–100x: This gray planetary nebula appears fairly bright. Its large circular disk contains a 13th magnitude central star. The disk is bright at center but fades noticeably toward its outer edges.
12/14″Scopes–125x: NGC 4361 has a conspicuous central star embedded in a bright 35″ central concentration surrounded by an outer halo that extends to a diameter double that of the inner

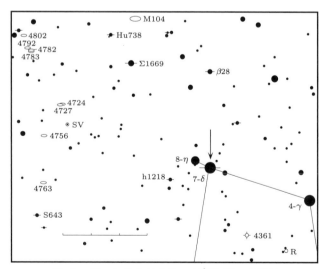

Finder Chart 40-4. 7–δ Crv: 12ʰ29.9ᵐ −16″31′

concentration. The halo seems cut off to the NW and therefore appears lopsided to the south. A 13th magnitude star lies 1.75′ NNW.

NGC 4462 H764³ Galaxy Type SB(r)ab
φ 2.8′ × 1.1′, m11.9v, SB13.0   12ʰ29.3ᵐ −23° 10′
Finder Chart 40-3, Figure 40-9   ★★★
8/10″Scopes–100x: NGC 4462, located 2′ WNW of a 9.5 magnitude star, is a faint hazy 2.5′ × 1.25′ NW–SE streak.
16/18″Scopes–150x: NGC 4462 has a fairly faint 3′ × 1.25′ NW–SE envelope containing a weakly concentrated core with tiny prolongations NE and SW along the halo's major axis.

NGC 4724 H280³ Galaxy Type SB0°
φ 0.9′ × 0.5′, m13.9v, SB12.9   12ʰ50.9ᵐ −14° 20′

NGC 4727 H298² Galaxy Type SAB(r)bc pec II-III?
φ 1.1′ × 0.9′, m13.0v, SB12.8   12ʰ51.0ᵐ −14° 20′
Finder Chart 40-4, Figure 40-10   ★/★★
16/18″Scopes–150x: NGC 4724 and NGC 4727 are a faint E–W galaxy pair with touching halos. The eastern galaxy, NGC 4727, is the larger and brighter of the two: its 1.5′ × 1′ NW–SE halo brightens slightly in toward its stellar nucleus. NGC 4724, joined to NGC 4727 at the latter's west edge, has a very faint, diffuse 30″ × 15″ E–W oval halo. 2.75′ NW of NGC 4727 is a magnitude 11.5 star, which forms a flat E–W triangle with a second magnitude 11.5 star to its WNW and a magnitude 10.5 star to its west. Near the midpoint of the south side of the triangle is the very faint galaxy, NGC 4726, which can be glimpsed with averted vision as a 45″ × 10″ E–W streak. 10′ NE of NGC 4727+4724 is the

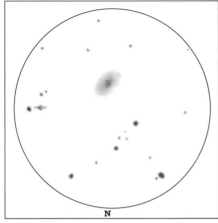

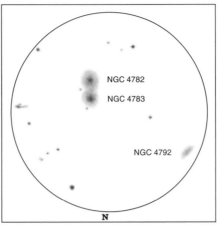

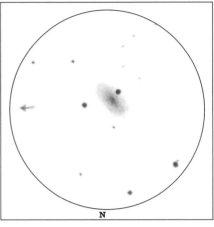

Figure 40-11. NGC 4763
17.5″, f4.5–225x, by G. R. Kepple

Figure 40-12. NGC 4782-83 and NGC 4792
17.5″, f4.5–225x, by Glen W. Sanner

Figure 40-13. NGC 4802
17.5″, f4.5–225x, by G. R. Kepple

galaxy NGC 4740, a faint, 45″ diameter glow slightly elongated NE–SW.

NGC 4756 H281³ Galaxy Type SAB(s:)0–
φ 1.8′ × 1.3′, m12.4v, SB13.2   **12ʰ52.8ᵐ −15° 25′**
Finder Chart 40-4, Figure 40-14   ★★

12/14″Scopes–125x: NGC 4756 is the brightest galaxy in the remote Abell 1631 galaxy cluster. It has a very faint, diffuse 1′ × 0.5′ ENE–WSW halo that is slightly brighter at its center.

16/18″Scopes–150x: NGC 4756 is faint, elongated 1.5′ × 1.25′ ENE–WSW, and has a broad, weak central concentration that contains a faint stellar nucleus. A 13th magnitude star is 2.5′ WSW of the galaxy, and a 14.5 magnitude star nearly touches the halo's ENE edge.

NGC 4763 Galaxy Type SB(r)a:
φ 1.7′ × 1.2′, m12.6v, SB13.2   **12ʰ53.4ᵐ −17° 00′**
Finder Chart 40-4, Figure 40-11   ★★

12/14″Scopes–125x: NGC 4763, located 7.5′ SSW of a 9th magnitude star and 2.5′ SSW of an 11th magnitude star, is a very faint, circular 45″ diameter glow with a slight central brightening.

16/18″Scopes–150x: NGC 4763 has a faint, ill-defined 1′ diameter halo which seems slightly elongated ESE–WNW. A very faint stellar nucleus is occasionally visible.

NGC 4782 Galaxy Type E/S0 pec
φ 1.8′ × 1.7′, m11.7v, SB12.8   **12ʰ54.6ᵐ −12° 34′**

NGC 4783 Galaxy Type S0 pec
φ 1.8′ × 1.7′, m11.5v, SB12.6   **12ʰ54.6ᵐ −12° 33′**
Finder Chart 40-4, Figure 40-12   ★★★/★★★

8/10″Scopes–100x: At 100x these two interacting galaxies have a faint common halo and therefore appear as one system. At 150x two diffuse but distinct N–S nodules may be discerned.

16/18″Scopes–150x: The interacting galaxy pair NGC 4782+NGC 4783 appear as a figure "8." Both galaxies are fairly bright, small, and round, and both are brighter in the center. NGC 4782, the southern galaxy, is the larger and brighter of the pair: its 1.5′ diameter halo contains a very faint stellar nucleus. NGC 4783, the northern component, is smaller, only about 1′ across, and is much more concentrated at its center, but its stellar nucleus is more pronounced than is that of its companion. 8′ NE of the interacting galaxies is NGC 4792, a faint, evenly concentrated 45″ × 15″ NNW–SSE streak.

NGC 4802 Galaxy Type SA:(r)0°
φ 2.3′ × 1.5′, m11.8v, SB13.0   **12ʰ55.8ᵐ −12° 03′**
Finder Chart 40-4, Figure 40-13   ★★★

8/10″Scopes–100x: At low power this galaxy is a faint, small, round glow that rather resembles a large, low surface brightness planetary nebula. It lies just east of the midpoint of a line joining a 2′ wide ESE–WNW pair of 11th magnitude stars. A 10th magnitude star lies 6′ NE of the galaxy, and a third 11th magnitude star is 6.5′ NNE.

16/18″Scopes–150x: NGC 4802 has a faint, diffuse 2′ × 1′ NE–SW oval halo that only slightly brightens in toward its center. On the SE edge of the galaxy's halo is an 11th magnitude star which forms a 2′ wide ESE–WNW pair with a second 11th magnitude star east of the galaxy's center.

Figure 40-14. *NGC 4756, a 12.4 magnitude galaxy, is the brightest object in the Abell 1631 Galaxy Cluster. This photograph may be used to identify the Abell 1631 members. Image courtesy of Jim Burnell.*

Chapter 41

Crater, the Cup

41.1 Overview

Crater the Cup represents a wine goblet. Though its stars are rather faint, none being brighter than magnitude 3.5, they form a pattern that really does suggest the footed goblet, or *Kantheros* of the early Greeks. However, the early Greeks probably named these stars *Kantheros* not only from the resemblance of their pattern to a wine goblet, but also because they rose just before the Sun at the beginning of the wine-making season. Having found its way into the heavens, the celestial Wine Goblet naturally found its way into the hands of the multitude of gods and heros, later Greek and Roman myth-spinners associating it with, among others, Apollo, Achilles, Bacchus, Hercules, and Medea.

Crater shares its stars Alpha and Beta, as well as a mythological story (for which see the introduction to Chapter 40, Corvus) with the constellation of Hydra the Water-Serpent. Though not a particularly small constellation – 35 constellations cover smaller areas than Crater's 282 square degrees – it is sparse in objects. Like all off-Milky Way constellations, it contains galaxies, but only eight of its galaxies are brighter than magnitude 12.0.

41.2 Interesting Stars

A1774 Double Star   **Spec. K0**
m5.6, 10.6; Sep. 3.7″; P.A. 271°   11ʰ03.2ᵐ −11° 18′
Constellation Chart 41-2   ★★
8/10″ Scopes–150x: Aitken 1774 is a very unequally bright double with a bright pale orange primary and a much fainter white secondary.

Gamma (γ) = 15 Crateris (h840) Double Star Spec. A5
m4.1, 9.6; Sep. 5.2″; P.A. 96°   11ʰ24.9ᵐ −17° 41′
Finder Chart 41-3   ★★
4/6″ Scopes–75x: Gamma Crateris is an unequally bright pair of white and blue stars.

> **Crater:** KRAY-ter
> **Genitive:** Crateris, KRAY-ter-is
> **Abbreviation:** Crt
> **Culmination:** 9pm–Apr. 26, midnight–Mar. 12
> **Area:** 282 square degrees
> **Best Deep-Sky Objects:** 15–γ Crt, Jc16, NGC 3511, NGC 3672, NGC 3887, NGC 3955, NGC 3962

Jc16 Double Star   **Spec. F1**
m5.8, 8.8; Sep. 8.2″; P.A. 80°   11ʰ29.8ᵐ −24° 29′
Finder Chart 41-3   ★★
8/10″ Scopes–125x: Jacob 16 is an easily separated pair of stars with subtle hues of yellowish-white and pale blue.

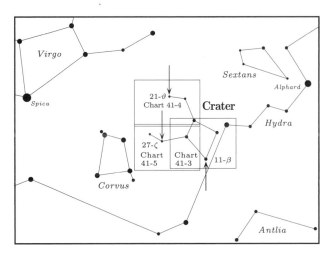

Master Finder Chart 41-1. Crater Chart Areas
Guide stars indicated by arrows.

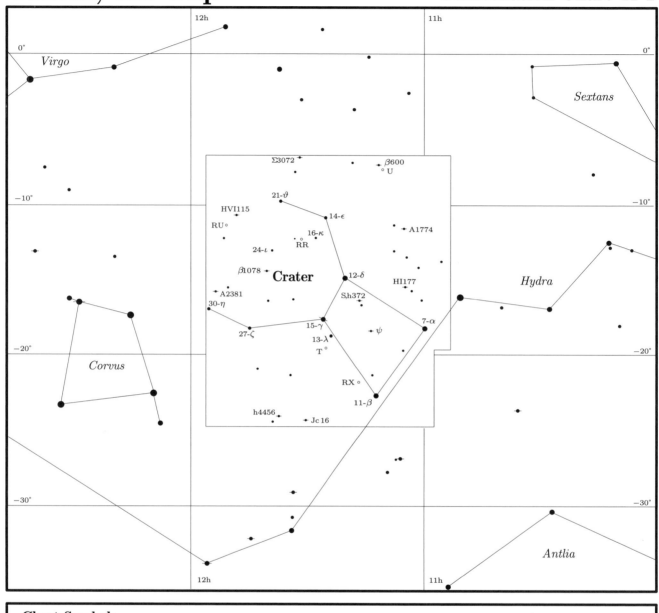

Chart Symbols

Constellation Chart	0	1	2	3	4	5	6	
Stellar Magnitudes								
Finder Charts	0/1	2	3	4	5	6	7	8 9
Master Finder Chart		0	1	2	3	4	5	

→ *Guide Star Pointer*

•—• *Double Stars*

Finder Chart Scale

(One degree tick marks)

◉ ○ *Variable Stars*

○ *Open Clusters*

⊕ *Globular Clusters*

⬭ *Galaxies*

⤫ *Planetary Nebulae*

□ *Small Bright Nebulae*

⬡ *Large Bright Nebulae*

▨ *Dark Nebulae*

Table 41-1: Selected Variable Stars in Crater

Name	HD No.	Type	Max.	Min.	Period (Days)	F*	Spec. Type	R.A. (2000)	Dec	Finder Chart No.	Notes
U Crt		M	9.5	>13.5	169	0.45	M0	11^{h}12.8^m	−07° 18′	41-2	
RX Crt	98218	SRb	7.3:	7.7:	300		M3	17.8	−22 09	41-3	
RR Crt		SRb	9.0	10.5	Irr.		M5	31.7	−12 23	41-4	
RU Crt	102946	Lb?	8.5	9.5	Irr.		M3	51.1	−11 12	41-4	

F* = The fraction of period taken up by the star's rise from min. to max. brightness, or the period spent in eclipse.

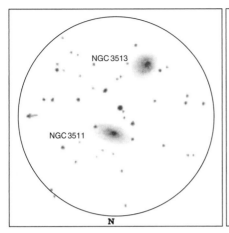

Figure 41-1. NGC 3511 and NGC 3513
13″, f5.6–165x, by Steve Coe

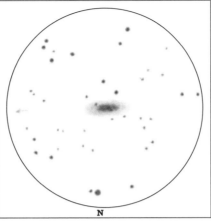

Figure 41-2. NGC 3571
12.5″, f5–200x, by G. R. Kepple

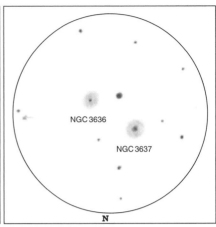

Figure 41-3. NGC 3636 and NGC 3637
13″, f5.6–165x, by Steve Coe

41.3 Deep-Sky Objects

NGC 3456 H29⁴ Galaxy Type SB(rs)c II
ϕ **1.6′ × 1.1′, m12.4v, SB12.9**   **10ʰ54.1ᵐ −16° 02′**
Finder Chart 41-3   ★★
12/14″ Scopes–125x: NGC 3456 has a faint 1.5′ × 1′ ESE–WNW halo that slightly brightens in toward its center. A 12th magnitude star touches its NE edge. 13th magnitude stars are 1′ east and 1.25′ SE of the galaxy's center.

NGC 3511 H39⁵ Galaxy Type SAB(s)c II
ϕ **5.5′ × 1.0′, m11.0v, SB12.7**   **11ʰ03.4ᵐ −23° 05′**
Finder Chart 41-3, Figure 41-1   ★★★★
12/14″ Scopes–125x: This galaxy has a faint 4′ × 1′ E–W halo that slightly brightens toward its center.

Magnitude 12.5 stars touch both the halo's east and west tips. Galaxy NGC 3513 lies 10′ SSE.
16/18″ Scopes–150x: NGC 3511 has a fairly bright 5′ × 1.5′ ENE–WSW oval halo containing a broad oval core. The magnitude 12.5 stars are clearly embedded in each tip.

NGC 3513 H40⁵ Galaxy Type SB(s)c II-III
ϕ **2.9′ × 2.3′, m11.5v, SB13.4**   **11ʰ03.8ᵐ −23° 15′**
Finder Chart 41-3, Figure 41-1   ★★★
12/14″ Scopes–125x: NGC 3513, located 10′ SSE of NGC 3511, has a faint, circular 1.5′ diameter halo with no discernible central brightening. An 11.5 magnitude star lies 4.5′ to the galaxy's SW.
16/18″ Scopes–150x: NGC 3513 appears faint, elongated 2.5′ × 1.5′ NW–SE, and has a faint 45″ × 10″ WNW–

Table 41-2: Selected Double Stars in Crater

Name	ADS No.	Pair	M1	M2	Sep.″	P.A.°	Spec	R.A. (2000	Dec.	Finder Chart No.	Notes
HI177	8025		8.5	8.9	2.9	18	F0	11ʰ02.1ᵐ	−15° 41′	41-3	
A1774	8037		5.6	10.6	3.7	271	K0	03.2	−11 18	41-2	Orange and white
S, h372			8.2	10.0	19.2	300	A3	15.7	−16 21	41-3	
β 600	8115	AB	6.1	11.6	1.0	210	F0	17.0	−07 08	41-2	
	8115	AC		9.9	57.2	98					
15–γ Crt	8153		4.1	9.6	5.2	96	A5	24.9	−17 41	41-3	White and blue
Jc 16	8183		5.8	8.8	8.2	80	F1	29.8	−24 29	41-3	Yellowish-white and bluish
	8183	AC		8.9	169.3	115	F2				
Σ3072	8190		7.7	10.7	9.4	33	F8	30.8	−06 43	41-2	
h4456	8240		7.2	10.9	15.2	122	K2	36.8	−24 26	41-2	
β 1078	8259		6.2	12.2	7.8	52	A0	39.9	−14 28	41-4	
HVI115		AB	6.3	9.6	88.4	67	G0	48.4	−10 19	41-4	
		AC		12.8	101.5	351					
A2381	8339	AB	7.5	12.0	4.4	356	K0	53.6	−16 07	41-5	
	8339	AC		11.1	68.7	321					

Footnotes: *= Year 2000, a = Near apogee, c = Closing, w = Widening. Finder Chart No: All stars listed in the tables are plotted in the large Constellation Chart, but when a star appears in a Finder Chart, this number is listed. Notes: When colors are subtle, the suffix *-ish* is used, e.g. *bluish*.

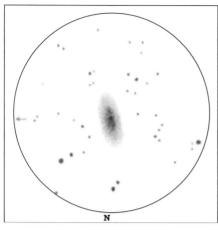

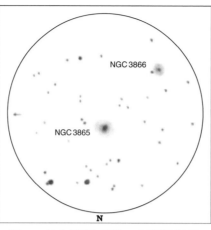

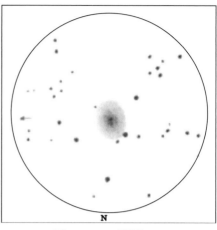

Figure 41-4. NGC 3672
18.5″, f5–200x, by Glen W. Sanner

Figure 41-5. NGC 3865 and NGC 3866
17.5″, f4.5–200x, by G. R. Kepple

Figure 41-6. NGC 3887
17.5″, f4.5–200x, by G. R. Kepple

ESE core. A 13th magnitude star lies 1.75′ east, and 14th magnitude stars are 1′ west and 1.5′ SSW of the galaxy.

IC 2627   A227   Galaxy Type SAB(s)c I-II
ϕ **2.6′ × 1.8′, m12.0v, SB 13.5** $11^h09.9^m -23°44'$
Finder Chart 41-3   ★★

16/18″ Scopes–150x: IC 2627, located 12′ SE of an 8th magnitude star, is a faint object elongated 1.75′ × 1.25′ ENE–WSW with ill-defined edges and no central brightening except for a very faint stellar nucleus. 9th magnitude stars are 3.5′ NE, 4′ NNE, 4′ north, and 4′ NW of the galaxy; and an 11th magnitude star lies 3.5′ to its SSW.

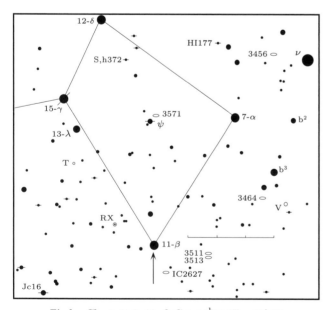

Finder Chart 41-3. 11–β Crt: $11^h11.6^m -22°50'$

NGC 3571=NGC 3544 H819² Galaxy Type SAB:(s)0/a
ϕ **3.4′ × 1.0′, m12.1v, SB 13.3** $11^h11.5^m -18°17'$
Finder Chart 41-3, Figure 41-2   ★★

12/14″ Scopes–125x: NGC 3571, located 18′ NW of 5.8 magnitude Psi (ψ) Crateris, is a faint, diffuse 2′ × 0.75′ E–W streak slightly brighter in the center. A 10th magnitude star lies 4.5′ north.

16/18″ Scopes–150x: NGC 3571 has a fairly faint 2.75′ × 1′ E–W halo containing a mottled, irregularly concentrated, extended core with a faint stellar nucleus. A 14th magnitude star lies 35″ south of the galaxy's nucleus.

NGC 3636   H550²   Galaxy Type SA?0–
ϕ **1.7′ × 1.7′, m12.4v, SB 13.4** $11^h20.4^m -10°17'$

NGC 3637   H551²   Galaxy Type (R′)SB(r:)0+
ϕ **1.7′ × 1.6′, m12.7v, SB 13.7** $11^h20.7^m -10°16'$
Finder Chart 41-4, Figure 41-3   ★★/★★

12/14″ Scopes–125x: NGC 3636 and NGC 3637 form a thin triangle with a magnitude 6.5 reddish star located somewhat SE of the line joining the galaxies. NGC 3637, located 3′ NE of the star, is the brighter and larger of the two: its circular 1.5′ diameter halo contains a faint, tiny core. NGC 3636, only 1.75′ WNW of the magnitude 6.5 star, is just half the size of its companion: its circular, uniformly concentrated halo contains a faint stellar nucleus.

NGC 3660   H635²   Galaxy Type SB(r)bc II
ϕ **2.9′ × 2.2′, m13.2v, SB 15.1** $11^h23.6^m -08°40'$
Finder Chart 41-4   ★

12/14″ Scopes–125x: NGC 3660 may be located by aiming the viewfinder midway between an 8th and

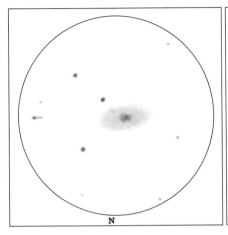

Figure 41-7. NGC 3892
12.5″, f5–200x, by G. R. Kepple

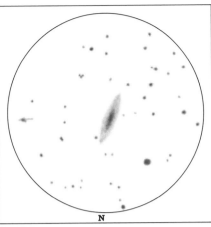

Figure 41-8. NGC 3955
12.5″, f5–200x, by G. R. Kepple

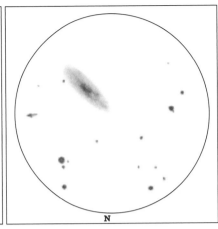

Figure 41-9. NGC 3956
13″, f5.6–250x, by Steve Coe

a 7th magnitude NE–SW star pair 40′ apart. The galaxy has a faint 1.5′ × 1.25′ ESE–WNW halo that slightly brightens in toward an inconspicuous stellar nucleus. A 14th magnitude star lies 1.25′ WNW, and a 12.5 magnitude star 2′ NE, of the galaxy.

NGC 3672 H131[1] Galaxy Type SA:(rs:)c I–II
φ **3.9′ × 1.8′, m11.4v, SB13.4**   11^{h}25.0^m −09° 48′
Finder Chart 41-4, Figure 41-4   ★★★

8/10″Scopes–100x: NGC 3672, located 20′ west of a 7.5 magnitude star, appears faint, evenly concentrated, and elongated 2.5′ × 1′ N–S. 12th magnitude stars are 3′ WNW and 4.5′ north of the galaxy.

16/18″Scopes–150x: NGC 3672 has a fairly bright halo elongated 3.5′ × 1.5′ slightly NNE–SSW containing a highly extended but weak core with a stellar nucleus. The halo is flanked by 13.5 magnitude stars 2′ to its west and 2.5′ to its east.

NGC 3732 H552[2] Galaxy Type Sa? pec?
φ **1.4′ × 1.2′, m12.5v, SB12.9**   11^{h}34.2^m −09° 51′
Finder Chart 41-4   ★★

16/18″Scopes–150x: NGC 3732 has a faint but conspicuous, circular halo less than 1′ in diameter containing a broad, prominent core with a very faint stellar nucleus. An 11th magnitude star lies 5.5′ WNW of the galaxy, and 12th magnitude stars are 1′ to its SW and 3.25′ to its north.

NGC 3865 Galaxy Type SB?(s)bc II:
φ **2.0′ × 1.6′, m12.0v, SB13.1**   11^{h}44.9^m −09° 14′
Finder Chart 41-4, Figure 41-5   ★★

16/18″Scopes–150x: NGC 3865, located 5′ SSE of a 9th magnitude star, is a faint, diffuse 2′ × 1.5′ ENE–WSW glow slightly brightening to a tiny core. 7′ to the SE of NGC 3865 is NGC 3866, a faint, tiny spot

with a stellar nucleus. A 13th magnitude star touches its west edge.

NGC 3887 Galaxy Type SAB(rs)bc II
φ **3.5′ × 2.4′, m10.6v, SB12.8**   11^{h}47.1^m −16° 51′
Finder Chart 41-5, Figure 41-6   ★★★★

12/14″Scopes–125x: NGC 3887 has a moderately bright, irregular halo elongated 3′ × 2′ N–S with a slight brightening at center. The galaxy protrudes from the mouth of a 5′ long "V" of 12.5 to 13th magnitude stars open to the south. The brightest star in this asterism touches the halo's edge 1.5′ NE of the galaxy's center.

16/18″Scopes–150x: The halo is considerably bright, elongated 3.5′ × 2.25′ NNE–SSW, and a little concentrated toward the center with a very faint stellar nucleus.

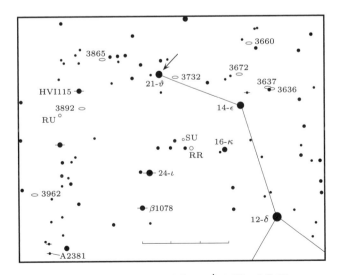

Finder Chart 41-4. 21-ϑ Crt: 11^{h}36.6^m −09° 48′

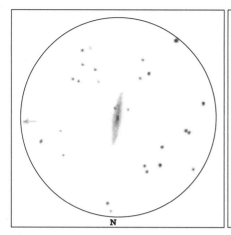

Figure 41-10. NGC 3957
12.5″, f5–200x, by G. R. Kepple

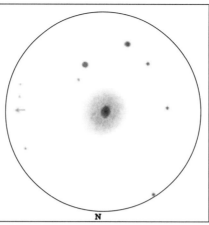

Figure 41-11. NGC 3962
17.5″, f4.5–250x, by G. R. Kepple

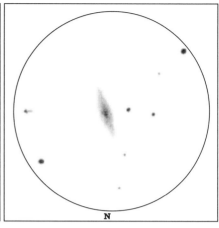

Figure 41-12. NGC 3981
17.5″, f4.5–250x, by G. R. Kepple

NGC 3892 H553² Galaxy Type (R:)SB(rs)0+
φ 3.4′ × 2.6′, m11.5v, SB13.7   11ʰ48.0ᵐ −10° 58′
Finder Chart 41-4, Figure 41-7   ★★★
12/14″ Scopes–125x: This galaxy has a fairly faint 2′
    diameter halo slightly elongated E–W containing a
    broad, weak central brightening.
16/18″ Scopes–150x: NGC 3892 has a fairly faint, diffuse
    2.25′ × 1.5′ E–W halo which slightly brightens to a
    faint, nonstellar nucleus. A 3′ × 1.5′ north-pointing
    triangle of magnitude 13.5 stars is west of the
    galaxy, the triangle's nearest star only 1′ SW of
    the galaxy's nucleus.

NGC 3955 H623² Galaxy Type S0/a pec
φ 3.7′ × 1.1′, m11.3v, SB12.7   11ʰ54.0ᵐ −23° 10′
Finder Chart 41-5, Figure 41-8   ★★★
12/14″ Scopes–125x: NGC 3955, located 5′ SSW of a 9.5

magnitude star, is a faint, highly elongated
1.5′ × 0.5′ NNW–SSE, lens-shaped object.
16/18″ Scopes–150x: NGC 3955 has a fairly bright,
    highly extended 2.5′ × 0.75′ NNW–SSE halo with a
    slight brightening through its center, in which is a
    faint nonstellar nucleus. A 13.5 magnitude star lies
    1′ NNW of the nucleus.

NGC 3956 H290³ Galaxy Type SAB:(rs)c II-III
φ 3.4′ × 1.0′, m12.2v, SB13.4   11ʰ54.0ᵐ −20° 34′
Finder Chart 41-5, Figure 41-9   ★★
12/14″ Scopes–125x: NGC 3956 is at the southern vertex
    of the 7.5′ × 4′ triangle it forms with magnitude 9.5
    stars to its NNW and ENE. This galaxy is faint,
    diffuse, and elongated 2.5′ × 0.75′ ENE–WSW.
16/18″ Scopes–150x: NGC 3956 has a faint oval core
    embedded in a faint, diffuse 3′ × 1′ ENE–WSW halo.
    A 12th magnitude star lies 4.5′ ENE.

NGC 3957 = IC 2965 H294² Galaxy Type Sa? sp
φ 3.1′ × 0.6′, m12.0v, SB12.5   11ʰ54.0ᵐ −19° 34′
Finder Chart 41-5, Figure 41-10   ★★
8/10″ Scopes–100x: This galaxy is visible as a very faint,
    small, lens-shaped object highly elongated 2′ × 0.5′
    N–S.
12/14″ Scopes–125x: NGC 3957 has a fairly faint, much
    elongated, 3′ × 0.5′ N–S halo with tapered ends. The
    core is highly extended and contains a faint stellar
    nucleus at its center. A fairly wide double of 13.5
    magnitude stars is 6′ east. A threshold star is 30″
    SSW of the galaxy's center on the halo's edge.

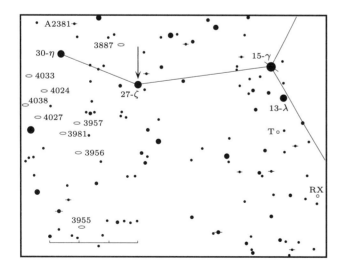

Finder Chart 41-5. 27-ζ Crt: 11ʰ44.7ᵐ −18° 21′

NGC 3962 H67[1] Galaxy Type E2/SA:(r?)0–
ϕ **2.6′ × 2.2′, m10.7v, SB 12.4** $11^h54.7^m -13° 58′$
Finder Chart 41-4, Figure 41-11   ★★★

8/10″ Scopes–100x: NGC 3962, a fairly bright galaxy, forms a triangle with two 10.5 magnitude stars 2.25′ to its SSW and 3.25′ to its SSE. It has a bright core embedded in a circular 1.5′ diameter halo.

12/14″ Scopes–125x: NGC 3962 has a bright 2′ × 1.5′ N–S halo containing a prominent core with a bright stellar nucleus.

NGC 3981 H274[3] Galaxy Type SAB?(rs:)c pec I-II
ϕ **3.3′ × 1.2′, m11.0v, SB 12.3** $11^h56.1^m -19° 54′$
Finder Chart 41-5, Figure 41-12   ★★★

12/14″ Scopes–125x: NGC 3981 is a faint 3′ × 1′ NNE–SSW streak with tapered ends and a uniform surface brightness. A 12th magnitude star is 1′ ESE, a 12.5 magnitude star 2.5′ east, and two 9th magnitude stars 4′ NW and 5′ SE, of the galaxy's center.

Chapter 42

Cygnus, the Swan

42.1 Overview

The northern Milky Way of summer is dominated by the oblong figure of Cygnus the Swan. The Swan's head is at Beta, the magnificent double star Albireo. Its wings stretch NW to Delta and SE to Epsilon. And its tail is marked by the 1st magnitude Alpha, whose name Deneb is from the Arabic word meaning "tail." This star-pattern is also known as the Northern Cross: during mid-evenings around Christmas the Northern Cross appears (as seen from mid-northern latitudes) to stand upright on the horizon. The Swan seems to be flying SW down the Milky Way toward Aquila the Eagle, which looks like it is flying NE up the Milky Way toward the Swan.

In classical mythology Cygnus was identified with the Swan into which Jupiter turned himself when he wished to seduce Leda, the wife of Tyndareus, King of Sparta, as she bathed in a pool. From their union was born Pollux and Helen, later to be Helen of Troy, "the face that launched a thousand ships." Castor was fathered by Leda's husband Tyndareus, and therefore, unlike Pollux, was not immortal.

Cygnus contains undoubtedly the most visually beautiful part of the entire 180° of the northern Milky Way. The Great Rift begins near Deneb and extends SW deep into the southern Milky Way, ending near Alpha Centauri. The dust clouds of the Great Rift are probably about 1,000 light years, or a little more, distant toward Cygnus and approach us in Aquila, Scutum, Sagittarius, and Scorpius, where they are only a few hundred light years away. The famous Coalsack in the Southern Cross is probably an outlying Great Rift dust cloud. The Cygnus Star Cloud, which stretches for 20° from Albireo NE to Gamma Cygni, is the single brightest Milky Way cloud north of the celestial equator. It is magnificent in any size binoculars; the SW half of the Star Cloud is remarkable for the star-gemmed brightness of its background glow, the NE half for the rich profusion of its 6th to 10th magnitude stars. When we look toward the Cygnus Star Cloud we look ahead down the length of our spiral arm where it begins to curve around the interior of our Galaxy.

Cygnus: SIG-nus
Genitive: Cygni, SIG-ni
Abbreviation: Cyg
Culmination: 9pm–Sept. 13, midnight–July 30
Area: 804 square degrees
Showpieces: 6–β Cyg, 18–δ Cyg, 61 Cyg, M29 (NGC 6913), M39 (NGC 7092), NGC 6826, *NGC 6960-92 Veil Nebula (*in larger telescopes with an O-III filter)
Binocular Objects: 6–β Cyg, 61 Cyg, 31–o^1 Cyg, B145, B164, B168, B343, B352, B361, Basel 6, Berk 86, Biur 2, Cr 419, Cr 428, IC 1369, IC 4996, IC 5067, IC 5146, M29 (NGC 6913), M39 (NGC 7092), NGC 6811, NGC 6819, NGC 6826, NGC 6834, NGC 6866, NGC 6871, NGC 6888, NGC 6910, NGC 6960, NGC 6992, NGC 7000, NGC 7039, NGC 7062, NGC 7063, NGC 7082, NGC 7086, Roslund 5, Ru 173

Cygnus also contains a multitude of individual objects which are aesthetically striking or astronomically interesting, or both. Beta Cygni, Albireo, is one of the most beautiful double stars in the entire sky. 61 Cygni is not far behind it – as well as being a near neighbor to the Solar System. The North America Nebula, just east of Deneb, is an easy binocular object and set in a star field that rivals that of the Cygnus Star Cloud. As often-photographed as the North America Nebula is the Veil Nebula, which also is a good binocular object. The Veil, however, is not an emission nebula like the North America but a supernova remnant, one of the two or three easiest to see in the sky. Cygnus has a large number of both planetary nebulae and open clusters; but none of its planetaries or open clusters are frontline examples of their species. Cygnus' two Messier objects are both open clusters: but M39, though large, is very loose; and M29 is small and not very populous. However, it is almost good not to have any open cluster distractions from the star-rich fields, the contorted dust clouds, and the subtly glowing nebulae of the Cygnus Milky Way,

Cygnus, the Swan

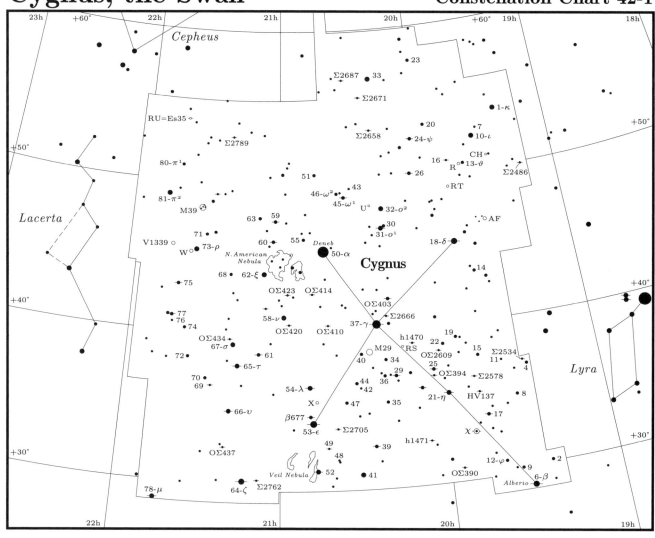

Chart Symbols

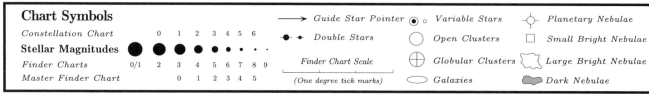

Table 42-1: Selected Variable Stars in Cygnus

Name	HD No.	Type	Max.	Min.	Period (Days)	F*	Spec. Type	R.A. (2000)	Dec.	Finder Chart No.	Notes
CH Cyg	182917	Z And	6.4	8.4	97		M7	$19^h24.5^m$	$+50°14'$	42-3	
AF Cyg	184008	SRb	7.4	9.4	94		M5	30.2	+46 09	42-3	
R Cyg	185456	M	6.1	14.2	426	0.35	S3-S6	36.8	+50 12	42-3	
RT Cyg	186686	M	6.4	12.7	190	0.44	M2-M8	43.6	+48 47	42-3	
X Cyg	187796	M	3.3	14.2	406	0.41	S6-S10	50.6	+32 55	42-6	
RS Cyg	192443	SRa	6.5	9.3	417		N0 ep	$20^h13.4^m$	+38 44	42-4	
U Cyg	193680	M	5.9	12.1	462	0.48	C7-C9	19.6	+47 54	42-3	
X Cyg	197572	Cd	5.8	6.8	16.38	0.35	F7-G8	43.4	+35 35	42-7	In OC Ru173
W Cyg	205730	SRb	6.8	8.9	126	0.50	M5	$21^h36.0^m$	+45 22	42-9	
V1339	206632	SRb	5.9	7.1	35		M4	42.1	+45 46	42-9	

F* = The fraction of period taken up by the star's rise from min. to max. brightness, or the period spent in eclipse.

Table 42-2: Selected Double Stars in Cygnus

Name	ADS No.	Pair	M1	M2	Sep."	P.A.°	Spec	R.A. (2000)	Dec.	Finder Chart No.	Notes
Σ2486	12169	AB	6.6	6.8	7.9	210	G5-G5	19ʰ12.1ᵐ	+49° 51′	42-1	
Σ2534	12478		7.6	7.8	6.9	64	A0	27.7	+36 32	42-1	
6–β Cyg	12540		3.1	5.1	34.0	54	K0-B8	30.7	+27 58	42-5	Albireo: Gold and blue
16 Cyg	12815		6.0	6.1	39.3	134	G0-G0	41.8	+50 32	42-3	
18–δ Cyg	12880	AB	2.9	6.3	w2.5	*221	A0	45.0	+45 08	42-4	
	12880	AC		11.9	65.7	66					
Σ2578	12893	AB	6.4	7.2	15.9	125	A0	45.7	+36 05	42-5	
	12893	AC		11.4	45.9	358					
HV137	12900	AB	6.2	9.2	38.7	27	K0	45.9	+35 01	42-5	
	12900	AC		8.5	44.6	77					
17 Cyg	12913	AB	5.0	9.2	26.0	69	F5-K5	46.4	+33 44	42-5	Fine yellow and orange pair
	12913	AC		9.0	134.6	138					
OΣ390	13117	AB	6.6	8.9	9.7	22	B9	55.1	+30 12	42-5	
	13117	AC		10.6	16.4	175					
24–ψ Cyg	13148	AB	4.9	7.4	3.2	178	A3	55.6	+52 26	42-3	
OΣ2609	13198		6.6	7.7	2.1	23	B5	58.6	+38 06	42-6	
OΣ394	13240		7.1	9.9	11.0	294	K0	20ʰ00.2ᵐ	+36 25	42-6	Beautiful orange and blue
26 Cyg	13278	AB	5.1	10.1	41.8	147	K0	01.4	+50 06	42-3	
	13278	AE		10.3	167.4	347					
	13278	BC		12.7	8.5	76					
h1470	13318		7.3	9.4	28.8	337	M	03.7	+38 20	42-4	
h1471	13335		5.6	11.2	31.2	7	B0	04.6	+32 13	42-5	
31–o¹ Cyg	13554	AC	3.8	6.7	107.0	173	K0 B9	13.6	+46 44	42-3	A = V695 (Variable)
	13554	AD		4.8	337.5	323	A2				
Σ2658	13560	AB	7.1	9.2	5.4	111	F5	13.7	+53 08	42-3	
OΣ403	13572	AB	7.4	7.6	0.8	173	B8	14.4	+42 06	42-4	
Σ2657	13572	AC		10.0	11.6	33					
29 Cyg		AB	5.0	6.6	212.4	153	A0 K5	14.5	+36 48	42-6	
Σ2666	13672	AB	5.8	8.0	2.7	245	B2	18.1	+40 44	42-4	
	13672	AC		8.5	34.1	208					
Σ2671	13692	AB	6.1	7.5	3.5	338	A0	18.4	+55 24	42-3	
Σ2687	13870		6.2	9.0	26.6	118	A0	26.4	+56 38	42-3	
Σ2705	14078	AB	7.4	8.4	3.1	261	K0	37.7	+33 22	42-1	
OΣ410	14126	AB	6.8	7.1	0.6	10	B8	39.6	+40 35	42-6	
	14126	ABxC		8.9	69.0	70					
49 Cyg	14158	AB	5.7	7.8	2.7	47	K0	41.0	+32 18	42-7	Golden and whitish
	14158	AC		11.6	68.3	91					
52 Cyg	14259		4.2	9.4	6.0	67	K0	45.7	+30 43	42-7	
OΣ414	14295	AB	7.6	8.7	10.0	95	B9	47.2	+42 25	42-8	
β 677	14290	AB	4.9	9.9	9.9	121	K0	47.2	+34 22	42-7	T Cyg
OΣ420	14413		6.5	10.7	5.8	3	B8	54.4	+40 42	42-8	
OΣ423	14432		7.0	9.5	2.9	80	B9	55.3	+42 31	42-8	
59 Cyg	14526	AB	4.7	9.6	20.2	352	B0	59.8	+47 31	42-8	
	14526	AC		11.5	26.7	141					
	14526	AD		11.0	38.3	220					
60 Cyg	14549		5.4	9.6	2.5	162	B3	21ʰ01.2ᵐ	+46 09	42-8	
61 Cyg	14636	AB	5.2	6.0	w30.3	*150	K5 K7	06.9	+38 45	42-7	Reddish-orange pair
Σ2762	14682	AB	5.8	7.8	3.4	306	A0	08.6	+30 12	42-7	V389
	14682	AC		8.9	57.7	226					
66–υ Cyg	14831	AB	4.4	10.0	15.1	220	B3	17.9	+34 54	42-7	
	14831	AC		10.0	21.5	181					
OΣ434	14850		6.7	9.5	24.7	122	A0	19.0	+39 45	42-1	
Σ2789	14878	AB	7.7	7.7	6.7	115	G5	20.0	+52 59	42-1	
OΣ437	14889	AB	6.2	6.9	2.1	28	G5	20.8	+32 27	42-7	Close yellow pair
69 Cyg	14969	AB	5.9	10.3	33.0	30	B0	25.8	+36 40	42-7	
	14969	AC		9.0	54.0	98					
Es35	15220	AB	6.8	11.5	11.1	224	M	40.7	+54 19	42-10	A = RU Cyg
	15220	AC		10.2	18.6	29					
78–μ Cyg	15270	AB	4.8	6.1	c1.2	*320	F5	44.1	+28 45	42-1	Bright yellow pair
	15270	AC		11.5	48.6	277					
	15270	AD		6.9	199.0	52	A5				

Footnotes: *= Year 2000, a = Near apogee, c = Closing, w = Widening. Finder Chart No: All stars listed in the tables are plotted in the large Constellation Chart, but when a star appears in a Finder Chart, this number is listed. Notes: When colors are subtle, the suffix *-ish* is used, e.g. *bluish*.

Figure 42-1. *The small planetary nebula PK64+5.1 is illuminated by a bright reddish-orange star known as Campbell's Hydrogen Star. Martin C. Germano made this five minute exposure on 2415 film with a 14.5″, f5 Newtonian.*

Figure 42-2. *NGC6811 is a coarse but attractive open cluster whose stars are distributed in arcs, chains, and knots. Image courtesy of Martin C. Germano.*

which repays countless hours of scanning with binoculars, richest-field telescopes, and low-power, wide-angle eyepieces

42.2 Interesting Stars

Beta (β) = 6 Cygni (ΣI43) Double Star   Spec. K3, B8
m3.1, 5.1; Sep. 34.0″; P.A. 54°   19ʰ30.7ᵐ +27° 58′
Finder Chart 42-5   ★★★★★

Albireo

2/3″ Scopes–50x: Beautiful! Albireo is a real celestial gem, its golden-yellow and blue stars embedded in the glittering background of the Cygnus Star Cloud. Albireo may well be the most observed of any double star because it is so lovely and easy to locate at the foot of the Northern Cross. It is 410 light years distant, so its primary has a luminosity of 760 suns and its secondary a luminosity of 120 suns.

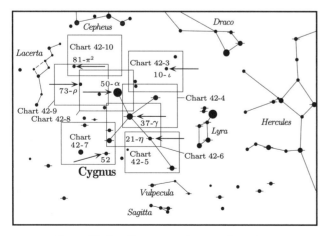

Master Finder Chart 42-2. Cygnus Chart Areas
Guide stars indicated by arrows.

Delta (δ) = 18 Cygni (Σ2579) Double Star Spec. B9
m2.9, 6.3; Sep. 2.5″; P.A. 221°   19ʰ45.0ᵐ +45° 08′
Finder Chart 42-4   ★★★★★

4/6″ Scopes–200x: Delta Cygni is a good test for telescopes of 4 to 6 inch aperture. It is easier to split in refractors than in reflectors of the same size. The primary has been reported as white, bluish-white, or greenish-blue, and the secondary as blue-white or bluish.

61 Cygni = Σ2758 Double Star   Spec. K5, K7
AB: m5.2, 6.1; Sep. 30.3″; P.A. 150° 21ʰ06.9ᵐ +38° 45′
Finder Chart 42-7   ★★★★★

61 Cygni, a wide, easily separated double of two orange K-type dwarfs, is only 11.2 light years distant, the twelfth nearest star or star pair to the Solar System. The two stars orbit each other in a period of 650 years, and will achieve maximum separation, 34″, about 2100 A.D. The components have luminosities of only 8% and 4% of the Sun's . Their color is probably at its best in binoculars, with which both stars are a stunning chrome orange-red.

4/6″ Scopes–75x: An easy target for small telescopes, 61 Cygni is a wide pair of bright orange stars.

42.3 Deep-Sky Objects

PK77+14.1 Abell 61 Planetary Nebula Type 2b
φ 190″, m13.5v, CS17.3v   19ʰ19.2ᵐ +46° 15′
Finder Chart 42-3, Figure 42-46   ★

16/18″ Scopes–100x: With an O-III filter Abell 61 appears as an extremely faint, diffuse 2′ diameter disk without a visible central star.

Figure 42-3. *NGC 6819 is a concentrated splash of faint stars contrasting nicely with the bright stars nearby. Image courtesy of Lee C. Coombs.*

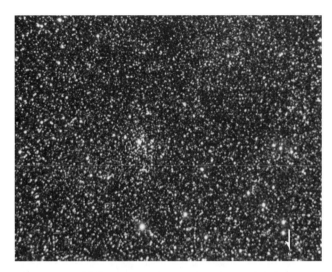

Figure 42-4. *NGC 6834 is a rich, irregular cluster of 60 faint stars surrounding a 9.5 magnitude star. Image courtesy of Martin C. Germano.*

PK64+5.1 Planetary Nebula Type 4
ϕ 8″, m11.3v, CS 10.0v   19^{h}34.8^m +30° 31′
Finder Chart 42-5, Figure 42-1   ★★★
Campbell's Hydrogen Star

8/10″Scopes–100x: Campbell's Hydrogen Star is the illuminating star of a very tiny planetary which requires high magnification to discern. The rich star field adds to the difficulty of identifying the nebula's stellar disk; look for the orange tone of Campbell's Hydrogen Star, then increase the magnification to see the faint enveloping haze.

12/14″Scopes–125x: The bright reddish-orange central star makes observation of this faint, 8″ diameter disk somewhat difficult.

Minkowski 92 Reflection Nebula
ϕ 0.2′ × 0.1′, Photo Br 2-5   19^{h}36.3^m +29° 33′
Finder Chart 42-5, Figure 42-6   ★★★
Footprint Nebula

12/14″Scopes–125x: At low power Minkowski 92 looks like a double star, but higher magnification reveals two nonstellar objects. The western of the two is larger and resembles a planetary nebula with a bright central area; but the eastern object remains a nearly stellar nodule. The two objects are oriented NW–SE and are in contact.

NGC 6811 Cr 402 Open Cluster 70★ Tr Type IV 3p
ϕ 20′, m6.8v, Br★ 9.88v   19^{h}36.9^m +46° 23′
Finder Chart 42-4, Figure 42-2   ★★★

8/10″Scopes–75x: This coarse open cluster has fifty 10th magnitude and fainter stars randomly scattered over a 20′ area. Fifteen 10th magnitude

and ten 11th magnitude stars stand out against the fainter members. Several of the cluster's star chains conspire to form a crude Greek omega (ω). Two relatively star-poor lanes cross the cluster NE–SW and NW–SE, the latter lane being the wider, and intersect at right angles. With a smaller telescope or perhaps your finder scope see if you can discern Walter Scott Houston's "hole in a cluster."

12/14″Scopes–100x: NGC 6811 is a loose but interesting cluster of 75 stars in a 20′ area. The majority of the stars are concentrated in the central 2′. The stars are arranged into some small groups, several star chains, and a number of doubles. A conspicuous double of 10th magnitude stars is on the east side of the cluster.

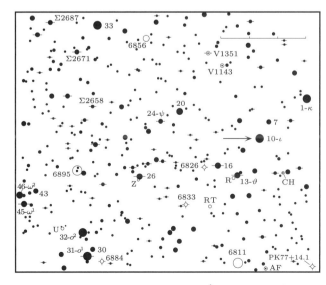

Finder Chart 42-3. 10–ι Cyg: 19^{h}29.4^m +51° 43′

Figure 42-5. *Emission nebula Sharpless 2-101 is visible as faint hazy areas around three 8th and 9th magnitude stars. Image courtesy of Dean Salman.*

NGC 6819 Cr 403 Open Cluster 150⋆ Tr Type I1r
φ 9.5′, m7.3v, Br⋆ 11.49v   **19ʰ41.3ᵐ +40° 11′**
Finder Chart 42-4, Figure 42-3   ★★★★

8/10″ Scopes–75x: NGC 6819 is a rich concentration of faint stars that contrasts with the field of the brighter Milky Way stars to its east. The cluster is centered 7′ SW of a magnitude 6.5 star and includes fifty magnitude 11.5 and fainter members in a 5′ area. Except for a large almost starless wedge missing from the north side, the cluster has an

almost square outline. (Photographs fill in this gap somewhat by recording faint stars which are not as noticeable visually.)

12/14″ Scopes–100x: NGC 6819 is a rich concentration of a hundred 11.5 to 15th magnitude stars in a 5′ area. The outline is irregular, but the fainter stars form a "U" open to the north. The brighter stars fall along chains and rows superimposed against the fainter members. The longest chain runs N–S and forms the U's western extension.

NGC 6826 H73⁴ PK83+12.1 Planetary Neb. Type 3a+2
φ >25″, m8.8v, CS 10.6v   **19ʰ44.8ᵐ +50° 31′**
Finder Chart 42-3, Figure 42-47   ★★★★★

The Blinking Planetary

8/10″ Scopes–75x: This bright, 25″ diameter planetary nebula lies just WSW of an 8.5 magnitude star convenient for producing the "blinking effect" with the planetary. Stare at the planetary's magnitude 10.6 central star through a medium or high power eyepiece until its brightness overwhelms the eye, and causes the nebula to fade. When you glance away and look at the nearby magnitude 8.5 star, the planetary's disk will reappear. This alteration between direct and averted vision of the planetary's nucleus thus causes the nebula to "blink." Many planetaries with a prominent central star will produce this phenomenon. The different combinations of central star and disk brightness in other planetary nebulae will require different magnifications to produce the blinking effect.

12/14″ Scopes–125x: NGC 6826 is a fine, bright, bluish-green planetary elongated 25″ × 20″ ESE–WNW with a bright magnitude 10.6 central star. A dark area is just perceptible west of the central star. A 12th magnitude star lies 1.5′ south.

NGC 6834 H16⁸ Open Cluster 50⋆ Tr Type II 2 m
φ 5′, m7.8v, Br⋆ 9.65v   **19ʰ52.2ᵐ +29° 25′**
Finder Chart 42-5, Figure 42-4   ★★★

8/10″ Scopes–75x: This cluster is a 5′ × 2′ E–W oblong streak of faint stars. A 7′ long E–W row of brighter stars stands out among forty fainter members.

12/14″ Scopes–125x: NGC 6834 is a faint but rich cluster of sixty faint stars in an 7′ area. The main body is elongated 5′ × 2′ E–W, and includes a chain of four evenly spaced magnitude 9.5–10.5 stars. The cluster's magnitude 9.5 lucida is near its center, with a 2′ knot of stars just to its west. Scattered around the central group is a thin halo of outlying stars, the outliers being numerous to the south.

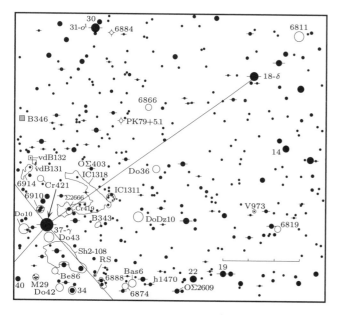

Finder Chart 42-4. 37–γ Cyg: 20ʰ22.2ᵐ +40° 15′

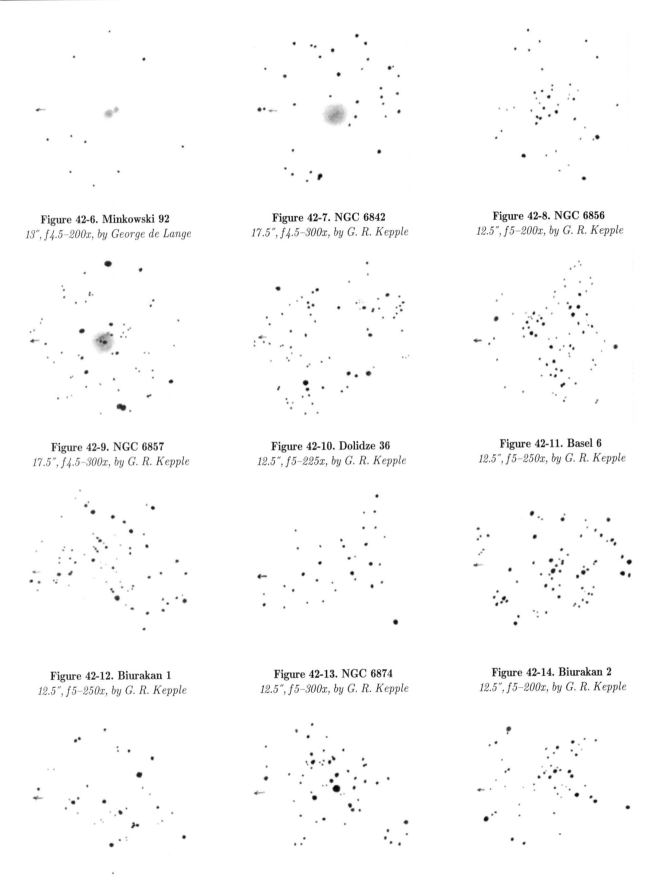

Figure 42-6. Minkowski 92
13″, f4.5–200x, by George de Lange

Figure 42-7. NGC 6842
17.5″, f4.5–300x, by G. R. Kepple

Figure 42-8. NGC 6856
12.5″, f5–200x, by G. R. Kepple

Figure 42-9. NGC 6857
17.5″, f4.5–300x, by G. R. Kepple

Figure 42-10. Dolidze 36
12.5″, f5–225x, by G. R. Kepple

Figure 42-11. Basel 6
12.5″, f5–250x, by G. R. Kepple

Figure 42-12. Biurakan 1
12.5″, f5–250x, by G. R. Kepple

Figure 42-13. NGC 6874
12.5″, f5–300x, by G. R. Kepple

Figure 42-14. Biurakan 2
12.5″, f5–200x, by G. R. Kepple

Figure 42-15. NGC 6896
12.5″, f5–250x, by G. R. Kepple

Figure 42-16. Collinder 419
12.5″, f5–250x, by G. R. Kepple

Figure 42-17. Berkeley 86
12.5″, f5–200x, by G. R. Kepple

Figure 42-18. *Barnard 145 stands out sharply in a profuse star field. Martin C. Germano made this 90 minute exposure on hypered 2415 film with an 8″, f5 Newtonian reflector.*

NGC 6842 PK65+0.1 Planetary Nebula Type 3b
ϕ 50″, m13.10v, CS16.2v   19^{h}55.0^m +29° 17′

Finder Chart 42-5, Figure 42-7   ★

16/18″Scopes–200x: NGC 6842, located in a rich star field, has a faint 50″ diameter disk with diffuse edges. 13th magnitude stars are 1′ east and 1.25′ SE of the planetary's center. Two doubles, each of magnitude 12.5 and 13 stars separated by about 15″, are 3.5′ west and 2.75′ NNW of the planetary.

Finder Chart 42-5. 21–η Cyg: 19^{h}56.3^m +35° 05′

NGC 6856 Open Cluster [15★]
[ϕ 4′, m –, Br★ 12.0v]   19^{h}59.3^m +56° 08′

Finder Chart 42-3, Figure 42-8   ★★

12/14″Scopes–175x: NGC 6856 is classified as "nonexistent" in the *RNGC*, but in fact can be seen at low power as a tiny, faint but distinct clump in the surrounding star field. 175x reveals a 3′ × 2′ NNW–SSE patch of fifteen 13th to 15th magnitude stars. The three brightest stars form a 1′ equilateral triangle NE of the cluster's center.

Sharpless 2-101 Emission Nebula
ϕ 18′ × 10′, Photo Br 1-5, Color 3-4 20^{h}00.0^m +35° 17′

Finder Chart 42-5, Figure 42-5   ★★

16/18″Scopes–100x: Sharpless 2-101 is 3/4° ENE of magnitude 3.9 Eta (η) = 21 Cygni, a multiple with four easily separated 10th to 11th magnitude companions. This emission nebula is a very faint haze around a thin NE-pointing triangle of one 9th and two 8th magnitude stars. The nebula is extended NNE–SSW and is brightest around each of the three stars, especially around the one on the SW, which has a wide companion. The O-III filter adds some contrast but diminishes the faint outer nebulosity.

NGC 6857 H144^3 Emission Nebula
ϕ 1′ × 1′, CS13.3:v   20^{h}01.9^m +33° 31′

Finder Chart 42-5, Figure 42-9   ★★

8/10″Scopes–75x: This faint, small emission nebula is within a distorted box of four stars that are progressively fainter in a counterclockwise direction, a 12th magnitude star to the SW, a 12.5 magnitude star to the NW, a 13th magnitude star to the NE, and a 13.5 magnitude star to the SE.

12/14″Scopes–125x: NGC 6857, located in a rich Milky Way field, is a faint, circular 45″ disk with a 13th magnitude central star slightly off-center to the NW. Its SW side is a little brighter and somewhat bloated outward. A 13th magnitude star is on the disk's SE edge. The nebula rather resembles a planetary.

Dolidze 36 Open Cluster Tr Type IV1p
ϕ 14′, m –   20^{h}02.5^m +42° 06′

Finder Chart 42-4, Figure 42-10   ★★★

12/14″Scopes–100x: Dolidze 36 is a moderately faint but fairly conspicuous loose, irregular splash of faint stars. Its brighter members are in two E–W streams along the cluster's northern and southern edges. At each end of a jagged 5′ long star-chain along the northern edge of the cluster is a wide double,

Figure 42-19. *NGC 6866 is a moderately rich cluster of 50 faint stars in knots and short chains. Image courtesy of Lee C. Coombs.*

Figure 42-20. *NGC 6871 is a highly irregular cluster of both bright and faint stars with the multiple ADS 13374 at its center. Image courtesy of Lee C. Coombs.*

magnitude 9.5 and 10 primaries with 12th magnitude secondaries. Along the southern edge of the cluster is a 12′ long curved star chain, concave to the south, with a 10th magnitude star at its west end.

Barnard 145 Dark Nebula
ϕ **35′ × 6′, Opacity 4**   20^{h}02.8^m +37° 40′
Finder Chart 42-6, Figure 42-18   ★★★
8/10″ Scopes–75x: Barnard 145 is a thin 35′ × 6′ E–W triangular dust cloud centered just south of a 7th magnitude star located at the midpoint of its long north side. It stands out well against the rich Milky Way star field around it. A sprinkling of faint stars shows through it, the brightest a magnitude 9.5 object 10′ south of the 7th magnitude star near the dark cloud's south corner.

NGC 6866 H59⁷ Open Cluster 80★ Tr Type II 2 m
ϕ **6′, m7.6v, Br★ 10.66v**   20^{h}03.8^m +44° 09′
Finder Chart 42-4, Figure 42-19   ★★★
8/10″ Scopes–75x: NGC 6866 is a fairly rich, irregular cluster of thirty stars in a 6′ area embedded in a rich Milky Way star field. A magnitude 6.5 star is 20′ west. A "V" of the cluster's brightest members stands out in its rather concentrated center. Other cluster stars are distributed along short N–S chains.
12/14″ Scopes–125x: NGC 6866 is a moderately rich cluster of fifty 11.5 magnitude and fainter stars irregularly distributed in an 8′ area. The western part of the cluster is more concentrated and contains

a bar formed by three NNW–SSE star chains. Two more star chains curve eastward from the bar's north and south ends toward each other but do not intersect. Several doubles are in the cluster, including an unequally bright pair north of its center, a pair near its NW edge, and a wide pair of magnitude 10 and 10.5 stars just to its north.

DoDz 10 Open Cluster 12★ Tr Type IV 2 pn
ϕ **20′, m –**   20^{h}05.7^m +40° 32′
Finder Chart 42-4   ★
12/14″ Scopes–100x: Nothing resembling the typical star cluster can be seen at the above coordinates. In the center of the area plotted in *Uranometria 2000.0* is a faint horseshoe-shaped asterism formed by a dozen faint stars, one of magnitude 12.5 and the others magnitude 14–15. A clump containing a dozen stars lies midway between the horseshoe and a 6.5 magnitude star to the north. A stream of thirty stars extends from the magnitude 6.5 star west to a magnitude 9.5 star.

NGC 6871 Cr 413 Open Cluster 15★ Tr Type II 2 pn
ϕ **20′, m5.2v, Br★ 6.83v**   20^{h}05.9^m +35° 47′
Finder Chart 42-5, Figure 42-20   ★★★
8/10″ Scopes–75x: NGC 6871 is a bright, irregular cluster of seventy-five 6.8 to 14th magnitude stars in a 20′ area just SSW of the bright 5.4 magnitude orange star 27 Cygni. The fourteen brightest members along with many fainter stars lie along a

Figure 42-21. *IC 1311, located in a profuse Milky Way field, is a mist of faint stars encircled by an irregular ring of bright stars. Image courtesy of Martin C. Germano.*

Figure 42-22. *NGC 6883 is a highly irregular cluster broken into at least five separate clumps. Image courtesy of Martin C. Germano.*

snaking N–S stream that extends from 23′ SSW of 27 Cygni south to a wide NW–SE pair of 8th and 9th magnitude stars. At the stream's center is the multiple ADS 13374, six of the eight components of which are in three doubles of magnitude 6.8 to 9 stars. A star-poor lane parallels the stream just to it east. The western edge is profuse with faint outlying stars. Open cluster Biurakan 1 lies to the east.

Basel 6 Open Cluster 40★ Tr Type IV1mn
ϕ 13′, m7.7v, Br★ 10.18v   20^{h}06.8^m +38° 21′
Finder Chart 42-6, Figure 42-11   ★★★
12/14″ Scopes–100x: Basel 6 is a fairly concentrated but irregular 10′ × 4′ E–W band of stars with an arm extending another 4′ north. It contains fifty stars,

the dozen brightest magnitude 11 and 12, divided into three subgroups to the north, west, and SE. A short star-chain extends NE from the SE subgroup, ending in a magnitude 11.5 star. A double of 10th magnitude stars lies to the SW.

Biurakan 1 Open Cluster 15★ Tr Type IV3pn
ϕ 14′, m –   20^{h}07.5^m +35° 41′
Finder Chart 42-5, Figure 42-12   ★★★
12/14″ Scopes–100x: Biurakan 1 is an irregular cluster of three dozen stars scattered over a 10′ area. Haze is visible around an 8th magnitude star on the cluster's northern edge and around a wide 9th magnitude pair on its southern edge. This wide double is at the SSW end of a star chain extending 8′ NNE that includes three magnitude 9 to 9.5 stars. A broad stream of mostly 11th to 13th magnitude stars stretches 12′ E–W. Open cluster NGC 6871 lies just to the west.

NGC 6874 H86⁸ Open Cluster 20★
ϕ 7′, m –, Br★ 10v   20^{h}07.8^m +38° 14′
Finder Chart 42-6, Figure 42-13   ★★★
12/14″ Scopes–125x: NGC 6874, though classed as "nonexistent" in the *RNGC*, is a 7′ wide triangular group of twenty 10th magnitude and fainter stars that stands out well from the surrounding Milky Way field. In fact NGC 6874 is more conspicuous than the open cluster Basel 6 to its NW. A 10th magnitude star marks the group's west corner. The triangle's sides are all concave, its southern edge being the

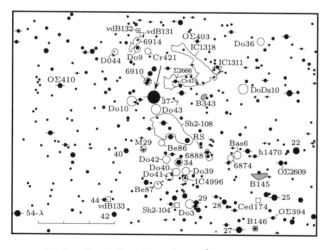

Finder Chart 42-6. 37–γ Cyg: 20^{h}22.2^m +40° 15′

most ambiguous. A 10th magnitude orange star stands out on the eastern side. At the center of the triangle is a starless void. A NE–SW double of 7th magnitude stars is to the cluster's SE.

PK79+5.1 Planetary Nebula Type 4+2
ϕ >19″, m14v, CS−   20^{h}09.1^m +43° 44′
Finder Chart 42-4, Figure 42-48   ★
16/18″Scopes–250x: PK79+5.1, located 8′ east of an 8th magnitude star, has a 19″ diameter disk with a slightly darker center. A wide E–W pair of 12th magnitude stars is centered 2.5′ west of the planetary, and a 13th magnitude star lies 1′ NE.

Biurakan 2 Open Cluster 10★ Tr Type III 2p
ϕ 19′, m6.3v, Br★ 7.87v   20^{h}09.2^m +35° 29′
Finder Chart 42-5, Figure 42-14   ★★★
12/14″Scopes–100x: Biur 2 is a loose, irregular group of three dozen stars in a 12′ area. A dozen members are concentrated around double star Σ 2639 (7.7, 8.7; 5.7″; 302°) located at the cluster's center. This double marks the NE corner of the parallelogram that includes one 8th and two 9th magnitude stars. The 8th magnitude star, at the parallelogram's NW corner, is in a 1′ knot of ten stars.

Roslund 5 Open Cluster 15★ Tr Type IV 2pn
ϕ 45′, m −   20^{h}10.0^m +33° 46′
Finder Chart 42-5   ★★★
12/14″Scopes–75x: Roslund 5 is a loose, irregular group of 15 bright stars spread over a 45′ area. Three dozen fainter stars are sprinkled about. Through the cluster center runs a prominent N–S star chain with west-curving ends. An E–W chain of fainter stars intersects the N–S chain at a wide 8th magnitude double near the cluster center. The cluster's best concentrations are in its NE and SW sections and include several doubles.

Berkeley 50 = IC 1310 Open Cluster 12★ Tr Type II 1pn
ϕ 4′, m −, Br★ 14.0p   20^{h}10.4^m +34° 46′
Finder Chart 42-5   ★★
12/14″Scopes–125x: Berkeley 50 is a very faint misty patch north of a tiny triangle of 13th magnitude stars. It contains four 14th magnitude members resolved against a twinkling background of threshold stars. At 175x a dainty pair of 14th and 15th magnitude star can be seen on its NNE edge. A brighter star group 10′ SE could be mistaken for this cluster.

IC 1311 Open Cluster 60★ Tr Type I 1 mn
ϕ 9′, m13.1p, Br★ 17.0p   20^{h}10.8^m +41° 11′
Finder Chart 42-6, Figure 42-21   ★
12/14″Scopes–125x: IC 1311 is a faint mist encircled by an irregular 10′ diameter ring of bright stars in a profuse field. On the ring are a 7th magnitude star 4.5′ north of the cluster-mist, an 8th magnitude star 6′ east, and several 9th magnitude stars. The cluster consists of an E–W row of four 13th and 14th magnitude stars resolved against a 3′ wide unresolved haze, around the perimeter of which eight more magnitude 13–14 stars can be made out. Two groups of 11th–12th magnitude stars NW of the 3′ haze could be mistaken as detached parts of the cluster; but their stars are too bright.

NGC 6883 Cr 415 Open Cluster 30★ Tr Type IV 2mn
ϕ 14′, m8.0p   20^{h}11.3^m +35° 51′
Finder Chart 42-5, Figure 42-22   ★★
12/14″Scopes–125x: NGC 6883 is a large, coarse, irregular cluster difficult to detect in the rich star field. It has at least five separate groupings scattered around the edges of its sparse center. The most prominent grouping, the one to the SE, could be mistaken as the entire cluster. On the east edge is a "V" of 10th and 11th magnitude stars, the southernmost a 17″ wide double of magnitude 10.5 objects. Many faint stars are scattered around the "V." On the cluster's SW edge is a triangle of magnitude 10.5 stars. Several star-knots are along the northern edge, and a scattered group around two magnitude 9.5 stars is WNW.

NGC 6888 H72^4 Emission Nebula
ϕ 18′ × 13′, Photo Br 1-5, Color 3-4 20^{h}12.0^m +38° 21′
Finder Chart 42-6, Figure 42-23   ★★★
Crescent Nebula

12/14″Scopes–100x: The Crescent Nebula is a faint, thin arc concave to the south. At the center of the arc is the unequally bright double ADS 13515 (7.2, 10.5; 14″; 60°). A UHC filter considerably enhances the nebula, pulling in its faint southern portions; but more aperture is needed for a really good view.
16/18″Scopes–125x: NGC 6888 is a visually interesting object especially in an O-III filter. Its 20′ × 10′ NE–SW halo is unevenly illuminated, the brightest portion an arc along the north side. The arc is most conspicuous on its NE, just where it begins a sharp curve to the south. Within and south of the arc the nebula-glow is much fainter. A multitude of Milky Way field stars shines through the nebula, including, in its NE section, a bright keystone with a 9th and 10th magnitude star forming the east

Figure 42-23. *NGC 6888, located 2.5 degrees SW of Gamma Cygni, is known as the Crescent Nebula. Image courtesy Jim Burnell.*

side and two 7th magnitude stars forming the west. The bright star embedded on the northernmost point of the arc of the nebula is a double with a magnitude 10.5 companion 14″ to its ENE.

Barnard 343 Dark Nebula
ϕ 13′ × 5′, Opacity 5   20^{h}13.5^m +40° 16′
Finder Chart 42-6   ★★★
8/10″Scopes–75x: Barnard 343 appears as a hole in the profuse Cygnus Star Cloud Milky Way. It is flanked by 8th and 9th magnitude stars, each a double with a fainter companion on its north. The dust cloud is elongated 10′ × 5′ NW–SE, its southern section more opaque. A 2′ clump of 12th–13th magnitude stars is on its SSW edge.

Dolidze 3 Open Cluster 40★ Tr Type III2mn
ϕ 14′, m −   20^{h}15.7^m +36° 47′
Finder Chart 42-6   ★★★
12/14″Scopes–100x: Dolidze 3 is a large cluster of 50 stars irregularly scattered over an E–W triangular area. It has three 10th magnitude stars, twenty 11th to 12th magnitude stars, and a 9th magnitude star on its east end. Its fainter stars appear as an enriched concentration of the Milky Way. Magnitude 4.9 star 29 Cygni, located near the cluster's west edge, is at the north end of a loose 40′ row of bright stars.

NGC 6895 H83^8 Open Cluster [30★]
[ϕ 15′, m −]   20^{h}16.4^m +50° 14′
Finder Chart 42-3   ★★★
12/14″Scopes–100x: NGC 6895 is classed as "nonexistent" in the *RNGC*, and indeed is not well detached from the surrounding Milky Way field. William Herschel saw it as a rather rich, 15′ wide cluster of scattered stars. We observed, 15′ NE of a 6th magnitude star that Herschel must have considered a cluster member, a patch of forty stars within a 9′ × 6′ triangle formed by one 9th and two 8th magnitude stars. 4.5′ east of the 6th magnitude star is a 2′ knot of six faint stars; and 6′ SE of the bright star is a 6′ × 2′ E–W group of twenty stars.

IC 1318 Emission Nebula
ϕ 50′ × 30′, Photo Br 1-5, Color 3-4   20^{h}16.4^m +41° 49′
Finder Chart 42-6, Figure 42-24   ★★
12/14″Scopes–60x: IC 1318 is a very faint, huge emission nebula located in the rich Milky Way field surrounding the bright star Gamma (γ) Cygni. There are five large segments with the more distinct patches flanking dark nebula LDN 889 that runs through the star field generally E–W with a concave bend to the north. The patient observer will see faint wisps and streaks spread over many degrees of sky. Use low power with a UHC filter to sweep the area. Also scan the area with binoculars.

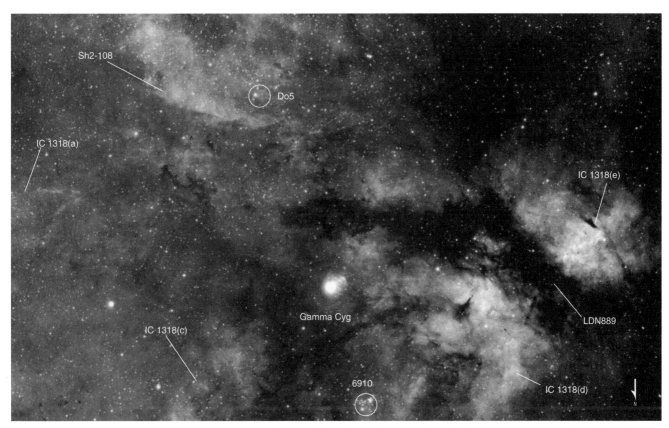

Figure 42-24. *IC 1318 surrounds the star Sadr (Gamma Cygni). The dark nebula is LDN 889. Image courtesy Jim Burnell.*

Dolidze 39 Open Cluster 40★ Tr Type IV 2 m
φ 12′, m –   **20ʰ16.4ᵐ +37° 52′**
Finder Chart 42-6, Figure 42-38   ★★★
12/14″ Scopes–100x: Dolidze 39 is 16′ SW of the irregular
    variable 34 = φ Cygni (mag range 3.0–6.0). It is a
    moderately faint, irregular, 12′ wide, cluster that
    consists of two distinct, roughly triangular, NE–SW
    groups joined near the cluster center. Each triangle
    has a starless void within. The group's lucida is a
    magnitude 9.5 star on its NE edge. Among its other
    thirty or so members are six 10th and a dozen 11th
    magnitude stars. A faint, small group detached to
    the NNW adds another ten stars.

**NGC 6894 H13⁴ PK69–2.1 Planetary Nebula Type
4+2**
φ >42″, m12.3v, CS17.6   **20ʰ16.4ᵐ +30° 34′**
Finder Chart 42-5, Figure 42-25   ★★★
8/10″ Scopes–200x: NGC 6894 has a fairly bright but
    diffuse, circular 40″ diameter halo without a visible
    central star.
12/14″ Scopes–250x: This planetary nebula has a smoky-
    gray disk slightly elongated 45″ × 40″ N–S within
    which is a vaguely darker center apparent only by
    averted vision. The periphery is brighter along the

northern and western edges. The planetary is
flanked by scattered groups of stars to its north and
south. A 12th magnitude star lies 2.5′ south.

Figure 42-25. *Planetary nebula NGC 6894 presents in medium size telescopes a smoky-gray, unevenly illuminated disk. Image courtesy of Adam Block NOAO/AURA/NSF.*

Figure 42-26. Berkeley 87
12.4″, f5-200x, by G. R. Kepple

Figure 42-27. Collinder 421
12.5″, f5-175x, by G. R. Kepple

Figure 42-28. Dolidze 9
12.5″, f5-250x, by G. R. Kepple

Figure 42-29. Dolidze 44
12.5″, f5-250x, by G. R. Kepple

Figure 42-30. Ruprecht 175
12.5″, f5-175x, by Glen W. Sanner

Figure 42-31. Collinder 428
12.5″, f5-200x, by G. R. Kepple

Figure 42-32. NGC 7024
12.5″, f5-225x, by G. R. Kepple

Figure 42-33. NGC 7058
12.5″, f5-225x, by G. R. Kepple

Figure 42-34. NGC 7093
12.5″, f5-225x, by G. R. Kepple

Figure 42-35. NGC 7127
12.5″, f5-300x, by G. R. Kepple

Figure 42-36. NGC 7150
12.5″, f5-225x, by G. R. Kepple

Figure 42-37. NGC 7175
12.5″, f5-200x, by G. R. Kepple

IC 4996 Open Cluster 15★ Tr Type II3pn
φ 5′, m7.3v, Br★ 8.51v   20^{h}16.5^m +37° 38′
Finder Chart 42-6, Figure 42-38   ★★★
8/10″Scopes–100x: IC 4996 is a little cluster 25′ SW of
   the explosive variable 34 = P Cygni (presently a
   5th magnitude object). At the center of a 3′ knot
   of faint cluster members is the magnitude 7.6 cluster
   lucida. Immediately to its north is the multiple
   Burnham 442, the magnitude 8.0 primary of which
   has a magnitude 9.0 companion 32″ away in P.A.
   77° and a magnitude 9.7 companion 19″ distant in
   P.A. 280°. These four stars form a distinct
   "trapezium." Faint outlying members are scattered
   east and north of this knot for a total of 30 stars
   over a 6′ diameter area. An 8th magnitude star lies
   6′ ENE, and a 9th magnitude star is 3′ NNE.

NGC 6896 Open Cluster [20★]
[φ 6′, m −]   20^{h}18.0^m +30° 39′
Finder Chart 42-5, Figure 42-15   ★★★
12/14″Scopes–100x: NGC 6896, though another open
   cluster classed as "nonexistent" in the *RNGC*,
   stands out fairly well against the background Milky
   Way field. Its brighter stars form a 6′ long arc
   concave to the SE just NW of a 9th magnitude star.
   Another dozen or so fainter stars are scattered
   about. At low power the arc consists of five 12th
   magnitude stars. 150x resolves the easternmost star
   of the arc into a knot of four 13th magnitude
   components.

Collinder 419 Open Cluster Tr Type IV2p
φ 4.5′, m5.4p   20^{h}18.1^m +40° 43′
Finder Chart 42-6, Figure 42-16   ★★
12/14″Scopes–125x: Collinder 419 is a faint, sparse
   cluster scattered around a 5th magnitude star. The
   brighter members are 2′ SW and 2′ WNW of the
   5th magnitude star, and a wide double is 2′ to its
   NE. A mist of 14th and 15th magnitude stars is
   concentrated south of the bright central star: two
   doubles with 14th magnitude components stand out
   in the mist. A 10th magnitude star lies 5.5′ NE.

Dolidze 40 Open Cluster 12★ Tr Type III2pn
φ 12′, m −   20^{h}18.2^m +37° 50′
Finder Chart 42-6, Figure 42-38   ★★
12/14″Scopes–100x: Dolidze 40, located 12′ south of the
   variable star 34 Cygni, is a faint irregular cluster
   not well detached from the surrounding star field.
   The brighter stars are in two N–S groups. The
   northern group has 16 stars, its more prominent
   members forming a conspicuous "Y" with the stem

Figure 42-38. *IC 4996 (at top) is a compact cluster 25′ SW of 34 Cygni (bottom right) with Dolidze 39 and 40 lying between them. Martin C. Germano made this 35 minute exposure on 2415 film with a 14.5″, f5 Newtonian.*

pointing WNW. The southern group contains 15
members in a triangular area, its brighter stars at
the south and NW vertices of the triangle. A
concentration of very faint stars lies SW of the
southern group.

Dolidze 41 Open Cluster Tr Type IV1p
φ 11′, m −   20^{h}19.3^m +37° 44′
Finder Chart 42-6   ★★★
12/14″Scopes–100x: Dolidze 41 is a fairly bright, loose,
   irregular cluster. It consists of three concentrations.
   The NW concentration includes a parallelogram of
   9th magnitude stars, a 10th magnitude star, and a
   scattering of fainter stars, especially on its south.
   The western concentration is a triangular gathering
   of faint stars. And the SE concentration is around
   an irregular NE–SW chain of four bright stars.

Dolidze 42 Open Cluster 20★ Tr Type III1pn
φ 11′, m −   20^{h}19.7^m +38° 08′
Finder Chart 42-6   ★★
12/14″Scopes–100x: Dolidze 42 is a faint, irregular E–
   W group of 30 stars. The brighter members form
   a triangle in the western part of the cluster, an
   8th magnitude star at its western corner and a
   pair of magnitude 12 and 14 stars at its south
   corner. A row of three stars is just north of the
   triangle. Within it are two dozen stars.

Figure 42-39. *NGC 6910 is a compact, but irregular cluster of bright stars that stands out well from the surrounding star field. Image courtesy of Chris Schur.*

Figure 42-40. *Messier 29 is a fine compact cluster of bright and faint stars. Image courtesy of Martin C. Germano.*

Berkeley 86 Open Cluster 30★ Tr Type IV2mn
φ 5′, m7.9v, Br★ 9.50v   20ʰ20.4ᵐ +38° 42′
Finder Chart 42-6, Figure 42-17   ★★★
12/14″Scopes–125x: Berkeley 86 is a loose, unconcentrated 8′ × 6′ E–W triangular scattering of two dozen stars. The seven brightest members, magnitude 9.5 to 11 objects, form an asterism resembling a tiny version of Lepus. Fainter cluster stars are sprinkled around them in all directions except to the south.

Berkeley 87 Open Cluster 30★ Tr Type IV2m
φ 12′, m –, Br★ 13.0p   20ʰ21.7ᵐ +37° 22′
Finder Chart 42-6, Figure 42-26   ★★★
12/14″Scopes–125x: Berkeley 87 is a visually interesting group of 30 stars scattered over a 10′ area. It is just east of a NW-pointing isosceles triangle formed by three 9th magnitude stars. In the eastern part of the cluster two magnitude 9.5 and two magnitude 10 stars form a kite-shaped asterism. Numerous magnitude 11–12.5 stars, including several variously-wide doubles, pepper the area between and around the triangle and the kite.

NGC 6910 H56⁸ Open Cluster 50★ Tr Type I2mn
φ 7′, m7.4v, Br★ 9.61v   20ʰ23.1ᵐ +40° 47′
Finder Chart 42-6, Figure 42-39   ★★★
8/10″Scopes–100x: NGC 6910, located half a degree NNE of magnitude 2.2 Gamma (γ) = 37 Cygni, is a 5′ × 2′ NW–SE band with magnitude 7.5 stars on its north and SE edges. The northern magnitude 7.5 star is yellow and at the base of a "Y" of five stars, with magnitude 13–14 stars scattered around.

The other magnitude 7.5 star lies in a small star-knot on the SE edge of the cluster. Two small groups detached to the NE and the SE enlarge the cluster to three dozen members in an 8′ area. 7′ south of the cluster is a NE–SW pair of magnitude 9.5 stars.

Collinder 421 Open Cluster 22★ Tr Type III1pn
φ 5′, m10.1p, Br★ 10.1p   20ʰ23.3ᵐ +41° 42′
Finder Chart 42-6, Figure 42-27   ★★★
12/14″Scopes–125x: Collinder 421 is a fairly conspicuous 6′ E–W splash of two dozen 10th to 14th magnitude stars. The brighter members are on the eastern side of the cluster, three of them in a 1.5′ wide triangle. The group includes fifteen 12th and 13th magnitude stars, including those in a parallelogram on the northern side of the cluster.

NGC 6913 Messier 29 OpenCluster 50★ Tr Type I2mn
φ 6′, m6.6v, Br★ 8.59v   20ʰ23.9ᵐ +38° 32′
Finder Chart 42-6, Figure 42-40   ★★★★★
    Charles Messier discovered this group on July 29, 1764, and described it as a cluster of 7 or 8 very small stars. M29 is 6,000 light years distant. It is not a particularly large cluster, only 11 light years in diameter, but its five brightest members are all B0 giants, so the cluster's absolute magnitude is a very impressive −8.2, a luminosity of 160,000 suns.
4/6″Scopes–75x: This nice little cluster is a compact group of eight bright stars standing out against a host of faint members. The four brightest stars form a square. Three of the other bright stars are in a north-pointing triangle. Twenty stars are visible in a 7′ area.

Figure 42-41. *The two patches of reflection nebulae Van den Bergh 131 and 132 may be seen as very faint patches of haze around its brighter stars. Open cluster Dolidze 8, at left, is the bright cluster of stars embedded in vdB131. Image courtesy of Josef Popsel and Stefan Binnewies.*

8/10"Scopes–100x: Messier 29 is a bright, moderately concentrated cluster of thirty stars in an 8' area. The brighter members give the cluster a boxy appearance. Eight 9th to 10th magnitude stars are in the main group and a couple more stars of similar brightness are isolated to the east. Two pairs of 9th to 10th magnitude stars are 10' west and 10' south of the cluster.

vdB131 NGC 6914A Reflection Nebula
ϕ 3' × 3', Photo Br 2-5, Color 1-4   20^{h}24.3^m +42° 18'

vdB132 NGC 6914B Reflection Nebula
ϕ 4' × 4', Photo Br 2-5, Color 1-4   20^{h}24.8^m +42° 23'

NGC 6914 DWB100-5-9 Emission Nebula
ϕ 40' × 15', Photo Br 4-5, Color 3-4 20^{h}26.7^m +42° 07'
Finder Chart 42-6, Figure 42-41   ★★/★★/★
12/14" Scopes–125x: Van den Bergh 31 and 32 are two faint milky areas surrounding bright stars. Dolidze 8, a 6' diameter cluster of 20 stars, is embedded in Van den Bergh 131, while van den Bergh 132, to the NE, surrounds a wide double of unequally bright stars. To the SE of the two van den Bergh nebulae is emission nebula DWB100-5-9, a very faint indefinite haze spreading 10' east from a 7th

magnitude star. All three nebulae are embedded in a rich Milky Way star field.

Dolidze 9 Open Cluster 8★ Tr Type II2pn
ϕ 5', m –   20^{h}25.8^m +41° 57'
Finder Chart 42-6, Figure 42-28   ★★★
12/14"Scopes–125x: Dolidze 9 is a bright cluster of a dozen stars in a 7' area. Its bright members are fairly well concentrated around its center, the magnitude 6.5 lucida being just west of the center, and two rather bright doubles, one of magnitude 9 and 9.5 components and the other a pair of 10th magnitude stars, lying in or just east of the center. Two more doubles, each with magnitude 11 and 12 members, are NE and NW of the interior of the cluster. The fainter cluster members are sprinkled about and blend into the rich Milky Way background.

Dolidze 44 Open Cluster 15★ Tr Type IV2pn
ϕ 12', m –   20^{h}29.7^m +41° 43'
Finder Chart 42-6, Figure 42-29   ★★★
12/14"Scopes–100x: Although faint, loose, and irregular, Dolidze 44 stands out fairly well from the Milky Way

Figure 42-42. *Centered on 52 Cygni, the western segment of the Veil Nebula, NGC 6960, is a delicately detailed north-south filamentary streamer. Image courtesy of Jim Burnell.*

background. It has three dozen members spread over a 12′ area, the two brightest being magnitude 8 and 9.5 stars. The cluster also contains ten 11th–12th magnitude stars. In the northern half is a wide E–W star-stream; and due west from a bright star on the SE corner of the group runs a chain of six or eight relatively faint stars.

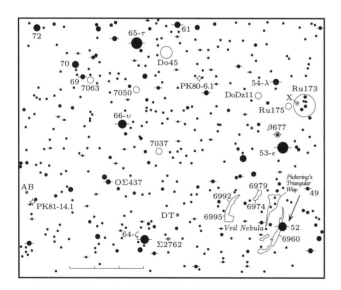

Finder Chart 42-7. 52 Cyg: 20ʰ45.7ᵐ +30° 43′

PK85+4.1 Abell 71 Planetary Nebula Type 3b
ϕ 157″, m14.0v, CS19.0v   20ʰ32.4ᵐ +47° 21′
Finder Chart 42-8, Figure 42-49   ★★
16/18″ Scopes–200x: Abell 71, located 14.5′ NW of an 8th magnitude star, has a very faint, tenuous 2′ diameter disk with many Milky Way stars superimposed upon it. A 13th magnitude star is 25″ WNW, and a 14th magnitude star 35″ SSE, of the nebula's center. Two more 13th magnitude stars lie outside the SSW edge, the nearest of which actually touches the halo. A 14th magnitude star touches the halo's NE edge. At least six threshold stars are in or near the halo.

Ruprecht 173 Open Cluster 20★ Tr Type II 2p
ϕ 50′, m −, Br★ 8.0p   20ʰ41.8ᵐ +35° 33′
Finder Chart 42-7   ★★★
8/10″ Scopes–35x: Ruprecht 173 is so large and so scattered that it requires low power for a good view. Its 75 stars are broadcast over nearly a degree of sky, the cluster's main body a brighter circlet with the Cepheid variable X Cygni (magnitude range 5.8–6.8; period 16.38 days) on its east edge. A secondary star-concentration is on the cluster's SW side.

Ruprecht 175 Open Cluster 30★ Tr Type IV 2 m
ϕ 9′, m −, Br★ 11.0p   20^{h}45.2^m +35° 30′
Finder Chart 42-7, Figure 42-30   ★★★
12/14″ Scopes–125x: Ruprecht 175 is a fairly faint, loose
group of thirty 11th magnitude and fainter stars
covering a 10′ area. The brighter stars are in an
irregular circlet around the interior of the cluster.
A magnitude 10.5 star is on the NE edge of the
circlet. A second magnitude 10.5 star is just outside
the circlet's SW edge. The majority of the faint
cluster stars are within the circlet just north of its
center. ESE of the center is a 12th magnitude star
with a 13th magnitude companion 12″ distant to
the WSW.

NGC 6960 SNR and Emission Nebula
ϕ 70′ × 6′, Photo Br 2-5   20^{h}45.7^m +30° 43′
Finder Chart 42-7, Figure 42-42   ★★★★
Veil Nebula–Western Segment
NGC 6960 is the western segment of the Great
Cygnus Loop, the remnants of a supernova explosion
estimated to have occurred 30 to 40 thousand years ago.
NGC 6960 is sometimes called the Network Nebula and
NGC 6962-95 the Filamentary Nebula; but often the
terms are switched, or refer to both as a whole. The
entire complex has three popular names: the Cirrus
Nebula, the Bridal Veil Nebula, or simply the Veil
Nebula. The last is now the most commonly used name.
All these titles refer to the nebula's wispy streaks and
elegant lace-like filamentary structure. William Herschel discovered the complex in 1784 with his 18-inch
reflector telescope.
8/10″ Scopes–100x: This dim nebula requires a very
dark, transparent sky and low power. It is elongated
30′ × 5′ N–S, the northern edge tapering to a point
as it arcs to the east. It is visible only north of the
double star 52 Cygni (4.2, 9.4; 6.0″; 67°), which
must be positioned out of the field of view to prevent
its bright light from interfering. A UHC filter makes
a phenomenal difference: the nebulosity becomes
visible south of 52 Cygni, and there is no need to
use averted vision. Even the glare of 52 Cygni does
not seem to interfere. A faint filamentary strand on
the west side is slightly brighter in three places.
The nebulosity south of 52 Cygni is traceable for
about 25′, where it widens to about 10′ before fading.
The nebula south of 52 Cygni is much brighter with
the filter, and two more strands are visible.
12/14″ Scopes–125x: With an O-III filter, NGC 6960 is
an impressive streamer of nebulosity over a degree
in length extending north and south of 52 Cygni, a
fine yellow and orange double not physically
associated with the nebula. The brighter part is a
long smooth streak flowing north and then curving
slightly east as it tapers to a point. The southern

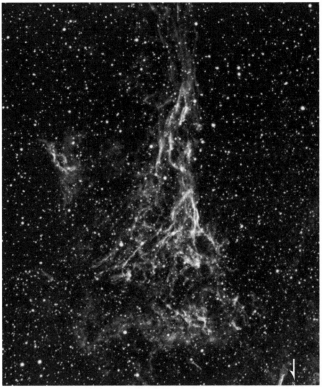

Figure 42-43. *The central segment of the Veil Nebula, known as Pickering's Triangular Wisp, is faint but quite visible with an O-III or UHC filter. Image courtesy of Jim Burnell.*

half is much fainter but full of wispy filaments
which, half a degree from 52 Cygni, widen and split.

Pickering's Triangular Wisp SNR and Emission Nebula
ϕ 45′ × 30′   20^{h}48.5^m +31° 09′

NGC 6974 SNR and Emission Nebula
ϕ 6′ × 4′   20^{h}50.8^m +31° 52′

NGC 6979 SNR and Emission Nebula
ϕ 7′ × 3′, Photo Br 2-5   20^{h}51.0^m +32° 09′
Finder Chart 42-7, Figure 42-43   ★★★/★★/★★
Veil Nebula–Central Segment
12/14″ Scopes–125x: The Veil's north central portion
is much fainter than the two outer sections but not
difficult with an O-III filter on a transparent night.
The portion without an NGC number, known as
Pickering's Triangular Wisp, is centered a degree
NE of 52 Cygni. It is a faint but easily visible
triangular haze measuring 30′ × 15′ N–S and
tapering south to a point. A few delicate diffuse
filamentary details may be detected. Further NE
are NGC 6974 and NGC 6979, the northernmost
segments of the Great Cygnus Loop. They appear
as two irregular NW–SE patches. The NW patch,
NGC 6979, is elongated 5′ × 2′ NW–SE and the more
concentrated of the two. NGC 6974 to its SE is a
4′ long irregular S-shaped haze.

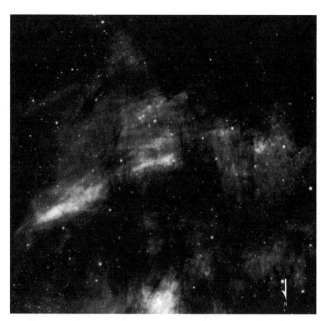

Figure 42-44. *In an O-III filter IC5068 is a very faint haze around the brighter stars embedded within it. Image courtesy Jim Burnell.*

IC 5067 Emission Nebula
25′ × 10′, Photo Br 1-5, Color 3-4   20ʰ50.8ᵐ +44° 21′

IC 5070 Emission Nebula
60′ × 50′, Photo Br 3-5, Color 3-4   20ʰ50.8ᵐ +44° 11′
Finder Chart 42-8, Figure 42-58   ★/★
The Pelican Nebula

4/6″Scopes–25x: The Pelican Nebula is less conspicuous than the North American Nebula; but we were able to glimpse it with the naked eye at the Texas Star Party. My 5″, f5 refractor at 25x revealed a very faint 60′×30′ N–S haze. The easiest portion, IC5067, lies north of the 5th magnitude stars 56 and 57 Cygni. It is a very faint, diffuse triangular area of nebulosity tapered to the north and more defined on the western edge. The view without filters required averted vision but revealed more of the nebula. The O-III filter added some contrast to the brighter portions but eliminated the faint outer wisps.

IC 5068 Emission Nebula
φ 40′ × 30′, Photo Br 2-5, Color 3-4 20ʰ50.8ᵐ +42° 31′
Finder Chart 42-8, Figure 42-44   ★
12/14″Scopes–75x: IC5068 is a very faint haze that is visible particularly around the brighter stars embedded within it. The most conspicuous portion is concentrated around a 7th magnitude star and spreads to the 9th and 10th magnitude stars in the area. Two more nebulous patches can be seen around 8th and 10th magnitude stars to the east.

Dolidze-Dzimselejsvili 11 Open Cl. 12★ Tr Type IV 2 p
φ 12′, m –   20ʰ51.0ᵐ +35° 57′
Finder Chart 42-7   ★★★
12/14″Scopes–100x: This open cluster, located 50′ SE of Lambda (λ) = 54 Cygni, is a fairly faint, irregular group with an 8th and two 9th magnitude stars on its southern edge. Three dozen stars span a 13′ E–W area, a concentration on each end. The western concentration is looser but contains the brighter stars. The eastern group is faint but more compressed. The cluster contains eight 12th and two dozen 13th to 15th magnitude stars. A boomerang-shaped concentration of stars is SSE.

Barkhatova 1 Open Cluster 12★ Tr Type IV 2 p
φ 20′, m –   20ʰ53.7ᵐ +46° 02′
Finder Chart 42-8   ★★★
12/14″Scopes–100x: Barkhatova 1 is a loose scattering of 70 stars in a triangular 20′ area. A 9th magnitude star marks the triangle's NW vertex and a magnitude 9.5 star its NE vertex. A jagged chain of five magnitude 10.5 stars links the cluster's two brightest stars. A wide pair of magnitude 9 and 9.5 stars in the southern portion of the cluster is surrounded by a scattering of faint stars.

NGC 6989 H82⁸ Open Cluster 17★
φ 10′, m –, Br★ 10.v   20ʰ54.1ᵐ +45° 17′
Finder Chart 42-8   ★★★
12/14″Scopes–100x: NGC 6989 is classed as "nonexistent" by the *Revised NGC*, and probably indeed is only a rich Milky Way concentration. However, it stands out well from the surrounding star field. It contains about twenty 10th magnitude and fainter stars in a 10′ area, including a fairly conspicuous E–W star row.

NGC 6992 SNR and Emission Nebula
φ 60′ × 8′, Photo Br 2-5   20ʰ56.4ᵐ +31° 43′

NGC 6995 SNR and Emission Nebula
φ 12′, Photo Br 2-5   20ʰ57.1ᵐ +31° 13′
Finder Chart 42-7, Figure 42-45   ★★★★/★★★★
Veil Nebula–Eastern Segment

Awesome! The Veil Nebula, especially the eastern segment NGC 6992-95, is the favorite summer celestial showpiece of both editors in the nebulae category. However, we could not say this if it were not for O-III filters. Needless to say, the more aperture you use the better the view; but a O-III filter makes the real difference.

8×50 Binoculars: NGC 6992+6995, the eastern segment

Figure 42-45. *Through an O-III filter, NGC 6992-95, the eastern segment of the Veil Nebula, is a magnificent streak of nebulosity full of wisps and strands. Image courtesy of Jim Burnell.*

of the Great Cygnus Loop, is the only part of the supernova remnant that can be unmistakably seen in binoculars. Indeed, it is fairly easy in 10×50 glasses. Look for it 3.5° SSE of Epsilon (ε) = 53 Cygni and 2.5° ENE of 52 Cygni. It appears as a faint, hazy, somewhat bloated fishhook, the shaft of which points ENE directly at Epsilon Cygni. It is brightest in the northern, NGC 6992, end and fades southward toward the west curving hook, the NGC 6995 end.

8/10″ Scopes–75x: This segment of the Veil Nebula is the longest and brightest. With an O-III filter it appears as an incredible N–S swath of nebulosity spanning 1.25° and arcing westward at both ends. 100x reveals subtle lacy filaments broken into unevenly illuminated patches. The nebula is brighter to the NNW. The southern end has two faint but distinct prongs extending west.

12/14″ Scopes–125x: In an O-III filter NGC 6992-95, the eastern portion of the Veil Nebula, is a magnificent streak of nebulosity full of fibrous strands from which it has been named the "Filamentary Nebula." Only a quarter of its length will fit the 75x field of view: the telescope must be panned to see the entire nebula. The lacy patches and swirls have a three

dimensional effect against the star studded background. The northern, NGC 6992, area is brightest and has a prominent patch along its eastern edge. To the south, near a 9th magnitude star on its eastern edge, NGC 6992 is pinched. It connects to NGC 6995, the southern segment of the Filamentary Nebula, by a narrow channel just south of an 8th magnitude star. NGC 6995 is particularly well embellished with wisps and laces that broaden out as it hooks and fans away toward the west.

NGC 6996 Open Cluster 40★ Tr Type III 2 mn
φ 6′, m10.0p   20ʰ56.4ᵐ +45° 28′
Finder Chart 42-8, Figure 42-58   ★★★

12/14″ Scopes–100x: The open cluster NGC 6996 is positioned within the North America Nebula, NGC 7000, at a spot equivalent to Lake Superior. Its forty faint stars are irregularly distributed over a 10′ E–W area formed by three 5th magnitude stars. In the center of the cluster is a star-spiral that makes one-and-a-half inward turns. A chain of five faint stars extends north from the circlet. Near the west edge of the cluster is a pentagon-shaped asterism with magnitude 9.5 and 10 stars on its south side. Outlying stars trail west from NGC 6996 to a semi-detached

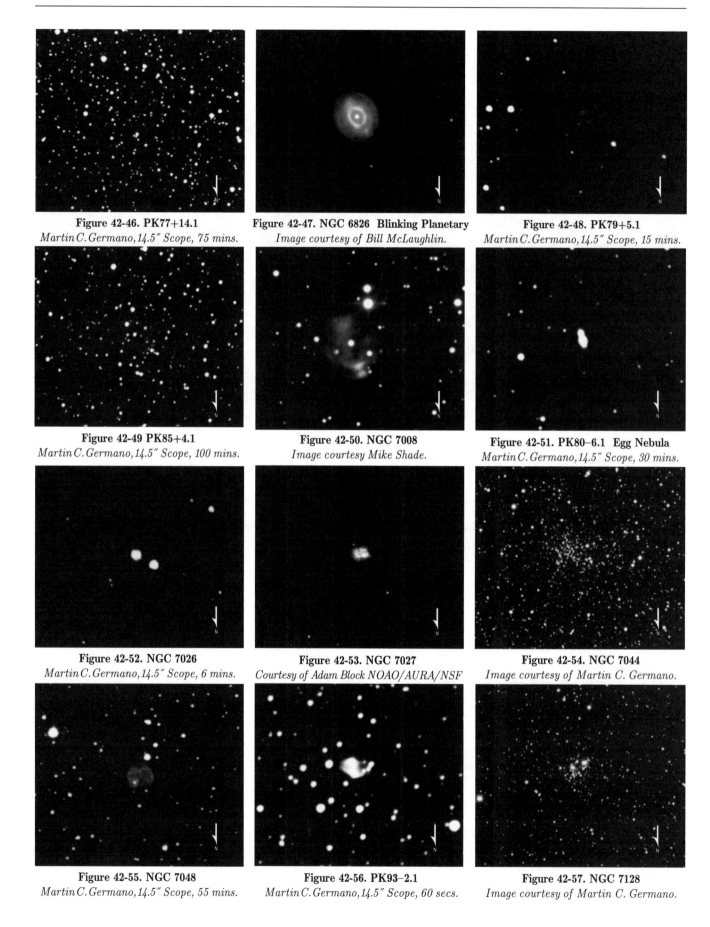

Figure 42-46. PK77+14.1
Martin C. Germano, 14.5″ Scope, 75 mins.

Figure 42-47. NGC 6826 Blinking Planetary
Image courtesy of Bill McLaughlin.

Figure 42-48. PK79+5.1
Martin C. Germano, 14.5″ Scope, 15 mins.

Figure 42-49 PK85+4.1
Martin C. Germano, 14.5″ Scope, 100 mins.

Figure 42-50. NGC 7008
Image courtesy Mike Shade.

Figure 42-51. PK80–6.1 Egg Nebula
Martin C. Germano, 14.5″ Scope, 30 mins.

Figure 42-52. NGC 7026
Martin C. Germano, 14.5″ Scope, 6 mins.

Figure 42-53. NGC 7027
Courtesy of Adam Block NOAO/AURA/NSF

Figure 42-54. NGC 7044
Image courtesy of Martin C. Germano.

Figure 42-55. NGC 7048
Martin C. Germano, 14.5″ Scope, 55 mins.

Figure 42-56. PK93–2.1
Martin C. Germano, 14.5″ Scope, 60 secs.

Figure 42-57. NGC 7128
Image courtesy of Martin C. Germano.

group. Numerous star-pairs and star-chains make this a visually interesting group.

NGC 6991 H76[8] Open Cluster 35★
Tr Type III 3pn, ϕ 25′, m − 20^{h}56.6^m +47° 25′
Finder Chart 42-8   ★★★

12/14″ Scopes–100x: NGC 6991 is classified as "nonexistent" and indeed probably is nothing more than an enrichment of the Milky Way background. It lies 8′ west of a 6th magnitude star and contains 35 stars that stand out from the rich Milky Way.

Barnard 352 Dark Nebula
ϕ 20′ × 10′, Opacity 5   20^{h}57.1^m +45° 54′
Finder Chart 42-8   ★★★

8/10″ Scopes–50x: Barnard 352, located on the north edge of the North America Nebula, is a well defined, triangular, 20′ × 10′ E–W dark dust cloud. Along its rather indistinct northern edge is an E–W arc of four 9th–10th magnitude stars. A N–S row of five stars is near the dark nebula's SSE corner, where it is at its most opaque and most sharply defined.

Figure 42-58. *NGC 7000, the North America Nebula, and IC 5067-70, the Pelican Nebula to its west (right), are huge faint emission nebulae best seen in binoculars. Image courtesy of Dean Salman.*

NGC 7000 H37[5]? Emission Nebula
ϕ 120′ × 100′, PhotoBr 1-5, Color 3-4   20^{h}58.8^m+44° 20′
Finder Chart 42-8, Figure 42-58   ★

The North America Nebula

The North America Nebula, NGC 7000, measures 3° N–S and 2.3° E–W. It can be seen with the unaided eye under dark, transparent skies as a conspicuous Milky Way patch due east of Deneb. Its full photographic extent and entire outline, except for the narrowest part of the Isthmus of Panama, is visible in 10 × 50 binoculars. To its north the nebula-glow merges imperceptibly into a brilliant Milky Way background glow – a stunning region in giant binoculars and richest-field telescopes. The distance to NGC 7000 is uncertain but seems to be on the order of 3,000 light years, not quite twice the 1,600 light years of Deneb.

4/6″ Scopes–25x: With a UHC filter the North America shape of NGC 7000 is vaguely visible. The nebula is brightest in the narrow portion corresponding to Mexico. The dark notch that forms the Gulf of Mexico is obvious.

12/14″ Scopes–60x: The North American Nebula is incredibly large and extremely faint, but the O-III

filter brings out some details. The opacity of the Gulf of Mexico is conspicuous: it is flanked by 7th magnitude stars, one at the tip of Florida and the other at Brownsville. The northern portion of NGC 7000 is very tenuous. Lake Superior is marked by the open cluster NGC 6996, a 15′ diameter group of fifty

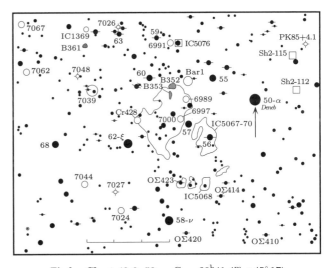

Finder Chart 42-8. 50–α Cyg: 20^{h}41.4^m +45° 17′

faint stars. A less conspicuous cluster, Collinder 428, consisting of 25 stars concentrated west of an 8th magnitude star, is near the Pacific Coast of British Columbia.

NGC 7008 PK93+5.2 Planetary Nebula Type 3
ϕ 83″, m10.7v, CS13.2v $21^h00.6^m$ +54° 33′
Finder Chart 42-10, Figure 42-50   ★★★★
12/14″Scopes–125x: NGC 7008 is an interesting planetary nebula just north of the double star h1606, the beautiful magnitude 9.3 and 10.2 blue and gold components of which are 18″ apart in a N–S direction. This bluish planetary has a 1.5′ × 1.25′ NNE–SSW halo that is irregular in brightness and contains two conspicuous nodules on its NE edge. Two magnitude 13 and 14 stars are superimposed upon the halo; and a NE–SW pair of magnitude 14.5 stars are just to its west, the NE component of which virtually touches the halo. South of the planetary is an E–W row of six wide doubles.

PK80–6.1 Planetary Nebula Protoplanetary?
[ϕ 19″ × 14″] $21^h02.3^m$ +36° 42′
Finder Chart 42-7, Figure 42-51   ★
                  The Egg Nebula
16/18″Scopes–250x: PK80–6.1, the Egg Nebula, is just 4′ east of an 8th magnitude star. Its faint disk is elongated 19″ × 14″ in position angle 15°. A 12th magnitude star, the glare of which makes this already small and faint object that much more difficult to see, touches the southern tip. A second magnitude 12 star lies 1.5′ WNW of the planetary.

Collinder 428 Open Cluster 20★ Tr Type IV1pn
ϕ 13′, m8.7p $21^h03.2^m$ +44° 35′
Finder Chart 42-8, Figure 42-31   ★★★
12/14″Scopes–100x: Collinder 428 lies in the NE part of the North America Nebula near the object's "Pacific Coast." It consists of several dozen mostly faint stars spread over a 14′ area. On its NW side is a 9th magnitude star. A N–S chain of five 12th magnitude stars passes just east of the 9th magnitude star. Further east is a rectangle of 12th magnitude stars.

NGC 7024 H57[8] Open Cluster [14★]
[ϕ 10′, m –, Br★ 10.v] $21^h06.0^m$ +41° 30′
Finder Chart 42-8, Figure 42-32   ★★★
12/14″Scopes–100x: NGC 7024, another "nonexistent" *RNGC* open cluster, is a loose scattering of a dozen 10th magnitude and fainter stars covering a 10′ area. The three brightest stars form a triangle on the southern edge. Herschel mentions this triangle in his observation: "A loose straggling coarse cluster of stars 10–11 magnitude, place that of three stars of 10th magnitude in a triangle in the closest part. Several stars precede the cluster which seems to be an outlier of the second band of the Milky Way."

NGC 7026 PK89+0.1 Planetary Nebula Type 3a
ϕ 21″, m10.9v, CS14.8v $21^h06.3^m$ +47° 51′
Finder Chart 42-8, Figure 42-52   ★★★
8/10″Scopes–250x: This bright bluish-green planetary nebula lies less than 30″ SW of a 10th magnitude star in a field of bright stars, including a 5th magnitude star 11′ south. Its 15″ diameter disk has a slightly brighter center but no visible central star.
16/18″Scopes–300x: NGC 7026 has an unevenly illuminated but bright 20″ × 15″ N–S disk. On the NE and SW edges are two slightly brighter nodules, the part of the disk between them somewhat darker. Occasional twinkles of the central star can be seen. 1′ to the NW of the nebula is a wide pair of magnitude 13.5 stars oriented in P.A. 10°. The double star B158 (7.5, 12.0; 11.1″; 310°) is 6′ SW. Another double, Es817 (7.3, 11.8; 11.4″; 352°) is 10′ SE.

NGC 7027 PK84+3.1 Planetary Nebula Type 3a
ϕ 15″, m8.4v, CS16.32v $21^h07.1^m$ +42° 14′
Finder Chart 42-8, Figure 42-53   ★★★
8/10″Scopes–100x: NGC 7027, located 2′ east of a 12th magnitude star, is a bluish-green 10″ × 5″ NW–SE ellipse with diffuse edges.
16/18″Scopes–150x: NGC 7027 has a bright blue oval disk elongated 15″ × 10″ NW–SE. A threshold star lies 45″ WSW. The O-III filter reveals a very faint outer shell and a bright spot on the NW edge.

Dolidze 45 Open Cluster 35★ Tr Type III2mn
ϕ 18′, m – $21^h09.0^m$ +37° 36′
Finder Chart 42-7   ★★★
12/14″Scopes–75x: Dolidze 45 is a large, loose, irregular cluster of two dozen stars in a rectangular area elongated ESE–WNW. A 9.5 magnitude star near the cluster's center forms a 10′ × 5′ triangle with two other magnitude 9.5 stars to the west. A few threshold stars are scattered in the background haze around the 9th magnitude central star. A dozen 11th to 12.5 magnitude stars are concentrated in the cluster's ESE portion.

NGC 7037 Open Cluster 10★
[ϕ 7′, m –, Br★ 12.v] $21^h10.7^m$ +33° 43′
Finder Chart 42-7   ★★
12/14″Scopes–125x: NGC 7037 is another open cluster

which the *Revised NGC* classified as "nonexistent" – and for good reason, because it does not stand out at all well from its Milky Way field. All that appears at the catalogue position are a dozen 12th magnitude and fainter stars loosely scattered over a 7′ area. Other stellar configurations in the vicinity look more like open clusters – especially to the NW where two 9th magnitude stars are part of a box-shaped group, with some fainter stars just to its east.

NGC 7039 Open Cluster 50★ Tr Type IV 2m
ϕ 16′, m7.6v, Br★ 11.26v $21^h11.2^m$ $+45°$ 39′
Finder Chart 42-8   ★★★
12/14″ Scopes–100x: NGC 7039 is a loose concentration between two 7th magnitude stars in a well populated field. Twenty members can be seen in a NE–SW 10′×5′ area, but outliers straggle around a 20′ area. The majority of the cluster stars are 11th–12th magnitude objects.

IC 1369 Open Cluster 40★ Tr Type II 2m
ϕ 8′, m8.8v, Br★ 12.14v $21^h12.1^m$ $+47°$ 44′

Barnard 361 Dark Nebula
ϕ 17′, Opacity 4 $21^h12.9^m$ $+47°$ 22′
Finder Chart 42-8, Figure 42-59   ★★★/★★★
12/14″ Scopes–125x: IC 1369, located 20′ east of a wide pair of 6th magnitude stars, is a rich 4′ concentration of 13th to 14th magnitude stars, a lone 12th magnitude member near its NW edge. This group is enclosed by an irregular circlet of 11th to 12th magnitude stars. Half a degree south is the dust cloud Barnard 361, a 20′ diameter starless gap in the rich Milky Way star field.

NGC 7044 H24⁶ Open Cluster 60★ Tr Type I 1m
ϕ 3.5′, m12.0p $21^h12.9^m$ $+42°$ 29′
Finder Chart 42-8, Figure 42-54   ★★
12/14″ Scopes–125x: NGC 7044 is a mist of very faint stars just east of the center of a 13′×10′ right triangle of 9.5 magnitude stars. A dozen threshold stars compressed into a 3′ area are visible against a hazy background. The two brightest stars are on the cluster's ENE and ESE edges, and both are wide doubles, the ENE star with a more equally matched companion than the ESE star.

NGC 7048 Planetary Nebula Type 3b
ϕ 61′, m12.1v, CS18.0v $21^h14.2^m$ $+46°$ 16′
Finder Chart 42-8, Figure 42-55   ★★★
8/10″ Scopes–150x: NGC 7048, located 3.5′ NE of a 9th magnitude star, has a faint 1′ diameter disk with a

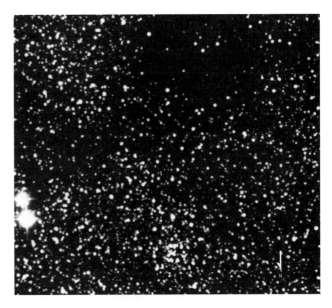

Figure 42-59. *IC 1369 (bottom) is a rich, compact cluster that starkly contrasts with the starless darkness of the dust cloud Barnard 361 to its south (top). Martin C. Germano made this 75 minute exposure on hypered 2415 film with an 8″, f5 Newtonian reflector.*

diffuse periphery. An 11th magnitude star just beyond the SSE edge of the planetary is at the foot of a Y-shaped asterism. A 12th magnitude star lies 2.5′ NNE.

16/18″ Scopes–175x: NGC 7048 has a fairly faint, evenly illuminated smoky-gray disk slightly elongated N–S. A very faint star is superimposed upon the disk 15″ NW of the planetary's center. Threshold stars touch the disk's NNE and NNW edges, the latter star being fainter.

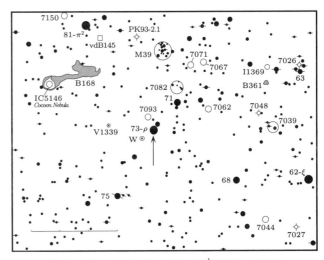

Finder Chart 42-9. 73–ϱ Cyg: $21^h34.0^m$ $+45°$ 36′

Figure 42-60. *NGC 7062 is a moderately faint but compact cluster that stands out well from the surrounding Milky Way star field. Image courtesy of Martin C. Germano.*

Figure 42-61. *NGC 7063 is a loose open cluster in a rich Milky Way star field. Image courtesy of Martin C. Germano.*

NGC 7050 Open Cluster [20★]
[φ 10′, m –, Br★ 12.v]   **21ʰ15.3ᵐ +36° 11′**
Finder Chart 42-7   ★★★
12/14″ Scopes–125x: NGC 7050 is yet another Cygnus
open cluster officially classified as "nonexistent."
However, at low power it stands out nicely as a
loose, triangular group of 20 stars 7′ south of a 9th
magnitude star. The cluster's brighter stars are on
the corners of the triangle, and at each corner is a
small group of stars: at the south corner is a wide
N–S star pair, at the west corner a tiny triangle,
and at the east corner a group of seven faint stars
around the brighter star. A wide pair of faint stars

lies on the SW side of the triangle. To the NE of
the cluster is a detached clump of five faint stars.

NGC 7058 Open Cluster [17★]
[φ 10′, m –, Br★ 8.09v]   **21ʰ21.8ᵐ +50° 48′**
Finder Chart 42-10, Figure 42-33   ★★★
12/14″ Scopes–125x: NGC 7058, though officially
"nonexistent," stands out nicely at low power as a
bright 10′ concentration of 15 stars. The brighter
members, 8th to 10th magnitude stars, are aligned
NW–SE through the cluster's center, and four of
them form a trapezium on its NW edge. The fainter
members are concentrated along the southern edge.
At 175x a very faint knot of threshold stars is visible
just south of the 9.5 magnitude star at the cluster
center.

NGC 7062 Open Cluster 30★ Tr Type II 2m
φ 6′, m8.3v, Br★ 10.10v   **21ʰ23.2ᵐ +46° 23′**
Finder Chart 42-9, Figure 42-60   ★★★
12/14″ Scopes–100x: NGC 7062 is moderately faint but
stands out well from the surrounding star field. It is
just north of the line joining 10th magnitude stars to
its east and west. Two magnitude 11 and 11.5 stars
combine with the 10th magnitude pair to enclose the
cluster in a stellar box or diamond. The cluster is a
7′ × 5′ E–W rectangle with 10th magnitude stars at
the east and west corners, and 11th and 13th
magnitude stars at the south and north corners.
Thirty 12th–15th magnitude stars are within the

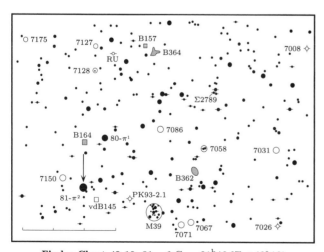

Finder Chart 42-10. 81–π ² Cyg: 21ʰ46.8ᵐ +49° 19′

Figure 42-62. *NGC 7086 is a well concentrated cluster with a starless oval in its NE section and a starless void in the Milky Way to its north. Lee C. Coombs made this 10 minute exposure on 103a-O film with a 10″, f5 Newtonian reflector.*

Figure 42-63. *Messier 39 is a large, loose cluster, the bright stars of which stand out attractively against a rich Milky Way field of faint stars. Image courtesy of Lee C. Coombs.*

rectangle, but an oblong starless gap runs through its center. A string of 9th and 11th magnitude stars lies to the NW; and a wide 9th magnitude pair is 13′ NNW of the cluster.

NGC 7063 Open Cluster 12★ Tr Type III 1 p
ϕ 7′, m7.0v, Br★ 8.89v   21^{h}24.4^m +36° 30′
Finder Chart 42-7, Figure 42-61   ★★★
12/14″ Scopes–100x: NGC 7063 is 19′ SW of the magnitude 5.9 star 69 Cygni, which has two companions (B: 10.3; 33″; 30°, and C: 9.0; 55″; 98°). The cluster contains twenty stars loosely concentrated in an 8′ × 4′ NNW–SSW area. Its three brightest members, magnitude 9.5 objects, are at the east end of a row of 10th magnitude stars which runs along the southern edge of the cluster. On the northern edge is a triangle of magnitude 10–11 stars. Detached 6′ south is a 9th magnitude star.

NGC 7071 Open Cluster [15★]
[ϕ 4′, m −, Br★ 12.v]   21^{h}26.5^m +47° 57′
Finder Chart 42-9   ★★
12/14″ Scopes–125x: Though classified as "nonexistent" in the *RNGC*, NGC 7071 stands out well from its surrounding star field. It is a faint 4′ NW–SE string of 14 stars 6′ SE of a 9th magnitude star. At the NW end of the string are three wide NE–SW star-pairs. The cluster's lucida, also a 9th magnitude star, is near its SE edge, and forms a short row with two very faint stars.

NGC 7086 H32^6 Open Cluster 50★ Tr Type II 2 m
ϕ 9′, m8.4v, Br★ 10.19v   21^{h}30.5^m +51° 35′
Finder Chart 42-10, Figure 42-62   ★★★
8/10″ Scopes–100x: This cluster is a fairly well concentrated group of forty 10th magnitude and fainter stars in a 10′ area. The SE part is the most concentrated, with outlying stars scattered to the NNW. A peculiar starless area is 15′ north of the cluster.
12/14″ Scopes–100x: NGC 7086 is a conspicuous cluster of fifty stars irregularly concentrated over a 12′ × 8′ NW–SE area. Two dozen of the brighter cluster members are gathered in a 6′ × 4′ NW–SE area in the SW part of the cluster. Within the NE perimeter of the group is a starless oval. A 9th magnitude star lies 9′ NE of the cluster center.

NGC 7092 Messier 39 Open Cluster 30★ Tr Type III 2 m
ϕ 31′, m4.6v. Br★ 6.83v   21^{h}32.2^m +48° 26′
Finder Chart 42-9, Figure 42-63   ★★★★★
Messier 39 was discovered by Le Gentil in 1750. Messier added it to his catalogue in 1764. The cluster is 830 light years distant. It is poor and sparse, its absolute magnitude only −2.5, a luminosity of just 830 suns. Its true diameter is about 7.5 light years.
8/10″ Scopes–50x: Messier 39 is a large cluster which fills a low power eyepiece field. Twenty bright stars form a 30′ triangle, a 9th magnitude star at its northern corner and 7th magnitude stars at its SE and SW corners. Though it is loose, the cluster's

Figure 42-64. *Abell 78, located midway between two 7th magnitude stars (upper right and lower left), is a challenging low surface brightness planetary nebula even for larger telescopes. Image courtesy of Adam block NOAO/AURA/NSF.*

bright stars stand out well against the rich Milky Way background of faint stars. A conspicuous double is just north of the triangle's center.

Barnard 364 Dark Nebula
ϕ 40′, Opacity 5   21ʰ33.6ᵐ +54° 33′

Barnard 157 Dark Nebula
ϕ 4′, Opacity 4   21ʰ33.7ᵐ +54° 40′
Finder Chart 42-10   ★★★/★★★
8/10″Scopes-50x: Barnard 364 and Barnard 157 are two dust clouds silhouetted against a Milky Way field profuse with faint stars. Barnard 157, located 8′ west of a magnitude 8.3 star, is a 4′ × 3′ teardrop-shaped opacity tapering north. Barnard 364, 24′ SW of B157 and centered 15′ NW of a 7th magnitude star, is an irregular checkmark-shaped patch, its most prominent part elongated 20′ × 5′ NW–SE. The SE end has an extension to the north.

NGC 7093 Open Cluster [23★]
[ϕ 7′, m −, Br★ 8.v]   21ʰ34.8ᵐ +46° 01′
Finder Chart 42-9, Figure 42-34   ★★★
12/14″Scopes-125x: NGC 7093 is a fairly nice group for a cluster officially classified as "nonexistent." Two dozen faint stars are loosely concentrated within a 5′ long right triangle with an 8th magnitude star

at its NW corner, a 9th magnitude star at its SSW corner, and a magnitude 10.5 star at its NNE corner. Most of the cluster members are scattered along the northern and western sides of the triangle. Some outliers scatter to the north and east.

PK81–14.1 Abell 78 Planetary Nebula Type 4
ϕ 101″, m13.4v, CS12.3v   21ʰ35.6ᵐ +31° 41′
Finder Chart 42-7, Figure 42-64   ★
20/22″Scopes-100x: Abell 78 is an extremely faint planetary nebula situated between two 7th magnitude stars the glare of which interferes with the pale nebula-glow. An O-III filter shows a 1.5′ diameter disk around the magnitude 12.3 central star. Along the NE edge runs a NW–SE row of three 13th magnitude stars.

PK93–2.1 M1-79 Planetary Nebula Type 4
ϕ 32″, m13.2v, CS>14.4v   21ʰ37.0ᵐ +48° 57′
Finder Charts 42-9, 42-10, Figure 42-56   ★
16/18″Scopes-200x: Minkowski 1-79, located 5′ NNE of a 9th magnitude star, has a faint, diffuse 30″ diameter disk surrounded by faint field stars, the brightest a magnitude 12.5 object 35″ west of the planetary's center. 13th magnitude stars are about half a minute east and north of the nebula's center. The disk seems slightly elongated NNE–SSW.

NGC 7127 Open Cluster 12★ Tr Type IV1p
ϕ 2.8′, m −   21ʰ43.9ᵐ +54° 37′
Finder Chart 42-10, Figure 42-35   ★★★
12/14″Scopes-125x: NGC 7127, located 15′ ENE of an orange 7.5 magnitude star, is a faint 3′ diameter concentration of twenty magnitude 10 to 15 stars sprinkled around, but mostly NW of, a magnitude 9.5 star. The five brightest stars form a figure like the "5" on a die. The magnitude 9.5 star is at the SE corner of the "5."

NGC 7128 H40⁷ Open Cluster 35★ Tr Type I3m
ϕ 3.1′, m9.7v, Br★ 11.50v   21ʰ44.0ᵐ +53° 43′
Finder Chart 42-10, Figure 42-57   ★★★
8/10″Scopes-100x: NGC 7128 is a small, faint, nebulous object. At low power only half a dozen stars resolve. At 100x a dozen 12th and 12th magnitude members can be seen in a 2′ area. A magnitude 11.5 star stands out on the cluster's SE edge.
12/14″Scopes-125x: NGC 7128 is a pretty cluster of thirty faint stars in a 3′ area. Ten of the brighter stars, most 12.5 to 13th magnitude objects, are in a ring on the SW side of the cluster. The magnitude

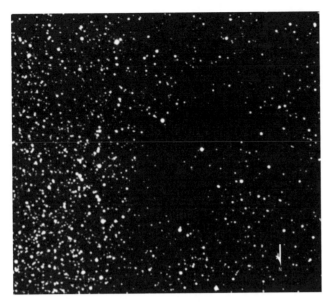

Figure 42-65. *Barnard 164 is a conspicuous starless C in a rich Milky Way field. Martin C. Germano made this 90 minute exposure on hypered 2415 film with a 8″, f5 Newtonian reflector at prime focus.*

Figure 42-66. *IC 5146, the Cocoon Nebula, is at the ESE end of the two degree long dark lane Barnard 168. Image courtesy of Chris Schur.*

11.5 cluster lucida, a reddish star on the group's SE edge, is the ring's gemstone. The other cluster members, magnitude 13.5 to 15 stars, are scattered around the ring, but particularly concentrated to its NW.

Barnard 164 Dark Nebula
ϕ 12′ × 6′, Opacity 5   21^{h}46.5^m +51° 04′
Finder Chart 42-10, Figure 42-65   ★★★
8/10″Scopes–75x: The dust cloud Barnard 164, located 40′ ESE of the magnitude 4.7 Pi-1 (π^1) = 80 Cygni, is a 12′ × 5′ NNW–SSE C-shaped star-void concave to the NE. A magnitude 10.5 star lies at the center of the inner arc of the C. A second magnitude 10.5 star lies near the center of the outer arc of the C opposite the first star. The star field is well populated to the west but thins noticeably to the east.

NGC 7150 Open Cluster [5★]
[ϕ 1′, m −, Br★ 15.v]   21^{h}50.4^m +49° 45′
Finder Chart 42-10, Figure 42-36   ★
12/14″Scopes–125x: The "nonexistent" open cluster NGC 7150, located 10′ NE of an 8th magnitude star, appears as a tiny, horseshoe-shaped arc of extremely faint stars open to the south. The star field includes half a dozen pairs of varying separations.

Barnard 168 Dark Nebula
ϕ 100′ × 10′, Opacity 4   21^{h}53.3^m +47° 12′

IC 5146 E. Nebula and Open Cluster 20★ Tr Type III2p
ϕ en10′ × 10′, oc9′, m7.2v, Br★ 9.64v 21^{h}53.4^m +47° 16′
Finder Chart 42-9, Figure 42-66   ★★★/★★
IC 5146 = Cocoon Nebula
12/14″Scopes–125x: The very faint Cocoon Nebula is at the ESE end of the two degree long dark lane Barnard 168, which is particularly conspicuous because of the rich Milky Way star field through which it runs. B168 is blotchy and irregular, its northern edge being more sharply defined. IC 5146 is a haze around a N–S pair of magnitude 9.5 stars. Its edges are distinct but the nebula extends noticeably more to the north of the star-pair. Embedded in the nebula-glow are five fainter stars, four of them in its SE section and one to the WSW.

NGC 7175 Open Cluster [35★]
[ϕ 8′, m −, Br★ 9.v]   21^{h}58.8^m +54° 49′
Finder Chart 42-10, Figure 42-37   ★★★
12/14″Scopes–125x: NGC 7175, though one of the *RNGC*'s "nonexistent" open clusters, is plotted in *Norton's Star Atlas* – and justifiably so, for it is one of the more conspicuous of the *RNGC* "nonexistent" groups. At lower power three dozen stars can be seen loosely scattered over an 8′ area. The group is somewhat elongated E–W, the majority of its

members in a circlet around a central starless void.
To the SE are two 9th magnitude stars 6′ apart,
the nearer one part of a short row of four stars.
Detached to the north of the cluster is a short row
of three stars.

Chapter 43

Delphinus, the Dolphin

43.1 Overview

Delphinus is a small but conspicuous constellation on the SE edge of the summer Milky Way. The distinctive curve of its star-pattern – Gamma (γ), Delta (δ), Alpha (α), Beta (β), Eta (ϵ), Epsilon (ζ) Delphini – is indeed evocative of a dolphin leaping out from the Milky Way stream. The identification of this star-pattern with a celestial Dolphin would have been almost inevitable for a maritime people like the early Greeks. However, the landlocked agrarian Babylonians had seen a mere Pig in these stars – but the same star-curve which resembles the arc of a dolphin's back as it leaps from the waves also resembles the arc of a pig's back as it feeds, and what creature you will see in these stars depends upon what creature is a part of your daily life. The Bedouin of the Arabian Desert had known these stars as Al Ka' ud, "The Riding Camel," because the curve suggested to them a camel's hump.

In classical mythology dolphins were the messengers of the Ocean-god Poseidon. According to one story the Dolphin was raised to the heavens because it had persuaded Amphitrite to become the wife of Poseidon. In another story the Dolphin was enconstellated because he had carried the poet Arion to shore after the latter had been cast overboard into the Mediterranean by a hostile ship's-crew.

Though the tight little star-pattern of Delphinus looks like it might be an open cluster, it is not: Gamma (γ) Delphini is 100 light years distant, Alpha (α) 180, and Epsilon (ϵ) 950. Indeed, though Delphinus is on the fringe of the Milky Way, it boasts no true Milky Way-type objects – such as open clusters and emission nebulae. On the contrary, it has off-Milky Way objects: planetary nebulae, globular clusters, and a few galaxies. Probably its finest object is the beautiful star Gamma.

Delphinus: Del-FY-nus
Genitive: Delphini, Del-FY-ni
Abbreviation: Del
Culmination: 9 pm–Sept. 14, midnight–Jul. 31
Area: 189 square degrees
Showpieces: 12–γ Del. NGC 6905, NGC 6934
Binocular Objects: S752, NGC 6934

43.2 Interesting Stars

Kappa (κ) = 7 Delphini (OΣ533) Triple Star Spec. G5
AB: m5.1, 11.7; Sep. 28.8″; P.A. 286° 20^{h}39.1^m +10° 05′
Constellation Chart 29-1　　　　　　　　　★★★★
4/6″ Scopes–100x: Kappa Delphini is a pretty triple: the closer components appear yellow and the more distant member reddish.

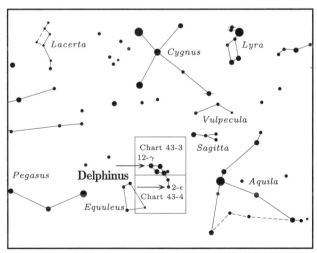

Master Finder Chart 43-1. Delphinus Chart Areas
Guide stars indicated by arrows.

Delphinus, the Dolphin

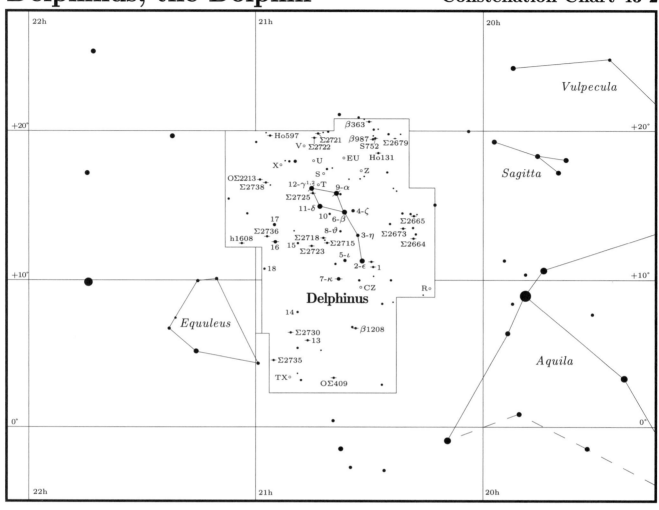

Chart Symbols

	0 1 2 3 4 5 6	
Constellation Chart		
Stellar Magnitudes		
Finder Charts	0/1 2 3 4 5 6 7 8 9	
Master Finder Chart	0 1 2 3 4 5	

→ Guide Star Pointer   ⊙ ∘ Variable Stars   Planetary Nebulae

●—• •—• Double Stars   ◯ Open Clusters   ☐ Small Bright Nebulae

Finder Chart Scale   ⊕ Globular Clusters   Large Bright Nebulae

(One degree tick marks)   ⬭ Galaxies   Dark Nebulae

Table 43-1: Selected Variable Stars in Delphinus

Name	HD No.	Type	Max.	Min.	Period (Days)	F*	Spec. Type	R.A. (2000) Dec.		Finder Chart No.	Notes
R Del	192502	M	7.6	13.8	284	0.45	M5-M6	20h14.9m	+09° 05′	43-4	
Z Del	195763	M	8.3	15.3	304	0.48	S5-S7	32.7	+17 27	43-3	
CZ Del	195876	SRb	9.0	10.2	123		M5	33.6	+09 31	43-4	
EU Del	196610	SRb	5.8	6.9	59		M6	37.9	+18 16	43-3	
S Del	197420	M	8.3	12.4	277	0.52	M5-M8	43.1	+17 05	43-3	
T Del	197772	M	8.5	15.2	332	0.45	M3-M6	45.3	+16 24	43-3	25′ NW of 12-γ Del
U Del	197812	SRb	7.6	8.9	110		M5	45.5	+18 05	43-3	
V Del	198288	M	8.1	16.0	533	0.42	M4-M6	47.8	+19 20	43-3	
TX Del		CW	8.85	9.54	6.16	0.33	G0 G5	50.2	+03 39	43-4	
X Del	199170	M	8.2	14.8	281	0.42	M4-M6	54.9	+17 39	43-3	

F* = The fraction of period taken up by the star's rise from min. to max. brightness, or the period spent in eclipse.

Table 43-2: Selected Double Stars in Delphinus

Name	ADS No.	Pair	M1	M2	Sep.*	P.A.*	Spec	R.A. (2000) Dec.		Finder Chart No.	Notes
Σ 2665	13688	AxBC	6.8	9.5	3.3	17	A0 G	20ʰ19.4ᵐ	+14° 22′	43-3	White and yellow
Σ 2664			8.4	8.9	27.7	322	K0	19.6	+13 00	43-3	
Σ 2673	13767	AB	8.6	10.1	2.5	331	F2	22.7	+13 20	43-3	Yellowish-white pair
		AC		8.7	76.0	103					
Σ 2679	13808	AB	7.9	9.2	23.5	78	A2	24.4	+19 35	43-3	Yellowish and blue
Ho131	13886	AB	6.8	10.2	4.1	324	G2	28.3	+18 46	43-3	
β 987	13921	AB	6.6	10.9	2.4	128	B9	30.2	+19 25	43-3	White pair
S752	13921	AC		7.0	105.9	288	B9				
	13921	AD		10.9	56.4	296					
	13921	Aa		10.5	22.1	71					
1 Del	13920	AB	6.1	8.1	0.9	346	A0	30.3	+10 54	43-4	
β 363	13913	AB	6.0	10.0	16.7	64	A2	31.0	+20 36	43-3	
β 1208	14017		7.0	11.8	3.0	333	B5	34.5	+06 53	43-4	
7-κ Del	14101	AB	5.1	11.7	28.8	286	G5	39.1	+10 05	43-4	AB: pretty yellow pair
	14101	AC		9:	214.4	101					C: reddish
OΣ 409	14133	AB	6.9	10.4	16.9	84	K0	40.3	+03 26	43-4	
	14133	AC		8.4	65.3	334					
Σ 2715	14168		7.7	10.3	12.3	2	F8	41.8	+12 31	43-3	
Σ 2718	14184	AB	8.0	8.0	8.5	86	F5 F5	42.6	+12 44	43-3	
	14184	AC		8.7	167.0	345					
Σ 2721	14205		7.8	9.9	2.6	28	G5	43.5	+19 53	43-3	
Σ 2722	14209		8.4	8.9	7.2	307	G5	43.6	+19 44	43-3	
Σ 2723	14233	AB	6.9	8.7	1.2	116	A0	44.9	+12 19	43-3	
Σ 2725	14270		7.6	8.4	5.8	8	K0	46.2	+15 54	43-3	In field with 12-γ Del
12-γ Del	14279		4.5	5.5	9.6	268	G5	46.7	+16 07	43-3	Beautiful yellow and green
13 Del	14293		5.6	9.2	1.6	194	A0	47.8	+06 00	43-4	
Σ 2730	14359		8.6	8.7	3.4	335	K0	51.1	+06 23	43-4	
Ho597	14402		7.6	11.9	10.0	221	A3	53.6	+19 36	43-3	
16 Del	14429		5.5	11.8	38.2	21	A2	55.6	+12 34	43-4	
Σ 2735	14430		6.1	7.6	2.1	284	G0	55.7	+04 32	43-4	Yellow and reddish
Σ 2736	14453		8.2	10.1	5.1	218	F2	56.7	+13 00	43-3	Yellowish pair
Σ 2738	14490	AB	6.6	8.7	14.9	254	A0	58.5	+16 26	43-3	White and bluish-white
	14490	AC		9.2	210.5	103					
OΣΣ 213			6.7	9.4	70.7	37	F2	59.8	+16 49	43-3	
h1608	14607		7.6	11.4	19.8	258	F2	21ʰ04.9ᵐ	+12 27	43-3	

Footnotes: *= Year 2000, a = Near apogee, c = Closing, w = Widening. Finder Chart No: All stars listed in the tables are plotted in the large Constellation Chart, but when a star appears in a Finder Chart, this number is listed. Notes: When colors are subtle, the suffix *-ish* is used, e.g. *bluish.*

Gamma (γ) = 12 Delphini (Σ 2727) Dbl Star Spec. K2, F8
m4.3, 5.1; Sep. 9.6″; P.A. 268°   20ʰ46.7ᵐ +16° 07′
Constellation Chart 43-2   ★★★★★

Gamma Delphini, at the nose of the Dolphin, is a beautiful double star easily split in small telescopes. This binary system lies about 100 light years away and is composed of two stars with luminosities 16 and 8 times greater than that of our Sun. Struve 2725, a close, fainter double, lies in the same field with Gamma Delphini 15′ to its south.

4/6″ Scopes-100x: Gamma Delphini has a yellow primary with a green companion, the latter a rather rare stellar color. Some observers however see the companion as bluish. The spectral type suggests a true color for the companion of yellow-white: Gamma Delphini B probably appears greenish or bluish only by contrast with its deeply yellow primary.

43.3 Deep-Sky Objects

NGC 6891 PK54–12.1 Planetary Nebula Type 2a+2b
φ >14″, m10.5v, CS12.44v   20ʰ15.2ᵐ +12° 42′
Finder Chart 43-3, Figure 43-3   ★★★★

4/6″ Scopes-150x: This planetary nebula has a fairly bright but small, round disk that appears stellar at low power.

8/10″ Scopes-200x: NGC 6891 displays a bright, round 10″ disk with a 12.4 magnitude central star.

12/14″ Scopes-250x: This planetary has a bright bluish-green 15″ disk with well-defined edges and a uniform surface brightness. Embedded in it is a 12.4 magnitude central star. 13th magnitude stars are 1′ WNW and 1.25′ SE of the planetary, and a 14th magnitude star is on its east edge.

Figure 43-1. *Planetary nebula NGC 6905 has a blue disk and a faint central star. Image courtesy of Bill McLaughlin.*

Figure 43-2. *Globular cluster NGC 6934 has a bright mottled halo with a well concentrated core. Image courtesy of Martin C. Germano.*

NGC 6905 H16⁴ PK61–9.1 Planetary Neb. Type 3+3
ϕ >39″, m11.1v, CS15.5v   20ʰ22.4ᵐ +20° 05′
Finder Chart 43-3, Figure 43-1   ★★★★
Blue Flash Nebula

8/10″Scopes–200x: NGC 6905 protrudes from the west side of a 1.5′ × 1′ keystone of 11th to 12.5 magnitude stars. Its 35″ diameter disk has a fine blue glow, and increases in surface brightness toward the center. The central star twinkles in and out of resolution, depending on seeing conditions. A 10th magnitude star lies 3′ NW.

12/14″Scopes–250x: This planetary nebula displays a bright, bluish, unevenly illuminated disk slightly

elongated 40″ × 35″ N–S. The disk is significantly brighter at its center and along its east edge, and just slightly brighter along its west edge. The northern and southern edges bulge out noticeably, but are more diffuse. The central star is steadily resolved at this aperture.

NGC 6928   Galaxy Type SB(s)ab
ϕ 2.0′ × 0.6′, m12.2v, SB12.3   20ʰ32.8ᵐ +09° 56′

NGC 6930   Galaxy Type SB(s)ab?
ϕ 1.1′ × 0.5′, m12.8v, SB12.0   20ʰ33.0ᵐ +09° 52′
Finder Chart 43-4, Figure 43-4   ★★/★★

12/14″Scopes–250x: These two faint galaxies are a 4′ wide NNW–SSE pair. NGC 6928, the northern galaxy, has a faint 1.25′ × 0.5′ ESE–WNW halo containing a poorly concentrated oval core. A 13th magnitude star lies 1.5′ ENE of the galaxy's center, and a very faint star is on the NE edge of its halo. The fainter NGC 6930 on the south is a faint, diffuse 1′ × 0.25′ N–S streak. Its southern tip almost touches the NNW corner of a thin NNW–SSE isosceles triangle of magnitude 12.5 stars. 3′ WSW of NGC 6928 is the galaxy NGC 6927, a very faint, tiny glow slightly elongated N–S.

NGC 6934 H103¹ Globular Cluster Class VIII
ϕ 5.9′, m8.7v   20ʰ34.2ᵐ +07° 24′
Finder Chart 43-4, Figure 43-2   ★★★

4/6″Scopes–100x: NGC 6934, located 2′ east of a 9.5 magnitude star, appears fairly bright, small, and round, and has a concentrated center. It is unre-

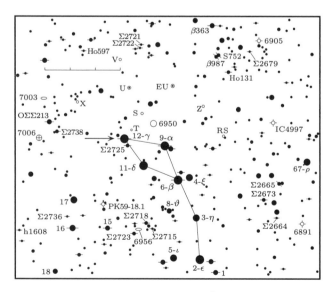

Finder Chart 43-3. 12–γ Del: 20ʰ46.7ᵐ +16° 07′

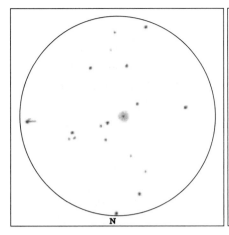

Figure 43-3. NGC 6891
13″, f4.5-300x, by Tom Polakis

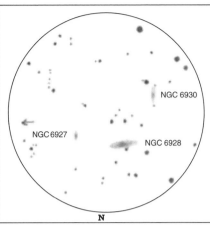

Figure 43-4. NGC 6927, 6928, 6930
17.5″, f4.5-250x, by G. R. Kepple

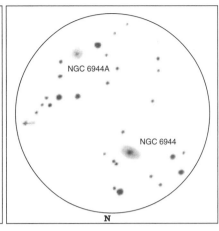

Figure 43-5. NGC 6944 and NGC 6944A
17.5″, f4.5-250x, by G. R. Kepple

solved at all powers.

8/10″Scopes-125x: NGC 6934 has a bright unresolved core surrounded by a granular 3′ diameter halo with three dozen discernible stars. Three magnitude 9.5 field stars lie to the west of the globular, one of them only 2′ away and the other two 8′ and 10′ distant.

12/14″Scopes-150x: This globular has a bright, mottled 4′ diameter halo around a well concentrated core. A few dozen stars stand out against the granular background of the halo: the core twinkles but remains unresolved, except for a lone star standing out on the NE edge.

NGC 6944A Galaxy Type SB(rs)d pec:
ϕ 0.9′ × 0.7′, m14.1v, SB13.5   20^{h}38.2^m +06° 55′

NGC 6944 Galaxy Type S0–:
ϕ 1.5′ × 0.6′, m13.8v, SB13.5   20^{h}38.4^m +07° 00′
Finder Chart 43-4, Figure 43-5   ★/★
16/18″Scopes-150x: NGC 6944 is 2′ SW of a 3.5′ × 1′ isosceles triangle of one 8th and two 10th magnitude stars, the bright star at the triangle's WNW corner. The galaxy is a 1′ × 0.5′ NE–SW oval glow containing a faint stellar nucleus. 6.5′ SSW of NGC 6944, and 1.5′ WNW of a 9th magnitude star, is NGC 6944A, an extremely faint circular glow that can be glimpsed in the glare of the 9th magnitude star only with averted vision.

NGC 6950 H23^8 Open Cluster
[ϕ 15′, m –, Br★ 11.5.v]   20^{h}41.2^m +16° 38′
Finder Chart 43-3   ★★
12/14″Scopes-100x: NGC 6950 is classified as a "nonexistent" open cluster. At the catalogue position is a large group of forty 12th magnitude and fainter stars rather evenly distributed over a 15′ area. A

magnitude 11.5 star near the cluster center is at the north end of a jagged 8′ long NNE–SSW string of a dozen stars, eight of the 12th magnitude and the rest magnitude 12.5–13. A second, widely-spaced star-string extends to the west from the magnitude 11.5 star to form a large "V" with the other string.

NGC 6956 H219^3 Galaxy Type SBb
ϕ 1.6′ × 1.5′, m12.3v, SB13.1   20^{h}44.0^m +12° 31′
Finder Chart 43-3, Figure 43-6   ★★
16/18″Scopes-150x: NGC 6956, located just west of an 11th magnitude star touching its halo, has a fairly bright, circular 1′ diameter halo containing a stellar nucleus. 200x reveals a faint core elongated N–S. A magnitude 9.5 star lies 3.5′ NNE of the galaxy.

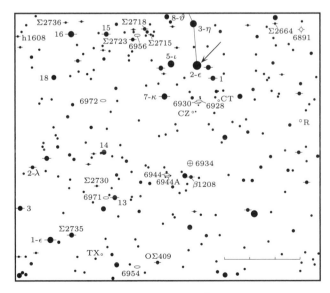

Finder Chart 43-4. 2–ϵ Del: 20^{h}33.2^m +11° 18′

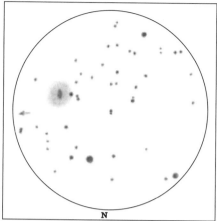

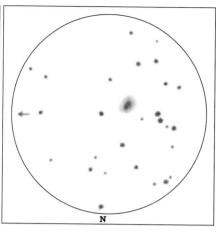

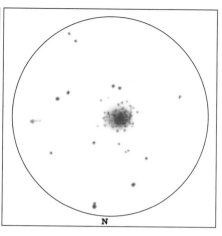

Figure 43-6. NGC 6956
17.5", f4.5–250x, by G. R. Kepple

Figure 43-7. NGC 6972
17.5", f4.5–250x, by G. R. Kepple

Figure 43-8. NGC 7006
17.5", f4.5–250x, by G. R. Kepple

NGC 6954 Galaxy Type SA?0°:
ϕ 0.8′ × 0.5′, m13.2v, SB 12.1   20^{h}44.1^m +03° 13′
Finder Chart 43-4   ★★
16/18″ Scopes–150x: NGC 6954 is a faint oval glow
slightly brighter toward its center. A very faint star
is on the halo's north edge. A magnitude 12.5 star
is 1.5′ south of the galaxy. Two wide pairs of
magnitude 14 and 15 stars are between the magnitude 12.5 star and the galaxy's halo. A 13th
magnitude star is 2.5′ WSW of the galaxy.

NGC 6972 Galaxy Type SA/a
ϕ 1.1′ × 0.5′, m13.2v, SB 12.5   20^{h}50.0^m +09° 54′
Finder Chart 43-4, Figure 43-7   ★★
16/18″ Scopes–150x: NGC 6972 has a faint, circular 1′
diameter halo containing a small, faint NNW–SSE
oval core. At 200x, the halo seems elongated in the
same direction as the core. The galaxy is within a
4.5′ × 3′ NW–SE circlet of magnitude 12 and 13
stars. A wide pair of magnitude 12 stars centered
2′ ENE of the galaxy is part of the circlet.

PK59–18.1 Abell 72 Planetary Nebula Type 3b
ϕ 130″, m13.8v, CS 15.0   20^{h}50.1^m +13° 33′
Finder Chart 43-3   ★
12/14″ Scopes–150x: Abell 72, a very faint planetary
nebula, is just ENE of an 8th magnitude star and
4′ SSW of a 9th magnitude star. The glare of the
two stars makes the planetary that much more
difficult to see. The 1.5′ nebula-disk is diffuse, ill-
defined, and seems elongated somewhat N–S. Even
in an O-III filter the disk is dim and transparent.

Seven stars are superimposed upon it; but they are
more conspicuous without the filter.

NGC 7003 Galaxy Type Sbc
ϕ 1.0′ × 0.6′, m13.0v, SB 12.3   21^{h}00.8^m +17° 48′
Finder Chart 43-3   ★
16/18″ Scopes–150x: NGC 7003 has a faint, circular 30″
diameter halo with a slight central brightening.
Very faint stars touch the NE and SW edges of the
halo. A tiny triangle of 13th magnitude stars is
visible 3′ west, and a 12th magnitude star 7′ south,
of the galaxy.

NGC 7006 H103^1 Globular Cluster Class I
ϕ 2.8′, m10.5v   21^{h}01.5^m +16° 11′
Finder Chart 43-3, Figure 43-8   ★★★
    NGC 7006 is one of the more distant globular
clusters associated with our Galaxy, located perhaps
185,000 light years from the Earth and 150,000 light-
years from the Galactic Center.
4/6″ Scopes–100x: NGC 7006 has a faint, small, unresolved uniform disk and appears more like a planetary nebula than a globular cluster.
8/10″ Scopes–125x: NGC 7006 has a moderately faint,
round 1.5′ diameter halo containing a broad central
brightening.
12/14″ Scopes–150x: At this aperture, the 1.75′ diameter
halo is fairly bright, has a granular texture, but
remains unresolved. The core is well concentrated
but not as bright as the typical globular cluster
core. 1.5′ south of the cluster's periphery is a wide
ENE–WSW pair of 14th magnitude stars.

Chapter 44

Draco, the Dragon

44.1 Overview

Draco the Dragon is, for mid-northern observers, a circumpolar constellation. Its stars are not particularly bright; therefore its 108°-long reverse-S pattern can be difficult to trace, especially on moonlit nights. The Head of the Dragon, consisting of Beta (β), Gamma (γ), Nu (ν), and Xi (ξ) Draconis, is, however, a fairly conspicuous asterism. The magnitude 2.2 Gamma, named Eltanin, is a lovely orange-tinted K-type star. Within the first coil of the Dragon's body, not far from the splendid planetary nebula NGC 6543, is the north pole of the ecliptic, one of the two points 90° from the Sun's path among the stars. The Tail of the Dragon stretches between the two Dippers, and halfway along it, between Beta Ursae Minoris in the Little Dipper and the famous multiple Mizar, Zeta Ursa Majoris, in the handle of the Big Dipper, is Thuban, Alpha (α) Draconis, often mentioned for having been the Pole Star during the Pyramid Age in Egypt around 2600 B.C.

The Greeks had several myths involving dragons. A dragon guarded the Golden Fleece sought by the Argonauts and was put to sleep by a potion given to Jason by the sorceress Medea. During the war between the Titans and the gods, which would lead to Jupiter's usurpation of the throne of Saturn, Minerva hurled a dragon into the sky. To obtain the golden apples of the Hesperides, one of his Twelve Labors, Hercules had to fight and kill a dragon. Probably the only certain personification of the celestial Dragon in classical mythology, however, are the winged dragons that drew Medea's celestial chariot, which was our Big Dipper and an immediate neighbor of the constellation of the Dragon. A winged Dragon drawing a four-wheeled Chariot was frequently shown in ancient, pre-Greek, Mesopotamian art and was undoubtedly the prototype of the Greek Dragon + Big Dipper (as a Wagon) constellation-pair.

Draco, with 1,083 square degrees, is the eighth largest of the constellations. Though it is far off the Milky Way, it is rich in objects. Most are galaxies, many of interesting appearance; but the constellation also

Draco: DRAY-ko
Genitive: Draconis, DRAY-Ko-nis
Abbreviation: Dra
Culmination: 9 pm–Jul. 8, midnight–May 24
Area: 1,083 square degrees
Best Deep-Sky Objects: NGC 4125, NGC 4256, NGC 5866 (M102), NGC 5907, NGC 5965, NGC 6015, NGC 6140, NGC 6503, NGC 6543, NGC 6643
Binocular Objects: OΣΣ123, 16 & 17 Dra, 25–ν Dra, NGC 4125, NGC 4256, NGC 5866 (M102), NGC 5907, NGC 6503, NGC 6543

contains several beautiful double stars and an exceptionally bright planetary nebula, NGC 6543, the Cat's Eye Nebula.

44.2 Interesting Stars

RY Draconis Variable Star Type SRb Spec. C3, 4
m9.4 to 11.4; Per. 172 days $12^h56.4^m$ +66° 00′
Finder Chart 44-4   ★★★
12/14″ Scopes–125x: RY Draconis is a variable star with a deep red tint. It is one of the cool "carbon stars," remarkable for the carbon compounds in their atmospheres. RY Draco varies by about 2 magnitudes in a period of roughly six months. It can be found near the midpoint of the SE side of the 1° equilateral triangle formed by 7, 8, and 9 Draconis.

17 and 16 Draconis Triple Star   Spec. A2, A0
AC: m5.4, 5.5; Sep. 90.3″; P.A. 194° $16^h36.2^m$ +52° 55′
Constellation Chart 44-1   ★★★★
2/3″ Scopes–50x: 17 and 16 Draconis is a fine, wide double that can be split in binoculars and at low power with small telescopes. 17 Draconis also has a close 3.4″ companion in position angle 108°. All three stars are bright white.

Draco, the Dragon

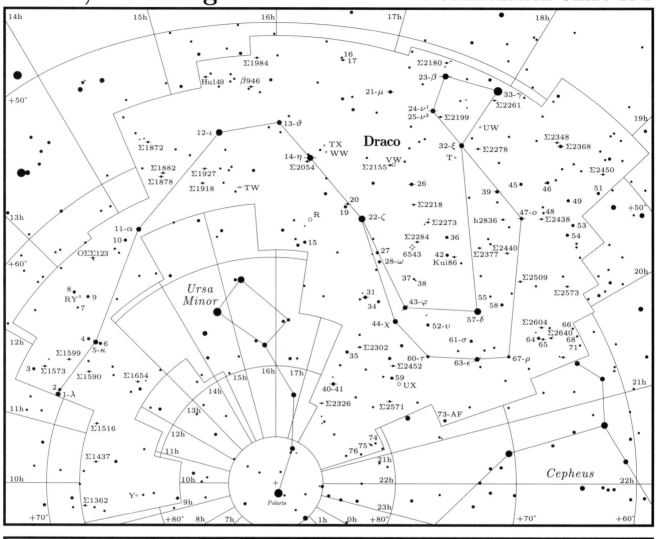

Chart Symbols

Constellation Chart		0	1	2	3	4	5	6
Stellar Magnitudes								
Finder Charts	0/1	2	3	4	5	6	7	8	9
Master Finder Chart		0	1	2	3	4	5

→ Guide Star Pointer ◉ ○ Variable Stars ⟡ Planetary Nebulae

●—● ● Double Stars ◯ Open Clusters ▢ Small Bright Nebulae

Finder Chart Scale ⊕ Globular Clusters ⌬ Large Bright Nebulae

(One degree tick marks) ⬭ Galaxies ☁ Dark Nebulae

Table 44-1: Selected Variable Stars in Draco

Name	HD No.	Type	Max.	Min.	Period (Days)	F*	Spec. Type	R.A. (2000)	Dec.	Finder Chart No.	& Notes
Y Dra	83114	M	6.2	15.0	325	0.45	M5	$09^h42.4^m$	+77° 51′	44-1	
RY Dra	112559	SBb	9.4	11.4	v172		C3,4	$12^h56.4^m$	+66 00	44-4	Deep red tint
R Dra	149880	M	6.7	13.0	245	0.45	M5-M9	$16^h32.7^m$	+66 45	44-1	
TX Dra	150077	SRb	7.9	10.2	78	0.50	M4-M5	35.0	+60 28	44-1	
WW Dra	150708	EA/RS	8.2	9.4	4.62	0.12	G2+K0	39.1	+60 42	44-1	
VW Dra	156947	SRd	6.0	6.5	170		K1.5	$17^h16.5^m$	+60 40	44-3	Orange
T Dra		M	7.2	13.5	421	0.44	C6-C8	56.4	+58 13	44-1	Deep red star
UW Dra	164345	Lb?	7.0	8.0			K5	57.5	+54 40	44-1	
UX Dra	183556	SRa	5.9	7.1	168		C7,3	$19^h21.6^m$	+76 34	44-1	Nice crimson color

F* = The fraction of period taken up by the star's rise from min. to max. brightness, or the period spent in eclipse.

Table 44-2: Selected Double Stars in Draco

Name	ADS No.	Pair	M1	M2	Sep."	P.A.°	Spec	R.A. (2000) Dec	Finder Chart No.	Notes
Σ1362	7446		7.2	7.2	4.9	129	F0	09^{h}37.9^m +73° 05′	44-3	
Σ1437	7824		7.6	10.1	23.5	290	A3	10^{h}34.2^m +73 50	44-3	
Σ1516	8100	AB	7.6	8.1	36.2	102	K5	11^{h}15.4^m +73 28	44-3	
	8100	AC		11.1	6.7	317				
Σ1573	8313		7.6	8.6	11.2	178	F8	49.2 +67 20	44-4	
Σ1590	8395		7.5	10.5	5.1	235	K0	12^{h}01.7^m +07 41	44-5	
Σ1599	8413	AB	7.4	10.4	10.2	167	K5	05.6 +68 48	44-4	
Σ1654	8591		7.6	9.1	3.7	24	K0	32.1 +74 49	44-5	
OΣΣ123		AB	6.7	7.0	68.9	147	F0 F0	13^{h}27.1^m +64 44	44-1	Nice yellowish pair
Σ1872	9346	AB	7.4	8.4	7.6	47	K0	14^{h}41.0^m +57 57	44-6	
Σ1878	9357		6.3	8.5	4.1	319	F2	42.1 +61 16	44-7	
Σ1882	9371	AB	6.9	8.4	12.2	2	F2	44.1 +61 06	44-7	
	9371	Aa		10.5	9.1	83				
Σ1918	9520		6.8	10.8	17.9	21	F2	15^{h}07.8^m +63 07	44-7	
Σ1927	9537		7.8	8.7	16.1	354	G0	11.8 +61 52	44-7	BV Dra
Hu149	9628		7.5	7.6	0.5	279	K0	24.6 +54 13	44-6	
β946	9793		5.8	11.5	1.8	136	A2	47.6 +55 23	44-6	
Σ1984	9816	AB	6.6	8.9	6.5	273	A0	51.2 +52 54	44-1	Pale and deep yellow
Σ2054	10052		6.0	7.2	1.0	355	G5	16^{h}23.8^m +61 42	44-1	Close yellow pair
14–η Dra	10058	AB	2.7	8.7	5.2	142	G5	24.0 +61 31	44-1	Fine yellow pair
17 Dra	10129	AB	5.4	6.4	3.4	108	A2	36.2 +52 55	44-1	Attractive white trio
17–16 Dra	10129	AC		5.5	90.3	194	A0			
20 Dra	10279		7.1	7.3	1.4w	*67	F0	56.4 +65 02	44-1	
21–μ Dra	10345	AB	5.6	5.7	1.9w	* 8	F5	17^{h}05.3^m +54 28	44-1	Yellowish-white pair
Σ2155	10448		6.8	10.1	9.8	114		16.1 +60 43	44-1	Yellowish and bluish
Σ2180	10597		7.7	7.9	3.2	262	F0	29.0 +50 52	44-1	
25–ν^{1,2}	10628		4.9	4.9	61.9	312	A5 A5	32.2 +55 11	44-1	Bright white pair
26 Dra	10660	AB	5.3	8.0	1.7	*330	F8	35.0 +61 52	44-1	
Σ2199	10699		7.8	8.4	1.8	71	F5	38.6 +55 46	44-1	
Σ2218	10728		7.1	8.3	1.7	326	F5	40.3 +63 41	44-9	
31–ψ Dra	10759	AB	4.9	6.1	30.3	15	F5 F5	41.9 +72 09	44-8	Fine yellowish pair
Σ2261	10953		7.7	9.7	9.5	262	A2	58.1 +52 13	44-10	
Σ2273	10985	AB	7.5	7.8	21.1	284	F2 F2	59.2 +64 09	44-9	
	10985	AC		12.7	23.7	266				
41–40 Dra	11061	AB	5.7	6.1	19.3	232	F6 F5	18^{h}00.2^m +80 00	44-1	Light yellow stars
Σ2284	11016		7.8	9.4	3.5	190	F5	18^{h}01.4^m +65 57	44-9	
Σ2302	11072	AB	6.9	9.9	5.8	247	A0	02.8 +75 47	44-8	
	11072	AC		9.4	23.1	280				
Σ2278	11035	AB	7.1	8.1	36.9	26	A5 A0	02.9 +56 26	44-10	
	11035	AC		8.5	34.3	35				
Σ2326	11156		7.7	10.0	16.4	196	A5	05.3 +81 29	44-1	
39 Dra	11336	AB	5.0	8.0	3.8	351	A2	23.9 +58 48	44-1	White and bluish-white
Kui 86			6.3	10.5	26.6	36	A3	31.2 +65 26	44-9	
Σ2348	11468	ABxC	6.1	8.8	25.7	272	K0	33.9 +52 21	44-10	Deep yellow and blue
Σ2377	11559		7.1	8.7	16.5	340	K0	38.4 +63 32	44-9	
h2836		AB	6.7	9.9	36.9	324	F2	38.4 +60 43	44-1	
		AC		9.9	54.7	259				
Σ2368	11558	AB	7.6	7.8	1.9	323	A2	38.9 +52 21	44-10	
	11558	AC		10.7	36.6	125				
47–o Dra	11779	AB	4.8	7.8	34.2	326	K0	51.2 +59 23	44-1	Yellow and greenish-blue
Σ2452	11870		6.6	7.4	5.7	218	A0	35.6 +75 47	44-8	
Σ2440	11901		6.5	9.0	17.0	123	K0	57.3 +62 24	44-1	
Σ2438	11897		7.1	7.4	0.9w	*359	A2	57.5 +58 14	44-1	
Σ2450	11979	AB	6.4	8.6	5.1	302	K2	19^{h}02.1^m +52 16	44-10	
Σ2509	12296		7.2	8.3	1.7	330	F5	16.9 +63 12	44-1	
Σ2571	12608		7.6	8.3	11.3	20	F0	29.5 +78 16	44-1	
Σ2573	12789		6.2	9.5	18.2	27	A2	40.2 +60 30	44-1	White and blue
63–ε Dra	13007		3.8	7.4	3.1	15	K0	48.2 +70 16	44-1	Deep and pale yellow
Σ2604	13092		6.9	9.1	27.8	184	G5	52.8 +64 11	44-1	
65 Dra		AB	6.6	8.7	96.8	336	G5	20^{h}02.3^m +64 38	44-1	
		Aa		11.9	26.7	192				
Σ2640	13371		6.3	10.2	5.6	16	A2	04.7 +63 53	44-1	

Footnotes: *= Year 2000, a = Near apogee, c = Closing, w = Widening. Finder Chart No: All stars listed in the tables are plotted in the large Constellation Chart, but when a star appears in a Finder Chart, this number is listed. Notes: When colors are subtle, the suffix *-ish* is used, e.g. *bluish*.

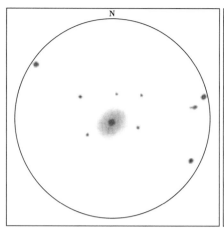

Figure 44-1. NGC 3147
18.5″, f5-150x, by Glen W. Sanner

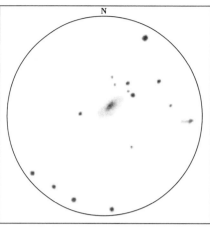

Figure 44-2. NGC 3183
16″, f5-185x, by Bob Erdmann

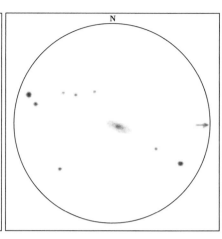

Figure 44-3. NGC 3403
17.5″, f4.5-250x, by G. R. Kepple

Mu (μ) = 21 Draconis (Σ 2130) Triple Star Spec. A2, A0
AB: m5.6, 5.7; Sep.1.9″; P.A.8°   17^{h}05.3^m +54° 28′
Constellation Chart 44-1   ★★★★
4/6″Scopes-175x: Mu Draconis consists of two equally
    bright white stars but requires high power to split.
    A faint 13th magnitude companion lies 13.2″ away
    in position angle 175°.

Σ2155 Double Star   **Spec. F0**
m6.8, 10.1; Sep.9.8″; P.A.114°   17^{h}16.1^m +60° 43′
Constellation Chart 44-1   ★★★★
4/6″Scopes-175x: Struve 2155 is an easily split pair of
    pale yellow and blue stars. To the SW of the double
    in the same field of view is the orange K-type semi-
    regular variable VW Draconis, a fine color contrast
    to the Struve 2155 stars.

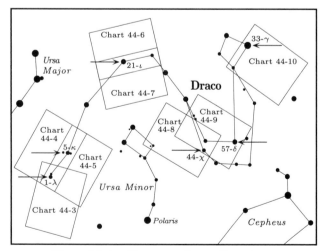

Master Finder Chart 44-2. Draco Chart Areas
Guide stars indicated by arrows.

Nu-1 (ν^1)=24, Nu-2(ν^2)=25 Draconis   Spec. A5, A5
m4.9, 4.9; Sep.61.9″; P.A.312°   17^{h}32.2^m +55° 11′
Constellation Chart 44-1   ★★★★★
4/6″Scopes-50x: The Nu Draconis pair is two very wide
    but exactly equally bright white stars attractive in
    both small and large telescopes.

Psi (ψ) = 31 Draconis (Σ 2241) Double Star Spec. F5, F5
AB: m4.9, 6.1; Sep.30.3″; P.A.15° 17^{h}41.9^m +72° 09′
Finder Chart 44-8   ★★★★
4/6″Scopes-150x: Psi Draconis is a wide pair of yellow-
    ish stars, the brighter one having a more subtle tint.

41 and 40 Draconis (Σ2308) Triple Star   Spec. F6, F5
AB: m5.7, 6.1; Sep.19.3″; P.A.232° 18^{h}00.2^m +80° 00′
Constellation Chart 44-1   ★★★★
4/6″Scopes-100x: 41 and 40 Draconis are a nearly
    equally bright pair of light yellow stars.

44.3 Deep-Sky Objects

NGC 2977 H282^1 Galaxy Type Sb:
ϕ 1.5′ × 0.6′, m12.5v, SB12.2   09^{h}43.8^m +74° 52′
Finder Chart 44-3   ★★
8/10″Scopes-100x: NGC 2977, located 20′ north of a
    7th magnitude star and 5.5′ north of a 10th mag-
    nitude star, is a faint, small, uniformly bright oval
    glow elongated 1′ × 0.5′ NE–SW.
16/18″Scopes-150x: NGC 2977 has a moderately faint
    1.5′ × 0.75′ NE–SW halo somewhat brighter in the
    core. A 13th magnitude star is 1.5′ ESE.

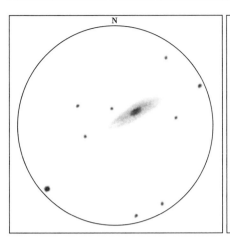

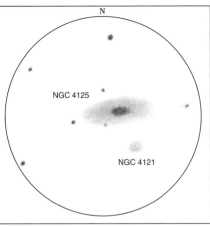

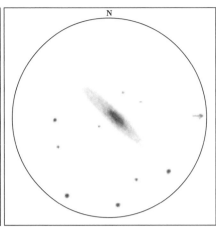

Figure 44-4. NGC 3735
17.5″, ƒ4.5–250x, by G. R. Kepple

Figure 44-5. NGC 4125
16″, ƒ5–185x, by Bob Erdmann

Figure 44-6. NGC 4256
16″, ƒ5–185x, by Bob Erdmann

NGC 3147 H79[1] Galaxy Type SA(rs)bc II
ϕ **4.3′ × 3.7′, m10.6v, SB13.5** $10^h16.9^m$ +73° 24′
Finder Chart 44-3, Figure 44-1   ★★★★

4/6″Scopes–75x: NGC 3147, located 23′ north of a 6th
magnitude star, is a faint oval glow with a bright
center.

12/14″Scopes–125x: NGC 3147 is a bright 2.5′ × 1.75′
NW–SE oval containing a large, well concentrated
core. The galaxy lies within the rectangle formed
by a row of three 13th magnitude stars to the north
and two more 13th magnitude stars to the south.

16/18″Scopes–150x: Larger instruments show a bright
nucleus embedded in a large, slightly extended core
surrounded by a smooth 3.5′ × 3′ NW–SE halo.

NGC 3183 Galaxy Type SB(s)bc:
ϕ **2.2′ × 1.2′, m11.9v, SB12.8** $10^h21.8^m$ +74° 10′
Finder Chart 44-3, Figure 44-2   ★★★

16/18″Scopes–150x: NGC 3183 has a fairly conspicuous
2′ × 1′ NW–SE halo that gradually brightens into
its core area. Four 13th and 14th magnitude lie to
the galaxy's north, the two nearest touching the
halo's edge. A 13th magnitude star is 1.25′ east.
An ENE–WSW chain of four 11th magnitude stars
is 10′ SSE of the galaxy.

NGC 3329 Galaxy Type (R)SA(r)b:
ϕ **2.0′ × 1.2′, m12.2v, SB13.0** $10^h44.7^m$ +76° 49′
Finder Chart 44-3   ★★

16/18″Scopes–150x: NGC 3329, located 7.5′ SE of a
10th magnitude star, has a faint but conspicuous
1.5′ × 0.75′ NW–SE halo containing a broad, poorly
concentrated core. A 13th magnitude star lies 2.5′
NW, and a 14th magnitude star 1.5′ north, of the
galaxy.

NGC 3403 H335[2] Galaxy Type SAbc: III
ϕ **3.2′ × 1.4′, m12.2v, SB13.6** $10^h53.9^m$ +73° 41′
Finder Chart 44-3, Figure 44-3   ★★★

8/10″Scopes–100x: NGC 3403, located between 10.5
magnitude stars 3′ to its WSW and 4′ to its ENE,
is a fairly faint, thin ray elongated 2′ × 0.5′ ENE–
WSW and containing a bright core.

16/18″Scopes–150x: NGC 3403 is a fine spindle-shaped
object. The halo is much elongated 3′ × 0.75′ ENE–
WSW and contains a bright 30″ × 20″ oval core.
Some faint knots are along the halo's major axis
on each side of the core. A 13th magnitude star lies
off the west tip of the halo 3′ from the galaxy's
center, and a second 13th magnitude star is 4.5′
ENE.

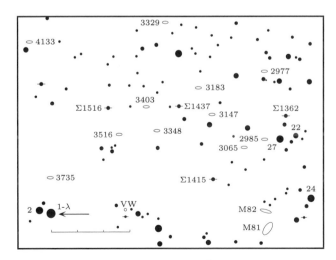

Finder Chart 44-3. 1–λ Dra: $11^h31.4^m$ +69° 20′

Figure 44-7. *NGC 4236 is a huge, extremely faint galaxy requiring low power and averted vision with large instruments. Image courtesy of Bernhard Hubl.*

NGC 3735 H287[1] Galaxy Type SAc: sp II-III
ϕ **3.9′ × 0.9′, m11.8v, SB 13.0**   11^{h}36.0^m +70° 32′
Finder Chart 44-3, Figure 44-4   ★★★
8/10″Scopes–100x: NGC 3735, located 1.25° NNE of
    3.8 magnitude Lambda (λ) = 1 Draconis, has a
    fairly faint 2.5′ × 0.5′ NW–SE halo containing a
    bright core.
16/18″Scopes–150x: NGC 3735 is a nice bright streak
    in larger telescopes. The 3.5′ × 0.75′ NW–SE halo
    contains a small, bright oval core. A 14th magnitude
    star lies 1′ NE and a 13th magnitude star is 2.75′
    west.

NGC 4121 Galaxy Type E
ϕ **1.0′ × 0.8′, m13.5v, SB 13.1**   12^{h}07.9^m +65° 07′

NGC 4125 U7118 Galaxy Type E6 pec
ϕ **6.1′ × 5.1′, m9.7v, SB 13.3**   12^{h}08.1^m +65° 11′
Finder Chart 44-4, Figure 44-5   ★/★★★★
8/10″Scopes–100x: NGC 4125, located 9′ SSW of an
    8th magnitude star, is a bright galaxy with a cigar-
    shaped 2.5′ × 1′ E–W halo containing an extended
    core. A magnitude 10.5 star lies just beyond the
    halo's east tip.
16/18″Scopes–150x: NGC 4125 is a bright edge-on
    galaxy elongated 4′ × 2′ E–W containing an oval

core brightening to a brilliant nonstellar nucleus.
A 13th magnitude star lies 1.75′ NNE. The companion galaxy, NGC 4121, located 3.5′ SSW of NGC
4125, is a faint, diffuse, circular 45″ diameter glow.

NGC 4128 H263[1] Galaxy Type SA0: sp
ϕ **2.5′ × 1.0′, m12.0v, SB 12.8**   12^{h}08.5^m +68° 46′
Finder Chart 44-4   ★★★
8/10″Scopes–100x: NGC 4128 lies 4.5′ SE of an 11th
    magnitude star, the brightest in a circlet of 11th to
    12th magnitude stars surrounding the galaxy. It is
    a small, well concentrated capsule-shaped object
    elongated 1.5′ × 0.5′ ENE–WSW and containing a
    prominent stellar nucleus. 15′ west of the galaxy is
    a bright diamond-shaped asterism of magnitude
    7.5–10 stars.
16/18″Scopes–150x: NGC 4128 displays a bright non-
    stellar nucleus embedded in a small circular core
    surrounded by a fairly bright 2′ × 0.75′ halo. A very
    faint, nearly stellar companion galaxy lies only 2′
    NW.

NGC 4133 H278[1] Galaxy Type SABb:
ϕ **1.8′ × 1.5′, m12.3v, SB 13.2**   12^{h}08.6^m +74° 56′
Finder Chart 44-5   ★★
8/10″Scopes–100x: This dim galaxy is 20′ north of a 6th

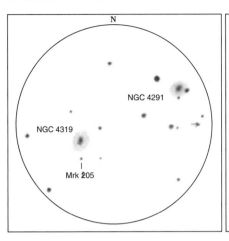

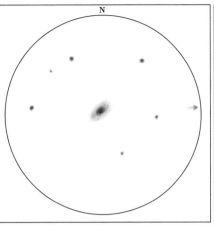

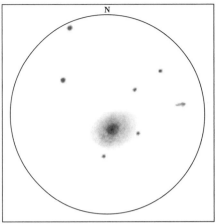

Figure 44-8. NGC 4291 and NGC 4319
17.5″, f4.5–250x, by G. R. Kepple

Figure 44-9. NGC 4386
17.5″, f4.5–250x, by G. R. Kepple

Figure 44-10. NGC 4589
16″, f5–185x, by Bob Erdmann

magnitude star and just south of a triangle of 10th and 11th magnitude stars. The halo is a small, faint, diffuse spot slightly brighter in its center.

16/18″Scopes–150x: NGC 4133 has a faint 1.5′ × 0.75′ NW–SE oval halo containing a sudden brightening in the core. The northern edge of the halo protrudes into the triangle of 10th magnitude stars.

NGC 4236 H51⁵ Galaxy Type SB(s)dm IV–V
ϕ **21.0′ × 7.5′, m9.6v, SB15.0**   **12ʰ16.7ᵐ +69° 28′**
Finder Chart 44-4, Figure 44-7   ★

8/10″Scopes–75x: This extremely faint galaxy lies in a field of bright stars, its northern tip just 5′ SSW of a 7.5 magnitude star. The halo is a very diffuse 4′ × 1.5′ NNW–SSE glow containing a broad central brightening, and requires averted vision to be seen well.

12/14″Scopes–100x: NGC 4236 has a very large, low surface brightness halo elongated 17′ × 4′ NNW–SSE and containing an irregularly concentrated 5′ × 1′ inner region that shows a slight mottling through its center.

16/18″Scopes–125x: This ghostly streak is best seen at low power. The haze is very faint and diffuse, elongated 20′ × 4′ NNW–SSE, and extends nearly to a 10th magnitude star at its southern tip. The central region is broadly brighter but irregularly illuminated, and contains a few indistinct patches at center and 5′ north of its center. Several knots or faint stars are 5′ SE of the galaxy's center, and half a dozen faint stars are embedded in the halo's southern extension. A 13th magnitude star lies 3′ WSW of the galaxy's center.

NGC 4250 H264¹ Galaxy Type SAB(r)0+
ϕ **2.3′ × 1.8′, m11.8v, SB13.2**   **12ʰ17.4ᵐ +70° 48′**
Finder Chart 44-4   ★★★

8/10″Scopes–100x: NGC 4250 displays a bright, tiny core embedded in a faint, circular 1.5′ diameter halo. A 13th magnitude star lies 4′ NNW.

NGC 4256 H846² Galaxy Type SA(s)b: sp
ϕ **4.1′ × 0.8′, m11.9v, SB13.0**   **12ʰ18.7ᵐ +65° 54′**
Finder Chart 44-4, Figure 44-6   ★★★

8/10″Scopes–100x: This galaxy is a faint, thin shaft of light elongated 3.5′ × 0.5′ NE–SW and moderately brighter along its center.

16/18″Scopes–150x: NGC 4256 is a thinly-tapered 4′ × 0.5′ NE–SW streak containing a bright, extended core. The galaxy is NE of the mouth of a "funnel", of six 12th magnitude stars, three on each side.

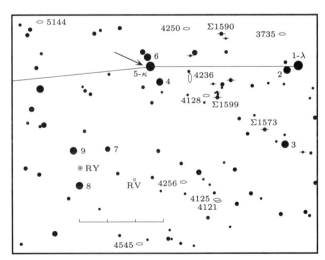

Finder Chart 44-4. 5–κ Dra: 12ʰ33.5ᵐ +69° 47′

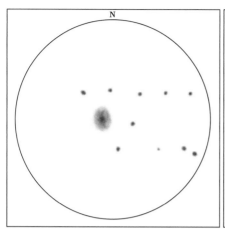

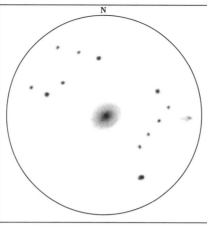

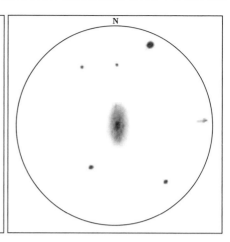

Figure 44-11. NGC 4648
16″, f5–185x, by Bob Erdmann

Figure 44-12. NGC 4750
16″, f5–185x, by Bob Erdmann

Figure 44-13. NGC 5678
17.5″, f4.5–250x, by G. R. Kepple

NGC 4291 H275[1] Galaxy Type E
φ **2.0′ × 1.7′, m11.5v, SB 12.6**   12ʰ20.3ᵐ +75° 22′
Finder Chart 44-5, Figure 44-8   ★★★

8/10″ Scopes–100x: NGC 4291, located 13′ NNE of a
5.5 magnitude star, displays a conspicuous core
surrounded by a faint, smooth 1′ diameter halo.
The galaxy is at the NW corner of a rectangle with
a 9.5 magnitude star 1.5′ to its ENE and 11th
magnitude stars 2′ to its SSE and 2.5′ to its SE.
The two galaxies NGC 4319 and NGC 4386, respectively 6.5′ SE and 15′ NE of NGC 4291, form a large
triangle with it.

16/18″ Scopes–150x: NGC 4291 has a bright, circular
1.5′ diameter halo containing a bright, tiny core. A
13th magnitude star is superimposed upon the halo
west of the core, and a 14th magnitude star is on
the halo's south edge. At low power this galaxy
resembles a planetary nebula.

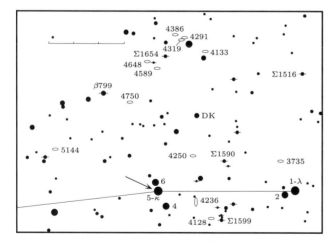

Finder Chart 44-5. 5–κ Dra: 12ʰ33.5ᵐ +69° 47′

NGC 4319 H276[1] Galaxy Type SB(r)ab
φ **2.8′ × 2.1′, m11.9v, SB 13.7**   12ʰ21.7ᵐ +75° 19′

Markarian 205 Quasar
m14.5v   12ʰ21.7ᵐ +75° 19′
Finder Chart 44-5, Figure 44-8   ★★★/★

8/10″ Scopes–100x: NGC 4319, located 13′ ENE of a
5th magnitude star, is at the southern vertex of the
triangle it forms with galaxies NGC 4291 and NGC
4386. NGC 4319 appears fainter and a little larger
than NGC 4291. It is elongated 1.5′ × 1.25′ N–S and
contains a prominent oval core.

16/18″ Scopes–150x: NGC 4319 has a well concentrated
2.5′ × 2′ N–S oval halo containing a bright extended
core. Quasar Markarian 205, lying 40″ south of the
galaxy's center, has the appearance of a 14th
magnitude star. Mark 205 has a redshift of 0.072,
implying a recessional velocity of 21,000 kilometers
per second. If the Hubble constant is 50km/sec/
megaparsec, the distance to the quasar is 1.3 billion
light years. The object's absolute magnitude therefore would be nearly −24, a luminosity of 330 billion
suns.

NGC 4386 H277[1] Galaxy Type SAB0° :
φ **2.8′ × 1.8′, m11.7v, SB 13.3**   12ʰ24.5ᵐ +75° 32′
Finder Chart 44-5, Figure 44-9   ★★★

8/10″ Scopes–100x: This galaxy is at the NE vertex of
the triangle it forms with NGC 4291 and NGC 4319.
It is nearly equal to NGC 4291 in brightness and
has a 1.25′ × 0.75′ NW–SE halo that contains a
prominent nonstellar nucleus. Two 12th magnitude
stars lying 3′ to its NE and NW form an equilateral
triangle with the galaxy.

16/18″Scopes–150x: NGC 4386 shows a conspicuous nonstellar nucleus embedded in an extended core surrounded by a 1.5′×0.75′ NW–SE halo.

NGC 4545   H850² Galaxy Type SB(s)cd: II
φ 2.7′×1.5′, m12.3v, SB13.7   12ʰ34.6ᵐ +63° 31′
Finder Chart 44-4   ★★

16/18″Scopes–150x: NGC 4545 has a rather faint, diffuse 2.5′×1′ N–S halo that gradually brightens toward its center. A 14th magnitude star is 1′ NE, and a 13th magnitude star 2.5′ WSW, of the galaxy.

NGC 4589   H273¹ Galaxy Type E2
φ 3.0′×2.7′, m10.7v, SB12.9   12ʰ37.4ᵐ +74° 12′
Finder Chart 44-5, Figure 44-10   ★★★

8/10″Scopes–100x: NGC 4589, located 3′ SW of an 11th magnitude star, has a faint, circular 2′ diameter halo surrounding a prominent core.

16/18″Scopes–150x: NGC 4589 displays a small, conspicuous core that contains a stellar nucleus surrounded by a 2.25′×1.75′ ESE–WNW halo. A 14th magnitude star is on the WNW edge of the halo. 7.5′ west of NGC 4589 is its companion, NGC 4572, a very faint, slender 1.5′×0.25′ NW–SE streak.

NGC 4648   H274¹ Galaxy Type E3
φ 1.7′×1.3′, m12.0v, SB12.8   12ʰ41.8ᵐ +74° 25′
Finder Chart 44-5, Figure 44-11   ★★★

8/10″Scopes–100x: This faint galaxy is located between the bottom legs of a Lambda-shaped asterism. 7.5′ to its west is an attractive double of blue and gold 10th magnitude stars. NGC 4648 has a small 1.25′×0.75′ ENE–WSW halo that contains a conspicuous stellar nucleus.

16/18″Scopes–150x: NGC 4648, situated in the opening of a V-shaped asterism, has a sharp nucleus embedded in a very faint 1.5′×1′ ENE–WSW halo.

NGC 4750   H78⁴ Galaxy Type (R)SA(rs)ab II-III
φ 2.1′×2.0′, m11.2v, SB12.6   12ʰ50.1ᵐ +72° 52′
Finder Chart 44-5, Figure 44-12   ★★★

8/10″Scopes–100x: This galaxy is a faint 2′×1.5′ NW–SE oval with a slight brightening at its center. Running roughly N–S about 4′ west of the galaxy is a chain of six stars, the middle stars 12th magnitude objects and the two end stars, bending from the line of the 12th magnitude stars in opposite directions, somewhat brighter.

16/18″Scopes–150x: NGC 4750 has a moderately concentrated 50″×30″ NNW–SSE core embedded in a faint 2′ diameter halo. An 11th magnitude star lies 5′ north of the galaxy.

Figure 44-14. *NGC5866 has been suggested to fill the position of M102, the missing entry in Messier's catalogue. Image courtesy Martin C. Germano.*

NGC 5678   H237¹ Galaxy Type SAB(rs)b II-III
φ 3.2′×1.6′, m11.3v, SB13.0   14ʰ32.1ᵐ +57° 55′
Finder Chart 44-6, Figure 44-13   ★★★

12/14″Scopes–125x: NGC 5678, located 2.75′ SSE of a 9th magnitude star, has a fairly bright 3′×1.5′ N–S oval halo containing a small, inconspicuous oval core. Two 13th magnitude stars are 1.75′ SE and 2.5′ SSW, and a 14th magnitude star is 2.25′ NNE, of the galaxy.

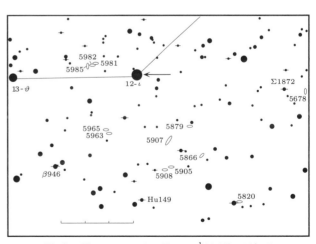

Finder Chart 44-6. 12–ι Dra: 15ʰ24.9ᵐ +58° 58′

Figure 44-15. *NGC 5907 is a beautiful edge-on galaxy with an elongated core and a faint dark lane along its western flank. Image courtesy of Bill McLaughlin.*

NGC 5866 H215[1] Messier 102 Galaxy Type SA0+
φ 6.6′ × 3.2′, m9.9v, SB 13.1   **15ʰ06.5ᵐ +55° 46′**
Finder Chart 44-6, Figure 44-14   ★★★★

M102 is one of the missing Messier objects. Mechain, in a 1783 letter to Bernoulli in Berlin, stated that M102 was a duplicate observation of M101. Owen Gingerich has suggested NGC 5866 as a worthy object with which to fill this blank in Messier's catalogue.

8/10″Scopes–100x: Messier 102 forms a triangle with an 11.5 magnitude star 1.5′ to its NNW and a magnitude 12.5 star 1.5′ to its SW. It is a bright lenticular galaxy elongated 2.75′ × 1′ NW–SE and brightening smoothly to its center.

12/14″Scopes–125x: This galaxy is a fine, bright object elongated 3.25′ × 1.25′ NW–SE and containing a broad bright core. An inconspicuous stellar nucleus is just discernible at the center of the grainy envelope. On good nights both a bright spot on the western side and the galaxy's dust lane are just visible.

20/22″Scopes–175x: Impressive! Messier 102 is a very bright, distinctive spindle-shaped galaxy elongated 4′ × 1.5′ NW–SE. A narrow dust lane cuts across the bright bulging core.

NGC 5879 H757[2] Galaxy Type SA(rs)bc:? II-III
φ 4.4′ × 1.6′, m11.6v, SB 13.5   **15ʰ09.8ᵐ +57° 00′**
Finder Chart 44-6   ★★★

8/10″Scopes–100x: NGC 5879, located 7′ SSE of a 7th magnitude star, is a thin, faint glowing streak elongated 2′ × 0.5′ N–S and containing a moderate brightening along its center.

16/18″Scopes–150x: NGC 5879 has a well concentrated, highly extended core that contains a bright non-stellar nucleus and is surrounded by a much fainter, diffuse outer envelope elongated 3.5′ × 1′ N–S. A magnitude 14.5 star lies near the halo's WNW edge 50″ from the galaxy's center.

NGC 5905 H758[2] Galaxy Type SB(r)b I
φ 4.3′ × 3.3′, m11.7v, SB 14.4   **15ʰ15.4ᵐ +55° 31′**
Finder Chart 44-6, Figure 44-16   ★★★

8/10″Scopes–100x: NGC 5905 is the fainter member of a pair with NGC 5908 lying 13′ to its SE. It has a fairly faint, 2′ diameter halo that is slightly brighter in its center.

16/18″Scopes–150x: NGC 5905 has a 2.5′ diameter halo slightly elongated NW–SE containing a well

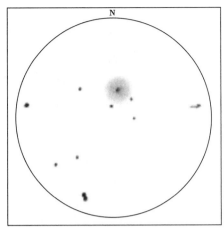

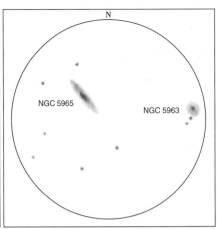

Figure 44-16. NGC 5905
18.5″, f5–250x, by Glen W. Sanner

Figure 44-17. NGC 5908
17.5″, f4.5–250x, by G. R. Kepple

Figure 44-18. NGC 5963 and NGC 5965
17.5″, f4.5–185x, by Richard Jakiel

concentrated but irregularly bright mottled core. A 13th magnitude star is 1.5′ east, and a close NNE–SSW pair of 11th magnitude stars is 4′ SSE.

NGC 5907 H259[2] Galaxy Type SA(s)c: sp II
φ 11.5′ × 1.7′, m10.3v, SB13.4 $15^h15.9^m$ +56° 19′
Finder Chart 44-6, Figure 44-15 ★★★★

4/6″Scopes–75x: This galaxy is a faint shaft of light elongated 7′ × 0.5′ NNW–SSE.

8/10″Scopes–100x: NGC 5907 appears moderately faint, elongated 9′ × 0.75′ NNW–SSE, and has an extended 2′ long core. The eastern edge is better defined than the western.

16/18″Scopes–150x: This is a beautiful edge-on galaxy with a fairly bright 10′ × 0.75′ NNW–SSE halo. The core is highly elongated 2.5′ × 0.25′. A faint dark dust lane extends along the west side of the galaxy's halo, except where it is drowned out in the core's light. The western flank of the galaxy is more diffuse, but wider, than the eastern flank. A 14th magnitude star is on the western edge of the halo 1′ WSW of the galaxy's center. Another 14th magnitude star is just east of the halo's northern tip 3.5′ from the galaxy's center.

NGC 5908 H260[2] Galaxy Type SA(s)b: sp II-III
φ 2.7′ × 1.2′, m11.8v, SB13.0 $15^h16.7^m$ +55° 25′
Finder Chart 44-6, Figure 44-17 ★★★

8/10″Scopes–100x: NGC 5908 is the brighter of an interesting galaxy pair with NGC 5905 13′ to its NW. The halo, smaller than its companion's, is elongated 2′ × 1′ NNW–SSE and contains a well concentrated center.

16/18″Scopes–150x: NGC 5908 has a fairly bright 2.25′ × 1.25′ NNW–SSE halo containing an extended core and some brightening along the center of the major axis of the halo. A fairly rich stream of 12th and 13th magnitude stars meanders between NGC 5908 and NGC 5905.

NGC 5949 H906[2] Galaxy Type SA(r)bc?
φ 2.1′ × 1.0′, m12.0v, SB12.7 $15^h28.0^m$ +64° 46′
Finder Chart 44-7 ★★★

12/14″Scopes–125x: NGC 5949 lies 8′ SE of a 9.5 magnitude star with an 11th magnitude companion 20″ NE. The galaxy is faint and diffuse but conspicuous. Its 1.75′ × 1′ halo is elongated NW–SE and lacks any central brightening. 13th magnitude stars are 2′ and 3′ ESE of the galaxy.

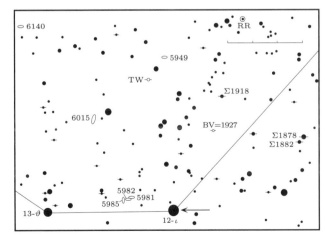

Finder Chart 44-7. 12-ι Dra: $15^h24.9^m$ +58° 58′

Figure 44-19. *NGC 5985, and NGC 5982, are part of a nice pair of galaxies with NGC 5981 (not in photo). Two very faint 16th magnitude galaxies are visible in the photo. Image courtesy of Bill McLaughlin.*

Figure 44-20. *NGC 6140 has a bright oval core embedded in a much fainter diffuse halo. Martin C. Germano took this 110 minute exposure on hypered 2415 Kodak Tech Pan film with a 14.5″, f5 Newtonian reflector.*

NGC 5963 H761² Galaxy Type S pec
φ 3.7′ × 2.8′, m12.5v, SB14.9   15ʰ33.5ᵐ +56° 35′

NGC 5965 H762² Galaxy Type
φ 5.5′ × 0.9′, m11.7v, SB13.3   15ʰ34.0ᵐ +56° 42′
Finder Chart 44-6, Figure 44-18   ★★/★★★
8/10″ Scopes–100x: NGC 5963 and NGC 5965 are an interesting 7′ wide E–W galaxy pair. NGC 5963 on the west is the brighter but smaller of the pair: its 1′ × 0.5′ NE–SW halo has a bright center. 12th and 13th magnitude stars are respectively 1′ and 1.5′ SSE of the galaxy's center. NGC 5965 appears much larger but is significantly fainter than NGC 5963: its much-elongated, diffuse 2.5′ × 0.5′ NE–SW halo contains a faint stellar nucleus.

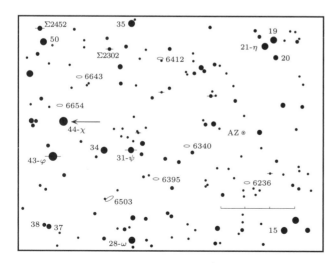

Finder Chart 44-8. 44–χ Dra: 18ʰ21.0ᵐ +72° 44′

16/18″ Scopes–150x: NGC 5963 is a well concentrated 1.5′ × 1′ NE–SW oval containing a bright nonstellar core. NGC 5965 is a large, fairly bright 4.5′ × 0.75′ NE–SW streak with a faint elongated core that surrounds a stellar nucleus. With averted vision a dark dust lane can be seen extending along the eastern flank of the galaxy from each end of the core to a third of the each extension.

NGC 5981 U9948 Galaxy Type Sc? sp
φ 2.6′ × 0.3′, m13.0v, SB12.6   15ʰ37.9ᵐ +59° 23′
Finder Chart 44-7   ★★
16/18″ Scopes–150x: NGC 5981 is the faintest, and farthest west, of a row of three galaxies that includes NGC 5982 and NGC 5985, respectively 6′ and 13′ to its east. NGC 5981 is a faint, narrow, delicate 2.5′ × 0.25′ NW–SE ray that contains a small faint core. At 175x some mottling is visible along the galaxy's major axis.

NGC 5982 H764² Galaxy Type E3
φ 3.0′ × 2.2′, m11.1v, SB13.0   15ʰ38.7ᵐ +59° 21′
Finder Chart 44-7, Figure 44-19   ★★★
8/10″ Scopes–100x: NGC 5982 is the brightest in the E–W galaxy row it forms with NGC 5981 6′ to its west and NGC 5985 7′ to its east. It has a bright 45″ × 30″ ESE–WNW oval halo that contains a bright core with a stellar nucleus.
16/18″ Scopes–150x: NGC 5982 has an intense oval core extended 1′ × 0.75′ ESE–WNW within a very

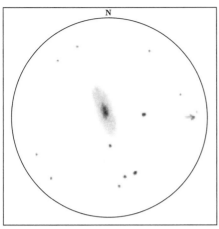

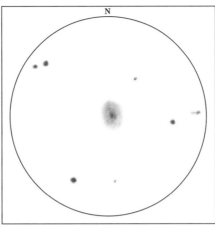

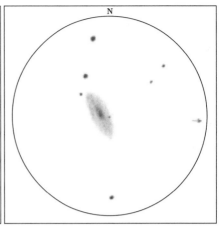

Figure 44-21. NGC 6015
13″, ƒ5.6–165x, by Steve Coe

Figure 44-22. NGC 6236
17.5″, ƒ4.5–250x, by G. R. Kepple

Figure 44-23. NGC 6395
17.5″, ƒ4.5–250x, by G. R. Kepple

faint diffuse outer halo indefinitely elongated 2′ × 1.5′ ESE–WNW. The halo extends to two 13th magnitude stars 1′ ESE and 1′ west of the galaxy core. Beyond and along the line of 13th magnitude stars are two slightly brighter stars near the halos of NGC 5981 and NGC 5985.

NGC 5985 H766² Galaxy Type SAB(r)b I
φ 5.3′ × 2.9′, m11.1v, SB 13.9   15ʰ39.6ᵐ +59° 20′
Finder Chart 44-7, Figure 44-19   ★★★
8/10″ Scopes–100x: NGC 5985 is the easternmost in a galaxy row with NGC 5982 and NGC 5981, 7′ and 13′ to its west, respectively. It has a fairly faint, diffuse 3′ × 1.5′ NNE–SSW halo around an inconspicuous core. The galaxy is enclosed within a triangle of fairly bright stars, a 10th magnitude star 3′ to its north, an 11th magnitude star 3.5′ to its west, and a 10th magnitude star 3′ to its east, the last flanked by 13th magnitude companions. A 9th magnitude star lies 6.5′ NNE of the galaxy.
16/18″ Scopes–150x: In larger telescopes, NGC 5985 shows a 4′ × 2′ NNE–SSW halo with diffuse edges and a mottled interior. The core is a bright 30″ × 20″ oval.

NGC 6015 H739¹ Galaxy Type SA(s)cd II-III
φ 6.4′ × 2.2′, m11.1v, SB 13.8   15ʰ51.4ᵐ +62° 19′
Finder Chart 44-7, Figure 44-21   ★★★
8/10″ Scopes–100x: This bright galaxy, 2.5′ east of an 11th magnitude star, is elongated 3.5′11.5′ NNE–SSW, and smoothly brightens in towards its center.
16/18″ Scopes–150x: In larger telescopes NGC 6015

appears bright, elongated 5.5′ × 2′ NNE–SSW, and broadly and slightly brighter in its core. Several bright spots are SW of the core. A 13.5 magnitude star is superimposed upon the halo 2′ south of the galaxy's center.

NGC 6140 H740³ Galaxy Type SB(s)cd pec
φ 7.3′ × 5.3′, m11.3v, SB 15.1   16ʰ20.9ᵐ +65° 23′
Finder Chart 44-7, Figure 44-20   ★★★
12/14″ Scopes–125x: NGC 6140, located 2.25′ SE of a 9.5 magnitude star, is fairly faint with a circular 3′ diameter halo that moderately brightens in toward its center.
16/18″ Scopes–150x: NGC 6140 has a bright extended 30″ × 10″ NE–SW core embedded in a much fainter, diffuse halo extending 4.5′ × 3.5′ E–W. The galaxy is surrounded by five 14.5 magnitude stars.

NGC 6236 U11218 Galaxy Type SAB(s)cd
φ 2.7′ × 1.7′, m11.9v, SB 13.4   16ʰ44.5ᵐ +70° 48′
Finder Chart 44-8, Figure 44-22   ★★
8/10″ Scopes–100x: NGC 6236, located 3.5′ east of a 9.5 magnitude star, appears faint, elongated 1.5′ × 1′ NNE–SSW, and slightly brighter at its center. A 10th magnitude star lies 3′ SSW, a 10th magnitude star with a 30″ distant magnitude 12.5 companion is 4′ NE.
16/18″ Scopes–150x: NGC 6236 has a fairly faint 2.5′ × 1.25′ NNE–SSW halo that gradually brightens in toward its center. Galaxy NGC 6232 lies 12′ SW.

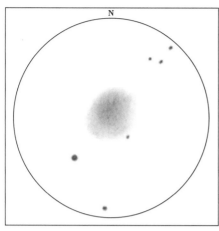

Figure 44-24. NGC 6412
17.5″, f4.5–250x, by G. R. Kepple

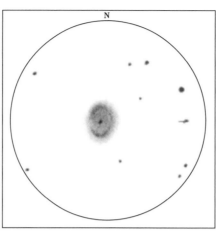

Figure 44-25. NGC 6543
13″, f5.6–165x, by Steve Coe

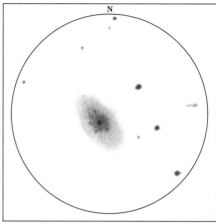

Figure 44-26. NGC 6643
17.5″, f4.5–250x, by G. R. Kepple

NGC 6340 H767² Galaxy Type SA(s)0/a
φ **3.0′ × 2.8′, m11.0v, SB13.2**   17ʰ10.4ᵐ +72° 18′
Finder Chart 44-8   ★★★
8/10″ Scopes–100x: This galaxy lies 2.5′ SE of an 10th
   magnitude star with a magnitude 12.5 companion
   30″ to its WNW. NGC 6340 has a fairly faint, 1.5′
   diameter halo that is suddenly brighter towards its
   center.
16/18″ Scopes–150x: NGC 6340 has a smooth, fairly
   bright, circular 2.5′ diameter halo that contains a
   bright nonstellar nucleus.

NGC 6395 U10876 Galaxy Type Scd:
φ **1.6′ × 0.7′, m12.3v, SB12.3**   17ʰ26.4ᵐ +71° 06′
Finder Chart 44-9, Figure 44-23   ★★
8/10″ Scopes–100x: NGC 6395 is SSW of two 11th
   magnitude stars, the nearest 1.5′ from the galaxy's
   center. It is a faint, diffuse 1.5′ × 0.5′ NNE–SSW
   streak.
16/18″ Scopes–150x: NGC 6395 appears fairly faint,
   elongated 2′ × 0.75′ NNE–SSW, and slightly
   brighter through its center. A 14th magnitude star
   almost touches the halo's edge 1′ NE of the galaxy's
   center.

Figure 44-27. *NGC 6503 has a bright lens-shaped halo that contains a broad, mottled core. Image courtesy of Chris Schur.*

Figure 44-28. *Kohoutek 1-16 is an extremely faint planetary nebula challenging even for large telescopes. Martin C. Germano took this two hour exposure on 2415 film with a 14.5″, f5 Newtonian.*

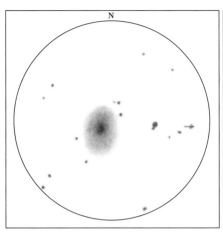

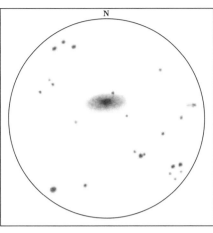

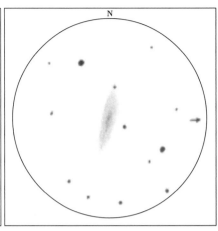

Figure 44-29. NGC 6654
17.5″, f4.5–225x, by G. R. Kepple

Figure 44-30. NGC 6667
18.5″, f5–250x, by Glen W. Sanner

Figure 44-31. NGC 6690
17.5″, f4.5–275x, by G. R. Kepple

NGC 6412 H41⁶ Galaxy Type SA(s)c II
φ **2.1′× 2.1′, m11.8v, SB 13.2**   **17ʰ29.6ᵐ +75° 42′**
Finder Chart 44-8, Figure 44-24   ★★★
8/10″ Scopes–100x: NGC 6412 is 2′ NW of an 11th magnitude star and north of a NNE–SSW row of 9th and 11th magnitude stars. It is a fairly faint, diffuse 1.5′ diameter glow without any central brightening.
16/18″ Scopes–150x: NGC 6412 has a fairly bright, circular 2′ diameter halo of uniform surface brightness. A 14th magnitude star lies 1′ SSW of the galaxy's center.

NGC 6503 U11012 Galaxy Type SA(s)sd III
φ **7.3′× 2.4′, m10.2v, SB 13.2**   **17ʰ49.4ᵐ +70° 09′**
Finder Chart 44-9, Figure 44-27   ★★★★
8/10″ Scopes–100x: NGC 6503, located 4′ west of an 8th magnitude star, has a bright 4′ × 1′ ESE–WNW lens-shaped halo that is slightly brighter along its center.
16/18″ Scopes–150x: NGC 6503 has a bright 5′ × 1.5′ ESE–WNW lenticular halo with a diffuse periphery and a somewhat mottled 2′ × 0.5′ core. An elegant double (14, 15; 10″; 225°) is 2.25′ NNE.

NGC 6543 H37⁴ PK96+29.1 Planetary Neb. Type 3a+2
φ **18/350″, m8.1v, CS 10.9v**   **17ʰ58.6ᵐ +66° 38′**
Finder Chart 44-9, Figure 44-25   ★★★★★
Cat's Eye Nebula
4/6″ Scopes–75x: NGC 6543, located 3′ ESE of an 8th magnitude star, has a bright, small disk with a greenish cat's eye tint.
8/10″ Scopes–100x: The Cat's Eye Nebula is the showpiece object of Draco. It has a bright, small, round greenish disk surrounding the 11th magnitude central star. Averted vision reveals a fainter outer haze

that is more conspicuous on its NE and SW.
16/18″ Scopes–150x: NGC 6543 is a fine, bright bluish-green disk which provides excellent color contrast to the bright, yellowish 10.9 magnitude central star. The inner halo is elongated 20″ × 15″ and surrounded by a faint outer shell that has two helical ribbons visually resembling the arcing arm of spiral galaxies. The central portion is slightly darker around the central star because of a small central "hole" in the nebula itself.

NGC 6643 U11218 Galaxy Type SA(rs)c II
φ **3.7′× 1.8′, m11.1v, SB 13.0**   **18ʰ19.8ᵐ +74° 34′**
Finder Chart 44-8, Figure 44-26   ★★★
8/10″ Scopes–100x: NGC 6643 is at the eastern corner of a small triangle with two 12th magnitude stars 2′ to its west and 1.75′ to its NW. The galaxy has a

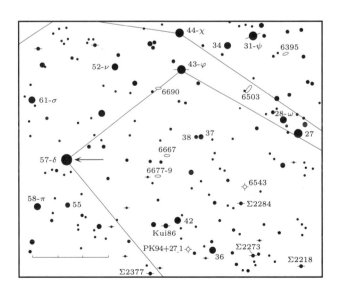

Finder Chart 44-9. 57-δ Dra: 19ʰ12.5ᵐ +67° 40′

Figure 44-32. *NGC 6742 has a faint, but obvious disk of uniform surface brightness. Image courtesy of Bill McLaughlin.*

fairly bright but diffuse 3′ × 1.25′ NE–SW halo.

16/18″ Scopes–150x: NGC 6643 has a moderately bright 3.5′ 11.5′ NE–SW oval halo with a mottled texture and a broad, unconcentrated core that contains a stellar nucleus. A faint knot is on the core's SW edge.

PK 94+27.1 K1-16 Planetary Nebula Type 3
φ 115″, m14.2v, CS 15.09v   18ʰ21.9ᵐ +64° 22′
Finder Chart 44-9, Figure 44-28   ★

16/18″ Scopes–150x: Kohoutek 1-16, located 12′ NE of a 7th magnitude star, is a challenging object even for large instruments. Under the clear, dark western skies of the Texas Star Party, we were able to

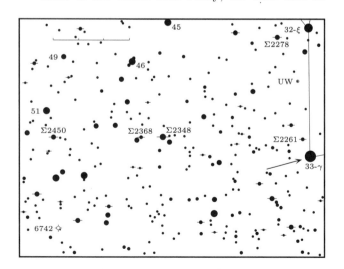

Finder Chart 44-10. 33–γ Dra: 17ʰ56.6ᵐ +51° 29′

glimpse with averted vision an extremely faint, smooth 2′ diameter disk. The 15th magnitude central star was also just visible. Threshold stars lie just beyond the south and east edges; and 13th magnitude stars are 2′ west and 3′ north of the planetary.

NGC 6654 U11238 Galaxy Type (R′)SB(s)0/a
φ 2.8′ × 2.4′, m12.0v, SB 13.9   18ʰ24.1ᵐ +73° 11′
Finder Chart 44-8, Figure 44-29   ★★

12/14″ Scopes–125x: This galaxy lies 2.5′ east of an 11th magnitude star with a faint 14th magnitude companion 6″ SSE. The 1.5′ diameter halo is fairly bright at its center but fades suddenly at the periphery.

16/18″ Scopes–150x: NGC 6654 has a moderately bright nonstellar nucleus surrounded by a faint, fat, oval halo elongated 2.5′ × 1.75′ N–S. Three 14th magnitude stars touch the halo's edge 1′ NW, 1.25′ NNW, and 1.25′ ESE of its center.

NGC 6667 U11269 Galaxy Type SABab? pec
φ 2.9′ × 2.1′, m12.7v, SB 14.5   18ʰ30.7ᵐ +67° 59′
Finder Chart 44-9, Figure 44-30   ★★

12/14″ Scopes–125x: NGC 6667 has a fairly faint 2.5′ × 1′ E–W oval halo around a poorly concentrated oval core. A threshold star touches the halo's edge 30″ NW of the galaxy's center.

NGC 6690 U11300 Galaxy Type Sd? sp
φ 3.8′ × 1.4′, m12.5v, SB 14.1   18ʰ34.8ᵐ +70° 32′
Finder Chart 44-9, Figure 44-31   ★★

12/14″ Scopes–125x: NGC 6690 is midway between a 12th magnitude star 3′ to the NNE and a magnitude 12.5 star 3′ to the SW. It has a fairly bright, highly elongated 3.25′ × 0.75′ NNW–SSE (or more nearly N–S) halo that is slightly brighter along its major axis. A 13th magnitude star is just off the galaxy's west edge 45″ from its center. A 14th magnitude star is near the halo's NNW tip, 1.5′ from the galaxy's center.

NGC 6742 H742³ Abell 50 Planetary Neb. Type 2c
φ 30″, m13.4v, CS 19.4v   18ʰ59.3ᵐ +48° 28′
Finder Chart 44-10, Figure 44-32   ★★

16/18″ Scopes–250x: NGC 6742, located 3.25′ SW of a 9th magnitude star, has a faint, but conspicuous 30″ diameter disk of uniform surface brightness. A threshold star touches the disk's east edge and a 13th magnitude star lies 70″ to its SW. A scattered group of fifteen 11th to 13th magnitude stars is just north of the 9th magnitude star.

Chapter 45

Equuleus, the Colt

45.1 Overview

Equuleus, occupying only 72 square degrees of sky, is the second smallest constellation of the 88. Only the bright-star-rich Crux in the southern Milky Way is smaller. The faint stars of Equuleus form a trapezoid between Delphinus and the nose of Pegasus. Though Equuleus is one of the constellations we have inherited from the Greco-Roman civilization, no ancient myths are associated with it. The reason is that it was one of the last-formed of the ancient constellations, its invention being credited to the great Greek astronomer Hipparchos, discoverer of the precession of the equinoxes, who lived in the mid and late 2nd century B.C. His actual name for it was "The Forepart of a Horse."

Equuleus is as sparse in interesting objects as it is in stars. It contains only a handful of doubles and a few very faint galaxies.

45.2 Interesting Stars

Epsilon (ϵ) = 1 Equulei (Σ2737) Triple Star Spec. F5
ABxC: m6.0, 7.1; Sep.10.7″; P.A.70° 20^{h}59.1^m +04° 18′
Finder Chart 45-2   ★★★★
8/10″ Scopes–200x: At low power the AB primary appears as one pale yellow star. The C companion is blue and therefore a good color contrast to AB. At high power the 0.8″ wide AB pair is oblong. This binary is closing in toward periastron, which will occur in 2021, and therefore will remain difficult for quite some time. Its period is 101 years.

Lambda (λ) = 2 Equulei (Σ2742) Double Star Spec. F8
m7.4, 7.4; Sep.2.8″; P.A.218°   21^{h}02.2^m +07° 11′
Finder Chart 45-2   ★★★★
4/6″ Scopes–150x: Lambda Equulei is a close, equally matched pair of pale yellow stars in a well sprinkled star field.

Equuleus: Ee-KWOO-lee-us
Genitive: Equulei, ee-KWOO-lee-eye
Abbreviation: Equ
Culmination: 9pm–Sept. 22, midnight–Aug. 8
Area: 72 square degrees
Best Deep-Sky Objects: 1–ϵ Equ, 2–λ Equ, 7–δ Equ, NGC 7015

Σ2786 Double Star   Spec. A3
m7.2, 8.3; Sep.2.5″; P.A.185°   21^{h}19.7^m +09° 32′
Finder Chart 45-2   ★★★★
4/6″ Scopes–150x: Struve 2786 is just split at this power. It is a close, elegant pair of white stars.

Σ2793 Double Star   Spec. A2
ABxC: m7.8, 8.5; Sep.26.6″; P.A. 242° 21^{h}25.1^m +09° 23′
Finder Chart 45-2   ★★★★
2/3″ Scopes–75x: Struve 2793 is an easy double for small telescopes. The AB primary is yellow and the C companion bluish. The B component is only 0.4″ from the A component and therefore is unresolved even at high power.

45.3 Deep-Sky Objects

NGC 7015 Galaxy Type Sbc
ϕ 1.6′ × 1.6′, m11.5v, SB13.4   21^{h}05.7^m +11° 25′
Finder Chart 45-2, Figure 45-1   ★★★
12/14″ Scopes–125x: NGC 7015, located 1.75′ east of a 12.5 magnitude star, has a very faint 1′ × 0.75′ E–W halo that slightly brightens in toward its center. A 20″ wide NNW–SSE pair of magnitude 12.5 and 13.5 stars is 2.5′ south.

Equuleus, the Colt

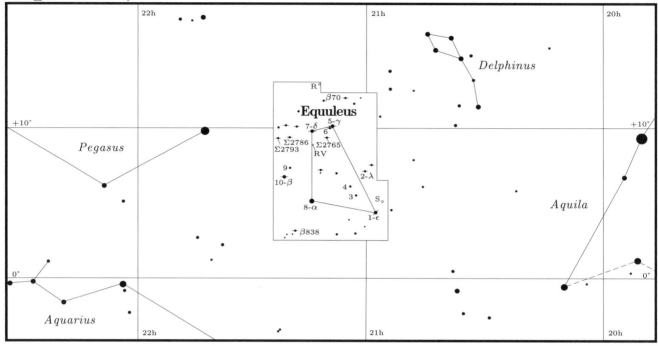

Chart Symbols

Constellation Chart	0 1 2 3 4 5 6
Stellar Magnitudes	● ● ● ● ● • • •
Finder Charts	0/1 2 3 4 5 6 7 8 9
Master Finder Chart	0 1 2 3 4 5

→ Guide Star Pointer   ◉ ○ Variable Stars   ⬦ Planetary Nebulae

●–• Double Stars   ○ Open Clusters   ☐ Small Bright Nebulae

Finder Chart Scale   ⊕ Globular Clusters   Large Bright Nebulae

(One degree tick marks)   ⬭ Galaxies   Dark Nebulae

Table 45-1: Selected Variable Stars in Equuleus

Name	HD No.	Type	Max.	Min.	Period (Days)	F*	Spec. Type	R.A. (2000) Dec.		Finder Chart No.	Notes
S Equ	199454	EA	8.0	10.08	3.44	0.13	B8+F0	20^{h}57.2^m	+05° 05′	45-2	
R Equ	202051	M	8.7	15.0	260	0.44	M3-M4	21^{h}13.2^m	+12 48	45-2	
RV Equ		Isb	9.0	9.7			K0	14.9	+09 00	45-2	

F* = The fraction of period taken up by the star's rise from min. to max. brightness, or the period spent in eclipse.

Table 45-2: Selected Double Stars in Equuleus

Name	ADS No.	Pair	M1	M2	Sep.′	P.A.°	Spec	R.A. (2000) Dec.		Finder Chart No.	Notes
1–ε Equ	14499	AB	6.0	6.3	c0.8	*284	F5	20^{h}59.1^m	+04° 18′	45-2	Pale yellow and blue
	14499	ABxC		7.1	10.7	70					
	14499	AD		12.4	74.8	280					
2–λ Equ	14556		7.4	7.4	2.8	218	F8	21^{h}02.2^m	+07 11	45-2	Matched pale yellow pair
Σ2765	14715		8.4	8.6	2.8	81	A3	11.0	+09 33	45-2	
β 70	14601	AB	7.6	9.8	78.8	239	K0	04.6	+12 01	45-2	
	14601	AC		10.0	75.0	237					
	14601	BC			5.3	96					
7–δ Equ	14773	ABxC	5.2	9.4	47.7	14	F5	14.5	+10 00	45-2	
Σ2786	14856		7.2	8.3	2.5	185	A3	19.7	+09 32	45-2	Elegant white pair
β 838	14880		8.1	10.0	1.6	130	F8	20.9	+03 08	45-2	
β 164	14954	AB	7.8	8.3	0.4	229	A2	25.1	+09 23	45-2	ABxC: yellowish and bluish
Σ2793	14954	AC		8.5	26.6	242					

Footnotes: *= Year 2000, a = Near apogee, c = Closing, w = Widening. Finder Chart No: All stars listed in the tables are plotted in the large Constellation Chart, but when a star appears in a Finder Chart, this number is listed. Notes: When colors are subtle, the suffix *-ish* is used, e.g. *bluish*.

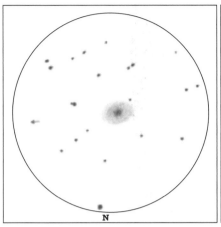

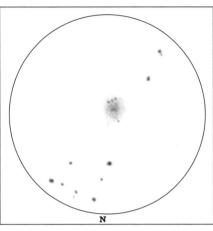

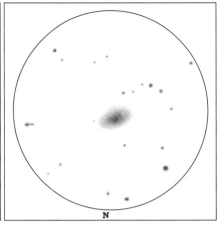

Figure 45-1. NGC 7015
16″, f5–300x, by George de Lange

Figure 45-2. NGC 7040
16″, f5–250x, by George de Lange

Figure 45-3. NGC 7046
16″, f5–125x, by George de Lange

16/18″Scopes–150x: NGC 7015 is a faint 1.5′ × 1.25′ E–W oval containing a moderately concentrated circular core. A 14.5 magnitude star is on the galaxy's SSE edge. The 12.5 magnitude star to the west of the galaxy has a very faint companion (14.5; 5″; 230°). A wider, even fainter pair lies 2′ to the galaxy's SSE.

NGC 7040 Galaxy Type Sb?
φ 1.0′ × 0.7′, m14.1v, SB13.5 **21ʰ13.2ᵐ +08° 51′**
Finder Chart 45-2, Figure 45-2 ★
16/18″Scopes–150x: NGC 7040 is 3′ WNW and 4′ south of 11th magnitude stars. It has a very faint, diffuse 45″ × 30″ N–S halo of smooth surface brightness. A threshold star lies on the galaxy's northern edge; and a row of three threshold stars is on the south edge.

IC 1367 Galaxy Type S?
φ 0.3′ × 0.2′, m15p **21ʰ14.2ᵐ +02° 59′**
Finder Chart 45-2 ★
12/14″Scopes–125x: IC 1367, located 1.75′ NNW of a 10.5 magnitude star, is a very faint, indistinct 15″ diameter smudge. A Y-shaped asterism of five 12.5 to 13th magnitude stars, its stem pointing SW, is 2′ east of the 10.5 magnitude star.

NGC 7046 H858³ Galaxy Type SB(rs)c II-III
φ 1.6′ × 1.4′, m13.1v, SB13.8 **21ʰ14.9ᵐ +02° 50′**
Finder Chart 45-2, Figure 45-3 ★★
12/14″Scopes–125x: NGC 7046, located 3.5′ SW of a 10th magnitude star, is a very faint, diffuse glow about 1′ in diameter and without central brightening.

16/18″Scopes–150x: NGC 7046 has a faint, diffuse 1.5′ × 1′ ESE–WNW halo. A 14th magnitude star is 1.25′ NNE of the galaxy. To the SE is a 2′ long arc, concave to the north, of half a dozen 13th and 14th magnitude stars, the nearest a magnitude 14 object just 1.25′ SSE of the galaxy.

IC 1375 Galaxy Type S?
φ 0.4′ × 0.4′, m15p **21ʰ21.0ᵐ +04° 00′**
Finder Chart 45-2, Figure 45-4 ★
12/14″Scopes–125x: IC1375 lies 5′ south of an 11th magnitude double star with a 13th magnitude companion 20″ NE. A 12th magnitude star 2.75′ north and a 13th magnitude star 2′ NNE form a

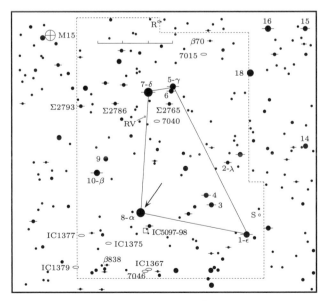

Finder Chart 45-2. 8–α Equ: 21ʰ15.8ᵐ +05° 15′
Guide star indicated by arrow.

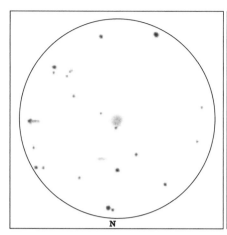

Figure 45-4. IC 1375
16", f5–250x, by G. R. Kepple

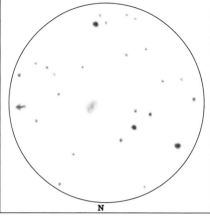

Figure 45-5. IC 1377
16", f5–250x, by Glen W. Sanner

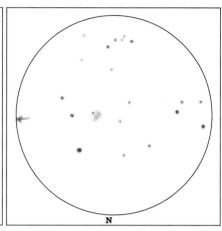

Figure 45-6. IC 1379
16", f5–250x, by G. R. Kepple

triangle with the galaxy. IC 1375 is a very faint 30″ diameter glow without central brightening. A threshold star touches the galaxy's north edge. 2′ to the NNW is an extremely faint companion galaxy that with averted vision can be seen to be elongated 20″ × 5″ E–W.

IC 1377 Galaxy Type Sc
φ 0.6′ × 0.4′, m14p   21^{h}25.4^m +04° 19′
Finder Chart 45-2, Figure 45-5   ★
12/14″ Scopes–125x: IC 1377, located 5′ SW of a 10.5 magnitude star, is a very faint, small, round 30″

diameter haze. An 11th magnitude star lies 4.25′ south, and a 12th magnitude star 2.25′ NE.

IC 1379 Galaxy Type S?
φ 0.7′ × 0.4′, m15.7p   21^{h}26.0^m +03° 06′
Finder Chart 45-2, Figure 45-6   ★
16/18″ Scopes–150x: IC 1379 is a very dim circular 15″ diameter smudge 1.75′ SSE of a 12th magnitude star. A threshold star touches the galaxy's NW edge, and 13th magnitude stars are 1′ to its WSW and 1.75′ to its SW.

Chapter 46

Hercules, the Strongman

46.1 Overview

The demigod Hercules was the issue of an illicit union between the great Zeus himself and a mortal, Alcmene, whom he seduced by coming to her in the guise of her husband Amphytrion. However, the super-human strength of the young Hercules aroused the suspicions of the jealous Hera, Zeus' wife – who often enough had good reason to be suspicious. She therefore resolved to make Hercules' life miserable. (The special, though maligned, relationship between the hero and Hera is expressed in the Greek form of Hercules' name: Heracles.) First she sent two snakes to attack Hercules; but he merely wrung their necks. Later she cast him under a spell of madness. During his seizure he committed the crime for which he was condemned to the service of King Eurytheos, who ordered Hercules to perform the Twelve Labors.

The connection between the Twelve Labors of Hercules and the twelve constellations of the zodiac, of which so much is made in misguided discussions on the history of the constellations, was an afterthought of ancient mythology; both traditions had developed independently. Indeed, the identification of the demigod Hercules with the star-pattern was also an afterthought of ancient mythology: before the second century A.D. this constellation had been called simply "The Kneeler," and Aratos, a Greek writer of the 3rd century B.C., says of the Kneeler "Of it can no one clearly speak, nor to what toil he is attached." The early Greeks had inherited a celestial Kneeler from the Babylonians; but the figure's real name (Ninurta, the war god) and all the associated mythology had been lost en route. (The oft repeated identification of Hercules, both as a constellation and as a mythological hero, with the Babylonian hero Gilgamesh, is also an error and has absolutely no support in ancient texts or art.)

Hercules, covering an impressive 1,225 square degrees, is the fifth largest of the 88 constellations. Though its constellation-pattern is quite distinctive, it has no really bright stars. Its most conspicuous asterism is the famous Keystone, Epsilon (ϵ), Zeta (ζ), Eta (η), and Pi (π) Herculis. On the western side of the Keystone,

Hercules: HER-cue-leez **Genitive:** Herculis, HER-cue-lis **Abbreviation:** Her **Culmination:** 9pm–July 28, midnight–June 13 **Area:** 1,225 square degrees **Showpieces:** 64–α Her, 65–δ Her, 75–ϱ Her, M13 (NGC 6205), M92 (NGC 6341) **Binocular Objects:** DoDz 9, M13 (NGC 6205), M92 (NGC 6341)

about two-thirds of the way from Zeta to Eta Herculis, is the constellation's finest object, the Great Hercules Globular Cluster Messier 13, the brightest globular in the northern celestial hemisphere. Hercules contains a second outstanding globular, M92, often neglected because it is far from any bright guide star. The constellation also has a large number of colorful double stars, the lovely bluish-green planetary nebula NGC 6210, and numerous galaxies, many of which are members of the remote Hercules Galaxy Cluster.

46.2 Interesting Stars

Kappa (κ) = 7 Herculis (Σ 2010) Triple Star Spec. G5, G5
AB: m5.3, 6.5; Sep. 28.4″; P.A. 12°   16^{h}08.1^m +17° 03′
Finder Chart 46-3   ★★★★
2/3″ Scopes–75x: Kappa Herculis is a fine double of
   yellow stars easily separated by small telescopes. A
   magnitude 13.6 companion lies 63″ SSW of the
   bright pair.

Gamma (γ) = 20 Herculis (S,h227) Triple Star Spec. F0
AB: m3.8, 9.8; Sep. 41.6″; P.A. 233°   16^{h}21.9^m +19° 09′
Finder Chart 46-3   ★★★★
2/3″ Scopes–50x: Gamma Herculis is an unequally
   bright pair of yellow stars easily separated by small
   telescopes at low power. A 12th magnitude companion lies 85″ distant in position angle 298°.

Hercules, the Strongman

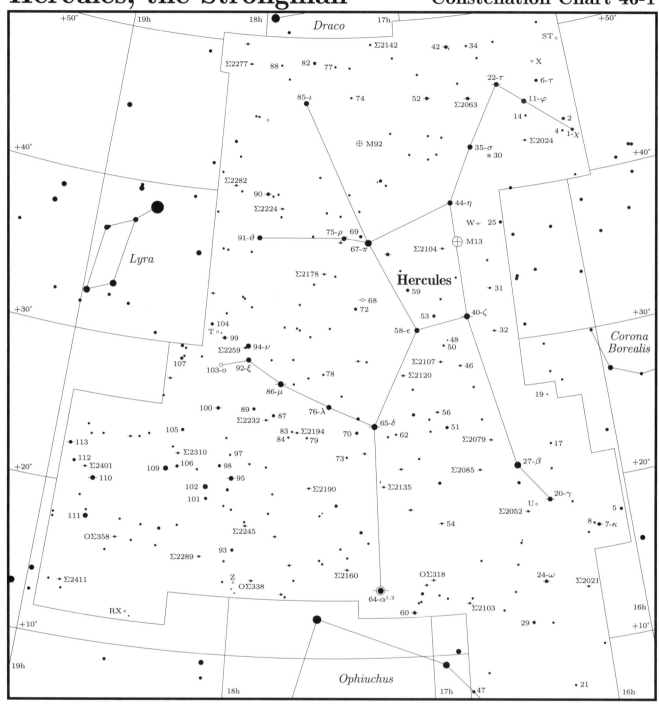

Draco

Lyra

Hercules

Corona Borealis

Ophiuchus

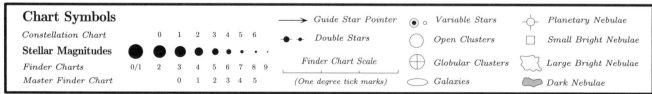

Chart Symbols

Constellation Chart		0	1	2	3 4 5 6		

Stellar Magnitudes

Finder Charts   0/1   2   3   4   5 6 7 8 9

Master Finder Chart   0   1   2 3 4 5

→ Guide Star Pointer

●–● Double Stars

Finder Chart Scale

(One degree tick marks)

◉ ○ Variable Stars

○ Open Clusters

⊕ Globular Clusters

⬭ Galaxies

⊕ Planetary Nebulae

☐ Small Bright Nebulae

Large Bright Nebulae

Dark Nebulae

Table 46-1: Selected Variable Stars in Hercules

Name	HD No.	Type	Max.	Min.	Period (Days)	F*	Spec. Type	R.A. (2000) Dec.		Finder Chart No.	Notes
X Her	144205	Srb	7.5	8.6	95	0.50	M6	16^{h}02.7^m	+47° 14′	46-1	
U Her	148206	M	6.5	13.4	406	0.40	M7	25.8	+18 54	46-3	
30 Her	148783	SRb	5.7	7.2	70		M6	28.6	+41 53	46-4	
64–α^{1,2} Her	156014	SRc	3.1	3.9			M5	17^{h}14.6^m	+14 23	46-9	Ras Algethi
68 Her	156633	EB	4.6	5.3	2.05		B1-B5	17.3	+33 06	46-6	U Herculis
Z Her	163930	EA/RS	7.3	8.1	3.99	0.11	F4-K0	58.1	+15 08	46-11	
T Her	166382	M	6.8	13.9	165	0.47	M2-M8	18^{h}09.1^m	+31 01	46-10	
RX Her	170757	EA	7.2	7.8	1.77	0.14	A0-A0	30.7	+12 37	46-1	

F* = The fraction of period taken up by the star's rise from min. to max. brightness, or the period spent in eclipse.

Table 46-2: Selected Double Stars in Hercules

Name	ADS No.	Pair	M1	M2	Sep.′	P.A.°	Spec	R.A. (2000) Dec.		Finder Chart No.	Notes
7–κ Her	9933	AB	5.3	6.5	28.4	12	G5 G5	16^{h}08.1^m	+17° 03	46-3	Fine yellow pair
Σ2024	9962		5.9	9.6	23.6	44	K5	11.8	+42 22	46-4	
Σ2021	9969	AB	7.4	7.5	4.1	348	K5	13.3	+13 32	46-5	
20–γ Her	10022	AB	3.8	9.8	41.6	233	F0	21.9	+19 09	46-3	Yellow and purple
		BC		12.2	84.7	298					
Σ2052	10075		7.7	7.8	w2.0	*124	K0	28.9	+18 25	46-3	
Σ2063	10105		5.7	8.2	16.4	195	A0	31.8	+45 36	46-7	White and yellow
W Her	10121		7.3	Var	6.4	331	M	35.2	+37 21	46-4	B: 7.6 to 14.4 in 280 days
42 Her	10144		5.1	11.8	25.6	92	M	38.7	+48 56	46-7	
Σ2079	10146		7.4	8.2	16.8	91	F0	39.6	+23 00	46-3	
40–ζ Her	10157		2.9	5.5	1.6	70	G0	41.3	+31 36	46-6	Yellow and greenish
Σ2085	10167		7.3	8.8	6.1	309	A0	42.4	+21 36	46-3	
46 Her	10194		7.3	9.3	5.1	162	F5	45.1	+28 21	46-1	
Σ2104	10224		7.3	9.1	5.8	19	F2	48.7	+35 55	46-6	
Σ2103	10225	AB	6.0	10.8	5.7	43	A0	49.6	+13 16	46-5	
Σ2107	10235	AB	6.8	8.2	w1.4	*98	F5	51.8	+28 40	46-1	Yellow pair
56 Her	10259		6.1	10.6	18.1	93	K0	55.0	+25 44	46-1	Pretty orange and blue pair
OΣ318	10270		7.0	9.6	2.7	247	K0	56.7	+14 08	46-5	
Σ2120	10332	AB	7.3	10.1	16.3	234	K0	17^{h}04.8^m	+28 05	46-1	Orange and bluish
Σ2142	10397		6.0	9.8	5.2	114	A2	11.7	+49 45	46-7	
Σ2135	10394		7.4	8.7	8.0	188	K0	12.1	+21 14	46-8	
64–α^{1,2} Her	10418	AB	3.5	5.4	4.7	107	M	14.6	+14 23	46-9	Orange and bluish-green
65–δ Her	10424	AB	3.1	8.2	8.9	236	A2	15.0	+24 50	46-8	White and bluish-purple
68–U Her	10449		4.8	10.2	4.4	60	B3	17.3	+33 06	46-6	
75–ρ Her	10526	AB	4.6	5.6	4.1	316	A0	23.7	+37 09	46-6	Yellowish-white pair
Σ2160	10528		6.2	10.7	3.9	66	B9	24.6	+15 36	46-9	
Σ2178	10594		7.5	9.1	10.7	130	K0	29.5	+34 56	46-1	
Σ2190	10655		5.8	9.3	10.3	23	A2	36.0	+21 00	46-8	
Σ2194	10715		6.6	8.9	16.3	8	K0	41.1	+24 31	46-8	
Σ2224	10782		6.7	9.9	7.6	350	K0	46.0	+39 19	46-1	
86–μ Her	10786	AB	3.4	10.1	33.8	247	G5	46.5	+27 43	46-1	Yellow and reddish
Σ2232	10827		6.8	8.3	6.4	141	A2	50.2	+25 17	46-8	
OΣ338	10850	AB	6.8	7.1	0.7	357	K0	52.0	+15 20	46-11	
90 Her	10875		5.2	8.5	1.6	116	K0	53.0	+40 00	46-1	Orange and white
Σ2245	10905		7.4	7.4	2.6	293	A2	56.4	+18 20	46-1	White pair
Σ2259	10955		7.3	8.3	19.6	278	A0	59.1	+30 03	46-10	
95 Her	10993		5.0	5.1	6.3	258	A3 G5	18^{h}01.5^m	+21 36	46-8	White and yellow
Σ2277	11028	AB	6.4	8.3	26.8	125	A0	03.1	+48 28	46-1	
Σ2282	11074		7.4	8.4	2.5	86	A0	06.5	+40 22	46-1	
100 Her	11089		5.9	6.0	14.2	183	A3 A3	07.8	+26 06	46-10	White pair
Σ2289	11123		6.5	7.2	1.2	224	F2	10.1	+16 29	46-11	Deep and pale yellow
Σ2310	11273		6.8	10.1	5.1	236	B9	20.6	+22 48	46-1	
OΣ358	11483		6.8	7.0	1.3	147	F0	35.9	+16 59	46-1	Yellow pair
Σ2401	11715	AB	7.1	8.7	4.3	38	B5	49.0	+21 10	46-1	
Σ2411	11773		6.6	9.4	13.5	95	K0	52.3	+14 32	46-1	Orange and ashy

Footnotes: *= Year 2000, a = Near apogee, c = Closing, w = Widening. Finder Chart No: All stars listed in the tables are plotted in the large Constellation Chart, but when a star appears in a Finder Chart, this number is listed. Notes: When colors are subtle, the suffix -ish is used, e.g. *blueish*.

Figure 46-1. *Abell 2151, the Hercules Cluster, is a remote group of galaxies located 700 million light years distant. Its brightest members are only magnitude 13.5 objects and therefore are challenging even for large amateur instruments. This photo along with Table 46-3 and Chart 46-3a helps identify the objects. Image courtesy of Jim Burnell.*

56 Herculis = Σ2110 Double Star   **Spec. K0**
m6.1, 10.6; Sep. 18.1″; P.A. 93°   16ʰ55.0ᵐ +25° 44′
Constellation Chart 46-1   ★★★★
2/3″ Scopes–75x: 56 Herculis is a beautiful color-contrast double of orange and blue stars.

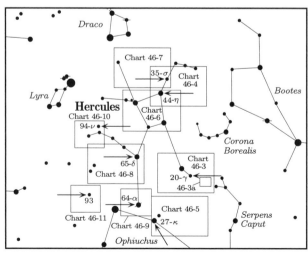

Master Finder Chart 46-2. Hercules Chart Areas
Guide stars indicated by arrows.

Alpha (α) = 64 Herculis (Σ2140) Double and Variable Star
Spec. M5 II, G5 IV+F2
AB: m3.5, 5.4; Sep. 4.7″; P.A. 107°   17ʰ14.6ᵐ +14° 23′
Finder Chart 46-9   ★★★★★
Ras Algethi

4/6″ Scopes–125x: Alpha Herculis is a beautiful double of an orange primary with a greenish secondary. The primary is a semi-regular M-type variable with a magnitude range of 3.1 to 3.9 and a period that very roughly averages 90 days. The secondary is a spectroscopic binary. To follow the light variation of Alpha Herculis compare it to Iota (ι) and Kappa (κ) Ophiuchi, which lie about 6.5° to its SW and have magnitudes of 4.3 and 3.2, respectively. Alpha Herculis is some 410 light-years away; the M giant therefore has a maximum absolute magnitude of −2.4, a luminosity of 760 suns.

Delta (δ) = 65 Herculis Multiple Star   Spec. A2
AB: m3.1, 8.2; Sep. 8.9″; P.A. 236°   17ʰ15.0ᵐ +24° 50′
Finder Chart 46-8   ★★★★★
2/3″ Scopes–50x: Delta Herculis AB is a fine double of a brilliant white primary with a bluish-purple companion.

Rho (ϱ) = 75 Herculis (Σ2161) Triple Star Spec.A0
AB:m4.6, 5.6; Sep.4.1″; P.A.316° 17h23.7m +37° 09′
Finder Chart 46-6 ★★★★★
2/3″Scopes–125x: Rho Herculis AB are a fine
white pair.

Mu (μ) = 86 Herculis (Σ2220) Quad. Star Spec. G5
AB:m3.4, 10.1; Sep.33.8″; P.A.247° 17^{h}46.5^m +27° 43′
Constellation Chart 46-1 ★★★★
8/10″Scopes–200x: Mu Herculis has a bright
yellow primary. The secondary is a 1″ wide
pair of faint red dwarfs. A fourth companion
lies 256″ distant to the north.

100 Herculis = Σ2280 Double StarSpec. A3, A3
m5.9, 6.0; Sep.14.2″; P.A.183° 18^{h}07.8^m +26° 06′
Finder Chart 46-10 ★★★★
2/3″Scopes–75x: 100 Herculis is an attractive pair of
virtually equally bright white stars easily separated
by small telescopes.

46.3 Deep-Sky Objects

Abell 2151 Hercules Galaxy Cluster
NGC 6042 Galaxy Type SA0− (Brightest of group)
ϕ 0.7′ × 0.7′, m13.9v, SB13.0 16^{h}04.6^m +17° 42′
Finder Chart 46-3a, Figures 46-1, 46-2 ★

Abell 2151, the Hercules Galaxy Cluster, is one of
the four groups which together comprise the huge
Hercules Supercluster. This vast aggregation of galaxies
is extremely remote; hence its members, though many
are intrinsically extremely luminous, are no brighter
than magnitude 13.5. Assuming a Hubble Constant of
50 kilometers per second recessional velocity for every
million parsecs (3.26 million light years) of distance, the

Table 46-3: Brighter Galaxies in Abell 2151

Name	Type	Size	Mag.	S.B.	R.A. (2000)	Dec.
6040	SAB(s)c	1.3′ × 0.5′	14.2	13.6	16^{h}04.4^m	+17° 45′
6041	SB0°	1.4′ × 1.4′	13.3	13.9	1604.6	+17 43
6042	SA0−	0.7′ × 0.7′	13.9	13.0	1604.6	+17 42
6043	SAB0−	0.5′ × 0.2′	14.3	11.6	1604.9	+17 47
6044	SA0°	0.5′ × 0.5′	14.2	12.6	1605.0	+17 52
6045	SB(s)c	1.0′ × 0.2′	13.9	12.0	1605.1	+17 45
6047	E+	1.0′ × 1.0′	13.5	13.4	1605.1	+17 43
6050	SA(s)c	0.9′ × 0.6′	14.7	13.9	1605.4	+17 46
6054	(R′)SAB(s)b	1.0′ × 1.0′	13.5	13.4	1605.4	+17 47
IC1178	S0−pec	1.1′ × 0.7′	14.1	13.7	1605.5	+17 35
IC1181	SAB(rs)0/a	1.0′ × 0.7′	14.8	14.3	1605.5	+17 35
IC1182	SA0+pec	1.5′ × 0.5′	14.2	13.7	1605.6	+17 49
IC1183	SAB0−	0.5′ × 0.5′	14.2	12.6	1605.6	+17 47
IC1185	SA(rs)ab:	0.8′ × 0.5′	13.9	12.7	1605.7	+17 43

red shift of the Hercules Supercluster galaxies implies
that they average around 700 million light years away.
At this distance a 7mm eyepiece with a 15′ apparent
field spans an actual field width of 3 million light-years
greater than the distance between the Milky Way and
the Great Andromeda Spiral M31! The observations
reported below were made with an 18.5″ *f*5 Newtonian
on a Dobsonian mount. The conditions on the observing
night were not pristine, but very good for western
Pennsylvania. Seeing was 7 on a scale of 10, and the
faintest star visible to the naked eye was magnitude
5.75. Elevation of the observing site was 1,200 feet above
sea level.

16/18″ Scopes–150x: NGC 6041A-B, located toward the
west edge of the Abell 2151 galaxy cluster 10′ SE
of a 7th magnitude star, is a double galaxy seen as
one 1′ × 0.5′ NE–SW halo with a slightly brighter
center. To its SSE is a 2′ wide pair of 10th magnitude
stars. Only 2.75′ NW of NGC 6041A-B is another
double galaxy, NGC 6040A-B, which also appears
as one 1′ × 0.5′ NE-SW halo with (using averted
vision) a slightly brighter center. Just 1.5′ SE of

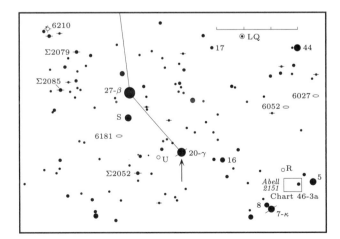

Finder Chart 46-3. 20–γ Her: 16^{h}21.9^m +19° 09′

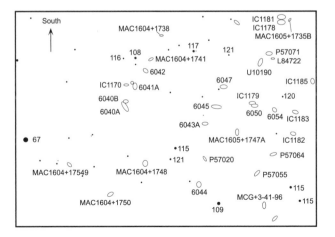

Finder Chart 46-3a. Enlarged area of Abell 2151

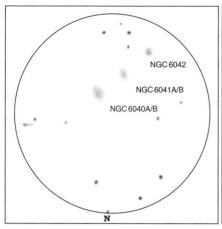
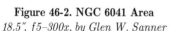

Figure 46-2. NGC 6041 Area
18.5″, f5–300x, by Glen W. Sanner

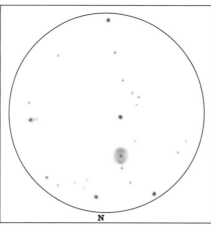

Figure 46-3. NGC 6058
17.5″, f4.5–150x, by G. R. Kepple

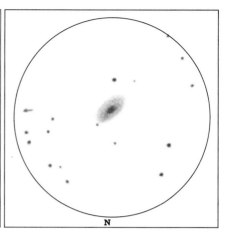

Figure 46-4. NGC 6106
17.5″, f4.5–150x, by G. R. Kepple

6041A-B is NGC 6042, a round, 30″ diameter halo without any central brightening. Many more of the very faint Abell 2151 galaxies were identified with Jim Burnell's photograph of the cluster (Figure 46-1) and averted vision.

NGC 6052 Galaxy Type Sc
ϕ 0.7′ × 0.5′, m13.0v, SB11.7   **16^{h}05.2^m +20° 32′**
Finder Chart 46-3   ★★

12/14″Scopes–125x: NGC 6502 is midway between a magnitude 11.5 star 2.5′ to its NNW and a magnitude 12.5 star 2.5′ to its SSE. The galaxy has a faint, circular 45″ diameter halo that contains a faint stellar nucleus.

16/18″Scopes–150x: NGC 6052 has a starlike nucleus embedded in a faint outer glow elongated 1′ × 0.75′ N–S. A 14th magnitude star lies just beyond the halo's west edge.

NGC 6058 PK64+48.1 Planetary Nebula Type3+2
ϕ >23″, m12.9v, CS13.6   **16^{h}04.4^m +40° 41′**
Finder Chart 46-4, Figure 46-3   ★★★

8/10″Scopes–150x: This faint planetary nebula has a 15″ diameter disk with a faint central star. Two 9.5 magnitude stars 6′ NE and 5′ NW, and a 10th magnitude star 3.5′ south, form a large triangle with the nebula near its center.

12/14″Scopes–200x: The conspicuous 13.6 magnitude central star is surrounded by a fairly faint 20″ diameter disk slightly elongated N–S.

16/18″Scopes–250x: NGC 6058 has a ghostly-white 25″ diameter disk which seems slightly elongated N–S and brighter along its north and south edges. The central star is faint but conspicuous. A 13th magnitude star lies 3′ ESE of the planetary, and a threshold star is 30″ north of the nebula's center.

IC 4593 PK25+40.1 Planetary Neb. Type2+2
ϕ >12″, m10.7v, CS11.13v   **16^{h}12.2^m +12° 04′**
Finder Chart 46-5   ★★★

8/10″Scopes–150x: This planetary nebula is 9′ north of an 8.5 magnitude double with a 9.5 magnitude companion 7″ SSE. The 10″ diameter disk is fairly faint but has a distinct bluish color and a well concentrated center. To the east of the planetary is a long NNW–SSE star chain.

12/14″Scopes–200x: IC4593 has a small, moderately faint, slightly oval 12″ × 10″ N–S bluish disk around a prominent central star. The nebula's center is sharply concentrated but fades rapidly to a diffuse periphery.

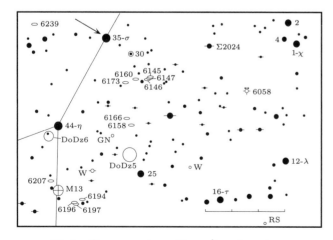

Finder Chart 46-4. 35–σ Her: 16^{h}42.8^m +38° 55′

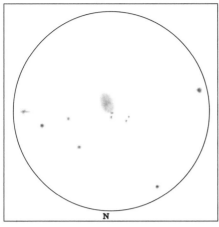

Figure 46-5. NGC 6160
18.5″, f5–300x, by Glen W. Sanner

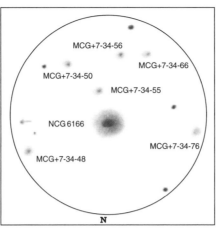

Figure 46-6. Abell 2199 Central Area
17.5″, f4.5–300x, by G. R. Kepple

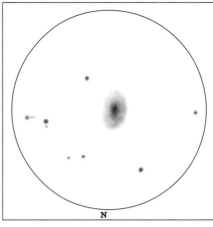

Figure 46-7. NGC 6181
17.5″, f4.5–300x, by G. R. Kepple

NGC 6106 H151² Galaxy Type SA(s)c II-III

ϕ 2.3′ × 1.2′, m12.2v, SB13.2   16ʰ18.8ᵐ +07° 25′

Finder Chart 46-5, Figure 46-4   ★★★

12/14″Scopes–125x: NGC 6106, located 9′ NNE of a 7.5 magnitude star, appears moderately faint, is elongated 1.5′ × 0.75′ NNW–SSE, and contains a broad oval core. A 13th magnitude star lies 1′ south. A 2′ long isosceles triangle of 13th magnitude stars points toward the galaxy from the WNW.

16/18″Scopes–150x: NGC 6106 has a fairly conspicuous 2′ × 1′ NNW–SSE halo containing a large moderately faint core with a faint stellar nucleus. A threshold star is at the halo's NNW tip.

NGC 6146 H638³ Galaxy Type E?

ϕ 1.3′ × 1.0′, m12.5v, SB12.7   16ʰ25.2ᵐ +40° 53′

Finder Chart 46-4   ★★

16/18″Scopes–150x: NGC 6146, located 12′ west of a 7th magnitude star, has a moderately faint 1′ × 0.75′ ENE–WSW halo that contains a small circular core with a faint stellar nucleus. A 12.5 magnitude star lies 1′ east. The two galaxies NGC 6147 and NGC 6145, respectively 1.5′ and 3.5′ NW of NGC 6146, require averted vision to be seen as two indistinct hazy patches.

DoDz5 Open Cluster Tr Type III1p

ϕ 27′, m –   16ʰ27.4ᵐ +38° 04′

Finder Chart 46-4   ★★

12/14″Scopes–75x: DoDz5 is a large, fairly bright, loosely scattered group. Its most conspicuous feature is an irregular ENE–WSW "S" of six 10th to 12th magnitude stars. Three magnitude 9.5 stars are on the NNE edge of the cluster. Another half dozen stars

are scattered about. Two 8th magnitude field stars are 20′ west and 20′ SW of the cluster center.

NGC 6158 H647² Galaxy Type E?

ϕ –, m13.7v, SB–   16ʰ27.7ᵐ +39° 23′

Finder Chart 46-4   ★★

16/18″Scopes–150x: NGC 6158 is located 12′ north of a 9.5 magnitude star in a "Y" with a magnitude 13.5 star to its east and a N–S pair of 12th magnitude stars. The galaxy is a faint, diffuse 30″ diameter glow with a faint stellar nucleus.

NGC 6160 Galaxy Type E

ϕ 1.8′ × 1.5′, m13.2v, SB14.1   16ʰ27.7ᵐ +40° 55′

Finder Chart 46-4, Figure 46-5   ★

NGC 6160 is a member of Abell 2197, one of the constituent galaxy groups of the Hercules Supercluster. Abell 2197, 25° north of the Abell 2151 core of the Supercluster, has over 30 members. If Abell 2197 is 500

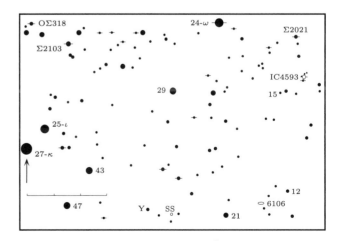

Finder Chart 46-5. 27–κ Oph: 16ʰ57.7ᵐ +09° 23′

million light years distant, which is probably an under-estimation, NGC 6160 has an absolute magnitude of nearly −23, a luminosity of 130 billion suns, and a true diameter of 260,000 light years.

16/18″Scopes–150x: In this size telescope NGC 6160 is a faint but conspicuous diffuse 45″×30″ NE–SW oval around a faint core. Centered 2.5′ NW of the galaxy is a 2′×1.5′ triangle of one 12th and two 13th magnitude stars. Two magnitude 13.5 stars touch the halo's NNE tip; 1.5′ ENE is a second magnitude 13.5 star pair. NGC 6160 is in a 2° long E–W chain of faint galaxies.

NGC 6166 H875[2] Galaxy Type E+2 pec
ϕ **2.2′ × 1.7′, m11.8v, SB 13.1**   **16^{h}28.6^m +39° 33′**
Finder Chart 46-4, Figure 46-6   ★★★

NGC 6166 is the brightest member of Abell 2199, another galaxy group in the extensive Hercules Super-cluster. It is 1.5° south of the Abell 2197 galaxy group. Abell 2199 has over 40 members. NGC 6166 is an even larger and brighter supergiant elliptical system than the impressive NGC 6160 in Abell 2197: its absolute magnitude must exceed −24, a luminosity of 330 billion suns, and its true diameter is at least 310,000 light years.

12/14″Scopes–125x: NGC 6166 has a fairly faint 1.25′ × 1′ NE–SW halo containing a very faint core. Averted vision reveals some very faint companion galaxies in the vicinity.

16/18″Scopes–150x: NGC 6166, located at the center of the Abell 2199 galaxy cluster, has a fairly conspicuous 2′ × 1.5′ NE–SW halo containing a faint core. At least five extremely faint companions are nearby, visible as fuzzy "stars" that require averted vision to be seen: 3′ NW is MCG+7-34-48; a mere 2′ SW is MCG+7-34-50; 2.5′ SE is MCG+7-34-66; and 1.25′ SSW is MCG+7-34-55 and 3′ south is NCG +7-34-56.

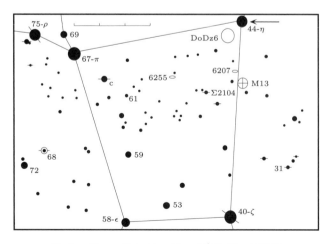

Finder Chart 46-6. 44–η Her: 16^{h}42.8^m +38° 55′

NGC 6173 H640[3] Galaxy Type E
ϕ **1.9′ × 1.4′, m12.1v, SB 13.0**   **16^{h}29.8^m +40° 49′**
Finder Chart 46-4   ★★★

16/18″Scopes–150x: NGC 6173, located 9′ NW of an 8th magnitude star, has a faint, diffuse 1′ × 0.75′ NW–SE halo containing a poor central concentration. Its companion galaxy NGC 6174 is an extremely faint hazy spot lying due north.

NGC 6181 H753[2] Galaxy Type SAB(rs)c I-II
ϕ **2.3′ × 0.9′, m11.9v, SB 12.5**   **16^{h}32.3^m +19° 50′**
Finder Chart 46-3, Figure 46-7   ★★★

8/10″Scopes–100x: This conspicuous galaxy forms a triangle with an 11th magnitude star 2.75′ to its west and a 12th magnitude star 3′ to its NNE. The halo is fairly bright, elongated 1.5′ × 1′ N–S, and contains a well concentrated core.

16/18″Scopes–150x: NGC 6181 has a moderately bright, irregular 2′ × 1′ N–S halo containing a 45″ × 30″ NNW–SSE oval core with a mottled texture and a faint stellar nucleus. A 13th magnitude star lies 1.5′ SSW.

NGC 6194 Galaxy Type –
ϕ **0.6′ × 0.5′, m13.6v, SB 12.1**   **16^{h}36.6^m +36° 11′**
Finder Chart 46-4   ★★

16/18″Scopes–150x: NGC 6194 is a degree east of Messier 13 and 9′ north of a 7th magnitude star. It is similar in appearance to NGC 6196 but slightly fainter and smaller, with a 30″ diameter halo containing a stellar nucleus.

NGC 6196 Galaxy Type SAB0–: pec
ϕ **1.4′ × 1.0′, m12.9v, SB 13.1**   **16^{h}37.9^m +36° 04′**
Finder Chart 46-4   ★★

12/14″Scopes–125x: NGC 6196 is nearly 1° WSW of Messier 13 and 15′ east of a 7th magnitude star. It has a prominent stellar nucleus embedded in a faint 45″ × 30″ N–S halo. 1′ to its south and SSE are magnitude 14.5 stars. 5′ SSE of NGC 6196 and 1′ NW of a 13th magnitude star is the galaxy NGC 6197, a tiny, faint smudge containing a faint stellar nucleus. Also in the neighborhood of NGC 6196, located 3′ to its NNW, is the galaxy IC 4614, a very small, extremely faint undistinguished glow.

NGC 6205 Messier 13 Globular Cluster Class V
ϕ **16.6′, m5.7v**   **16^{h}41.7^m +36° 28′**
Finder Chart 46-6, Figure 46-8   ★★★★★
Great Hercules Cluster

Messier 13 was discovered in 1714 by Edmond Halley who noticed it as a naked eye object when, as he

Figure 46-8. *Messier 13 (NGC6205), the Great Hercules Cluster, is one of the finest globular clusters in the northern hemisphere. Image courtesy of Martin C. Germano.*

expressed it, "the sky was serene and the Moon absent." It is generally considered to be the finest globular cluster in the northern celestial hemisphere. One of the reasons M13 is so large and so bright and so well resolved even in small telescopes is that it is relatively near to us, about 21,000 light years distant. The globular also looks bright and large because it *is* bright and large intrinsically: M13 has an absolute magnitude of −8.7, which corresponds to a luminosity of a quarter million suns, and a true diameter of over 140 light years, both values above average for a globular cluster. It must contain several hundred thousand stars. In the globular's center the density is probably several stars per cubic light year, some 500 times that of the Sun's vicinity. The probability of collisions between stars even in such a "crowded" milieu is negligible; but if we were on a planet orbiting a star near the center of a globular cluster, our sky would be ablaze with stars as bright as Sirius.

4/6″Scopes–75x: Messier 13, visible to the naked eye under dark skies, is a splendid object in small telescopes. It appears quite bright, large, round, and rich, and has a large, bright core. The cluster resolves nicely even across the core, in which starless gaps are mingled with rich regions. The periphery has irregular extensions.

8/10″Scopes–100x: This bright, magnificent globular cluster is a glittering sphere of stars with a dense 7′ diameter core embedded in a thinner, irregular halo spanning 12′. The periphery displays streamers in all directions except the NE. Most of them arc from the ESE edge toward the south and SW. At 150x hundreds of stars can be resolved right into the densest part of the core, where they twinkle in and out of resolution. The southern and western edges have an abundance of short star chains.

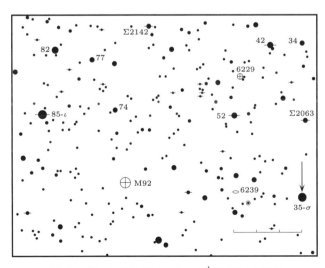

Finder Chart 46-7. 35–σ Her: $16^h34.1^m$ +42° 26′

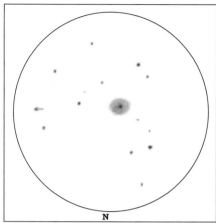

Figure 46-9. NGC 6210
17.5″, f4.5–300x, by G. R. Kepple

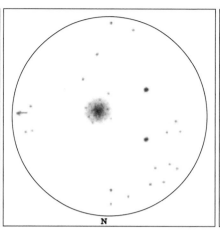

Figure 46-10. NGC 6229
17.5″, f4.5–300x, by G. R. Kepple

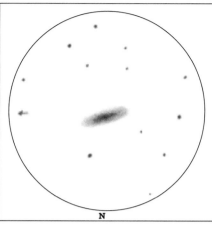

Figure 46-11. NGC 6239
17.5″, f4.5–300x, by G. R. Kepple

12/14″ Scopes–125x: This cluster is breath-taking in medium and large instruments! It has a bright, dense 5′ diameter core that resolves into hundreds of stars. Three relatively starless lanes divide the cluster into three unequal sections that resemble the blades of a propeller. The most conspicuous lane is a dark wedge cutting into the cluster from the SE. The other two lanes intrude from the NE and NW. These dark lanes are more striking in a telescope than in any photograph, which tend to burn the lanes out. With outlying stars the cluster's diameter is 15′. Star-branches extend in all directions from the halo. 200x gives a dramatic three-dimensional effect, the resolved cluster members standing out against the partially resolved background glitter. Perimeter stars radiate from the halo to the edge of the field, and the blazing, star-encrusted core occupies fully a fourth of the field. NGC 6207 is located 28′ NNE while IC 4617 (M15V, φ 1.1′×0.4′) lies 15′ NNE, about halfway between M13 and NGC 6207 and slightly west of a line between them.

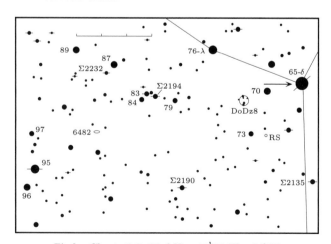

Finder Chart 46-8. 65-δ Her: 17ʰ15.0ᵐ +24° 50′

NGC 6207 H701² Galaxy Type SA(s)c III
φ 3.0′×1.1′, m11.6v, SB12.8   16ʰ43.1ᵐ +36° 50′
Finder Chart 46-6   ★★★
8/10″ Scopes–100x: NGC 6207, located 28′ NNE of Messier 13, is a lens-shaped galaxy with a 1.5′×0.5′ NNE–SSW halo that contains a stellar nucleus. 20′ to the NW of the galaxy is a fine double with a yellow 8th magnitude primary and an 11th magnitude secondary.

12/14″ Scopes–125x: NGC 6207 is enclosed in a triangle of 12th magnitude stars. Its fairly bright 2′×0.75′ NNE–SSW halo has tapered ends and contains a stellar nucleus.

NGC 6210 PK43+37.1 Planetary Nebula Type 2+3b
φ 14″, m8.8v, CS13.7v   16ʰ44.5ᵐ +23° 49′
Finder Chart 46-3, Figure 46-9   ★★★★
8/10″ Scopes–175x: This planetary nebula forms a thin triangle with a yellow 7.5 magnitude star 8′ to its SE and a 9.5 magnitude star 4′ to its NE. It has a bright blue 25″×15″ E–W oval disk.

12/14″ Scopes–225x: NGC 6210 is a bright blue 30″×20″ E–W ellipse enveloping a central star that fades in and out of view with the changing air currents. 20′ SSW of the planetary is the triple star Σ2094, which appears as two yellow disks in contact (AB: 7.4, 7.7; 1.3″; 77°), with a faint, distant third component (AC: 11.0; 24.9″; 312°).

DoDz6 Open Cluster 5★ Tr Type IV 2p
φ 27′, m −   16ʰ45.3ᵐ +38° 17′
Finder Chart 46-4   ★★
12/14″ Scopes–75x: DoDz6 consists of two irregular concentrations lying N–S of each other. The north-

ern group has two 9th magnitude, five 10–11th magnitude, and three fainter stars in a 15′×5′ E–W area. The southern group includes eleven stars in a thin 8′×3′ NE–SW oval around a starless center. Two 10th magnitude stars are on the oval's NE tip.

NGC 6229 H50⁴ Globular Cluster Class IV

φ 4.5′, m9.4v   16ʰ47.0ᵐ +47° 32′

Finder Chart 46-7, Figure 46-10   ★★★

8/10″Scopes–125x: This globular cluster is at the western corner of the 5′ long triangle it forms with 8th magnitude stars to its ENE and ESE. It is an unresolved 1′ diameter glow that is slightly brighter in its center.

16/18″Scopes–150x: NGC 6229 has a 2′ diameter halo with a granular texture enveloping a broad central concentration. A few stars may be resolved around the periphery.

NGC 6239 H727³ Galaxy Type SB(s)b pec? III-IV

φ 2.3′×1.0′, m12.4v, SB13.2   16ʰ50.1ᵐ +42° 44′

Finder Chart 46-7, Figure 46-11   ★★

12/14″Scopes–125x: This faint galaxy is in a field of bright stars and enclosed by an irregular 1.5° pentagon of 6th magnitude stars. It is a highly elongated 1.5′×0.75′ ESE–WNW streak containing a brighter elongated core.

16/18″Scopes–150x: NGC 6239 has a fairly faint 2′×0.75′ ESE–WNW halo that contains a broad central brightening which spans nearly half the length of the major axis. With averted vision a very faint stellar nucleus is suspected. A 12.5 magnitude star lies 2′ north, and a 13th magnitude star 2.5′ NE, of the galaxy.

NGC 6255 H689³ Galaxy Type SBcd:

φ 3.2′×1.3′, m12.7v, SB14.1   16ʰ54.8ᵐ +36° 30′

Finder Chart 46-6   ★★

16/18″Scopes–150x: NGC 6255, located 10′ south of an 8th magnitude star, has a faint 3′×1′ E–W halo that contains a poorly concentrated, somewhat mottled center.

DoDz7 Open Cluster 6★ Tr Type IV1p

φ 20′, m –   17ʰ10.6ᵐ +15° 32′

Finder Chart 46-9, Figure 46-13   ★★

12/14″Scopes–125x: DoDz7, located 1.5° NW of Alpha (α) = 64 Herculis, is a loose, irregular cluster of 30 stars spread over a 20′×10′ E–W area. A rectangular asterism stands out at the cluster's center. A dozen stars, including those in the rectangle, are

Figure 46-12. *Messier 92 (NGC 6341) lies in a field well away from any bright guide stars and therefore can be difficult to find, however, this beautiful cluster deserves attention. Image courtesy of Martin C. Germano.*

11th magnitude objects. A 10th magnitude field star lies 20′ west of the cluster.

NGC 6341 Messier 92 Globular Cluster Class IV

φ 11.2′, m6.4v   17ʰ17.1ᵐ +43° 08′

Finder Chart 46-7, Figure 46-12   ★★★★★

The beautiful globular cluster Messier 92 deserves more attention but is outclassed by the great Hercules Cluster Messier 13 to its SW. One of its problems is that it is harder to locate than its more famous cousin: M92 is in a bright-star-poor region 6° due north of Pi (π) = 67 Herculis, the star at the NE corner of the Keystone. Look for the cluster about 1/3 of the way from Iota (ι) = 85 Her to Eta (η) = 44 Her, the star at the NW corner of the Keystone.

J. E. Bode discovered this globular in 1777, and Messier added it as his 92nd catalog entry in 1781. It lies about 25,000 light years distant. M92 is intrinsically fainter and smaller than M13: its absolute magnitude is −8.1, a luminosity of 150,000 suns (only 60% that of M13), and its diameter is 80 light years. Its most outstanding feature is that its stars are exceptionally poor in iron and other elements heavier than basic hydrogen and helium. This suggests that M92 was formed before the gas and dust of our Galaxy were enriched with heavy elements and that it therefore is exceptionally old even for a globular cluster.

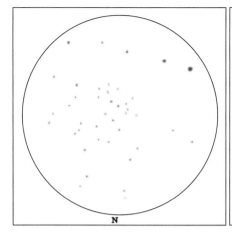

Figure 46-13. DoDz 7
17.5″, f4.5–135x, by G. R. Kepple

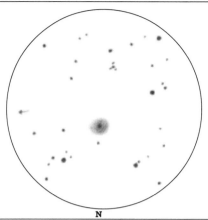

Figure 46-14. NGC 6482
17.5″, f4.5–300x, by G. R. Kepple

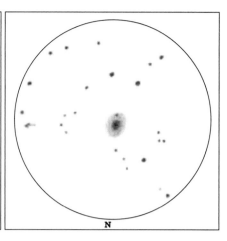

Figure 46-15. NGC 6574
17.5″, f4.5–300x, by G. R. Kepple

4/6″ Scopes–75x: Messier 92 is a little fainter and smaller but more concentrated than Messier 13. Small telescopes show a bright unresolved core that fades gradually to an irregular periphery well resolved with faint stars.

8/10″ Scopes–100x: Messier 92 is a fine globular cluster with a bright, strongly concentrated 3′ diameter core surrounded by an irregular 9′ diameter periphery which thins gradually outward. 6′ to the east is a row of 10th magnitude stars that is part of a longer string of moderately bright stars leading NE.

12/14″ Scopes–125x: Messier 92 is a bright, large globular cluster which compares well with the more celebrated Messier 13. It has a blazing 1.5′ diameter inner core embedded in a dense 3′ diameter outer core beyond which the stars thin noticeably but gradually for the 2′ width of the inner halo. An even thinner outer halo, the stars of which are distributed in attractive chains, extends out to the cluster's full 11′ diameter. A 12th magnitude star is near the halo's SW periphery. The stars resolve quite nicely right into the core. A dark area runs E–W just SW of the core, and a smaller dark area is on the cluster's east side.

DoDz 8 Open Cluster 6★ Tr Type IV 2p
φ 13′, m –   17^h26.2^m +24° 11′
Finder Chart 46-8   ★★★
12/14″ Scopes–75x: DoDz 8 is a loose, sparse 13′ diameter cluster containing three 8th magnitude, four 9th magnitude, and a dozen fainter stars. The brighter cluster members trace two triangles on its north and south edges.

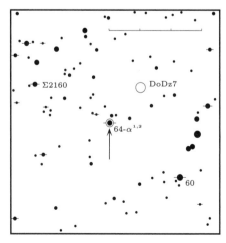

Finder Chart 46-9.
64–α ^{1,2} Her: 17^h14.7^m +14° 23′

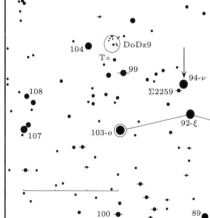

Finder Chart 46-10.
94–ν Her: 17^h58.5^m +30° 11′

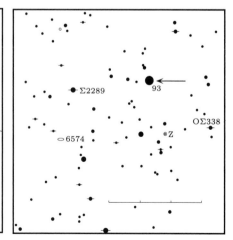

Finder Chart 46-11.
93 Her: 18^h00.0^m +16° 45′

NGC 6482 Galaxy Type E:
ϕ 2.1′ × 1.8′, m11.4v, SB12.7   17ʰ51.8ᵐ +23° 04′

Finder Chart 46-8, Figure 46-14   ★★★

8/10″Scopes–100x: NGC 6482, located 5.5′ NW of a 9th magnitude star, is at the southern vertex of a 2.5′ triangle with two 12th magnitude stars. It has a fairly faint, small 45″ × 30″ E–W oval halo that contains a bright stellar nucleus.

16/18″Scopes–150x: In larger instruments the faint halo is elongated about 1.25′ × 1′ E–W and has twin nuclei, the one at the halo's center the true galactic nucleus and the other, just west of the halo's center, merely a superimposed foreground star. The 12th magnitude star to the NE of the galaxy has a 14th magnitude companion 6″ from it in position angle 130°.

DoDz9 Open Cluster 15★ Tr Type III2p
ϕ 34′, m –   18ʰ08.8ᵐ +31° 32′

Finder Chart 46-10   ★★★

12/14″Scopes–75x: DoDz9 stands out better than one would expect for a loose, uncompressed cluster of only 50 stars in a 34′ area. The brighter members form distinctive asterisms around the cluster periphery. On the SSW edge is a 7′ long box of one

8th and four 9th–10th magnitude stars. On the NE edge five magnitude 9.5 stars form a 12′ × 5′ pattern that resembles the house-shape of the constellation Cepheus. On the NW edge a 12th, a 13th, and two 9th magnitude stars are arranged in a 4′ × 3′ diamond. The area around and between these asterisms is sprinkled generously with 13th and half a dozen 12th magnitude stars. Three more 9th magnitude stars, not a part of the asterisms, are distributed around the cluster's edges.

NGC 6574 Galaxy Type SAB(rs)bc: II-III
ϕ 1.2′ × 0.8′, m12.0v, SB11.8   18ʰ11.9ᵐ +14° 59′

Finder Chart 46-11, Figure 46-15   ★★★

8/10″Scopes–100x: This faint galaxy is 14′ SW of a wide NE–SW pair of magnitude 10.5 stars and 2.25′ SW of a magnitude 11.5 star. Its 1′ diameter halo appears slightly elongated N–S and just a little brighter at the center.

16/18″Scopes–150x: NGC 6574 has a moderately faint 1.25′ × 0.75′ NNW–SSE halo containing a broad, faint central core. A very faint star is embedded in the halo on its south edge. The star field is moderately well populated: a jagged chain of five stars lies south of the galaxy.

Chapter 47

Hydra, the Female Water Snake

47.1 Overview

Hydra, the Water Serpent, is the largest and the longest of the constellations. Its star-pattern from its Head to its Tail-tip extends for nearly 100°, and the constellation as a whole covers 1303 square degrees. The Head is a very attractive, conspicuous asterism (Delta (δ), Epsilon (ε), Zeta (ζ), Eta (η), Rho (ρ), and Sigma (σ) Hydrae) that fits in the field of most 7x to 10x binoculars. The heart of the Water Serpent is the 2nd magnitude orange-red Alpha (α), the name of which, Alphard, "The Solitary One," refers to the lack of bright stars in its vicinity. The curves of the Water Serpent's body, best traced on dark clear nights because of its many 4th and 5th magnitude stars, ends at 58 Hydrae SW of Sigma Librae. Thus Hydra extends from the eastern edge of the constellations of the winter to the western edge of the constellations of summer.

Hydra represents the multi-headed serpent which would grow two new heads for every one that would be cut off. Killing it therefore was a bit of a problem. However, Hercules got around this difficulty by *burning* Hydra's heads. The story of a hero killing a multi-headed serpent is ancient: it is pictured in Mesopotamian art of about 2500 B.C. The constellation of Hydra was also a Greek inheritance from Mesopotamia: the "Snake of Heaven," which refers to the same star-pattern as our Hydra, is mentioned on a Mesopotamian tablet written in 2400 B.C. The Mesopotamian deity who was particularly known as a serpent-slayer was Ninurta, the god of war and agriculture, who was figured in the stars of our Sagittarius.

Though it is well off the Milky Way, Hydra, in part because of its size, has a large number and a remarkable variety of objects. The majority of its objects are of course galaxies, but the constellation also contains some fine planetary nebulae, a couple globular clusters, and even a good open cluster. It has three Messier objects: the open cluster M48, the globular cluster M68, and the spiral galaxy M83. Because Hydra extends through nearly seven hours of right ascension, it should be observed in separate sessions as first the western and then its eastern sections culminate:

> **Hydra:** HIGH-dra
> **Genitive:** Hydrae, HIGH-dree
> **Abbreviation:** Hya
> **Culmination:** 9pm–Apr. 29, midnight–Mar. 15
> **Area:** 1,303 square degrees
> **Showpieces:** U Hya, M48 (NGC 2548), M68 (NGC 4590), M83 (NGC 5236), NGC 3242
> **Binocular Objects:** R Hya, U Hya, V Hya, M48 (NGC 2548), M68 (NGC 4590), M83 (NGC 5236), NGC 3242

the western part of the constellation, with the Head and the Alphard region, transits the meridian during the early evenings of March; the eastern part of the constellation, which consists of its long-trailing Tail, can best be observed after midnight in March.

47.2 Interesting Stars

U Hydrae Variable Star Type SRb   Spec. N2
m4.7 to 6.2, Per 450 days $10^h37.6^m -13° 23'$
Finder Chart 47-9   ★★★★
2/3″ Scopes–75x: U Hydrae, located about 4° NW of Nu (ν) Hya, is one of the brightest of the unusual deep hued carbon stars. Its color is a remarkable poppy red and is obvious even in 35mm binoculars. The ruddy tone of carbon stars is a consequence of the abundance of carbon molecules in their atmospheres, such molecules being exceptionally efficient absorbers of blue light.

N Hydrae=17 Crt (HIII96) Double Star Spec. F6, F7
m5.8, 5.9; Sep. 9.2″; P.A.210° $11^h32.3^m -29° 16'$
Finder Chart 47-10   ★★★★
2/3″ Scopes–75x: N Hydrae is a fine equally bright yellow pair easily separated by small telescopes. A reddish-orange star is in the same field as N Hya 8′ to its NE.

Hydra, the Female Water Snake Constellation Chart 47-1

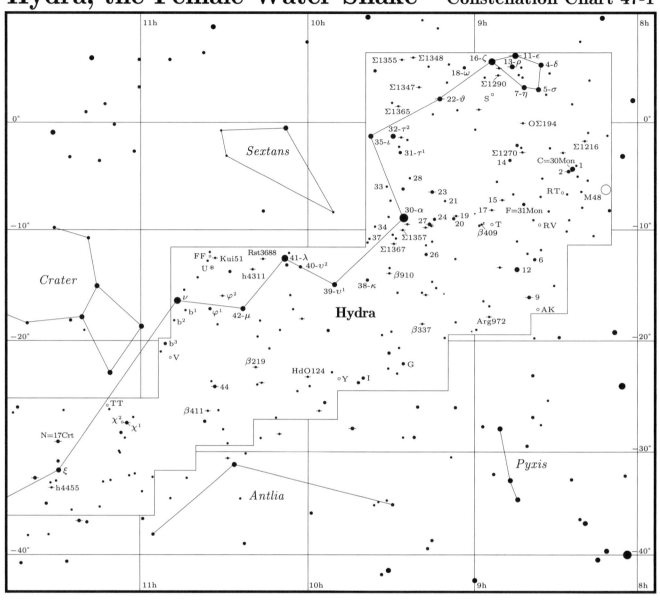

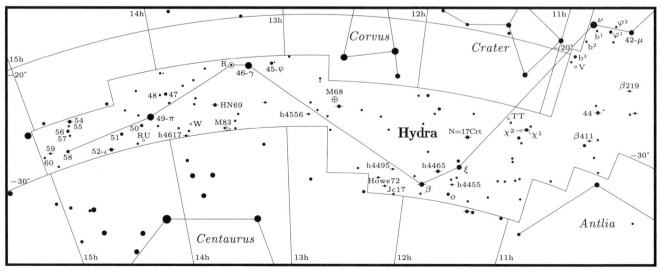

Table 47-1: Selected Variable Stars in Hydra

Name	HD No.	Type	Max.	Min.	Period (Days)	F*	Spec. Type	R.A. (2000) Dec.		Finder Chart No.	Notes
RT Hya	71887	SRb	7.0	11.0	253	0.46	M6-M7	$08^h29.7^m$	$-06°\,19'$	47-3	
S Hya	76011	M	7.4	13.3	256	0.49	M4-M6	53.6	$+03\,04$	47-5	
T Hya	76400	M	6.7	13.2	289	0.49	M3-M9	55.7	$-09\,08$	47-1	
U Hya	92055	SRb	4.7	6.2	450		N2	$10^h37.6^m$	$-13\,23$	47-9	Carbon star
FF Hya	92096	SRb	8.2	10.3	85		Mb	37.9	$-12\,01$	47-9	
V Hya		SR	6.5	12.	533		N6e	51.6	$-21\,15$	47-9	Carbon star
TT Hya	97528	EA	7.5	9.5	6.95	0.10	A3+G6	$11^h13.2^m$	$-26\,28$	47-10	
R Hya	117287	M	3.0	11.0	389	0.48	M7	$13^h29.7^m$	$-23\,17$	47-12	Reddish-orange
W Hya	120285	SRa	7.7	11.6	397	0.50	M7-M9		$-28\,22$	47-12	Orange and blue pair
RU Hya		M	7.2	14.3	333	0.35	M6	$14^h11.6^m$	$-28\,53$	47-13	

F* = The fraction of period taken up by the star's rise from min. to max. brightness, or the period spent in eclipse.

Table 47-2: Selected Double Stars in Hydra

Name	ADS No.	Pair	M1	M2	Sep."	P.A.°	Spec	R.A. (2000) Dec.		Finder Chart No.	Notes
Σ1216	6762		7.1	7.4	*0.7	287	A0	$08^h21.3^m$	$-01°\,36'$	47-3	
2 Hya			5.6	9.4	72.8	3	A5	26.5	$-03\,59$	47-3	
9 Hya	6937		4.9	11.7	31.0	112	K0	41.7	$-15\,57$	47-4	
Σ1270	6977		6.4	7.4	4.7	262	F5	45.3	$-02\,36$	47-3	White and blue
11–ε Hya	6993	ABxC	3.8	6.8	2.8	281	F8	46.8	$+06\,25$	47-1	Yellow and blue
13–ϱ Hya	7006		4.4	11.9	12.4	145	A0	48.4	$+05\,50$	47-1	
OΣ194	7004		7.3	10.8	12.6	56	K2	48.3	$+00\,33$	47-1	Yellowish-orange and orange
15 Hya	7050	AB	5.6	8.6	0.9	125	A2	51.6	$-07\,11$	47-3	Yellowish-white primary
HV20	7050	AC		9.6	45.7	358					C and D bluish
β 587	7050	AD		10.7	51.9	54					
Σ1290	7055		7.5	9.4	3.0	320	A2	52.1	$+0\,428$	47-1	
17 Hya	7093		6.8	7.0	4.1	2	A3	55.5	$-07\,58$	47-1	White pair
Arg 72	7103		7.3	7.5	3.0	183	F2	56.8	$-17\,26$	47-4	
β 409	7136		7.3	9.8	9.7	185	A0	$09^h00.8^m$	$-09\,11$	47-1	
22–ϑ Hya	7253		3.9	9.9	29.4	197	A0	14.4	$+02\,19$	47-5	
27 Hya	7311	AB	5.0	6.9	229.4	211	G5 F2	20.5	$-09\,33$	47-6	Yellow and white
	7311	BC		9.1	9.3	198					C: bluish
β 337	7331		6.8	10.8	8.3	334	F2	22.5	$-17\,54$	47-7	
Σ1347	7342		7.3	8.6	21.2	311	F0	23.3	$+03\,30$	47-5	Yellowish and bluish
Σ1348	7352		7.5	7.6	1.9	317	F5	24.5	$+06\,21$	47-5	
Σ1355	7380		7.5	7.5	2.5	345	F5	27.3	$+06\,14$	47-5	
Σ1357	7393		6.9	10.4	7.5	54	K0	28.3	$-09\,59$	47-6	Orange pair
Σ1365	7412		7.4	8.4	3.4	158	F8	31.5	$+01\,28$	47-5	Yellowish and yellow
β 910	7427		7.2	9.7	6.8	305	G5	32.9	$-14\,00$	47-6	
HdO124	7610	AB	7.6	10.3	13.2	8	A0	$10^h01.3^m$	$-22\,46$	47-8	
	7610	AC		11.9	42.0	50					
Rst 3688			6.4	7.7	0.5	314	F0	19.3	$-12\,32$	47-9	
β 219	7739		6.7	8.2	1.8	187	A0	21.6	$-22\,32$	47-8	White pair
h4311	7749		6.6	9.7	4.2	122	F8	23.3	$-13\,23$	47-9	
β 411	7846		6.7	7.5	w1.4	315	F3	36.1	$-26\,40$	47-8	
Kui51			5.4	10.5	14.4	75	F8	36.5	$-12\,14$	47-9	
17 Crt			5.8	5.9	9.2	210	F6 F7	$11^h32.2^m$	$-29\,16$	47-10	N Hya, yellowish pair
h4455		AB	5.8	7.9	3.3	243	K0	36.6	$-33\,34$	47-10	Orangish and bluish
h4465		AB	5.3	12.8	26.6	346	M1	41.7	$-32\,30$	47-11	Orange v bluish
		AC		8.4	67.0	44					
β Hya			4.7	5.5	0.9	8	B9	52.9	$-33\,54$	47-11	
h4495		AB	6.7	8.9	6.6	317	G0	$12^h06.1^m$	$-32\,58$	47-11	
Jc 17			6.4	8.2	3.4	20	A0	10.0	$-34\,42$	47-11	
Howe 72			6.5	8.3	1.4	164	B9	13.6	$-33\,48$	47-11	
h4556	8700		7.4	8.9	6.0	82	G0	54.2	$-27\,58$	47-1	
HN69	8966	AB	5.9	6.8	10.1	191	A2 A	$13^h36.8^m$	$-26\,30$	47-12	Fine white pair
h4617			7.7	9.6	4.9	261	G5	50.7	$-29\,52$	47-12	
54 Hya	9375		5.1	7.1	8.6	126	F1 F9	$14^h46.0^m$	$-25\,27$	47-13	Yellowish pair
59 Hya	9453		6.3	6.6	0.8	335	A5	58.7	$-27\,39$	47-1	

Footnotes: *= Year 2000, a = Near apogee, c = Closing, w = Widening. Finder Chart No: All stars listed in the tables are plotted in the large Constellation Chart, but when a star appears in a Finder Chart, this number is listed. Notes: When colors are subtle, the suffix -*ish* is used, e.g. *bluish*.

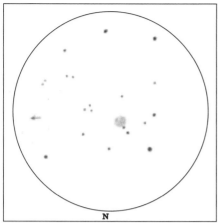

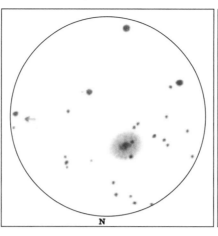

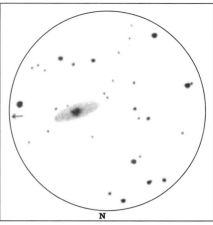

Figure 47-1. NGC 2610
13″, f4.5–312x, by Tom Polakis

Figure 47-2. NGC 2642
17.5″, f4.5–250x, by G. R. Kepple

Figure 47-3. NGC 2713
12.5″, f5–100x, by G. R. Kepple

R Hydrae Variable Star Type M   Spec. M7
m3.0 to 11.0, Per. 389.6 days   13ʰ29.7ᵐ −23° 17′
Finder Chart 47-12   ★★★★

2/3″ Scopes–75x: R Hydrae, 2.6° east of magnitude 3.0 Gamma (γ) = 46 Hya, is one of the brightest long-period variables (LPVs) in the sky. At extreme maxima it reaches magnitude 3.0. Near maximum its ruddy color is obvious even in binoculars; but the star's hue is deepest near its 10th–11th magnitude minimum, when it requires telescopes to be seen. R Hydrae is about 325 light years distant, and at high maximum is perhaps 500 times as luminous as the Sun.

54 Hydrae = HIII97 Double Star   Spec. F1, F9
m5.1, 7.1; Sep. 8.6″; P.A. 126°   14ʰ46.0ᵐ −25° 27′
Finder Chart 47-13   ★★★★

2/3″ Scopes–100x: Easily separated in small telescopes, 54 Hyrae is a pretty pair of pale and deep yellow stars.

47.3 Deep-Sky Objects

NGC 2548 M48 H22⁶ Open Cl. 80★ Tr Type I3r
φ 54′, m5.8v, Br★ 8.23v   08ʰ13.8ᵐ −05° 48′
Finder Chart 47-3, Figure 47-4   ★★★★★

NGC 2548 fits the description of the missing Messier 48 and therefore is generally accepted as being the object Messier described in 1771, though it is four degrees south of his position. It is an ideal object for high power binoculars. M48 is around 1,500 light years away, 24 light years in diameter, and as luminous as one thousand suns.

4/6″ Scopes–35x: Messier 48 is a beautiful cluster that stands out well at low power in small telescopes. It is large but rich, containing 50 stars in a 50′ area. The brighter members fall along a N–S stream.

8/10″ Scopes–50x: This fine cluster is bright, rich, and irregular, its 65 stars broadcast over a degree of sky.

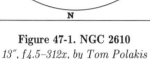

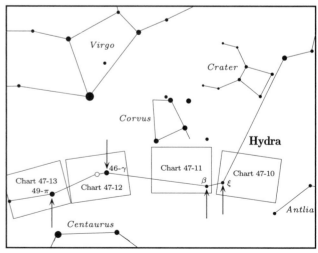

Master Finder Chart 47-2a. Hydra Chart Areas
Guide stars indicated by arrows.

Master Finder Chart 47-2b. Hydra Chart Areas
Guide stars indicated by arrows.

The brighter stars, most of which are 9th and 10th magnitude objects, fall along two broad, half-degree-long NNE–SSW streams divided by a starless channel. The western stream is the brighter and denser of the two, and has a prong at the southern end that diverges to the SW. The two streams join at a 15′ × 7′ circlet on their northern end. A third star stream runs NW–SE from the NE edge of the circlet. 100x brings the star count up to over a hundred, many of the members in interesting pairs. The wide range of stellar magnitudes give the cluster the illusion of depth, for its brighter members seem to be in front of its fainter "background" stars.

NGC 2610 PK239+13.1 Planetary Neb.
Type 4+2, ϕ 37″, m12.8v, CS15.90v
08ʰ33.4ᵐ −16° 09′
Finder Chart 47-4, Figure 47-1   ★★★

8/10″Scopes–100x: NGC 2610, located 3.5′ SW of a yellowish 6.5 magnitude star, has a faint, round, evenly concentrated 35″ diameter disk. The NNE edge touches the western tip of a 2′×1′ triangle of 12th magnitude stars.

16/18″Scopes–150x: NGC 2610 has a fairly bright, gray 40″ diameter disk which flares to the SW. This flare, and the 12th magnitude field star embedded in the disk's NE edge, makes the planetary mimic a comet. The 16th magnitude central star can be just glimpsed at 275x. An O-III filter reveals a slight central void.

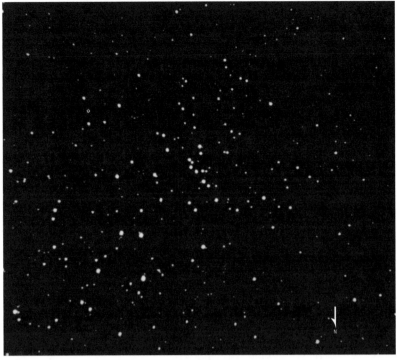

Figure 47-4. *Messier 48 (NGC 2548) is a large, beautiful cluster that stands out well at low power in small telescopes. Lee C. Coombs made this five minute exposure on 103a-0 film with a 10″, f5 Newtonian.*

NGC 2642 Galaxy Type SB(rs)bc I-II
ϕ 2.2′×1.8′, m12.6v, SB13.9   08ʰ40.7ᵐ +04° 07′
Finder Chart 47-3, Figure 47-2   ★★

8/10″Scopes–100x: NGC 2642 lies 2.5′ NNE of the closest member of a 4′ equilateral triangle of 8th magnitude stars. This galaxy is a faint, small, round glow containing a dim stellar nucleus.

16/18″Scopes–150x: NGC 2642 has a fairly faint, circular 1.5′ diameter halo with twin nuclei, the SE of which is in fact just a superimposed foreground star.

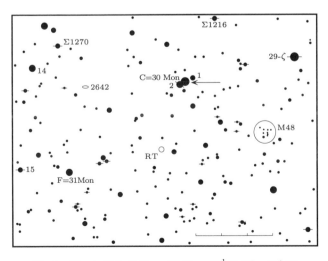

Finder Chart 47-3. C Hya=30 Mon: 08ʰ25.6ᵐ −03° 54′

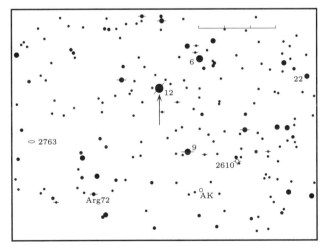

Finder Chart 47-4. 12 Hya: 08ʰ46.2ᵐ −13° 33′

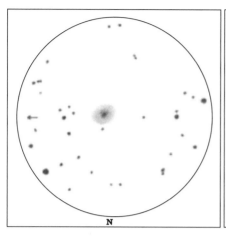

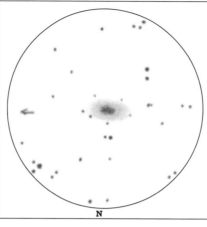

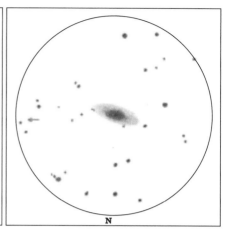

Figure 47-5. NGC 2763
17.5″, ƒ4.5–250x, by G. R. Kepple

Figure 47-6. NGC 2781
17.5″, ƒ4.5–250x, by G. R. Kepple

Figure 47-7 NGC 2784
17.5″, ƒ4.5–250x, by G. R. Kepple

A magnitude 12.5 star lies near the halo's north edge, and a 10″ wide NW–SE pair of 10th magnitude stars is 1′ SE of the galaxy's center.

NGC 2713 Galaxy Type SB(rs)ab I-II
φ **3.7′×1.3′, m11.8v, SB13.3**   08ʰ57.3ᵐ +02° 55′
Finder Chart 47-5, Figure 47-3   ★★★
12/14″Scopes–100x: NGC 2713, located 4.5′ ENE of a 9.5 magnitude star, has a fairly bright 3′×1.25′ ESE–WNW oval halo that contains a round bright core. Galaxy NGC 2716 lies 11′ north.

NGC 2716 Galaxy Type (R)SB(r)0+
φ **1.6′×1.2′, m11.8v, SB12.4**   08ʰ57.6ᵐ +03° 05′
Finder Chart 47-5   ★★★
12/14″Scopes–125x: NGC 2716 is as bright as, but

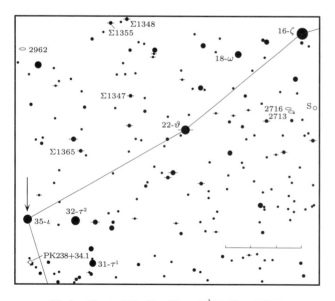

Finder Chart 47-5. 35–ι Hya: 09ʰ39.8ᵐ −10° 34′

smaller than, NGC 2713 lying 11′ to its south. The galaxy has a circular 1.5′ diameter halo slightly elongated NNE–SSW and containing a conspicuous core.

NGC 2763 H275³ Galaxy Type SAB(rs)c II
φ **2.3′×1.9′, m12.0v, SB13.5**   09ʰ06.8ᵐ −15° 30′
Finder Chart 47-4, Figure 47-5   ★★
8/10″Scopes–100x: NGC 2763 is 5′ SE and 5.5′ west of 10th magnitude stars. This faint galaxy is elongated 1.25′×1′ E–W and slightly brighter at its center.
16/18″Scopes–150x: NGC 2763 has a fairly faint 1.5′ diameter halo that contains a weakly concentrated core with a faint stellar nucleus. A group of 12th and 13th magnitude stars is centered 2′ west of the halo, and a 14th magnitude star is 1′ north of the halo's edge.

NGC 2781 H66¹ Galaxy Type (R)SAB:(r)0+
φ **3.0′×1.7′, m11.6v, SB13.2**   09ʰ11.5ᵐ −14° 49′
Finder Chart 47-6, Figure 47-6   ★★★
8/10″Scopes–100x: NGC 2781, located 9′ NNE of an 8th magnitude star, is elongated 1.5′×1′ E–W and slightly brighter at its center. 2.25′ to its north is a 27″ wide E–W pair of 12th and 13th magnitude stars.
16/18″Scopes–150x: NGC 2781 has a fairly faint 3′×1.5′ ENE–WSW halo containing an oval core with a faint stellar nucleus. 14th magnitude stars are 1′ WNW, and 2′ west, of the galaxy, and three threshold stars are distributed around its periphery.

NGC 2784 H59¹ Galaxy Type S0°
φ **5.5′×2.4′, m10.0v, SB12.7**   09ʰ12.3ᵐ −24° 10′
Finder Chart 47-7, Figure 47-7   ★★★★
8/10″Scopes–100x: NGC 2784 forms a triangle with

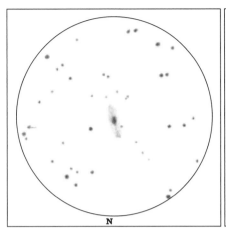

Figure 47-8. NGC 2811
17.5″, f4.5–250x, by G. R. Kepple

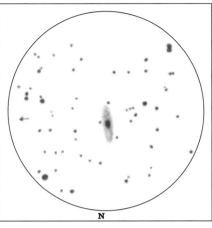

Figure 47-9. NGC 2815
17.5″, f4.5–250x, by G. R. Kepple

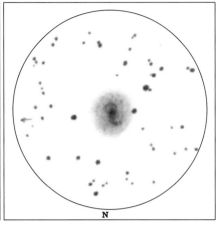

Figure 47-10. NGC 2835
17.5″, f4.5–250x, by G. R. Kepple

two 9th magnitude stars 3.5′ to its ESE and 5′ to its NNW. It is bright and highly elongated 3′ × 1′ E–W, and contains a bright center.

16/18″Scopes–150x: A very bright core containing a stellar nucleus is embedded in a fainter halo elongated 4.5′ × 2′ ENE–WSW, the southern edge of the halo appearing more distinct than the northern. A 14th magnitude star lies on the halo's edge 1.25′ NE of the galaxy's center, and 13th magnitude stars are 2.5′ NE and 2.75′ west.

NGC 2811 H505² Galaxy Type SB(r)0+
ϕ **1.9′×0.6′, m11.3v, SB11.3**   **09ʰ16.2ᵐ −16° 19′**
Finder Chart 47-6, Figure 47-8   ★★★

8/10″Scopes–100x: NGC 2811, located 7.5′ SSW of a 9th magnitude star, is a faint, circular 1′ diameter glow that is slightly brighter at its center.

16/18″Scopes–150x: NGC 2811 has a fairly bright 2′ × 1′ NNE–SSW halo containing a well concentrated oval core. A 14th magnitude star is superimposed upon the halo 40″ NE of the galaxy's center, and a 12th magnitude star lies 2′ to the WNW.

NGC 2815 H242³ Galaxy Type (R′)SB(r)ab
ϕ **3.4′×1.2′, m11.8v, SB13.2**   **09ʰ16.3ᵐ −23° 38′**
Finder Chart 47-7, Figure 47-9   ★★★

12/14″Scopes–125x: NGC 2815, located 10′ SE of an 8th magnitude star, has a large, bright core embedded in a faint 3′ × 1′ NNE–SSW halo. A 13th magnitude star touches the halo's southern tip, and a 13.5 magnitude star is just east of its northern tip 1.25′ NNE of the galaxy's center.

NGC 2835 Galaxy Type SAB(rs)c I-II
ϕ **6.3′×4.5′, m10.4v, SB13.9**   **09ʰ17.9ᵐ −22° 21′**
Finder Chart 47-7, Figure 47-10   ★★★★

12/14″Scopes–125x: NGC 2835 lies between a 9th magnitude star 2.75′ to its west and an 11th magnitude star 1.5′ to its east, the latter at the northern end of a NW–SE chain of six stars. The galaxy's halo has uniformly low surface brightness, is 3.5′ in diameter, and touches the 11th magnitude star to its east.

16/18″Scopes–150x: An increase in aperture reveals a faint 5′ × 3.5′ N–S halo containing a faint stellar nucleus and a hint of spiral structure. An 11th magnitude star touches the halo's east edge. The star field is rather abundant in brighter stars. A 9th magnitude star 3.5′ SE of the galaxy has a magnitude 12.5 companion 15″ distant in position angle 45°.

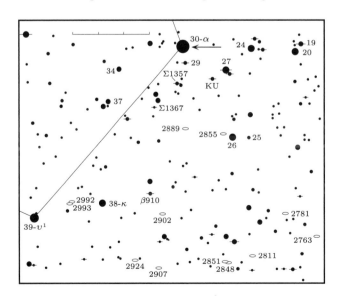

Finder Chart 47-6. 30–α Hya: 09ʰ27.5ᵐ −08° 40′

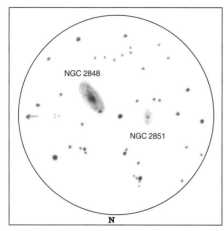

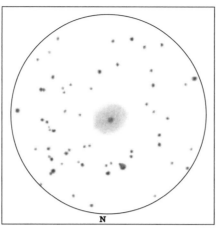

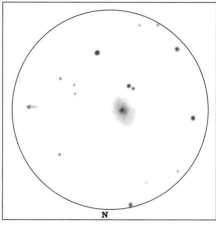

Figure 47-11. NGC 2848 and NGC 2851
13″, f5.6–165x, by Steve Coe

Figure 47-12. NGC 2855
17.5″, f4.5–250x, by G. R. Kepple

Figure 47-13. NGC 2889
17.5″, f4.5–250x, by G. R. Kepple

NGC 2848 H488³ Galaxy Type SB(s)cd II-III
ϕ **2.4′×1.7′, m11.8v, SB13.2**   09ʰ20.2ᵐ −16° 32′

NGC 2851 Galaxy Type SA:0°
ϕ **1.4′×0.5′, m13.6v, SB13.1**   09ʰ20.6ᵐ −16° 28′
Finder Chart 47-6, Figure 47-11   ★★★/★★

8/10″Scopes–100x: NGC 2848 is a very faint diffuse glow 2.5′ SW of a 12.5 magnitude star.

16/18″Scopes–150x: NGC 2848 has a fairly faint 2′×1′ NNE–SSW halo that is slightly brighter at its center. A 30″×15″ triangle of 14.5 magnitude stars lies on the halo's NNE tip. 5′ ENE of NGC 2848 is galaxy NGC 2851, a very faint 1′×0.5′ N–S smudge containing a stellar nucleus.

NGC 2855 H132¹ Galaxy Type (R′?)SA(r)0°
ϕ **3.6′×2.8′, m11.7v, SB14.0**   09ʰ21.5ᵐ −11° 55′
Finder Chart 47-6, Figure 47-12   ★★★

8/10″Scopes–100x: NGC 2855, located 4′ south of a 9th magnitude star, is a fairly obvious circular 1.5′ diameter glow slightly elongated NW–SE and containing a small, weakly concentrated core.

16/18″Scopes–150x: NGC 2855 has a large, moderately concentrated core containing an intermittently visible stellar nucleus, the two surrounded by a diffuse 2.25′×2′ NW–SE halo.

NGC 2865 Galaxy Type (R′)SAB(rs)0° pec
ϕ **2.4′×1.9′, m11.4v, SB12.9**   09ʰ23.5ᵐ −23° 10′
Finder Chart 47-7   ★★★

12/14″Scopes–125x: NGC 2865, located 6′ south of a 9th magnitude star, shows a bright stellar nucleus embedded in a fairly faint, circular 1.5′ diameter halo with a diffuse periphery.

NGC 2889 H555² Galaxy Type SA(s)bc I:
ϕ **2.0′×1.7′, m11.7v, SB12.9**   09ʰ27.2ᵐ −11° 38′
Finder Chart 47-6, Figure 47-13   ★★★

8/10″Scopes–100x: NGC 2889, located 3.25′ NNE of a 10th magnitude star, is a faint, circular 1.25′ diameter haze containing a slight brightening at its center. An 11th magnitude star lies 1.5′ south.

16/18″Scopes–150x: NGC 2889 has a fairly bright 1.5′×1′ N–S halo containing a small core off center to the east. The 11.5 magnitude star 1.5′ to the south has a 14th magnitude companion 20″ away in position angle 45°. Galaxy NGC 2884 lies 13′ WNW.

NGC 2902 H276³ Galaxy Type (R)SA(rs:)0−
ϕ **1.5′×1.2′, m12.2v, SB12.7**   09ʰ30.9ᵐ −14° 44′
Finder Charts 47-6 and 47-7   ★★

8/10″Scopes–100x: NGC 2902, located 6′ NNW of a 9th magnitude star, is a faint 30″ diameter glow surrounding a faint diffuse core.

16/18″Scopes–150x: NGC 2902 has a diffuse, round 1′ diameter halo containing a well concentrated center with a very faint stellar nucleus. A 15th magnitude star lies on the NNW edge of the halo.

NGC 2907 H506² Galaxy Type S0+: sp
ϕ **2.1′×1.2′, m11.7v, SB12.5**   09ʰ31.6ᵐ −16° 44′
Finder Charts 47-6, 47-7   ★★★

8/10″Scopes–100x: NGC 2907 is 6.5′ and 10′ NNW of two 9th magnitude stars that act as pointers toward it. It has a lens-shaped 1.5′×0.5′ ESE–WNW halo that contains a slight central brightening.

16/18″Scopes–150x: NGC 2907 has a bright lenticular 1.5′×0.75′ ESE–WNW halo elongated to tapered ends. The extended core is mottled but lacks a sharp

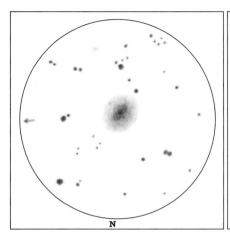

Figure 47-14. NGC 2935
17.5″, ƒ4.5–250x, by G. R. Kepple

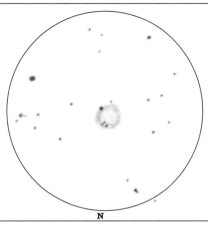

Figure 47-15. PK238+34.1
18″, ƒ4.5–100x, by Dr. Jack Marling

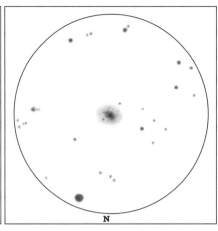

Figure 47-16. NGC 2983
17.5″, ƒ4.5–200x, by G. R. Kepple

stellar nucleus. Along the major axis of the halo are several faint knots. A 13th magnitude star is 1.5′ NW, and a pair of fainter stars are 2.5′ ESE of the galaxy.

NGC 2924 Galaxy Type SA(r?)0–
ϕ 1.3′×1.2′, m12.0v, SB12.3　　　09^{h}35.2^m −16° 24′
Finder Charts 47-6, 47-7　　　　　　★★★

8/10″Scopes–100x: NGC 2924 is situated within a nearly equilateral triangle of one 8th and two 9th magnitude stars, the former at the triangle's western corner. The galaxy has a faint 30″ diameter halo containing a small faint core.

16/18″Scopes–150x: NGC 2924 has a fairly faint, diffuse 1′ diameter halo around a mottled oval core that contains several faint knots. A 14th magnitude star lies 1′ SW of the galaxy's center, and a 15th magnitude star is just visible at the core's SW edge.

NGC 2935 H556^2 Galaxy Type (R′)SB(rs)ab
ϕ 4.3′×3.2′, m11.1v, SB13.8　　　09^{h}36.7^m −21° 08′
Finder Chart 47-7, Figure 47-14　　　　★★★

8/10″Scopes–100x: NGC 2935 has an extended core containing a stellar nucleus and surrounded by a faint 2.5′×2′ N–S halo. A 12th magnitude star lies 2′ SSE of the galaxy's center, and 10th magnitude stars are 4′ to its south and west.

16/18″Scopes–150x: Larger instruments show a moderately bright 3′×2.5′ N–S halo containing a well concentrated center. Several threshold knots or stars are superimposed upon the central area, the most conspicuous of them just NNE of the nucleus. The 10th magnitude star to the west of the galaxy has a 12.5 magnitude companion 20″ away in position angle 135°.

PK238+34.1 Abell 33 Planetary Nebula Type 2b
ϕ 268″, m12.4v, CS15.66v　　　　09^{h}39.1^m −02° 48′
Finder Chart 47-5, Figure 47-15　　　★★★

12/14″Scopes–150x: Abell 33 has a very faint 4′ diameter disk slightly elongated N–S and containing a slightly darker center. The rim's NW edge seems slightly brighter. A 7.2 magnitude star lies 5′ SW of the planetary's center.

16/18″Scopes–175x: In an O-III filter, PK238+34.1 is an eerie, ghostly ring slightly elongated 4.5′×4′ in position angle 30°. The darker interior region occupies more than 75% of the disk. The inner edge of the ring is diffuse all around, but is particularly ambiguous on the east. The glow of the nebula is not any easier to see for the glare of the magnitude 7.2 star to the SW. Three 13th and 14th magnitude stars

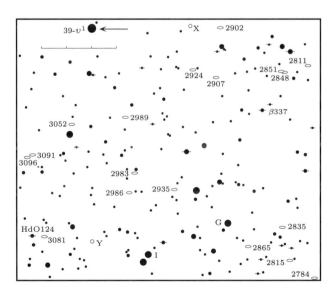

Finder Chart 47-7. 39– v^1 Hya: 09^{h}51.5^m −14° 51′

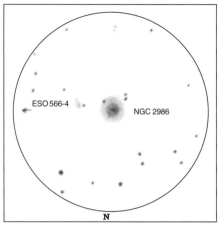

Figure 47-17. NGC 2986
20″, f4.5–175x, by Richard W. Jakiel

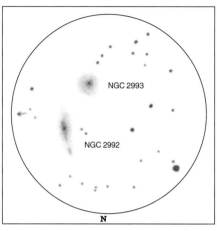

Figure 47-18. NGC 2992 and NGC 2993
20″, f4.5–175x, by Richard W. Jakiel

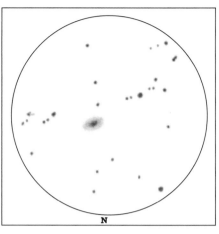

Figure 47-19. NGC 3052
17.5″, f4.5–200x, by G. R. Kepple

are superimposed upon the planetary's NNW section, and a faint star lies outside its south edge.

NGC 2962 Galaxy Type (R)SAB(rs)0+
φ 2.7′×2.0′, m11.9v, SB13.6   09ʰ40.9ᵐ +05° 10′
Finder Chart 47-5   ★★★

8/10″Scopes–100x: NGC 2962 lies 5′ north of a short row of three stars, the middle star the brightest. The galaxy's faint 2′×1′ N–S halo is slightly brighter toward its center.

16/18″Scopes–150x: A bright stellar nucleus is embedded in a very faint diffuse halo elongated 2.5′×2′ N–S. A 12th magnitude star 2′ north has a 13th magnitude companion 23″ away toward the galaxy.

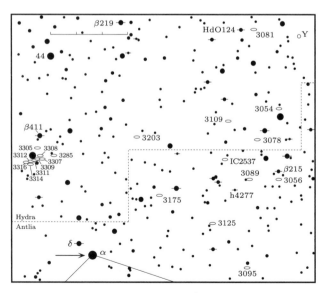

Finder Chart 47-8. α Ant: 10ʰ27.2ᵐ −31° 04′

NGC 2983 H289³ Galaxy Type SB(r)0+
φ 2.4′×1.5′, m11.8v, SB13.0   09ʰ43.7ᵐ −20° 29′
Finder Chart 47-7, Figure 47-16   ★★★

8/10″Scopes–100x: NGC 2983, located 7′ SSE of a 6.5 magnitude star, is faint but conspicuous. Its 1.5′×1′ NE–SW halo contains a tiny core that is only slightly brighter than the halo but has a dim stellar nucleus.

16/18″Scopes–150x: NGC 2983 has a small but bright core embedded in a faint 2′×1.5′ NE–SW halo. A magnitude 14.5 star is 1′ SE of the galaxy's center, and a threshold star is 30″ NW of the center within the halo.

NGC 2986 H311² Galaxy Type SAB(s:)0°
φ 4.1′×3.4′, m10.6v, SB13.3   09ʰ44.3ᵐ −21° 17′
Finder Chart 47-7, Figure 47-17   ★★★

8/10″Scopes–100x: NGC 2986, located 10′ SE of an 8.5 magnitude star, has a stellar nucleus embedded in a faint, diffuse 1′ diameter glow. A wide pair of 13th magnitude stars is 1.5′ SE of the galaxy's center.

16/18″Scopes–150x: In larger telescopes NGC 2986 shows a circular 2′ diameter halo that contains a broad core, smooth in texture except for its stellar nucleus. 2′ to the WSW of NGC 2986 is its companion galaxy ESO 566-4, a faint 1′×0.5′ NNE–SSW seed-shaped glow.

NGC 2989 Galaxy Type SB(s:)c I-II
φ 1.9′×1.1′, m12.7v, SB13.4   09ʰ45.4ᵐ −18° 23′
Finder Chart 47-7   ★★

12/14″Scopes–125x: NGC 2989, located 2′ NW of a 9th magnitude star, has a faint, circular 1′ diameter halo which is slightly brighter in its center. Another 9th magnitude star is 6′ NE of the galaxy.

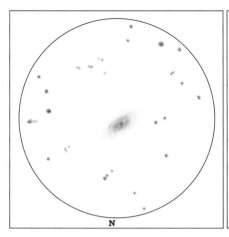

Figure 47-20. NGC 3054
17.5″, f4.5–200x, by G. R. Kepple

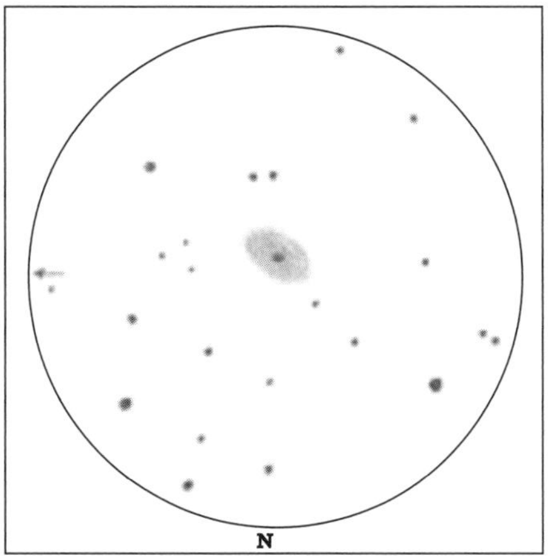

Figure 47-21. NGC 3081
17.5″, f4.5–200x, by G. R. Kepple

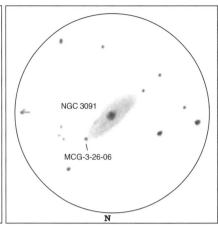

Figure 47-22. NGC 3091
17.5″, f4.5–200x, by G. R. Kepple

NGC 2992 H277³ Galaxy Type S0 pec sp
ϕ **4.0′×1.2′, m12.2v, SB13.7**   **09ʰ45.7ᵐ −14° 20′**

NGC 2993 H278³ Galaxy Type I0? pec
ϕ **3.3′×1.8′, m12.6v, SB14.4**   **09ʰ45.8ᵐ −14° 22′**
Finder Chart 47-6, Figure 47-18   ★★★/★★
12/14″Scopes–125x: NGC 2992 and NGC 2993 are
   interacting galaxies 3′ apart in a NE–SW direction.
   NGC 2992 on the NW is the brighter and larger of
   the two: its moderately concentrated 2′×1′ NNE–
   SSW halo contains a stellar nucleus. The smaller
   NGC 2993 on the SE has a halo that measures only
   1′×0.5′ N–S, but also contains a stellar nucleus.
20/22″Scopes–175x: NGC 2992 is a fairly bright teardrop-shaped object elongated 3.5′×1′ NNE–SSW
   containing a broadly concentrated core extending
   along the major axis. A faint wisp bridges toward
   its smaller companion, NGC 2993, which has a tiny
   core surrounded by a well concentrated 1.5′ diameter halo.

NGC 3052 H272³ Galaxy Type SA:(rs)c I-II
ϕ **2.1′×1.4′, m12.2v, SB13.2**   **09ʰ54.5ᵐ −18° 38′**
Finder Chart 47-7, Figure 47-19   ★★★
12/14″Scopes–125x: NGC 3052 is 23′ north and slightly
   west of an attractive red 5th magnitude star. The
   galaxy has a bright core embedded in a faint 1.5′×1′
   ESE–WNW halo. A magnitude 11.5 star lies 3.5′
   west of the galaxy's center, and a 10th magnitude
   star is 5′ SE.

NGC 3054 Galaxy Type SAB(rs)bc IC
ϕ **3.4′×1.9′, m11.5v, SB13.4**   **09ʰ54.5ᵐ −25° 42′**
Finder Chart 47-8, Figure 47-20   ★★★
12/14″Scopes–125x: NGC 3054, located 12′ north of a

5th magnitude star, has a fairly faint 3′×2′ ESE–
   WNW halo containing a faint stellar nucleus. A
   12.5 magnitude star lies 2.75′ east of the galaxy's
   center, and a 10th magnitude star is 6.5′ SSE.

NGC 3078 H268² Galaxy Type E3:
ϕ **3.0′×2.4′, m11.0v, SB13.0**   **09ʰ58.4ᵐ −26° 56′**
Finder Chart 47-8   ★★★
8/10″Scopes–100x: NGC 3078 has a fairly bright, circular 1.5′ diameter halo containing a bright core. In
   appearance the galaxy resembles a diffuse globular
   cluster.
12/14″Scopes–125x: NGC 3078 has a very bright core
   containing a stellar nucleus and surrounded by a
   well concentrated 2′×1.5′ N–S halo. A 13th magnitude star touches the halo's west edge.

NGC 3081 H596³ Galaxy Type (R)SAB(r)0/a
ϕ **2.0′×1.2′, m12.0v, SB12.8**   **09ʰ59.5ᵐ −22° 50′**
Finder Chart 47-8, Figure 47-21   ★★★
12/14″Scopes–125x: NGC 3081 forms a triangle with
   two 9th magnitude stars 4′ NW and 4′ NE of its
   center. It has a fairly faint 1.5′ diameter halo
   containing a dim stellar nucleus.
16/18″Scopes–150x: NGC 3081 has a moderately concentrated 20″ diameter core containing a stellar
   nucleus. The faint halo is elongated 1.75′×1.50′
   ENE–WSW.

NGC 3091 H293² Galaxy Type E+3
ϕ **3.5′×2.3′, m11.0v, SB13.1**   **10ʰ00.2ᵐ −19° 38′**
Finder Chart 47-7, Figure 47-22   ★★★
8/10″Scopes–100x: NGC 3091, located 3′ west of a 10.5
   magnitude star, has a bright core embedded in a
   moderately faint 2′×0.75′ NW–SE halo.

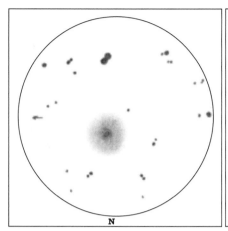

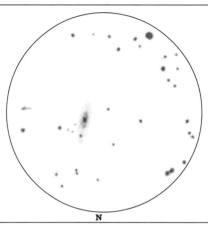

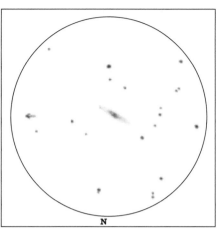

Figure 47-23. NGC 3124
17.5″, ƒ4.5–200x, by G. R. Kepple

Figure 47-24. NGC 3200
17.5″, ƒ4.5–200x, by G. R. Kepple

Figure 47-25. NGC 3203
17.5″, ƒ4.5–200x, by G. R. Kepple

16/18″Scopes–150x: NGC 3091 has a well concentrated 2.25′×1′ NW–SE halo containing a bright, circular 30″ core with a stellar nucleus. A 13th magnitude star lies 2′ SE of the galaxy's center just beyond the halo's SE tip. Almost touching the NW tip is the galaxy MCG–3-26-06, a tiny fuzzy dot which at first glance might be mistaken for a very faint star. 4.75′ to the ESE of NGC 3091 is another companion galaxy, NGC 3096, appearing merely as a faint 30″ halo around a dim stellar nucleus. NGC 3096 is at the southern corner of the 2.5′×1.25′ triangle which it forms with two magnitude 10.5 stars.

NGC 3109 Galaxy Type SB(s)m IV-V
ϕ **16.0′×2.9′, m9.8v, SB13.8**   **10ʰ03.1ᵐ −26° 09′**
Finder Chart 47-8, Figure 47-26   ★★
8/10″Scopes–100x: NGC 3109 is a very faint, highly

elongated 12′×2′ E–W ghostly streak containing a bright center. On the halo's edge NE of the galaxy's center is a wide pair of magnitude 12 and 12.5 stars. 3′ south of the center begins a 16′ chain of stars which arcs SW and then west away from the galaxy. The chain includes two 9th, three 10th, two 11th, one 12.5, and one 13th magnitude star.

16/18″Scopes–150x: In large telescopes the halo of NGC 3109 is fairly faint, diffuse, irregularly-outlined, and elongated 14′×3′ E–W. The irregularly extended core is mottled and peppered with faint knots. The halo extends beyond the western edge of a 7′×3.5′ "L" of magnitude 11.5 to 13 stars. The L's long side, composed of six unequally spaced stars, points toward a 45″ wide pair of 11th and 13th magnitude stars on the halo's edge 7′ ENE of the galaxy's center.

NGC 3124 Galaxy Type SB(r)bc I
ϕ **2.6′×1.9′, m12.0v, SB13.6**   **10ʰ06.7ᵐ −19° 13′**
Finder Chart 47-9, Figure 47-23   ★★
12/14″Scopes–125x: NGC 3124, located 5′ north of an attractive double of white stars (S607: 8.8, 10.0; 9.5″; 146°), is a dim, circular smudge about 1.5′ across.
16/18″Scopes–150x: NGC 3124 has a fairly faint, diffuse 2′ diameter halo which is slightly brighter toward its center. One 13th magnitude star is 2.5′ north, and a second is 3.5′ ENE, of the galaxy's center.

NGC 3145 Galaxy Type SB(rs)bc I
ϕ **2.3′×1.8′, m11.7v, SB13.1**   **10ʰ10.2ᵐ −12° 26′**
Finder Chart 47-9   ★★★
12/14″Scopes–125x: NGC 3145 appears fairly faint, elongated 2′×1.5′ NNE–SSW, and has a faint core. It is virtually overpowered by the glare of the

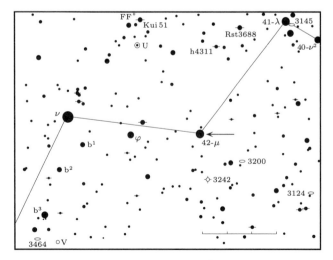

Finder Chart 47-9. 42–μ Hya: 10ʰ26.1ᵐ −16° 50′

Figure 47-26. *NGC 3109 has a diffuse, mottled halo without a distinct core. Image courtesy of Steven Juchnowski.*

Figure 47-27. *In larger instruments, NGC 3242, the Ghost of Jupiter, shows a bright bluish disk with a dark central region. Image courtesy of Josef Pöpsel and Stefan Binnewies.*

magnitude 3.6 Lambda (λ) = 41 Hydrae, located only 8′ to the NE. A 12th magnitude star lies 3.5′ SW of the galaxy's center.

NGC 3200 Galaxy Type SB(rs)c II
ϕ **4.1′×1.2′, m12.2v, SB13.8** $10^h18.6^m -17° 59′$
Finder Chart 47-9, Figure 47-24   ★★

12/14″ Scopes–125x: NGC 3200, located 9′ NW of an 8th and 2′ east of an 11th magnitude star, appears faint, of low surface brightness, and elongated 2.5′×0.75′ N–S.

16/18″ Scopes–150x: In larger telescopes NGC 3200 has a 4′×1′ NNW–SSE halo containing a weakly concentrated core with a stellar nucleus. A magnitude 13.5 star is inside the north edge of the halo 50″ from the galaxy's center. A 15″ wide NNE–SSW pair of 13th magnitude stars is 3.5′ north of the galaxy's center.

NGC 3203 Galaxy Type S0
ϕ **2.8′×0.6′, m12.2v, SB12.6** $10^h19.6^m -26° 42′$
Finder Chart 47-8, Figure 47-25   ★★★

8/10″ Scopes–100x: NGC 3203 is 4′ north of an 11th magnitude and 6.5′ west of a 10th magnitude star. It has a faint, small 2′×0.5′ ENE–WSW lens-shaped halo that contains an inconspicuous core.

16/18″ Scopes–150x: NGC 3203 has a moderately faint 2.5′×0.75′ ENE–WSW halo that elongates to tapered ends. The halo brightens suddenly into a well concentrated 45″×15″ core containing a possible threshold stellar nucleus.

NGC 3242 PK261+32.1 H27⁴ Plan. Neb. Type 4+3b
ϕ **>16″, m7.8v, CS12.10v** $10^h24.8^m -18° 38′$
Finder Chart 47-9, Figure 47-27   ★★★★★
Ghost of Jupiter

4/6″ Scopes–150x: The Ghost of Jupiter has a fine blue color and appears nearly the same size as Jupiter's disk – hence its name. The disk is bright with diffuse edges.

8/10″ Scopes–175x: This fine planetary nebula has an irregularly round disk. Faint extensions to the east and west bring the overall size to about 35″×30″. The central star is quite prominent.

12/14″ Scopes–200x: The magnitude 12.1 central star is surrounded by a small circular dark area. About 10″ from the star is a bright oval inner ring. The inner ring, dark area, and central star resemble an eye. Surrounding the inner ring is a faint diffuse outer shell elongated NW–SE.

16/18″ Scopes–250x: This fine, bright planetary nebula has in intense bluish hue with a prominent whitish central star. The star is embedded in a 20″×15″ NNW–SSE oval dark region that is surrounded by a bright inner ring. The faint outer ring is elongated 45″×35″ and has several bright spots on its NW and SE.

NGC 3285 Galaxy Type (R′)SAB(rs)a pec:
ϕ **2.5′×1.3′, m12.0v, SB13.1** $10^h33.6^m -27° 27′$
Finder Chart 47-8   ★★★
12/14″ Scopes–125x: NGC 3285 is 7′ SW of a 7.5 magnitude star and about half a degree west of the

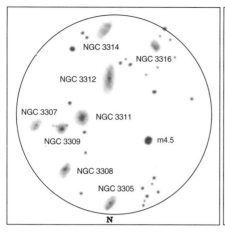

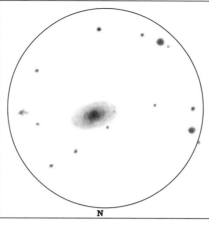

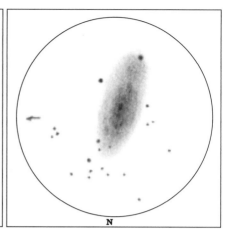

Figure 47-28. Hydra I Galaxy Cluster
17.5″, f4.5–125x, by G. R. Kepple

Figure 47-29. NGC 3585
17.5″, f4.5–175x, by G. R. Kepple

Figure 47-30. NGC 3621
17.5″, f4.5–225x, by G. R. Kepple

Hydra I Galaxy Cluster. The faint 2′×1′ ESE–WNW oval halo contains a faint stellar nucleus.

NGC 3305 Galaxy Type E0
φ 1.1′×1.0′, m12.9v, SB12.9   10ʰ36.3ᵐ −27° 10′
Finder Chart 47-8, Figure 47-28   ★★

16/18″Scopes–150x: NGC 3305, the northernmost member of the Hydra I Galaxy Cluster (Abell 1060), is 14′ NNW of a 4.5 magnitude star. It has a very faint diffuse 1′×0.5′ NW–SE halo containing a faint stellar nucleus. A 13th magnitude star lies 2′ NNE, and a 12th magnitude star 3.5′ NNE, of the galaxy's center.

NGC 3307 Galaxy Type SB(r)0+:
φ 1.0′×0.4′, m14.2v, SB13.1   10ʰ36.3ᵐ −27° 32′
Finder Chart 47-8, Figure 47-28   ★

16/18″Scopes–150x: This extremely dim object is the westernmost member of the Hydra I Galaxy Cluster (Abell 1060). It is located 4′ due west of the bright Hydra I galaxy pair, NGC 3309 + NGC 3311. NGC 3307 is a 1′×0.5′ NW–SE oval glow containing a faint stellar nucleus.

NGC 3308 Galaxy Type SB(s)0°
φ 1.8′×1.4′, m12.3v, SB13.2   10ʰ36.4ᵐ −27° 26′
Finder Chart 47-8, Figure 47-28   ★★

8/10″Scopes–100x: NGC 3308 is in the Hydra I Galaxy Cluster 12′ WNW of a 4.5 magnitude star and 5′ SSW of a 12th magnitude star. It has a faint, small NNE–SSW halo that is slightly brighter in its center.

16/18″Scopes–150x: NGC 3308 has a small, mottled core embedded within a poorly concentrated 2′×1′ NNW–SSE halo.

NGC 3309 Galaxy Type E1
φ 4.4′×3.1′, m11.0v, SB13.7   10ʰ36.6ᵐ −27° 31′
Finder Chart 47-8, Figure 47-28   ★★★

8/10″Scopes–100x: NGC 3309, the second brightest member of the Hydra I Galaxy Cluster, is at the NW vertex of the equilateral triangle it forms with 12th magnitude stars 3′ to its ENE and SSE. Only 1.5′ to the galaxy's ESE, between the 12th magnitude stars, is the brightest object of the Hydra I system, NGC 3311. NGC 3309 has a faint, small round halo that is slightly brighter at its center. A 13th magnitude star is just 30″ SE of the galaxy's center.

12/14″Scopes–125x: In medium-size instruments, NGC 3309 shows a fairly bright 1.5′ diameter halo slightly elongated N–S and containing a broad but weakly concentrated core.

NGC 3311 Galaxy Type SA(r)0° ?
φ 4.0′×3.6′, m10.9v, SB13.6   10ʰ36.7ᵐ −27° 32′
Finder Chart 47-8, Figure 47-28   ★★★

8/10″Scopes–100x: NGC 3311, the brightest member of the Hydra I Galaxy Cluster, is between a NNE–SSW pair of 12th magnitude stars. Just 1.5′ to the WNW is another bright Hydra I galaxy, NGC 3309. NGC 3311 appears slightly larger than the latter. Its circular 1.5′ diameter halo has smooth surface brightness. The Hydra I Galaxy Cluster is around 200 million light years distant. Hence both NGC 3309 and NGC 3311 have absolute magnitudes of at least −23, which corresponds to luminosities of about 130 billion suns. Their true diameters are around a quarter of a million light years.

16/18″Scopes–150x: In larger instruments, NGC 3311 has a 2′ diameter halo that is slightly elongated NNE–SSW and contains a very faint stellar nucleus.

NGC 3312 Galaxy Type SA(s)b pec
φ 3.4′×1.1′, m11.8v, SB13.1   10ʰ37.0ᵐ −27° 34′
Finder Chart 47-8, Figure 47-28   ★★★
8/10″ Scopes–100x: NGC 3312 is a Hydra I Cluster
    member located 5′ SE of NGC 3311, 7′ NNE of a
    6th magnitude star, and 10′ SSW of a magnitude
    4.5 star. The halo is rather faint, elongated 2′×1′
    N–S, and contains a faint stellar nucleus. 2.5′ SE
    of the galaxy's center is a triangle of one 12.5 and
    two 12th magnitude stars.
16/18″ Scopes–150x: NGC 3312 has a large, moderately
    concentrated core containing a stellar nucleus
    embedded in a much fainter 3′×1.5′ N–S halo.

NGC 3314 Galaxy Type Sab: sp
φ 1.5′×0.8′, m12.8v, SB12.8   10ʰ37.2ᵐ −27° 41′
Finder Chart 47-8, Figure 47-28   ★★
16/18″ Scopes–150x: NGC 3314, a dim object, is the
    southernmost member of the Hydra I Galaxy Clus-
    ter. It is located 7′ ESE of a 6th magnitude star
    and 7.5′ south of galaxy NGC 3312. NGC 3314 has
    a faint 1′×0.5′ NW–SE halo of even surface bright-
    ness. A 13th magnitude star touches the galaxy's
    NW tip.

NGC 3316 Galaxy Type SB(rs)0+:
φ 1.4′×1.2′, m12.6v, SB13.0   10ʰ37.6ᵐ −27° 36′
Finder Chart 47-8, Figure 47-28   ★★
16/18″ Scopes–150x: NGC 3316 is near the eastern edge
    of the Hydra I Galaxy Cluster 8′ ESE of Hydra I
    galaxy NGC 3312. NGC 3316 is a dim 30″ diameter
    glow slightly elongated NNE–SSW. A 12.5 magni-
    tude star lies 3′ to its SSE, and a 14th magnitude
    star is on its SSE edge. Many more Hydra I Cluster
    galaxies are within reach of large reflectors.

NGC 3390 Galaxy Type Sb
φ 3.1′×0.7′, m12.4v, SB13.1   10ʰ48.1ᵐ −31° 32′
Finder Chart 47-10   ★★★
8/10″ Scopes–100x: NGC 3390, nestled in a moderately
    rich field of bright stars, forms a triangle with a 6th
    magnitude star 10′ to its south and a 7.5 magnitude
    star 8′ to its SW. The galaxy has a fairly faint
    2′×0.5′ N–S halo that contains a well concentrated
    center.
16/18″ Scopes–150x: In larger telescopes NGC 3390
    reveals a large, unevenly bright oval core embedded
    in a much fainter 4′×0.5′ N–S halo that fades to
    diffuse edges. 1′ north and 2′ south of the galaxy,
    near each of the halo's tips, is a 14th magnitude
    star.

NGC 3464 Galaxy Type SB(rs)cd II
φ 2.3′×1.5′, m12.5v, SB13.7   10ʰ54.7ᵐ −21° 04′
Finder Chart 47-9   ★★
12/14″ Scopes–125x: NGC 3464, located 12′ east of a
    9th magnitude star, is faint, elongated 1.5′×1.0′
    ESE–WNW, and slightly brighter in its center. Not
    quite a degree to the galaxy's WSW is the carbon
    star V Hydrae, one of the most deeply red-hued
    objects in the entire sky. However, the immediate
    area around NGC 3464 is rather star poor.

NGC 3585 H269² Galaxy Type SAB(s)0−: pec
φ 6.9′×4.2′, m9.7v, SB13.2   11ʰ13.3ᵐ −26° 45′
Finder Chart 47-10, Figure 47-29   ★★★★
8/10″ Scopes–100x: NGC 3585 is 19′ east of a 5.5
    magnitude star at the west vertex of an equilateral
    triangle with a 7.5 magnitude star 8.5′ to the
    galaxy's SE and a magnitude 8.5 star 8.25′ to its
    ENE. Its bright 2′×1′ ESE–WNW halo contains a
    large, well concentrated core with a stellar nucleus.
16/18″ Scopes–150x: NGC 3585 has a fairly bright 5′×3′
    ESE–WNW oval halo that brightens smoothly to
    a 1′×0.45′ core containing a brilliant nucleus. 13th
    magnitude stars are 2.5′ NE, 3′ NNW, and 4′ WNW
    of the galaxy's center.

NGC 3621 H241¹ Galaxy Type SA(s)d III
φ 9.8′×4.6′, m8.9v, SB12.9   11ʰ18.3ᵐ −32° 49′
Finder Chart 47-10, Figure 47-30   ★★★★★
8/10″ Scopes–100x: NGC 3621, located within a large
    kite-shaped asterism, is a fine galaxy with a large,
    bright core embedded in a diffuse 8″×5″ N–S halo.
12/14″ Scopes–125x: NGC 3621 is an impressive object.
    It's large, bright 9′×6′ NNW–SSE halo brightens
    gradually toward the large, diffuse core, at the
    center of which is some mottling. A 10th magnitude

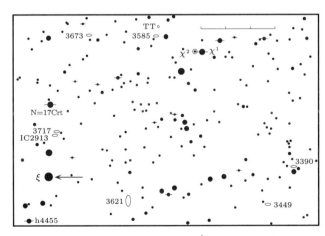

Finder Chart 47-10. α Hya: 11ʰ33.0ᵐ −31° 51′

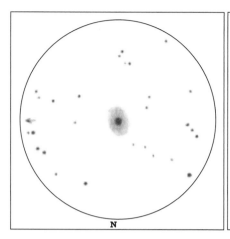

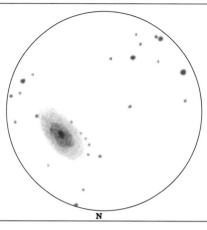

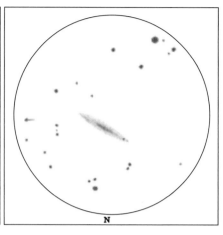

Figure 47-31. NGC 3904
17.5″, f4.5–200x, by G. R. Kepple

Figure 47-32. NGC 3923
17.5″, f4.5–175x, by G. R. Kepple

Figure 47-33. NGC 3936
17.5″, f4.5–225x, by G. R. Kepple

star touches the halo 3.5′ SSW of the galaxy's center, and an 11th magnitude touches the halo 5′ SSE of the center. At least ten foreground stars are superimposed upon the northern half of the halo.

20/22″ Scopes–175x: In large telescopes NGC 3621 is a bright 10′×6′ NNW–SSE oval patch containing a 2′×1′ core with a stellar nucleus. The outer halo is diffuse. With averted vision faint spiral features can be glimpsed as brightenings outside the east and west edges of the core.

NGC 3673 Galaxy Type SB(r)b II
ϕ 3.5′×1.8′, m11.5v, SB13.3   11^{h}25.2^m −26° 44′
Finder Chart 47-10   ★★★

12/14″ Scopes–125x: NGC 3673 is located 8′ north of a 7.5 magnitude star and 1.5′ west of a 40″ wide NE–SW double of 10.5 and 12th magnitude stars. The

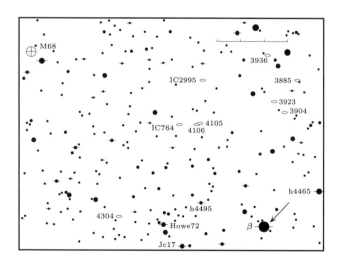

Finder Chart 47-11. β Hya: 11^{h}52.9^m −33° 54′

halo is rather faint elongated 2′×1′ ENE–WSW, and slightly brighter in its center.

NGC 3717 Galaxy Type SAb
ϕ 6.6′×1.5′, m11.4v, SB13.7   11^{h}31.5^m −30° 19′
Finder Chart 47-10   ★★★★

8/10″ Scopes–100x: NGC 3717 is located 7′ ESE of an 8th magnitude star, appears faint and elongated 3′×0.5′ NE–SW.

12/14″ Scopes–125x: NGC 3717 is a faint nebulous streak elongated 4.5′×1′ NE–SW and containing moderate central brightening. A 13th magnitude star is at the galaxy's northern tip.

16/18″ Scopes–150x: In larger telescopes NGC 3717 shows a fine 6′×1.25′ NE–SW lens-shaped halo that elongates to tapered ends and contains a highly extended core with a faint stellar nucleus. A 13th magnitude star is superimposed upon the halo 45″ north of the core's center. 7.5′ SE of NGC 3717 is its companion galaxy IC 2913, a fairly bright 30″ diameter halo that is uniformly illuminated but for a stellar nucleus.

NGC 3885 H828³ Galaxy Type SAB(rs)a ?
ϕ 3.2′×1.3′, m11.8v, SB13.2   11^{h}46.8^m −27° 55′
Finder Chart 47-11   ★★★

12/14″ Scopes–125x: NGC 3885 is midway between two 9th magnitude stars that form the eastern side of an equilateral triangle with an 8th magnitude star 6′ to their west. The galaxy's circular 1′ diameter halo appears faint and diffuse and evenly illuminated.

16/18″ Scopes–150x: At this aperture NGC 3885 has a fairly faint 1.5′×1′ ESE–WNW halo that is moderately brighter in its center.

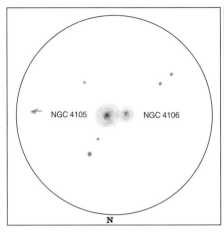

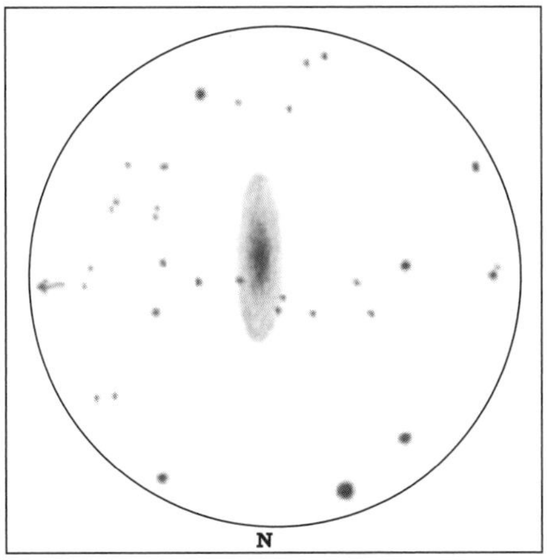

Figure 47-34. NGC 4105 and NGC 4106
17.5", f4.5–200x, by G. R. Kepple

Figure 47-35. IC 764
17.5", f4.5–175x, by G. R. Kepple

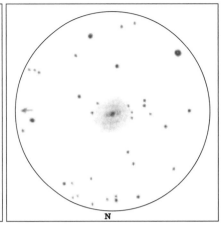

Figure 47-36. NGC 4304
17.5", f4.5–225x, by G. R. Kepple

NGC 3904 H864[2] Galaxy Type SA0–:
φ 3.1′×2.2′, m10.8v, SB12.7   11^{h}49.2^m −29° 17′
Finder Chart 47-11, Figure 47-31   ★★★
8/10″Scopes–100x: This galaxy has a fairly faint, circular 1.25′ diameter halo that surrounds a bright core. NGC 3904 is 40′ SW of the much brighter and larger galaxy NGC 3923.
16/18″Scopes–150x: NGC 3904 has a fairly bright halo elongated 2.5′×2′ in position angle 15° and contains a well concentrated core. A 9th magnitude star is 10′ ESE of the galaxy.

NGC 3923 H259[1] Galaxy Type SAB(s)0–? pec
φ 6.9′×4.8′, m9.6v, SB13.3   11^{h}51.0^m −28° 48′
Finder Chart 47-11, Figure 47-32   ★★★★
8/10″Scopes–100x: NGC 3923 has a bright nucleus embedded in a fairly bright 2.5′×2′ NE–SW halo. A triangle of 9th magnitude stars lies 9′ to the galaxy's SE.
16/18″Scopes–150x: NGC 3923 is bright, elongated 3.5′×2.5′ NE–SW, and contains a well concentrated core with a stellar nucleus. One 14th magnitude star lies just west of the nucleus, and another is on the halo's SW edge.

NGC 3936 Galaxy Type Sbc: sp I-II
φ 4.7′×0.9′, m11.8v, SB13.2   11^{h}52.3^m −26° 54′
Finder Chart 47-11, Figure 47-33   ★★★
12/14″Scopes–125x: NGC 3936, located 4.75′ south of a 9th magnitude star, is a faint 3.5′×0.5′ ENE–WSW streak containing a thin, poorly concentrated 1′ long core. A threshold star is embedded in the ENE tip. Another 9th magnitude star is 8′ SSE of the galaxy.

IC 2995 Galaxy Type SB(s)cd II-III
φ 3.5′×0.9′, m12.4v, SB13.5   12^{h}05.8^m −27° 56′
Finder Chart 47-11   ★★
12/14″Scopes–125x: IC 2995 is at the WNW corner of the triangle it forms with a 9th magnitude star 5.5′ to its ESE and a double of 9th and 12.5 magnitude stars 8′ to its SE. The galaxy's halo is extremely faint, elongated 2′×1′ NW–SE, and a little brighter in its center.
20/22″Scopes–175x: IC 2995 appears faint, diffuse, and elongated 3′×1′ ESE–WNW, and contains a faint central bar. A 13th magnitude star lies 45″ SW of the galaxy's center.

NGC 4105 H865[2] Galaxy Type E1: pec
φ 3.7′×1.7′, m10.4v, SB12.2   12^{h}06.7^m −29° 46′

NGC 4106 H866[2] Galaxy Type SAB(s)0°: pec
φ 4.0′×2.6′, m10.6v, SB13.0   12^{h}06.8^m −29° 46′
Finder Chart 47-11, Figure 47-34   ★★★/★★★
8/10″Scopes–100x: These two galaxies form a close 2′ E–W pair. NGC 4105, the western system, is the brighter and larger of the two, its halo 1.5′ in diameter. The eastern galaxy, NGC 4106, is similar in appearance to NGC 4105 but only 1′ across.
16/18″Scopes–150x: In larger telescopes NGC 4105 and NGC 4106 are an attractive double galaxy with touching halos. NGC 4105 is distinctly larger, with a slightly elongated 2′×1.75′ ESE–WNW halo that contains a bright nonstellar nucleus. NGC 4106 to the east is a 1.75′×1.5′ E–W oval with a tiny bright core. A 9th magnitude star is 6′ NNW of NGC 4105.

Figure 47-37. *Messier 68 (NGC 4590) is a rather large and bright, but poorly concentrated, class X globular cluster. Image courtesy of Jim Burnell.*

IC 764 Galaxy Type SAB(rs)c: II
ϕ **4.0′×1.5′, m12.3v, SB14.1**   **12ʰ10.2ᵐ −29° 44′**
Finder Chart 47-11, Figure 47-35   ★★
12/14″Scopes–125x: IC764 lies 7.5′ SSW of an 8th magnitude star which forms a wide double with a 10th magnitude companion 2′ SE. The galaxy has an extremely faint, diffuse 2.5′×1.25′ N–S halo.
20/22″Scopes–175x: This galaxy appears very faint and diffuse, its 4.5′×1.75′ N–S halo containing only a slight central concentration. The surrounding field is lightly sprinkled with faint stars, two of which lie on the NE edge of the halo and a third on the west edge of the halo 1′ NW of the galaxy's center.

NGC 4304 Galaxy Type SB(s)c pec: I-II
ϕ **2.5′×1.1′, m11.7v, SB12.6**   **12ʰ22.2ᵐ −33° 29′**
Finder Chart 47-11, Figure 47-36   ★★★
8/10″Scopes–100x: NGC 4304 is between a 7th magni-

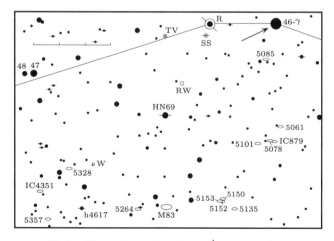

Finder Chart 47-12. 46–γ Hya: 13ʰ18.9ᵐ −23° 11′

tude star 7′ to its SE and a 9.5 magnitude star 6′ to its west. The galaxy has a very faint, round 1.5′ diameter halo that is slightly brighter in the center.
16/18″Scopes–150x: NGC 4304 appears faint and diffuse with a circular 2.5′ diameter halo. 200x shows a faint central bar extended 1′×0.25′ ESE–WNW. A 12.5 magnitude star is 2′ SW of the galaxy's center, and five threshold stars lie along the WSW and eastern edges of its halo.

NGC 4590 Messier 68 Globular Cluster Class X
ϕ **12′, m7.7v**   **12ʰ39.5ᵐ −26° 45′**
Finder Chart 47-11, Figure 47-37   ★★★★
  This globular cluster was first seen by Mechain and Messier in 1780. It lies 31,000 light years distant.
8/10″Scopes–100x: Messier 68 is a fairly bright globular cluster with a mottled core embedded in a loose 10′ diameter halo which resolves well around its periphery.
16/18″Scopes–150x: Messier 68 is a fine globular with a bright 3′ diameter core that is poorly resolved at 125x, but rich at 175x. The core is embedded in a 12′ diameter halo of faint stars scattered in outcurving streamers reminiscent of the spray of a lawn sprinkler.

NGC 5061 H138¹ Galaxy Type SA0–
ϕ **4.1′×3.5′, m10.2v, SB12.9**   **13ʰ18.1ᵐ −26° 50′**
Finder Chart 47-12   ★★★★
8/10″Scopes–100x: NGC 5061 is at the NW corner of the isosceles triangle it forms with 10th and 10.5 magnitude stars. It is a moderately concentrated 2′×1.5′ NE–SW oval containing a stellar nucleus. A 12th magnitude star lies 1′ ENE of the galaxy's center.
12/14″Scopes–125x: NGC 5061 has a very luminous core embedded in a bright 2.5′×2′ NE–SW halo. A 12th magnitude star nearly touches the NE tip of the halo. Galaxy NGC 5078 lies 39′ SE.

NGC 5078 H566² Galaxy Type SA(s)a: sp
ϕ **4.8′×2.6′, m10.6v, SB13.2**   **13ʰ19.8ᵐ −27° 24′**
Finder Chart 47-12, Figure 47-38   ★★★★
8/10″Scopes–100x: NGC 5078 and NGC 5101 are a comparably bright and large galaxy-pair 25′ apart in an E–W direction. A NW–SE pair of 8th magnitude stars are between the galaxies. NGC 5078 is a fairly faint, smoothly illuminated 2′×1′ NNW–SSE oval.
16/18″Scopes–150x: NGC 5078 has a moderately concentrated, extended core embedded in a faint 3′×1.5′

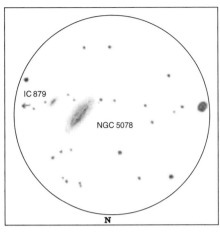

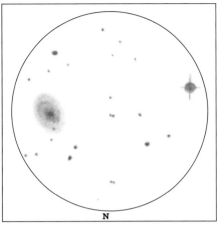

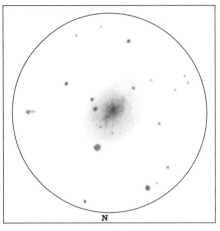

Figure 47-38. NGC 5078 and IC 879
17.5″, f4.5–200x, by G. R. Kepple

Figure 47-39. NGC 5085
17.5″, f4.5–200x, by G. R. Kepple

Figure 47-40. NGC 5101
17.5″, f4.5–200x, by G. R. Kepple

NW–SE halo. The eastern edge of the halo is more sharply defined because a dust lane is just visible paralleling the western edge. At 200x the stellar nucleus glitters in and out of view. 2.5′ SW of NGC 5078 is its companion galaxy IC 879, a very faint 45″×30″ NW–SE oval smudge with a faint stellar nucleus.

NGC 5085 H780² Galaxy Type SA(s)c I-II
φ 3.2′×2.7′, m11.3v, SB 13.5   13ʰ20.3ᵐ −24° 26′
Finder Chart 47-12, Figure 47-39   ★★★
12/14″Scopes–125x: NGC 5085, located 11′ west of a 5th magnitude star and 4′ north of a magnitude 8.5 star, is a faint, diffuse galaxy with a circular 2′ diameter halo that contains a faint central core. 3.5′ to the NNE of the galaxy is a 50″ wide NNW–SSE pair of 12th magnitude stars.

NGC 5101 H567² Galaxy Type (R′)SB(rs)a
φ 6.0′×4.1′, m10.4v, SB 13.7   13ʰ21.8ᵐ −27° 26′
Finder Chart 47-12, Figure 47-40   ★★★★
8/10″Scopes–100x: NGC 5101 is 3′ SSE of a 9th magnitude member of a large semicircle asterism. The galaxy has a fairly faint, circular 2′ diameter halo with slight central brightening.
16/18″Scopes–150x: NGC 5101 has a fairly bright 2′×1′ core surrounded by a much fainter 6′×5′ NW–SE halo. A very faint stellar nucleus is embedded in a conspicuous nuclear bulge. Superimposed upon the halo are a 12.5 magnitude star 2′ west, and a 13.5 magnitude star 2.5′ WSW, of the galaxy's center.

NGC 5135 Galaxy Type SAB(s)b
φ 2.3′×1.5′, m11.8v, SB 13.0   13ʰ25.7ᵐ −29° 50′
Finder Chart 47-12   ★★★
12/14″Scopes–125x: NGC 5135 is at the western corner of the triangle it forms with a magnitude 9.5 star 7′ to its east and a 10th magnitude star 7′ SE. It has a fairly faint 2′×1′ ESE–WNW halo containing a very faint ESE–WNW bar with a conspicuous stellar nucleus.

NGC 5150 Galaxy Type Sbc II
φ 1.5′×1.1′, m12.6v, SB 13.0   13ʰ27.6ᵐ −29° 34′
Finder Chart 47-12, Figure 47-42   ★★★
12/14″Scopes–125x: NGC 5150, located 1.75′ WSW of a 9th magnitude star, has a faint, round 1′ diameter halo containing a well concentrated core with a double nucleus. Galaxies NGC 5152-53 form a contact pair 5′ SE of NGC 5150.

NGC 5152 Galaxy Type SB(s)b
φ 3.0′×1.0′, m12.5v, SB 13.5   13ʰ27.9ᵐ −29° 37′
NGC 5153 Galaxy Type E1 pec
φ 1.7′×1.3′, m12.3v, SB 13.0   13ʰ28.0ᵐ −29° 37′
Finder Chart 47-12, Figure 47-42   ★★/★★
12/14″Scopes–125x: NGC 5152 and NGC 5153, located 3′ WNW of a 9th magnitude star, appear as two very faint, small, nearly merged circular nodules. The eastern nodule, NGC 5153, has a 1′ diameter halo around a well concentrated center. The western galaxy, NGC 5152, is diffuse and elongated 1.5′×0.5′ ESE-WNW. Galaxy NGC 5150 lies 5′ NW.

Figure 47-41. *Messier 83 (NGC 5236) is a magnificent galaxy displaying in medium-size telescopes a bright core and bar around which are spiral arms. Image courtesy of Dean Salman.*

NGC 5236 Messier 83 Galaxy Type SAB(s)c II
ϕ **15.5′×13.0′, m7.6v, SB 13.2**   **13ʰ37.0ᵐ −29° 52′**
Finder Chart 47-12, Figure 47-41   ★★★★★

Messier 83 was discovered by Lacaille at the Cape of Good Hope in 1752, and Messier added it to his catalogue in March 1781. It lies 22 million light years distant and is part of the Centaurus Galaxy Group with

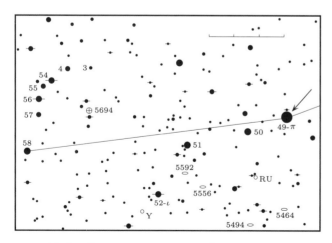

Finder Chart 47-13. 49–π Hya: 14ʰ06.3ᵐ −26° 41′

NGC 4945, NGC 5102, and NGC 5253 in Centaurus to its south, and NGC 5068 in Virgo to its north. M83's absolute magnitude is −21.6, a luminosity of 36 billion suns. Its true diameter is over 100,000 light years.

8/10″Scopes–100x: This magnificent galaxy forms a large triangle with a 7th magnitude star 15′ to its east and a 6th magnitude star 25′ to its NE. Messier 83 has a bright, circular core in a NE–SW bar with spiral arms arcing from either end of the bar within a 14′ diameter halo. The arm from the NE end of the bar curves east and then south; the arm from the SW end of the bar curves west and north. With averted vision the two arms appear to curve into each other. The interarm zones are sprinkled with marginally resolved objects that are either threshold foreground stars of our own Galaxy or actual M83 giant emission nebulae.

12/14″Scopes–125x: Messier 83 is a fine face-on barred spiral galaxy with an oval core and a bright bar encircled by an interesting spiral arm pattern. The irregular halo has a profile similar to that of the gibbous Moon, its periphery circular on the east side

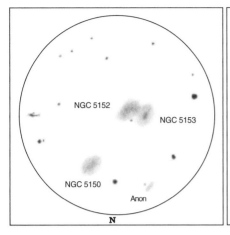

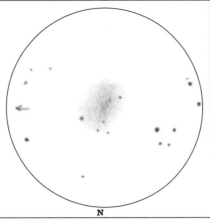

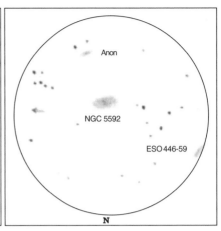

Figure 47-42. NGC 5150 and NGC 5152-53
17.5", f4.5–200x, by G. R. Kepple

Figure 47-43. NGC 5556
17.5", f4.5–200x, by G. R. Kepple

Figure 47-44. NGC 5592
17.5", f4.5–200x, by Glen W. Sanner

but raggedly linear on the west. The spiral arm that springs from the NE end of the bar arcs through only 90°, ending south of the galaxy's center; but the arm that springs from the bar's SW end wraps all the way around the north side of the galaxy to its east, thus giving the galaxy an asymmetrical look. The dark lanes divide the spiral arms, the most conspicuous NNE and SSE of the bar. A dozen foreground stars are superimposed upon the halo. The star field is richest to the south and SE of the galaxy. Three 9th magnitude stars are near M83, one just outside its south edge, a second 7' to its south, and the third 9' to the ESE. A 12th magnitude star is on the outer edge of the WSW spiral arm.

NGC 5264 Galaxy Type IB(s)m
ϕ 3.4'×2.1', m12.1v, SB14.1   13^{h}41.6^m −29° 55'
Finder Chart 47-12   ★★
12/14"Scopes–125x: NGC 5264 is a degree east of Messier 83 and 4.5' west of a 9th magnitude star with an 11th magnitude companion 16" distant in position angle 280°. The galaxy has a very faint 1.5'×1' NE–SW halo that is slightly brighter at its center. A 13th magnitude star is 1.5' ENE of the galaxy's center.

NGC 5328 H923³ Galaxy Type E4-5:
ϕ 2.5'×1.7', m11.7v, SB13.1   13^{h}52.9^m −28° 29'
Finder Chart 47-12   ★★★
8/10"Scopes–100x: NGC 5328, located 19' WNW of a 6th magnitude star, appears moderately faint with a 1' diameter halo containing a very small, but conspicuous core.
12/14"Scopes–125x: NGC 5328 has a fairly bright, circular 1.5' diameter halo which grows smoothly brighter to a nonstellar nucleus. Two 13th magni-

tude stars to the south point toward the galaxy. Only 1.5' to the NE is galaxy NGC 5330, even with averted vision nothing more than a faint smudge.

IC 4351 Galaxy Type SAbc: sp
ϕ 6.0'×1.1', m11.8v, SB13.7   13^{h}57.9^m −29° 19'
Finder Chart 47-12   ★★★
8/10"Scopes–100x: IC 4351 is 7' east of a 9th magnitude and 11.5' NE of an 8th magnitude star. It has a faint halo highly elongated 3'×0.5' NNE–SSW containing a slight brightening at its core.
16/18"Scopes–150x: In larger telescopes the halo appears moderately concentrated, elongated 4'×0.75' NNE–SSW, and has a patchy center but no discernible nucleus. A 14th magnitude star is on the halo's ESE edge. A wide WNW–ESE pair of magnitude 13 and 13.5 stars is 3' SW of the galaxy's center.

NGC 5556 Galaxy Type SB(s)d IV
ϕ 3.4'×2.1', m11.8v, SB13.8   14^{h}20.6^m −29° 15'
Finder Chart 47-13, Figure 47-43   ★★
12/14"Scopes–125x: NGC 5556 lies 4' SW of an 11th magnitude star which is the westernmost and brightest member of a 4'×1' stellar trapezoid, the other three stars 12th and 13th magnitude objects. The galaxy has a very dim 2.5' diameter halo slightly elongated NNW–SSE but with no central brightening. A magnitude 12.5 star is on the halo's NW edge, a tiny triangle of faint stars on its northern edge, and a fourth faint star superimposed upon the halo 1' SE of the galaxy's center.

NGC 5592 H924³ Galaxy Type SB(s)c: II
φ 1.6′×1.0′, m12.9v, SB 13.3   14ʰ23.9ᵐ −28° 41′
Finder Chart 47-13, Figure 47-44   ★★
12/14″Scopes–125x: NGC 5592 is located 2.5′ WSW of
   the SW member of a 2.5′×1.5′ triangle of 12th
   magnitude stars. It is a dim 1.5′×0.75′ E–W smudge
   containing a slightly brighter center. 7′ to its WSW
   is a small asterism reminiscent of the Little Dipper.
   7′ to the ENE of NGC 5592 is the galaxy ESO 446-
   59, a very faint 1′×0.25′ NW–SE streak.

NGC 5694 H196² Globular Cluster Class VII
φ 3.6′, m9.2:v   14ʰ39.6ᵐ −26° 32′
Finder Chart 47-13   ★★
8/10″Scopes–150x: This globular cluster lies 1.5′ NE of
   the northernmost member of a 1.25′ wide N–S pair
   of 9th magnitude stars. It has a fairly faint, fuzzy,
   unresolved 2′ diameter halo with a bright center.
16/18″Scopes–200x: NGC 5694 shows a well concentrated 1′ diameter core embedded in a fainter 2.5′
   granular but unresolved halo.

Chapter 48

Leo, the Lion

48.1 Overview

Leo, the Lion has one of the most conspicuous and distinctive constellation patterns – though in all truth it has no special resemblance to the figure of a lion. The head and forequarters of the Lion are marked by the striking asterism called the Sickle, comprised of Epsilon (ϵ), Mu (μ), Zeta (ζ), Gamma (γ), Eta (η), and Alpha (α) Leonis. The Lion's hindquarter is the large right triangle of Beta (β), Delta (δ), and Theta (ϑ) Leonis. Before it became the Hair of Queen Berenice, the Coma Berenices Star Cluster probably was considered to be the tuft at the end of the Lion's tail. In Greek astromythology the celestial Lion was associated with the Nemean Lion slain by Hercules as the first of his Twelve Labors. The Greeks inherited the celestial Lion from the Babylonians before them. It was especially sacred to the goddess of love and war, Ishtar, who was in the course of time absorbed into the Greek Aphrodite. A very common motif in Babylonian art is a combat between a lion and a bull, the lion always getting the better of it: this apparently was their expression of the astronomical fact that the celestial Bull, Taurus, sets as the celestial Lion transits the meridian.

The constellation of Leo contains the radiant of the Leonid meteor shower, which peaks every year around November 17. The normal peak rate for the Leonids is only 10 per hour. But every 33 years the shower produces a spectacular storm of up to a hundred thousand meteors per hour. The last outbursts were in 1966 and 2001. These mega-storms are a consequence of the fact that the head of the parent comet of the shower has just recently broken up and its debris is not yet well distributed around the comet/shower orbit.

Leo, as is typical for off-Milky Way constellations, is well-provisioned with galaxies. However, many of its galaxies are large, bright objects in relatively nearby galaxy groups. Consequently Leo has five galaxies with Messier numbers: M65, M66, M95, M96, and M105. Several other Leo galaxies would not have been out of place in the Messier catalogue. The constellation also has several exceptionally interesting stars, one of them Algieba, Gamma (γ) Leonis, is one of the finest double stars in the sky.

Leo: LEE-oh
Genitive: Leonis, LEE-oh-nis
Abbreviation: Leo
Culmination: 9pm–Apr. 15, midnight–Mar. 1
Area: 947 square degrees
Showpieces: 41–γ Leo, 54 Leo, 65 Leo, 90 Leo, M65 (NGC 3623), M66 (NGC 3627), M95 (NGC 3351), M96 (NGC 3368), M105 (NGC 3379), NGC 2903, NGC 3521, NGC 3628
Binocular Objects: 14 Leo, 32–α Leo, 84 Leo, 93 Leo, M65 (NGC 3623), M66 (NGC 3627), M95 (NGC 3351), M96 (NGC 3368), M105 (NGC 3379), NGC 2903, NGC 3521, NGC 3628

48.2 Interesting Stars

R Leonis Variable Star   **Spec. M8 IIIe**
m4.4 to 11.3, Per 312.43 days $09^h47.6^m$ +11° 26′
Finder Chart 48-3   ★★★★

R Leonis is a pulsating red giant of the Mira class varying between the 4th and 11th magnitudes in an average period of 312 days. This star is one of the brightest of the long-period variables (LPVs). It is conveniently placed 8′ south of 19 Leonis, its red hue contrasting nicely with the white of 19 Leonis. Long-period variables are thought to have peak absolute magnitudes of −1.5, a luminosity of 330 suns. This implies that the distance to R Leo is around 520 light years.

Alpha (α) = 32 Leonis (ΣII6) Double Star Spec. B7, G
m1.4, 7.7; Sep. 176.9″; P.A. 307° $10^h08.3^m$ +11° 58′
Finder Chart 48-3   ★★★★

Regulus

"The Lion's Heart." Regulus is a diminutive form of the Latin word "Rex" or "King." The modern name Regulus was given to the star by Copernicus. The star also was known both as "The Lion's Heart" and as "The Kingly Star" to the ancient Babylonians, and is shown on the shoulder of lion statues carved around 2500 BC.

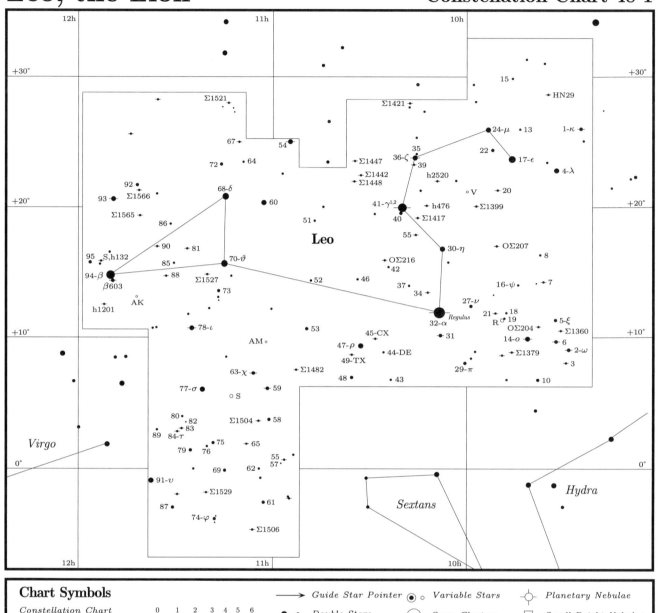

Chart Symbols

| Constellation Chart | 0 | 1 | 2 | 3 | 4 | 5 | 6 |

Stellar Magnitudes

Finder Charts   0/1   2   3   4   5   6   7   8   9

Master Finder Chart   0   1   2   3   4   5

→ Guide Star Pointer

●—• Double Stars

Finder Chart Scale

(One degree tick marks)

◉ ○ Variable Stars

◯ Open Clusters

⊕ Globular Clusters

⬯ Galaxies

⬡ Planetary Nebulae

☐ Small Bright Nebulae

⬭ Large Bright Nebulae

▨ Dark Nebulae

Table 48-1: Selected Variable Stars in Leo

Name	HD No.	Type	Max.	Min.	Period (Days)	F*	Spec. Type	R.A. (2000) Dec.		Finder Chart No.	Notes
R Leo	84748	M	4.4	11.3	312	0.43	M8	09h47.6m	+11° 26′	48-3	
V Leo	86608	M	8.4	14.6	273	0.44	M5	10h00.0m	+21 16	48-5	
AM Leo		EW	8.2	8.9	0.36		F8	11h02.2m	+09 54	48-9	
S Leo		M	9.0	14.5	189	0.48	M3-M6	10.8	+05 28	48-10	
AK Leo	101487	Lb	8.4	9.4	60		M5	40.8	+13 05	48-1	

F* = The fraction of period taken up by the star's rise from min. to max. brightness, or the period spent in eclipse.

Table 48-2: Selected Double Stars in Leo

Name	ADS No.	Pair	M1	M2	Sep.″	P.A.°	Spec	R.A. (2000) Dec	Finder Chart No.	Notes
2–ω Leo	7390		5.9	6.5	w0.6	*84	G0	09ʰ28.5ᵐ +09° 03′	48-3	118 year binary
3 Leo	7391		5.7	10.4	25.2	80	K0	28.5 +08 11	48-3	Yellow and blue
Σ1360	7406	AB	8.3	8.6	14.2	242	G5	30.5 +10 35	48-3	Equal yellow stars
6 Leo	7416		5.2	8.2	37.4	75	K0	32.0 +09 43	48-3	Gold and blue pair
HN 29	7426		6.5	10.5	30.5	260	A2	33.3 +28 22	48-6	
7 Leo	7448		6.2	10.0	41.2	80	A0	35.9 +14 23	48-4	
OΣ204	7471		7.6	11.6	8.4	102	A3	38.8 +10 47	48-3	
14–o Leo	7480		3.5	9.5	85.4	44	F5	41.2 +09 54	48-3	Yellow and blue
Σ1379	7508		7.9	11.6	9.6	173	F5	45.3 +08 53	48-3	
OΣ207			8.0	11.1	20.4	322	K2	49.9 +16 50	48-4	
Σ1399	7589		7.7	9.6	30.3	175	G0	57.0 +19 46	48-5	
31 Leo	7649		4.4	13.4	7.9	44	K2	10ʰ07.9ᵐ +10 00	48-3	
32–α Leo	7654	AB	1.4	7.7	176.9	307	B8 G	08.4 +11 58	48-3	Blue-white, yellowish
HdO 127		BC		13.2	2.5	86				
h2520			8.0	11.9	34.0	343	A0	09.2 +21 47	48-7	
h476			8.0	10.3	24.2	49	G5	12.0 +20 07	48-7	
Σ1417	7695		8.8	8.8	2.4	259	F2	15.2 +19 07	48-8	
OΣ215	7704		7.2	7.5	1.5	179	F0	16.3 +17 44	48-8	Yellow pair (552 yr)
36–ζ Leo			3.5	5.8	325.9	v340	F0 G0	16.7 +23 25	48-7	
39 Leo	7712		5.8	11.4	7.4	299	F5	17.2 +23 06	48-7	
Σ1421	7715		8.3	9.3	4.4	330	F2	18.1 +27 31	48-7	
41–γ Leo	7724	AB	2.2	3.5	w4.4	*125	K0 G7	20.0 +19 51	48-7	Deep and pale yellow
OΣ216	7744		7.5	9.6	w1.9	*238	G5	22.7 +15 21	48-8	618 year binary
45–CX Leo	7781		6.0	11.0	37.2	132	A0	27.6 +09 46	48-9	
Σ1442	7817		8.0	8.6	13.4	155	F0	32.0 +22 02	48-7	
Σ1447	7833		7.3	9.1	4.2	124	A2	33.8 +23 21	48-7	
Hu 1338	7836	AB	7.3	13.4	3.6	180	K0	34.4 +21 36	48-7	
Σ1448	7836	AC		9.0	11.0	259				
49–TX Leo	7837		5.8	8.5	2.4	157	A0	35.0 +08 39	48-9	White pair
Σ1482	7955		8.3	9.2	11.7	305	G5	52.2 +07 28	48-9	
54 Leo	7979		4.5	6.3	6.5	110	A0	55.6 +24 45	48-7	Yellowish and white
55 Leo	7982		6.1	8.0	1.1	*53	F2	55.7 +00 44	48-10	128 year binary
Σ1504	8043		7.8	7.9	1.2	296	F0	11ʰ04.0ᵐ +03 38	48-10	
Σ1506	8048	AxBC	7.6	10.1	11.4	220	G5	04.7 −04 13	48-1	
63–χ Leo		AB	4.6	10.9	3.3	262	F0	05.0 +07 20	48-9	
65 Leo	8060		5.5	9.3	2.4	102	A0	06.9 +01 57	48-10	
Σ1521	8105		7.7	8.0	3.7	96	A5	15.3 +27 34	48-13	
Σ1527	8128		7.0	8.1	1.7	30	G0	19.0 +14 16	48-12	Yellow pair
Σ1529	8131		7.0	8.0	9.6	252	F8	19.4 −01 39	48-10	
78–ι Leo	8148		4.0	6.7	w1.7	*117	F5	23.9 +10 32	48-11	Yellow and white, (192 yr)
81 Leo			5.6	9.2	55.7	351	F2	25.6 +16 27	48-12	
83 Leo	8162	AB	6.2	7.9	28.5	150	K0 K0	26.8 +03 01	48-10	
		AC		9.9	90.3					
84–τ Leo		AB	5.1	8.0	91.1	176	K0 G5	27.9 +02 51	48-10	
88 Leo	8196		6.4	8.4	15.4	328	G0	31.7 +14 22	48-12	Yellow and blue
90 Leo	8220	AB	6.0	7.3	3.3	209	B3	34.7 +16 48	48-12	Close white pair
		AC		8.7	63.1	234				C: blue
Σ1565	8257		7.0	8.9	21.6	304	F5 F5	39.6 +19 00	48-12	
Σ1566			8.2	9.7	2.7	349	G5	40.6 +21 02	48-13	
93 Leo			4.5	9.6	74.3	355	F8	48.0 +20 13	48-13	
β 603	8311		6.0	8.3	1.1	*342	A5	48.6 +14 17	48-1	122 year binary
h1201	8320		6.4	11.2	14.9	190	A3	50.9 +12 17	48-1	
S, h132			6.9	9.9	38.9	14	A2	52.8 +15 26	48-1	

Footnotes: *= Year 2000, a = Near apogee, c = Closing, w = Widening. Finder Chart No: All stars listed in the tables are plotted in the large Constellation Chart, but when a star appears in a Finder Chart, this number is listed. Notes: When colors are subtle, the suffix *-ish* is used, e.g. *bluish*.

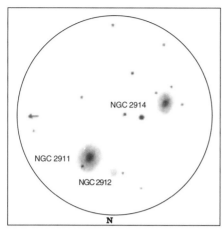

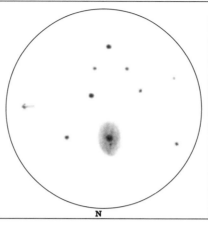

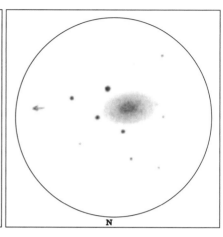

Figure 48-1. NGC 2911 Group
17.5", f4.5–250x, by G. R. Kepple

Figure 48-2. NGC 2916
18.5", f5–300x, by Glen W. Sanner

Figure 48-3. NGC 3041
17.5", f5–300x, by G. R. Kepple

Regulus is at the base of the "Sickle" asterism only half a degree from the ecliptic and therefore is often occulted by the Moon and even sometimes a planet. At magnitude 1.36, Regulus is the 21st brightest star in the sky. It is only about 85 light years from us and therefore has an absolute magnitude of −0.7, a luminosity of 160 suns. The magnitude 7.7 dwarf companion is 177″, almost 3′, from the primary toward the WNW and therefore is an easy binocular target.

4/6″ Scopes–75x: Regulus shines like a brilliant blue-white diamond with a tiny yellowish companion.

Gamma (γ) = 41 Leonis (1424) Dbl Star Spec. K0, G7
m2.2, 3.5; Sep. 4.4″; P.A. 127°   10ʰ20.0ᵐ +19° 51′
Finder Chart 48-7   ★★★★★

Algieba

The name Algieba is from the Arabic Al Jabha, "The Forehead." Gamma Leonis lies in the curve of the sickle 8° NNE of Regulus. It is an attractive binary star with a close companion discovered in 1782 by William

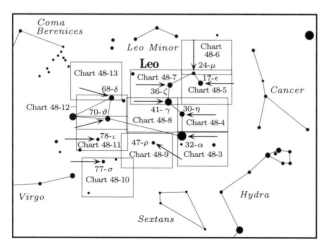

Master Finder Chart 48-2. Leo Chart Areas
Guide stars indicated by arrows.

Herschel. Gamma Leo is about 90 light years from us, so its stars have actual luminosities of about 90 and 30 times the Sun's.

4/6″ Scopes–125x: Gamma Leonis is a fine close pair of deep yellow and pale yellow stars. Some observers have reported the companion to be greenish – but that is at least in part an optical illusion caused by the contrast of the deeper yellow of the primary with the paler yellow of the secondary. 40 Leonis is in the same field 22′ south.

Wolf 359 Red Dwarf Star   Spec. M6.5 Ve
m13.46v   10ʰ56.0ᵐ +07° 01′
Finder Chart 48-9   ★

Wolf 359 is a magnitude 13.66 star that called attention to itself in the proper motion survey of Max Wolf at Heidelburg University early in the 20th century. It moves 4.71″ per year toward position angle 235°, a rate of 8′ per century. One of the reasons for the star's apparent motion is its proximity to us: it lies only 7.75 light years away, the third nearest star or star system (after Alpha Centauri and Barnard's Star in Ophiuchus) to the Sun. Wolf 359 is an extremely cool, extremely faint red dwarf: its absolute magnitude is just +16.8, a luminosity of 1/63,000th the Sun's. Its mass and radius are both probably about 10% of the Sun's. It can be found 1.4° NW of the 5th magnitude 59 Leonis and 20′ south of a 7th magnitude star, and is best identified in large telescopes by its ruddy color.

54 Leonis = Σ1487 Double Star   Spec. A0
m4.5, 6.3; Sep. 6.5″; P.A. 110°   10ʰ55.6ᵐ +24° 45′
Finder Chart 48-7   ★★★★★

4/6″ Scopes–100x: 54 Leonis is an unequally bright color-contrast double. The majority of observers report the primary as yellowish-white and the companion as either bluish or greenish.

Figure 48-4. *NGC 2903 is one of the better objects missed by Charles Messier. It is a nice object for small and medium size telescopes with a large, bright halo and a intense core. Image courtesy of Chris Schur.*

88 Leonis = Σ1547 Double Star Spec. G0
m6.4,8.4; Sep.15.4″; P.A.328°   **11ʰ31.7ᵐ +14° 22′**
Finder Chart 48-12   ★★★★
4/6″Scopes-75x: 88 Leonis is an easy pair for small
    telescopes to split. Its primary is yellow and its
    secondary blue. 88 Leonis is flanked by two faint,
    wide pairs.

90 Leonis = Σ1552 Triple Star   Spec. B3
AB: m6.0,7.3; Sep.3.3″; P.A.209° **11ʰ34.7ᵐ +16° 48′**
Finder Chart 48-12   ★★★★★
4/6″Scopes-100x: 90 Leonis is a fine 3″ wide pair of
    bluish-white stars. The third member of the system,
    an 8.7 magnitude object 63″ distant in position angle
    234°, appears to have a somewhat deeper blue tone.

48.3 Deep-Sky Objects

NGC 2903 H56[1] Galaxy Type SAB(rs)bc I-II
φ 12.0′ × 5.6′, m9.0v, SB13.4   **09ʰ32.2ᵐ +21° 30′**
Finder Chart 48-5, Figure 48-4   ★★★★★
    The large bright galaxy NGC 2903 is unusual for
being one of the few nearby galaxies unattached to any
of the local galaxy groups. It is around 31 million light

years away. Its absolute magnitude is therefore −20.9,
a luminosity of 19 billion suns, and its true size over
110,000 light years.
4/6″Scopes-75x: NGC 2903, centered 20′ south of a
    7th magnitude star, is a fine bright galaxy for small
    telescopes. It is elongated 8′×4′ NNE–SSW, has a
    well concentrated oval core, and is positioned in the
    mouth of a west-opening irregular semicircle of

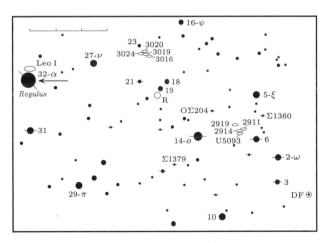

Finder Chart 48-3. 32–α Leo: 10ʰ08.3ᵐ +11° 58′

Figure 48-5. *NGC 2964 and NGC 2968 form a nice pair for medium and large telescopes. Image courtesy of Bill Logan.*

stars, including two of the 10th magnitude 4.5′ SSE and 6′ SSW of the galaxy's halo.

8/10″Scopes–100x: This is one of the better objects missed by Charles Messier. A bright stellar nucleus is embedded in a large, extended core surrounded by a mottled halo that is elongated 9′×4′ NNE–SSW and has diffuse edges.

12/14″Scopes–125x: Superb! NGC 2903 has a bright 10′×5′ halo elongated in position angle 15° and containing an intense 1′×0.5′ core. The halo is mottled throughout, with bright and dark patches. Two particularly bright patches are about 1.25′ north and south of the galaxy's center. The diffuse periphery of the halo extends farther east than west from the core. A 13th magnitude star lies near the halo's edge 2′ ESE of the galaxy's center.

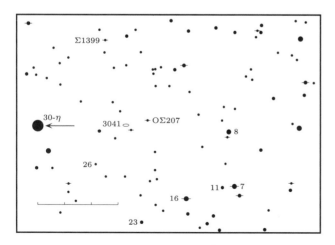

Finder Chart 48-4. 30–η Leo: 10^{h}07.3^m +16° 46′

NGC 2911 H40^2 Galaxy Type SA(s)0: pec
φ 3.7′×2.8′, m11.5v, SB13.9   09^{h}33.8^m +10° 09′

NGC 2914 H513^3 Galaxy Type SB(s)ab
φ 1.0′×0.6′, m13.2v, SB12.4   09^{h}34.0^m +10° 17′

NGC 2919 Galaxy Type SAB(r)b:
φ 1.6′×0.5′, m12.8v, SB12.5   09^{h}34.8^m +10° 17′
Finder Chart 48-3, Figure 48-1   ★★/★★/★★

16/18″Scopes–150x: NGC 2911, located half a degree NE of the double star 6 Leonis (5.1, 8.2; 37.4″; 75°), is the largest and brightest in a group of faint galaxies. Its faint, diffuse 1.5′ diameter halo contains a poorly concentrated core. A threshold star lies on its NW edge. 5′ to the SE is galaxy NGC 2914, a faint oval smudge. A 12th magnitude star lies between NGC 2914 and NGC 2911. 1.5′ WNW of the former, 5.5′ SSE of the 12th magnitude star is galaxy UGC 5093, a faint, circular glow that requires averted vision. 19′ ENE of NGC 2911 is NGC 2919, a faint, diffuse glow elongated 1.25′×0.5′ NNW–SSE.

NGC 2916 H260^2 Galaxy Type SA(rs)b?
φ 2.3′×1.6′, m12.1v, SB13.3   09^{h}35.0^m +21° 42′
Finder Chart 48-5, Figure 48-2   ★★★

16/18″Scopes–150x: NGC 2916, located 40′ ENE of NGC 2903, has a fairly bright 2′×1′ NNE–SSW halo containing a stellar nucleus. The galaxy is situated north of the opening of a 2.5′ long V-shaped asterism, the two brightest stars of which (12th magnitude objects) are at the south angle and NW point of the "V." A 12.5 magnitude star lies 2′ west of the galaxy.

NGC 2964 H114^2 Galaxy Type SAB(r)bc: II-III
φ 3.2′×1.8′, m11.3v, SB13.1   09^{h}42.9^m +31° 51′

NGC 2968 H491^2 Galaxy Type I0
φ 2.2′×1.6′, m11.7v, SB12.9   09^{h}43.2^m +31° 56′
Finder Chart 48-6, Figure 48-5   ★★★/★★★

8/10″Scopes–100x: NGC 2964 and NGC 2968 are a fine 6′ wide NE–SW galaxy-pair. The SW galaxy, NGC 2964, is the larger and brighter of the two: it is moderately bright and quite conspicuous, its 2′×1′ E–W oval halo distinctly outlined but very little brighter in its center. NGC 2968 is not as well defined as its companion: a stellar nucleus is suspected in its small 1′×0.5′ NE–SW halo.

16/18″Scopes–150x: NGC 2964 has a fairly faint somewhat irregular 2.5′×1.25′ E–W oval halo containing a faint weakly concentrated core with a faint stellar nucleus. At 175x some slightly brighter areas and dark patches can be seen throughout its mottled halo. A 14th magnitude star lies 1.5′ WNW of the galaxy's center. NGC 2968 shows a fairly faint

1.5′×1′ E–W halo containing a small, moderately concentrated extended core with a faint stellar nucleus. 3.5′ to the galaxy's NNE is a pair of magnitude 11.5 and 13 stars 25″ apart in position angle 45°. 5′ NE of NGC 2968 is the galaxy NGC 2970, a very faint, small round glow with a faint core.

NGC 3016 Galaxy Type Sb III
ϕ 1.1′×0.9′, m12.9v, SB12.8 $09^h49.7^m$ +12° 42′

NGC 3019 Galaxy Type?
ϕ 0.8′×0.5′, m14.0v, SB12.9 $09^h50.0^m$ +12° 44′

NGC 3020 H51[3] Galaxy Type SB(r)cd:
ϕ 2.9′×1.7′, m11.9v, SB13.5 $09^h50.1^m$ +12° 49′

NGC 3024 H52[3] Galaxy Type Sc: sp
ϕ 1.8′×0.5′, m13.1v, SB12.8 $09^h50.5^m$ +12° 46′
Finder Chart 48-3   ★★/★/★★★/★
16/18″Scopes–150x: NGC 3020, located 19′ SW of 6.6 magnitude 23 Leonis, is the brightest, largest, and most northerly in a triangular group of four galaxies. It has a fairly bright 1.5′×0.75′ E–W halo with an evenly mottled texture. NGC 3016, at the SW corner of the group, is the second brightest member and has a diffuse halo slightly elongated 1′×0.75′ ENE–WSW. At the SE corner of the group is NGC 3024, a 1.5′×0.25′ ESE–WNW streak with a magnitude 12.5 star 2′ to its SW. Finally NGC 3019, the faintest member of the galaxy group and located at the center of the triangle of the other three galaxies 3.75′ WNW of the magnitude 12.5 star, can be seen with averted vision as a faint smudge 50″ NE of a magnitude 13.5 star.

NGC 3032 Galaxy Type SAB(r)0°
ϕ 2.0′×1.7′, m12.5v, SB13.7 $09^h52.1^m$ +29° 14′
Finder Chart 48-6   ★★
12/14″Scopes–125x: NGC 3032, located between 9th

and 10th magnitude stars 1.75′ to its north and south respectively, has a conspicuous stellar nucleus embedded in a tiny core surrounded by a fairly faint, diffuse 1.5′ diameter halo.

NGC 3041 H98[2] Galaxy Type SAB(rs)c II-III
ϕ 3.4′×2.2′, m11.5v, SB13.6 $09^h53.1^m$ +16° 41′
Finder Chart 48-4, Figure 48-3   ★★
12/14″Scopes–125x: NGC 3041 has a low surface brightness 3′×2′ E–W halo containing a broad, poorly concentrated central area without a nucleus. A 12th magnitude star 1.5′ SW, and 14th magnitude stars 1.25′ west and 1′ north, of the galaxy's center form a triangle that caps the halo's western tip.

NGC 3067 H49[2] Galaxy Type SAB(s)ab? III
ϕ 2.0′×0.7′, m12.1v, SB12.3 $09^h58.4^m$ +32° 22′
Finder Chart 48-6   ★★★
12/14″Scopes–125x: NGC 3067, located 2′ SW of a 9th magnitude star, has a fairly faint 2′×0.5′ ESE–WNW halo containing an unevenly concentrated core without a visible nucleus.

NGC 3098 Galaxy Type S0
ϕ 2.1′×0.6′, m12.0v, SB12.1 $10^h02.3^m$ +24° 43′
Finder Chart 48-5   ★★★
12/14″Scopes–125x: NGC 3098, located in a sparse star field, is a fairly bright edge-on galaxy elongated 2′×0.75′ E–W containing a small extended core with a stellar nucleus. A 13th magnitude star lies 2.5′ east of the center of the galaxy.

NGC 3162 H43[2] Galaxy Type SAB(rs)bc II
ϕ 3.1′×2.6′, m11.6v, SB13.8 $10^h13.5^m$ +22° 44′
Finder Chart 48-7, Figure 48-6   ★★★
8/10″Scopes–100x: NGC 3162, located 9′ SE of an 8th

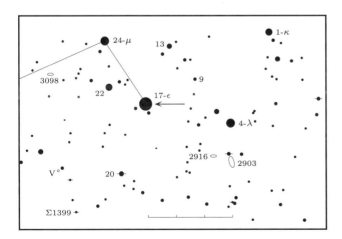

Finder Chart 48-5. 17–ε Leo: $09^h45.8^m$ +23° 46′

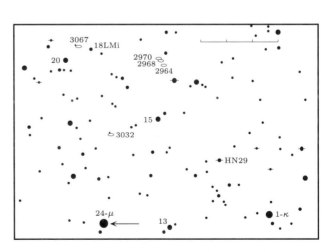

Finder Chart 48-6. 24–μ Leo: $09^h52.8^m$ +26° 00′

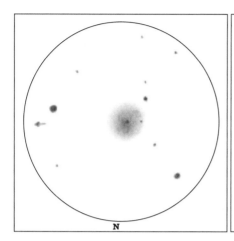

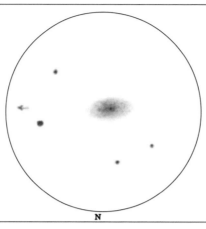

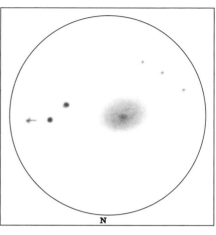

Figure 48-6. NGC 3162
17.5", f4.5–300x, by G. R. Kepple

Figure 48-7. NGC 3338
18.5", f5–300x, by Glen W. Sanner

Figure 48-8. NGC 3346
17.5", f5–300x, by G. R. Kepple

magnitude star, is a faint, circular 1′ diameter glow containing a broad core with a stellar nucleus. 11th magnitude stars lie 4′ NE and 3.5′ west of the galaxy's center.

16/18″ Scopes–150x: The halo appears moderately faint, elongated 1.5′×1′ NNE–SSW, and broadly concentrated with an unevenly illuminated surface around a faint stellar nucleus. A 13th magnitude star lies 1′ SE.

NGC 3177 H25³ Galaxy Type SA(rs)b II-III
φ 1.5′×1.2′, m12.4v, SB 12.9   10ʰ16.6ᵐ +21° 07′
Finder Chart 48-7   ★★★
12/14″ Scopes–125x: NGC 3177, located in the center of a triangle of 10th and 11th magnitude stars, has a moderately faint, circular 1′ diameter halo containing a small core with a nonstellar nucleus.

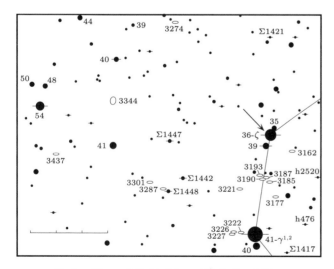

Finder Chart 48-7. 36–ζ Leo: 10ʰ16.7ᵐ +23° 25′

NGC 3185 Galaxy Type (R)SB(r)a
φ 1.8′×1.1′, m12.1v, SB 12.8   10ʰ17.6ᵐ +21° 41′
Finder Chart 48-7, Figure 48-9   ★★★
8/10″ Scopes–100x: NGC 3185 lies 11′ SW of NGC 3190, the brightest member of a small galaxy group a little more than halfway from Gamma (γ) = 41 to Zeta (ζ) = 36 Leonis. NGC 3185 has a fairly faint 1′ diameter halo containing a stellar nucleus.

16/18″ Scopes–150x: NGC 3185 has a small, faint core containing a stellar nucleus surrounded by a conspicuous 1.5′×1′ NW–SE oval halo. The halo's SW edge is almost touched by the nearest of a 40″ wide NE–SW pair of magnitude 13.5 stars.

NGC 3187 Galaxy Type SB(s)c pec
φ 3.2′×1.4′, m13.4v, SB 14.9   10ʰ17.8ᵐ +21° 52′
Finder Chart 48-7, Figure 48-9   ★
16/18″ Scopes–150x: NGC 3187, located 5′ NW of NGC 3190, is the faintest member in a group of four galaxies between Gamma (γ) = 41 and Zeta (ζ) = 36 Leonis. It is a faint, diffuse glow elongated 1.5′×0.5′ ESE–WNW containing a slight central brightening. Both NGC 3187 and NGC 3190 are oriented in the same position angle, their major axis practically on the same ESE–WNW line. 13th magnitude stars are 1′ SW and 1.25′ SE of the galaxy's center.

NGC 3190 H44² Galaxy Type SA(s)a pec sp
φ 4.1′×1.6′, m11.2v, SB 13.0   10ʰ18.1ᵐ +21° 50′
Finder Chart 48-7, Figure 48-9   ★★★★
8/10″ Scopes–100x: NGC 3190 is the flagship of a small group of galaxies which includes NGC 3185 located 11′ to the SW, NGC 3187 lying 5′ NW, and NGC 3193 lying 6′ NE. NGC 3190 has a bright oval core

Figure 48-9. *The peculiar spiral galaxy NGC 3190, at center, is the brightest member of a close trio with the barred spiral NGC 3187 to its lower left and the elliptical galaxy NGC 3193 to the lower right. NGC 3185, a ringed barred spiral type, is at the top. Image courtesy of Jim Burnell.*

containing a stellar nucleus surrounded by a much fainter, diffuse 2′×0.5′ NW–SE halo. A 13th magnitude star lies 1.25′ WSW of the galaxy's center.

16/18″ Scopes–150x: NGC 3190 is an interesting object elongated 3′×1.25′ ESE–WNW containing a bright extended core with a stellar nucleus. A dark dust lane running along the SW side of the halo can be glimpsed with averted vision.

NGC 3193 H45² Galaxy Type E2
ϕ **2.5′×2.5′, m10.9v, SB 12.7**   **10ʰ18.4ᵐ +21° 54′**
Finder Chart 48-7, Figure 48-9   ★★★
8/10″ Scopes–100x: NGC 3193 is at the NE edge of the NGC 3190 galaxy group just 1.5′ south of a 9th magnitude star. It is the second brightest galaxy of the group, but appears only as a bright, small, round 1′ diameter object.

16/18″ Scopes–150x: A prominent core with a stellar nucleus are embedded in a bright 2′ diameter halo elongated slightly N–S.

NGC 3221 Galaxy Type SB(s)cd: sp III-IV
ϕ **3.0′×0.8′, m13.1v, SB 13.9**   **10ʰ22.3ᵐ +21° 34′**
Finder Chart 48-7   ★★
16/18″ Scopes–150x: NGC 3221, located 5′ north of an

11.5 magnitude star, is a faint 3′×0.5′ N–S spindle containing a slight brightening along its center.

NGC 3222 Galaxy Type SB0:
ϕ **0.9′×0.8′, m11.8v, SB 12.3**   **10ʰ22.6ᵐ +19° 53′**
Finder Chart 48-7   ★★
12/14″ Scopes–125x: NGC 3222 is 35′ east of magnitude 2.3 Gamma (γ) = 41 Leonis and 12′ west of galaxy NGC 3226. It is a moderately faint 45″×30″ oval glow surrounding a faint nonstellar nucleus. A 12th magnitude star lies 3′ south of the galaxy's center.

NGC 3226 H28² Galaxy Type E2: pec
ϕ **2.5′×2.2′, m11.4v, SB 13.1**   **10ʰ23.4ᵐ +19° 54′**

NGC 3227 H29² Galaxy Type SAB(s)pec II-III
ϕ **6.9′×5.4′, m10.3v, SB 14.1**   **10ʰ23.5ᵐ +19° 52′**
Finder Chart 48-7, Figure 48-10   ★★★/★★★
8/10″ Scopes–100x: NGC 3226 and NGC 3227, located about 40′ east of the magnitude 2.3 Gamma (γ) = 41 Leonis, is a contact pair of contrasting galaxies. NGC 3227 is the larger of the two but has noticeably lower surface brightness: its stellar nucleus is embedded in a diffuse halo elongated 2′×1.5′ NNW–SSE in the direction of its more compact companion. NGC 3226, touching the northern tip of

Figure 48-10. *NGC 3226 and NGC 3227 (at top) are a visually interesting pair of morphologically contrasting galaxies. Image courtesy of Jim Burnell.*

Figure 48-11. *In large telescopes, Messier 95 (NGC 3351) shows a bar with a bright core forming the crosspiece in a very faint "θ." Image courtesy of Jim Burnell.*

NGC 3227, has a prominent stellar nucleus within a fairly bright but small 1′ diameter halo. The contrast in appearance between the two galaxies is the consequence of their difference in intrinsic structure: NGC 3226 is a compact, spherical elliptical type galaxy whereas NGC 3227 is a disk-like spiral tilted somewhat to the line of sight.

16/18″Scopes–150x: NGC 3227 is a spiral galaxy highly elongated 3′×1.5′ NNW–SSE containing a faint extended core with a bright stellar nucleus. A 13th magnitude star lies beyond the halo's SSE edge 2.25′ from the galaxy's center. By contrast, NGC 3226 is a typical elliptical galaxy with a bright, smooth, circular 1.5′ diameter halo containing a stellar nucleus.

NGC 3274 H358² Galaxy Type SABd? IV-V
φ 1.9′×1.0′, m12.8v, SB13.4   10ʰ32.3ᵐ +27° 40′
Finder Chart 48-7   ★★
  NGC 3274 is a member of the NGC 3245 group, centered across the border in Leo Minor. The group is about 31 million light years distant; thus NGC 3274 has an absolute magnitude of −17.1, a luminosity of 580 million suns, and a true diameter of over 17,000 light years.

12/14″Scopes–125x: NGC 3274 is near Leo's northern border 12′ SW of an 8th magnitude star and 4′ WNW of an 11th magnitude star. The halo is moderately faint, elongated 1.25′×0.75′ E–W, and

contains a faint stellar nucleus. 13th magnitude stars are 2′ NNW and 2′ SW of the galaxy's center.

NGC 3287 Galaxy Type SB(s)d III-IV
φ 1.9′×0.9′, m12.3v, SB12.7   10ʰ34.8ᵐ +21° 39′
Finder Chart 48-7   ★★
12/14″Scopes–125x: NGC 3287 lies 6′ NE of Σ1448, a fine double of orange and bluish stars (7.3, 9.0; 11.0″; 259°). It has a fairly faint 2′×0.75′ NNE–SSW halo that gradually brightens to a faint stellar nucleus.

NGC 3300 H55³ Galaxy Type SAB(r)0° :?
φ 1.8′×0.9′, m12.1v, SB12.5   10ʰ36.6ᵐ +14° 10′
Finder Chart 48-8   ★★★
12/14″Scopes–125x: NGC 3300 may be found a degree east of magnitude 5.5 star 46 Leonis, lying within a 10′ long box of five 8th to 12th magnitude stars. It has a fairly faint 2′×1′ N–S halo containing a moderately bright core.

NGC 3301 H46² Galaxy Type (R′)SB(rs)0/a
φ 3.4′×1.2′, m11.4v, SB12.8   10ʰ36.9ᵐ +21° 53′
Finder Chart 48-7   ★★★
12/14″Scopes–125x: NGC 3301 is south of a 3′ wide triangle of 10th magnitude stars. It has a prominent stellar nucleus embedded in an irregularly concentrated 3′×0.75′ NE–SW halo. Brighter patches can

be seen on the NE and SW edges of the core. Galaxy NGC 3287 lies 34′ WSW.

NGC 3338 H77[2] Galaxy Type SA(s)c I-II
ϕ 4.8′×3.2′, m11.1v, SB13.9 $10^h42.1^m$ +13° 45′
Finder Chart 48-8, Figure 48-7   ★★★
8/10″Scopes–100x: NGC 3338 is 2.75′ east of a 9th magnitude star and 5′ south of an 11.5 magnitude star. It has a moderately faint 3.5′×1.5′ E–W halo that gradually brightens toward its center.
12/14″Scopes–125x: NGC 3338 is rather faint, diffuse, and elongated 4.5′×2.5′ E–W. Its center is broadly but only slightly brighter than its halo, and contains a faint stellar nucleus. Because of its low surface brightness, the glow of NGC 3338 is almost lost in the glare of the 9th magnitude star off its western tip. 13th magnitude stars are 2.25′ north and 3′ SW of the galaxy's center.

NGC 3346 H7[5] Galaxy Type SB(rs)cd II-III
ϕ 2.4′×2.3′, m11.7v, SB13.4 $10^h43.7^m$ +14° 52′
Finder Chart 48-8, Figure 48-8   ★★★
8/10″Scopes–100x: NGC 3346 is 3.5′ east and 2.5′ ENE of a ESE–WNW pair of 11th magnitude stars. It has a fairly faint, diffuse 2′ diameter halo of even surface brightness.
16/18″Scopes–150x: The faint halo is elongated 2.5′×2′ E–W but, apart from a little central brightening, remains diffuse and featureless. 5′ east of NGC 3346 is a very faint anonymous companion galaxy that requires averted vision.

NGC 3351 Messier 95 Galaxy Type SB(r)b II
ϕ 7.8′×4.6′, m9.7v, SB13.5 $10^h44.0^m$ +11° 42′
Finder Charts 48-8, 48-9, Figs. 48-11, 48-12   ★★★★
   Messier 95 and Messier 96 were discovered by P. Mechain in 1781. They lie some 31 million light years away and are members of the M96 subgroup of the Leo I Cloud. The Leo I Cloud includes the M65–M66 Galaxy Group in western Leo. The M96 Group's brightest members are M95, M96, the giant ellipticals M105 and NGC 3377, and the lenticular system NGC 3384. The M96 Group is extremely compact, its core covering a $3° ×1.5° = 13 × 6.5$ million light year area. M96 has an absolute magnitude of −20.2, a luminosity of 10 billion suns, and a true diameter of over 70,000 light years.
4/6″Scopes–75x: Messier 95 has a bright, circular 3′ diameter halo of granular texture. The core is very bright and contains a brilliant stellar nucleus. A 10′ wide triangle of 10th and 11th magnitude stars is centered 7′ west of the galaxy.

8/10″Scopes–100x: This galaxy appears slightly fainter than Messier 96 in the same low power field 40′ west. Messier 95 has a bright, circular 3.5′ diameter halo that contains a bright core with a sharp stellar nucleus.
16/18″Scopes–150x: In larger telescopes M95 has an unevenly illuminated, slightly elongated, 5′×4′ ESE–WNW halo with darker zones north and south of a NW–SE bar containing a bright oval core. The bar and the darker zones north and south of it give the galaxy the appearance of the Greek letter theta, "θ" – an effect most pronounced with averted vision.

NGC 3367 H78[2] Galaxy Type SB(rs)c I-II
ϕ 2.1′×2.0′, m11.5v, SB12.9 $10^h46.6^m$ +13° 45′
Finder Chart 48-8   ★★★★
8/10″Scopes–100x: NGC 3367 is 25′ south of the magnitude 5.5 52 Leonis and 10′ north of a wide E–W pair of 9th magnitude stars. It has a fairly bright, circular 1.25′ diameter halo that contains a very faint stellar nucleus.
16/18″Scopes–150x: A faint but well concentrated 1.5′ diameter halo contains a bar-like ENE–WSW core in which is embedded a very faint stellar nucleus. 12th magnitude stars are 2.25′ WSW and 2.75′ SSW of the galaxy's center.

NGC 3368 Messier 96 Galaxy Type SAB(rs)ab II
ϕ 6.9′×4.6′, m9.2v, SB12.9 $10^h46.8^m$ +11° 49′
Finder Charts 48-8, 48-9, Figure 48-12   ★★★★
   Messier 96, discovered by Mechain in 1781, is the eastern component of a fine 40′ wide galaxy pair. Both belong to the M96 subgroup of the 31 million light year distant Leo I Galaxy Cloud. M96 has an absolute magnitude of −20.7, a luminosity of 16 billion suns, and a true diameter of over 62,000 light years.

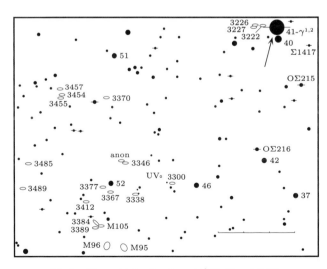

Finder Chart 48-8. 41–γ Leo: $10^h20.0^m$ +19° 50′

Figure 48-12. *Messier 95 (left) and Messier 96 (right) are in the same field of view only 40 arc minutes apart. Image courtesy of Jim Burnell.*

4/6″Scopes–75x: Messier 96 is the brightest galaxy in the Messier 95–96 group. Messier 95 lies 40′ west and Messier 105 is located 50′ NNE, and all three may be seen in the same 50x field. Messier 96 has a bright extended core with a stellar nucleus embedded in a 4′×3′ NW–SE halo.

8/10″Scopes–100x: This galaxy has a bright 5′×3.5′ NW–SE halo containing a large extended core with a stellar nucleus.

16/18″Scopes–150x: Messier 96 is a bright 6′×4′ NW–SE oval containing a brilliant 2′×1′ oval core with a nonstellar nucleus. The halo's periphery is irreg-

ular both in brightness and in shape, and bulges noticeably more toward the SE.

NGC 3370 H81[2] Galaxy Type SA(s)c II
ϕ **2.7′×1.6′, m11.6v, SB13.0**   **10^h47.1^m +17° 16′**

Finder Chart 48-8   ★★

12/14″Scopes–125x: NGC 3370 is a faint, circular 1.5′ diameter glow that is slightly brighter toward its center.

NGC 3377 H99[2] Galaxy Type E5-6
ϕ **4.1′×2.6′, m10.4v, SB12.8**   **10^h47.7^m +13° 59′**

Finder Chart 48-8, Figure 48-14   ★★★★

8/10″Scopes–100x: NGC 3377, located 20′ SE of the 5.5 magnitude 52 Leonis, has a bright 2.5′×1.25′ NE–SW halo containing a bright circular core. It is a member of the 31 million light year distant M96 Galaxy Group and has an absolute magnitude of –19.5, corresponding to a true luminosity of 5.2 billion suns, and a true diameter of 50,000 light years.

16/18″Scopes–150x: In larger telescopes NGC 3377 shows a well concentrated 4.5′×2.5′ NE–SW halo around a bright, extended oval central area containing a brilliant nucleus. 14th magnitude stars are 2′ east, 2.5′ SE, and 1.5′ west of the galaxy.

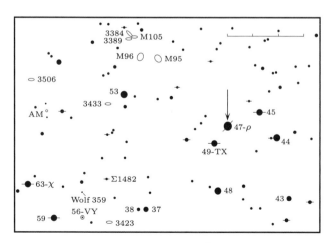

Finder Chart 48-9. 47–ρ Leo: 10^h32.8^m +09° 18′

NGC 3379 Messier 105 Galaxy Type E1
ϕ 3.9′×3.9′, m9.3v, SB12.1 10^{h}47.8^m+12° 35′
Finder Chart 48-9, Figure 48-13   ★★★★★

Messier 105, discovered by Mechain in 1781, is the brightest of a fine 8′ wide triangle of galaxies that includes NGC 3384 and NGC 3389. This trio is part of the M96 Galaxy Group, the western half of the 31 million light year distant Leo I Cloud. M105 is a giant elliptical with an absolute magnitude of −20.6, corresponding to a luminosity of 15 billion suns. Its true diameter is in excess of 35,000 light years.

4/6″Scopes–75x: Messier 105 is at the west corner of a triangle with NGC 3384 and NGC 3389. It has a bright circular 2′ diameter halo with a homogeneous center that fades gradually to the periphery.

8/10″Scopes–100x: The bright halo appears slightly elongated 2.5′×2.25′ ENE–WSW and smoothly brightens to a moderately concentrated core containing a stellar nucleus.

16/18″Scopes–150x: In large telescopes M105 shows a well concentrated 4′×3′ ENE–WSW halo growing smoothly brighter toward a bright but tiny nucleus. A magnitude 14.5 star lies on the halo's NE edge 1.5′ from the galaxy's center.

NGC 3384 H18[1] Galaxy Type SB(s)0–:
ϕ 5.5′×2.9′, m9.9v, SB12.8   10^{h}48.3^m +12° 38′
Finder Chart 48-9, Figure 48-13   ★★★★

8/10″Scopes–100x: NGC 3384 is the northernmost member of a galaxy triangle with Messier 105 and NGC 3389, and like them a member of the 31 million light year distant M96 Galaxy Group. Its absolute magnitude is −20, a luminosity of 8.4 billion suns, and its true diameter over 50,000 light years. NGC 3384 is noticeably fainter than M105, but its halo is well concentrated, elongated 3′×1′ NE–SW, and contains a bright, circular core with a stellar nucleus.

16/18″Scopes–150x: NGC 3384 displays a fairly bright 5′×2′ NE–SW halo with diffuse edges. The central area suddenly brightens to a circular core with a stellar nucleus. A 14.5 magnitude star is superimposed upon the halo SW of the core. A 13th magnitude star lies 2.25′ SE of the galaxy's center.

NGC 3389 H41[2] Galaxy Type SA(s)c II-III
ϕ 2.7′×1.1′, m11.9v, SB12.9   10^{h}48.5^m +12° 32′
Finder Chart 48-9, Figure 48-13   ★★★

8/10″Scopes–100x: NGC 3389 is at the SE corner of a

Figure 48-13. *Messier 105 (NGC 3379), NGC 3384, and NGC 3389 (left to right) are a morphologically contrasting galaxy triangle: M105 is an almost spherical elliptical, NGC 3384 a smooth lenticular, and NGC 3389 a loosely-wound spiral. Image courtesy Martin C. Germano*

galaxy triangle with Messier 105 and NGC 3384. It is the smallest and faintest of the three, its uniformly illuminated halo elongated 2′×1′ ESE–WNW. NGC 3389 is another member of the 31 million light years distant M96 Galaxy Group. Its absolute magnitude is −18, a luminosity of 1.3 billion suns, and its true diameter around 25,000 light years.

16/18″Scopes–150x: This galaxy has a moderately faint 2.5′×1′ ESE–WNW halo that contains a much brighter, slightly mottled central area. A 14th magnitude star lies 45″ south of the galaxy's center. A string of stars about 15′ in length lies to the galaxy's east and curves SE.

NGC 3412 H27[1] Galaxy Type SB(s)0°
ϕ 3.3′×2.0′, m10.5v, SB12.4   10^{h}50.9^m +13° 25′
Finder Chart 48-8, Figure 48-15   ★★★★

8/10″Scopes–100x: NGC 3412 has a fairly bright 2.5′×1.5′ NNW–SSE halo containing a bright but small circular core. It is one of the fainter and smaller members of the M96 Galaxy Group, its absolute magnitude about −19.4, a luminosity of 4.8 billion suns, and its diameter 30,000 light years.

16/18″Scopes–150x: NGC 3412 displays a prominent 45″ core containing a bright nucleus and surrounded by a diffuse 3′×1.5′ NNW–SSE halo. The west edge of the galaxy seems somewhat brighter than the east

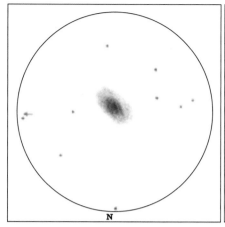
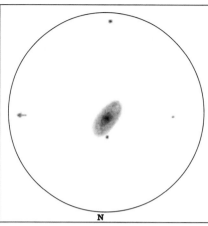
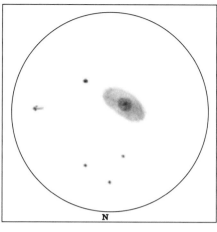

Figure 48-14. NGC 3377
17.5″, f4.5–300x, by G. R. Kepple

Figure 48-15. NGC 3412
18.5″, f5–300x, by Glen W. Sanner

Figure 48-16. NGC 3489
17.5″, f5–300x, by G. R. Kepple

edge. A 13.5 magnitude star touches the halo 1.25′ north of the galaxy's center.

NGC 3433 H20² Galaxy Type SA(s) I-II
φ 3.7′×3.3′, m11.6v, SB14.2   10ʰ52.1ᵐ +10° 09′
Finder Chart 48-9   ★★
12/14″Scopes–125x: NGC 3433, located about 45′ SE of the magnitude 5.25 star 53 Leonis, is a faint, diffuse 2′ diameter glow containing a faint stellar nucleus. A 12th magnitude star lies 4′ NNW of the galaxy.

NGC 3437 H47² Galaxy Type SAB(rs)c: III
φ 2.6′×0.8′, m12.1v, SB12.7   10ʰ52.6ᵐ +22° 56′
Finder Chart 48-7   ★★★
12/14″Scopes–125x: NGC 3437 has a moderately faint 2′×0.5′ ESE–WNW halo containing a broad concentration through its center. No nucleus is visible, but at 175x several faint, tiny knots can be seen. A 14th magnitude star lies just beyond the halo's WNW tip, and 13th magnitude stars are 2.25′ SE and 3′ NE of the galaxy's center.

NGC 3455 H82² Galaxy Type
φ 2.6′×1.7′, m12.0v, SB13.5   10ʰ54.5ᵐ +17° 17′
Finder Chart 48-8   ★★
12/14″Scopes–125x: NGC 3455, located 2′ south of a 10.5 magnitude star, has a faint 1.25′×1′ ENE–WSW halo containing a slight broad central brightening. 1.5′ NNW of the same 10.5 magnitude star is NGC 3454, a much fainter 1.5′×0.25′ ESE–WNW spindle-shaped galaxy which is slightly brighter along the center of its major axis.

NGC 3457 Galaxy Type S?
φ 0.9′×0.9′, m12.6v, SB12.2   10ʰ54.7ᵐ +17° 37′
Finder Chart 48-8   ★★
12/14″Scopes–125x: NGC 3457 has a prominent stellar nucleus in a well concentrated core surrounded by a faint, circular 45″ diameter halo. A 12th magnitude star lies 4′ south, and a knot of very faint stars is 4.5′ east. Galaxy NGC 3455 lies 19′ south.

NGC 3485 H100² Galaxy Type SB(r)b: II
φ 2.4′×2.2′, m11.8v, SB13.4   11ʰ00.0ᵐ +14° 50′
Finder Charts 48-8, 48-11   ★★
12/14″Scopes–125x: NGC 3485, located 1.5′ east of an 11.5 magnitude star, is a moderately faint, 1.5′ diameter glow containing a slight brightening at its center.

NGC 3489 H101² Galaxy Type SAB(rs)0+
φ 3.2′×2.0′, m10.3v, SB12.2   11ʰ00.3ᵐ +13° 54′
Finder Chart 48-11, Figure 48-16   ★★★
12/14″Scopes–125x: NGC 3489 has a bright core and a stellar nucleus embedded in a tapered halo elongated 2.5′×1′ ENE–WSW. A 12th magnitude star lies south of the halo's WSW tip 1.75′ from center.

NGC 3495 H498³ Galaxy Type Sd: III
φ 4.4′×0.9′, m11.8v, SB13.2   11ʰ01.3ᵐ +03° 38′
Finder Chart 48-10   ★★★
12/14″Scopes–125x: NGC 3495, located 10′ east of the magnitude 4.8 star 58 Leonis, is a moderately faint edge-on galaxy highly elongated 3.75′×0.75′ NNE–SSW without central brightening. A 13th magnitude star lies 1.5′ SSE of the galaxy's center. NGC 3495 is enclosed by a 4.5′ equilateral triangle

of 12th magnitude stars, the nearest 2′ north of the galaxy's center.

NGC 3501 Galaxy Type Scd:
φ 3.5′×0.5′, m12.9v, SB13.3   11ʰ02.9ᵐ +17° 57′
Finder Chart 48-12   ★★★

12/14″ Scopes–125x: NGC 3501, located 7′ SE of a 9.5 magnitude star, is a faint, thin streak elongated 4′×0.5′ NNE–SSW. It has no nucleus, but the halo is mottled with a few knots along the major axis. A 13th magnitude star is visible 2.5′ SE of the galaxy's center. NGC 3507 lies 12′ NE.

NGC 3506 H22³ Galaxy Type Sc: I-II
φ 1.2′×1.2′, m12.5v, SB12.7   11ʰ03.2ᵐ +11° 05′
Finder Chart 48-9   ★★

12/14″ Scopes–125x: NGC 3506 has a faint, circular 1.25′ diameter halo containing a broad, slightly brighter central concentration with a faint stellar nucleus. The galaxy is virtually surrounded by 12.5 magnitude stars 4′ south, 3.5′ west, 4.5′ NW, 3′ NNW, and 4.5′ NE.

NGC 3507 H7⁴ Galaxy Type SB(s)b
φ 3.1′×2.6′, m10.9v, SB13.0   11ʰ03.5ᵐ +18° 08′
Finder Chart 48-12, Figure 48-18   ★★★

12/14″ Scopes–125x: NGC 3507, located 3′ north of a 9th magnitude star, displays a fairly bright but diffuse 3′×2.5′ E–W halo with an irregularly brighter inner portion containing a small but prominent core. A bright star is superimposed 30″ NE of the galaxy's center.

NGC 3521 H13¹ Galaxy Type SA:(s:)b II
φ 12.5′×6.5′, m9.0v, SB13.6   11ʰ05.8ᵐ +00° 02′
Finder Chart 48-10, Figure 48-17   ★★★★★

8/10″ Scopes–100x: NGC 3521 is 30′ east of 62 Leonis (m5.9) and 11′ NW of an 8th magnitude star. This fine galaxy shows a well concentrated oval core containing a bright stellar nucleus surrounded by a much fainter somewhat diffuse 5′×2′ NNW–SSE halo.

16/18″ Scopes–150x: NGC 3521 is a fabulous object for larger instruments! The halo is bright, elongated 8′×3′ NNW–SSE, and contains a large, bright, extended core with a stellar nucleus. Both the core and halo are mottled. The halo's periphery is irregular in brightness and extends further west then east from the galaxy's center. With averted vision a patchy dark lane can be seen along the halo's west edge. A 14th magnitude star is 3′ NW of the galaxy's center with a 13th magnitude star just beyond.

Figure 48-17. *NGC 3521 is a fine galaxy that reveals detail in large instruments. Image courtesy of Steven Juchnowski.*

NGC 3547 H42² Galaxy Type Sb: II-IV
φ 1.9′×0.8′, m12.8v, SB13.1   11ʰ09.9ᵐ +10° 43′
Finder Chart 48-11   ★★

16/18″ Scopes–150x: NGC 3547 lies 4′ NNE of a 10th magnitude star with a 13th magnitude companion 12″ away from it in position angle 170°. The galaxy has a fairly faint 1.5′×0.75′ N–S halo containing a large, faint oval core. Other wide double stars in the vicinity are 3.5′ NNE of the galaxy (12.5, 14; 10″; 345°), 2′ to its west (13, 13.5; 18″; 170°), and 4.5′ to its ENE (12, 13.5; 20″; 280°).

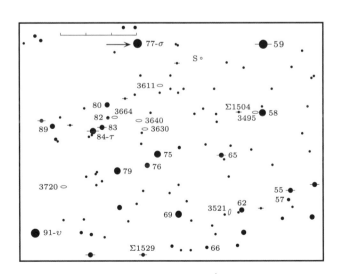

Finder Chart 48-10. 77–σ Leo: 11ʰ21.1ᵐ +06° 02′

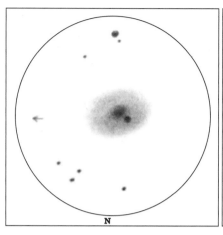

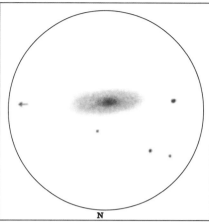

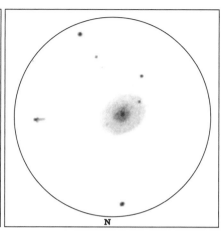

Figure 48-18. NGC 3507
17.5″, f4.5–300x, by G. R. Kepple

Figure 48-19. NGC 3593
17.5″, f4.5–300x, by G. R. Kepple

Figure 48-20. NGC 3596
17.5″, f4.5–300x, by G. R. Kepple

NGC 3593 H29[1] Galaxy Type SA(s)0/a:
φ **5.3′×2.2′, m10.9v, SB13.4**   **11ʰ14.6ᵐ +12° 49′**
Finder Chart 48-11, Figure 48-19   ★★★★
8/10″Scopes–100x: NGC 3593 is half a degree SW of
the magnitude 5.3 star 73 Leonis and 18′ west of
a 6.5 magnitude star. It has a fairly faint 3′×1.5′
E–W halo containing a circular core.
16/18″Scopes–150x: This galaxy has a diffuse, nearly
uniformly bright halo elongated 4′×1.5′ E–W. A
narrow dark lane visible with averted vision passes
just north of the 1′×0.25′ core. At 300x the halo
may be traced with averted vision out to a 13th
magnitude star 2.5′ east of the galaxy's center.

NGC 3596 H102[2] Galaxy Type SAB(rs)c II-III
φ **4.0′×4.0′, m11.2v, SB14.1**   **11ʰ15.1ᵐ +14° 47′**
Finder Chart 48-11, Figure 48-20   ★★
12/14″Scopes–125x: NGC 3596 is 40′ SSE of the magnitude 3.3 Theta (ϑ) = 70 Leonis and 18′ south of
a magnitude 7.3 star. It has a faint, circular 2.5′
diameter halo containing a very faint stellar nucleus.
It is enclosed by a 7′ wide equilateral triangle of
13th magnitude stars. A threshold star is embedded
just inside the halo's SE edge.

NGC 3599 H49[2] Galaxy Type SA0:
φ **2.5′×2.5′, m11.9v, SB13.8**   **11ʰ15.4ᵐ +18° 07′**
Finder Chart 48-12   ★★
12/14″Scopes–125x: NGC 3599, located in a blank star
field, displays a fairly bright stellar nucleus embedded in a faint 30″ core surrounded by a faint, diffuse
2′ diameter halo.

NGC 3605 H27[3] Galaxy Type E4-5
φ **1.2′×0.6′, m12.3v, SB11.8**   **11ʰ16.8ᵐ +18° 01′**

NGC 3607 H50[2] Galaxy Type SA(s)0° :
φ **4.6′×4.1′, m9.9v, SB12.9**   **11ʰ16.9ᵐ +18° 03′**
Finder Chart 48-12, Figure 48-21   ★★/★★★
8/10″Scopes–100x: NGC 3607 is the largest and brightest in a small galaxy group with NGC 3605 only
2.5′ to its SW, NGC 3608 located 6′ to its north,
and NGC 3599 lying 20′ to its west. NGC 3607 has
a bright 1.5′×1′ halo that contains a stellar nucleus.
Its near neighbor NGC 3507 is merely a faint 30″
diameter glow. A 2′ wide keystone of 12th magnitude stars is centered 4′ SE of the brighter galaxy.

Figure 48-21. *NGC3607 (center) and NGC3608 (lower right)
form a bright galaxy pair, but NGC3605 (at left) is merely a
small, faint glow. Image courtesy of Jim Burnell.*

Figure 48-22. *Messier 65 (bottom left), Messier 66 (top left), and NGC 3628 (at right) are a trio of spiral galaxies viewed at different angles of inclination to our line of sight. Low power must be used to see all three at once. Image courtesy of Jim Burnell.*

NGC 3608 H51² Galaxy Type E2
φ 2.7′×2.3′, m10.8v, SB 12.6   11ʰ17.0ᵐ +18° 09′
Finder Chart 48-12, Figure 48-21   ★★★
8/10″Scopes–100x: NGC 3608 is a fainter and smaller version of NGC 3607 located 6′ to its south. Its faint 1′ diameter halo contains a faint stellar nucleus. Centered 2′ to the galaxy's NW is a 2′×1.5′ triangle of magnitude 12.5 stars.

NGC 3611 H521² Galaxy Type SA(s)a pec
φ 2.5′×2.5′, m12.2v, SB 14.0   11ʰ17.5ᵐ +04° 33′
Finder Chart 48-10   ★★
8/10″Scopes–100x: NGC 3611 is 19′ north of an 8th magnitude star. A 1′ wide pair of 11th magnitude stars is situated between the 8th magnitude star and the galaxy. NGC 3611 has a small bright core embedded in a moderately faint 1.25′×0.75′ NNE–SSW halo. A 10th magnitude star lies 3′ NNW.

NGC 3623 Messier 65 Galaxy Type SAB(rs)a II
φ 8.7′×2.2′, m9.3v, SB 12.4   11ʰ18.9ᵐ +13° 05′
Finder Chart 48-11, Figures 48-22, 48-23   ★★★★★
Messier 65 and Messier 66 were discovered by P. Mechain in 1780. They are an easy pair for 10x and

higher binoculars. M65 and M66 with NGC 3628 to the north are the core of the M66 subgroup of the 31 million light year distant Leo I Galaxy Cloud. Other members of the M66 Group include NGCs 3489, 3593, 3596, and 3666. M65 has an absolute magnitude of −20.6, corresponding to a luminosity of 15 billion suns, and a true diameter of over 80,000 light years.

4/6″Scopes–75x: Messier 65 forms an impressive trio with Messier 66 lying 20′ east and NGC 3628 located 35′ NNE. Its bright halo is elongated 6′×2′ N–S and contains a bright, large 3′×2′ core.

8/10″Scopes–100x: Messier 65 is a fine, bright galaxy elongated 7′×2′ in position angle 170°, the halo mottled and unevenly bright in its northern wing. The bulging core narrows to rounded ends. A 12th magnitude star lies 2′ SSW, and a 13th magnitude star 2′ NE, of the galaxy's center.

16/18″Scopes–150x: Exquisite! Messier 65 has a bright, mottled 3′×2′ core containing a brilliant nonstellar nucleus surrounded by a diffuse 8′×2′ halo. The southern tip of the halo is somewhat more extended and pointed than the northern. The eastern side of the halo is better defined than the western side, which is more diffuse because along it runs a tiny dark dust lane. A very faint foreground star is

Figure 48-23. *Messier 65 (NGC 3623) presents a bright unevenly concentrated halo with a faint dark lane and a bulged central region. Image courtesy of Chris Schur.*

Figure 48-24. *Messier 66 (NGC 3627) is a beautiful galaxy with an unevenly bright halo containing a broad central region. Image courtesy of Chris Schur.*

superimposed upon the dark lane due east of the galaxy's core. Another faint star, or tiny bright knot, is on the halo's SW edge. 1.5′ beyond the star or knot, outside of the halo, is a 12th magnitude star.

NGC 3626 H52² Galaxy Type (R)SA(rs)0+
φ **2.6′×1.8′, m11.0v, SB12.5**   11ʰ20.1ᵐ +18° 21′
Finder Chart 48-12, Figure 48-26   ★★★
8/10″Scopes–100x: This galaxy has a bright stellar nucleus embedded in a faint, diffuse circular 1.5′ diameter halo.

16/18″Scopes–150x: NGC 3626 appears bright but fades rapidly outward from its bright nonstellar nucleus. The halo is elongated 2′×1.5′ N–S. A 14th magnitude star is 1.5′ east, and a 13.5 magnitude star 2.5′ WSW, of the galaxy.

NGC 3627 Messier 66 Galaxy Type SAB(s)b II
φ **8.2′×3.9′, m8.9v, SB12.5**   11ʰ20.2ᵐ +12° 59′
Finder Chart 48-11, Figures 48-22, 48-24   ★★★★★

Messier 66 was discovered by Mechain in March 1780. The comet of 1773 had passed directly through the field on November 2 of that year; but in his preoccupation with the comet Messier apparently had failed to notice M66. M65 and M66, with NGC 3628 to the north, are the core of the M66 Galaxy Group, the eastern half of the 31 million light year distant Leo I Galaxy Cloud. M66 has an absolute magnitude of −21, a luminosity of 21 billion suns, and a true diameter of at least 75,000 light years. The 21′ apparent separation between M65 and M66 corresponds to a projected separation, at a distance of 31 million light years, of 190,000 light years; but the true separation is no doubt considerably greater because it is very unlikely that both galaxies are precisely the same distance from us.
4/6″Scopes–75x: Messier 66 is the brightest of a fine trio of galaxies with Messier 65 and NGC 3628. It has a large, bright 5′×2′ N–S halo containing a bright, extended core. A row of three stars runs past

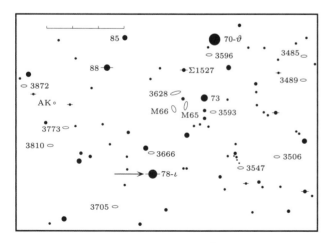

Finder Chart 48-11. 78–ι Leo: 11ʰ23.9ᵐ +10° 32′

Figure 48-25. *Although much fainter than M65 and M66, NGC 3628 is a grand sight in larger instruments. Its extremely long, thin halo contains a detailed dust lane. Image courtesy of Bill McLaughlin.*

the western side of the halo and curves toward the NW, where it connects to a triangle. The brightest star of the six in the row and the triangle is a 9th magnitude object 2.75′ NW of the galaxy's center.

8/10″Scopes–100x: This galaxy has a bright 2′×0.75′ core containing a 30″ diameter nucleus surrounded by an irregularly-shaped mottled halo elongated 5′×2.5′ N–S. A 14th magnitude star lies 3.5′ SW of the galaxy's center.

16/18″Scopes–150x: Beautiful! Messier 66 has a bright, highly irregular 7′×3′ N–S halo containing a well concentrated oval core that brightens smoothly to a nonstellar nucleus. Averted vision reveals dark areas just NE and SW of the core. The southern wing of the halo is very uneven in surface brightness with hints of spiral structure. The northern wing of the halo has a more rounded periphery and is mottled along its NE edge.

NGC 3628 H8⁵ Galaxy Type Sb pec sp III
φ 14.0′×4.0′, m9.5v, SB13.7   11ʰ20.3ᵐ +13° 36′
Finder Chart 48-11, Figures 48-22, 48-25   ★★★★
4/6″Scopes–75x: NGC 3628 is the largest but faintest of a beautiful galaxy trio with Messier 65 and Messier 66. It is a fairly faint edge-on spiral elongated 9′×1′ E–W. A slight brightening along the

major axis interrupts the galaxy's otherwise uniform surface brightness. A 12.5 magnitude star lies south of the eastern tip.

8/10″Scopes–100x: This galaxy has a fairly bright, thin, much elongated 10′×1.5′ E–W halo containing a highly extended 3′×0.5′ core.

16/18″Scopes–150x: NGC 3628 is a grand sight in larger instruments! The envelope extends 13′×2.5′ in position angle 105°. The highly elongated 4′×0.75′ core is displaced just to the north of the halo's center because of the indistinct dark lane passing to its south. The halo is irregularly bright and mottled along the dust lane but flares and becomes very diffuse near the ends of the major axis. Very faint stars can be glimpsed near the halo's edge 2.5′ NE and 1′ NNE of the galaxy's center.

NGC 3629 H338² Galaxy Type SA(s)cd: III
φ 1.9′×1.5′, m12.1v, SB13.1   11ʰ20.5ᵐ +26° 58′
Finder Chart 48-13   ★★
12/14″Scopes–125x: NGC 3629, located 1′ NW of an 11.5 magnitude star, has a faint, circular 1.25′ diameter halo that slightly brightens to an inconspicuous stellar nucleus. 10th magnitude stars are 6′ ENE, 6.5′ SSE, 7′ SSW, and 8′ NNW of the galaxy.

NGC 3630 Galaxy Type S0
φ 1.7′×0.7′, m11.9v, SB11.9   11ʰ20.3ᵐ +02° 58′
Finder Chart 48-10   ★★★
12/14″Scopes–125x: NGC 3630 is centered in a triangle
    of three stars, the brightest an 8th magnitude object
    9′ to the galaxy's SE. The halo is fairly faint,
    elongated 1.5′×0.5′ NE–SW, and contains an oval
    core with a distinct stellar nucleus. This galaxy is
    west of a 50′ long N–S row of galaxies, the brightest
    of which is NGC 3640.

NGC 3640 H33[2] Galaxy Type E3
φ 4.6′×4.1′, m10.4v, SB13.5   11ʰ21.1ᵐ +03° 14′
Finder Chart 48-10, Figure 48-27   ★★★
8/10″Scopes–100x: NGC 3640, located 5′ NNE of an
    11th magnitude star, has a faint, circular 2′ diameter
    halo that is slightly brighter at its center.
12/14″Scopes–125x: The moderately faint, circular 2.5′
    diameter halo surrounds a small, well concentrated
    core containing an inconspicuous stellar nucleus.
    2.5′ south of NGC 3640 is galaxy NGC 3641, a faint,
    circular 1′ diameter glow with a faint stellar nucleus.
    An 11th magnitude star lies 5′ SSW of NGC 3640.

NGC 3646 H15[3] Galaxy Type Ring I-II
φ 3.5′×2.0′, m11.1v, SB13.1   11ʰ21.7ᵐ +20° 10′
Finder Charts 48-12, 48-13   ★★★
12/14″Scopes–125x: NGC 3646 has a faint, diffuse
    3′×1.5′ NE–SW halo containing a broad slight
    central brightening. 8′ to the ENE of NGC 3646 is
    the galaxy NGC 3649, an extremely faint smudge
    30″ north of a 13th magnitude star.

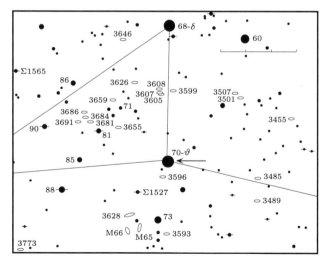

Finder Chart 48-12. 70–ϑ Leo: 11ʰ14.2ᵐ +15° 26′

NGC 3655 H5[1] Galaxy Type SA(s)c: III-IV
φ 1.5′×0.9′, m11.7v, SB11.8   11ʰ22.9ᵐ +16° 35′
Finder Chart 48-12   ★★★
12/14″Scopes–125x: NGC 3655, located 35′ west of the
    double star 81 Leonis (5.6, 9.2; 55.7″; 351°), has a
    moderately bright envelope elongated 1.5′×1′ NE–
    SW which contains a brighter center. A 12.5 mag-
    nitude star lies 2.5′ east.

NGC 3659 H53[2] Galaxy Type SB(s)m? III-IV
φ 1.8′×0.9′, m12.3v, SB12.6   11ʰ23.9ᵐ +17° 49′
Finder Chart 48-12   ★★
12/14″Scopes–125x: NGC 3659, located 25′ NE of the
    magnitude 7.0 star 71 Leonis, is a faint, featureless
    1.25′×0.5′ NE–SW oval glow. A 14th magnitude
    star lies 45″ SE of the galaxy's center.

NGC 3664 Galaxy Type SB(s)m pec IV-V
φ 1.7′×1.6′, m12.8v, SB13.7   11ʰ24.4ᵐ +03° 20′
Finder Chart 48-10   ★★
8/10″Scopes–100x: NGC 3664, located 25′ west of the
    magnitude 6.7 star 82 Leonis, has a 2′ diameter low
    surface brightness halo containing very little central
    brightening. The galaxy lies NW of an east-pointing
    right triangle of 11.5 to 13.5 magnitude stars.

NGC 3666 H20[1] Galaxy Type SA(rs)c: III
φ 4.1′×1.1′, m12.0v, SB13.5   11ʰ24.4ᵐ +11° 21′
Finder Chart 48-11   ★★★
12/14″Scopes–125x: NGC 3666 is about 40′ north of the
    magnitude 3.9 Iota (ι) = 78 Leonis and just 9′ SW
    of a yellow magnitude 5.8 star. The glare of the
    latter makes this low surface brightness object even
    more difficult to see. The galaxy's halo appears
    faint, elongated 3′×1′ ESE–WNW, and has a bright
    granular center. A 14th magnitude star lies 1.5′ NE,
    and a threshold star is just visible 30″ SSW, of the
    galaxy's center.

NGC 3681 H159[2] Galaxy Type SAB(r)bc I-II
φ 2.5′×2.5′, m11.2v, SB13.0   11ʰ26.5ᵐ +16° 52′
Finder Chart 48-12   ★★★
12/14″Scopes–125x: NGC 3681, located 25′ NE of the
    magnitude 5.6 star 81 Leonis, is west of the southern
    side of an isosceles triangle of fairly bright stars,
    the nearest of which is 3′ NE of the galaxy. Its fairly
    faint 1.5′ diameter halo contains a moderately
    concentrated N–S core. NGC 3681 is at the SW
    edge of a loose galaxy group with NGCs 3684, 3686,
    and 3691.

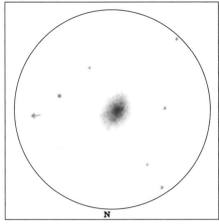

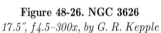

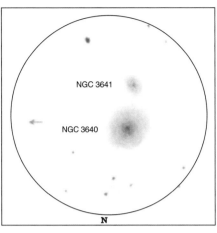

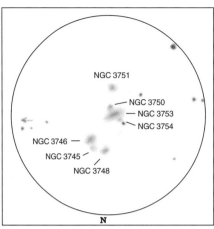

Figure 48-26. NGC 3626
17.5″, f4.5–300x, by G. R. Kepple

Figure 48-27. NGC 3640 and NGC 3641
17.5″, f4.5–300x, by Glen W. Sanner

Figure 48-28. Copeland's Septet
18.5″, f5–300x, Greg Bargerstock

NGC 3684 Galaxy Type SA(rs)bc II-III
ϕ **3.2′×2.2′, m11.4v, SB13.3**   **11ʰ27.2ᵐ +17° 02′**
Finder Chart 48-12   ★★★
8/10″Scopes–100x: NGC 3684 is at the center of a galaxy group with NGC 3681 lying 14′ to its SW, NGC 3686 lying 14′ NE, and NGC 3691 lying 13′ ESE. It has a fairly faint, circular 2′ diameter halo.
16/18″Scopes–150x: NGC 3684 is a little fainter, but larger, than NGC 3681. Its 2.5′×1.5′ oval halo contains a faint stellar nucleus. A 12.5 magnitude star lies 4.5′ NNE of the galaxy's center.

NGC 3686 H160² Galaxy Type SB(s)bcII
ϕ **2.8′×2.3′, m11.3v, SB13.2**   **11ʰ27.7ᵐ +17° 13′**
Finder Chart 48-12   ★★★
8/10″Scopes–100x: NGC 3686, located 2.75′ south of a 10.5 magnitude star, is the northernmost in a small galaxy group with NGC 3681, NGC 3684, and NGC 3691. It is the brightest and largest of the group, with a uniformly bright circular halo 2′ in diameter.
16/18″Scopes–150x: NGC 3686 has a fairly bright 3′×2′ NNE–SSW halo lacking any central brightening. At 200x a few faint knots can be glimpsed. A 13th magnitude star touches the halo's south edge. A second 13th magnitude star is 1.75′ west of the galaxy's center.

NGC 3689 H339² Galaxy Type SAB(rs)c II
ϕ **1.5′×0.9′, m12.3v, SB12.5**   **11ʰ28.2ᵐ +25° 40′**
Finder Chart 48-13   ★★
12/14″Scopes–125x: NGC 3689, located 4.5′ north of a 10th magnitude star, has a faint 1′×0.5′ E–W halo with a brighter streak along its major axis. A

conspicuous 10″ wide N–S pair of 10th magnitude stars is 6′ SSW of the galaxy.

NGC 3691 H54² Galaxy Type SBb?
ϕ **1.0′×0.8′, m11.8v, SB11.4**   **11ʰ28.2ᵐ +16° 55′**
Finder Chart 48-12   ★★★
12/14″Scopes–125x: NGC 3691, located south of a triangle of 10th magnitude stars, is the easternmost of a small galaxy group that includes NGC 3681, NGC 3684, and 3686. It is the smallest and faintest of the four. Its faint, circular 1′ diameter halo is slightly elongated N–S and slightly brighter in the center. A 14th magnitude star is 1.25′ ESE, a 13th magnitude star 2.5′ NNE, and an 11th magnitude star 4.25′ SW of the galaxy's center.

NGC 3705 H13² Galaxy Type SAB(r)ab II
ϕ **4.6′×2.0′, m11.1v, SB13.3**   **11ʰ30.1ᵐ +09° 17′**
Finder Chart 48-11   ★★★★
8/10″Scopes–100x: NGC 3705 has a fairly bright 2.5′×1′ NW–SE oval halo containing a prominent stellar nucleus.
16/18″Scopes–150x: In large telescopes NGC 3705 is a visually interesting object. Its much elongated 4′×1.5′ ESE–WNW halo contains a mottled oval core with a bright stellar nucleus. A magnitude 12.5 star lies 4′ NW.

NGC 3720 H27³ Galaxy Type S0/a:
ϕ **0.9′×0.8′, m12.9v, SB12.4**   **11ʰ32.4ᵐ+00° 48′**
Finder Chart 48-10   ★★
16/18″Scopes–150x: NGC 3720, located 6′ NNE of a 9.5 magnitude star, has a faint 45″ diameter halo that contains a tiny core with a very faint stellar

Figure 48-29. *Abell 1367 is a distant cluster of faint galaxies that require large telescopes to be observed. NGC 3842, near the lower left, is its brightest member. Image courtesy Jim Burnell.*

nucleus. A 13.5 magnitude star lies 1′ SSW of the nucleus. 2.25′ NW of NGC 3720 is its companion galaxy NGC 3719, much fainter but larger, measuring 1.25′×0.75′ N–S.

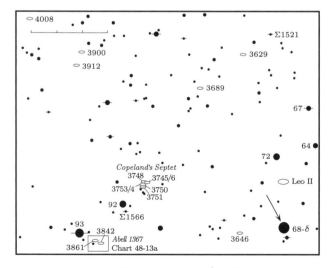

Finder Chart 48-13. 68–δ Leo: 11ʰ14.1ᵐ +20° 31′

NGC 3745 Galaxy Type SB(s)0–:
φ 0.3′×0.2′, m15.2v, SB12.0 11ʰ37.7ᵐ+22° 01′

NGC 3746 Galaxy Type SB(r)b
φ 1.1′×0.6′, m14.2v, SB13.6 11ʰ37.7ᵐ+22° 00′

NGC 3748 Galaxy Type SB0° ? sp
φ 0.8′×0.4′, m14.8v, SB13.4 11ʰ37.8ᵐ+22° 02′

NGC 3750 Galaxy Type SAB0–?
φ 0.7′×0.6′, m13.9v, SB12.8 11ʰ37.9ᵐ+21° 58′

NGC 3751 Galaxy Type S0– pec?
φ 1.1′×0.5′, m13.9v, SB13.1 11ʰ37.9ᵐ+21° 56′

NGC 3753 Galaxy Type Sab? pec sp
φ 1.8′×0.5′, m13.6v, SB13.4   11ʰ37.9ᵐ +21° 59′

NGC 3754 Galaxy Type SBb? pec
φ 0.5′×0.4′, m14.3v, SB12.411ʰ37.9ᵐ +21° 59′
Finder Chart 48-13, Fig.48-28★/*/*/*/*/*/*
Copeland's Septet

16/18″ Scopes–150x: Even in 16-inch and larger telescopes Copeland's Septet is just visible under dark, transparent skies. To find the group start at the magnitude 5.2 star 92 Leonis and sweep 45′ NW to a NE–SW line of three 8th magnitude stars. 9′ NNW of the northernmost of these 8th magnitude stars is a 12th magnitude star: the galaxy group is scattered in a 6′ diameter area centered on this 12th magnitude star. Spread 1.5′ SW from the 12th magnitude star in a close NE–SW line are the three galaxies NGCs 3750, 3754, and 3755: at low power the three appear as one NE–SW halo; but 250x resolves 3750 and 3754-55 as two NE–SW stellar spots. 2.5′ south of this galaxy trio is NGC 3751, a very faint, slightly N–S elongated, spot. 2.5′ west of the 12th magnitude star is the 1.5′ long NE–SW arc of NGC 3748, NGC 3745, and NGC 3746, the last being the most conspicuous of the three. NGC 3745 and NGC 3748 appear only as extremely faint spots.

NGC 3773 H81³ Galaxy Type SA0:
φ 1.4′×1.1′, m12.0v, SB12.3   11ʰ38.2ᵐ +12° 07′
Finder Chart 48-11   ★★
12/14″ Scopes–125x: NGC 3773, located 5.25′ NW of a 10th magnitude star, shows a conspicuous stellar nucleus embedded in a tenuous 1′ diameter halo. 11.5 magnitude stars are 3.25′ north and 6′ NW.

NGC 3810 H21¹ Galaxy Type SA(rs)c I-II
φ 3.8′×2.6′, m10.8v, SB13.1   11ʰ41.0ᵐ +11° 28′
Finder Chart 48-11   ★★★
8/10″ Scopes–100x: NGC 3810 has a fairly bright 2′×1.5′ NNE–SSW halo containing a brighter center. A triangle of 11th and 12th magnitude stars is centered 9′ south of the galaxy.

16/18″Scopes–150x: This galaxy has a 3.5′×2.5′ NNE–SSW halo containing a mottled core with a faint stellar nucleus. Several faint knots are visible in the halo's NE portion.

Abell 1367 Galaxy Cluster

Abell 1367, 400 million light years distant, is one of the richest of the Abell clusters, including over 60 members within little more than one square degree of sky. The following are but a few of the Abell 1367 galaxies observable with large instruments:

UGC 6697 Galaxy Type SB(s)m: sp

ϕ 1.7′×0.4′, m14.3v $11^h43.8^m +19°58′$
Finder Chart 48-13a, Figure 48-29   ★

16/18″Scopes–150x: UGC 6697, located 3.5′ NW of NGC 3842, is a faint member of the Abell 1367 galaxy cluster. It appears merely as a very faint 1.25′×0.1′ NW–SE spindle of light.

NGC 3837 Galaxy Type E

ϕ 0.8′×0.7′, m13.2v, SB12.5 $11^h43.9^m +19°54′$
Finder Chart 48-13a, Figure 48-29   ★

16/18″Scopes–150x: NGC 3837 lies 3.5′ SSW of NGC 3842 in the Abell 1367 galaxy cluster. It is just a little fainter than, but only half the size of, NGC 3842. Its 30″ diameter halo is diffuse and broadly concentrated without much central brightening.

NGC 3840 Galaxy Type Sa

ϕ 1.0′×0.6′, m13.8v, SB13.1 $11^h43.9^m +20°05′$
Finder Chart 48-13a, Figure 48-29   ★

16/18″Scopes–150x: NGC 3840 is the northernmost in a string of four faint Abell 1367 galaxies extending north from NGC 3842, the galaxy cluster lucida. NGC 3840 is a very faint 30″ diameter glow with only a slight central brightening. Abell 1367 galaxy NGC 3844 lies 3′ south.

NGC 3841 Galaxy Type S?

ϕ 0.7′×0.7′, m13.6v, SB12.7 $11^h44.0^m +19°59′$

NGC 3842 H377[3] Galaxy Type E

ϕ 1.4′×1.0′, m11.8v, SB12.0 $11^h44.0^m +19°57′$
Finder Chart 48-13a, Figure 48-29   ★/★★★

16/18″Scopes–150x: NGC 3842 lies 2.75′ SW of an 11th magnitude star in the heart of the Abell 1367 galaxy cluster. It is the brightest object of the group. Its 45″ diameter halo is slightly elongated N–S and contains a diffuse core with a stellar nucleus. A 13th magnitude star is 40″ SE of the galaxy's center. Only 1.25′ to the north of NGC 3842 is its companion galaxy NGC 3841, a faint but reasonably

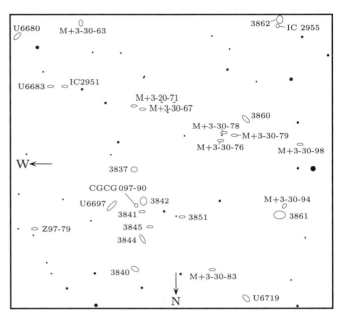

Finder Chart 48-13a. Abell 1367 Galaxy Cluster
See Figure 48-29

conspicuous 20″ diameter glow. 1′ to the west of NGC 3842 is a second faint, nearly stellar, companion galaxy, CGCG 097-90. Such crowding of smaller systems around the giant elliptical at the center of a galaxy group is the rule rather than the exception. Given the 400 million light year distance to Abell 1367, NGC 3842 must have an absolute magnitude of −23.7, which corresponds to a luminosity of 250 billion suns, and a true diameter in excess of 160,000 light years.

NGC 3844 Galaxy Type S0/a

ϕ 1.3′×0.2′, m13.9v, SB12.3 $11^h44.0^m +20°02′$
Finder Chart 48-13a, Figure 48-29   ★

16/18″Scopes–150x: NGC 3844 lies 5.5′ north of NGC 3842, the brightest galaxy in the Abell 1367 galaxy cluster. It is a very faint 40″×30″ NNE–SSW glow containing a very faint stellar nucleus.

NGC 3860 H386[3] Galaxy Type S?

ϕ 1.1′×0.6′, m13.4v, SB12.8 $11^h44.8^m +19°48′$
Finder Chart 48-13a, Figure 48-29   ★

16/18″Scopes–150x: NGC 3860, though a moderately faint Abell 1367 galaxy cluster member, is easily found 10′ SW of an 8th magnitude star. It has a faint 45″×30″ NE–SW halo containing a broad central concentration.

NGC 3861 H386³ Galaxy Type (R′)SAB(r)b III
ϕ **2.2′×1.3′, m12.7v, SB13.7   11ʰ45.1ᵐ +19° 59′**
Finder Chart 48-13a, Figure 48-29   ★★
16/18″Scopes–150x: NGC 3861, a bright member of the
Abell 1367 galaxy cluster, is 7′ NW of an 8th
magnitude star. It is easily spotted as a large, diffuse
1.5′×1′ ENE–WSW patch surrounding a small, well
concentrated core. On its SE edge is its companion
galaxy, M+03-30-94, which can be just glimpsed
with averted vision on good nights. NGC 3861 has
an absolute magnitude of −22.8, a luminosity of
110 billion suns, and a true diameter of over 250,000
light years.

NGC 3862 H385³ Galaxy Type E
ϕ **1.0′×1.0′, m12.7v, SB12.5   11ʰ45.1ᵐ +19° 36′**
Finder Chart 48-13a, Figure 48-29   ★★
16/18″Scopes–150x: NGC 3862, one of the brighter
members of the Abell 1367 galaxy cluster, is easily
identified 7′ north of an 8th magnitude star. It has
a 45″ diameter halo in which is embedded a very
faint stellar nucleus. Only 1′ to its NNW is its
companion galaxy IC 2955, merely a small, faint
diffuse spot. NGC 3862 has an absolute magnitude
of −22.8, a luminosity of 110 billion suns, corresponding to a true diameter in excess of 120,000
light years.

NGC 3872 H104² Galaxy Type E5
ϕ **2.3′×1.7′, m11.7v, SB13.1   11ʰ45.8ᵐ +13° 46′**
Finder Chart 48-11   ★★★
12/14″Scopes–125x: NGC 3872, lying in a barren star
field, has a bright stellar nucleus with a small core

surrounded by a well concentrated 1.25′×1′ NNE–
SSW halo. Two 12.5 magnitude stars are 3.25′ SSW
and 4.25′ WSW of the galaxy's nucleus.

NGC 3900 H82¹ Galaxy Type SA(r)0+
ϕ **2.9′×1.5′, m11.3v, SB12.8   11ʰ49.2ᵐ +27° 01′**
Finder Chart 48-13   ★★★
12/14″Scopes–125x: NGC 3900, located west of a triangle of 10th to 12th magnitude stars, has a fairly
bright 2.5′×1.5′ N–S halo surrounding a broad
central brightening containing a faint stellar
nucleus. A threshold star lies on the halo's edge
50″ ENE of the galaxy's center.

NGC 3912 H34² Galaxy Type SAB(s)b? pec III
ϕ **1.6′×0.9′, m12.7v, SB12.7   11ʰ50.1ᵐ +26° 29′**
Finder Chart 48-13   ★★
12/14″Scopes–125x: NGC 3912, located in a poor star
field, has a faint 1′×0.5′ N–S oval halo containing
a stellar nucleus. A 13th magnitude star lies 2.75′
SE, and a wide double (13, 13.5; 20″; 275°) is 4.5′
SE, of the galaxy's center.

NGC 4008 H368² Galaxy Type E5
ϕ **2.4′×1.4′, m12.0v, SB13.2   11ʰ58.3ᵐ +28° 12′**
Finder Chart 48-13   ★★★
12/14″Scopes–125x: NGC 4008 has a moderately faint
1.5′×0.75′ NNW–SSE lens-shaped halo surrounding
a well concentrated core that contains a bright
stellar nucleus. 20′ SSW is the galaxy NGC 4004;
and 40′–45′ SSE is the galaxy-pair NGC 4016+NGC
4017.

Chapter 49

Leo Minor, the Small Lion

49.1 Overview

Leo Minor, the Little Lion, is an inconspicuous diamond of faint stars (21, 30, $\beta = 31$, and $\sigma = 46$ Leo Minoris) between the Sickle of Leo on the south, the SE end of Lynx on the west, and the back legs of Ursa Major on the north and east. It was introduced in the late 17th century by the imaginative Johannes Hevelius. The NW–SE 232 square degree area of the celestial sphere assigned to the constellation by the International Astronomical Union early in the 20th century is strewn with faint galaxies, but does not contain much else of interest.

49.2 Interesting Stars

R Leo Minoris Variable Star　　　　**Spec. M6.5-M9**
m6.3 to 13.2, Per. 372 days　　　　$09^h45.6^m +34° 31'$
Finder Chart 49-3　　　　　　　　　　★★★★
4/6″Scopes–100x: R Leo Minoris, the brightest of the red giant long-period variables (LPVs) in the constellation, is located about 45′ SE of the magnitude 6.2 star 13 LMi. At extreme maximum R nearly equals the brightness of 13 LMi; but at minimum the star fades to the limit of visibility of 6″ telescopes.

49.3 Deep-Sky Objects

NGC 2859 H137[1] Galaxy Type (R)SB(r)0+
ϕ **4.6′ × 4.1′, m10.9v, SB13.9**　　　$09^h24.3^m +34° 31'$
Finder Chart 49-3, Figure 49-1　　　　★★★
8/10″Scopes–100x: NGC 2859, located 6.5′ ESE of a 7th magnitude star, has a fairly faint 2′ × 1′ N–S halo containing a bright core.
16/18″Scopes–150x: NGC 2859 exhibits a bright core embedded in a fainter halo extending 2.5′ × 1.75′ NNW–SSE. A 13th magnitude star lies 2.75′ ENE of the galaxy, and an ESE–WNW pair of threshold stars are superimposed upon the halo's northern edge.

NGC 2942 Galaxy Type SA(s)c: I-II
ϕ **1.9′ × 1.5′, m12.6v, SB13.6**　　　$09^h39.1^m +34° 00'$
Finder Chart 49-3　　　　　　　　　　★★
16/18″Scopes–150x: NGC 2942 is in the northern portion of a large WNW-pointing triangle of 11th

Figure 49-1. *NGC 2859 exhibits a well concentrated core surrounded by a very faint halo. Image courtesy of Dean Salman.*

249

Leo Minor, the Small Lion

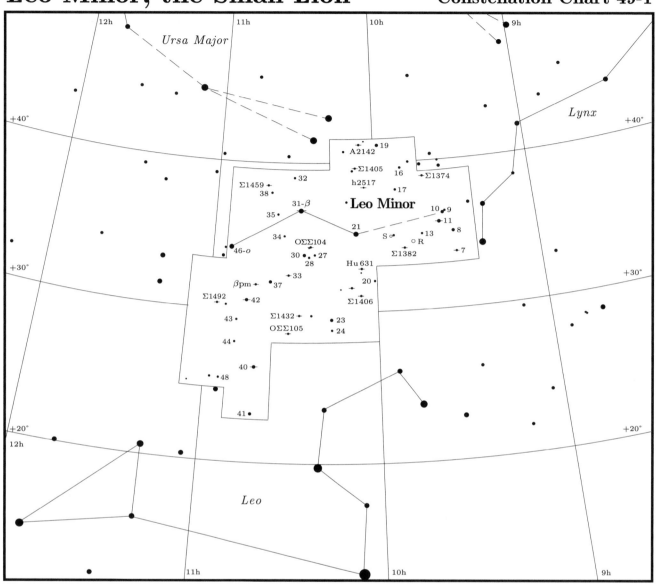

Chart Symbols

Constellation Chart

Stellar Magnitudes   0   1   2   3 4 5 6

Finder Charts   0/1   2   3   4   5 6 7 8 9

Master Finder Chart   0   1   2   3   4   5

→ *Guide Star Pointer*

●—● *Double Stars*

Finder Chart Scale

(One degree tick marks)

⊙ ○ *Variable Stars*

◯ *Open Clusters*

⊕ *Globular Clusters*

⬭ *Galaxies*

⬦ *Planetary Nebulae*

☐ *Small Bright Nebulae*

Large Bright Nebulae

Dark Nebulae

Table 49-1: Selected Variable Stars in Leo Minor

Name	HD No.	Type	Max.	Min.	Period (Days)	F*	Spec. Type	R.A. (2000) Dec.		Finder Chart No.	Notes
R LMi	84346	M	6.3	13.2	372	0.41	M6.5-M9	09^{h}45.6^m	+34° 31′	49-3	
S LMi	85597	M	7.9	14.3	233	0.42	M4-M7	53.7	+34 55	49-3	

F* = The fraction of period taken up by the star's rise from min. to max. brightness, or the period spent in eclipse.

Table 49-2: Selected Double Stars in Leo Minor

Name	ADS No.	Pair	M1	M2	Sep."	P.A.°	Spec	R.A. (2000 Dec.		Finder Chart No.	Notes
7 LMi		AB	6.0	9.3	62.8	130	K0	09ʰ30.7ᵐ	+33° 39′	49-3	
		AC		9.7	97.8	213					
Σ1374	7477		7.3	8.6	2.9	301	G5	41.4	+38 57	49-3	Yellow and deep blue
Σ1382		AB	7.1	11.1	27.8	106	A3	49.0	+34 05	49-3	
		AC		11.8	32.7	255					
h2517	7621		6.8	11.6	44.3	153	F5	10ʰ03.9ᵐ	+38 01	49-3	
Hu 631	7624		7.8	9.4	0.8	263	F8	04.0	+32 39	49-4	
Σ1406	7632		8.4	9.1	1.0	227	A3	05.7	+31 05	49-4	
A2142	7631		8.0	8.9	0.9	304	F0	05.7	+41 03	49-3	
Σ1405	7633		7.3	10.5	21.9	251		05.9	+39 35	49-3	
OΣΣ104			7.8	8.3	207.8	286	M K0	24.4	+34 11	49-4	
Σ1432			8.0	10.0	29.3	123	F2	27.0	+29 40	49-5	
OΣΣ105			7.3	8.3	131.3	225	K0	29.9	+28 35	49-5	
33 LMi	7813		5.8	11.8	43.3	245		31.9	+32 23	49-4	
Σ1459	7873		8.5	9.0	5.2	153	K0	40.2	+38 24	49-4	
β pm			6.0	10.0	116.8	173	M	42.2	+31 42	49-4	
40 LMi	7899	AB	5.5	12.5	18.5	112	A2	43.0	+26 20	49-5	
42 LMi			5.3	8.1	197.1	173	B9 K2	45.9	+30 41	49-4	
Σ1492	7988		8.1	10.0	21.5	165	A2	57.6	+30 39	49-5	

Footnotes: *= Year 2000, a = Near apogee, c = Closing, w = Widening. Finder Chart No: All stars listed in the tables are plotted in the large Constellation Chart, but when a star appears in a Finder Chart, this number is listed. Notes: When colors are subtle, the suffix *-ish* is used, e.g. *bluish.*

and 12th magnitude stars. Its circular 1′ diameter halo is faint and diffuse. A 13.5 magnitude star lies 1.5′ west of the galaxy's center, and a threshold star touches the halo's northern edge.

NGC 2955 H541³ Galaxy Type (R′)SA(r)b II
φ 1.4′×0.7′, m12.9v, SB12.7   09ʰ41.3ᵐ +35° 53′
Finder Chart 49-3, Figure 49-15   ★★
12/14″Scopes-125x: NGC 2955 has a faint, diffuse 1′×0.5′ NNW–SSE halo with very little central brightening, though a very faint stellar nucleus can be seen with averted vision. A 12th magnitude star lies 2.25′ south of the galaxy, and threshold stars are 30″ west and 35″ east of its center.

NGC 3003 H26⁵ Galaxy Type Sbc? III-IV
φ 5.2′×1.6′, m11.9v, SB14.1   09ʰ48.6ᵐ +33° 25′
Finder Chart 49-3, Figure 49-2   ★★★★
8/10″Scopes-100x: NGC 3003 is a faint 3′×0.5′ E–W streak that is slightly brighter along its major axis.
16/18″Scopes-150x: This galaxy responds well to an increase in aperture. The halo is extended 5′×1.5′ ENE–WSW to tapered ends. The bulging center contains a thin faint core. Along the major axis is a line of tiny bright spots. 5.5′ to the WSW of the galaxy is a 40″ wide pair of 13th and 14th magnitude stars.

NGC 3021 H115¹ Galaxy Type SA(rs)bc: II
φ 1.4′×0.8′, m12.1v, SB12.1   09ʰ51.0ᵐ +33° 33′
Finder Chart 49-3, Figure 49-16   ★★★
12/14″Scopes-125x: NGC 3021, located 1′ NW of a 10.5 magnitude star, is a fairly conspicuous galaxy with a well defined 1.25′×0.75′ ESE–WNW halo containing a faint extended core. 175x reveals a vague bar along the major axis. A 14th magnitude star lies on the halo's NE edge; and a 10th magnitude star is 4.5′ SW of the galaxy's center.

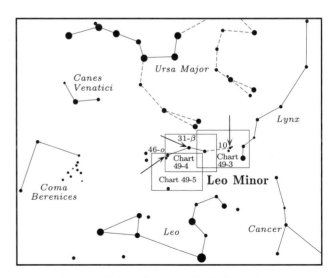

Master Finder Chart 49-2. LMi Chart Areas
Guide stars indicated by arrows.

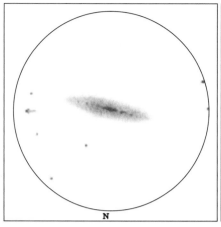

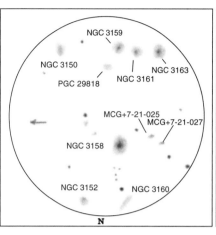

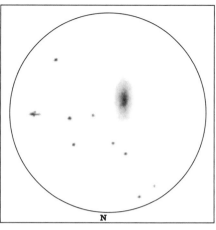

Figure 49-2. NGC 3003
17.5″, f4.5–300x, by G. R. Kepple

Figure 49-3. NGC 3158 Group
17.5″, f4.5–200x, by G. R. Kepple

Figure 49-4. NGC 3245
20″, f4.5–175x, by Richard W. Jakiel

NGC 3158 H639² Galaxy Type E3:
φ 2.3′ × 2.2′, m11.9v, SB 13.5   10ʰ13.8ᵐ +38° 46′
Finder Charts 49-3, 49-4, Figure 49-3   ★★

8/10″ Scopes–100x: NGC 3158, located within a NE-opening V-shaped asterism, has a moderately faint, circular 1′ diameter halo containing a stellar nucleus.

16/18″ Scopes–150x: NGC 3158, situated within a triangle of 13th magnitude stars, is the brightest of a 15′ diameter group of eight galaxies. Its 1.5′ × 1.25′ NNW–SSE halo contains a faint core with a stellar nucleus. 7.5′ SSE of NGC 3158 is NGC 3163, the brightest and most easterly in an E–W row of six galaxies that includes (going west from NGC 3163) NGCs 3161, 3159, and 3150. NGC 3163 is a faint 45″ diameter glow with a bright center; but the other galaxies in the line require averted vision to be seen at all. Two faint galaxies are an E–W pair

north of NGC 3158: NGC 3160 is 4.5′ due north of NGC 3158, and NGC 3152 is 5.75′ NNW of the bright galaxy.

NGC 3245 H86¹ Galaxy Type SA(r)0° :?
φ 2.9′ × 2.0′, m10.8v, SB 12.5   10ʰ27.3ᵐ +28° 30′
Finder Chart 49-5, Figure 49-4   ★★★

12/14″ Scopes–125x: NGC 3245 has a 1.5′ × 0.75′ N–S oval halo containing a bright core with a stellar nucleus. A 13th magnitude star lies 3′ WNW.

16/18″ Scopes–150x: This galaxy has a bright 2.25′ × 1′ N–S lens-shaped halo that fades outward to tapered tips. The well defined 30″ × 20″ N–S oval core contains a stellar nucleus.

NGC 3254 H72¹ Galaxy Type SA(s)bc II
φ 4.9′ × 1.4′, m11.7v, SB 13.7   10ʰ29.3ᵐ +29° 30′
Finder Chart 49-5, Figure 49-5   ★★★

8/10″ Scopes–100x: NGC 3254, located 6′ west of a pair of 10th magnitude stars, is a hazy 2′ × 0.75′ NE–SW patch containing a stellar nucleus.

16/18″ Scopes–150x: The 5′ × 1.25′ NE–SW halo contains a nonstellar nucleus. A few faint knots can be glimpsed in the central area. A 13.5 magnitude star lies 3′ west of the galaxy.

NGC 3277 H359² Galaxy Type SA(r)ab II
φ 2.2′ × 2.0′, m11.7v, SB 13.1   10ʰ32.9ᵐ +28° 31′
Finder Chart 49-5, Figure 49-17   ★★★

8/10″ Scopes–100x: NGC 3277, located some distance south of a 10th magnitude star, has a moderately faint, circular 1′ diameter halo containing a bright center.

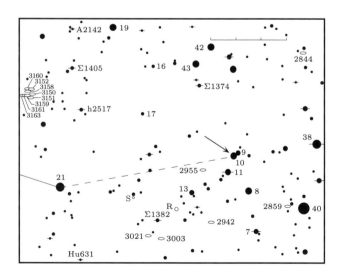

Finder Chart 49-3. 10 LMi: 09ʰ34.2ᵐ +36° 24′

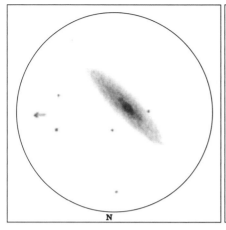

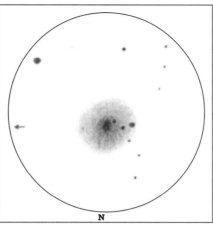

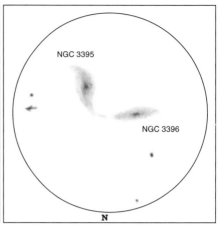

Figure 49-5. NGC 3254
17.5″, f4.5-300x, by G. R. Kepple

Figure 49-6. NGC 3344
17.5″, f4.5-250x, by G. R. Kepple

Figure 49-7. NGC 3395-96
20″, f4.5-175x, by Richard W. Jakiel

12/14″Scopes–125x: A well concentrated 45″ diameter core containing a stellar nucleus is surrounded by a 1.5′ diameter halo with diffuse edges. A 13.5 magnitude star is 1.5′ NE, and just about as bright as the nucleus. An 11th magnitude star lies 5′ WSW, and a 10.5 magnitude star 7′ SW, of the galaxy.

NGC 3294 H164[1] Galaxy Type SA(s)c I-II
ϕ **3.5′× 1.7′, m11.8v, SB13.6**   **10ʰ36.3ᵐ +37° 20′**
Finder Chart 49-4, Figure 49-18   ★★★

8/10″Scopes–100x: NGC 3294, located 5′ south of an 11th magnitude star, is a featureless glow elongated 2.5′ × 1′ NW–SE.

16/18″Scopes–150x: Larger telescopes reveal a moderately faint 3′× 1.25′ ESE–WNW halo containing a broad, mottled core but no definite nucleus. A 13th magnitude star lies 2.5′ west of the galaxy's center.

NGC 3344 H81[1] Galaxy Type (R)SAB(r)bc I-II
ϕ **6.9′× 6.4′, m9.9v, SB13.8**   **10ʰ43.5ᵐ +24° 55′**
Finder Chart 49-5, Figure 49-6   ★★★

8/10″Scopes–100x: NGC 3344 is a fairly bright face-on galaxy with a 4′ diameter halo around a brighter center. A 10.5 magnitude star just touches the halo's east edge. A fainter star is superimposed upon the halo a little closer to the galaxy's center.

16/18″Scopes–150x: The halo does not gain much in size with an increase in aperture, but the two stars east of the galaxy's center are now distinctly within its periphery. The central area has a mottled texture and a small 25″ core with a nonstellar nucleus. 30″ SSE of the galaxy's center is a 14th magnitude star that appears about as bright as the nucleus.

NGC 3395 H116[1] Galaxy Type SAB(rs)cd pec: III
ϕ **1.6′× 0.9′, m12.1v, SB12.3**   **10ʰ49.8ᵐ +32° 59′**

NGC 3396 H117[1] Galaxy Type IBm pec
ϕ **3.4′× 1.3′, m12.1v, SB13.6**   **10ʰ49.9ᵐ +32° 59′**
Finder Chart 49-4, Figure 49-7   ★★★/★★★

16/18″Scopes–150x: This fairly bright interacting NE–SW galaxy pair consists of two much-elongated systems in contact at their tips. They therefore have the appearance of a butterfly. The southwestern galaxy, NGC 3395, is larger and more concentrated than its companion: its 1.5′× 0.75′ NNE–SSW halo contains a nonstellar nucleus. A 14th magnitude star is 1.5′ due west of the galaxy. The other system, NGC 3396, is attached by its western end to the northern tip of NGC 3395: it has a more conspicuous stellar nucleus than its SW associate but only a

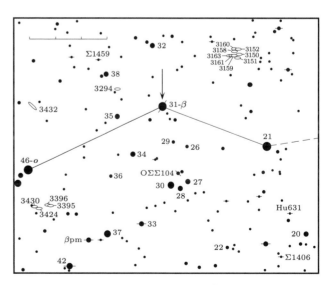

Finder Chart 49-4. 31-β LMi: 10ʰ27.8ᵐ +36° 42′

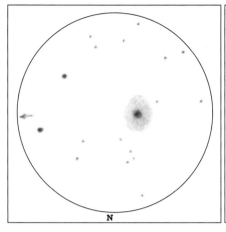

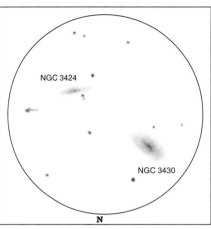

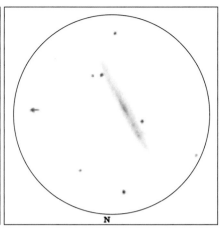

Figure 49-8. NGC 3414
17.5″, f4.5–250x, by G. R. Kepple

Figure 49-9. NGC 3424-30
20″, f4.5–175x, by Richard W. Jakiel

Figure 49-10. NGC 3432
20″, f4.5–175x, by Richard W. Jakiel

poorly concentrated 1.5′×0.5′ E–W halo. A 14th magnitude star is 1.25′ NNE of the nucleus of NGC 3396.

NGC 3414 H362² Galaxy Type S0 pec
φ **3.2′×2.7′, m11.0v, SB 13.1**   10ʰ51.3ᵐ +27° 19′
Finder Chart 49-5, Figure 49-8   ★★★

8/10″ Scopes–100x: NGC 3414 exhibits a very bright but small core embedded in a 1.5′ diameter halo which fades rapidly from its center out to a diffuse periphery.

12/14″ Scopes–125x: A bright 1′ diameter core with a stellar nucleus is embedded in a fainter halo elongated 2.5′×1.5′ NNE–SSW. Two 12.5 magnitude stars 5.5′ WSW and 6.5′ WNW of the galaxy form a triangle with it. Galaxy NGC 3418 lies 8′ north.

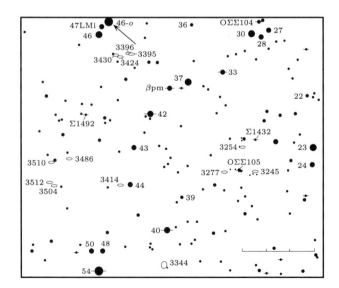

Finder Chart 49-5. 46-o LMi: 10ʰ53.3ᵐ +34° 13′

NGC 3424 H494² Galaxy Type SB(s)b:?
φ **2.5′×0.8′, m12.4v, SB 13.0**   10ʰ51.8ᵐ +32° 54′

NGC 3430 H118¹ Galaxy Type SAB(rs)c II
φ **4.1′×2.2′, m11.6v, SB 13.8**   10ʰ52.2ᵐ +32° 57′
Finder Chart 49-4, 49-5, Figure 49-9   ★★/★★

16/18″ Scopes–150x: NGC 3430, located 8′ WSW of an 8th magnitude star, is a fairly large low surface brightness oval elongated 3′×1.75′ NE–SW with very little central brightening. A threshold stellar nucleus is intermittently visible. A magnitude 13.5 star lies 1.5′ SSE, and a magnitude 9.5 star lies 2.75′ NW of the galaxy's center. 6′ SW of NGC 3430 is the galaxy NGC 3424, a faint 2.5′×0.75′ WNW–ESE streak with an extended brighter core. A 13th magnitude star touches the north edge of the halo 30″ east of the galaxy's center. A magnitude 10.5 star is 1.5′ SE of the center. 10′ SW of NGC 3424 lies NGC 3413.

NGC 3432 H172¹ Galaxy Type SB(s)m III
φ **6.9′×1.9′, m11.2v, SB 13.9**   10ʰ52.5ᵐ +36° 37′
Finder Chart 49-4, Figure 49-10   ★★★★

8/10″ Scopes–100x: NGC 3432 has a moderately bright spindle-shaped halo elongated 3.5′×0.75′ NE–SW. A very thin 2′ long core runs through the galaxy's center along the halo's major axis. An E–W pair of 12.5 and 13th magnitude stars lies west of the halo's SW tip, and a 12.5 magnitude star lies 1′ ENE of the galaxy's center.

16/18″ Scopes–150x: In larger telescopes NGC 3432 has a much-elongated 5′×1′ NE–SW envelope with a mottled texture and a highly irregular central bar, the NE half of which is broken into knots. A 14th magnitude star is on the NW edge of the envelope 1.25′ north of the galaxy's center. Opposite it, on

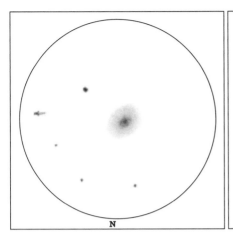

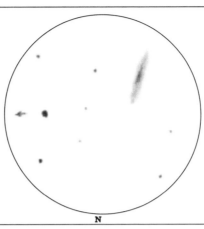

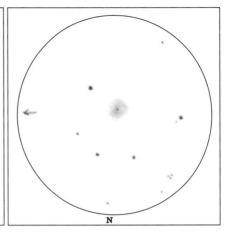

Figure 49-11. NGC 3504
20″, f4.5-175x, by Richard W. Jakiel

Figure 49-12. NGC 3510
17.5″, f4.5-250x, by G. R. Kepple

Figure 49-13. NGC 3512
17.5″, f4.5-250x, by G. R. Kepple

the other flank, is a magnitude 12.5 star.

NGC 3486 H87[1] Galaxy Type SAB(r)c II
ϕ **6.6′ × 4.7′, m10.5v, SB14.1**   **11ʰ00.4ᵐ +28° 58′**
Finder Chart 49-5, Figure 49-14   ★★★

8/10″ Scopes-100x: NGC 3486 has a fairly bright core embedded in a faint diffuse 3′ × 2′ E–W halo.

16/18″ Scopes-150x: In larger telescopes NGC 3486 shows a stellar nucleus embedded in a bright mottled 1′ × 0.5′ ENE–WSW core surrounded by a much fainter 5′ × 4′ E–W oval halo. A few faint knots can be glimpsed around the core. 13th magnitude stars are 5.5′ north and 6′ west of the galaxy.

NGC 3504 H88[1] Galaxy Type (R)SAB(s)ab I-II
ϕ **2.3′ × 2.3′, m10.9v, SB12.6**   **11ʰ03.2ᵐ +27° 58′**
Finder Chart 49-5, Figure 49-11   ★★★

12/14″ Scopes-125x: NGC 3504 has a bright nonstellar nucleus embedded in a much fainter unconcentrated 1.5′ × 1′ NNW–SSE halo. At 175x a slight mottled texture may be seen near the nucleus. A 12th magnitude star lies 2′ SW, and two 14.5 magnitude stars are 2.5′ NNW and 2.75′ NNE of the galaxy's center. 12′ ENE is galaxy NGC 3512.

NGC 3510 H365[2] Galaxy Type SB(s)m
ϕ **3.8′ × 0.9′, m12.2v, SB13.4**   **11ʰ03.7ᵐ +28° 53′**
Finder Chart 49-5, Figure 49-12   ★★

12/14″ Scopes-125x: NGC 3510 lies 8′ ESE of a 7.5 magnitude star with a magnitude 9.5 companion 3.5′ to its north. The galaxy is a faint featureless 3′ × 0.5′ NNW–SSE streak with a slight brightening along its major axis. A 12th magnitude star lies 4.5′ to the galaxy's WSW.

NGC 3512 H366[2] Galaxy Type SAB(rs)c II
ϕ **1.6′ × 1.5′, m12.3v, SB13.1**   **11ʰ04.0ᵐ +28° 02′**
Finder Chart 49-5, Figure 49-13   ★★

12/14″ Scopes-125x: NGC 3512, located 12′ ENE of the galaxy NGC 3504, appears much fainter and smaller than its companion. Its circular 1.5′ halo is very little brighter in its center. At 175x the halo looks slightly elongated NW–SE and contains a faint stellar nucleus. 12.5 magnitude stars lie 2′ SW and 3.75′ east, and 13th magnitude stars are 3′ NNE and 2.5′ NNW, of the galaxy's center.

Figure 49-14 *NGC 3486 shows a stellar nucleus embedded in a bright mottled core surrounded by a much fainter oval halo. Image courtesy of Adam Block NOAO/AURA/NSF.*

Figure 49-15. *NGC 2955 is a 12.9 magnitude galaxy with a faint stellar nucleus. Image courtesy of Bill Logan.*

Figure 49-16. *NGC 3021 is an edge-on galaxy containing a faint extended core. Image courtesy of Bill Logan.*

Figure 49-17 *NGC 3277 is a circular SA galaxy with a well concentrated core. Image courtesy of Bill Logan.*

Figure 49-18. *NGC 3294 displays broad, mottled core in an oval-shaped halo. Image courtesy of Bill Logan.*

Chapter 50

Libra, the Scales

50.1 Overview

The word "Zodiac" is derived from an ancient Greek phrase meaning "Circle of Animals." Libra the Scales is the only inanimate object in the Zodiac and is there because it is one of the many constellations which the early Greeks had inherited from the Babylonians. However, a couple of the ancient Greek astronomers, to make the Zodiac purely zoological, turned the Scales into the Claws of the Scorpion. Nevertheless the celestial Scales is of very high antiquity: an ancient Mesopotamian carving of about 2200 B.C. shows a priest holding a balance-beam scale out over an altar in front of the enthroned sun-god Shamash. Because Shamash was also the god of justice, even at that early date scales symbolized the "weighing of justice." This idea was inherited by the Greeks, though in Greek mythology it was a goddess, Astraea, who held the Scales of Justice. She was identified with the constellation of Virgo, which is in the Zodiac immediately NW of Libra.

Libra is just west and northwest of the Scorpius Milky Way. Consequently it lacks such Milky Way objects as open and diffuse nebulae. It is fairly rich in galaxies, as indeed are most off-Milky Way constellations. It also has a couple of attractive double stars and a very loose Class XI globular cluster.

50.2 Interesting Stars

Mu (μ) = 7 Librae (β 106) Double Star   Spec. A2
m5.8,6.7; Sep. 1.8″; P.A. 355° $14^h49.3^m -14° 09'$
Finder Chart 50-3   ★★★★
4/6″ Scopes–200x: Mu Librae is a close pair of white stars which appear as two disks in contact. The stars may be completely split when air currents are calm.

Libra: LIE-bra, or LEE-bra
Genitive: Librae, LIE-bree, or LEE-bree
Abbreviation: Lib
Culmination: 9pm–June 23, midnight–May 9
Area: 538 square degrees
Best Deep-Sky Objects: NGC 5728, NGC 5792, NGC 5812, NGC 5878, NGC 5898–NGC 5903
Binocular Objects: 9–$\alpha^{1,2}$ Lib, 19–δ Lib, 24–ι Lib, NGC 5897

Alpha (α) = 9 Librae (S,h186) Double Star Spec. A2, F5
m2.8,5.2; Sep. 231.0″; P.A. 314° $14^h50.9^m -16° 02'$
Finder Chart 50-3   ★★★★

Zubenelgenubi

2/3″ Scopes–25x: Alpha Librae is easily seen in binoculars as a bright, wide pair of white and yellow stars.

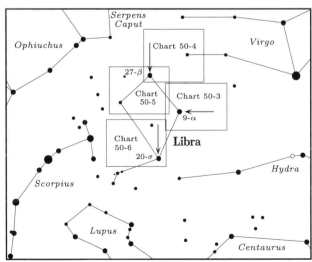

Master Finder Chart 50-1. Libra Chart Areas
Guide stars indicated by arrows.

257

Libra, the Scales

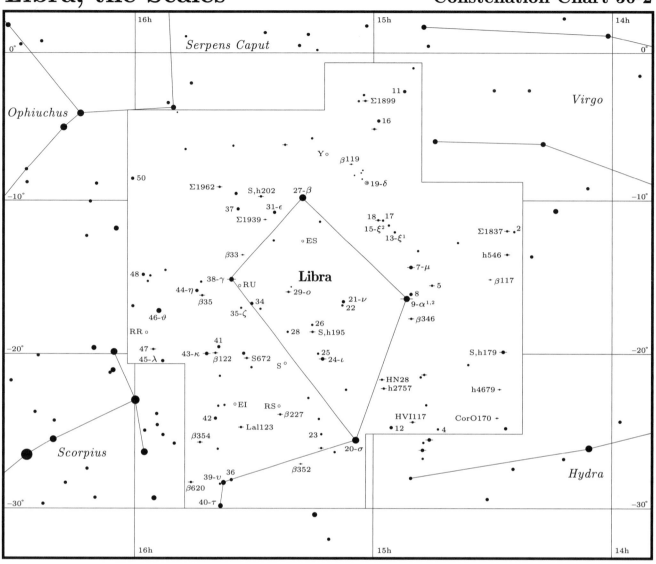

Chart Symbols

Constellation Chart	0 1 2 3 4 5 6
Stellar Magnitudes	
Finder Charts	0/1 2 3 4 5 6 7 8 9
Master Finder Chart	0 1 2 3 4 5

→ Guide Star Pointer ◉ ○ Variable Stars ✦ Planetary Nebulae

●—● Double Stars ◯ Open Clusters ☐ Small Bright Nebulae

Finder Chart Scale ⊕ Globular Clusters Large Bright Nebulae

(One degree tick marks) ⬯ Galaxies Dark Nebulae

Table 50-1: Selected Variable Stars in Libra

Name	HD No.	Type	Max.	Min.	Period (Days)	F*	Spec. Type	R.A. (2000) Dec.		Finder Chart No.	Notes
19–δ Lib	126289	EA	4.92	5.90	2.32	0.23	B9.5V	15h01.0m	−08° 31′	50-4	
Y Lib	134739	M	7.6	14.7	275	0.41	M5e	11.7	−06 01	50-4	
ES Lib	135681	EB	7.10	7.57	0.88		A2-A3V	16.8	−13 02	50-5	
S Lib	136753	M	7.5	13.0	192	0.49	M2e	21.4	−20 23	50-6	
RS Lib	136986	M	7.0	13.02	217	0.48	M7e-M8e	24.3	−22 55	50-6	
EI Lib	138672	EA	9.5	10.5	1.98	0.13	A2	34.4	−23 00	50-6	
RR Lib	142641	M	7.8	15.0	276	0.47	M4e-M5.5e	56.4	−18 18	50-1	

F* = The fraction of period taken up by the star's rise from min. to max. brightness, or the period spent in eclipse.

Table 50-2: Selected Double Stars in Libra

Name	ADS No.	Pair	M1	M2	Sep.′	P.A.°	Spec	R.A. (2000) Dec.		Finder Chart No.	Notes
Σ1837	9254		6.7	8.3	1.2	292	F2	14ʰ24.7ᵐ	−11° 40′	50-3	
h546			6.6	10.0	39.7	42	K0	25.3	−13 21	50-3	
S, h179	9258	AB	6.4	7.6	35.1	296	A0 A0	25.5	−19 58	50-3	Two white stars
β 225	9258	BC		8.8	1.2	93					
h4679	9260		8.2	9.3	16.6	306	F2	25.9	−22 08	50-2	
CorO170	9261		8.4	9.2	2.4	132	F8	26.3	−24 13	50-2	
β 117	9291	AB	8.3	9.2	2.1	84	G5	31.3	−15 38	50-3	
	9291	AC		12.0	107.3	335					
5 Lib	9376		6.6	11.3	2.7	246	K0	46.0	−15 28	50-3	
β 346	9387		7.4	8.2	2.0	269	G0	48.5	−17 20	50-3	
7−μ Lib	9396	AB	5.8	6.7	1.8	355	A2	49.3	−14 09	50-3	Close white pair
HVI117	9394	AB	5.8	8.7	61.0	220	K0 F8	49.3	−24 15	50-2	
β 617	9394	BC		11.1	2.7	338					
α², α¹ Lib			2.8	5.2	231.0	314	A2 F5	50.9	−16 02	50-3	White and yellowish
HN28	9446	AB	5.7	8.0	23.0	303	K5 M0	57.5	−21 25	50-2	Beautiful orange and red
h2757			7.7	9.9	12.0	95	F5	58.7	−22 24	50-2	Lovely orange and red pair
18 Lib	9456	AB	5.8	10.0	19.7	39	K0	58.9	−11 09	50-2	
	9456	AC		11.3	162.3	41					
Σ1899	9479		6.8	9.3	28.2	67	K2	15ʰ01.6ᵐ	−03 10	50-4	
β 119	9497		8.0	8.5	1.9	287	G0	05.5	−07 01	50-4	
24−ι Lib	9532	AB	5.1	9.4	57.8	111	A0	12.2	−19 47	50-6	White
	9532	BC		11.1	1.9	17					Reddish-purple companions
S,h195			7.1	8.1	47.4	140	F5	14.5	−18 26	50-2	
β 352	9569		7.8	9.8	14.0	66	K2	17.9	−27 00	50-2	
β 227	9579		7.5	8.8	1.9	168	A2	19.2	−24 16	50-6	
29−o Lib			6.2	8.4	44.4	350	F5	21.0	−15 33	50-5	Yellowish and purplish
Σ1939	9640		8.1	9.1	9.4	130	G0	27.5	−10 58	50-5	Yellowish and bluish
S, h202			6.8	8.1	51.9	133	K0 K0	28.2	−09 21	50-5	Nice yellow pair
β 33	9680	AB	7.7	10.0	3.0	40	F8	31.3	−13 00	50-5	
S672	9681		6.2	8.5	11.1	281	A5 F0	31.7	−20 10	50-6	White and yellowish
Lal123	9689	AxBC	7.5	7.8	9.2	300	A3 A3	33.2	−24 29	50-6	
38−γ Lib	9704	AB	3.9	11.1	41.7	153	K0	35.5	−14 47	50-5	
Σ1962	9728		6.5	6.6	11.9	188	F8 F8	38.7	−08 47	50-5	Matched pale yellow pair
β 122	9735		7.6	7.8	1.7	218	F2	39.9	−19 46	50-6	Close yellowish pair
43−κ Lib			4.7	9.7	172.0	279	M0	41.9	−19 41	50-6	
β 35	9751	AB	7.3	8.4	2.3	104	G4	42.8	−16 01	50-5	
	9751	AC		10.0	112.9	36					
β 354	9754		7.3	9.4	5.6	289	F0	43.2	−25 25	50-6	
β 620	9775	AB	7.2	7.2	0.5	164	A5	46.2	−28 04	50-2	
h4803		ABxC		9.1	50.7	214					

Footnotes: *= Year 2000, a = Near apogee, c = Closing, w = Widening. Finder Chart No: All stars listed in the tables are plotted in the large Constellation Chart, but when a star appears in a Finder Chart, this number is listed. Notes: When colors are subtle, the suffix *-ish* is used, e.g. *bluish*.

HN28 Double Star Spec. K5, M0
m5.7,8.0; Sep.23.0″; P.A.303° 14ʰ57.5ᵐ −21° 25′
Constellation Chart 50-2 ★★★★★
4/6″Scopes–75x: HN28 (William Herschel's 1821 catalogue) is an unusually beautiful combination of bright orange and red stars easily resolved in small telescopes.

Delta (δ) = 19 Librae Variable Star Spec. B9.5
m4.92,5.90; Per2.33 days 15ʰ01.0ᵐ −08° 31′
Finder Chart 50-4 ★★★★
8/10″Scopes–100x: Delta is an Algol-type eclipsing binary, the brighter blue B-type star being partially, but not completely, occulted by a yellowish B-type subgiant every 2.33 days. The one magnitude fall to minimum takes only six hours, and therefore can often be observed in the course of a single evening. The Delta Librae system is around 200 light years distant.

Σ1962 Double Star Spec. F8, F8
m6.5,6.6; Sep.11.9″; P.A.188° 15ʰ38.7ᵐ −08° 47′
Finder Chart 50-5 ★★★★
4/6″Scopes–100x: Struve 1962 is a fine pair of yellow stars especially well suited for small telescopes: the color appears much paler in larger aperture instruments.

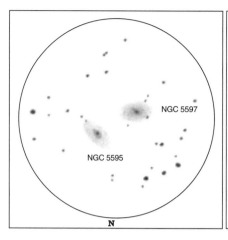
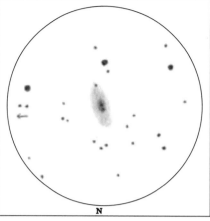
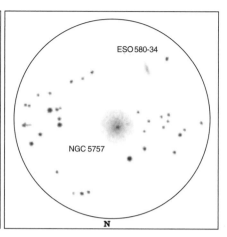

Figure 50-1. NGC 5595 and NGC 5597
16″, f5–165x, by G. R. Kepple

Figure 50-2. NGC 5728
13″, f5.6–165x, by Steve Coe

Figure 50-3. NGC 5757
12.5″, f5–150x, by G. R. Kepple

50.3 Deep-Sky Objects

NGC 5595 H121³ Galaxy Type SAB:(rs)c pec II?
ϕ **2.2′ × 1.2′, m12.0v, SB 12.9** $14^h24.2^m -16° 43'$

NGC 5597 H122³ Galaxy Type (R′)SB(s)cd pec II:
ϕ **2.4′ × 1.8′, m12.0v, SB 13.5** $14^h24.5^m -16° 46'$
Finder Chart 50-3, Figure 50-1   ★★/★★
12/14″ Scopes–125x: NGC 5595 and NGC 5597 are a
4′ wide NW–SE pair of faint galaxies. The NW
object, NGC 5595, has a faint 2′ × 1.25′ NE–SW
halo containing a somewhat brighter circular core
with a stellar nucleus. The SE galaxy, NGC 5597,
is slightly fainter, its 1.75′ halo slightly elongated
E–W, and has a faint stellar nucleus but no core
around it.

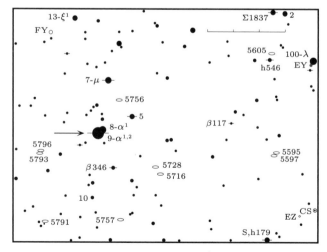

Finder Chart 50-3. 9–$\alpha^{1,2}$ Lib: $14^h50.8^m -16° 03'$

NGC 5605 H120³ Galaxy Type (R′)SAB(rs)bc pec II:
ϕ **1.4′ × 1.4′, m12.3v, SB 12.9** $14^h25.1^m -13° 10'$
Finder Chart 50-3   ★★
12/14″ Scopes–125x: NGC 5605 has a moderately faint,
circular 1.5′ diameter halo that is slightly brighter
in the center.

16/18″ Scopes–150x: Larger telescopes show a low
surface brightness object slightly elongated
1.75′ × 1.5′ E–W halo containing a broad, faint
slightly mottled core. A magnitude 12.5 star is 3′
west, and a magnitude 13.5 star 4′ SSW, of the
galaxy's center.

NGC 5716 H671³ Galaxy Type SB(s)cd II-III
ϕ **2.0′ × 1.2′, m12.9v, SB 13.7** $14^h41.1^m -17° 29'$
Finder Chart 50-3   ★★
12/14″ Scopes–125x: NGC 5716 has a faint, diffuse 1.25′
halo with no central concentration. A 40″ wide pair
of magnitude 11 and 12 stars touch the NE edge of
the halo. 23′ to the NE of NGC 5716 is the galaxy
NGC 5728.

NGC 5728 H184¹ Galaxy Type (R)SB(rs)a
ϕ **3.7′ × 2.6′, m11.5v, SB 13.8** $14^h42.4^m -17° 15'$
Finder Chart 50-3, Figure 50-2   ★★★
12/14″ Scopes–125x: NGC 5728 is just north of a 17′
long E–W row of 9th magnitude stars. It has a fairly
bright 2.5′ × 1′ NNE–SSW halo containing a broad
central brightening. The core is irregularly bright,
extended 1′ × 0.5′, and has two stellar points, the
one 12″ NE of the galaxy's true central nucleus
merely a superimposed 14th magnitude star. A
second 14th magnitude star lies at the halo's
southern tip 1′ SSW of the nucleus.

Figure 50-4. *NGC 5792 has a low surface brightness halo with a broad, irregular core. Large instruments are needed to see any detail due to the 9.5 magnitude star at its NE edge. Image courtesy of Josef Pöpsel and Stefan Binnewies.*

NGC 5756 Galaxy Type (R′)SB(s)bc pec II:
ϕ **2.6′×1.0′, m12.3v, SB13.2   14^{h}47.6^m −14° 51′**
Finder Chart 50-3   ★★
12/14″ Scopes–125x: NGC 5756 has a faint 2′ × 1′ NE–SW halo containing a broad, slightly brighter core. 175x reveals a few faint knots spread along the center of the galaxy's major axis.

NGC 5757 H690³ Galaxy Type (R)SB(rs)b: pec II:
ϕ **2.3′×1.5′, m12.0v, SB13.2   14^{h}47.8^m −19° 05′**
Finder Chart 50-3, Figure 50-3   ★★
12/14″ Scopes–125x: NGC 5757, located 1.5′ south of a 12.5 magnitude star, appears moderately faint and has a circular 1.5′ diameter halo which brightens slightly to a tiny core with a very faint stellar nucleus. 3.5′ to the SE of NGC 5757 is its companion galaxy ESO 580-34, a very faint 45″ × 10″ NE–SW streak.

NGC 5768 H373³ Galaxy Type SB:(s)m: III-IV
ϕ **1.8′×1.6′, m12.5v, SB13.5   14^{h}52.1^m −02° 32′**
Finder Chart 50-4   ★★
8/10″ Scopes–100x: NGC 5768 is a very faint featureless glow about 1′ in diameter. A 12th magnitude star is on the south edge of its halo. The 12th magnitude

star forms a triangle with two stars to its east and SE.
16/18″ Scopes–150x: The halo appears faint, is elongated 1.5′ × 1′ E–W, and contains a weak central concentration.

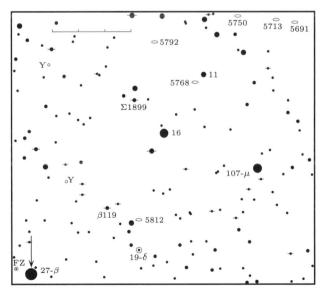

Finder Chart 50-4. 27–β Lib: 15^{h}17.0^m −09° 23′

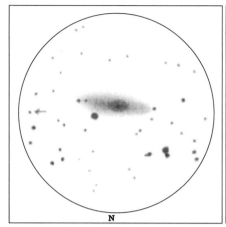
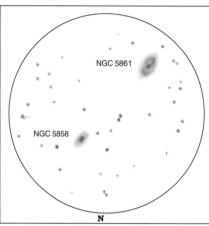
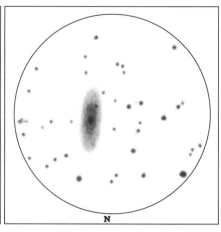

Figure 50-5. NGC 5792
16″, f5–100x, by G. R. Kepple

Figure 50-6. NGC 5858 and NGC 5861
16″, f5–150x, by G. R. Kepple

Figure 50-7. NGC 5878
13″, f5.6–100x, by Steve Coe

NGC 5792 H671³ Galaxy Type (R′)SAB(rs)b: II?
ϕ **7.3′×1.9′, m11.2v, SB14.0**   14^{h}58.4^m −01° 05′
Finder Chart 50-4, Figures 50-4, 50-5   ★★
12/14″Scopes–125x: NGC 5792 is a faint featureless
   2.5′×1′ E–W glow with a 9.5 magnitude star on its
   NW edge.
20/22″Scopes–175x: Despite the glare of the
   magnitude 9.5 star on its NW edge, with averted
   vision NGC 5792 appears as a low surface
   brightness 6′×1.5′ E–W halo containing a broad,
   irregular core with an extremely faint stellar
   nucleus. A 13th magnitude star lies at the eastern
   tip 3.5′ east of the galaxy's center.

NGC 5791 H691³ Galaxy Type E4/S0⁻:
ϕ **2.4′×1.3′, m11.9v, SB13.0**   14^{h}58.8^m −19° 16′
Finder Chart 50-3   ★★★
12/14″Scopes–125x: NGC 5791 is NW of a 10′ triangle
   of 8th and 9th magnitude stars. A bright stellar
   nucleus is embedded in a small, round core
   surrounded by an irregular 1′×0.5′ NNW–SSE halo.
   An 11th magnitude star lies 3′ SE of the galaxy's
   center. IC 1081 lies 2′ NE of 5791 and appears as
   a small version of 5791.

NGC 5793 Galaxy Type SA?b:
ϕ **1.8′×0.8′, m13.2v, SB13.5**   14^{h}59.4^m −16° 42′
Finder Chart 50-3   ★★
16/18″Scopes–150x: NGC 5793, located 4′ south of NGC
   5796, has a fairly faint, diffuse 1′×0.5′ NNE–SSW
   halo containing a very faint, small core. A 13th
   magnitude star lies 1.25′ SE of the galaxy's center.

NGC 5796 Galaxy Type SA0⁻:
ϕ **2.7′×1.7′, m11.6v, SB13.1**   14^{h}59.4^m −16° 37′
Finder Chart 50-3   ★★★
12/14″Scopes–125x: NGC 5796 has a broad core
   containing a stellar nucleus embedded in a fairly
   concentrated, circular 1′ diameter halo which fades
   smoothly to its periphery. Galaxy NGC 5793 lies
   4′ south.

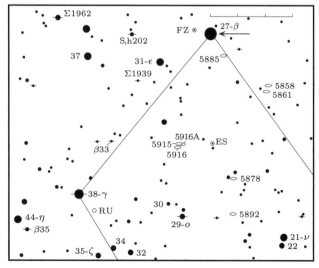

Finder Chart 50-5. 27–β Lib: 15^{h}17.0^m −09° 23′

NGC 5812 H71¹ Galaxy Type E1/S0⁻
ϕ **2.3′×1.9′, m11.2v, SB12.6**   15^{h}01.0^m −07° 27′
Finder Chart 50-4   ★★★
8/10″Scopes–100x: NGC 5812 has a fairly bright,
   circular 1′ diameter halo containing a stellar
   nucleus.

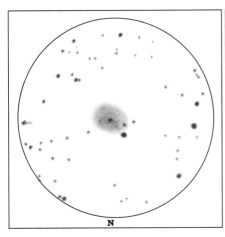

Figure 50-8. NGC 5885
16″, f5–200x, by G. R. Kepple

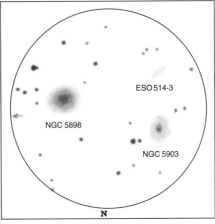

Figure 50-9. NGC 5898 and NGC 5903
13″, f5.6–100x, by Steve Coe

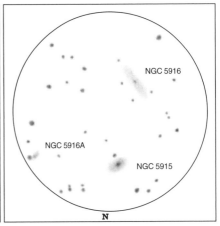

Figure 50-10. NGC 5915 and NGC 5916
16″, f5–200x, by G. R. Kepple

16/18″ Scopes–150x: The halo appears fairly well defined, is elongated 1.5′ × 1.25′ ENE–WSW, and contains a nonstellar nucleus.

NGC 5858 Galaxy Type S0°
ϕ 1.4′ × 0.8′, m12.8v, SB 12.8   15ʰ08.8ᵐ −11° 13′
Finder Chart 50-5, Figure 50-6   ★★

12/14″ Scopes–125x: NGC 5858 has a faint, circular 45″ diameter halo that brightens smoothly to a small core containing a stellar nucleus. Galaxy NGC 5861 lies 9′ SE.

16/18″ Scopes–150x: The halo is elongated 1.25′ × 0.5′ NNW–SSE and contains a small oval core. A 12th magnitude star lies 2′ west. The very faint galaxy IC 1091 lies 10′ NW.

NGC 5861 H192² Galaxy Type SB(rs)c I or I-II
ϕ 2.8′ × 1.8′, m11.6v, SB 13.2   15ʰ09.3ᵐ −11° 19′
Finder Chart 50-5, Figure 50-6   ★★★

12/14″ Scopes–125x: NGC 5861, located 2.5′ NNE of a 10th magnitude star, is a faint, uniformly illuminated, 2′ × 1′ NNW–SSE oval glow. The faint, small galaxy NGC 5858 is 9′ to the NW. A 15″ wide pair of magnitude 11 and 11.5 stars, aligned with the major axis of NGC 5861, lies midway between the two galaxies.

16/18″ Scopes–150x: NGC 5861 is elongated 2.5′ × 1.25′ NNW–SSE and contains a faint core. A vague spiral structure can be glimpsed in the halo with averted vision. A NE–SW pair of 11th and 13th magnitude stars is 2.5′ ESE of the galaxy's center.

NGC 5878 H736³ Galaxy Type SAB:(s)bc II or II-III
ϕ 3.0′ × 1.4′, m11.5v, SB 12.9   15ʰ13.8ᵐ −14° 16′
Finder Chart 50-5, Figure 50-7   ★★★

8/10″ Scopes–100x: NGC 5878, located 9′ WSW of a 7th magnitude star in a well populated star field, is a bright, thin 1.75′ × 0.5′ N–S oval containing a small core with a stellar nucleus. A 10th magnitude star lies 2.75′ north of the galaxy's center.

16/18″ Scopes–150x: The fairly bright 3′ × 1′ N–S halo contains a small oval core with a stellar nucleus. The halo is unevenly concentrated near the core. A 13.5 magnitude star lies on the edge of the halo 45″ SSE of the galaxy's center. A chain of 9th to 12th magnitude stars within 1.75′ to 2.75′ of the galaxy loops around its northern and eastern sides to a hook at the SE end of the chain.

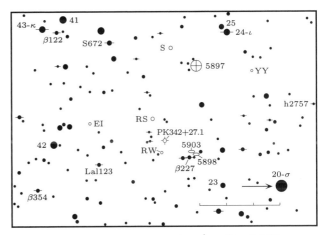

Finder Chart 50-6. 20-σ Lib: 15ʰ04.1ᵐ −25° 17′

NGC 5885 H116³ Galaxy Type SB(r)cd II-III
φ 3.2′ × 2.6′, m11.8v, SB13.1   15ʰ15.1ᵐ −10° 05′
Finder Chart 50-5, Figure 50-8   ★★
12/14″Scopes-125x: NGC 5885 is a diffuse 3′ × 2′ NE–
    SW oval containing a faint stellar nucleus. A
    magnitude 8.5 star is on the halo's NE tip. 2′ WNW
    of the galaxy's center, just outside of the halo's
    periphery, is a 12th magnitude star. Two slightly
    fainter stars are on the halo's east edge.

NGC 5897 H19⁶ Globular Cluster Class XI
φ 12.6′, m8.6v   15ʰ17.4ᵐ −21° 01′
Finder Chart 50-6   ★★★
8/10″Scopes-100x: This globular cluster has a diffuse,
    low surface brightness halo about 8′ in diameter
    and slightly elongated E–W. The center is poorly
    concentrated and the periphery uneven. A few
    dozen stars may be glimpsed with averted vision,
    the brightest located on the globular's NW edge.
16/18″Scopes-150x: NGC 5897 is a large, loosely
    concentrated globular cluster that resolves well,
    there are four dozen stars visible against a nebulous
    background glow. The center is only very slightly
    compressed. Outlying members bring the globular's
    overall dimension's to 11′ × 9′ E–W.

NGC 5898 H138³ Galaxy Type SAB0⁻
φ 2.6′ × 2.3′, m11.4v, SB13.2   15ʰ18.2ᵐ −24° 06′

NGC 5903 H139³ Galaxy Type SA(s)0⁻:
φ 3.4′ × 2.7′, m11.1v, SB13.4   15ʰ18.6ᵐ −24° 04′
Finder Chart 50-6, Figure 50-9   ★★★/★★★
8/10″Scopes-100x: NGC 5898 has a fairly faint, round
    1.25′ diameter halo with only a slight central
    brightening. 5.5′ to the ENE of NGC 5898 is galaxy
    NGC 5903, similar in brightness but with a halo
    elongated 1.25′ × 0.75′ N–S a stellar nucleus.

16/18″Scopes-150x: NGC 5898 has a broadly
    concentrated 2′ diameter halo that grows smoothly
    brighter toward a center that lacks a stellar nucleus.
    3′ to the galaxy's SW is a 12th magnitude star with
    a 13th magnitude companion 7″ away in PA 90°.
    NGC 5903, 5.5′ to the ENE of NGC 5898, is slightly
    smaller than the latter: its 2′ × 1.5′ NE–SW halo
    contains an extended core with a stellar nucleus.
    1.5′ to the NW of NGC 5903 is a 12th magnitude
    star; and 3′ to its south is the galaxy ESO 514-3,
    a faint object elongated 45″ × 15″ NW–SE.

NGC 5915 A407 Galaxy Type SB?b? pec
φ 1.4′ × 1.1′, m12.3v, SB12.6   15ʰ21.6ᵐ −13° 06′

NGC 5916 Galaxy Type (R′)SB:(s:)b pec
φ 2.5′ × 1.1′, m13.4v, SB14.3   15ʰ21.6ᵐ −13° 10′
Finder Chart 50-5, Figure 50-10   ★★/★
12/14″Scopes-125x: NGC 5915, located 2′ SE of a 12th
    magnitude star, displays a prominent stellar nucleus
    within a small, circular core surrounded by a
    1′ × 0.75′ ESE–WNW halo. A 14th magnitude star
    lies on the halo's SSW edge. 5′ south of NGC 5915
    is its companion galaxy NGC 5916, which has a
    faint 2′ × 0.5′ NE–SW halo containing a faint stellar
    nucleus. 5′ west of NGC 5915 is another companion,
    NGC 5916A, a very faint smudge with a 12th
    magnitude star on its NW edge.

PK342+27.1 Merrill 2-1 Planetary Nebula Type 2
φ 7″, m11.6v, CS16.03v   15ʰ22.3ᵐ −23° 38′
Finder Chart 50-6   ★★★
16/18″Scopes-300x: PK342+27.1, located 50″ SE of a
    9.5 magnitude star, appears merely stellar at low
    power: 300x is necessary to glimpse the small 7″
    diameter disk surrounding a starlike center.

Chapter 51

Lupus, the Wolf

51.1 Overview

Greek and Roman astronomical texts describe, and the Farnese Globe (1st century B.C.) shows, this constellation as an unspecified animal being carried by the Centaur east toward Ara the Altar as a sacrifice. The Greeks called the constellation *Therion*, "Wild Beast," and the Romans *Bestia*: only early in the Middle Ages was the type of Beast in the constellation represented particularly as a Wolf. Despite this ambiguity, the early Greeks had inherited the constellation from Babylonia, where it was known as Ur-idim, "Wild Dog."

Lupus lies on the NE edge of the Milky Way. Its constellation pattern is rich in 2nd and 3rd magnitude stars, most of which are members of the extensive Scorpio-Centaurus Stellar Association. Many of the Sco-Cen Association stars are doubles and multiples; hence several of the brighter stars are fine binaries of bluish or white components. Like other Milky Way constellations, Lupus contains open clusters: but they are too far south in the constellation to be seen by European and U.S. observers. However, northern Lupus has an assortment of planetary nebulae, globular clusters, and even, out of the Milky Way, galaxies.

51.2 Interesting Stars

R244 Double Star   **Spec. B2**
AB: m6.1, 9.8; Sep. 4.4″; P.A. 122°   14^{h}22.6^m −48° 19′
Finder Chart 51-3   ★★★★
4/6″Scopes–150x: Russell 244 is a close, unequally bright pair of white stars requiring medium power to be well separated.

h4690 Double Star   **Spec. K0, A**
ABxC: m6.2, 9.2; Sep. 19.3″; P.A. 25°   14^{h}37.3^m −46° 08′
Finder Chart 51-3   ★★★★
4/6″Scopes–75x: (John) Herschel 4690 is a beautiful color-contrast pair, the primary orange and the companion bluish-white.

Lupus: LEW-puss
Genitive: Lupi, LEW-pie
Abbreviation: Lup
Culmination: 9pm–June 23, midnight–May 9
Area: 334 square degrees
Showpieces: IC 4406, NGC 5986
Binocular Objects: B228, NGC 5986

Pi (π) Lupi = h4728 Double Star   **Spec. B5, B5**
m4.6, 4.7; Sep. 1.4″; P.A. 73°   15^{h}05.1^m −47° 03′
Finder Chart 51-3   ★★★★
8/10″Scopes–200x: Pi Lupi is a beautiful binary of equally bright bluish-white stars. Fairly high power is required to split the system.

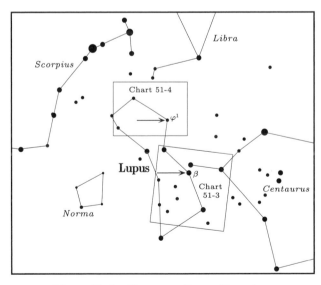

Master Finder Chart 51-1. Lupus Chart Areas
Guide stars indicated by arrows.

Lupus, the Wolf

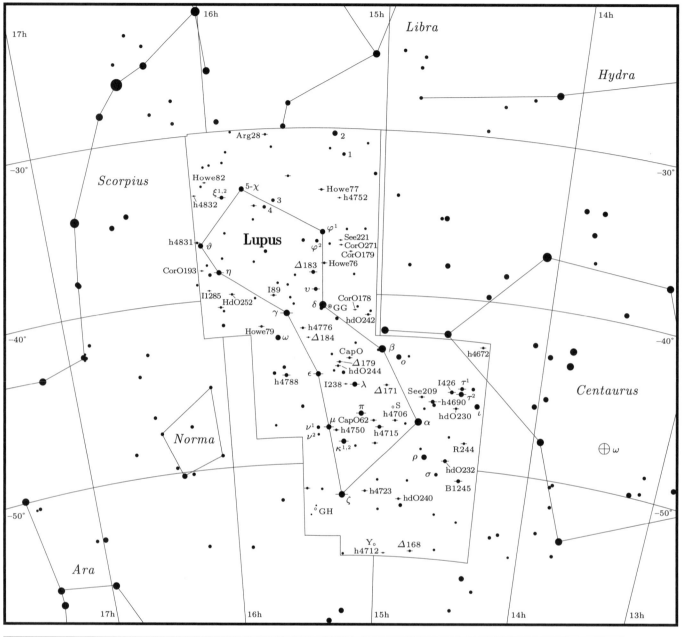

Chart Symbols

Constellation Chart

Stellar Magnitudes   0 1 2 3 4 5 6

Finder Charts   0/1 2 3 4 5 6 7 8 9

Master Finder Chart   0 1 2 3 4 5

→ *Guide Star Pointer*

●—● *Double Stars*

Finder Chart Scale

(One degree tick marks)

⊙ ○ *Variable Stars*

○ *Open Clusters*

⊕ *Globular Clusters*

◯ *Galaxies*

⟡ *Planetary Nebulae*

□ *Small Bright Nebulae*

⬡ *Large Bright Nebulae*

▨ *Dark Nebulae*

Table 51-1: Selected Variable Stars in Lupus

Name	HD No.	Type	Max.	Min.	Period (Days)	F*	Spec. Type	R.A. (2000) Dec.		Finder Chart No.	Notes
S Lup	131169	M	7.8	13.5	342	0.52	Se	$14^h53.4^m$	$-46°\ 37'$	51-3	
Y Lup	132125	M	8.2	15.2	401	0.37	M7e	59.6	$-54\ 57$	51-2	
GG Lup	135876	EB	5.4	6.0	2.16		B5+A0	$15^h18.9^m$	$-40\ 47$	51-3	
GH Lup	136739	Cep	8.6	9.05	9.28	0.50	G5-K2	24.7	$-52\ 51$	51-2	

F* = The fraction of period taken up by the star's rise from min. to max. brightness, or the period spent in eclipse.

Table 51-2: Selected Double Stars in Lupus

Name	ADS No.	Pair	M1	M2	Sep.′	P.A.°	Spec	R.A. (2000) Dec		Finder Chart No.	Notes
h4672			5.7	8.1	3.7	302	G5	14ʰ20.2ᵐ	−43° 04′	51-3	
R244		AB	6.1	9.8	4.4	122	B2	22.6	−48 19	51-3	Close, unequal white pair
B1245			6.0	9.6	1.3	145	K0	23.3	−50 46	51-2	
τ¹ Lup			4.6	9.3	158.2	204	B3 M0	26.1	−45 13	51-3	
HdO230			5.8	11.4	26.9	143	A3	27.2	−46 08	51-3	
I426			5.5	11.8	10.5	310	B9	30.1	−45 19	51-3	
HdO232			5.4	11.9	22.1	18	A2	30.3	−49 31	51-3	
h4690		ABxC	6.2	9.2	19.3	25	K0 A	37.3	−46 08	51-3	Beautiful yellow and blue
See209			6.6	12.4	10.4	244	A0	40.3	−45 48	51-3	
Δ168			8.3	8.6	5.7	202	F5	42.8	−55 11	51-2	
HdO240			6.3	11.6	39.1	290	A0	47.2	−52 12	51-2	
h4706			8.0	8.9	6.7	220	K0	51.3	−47 24	51-3	
Δ171		AB	7.1	9.5	17.5	226	B8	53.4	−45 51	51-3	
		AC		12.6	17.0	332					
h4712			8.3	9.1	7.1	228	A2	55.4	−55 26	51-2	
h4715			6.0	6.8	2.4	278	B9	56.5	−47 53	51-3	
CapO62			7.3	8.9	25.1	162	G A	58.5	−47 26	51-3	
h4723			7.1	10.5	5.5	v169	K0	15ʰ02.0ᵐ	−51 55	51-2	
π Lup			4.6	4.7	1.4	73	B5 B5	05.1	−47 03	51-3	Beautiful white pair
HdO242		AB	5.3	12.5	25.0	75	G5	05.3	−41 04	51-3	
		AC		9.0	30.0	180					
CorO178			8.2	8.8	4.9	75	A0	10.3	−41 01	51-3	
CapO			7.3	7.8	50.6	22	G0 G0	10.7	−43 44	51-3	
κ Lup (Δ177)			3.9	5.8	26.8	144	B9 A0	11.9	−48 44	51-3	Bluish and yellowish
I238			8.0	11.0	3.2	139	B9	12.1	−45 01	51-3	
ζ Lup			3.4	7.0	71.9	249	G5 F8	12.3	−52 06	51-2	
CorO179			8.0	8.2	6.5	227	A3	13.1	−37 15	51-4	
Δ179			7.1	8.6	10.5	46	A2	14.5	−43 23	51-3	White and bluish
HdO244			6.8	9.5	13.9	39	B9	15.3	−44 09	51-3	White and bluish
CorO271			7.9	8.7	21.4	197	A2	15.8	−37 09	51-4	
See221			7.9	10.9	5.3	42	F2	15.9	−37 00	51-4	
h4750			6.0	10.2	13.3	19	A2	15.9	−48 04	51-3	
h4752			8.0	10.8	18.2	6	A2	17.2	−34 35	51-4	
μ Lup		AB	5.1	5.2	1.2	142	B8	18.5	−47 53	51-3	Equal white and blue pair
(Δ180)		AC	7.2	23.7	130	A					
Howe 76			6.6	9.1	5.6	123	A0	21.5	−38 13	51-4	Unequal white pair
Howe 77			7.7	9.7	8.9	251	A0	22.5	−34 09	51-4	
ε Lup		AB	3.7	5.2	0.6	247	B2	22.7	−44 41	51-3	White and purple
(Σ 182)		AC		8.8	26.5	171					
κ = Δ183		AD	4.7	9.3	148.5	134	F0	25.3	−38 44	51-4	
I 87		AE		11.0	30.0						
κ = Δ183		AxBC			92.4	205	A0				
I 87		BC	9.3	9.6	1.3	230	G0				
Δ184			8.2	9.8	18.7	101	G0	26.3	−42 52	51-2	
h 4776			6.8	8.5	5.8	229	A0	30.4	−41 55	51-2	
γ Lup			3.5	3.6	c0.7	*274	B2	35.1	−41 10	51-2	Close white pair
h 4788			4.7	6.7	2.2	4	B3	35.9	−44 58	51-2	White and yellowish stars
I 89			7.0	7.9	1.2	158	F5	41.1	−39 59	51-2	
Arg 28		AB	7.7	9.2	35.0	24	K0 F5	41.9	−30 09	51-4	
		AC		11.4	35.6	331					
		AD		9.9	88.8						
Howe79			6.1	7.7	3.7	343	A0	44.4	−41 49	51-2	Pale and deep yellow pair
HdO252			6.0	11.9	18.0	300	B9	56.1	−39 52	51-2	
ξ Lup			5.3	5.8	10.4	49	A0 A0	56.9	−33 58	51-4	White and greenish-white
η Lup		AB	3.6	7.8	15.0	20	B2	16ʰ00.1ᵐ	−38 25	51-4	Bluish-white and deep blue
		AC		9.3	115.0	248	F5				
Howe82			7.8	7.9	2.6	346	F0	03.8	−33 04	51-2	
I1285			8.2	9.7	1.7	271	A3	05.8	−39 51	51-2	
h4832		AB	8.0	10.1	37.7	354	A0	07.3	−33 43	51-2	
		BC		10.8	23.7	20					
h4831			5.7	11.7	40.7	358	F0	07.3	−36 45	51-2	
CorO193			8.4	8.5	2.5	102	G5	07.7	−38 02	51-2	

Footnotes: *= Year 2000, a = Near apogee, c = Closing, w = Widening. Finder Chart No: All stars listed in the tables are plotted in the large Constellation Chart, but when a star appears in a Finder Chart, this number is listed. Notes: When colors are subtle, the suffix *-ish* is used, e.g. *bluish*.

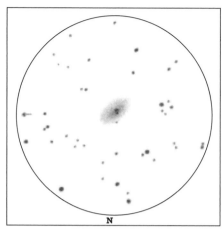

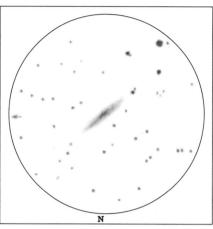

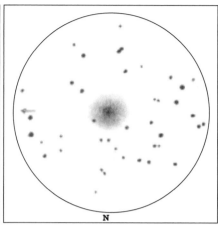

Figure 51-1. NGC 5530
16", f5–200x, by G. R. Kepple

Figure 51-2. IC 4402
16", f5–200x, by G. R. Kepple

Figure 51-3. IC 4444
16", f5–200x, by G. R. Kepple

Kappa (κ) Lupi = Δ 177 Double Star   Spec. B9, A0
m3.9, 5.8; Sep. 26.8″; P.A. 144°   15ʰ11.9ᵐ −48° 44′
Finder Chart 51-3   ★★★★
4/6″ Scopes–100x: Kappa Lupi is a beautiful, easily separated double of white or bluish-white stars.

Mu (μ) Lupi = h4753 Triple Star   Spec. B8
AB: m5.1, 5.2; Sep. 1.2″; P.A. 142°   15ʰ18.5ᵐ −47° 53′
Finder Chart 51-3   ★★★★
8/10″ Scopes–200x: Mu Lupi is a tight, equally matched binary of bright white or bluish-white stars. A third member at 7.3 magnitude lying 23″ distant in position angle 130° appears somewhat yellowish.

Xi (ξ) Lupi Double Star   Spec. A0, A0
m5.3, 5.8; Sep. 10.4″; P.A. 49°   15ʰ56.9ᵐ −33° 58′
Finder Chart 51-4   ★★★★
2/3″ Scopes–75x: Xi Lupi is a bright, rather wide pair easily resolved in small telescopes. The colors are subtle, and different observers see different hues: some report both stars to be pale yellow; others see the components as white and greenish. In general, however, stars with AO spectra like the components of Xi Lupi appear white or bluish-white.

h4788 Double Star   Spec. B3
m4.7, 6.7; Sep. 2.2″; P.A. 4°   15ʰ35.9ᵐ −44° 58′
Constellation Chart 51-2   ★★★★
4/6″ Scopes–200x: This double provides a good test for small and medium telescopes. Under steady skies these unequally bright white and yellowish stars appear as two disks in contact; but with any atmospheric turbulence the two stars merge into one oblong blob.

Eta (η) Lupi = Rmk 21 Triple Star   Spec. B3
AB: m3.6, 7.8; Sep. 15.0″; P.A. 20° 16ʰ00.1ᵐ −38° 24′
Finder Chart 51-4   ★★★★
2/3″ Scopes–75x: Eta Lupi has a brilliant bluish-white primary and a deep blue secondary. A magnitude 9.4 component lies 115″ distant from the primary in P.A. 248°. Two 20″ wide pairs of white stars are in the field 15″ ENE and 10′ NNE of Eta Lupi AB.

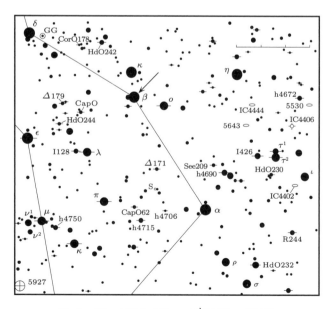

Finder Chart 51-3. *β* Lup: 14ʰ58.5ᵐ −43° 08′

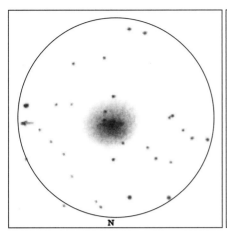

Figure 51-4. NGC 5643
16″, f5–200x, by G. R. Kepple

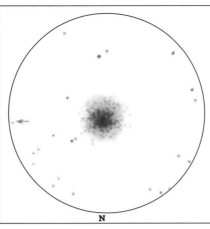

Figure 51-5. NGC 5927
16″, f5–200x, by G. R. Kepple

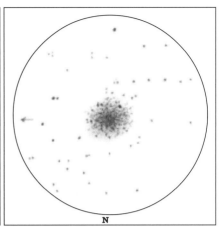

Figure 51-6. NGC 5986
16″, f5–200x, by G. R. Kepple

51.3 Deep-Sky Objects

NGC 5530 Galaxy Type SAB(rs)c? II-III
ϕ **4.9′ × 2.2′, m11.1v, SB 13.5**   14^{h}18.5^m −43° 24′
Finder Chart 51-3, Figure 51-1   ★★★
12/14″ Scopes–125x: This galaxy is a faint, diffuse glow elongated 2′ × 1.25′ NW–SE and containing a broad central brightening.

16/18″ Scopes–150x: NGC 5530 has a faint 2.5′ × 1.5′ NW–SE oval halo with diffuse edges and a faint stellar nucleus. A 12th magnitude star is superimposed upon the halo NE of the nucleus. A 13th magnitude star is 2.75′ east, and a 12.5 magnitude star 3.75′ NNE, of the galaxy's center.

IC 4402 Galaxy Type SB:
ϕ **3.4′ × 0.5′**   14^{h}21.2^m −46° 18′
Finder Chart 51-3, Figure 51-2   ★★
16/18″ Scopes–150x: IC 4402, located 5.5′ NW of a 9.5 magnitude star, has a very faint 2.5′ × 0.5′ NW-SE spindle-shaped halo containing a poorly concentrated 1′ × 0.25′ core. The NW tip of the halo is more distinct than the SE: it tapers to a point whereas to the SE the halo fans out to a diffuse edge. 13th magnitude stars are 1′ NE and 2′ SE of the galaxy's center in a field well populated with faint stars.

IC 4406 Planetary Nebula Type 4+3
ϕ **>28″, m10.2v, CS 14.7**   14^{h}22.4^m −44° 09′
Finder Chart 51-3   ★★★★
16/18″ Scopes–150x: IC 4406 has an irregularly bright 30″ diameter disk with faint extensions to the east and west. The brighter core area, around the just visible central star, is slightly elongated N–S. A 13th magnitude star is at the planetary's western edge.

IC 4444 Galaxy Type Sbc
ϕ **2.0′ × 1.5′, m11.4v, SB 12.4**   14^{h}31.7^m −43° 25′
Finder Chart 51-3, Figure 51-3   ★★★
16/18″ Scopes–150x: IC 1444 has a faint, circular 2′ diameter halo surrounding a broad central brightening with a stellar nucleus. A 14th magnitude star is superimposed upon the halo just inside its WNW edge. The field is well sprinkled with faint stars, many in wide pairs. The most conspicuous of these doubles is 4′ west of the galaxy.

NGC 5643 Galaxy Type SB(rs)c II-III
ϕ **5.1′ × 4.3′, m10.4v, SB 13.6**   14^{h}32.7^m −44° 10′
Finder Chart 51-3, Figure 51-4   ★★★
12/14″ Scopes–125x: This fairly bright galaxy has a circular 2.5′ diameter halo with diffuse edges and a gradual brightening toward its center.

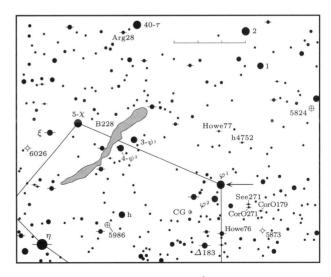

Finder Chart 51-4. φ^1 Lup: 15^{h}21.8^m −36° 16′

16/18″Scopes–150x: NGC 5643 has a fairly well concentrated 3′ diameter halo that contains a faint nonstellar nucleus with a vague E–W bar-like brightening. A very faint star is superimposed upon the halo 45″ SW of the galaxy's center. A 14th magnitude star is on the halo's NNE edge, and a 13th magnitude star lies 1.75′ south of the galaxy's center.

NGC 5824 Globular Cluster Class I
φ 6.2′, m7.8:v   15ʰ04.0ᵐ −33° 04′
Finder Chart 51-4   ★★★
12/14″Scopes–125x: NGC 5824 has a bright 1′ diameter core embedded in a 3′ diameter halo with only a few stars resolved around its edges.

NGC 5873 PK331+16.1 Planetary Nebula Type 2
φ 3″, m11.0v, CS 15.52:v   15ʰ12.8ᵐ −38° 08′
Finder Chart 51-4   ★
16/18″Scopes–300x: NGC 5873 is at the northern vertex of the 2′ equilateral triangle it forms with an 11th and a 12th magnitude star. This tiny 3″ diameter planetary appears stellar even at high power: it can be identified only by "blinking" with an O-III filter.

NGC 5927 Globular Cluster Class 8
φ 12.0′, m8.0v   15ʰ28.0ᵐ −50° 40′
Finder Chart 51-3, Figure 51-5   ★★★★
16/18″Scopes–150x: At the Texas Star Party we observed globular cluster NGC 5927, located 14′ WNW of a magnitude 7.5 star, just above the southern horizon. It displayed a 4′ diameter granular halo around a bright 1′ diameter core. Globular cluster NGC 5946, 1′ east of NGC 5927 in Norma, appeared smaller and fainter with an unresolved 2′ diameter halo containing a tiny 30″ core.

Barnard 228 Dark Nebula
φ 240′×20′, Opacity 6   15ʰ45.5:ᵐ −34° 24′
Finder Chart 51-4   ★★★★
4/6″Scopes–25x: Barnard 228 is a thin 4° long NW–SE dust lane running from north to SE of Psi-one (ψ^1) = 3 and Psi-two (ψ^2) = 4 Lupi, and parallel to the line joining the two stars. It appears as a narrow dark channel in the star field and is best observed in such wide-field, low-power instruments as giant binoculars and richest-field telescopes, which heighten the contrast between dust clouds like B228 and the surrounding Milky Way glow. To spot it in telescopes slowly sweep north, NE, or SE from Psi-1 and Psi-2 Lupi: each sweep will cross one section of the dark nebula.

NGC 5986 Globular Cluster Class VII
φ 9.8′, m7.5v   15ʰ46.1ᵐ −37° 47′
Finder Chart 51-4, Figure 51-6   ★★★★
12/14″Scopes–125x: NGC 5986 is a fairly well concentrated globular cluster about 5′ in diameter and containing a broad core. Its periphery is well resolved: a 12th magnitude star stands out on its SE edge, and two 13th magnitude stars can be seen within its NE side.

NGC 6026 PK341+13.1 Planetary Nebula Type 4
φ 45″, m12.9v, CS 13.29v   16ʰ01.4ᵐ −34° 32′
Finder Chart 51-4   ★★★
16/18″Scopes–200x: NGC 6026, located 7.5′ NW of an 8th magnitude star, has a 50″×35″ E–W disk around a prominent 13th magnitude central star. The disk is smooth and uniformly bright, but has a diffuse, ill-defined periphery.

Chapter 52

Lyra, the Lyre

52.1 Overview

Though Lyra the Lyre is one of the smallest of the constellations, it has one of the most distinctive and attractive star-patterns: the remarkably precise parallelogram of Beta (β), Gamma (γ), Delta (δ), and Zeta (ζ) Lyrae has attached to its NW corner the nearly equilateral triangle of Zeta (ζ), Epsilon (ϵ), and Alpha (α) = Vega. Vega itself is a beautiful object, a blue white magnitude 0.0 star, the fifth brightest in the sky. Small wonder that such a beautiful celestial configuration should have been associated with the Lyre of Orpheus! It is a tribute to the good taste of the early Greeks that they saw Orpheus' sublime instrument in these stars: the Babylonians, by contrast, identified this exquisite star-pattern with the Goat of the goddess Bau, consort of the war-god Ninurta.

The early form of the Greek lyre was a tortoise shell with strings attached across its hollow opening, and as such was the constellation Lyra described by the Greek and Roman astronomical writers. The names of Beta and Gamma Lyrae, Sheliak and Sulafat, are respectively from the Persian and the Arabic words for "Tortoise." Vega, however, is from the Arabic phrase meaning "The Plunging Eagle," and derives from the Arab's conception of Alpha, Epsilon, and Zeta Lyrae as an Eagle with outstretched wings.

Lyra is on the fringes of the summer Milky Way. It is remarkably rich in beautiful and interesting objects. The Ring Nebula, Messier 57, is almost the archetype planetary nebula. Beta Lyrae is the prototype of the Lyrid eclipsing binary stars. Epsilon Lyrae is one of the most observed multiple star systems in the entire sky – and for good reason. Delta and Zeta Lyrae are exceptionally attractive doubles for small aperture instruments. NGC 6791 is a splendid open cluster for large aperture instruments. And the constellation even has a number of galaxies!

Lyra: LIE-ra
Genitive: Lyrae, LIE-re
Abbreviation: Lyr
Culmination: 9 pm–Aug. 18, midnight–July 4
Area: 286 square degrees
Showpieces: 3–α Lyr, 4,5–$\epsilon^{1,2}$ Lyr, M56 (NGC 6779), M57 (NGC 6720)
Binocular Objects: 7–ζ^2 Lyr, 10–β Lyr, 11,12–$\delta^{1,2}$ Lyr, $O\Sigma$525, $O\Sigma\Sigma$181, M56 (NGC 6779), M57 (NGC 6720), NGC 6791

52.2 Interesting Stars

Alpha (α) = 3 Lyrae Multiple Star   Spec. A0 V
AB: m0.04, 9.5; Sep. 62.8″; P.A. 173° $18^h 36.9^m +38° 47'$
Finder Chart 52-3   Vega   ★★★★

Vega, the fifth brightest star in the sky, is only 27 light years away. It has the distinction of having been the first star to be photographed (in 1850, at Harvard Observatory with a 15-inch refractor). It is a blue-white A0 main sequence object with an absolute magnitude of +0.5, a luminosity of 53 suns. It is estimated to contain 3 solar masses of material and to be 2.7 million miles in diameter. The two faint companions are not physically connected to the star. Recent measurements of infrared emissions from Vega by the Infrared Astronomical Satellite (IRAS) have detected solid matter which could be planetary or protoplanetary material around the star.

Epsilon-1(ϵ^1) = 4 + Epsilon-2 (ϵ^2) = 5 Lyrae Quad. Star
AB: Spec. A2 A4 CD: Spec A3 A5
AB: m5.4, 6.5; Sep. 2.6″; P.A. 357°
CD: m5.1, 5.3; Sep. 2.3″; P.A. 94° $18^h 44.3^m +39° 40'$
Finder Chart 52-3   The Double–Double   ★★★★★
4/6″ Scopes–150x: Epsilon Lyrae, known as the Double-Double, is one of the most popular of all double stars in the summer sky. The 208″ wide ϵ^1–ϵ^2 pair splits

---

271

Lyra, the Lyre

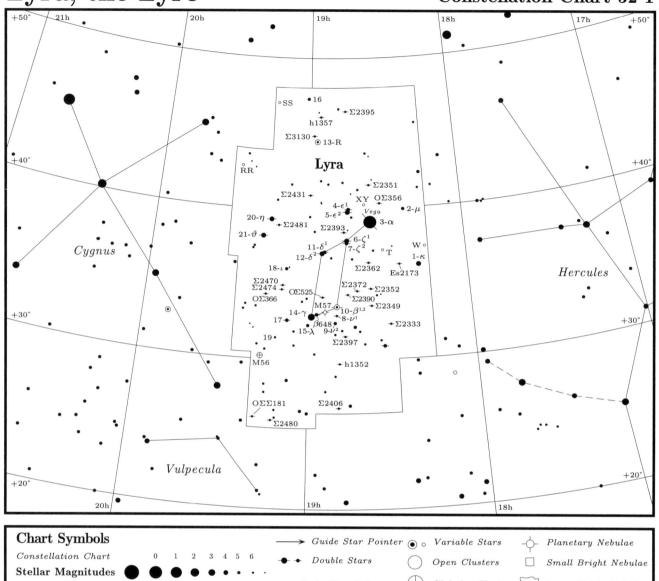

Chart Symbols

Constellation Chart

Stellar Magnitudes 0 1 2 3 4 5 6

Finder Charts 0/1 2 3 4 5 6 7 8 9

Master Finder Chart 0 1 2 3 4 5

→ Guide Star Pointer
●–•–• Double Stars
Finder Chart Scale
(One degree tick marks)

◉ ○ Variable Stars
○ Open Clusters
⊕ Globular Clusters
⬭ Galaxies

⬦ Planetary Nebulae
▫ Small Bright Nebulae
Large Bright Nebulae
Dark Nebulae

Table 52-1: Selected Variable Stars in Lyra

Name	HD No.	Type	Max.	Min.	Period (Days)	F*	Spec. Type	R.A. (2000) Dec.		Finder Chart No.	Notes
W Lyr	167740	M	7.3	13.0	196	0.48	M2-M8	18h14.9m	+36° 40′	52-1	
T Lyr		Lb	7.8	9.6			R6	32.3	+37 00	52-3	
XY Lyr	172380	Lc	7.3	7.8			M4-M5	38.1	+39 40	52-3	
10-β Lyr	174639	EB	3.4	4.4	12.91		B7-A8	50.1	+03 22	52-4	
13-R Lyr	175865	SRb	3.8	5.0	46		M5	55.3	+43 57	52-3	
SS Lyr	180162	M	8.4	13.0	350		M5	18h13.3m	+46 59	52-3	
RR Lyr	182989	RRab	7.0	8.1	0.56	0.19	A8-F7	25.5	+42 47	52-3	

F* = The fraction of period taken up by the star's rise from min. to max. brightness, or the period spent in eclipse.

Table 52-2: Selected Double Stars in Lyra

Name	ADS No.	Pair	M1	M2	Sep."	P.A.°	Spec	R.A. (2000) Dec.		Finder Chart No.	Notes
Es 2173	11361		7.7	11.9	5.6	300	K0	18ʰ26.7ᵐ	+36° 10′	52-1	
Σ2333	11424	AB	7.8	8.4	6.4	334	A0	31.1	+32 15	52-1	
OΣ356		AB	7.3	9.9	35.2	305	F5	33.2	+40 10	52-3	
		AC		9.7	52.2	4					
Σ2351	11500		7.7	7.7	5.2	340	A0	36.2	+41 17	52-3	
Σ2349	11504		5.4	10.6	7.3	205	B8	36.6	+33 28	52-4	White and light blue
3–α Lyr	11510	AB	0.0	9.5	62.8	173	A0	36.9	+38 47	52-3	Brilliant white and bluish
	11510	AC		11.0	54.4	285					
	11510	AE		9.5	118.5	39					
Σ2352	11511	AB	8.1	11.1	15.3	284	K0	37.0	+34 52	52-4	
		AC		11.0	210.2	161					
Σ2362	11534		7.5	8.8	4.2	183	A5	38.4	+36 03	52-4	
Σ2372	11593	AbxB	6.6	8.4	25.0	83	B5	42.1	+34 45	52-4	White and bluish
4–ε¹ Lyr	11635	AB	5.4	6.5	2.6	357	A3	44.3	+39 40	52-3	Double-double
5–ε² Lyr	11635	CD	5.1	5.3	2.3	94					All four stars appear
	11635	AB-CD			207.7	173					white or slightly yellow
ζ² Lyr	11639	AD	4.3	5.9	43.7	150	A3 A3	44.8	+37 36	52-3	Yellowish pair
	11639	AE		11.5	61.8	301					
Σ2395	11660		8.0	10.4	8.3	309	A0	45.1	+46 08	52-3	
Σ2393	11656	AB	7.7	10.4	14.6	23	K0	45.2	+38 19	52-3	
Σ2390	11669		7.2	8.6	4.2	157	A5	45.8	+34 31	52-4	
Σ2397	11685		7.2	9.5	3.9	267	G5	47.2	+31 24	52-4	
8–ν¹ Lyr	11732	AB	5.9	11.4	34.8	73	B2	49.8	+32 49	52-4	
	11732	AC		10.4	58.7	122					
	11732	CD		11.6	18.1	213					
Σ2406	11733		6.9	10.9	4.8	2	A2	49.9	+26 26	52-4	
10–β Lyr	11745	AB	3.4	8.6	45.7	149	B8	50.1	+33 22	52-4	AB: white pair
	11745	AC		13.0	46.6	248					E and F: bluish
	11745	AD		13.0	46.6	248					
	11745	AE		9.9	66.9	318					
	11745	AF		9.9	85.8	19					
h1352	11741		7.5	11.7	11.9	243	B8	50.1	+29 49	52-4	
δ¹,² Lyr			5.6	4.5	630.0					52-3	Binocular pair
11–δ¹ Lyr			5.6	9.3	174.6	20	B3	53.7	+36 58	52-3	
12–δ² Lyr	11825	AB	4.5	11.2	86.2	349	M	54.5	+36 54	52-3	
	11825	BC		11.6	2.2	138					
OΣ525	11834	AB	6.0	10.2	1.7	128	G0	54.9	+33 58	52-4	Yellow and blue
(S,h282)	11834	AC		7.7	45.4	350	A				
Σ3130	11863	AC	7.2	10.6	2.7	262	A2	55.9	+44 14	52-3	
h1357			7.3	9.8	26.8	212		57.0	+45 51	52-3	
β648	11871	AB	5.4	7.5	0.7	*317	G0	57.0	+32 54	52-4	
Σ2431	11910		6.2	8.5	18.9	236		58.8	+40 41	52-3	
17 Lyr	12061	AB	5.2	9.3	3.4	300	F0	19ʰ07.4ᵐ	+32 30	52-4	
Σ2470	12093		6.6	8.6	13.4	271	B3	08.8	+34 46	52-4	White pair
Σ2474	12101		6.7	8.8	16.2	262	G5	09.1	+34 36	52-4	Yellow pair
Σ2481	12145	AB	8.5	8.5	4.6	206	G5	11.1	+38 47	52-3	Equal yellowish pair
Σ2480	12153		7.5	10.8	15.3	24	A3	11.7	+26 15	52-4	
20–η Lyr	12197	AB	4.4	9.1	28.1	82	B3	13.8	+39 09	52-3	Bluish-white and blue
OΣ366	12211		7.7	10.3	21.3	230	B9	14.2	+34 13	52-4	
21–ϑ Lyr		AB	4.4	9.1	99.8	71	K0	16.4	+38 08	52-3	Orange and bluish
		AC		10.9	99.9	127					
OΣΣ181		AB	7.6	7.4	57.8	3	F5 K	20.1	+26 39	52-4	

Footnotes: *= Year 2000, a = Near apogee, c = Closing, w = Widening. Finder Chart No: All stars listed in the tables are plotted in the large Constellation Chart, but when a star appears in a Finder Chart, this number is listed. Notes: When colors are subtle, the suffix *-ish* is used, e.g. *bluish*.

with the slightest optical aid: but each of these stars requires medium to high powers to be resolved. The components of ε¹ and ε² are aligned perpendicular to each other. All four stars are early-to-mid A-type objects that appear white or cream. The Epsilon Lyrae system is 180 light years distant; so the wide pair is at least 1/5 light year apart, and must have an orbital period thousands of years long. The periods of ε¹ and ε² are around 600 and 1200 years, respectively.

Beta (β) = 10 Lyrae Variable Star   Spec. B7+A8
m3.4 to 4.4; Per. 12.91 days   18ʰ50.1ᵐ +33° 22′
Finder Chart 52-4   ★★★★

Sheliak

Beta Lyrae, at the SW corner of the parallelogram that forms the tortoise shell of the Lyre, is both a visual multiple and an eclipsing binary. Its light range is from magnitude 3.4 to magnitude 4.4 in a period of 12.91 days. The light changes can be followed by comparing Beta to nearby Gamma (γ) = 14 Lyrae, which is a constant magnitude 3.25. The variations of Beta are caused by the orbiting of two very massive but close stars around each other: not only do the stars mutually eclipse, primary eclipse occurring when the B8 object is obscured by the cooler A star and a secondary, shallower, eclipse when the B8 star passes in front of its A companion, but the stars' gravitational fields have actually distorted them both into ellipsoids so they present continuously changing radiating surface areas to the line of sight. The sinusoidal – that is, constantly arcing – light curves that are characteristic of Beta Lyrae variables is a consequence of the components' ovoid shapes.

Beta Lyrae is also a visual multiple star, with a magnitude 7.8, two magnitude 9.9, and two magnitude 13.0 companions. The magnitude 7.8 star at least seems to be a physical member of the Beta Lyr system. Its B7 V spectrum suggests a distance of 1,500 light years.

13-R Lyrae Variable Star Type SRb   Spec. M5
m3.8 to 5.0; Per. 46.0 days   18ʰ55.3ᵐ +43° 57′
Finder Chart 52-3   ★★★★

R Lyrae is a beautiful deeply red-orange semi-regular variable suitable for binoculars and small telescopes. It fluctuates between magnitudes 3.8 and 5.0 in an average period of 46 days.

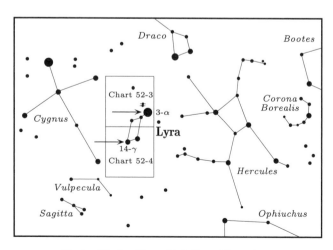

Master Finder Chart 52-2. Lyra Chart Areas
Guide stars indicated by arrows.

Σ2470 Double Star   Spec. B3
m6.6,8.6; Sep. 13.4″; P.A. 271°   19ʰ08.8ᵐ +34° 46′
Σ2474 Double Star   Spec. G5
m6.7,8.8; Sep. 16.2″; P.A. 262°   19ʰ09.1ᵐ +34° 36′
Finder Chart 52-4   ★★★★/★★★★
4/6″Scopes–75x: Struve 2470 and Struve 2474, located NE of Gamma (γ) Lyrae, is Lyra's other "double-double," the two binaries being only a dozen minutes apart almost N–S. The Σ 2470 stars are white and blue-white, and the Σ 2474 members both pale yellow.

RR Lyrae Variable Star Type RRab   Spec. A8-F7
m7.0 to 8.1; Per. 0.56 days   19ʰ25.5ᵐ +42° 47′
Finder Chart 52-3   ★★★★

RR Lyrae is the prototype of the "cluster variables," so-called because large numbers of them are found inside many globular clusters. RR Lyrae stars are similar to Cepheid variables in the clockwork regularity of their light curve, but they have shorter periods and lower luminosities. They are all nearly equal in luminosity and therefore a valuable tool for determining the distances to the globular clusters that contain them. The majority of RR Lyrae variables have periods of less than a day and are characterized by a rapid rise to maximum, often in less than an hour, followed by a gradual fade back to minimum. With a period of only 13 hours and 36 minutes, RR Lyra may be observed over a good portion of its cycle in one night. It appears white near maxima but is somewhat yellowish near minima.

52.3 Deep-Sky Objects

NGC 6646 H907² Galaxy Type Sa
φ 1.2′ × 1.2′, m12.6v, SB12.8   18ʰ29.6ᵐ +39° 52′
Finder Chart 52-3, Figure 52-1   ★★
16/18″Scopes–200x: NGC 6646 is located near the center of a 6′ wide, 10′ long isosceles triangle of stars, an 8th magnitude star at its SW vertex, and two 8th magnitude stars at its north and east corners. The galaxy has a faint, diffuse, circular 1′ diameter halo with a very slight NE-SW elongation and a faint nonstellar nucleus. 13th magnitude and fainter stars are sprinkled throughout the area, and two 11th magnitude field stars are 7′ SSE of the galaxy.

NGC 6671 Galaxy Type Sbc
φ 1.7′ × 1.7′, m12.9v, SB13.9   18ʰ37.4ᵐ +26° 24′
Finder Chart 52-4, Figure 52-2   ★★
16/18″Scopes–250x: NGC 6671, located 4′ west of a 9th magnitude star, has a very faint circular halo

containing a threshold nucleus. The galaxy lies at the SSE end of a 4′ long NNW–SSE row of four 13th magnitude stars. A 14th magnitude star touches the halo's ENE periphery.

NGC 6675 Galaxy Sbc
φ 1.8′ × 1.3′, m12.4v, SB13.2   18ʰ37.4ᵐ +40° 04′
Finder Chart 52-3, Figure 52-3   ★★
16/18″ Scopes-150x: NGC 6675, located 1.25° north of Vega (α = 3 Lyrae), has a faint, diffuse, circular 1.25′ diameter halo containing a very faint stellar nucleus. A jagged NE–SW string of 12th to 13th magnitude stars passes the NW edge of the halo, and a rectangular 2′ × 1.5′ group of seven stars lies to the SE of the galaxy.

NGC 6685 Galaxy Type S0–:
φ 1.1′ × 0.9′, m13.4v, SB13.3   18ʰ39.9ᵐ +39° 59′
Finder Chart 52-3   ★
16/18″ Scopes-150x: NGC 6685 is between 10.5 magnitude stars located 6′ ENE and 5.5′ to its SW. Even with averted vision the galaxy is merely a very faint 1′ circular glow. One 12.5 magnitude star lies 2.5′ north of the galaxy and another is 3.5′ to its SE.

NGC 6688 Galaxy Type SA0+
φ 1.6′ × 1.6′, m12.6v, SB13.5   18ʰ40.7ᵐ +36° 16′

UGC 11325 Galaxy Type Sb III
φ 2.1′ × 0.5′, m13.6v, SB13.5   18ʰ40.7ᵐ +36° 09′
Finder Chart 52-3, Figure 52-4   ★★/★
16/18″ Scopes-200x: NGC 6688 is at the midpoint of the south-opening mouth of a semicircle of one 10th and four 11th magnitude stars. The 10th magnitude star is 6.5′ NE of the galaxy, and the 11th magnitude stars are 5′ ENE, 4′ north, 6′ WNW, and 6′ WSW. NGC 6688 has a conspicuous core surrounded by a very faint 1′ diameter halo. 7.5′ to the south of NGC 6688 is the galaxy UGC 11325, a very faint 1′ NW–SE streak with no central brightening. A 10th magnitude star is 1′ west of this system.

NGC 6695 Galaxy Type SBb
φ 1.0′ × 0.6′, m13.5v, SB12.8   18ʰ42.7ᵐ +40° 24′
Finder Chart 52-3   ★
16/18″ Scopes-150x: NGC 6695, located 45′ NNW of Epsilon Lyrae, is a very faint 45″ × 30″ N–S glow without central brightening. An isosceles triangle of 12th magnitude stars is centered 5′ north of the galaxy. An L-shaped asterism of 12th magnitude stars lies 9′ NW of the triangle.

NGC 6702 Galaxy Type E:
φ 1.9′ × 1.5′, m12.2v, SB13.2   18ʰ47.0ᵐ +45° 42′
Finder Chart 52-3, Figure 52-5   ★★
8/10″ Scopes-100x: NGC 6702 appears much fainter and a little smaller than galaxy NGC 6703 lying 12′ to the SSE. Its 45″ diameter halo is diffuse except for a slight brightening at its featureless center.
16/18″ Scopes-150x: In larger telescopes NGC 6702 has a 1′ × 0.75″ ENE–WSW halo surrounding a small, poorly concentrated core. Just outside the halo's NNE edge springs a chain of five magnitude 13.5– 14 stars which arcs north and NW, ending with a 13th magnitude star 3′ north of the galaxy. Centered 2′ WNW of NGC 6702 is an equilateral triangle of magnitude 13.5 stars, the eastern vertex of which is just NW of the galaxy's halo.

NGC 6703 Galaxy Type SA0–
φ 2.3′ × 2.3′, m11.3v, SB13.0   18ʰ47.3ᵐ +45° 33′
Finder Chart 52-3, Figure 52-6   ★★★
8/10″ Scopes-100x: This galaxy is the third object from the southern end of a 10′ long, rather jagged, N–S star chain. A magnitude 9.5 star is at the northern, and two magnitude 12.5 stars at the southern, end of the chain. The galaxy has a fairly bright, circular 1.25′ diameter halo containing a stellar nucleus.
16/18″ Scopes-150x: A fairly bright stellar nucleus is embedded in a 30″ diameter core surrounded by a moderately bright 1.75′ diameter halo which fades smoothly to a diffuse periphery.

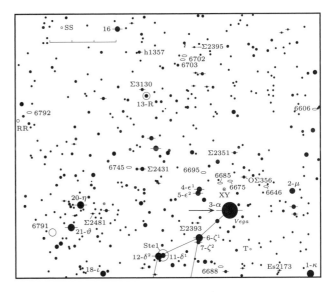

Finder Chart 52-3. 3–α Lyr: 18ʰ36.9ᵐ +38° 47′

Figure 52-1. NGC 6646
18.5″, f5–175x, by Glen W. Sanner

Figure 52-2. NGC 6671
18.5″, f5–175x, by Glen W. Sanner

Figure 52-3. NGC 6675
17.5″, f4.5–200x, by G. R. Kepple

Figure 52-4. NGC 6688 and UGC 11325
18.5″, f5–150x, by Glen W. Sanner

Figure 52-5. NGC 6702
17.5″, f4.5–200x, by G. R. Kepple

Figure 52-6. NGC 6703
17.5″, f4.5–200x, by G. R. Kepple

Figure 52-7. NGC 6710
18.5″, f5–250x, by Glen W. Sanner

Figure 52-8. PK64+15.1
13.5″, f5.6–165x, by Steve Coe

Figure 52-9. NGC 6745
18.5″, f5–200x, by Glen W. Sanner

Figure 52-10. NGC 6765
17.5″, f4.5–300x, by G. R. Kepple

Figure 52-11. NGC 6791
12.5″, f5–200x, by G. R. Kepple

Figure 52-12. NGC 6792
18.5″, f5–200x, by Glen W. Sanner

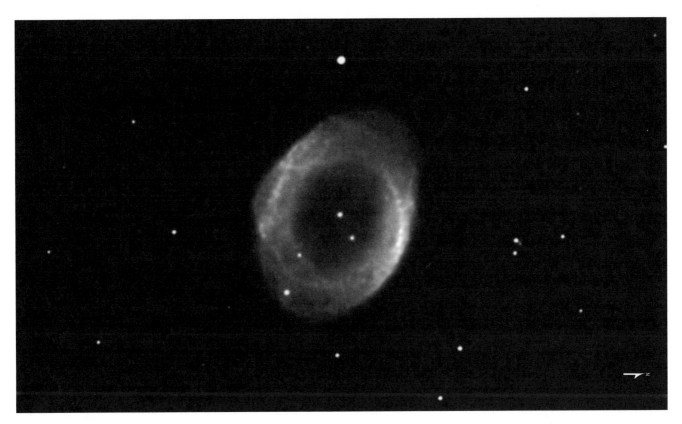

Figure 52-13. *Messier 57 (NGC 6720), the famous Ring Nebula, appears in all telescopes as a beautiful little smoke ring. Modest aperture shows the center filled with faint nebulosity, but large aperture is needed to reveal the central star. Image courtesy of Bill McLaughlin.*

NGC 6710 Galaxy Type SA0+?
ϕ 1.5′ × 0.8′, m13.1v, SB 13.1   18^{h}50.6^m +26° 50′
Finder Chart 52-4, Figure 52-7   ★

16/18″ Scopes–250x: NGC 6710 is a faint, diffuse, circular 1′ diameter haze around a slight central brightening that contains a threshold nucleus. An L-shaped asterism lies east of the galaxy.

PK 64+15.1 Planetary Nebula Type 4
ϕ 17″, m13.3v, CS–   18^{h}50.0^m +35° 15′
Finder Chart 52-4, Figure 52-8   ★★

8/10″ Scopes–175x: This planetary has a very faint, round 10″ diameter disk. The field includes a triangle of 9th magnitude stars.

12/14″ Scopes–200x: PK 64+15.1 has a faint 15″ diameter disk containing a very faint central star that is sporadically visible as seeing conditions change.

Stephenson 1 Open Cluster 15★ Tr Type IV 3p
ϕ 20″, m3.8v, Br★ 4.30v   18^{h}53.5^m +36° 55′
Finder Chart 52-3   ★★★★

4/6″ Scopes–50x: Stephenson 1 is a large but loose group for small telescopes and binoculars located between Delta-1 (δ^1) = 11 and Delta-2 (δ^2) = 12 Lyrae,

which are considered to be true cluster members. The two Deltas are a splendid color-contrast pair: the magnitude 4.5 Delta-two is an orange M4 giant and the magnitude 5.5 Delta-one is a blue-white B3 main sequence star. The fainter cluster members are scattered between the two lucidae, but are particularly concentrated west of Delta-two. A modest increase in power pulls in another score of cluster stars. Stephenson 1 is one of the nearer open clusters, lying only about 800 light years away. The group's total luminosity is a very modest 2,100 suns.

NGC 6720 Messier 57 Planetary Nebula Type 4+3
ϕ >71″, m8.8v, CS 15.29v   18^{h}53.6^m +33° 02′
Finder Chart 52-4, Figure 52-13   ★★★★★
The Ring Nebula

4/6″ Scopes–100x: The Ring Nebula is fine object for small telescopes! The fairly bright doughnut-shaped disk has a dark center. A 12th magnitude star lies 1′ east of the planetary's center.

8/10″ Scopes–150x: Messier 57 has a beautiful bright 70″ × 50″ ENE–WSW oval disk containing a dark, though not completely black, center. The perimeter of the ring at the ends of its long axis is noticeably fainter.

Figure 52-14. *Messier 56, a class X globular cluster, has a loose concentration of stars surrounding a broad core. Image courtesy of Adam Block NAOA/AURA/NSF.*

12/14″ Scopes–175x: The Ring Nebula is a truly magnificent object in instruments of moderate aperture. It is a bright oval smoke ring, the center filled with a faint ghostly haze. The very faint central star is visible only under ideal conditions even in large telescopes. At high power, the edges of the major axis appear ragged with wisps of faint nebulosity. Some subtle variation in surface brightness may be glimpsed in the ring: in particular the periphery of the ring at the ends of the minor axis is slightly brighter. Very faint stars can be seen 1.25′ north and NW of the center.

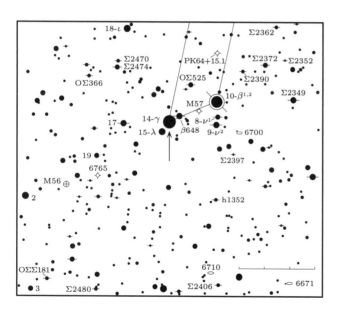

Finder Chart 52-4. 14–γ Lyr: $18^h58.9^m$ +32° 41′

NGC 6745 Galaxy Type?
φ 1.4′ × 0.7′, m12.3v, SB 12.1 $19^h01.6^m$ +40° 45′
Finder Chart 52-3, Figure 52-9   ★★
16/18″ Scopes–150x: NGC 6745, located 5′ WNW of a 9th magnitude star, is actually three galaxies that appear as one faint 1.25′ × 0.5′ NNE–SSW object. Its wispy halo has a slightly bulged center with curved ends, the SSW tip curved west and the NNE tip is curved north. Four stars are near the NNE tip, the three brightest in a N–S, east-opening arc. Beyond the SSW tip, 1.5′ from the center of the halo, is a NE–SW pair of 13th magnitude stars.

NGC 6765 PK62+9.1 Planetary Nebula Type 5
φ 38″, m12.9v, CS– $19^h11.1^m$ +30° 33′
Finder Chart 52-4, Figure 52-10   ★★
12/14″ Scopes–150x: NGC 6765 resembles a face-on galaxy, its faint, slightly N–S elongated, 35″ disk containing a slight central brightening reminiscent of a galaxy core. A UHC filter accentuates the planetary's oval shape and makes its halo appear brighter north of its center. The nebula is just NNW of a horseshoe-shaped asterism open to the south. 3.5′ to the SSW of NGC 6765 is a 45″ wide NNE–SSW pair of 12th magnitude stars pointing toward the planetary.

NGC 6779 Messier 56 Globular Cluster Class 10
φ 7.1′, m8.3v $19^h16.6^m$ +30° 11′
Finder Chart 52-4, Figure 52-14   ★★★★
    Messier discovered M56 on January 19, 1779, the same night he found the comet of 1779. The globular lies 31,000 light years distant.
4/6″ Scopes–100x: M56, located in a rich star field, is a fairly bright, fuzzy, unresolved ball. Its bright core fades gradually outward to an irregular periphery. A 10th magnitude star is 3′ west, and an 11.5 magnitude star 3′ NE, of the globular's center.
8/10″ Scopes–125x: M56 is a bright, 3′ diameter, but poorly concentrated, globular cluster. Its well resolved periphery surrounds a broad core in which half a dozen stars stand out on the hazy background glow. The periphery is slightly elongated N–S.
12/14″ Scopes–150x: M56 is a 5′ diameter disk of tiny twinkling stars well resolved except at the very center of its 1.5′ diameter core. The 11th magnitude foreground star on the west edge of the cluster has a faint companion 10″ away in position angle 45°.

NGC 6791 Open Cluster 300★ Tr Type I2r
ϕ 15′, m9.5v, Br★ 13.00v   19^{h}20.7^m +37° 51′
Finder Chart 52-3, Figure 52-11   ★★

8/10″Scopes–100x: NGC 6791 is a rich aggregation of faint stars covering a 10′ diameter area. Several dozen 11th to 13th magnitude members can be resolved against a hazy background glow. A line of three 11th magnitude field stars runs along the south side of the cluster.

16/18″Scopes–150x: NGC 6791 is a very faint granular concentration of 11th to 15th magnitude stars covering a 16′ area. At 175x, in moments of good seeing, hundreds of cluster members may be partially resolved. At least three dozen 11th to 13th magnitude stars can be counted. Near the east edge of the cluster is a wide double of foreground stars (12, 12.5; 25″; 112°).

NGC 6792 Galaxy Type SBb
ϕ 2.2′ × 1.2′, m12.1v, SB13.0   19^{h}21.0^m +43° 08′
Finder Chart 52-3, Figure 52-12   ★★

16/18″Scopes–150x: NGC 6792 has a faint, much elongated NNE–SSW lens-shaped halo with diffuse edges and a more concentrated center. A 10th magnitude star is just outside the NW edge of the halo. To the west and WSW of the galaxy are three wide pairs of 13th magnitude stars.

Chapter 53

Microscopium, the Microscope

53.1 Overview

Microscopium was created by the French astronomer Nicolas Louis de Lacaille in the 1750s along with thirteen other small constellations designed to occupy spaces between the larger southern constellations that had been introduced by the German Johannes Bayer in 1603. Most of Lacaille's groups commemorate scientific instruments invented during Europe's Enlightenment. Lacaille also honored the Telescope with a place in the heavens, situating it immediately to the SW of the Microscope. Thus the instruments for exploring both the Microcosm and Macrocosm are adjacent to each other in the celestial sphere – a juxtaposition and balance characteristic of Enlightenment thinking. Of course the scatterings of faint stars which occupy the Lacaille constellations usually have absolutely no resemblance to the objects after which they have been named.

Microscopium is a star-poor rectangle of sky due south of the "keel" of the boat-shaped constellation outline of Capricornus the Goat-Fish. It has no stars brighter than magnitude 4.7 and contains nothing more than a couple of moderately attractive doubles and a handful of faint galaxies.

53.2 Interesting Stars

Alpha (α) Microscopii = h5224 Double Star Spec. G6
m5.0, 10.0; Sep. 20.5″; P.A. 166°   20^{h}50.0^m −33° 47′
Finder Charts 53-3, 53-4   ★★★★
4/6″ Scopes–75x: Alpha Microscopii has a bright yellow primary with a grayish-white companion.

Δ236 Double Star   Spec. G5, G5
m6.5, 6.9; Sep. 57.4″; P.A. 73°   21^{h}02.2^m −43° 00′
Constellation Chart 53-2   ★★★★
4/6″ Scopes–50x: Dunlop 236 is a beautiful wide pair of two nearly equally bright yellow stars. It is particularly well suited to binoculars and small telescopes.

> **Microscopium:** Micro-SCOPE-ee-um
> **Genitive:** Microscopii, Micro-SCOPE-ee-eye
> **Abbreviation:** Mic
> **Culmination:** 9pm–Sept. 18, midnight–Aug. 4
> **Area:** 210 square degrees
> **Best Deep-Sky Objects:** NGC 6925, NGC 6958, IC 5105

Theta-2 (ϑ^2) Microscopii = β766 Double Star Spec. A0
AB: m6.4, 7.0; Sep. 0.5″; P.A. 267° 21^{h}24.4^m −41° 00′
Finder Chart 53-4   ★★★★
8/10″ Scopes–250x: Theta-2 Microscopii is a test of telescope optics and atmospheric conditions: high power in a good telescope under steady skies are necessary to show this tight yellow pair as two disks in contact.

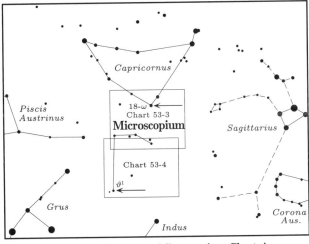

Master Finder Chart 53-1. Microscopium Chart Areas
Guide stars indicated by arrows.

Microscopium, the Microscope

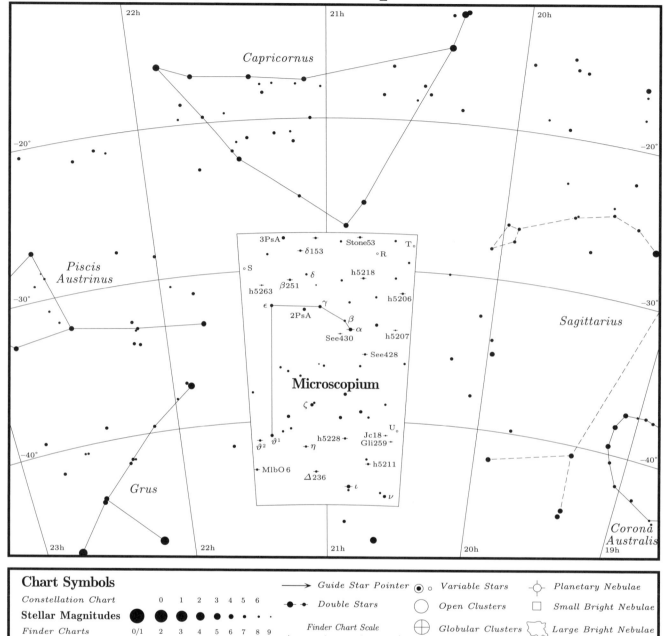

Table 53-1: Selected Variable Stars in Microscopium

Name	HD No.	Type	Max.	Min.	Period (Days)	F*	Spec. Type	R.A. (2000)	Dec.	Finder Chart No.	Notes
T Mic	194676	SRb	7.7	9.6	344		M6e	$20^h27.9^m$	$-28°\,16'$	53-3	
U Mic	194814	M	7.0	14.4	334	0.39	M6e	29.2	-4025	53-4	
R Mic	196717	M	8.3	13.8	138	0.46	M4e	40.0	-2847	53-3	
S Mic	204045	M	7.8	14.3	208	0.43	M3-M5.5	$21^h26.7^m$	-2951	53-1	

F* = The fraction of period taken up by the star's rise from min. to max. brightness, or the period spent in eclipse.

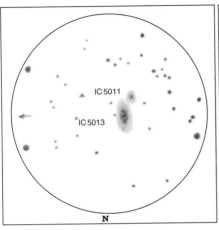

Figure 53-1. IC 5011 — 5013
16″, f5–200x, by G. R. Kepple

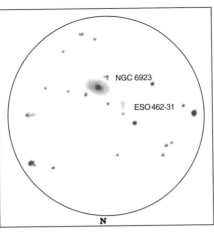

Figure 53-2. NGC 6923
16″, f5–200x, by G. R. Kepple

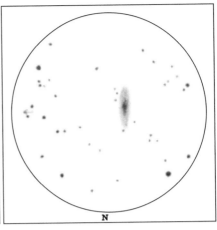

Figure 53-3. NGC 6925
16″, f5–200x, by G. R. Kepple

53.3 Deep-Sky Objects

IC 5013 Galaxy Type SB(s)0: pec
φ 2.4′ × 1.2′, m12.7p   **20ʰ28.6ᵐ −36° 02′**

IC 5011 Galaxy Type S0?
φ 0.6′ × 0.4′, m13.8p   **20ʰ28.6ᵐ −36° 02′**
Finder Chart 53-4, Figure 53-1   ★★/★
16/18″ Scopes–150x: IC 5013 is located just east of the center of a 10′ × 5′ E–W right triangle of 8th magnitude stars. Its faint 2.5′ × 1.25′ NNE–SSW oval halo contains a moderately well concentrated 1′ × 0.5′ core. A magnitude 13.5 star lies 45″ west of the galaxy's center. Touching the SSE edge of the halo of IC 5013 is its companion galaxy IC 5011, the very faint 30″ diameter halo of which contains a faint stellar nucleus.

NGC 6923 Galaxy Type SB(rs)b II
φ 2.4′ × 1.2′, m12.0v, SB13.0   **20ʰ31.7ᵐ −30° 50′**
Finder Chart 53-3, Figure 53-2   ★★
16/18″ Scopes–150x: NGC 6923 is at the southern corner of the large 16′ × 10′ triangle that it forms with two 9th magnitude stars. It has a fairly faint 1.75′ × 0.75′ ENE–WSW halo containing an oval

Table 53-2: Selected Double Stars in Microscopium

Name	ADS No.	Pair	M1	M2	Sep.″	P.A.°	Spec	R.A. (2000)	Dec.	Finder Chart No.	Notes
Gli259		AB	8.2	8.3	3.8	156	G0	20ʰ31.9ᵐ	−40° 54′	53-4	
		AC		12.5	10.3	356					
h5206			7.7	12.2	16.4	192	A2	32.7	−31 23	53-3	
Jc18		AB	7.9	8.5	4.4	225	A0	33.8	−40 33	53-4	
		AC		10.5	10.6	144					
h5207			7.8	10.2	10.2	258	F5	34.8	−33 55	53-3	
h5211		AB	6.5	10.4	20.3	300	G5	40.9	−42 24	53-4	
See428			6.9	10.9	4.4	185	F0	45.2	−35 10	53-4	
h5218			6.6	11.0	9.8	192	F0	45.4	−30 29	53-3	
Stone 53	14288		7.5	10.5	17.3	177	G5		−27 45	53-3	
α Mic			5.0	10.0	20.5	166	G6	50.0	−33 47	53-3	Yellow and grayish-white
h5228			7.2	9.2	32.1	104	K0	51.7	−40 54	53-4	
See430			7.8	12.6	13.7	347	K5	52.1	−33 53	53-3	
Δ 236			6.5	6.9	57.4	73	G5 G5	21ʰ02.2ᵐ	−43 00	53-1	Fine yellow pair
η Mic	(See437)	AB	5.6	14.5	44.1	56	K0	06.4	−41 23	53-4	
		AC		8.4	132.9	88	F8				
δ 153	14674		7.0	11.7	3.5	280	G5	09.0	−28 29	53-3	
β 251			7.5	8.8	2.5	233	F5	12.1	−30 35	53-3	
h5263			8.0	12.4	27.9	94	K2	20.9	−30 54	53-1	
ϑ² Mic	(τ 766)	AB	6.4	7.0	0.5	267	A0	24.4	−41 00	53-4	Yellowish pair
		AC		10.5	78.4	66					
MlbO6			5.6	7.9	2.9	147	A3	27.0	−42 33	53-4	Yellowish and white

Footnotes: *= Year 2000, a = Near apogee, c = Closing, w = Widening. Finder Chart No: All stars listed in the tables are plotted in the large Constellation Chart, but when a star appears in a Finder Chart, this number is listed. Notes: When colors are subtle, the suffix *-ish* is used, e.g. *bluish*.

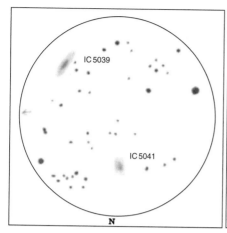

Figure 53-4. IC 5039 and IC 5041
16″, f5–200x, by G. R. Kepple

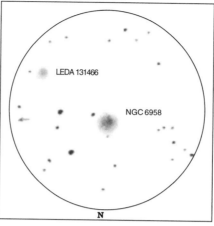

Figure 53-5. NGC 6958
13″, f5.6–135x, by Steve Coe

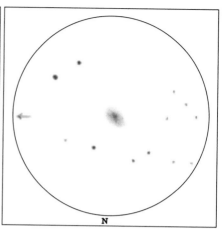

Figure 53-6. IC 5105
16″, f5–200x, by G. R. Kepple

core. A 13th magnitude star lies 1′ NW of the galaxy's center. 2′ NE of NGC 6923 is its companion galaxy ESO 462-31, a faint 45″×15″ N–S smudge.

NGC 6925 Galaxy Type SA(s)bc: I-II

φ 4.7′×1.3′, m11.3v, SB 13.1   20ʰ34.3ᵐ −13° 59′

Finder Chart 53-3, Figure 53-3   ★★★

12/14″ Scopes–125x: NGC 6925 is located between the two southernmost members of a 3/4° long NE–SW chain of 11th magnitude stars. It has a fairly bright mottled halo elongated 3′×1′ N–S and containing an irregularly illuminated core with a stellar nucleus. A 14th magnitude star lies just beyond the galaxy's northern tip.

IC 5039 Galaxy Type Sb

φ 2.3′×0.7′, m12.6v, SB 13.0   20ʰ43.2ᵐ −29° 51′

IC 5041 Galaxy Type SAB(s)d III-IV

φ 2.5′×1.3′, m12.5v, SB 13.6   20ʰ43.6ᵐ −29° 42′

Finder Chart 53-3, Figure 53-4   ★★★/★★★

16/18″Scopes–150x: IC 5039 and IC 5041 are located in a relatively well-populated off-Milky Way star field and together form a large triangle with an 8th magnitude star 10′ SE of IC 5041 and 12′ east of IC 5039. A 10th magnitude star lies within the triangle SE of its center. IC 5039, at the SW corner of the triangle, consists of a faint 2′×0.5′NNW–SSE halo containing an oval core: a 13th magnitude star on the halo's NE edge 45″ SE of the galaxy's center is at the south corner of a triangle of 13th magnitude stars, its two associates 50″ and 1.75′ ENE of the

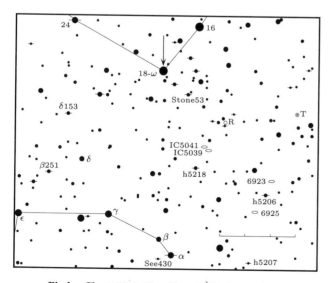

Finder Chart 53-3. 18–ω Cap: 20ʰ51.8ᵐ −26° 55′

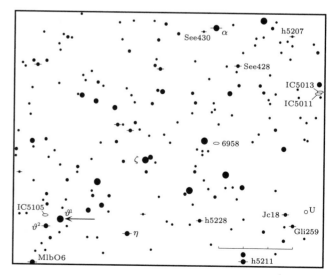

Finder Chart 53-4. ϑ¹ Mic: 21ʰ20.8ᵐ −40° 49′

galaxy's center. IC 5041, located 10′ NNE of IC 5039, has a faint 2′ × 1.25′ NNE–SSW halo containing a poorly concentrated oval core. A 13th magnitude star lies 2′ east of the galaxy's center.

NGC 6958 Galaxy Type SA(rs)0°

ϕ **2.5′ × 2.1′, m11.3v, SB 13.0** $20^{\text{h}}48.6^{\text{m}} -38° 00′$
Finder Chart 53-4, Figure 53-5 ★★★
12/14″ Scopes–125x: NGC 6958 is at the eastern vertex of the 3′ equilateral triangle it forms with two 10th magnitude stars. The galaxy has a faint, circular 2′ diameter halo containing a broad, poorly concentrated core. LEDA 131446, a very faint 1′ diameter companion, lies 5.75′ to its SW.

IC 5105 Galaxy Type E⁺

ϕ **2.8′ × 1.7′, m11.4v, SB 12.9** $21^{\text{h}}24.4^{\text{m}} -40° 37′$
Finder Chart 53-4, Figure 53-6 ★★★
12/14″ Scopes–125x: IC 5105 lies 3.5′ NE of a 10th magnitude star with an 11.5 magnitude companion 1.5′ to its ESE. The galaxy's rather faint 1.5′ × 1′ NE–SW halo contains a faint core with a stellar nucleus. 12th magnitude stars are 1.5′ NW and 2.5′ NNE of the galaxy's nucleus.

Chapter 54

Ophiuchus, the Serpent Bearer

54.1 Overview

In Greco-Roman astromythology the constellation of Ophiuchus represented the god of medicine Aesculapius, son of Apollo. Aesculapius/Ophiuchus was taught the art of healing by the wise and gentle Chiron, the centaur embodied in the constellation Centaurus, who also was the tutor of Jason, captain of the ship Argo: thus Ophiuchus is one of the several constellations with Argonautic associations and it may well have been created when one of the early Greeks consciously attempted to coordinate the Argonautic legend with the stars. According to one story, when Aesculapius once killed a snake another came along with a medicinal herb in its mouth that revived the first serpent: Aesculapius snatched some of the herb and thereby gained the power to restore life. Hence the symbol of Aesculapius in particular, and medicine in general, is the staff of two intertwined serpents, the caduceus. Aesculapius was so successful in the new art that the kingdom of Pluto, god of the Nether World, was threatened. Pluto appealed to Zeus, who killed Aesculapius with a thunderbolt. Apollo interceded on his dead son's behalf with Zeus, who relented to the extent that he immortalized Aesculapius in the heavens as the constellation Ophiuchus.

The Greeks may have inherited the constellation of the Serpent Bearer from the Babylonians, for Serpent Bearers and Serpent Wrestlers are conspicuous in ancient Mesopotamian art all the way back to the centuries around 3000 B.C. In any case the caduceus was an ancient Mesopotamian symbol particularly associated with the war-god Ninurta, who was embodied in the stars of our Sagittarius immediately SE of the later Greek celestial Serpent Bearer.

Ophiuchus is extremely large: its 948 square degrees make it eleventh in area out of the 88 constellations. Most of it lies just NW of the southern part of the summer Milky Way. However the SE wing of the constellation extends into the Milky Way almost to the direction toward the Galactic Center, which is in extreme SW Sagittarius. Therefore, because most of our Galaxy's family of globular clusters are distributed

Ophiuchus: Oh-fee-YOU-kus
Genitive: Ophiuchi, Oh-fee-YOU-ki
Abbreviation: Oph
Culmination: 9 pm–July 26, midnight–June 11
Area: 948 square degrees
Showpieces: 5–ϱ Oph, 36 Oph, 39–o Oph, 61 Oph, 69–τ Oph, 70 Oph, M9 (NGC 6333), M10 (NGC 6254), M12 (NGC 6218), M14 (NGC 6402), M19 (NGC 6273), M62 (NGC 6266), NGC 6369
Binocular Objects: 30 Oph, 53 Oph, S,h251, B72 (Snake Nebula), IC 4665, LDN 1773 (Pipe Nebula), M9 (NGC 6333), M10 (NGC 6254), M12 (NGC 6218), M14 (NGC 6402), M19 (NGC 6273), M62 (NGC 6266), NGC 6356, NGC 6355, NGC 6633.

toward the Galactic Center, Ophiuchus is rich in globular clusters: only Sagittarius and Scorpius, in this same area of the Milky Way, rival its number of globular clusters. Ophiuchus also has a selection of typical Milky Way objects: open clusters, emission nebulae, and dark nebulae. The ecliptic, the Sun's path among the stars, also crosses extreme SE Ophiuchus between the Head of the Scorpion and the Bow of Sagittarius; however, not even in ancient times was the constellation considered part of the Zodiac.

54.2 Interesting Stars

Rho (ϱ) = 5 Ophiuchi Double Star   Spec. B2, B2
m5.3, 6.0; Sep. 3.1″; P.A. 344°   16^{h}25.6^m −23° 27′
Constellation Chart 54-1   ★★★★★
4/6″ Scopes–150x: Rho Ophiuchi, located 3.25° NNW of Antares (α = 21 Scorpii), is the easternmost and brightest star of a nice binocular trio. It is a tight 3″ pair of blue stars. Barnard 42, a dark nebula elongated 20′ × 5′ N–S, is just west. B42 is silhouetted upon the very low surface brightness glow of the nebula IC 4604, which shines by light reflected from Rho.

Ophiuchus, the Serpent Bearer   Constellation Chart 54-1

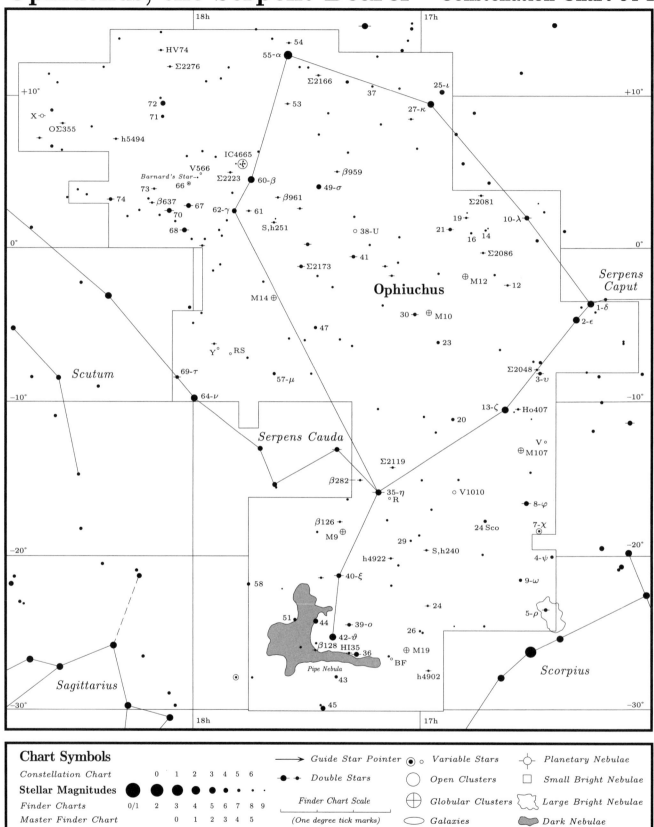

18h

17h

HV74

Σ2276

54

55-α

+10°

72

71

X

OΣ355

h5494

Σ2166

37

53

25-ι

27-κ

+10°

IC4665

V566

Barnard's Star

66

73

74

β637

70

68

67

62-γ

61

Σ2223

60-β

β961

S,h251

β959

49-σ

38-U

41

Σ2173

Σ2081

19

21

16 14

Σ2086

M12

12

10-λ

Serpens
Caput

Ophiuchus

0°

M14

M10

30

23

47

Y

RS

69-τ

64-ν

57-μ

Scutum

Serpens Cauda

Σ2119

β282

1-δ

2-ε

Σ2048

3-υ

13-ζ

Ho407

20

V
M107

-10°

35-η
R

β126

M9

29

h4922

40-ξ

58

51

44

39-ο

42-ϑ

β128

HI35 36

Pipe Nebula

43

45

V1010

24 Sco

8-φ

7-χ

4-ψ

9-ω

5-ρ

S,h240

24

26

M19

BF

h4902

Scorpius

Sagittarius

-20°

-30°

18h

17h

Chart Symbols

Constellation Chart

Stellar Magnitudes

    0 1 2 3 4 5 6

Finder Charts   0/1 2 3 4 5 6 7 8 9

Master Finder Chart   0 1 2 3 4 5

⟶ *Guide Star Pointer*

⊶ *Double Stars*

Finder Chart Scale

(One degree tick marks)

⊙ ○ *Variable Stars*

◯ *Open Clusters*

⊕ *Globular Clusters*

⬭ *Galaxies*

✦ *Planetary Nebulae*

☐ *Small Bright Nebulae*

Large Bright Nebulae

Dark Nebulae

Table 54-1: Selected Variable Stars in Ophiuchus

Name	HD No.	Type	Max.	Min.	Period (Days)	F*	Spec. Type	R.A. (2000)	Dec.	Finder Chart No.	Notes
V Oph	148182	M	7.3	11.6	297	0.48	N3e	$16^h26.7^m$	$-12°26'$	54-3	
$7-\chi$ Oph	148184	γ C	4.1	5.0	334		B2	27.0	-18 27	54-1	
V1010	151676	EB	6.1	7.0	0.66		A5	49.5	-15 40	54-3	
BF Oph	154365	C'	6.9	7.6	4.06	0.30	F6-G2	$17^h06.1^m$	-26 35	54-5	
R Oph	154721	M	7.0	13.8	302	0.45	M4e-M6e	07.8	-16 06	54-6	
$38-$U Oph	156247	EA	5.8	6.5	1.67	0.17	B5+B5	16.5	$+01$ 13	54-8	
RS Oph	162214	Nr	5.3	12.3			Ocp+M2ep	50.2	-06 43	54-7	
Y Oph	162714	Cep	5.9	6.3	17.12	0.44	F8-G3	52.6	-06 09	54-7	
V566	163611	EW	7.5	7.96	0.41		F4	56.9	$+04$ 59	54-8	
X Oph	172171	M	5.9	9.2	334	0.53	M6+K1	$18^h38.3^m$	$+08$ 50	54-9	

F* = The fraction of period taken up by the star's rise from min. to max. brightness, or the period spent in eclipse.

Table 54-2: Selected Double Stars in Ophiuchus

Name	ADS No.	Pair	M1	M2	Sep.″	P.A.°	Spec	R.A. (2000)	Dec.	Finder Chart No.	Notes
$5-\varrho$ Oph	10049	AB	5.3	6.0	3.1	344	B2 B2	$16^h25.6^m$	$-23°27'$	54-1	Fine bluish-white pair
$3-\upsilon$ Oph			4.6	7.8	1.0	95	A2	27.8	-08 22	54-3	
Σ 2048	10072	AB	6.5	9.2	5.3	299	F0	28.8	-08 08	54-3	Yellow and orange
$10-\lambda$ Oph	10087	AB	4.2	5.2	1.5	*30	A0	30.9	$+01$ 59	54-4	White and pale yellow
Ho 407	10104		6.8	11.8	14.2	217	A5	32.9	-10 34	54-3	
Σ 2081			7.8	10.5	21.1	322	A5	43.0	$+03$ 27	54-1	
Σ 2086	10180		7.5	10.0	13.9	157	A0	44.3	-00 33	54-4	
19 Oph	10207	AB	6.1	9.4	23.4	89	A2	47.2	$+02$ 04	54-4	
24 Oph	10265	AB	6.2	6.5	0.8	294	A0	56.8	-23 09	54-5	White and pale yellow
S,h 240	10266		6.3	8.3	4.7	231	B8	57.1	-19 32	54-6	
h 4902	10271		7.6	10.3	11.2	31	A0	57.9	-27 37	54-5	
30 Oph			4.8	9.6	94.1	69	K0	$17^h01.1^m$	-04 13	54-4	
Σ 2119	10331		8.2	8.2	2.3	11	F8	06.5	-13 56	54-6	
h 4922		AB	7.5	10.7	21.8	310	A0	08.5	-20 13	54-6	
$35-\eta$ Oph	10374	AB	3.0	3.5	0.6	*237	A2	10.4	-15 43	54-6	Close, bright white pair
β 282	10419		6.2	11.3	4.2	153	K0	15.3	-14 35	54-6	
36 Oph	10417	AB	5.1	5.1	w4.9	*146	K0 K1	15.3	-26 36	54-5	Fine orange pair
HI 35	10436		7.1	8.6	5.7	335	A0	17.7	-26 38	54-5	
$39-o$ Oph	10442		5.4	6.9	10.3	355	K2 F6	18.0	-24 17	54-5	Orange and yellow
β 126	10465	AB	6.3	7.4	1.9	262	A0	19.9	-17 45	54-6	White triplet
	10465	AC		11.3	11.4	40					
β 959	10498		6.7	11.6	3.4	257	G5	22.1	$+05$ 00	54-8	
β 128	10547		7.5	9.7	4.0	324	B9	26.8	-26 20	54-5	
Σ 2166	10562		7.1	8.9	27.3	283	A	27.9	$+11$ 23	54-1	White and bluish
Σ 2173	10598		6.0	6.1	1.1	330	G5	30.4	-01 04	54-7	Deep yellow pair
53 Oph	10635	AB	5.8	8.5	41.2	191	A2	34.6	$+09$ 35	54-8	
	10635	AC		10.8	94.0	34.5					
	10635	AD		10.8	91.4	223					
S,h 251		AB	6.3	7.4	111.2	328	K0 F0	39.1	$+02$ 02	54-8	
β 961	10688	AB	6.8	11.4	8.0	141	K0	39.5	$+03$ 24	54-8	
61 Oph	10750	AB	6.2	6.6	20.6	93	A0 A0	44.6	$+02$ 35	54-8	White stars
Σ 2223	10813		7.3	8.6	18.3	211	F0	48.9	$+04$ 58	54-8	
67 Oph	10966	AB	4.0	13.8	6.6	196	B5	$18^h00.6^m$	$+02$ 56	54-8	AC: bluish-white pair
	10966	AC		8.6	54.5	143					
$69-\tau$ Oph	11005	AB	5.2	5.9	c1.7	*283	F0 F3	03.1	-08 11	54-7	Close yellow pair
	11005	AC		9.3	100.3	127					
70 Oph	11046	AB	4.2	6.0	w3.8	*148	K0	05.5	$+02$ 30	54-9	Yellow-orange and red
Σ 2276	11056	AB	7.0	7.4	6.9	257	A0	05.7	$+12$ 00	54-9	Fine white pair
HV 74	11086		6.6	9.6	42.3	138	A0	07.8	$+13$ 04	54-1	
β 637	11113		5.7	11.7	7.3	194	F5	09.9	$+03$ 07	54-9	
h 5494			5.4	11.2	39.6	70	K0	19.2	$+07$ 16	54-9	
74 Oph	11271	AB	4.9	11.5	28.1	286	G5	20.9	$+03$ 23	54-9	
	11271	AC		11.9	57.8	80					
$O\Sigma$ 355	11448		6.4	9.7	38.7	248	B8	33.4	$+08$ 16	54-9	

Footnotes: *= Year 2000, a = Near apogee, c = Closing, w = Widening. Finder Chart No: All stars listed in the tables are plotted in the large Constellation Chart, but when a star appears in a Finder Chart, this number is listed. Notes: When colors are subtle, the suffix *-ish* is used, e.g. *bluish*.

Lambda (λ) = 10 Ophiuchi Quadruple Star Spec. A0
AB: m4.2, 5.2; Sep.1.5″; P.A.30°   16ʰ30.9ᵐ +01° 59′
Finder Chart 54-4   ★★★★
4/6″Scopes–150x: Lambda Ophiuchi is a fine binary
    with a period of 130 years. These white and pale
    yellow stars are a test for small telescopes. There
    are also two wide companions: a magnitude 11.1
    star 119.2″ away from AB in PA 170°, and a
    magnitude 9.5 component 313.8″ distant in PA
    246°.

24 Ophiuchi Double Star   Spec. A0
m6.2, 6.5; Sep.0.8″; P.A.294°   16ʰ56.8ᵐ −23° 09′
Finder Chart 54-5   ★★★★
8/10″Scopes–200x: 24 Ophiuchi is a very close, equally
    bright pair of white and pale yellow stars. It is a
    challenge for medium-size telescopes.

36 Ophiuchi Multiple Star   Spec. K0, K1
AB: m5.1, 5.1; Sep.4.9″; P.A.146°   17ʰ15.3ᵐ −26° 36′
Finder Chart 54-5   ★★★★
4/6″Scopes–125x: 36 Ophiuchi is a beautiful double of
    orange stars easily split even in small telescopes.
    Two distant components can also be seen: an orange
    magnitude 8.1 star is 208″ away from the close pair
    to their NW; and a magnitude 6.6 star is 12.2′ away.
    In large telescopes a magnitude 13.4 star can be
    glimpsed 38.6″ away from the AB pair in PA 298°.

Omicron (o) = 39 Ophiuchi Double Star Spec. K2, F6
m5.4, 6.9; Sep.10.3″; P.A.355°   17ʰ18.0ᵐ −24° 17′
Finder Chart 54-5   ★★★★
4/6″Scopes–100x: Omicron Ophiuchi is an orange and
    yellow color contrast double in a field of bright stars.

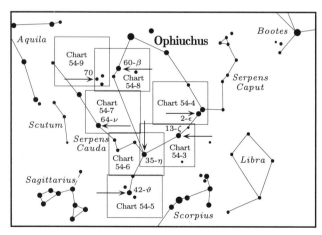

Master Finder Chart 54-2. Ophiuchus Chart Areas
Guide stars indicated by arrows.

β126 Triple Star   Spec. A0
AB: m6.3, 7.4; Sep.1.9″; P.A.262°   17ʰ19.9ᵐ −17° 45′
Finder Chart 54-6   ★★★★
4/6″Scopes–150x: Burnham 126, located in an attrac-
    tive Milky Way field, is an elegant triple of all white
    stars.

Barnard's Star Red Dwarf   Spec. M5 V
m9.5;   17ʰ58ᵐ +04° 41′
Finder Chart 54-8   ★★★
    Barnard's "Runaway Star" has the largest proper
motion of any star in the sky, moving 10.31″ per year
in position angle 356° – almost due north. Since its
discovery in 1916 the star has moved over 12′, almost
half the apparent diameter of the Moon. One of the
reasons for the star's large proper motion is that it is
the second nearest star to the Solar System, only 6.0
light years away. Like all red dwarfs, it is intrinsically
a very faint object, its absolute magnitude of +13.4
corresponding to a luminosity of a mere 1/2500 Sun.
large planets are suspected to be orbiting this red dwarf.
    Recording the movement of Barnard's Star can be
very interesting; a drawing of the star field made once
a year will dramatically reveal the object's path across the
heavens. To locate Barnard's Star, sweep 40′ NW of 66
Ophiuchi until you spot a 9.5 magnitude reddish glow.
    The search for exoplanets is rapidly moving for-
ward, and their is still much controversy about planets
circling Barnard's Star. Many amateur astronomers
with the right equipment can detect the periodic dim-
ming of stars due to planetary transits. Here is a great
opportunity to do real research. A good place to start
is the transit web site (www.transitsearch.org).

Tau (τ) = 69 Ophiuchi Triple Star   Spec. F0, F3
m5.2, 5.9; Sep.1.7″; P.A.283°   18ʰ03.1ᵐ −08° 11′
Finder Chart 54-7   ★★★★
4/6″Scopes–150x: Tau Ophiuchi is a fine but close pair
    of yellow stars. The system's period is 280 years,
    the components presently decreasing in separation.
    Another companion of magnitude 9.3 lies 100″
    distant in position angle 127°.

70 Ophiuchi Multiple Star   Spec. K0
AB: m4.2, 6.0; Sep.3.8″; P.A.148°   18ʰ05.5ᵐ +02° 30′
Finder Chart 54-8   ★★★★★
4/6″Scopes–150x: 70 Ophiuchi is a beautiful pair of
    yellowish-orange and reddish stars only 17 light
    years away. Because the system's period is only 88
    years, the changes in position angle and separation
    are noticeable in just a few years. The two stars were
    closest at 1.5″ in 1989 and will open to 6.8″ in 2024.
    There are eight more companions of various magni-
    tudes and separations near 70 Ophiuchi, but none of

Figure 54-1. *Messier 107 (NGC 6171) is a class X globular cluster with an unconcentrated periphery which grows denser to the core. Image courtesy Martin C. Germano.*

Figure 54-2. *Messier 12 (NGC 6218) is a large, beautiful globular cluster that resolves well even in small telescopes. Image courtesy Martin C. Germano.*

these stars are actually physically involved with the binary.

54.3 Deep-Sky Objects

NGC 6171 Messier 107 Globular Cluster Class 10
φ 10′, m8.1v   16ʰ32.5ᵐ −13° 03′
Finder Chart 54-3, Figure 54-1   ★★★★

This globular cluster was discovered in April 1782 by Mechain. It lies at a distance of 19,000 light years.

4/6″ Scopes–100x: Messier 107 is fairly faint, unresolved 4′ disk of granular texture with a slightly brighter core.

8/10″ Scopes–125x: A large core is embedded in an unconcentrated 5′×4′ halo, the southern edge of which is noticeably flattened. It is encircled by four field stars, the brightest an 11th magnitude star 4.5′ to its west.

12/14″ Scopes–150x: Although not aesthetically overpowering, Messier 107 is interesting and well worth careful study. 150x shows an unconcentrated 5′ diameter halo of shimmering threshold stars growing abruptly denser to a 2′ diameter core. The core is unresolved but has a granular texture and star clumps on its NW and SW sides. Star poor lanes are visible on the west and NNE sides.

NGC 6218 Messier 12 Globular Cluster Class IX
φ 14.5′, m6.8v   16ʰ47.2ᵐ −01° 57′
Finder Chart 54-4, Figure 54-2   ★★★★

Discovered on May 30, 1764 by Charles Messier, M12 is one of eight globular clusters in Ophiuchus that

he entered in his catalogue. It is estimated to be 19,500 light years distant.

4/6″ Scopes–100x: Messier 12 is nearly the twin of Messier 10 lying 3° to its SE, though less concentrated and with a small core. The 10′ diameter halo resolves well to the edge of the core. A magnitude 10.5 star lies 15′ WSW, and a magnitude 11 star 14′ SSE, of the globular's center.

8/10″ Scopes–125x: Messier 12 is an impressive object with hundreds of stars resolved against a background glow. The core is 3′ across; but outlying stars extend the cluster to a diameter of 11′. Two dozen brighter members stand out against the other cluster stars. A 12th magnitude star is on the south side of the core.

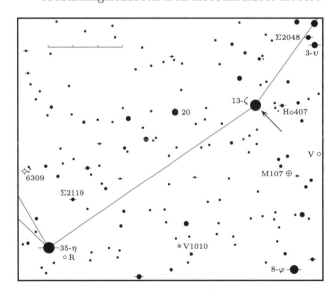

Finder Chart 54-3. 13–ζ Oph: 16ʰ37.2ᵐ −10° 34′

Figure 54-3. *Messier 10 (NGC 6254) is a splendid globular cluster with a large, bright core and a well resolved halo. Image courtesy of Jim Burnell.*

Figure 54-4. *Messier 62 (NGC 6266) is an interesting globular cluster with an irregular periphery and many star chains in its halo. Image courtesy of Josef Pöpsel and Stefan Binnewies.*

12/14″ Scopes–150x: Beautiful! This well resolved globular cluster has a bright 3′ diameter core that thins evenly out to a 5′ diameter inner halo. The outer halo has an irregular distribution of star chains and arms separated by dark areas. Peripheral members bring the globular's full diameter to 12′.

NGC 6235 H584² Globular Cluster Class 10
φ 5′, m10.0v   **16ʰ53.4ᵐ −22° 11′**
Finder Chart 54-5, Figure 54-15   ★★
8/10″ Scopes–100x: NGC 6235, situated within a triangle of 12th magnitude stars, is a small, faint, hazy spot.

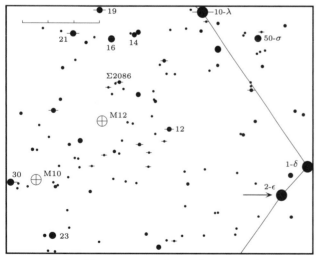

Finder Chart 54-4. 2–ε Oph: 16ʰ18.3ᵐ −04° 42′

16/18″ Scopes–150x: NGC 6235 has a 3′ diameter, moderately faint, poorly concentrated halo containing a slightly brighter core. The halo has a granular texture and its periphery is uniform. 175x resolves a few dozen stars around the edges of the periphery. The field east and south of the globular is star poor.

NGC 6254 Messier 10 Globular Cluster Class VII
φ 15.1′, m6.6v   **16ʰ57.1ᵐ −04° 06′**
Finder Chart 54-4, Figure 54-3   ★★★★★
    Messier discovered this globular cluster on May 29, 1764, a day before finding M12. M10, about 15,000 light years away, is the nearest of the Messier globulars in Ophiuchus.

4/6″ Scopes–100x: Messier 10 is similar in appearance to M12, located 3° to its NW, but a little more concentrated and slightly brighter. The bright core has a granular texture and is embedded in a fairly well resolved halo, three or four dozen stars of which stand out against a background haze.

8/10″ Scopes–125x: This bright globular cluster is a disk of sparkling pinpoints that resolves well right up to the core's center. The peripheral members extend the cluster's diameter to 12′ and are more smoothly distributed than those of Messier 12.

12/14″ Scopes–150x: Splendid! The bright 5′ diameter central core of Messier 10 is ablaze with a maze of glittering points. The globular's peripheral stars give its halo a full diameter of 15′. Two conspicuous star streams extend north and south of the core. At

Figure 54-5. *Barnard 47 (lower right) and Barnard 51 (upper left) are two of the many star-obscuring dark nebulae that run E–W through the southern portion of Ophiuchus. Globular cluster NGC 6287 is at the lower left. Martin C. Germano made this 65 minute exposure on hypered 2415 Kodak Tech Pan film with an 8″, f5 Newtonian. The photo is shown with north up for binocular users.*

175x an evenly distributed overlay of bright stars is sprinkled over the glittered background of threshold points. A bright 8th magnitude foreground star is NE of the cluster, and four other bright stars are just off its west side.

Barnard 47 Dark Nebula
ϕ **15′, Opacity 5**　　　　　　　$16^h59.7^m -22°\,39'$

Barnard 51 Dark Nebula
ϕ **20′, Opacity 6**　　　　　　　$17^h04.7^m -22°\,16'$
Finder Chart 54-5, Figure 54-5　　　★★★/★★★
4/6″Scopes–50x: Barnard 47 and 51 are two of the several dark nebulae running E–W through the southern portion of Ophiuchus from Rho (ϱ) = 5 Ophiuchi region east to the Pipe Nebula past Theta (ϑ) = 42 Ophiuchi. Barnard 47 is a circular 5′ diameter dust cloud which becomes gradually more opaque toward its center. Two indefinite dark lanes lead eastward from B47 toward Barnard 51, which lies just WSW of a 7th magnitude star. B51's darkest portion is elongated 20′ × 5′ NE–SW. Globular cluster NGC 6287 lies 25′ SSE of the dark nebula's center.

NGC 6266 Messier 62 Globular Cluster Class IV
ϕ **14.1′, m6.7v**　　　　　　$17^h01.2^m -30°\,07'$
Finder Chart 54-5, Figure 54-4　　　★★★★★
　　M62 was noticed by Charles Messier on June 7, 1771, seven years after his discoveries of M9, M10, M12, M14, and M19. It lies about 20,500 light years distant,

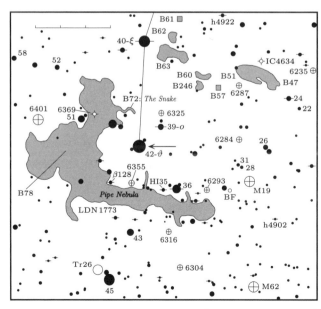

Finder Chart 54-5. 42–ϑ Oph: $17^h22.0^m -25°\,00'$

Figure 54-6. *Messier 19 (NGC 6273) is an attractive globular with a well resolved egg-shaped halo. Image courtesy of Jim Burnell.*

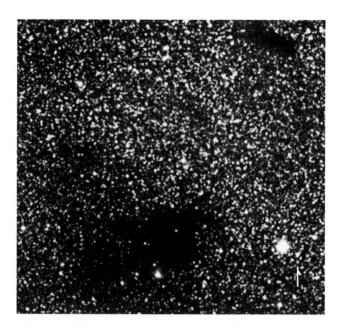

Figure 54-7. *Barnard 61 (upper right) and Barnard 62 (lower left) are small, dense dust clouds in front of a profuse Milky Way star field. Martin C. Germano made this 65 minute exposure on 2415 film with an 8", f5 Newtonian.*

and is a brighter than average globular, its absolute magnitude of −8.8 corresponding to a luminosity of 276,000 suns.

8/10″Scopes–125x: Messier 62 has a bright core noticeably off center to the NW. At low power the core's asymmetry gives the globular a cometary appearance. The fainter halo extends to a diameter of about 7′.

12/14″Scopes–150x: This interesting globular cluster has a bright core surrounded by an irregular 12′ diameter halo noticeably flattened on its SE side. The core lies NW of center with many star strings or chains extending from it toward the NW; the effect is similar to streams from a water sprinkler blowing downwind. A bright star lies just beyond the halo's NW edge.

IC 4634   Planetary Nebula   Type 2a+3
φ >9″, m10.9v, CS13.95v   17ʰ01.6ᵐ −21° 50′
Finder Chart 54-5   ★★★

12/14″Scopes–225x: IC 4634 is at the western corner of the triangle it forms with two 12th magnitude stars. At low power it appears stellar; but 225x permits the planetary's fairly bright 9″ diameter disk to be seen. The 14th magnitude central star, however, requires more aperture.

16/18″Scopes–250x: With larger telescopes IC 4634 shows a bright, slightly oval 10″×8″ N–S disk with a very pale greenish-blue tint. The central star can be glimpsed with averted vision.

NGC 6273   Messier 19   Globular Cluster   Class VIII
φ 13.5′, m6.7v   17ʰ02.6ᵐ −26° 16′
Finder Chart 54-5, Figure 54-6   ★★★★★

Discovered on June 5, 1764, M19 was the fifth globular cluster found in the span of one week by Messier. It is roughly 28,000 light years distant, and much brighter than average for a globular cluster, its absolute magnitude of −9.2 corresponding to a luminosity of nearly 400,000 suns.

4/6″Scopes–100x: Messier 19 is a bright but small globular cluster with a N–S elongated oval halo. The core is off center to the north. A few scattered stars resolve around the globular's periphery, particularly on its southern edge.

12/14″Scopes–150x: Messier 19, perhaps the most attractive object in Ophiuchus, has a well resolved 8′×6′ NNE–SSW egg-shaped halo containing a 4′×3′ oval core that is highly uneven in concentration. High powers reveal a mix of bright clumps and dark patches. Hundreds of irregularly distributed partially resolved stars are embedded in the luminous background haze. A star chain arcs around the core's southern side. Magnitude 12 and 12.5 foreground stars are in the halo just NE and NW, respectively, of the core. A 40′ long chain of 11th and 12th magnitude field stars passes among the cluster's outliers on the northern extremities of its halo. A shorter ESE–WNW chain of field stars is on the globular's southern periphery.

Figure 54-8. *Barnard 246, 60, and 57 (left to right) are starless patches silhouetted against the profuse southern Ophiuchus Milky Way. Martin C. Germano made this 65 minute exposure on 2415 film with an 8", f5 Newtonian. North is up for binocular users.*

NGC 6284 H11[6] Globular Cluster Class IX
ϕ **5.6′, m8.9v**   **17ʰ04.5ᵐ −24° 46′**
Finder Chart 54-5, Figure 54-16   ★★
12/14″Scopes–150x: NGC 6284, located 10′ ENE of a wide pair of 8.5 magnitude stars, displays a moderately faint, evenly concentrated 2′ diameter halo that is slightly elongated ESE–WNW and has irregular edges. The core appears granular but condenses to a bright, nearly stellar center. A few stars resolve around the globular's periphery, including a 12th magnitude field star 1.5′ east of the core's center.

NGC 6287 H195[2] Globular Cluster Class IV
ϕ **5.1′, m8.2:v**   **17ʰ05.2ᵐ −22° 42′**
Finder Chart 54-5, Figure 54-17   ★★
8/10″Scopes–125x: NGC 6287 is located south of a dark star-obscuring dust cloud. It appears as a faint 2′ blob of even-textured glow slightly brighter in the center. A peculiar T-shaped asterism is in the field near the globular: four 11th magnitude stars form the crossbar to an upright of five 12th magnitude stars, a single 11th magnitude star located at its base.
16/18″Scopes–150x: NGC 6287 appears granular, only a sprinkling of stars resolving around its periphery. The cluster's 3′ halo has a broad central area with a slightly brighter core.

Barnard 57 LDN11 Dark Nebula
ϕ **5′, Opacity 6**   **17ʰ08.3ᵐ −22° 50′**

Barnard 60 LDN17 Dark Nebula
[ϕ **30′**], **Opacity 3**   **17ʰ11.8ᵐ −22° 26′**

Barnard 246 LDN17 Dark Nebula
ϕ **20′, Opacity 3**   **17ʰ12.0ᵐ −22° 40′**
Finder Chart 54-5, Figure 54-8   ★★★★/★★★★/★★★
4/6″Scopes–50x: These three dark nebulae are conspicuous starless blotches silhouetted on a very rich Milky Way background. Barnard 57 is a distinct 5′×2′ NE–SW dark oval. Barnard 60, located about 3/4° ENE of B57 and 12′ south of a 9th magnitude star, is a less distinct 13′×5′ ENE–WSW curved patch. Barnard 246, just SSE of B60, is even less distinct, its rather irregular form elongated N–S and more opaque at its northern end.

NGC 6293 H12[6] Globular Cluster Class IV
ϕ **7.9′, m8.2v**   **17ʰ10.2ᵐ −26° 35′**
Finder Chart 54-5, Figure 54-18   ★★★
12/14″Scopes–125x: NGC 6293, located just north of dark nebula Barnard 59, the west end of the stem of the Pipe Nebula, has a 3′ diameter halo with an irregular periphery. A few outlying globular members can be resolved; but the central core retains a granular, partially resolved texture. 1.5′ ENE from the cluster's center is a 12th magnitude field star with a 13th magnitude companion 15″ distant in position angle 315°.

Figure 54-9. *Barnard 63 is a conspicuous dust lane over 1.5° in length silhouetted against a spectacular Milky Way star field. It is best observed in binoculars and richest-field telescopes. Martin C. Germano made this 65 minute exposure on 2415 film with an 8″, f5 Newtonian.*

Figure 54-10. *(Left) The Pipe Nebula, in the lower half of the field, is a 7° long E–W series of dust clouds. Martin C. Germano made this 30 minute exposure on 2415 film with a 135mm telephoto lens.*

Figure 54-11. *(Above) Globular cluster Messier 9 (NGC 6333) is an attractive globular cluster with a large bright core. Barnard 64 is the starless area to the upper left. Image courtesy of Jim Burnell.*

NGC 6309 PK9+14.1 Planetary Nebula Type 3b+6
ϕ >16″, m11.5v, CS13.0v 17^{h}14.1^m −12° 55′
Finder Chart 54-6, Figure 54-20 ★★★★
8/10″ Scopes–200x: NGC 6309 is centered only 25″ south of a magnitude 11.5 field star, and at low power looks like a component of a binary system. At 200x this planetary nebula appears rectangular in shape and therefore is often called the "Box Nebula." Its disk is greenish and its magnitude 13.0 central star intermittently visible.
16/18″ Scopes–250x: With large aperture and an O-III filter NGC 6309 has a bright 25″×15″ NNW–SSE oblong disk with a pinched center. The northern lobe of the disk is longer and more distinct than the southern. The bright central structure is surrounded by a much fainter outer nebulosity.

NGC 6304 H147[1] Globular Cluster Class VI
ϕ 6.8′, m8.4v 17^{h}14.5^m −29° 28′
Finder Chart 54-5, Figure 54-19 ★★★
8/10″ Scopes–125x: NGC 6304 appears a little brighter and slightly larger than its neighbor NGC 6316. Its 2′ diameter halo has a broad concentration at center. Only a few stars around the globular's periphery can be resolved.
16/18″ Scopes–150x: In larger telescopes the periphery of the halo extends to a diameter of 3′ and partially resolves. The core is slightly oval ESE–WNW, weakly concentrated and somewhat granular with partial resolution.

Barnard 61 Dark Nebula
ϕ 10′×4′, Opacity 6 17^{h}15.2^m −20° 21′

Barnard 62 LDN100 Dark Nebula
ϕ 19′, Opacity 6 17^{h}16.2^m −22° 53′
Finder Chart 54-5, Figure 54-7 ★★★★/★★★★
4/6″ Scopes–50x: Barnard 61, located 1.5′ NW of Xi $(\xi) = 40$ Ophiuchi, is a small but conspicuous 7′×3′ E–W "halo" in a profuse Milky Way star field. Its companion dust cloud Barnard 62, lying 70′ west of Xi, is a circular patch darkest toward its NE edge and with a 12th magnitude star on its south edge and a magnitude 9.4 star 15′ to its west. To the south lies the much larger dust cloud Barnard 63.

Barnard 63 LDN99 Dark Nebula
ϕ 100′×20′, Opacity 3 17^{h}16.5^m −21° 29′
Finder Chart 54-5, Figure 54-9 ★★★★
4/6″ Scopes–50x: Barnard 63, centered a degree WSW of Xi $(\xi) = 40$ Ophiuchi, is a large, distinct dust lane over 1.5° in length E–W and concave to the south. The east end is irregular but the west end abrupt. 20′ to its south is a 7th magnitude star.

NGC 6316 H45[1] Globular Cluster Class III
ϕ 4.9′, m8.8v 17^{h}16.6^m −28° 08′
Finder Chart 54-5, Figure 54-21 ★★
8/10″ Scopes–125x: NGC 6316 is almost surrounded by five faint field stars, the brightest an 11.5 magnitude object on the cluster's SE edge 1′ from its center. The cluster has an unresolved 2′ diameter halo containing a weak central brightening.
16/18″ Scopes–175x: The globular's core is broad, moderately concentrated, and granular. The 3′ diameter periphery displays only a few stars. In addition to the 11.5 magnitude star, 12th magnitude field stars are 1.25′ ESE and 1.75′ west of the cluster center.

Barnard 64 LDN173 Dark Nebula
ϕ 20′, Opacity 6 17^{h}17.2^m −18° 32′

NGC 6333 Messier 9 Globular Cluster Class VIII
ϕ 9.3′, m7.6v 17^{h}19.2^m −18° 31′
Finder Chart 54-6, Figure 54-11 ★★★★/★★★★
Messier 9 was the first of five globular clusters discovered by Charles Messier between May 28 and June 5th 1764. It is about 19,000 light years distant, and below average in luminosity for a globular cluster, its absolute magnitude of −7.4 corresponding to a brightness of just 76,000 suns.
8/10″ Scopes–125x: Messier 9 is a bright globular cluster with a large bright core and a 4′ diameter halo. The periphery is concentrated, but a few streamers of outlying stars can be resolved. 25′ due west of M9

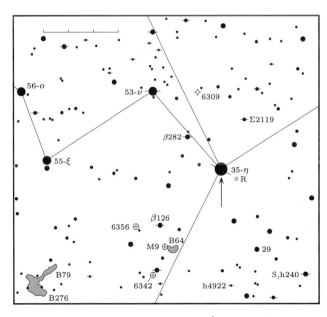

Finder Chart 54-6. 35-η Oph: 17^{h}10.4^m −15° 44′

Figure 54-12. *Barnard 72, a small but conspicuous S-shaped dust lane appropriately named the Snake Nebula, meanders to the WNW edge of the bowl of the Pipe Nebula. Image courtesy of Dean Salman.*

is the dark core of the dust cloud Barnard 64, a comet-shaped obscuring nebula with an ambiguous "tail" fanning and fading into the rich star field SE of the dark core.

12/14″ Scopes–150x: M9 is an attractive, concentrated, well resolved 5′ diameter globular. It is peculiarly triangle-shaped, one corner pointing north. Two wide pairs of bright field stars are south and SW of the cluster.

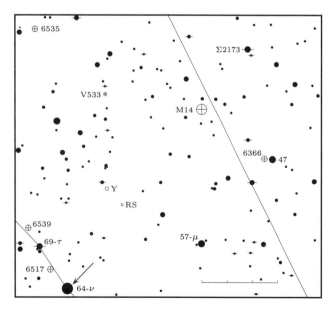

Finder Chart 54-7. 64–ν Oph: $17^h59.0^m$ $-09°$ 46′

NGC 6325 Globular Cluster Class IV
ϕ **4.3′, m10.6v** $17^h18.0^m$ $-23°$ 46′
Finder Chart 54-5, Figure 54-22   ★★
12/14″ Scopes–125x: NGC 6325 is a faint globular cluster with a diffuse, unresolved 1.5′ diameter halo containing a weak central concentration. A 13th magnitude star lies 1.25′ SW, and a 14th magnitude star is 2.25′ north, of the globular's center.

Barnard 59, 65-7 LDN 1773 Dark Neb. (Stem of Pipe)
ϕ **300′ × 60′, Opacity 6** $17^h21.^m$ $-27°$ 23′

Barnard 78 LDN 42 Dark Neb. (Bowl of Pipe Nebula)
ϕ **200′ × 140′, Opacity 5** $17^h33.^m$ $-26°$ 30′
Finder Chart 54-5, Figure 54-10   ★★★★/★★★★
                    The Pipe Nebula

7 × 50 Binoculars: The series of dark dust clouds Barnard 59, 65–7, and 78 form the 7° long Pipe Nebula, extending from SW to SE and east of Theta (ϑ) = 42 Ophiuchi in the rich southern Ophiuchus Milky Way. It is clearly visible to the unaided eye under clear, dark skies in the southern United States, and is at its best in 7x binoculars. The Pipe's bowl is Barnard 78, also catalogued as LDN (Lynds Dark Nebula) 42, a 2° diameter, N–S elongated dust cloud centered 2.5° SE of Theta Ophiuchi. A conspicuous magnitude 6.2 star is superimposed upon B78 just

Figure 54-13. *NGC 6366 is a faint, loosely concentrated class XI globular cluster. Martin C. Germano made this 45 minute exposure on hypered 2415 film with an 8″, f5 Newtonian.*

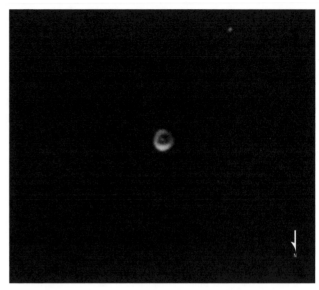

Figure 54-14. *NGC 6369 is a bright annular planetary known as the "Little Ghost Nebula." Martin C. Germano made this 20 minute exposure on 2415 film with an 8″, f5 Newtonian.*

south of its center. The Pipe's stem is the E–W line of Barnard's 59, 65–67 (together LDN 1773), some 5° long and connected to the SW edge of B78. This whole region, with its mix of dark nebulae of various sizes and shapes silhouetted upon brilliant, billowy Milky Way background clouds, is a stunning field to scan with binoculars and richest-field telescopes. The Pipe Nebula no doubt is part of the same general dust cloud complex with the dark nebulae around Rho Ophiuchi and Antares to its west, and therefore must lie 600-700 light years away.

NGC 6342 H149[1] Globular Cluster Class 4
ϕ **3′, m9.8v**   **17^{h}21.2^m −19° 35′**
Finder Chart 54-6, Figure 54-23   ★★★
8/10″Scopes–125x: NGC 6342, located 1.25′ north of a 12th magnitude star, is a rather faint globular with an irregular 1′ diameter outer envelope containing a fairly well compressed center.
16/18″Scopes–150x: The halo appears granular, about 1.5′ diameter and slightly elongated NE–SW, and contains a gradually brighter core.

Barnard 72 LDN 66 Dark Nebula
ϕ **4′, Opacity 6**   **17^{h}23.5^m −23° 38′**
Finder Chart 54-5, Figure 54-12   ★★★★★
                The Snake Nebula
4/6″Scopes–100x: Barnard 72 is a small but conspicuous S-shaped dust lane snaking out into the Milky Way star clouds from the NNW edge of the bowl of the Pipe Nebula. It averages 2′ to 3′ in thickness, and

extends about 6′ NW–SE. As with all nebulae, clear, dark skies are absolutely necessary for a good view.

NGC 6356 H48[1] Globular Cluster Class II
ϕ **7.2′, m8.2v**   **17^{h}23.6^m −17° 49′**
Finder Chart 54-6, Figure 54-25   ★★★
8/10″Scopes–125x: NGC 6356 is an unresolved, moderately faint 2′ diameter disk of haze having a smooth surface brightness.
16/18″Scopes–150x: The compact core fades gradually out to an irregular periphery. A few stars resolve around the edges of the 3′ diameter, somewhat ENE–WSW elongated halo; but the core remains merely granular. An 11th magnitude field star lies 2.5′ west of the cluster center.

NGC 6355 H46[1] Globular Cluster Class –
ϕ **5′, m9.7v**   **17^{h}24.0^m −26° 21′**
Finder Chart 54-5, Figure 54-24   ★★
12/14″Scopes–150x: NGC 6355 has a 2′ diameter halo containing a broad, moderately concentrated core with a granular texture. A few stars can be resolved on the NNE and SE edges of the halo.

NGC 6366 Globular Cluster Class XI
ϕ **8.3′, m8.9:v**   **17^{h}27.7^m −05° 05′**
Finder Chart 54-7, Figures 54-13, 54-26   ★★★
8/10″Scopes–125x: NGC 6366 is a faint, weakly concentrated globular, its low surface brightness typical of class XI globulars. Its uniformly faint glow covers

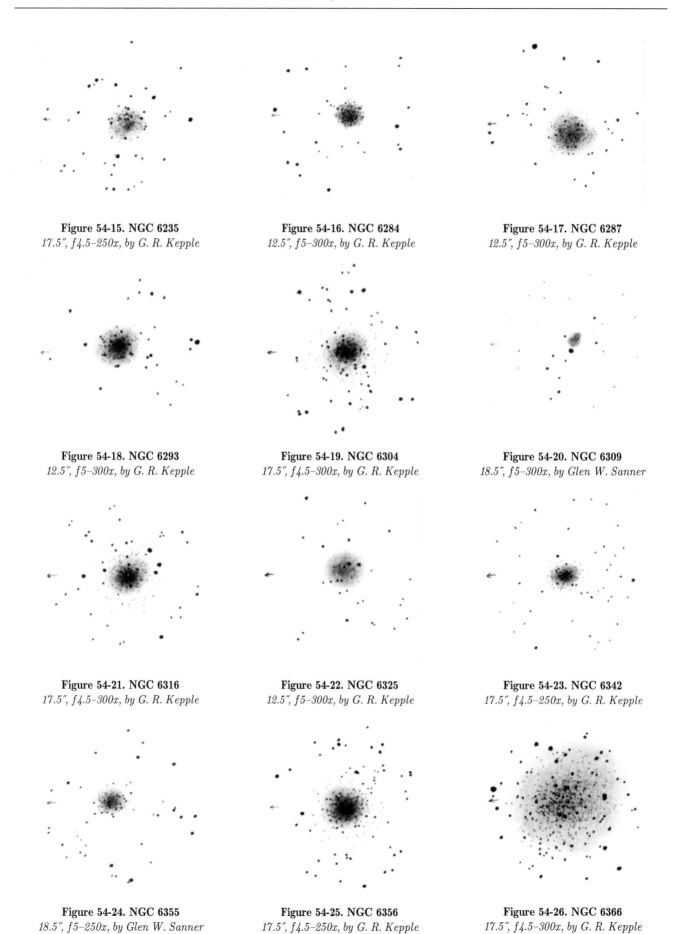

Figure 54-15. NGC 6235
17.5″, f4.5–250x, by G. R. Kepple

Figure 54-16. NGC 6284
12.5″, f5–300x, by G. R. Kepple

Figure 54-17. NGC 6287
12.5″, f5–300x, by G. R. Kepple

Figure 54-18. NGC 6293
12.5″, f5–300x, by G. R. Kepple

Figure 54-19. NGC 6304
17.5″, f4.5–300x, by G. R. Kepple

Figure 54-20. NGC 6309
18.5″, f5–300x, by Glen W. Sanner

Figure 54-21. NGC 6316
17.5″, f4.5–300x, by G. R. Kepple

Figure 54-22. NGC 6325
12.5″, f5–300x, by G. R. Kepple

Figure 54-23. NGC 6342
17.5″, f4.5–250x, by G. R. Kepple

Figure 54-24. NGC 6355
18.5″, f5–250x, by Glen W. Sanner

Figure 54-25. NGC 6356
17.5″, f4.5–250x, by G. R. Kepple

Figure 54-26. NGC 6366
17.5″, f4.5–300x, by G. R. Kepple

Figure 54-27. *NGC 6384 has a fairly bright halo around an irregularly concentrated core containing a stellar nucleus. Image courtesy of Dean Salman.*

Figure 54-28. *Barnard 276 is a large, broken region of dark matter with prongs extending into the star cloud to its west. Martin C. Germano made this 65 minute exposure on hypered 2415 film with an 8″, f5 Newtonian reflector.*

a 4′ area and has a granular texture. A NW–SE pair of 9th magnitude stars lies to the globular's west, the nearest star touching the halo's edge.

16/18″ Scopes–175x: In large telescopes the halo's diameter increases to 8′, extending out almost as far as the more distant of the two 9th magnitude field stars to the globular's west. A sprinkling of very faint cluster members resolves against a very pale background glow. The central area is slightly concentrated. A wide ENE–WSW pair of 11th magnitude stars is near the SSW edge of the halo.

Trumpler 26 Harvard 15 Open Cl. 40⋆ Tr Type II 1 m
φ 17′, m9.5p   17ʰ28.5ᵐ −29° 29′
Finder Chart 54-5, Figure 54-29   ★★★
4/6″ Scopes–75x: Trumpler 26, located 25′ NE of 4.3 magnitude star 45 Ophiuchi, is a 7′ diameter patch of 15 moderately bright, and about twice as many faint, stars loosely sprinkled about.

12/14″ Scopes–125x: Trumpler 26 is a loose but visually interesting scattering of some 40 stars in a 7′ area. Near the cluster's center is a close NNE–SSW triple of equally bright 11th magnitude stars. To its WNW is a Y-shaped asterism. Outlying stars to the NE and SW give the impression of being cluster members and, if so, double its diameter.

NGC 6369 H11⁶ PK2+5.1 Planetary Nebula Type 4+2
φ >30″, m11.4v, CS 15.56v   17ʰ29.3ᵐ −23° 46′
Finder Chart 54-5, Figure 54-14   ★★★★
Little Ghost Nebula

12/14″ Scopes–200x: NGC 6369, located in the Bowl of the Pipe Nebula, is a bright annular planetary nebula lying just south of a field star. The 30″ disk displays a darker center but does not approach the ring effect of Messier 57 in Lyra. The planetary is slightly brighter along its northern periphery.

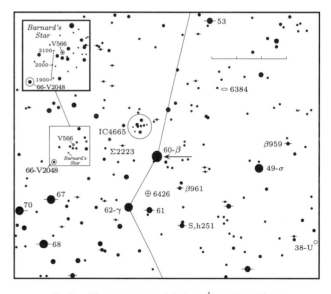

Finder Chart 54-8. 60–β Oph: 17ʰ43.5ᵐ +04° 34′

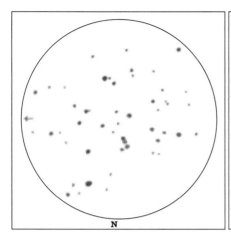

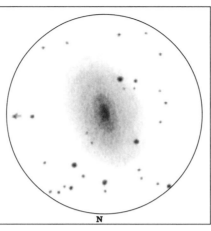

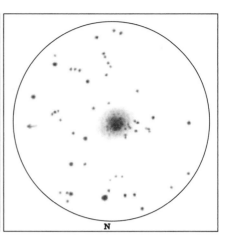

Figure 54-29. Trumpler 26
17.5″f4.5–300x, by G. R. Kepple

Figure 54-30. NGC 6384
17.5″f4.5–300x, by G. R. Kepple

Figure 54-31. NGC 6401
17.5″f4.5–250x, by G. R. Kepple

NGC 6384 Galaxy Type SAB(r)bc I
ϕ 6.4′ × 4.3′, m10.4v, SB13.9   17ʰ32.4ᵐ +07° 04′
Finder Chart 54-8, Figures 54-27, 54-30   ★★★
8/10″Scopes–125x: NGC 6384, located behind the
   peripheral star fields of the NW edge of the Ophiuchus Milky Way, is a faint 2′ × 1.5′ NE–SW oval
   haze.
16/18″Scopes–150x: In larger telescopes NGC 6834
   shows a moderately bright 5′ × 3.5′ NNE–SSW halo
   containing an irregularly concentrated core with a
   nonstellar nucleus. On the NNE edge of the halo is
   an 11th magnitude star which is at the SE vertex
   of a 2.5′ × 1.5′ triangle of 11th magnitude stars. A
   magnitude 12.5 star is on the SSE edge of the halo.

*Figure 54-32. Messier 14 (NGC 6402) requires large telescopes
even to begin to resolve. Image courtesy of Jim Burnell.*

Barnard 79 Dark Nebula
ϕ 30′, Opacity 6   17ʰ37.4ᵐ −19° 37′

Barnard 276 LDN 219 Dark Nebula
ϕ 40′, Opacity 6   17ʰ39.6ᵐ −19° 46′
Finder Chart 54-6, Figure 54-28   ★★★/★★★
4/6″Scopes–50x: Barnard 276, located 4.5° ENE of Xi
   (ξ) = 40 Ophiuchi, near the Sagittarius border, is
   a 40′ × 20′ N–S region of broken dust clouds. Its
   eastern edge is curved, and indistinct prongs extend
   from it west into a bright Milky Way star cloud.
   Detached from B276 to its NW, appearing as an
   extension from its prongs, is Barnard 79, a narrow
   30′ NW–SE dark streak.

NGC 6402 Messier 14 Globular Cluster Class VIII
ϕ 11.7′, m7.6v   17ʰ37.6ᵐ −03° 15′
Finder Chart 54-7, Figure 54-32   ★★★★
   Found on June 1, 1764, M14 was the fourth of five
globular clusters discovered by Messier from May 28 to
June 5. Its distance is about 33,000 light years, which
makes it the most remote of the Messier globulars in
Ophiuchus. It is both exceptionally large and exceptionally bright for a globular: its true diameter is in excess
of 110 light years, and its absolute magnitude is −9.3,
a luminosity of 440,000 suns.
4/6″Scopes–75x: Messier 14, although fairly bright and
   large, cannot be resolved in small telescopes. The
   center of its hazy disk is broadly concentrated and
   is enveloped by a thin periphery.
12/14″Scopes–125x: M14 has a large, uniformly bright,
   3′ diameter core embedded in a 6′ diameter halo.
   The core has a granular texture from the partial
   resolution of its brighter stars.
16/18″Scopes–150x: Messier 14 has a thinly concen-

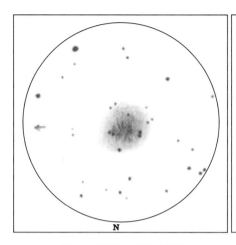

Figure 54-33. NGC 6426
17.5″f4.5–300x, by G. R. Kepple

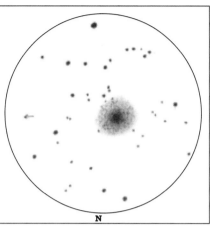

Figure 54-34. NGC 6517
17.5″f4.5–250x, by G. R. Kepple

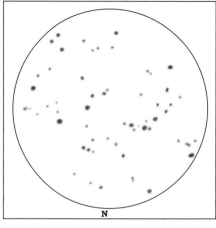

Figure 54-35. NGC 6633
12.5″f5–150x, by G. R. Kepple

trated 8′ diameter halo surrounding a broad core. The core remains granular at this aperture, but the halo becomes a rich shimmering of delicate, star-sparks. M14 requires large telescopes to bring it to life.

NGC 6401 H44[1] Globular Cluster Class VIII
φ 5.6′, m9.5:v   17ʰ38.6ᵐ −23° 55′
Finder Chart 54-5, Figure 54-31   ★★★

8/10″Scopes–125x: NGC 6401, located in an attractive Milky Way star field, is a small 1.5′ diameter globular cluster moderately concentrated in its center. It cannot be even partially resolved at this aperture. A magnitude 12.5 field star is superimposed upon the core's SE edge.

16/18″Scopes–175x: NGC 6401 has a 2′ diameter, slightly ESE–WNW elongated, halo containing a bright core that covers nearly half the area of the halo. The globular still cannot be resolved, but its periphery is granular and a few stars can be glimpsed beyond the east edge.

NGC 6426 H587[2] Globular Cluster Class IX
φ 3.2′, m11.1v   17ʰ44.9ᵐ +03° 00′
Finder Chart 54-8, Figure 54-33   ★★

16/18″Scopes–150x: NGC 6426 is a very faint globular located just south of the thin triangle formed by Beta (β), Gamma (γ), and 61 Ophiuchi. Its 2.5′ diameter halo has diffuse edges and is only weakly concentrated toward its center. The cluster cannot be even partially resolved. A 12th magnitude field star is 2.5′ SE of the globular's center.

IC 4665 Open Cluster 30★ Tr Type III 2 m
φ 40′, m4.2v   17ʰ46.3ᵐ +05° 43′
Finder Chart 54-8   ★★★

4/6″Scopes–50x: IC4665 is a large open cluster of 30 fairly bright stars evenly distributed over a circular one degree area. The group contains several star chains and some wide doubles. The brighter stars in the NW part of the cluster form a Y-shaped asterism.

NGC 6517 H199[2] Globular Cluster Class IV
φ 4.3′, m10.3v   18ʰ01.8ᵐ −08° 58′
Finder Chart 54-7, Figure 54-34   ★★

16/18″Scopes–150x: NGC 6517 is at the NE corner of the right triangle it forms with an 11.5 magnitude

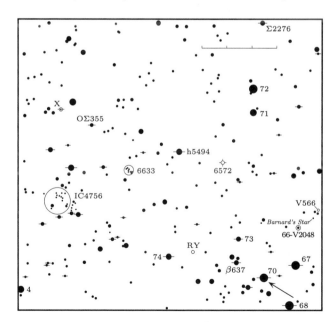

Finder Chart 54-9. 70 Oph: 18ʰ05.5ᵐ +02° 30′

Figure 54-36. *NGC 6633 is a large and bright but loose, open cluster which stands out well only at low power in small telescopes. Image courtesy of Lee C. Coombs.*

NGC 6572 PK34+11.1 Planetary Nebula Type 2a
ϕ 8″, m8.1v, CS12.88:v   18^{h}12.1^m +06° 51′
Finder Chart 54-9   ★★★★
8/10″Scopes–200x: NGC 6572, located less than 4′ west of a 9.5 magnitude star, is a fine bright greenish planetary nebulae with a 15″ diameter disk. The observed diameter is nearly twice that listed in the technical catalogues.
16/18″Scopes–250x: The intense bluish-green glow of the planetary's disk is an attractive contrast with the 9.5 magnitude stars to the west. The disk is slightly oval, about 18″ × 15″ N–S, and has diffuse edges but no central brightening. The central star is intermittently visible.

NGC 6633 H72⁸ Open Cluster 30★ Tr Type III 2 m
ϕ 27′, m4.6v, Br★ 7.57   18^{h}27.7^m +06° 34′
Finder Chart 54-9, Figures 54-35, 54-36   ★★★★
4/6″Scopes–75x: NGC 6633 is a large and bright, but loose, open cluster well suited for small telescopes. At 25x some twenty stars can be seen spreading NNW from a magnitude 5.5 star. 50x reveals 65 stars thinly scattered over a 50′ × 25′ NE–SW area. The cluster lacks any central condensation. A W-shaped asterism is conspicuous in its SW portion and a tight clump of six stars is on its west side. Near the northern edge lies an attractive triple.

star 2.5′ to its west and a 10th magnitude star 3.5′ to its south. The cluster has a fairly faint 1.5′ diameter halo containing a slightly brighter center. Even at higher powers it remains unresolved.

Chapter 55

Sagitta, the Arrow

55.1 Overview

The delicate little star-pattern of Sagitta really does resemble an arrow: Alpha (α) = 5, Beta (β) = 6, and Delta (δ) = 7 Sagittae are the Arrow's feather, Gamma (γ) = 12 Sagittae its tip. Though none of the stars are brighter than magnitude 3.7, its figure is so distinctive that it can be immediately recognized 10° NNE of Altair in Aquila. Sagitta had many associations in classical mythology: it was identified as the Arrow with which Apollo killed the Cyclops, the Arrow which Cupid shot into the heart of Apollo to make him fall in love with the nymph Daphne, and the Arrow with which Hercules killed Jupiter's Eagle, represented by Aquila. The last was a story concocted late in Roman times, for the constellation of the Kneeler was not identified with Hercules until about 200 A.D.

Sagitta is the third smallest of the constellations, only Equuleus and Crux being its inferiors. However, it lays across the eastern branch of the Summer Milky Way between Aquila and Vulpecula. Its star fields are splendid scans for binoculars and richest-field telescopes: a profusion of magnitude 6 to 9 stars are sprinkled over a pale, somewhat mottled background glow. The constellation contains one Messier object, the globular cluster M71, and a couple of interesting variable stars. However, its handful of clusters, emission nebulae, double stars, and planetary nebulae are rather routine.

55.2 Interesting Stars

U Sagittae Variable Star Type EA   Spec. B8, K
m6.6 to 9.2, Per. 3.38 days   19^{h}18.8^m +19° 37′
Finder Chart 55-3   ★★★★
4/6″ Scopes–100x: U Sagittae is a fine Algol-type eclipsing binary. Its light drop from magnitude 6.6 to 9.2 is easily followed with binoculars and small telescopes. Totality, which occurs every three and a half days, lasts about one hour and forty minutes. The primary is a bluish main sequence star while

Sagitta: Sa-JIH-ta
Genitive: Sagittae, Sa-JIH-tee
Abbreviation: Sge
Culmination: 9pm–Aug. 30, midnight–July 16
Area: 80 square degrees
Showpieces: M71 (NGC 6838)
Binocular Objects: $O\Sigma\Sigma$177, 2 & 3 Sge, 4–ϵ Sge, 15 Sge, 17–ϑ Sge, H20, M71 (NGC 6838)

the larger, but fainter, companion is a yellow subgiant.

HN 84 Double Star   Spec. K5
m6.5, 8.9; Sep. 28.2″; P.A. 302°   19^{h}39.4^m +16° 34′
Finder Chart 55-3   ★★★★★
4/6″ Scopes–100x: Herschel 84, which consists of a deep orange primary and a blue secondary, is by far the most beautiful double in Sagitta. Higher powers improve the color contrast by spreading the light over a larger area.

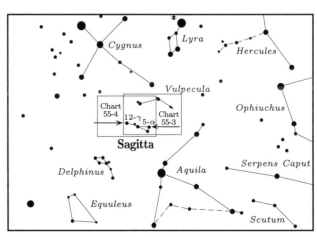

Master Finder Chart 55-1. Sagitta Chart Areas
Guide stars indicated by arrows.

305

Sagitta, the Arrow

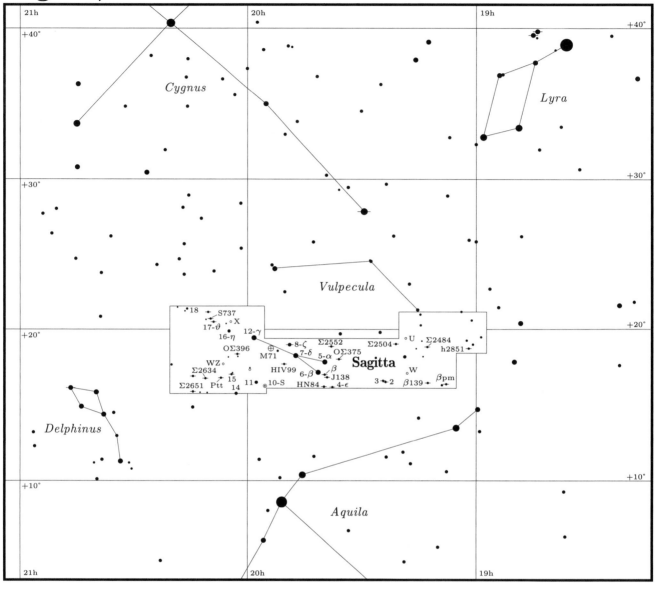

Chart Symbols

Constellation Chart
Stellar Magnitudes   0 1 2 3 4 5 6
Finder Charts   0/1 2 3 4 5 6 7 8 9
Master Finder Chart   0 1 2 3 4 5

→ *Guide Star Pointer*
●—● *Double Stars*
Finder Chart Scale
⊢———⊣
(One degree tick marks)

◉ ○ *Variable Stars*
○ *Open Clusters*
⊕ *Globular Clusters*
◯ *Galaxies*

⬡ *Planetary Nebulae*
▢ *Small Bright Nebulae*
⬭ *Large Bright Nebulae*
☁ *Dark Nebulae*

Table 55-1: Selected Variable Stars in Sagitta

Name	HD No.	Type	Max.	Min.	Period (Days)	F*	Spec. Type	R.A. (2000) Dec.		Finder Chart No.	Notes
U Sge	181182	EA	6.58	9.18	3.38	0.14	B8 + K	$19^h18.8^m$	$+19°37'$	55-3	Eclipsing Binary
W Sge	181332	M	8.8	13.2	278		M4	19.5	+17 12	55-3	
10–S Sge	188727	Cδ	5.28	6.04	8.38	0.31	F6-G5	56.0	+16 38	55-4	Cepheid Variable
X Sge	190606	SR	7.0	8.36	196	0.56	N (C5,5)	$20^h05.1^m$	+20 39	55-4	
WZ Sge		Nr (E)	7.0	15.5	11,900		P(Q)	07.6	+17 42	55-4	Recurrent nova

F* = The fraction of period taken up by the star's rise from min. to max. brightness, or the period spent in eclipse.

Table 55-2: Selected Double Stars in Sagitta

Name	ADS No.	Pair	M1	M2	Sep."	P.A.°	Spec	R.A. (2000) Dec.		Finder Chart No.	Notes
h2851	11957	AB	6.8	11.1	11.1	131	G5	19^{h}02.0^m	+19° 07′	55-2	
	11957	AC		9.2	44.2	298					
β pm			6.1	10.6	21.5	277	G5	08.0	+16 51	55-2	
β 139	12160	AB	6.7	8.0	0.7	140	B9	12.6	+16 51	55-3	
$O\Sigma\Sigma$177	12160	AC		7.9	113.4	285	G5				
Σ 2484	12201		7.9	9.4	2.5	234	F8	14.3	+19 04	55-3	Yellowish and bluish stars
Σ 2504	12336		7.0	8.7	8.9	285	F5	21.0	+19 09	55-3	
2 and 3 Sge			6.3	7.1	340.6	78	A0 A0	24.4	+16 56	55-3	
$O\Sigma$375	12623		7.5	8.7	0.6	165	G5	34.6	+18 08	55-3	
4-ϵ Sge	12693	AB	5.7	8.0	89.2	81	K0	37.3	+16 28	55-3	Yellow and pale blue
	12693	AC		12.5	99.4	280					
Σ 2552	12705		8.2	9.0	5.2	197	A2	37.9	+19 21	55-3	
J139	12711	AC	6.7	11.4	377	130	A0	38.2	+17 15	55-3	
β	12723		7.5	11.1	12.4	333	B3	38.5	+17 15	55-3	
HN84	12750		6.5	8.9	28.2	302	K5	39.4	+16 34	55-3	Beautiful orange and blue
8-ζ Sge	12973	ABxC	5.5	8.7	8.6	311	A2	49.0	+19 09	55-3	Yellowish and bluish
	12973	ABxD		11.0	76.0	247					
HIV99		AB	8.3	10.3	24.8	85	A0	50.0	+17 57	55-3	
		AC		9.3	68.7	256					
$O\Sigma$ 396			6.1	9.4	47.4	206	K2	20^{h}03.3^m	+18 30	55-4	Deep yellow and blue
	11957	AC		9.2	44.2	298					
15 Sge		AB	5.9	9.1	190.7	276	G0	04.1	+17 04	55-4	
		AC		6.8	203.7	320	A2				
		Aa		11.6	60.0	330	G0				
		Bb		8.9	183.4	231					
		Cc		11.6	93.4	184					
Ptt	13341		8.1	8.8	6.3	190	A0	05.1	+16 41	55-4	
Σ 2634	13434	AB	7.9	9.4	4.7	14	K0	09.6	+16 48	55-4	Orangish and yellowish
	13434	AC		12.6	74.8	312					
17-ϑ Sge	13442	AB	6.5	9.0	11.9	325	F2	09.9	+20 55	55-4	AB: Pale yellow pair
	13442	AC		7.4	83.9	223	K0				C: Orangish
S737			8.2	9.6	100.8	129	K0	09.9	+21 01	55-4	In oc NGC6873
Σ 2651	13542		8.5	8.5	1.4	279	F8	13.8	+16 09	55-4	

Footnotes: *= Year 2000, a = Near apogee, c = Closing, w = Widening. Finder Chart No: All stars listed in the tables are plotted in the large Constellation Chart, but when a star appears in a Finder Chart, this number is listed. Notes: When colors are subtle, the suffix *-ish* is used, e.g. *bluish*.

Zeta (ζ) = 8 Sagittae (AGC11) Multiple Star Spec. A2
ABxC: m5.5,8.7; Sep.8.6″; P.A.311°   19^{h}49.0^m +19° 09′
Finder Chart 55-3   ★★★★
4/6″Scopes-100x: The ABxC pair of Zeta Sagittae is an unequally bright pair comfortably separated in small telescopes. The AB primary, too close to be split in amateur instruments, appears pale yellowish and its C component appears bluish. A fourth D component, a magnitude 11.0 star, is 76″ distant in position angle 247°.

Theta (ϑ) = 17 Sagittae (Σ2637) Triple Star Spec. F2
AB: m6.5,9.0; Sep.11.9″; P.A.325°   20^{h}09.9^m +20° 55′
Finder Chart 55-4   ★★★★★
4/6″Scopes-100x: Theta Sagittae is located within the SW edge of the doubtfully existent open cluster NGC 6873. It has a pale yellow AB pair and a third magnitude 7.4 orangish companion 84″ away in position angle 223°. South 737 (8.2, 9.6; 100.8″; 129°) lies within the same field to Theta's NE. (See NGC 6873.)

55.3 Deep-Sky Objects

Palomar 10 Globular Cluster Class XII
ϕ 3.5′, m13.2v, SB13.9   19^{h}18.2^m +18° 34′
Finder Chart 55-3, Figure 55-3   ★
12/14″Scopes-125x: Palomar 10 is a very faint, diffuse patch about 2′ diameter containing a slight central concentration. At high power the globular appears granular but remains unresolved. It lies within a 7′×5′ isosceles triangle of one 11th and two 12th magnitude stars. A third 12th magnitude star lies within the triangle near the NE edge of the cluster.

Sharpless 2-82 Emission and Reflection Nebula
ϕ 7′×7′, Photo Br3-5, Color3-4   19^{h}30.3^m +18° 16′
Finder Chart 55-3, Figure 55-1   ★
12/14″Scopes-125x: In a UHC filter Sharpless 2-82 appears as two circular patches of haze around a N–S pair of rather faint stars. The southern patch is the more conspicuous of the two, for it is larger,

Figure 55-1. *Sharpless 2-82 is a N–S pair of nebulous patches around two faint stars. Image courtesy of Don Gordon.*

Figure 55-2. *M71 (NGC 6838) was previously thought to be a transition between a very loose globular cluster and a very dense open cluster. Image courtesy of Jim Burnell.*

about 5′ in diameter, and surrounds a brighter star, a magnitude 10.7 object. The northern patch is less than half the size of its companion. The southern nebula is just visible without filters. A 9th magnitude star 6.5′ to its east has a 10th magnitude companion 1.25′ to the SE.

Sharpless 2-84 Emission Nebula
φ 6′ × 3′, Photo Br 3-5, Color 3-4   19^{h}49.0^m +18° 24′
Finder Chart 55-3   ★

12/14″Scopes-125x: In a UHC filter Sharpless 2-84 appears as a faint, highly extended 12′ × 3′ E–W patch, its southern side convex and somewhat brighter. It is a smaller version of the California

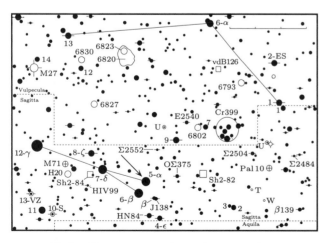

Finder Chart 55-3. 5–α Sge: 19^{h}40.1^m +18° 01′

Nebula in Perseus. A magnitude 9.5 star is near the nebula's east edge, and its glow extends 2′ west beyond the NW–SE line of three 13th magnitude stars. At least half a dozen stars are superimposed upon the nebula, the two brightest, 8th magnitude objects, located 3′ from its NE and SW edges.

Harvard 20 Open Cluster 15★ Tr Type IV 2p
φ 9′, m7.7v, Br★ 8.90v   19^{h}53.1^m +18° 20′
Finder Chart 55-3, Figure 55-4   ★★★

8/10″Scopes-100x: Harvard 20, located ESE of two 9th magnitude stars, has thirty 12th and 13th magnitude members spread over a 7′ × 4′ E–W area. The overall shape is triangular, the southern side being the longest. The cluster's stars are widely scattered without clumping or central concentration.

NGC 6838 Messier 71 Globular Cluster Class ?
φ 7.2′, m8.0v   19^{h}53.8^m +18° 47′
Finder Chart 55-3, Figure 55-2   ★★★★

Messier 71 was noticed by Koehler at Dresden about 1775, but may have been seen as early as 1746 by de Cheseaux. Up to the 1970s the classification of M71 was in doubt: it is very rich and compact but lacks the dense central compression of a normal globular cluster; its stars have more "metals" – that is, elements heavier than hydrogen and helium – than is usual for an ancient globular-cluster-type stellar population; and it lacks the RR Lyrae "cluster" variables that are so abundant in many globulars. With the information at hand it could

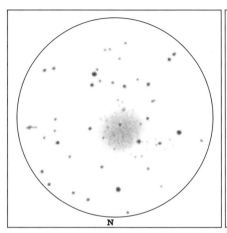

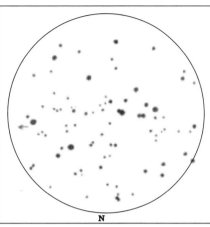

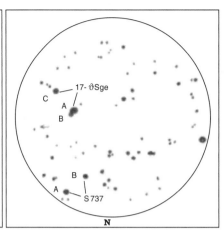

Figure 55-3. Palomar 10
17.5″, f4.5–285x, by G. R. Kepple

Figure 55-4. Harvard 20
12.5″, f5–250x, by G. R. Kepple

Figure 55-5. NGC 6873
17.5″, f4.5–285x, by G. R. Kepple

not be conclusively decided if M71 was an exceptionally rich open cluster or an exceptionally poor globular cluster. However, modern photometric photometry has found a short "horizontal branch" in the H-R diagram of M71, which is a typical globular cluster feature. In most globulars the horizontal branch is quite long and extends through and past the RR Lyrae variable instability strip: but apparently M71 is a relatively young globular cluster, only 9-10 billion years old, and does not yet possess any of the highly-evolved RR Lyrae variables. Its youth would also account for the abundance of "metals" in the stars. M71 is 12,000 light years distant. Its absolute magnitude is −5.5, a luminosity of 13,200 suns – respectable for an open cluster but pathetic for a globular.

8/10″Scopes–125x: Messier 71 lies 20′ ENE of an 8th magnitude star and 15′ east of a Y-shaped asterism with north-pointing prongs. The globular has an irregular 4′ diameter halo with numerous stars resolved against a broad, weakly concentrated center. An 11th magnitude field star is conspicuous near the edge of the globular's halo 2′ south of the cluster center.

12/14″Scopes–125x: This interesting cluster is bright and rich but loose for a globular. The 2′ diameter core is well resolved: some clumps of 12th magnitude stars extend ENE and NNE from its center. Around the core the brighter cluster members form a 4′ × 2.5′ arrowhead pointing SW. The well-resolved halo has a diameter of 7′, with star chains meandering from it toward the north, east, and SW: the west side of the halo appears more abrupt because it lacks bright outliers. At least fifty stars are resolved against a luminous background mixed with dark patches. The globular's surrounding Milky Way field is very rich and interesting. Some brighter field stars lie just NE of the cluster.

NGC 6873 Open Cluster 22⋆
φ 12′, m6.4v   20^{h}08.3^m +21° 06′
Finder Chart 55-4, Figure 55-5   ⋆⋆⋆

12/14″Scopes–100x: NGC 6873, catalogued as "nonexistent" in the *Revised NGC*, appears at the listed coordinates as a faint, loose, irregular scattering hardly discernible as a discreet star group. The official position seems to be an error, however: the stellar aggregation originally seen by William Herschel and included in the New General Catalogue as its number 6873 is most likely the scattering of stars just NE of Theta (ϑ) = 17 Sagittae, a stream of twenty 10th to 13th magnitude objects extending from an 8th magnitude star on its ESE to the wide double South 737 (8.2, 9.6; 100.8″; 129°) at its NW. Theta Sagittae, an attractive triple of a close yellow pair with an orangish companion to its SW, itself appears to be either a detached member of NGC 6873 or the core of a small triangular E–W cluster.

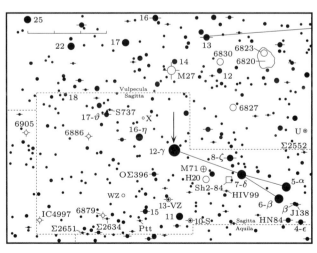

Finder Chart 55-4. 12–γ Sge: 19^{h}58.8^m +19° 30′

NGC 6879 PK57–8.1 Planetary Nebula Type 2a
ϕ 5″, m12.5v, CS15v $20^h10.5^m$ +16° 55′
Finder Chart 55-4   ★
12/14″ Scopes–125x: NGC 6879 is just south of a long
    straggling E–W star chain convex to the south. The
    planetary has a fairly bright, small 5″ disk
    containing a slight central brightening. Double star
    Σ2634 (7.9, 9.4; 4.7″; 14°) is 13′ to the nebula's SW.

NGC 6886 PK60–7.2 Planetary Nebula Type 2-3
ϕ 4″, m11.4v, CS18v $20^h12.7^m$ +19° 59′
Finder Chart 55-4   ★★
8/10″ Scopes–225x: This planetary nebula forms an
    equilateral triangle with two stars to its east that
    are also approximately magnitude 11.5 objects. It
is visible as a small, greenish disk at 250x but is
    stellar at lower power.
12/14″ Scopes–250x: NGC 6886 has a fairly bright but
    small 10″ diameter disk slightly elongated NW–SE.
    The disk has a nice greenish tint with a brighter
    center. The central star is not visible.

IC 4997 PK58–10.1 Planetary Nebula Type 1
ϕ 2″, m10.5v, CS15.4v $20^h20.2^m$ +16° 45′
Finder Chart 55-4   ★
12/14″ Scopes–300x: IC 4997 is a bright, extremely small
    planetary nebula that remains stellar even at high
    power. It can be found only by "blinking" with an
    O-III filter. A star that is slightly brighter than the
    nebula is located 1′ SW.

Chapter 56

Sagittarius, the Archer

56.1 Overview

Two of the composite monsters called centaurs – beings with the bodies of a horse but the upper torso, arms, and head of a human – were immortalized among the stars. The centaur represented by the constellation Centaurus was named Chiron, the tutor of Aesculapius and Jason, and famed for his gentle, humane intelligence. However, the centaurs as a group were savage, even bestial, and were more appropriately embodied in the constellation of Sagittarius, the Archer, which is described in ancient texts, and shown in the zodiacs carved on the Hellenistic Egyptian temple-ceilings and coffin-lids, as a centaur with a scorpion-tail and two faces, one of a lion, who is belligerently aiming an arrow at Scorpius, the next constellation to the west in the Zodiac. In Greco-Roman astromythology Sagittarius was the Archer-Centaur who slew the Scorpion that had killed Orion: Orion sets as Scorpius rises and Sagittarius soon follows Scorpius over the SE horizon.

The image of an archer-centaur – complete with the two heads and the scorpion-tail – was a figure the early Greeks had inherited from the Assyrians of Mesopotamia. There is no conclusive evidence that the Assyrians – or the Babylonians before them – had seen an archer-centaur in the stars of the celestial Sagittarius; but it is very likely that they did. In any case Sagittarius the constellation had come by his bellicose demeanor honestly, for the Assyrians, Babylonians, and – most ancient of all – the Sumerians had seen in these stars the figure of Ninurta, their god of war. Ninurta's principal weapons were named the Sharur and the Shargaz and are pictured in our Lambda (λ) and Upsilon (υ) Scorpii – the Sting of the Scorpion. Shargaz is remembered in the modern name for Theta (ϑ) Scorpii, "Sargaz." Ninurta's symbol was the spread-eagle, which, as the classical constellation Aquila, is the next major star-group NE up the Milky Way from Sagittarius. Because the earliest texts and artworks that mention or represent Ninurta, his Sharur and Shargaz, and his spread-eagle date from before 2500 B.C., the traditions behind our constellation Sagittarius are probably 5,000 years old.

Sagittarius: Sa-jih-TARE-ee-us
Genitive: Sagittarii, Sa-jih-TARE-ee-eye
Abbreviation: Sgr
Culmination: 9 pm–Aug. 21, midnight–July 7
Area: 867 square degrees
Showpieces: B86, M8 (NGC 6523), M17 (NGC 6618), M20 (NGC 6514), M21 (NGC 6531), M22 (NGC 6656), M23, (NGC 6494)M24 & NGC 6603, M25 (IC 4725), M28 (NGC 6626), M55 (NGC 6809), M75 (NGC 6864), NGC 6818
Binocular Objects: M8 (NGC 6523), M17 (NGC 6618), M20 (NGC 6514), M21 (NGC 6531), M22 (NGC 6656), M23, (NGC 6494)M24 and NGC 6603, M25 (IC 4725), M28 (NGC 6626), M54 (NGC 6715), M55 (NGC 6809), M69 (NGC 6637), M70 (NGC 6681), M75 (NGC 6864), NGC 6642, NGC 6652

The most important fact about the constellation Sagittarius is that toward it lies the center of our Galaxy. The precise direction toward the center is a spot about 4° WNW of Gamma (γ) = 10 Sagittarii. However, toward Sagittarius is the bulk of the cool dust that lies along the spiral plane of our Galaxy; hence the galactic center itself is obscured by the dark clouds of the Great Rift. In fact, astronomers have estimated that the stars at the galactic center are dimmed by 27 magnitudes – a factor of over 60 billion. The center can be observed only in long-wave radiation – radio waves, microwaves, and infrared light.

The Solar System lies about 30,000 light years out from the galactic center on the inner edge of the Orion-Cygnus Spiral Arm. Thus when we look toward Sagittarius we look across a relatively vacant interarm gap (a few old stars and open clusters are scattered through it) at the next spiral arm in toward the galactic interior, the Sagittarius-Carina Spiral Arm. Most of the famous and beautiful Messier nebulae and open clusters of Sagittarius are embedded in the Sagittarius-Carina Spiral Arm:

Sagittarius, the Archer

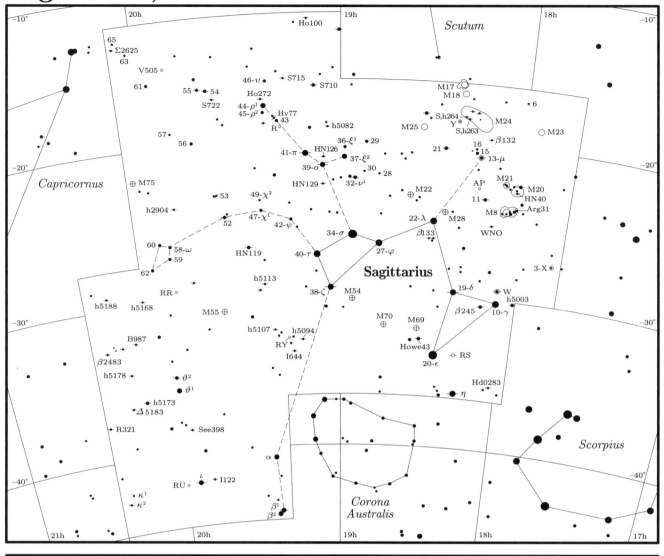

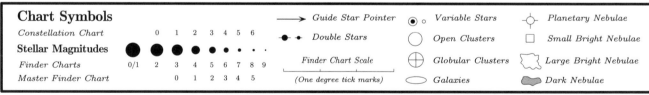

Table 56-1: Selected Variable Stars in Sagittarius

Name	HD No.	Type	Max.	Min.	Period (Days)	F*	Spec. Type	R.A. (2000) Dec.		Finder Chart No. Notes
3-X Sgr	161592	Cδ	4.2	4.8	7.01	0.36	F7	$17^h47.6^m$	$-27°\,50'$	56-4
W Sgr	164975	Cδ	4.3	5.0	7.59	0.32	F4-G1	$18^h05.0^m$	$-29\;35$	56-4
AP Sgr	166767	Cδ	6.5	7.4	5.05	0.30	F6-G1	13.0	$-23\;07$	56-4
RS Sgr	167647	EA	6.0	6.9	2.41	0.17	B3+A	17.6	$-34\;06$	56-5
Y Sgr	168608	Cδ	5.4	6.1	5.77	0.34	F8	21.4	$-18\;52$	56-3
RY Sgr	180093	RCB	6.0	15.0			G0	$19^h16.5^m$	$-33\;31$	56-1
R Sgr	180275	M	6.7	12.8	268	0.46	M4-M6	16.7	$-19\;18$	56-7
V505 Sgr	187949	EA	6.4	7.5	1.18	0.20	A0+F8	53.1	$-14\;36$	56-7
RU Sgr	188813	M	6.0	13.8	240	0.43	M3-M6	58.7	$-41\;51$	56-1

F* = The fraction of period taken up by the star's rise from min. to max. brightness, or the period spent in eclipse.

Table 56-2: Selected Double Stars in Sagittarius

Name	ADS No.	Pair	M1	M2	Sep.′	P.A.°	Spec	R.A. (2000)	Dec.	Finder Chart No.	Notes
h5003 (Pz)		AB	5.2	6.9	5.5	105	M0	17^{h}59.1^m	−30° 15′	56-4	Reddish orange pair
		AC		13.0	26.2	239					
HN 40	10991	AB	6.9	10.6	5.4	23	O8	18^{h}02.4^m	−23 02	56-4	In Trifid Nebula (M20)
HN 6	10991	AC		8.8	10.6	212					
	10991	CD		10.5	2.2	282					
	10991	CE		12.4	6.2	191					
Arg 31		AC	6.9	8.5	35.5	27	B3	02.6	−24 15	56-4	In Lagoon Nebula (M8)
HdO 283			5.8	11.0	12.5	290	K0	04.8	−35 54	56-5	
WNO	11069		6.6	8.6	13.3	64	B8	08.9	−25 28	56-4	
β 245			5.6	8.6	4.0	352	K0	10.1	−30 44	56-5	Orange and yellow pair
β 132	11127		6.9	7.3	1.0	203	A2	11.2	−19 51	56-3	Close white pair
11 Sgr	11133		5.0	10.7	42.1	287	K0	11.7	−23 42	56-4	
13–μ Sgr	11169	AB	3.9	11.4	16.9	258	B8	13.8	−21 04	56-4	
	11169	AC		13.4	25.8	119					
	11169	AD		9.8	48.5	312					
	11169	AE		9.3	50.0	115					
η Sgr		AB	3.2	7.8	3.6	105	M4	17.6	−36 46	56-5	Reddish-orange and white
S,h263	11232	AB	6.7	9.7	54.3	12	B5	17.8	−18 48	56-3	In field with S, h264
S,h264	11240	AC	6.8	9.3	17.2	52	B0	18.7	−18 37	56-3	In field with S, h263
21 Sgr	11325		4.9	7.4	1.8	289	K0 A0	25.3	−20 32	56-3	Orange and greenish pair
β 133	11354		6.9	7.0	1.3	251	A5	27.7	−26 38	56-4	Yellowish pair
Howe 43		AB	5.3	9.8	3.2	193	A3	31.1	−32 59	56-5	
38–ζ Sgr	11950	AB	3.2	3.4			A4	19^{h}02.6^m	−29 53	56-5	Binary with 21 yr period
		ABxC		9.9	75.0	302					
h5082	11972	AB	6.0	9.5	7.5	99	G5	03.1	−19 15	56-6	Elegant triple (h)
	11972	AC		10.7	20.2	113					
HN 129	11987		6.9	8.4	8.0	308	A0	04.2	−22 54	56-6	
HN 126	11989		7.7	7.9	w1.0	*171	G0	04.3	−21 32	56-6	Yellow binary
S 710	12039		5.9	9.9	6.4	2	B8	06.9	−16 14	56-1	
Ho 100	12119		7.7	10.7	4.8	327	A0	10.8	−12 09	56-1	
h5094		AB	7.3	7.9	23.6	191	A0 A0	12.7	−33 51	56-1	
I 644			7.9	10.1	8.1	173	K0	15.3	−34 17	56-1	
S 715	12266		7.0	7.5	8.5	15	A3	17.7	−15 58	56-7	
HV 77			6.8	9.0	39.7	159	B9	18.2	−18 52	56-7	
h5107			7.8	9.1	13.6	127	G0	20.9	−33 03	56-1	
Ho 272	12337	AB	7.4	11.9	12.3	52	F8	21.7	−17 15	56-7	
	12337	AC		12.4	4.9	301					
β¹ Sgr			4.0	7.1	28.3	77	B8 A3	22.6	−44 28	56-1	Ashy white and pale yellow
h5113	12400		6.1	10.5	12.2	160	K0	25.1	−29 19	56-8	
HN 119	12506		5.6	8.6	7.8	142	K3	29.9	−26 59	56-8	Orangish and blue
52 Sgr	12654		4.7	9.2	2.5	170	B9	36.7	−24 53	56-8	
S 722	12728		7.1	7.6	10.2	236	A2	39.2	−16 54	56-7	
54 Sgr	12767	AB	5.4	11.9	38.0	274	K0	40.7	−16 18	56-7	Deep yellow and pale blue
	12767	AC		8.9	45.6	42	G0				
I 122			7.6	10.6	5.1	339	A2	50.7	−41 52	56-1	
h2904	13072		6.2	10.2	28.9	49	K0	54.3	−23 56	56-8	
See 398			6.7	12.7	10.5	307	K5	56.2	−38 20	56-1	
ϑ² Sgr		AB	5.3	10.8	30.0	s.p.	A3	59.9	−34 42	56-1	
		BC		11.5	1.2	106					
Σ2625	13370		7.6	11.4	12.8	8	K0	20^{h}06.8^m	−12 56	56-1	
h5168			6.7	10.7	18.7	80	K0	07.4	−29 43	56-8	
B 987			7.6	11.8	5.1	25	A0	10.9	−32 19	56-1	
h5173			5.3	11.5	7.1	123	K4	11.2	−36 06	56-1	
h5178			7.0	8.5	2.7	10	G0	13.7	−34 07	56-1	
Δ 5183		AB	6.1	11.2	38.0	229	M	16.4	−36 27	56-1	
h5188	13702	AB	6.4	9.4	4.1	50	A0	20.5	−29 12	56-1	AB: White and reddish
	13702	AC		8.3	27.2	321	A0				
	13702	AD		10.2	106.3	32					
	13702	DE		10.2	4.7	186					
β 2483			7.6	11.0	12.0	s.f.	K5	23.1	−33 03	56-1	
κ² Sgr		AB	6.0	6.9	0.8	234	A3	23.9	−42 25	56-1	Close white pair
R 321			6.7	8.0	w1.6	*140	K1	26.9	−37 24	56-1	

Footnotes: * = Year 2000, a = Near apogee, c = Closing, w = Widening. Finder Chart No: All stars listed in the tables are plotted in the large Constellation Chart, but when a star appears in a Finder Chart, this number is listed. Notes: When colors are subtle, the suffix *-ish* is used, e.g. *bluish*.

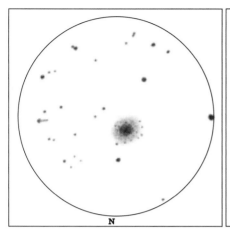

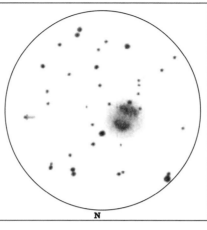

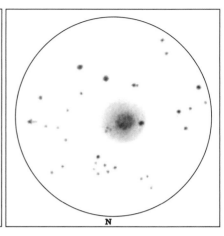

Figure 56-1. NGC 6440
12.5″, f5-250x, by G. R. Kepple

Figure 56-2. NGC 6445
17.5″, f4.5-300x, by G. R. Kepple

Figure 56-3. NGC 6522
17.5″, f4.5-300x, by G. R. Kepple

M8, the Lagoon Nebula; M17, the Swan Nebula; M20, the Trifid Nebula; and open clusters M18 and M21. (Open clusters M23 and M25 are in the interarm gap between our Orion-Cygnus Arm and the Sagittarius-Carina Arm.) Through a gap in the heavy dust lanes of the Sagittarius-Carina Arm we look deeper into the interior of our Galaxy at a rich star cloud of the Norma Spiral Arm, M24, the Small Sagittarius Star Cloud. Embedded in the Small Sagittarius Star Cloud is the distant but populous open cluster NGC 6603. Heavy dust prevents us from viewing much else of the interior spiral arms of our Galaxy. However, below the dust clouds bulges a portion of the 10,000 light year diameter central hub of our Galaxy, visible as the Great Sagittarius Star Cloud, which extends north from Gamma and Delta Sagittarii. Because most of our Galaxy's 150+ globular clusters are congregated in and around the central hub of the Galaxy, Sagittarius is exception-

ally rich in globulars, including seven in the Messier catalogue: M22, M28, M54, M55, M69, M70, and M75.

56.2 Interesting Stars

h5003 Triple Star   **Spec. M0**
AB: m5.2, 6.9; Sep.5.5″; P.A.105°   17ʰ59.1ᵐ −30° 15′
Finder Chart 56-4   ★★★★
4/6″Scopes-100x: J. Herschel 5003 AB is a beautiful pair of reddish-orange stars, the brighter star being the redder. The very faint magnitude 13.0 C component is 26.2″ away and might be glimpsed under good skies. h5003 lies in a splendid Milky Way star field.

Eta (η) Sagittarii = β760 Quadruple Star Spec. M4
AB: m3.2, 7.8; Sep.3.6″; P.A.105°   18ʰ17.6ᵐ −36° 46′
Finder Chart 56-5   ★★★★
4/6″Scopes-150x: Eta Sagittarii AB is an unequally bright double with a reddish-orange primary and a close white secondary. Two more companions are involved: a 10th magnitude star 93″ distant in position angle 303°, and a 13th magnitude star 33″ away in position angle 276°.

21 Sagittarii = Jc6 Double Star   **Spec. K0, A0**
m4.9, 7.4; Sep.1.8″; P.A.289°   18ʰ25.3ᵐ −20° 32′
Finder Chart 56-3   ★★★★
8/10″Scopes-175x: 21 Sagittarii is an unequally bright color contrast double of orange and bluish stars. Sometimes, because of the deep color of the primary, the secondary can seem greenish. The components are close enough to be a challenge for medium, and a severe test for small, telescopes.

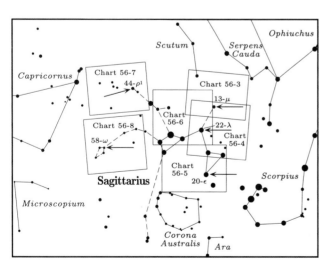

Master Finder Chart 56-2. Sagittarius Chart Areas
Guide stars indicated by arrows.

Figure 56-4. *NGC 6469 is a loose cluster just rich enough to stand out against the surrounding Milky Way. Martin C. Germano made this 35 minute exposure on hypered 2415 film with a 14.5", f5 Newtonian reflector.*

Figure 56-5. *Messier 23 (NGC 6494) is a large cluster of 150 stars spread over a 45' diameter area. Image courtesy of Lee C. Coombs.*

HN 119 Double Star   **Spec. K3**
m5.6, 8.6; Sep. 7.8″; P.A. 142° $19^h29.9^m$ **−26° 59′**
Finder Chart 56-8   ★★★★
4/6″ Scopes–125x: HN 119, a double originally in William Herschel's 1821 catalog, is a beautiful binary of orange and blue stars.

54 Sagittarii = h599 Triple Star   **Spec. K0**
AB: 5.4, 11.9; Sep. 38.0″; P.A. 274°
AC: 8.9; Sep. 45.6″; P.A. 42° $19^h40.7^m$ **−16° 18′**
Finder Chart 56-7   ★★★★
4/6″ Scopes–75x: 54 Sagittarii is a fine triple easily resolved in small telescopes. The primary is deep yellow, the secondary pale blue, and the C component pale yellow.

56.3 Deep-Sky Objects

NGC 6440 H150[1] Globular Cluster Class V
ϕ **5.4′, m9.1v** $17^h48.9^m$ **−20° 22′**
Finder Chart 56-3, Figure 56-1   ★★
12/14″ Scopes–150x: NGC 6440, located 5′ west of a 10th magnitude star, has a diffuse 2′ diameter halo which brightens to a small core. The edges are ragged, and less than a dozen of the principal cluster members can be discerned. The central core is unresolved and only slightly granular. The planetary nebula NGC 6445 lies 22′ north. An 11.5 magnitude star 3.25′ SSE, and a 12th magnitude star 1.75′ NNE, of the globular are part of a NNW–SSE star-chain.

NGC 6445 H586[2] PK8+3.1 Planetary Neb. Type 3b+3
ϕ **>34″, m11.2v, CS19v** $17^h49.2^m$ **−20° 01′**
Finder Chart 56-3, Figure 56-2   ★★★★
8/10″ Scopes–150x: NGC 6445 lies 5′ west of the wide, unequally bright double h2810 (7.7, 10.5; 40.8″; 189°). The planetary has a conspicuous 30″ diameter disk; it appears about half the size of, and only slightly fainter than, the globular cluster NGC 6440 located 22′ to its south. A 12th magnitude star lies 45″ west of the nebula's center.
16/18″ Scopes–200x: With an O-III filter NGC 6445 has a 45″ × 30″ NNW–SSE disk pinched in the middle and reminiscent of the Dumbbell Nebula, M27, in Vulpecula. The planetary is brighter at its north and south, the northern lobe more luminous than the southern. A very faint outer halo elongated NE–SW surrounds the main disk. Magnitude 10.5 stars are 2.5′ NNE and 2.25′ south of the planetary; and a magnitude 11.5 star 3′ to its SW has a magnitude 12.5 companion 10″ away in position angle 160°.

NGC 6469 Open Cluster 50★ Tr Type IV 2m
ϕ **12′, m8.2p** $17^h52.9^m$ **−22° 21′**
Finder Chart 56-3, Figure 56-4   ★★★
12/14″ Scopes–100x: NGC 6469 is just rich enough to stand out well from the surrounding Milky Way star field. It contains fifty 12th magnitude and fainter members loosely scattered over a 15′ × 10′ N–S area. The cluster lies in a semicircle, open to the north, of brighter field stars. At the center of the arc of the semicircle is the wide double h4990 (9.5, 11.0; 23″; 300°).

Figure 56-6. *The dark lanes of the Trifid Nebula, Messier 20 (NGC 6514) provides a nice contrast to the relatively high surface brightness of the nebulosity. An O-III or UHC filter provides a fine sight through medium-size telescopes. Image courtesy of Bill Logan.*

NGC 6494 Messier 23 Open Cl. 150★ Tr Type II 2r
φ 27′, m5.5v, Br★ 9.21v   17^{h}56.8^m −19° 01′
Finder Chart 56-3, Figure 56-5   ★★★★★

    This stunning cluster, discovered by Charles Messier in June 1764, fills an area the size of the full Moon. It lies 2,100 light years away, has an absolute magnitude of −4.7 (a luminosity of 6,300 suns), and is 300 million years old.

8/10″Scopes–50x: Messier 23, located just SE of a magnitude 6.5 star, is a beautiful open cluster of more than a hundred members evenly distributed over half a degree wide area. An 8th magnitude field star is conspicuous near the cluster's NE edge, but its brightest true members are the large number of 9th and 10th magnitude stars scattered in pairs, arcs, and short chains. These pairs, arcs, and chains are themselves gathered into large, irregular loose clumps interspersed with relatively starless voids

12/14″Scopes–75x: Messier 23, a splash of glittering jewels against the black velvet of the sky, packs 150 stars into a 45′ area. Star chains curve around the periphery like gems around the cornice of a crown. The cluster is narrower E–W on its north than on its south, where its full width approaches one degree.

Ruprecht 136 Open Cl. 40★   Tr Type IV 1m
φ 3′, m −, Br★ 13v   17^{h}59.3^m −24° 42′
Finder Chart 56-4   ★★

12/14″Scopes–150x: Ruprecht 136 is a faint 3′ wide open cluster with only about ten 13th magnitude and fainter stars resolved against a background haze. Open cluster NGC 6506 lies 7′ east.

NGC 6506 Open Cluster 20★ Tr Type IV 1p
φ 6′, m −   17^{h}59.9^m −24° 46′
Finder Chart 56-4   ★★★

12/14″Scopes–150x: NGC 6506 has thirty 11th to 14th magnitude stars in a 7′ area. The cluster has no central concentration, its members being loosely scattered about. However, several star-strings stand out. Open cluster Ruprecht 136 lies only 7′ west.

NGC 6514 Messier 20 Emission and Reflection Nebula
φ 20′×20′, Photo Br 1-5, Color 3-4   18^{h}02.3^m −23° 02′
Finder Chart 56-4, Figure 56-6   ★★★★★
Trifid Nebula

    M20 was discovered by Le Gentil before the year 1750, and Messier added it to his catalog on June 5, 1764. It is easily spotted in 10×50 binoculars as a N–S ellipse of haze. M20 is estimated to lie about 6,700 light years distant on the far side of the same complex of bright and dark nebulosity to which belongs the nearer Lagoon Nebula, M8.

4/6" Scopes-75x: Messier 20 is fairly obvious at this aperture as an irregular 20′ long oval patch surrounding magnitude 7 and 7.5 stars about 8′ apart N–S. The haze around the northern star, because it is reflection nebulosity, is much fainter and more diffuse than the glow around the southern star, which is the Trifid Nebula proper. The three dark lanes from which the nebula has been named are conspicuous: they radiate from the object's center near the central star (the hot O8 fluorescing star powering the Trifid's glow) toward its NE, south, and west edges. The NE lane is the easiest; but the west lane is broadest.

12/14" Scopes-100x: The Trifid Nebula is an outstanding object when viewed with an O-III filter on a medium size telescope. The Trifid proper spans a diameter of 15′ around its magnitude 6.9 central star. The fainter reflection nebula surrounding the yellowish magnitude 7.5 star to the north appears about half this size. Both sections of the nebula are enveloped by a fainter outer haze that reaches a diameter of 30′ around the Trifid proper and is more extensive to the east. The relatively high surface brightness of M20 provides good contrast for its three radial dark dust lanes. The three sections into which the dark lanes divide the nebula are unequal in area, the northern being the largest and the SW the smallest. The dark lanes themselves are unequal in length and width: the NE lane is longest and most distinct; the west lane is broad and short; and the south lane is thin and short. The lanes do not converge directly but lead to a circular, mottled central area. High power reveals a short and very thin lane headed straight north from the inner half of the west lane. The central star is not located in the mottled central area, but on the tip of the nebula's eastern segment. It is a sextuple, each of its two bright components (AC: 6.9, 8.8; 10.6″; 212°) having two faint companions.

Barnard 86 LDN 93 Dark Nebula "Ink Spot"
ϕ **5′, Opacity 5**   **18ʰ03.0ᵐ −27° 53′**

NGC 6520 H7⁷ Open Cl. 60★ Tr Type I2rn
ϕ **6′, m7.6p, Br★ 9.0p**   **18ʰ03.4ᵐ −27° 54′**
Finder Chart 56-4, Figure 56-7   ★★★★/★★★★

8/10" Scopes-100x: NGC 6520 is situated in a most interesting and spectacular star field within the Great Sagittarius Star Cloud. It contains thirty faint stars sprinkled over a 5′ area, mostly NE of a conspicuous NW–SE pair of cluster stars. A few

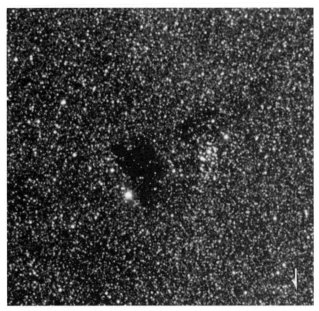

Figure 56-7. *Barnard 86, the Ink Spot, is a distinct dark cloud just west of open cluster NGC 6520. Image courtesy of Martin C. Germano.*

minutes to its west is the virtually opaque, 5′ diameter dust cloud named the "Ink Spot."

12/14" Scopes-150x: NGC 6520 contains fifty faint stars in a 5′ × 2′ N–S area, over half the cluster members concentrated in a 1.5′ area around a bright reddish-orange star. A second orange star lies near the cluster's NW edge. A thin dark lane winds its way from south of NGC 6520 WNW to the very dark dust cloud Barnard 86 due west of the cluster. B86 is elongated 5′ × 3′ N–S and tapers north to a point. It is darkest along its southern edge, and an especially opaque extension juts from its SSW edge. An orange magnitude 6.9 star is on the NNW edge. A few very faint stars are superimposed upon the cloud.

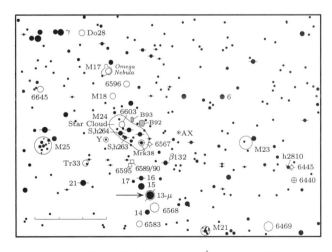

Finder Chart 56-3. 13–μ Sgr: 18ʰ13.8ᵐ −21° 04′

Figure 56-8. *Messier 8 (NGC 6523), the Lagoon Nebula, features a large, bright, rich open cluster embedded in a nebula divided in two by a broad lane of foreground dust. Image courtesy of Jim Burnell*

NGC 6522 H49[1] Globular Cluster Class VI
ϕ **5.6′, m8.6v**   **18^{h}03.6^m −30° 02′**
Finder Chart 56-4, Figure 56-3   ★★
8/10″ Scopes–100x: NGC 6522, located about 40′ NW
    of Gamma (γ) = 10 Sagittarii, has a small, bright
    core embedded in an unresolved 1.5′ diameter halo.
    A 12th magnitude star lies on the globular's NE
    edge.
16/18″ Scopes–150x: This globular has a granular 2.5′
    diameter halo surrounding a bright, irregularly
    concentrated, somewhat elongated ENE–WSW
    core. Even at higher powers neither halo nor core
    resolves. Globular cluster NGC 6528 lies 16′ east.

NGC 6523 M8 Emission Nebula "Lagoon Nebula"
ϕ **45′ × 30′, Photo Br 1-5, Color 2-4 18^{h}03.8^m −24° 23′**

NGC 6530 Open Cluster 113★ Tr Type II 2 mn
ϕ **14′, m4.6p, Br★ 6.87v**   **18^{h}04.8^m −24° 20′**
Finder Chart 56-4, Figure 56-8   ★★★★/★★★★★
    The earliest records of Messier 8 were by Flamsteed
in 1680 and de Cheseaux in 1745-46. The open cluster
NGC 6530 is actually embedded in the Lagoon Nebula
and its brightest stars, hot O-type objects, are fluorescing the eastern part of the nebula. The western half of

M8 is primarily illuminated by the magnitude 6.0 star
9 Sagittarii, an extremely hot O4 object which radiates
44 times more high-energy ultraviolet light than it does
visual light – and even at visual wavelengths 9 Sagittarii
is 23,000 times brighter than our Sun! The Lagoon
Nebula is 5,200 light years distant in the heart of the
Sagittarius-Carina Spiral Arm. Its true size is about
60 × 38 light years.
4/6″ Scopes–75x: Small telescopes show a large oval
    wisp of greenish light split into two distinct sections
    by an irregular dark lane. The open cluster NGC
    6530, centered in the northern part of the eastern
    wing of the nebula, contains thirty members in a
    10′ area.
12/14″ Scopes–125x: Though large and bright and de-
    tailed even without filters, the Lagoon Nebula is at
    its best in an O-III filter, which triples the lumines-
    cence of the nebula glow while blunting the glare of
    9 Sagittarii and the NGC 6530 stars. The brightest
    part of the Lagoon is west of the dark lane SW of 9
    Sagittarii and the 7th magnitude star 3′ to its NNE.
    The wide, curved dark lane slashes through the
    middle of the nebula from NE to SW. Several thinner
    dark bands, also running NE–SW, are east of NGC
    6530. A broad dark area extends E–W north of both

the western and eastern wings of the nebula. Some nebulous haze can be observed around a 7th magnitude star 15′ east of NGC 6530; and the outlying nebulosity of M8 covers an area more than a degree wide. The glittering star points of NGC 6530 contrast vividly with the smooth nebula-glow in which they are embedded. The cluster has over fifty members loosely spread over half a degree; but the rich-appearing central concentration contains two dozen stars in just 5′.

Barnard 87 LDN1771 Dark Nebula
φ 12′, Opacity 4   18^{h}04.3^m −32° 30′
Finder Chart 56-5   ★★★
Parrot's Head Nebula

4/6″Scopes-75x: Barnard 87, located 2′ south and slightly west of Gamma (γ) = 10 Sagittarii in a rich Milky Way field, is an irregular, somewhat circular dark area surrounding a 9.3 magnitude star. Although not as distinct as other dark nebulae in the area, it stands out fairly well because of the rich stellar background. The dark cloud's NE periphery is its most distinct edge. A projection to the SE defines the Parrot's beak, the magnitude 9.3 star in the main body of the nebula representing the bird's eye. Along the SSE edge of B87 is a row of three magnitude 9.5–10 stars, and a knot of faint stars is on its NNW edge.

NGC 6531 Messier 21 Open Cluster 70★ Tr Type I3r
φ 13′, m5.9v, Br★ 7.25v   18^{h}04.6^m −22° 30′
Finder Chart 56-4, Figure 56-9   ★★★★
   Messier discovered M21 in June, 1764 while he was observing the Trifid Nebula. Estimates place this cluster at a distance of 5,200 light years, the same as the Lagoon Nebula. Its true diameter is about 20 light years and it has an absolute magnitude of −5.9, a luminosity of 20,000 suns. The brightest star of M21 is a hot luminous B0 giant, so it must be a very young group.

8/10″Scopes-100x: Messier 21 is a compact round cluster of fifty stars, many of them quite bright, concentrated in a 15′ area. A double of 9th and 10th magnitude stars is at the center of the group. Two strings of fairly bright stars trail toward the Trifid Nebula, located less than half a degree from M21 to its SW.

12/14″Scopes-125x: M21 has seventy members distributed in irregular clumps over a 15′ area. The NE part of the cluster has the brighter stars and is the most concentrated. At the cluster's center is a short E–W chain of bright stars, a wide pair of magnitude 7.5 and 8 stars at its west end. This pair is within a knot that includes four fainter stars. Immediately north of the short star chain is a circlet of ten stars

Figure 56-9. *Messier 21 (NGC 6531) is a bright, irregular cluster of 70 stars. Image courtesy of Martin C. Germano.*

surrounding a blank area. From the SW part of the cluster fainter members straggle out into and blend with the surrounding star field. The cluster's brighter stars appear bluish-white.

NGC 6528 H200^2 Globular Cluster Class V
φ 3.7′, m9.5v   18^{h}04.8^m −30° 03′
Finder Charts 56-4, 56-5, Figure 56-11   ★★
8/10″Scopes-125x: NGC 6528 is fainter and smaller than its companion globular cluster NGC 6522 lying 16′ west. It has a 1′ diameter halo containing a brighter center. Neither halo nor core can be resolved, and no outlying stars are visible. A small dark dust cloud obscures the Milky Way glow between the two globulars.

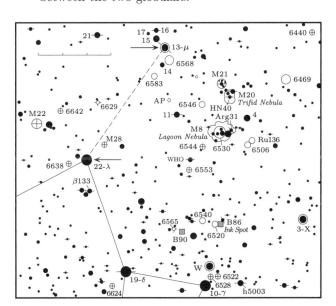

Finder Chart 56-4. 22–λ Sgr: 18^{h}27.9^m −25° 25′

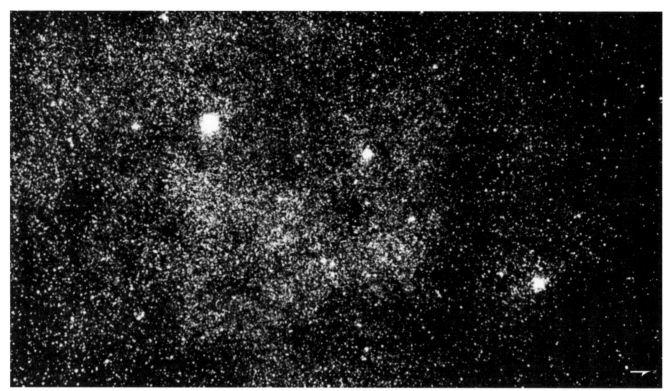

Figure 56-10. *The globular clusters NGC 6544, at lower right, and NGC 6553, at upper left, lie less than a degree apart SSE of the Lagoon Nebula in a profuse star field. Martin C. Germano made this 60 minute exposure on hypered 2415 film with an 8″, f5 Newtonian reflector.*

12/14″ Scopes–175x: NGC 6528 remains unresolved in larger instruments. Its 1.5′ diameter halo contains a poorly concentrated center. A 13th magnitude field star is on the SW edge of the halo.

NGC 6540 H198[2] Open Cluster 10★ Tr Type I1pn
ϕ 0.8′, m14.6p   18^{h}06.3^m −27° 49′
Finder Charts 56-4, 56-5, Figure 56-12   ★
12/14″ Scopes–150x: At low power NGC 6540, lying 3.5′ NE of a 10th magnitude star, is a very faint, 1′ diameter patch of haze. 150x reveals an E–W arc of five cluster members, concave to the north. At the center of the arc is an unresolved knot of threshold stars.

NGC 6544 H197[2] Globular Cluster Class –
ϕ 8.9′, m8.1v   18^{h}07.3^m −25° 00′
Finder Chart 56-4, Figures 56-10 and 56-13   ★★
8/10″ Scopes–125x: NGC 6544, located in a profuse star field 6′ NNW of an 8th magnitude star, is a moderately concentrated 1.5′ diameter globular cluster with a granular texture. A few stars can be resolved around its edges.
12/14″ Scopes–150x: At low power NGC 6544 is only marginally resolved; but 150x reveals a twinkling 2.5′ diameter disk of very faint stars, the most conspicuous at the cluster's center and on its west

edge. 1.5′ SW of the globular is an E–W pair of magnitude 11.5 stars separated by 15″, the eastern component with a very faint companion just to its south. A halo of brighter field stars surrounds the cluster. Messier 8, the Lagoon Nebula, lies to the NW.

NGC 6546 Open Cluster 150★ Tr Type II1m
ϕ 13′, m8.0v, Br★ 10.62v   18^{h}07.2^m −23° 20′
Finder Chart 56-4, Figure 56-14   ★★★
12/14″ Scopes–125x: NGC 6546 lies in the rich and interesting Milky Way field NE of the Lagoon Nebula, Messier 8. It is a fairly bright, irregularly scattered group of 11th magnitude and fainter stars in a 14′ area. The cluster has no central condensation of members, but most of its brighter stars are in its eastern section. Also in its eastern part is a triangle of 9th magnitude field stars, two of which have an attractive orange color.

NGC 6553 H12[4] Globular Cluster Class XI
ϕ 8.1′, m8.1v   18^{h}09.3^m −25° 54′
Finder Chart 56-4, Figures 56-10, 56-15   ★★
8/10″ Scopes–125x: NGC 6553 has a fairly bright 2′ diameter halo with diffuse, irregular edges. It is not conspicuously brighter toward its center. An 11th magnitude field star lying on the halo's NW edge

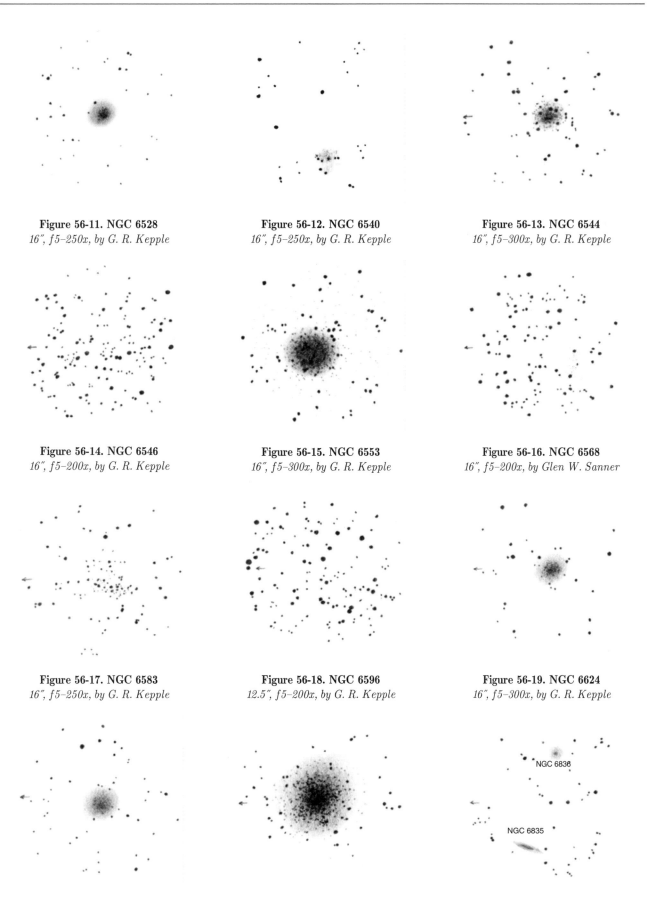

Figure 56-11. NGC 6528
16″, f5–250x, by G. R. Kepple

Figure 56-12. NGC 6540
16″, f5–250x, by G. R. Kepple

Figure 56-13. NGC 6544
16″, f5–300x, by G. R. Kepple

Figure 56-14. NGC 6546
16″, f5–200x, by G. R. Kepple

Figure 56-15. NGC 6553
16″, f5–300x, by G. R. Kepple

Figure 56-16. NGC 6568
16″, f5–200x, by Glen W. Sanner

Figure 56-17. NGC 6583
16″, f5–250x, by G. R. Kepple

Figure 56-18. NGC 6596
12.5″, f5–200x, by G. R. Kepple

Figure 56-19. NGC 6624
16″, f5–300x, by G. R. Kepple

Figure 56-20. NGC 6638
16″, f5–300x, by Glen W. Sanner

Figure 56-21. NGC 6723
16″, f5–300x, by G. R. Kepple

Figure 56-22. NGC 6835 and NGC 6836
12.5″, f5–200x, by G. R. Kepple

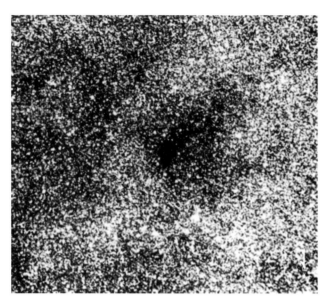

Figure 56-23. *Barnard 90 is a distinct dark dust cloud silhouetted upon a profuse Milky Way star field. Martin C. Germano made this 60 minute exposure on 2415 film with an 8", f5 Newtonian.*

makes the cluster appear elongated NNW–SSE.

16/18"Scopes–175x: Instruments of larger aperture show a granular-textured, poorly concentrated 2.5′ diameter disk with half a dozen faint stars resolved around its periphery.

Barnard 90 LDN108 Dark Nebula
[φ 3′], Opacity 5   **$18^h10.2^m$ −28° 19′**
Finder Chart 56-4, Figure 56-23   ★★★★
4/6"Scopes–75x: Barnard 90, located half a degree ENE of a 5th magnitude star in a profusely populated field of the Great Sagittarius Star Cloud, is a fairly distinct, irregular inky patch elongated 3′ × 2′ N–S. It is the densest section of a 13′ wide irregular region of dust superimposed upon the Great Sagittarius Star Cloud.

NGC 6558 Globular Cluster Class –
φ 3.7′, m9.8v   **$18^h10.3^m$ −31° 46′**
Finder Chart 56-5   ★★
12/14"Scopes–150x: NGC 6558 has a moderately faint 1.5′ diameter halo of granular texture surrounding a faint, tiny core. The irregular periphery is somewhat elongated NNE–SSW.

NGC 6565 PK3–4.5 Planetary Nebula Type 4
φ 9″, m11.6v, CS15.88:v   **$18^h11.9^m$ −28° 11′**
Finder Chart 56-4, 56-5   ★★
8/10"Scopes–250x: This planetary nebula has a dim round 5″ disk of a light bluish tint.

16/18"Scopes–300x: In an O-III filter NGC 6565 appears as a fairly bright 10″ diameter disk slightly elongated N–S. With averted vision the disk seems subtly annular.

NGC 6563 PK358–7.1 Planetary Nebula Type 3a
φ 48″, m11.0v, CS15.38v   **$18^h12.0^m$ −33° 52′**
Finder Chart 56-5   ★★★
8/10"Scopes–200x: NGC 6563 lies in a dense Milky Way field, and forms a right triangle with two stars. It has an evenly illuminated pale gray 40″ diameter disk.

16/18"Scopes–250x: In an O-III filter the planetary's disk appears unevenly bright with a hint of annularity and a slightly brighter NW rim. It is elongated 50″ × 40″ NE–SW. A faint star lies just beyond the south edge.

NGC 6567 PK11–0.2 Planetary Nebula Type 2a+3
φ >8″, m11.0v, CS14.43:v   **$18^h13.7^m$ −19° 05′**
Finder Chart 56-3   ★★
12/14"Scopes–250x: NGC 6567 can be difficult to spot because it lies within the crowded star fields of the Small Sagittarius Star Cloud. The nebula is located 1.25′ SE of a magnitude 11.5 star and has a hazy, but fairly bright, 10″ diameter disk which brightens noticeably toward its center. 13th magnitude stars lie on the planetary's east edge and 30″ WNW of its center. A dark dust cloud to the west of the field contrasts starkly with the rich Small Sagittarius Star Cloud field around the nebula.

NGC 6568 H30[7] Open Cluster 50★ Tr Type IV1m
φ 12′, m8.6p   **$18^h12.8^m$ −21° 36′**
Finder Chart 56-3, Figure 56-16   ★★
12/14"Scopes–100x: NGC 6568 is situated half a degree SW of magnitude 3.9 Mu (μ) Sagittarii and 20′ NW of the magnitude 5.4 star 14 Sagittarii. The cluster contains some fifty stars, thirty of them 11th and 12th magnitude objects, irregularly and loosely scattered over a 15′ × 10′ N–S area. North of the group's comparatively star-poor center is a conspicuous E–W S-shaped asterism.

NGC 6569 H201[2] Globular Cluster Class 8
φ 5.8′, m8.7v   **$18^h13.6^m$ −31° 50′**
Finder Chart 56-5   ★★
12/14"Scopes–150x: NGC 6569, located 8.5′ north of a 7.5 magnitude star, shows a moderately faint, unresolved 2′ diameter halo containing a broad core. Around its edges the globular partially resolves to a granulated texture.

Figure 56-24. *Barnard 92 and Barnard 93 (left to right) are two equally distinct and dense dust patches silhouetted upon the NW edge of the Small Sagittarius Star Cloud. Open cluster NGC 6603 is visible near center. Image courtesy of Jim Burnell.*

Figure 56-25. *Open cluster NGC 6603 is a rich but tiny splash of faint stars embedded in the NE portion of the Small Sagittarius Star Cloud. Lee C. Coombs made this 10 minute exposure on 103a-O film with a 10", f5 Newtonian reflector.*

Markarian 38 Open Cluster 14★ Tr Type I1p
φ 2′, m6.9v   18ʰ15.2ᵐ −19° 00′
Finder Chart 56-3   ★★★
12/14″Scopes–125x: Markarian 38, lying within M24, the Small Sagittarius Star Cloud, is a 2′ × 1′ N–S sprinkling of a dozen faint stars around the group's bright 7th magnitude lucida. On the cluster's north edge is a 5″ wide NW–SE double of magnitude 11.5 and 12.5 stars.

Barnard 92 LDN 323 Dark Nebula
φ 15′ × 9′, Opacity 6   18ʰ15.5ᵐ −18° 14′

Barnard 93 LDN 327 Dark Nebula
[φ 12′ × 2′], Opacity 4   18ʰ16.9ᵐ −18° 04′
Finder Chart 56-3, Figure 56-24   ★★★★/★★★★
4/6″Scopes–75x: Barnard 92 and Barnard 93 are two dark dust clouds silhouetted conspicuously on the NW side of the 120′ × 45′ NE–SW rectangle of M24, the Small Sagittarius Star Cloud. Barnard 92, the westernmost of the two dark nebulae, is the larger and more distinct: it measures 15′ × 7′ N–S and has a single 12th magnitude foreground star near its center and an 8th magnitude field star just outside its east edge. The eastern side of B92 is more well defined than its western, which dissipates imperceptibly into the star field west of M24. Barnard 93, 17′ ENE of B92, is less opaque and sharp-edged than its companion: it is elongated 15′ × 3′ N–S with something of a cometary appearance, the main body of the nebula trailing south from the very well

defined circular 2′ diameter black cloudlet on its northern edge.

NGC 6583 H31⁷ Open Cluster 35★ Tr Type I2m
φ 2.8′, m10.0p   18ʰ15.8ᵐ −22° 08′
Finder Chart 56-4, Figure 56-17   ★★★
12/14″Scopes–125x: NGC 6583 is a 5′ diameter cluster of thirty 12th magnitude and fainter stars, twenty concentrated in a 2.5′ area. 2.5′ south of the central condensation is a 1.5′ long ESE–WNW arc of three stars, from west to east of magnitudes 11, 13, and 12.

Messier 24 Small Sagittarius Star Cloud
φ 95′ × 35′, m4.6v   18ʰ16.5ᵐ −18° 50′

NGC 6603 Open Cluster 100★ Tr Type I2rn
φ 5′, m11.1p, Br★ 14.0p   18ʰ18.4ᵐ −18° 25′
Finder Chart 56-3, Figure 56-25   ★★★★/★★★★
　　Though the Small Sagittarius Star Cloud, located NE of Mu (μ) Sagittarii, is a conspicuous unaided eye object four times the size of the full Moon, hardly the sort of thing that could be mistaken for a comet, Messier mentioned it in 1764 as a star cluster and saw fit to include it as number 24 in his catalogue of comet imposters. It is a stunning sight in richest-field telescopes and binoculars, and one of the most interesting star clouds in the entire Milky Way: M24 is a section of a far interior spiral arm of our Galaxy, the Norma Spiral Arm, which we see framed by the dust clouds of the nearer Sagittarius-Carina Spiral Arm. The dust clouds

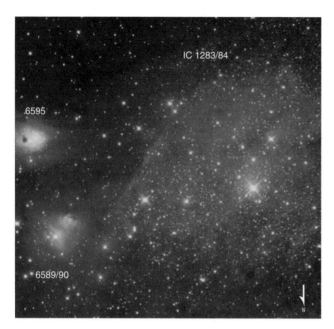

Figure 56-26. *Reflection nebulae NGC 6595 (top) and NGC 6589-90 (lower center) are faint haze around double stars. IC 1283/84 is the very faint nebula at lower right. Image courtesy of Josef Pöpsel and Stefan Binnewies.*

Figure 56-27. *Open cluster Messier 18 (NGC 6613), located a degree south of the Messier 17, the Omega Nebula, is an irregular group of 40 faint stars. Image courtesy of Martin C. Germano.*

of the Sagittarius-Carina Arm, in which are embedded the Lagoon, the Trifid, and the Swan emission nebulae, lie from about 5,000 to around 7,000 light years from us: the stars which comprise the M24 Star Cloud are probably from 12,000 to 16,000 light years distant. The small open cluster NGC 6603 seems to be on the nearer edge of the Small Sagittarius Star Cloud.

4/6″ Scopes–50x: Messier 24 is a 90′ × 30′ NE–SW rectangular star cloud located just NE of Mu (μ) Sagittarii. It is best defined along its SE long side, its NE short side, and the NE half of its NW long side. The two conspicuous dust clouds Barnard 92 and 93 are near the midpoint of its NW long side. The Star Cloud is best viewed with binoculars and richest-field telescopes, in which its pale background glow is richly gemmed with glittering magnitude 6 to 10 stars and a profusion of momentarily-resolved fainter star-sparks – the impression of depth is breathtaking. In giant binoculars M24 is one of the most beautiful sights the heavens has to offer any astronomical instrument, no matter how large. Photographs do not even begin to do it justice. It is an even superior sight to the Great Sagittarius Star Cloud to its south, which lacks M24's combination of brighter star diamonds with fainter star scintillations. NGC 6603, for which some magnification is necessary, is a dense knot of faint stars near the "bend" in M24: it forms a triangle with magnitude 6.5 stars 15′ to its west and south.

12/14″ Scopes–125x: NGC 6603 is a very rich splash of faint stars within Messier 24, the Small Sagittarius Star Cloud. It contains seventy-five 12th magnitude and fainter members concentrated in a 10′ area, and stands out very well from the surrounding star field. A chain of slightly brighter cluster stars runs from its center to its NW edge. A second star chains arcs across the southern part of the group. South of the NW star chain is a dark gap in the cluster. A vivid red 9th magnitude field star is 4′ SSW of the group.

NGC 6589-90 Reflection Nebula
φ 5′× 3′, Photo Br 1-5, Color 1-4   18ʰ16.9ᵐ −19° 47′

NGC 6595 Reflection Nebula
φ 4′× 3′, Photo Br 1-5, Color 1-4   18ʰ17.1ᵐ −19° 52′
Finder Chart 56-3, Figure 56-26   ★★/★★
8/10″ Scopes–100x: NGC 6589–90 and NGC 6595, located just outside the southern edge of the Small Sagittarius Star Cloud, are two patches of reflection nebulae around fairly bright stars. NGC 6589–90 is a faint 1′ diameter glow around a magnitude 9.5 star with a faint companion 25″ to its SW. 6′ SSE of NGC 6589–90 is NGC 6595, another hazy 1′ diameter patch: it surrounds a 20″ wide ENE–WSW pair of 10th magnitude stars. To the NE of NGCs 6589–90 and 6595 is IC 1283–84, a very faint haze around several of the brighter stars in that area. Many dark dust patches are scattered in the region around these small nebulae.

Figure 56-28. *Festooned with bright and dark material, Messier 17 (NGC 6618), the Omega or Swan Nebula, rivals Messier 42, the Orion Nebula, in splendor. Image courtesy Martin C. Germano.*

NGC 6596 H55⁸ Open Cluster 30★ Tr Type II2mn
ϕ 10′, m –   18^{h}17.5^m −16° 40′
Finder Chart 56-3, Figure 56-18   ★★★
12/14″Scopes–100x: NGC 6596, located in an interesting field of bright stars among which snake small dark dust lanes, is a 7′ × 4′ N–S oval with a starless center. The oval is broken on its east side, but a 6′ long NNW–SSE string of stars runs along its west. 8′ to the west of the oval is another jagged string of stars, including one of the 10th magnitude.

NGC 6613 M18 Open Cluster 20★ Tr Type II3pn
ϕ 10′, m6.9v, Br★ 8.65v   18^{h}19.9^m −17° 08′
Finder Chart 56-3, Figure 56-27   ★★★★
   Charles Messier discovered M18 on June 3, 1764, calling it "a cluster of small stars, a little below M17; surrounded by slight nebulosity." Its distance is estimated to be about 4,100 light years, and its absolute magnitude is −5, a luminosity of 8,300 suns.
8/10″Scopes–100x: Messier 18 is an irregular group of thirty 9th magnitude and fainter stars in an 8′ area. The seven brightest stars are concentrated in a 3.5′ × 2′ NE–SW oval.
12/14″Scopes–125x: Messier 18, visible in the same low power field with the Omega Nebula, is a cluster of forty 8.6 magnitude and fainter stars in a 10′ area.

Most of the brighter members lie in an irregular NE–SW 3.5′ × 2′ oval. The cluster's magnitude 8.6 lucida is on the NW edge of the oval. Five of the stars in the oval have fainter companions. An isolated 4′ × 3′ triangle of cluster members lies 4′ SW of the oval. Faint outlying stars spread 8′ ESE to a wide NE–SW pair of 9th magnitude field stars. A third 9th magnitude field star lies 7′ NE of the oval.

NGC 6618 Messier 17 Emission Nebula
ϕ 20′× 15′, Photo Br1-5, Color 3-4 18^{h}20.8^m −16° 11′

NGC 6618 Messier 17 Open Cl. 40★ Tr Type III3mn
ϕ 11′, m6.0v, Br★ 9.28v   18^{h}20.8^m −16° 11′
Finder Chart 56-3, Figure 56-28   ★★★★★
Omega or Swan Nebula

   M17 was first noted by de Cheseaux in the spring of 1746 and discovered independently again by Messier in June of the same year. The former wrote that the nebula has the "perfect form of a ray or the tail of a comet." M17 lies about 6,800 light years away.
4/6″Scopes–75x: Messier 17 rivals Messier 42, the Orion Nebula, in splendor. The core of the nebula is a checkmark, the bar of which is extended 12′ ESE–WNW. The check projects SSW from the

Figure 56-29. *Messier 28 (NGC 6626) is a class IV globular cluster with an intense core and extensive outer halo. Image courtesy of Jim Burnell.*

WNW end of the bar. Fainter nebulosity loops west from the check, forming a figure "2" and enclosing a dark mass popularly called the "Fish's Mouth." The involved cluster is poorly concentrated, its fifty stars spread over a 25' area.

12/14"Scopes–100x: Splendid! In an O-III filter the Omega Nebula displays much more contrast between its dark and bright areas of nebulosity than does the Great Orion Nebula. The brighter core that forms the checkmark or number "2" is festooned with irregular extensions to the south. The western portion of the core is especially impressive, with wisps and arcs surrounding a mottled dark mass sprinkled by a glittering concentration of stars. The base of the "2" is formed by a well defined bright bar of nebulosity elongated 15' ESE–WNW. The O-III filter brings out the otherwise invisible feathered area of faint nebulosity that extends east and SE from the box. Some nebula haze can be glimpsed north of the bar, where most of the brighter stars of the complex's open cluster are embedded. The cluster has at least 75 members loosely scattered around a 25' area.

NGC 6624 H50[1] Globular Cluster Class VI
ϕ 5.9', m8.0v   18h23.7m −30° 22'
Finder Chart 56-5, Figure 56-19   ★★★
12/14"Scopes–150x: NGC 6624 is a fairly bright globular cluster with a small core embedded in a 2.5'

diameter halo. A few faint stars are resolved around the periphery; but even with good seeing the core appears only granular. 12th magnitude stars are 1.75' WSW and 2.25' ESE of the globular's halo.

NGC 6626 M28 Globular Cluster Class IV
ϕ 11.2', m6.8v   18h24.5m −24° 52'
Finder Chart 56-6, Figure 56-29   ★★★★★

Messier 28 was noted by Charles Messier on July 27, 1764, as a "nebula containing no star... round, seen with difficulty in 3.5" telescope." Estimates place it about 19,000 light years distant.

4/6"Scopes–100x: Messier 28 has a glowing core which fades rapidly outward into a halo that extends to a diameter of 3'. A scattering of stars can be resolved around its rim.

8/10"Scopes–125x: Impressive! This globular cluster is well resolved 4' diameter halo of glittering stars surrounds a 2' core.

16/18"Scopes–175x: This fine globular cluster has an intense inner core within an extensive halo of stars that radiates outward in star chains to a diameter of 8'. The periphery, although irregular, is richly concentrated, and has fewer open starless gaps than most globular halos. Two prominent starless arms loop northward from the NE and NNW edges of the halo and merge 3' from globular's center. The halo and core are both well resolved, the star of the latter sprinkled like ice-chips across a soft snowy background glow.

NGC 6629 H204[2] PK9-5.1 Planetary Neb. Type 2a
ϕ 15", m11.3v, CS12.82v   18h25.7m −23° 12'
Finder Chart 56-4, 56-6   ★★★
8/10"Scopes–200x: At low power NGC 6629 appears stellar – merely the middle "star" in a row with two other field stars. However at 200x the planetary's 15" diameter disk is well defined and its magnitude 12.8 central star can occasionally be discerned.

12/14"Scopes–225x: NGC 6629 has a bright greenish 15" diameter disk of uniform brightness. The planetary's central star is plainly visible.

NGC 6638 H51[1] Globular Cluster Class VI
ϕ 5', m9.1v   18h30.9m −25° 30'
Finder Chart 56-6, Figure 56-20   ★★★
8/10"Scopes–125x: NGC 6638 is half a degree ESE of the magnitude 2.8 star Lambda (λ) = 22 Sagittarii and 3.5' north of a 10th magnitude star. It is a moderately faint 1.5' diameter, smooth-textured hazy disk with diffuse edges.

12/14"Scopes–150x: A small, well concentrated core is

Figure 56-30. *Messier 25 (IC4725) is an irregular open cluster with a hundred stars spanning half a degree. Image courtesy of Martin C. Germano.*

Figure 56-31. *NGC6645 is a rich open cluster of 70 faint stars, many of them in attractive pairs. Lee C. Coombs made this 10 minute exposure on 103a-O film with a 10", f5 Newtonian reflector.*

embedded in a 2' diameter halo of uniform brightness. The halo is unresolved, but hints of granulation can be glimpsed around its rim.

NGC 6637 Messier 69 Globular Cluster Class V
ϕ 7.1', m7.6v   18^{h}31.4^m −32° 21'
Finder Chart 56-5, Figure 56-33   ★★★

M69 was discovered at the Cape of Good Hope in 1752 by Lacaille who described it as similar to "the small nucleus of a comet." Messier added it to his catalogue in August 1780. Its distance is about 33,000 light years.

8/10" Scopes–125x: Messier 69, located 4.5' SE of an 8th magnitude star, appears similar to, but is slightly brighter and more concentrated than, Messier 70. It has a diameter of about 2.5' and contains a broadly concentrated center that intensifies to a bright, nearly stellar core.

16/18" Scopes–175x: In larger telescopes M69 has a broadly concentrated, granular core with a 3' diameter halo. Some very faint stars can be resolved around the highly irregular periphery: the eastern edge of the halo is especially ragged and is broken by a small notch. A 13th magnitude field star is in the halo east of the core.

IC 4725 Messier 25 Open Cluster 30★ Tr Type I3m
ϕ 32', m4.6v, Br★ 6.0v   18^{h}31.6^m −19° 15'
Finder Chart 56-6, Figure 56-30   ★★★★★

Messier 25, visible to the naked eye under dark skies as a blurry spot, is a fine open cluster for binoculars

and small telescopes. It was discovered by de Cheseaux in 1746 and re-observed by Messier in 1764. M25 lies about 3,000 light years away and has an absolute magnitude of −6.5, a luminosity of 33,000 suns. It is notable for containing a Cepheid, U Sagittarii, which varies between magnitudes 6.3 and 7.0 in a period of 6.75 days.

4/6" Scopes–50x: Messier 25 has three dozen bright stars irregularly scattered over a 30' area. The more prominent members form two E–W streams divided by a starless lane. The outlying stars are brighter to the north and south of the cluster's core than to the east and west.

8/10" Scopes–75x: This fine, bright cluster has a hundred stars in a 40' area. Two prominent streams of

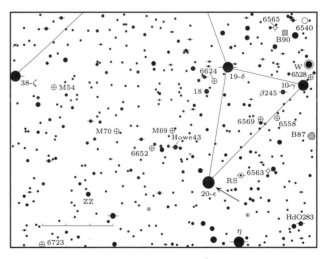

Finder Chart 56-5. 20–ϵ Sgr: 18^{h}24.2^m −34° 23'

Figure 56-32. *Messier 22 (NGC 6656) is a large, spectacular globular cluster outclassed only by Omega Centauri and 47 Tucana. Image courtesy of Martin C. Germano.*

stars running generally E–W dominate its central region. The northern stream, slightly concave to the north, is thicker and contains brighter stars. It is more concentrated in its western half where there is a dense knot of 6th to 8th magnitude stars. U Sagittarii is a conspicuous yellow object just east of the knot. In the northern part of the cluster is a longer and looser star stream. The area around the cluster is rich in little groups of field stars.

NGC 6642 H205² Globular Cluster Class –
ϕ 4.5′, m9.4v   18^{h}31.9^m –23° 29′
Finder Chart 56-6   ★★★
12/14″Scopes–150x: NGC 6642, located a degree NW of Messier 22 in a field profuse with faint stars, has an unresolved, but granular-textured, 1.5′ diameter halo containing a well-concentrated center. A 12th magnitude star 2.5′ north of the globular has a faint companion 10″ to its SSE.

NGC 6645 H23⁶ Open Cl. 40★ Tr Type IV1m
ϕ 10′, m8.5p, Br★ 12.0p   18^{h}32.6^m –16° 54′
Finder Chart 56-3, Figure 56-31   ★★★
12/14″Scopes–125x: NGC 6645 is a rich open cluster of seventy 11th to 14th magnitude stars scattered over a 20′×10′ E–W area. Most of the brighter stars are distributed along the group's northern edge. A short E–W row of three 12th magnitude stars is near the cluster's center. NGC 6645 has an abun-

dance of doubles, the two brightest lying near its east edge.

NGC 6652 Globular Cluster Class VI
ϕ 3.5′, m8.8v   18^{h}35.8^m –32° 59′
Finder Chart 56-5   ★★
12/14″Scopes–150x: NGC 6652, located 7′ SE of a 7th magnitude star, has a faint 2′ diameter halo containing a poorly concentrated core. A few faint stars can be resolved around its irregular periphery. A 13th magnitude field star is on the globular's west edge.

NGC 6656 Messier 22 Globular Cluster Class VII
ϕ 24′, m5.1v   18^{h}36.4^m –23° 54′
Finder Chart 56-6, Figure 56-32   ★★★★★
   The discoverer of M22 is uncertain. The first recorded sighting of it is usually credited to the obscure German astronomer Abraham Ihle in 1665, but it may have been spotted previously by Hevelius. In any event it was the first globular cluster to be seen as such: the Great Omega Centauri appears in the 1603 *Uranometria* of Bayer, and is catalogued in the *Almagest* of the 2nd century A.D. Greek astronomer Ptolemy, but in both instances only as a star. M22, at a distance of 10,000 light years, is one of the nearest globulars. Its absolute magnitude of −8.5, a luminosity of 210,000 suns, and its true diameter of 70 light years are both average for a globular cluster.

4/6″Scopes–75x: Messier 22, visible to the naked eye as a small fuzzy spot NE of Lambda (λ) Sagittarii, begins to resolve even in large binoculars and small telescopes. In 6″ telescopes at medium power it appears as a brilliant circle of tiny sparkling stars almost evenly crowded together over a huge 20′ area.

8/10″Scopes–75x: Spectacular! If Messier 22 were higher in declination, it would appear even more stunning to European and U.S. observers than the famous M13 in Hercules. The only globulars more beautiful than M22 are Omega Centauri and 47 Tucanae, both far southern objects. The halo, somewhat elongated NNE–SSW, has a multitude of well resolved stars. Outlying cluster members bring the halo's full diameter to 24′.

12/14″Scopes–100x: The relatively loose 5′ core is a mass of faint, well resolved, stars. Though the halo stars are in general uniformly distributed, they lie along a multitude of visually attractive arcs and streams and in several clumps, the most conspicuous of the latter NE and SW of the core. The globular's setting on the northern fringes of the Great Sagittarius Star Cloud adds to the richness of the scene.

Figure 56-33. Messier 69　　　**Figure 56-34. Messier 70**　　　**Figure 56-35. Messier 54**

Three globular clusters, Messier 69, 70, and 54 (in order of right ascension), lie along the southern base of the "Teapot" in Sagittarius. Images courtesy of Jim Burnell.

NGC 6681　Messier 70　Globular Cluster　Class V
ϕ 7.8′, m8.0v　　　　　　　　**18ʰ42.2ᵐ −32° 18′**

Finder Chart 56-5, Figure 56-34　　　　★★★

Messier 70 is the smallest and faintest of the three globular clusters distributed between Epsilon (ϵ) and Zeta (ζ) Sagittarii along the base of the "Teapot" asterism. Messier discovered this cluster in August 1780, calling it, as usual, a "nebula without a star." It lies some 34,000 light years distant. Its absolute magnitude of −7.3 (a luminosity of 70,000 suns) is about one magnitude less than average for a globular cluster.

8/10″Scopes–125x: Messier 70 has a small 2′ diameter halo containing a well concentrated core. The periphery is irregular, flattened on the NNW but richer with outlying stars on the south. A few dozen stars can be resolved around the edges. 10th and 11th magnitude field stars are respectively 5′ north and 6′ NNE of the cluster.

16/18″Scopes–175x: This globular cluster benefits greatly from an increase in aperture. The 3′ diameter halo shows a fair number of stars against a granular background. The halo's edges are irregular, some of its brighter stars lying along short chains, the most conspicuous leading NNE away from the cluster. The globular's core is small and poorly concentrated.

NGC 6715　Messier 54　Globular Cluster　Class III
ϕ 9.1′, m7.6v　　　　　　　　**18ʰ55.1ᵐ −30° 29′**

Finder Chart 56-5, Figure 56-35　　　　★★★

M54 was discovered in July 1778 by Messier, who described it as a "very bright nebula . . . It is bright in the centre and contains no star." It is about 68,000 light years away and therefore twice as distant as its neigh-

bors M69 and M70. It is much above average in luminosity for a globular cluster; its absolute magnitude is −9.4, a brilliance of 480,000 suns.

8/10″Scopes–125x: Messier 54 is the largest and most concentrated of the three globular clusters distributed along the base of Sagittarius' "Teapot." It has a diffuse 2′ diameter halo that contains an intense 1′ diameter core. Except for a few sparkles around its edges, the globular shows no resolution.

16/18″Scopes–175x: M54 is unresolved even in larger telescopes, showing only a granulation around the edges of its 3′ diameter halo. The core is bright but smooth. A 12th magnitude star is on the halo's SE edge.

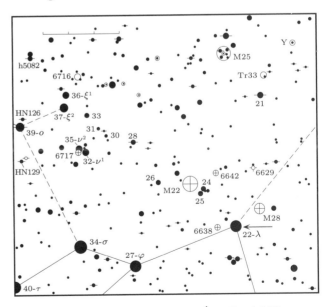

Finder Chart 56-6. 22–λ Sgr: 18ʰ27.9ᵐ −25° 25′

Figure 56-36. *Messier 55 (NGC6809) is an exquisite sight, resolving into hundreds of stars even with only medium-size telescopes. Image courtesy of Jim Burnell.*

NGC 6716   Open Cluster 20★   Tr Type IV 1p
φ 10′, m6.9v, Br★ 8.28v   18ʰ54.6ᵐ −19° 53′
Finder Chart 56-6   ★★★
12/14″ Scopes–125x: NGC 6716 is a loose, irregular group
of thirty 7th magnitude and fainter stars in a 10′×6′
NE–SW area. The cluster has two concentrations.
The SW concentration contains two brighter stars,
surrounded by a sprinkling of a dozen fainter members. The NE concentration is a circlet of faint stars,
the brighter of which are along its northern rim.

NGC 6717   Palomar 9   Globular Cluster   Class VIII
φ 3.9′, m9.2v   18ʰ55.1ᵐ −22° 42′
Finder Chart 56-6   ★★
12/14″ Scopes–150x: NGC 6717 lies 2′ south of magni-

tude 5.0 Nu-two (ν ²) Sagittarii, the glare of which
makes the relatively faint globular that much more
difficult to see. The cluster's 1′ diameter halo
sharply concentrates to a tiny, nearly stellar core.
A 13th magnitude star lies on the halo's WNW
edge, and a close double of 13th magnitude stars is
just outside the globular's NE periphery.

NGC 6723   Globular Cluster   Class VII
φ 11.0′, m7.2v   18ʰ59.6ᵐ −36° 38′
Finder Chart 56-5, Figure 56-21   ★★★★
8/10″ Scopes–125x: NGC 6723 is a fairly well resolved
globular cluster with a 4′ diameter halo containing
a broad, mildly concentrated core. A magnitude
10.5 field star is on the NE side of the halo.
12/14″ Scopes–150x: At moderate magnification NGC
6723 has a 6′ diameter halo that contains a uniformly concentrated 2′ diameter core. The cluster
is well resolved even across its core.

NGC 6809   Messier 55   Globular Cluster   Class XI
φ 19.0′, m6.4v   19ʰ40.0ᵐ −30° 58′
Finder Chart 56-8, Figure 56-36   ★★★★
4/6″ Scopes–75x: Messier 55 is a fine, bright, well
resolved globular cluster with a uniformly concentrated halo. Its outlying stars reach to a diameter
of 10′.
8/10″ Scopes–100x: This globular is an exquisite sight:
hundreds of resolved stars are spread evenly across
a 15′ diameter halo. A uniform spray of brighter
stars stands out, almost three-dimensionally,
against the myriad of fainter stars. Two jagged star
chains coming from the north and south edges join
10′ west of the cluster center. More peripheral stars
are visible to the north and south than to the east
and west.

NGC 6818   H51⁴   PK25−17.1   Planetary Nebula Type 4
φ 17″, m9.3v, CS15v   19ʰ44.0ᵐ −14° 09′
Finder Chart 56-7   ★★★★

Little Gem

8/10″ Scopes–225x: NGC 6818 has a bright bluish 15″
diameter disk with a slightly darker center. 12.5
magnitude stars lie 45″ NW and 1.25′ SW, and a
13.5 magnitude star 1′ ENE, of the planetary.
12/14″ Scopes–250x: The 20″×15″ N–S oval bluish disk
has a dark center, although the contrast between
the disk's brighter periphery and its fainter interior
is nowhere as distinct as in Messier 57 of Lyra. Very
faint segments of an outer halo can be glimpsed
beyond the edges of the long axis. An O-III filter
kills the bluish tint but enhances the sense of
annularity.

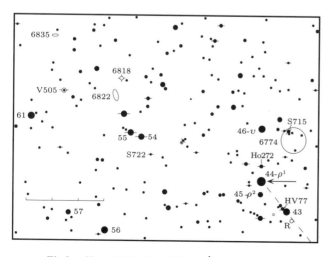

Finder Chart 56-7. 44–ρ ¹ Sgr: 19ʰ21.7ᵐ −17° 51′

Figure 56-37. *NGC 6822, an extremely faint glow in a rich star field, is a challenge even for large telescopes. Image courtesy of Chris Schur.*

Figure 56-38. *In medium-size telescopes globular cluster M75 (NGC 6864) resolves only around the periphery of its compact disk. Image courtesy of Josef Pöpsel and Stefan Binnewies.*

NGC 6822 Galaxy Type IB(s)m IV-V
φ 19.1′ × 14.9′, m8.8v, SB14.8   19ʰ44.9ᵐ −14° 48′
Finder Chart 56-7, Figure 56-37   ★
Barnard's Galaxy

16/18″ Scopes–100x: NGC 6822 is an irregular member of our Local Galaxy Group located about 2.2 million light years distant. Its absolute magnitude is a modest −15.4, a luminosity of just 200 million suns, and its true diameter is not much over 12,000 light years. Visually it is an extremely faint, extremely low surface brightness, ill defined glow in a field rich with faint stars. It needs no less than perfectly dark skies to be seen: nevertheless under good conditions it can be glimpsed even in mere 10×50 binoculars as a vague N–S smudge. At the Texas Star Party a larger telescope at 100x showed Barnard's Galaxy as a 12′ × 5′ N–S haze containing a NE–SW pair of brighter patches. The galaxy's meager glow tends to be camouflaged by the numerous foreground stars superimposed upon its halo.

NGC 6835 Galaxy Type Sb: sp
φ 2.2′ × 0.6′, m12.5v, SB12.7   19ʰ54.5ᵐ −12° 34′
Finder Chart 56-7, Figure 56-22   ★★★
12/14″ Scopes–125x: NGC 6835, located 3.25′ east of a 12th magnitude star, has a fairly faint 1.25′ × 1′ ENE–WSW halo containing a slight brightening at its center. 13th magnitude stars lie 1′ east and 1.5′ NE of the galaxy's center. NGC 6836 lies 7′ ESE.

NGC 6864 Messier 75 Globular Cluster Class I
φ 6′, m8.5v   20ʰ06.1ᵐ −21° 55′
Finder Chart 56-8, Figure 56-38   ★★★

M75 was probably first seen by Mechain in August, 1780, and confirmed by Messier two months later as "a nebula without star . . ." It lies about 59,000 light years distant.

8/10″ Scopes–125x: Messier 75 is a moderately faint globular cluster with a 2.5′ diameter halo that contains a bright core. A few stars can be resolved

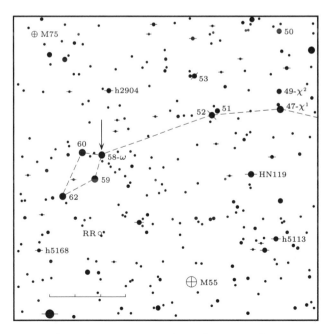

Finder Chart 56-8. 58–ω Sgr: 19ʰ55.8ᵐ −26° 18′

around the edges. A 12.5 magnitude star is 1.5′ SE of the cluster's center.

16/18″ Scopes–175x: Larger telescopes show a granular halo and resolve numerous stars around the halo's periphery. The outlying stars, rather uniformly distributed in all directions, bring the globular's full diameter to 5′. The core is well concentrated but remains unresolved.

Chapter 57

Scorpius, the Scorpion

57.1 Overview

In Greco-Roman mythology Scorpius represented the Scorpion sent to sting Orion in his heel. Some classical astronomers, to make a Zodiac that was completely animate (the word "zodiac," after all, came from the ancient Greek phrase meaning "circle of animals"), transformed Libra the Scales into the Claws of the Scorpion: Ptolemy, for example, in his *Almagest* of the mid-2nd century A.D., used Libra only in the astrological sections of his work, calling these stars the "Claws" in his purely astronomical chapters. Nevertheless the Greeks were thereby playing fast and loose with the constellations they had inherited from the Babylonians and Sumerians; for the celestial Scales is not only mentioned in Assyrian and Babylonian astronomical texts, it is actually illustrated on a Sumerian cylinder seal of about 2200 B.C.

The celestial Scorpion is every bit as venerable as the celestial Scales because its star-pattern actually does resemble the shape of a scorpion. The constellation is mentioned several times in a group of Mesopotamian tablets that have been dated to 2500 B.C.; and in ancient Mesopotamian art there are figures of scorpions and scorpion-men with starlike figures between their claws and within the curve of their tails. In Mesopotamian mythology scorpions were sacred to the fertility goddess Ishara. But the Sting of the Scorpion seems to have been sacred to the war-god Ninurta, represented in the stars of neighboring Sagittarius, for the star-pair Lambda (λ) and Upsilon (υ) Scorpii were identified with Ninurta's sacred weapons Sharur and Shargaz. (Late 19th century scholars incorrectly identified Theta Scorpii as Shargaz – hence its name Sargaz on many star charts.)

The star-pattern of Scorpius is not entirely an accident: most of the bright stars of the constellation are members of the sprawling Scorpio-Centaurus Association, a moving group that includes many of the brighter stars not only of Scorpius and Centaurus but also of Lupus and Crux. Antares is the only evolved red

Scorpius: SCORE-pee-us
Genitive: Scorpii, SCORE-pee-eye
Abbreviation: Sco
Culmination: 9 pm–July 18, midnight–June 3
Area: 497 square degrees
Showpieces: ξ Sco, β Sco, 14–ν Sco, M4 (NGC 6121), M6 (NGC 6405), M7 (NGC 6475),M80 (NGC 6093), NGC 6231
Binocular Objects: H16, M4 (NGC 6121), M6 (NGC 6405), M7 (NGC 6475),M80 (NGC 6093), NGC 6124, NGC 6178, NGC 6231, NGC 6242, NGC 6249, NGC 6281, NGC 6322, NGC 6383, NGC 6388, NGC 6400, NGC 6416, NGC 6441, NGC 6453, Tr 24, Tr 27, Tr 28, Tr 29, Tr 30

supergiant in the association: all its other bright members are B0, B1, B2, and B3 main sequence, subgiant, and giant stars. Many of the bright Scorpio-Centaurus members are attractive double and multiple stars: in Scorpius these include Antares, Beta (β), Mu (μ), and Nu (ν) Scorpii. In the Antares region are also some bright and dark nebulae involved with the NE end of the Scorpio-Centaurus Association.

Scorpius not only is a Milky Way constellation, it lies in the general direction of the center of our Galaxy, which is toward a spot near the Sagittarius/Scorpius border 4° WNW of Gamma (γ) Sagittarii due north of the Sting of the Scorpion. Because we lie on the interior edge of our Orion-Cygnus Spiral Arm – the Scorpio-Centaurus Association can be taken to mark the very inner edge of the Arm – we look through the Scorpio-Centaurus Association across an interarm gap at the next spiral arm toward the interior of our Galaxy, the Sagittarius-Carina Spiral Arm. Most of the numerous open clusters around the Tail of the Scorpion are embedded in the Scorpio-Centaurus Spiral Arm. A major Sagittarius-Carina Arm tracer is the magnificent open cluster NGC 6231, a beautiful object in any size

Scorpius, the Scorpion

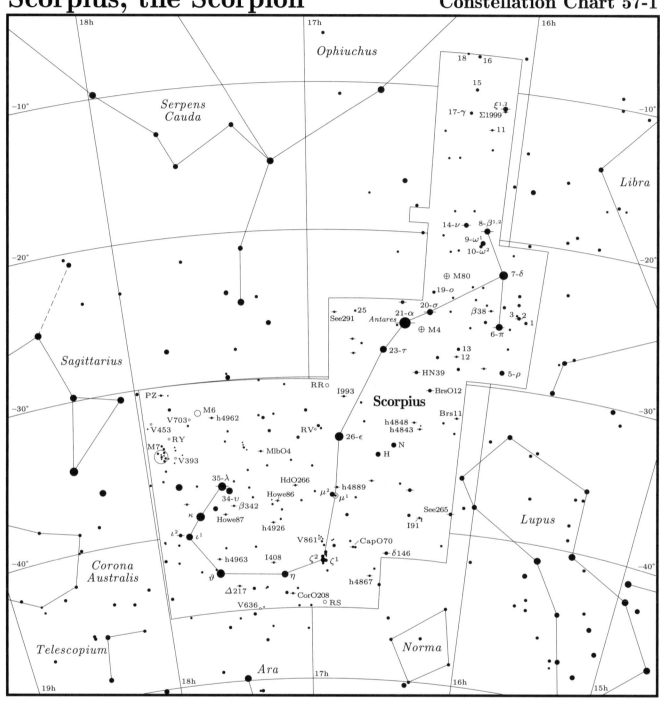

Ophiuchus

Serpens
Cauda

−10°

18h   17h   16h

18   16

15

17-γ   ξ¹·²
Σ1999

11

Libra

14-ν   8-β¹·²
9-ω¹
10-ω²

−20°

⊕ M80   7-δ
19-o

See291   25
Antares   21-α   20-σ   β38   3 · 2 · 1
⊕ M4   6-π

23-τ   13
12

HN39   5-ρ

RR○   I993   BrsO12

Scorpius

Brs11

Sagittarius

−30°

PZ

V703○   M6○   h4962   h4848
h4843

V453   RV○   26-ε   N
M7   RY   H

V393   MlbO4

35-λ   HdO266   μ²   h4889
Howe86   μ¹
34-υ   β342

κ   Howe87   See265
ι²   ι¹   h4926   I91

Lupus

V861   CapO70
h4963   I408   ζ²   ζ¹   δ146
−40°   ϑ   η
Δ217   h4867
CorO208
Corona   V636○   RS○
Australis

Telescopium

Norma

Ara   17h   16h

19h   18h   15h

−30°

−40°

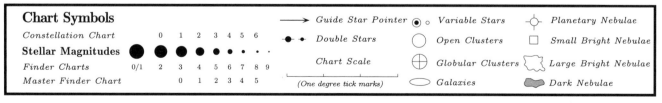

Table 57-1: Selected Variable Stars in Scorpius

Name	HD No.	Type	Max.	Min.	Period (Days)	F*	Spec. Type	R.A. (2000)	Dec.	Finder Chart No.	Notes
μ^1 Sco	151890	EB	2.80	3.08	1.44		B1.5-B6.5	$16^h51.9^m$	$-38°\,03'$	57-4	
RS Sco	152476	M	6.2	13.0	320		M5-M8	55.6	$-45\,06$	57-4	
RR Sco	152783	M	5.0	12.4	279	0.47	M6-M8	56.6	$-30\,35$	57-1	
V861	152667	EB	6.07	6.69	7.82		B0.5	56.6	$-40\,49$	57-4	In Tr24 (H12)
RV Sco	153004	Cδ	6.61	7.49	6.06	0.30	F5-G1	58.3	$-33\,37$	57-1	
V636	156979	Cδ	6.04	6.94	6.79	0.34	G5	$17^h22.8^m$	$-45\,37$	57-5	
V703	160589	δ Sct	7.28	8.50	0.11	0.40	F0-F5	42.3	$-32\,31$	57-6	
V393	161741	ES	7.7	8.6	7.71	0.12	B9	48.8	$-35\,03$	57-6	
RY Sco	162102	C'	7.52	8.44	20.31	0.37	F6-G2	50.9	$-33\,42$	57-6	
V453	163181	EB	6.36	6.73	12.00		B0.5	56.3	$-32\,29$	57-6	

F* = The fraction of period taken up by the star's rise from min. to max. brightness, or the period spent in eclipse.

Table 57-2: Selected Double Stars in Scorpius

Name	ADS No.	Pair	M1	M2	Sep.′	P.A.°	Spec	R.A. (2000)	Dec	Finder Chart No.	Notes
2 Sco	9823		4.7	7.4	2.5	274	B3	$15^h53.6^m$	$-25°\,20'$	57-3	Bluish-white
β 38	9899		7.4	9.4	4.4	348	A0	$16^h02.9^m$	$-25\,01$	57-3	
ξ Sco	9909	AB	4.8	5.1	0.5	61	F8	04.4	$-11\,22$	57-1	Bright yellow pair
	9909	AC		7.3	7.6	51					C: bluish. Σ1999 in field
Σ1999	9910	AB	7.4	8.1	11.6	99	K0	04.0	$-11\,27$	57-1	Deep yellow pair
8–$\beta^{1,2}$ Sco	9913	AC	2.6	4.9	13.6	21	B1	05.4	$-19\,48$	57-3	White and pale blue
11 Sco	9924		5.6	9.9	3.3	257	A0	07.6	$-12\,45$	57-1	
Brs 11			6.7	7.4	7.8	85	G5	09.5	$-32\,39$	57-1	Fine yellow pair
14–ν Sco	9951	AB	4.3	6.8	0.9	3	B3	12.0	$-19\,28$	57-3	Double-double
(HV6)	9951	AC		6.4	41.4	337					
	9951	CD		7.8	2.3	51	A				
12 Sco	9953		5.9	7.9	4.0	73	B9	12.3	$-28\,25$	57-3	Bluish pair
BrsO 12			5.4	6.9	22.8	320	F5 F8	19.5	$-30\,54$	57-1	
I91			6.1	10.1	15.1	293	A0	20.5	$-39\,26$	57-4	
20–σ Sco	10009		2.9	8.5	20.0	273	B1	21.2	$-25\,36$	57-3	Bluish-white and white
h4843			7.3	11.8	12.4	267	F5	21.4	$-33\,18$	57-1	
h4848		AB	7.1	7.6	6.2	153	A0	23.9	$-33\,12$	57-1	
		AC		9.0	92.0	357					
HN39	10035		5.9	6.6	5.4	354	G0 G0	24.7	$-29\,42$	57-1	
21–α Sco	10074		1.2	5.4	2.9	275	M1 B3	29.4	$-26\,26$	57-3	Reddish-orange and green
δ 146		AB	5.5	12.5	8.6	131	B1	31.7	$-41\,49$	57-4	
Δ 202		AC		9.8	58.0	180					
h4867			5.9	9.1	16.3	294	B3	38.4	$-43\,24$	57-4	
CapO 70			6.2	6.3	95.7	258	B8 A3	43.9	$-41\,07$	57-4	
I993			6.7	11.2	3.6	99	K0	49.6	$-31\,39$	57-1	
h4889			6.2	8.3	6.7	5	B9	51.0	$-37\,31$	57-4	
See 291			6.9	11.0	2.7	2	A0	52.3	$-25\,36$	57-1	
HdO 266		AB	6.0	11.4	5.9	86	A2	$17^h06.3^m$	$-37\,14$	57-6	
CorO 208			7.2	9.3	5.1	139	A0	07.4	$-44\,27$	57-5	
Howe 86			7.0	8.8	2.8	143	F5	13.9	$-38\,18$	57-5	Yellow and reddish
h4926		AB	6.3	10.5	14.4	334	K5	14.5	$-39\,46$	57-5	Reddish-orange and white
		AC		11.3	16.9	210					C: White
I408			7.0	9.0	1.7	168	B5	16.3	$-42\,20$	57-5	
MlbO 4		AB	6.1	7.6	2.0	271	K2	19.0	$-34\,59$	57-6	Close orange pair
		AC		10.0	30.8	136					
Δ 217			6.3	8.7	13.4	169	B9	29.0	$-43\,58$	57-5	
β 342			7.0	7.3	0.4	85	A2	29.4	$-38\,31$	57-5	
Howe 87			7.5	8.8	3.1	232	F8	31.3	$-39\,01$	57-5	
h4962			5.7	10.5	5.4	102	O5	34.7	$-32\,35$	57-6	In NGC6383
(Ho647)		AC		10.5	13.3	83					
h4963			8.0	10.5	6.9	312	K2	36.7	$-41\,56$	57-5	
ι^2 Sco			4.8	10.9	32.6	37	A3	50.2	$-40\,05$	57-5	
Pz			6.8	8.2	10.1	190	A0	51.2	$-30\,33$	57-6	

Footnotes: *= Year 2000, a = Near apogee, c = Closing, w = Widening. Finder Chart No: All stars listed in the tables are plotted in the large Constellation Chart, but when a star appears in a Finder Chart, this number is listed. Notes: When colors are subtle, the suffix *-ish* is used, e.g. *bluish*.

astronomical instrument and one of the richest aggregations of super-hot, super-luminous O-type and Wolf-Rayet stars anywhere along the Milky Way. Because our Galaxy's family of perhaps 200 globular clusters is concentrated toward the interior of the Galaxy, Scorpius (as well as neighboring Sagittarius and Ophiuchus) is rich in globulars, two of them, M4 and M80, being Messier objects.

57.2 Interesting Stars

Xi (ξ) Scorpii = Σ1998 Triple Star   Spec. F8
AB: m4.8, 5.1; Sep. 0.5″; P.A. 61°
AC: 7.3; Sep. 7.6″; P.A. 51°   16ʰ04.4ᵐ −11° 22′
Constellation Chart 57-1   ★★★★
8/10″ Scopes–200x: Xi Scorpii AB is a good test for medium and large telescopes, its close, nearly equal bright yellow components only 0.5″ apart. The C component, a bluish star 7.6″ from the primary, can be resolved even in small telescopes. In the same field of view with Xi Scorpii is the double Struve 1999, a deep yellow pair of magnitude 7.4 and 8.1 stars separated comfortably 11.6″ apart in position angle 99°.

Beta (β) = 8 Scorpii (HIII7) Double Star   Spec. B1
AC: m2.6, 4.9; Sep. 13.6″; P.A. 21°   16ʰ05.4ᵐ −19° 48′
Finder Chart 57-3   ★★★★
4/6″ Scopes–100x: A fine double for small telescopes, Beta Scorpii consists of a brilliant blue-white primary with a pale blue companion. The system's B component, a magnitude 10.3 star, is a mere 0.5″ from the primary and therefore cannot be split even with large amateur telescopes.

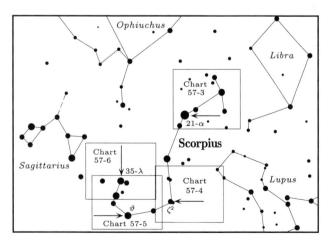

Master Finder Chart 57-2. Scorpius Chart Areas
Guide stars indicated by arrows.

Nu (ν) = 14 Scorpii Double-Double   Spec. B3
AB: m4.3, 6.8; Sep. 0.9″; P.A. 03°
CD: m6.4, 7.8; Sep. 2.3″; P.A. 51°   16ʰ12.0ᵐ −19° 28′
Finder Chart 57-3   ★★★★
8/10″ Scopes–200x: When air currents are steady, the AB pair appears as two white disks in contact: under poor atmospheric conditions it is just one oblong blob. The CD pair is less challenging, its two yellowish stars lying 2.3″ apart. The AB and CD pairs are separated by 44″ in a NNW–SSE direction.

12 Scorpii = h4839 Double Star   Spec. B9
m5.9, 7.9; Sep. 4.0″; P.A. 73°   16ʰ12.3ᵐ −28° 25′
Finder Chart 57-3   ★★★★
4/6″ Scopes–125x: 12 Scorpii is close but separates nicely in small telescopes. The colors are subtle, some observers seeing the stars as bluish and others as greenish.

Alpha (α) Scorpii Double Star   Spec. M1, B3
m1.2, 5.4; Sep. 2.9″; P.A. 275°   16ʰ29.4ᵐ −26° 26′
Finder Chart 57-3   Antares   ★★★★
The Greek name Antares is a combination of *anti* = against + Aries, the Greek name for Mars, the god of war. Antares was compared to Mars because of its red color: hence the name Antares, the "rival of Mars." The Romans called the star Cor Scorpionis, meaning "Heart of the Scorpion." However, they had been anticipated in this by the Assyrians, Babylonians, and Sumerians, who for at least two millennia had also known the star as the Heart of the Scorpion. Antares is the fifteenth brightest star in the sky. Of the 22 first magnitude stars Antares and Betelgeuse are the only red M-type supergiants. Both, like all M-type supergiants, are variable, Antares is less so than Betelgeuse: its range is between magnitudes 0.86 and 1.06, and its period is irregular. Antares is about 520 light years from us and has an absolute magnitude of −5.1, a luminosity of 9,900 suns.
8/10″ Scopes–250x: Antares is difficult to split because of the primary's brilliance. But even when not resolved, the companion can be detected as a greenish spike that contrasts nicely with the reddish-orange glare of Antares' airy disk. Several times we have split Antares at twilight when the air is normally at its steadiest and the background sky-glow prevents the primary's glare from being as overwhelming.
16/18″ Scopes–300x: On those rare nights when conditions are perfect, Antares is one of the most beautiful of all doubles. A tiny emerald point touches the edge of a brilliant reddish-orange disk.

Figure 57-1. *Dark nebula Bernes 149, located near the Lupus border, stretches a degree east of the colorful yellowish and reddish double star Dunlop 199. Martin C. Germano made a 60 minute exposure on 2415 film with an 8″, f5 Newtonian.*

57.3 Deep-Sky Objects

Bernes 149 Dark Nebula
φ 60′ × 12′, Opacity 6   16^h09.4^m −39° 08′
Finder Chart 57-4, Figure 57-1   ★★★

8/10″ Scopes–75x: Bernes 149 is near the Lupus border 2.25° ESE of magnitude 3.4 Eta (η) Lupi. It is an irregular, dark streak in the star field a degree long but only 12′ wide. The most distinct portion of the dust cloud is directly east of Dunlop 199, a wide, easy double of yellowish and reddish stars (AC: 6.9, 7.1; 44.1″; 184°). A branch of the nebula extends SW from the double.

NGC 6072 PK342+10.1 Planetary Nebula Type 3a
φ 40″, m11.7v, CS18.47:   16^h13.0^m −36° 14′
Finder Chart 57-4, Figure 57-4   ★★★★

8/10″ Scopes–150x: NGC 6072 is a fairly bright planetary nebula with a 50″ diameter disk of uniform surface brightness.

16/18″ Scopes–175x: The 60″ diameter disk seems slightly elongated N–S and has diffuse edges and a light green color. An O-III filter shows a slight central darkening. A 13th magnitude star is just within the NE edge of the disk. 11th magnitude stars are 2.25′ and 3.5′ WNW of the planetary.

NGC 6093 Messier 80 Globular Cluster Class II
φ 8.9′, m7.3v   16^h17.0^m −22° 59′
Finder Chart 57-3, Figure 57-2   ★★★★★

M80 was discovered by Charles Messier who observed it on January 4, 1781, three weeks earlier than his friendly rival Mechain. The cluster is about 28,000 light years distant, four times farther than M4.

4/6″ Scopes–100x: Messier 80 is 4.2° NNW of magnitude

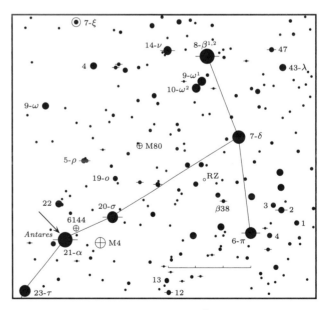

Finder Chart 57-3. 21–α Sco: 16^h29.4^m −26° 26′

Figure 57-2. *Messier 80 (NGC 6093) is a well resolved sphere of stars with a bright core. Image courtesy of Martin C. Germano.*

Figure 57-3. *Messier 4 (NGC 6121) is visible to the naked eye, and even in small telescopes becomes an impressive mass of glittering stars. Image courtesy of Jim Burnell.*

1.0 Antares (α = 21 Scorpii) and 4.5′ SSE of magnitude 2.6 Beta (β) = 8 Scorpii. It is a round, bright but unresolved 4′ diameter disk of haze. Immediately to the globular's NE is a magnitude 8.5 field star.

12/14″ Scopes–150x: Medium-size instruments show a well resolved 6′ diameter disk. The more prominent outliers fall along curved strings on the globular's northern and western edges. An E–W row of widely spaced stars passes along the southern edge.

NGC 6121 Messier 4 Globular Cluster Class IX
ϕ 26.3′, m5.8v $16^h23.6^m -26° 32′$
Finder Chart 57-3, Figure 57-3   ★★★★★

Discovery of Messier 4 is credited to de Cheseaux in 1746. It is estimated to be only 6,500 light years distant from us and therefore might well be the nearest globular to the Earth – though NGC 6397 in Ara and NGC 6366 in Ophiuchus, both thought to be 7,800 light years away are possible pretenders to the honor. M4 is decidedly below average in luminosity for a globular cluster, its absolute magnitude of -6.8 corresponding to a modest luminosity of 44,000 suns.

4/6″ Scopes–100x: Messier 4, visible to the unaided eye, forms a triangle with magnitude 1.0 Antares (α = 21 Scorpii) 1.25′ to its east and magnitude 2.9 Sigma (σ) = 20 Scorpii to its NW. It has a large, loosely concentrated 12′ diameter halo. The stars are irregularly distributed, but a few clumps of brighter stars stand out.

8/10″ Scopes–150x: Super! Messier 4 is a bright mass of glittering stars. Its many jagged star chains extend out to a diameter of 16′. The core is bright, though less concentrated than those of other globular clusters, and well resolved. A prominent lane of brighter stars runs N–S through the cluster center. Several other chains and clumps stand out against the profuse background of faint pinpoints, giving a 3-D effect. The field north and south of the globular's extreme outliers contains brighter stars.

NGC 6124 Cr 301 Open Cluster 100★ Tr Type I3r
ϕ 29′, m5.8:v, Br★ 8.67v $16^h25.6^m -40° 40′$
Finder Chart 57-4, Figure 57-5   ★★★★

8/10″ Scopes–75x: NGC 6124 is a bright, rich cluster of seventy-five 9th to 12th magnitude stars irregularly distributed over a 35′ area. The most concentrated part of the cluster, with the majority of its brighter members, is SW of its center and contains several dozen stars in a 10′ area.

12/14″ Scopes–100x: At 100x the cluster fills the field of view. Of the hundred stars visible, some two dozen are 9th and 10th magnitude objects bunched in conspicuous pairs and short rows. 10′ SE of the cluster center is a 20″ wide E–W pair of 10th magnitude stars. On the group's WNW edge is a wide equilateral triangle of brighter stars.

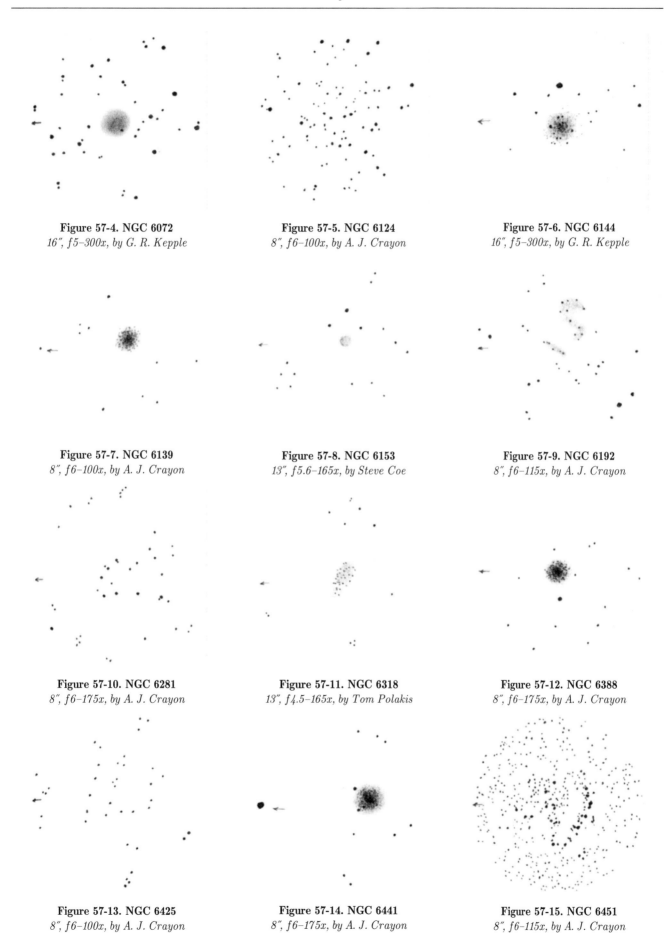

Figure 57-4. NGC 6072
16″, f5–300x, by G. R. Kepple

Figure 57-5. NGC 6124
8″, f6–100x, by A. J. Crayon

Figure 57-6. NGC 6144
16″, f5–300x, by G. R. Kepple

Figure 57-7. NGC 6139
8″, f6–100x, by A. J. Crayon

Figure 57-8. NGC 6153
13″, f5.6–165x, by Steve Coe

Figure 57-9. NGC 6192
8″, f6–115x, by A. J. Crayon

Figure 57-10. NGC 6281
8″, f6–175x, by A. J. Crayon

Figure 57-11. NGC 6318
13″, f4.5–165x, by Tom Polakis

Figure 57-12. NGC 6388
8″, f6–175x, by A. J. Crayon

Figure 57-13. NGC 6425
8″, f6–100x, by A. J. Crayon

Figure 57-14. NGC 6441
8″, f6–175x, by A. J. Crayon

Figure 57-15. NGC 6451
8″, f6–115x, by A. J. Crayon

NGC 6144 H10⁶ Globular Cluster Class XI
φ 9.3′, m9.0v   16ʰ27.3ᵐ −26° 02′
Finder Chart 57-3, Figure 57-6   ★★
8/10″Scopes–125x: NGC 6144 lies only 40′ NW of
   Antares (α = 21 Scorpii). This fairly faint globular
   cluster has an evenly concentrated 3′ diameter halo,
   a few stars resolved around its periphery. A 12th
   magnitude field star is on the west edge of the halo.
   The star field to the north is noticeably sparse.
16/18″Scopes–150x: This globular's soft glow dramatically contrasts with the stark hard orange rays of
   Antares to the SE. The 4′ diameter halo has a
   slightly brighter center. A dozen stars can be
   resolved around the halo. Outlying cluster members
   can be traced out 3′ from the globular's center.

NGC 6139 Δ536 Globular Cluster Class II
φ 5.5′, m8.9v   16ʰ27.7ᵐ −38° 51′
Finder Chart 57-4, Figure 57-7   ★★
8/10″Scopes–125x: NGC 6139 has a fairly bright, diffuse
   2′ diameter halo that contains a brighter central
   area.
16/18″Scopes–175x: The 3′ diameter halo contains a
   moderately concentrated core with a faint stellar
   nucleus. The halo has a granular texture, and in
   moments of good seeing a few stars can be resolved.

NGC 6153 PK341+5.1 Planetary Nebula Type 4
φ 25″, m10.9v, CS15.39v   16ʰ31.5ᵐ −40° 15′
Finder Chart 57-4, Figure 57-8   ★★★★
8/10″Scopes–200x: NGC 6153 is at the southern corner

of a diamond-shaped asterism with three 10th
magnitude stars. The figure is reminiscent of the
body of Delphinus. The planetary has a fairly bright,
circular 20″ diameter disk.
16/18″Scopes–250x: The disk has a greenish tint. With
   averted vision a slightly darker center is suspected.
   The O-III filter does not support this impression
   but shows a well defined 25″ disk.

NGC 6178 Cr308 Open Cluster 12★ Tr Type III3p
φ 4′, m7.2v, Br★ 8.41v   16ʰ35.7ᵐ −45° 38′
Finder Chart 57-4   ★★★
12/14″Scopes–125x: NGC 6178 contains a dozen stars
   in a 5′ area scattered around the northernmost of
   two 8.5 magnitude stars. Near the east edge of the
   cluster is a 12″ wide E–W pair of 10th and 12th
   magnitude stars.

NGC 6192 Cr309 Open Cluster 60★ Tr Type I2r
φ 7′, m8.5p, Br★ 11.0p   16ʰ40.3ᵐ −43° 22′
Finder Chart 57-4, Figure 57-9   ★★★
8/10″Scopes–100x: NGC 6192 is an attractive cluster
   of three dozen 11th to 14th magnitude stars grouped
   into three or four irregular clumps, the southernmost of which is an S-shaped formation.
12/14″Scopes–125x: This cluster has forty stars in a 10′
   area, the majority in a zone half that large. The
   stars are distributed in chains, small clumps, and
   pairs with large gaps between. NW and NNW of
   the cluster center are two NE–SW star strings.

NGC 6216=6222? Open Cluster 35★ Tr Type II2p
φ 4.0′, m10.2p   16ʰ49.4ᵐ −44° 44′
Finder Chart 57-4   ★★
12/14″Scopes–125x: At low power NGC 6216 is merely
   a hazy patch: 125x is required to resolve two dozen
   12th magnitude and fainter stars against a hazy 5′
   diameter background.

NGC 6231 Cr315 Open Cluster Tr Type I3p
φ 14′, m2.6v, Br★ 4.71v   16ʰ54.0ᵐ −41° 48′
Finder Chart 57-4, Figure 57-16   ★★★★★
   The compact NGC 6231 is one of the most beautiful
and interesting open clusters in the sky. It is about 2.5
magnitudes brighter than the NGC 869 and NGC 884
components of the Perseus Double Cluster, and only 1.4
magnitudes fainter than the Pleiades. And it is intrinsically bright as well: it is about 6,200 light years away
and has an absolute magnitude of −10.2, a luminosity
of one million suns! NGC 6231 is about as luminous as
the most brilliant globular cluster of our Galaxy, the

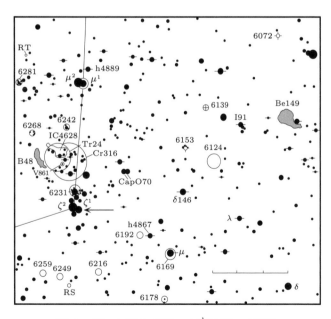

Finder Chart 57-4. ζ ² Sco: 16ʰ54.6ᵐ −42° 22′

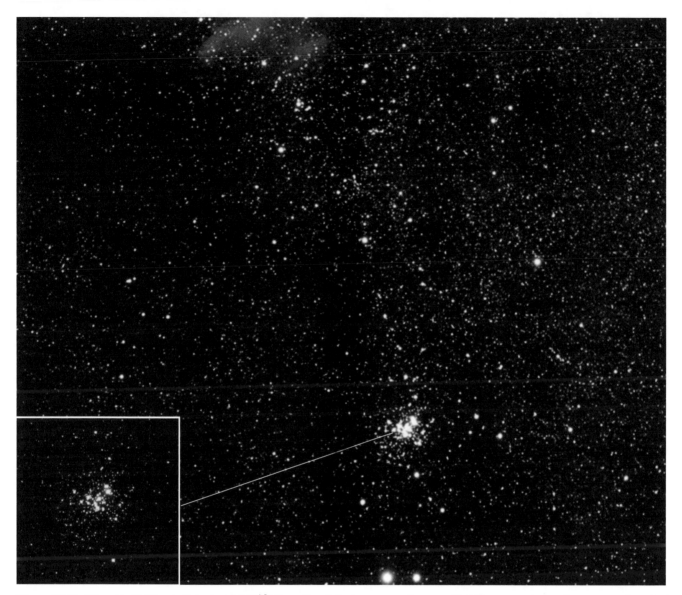

Figure 57-16. *The wide E–W pair Zeta-1 and 2 ($\zeta^{1,2}$) Scorpii and the large open clusters of bright stars to the north appear to the naked eye as a false comet. The Zeta pair is the "comet's" head or nucleus, and (from south to north) the compact NGC 6231 and the wider Collinder 316 and Trumpler 24 spread out as the "comet's" tail. Wide field image coursesy of Robert Reeves. The insert of open cluster NGC 6231 is courtesy of Tim Hunter and James McGaha.*

Great Omega Centauri, which has an absolute magnitude of −10.3. NGC 6231 is not, however, anywhere near as populous as Omega Centauri: the reason for its great luminosity is the brilliance of its individual stars – extremely hot, extremely luminous B0 and O-type giants and supergiants. The cluster also includes two of the rare Wolf-Rayet stars, objects with explosively expanding envelopes driven outward by the star's great radiation pressure and stellar winds. Zeta-1 (ζ^1) Scorpii is thought to be an outlying cluster member; it is a B1.5 Ia extreme supergiant with an absolute magnitude of −8.8, a luminosity of 276,000 suns. NGC 6231 is the core of the Scorpius OB1 association, which includes

the star fields of Collinder 316 and Trumpler 24 to the north.

4/6" Scopes–50x: NGC 6231 is less than a degree north of magnitude 4.8 Zeta-1 (ζ^1) and magnitude 3.6 Zeta-2 (ζ^2) Scorpii in a glorious N–S field of bright stars often called the "false comet." To the naked eye Zeta-1 and Zeta-2 form the "comet's" nucleus and the star clusters NGC 6231, Collinder 316, and Trumpler 24 fan out to the north as its tail. NGC 6231, a fine cluster for binoculars and small telescopes, is a compact, rich clump of bright stars. 50x shows eight 7th and 8th magnitude and fifty fainter stars. To the west of the cluster is a 1′ wide NE–

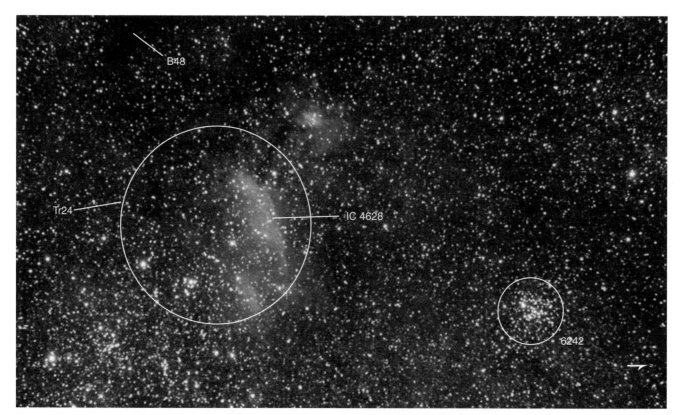

Figure 57-17. *The emission nebulae IC4628 arcs along the NE perimeter of open cluster Trumpler 24. A portion of dark nebula Barnard 48 is visible in the upper left of the field while open cluster NGC 6242 is obvious at the lower right. Image courtesy of Nicola Monteschiari.*

SW pair of magnitude 5.5 and 7.5 stars. To the south, between the cluster and the two Zeta stars, is a triangle of 4th, 5th and 6th magnitude stars. Trumpler 24 and Collinder 316, centered a degree NNE, form one huge merged sprawling cluster larger than the Pleiades in Taurus.

8/10″Scopes–75x: This fabulous cluster concentrates over a hundred stars in a 10′ area with a few dozen more out to a diameter of 15′. Many of the members are in attractive triangles and short rows. South of the cluster a rich star stream trails toward the northern corner of a triangle of bright stars. Many of the stars in the region are brilliantly colored, especially in blues, yellows, and oranges. An O-III or UHC brings out the faint nebulosity in which some of the cluster stars are embedded.

NGC 6242 Cr 317 Open Cluster Tr Type I 3m
φ 9′, m6.4v, Br★ 7.28v   16ʰ55.6ᵐ −39° 30′
Finder Chart 57-4   ★★★★
8/10″Scopes–100x: NGC 6242 is a bright cluster of fifty stars in a 10′ area. The brightest member, a magnitude 7.3 star, is at the SE corner of the triangle it forms with the group's two next brightest stars. The cluster has about a dozen 8th and 9th magnitude stars, but its remaining members are much fainter.

Trumpler 24 Harvard 12 Open Cl. 00★ Tr Type IV 2pn
φ 60′, m8.6p   16ʰ57.0ᵐ −40° 40′

IC 4628 Gum 56 Emission Nebula
φ 90′ × 60′, Photo Br 2-5, Color 2-4 16ʰ57.0ᵐ −40° 20′

Barnard 48 Dark Nebula
φ 40′ × 40′, Opacity 5   17ʰ01.0ᵐ −40° 47′
Finder Chart 57-4, Figures 57-16, 57-17   ★★★★/★★/★★★
7×50 Binoculars: Trumpler 24 is a scattered group of bright stars spread over an area one degree across. In *Uranometria 2000.0* Trumpler 24 is shown as the eastern portion of the even larger open cluster Collinder 316; but visually, the two groups appear as one huge cluster. And in fact they are simply the core of the major stellar association, Scorpius OB1, to which belongs the compact open cluster NGC 6231 south of Tr 24 + Cr 316. The outline of the Tr 24 + Cr 316 composite group is roughly triangular, a 7th magnitude star at its southern corner and a loose, jagged NE–SW star-stream forming its NW side. The stars are irregularly distributed in clumps and chains: the densest clump is near the NE corner of the cluster; a curved star chain convex to the north runs NW–SE through the southern part of the cluster from east to north of the 7th magnitude star; and a loose stellar grouping is

near the NW corner of the cluster's triangle. Even in binoculars over fifty cluster members can be counted against the profuse background of faint Milky Way stars. Half a degree east of Tr 24 is the dark nebula Barnard 48, a 40″ × 15″ NE–SW starless streak. NGC 6231 is a bright, dense knot to the south. Farther south is a brilliant triangle of stars that includes magnitudes 4.8 and 3.6 Zeta 1 and 2 Scorpii.

4/6″Scopes–50x: Low power shows more than a hundred stars irregularly broadcast over a 1.5′ field. The brighter members are clumped into small groups along the northern edge. A few more bright stars form pairs and triplets in the southern part of the cluster. A conspicuous ESE–WNW star chain runs from east to north of the 7th magnitude star at the southern corner of the group. A second star chain extends south from the 7th magnitude star to cluster NGC 6231. An O-III filter brings out IC 4628, a 30′ × 15′ E–W patch of faint nebula glow in the NE part of Tr 24. A degree east of the center of IC 4628 is the dust cloud Barnard 48, a dark 30′ × 10′ NE–SW streak.

NGC 6249 Cr 319 Open Cluster 30★ Tr Type II2m
φ 6′, m8.2v, Br★ 9.78v   16ʰ57.6ᵐ −44° 47′
Finder Chart 57-4   ★★★

8/10″Scopes–100x: NGC 6249 is a coarse group of fifteen 9th to 12th magnitude stars in a 6′ area. The more prominent members form a parallelogram, the other cluster stars trailing to the north and east.

NGC 6259 Cr 322 Open Cluster 120★ Tr Type II2r
φ 8′, m8.0v, Br★ 11.64v   17ʰ00.7ᵐ −44° 40′
Finder Chart 57-4   ★★★★

8/10″Scopes–100x: NGC 6259, located 17′ NNE of a 5th magnitude star, is a patch of a hundred 12th magnitude and fainter stars evenly distributed over a 16′ × 12′ E–W area. The uniformity of the star distribution is reminiscent of NGC 7789 in Cassiopeia or Messier 11 in Scutum. However, the cluster also has a few star chains intermingled with dark starless lanes.

NGC 6268 Cr 323 Open Cluster   Tr Type II2p
φ 6′, m9.5p   17ʰ02.4ᵐ −39° 44′
Finder Chart 57-4   ★★★

8/10″Scopes–100x: NGC 6268 is a moderately rich knot of two dozen 9th to 12th magnitude stars in a 7′ area. The stars are in two parallel NE–SW streams divided by a starless lane. The northern stream is the more concentrated of the two.

Figure 57-18. *Barnard 50, located 25′ SW of a 5th magnitude star, appears as a conspicuous "hole" in the Milky Way. Martin C. Germano made this 65 minute exposure on hypered 2415 film with an 8″, f5 Newtonian reflector.*

12/14″Scopes–125x: Three dozen 9th to 13th magnitude stars are visible in a 9′ area, the brighter members forming 5′ long chains in the cluster's northern section. A starless gap separates these chains from a rich patch of a dozen stars on the cluster's south edge. Outliers are scattered to the north of the chains.

Barnard 50 SL 30 Dark Nebula
φ 15′, Opacity 6   17ʰ02.9ᵐ −34° 24′

Barnard 53 SL 32 Dark Nebula
φ 30′ × 10′, Opacity 4   17ʰ06.1ᵐ −33° 35′
Finder Chart 57-6, Figure 57-18   ★★★★/★★★

8/10″Scopes–75x: Barnard 50, located 2.5° east of magnitude 2.3 Epsilon (ε) = 26 Scorpii and 25′ SW of a 5th magnitude star, appears as a "hole" in a particularly star-rich Milky Way field. It is darkest in an 8′ circular area on its SE side, from which vague wings extend north and west into the star field. A 10th magnitude foreground star is superimposed upon B50 in the north central part of the darkest zone, and two more 10th magnitude stars are on its eastern edge. To the NE of B50 are many small, dark dust clouds like it in appearance. One of the larger of these, half a degree NNE of a 5th magnitude star, is Barnard 53, a 30′ long N–S, boomerang-shaped dark area concave to the east. B53 is not as opaque as B50.

Figure 57-19. *Barnard 55 and 56 (left to right), typical of the many dark nebulae in the area, appear as two spots in the Milky Way. Martin C. Germano made this 60 minute exposure on 2415 film with an 8″, f5 Newtonian reflector.*

Figure 57-20. *The planetary NGC 6302 has been named the Bug Nebula because of the pinched appearance of its halo. Image courtesy of Steven Juchnowski.*

NGC 6281 Cr 324 Open Cluster Tr Type II 2p
φ 8′, m5.4v, Br★ 7.94v   17ʰ04.8ᵐ −37° 54′
Finder Chart 57-5, Figure 57-10   ★★★
*8/10″Scopes-100x:*NGC 6281 is a loose, irregular group
   of two dozen stars in a 7′ area. The brighter stars,
   magnitude 8 to 9.5 objects, fall along two slightly
   curved strings oriented E–W and NW–SE, that
   meet on the west side of the cluster to form a "V"
   open to the SE. The group's fainter, magnitude 11–
   12, stars spread from within the mouth of the V to
   the SE.

12/14″Scopes-125x: This cluster has three dozen stars
   in an 8′ wide triangular formation, the brighter
   members along the northern and SW sides of the
   triangle. The cluster has no central compression
   and its stars are not distributed in clumps. The
   group's lucida, a magnitude 7.9 object, is at the
   east end of the chain of stars that defines the
   northern side of the cluster triangle. The lucida has
   a magnitude 10.5 companion 7″ to its NNW.

Barnard 55 LDN 1682 Dark Nebula
φ 16′, Opacity 5   17ʰ06.6ᵐ −32° 00′

Barnard 56 LDN 1682 Dark Nebula
φ 3′, Opacity 5   17ʰ09.1ᵐ −32° 06′
Finder Chart 57-6, Figure 57-19   ★★★★/★★★★
8/10″Scopes-75x: The two small dark dust clouds
   Barnard 55 and Barnard 56 are 4.5° NE of magnitude 2.3 Epsilon (ε) = 26 Scorpii. B55, the western
   cloud, is an irregular 16′ × 5′ N–S dark patch with
   a 9th magnitude foreground star superimposed near
   its center. Its SE edge is its most distinct. Barnard
   56, 17′ east of B55, is much smaller, a 3′ circle, with
   9th and 10th magnitude stars on its west and SSW
   edges, respectively.

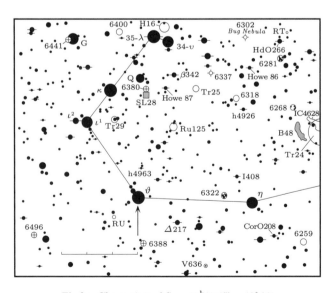

Finder Chart 57-5. *ϑ Sco: 17ʰ37.3ᵐ −43° 00′*

NGC 6302 PK349+1.1 Planetary Nebula Type 6
φ 50″, m9.6v, CS 21.1   17ʰ13.7ᵐ −37° 06′
Finder Chart 57-5, Figure 57-20   ★★★★
                    Bug Nebula
8/10″Scopes-175x: NGC 6302 is a visually interesting
   planetary with a bright central area flanked by faint

Figure 57-21. *NGC 6334, "The Cat's Paw" is complex emission nebula divided by four dark lanes surrounding a central cometary-shaped hub. Image courtesy of Robert Reeves.*

extensions to the ENE and WSW, the latter extension the longer. The nebula's overall dimensions are 1.5′ × 0.5′ ENE–WSW.

12/14″ Scopes–200x: This unusual nebula does indeed look like a "bug." The bright, slightly oval core is flanked by two faint hazy projections that are pinched near the core to form an irregular figure-8, resembling an ant or beetle. The longer WSW extension is the bug's thorax, and the shorter ENE extension is its head. Both extensions brighten slightly some distance from the core before fading at their ends. The nebula's full size is 2.25′ × 0.75′ ENE–WSW.

NGC 6318 Cr 325 Open Cluster Tr Type III 2p
φ 4′, m11.8p, Br★ 12.0p   17ʰ17.8ᵐ −39° 27′
Finder Chart 57-5, Figure 57-11   ★★★
8/10″ Scopes–100x: NGC 6318, located 10′ west of a 7th magnitude star, is a rich, concentrated group of three dozen faint stars in a 4′ × 3′ N–S area.

12/14″ Scopes–125x: NGC 6318, shaped something like a thumbprint, is an attractive 5′ × 3.5′ N–S concentration of 12th to 14th magnitude stars. An arc of

stars along the group's eastern side meets a shorter E–W row on the cluster's southern end.

NGC 6322 Cr 326 Open Cluster 30★ Tr Type I 2m
φ 10.0′, m6.0v, Br★ 7.50v   17ʰ18.5ᵐ −42° 57′
Finder Chart 57-5   ★★★
8/10″ Scopes–100x: NGC 6322 is a 6′ wide group of twenty faint stars contained by an equilateral triangle of magnitude 7.5 stars.

12/14″ Scopes–125x: Thirty stars are visible within a 6′ wide triangle of magnitude 7.5 stars. Outlying members spilling beyond the SE edge of the triangle bring the total star count to forty. Two doubles of nearly equally bright stars aligned NNE–SSW are in the cluster: a 9th magnitude pair 20″ apart and an 11th magnitude pair 10″ apart.

NGC 6334 RCW 127 Emission Nebula
φ 35′ × 20′, Photo Br 2-5, Color 3-4 17ʰ20.4ᵐ −35° 51′
Finder Chart 57-6, Figure 57-21 "Cat's Paw" ★★★
8/10″ Scopes–175x: NGC 6334 is an emission nebula complex located between a 1.25′ wide E–W pair of 6th magnitude stars. A series of dark lanes divide

Figure 57-22. *NGC 6357 is a large, faint irregular complex lying NW of a bright string of stars. Open cluster Pismis 24 is embedded in nebulosity at the center of the field. Image courtesy of Don Westergren.*

this irregular nebulous region into a trapezoid of four separate 7′ to 10′ wide nebulae with a small 3′×2′ N–S comet-shaped glow in the trapezoid's center. An O-III filter brings out the faint haze that extends NNW from the NW corner of the trapezoid.

Figure 57-23. *Planetary nebula NGC 6337 has a bright pale blue disk with a slightly darker center. Image courtesy of Josef Pöpsel and Stefan Binnewies.*

NGC 6337 PK 349–1.1 Planetary Nebula Type 4
φ 48″, m12.3v, CS 14.90v   17^{h}22.3^m −38° 29′
Finder Chart 57-5, Fig. 57-23 "Cheerio Neb"   ★★★★
12/14″Scopes–125x: NGC 6337 has a fairly bright 40″ diameter disk with a pale bluish glow and a slightly darker center. Three stars are visible within the nebula: the brightest, a 12th magnitude object, is just inside the planetary's ring NNE of its center, and two fainter stars are WSW of the center on the south edge of the ring. The actual central star, however, cannot be seen.

NGC 6357 Emission Nebula
φ 25′, Photo Br 2-5, Color 3-4   17^{h}24.7^m −34° 12′

Pismis 24 Open Cluster 15★ Tr Type III 2 pn
φ 4′, m9.6v, Br★ 10.43v   17^{h}24.7^m −34° 12′
Finder Chart 57-6, Figure 57-22   ★★/★★
12/14″Scopes–125x: In an O-III filter the emission nebula NGC 6357 appears as a faint 6′×3′ E–W glow at the northern end of a N–S chain of one 6th and four 7th magnitude stars. The open cluster Pismis 24, located between the two northernmost stars in the chain, is a faint cluster of twenty magnitude 10.5 and fainter stars spread over a 5′

Figure 57-24. *Harvard 16 is a concentrated stream of faint stars lying north of Lambda (35–λ) Scorpii (right) and Upsilon (34–υ) Scorpii (top). Martin C. Germano made this 10 minute exposure on hypered 2415 film with an 8″, f5 Newtonian reflector.*

Figure 57-25. *NGC 6380 (left of center) is a faint globular cluster lying north of the dark nebula Sandqvist-Lindroos 28. Martin C. Germano made this 50 minute exposure on 2415 film with an 8″, f5 Newtonian reflector.*

area. The magnitude 10.5 lucida is on the cluster's north edge. On the group's SE is a 4″ wide NW–SE double of magnitude 11.5 stars. The majority of the other cluster stars are much fainter.

Trumpler 25 Harvard 14 Open Cl. 40★ Tr Type II1m
φ 4′, m11.7p   17ʰ24.8ᵐ −39° 00′
Finder Chart 57-6   ★★★
12/14″ Scopes–125x: Trumpler 25, located 6.5′ north of two widely spaced 9.5 magnitude stars, is a loose, irregular scattering of three dozen very faint 14.5 and 15th magnitude stars in a 7′ area. Small dark dust clouds are north and south of the cluster.

Collinder 333 Open Cluster 30★ Tr Type II2m
φ 5′, m9.8p   17ʰ31.3ᵐ −34° 05′
Finder Chart 57-6   ★★★
12/14″ Scopes–125x: Collinder 333 is just west of the midpoint of the half degree long N–S line connecting two 6th magnitude stars. It contains twenty 10th to 13th magnitude members spread over a 6′ area. The magnitude 9.8 lucida is on the south edge of the group. In its NE part are two doubles of 11th magnitude stars.

Harvard 16 Open Cluster 70★ Tr Type III2r
φ 14′, m –   17ʰ31.4ᵐ −36° 51′
Finder Chart 57-6, Figure 57-24   ★★★
8/10″ Scopes–75x: Harvard 16 is 30″ NW of magnitude 1.6 Lambda (λ) = 35 Scorpii and 25″ NNE of magnitude 2.7 Upsilon (μ) = 34 Scorpii, the two stars in the Sting of the Scorpion. The cluster is a large, irregular group of fifty members spread over a 15′ area.
12/14″ Scopes–100x: Seventy magnitude 11 and fainter stars are in a 20′ area, most in a wide but concentrated ENE–WSW stream through the cluster's center. A large proportion of the stars are 12th magnitude objects, which gives the cluster a uniform, richly populated appearance. An 8th magnitude field star is on the stream's north edge.

NGC 6383 Cr 335 Open Cluster 40★ Tr Type II3mn
φ 20′, m5.5v, Br★ 5.64v   17ʰ34.8ᵐ −32° 34′
Finder Chart 57-6   ★★★
4/6″ Scopes–75x: NGC 6383 lies 1.25° WSW of Messier 6. It can be seen with the unaided eye as a faint, hazy spot due north of the Sting of the Scorpion, and at low power in small telescopes resolves to fifteen faint stars, scattered around, but mostly west, of the bright magnitude 5.6 cluster lucida.

8/10″ Scopes–100x: This cluster has several dozen faint members, most sprinkled west of the bright triple h4962, which consists of a 5.6 magnitude primary with two bluish 10.5 magnitude companions. Several 9.5 magnitude stars lie on the cluster's west edge 5′ from its center.

Sandqvist-Lindroos 28   Dark Nebula
ϕ 30′ × 15′, Opacity 5   17ʰ35.3ᵐ −39° 14′

NGC 6380   Globular Cluster
ϕ 3.9′, m11.1:v   17ʰ35.4ᵐ −39° 04′
Finder Chart 57-5, Figure 57-25   ★★★/★

16/18″ Scopes–150x: NGC 6380, located 28′ SW of magnitude 4.3 Q Scorpii, is an extremely faint globular cluster. At the Texas Star Party, under very transparent skies, it could be glimpsed as a faint, featureless smudge just north of an 11th magnitude star. Dark nebula SL 28 lies 10′ south of NGC 6380 and probably will be noticed before the globular is spotted. It is an irregular, somewhat circular blotch in the Milky Way with a few faint stars superimposed. A 10′ diameter clump of 11th and 12th magnitude stars is on its east edge.

NGC 6388   Globular Cluster Class III
ϕ 8.7′, m6.7v   17ʰ36.3ᵐ −44° 44′
Finder Chart 57-5, Figure 57-12   ★★★

8/10″ Scopes–125x: NGC 6388 has a very bright core surrounded by a 2.5′ diameter halo with a few stars resolved around its rim. A magnitude 10.5 field star is on the halo's north edge.

16/18″ Scopes–175x: Larger instruments show a granular 4′ diameter halo with perhaps a dozen faint

stars resolved around its periphery. The core is sharply concentrated at the cluster center.

Trumpler 27   Open Cluster 35★ Tr Type III 3 m
ϕ 6′, m6.7v, Br★ 8.39v   17ʰ36.2ᵐ −33° 29′
Finder Chart 57-6   ★★★

12/14″ Scopes–125x: Trumpler 27 has forty 9th magnitude and fainter stars irregularly scattered over an 8′ area around and SE of two 9th magnitude stars.

Trumpler 28   Open Cluster 30★ Tr Type III 2 m
ϕ 12.5′, m7.7, Br★ 9.84v   17ʰ36.8ᵐ −32° 29′
Finder Chart 57-6   ★★★

12/14″ Scopes–125x: Trumpler 28, located about halfway between Messier 6 and NGC 6383, is a loose scattering of thirty faint stars spread over a 10′ area. The magnitude 9.8 cluster lucida is just north of the group's center.

NGC 6396   Open Cluster 30★ Tr Type III 3 m
ϕ 3′, m8.5v, Br★ 9.79v   17ʰ38.1ᵐ −35° 00′
Finder Chart 57-6   ★★★

12/14″ Scopes–125x: NGC 6396 has twenty 10th magnitude and fainter stars concentrated in a 3′ area. A NW–SE row of stars runs through the cluster center, the faint but interesting quadruple star h4966 at the row's NW end. This quadruple consists of two pairs, each a close double of nearly equally bright components, separated by 12″ in an E–W direction; the brighter double is a tight 1.0″ wide pair of 10th magnitude stars appearing oblong ESE–WNW; and the fainter double is composed of magnitude 11.7 and 12.0 stars separated by 2.5″ in position angle 245°.

NGC 6404   Cr 340   Open Cluster 50★ Tr Type III 3 m
ϕ 5′, m10.6p   17ʰ39.6ᵐ −33° 15′
Finder Chart 57-6   ★★★

12/14″ Scopes–125x: NGC 6404, located a degree south of Messier 6, is a very faint but rich concentration of 13th magnitude and fainter stars in a 5′ × 3′ N–S ellipse. Forty cluster members can be resolved under clear, dark skies. A 10th magnitude star is on the group's west edge; and a slightly fainter star is conspicuous on its east edge.

NGC 6405   Messier 6   Open Cluster 80★ Tr Type II 3 r
ϕ 33′, m4.2v, Br★ 6.17v   17ʰ40.1ᵐ −32° 13′
Finder Chart 57-6, Figure 57-26   ★★★★★

The Butterfly Cluster

Messier 6, though first recognized as a star cluster by Hodierna sometime prior to 1654, had been men-

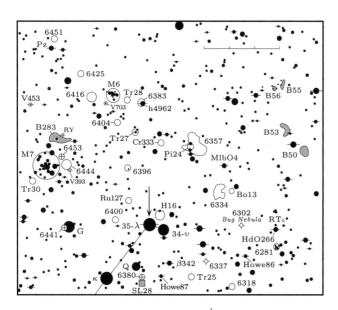

Finder Chart 57-6. 35–λ Sco: 17ʰ33.6ᵐ −37° 06′

tioned together with M7 by Ptolemy in the 2nd century A.D., who referred to the two as "small clouds" near the Sting of the Scorpion. M6 is 1,500 light years distant, has an absolute magnitude of −5.0 (a luminosity of 8,300 suns), and is 15 light years across.

4/6" Scopes-50x: Messier 6, visible to the unaided eye, is an attractive cluster of 6th to 10th magnitude stars spread across a half degree long, NE–SW rectangular area slightly pinched in the middle (hence its name, the "Butterfly Cluster"). The stars are distributed into small knots, strings and geometric patterns. The cluster lucida, a K-type long period variable BM Scorpii, is a conspicuous orange star on the group's ENE edge. The cluster is best at lower powers, which accentuate the contrast between its brighter and fainter members.

8/10" Scopes-75x: The Butterfly Cluster has a hundred stars spread over a 45' area, its brighter members concentrated in a 30' × 15' rectangle. The irregular parallel lines of stars that form the long side of the rectangle are the butterfly's wings, and its antennæ are a small but conspicuous "V" of 10th and 11th magnitude stars SSE of the cluster center.

NGC 6400 Cr 342 Open Cluster 60★ Tr Type II 2 m
ϕ 7', m8.8p, Br★ 9.0p   17^{h}40.8^m −36° 57'
Finder Chart 57-6   ★★★

8/10" Scopes-100x: NGC 6400, located near the tip of the stinger 1.25° east of magnitude 1.6 Lambda (λ) = 35 Scorpii, is an irregular group of twenty 10th magnitude and fainter stars covering an 8' area. Jagged star chains radiate outward from a central concentration.

12/14" Scopes-125x: NGC 6400, located north of two 9th magnitude stars, has forty members loosely distributed over a 10' × 5' N–S area. The most prominent of the cluster's several star chains can be seen extending NE–SW.

Trumpler 29 Harvard 17 Open Cl. 30★ Tr Type III 2 m
ϕ 9', m7.5p   17^{h}41.6^m −40° 06'
Finder Chart 57-5   ★★★

12/14" Scopes-125x: Trumpler 29 is within the curl of the Scorpion's tail west of magnitude 3.0 Iota-1 (ι^1) Scorpii. It consists of thirty faint stars in a 7' area around the eastern end of an 8' pair of 7th magnitude stars. Near the group's west edge is an E–W line of three 11th magnitude stars. To the cluster's east is a starless void.

Figure 57-26. *Visible to the naked eye, Messier 6 (NGC 6405), a large, bright cluster, is fine object for small telescopes. Image courtesy of Lee C. Coombs.*

NGC 6416 Cr 344 Open Cluster 40★ Tr Type III 2 m
ϕ 30', m5.7v, Br★ 8.43v   17^{h}44.4^m −32° 21'
Finder Chart 57-6   ★★★

8/10" Scopes-100x: NGC 6416 is an inconspicuous cluster half a degree ESE of Messier 6 containing twenty 8th to 11th magnitude, and forty 12th to 14th magnitude stars irregularly strewn over a 30' × 15' N–S area. The brighter members are in the northern part of the cluster. Many of the cluster's stars are in chains, generally running E–W. Two reddish stars are on the NE edge of the group and one on its SSW edge.

NGC 6425 Cr 384 Open Cluster 35★ Tr Type II 1 m
ϕ 15', m7.2v, Br★ 10.15v   17^{h}46.9^m −31° 32'
Finder Chart 57-6, Figure 57-13   ★★★

8/10" Scopes-100x: NGC 6425 has two dozen 10th to 12th magnitude stars in a roughly triangular 12' wide area. Three star chains join at the NNW edge, the two western chains running N–S and the eastern chain running first E–W then arcing south. The chains are separated by starless lanes. The middle chain contains three triangles, one triangle at the chain's center and the two others at each end.

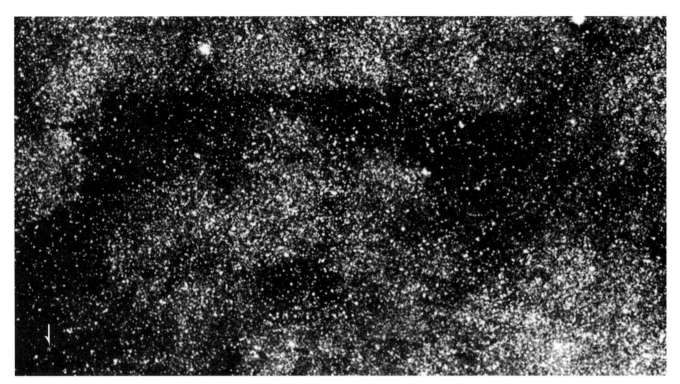

Figure 57-27. *Barnard 283, located a degree NNW of Messier 7, is a conspicuous dark lane in the Milky Way visible in binoculars and small telescopes. Martin C. Germano made this 20 minute exposure on hypered 2415 film with an 14.5″, f5 Newtonian reflector.*

NGC 6441 Δ557 Globular Cluster Class III
φ **7.8′, m7.2v**   17ʰ50.2ᵐ −37° 03′
Finder Chart 57-6, Figure 57-14   ★★★
12/14″Scopes–150x: NGC 6441, located 4′ east of the orange magnitude 3.2 G Scorpii, has a brilliant core embedded in a bright but unresolved 3′ diameter halo. A 10th magnitude field star touches the halo's SW edge, and a 12.5 magnitude star is on its NNW edge.

NGC 6444 Ru132 Open Cluster 8★ Tr Type IV1p
φ **12′, m −, Br★ 11.p**   17ʰ49.5ᵐ −34° 49′
Finder Chart 57-6   ★★★
12/14″Scopes–125x: NGC 6444, located nearly a degree west of open cluster Messier 7, contains three dozen magnitude 11.5 to 12.5 stars spread over a 15′ area. The cluster has no central compression, and its members are distributed in only a few star pairs and small clumps.

NGC 6451 Cr352 Open Cluster 80★ Tr Type I2rn
φ **7′, m8.2p, Br★ 12.0p**   17ʰ50.7ᵐ −30° 13′
Finder Chart 57-6, Figure 57-15   ★★★
4/6″Scopes–75x: NGC 6451 is a triangular patch of faint stars at the edge of a rich Milky Way field. An extensive network of dark nebulosity lies to the west of the cluster.

8/10″Scopes–100x: This rich cluster has three dozen 11th to 13th magnitude stars in a roughly triangular 8′ area. A N–S starless arc divides the band of brighter cluster members along its east side from the broader area of fainter stars straggling away to its west.

NGC 6453 Globular Cluster Class IV
φ **3.5′, m9.8v**   17ʰ50.9ᵐ −34° 36′
Finder Chart 57-6   ★★
8/10″Scopes–125x: NGC 6453 lies among the NW outliers of open cluster Messier 7. This globular cluster has a faint 1.5′ diameter halo which at low power resembles a planetary nebula. The halo is smoothly illuminated, with no hint of resolution.
16/18″Scopes–175x: The 2′ diameter halo exhibits the granularity of partial resolution only around its periphery. The core is small and poorly concentrated. The few stars visible across the halo are probably foreground objects, members of M7.

Barnard 283 Dark Nebula
φ **90′× 60′, Opacity 5**   17ʰ51.3ᵐ −33° 53′
Finder Chart 57-6, Figure 57-27   ★★★
8/10″Scopes–75x: Barnard 283, located a degree NNW of the open cluster Messier 7, is a conspicuous E–W

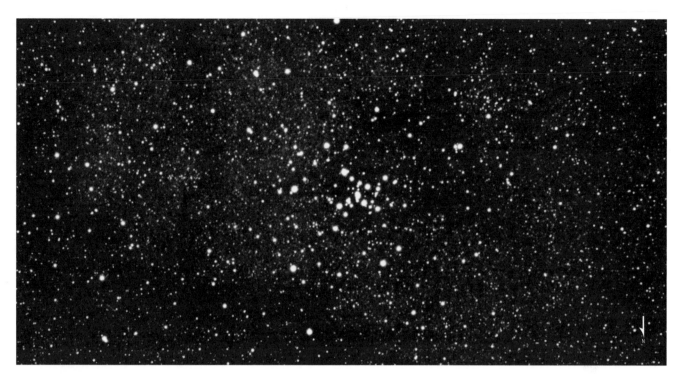

Figure 57-28. *Messier 7 (NGC 6475), visible to the unaided eye as a pale Milky Way patch, is a cluster of bright stars that contrast with its rich Milky Way background of faint stars. Image courtesy of Lee C. Coombs.*

dark dust lane. Toward the east the cloud broadens and diffuses into the star field. Toward the west the dark nebula narrows nearly to a point but then widens and continues many degrees to the NW.

NGC 6475 Messier 7 Open Cluster 80★ Tr Type I3r
φ 80′, m3.3v, Br★ 5.60v   17ʰ53.9ᵐ −34° 49′
Finder Chart 57-6, Figure 57-28   ★★★★★

Messier 7 was mentioned with Messier 6 by Ptolemy in the 2nd century A.D.: he called the two open clusters, visible to the unaided eye as visible shreds of haze, "little clouds" near the Sting of the Scorpion. M7 is about 820 light years away, a little more than half as far as M6. Its absolute magnitude is a rather modest −3.7, a luminosity of 2,500 suns, and its diameter about 20 light years.

4/6″Scopes–50x: Messier 7, located halfway between the Sting of the Scorpion and the "Teapot" asterism of Sagittarius, is a huge open cluster plainly visible to the naked eye as a concentrated patch in the Milky Way. Its seventy stars are loosely dispersed over a 70′ area. The cluster's brighter stars are arranged in a crushed box at its center, with jagged star chains, running generally E–W, attached to each box corner. From the SE corner two chains wander further SE, one shorter than the other.

8/10″Scopes–60x: Messier 7 is a very large cluster of bright stars set against a rich background of faint stars. In the cluster's center is a large, conspicuous keystone, nearly devoid of stars in its middle. Nearly all the other cluster stars are in chains, five of the chains attach to the corners of the keystone. Near the northern edge of the cluster is a moderately curved E–W chain of fainter stars, separated from the main group by a starless void. Many of the cluster members are in pairs and triplets; and many are bluish, contrasting sharply with the group's orange magnitude 5.6 lucida near its SW edge. Overall the cluster contains at least a hundred stars in a 90′ area, two dozen of them from magnitude 5.6 to magnitude 9. The peripheral stars blend into the surrounding star field, making the cluster's true borders difficult to distinguish.

Trumpler 30 Harvard 18 Open Cl. 20★ Tr Type IV1p
φ 10′, m8.8p   17ʰ56.5ᵐ −35° 19′
Finder Chart 57-6   ★★★

12/14″Scopes–125x: Trumpler 30 is a 10′ diameter group rich in faint stars. Its brighter members form a triangle, an 8th magnitude star at its northern corner. At least sixty stars are visible inside the triangle, but other faint stars spreading out to a diameter of 20′ double the star count. Outlying stars are more numerous to the south of the cluster.

Chapter 58

Scutum, the Shield

58.1 Overview

Scutum, the Shield, was introduced in 1690 by Johannes Hevelius to honor John III Sobieski, the king of Poland who defeated the Turks when they besieged Vienna in 1683. Hevelius' original name for the constellation was Scutum Sobiescianum: it was shortened to the present Scutum by Flamsteed in the 18th century.

Scutum is basically just a rectangular area in the Milky Way between Sagittarius on the south, Aquila to the NE, and Serpens Cauda to the west. It has no distinctive star pattern, and no individual stars as bright as the 3rd magnitude. Nevertheless because it is in the Milky Way it is rich in objects. Scutum's most outstanding feature is the Milky Way itself, which here is a remarkable mixture of extremely bright star clouds with the extremely dark dust clouds of the Great Rift, which grazes the NW corner of the constellation. The Scutum Star Cloud, in the NE quadrant of the constellation between Alpha (α) Scuti on the SW and Beta (β) Scuti on the NE, is one of the most brilliant star clouds anywhere along the Milky Way – in large part because our view in this direction is toward the star-rich interior of our Galaxy. In binoculars and richest field telescopes the star cloud's background haze is alive with the scintillation of momentarily resolved star-sparks. The edge of the foreground dust of the Great Rift creates visually striking bays into the star cloud. Some isolated islands of the star cloud are out in the Great Rift; and many distinctive patches of Great Rift dust are scattered around the constellation and have been given Barnard numbers. Scutum, like most Milky Way constellations, is rich in open clusters. Two of its open clusters are Messier objects, M11 and M26. M11 is one of the finest open clusters in the entire sky – not because it is especially bright and large, but because it is so uniform in magnitude.

58.2 Interesting Stars

Σ2306 Triple Star   **Spec. F5**
AB: 7.9, 8.6; Sep. 10.2″; P.A 221°   **18^{h}22.2^m −15° 05′**
Finder Chart 58-3   ★★★★
12/14″Scopes–200x: Struve 2306, located 1.75′ WSW

Scutum: SKOO-tum
Genitive: Scuti, SKOO-tee
Abbreviation: Sct
Culmination: 9pm–Aug. 15, midnight–July 1
Area: 109 square degrees
Showpieces: M11 (NGC 6705), M26 (NGC 6694)
Binocular Objects: B312, B100-1, B103, B104, B110, B111, B113, M11 (NGC 6705), M26 (NGC 6694), NGC 6664, NGC 6683, NGC 6712

of magnitude 4.7 Gamma (γ) Scuti, is a fine color contrast pair. We received observations calling the primary copper, gold, or yellow, and the secondary blue or cobalt blue. The secondary is a close 1.2″ pair requiring moderately high power to separate.

Delta (δ) Scuti = HV 36 Double and Var. Star Spec. F0
AC: 4.7, 9.2; Sep. 52.6″; P.A. 130°   **18^{h}42.3^m −09° 03′**
Finder Chart 58-4   ★★★★
4/6″Scopes–75x: Delta Scuti is the prototype of a class of short-period, small amplitude pulsating variables. The magnitude range of Delta Scuti stars is too slight to be followed visually. They are thought to be something on the nature of low-mass Cepheids. The brightest Delta Scuti stars include Rho (ρ) Puppis and Beta (β) Cassiopeiae. Delta Scuti is also a triple star (see Table 58-2), the blue of its brighter companion a nice contrast to the primary's yellow-white.

Σ2373 Double Star   **Spec. F2**
7.2, 8.2; Sep. 4.2″; P.A. 338°   **18^{h}45.9^m −10° 30′**
Finder Chart 58-3   ★★★★
4/6″Scopes–125x: Struve 2373 is a well-balanced double with pale and deep yellow stars set in a rich Milky Way field.

Scutum, the Shield

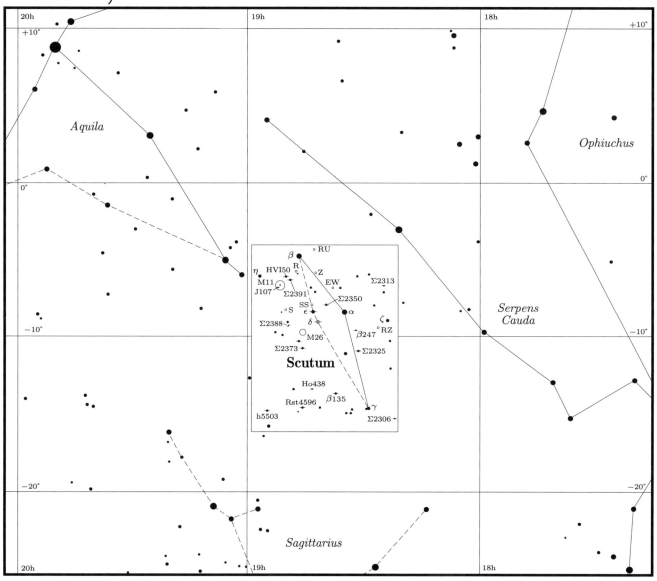

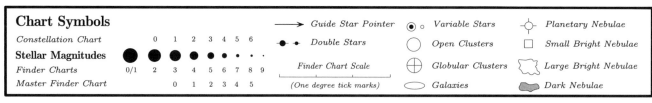

Chart Symbols

Constellation Chart

Stellar Magnitudes

Finder Charts

Master Finder Chart

→ *Guide Star Pointer*   ◉ ○ *Variable Stars*   ⊕ *Planetary Nebulae*

•—• *Double Stars*   ○ *Open Clusters*   □ *Small Bright Nebulae*

Finder Chart Scale   ⊕ *Globular Clusters*   *Large Bright Nebulae*

(One degree tick marks)   ◯ *Galaxies*   *Dark Nebulae*

Table 58-1: Selected Variable Stars in Scutum

Name	HD No.	Type	Max.	Min.	Period (Days)	F*	Spec. Type	R.A. (2000) Dec.		Finder Chart No.	Notes
RZ Sct	169753	EA	7.34	8.84	15.19	0.17	B3	18^{h}26.6^m	−09° 12′	58-4	
EW Sct	171955	Cep?	7.77	8.24	10:		K0	37.9	−06 48	58-4	
RU Sct	172730	Cδ	8.87	10.02	19.69	0.36:	F4-G5	41.9	−04 07	58-4	
Z Sct		Cep	9.1	10.1	12.90	0.40	F8-G4	42.9	−05 49	58-4	
SS Sct	173058	Cδ	7.97	8.43	3.67	0.37	F6-G0	43.7	−07 44	58-4	
R Sct	173819	RVa	4.9	8.2	140		G0-K0	47.5	−05 42	58-4	
S Sct	174325	SR	6.8	9	148		C5	50.3	−07 54	58-4	

F* = The fraction of period taken up by the star's rise from min. to max. brightness, or the period spent in eclipse.

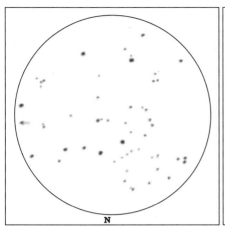

Figure 58-1. Dolidze 28
12.5″, f5–200x, by G. R. Kepple

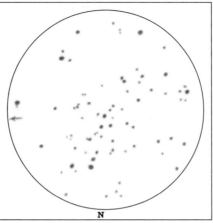

Figure 58-2. NGC 6631
12.5″, f5–200x, by G. R. Kepple

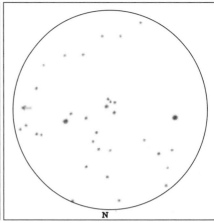

Figure 58-3. NGC 6639
12.5″, f5–200x, by G. R. Kepple

R Scuti Variable Star Type RVa   Spec. G0-K0
m4.9, 8.2; Per. 140 days   18ʰ47.5ᵐ −05° 42′
Finder Chart 58-4   ★★★★

R Scuti, a deep yellow star a degree south of magnitude 4.2 Beta (β) Scuti, is one of the brighter examples of a class of pulsating yellow supergiant variables known as RV Tauri stars. The variations of these stars are in general similar to those of long-period variables, but often show secondary pulsations which result in alternating deep and shallow minima. R Scuti, for example varies between the 5th and 6th magnitudes; but every fourth or fifth cycle it will drop to the 8th magnitude. RV Tauri stars are thought to have peak absolute magnitudes of −4.5 to 5, so the distance to R Scuti must be around 2500 light years. RV Tauri stars

are not found only in the Milky Way, like R Scuti itself, but even in globular clusters and in our Galaxy's central bulge.

58.3 Deep-Sky Objects

Dolidze 28 Open Cluster 20★ Tr Type IV1p
φ 12′, m −   18ʰ25.4ᵐ −14° 39′
Finder Chart 58-3, Figure 58-1   ★★
12/14″ Scopes–100x: Dolidze 28, located a degree west of magnitude 4.7 Gamma (γ) Scuti, is hardly recognizable as an open cluster, its two dozen members scattered in a 12′ area. Near the NE edge is a tiny 30″ triangle of 13th magnitude stars, and a string of magnitude 9.5 stars trails off to the west.

Table 58-2: Selected Double Stars in Scutum

Name	ADS No.	Pair	M1	M2	Sep.″	P.A.°	Spec	R.A. (2000) Dec.	Finder Chart No.	Notes
Σ 2306	11282	AB	7.9	8.6	10.2	221	F5	18ʰ22.2ᵐ −15° 05′	58-3	Gold and blue
	11282	AC		9.0	10.1	218				
		BC			1.2	70				
Σ 2313	11318		7.5	8.8	6.1	198	G0	24.7	−06 36	58-4	Yellow and pale blue
Σ 2325	11414		5.8	9.1	12.3	257	B3	31.4	−10 48	58-3	White and pale blue
β 247	11429		7.7	11.1	7.8	167	A0	32.2	−09 22	58-4	
β 135	11512	AB	6.4	11.2	2.4	186	B9	38.1	−14 00	38-3	
Σ 2350	11552		5.8	10.8	22.0	194	K0	40.0	−07 47	58-4	
δ Sct	11581	AB	4.7	12.2	15.2	46	F0	42.3	−09 03	58-4	Pale yellow and bluish
(HV36)	11581	AC		9.2	52.6	130				
Ho438	11637		8.0	10.8	2.7	75	F2	45.7	−13 40	58-3	
Σ 2373	11642		7.2	8.2	4.2	338	F2	45.9	−10 30	58-3	Pale and deep yellow
Rst4596			7.1	12.0	6.0	159	F8	46.8	−14 28	58-3	
Σ 2391	11695	AB	6.5	9.8	37.9	332	A2	48.7	−06 00	58-4	Yellowish-white and blue
Σ 2388		AB	7.8	10.0	53.7	345	B3	49.0	−08 28	58-4	
		BC		10.1	21.4	20				
HVI 50	11719	AB	6.1	12.2	23.3	0	K0	49.7	−05 55	58-4	
	11719	AC		8.6	113.7	171	K0			
J107	11752	AB	8.0	12.4	5.8	191	B8	51.1	−06 17	58-4	
h5503			7.2	10.8	38.0	79	B9	56.8	−14 51	58-3	

Footnotes: *= Year 2000, a = Near apogee, c = Closing, w = Widening. Finder Chart No: All stars listed in the tables are plotted in the large Constellation Chart, but when a star appears in a Finder Chart, this number is listed. Notes: When colors are subtle, the suffix *-ish* is used, e.g. *bluish*.

Figure 58-4. *Reflection nebula IC 1287 is a faint haze around the double star Struve 2325 (upper left of center). Open cluster NGC 6649 (at lower right) is a fairly well defined concentration of 12th and 13th magnitude stars. Image courtesy of Bernard Hubl.*

NGC 6631 Cr 379 Open Cluster 30★ Tr Type II1m
φ 5′, m11.7p   **18ʰ27.2ᵐ −12° 02′**
Finder Chart 58-3, Figure 58-2   ★★
8/10″ Scopes–100x: NGC 6631 is a 5′×3′ NNW–SSE
    stream of two dozen 12th to 15th magnitude stars.
    A 12″ wide NE–SW pair of magnitude 12 stars lies
    on the stream's SSE end, and a 1′×0.5′ right triangle
    of magnitude 10.5, 12, and 12.5 stars is at its NNE

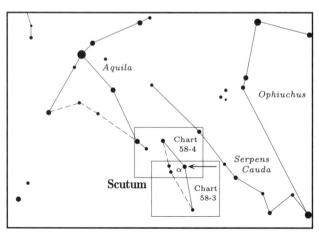

Master Finder Chart 58-2. Scutum Chart Areas
Guide stars indicated by arrows.

end. A rather conspicuous 30″ wide equilateral
triangle of stars is near the stream's center.

NGC 6639 Open Cluster [25★ Tr Type II2p]
[φ 5′, m11.v]   **18ʰ30.1ᵐ −13° 12′**
Finder Chart 58-3, Figure 58-3   ★★
12/14″ Scopes–125x: NGC 6639, classed as "nonexist-
    ent" in the *RNGC*, is a loose group of two dozen
    magnitude 11 and fainter stars in a 5′, somewhat
    N–S elongated, area between two magnitude 9.5
    field stars. On its western edge is a 3″ NW–SE
    magnitude 11.5 pair; and near its eastern edge is a
    5″ wide magnitude 11.5 and 12.5 double.

IC 1287 Reflection Nebula
φ 20′×10′, Photo Br 3-4, Color 1-4   18ʰ30.4ᵐ −10° 48′
Finder Chart 58-3, Figure 58-4   ★★
12/14″ Scopes–75x: IC 1287 is a faint but not difficult
    reflection nebula centered on the double Struve
    2325 (5.8, 9.1; 123″; 257°) and extending west to
    an 8th magnitude star. The haze is indefinite but
    more conspicuous around the two stars. Open
    cluster NGC 6649 lies 35′ NE.

Figure 58-5. *Barnard 312, located 1.5° SE of Gamma (γ) Scuti on the Sagittarius border, is a large dark nebula visible in binoculars. Martin C. Germano made this 65 minute exposure on 2415 film with an 8″, f5 Newtonian.*

Ruprecht 141 Open Cluster 20★ Tr Type IV1p
φ 6′, m −, Br★ 12.0p   18ʰ31.3ᵐ −12° 19′
Finder Chart 58-3   ★★
12/14″Scopes–125x: Ruprecht 141 is a 10′×6′ NNW–
SSE group of two dozen 11th magnitude and fainter
stars sprinkled around and north of an 8.5 magnitude star. It does not stand out well from the star-
rich Milky Way field around it. Many of its members
fall along six E–W, more-or-less 3′ long, rows.
Ruprecht 141, unimpressive as it is, is more conspicuous than Ruprecht 142 and Ruprecht 143,
respectively 14′ and 23′ to its NE.

Dolidze 29 Open Cluster (Asterism?)
φ 18′, m −   18ʰ31.4ᵐ −06° 38′
Finder Chart 58-4   ★★
12/14″Scopes–100x: Dolidze 29 is a poor cluster of a
mere handful of 12th and 13th magnitude stars.
Just to the north is a more impressive group of ten
magnitude 11.5–12 stars in an 8′ area.

Ruprecht 142 Open Cluster 15★ Tr Type IV1p
φ 5′, m −   18ʰ32.1ᵐ −12° 15′
Finder Chart 58-3   ★★
12/14″Scopes–125x: Ruprecht 142 is an inconspicuous
cluster between the not-much-more conspicuous
Ruprecht 141 and Ruprecht 143. It contains two

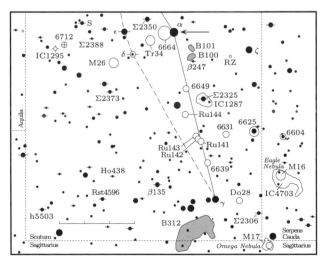

Finder Chart 58-3. α Sct: 18ʰ35.2ᵐ −08° 15′

Figure 58-6. *Dark nebulae Barnard 100 (top) and Barnard 101 (bottom), located a degree SW of Alpha (α) Scuti, together form a crescent split in its middle. Martin C. Germano made this 65 minute exposure on 2415 film with an 8", f5 Newtonian.*

Figure 58-7. *Barnard 103, located at the NE edge of the Scutum Star Cloud 2° NE of Alpha (α) Scuti, stands out well as a curved, irregular dark streak. Martin C. Germano made this 65 minute exposure on 2415 film with an 8", f5 Newtonian.*

10th magnitude, and a dozen 12th magnitude and fainter, stars irregularly concentrated in a 5′ area.

Barnard 312 LDN 379 Dark Nebula
φ 100′ × 30′, Opacity 4   18ʰ32.2ᵐ −15° 35′
Finder Chart 58-3, Figure 58-5   ★★★
4/6″ Scopes–35x: Barnard 312, located 1.5° SE of magnitude 4.7 Gamma (γ) Scuti, is a large dark nebula visible in binoculars. Its northern and NW edges are sharply defined, and meet at a blunt point at the cloud's NNW edge. The other sides are diffuse, especially to the south, their darkness compromised

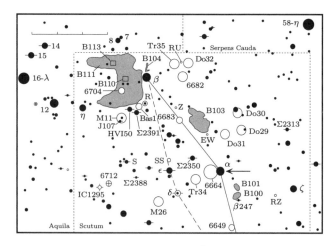

Finder Chart 58-4. α Sct: 18ʰ35.2ᵐ −08° 15′

by numerous faint stars superimposed upon them. Near the cloud's NNE edge is an 8th magnitude star and on its NW edge is a double with 12th magnitude components. Five 4th and 5th magnitude stars, of which Gamma Scuti is the westernmost, lie to the north of B312 in a field profuse with faint stars.

Barnard 100 LDN 443 Dark Nebula
φ 16′, Opacity 5   18ʰ32.6ᵐ −09° 12′

Barnard 101 LDN 443 Dark Nebula
φ 13′ × 4′, Opacity 5   18ʰ32.6ᵐ −08° 57′
Finder Chart 58-3, Figure 58-6   ★★★/★★★
4/6″ Scopes–35x: Barnard 100, located NE of a 9th magnitude star, is a 16′ long crescent-shaped starless area concave to the north. Its east end is broader, and a magnitude 12.5 star is near its SE edge. Barnard 101 to the north of B100 is a more elongated 13′ × 4′ streak slightly concave to the SE. A clump of faint stars lies on its northern edge, and another is to its west. These two dark patches are separated by a scattering of faint stars.

Ruprecht 143 Open Cluster 30★ Tr Type IV1m
φ 6′, m −   18ʰ32.6ᵐ −12° 08′
Finder Chart 58-3   ★★
12/14″ Scopes–125x: Ruprecht 143 is the northernmost of three Ruprecht clusters lying in a 23′ long NE–SW

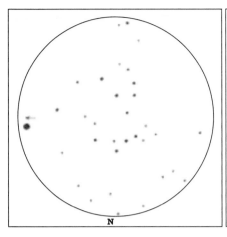

Figure 58-8. NGC 6664
12.5″, f5–200x, by G. R. Kepple

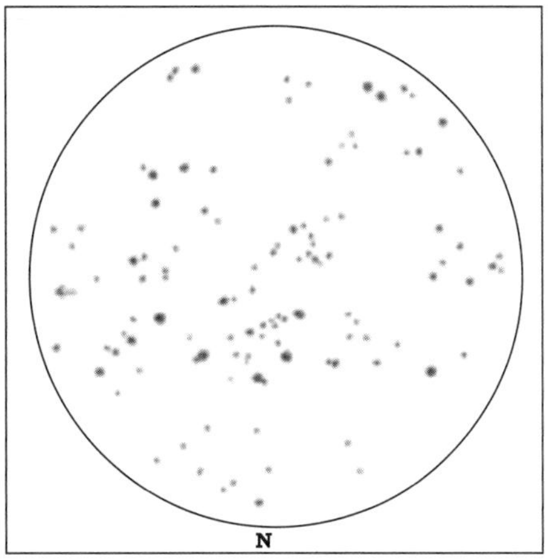

Figure 58-9. Dolidze 32
12.5″, f5–225x, by G. R. Kepple

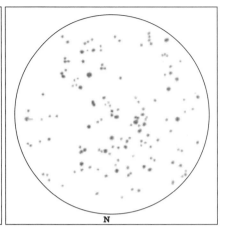

Figure 58-10. Basel 1
12.5″, f5–225x, by G. R. Kepple

row. It is a crescent-shaped group, concave to the west, of two dozen stars, the brightest at the center of the arc. Faint outliers spread to the north and south.

Dolidze 30 Open Cluster (Asterism?)
φ **18′, m –**   18ʰ32.9ᵐ −06° 02′
Finder Chart 58-4   ★★
12/14″Scopes–100x: Dolidze 30 is a 15′ wide group of fifty 12th and 13th magnitude stars loosely gathered around a magnitude 5.5 star.

Ruprecht 144 Open Cluster 30★ Tr Type IV1p
φ **2′, m –**   18ʰ33.4ᵐ −11° 26′
Finder Chart 58-3   ★★
12/14″Scopes–125x: Ruprecht 144, lying on the south edge of a large dark area in the Scutum Milky Way, is a loose, irregular group of twenty stars in a 4′ diameter area. The brightest member is a magnitude 10.5 object, but all the other cluster stars are 12th magnitude and fainter.

NGC 6649 Open Cluster 50★ Tr Type I2m
φ **6.6′, m8.9v, Br★ 11.56v**   18ʰ33.5ᵐ −10° 24′
Finder Chart 58-3, Figure 58-4   ★★★
8/10″Scopes–100x: NGC 6649 is a fairly well defined concentration of twenty magnitude 12 and fainter stars in a 5′ area just NNE of a magnitude 9.7 field star. It stands out the better for being in a sparse star field laced with diffuse dark nebulae. The magnitude 12 cluster lucida is conspicuous at its center.
16/18″Scopes–150x: NGC 6649 contains forty 12th to 15th magnitude stars in a 6′ square, the diagonals of the square oriented NE–SW and NW–SE. Four

of the cluster's magnitude 12–12.5 members are part of an oval on its NW edge. At the SSE edge is a 5.25′ long arc, concave to the south, of four magnitude 9 and 10 stars. The magnitude 9.7 star on the south has a magnitude 11.4 companion just 4″ to its east.

Dolidze 31 Open Cluster (Asterism?)
φ **18′, m –**   18ʰ34.9ᵐ −06° 51′
Finder Chart 58-4   ★★
12/14″Scopes–100x: Dolidze 31 is a scattered, unconcentrated 15′ wide group of two dozen 12.5 to 14th magnitude stars with two 11.5 magnitude stars on its southern edge and a 9th magnitude star on its NE edge. The majority of its stars are in a loose E–W stream along the cluster's northern side.

NGC 6664 H12⁸ Open Cluster 50★ Tr Type III2m
φ **16′, m7.8v, Br★ 10.15v**   18ʰ36.7ᵐ −08° 13′
Finder Chart 58-4, Figure 58-8   ★★★
8/10″Scopes–75x: NGC 6664, located 20′ NE of magnitude 3.9 Alpha (α) Scuti, is an unconcentrated cluster of two dozen 10th magnitude and fainter stars in a 15′ × 12′ N–S area. A N–S star chain runs along the east side of the group. The faintness of the group's members contrasts starkly with the nearby brightness of Alpha.
12/14″Scopes–100x: NGC 6664 is a very loose collection of three dozen 10th to 13th magnitude stars in a 16′ somewhat N–S area. Scattered outlying stars bring the total to 50 or 60 over a 25′ area. The brighter members are concentrated on the cluster's northern edge.

Figure 58-11. *Messier 26 (NGC 6694) is a rich patch of faint stars. Image courtesy of Lee C. Coombs.*

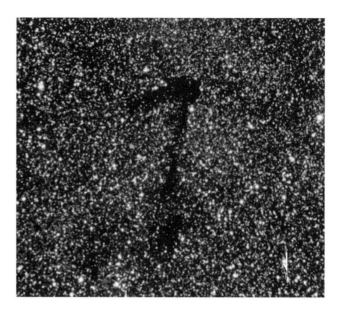

Figure 58-12. *Barnard 104 is a hook silhouetted against the northern edge of the Scutum Star Cloud. Image courtesy of Martin C. Germano.*

Barnard 103 LDN 497 Dark Nebula
ϕ [45′× 15′], Opacity 6   18^{h}39.4^m −06° 41′
Finder Chart 58-4, Figure 58-7   ★★★
4/6″Scopes–35x: Barnard 103, located on the NE edge of the Scutum Star Cloud, is a 45′× 15′ ENE–WSW curved dark streak, concave to the north. It is darkest to the SW. Just beyond its SW edge is the deep golden Cepheid variable EW Scuti (mags 7.77 to 8.24 in a 10 day period). EW Scuti has a magnitude 9.5 companion just to its east.

Trumpler 34 Cr 387 Open Cluster 40★ Tr Type II 2 m
ϕ 7′, m8.6v, Br★ 11.17v   18^{h}39.8^m −08° 29′
Finder Chart 58-4   ★★
12/14″Scopes–125x: Trumpler 34 is a small 5′ cluster of twenty faint 13th to 15th magnitude stars gathered around and to the east of a 3′ long E–W arc, concave to the south, of magnitude 12.5–13 stars. A magnitude 9.5 star is on the western edge of the group.

Dolidze 32 Open Cluster 40★ Tr Type II 2 p
ϕ 12′, m −   18^{h}40.4^m −04° 06′
Finder Chart 58-4, Figure 58-9   ★★
12/14″Scopes–100x: Dolidze 32 contains fifteen 11.5 magnitude and fainter stars in a 12′ area. At the cluster's center is a 2.5′× 2′ triangle of magnitude 11.5–12 stars. West of the triangle is a 2′ long NW–SE row of four magnitude 13–14 stars. A 9th magnitude star lies to the east. Other than this bright star and the asterisms, there is little resembling a cluster here.

NGC 6683 Open Cluster 20★ Tr Type I 2 p n
ϕ 11′, m9.9v, Br★ 11.71v   18^{h}42.2^m −06° 17′
Finder Chart 58-4   ★★★
12/14″Scopes–125x: NGC 6683 is located in an interesting region near the NW edge of the Scutum Star Cloud. The cluster has two dozen faint stars in a 5′× 3′ NE–SW area but is not well detached from the Star Cloud. Medium power shows the cluster best, but low power brings out the star-rich beauty of the surrounding Scutum Star Cloud and heightens the contrast between the Star Cloud and the Great Rift just to the cluster's NW.

Trumpler 35 Open Cluster 35★ Tr Type I 2 p
ϕ 9′, m9.2v, Br★ 11.41v   18^{h}42.9^m −04° 08′
Finder Chart 58-4   ★★★
12/14″Scopes–125x: Trumpler 35 is a mildly concentrated group of thirty 10th magnitude and fainter stars covering a 9′× 5′ E–W area. It stands out well from the surrounding star field. The cluster's brighter stars are along its southern edge, and in its center is a circular 2.5′ diameter concentration of its fainter members.

NGC 6694 Messier 26 Open Cluster 30★ Tr Type I 2 m
ϕ 14′, m8.0v, Br★ 10.30v   18^{h}45.2^m −09° 24′
Finder Chart 58-4, Figure 58-11   ★★★★
4/6″Scopes–75x: Messier 26 is a rich 5′ diameter group of two dozen 11th to 13th magnitude stars standing out against the background haze of unresolved members. A yellow 9th magnitude field star lies on the cluster's SW edge.

8/10"Scopes–100x: M26 is a compact, rich open cluster that stands out well from the surrounding field of faint stars. It contains forty mostly 12th to 14th magnitude members concentrated in an 8′ area, its brighter stars south of the cluster center. A 9th magnitude field star is on the SW edge and a dark, starless notch juts into the northern edge. A chain of faint stars curves from the northern edge around the cluster's eastern perimeter to the southern edge. A star-clump is semi detached at the southern edge. The cluster's members are more evenly distributed in its northern part.

Barnard 104 LDN 532 Dark Nebula
ϕ 16′ × 1′, Opacity 5 18^{h}47.3^m −04° 32′
Finder Chart 58-4, Figure 58-12   ★★★
4/6"Scopes–50x: Barnard 104, a dust cloud located 20′ north of magnitude 4.2 Beta (β) Scuti, is hook-shaped, its shaft a thin 16′ × 1′ N–S streak and its prong a 5′ WNW line from the shaft's southern end. Because B104 is on the northern edge of the Scutum Star Cloud, its field is profuse with faint stars.

Basel 1 Open Cl. 15★ Tr Type IV 1 p
ϕ 8′, m8.9v, Br★ 12.58v   18h48.2m −05° 51′
Finder Chart 58-4, Figure 58-10   ★★★
12/14"Scopes–125x: Basel 1 is near the center of a 35′ × 15′ WNW–ESE trapezoid of 6th and 7th magnitude stars. Low power shows two dozen stars in an irregular 8′ area. At 125x twenty faint stars are visible in the cluster's central 2′ × 1′ E–W concentration. A loose group is NNW of the cluster center.

Barnard 110 Dark Nebula
ϕ 11′, Opacity 6   18^{h}50.1^m −04° 48′

Barnard 111 Dark Nebula
ϕ [15′ × 5′], Opacity 3   18^{h}50.1^m −04° 48′

Barnard 113 Dark Nebula
ϕ 11′, Opacity 5   18^{h}51.4^m −04° 19′
Finder Chart 58-4, Figure 58-13   ★★★★/★★★/★★★
4/6"Scopes–35x: The Barnard 111 dark nebula complex, east of magnitude 4.2 Beta (β) Scuti and immediately north of the rich open cluster M11, is a dark bay that extends south from the Great Rift down into the northern part of the Scutum Star

Figure 58-13. *Located north of Messier 11 (at bottom), Barnard 113 (at top) and Barnard 110 (upper right of center) are the two most opaque areas within the larger, less distinct dark complex of Barnard 111, which encompasses all the dark area within this photo. Open cluster NGC 6704 is the small knot of stars at center. Chris Schur made this ten minute exposure on hypered 2415 film with an 8″, f1.5 Schmidt camera.*

Cloud. Barnard 110 and 113 are the darkest patches of B111, and their contrast with the surrounding Milky Way glow is so good that both are visible in binoculars. Barnard 110 is just NNW of an 8′ wide E–W pair of 8th magnitude stars: it is darkest just north of the western 8th magnitude star and becomes broader and less distinct to its north. An irregular prong extends west from its southern edge. Barnard 113 is an irregular 15′ × 5′ N–S dark patch separated from B110 to its SW by a streak of faint stars.

NGC 6704 Cr 390 Open Cluster 30★ Tr Type I 2 m
ϕ 6′, m9.2v, Br★ 12.20v   18^{h}50.9^m −05° 12′
Finder Chart 58-4, Figure 58-13   ★★
8/10"Scopes–100x: NGC 6704 is a granular patch 2′ NNW of a fine reddish colored 11.5 magnitude star. Fifteen 12th to 13th magnitude cluster members are in a 6′ area.
12/14"Scopes–125x: This cluster is a faint, irregularly scattered group of two 11.5 magnitude, and three

Figure 58-14. *Messier 11 (NGC 6705) is a large, rich impressive open cluster, its several dozen brightest members of remarkably uniform magnitude. Image courtesy of Martin C. Germano.*

Figure 58-15. *In large telescopes NGC 6712 has a large granular core within a well-resolved halo. Image courtesy of Lee C. Coombs.*

dozen 12th to 15th magnitude, stars in a 6′ area. It is divided into three distinct groups. The SSE concentration contains twenty stars, including a conspicuous NE–SW row of one red 11.5 and three 12th magnitude stars. The SW concentration is an irregular semicircle open to the NE. The northern concentration is an E–W row of one 11.5 and two 12th magnitude stars with a kite-shaped asterism of four 13th magnitude stars SW of the west end of the row.

NGC 6705 Messier 11 Open Cluster 200★ Tr Type I2r
ϕ 13′, m5.8v, Br★ 8.00v   18^{h}51.1^m −06° 16′
Finder Chart 58-4, Figure 58-14   ★★★★★
Wild Duck Cluster

Messier 11 is an extremely populous open cluster 6,200 light years distant. It is so rich that it resembles the looser globular clusters, but it is in fact an intermediate age open cluster 250 million years old. It is extremely luminous for a somewhat evolved open cluster, its absolute magnitude being −6.9, a brightness of 48,000 suns.

4/6″ Scopes–75x: Messier 11, one of the finest open clusters in the sky, is visible in binoculars and small telescopes as a uniform patch of moderately faint stars surrounding a single bright magnitude 8.0 star. At least a hundred 11th to 12.5 magnitude stars are evenly concentrated over a 14′ area. The concentration and uniform magnitude of the cluster's couple dozen brightest stars makes M11 visually impressive.

8/10″ Scopes–100x: Exquisite! This cluster is a favorite of many amateur astronomers. 50x to 75x shows a cluster the brightest stars of which are uniform both in distribution and brightness. At 100x, 150 magnitude 11 to 14 stars are seen in a 15′ area, the lone magnitude 8.0 bright star at the center giving the impression of being a foreground object (which it indeed seems to be). At 150x the cluster stars are noticeably distributed in a network of knots and clumps mixed with some meandering dark lanes, the two most conspicuous winding from the cluster's center to its north and west edges. Although difficult to discern amongst the profusion of stars, careful scrutiny shows the east-pointing "V" of brighter cluster members that resembles the V-formation "Wild Ducks" form when flying.

NGC 6712 Globular Cluster Class IX
ϕ 7.2′, m8.2v   18^{h}53.1^m −08° 42′
Finder Chart 58-4, Figure 58-15   ★★
8/10″ Scopes–125x: Globular cluster NGC 6712 is in the same field as planetary nebula IC 1295. The globular is moderately faint and unresolved, its 3′ diameter halo containing a slightly brighter core.
16/18″ Scopes–175x: In larger telescopes NGC 6712 has a large granular core within a 5′ diameter well resolved halo. The outline of the globular's periphery is irregular and somewhat flattened on its SSW side. The surrounding Milky Way field is very rich.

IC 1295 PK25+4.2 Planetary Nebula Type 3b+2
φ >86″, m15.0p, CS15.0v   18ʰ54.6ᵐ −08° 50′
Finder Chart 58-4   ★

8/10″Scopes–150x: IC1295, located less than half a
  degree ESE of globular cluster NGC 6712, is a large,
  diffuse, featureless blob with two faint stars superimposed near the SW edge of its disk.

16/18″Scopes–175x: IC1295 is a dim, pale white glow
  with three 13.5 magnitude stars just within the halo
  near its SW edge. A 12th magnitude star lies 1.5′
  WSW of the nebula's center. The central star is
  occasionally visible as a faint twinkle. In an O-III
  filter the halo seems elongated 1.75′ × 1.5′ E–W and
  vaguely annular.

Chapter 59

Serpens Caput, the Snake's Head

59.1 Overview

Serpens is the Serpent with which the Serpent-Bearer, Ophiuchus wrestles. Serpens writhes across the Serpent-Bearer's waist, and is firmly grasped by the giant at Delta (δ) and Epsilon (ϵ) Ophiuchi on the west and Nu (ν) Ophiuchi on the east. Consequently Serpens is the only constellation that is in two separate sections: Serpens Caput, the Serpent's Head, is west of Ophiuchus, extending west and north from Delta + Epsilon Ophiuchi through Mu (v), Epsilon, Lambda (λ), and Delta Serpentis up to the conspicuous asterism of the Serpent's upraised head, Beta (β), Gamma (γ), Kappa (κ), and Iota (ι) Serpentis; and Serpens Cauda, the Serpent's Tail, is east of Ophiuchus, extending NE up the Great Rift in the summer Milky Way. The celestial combination of Serpent and Serpent-Wrestler was explained in Greek mythology by identifying Ophiuchus with Aesculapius, fabled founder of the art of medicine who was said to have obtained an herb which restored life to the dead from a snake. This legend derived from the apparent return to youth which snakes experience when they slough off their skin. But the celestial pair of Serpent + Serpent-Wrestler probably originated in ancient Babylonia, for Serpent-Wrestlers which bear an uncanny similarity to the Greek constellation-figure of Ophiuchus were common in Mesopotamian art of the 3rd millennium B.C.

Like all off-Milky Way constellations, Serpens Caput features galaxies, though most of them are rather small and faint. It also has a couple of globular clusters, one of which, Messier 5, rivals the Hercules Cluster M13 as the finest globular in the northern celestial hemisphere.

59.2 Interesting Stars

5 Serpentis = Σ1930 Triple Star   Spec. G0
AB: m5.1, 10.1; Sep. 11.2″; P.A. 36° $15^h19.3^m$ +01° 46′
Finder Chart 59-3   ★★★★
4/6″ Scopes–100x: 5 Serpentis is an unequally bright pair of yellow and reddish stars. A third companion

Serpens: SIR-pens
Genitive: Serpentis, SIR-pen-tis
Abbreviation: SerCp
Culmination: 9 pm–July 1, midnight–May 15
Area: 637 square degrees (Caput and Cauda combined)
Showpieces: 5 Ser, 13–δ Ser, $O\Sigma$300, M5 (NGC 5904)
Binocular Objects: 41–γ Ser, M5 (NGC 5904)

at 9.1 magnitude lies 127″ distant in position angle 40°. The globular cluster Messier 5 is in the same field of view to the NW.

Delta (δ)=13 Ser (Σ1954) Quadruple Star   Spec. F0
AB: m4.2, 5.2; Sep. 4.4″; P.A. 176° $15^h34.8^m$ +10° 32′
Finder Chart 59-4   ★★★★★
4/6″ Scopes–100x: Delta Serpentis is a close pair of pale yellow stars orbiting each other in a period of nearly 3,170 years. Two faint magnitude 14.7 and 15 stars are near the bright binary.

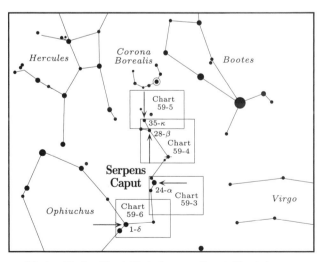

Master Finder Chart 59-1. Serpens Caput Chart Areas
Guide stars indicated by arrows.

Serpens Caput, the Snake's Head Constellation Chart 59-2

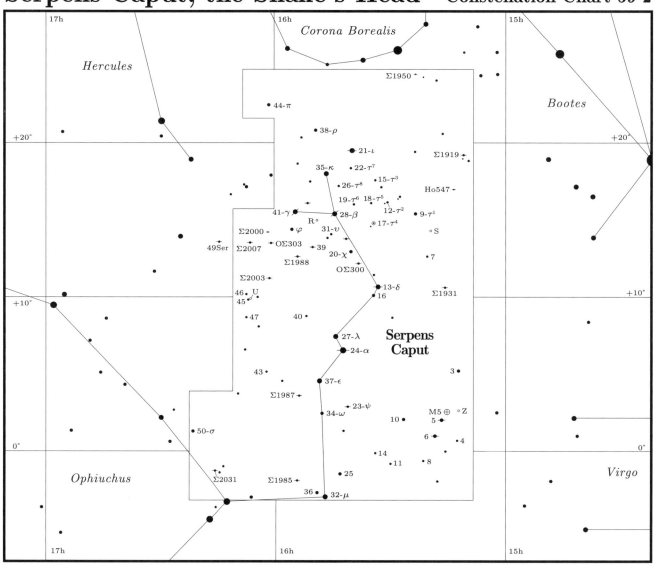

Chart Symbols

Constellation Chart   0 1 2 3 4 5 6

Stellar Magnitudes   ● ● ● ● ● • • •

Finder Charts   0/1 2 3 4 5 6 7 8 9

Master Finder Chart   0 1 2 3 4 5

→ Guide Star Pointer   ⊙ ○ Variable Stars   ⟡ Planetary Nebulae

●—• Double Stars   ○ Open Clusters   □ Small Bright Nebulae

Finder Chart Scale   ⊕ Globular Clusters   Large Bright Nebulae

(One degree tick marks)   ⬭ Galaxies   Dark Nebulae

Table 59-1: Selected Variable Stars in Serpens Caput

Name	HD No.	Type	Max.	Min.	Period (Days)	F*	Spec. Type	R.A. (2000)	Dec.	Finder Chart No.	Notes
Z Ser		SRa	9.4	10.9	87		M5	$15^h16.0^m$	$+02°\,10'$	59-3	
S Ser	136695	M	7.0	14.1	368	0.43	M5e-M6e	21.7	+14 19	59-4	
17–τ^4 Ser	139216	Lb	7.5	8.9			M5	36.5	+15 06	59-4	
R Ser	141850	M	5.16	14.4	356	0.41	M7	50.7	+15 08	59-4	
U Ser	144782	M	7.8	14.7	237	0.47	M4e-M6e	$16^h07.3^m$	+09 56	59-2	

F* = The fraction of period taken up by the star's rise from min. to max. brightness, or the period spent in eclipse.

Table 59-2: Selected Double Stars in Serpens Caput

Name	ADS No.	Pair	M1	M2	Sep."	P.A.°	Spec	R.A. (2000)	Dec.	Finder Chart No.	Notes
Σ1919	9535		6.7	7.6	23.9	10	G5	15ʰ12.7ᵐ	+19° 18′	59-2	Yellow and bluish
Ho547	9562		7.9	12.0	5.2	298	G0	16.4	+16 48	59-4	Yellowish pair
Σ1931	9580		7.1	8.5	13.4	168	F8	18.7	+10 25	59-4	
5 Ser	9584	AB	5.1	10.1	11.2	36	G0	19.3	+01 46	59-3	Yellow and reddish
	9584	AC		9.1	127.2	40					
6 Ser	9596		5.4	10.0	3.1	20	K0	21.0	+00 43	59-3	Close yellow pair
Σ1950	9675		8.1	9.6	3.2	93	K2	30.0	+25 30	59-5	Deep yellow and blue
13-δ Ser	9701	AB	4.2	5.2	w4.4	*176	F0	34.8	+10 32	59-4	Pale yellowish pair
OΣ300	9740		6.4	9.5	15.3	261	G5	40.2	+12 03	59-4	Yellow and blue
23-ξ Ser	9763	AB	5.9	12.1	4.4	48					
	9763	AC		8.9	207.3	208					
	9763	AD		10.5	171.5	281					
	9763			7.2	171.9	236					
24-α Ser	9765	AB	2.7	11.7	58.2	350	K0	44.3	+06 26	59-3	
28-β Ser	9778	AB	3.7	9.9	30.6	265	A2	46.2	+15 25	59-4	Blue and yellow
	9778	AC		10.7	201.1	210					
39 Ser			6.2	11.8	98.3	116	G0	53.2	+13 12	59-4	
Σ1985	9842		7.0	8.1	5.9	348	G0	55.9	−02 10	59-6	Yellow and white
41-γ Ser		AB	3.9	10.5	201.5	315	F5	56.5	+15 40	59-4	
		BC		10.9	177.1	165					
Σ1988	9850		7.4	8.1	2.1	259	F2	56.8	+12 29	59-4	
Σ1987			7.2	8.7	10.4	322	A0	57.2	+03 24	59-3	
OΣ303	9880		7.5	8.0	1.2	164	F5	16ʰ00.9ᵐ	+13 16	59-4	
Σ2000	9904		8.4	9.2	2.6	228	F2	03.0	+14 00	59-2	
Σ2003	9908		7.3	11.3	14.4	171	K2	03.7	+11 26	59-2	
Σ2007	9922	AB	6.9	8.4	36.6	323	K0	06.0	+13 19	59-2	
	9922	AC		10.5	167.6	138					
49 Ser	9969	AB	7.4	7.5	4.1	348	K0	13.3	+13 32	59-2	
(In Her)	9969	AC		10.5	236.2	123					
Σ2031	9984	AB	7.0	9.1	20.8	230	F8	16.3	−01 39	59-6	
	9984	AC		11.1	93.4	21					

Footnotes: *= Year 2000, a = Near apogee, c = Closing, w = Widening. Finder Chart No: All stars listed in the tables are plotted in the large Constellation Chart, but when a star appears in a Finder Chart, this number is listed. Notes: When colors are subtle, the suffix *-ish* is used, e.g. *bluish*.

OΣ300 Double Star   **Spec. G5**
m6.4,9.5; Sep.15.3″; P.A.261°   **15ʰ40.2ᵐ +12° 03′**
Finder Chart 59-4   ★★★★
4/6″Scopes–100x: Otto Struve 300 is a color contrast double of unequally bright yellow and blue stars.

Beta (β) = 28 Serpentis (Σ1970) Triple Star Spec. A2
AB: m3.7,9.9; Sep.30.6″; P.A.265° 15ʰ46.2ᵐ +15° 25′
Finder Chart 59-4   ★★★★
4/6″Scopes–75x: Beta Serpentis is a wide, easily resolved triple for small telescopes. The closer AB pair is pale yellow and blue. The third star, a magnitude 10.7 object, lies 201″ distant from the primary in position angle 210°.

59.3 Deep-Sky Objects

Palomar 5 Globular Cluster Class XII
φ 6.9′, m11.8v   **15ʰ16.1ᵐ −00° 07′**
Finder Chart 59-3, Figure 59-1   ★
20/22″Scopes–100x: Palomar 5, located half a degree south of the magnitude 5.6 star 4 Serpentis, is a challenge to detect even with large instruments. Ideal sky conditions and averted vision are necessary to glimpse its extremely faint, hazy 5′ diameter patch. Three or four of its brightest members, 15th magnitude objects, may be just resolved. A 9th magnitude foreground star is on the globular's SE

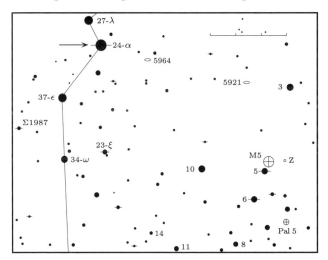

Finder Chart 59-3. 24–α SerCp: 15ʰ44.3ᵐ +06° 26′

Figure 59-1. *Palomar 5, a challenge even in large telescopes, is an extremely faint globular cluster of the lowest concentration class. Martin C. Germano made this 80 minute exposure on hypered 2415 film with an 8″, f5 Newtonian.*

Figure 59-2. *In large telescopes the halo of NGC 5921 can be seen to have a faint bar extending out of a bright core surrounded by a faint halo. Image courtesy of Mike Schade.*

edge. Palomar 5 is so faint because it is very distant, about 70,000 light years away beyond not only our galaxy's central bulge but even beyond the far edge of its spiral disk.

NGC 5904 Messier 5 Globular Cluster Class V
ϕ 17.4′, m5.7v   15^{h}18.6^m +02° 05′
Finder Chart 59-3, Figure 59-3   ★★★★★
4/6″ Scopes–100x: Messier 5, located 22′ NNW of the double star 5 Serpentis (5.1, 10.1; 11.2″; 36°), is a fine globular cluster nearly as impressive as the great Hercules Cluster, Messier 13. At low power M5 shows a well concentrated core and some

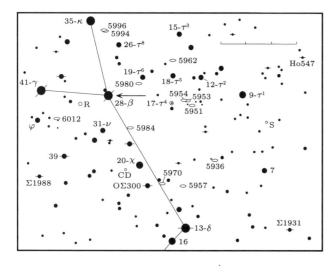

Finder Chart 59-4. 28–β SerCp: 15^{h}46.2^m +15° 25′

resolution around the periphery of its halo. At 100x the outer halo is well resolved and can be seen to extend out to a diameter of 10′.

8/10″ Scopes–125x: This splendid globular cluster has a bright granular core with an irregular 12′ diameter well resolved halo. Chains of faint stars radiate from the periphery outward in all directions save east, on which side the globular's halo is somewhat flattened.

12/14″ Scopes–150x: Messier 5, one of the finest globular clusters in the northern celestial hemisphere, is a spectacular sight in 12″ and larger telescopes! Hundreds of white and yellowish stars can be resolved from the extremities of the 15′ diameter halo right into the dense core. The view is breathtakingly (but falsely) three-dimensional: an overlay of resolved stars stands out against a luminous background glow broken by a few dark gaps. At high power numerous star chains can be traced across the face of the halo and from the halo's perimeter outward in all directions but east, toward which the cluster outliers are thinner. Conspicuous on the globular's SW edge is a 10th magnitude foreground star. To the SE of M5 is the double 5 Serpentis, a magnitude 5.1 yellow star with a 10th magnitude reddish companion 11″ distant.

NGC 5921 H148[1] Galaxy Type SB(r)bc I-II
ϕ 4.9′ × 4.2′, m10.8v, SB14.0   15^{h}21.9^m +05° 04′
Finder Chart 59-3, Figures 59-2, 59-4   ★★★
12/14″ Scopes–125x: NGC 5921, located 3′ WNW of a

9th magnitude star, displays a bright core embedded in a moderately faint 2′ × 1.75′ NNE–SSW halo. A 12th magnitude star is at the halo's SW edge.

16/18″Scopes–150x: In large telescopes NGC 5921 shows a 4′ × 3′ halo containing a faint NNE–SSW bar that extends from the major axis of a 45″ × 30″ oval core with a stellar nucleus.

NGC 5936 H130² Galaxy Type SB(rs)b I-II
ϕ 1.2′ × 1.1′, m12.5v, SB12.7   15^{h}30.0^m +12° 59′
Finder Chart 59-4   ★★
12/14″Scopes–125x: NGC 5936, located 10′ NW of a 7th magnitude star, is a fairly faint 1.25′ diameter glow. The poorly concentrated core covers a third of the halo. A 14th magnitude star lies 2′ west.

NGC 5951 H654² Galaxy Type SBc: sp
ϕ 3.2′ × 0.7′, m12.7v, SB13.4   15^{h}33.7^m +15° 00′
Finder Chart 59-4   ★★★
16/18″Scopes–150x: NGC 5951, located 6′ WSW of a 9.5 magnitude star, is a faint 3′ × 0.75′ streak that is slightly brighter along its major axis. A 14th magnitude star lies 2′ SE. The galaxy-pair NGC 5953-54 is 12′ NE.

NGC 5953 H178² Galaxy Type SAa: pec
ϕ 1.7′ × 1.3′, m12.1v, SB12.8   15^{h}34.5^m +15° 12′
NGC 5954 H179² Galaxy Type SAB(rs)cd: pec
ϕ 1.0′ × 0.5′, m12.1v, SB11.2   15^{h}34.6^m +15° 12′
Finder Chart 59-4, Figure 59-5   ★★/★★
16/18″Scopes–150x: NGC 5953 and NGC 5954 are a close NE–SW galaxy pair with touching halos. NGC 5953, the southwestern galaxy, is the brighter of the two and has a very faint circular 1.25′ diameter halo containing a small 20″ diameter core. A 14th magnitude star touches the halo's SW edge. NGC 5954 to the NE is much fainter and its 1.25′ × 0.5′ N–S halo surrounds only a poorly concentrated center. Two magnitude 12.5 stars are 1.25′ and 1.5′ SE of the galaxy-pair.

NGC 5957 Galaxy Type (R′)SAB(r)b
ϕ 2.6′ × 2.6′, m11.7v, SB13.6   15^{h}35.4^m +12° 03′
Finder Chart 59-4, Figure 59-6   ★★★
12/14″Scopes–125x: NGC 5957 forms a triangle with a 10th magnitude star 2.5′ to the galaxy's NNW and a 10.5 magnitude star 2.5′ to its SW. It has a fairly faint, circular 1.75′ diameter halo that slightly brightens to a small core. A threshold star touches the halo's SE edge.

Figure 59-3. *Messier 5 (NGC5904) is a splendid globular cluster nearly as fine as the Hercules Cluster Messier 13. Image courtesy of Jim Burnell.*

NGC 5962 H96² Galaxy Type SA(r)c II-III
ϕ 2.6′ × 1.8′, m11.3v, SB12.9   15^{h}36.5^m +16° 37′
Finder Chart 59-4, Figure 59-7   ★★★
8/10″Scopes–100x: NGC 5962 has a fairly faint 1.5′ × 1′ ESE–WNW halo that gradually brightens toward its center.

16/18″Scopes–150x: A prominent stellar nucleus is embedded in a broad core surrounded by a fairly bright 2′ × 1.25′ ESE–WNW halo. A 14th magnitude

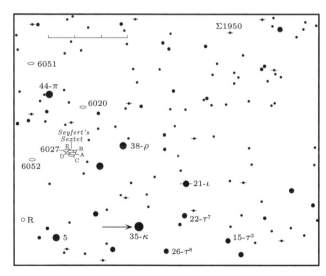

Finder Chart 59-5. 35-κ SerCp: 15^{h}48.7^m +18° 08′

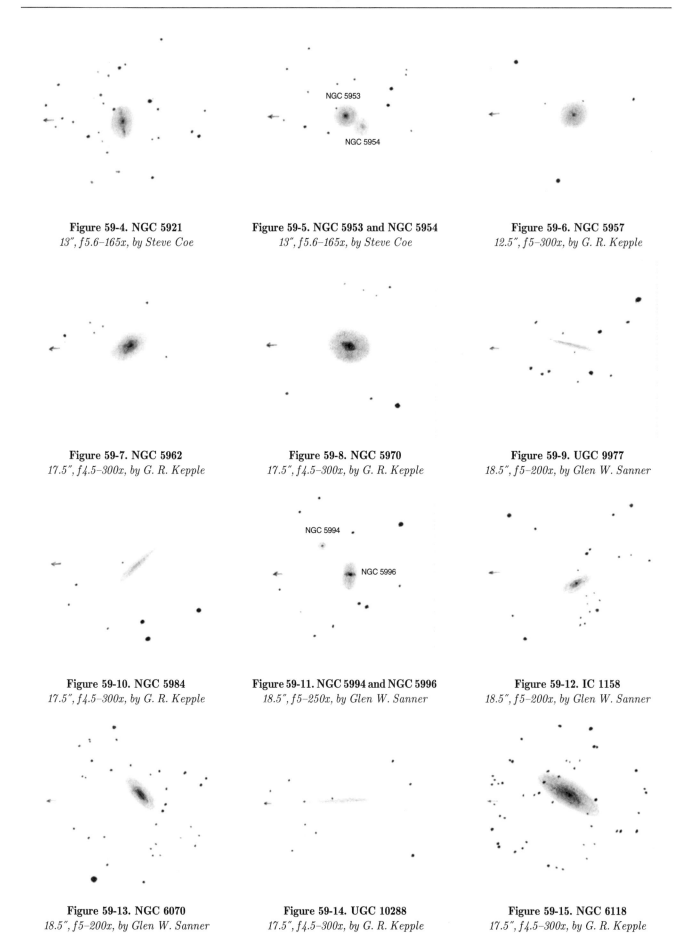

Figure 59-4. NGC 5921
13″, ƒ5.6–165x, by Steve Coe

Figure 59-5. NGC 5953 and NGC 5954
13″, ƒ5.6–165x, by Steve Coe

Figure 59-6. NGC 5957
12.5″, ƒ5–300x, by G. R. Kepple

Figure 59-7. NGC 5962
17.5″, ƒ4.5–300x, by G. R. Kepple

Figure 59-8. NGC 5970
17.5″, ƒ4.5–300x, by G. R. Kepple

Figure 59-9. UGC 9977
18.5″, ƒ5–200x, by Glen W. Sanner

Figure 59-10. NGC 5984
17.5″, ƒ4.5–300x, by G. R. Kepple

Figure 59-11. NGC 5994 and NGC 5996
18.5″, ƒ5–250x, by Glen W. Sanner

Figure 59-12. IC 1158
18.5″, ƒ5–200x, by Glen W. Sanner

Figure 59-13. NGC 6070
18.5″, ƒ5–200x, by Glen W. Sanner

Figure 59-14. UGC 10288
17.5″, ƒ4.5–300x, by G. R. Kepple

Figure 59-15. NGC 6118
17.5″, ƒ4.5–300x, by G. R. Kepple

star lies 2.5′ west of the galaxy's center and several threshold stars are just visible on its SW edge.

NGC 5970 H76² Galaxy Type SB(r)c II-III
ϕ **2.7′×1.8′, m11.5v, SB13.2**   15ʰ38.5ᵐ +12° 11′
Finder Chart 59-4, Figure 59-8   ★★★
8/10″Scopes–100x: NGC 5970 is situated among three bright stars, a magnitude 6.5 star 20′ WNW, a magnitude 7 star 15′ ESE, and a magnitude 7.5 star 6′ SW. It has a fairly faint 1.5′×0.75′ E–W halo containing a slight brightening at its center.
16/18″Scopes–150x: This fairly bright galaxy has a 2.5′×2′ ENE–WSW halo that contains a highly extended 40″×20″ core with a faint stellar nucleus. A 9th magnitude star lies 3.25′ NE.

NGC 5980 H655² Galaxy Type S
ϕ **1.7′×0.6′, m12.6v, SB12.4**   15ʰ41.4ᵐ +15° 47′
Finder Chart 59-4   ★★
16/18″Scopes–150x: NGC 5980, located 3′ NNW of an 11th magnitude star, has a faint halo elongated 1.5′×0.5′ in position angle 13° and surrounding a poorly concentrated core.

UGC 9977 Galaxy Type Sc: sp
ϕ **3.6′×0.4′, m13.2v, SB13.4**   15ʰ42.0ᵐ +00° 42′
Finder Chart 59-6, Figure 59-9   ★★
16/18″Scopes–150x: UGC 9977 is a very faint, thin shaft of light highly elongated 3.5′×0.25′ ENE–WSW and requiring averted vision. A 12th magnitude star is 2.5′ NE, a 13th magnitude star 2′ SE, and a 10th magnitude star 5′ SE, of the galaxy's center.

NGC 5984 H656² Galaxy Type SB(rs)d: III
ϕ **2.7′×0.6′, m12.5v, SB12.9**   15ʰ42.9ᵐ +14° 14′
Finder Chart 59-4, Figure 59-10   ★★
16/18″Scopes–150x: NGC 5984 has a faint, highly elongated 3′×0.5′ NW–SE halo containing a faint stellar nucleus. Centered about 2′ to its NNE is a 2′×0.75′ E–W isosceles triangle of magnitude 12.5 stars. The surrounding field is relatively rich, well mixed with both bright and faint stars.

NGC 5996 H97² Galaxy Type S?
ϕ **1.8′×1.0′, m12.8v, SB13.3**   15ʰ46.9ᵐ +17° 52′
Finder Chart 59-4, Figure 59-11   ★★
16/18″Scopes–150x: NGC 5996, located half a degree SW of magnitude 4.1 Kappa (κ) = 35 Serpentis, has a very faint 1′×0.5′ N–S halo containing a faint E–W bar. Its companion galaxy NGC 5994, 1.5′ SW of its center, is an extremely faint stellar object. 2.75′ SE of NGC 5996 is a magnitude 10.5 star, and

2′ to its NNE a 30″ wide ENE–WSW pair of magnitude 12.5 stars.

NGC 6012 H957² Galaxy Type (R)SB(r)ab:
ϕ **1.9′×1.5′, m12.0v, SB13.0**   15ʰ54.2ᵐ +14° 35′
Finder Chart 59-4   ★★
16/18″Scopes–150x: NGC 6012 forms a triangle with a 9th magnitude star 2′ to its south and a 9.5 magnitude star 1.5′ to its NE, the latter with a magnitude 12 companion 10″ away in P.A. 350°. The galaxy has a very faint, circular 1.5′ diameter halo slightly elongated NW–SE and containing a poorly concentrated center.

NGC 6027 Galaxy Type S0 pec
ϕ **0.5′×0.2′, m14.3v, SB11.7**   15ʰ59ᵐ11.9ˢ +20°45′55″
NGC 6027A Galaxy Type Sa pec
ϕ **0.7′×0.5′, m13.9v, SB12.6**   15ʰ59ᵐ11.2ˢ +20°45′13″
NGC 6027B Galaxy Type S0 pec
ϕ **0.3′×0.2′, m14.5v, SB11.3**   15ʰ59ᵐ10.9ˢ +20°45′43″
NGC 6027C Galaxy Type SB(s)c? sp
ϕ **0.9′×0.2′, m15.7v, SB13.7**   15ʰ59ᵐ14.4ˢ +20°45′52″
NGC 6027D Galaxy Type S?
ϕ **0.2′×0.2′, m15.5v, SB11.8**   15ʰ59ᵐ13.0ˢ +20°45′32″
NGC 6027E Galaxy Type S0?
ϕ **0.7′×0.4′, m13.4v, SB11.8**   15ʰ59ᵐ12.6ˢ +20°45′46″
Finder Chart 59-5   ★/★/★/★/★/★
Seyfert's Sextet
16/18″Scopes–150x: Seyfert's Sextet is an extremely compact cluster of six galaxies superimposed upon one another and therefore appearing as one bizarre object with three separate faint stellar nuclei. The composite halo is exceedingly irregular in profile and no larger than 2′ across its largest dimension. The southernmost nucleus is of NGC 6027A, the

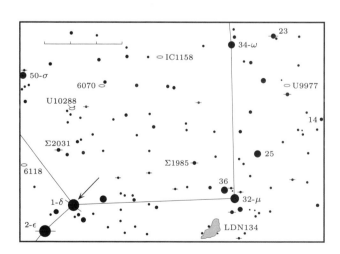

Finder Chart 59-6. 1–δ Oph: 16ʰ14.2ᵐ −03° 41′

NNE nucleus of NGC 6027E, and the NW, and faintest, nucleus of NGC 6027B. The halo of NGC 6027 itself is visible as a spike that protrudes from the fuzzy blob to the NE. The halo of NGC 6027C is an extension to the south. NGC 6027D is entirely superimposed upon the others and at this aperture cannot be distinguished as a separate entity. 14th magnitude stars lie 1.5′ west, and 1.25′ and 1.5′ ESE, of the galaxy cluster.

IC 1158   Galaxy Type SB:(r:)c II-III
ϕ 2.6′ × 1.6′, m12.6v, SB 14.0   16ʰ01.5ᵐ +01° 43′
Finder Chart 59-6, Figure 59-12   ★★
16/18″ Scopes–150x: IC 1158, located 2.5′ SW of a 10.5 magnitude star, is a very faint, diffuse 2′ × 1.5′ NW–SE oval without central brightening.

NGC 6051   Galaxy Type E
ϕ 1.6′ × 1.0′, m13.1v, SB 13.4   16ʰ04.9ᵐ +23° 56′
Finder Chart 59-5   ★★
16/18″ Scopes–150x: NGC 6051, located just 1.25′ NNW of a 10th magnitude star, has an extremely faint, circular 1′ diameter halo that contains a faint stellar nucleus. The glare of the 10th magnitude star makes this already low surface brightness galaxy even that much harder to see.

NGC 6070   H553²   Galaxy Type SA(r)c I-II
ϕ 3.6′ × 1.9′, m11.8v, SB 13.7   16ʰ10.0ᵐ +00° 43′
Finder Chart 59-6, Figure 59-13   ★★★
12/14″ Scopes–125x: NGC 6070, located 7′ SSE of a 7th magnitude star, is a faint 2.5′ × 1′ NE–SW glow containing a slight central brightening.

16/18″ Scopes–150x: The halo is a fairly bright 3′ × 1.5′ ENE–WSW oval that contains a large bright core but no stellar nucleus. A 12.5 magnitude star 2.25′ NE of the galaxy's core is the brightest in an arc of stars that curves around the halo from its NE to its SSW.

UGC 10288   Galaxy Type Sc: sp
ϕ 4.9′ × 0.6′, m13.3v, SB 14.3   16ʰ14.4ᵐ −00° 13′
Finder Chart 59-6, Figure 59-14   ★★
16/18″ Scopes–150x: UGC 10288 lies 8′ WNW of an 8th magnitude star and 3.5′ SSE of a 9th magnitude star. It is a very faint, diffuse ghostly streak elongated 4.5′ × 0.5′ E–W without central brightening. Two threshold stars are superimposed upon the halo, one at its western tip and the other 30″ SW of its center.

NGC 6118   H402²   Galaxy Type SA(s)c I
ϕ 4.6′ × 1.9′, m11.7v, SB 13.9   16ʰ21.8ᵐ −02° 17′
Finder Chart 59-6, Figure 59-15   ★★
12/14″ Scopes–125x: NGC 6118 is 7′ south of a 7th magnitude star and 3.5′ NNW of an 11.5 magnitude star. It has a faint, diffuse 3′ × 2′ NE–SW halo.

16/18″ Scopes–150x: With averted vision the moderately faint halo appears elongated 4′ × 2′ NE–SW without any central brightening, though a very faint stellar nucleus is intermittently visible. Two very faint stars lie on the halo's edge 1′ SW and 1.5′ ENE of the galaxy's center.

Chapter 60

Serpens Cauda, the Snake's Tail

60.1 Overview

Serpens Cauda is the Tail of the Serpent wrestled by the Serpent-Bearer, Ophiuchus. The Serpent's Head, Serpens Caput, is on the western side of Ophiuchus: thus the Serpent is the only two-part constellation. Some of the history and mythology of the celestial Serpent-Bearer and his Serpent is given in the Overviews to Chapters 59 and 54. Suffice it here to repeat only that in classical mythology the constellation Ophiuchus was identified with the god Aesculapius, legendary founder of medicine, whose sacred icon was the caduceus – the staff with two serpents coiled around it.

As regions of the celestial sphere Serpens Cauda and Serpens Caput are as different as they can get. Serpens Caput is well out of the Milky Way and therefore rich in external galaxies. Serpens Cauda, on the other hand, runs along the very heart of the Milky Way, the galactic equator, and therefore contains such typical Milky Way objects as open clusters, emission nebulae, and obscuring dust clouds. In fact Serpens Cauda does a little too good of a job of running along the heart of the Milky Way, for most of the constellation is covered by the virtually opaque Great Rift that divides the Milky Way in two from Cygnus SW all the way to Centaurus. Thus Serpens Cauda has rather fewer open clusters and emission nebulae than we would have a right to expect from a Milky Way group. However, one of its objects is Messier 16, an impressive open cluster + emission nebula complex known as the Eagle or Star Queen Nebula.

60.2 Interesting Stars

Nu (ν) = 53 Ser (S,h247) Double Star   **Spec. A0**
m4.3, 8.3; Sep. 46.3″; P.A. 28° $17^h20.8^m -12° 51'$
Constellation Chart 60-2   ★★★★
4/6″ Scopes–75x: Nu Serpentis is a very wide double, easily split with small telescopes, of attractive green and pale blue components.

> **Serpens:** SIR-pens
> **Genitive:** Serpentis, SIR-pen-tis
> **Abbreviation:** SerCd
> **Culmination:** 9 pm–Aug. 1, midnight–June 15
> **Area:** 637 square degrees (Caput and Cauda combined)
> **Showpieces:** 53–ν Ser, 59 Ser, 63–ϑ Ser, IC 4703, M16 (NGC 6611)
> **Binocular Objects:** 53–ν Ser, 59 Ser, 63–ϑ Ser, IC 4703, IC 4756, M16 (NGC 6611), NGC 6539, NGC 6604

Σ2303 Double Star   **Spec. F5**
m6.6, 9.1; Sep. 2.1″; P.A. 236° $18^h20.1^m -07° 59'$
Finder Chart 60-3   ★★★★
4/6″ Scopes–150x: Struve 2303, located in a Milky Way field laced with dark nebulae, is a close double which provides a good optical test for small instruments.

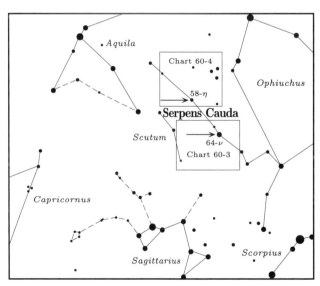

Master Finder Chart 60-1. Serpens Cauda Chart Areas
Guide stars indicated by arrows.

Serpens Cauda, the Snake's Tail

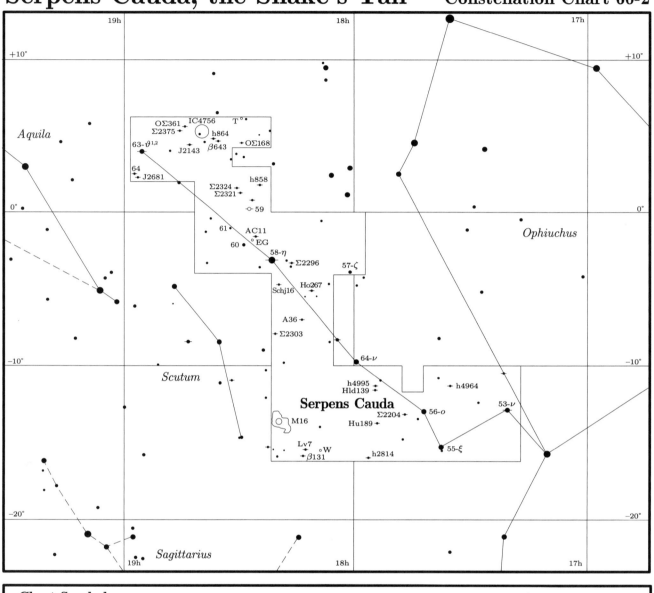

Chart Symbols

Constellation Chart	0 1 2 3 4 5 6	
Stellar Magnitudes	● ● ● ● ● • • •	
Finder Charts	0/1 2 3 4 5 6 7 8 9	
Master Finder Chart	0 1 2 3 4 5	

→ Guide Star Pointer
●—● Double Stars
Finder Chart Scale
(One degree tick marks)

⊙ ○ Variable Stars
◯ Open Clusters
⊕ Globular Clusters
⬯ Galaxies

⬙ Planetary Nebulae
▢ Small Bright Nebulae
Large Bright Nebulae
Dark Nebulae

Table 60-1: Selected Variable Stars in Serpens Cauda

Name	HD No.	Type	Max.	Min.	Period (Days)	F*	Spec. Type	R.A. (2000) Dec.		Finder Chart No.	Notes
W Ser	166126	E	8.42	10.20	14.16	0.20	CF5ep	$18^{\mathrm{h}}09.8^{\mathrm{m}}$	$-15°\,33'$	60-3	
59 Ser	169986	?	7.2	14.8	317	0.47	M5e-M9	27.2	$+00\,12$	60-4	
EG Ser	169691	EA	8.7	9.5	497	0.05	A0	26.0	$-01\,41$	60-4	
T Ser		M	9.1	15.5	340	0.47	M7e	28.8	$+06\,18$	60-4	

F* = The fraction of period taken up by the star's rise from min. to max. brightness, or the period spent in eclipse.

Table 60-2: Selected Double Stars in Serpens Cauda

Name	ADS No.	Pair	M1	M2	Sep."	P.A.°	Spec	R.A. (2000)	Dec.	Finder Chart No.	Notes
53–ν Ser	10481		4.3	8.3	46.3	28	A0	17^{h}20.8^m	−12° 51′	60-2	Green and pale blue
h4964			5.7	8.7	54.6	225	B8	34.8	−11 15	60-2	
Σ2204	10771		8.1	8.2	14.4	25	A0	46.3	−13 19	60-3	
Hu189	10856		7.5	8.7	1.5	241	F5	53.1	−13 39	60-3	
h4995	10872		6.6	11.6	28.6	155	K0	54.1	−11 20	60-3	
Hld139	10878	AB	7.0	10.8	3.5	152	F2	54.9	−11 38	60-3	
	10878	AC		12.5	65.6	94					
h2814	10891	AB	6.1	8.6	20.8	157	A0	56.3	−15 49	60-3	
	10891	AC		11.5	33.7	349					
Ho267	11135		6.6	12.6	19.0	355	B9	18^{h}11.4^m	−05 12	60-2	
A36	11165	AxBC	7.6		65.6	42	G0	12.4	−07 18	60-3	
	11165	BC	11.0	11.3	1.3	196					
Lv7	11146	AB	8.0	11.6	3.8	278	B5	12.5	−15 22	60-3	
	11146	AC		11.6	33.6	240					
β131	11166	AB	7.3	9.3	2.8	278	F5	13.6	−15 37	60-3	
	11166	AC		11.5	8.4	289					
Σ2296	11205		7.3	10.9	3.2	8	K0	15.7	−03 21	60-4	
Schj16	11257		8.1	9.4	2.9	203	G0	19.7	−04 57	60-2	
Σ2303	11262		6.6	9.1	2.1	236	F5	20.1	−07 59	60-3	Unequal yellowish pair
h858			8.2	9.5	12.8	229	F5	24.0	+01 30	60-4	
AC11	11324		6.8	7.0	0.8	*355	F5	24.9	−01 35	60-4	Close yellow pair
59 Ser	11353	AB	5.3	7.6	3.8	318	A0	27.2	+00 12	60-4	Yellowish and white
OΣ168		AB	7.7	8.4	47.6	164	A0	28.6	+04 51	60-4	
Σ2321	11396		8.2	9.8	6.8	190	A0	30.0	+01 11	60-4	
Σ2324	11410	AB	8.4	8.7	2.4	146	B8	31.0	+01 23	60-4	
β643	11477	AB	6.5	12.3	10.5	330	A0	35.6	+04 56	60-4	
Σ2342	11477	AC		9.1	30.5	5					
h864	11494		6.8	11.0	18.2	323	K2	36.5	+04 57	60-4	
J2143			7.1	12.1	10.0	315	F8	41.3	+04 33	60-4	
Σ2375	11640	ABxCD	6.9	7.9	2.5	118	A0	45.5	+05 30	60-4	
63–ϑ	11853		4.6	5.0	22.3	104	A5 A5	56.2	+04 12	60-2	Bluish-white pair

Footnotes: *= Year 2000, a = Near apogee, c = Closing, w = Widening. Finder Chart No: All stars listed in the tables are plotted in the large Constellation Chart, but when a star appears in a Finder Chart, this number is listed. Notes: When colors are subtle, the suffix *-ish* is used, e.g. *bluish*.

150x is required to separate this unequally bright pair of yellowish stars.

AC11 Double Star **Spec. F5**
m6.8,7.0; Sep.0.8″; P.A.355° **18^{h}24.9^m −01° 35′**
Finder Chart 60-4 ★★★★
8/10″ Scopes–250x: Alvan Clark 11 is a very close binary that provides a good test for medium and large telescopes. 250x shows two yellow disks in contact. The two stars orbit each other in a 240 year period.

59 Serpentis = Σ2316 Double Star **Spec. A0**
m5.3,7.6; Sep.3.8″; P.A.318° **18^{h}27.2^m +00° 12′**
Finder Chart 60-4 ★★★★
4/6″ Scopes–150x: 59 Serpentis is an unequally bright but attractive double of yellowish and white stars superimposed upon a particularly dark area of the Great Rift.

Theta (ϑ) = 63 Serpentis Double Star **Spec. A5, A5**
m4.6,5.0; Sep.22.3″; P.A.104° **18^{h}56.2^m +04° 12′**
Constellation Chart 60-2 ★★★★★
4/6″ Scopes–75x: Theta Serpentis is a moderately wide but easily resolved double of comparably bright bluish-white stars. The components can be split even in 10 × 50 binoculars, and are surprisingly blue for stars of mid-A spectra.

60.3 Deep-Sky Objects

Ruprecht 135 Open Cluster 20★ Tr Type IV 2p
φ 11′, m – **17^{h}58.2^m −11° 41′**
Finder Chart 60-3 ★★★
12/14″ Scopes–100x: Ruprecht 135, located 2° south of Nu (ν) = 64 Ophiuchi, is a highly irregular cluster of star-knots and star groups that do not stand out well from the surrounding Milky Way field. The cluster contains forty 9th to 13th magnitude members in a

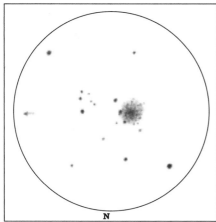

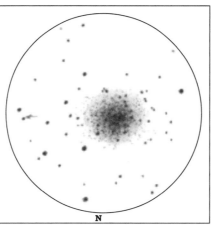

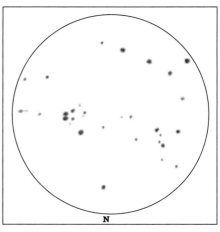

Figure 60-1. NGC 6535
12.5″, f5–275x, by G. R. Kepple

Figure 60-2. NGC 6539
12.5″, f5–300x, by G. R. Kepple

Figure 60-3. NGC 6604
12.5″, f5–300x, by G. R. Kepple

11′×5′ E–W area. On its west edge is a 1.5′ wide knot of nine 9th to 12th magnitude stars. 4.5′ east of this knot is a 4′×2′ N–S group of two dozen stars, nine of which are in a horseshoe-shaped asterism open to the NNE. At the horseshoe's south edge is a double with magnitude 10.5 components. Two stars lie north of center within the horseshoe. A chain of eight more stars zigzag east from the horseshoe and end at a magnitude 9.5 star on the east edge of the cluster.

NGC 6535 Globular Cluster Class XI
φ 3.6′, m10.6v   18ʰ03.9ᵐ −00° 18′
Finder Chart 60-4, Figure 60-1   ★★
12/14″Scopes–150x: NGC 6535 is a small globular cluster located 2.5° south of the triangle of 67, 68,

and 70 Ophiuchi. It has a poorly concentrated 2.5′ diameter halo with a few members resolved on its east edge. A 1′ long NNE–SSW row of 12.5 to 13th magnitude foreground stars runs tangent to the WNW edge of the halo.

NGC 6539 Globular Cluster Class X
φ 6.9′, m9.8v   18ʰ04.8ᵐ −07° 35′
Finder Chart 60-3, Figure 60-2   ★★
12/14″Scopes–150x: NGC 6539 is a faint, round 4′ diameter haze of uniform brightness. At 200x, the globular seems on the verge of resolution; but only half a dozen stars can be glimpsed around the periphery, the most conspicuous a 12.5 magnitude foreground star on the cluster's NW edge.

NGC 6605 Open Cluster [15★]
[φ 7′, m −, Br★ 10:]   18ʰ17.0ᵐ −14° 57′
Finder Chart 60-3   ★★★
12/14″Scopes–150x: NGC 6605 is classified as "nonexistent" in the *RNGC*. However, William Herschel had called it a "Loose straggling cluster; stars of 10–12 magnitude," and a group fitting Hershel's description is just slightly west of the listed coordinates, which are SW of an 8th magnitude star. Fifteen 10th to 12th magnitude stars can be seen rather evenly distributed over a 7′ area. If you include the 8th magnitude star and stars to its south and east, which look like a continuation of the main group, the cluster, if it does exist, would contain three dozen stars in a 15′ area.

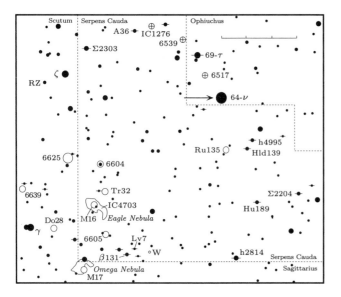

Finder Chart 60-3. 64–ν Oph: 17ʰ59.0ᵐ −09° 46′

Trumpler 32 Harvard 19 Open Cl. 50★ Tr Type I2m
φ 6′, m12.2p   18ʰ17.5ᵐ −13° 21′
Finder Chart 60-3   ★★
12/14″Scopes–125x: Trumpler 32 has thirty 12th mag-

Figure 60-4. *The open cluster of M16 (NGC 6611) is embedded in a large emission nebula separately catalogued as IC 4703 and popularly known as the Eagle or Star Queen Nebula. The "Eagle" or "Pillar" feature, formed by foreground dust outlined by rim nebulae, is difficult to discern visually but may be seen under very clear, dark skies in large amateur telescopes. Image courtesy Martin C. Germano.*

nitude and fainter members scattered over a 6′ area. A wide NW–SE starless streak separates the cluster into two groups, the northern group containing twenty stars and the southern ten.

NGC 6604 H15[8] Open Cluster 30★ Tr Type I3mn
φ 4′, m6.5v, Br★ 7.48   18ʰ18.1ᵐ −12° 14′
Finder Chart 60-3, Figure 60-3   ★★★
12/14″ Scopes–150x: NGC 6604, located half a degree

NW of Messier 16, consists of a 1′ wide triangular group of six 7.5 magnitude and fainter stars within a larger group of 9th to 11th magnitude stars. The cluster's most conspicuous members fall along a tiny arc concave to the east, its lucida the second star from the arc's east end. NGC 6604 is about the same distance from us as M16, and is embedded in an M16-type nebula, but it is much dimmed by Great Rift dust.

IC 4703 Emission Nebula
ϕ 35′ × 28′, Photo Br 1-5, Color 3-4 18^{h}18.6^m −13° 58′

NGC 6611 Messier 16 Open Cluster Tr Type II3mn
ϕ 21′, m6.0v, Br★ 8.24v   18^{h}18.8^m −13° 47′
Finder Chart 60-3, Figure 60-4   ★★★/★★★★
IC 4703: The Eagle or Star Queen Nebula

The M16 + IC 4703 open cluster + emission nebula complex lies 6,500 light years away in the Sagittarius–Carina Spiral Arm. It might form one giant complex with M17, the Swan Nebula, in Sagittarius to its south. The brightest stars of the M16 cluster are very hot, very luminous O-type stars emitting the ultraviolet photons which fluoresce the nebula. The cluster is about 40 light years across, and the full extent of the nebula about 66×53 light years.

8/10″Scopes–100x: Messier 16 is a large, loose 20′ diameter cluster of fifty 8th magnitude and fainter stars immersed in the Eagle Nebula, a vast network of emission nebulosity. An O-III filter effectively enhances the nebula-glow. The nebulosity surrounds the cluster and spreads south, but a dark, triangular wedge of obscuring dust juts into it from the north.

12/14″Scopes–125x: The IC 4703 nebulosity is a 30′ wide fan-shaped area flattened on the north by the sharp edge of a foreground dust cloud, a wedge of which penetrates south into the embedded open cluster of sixty stars spread over a 15′ area. The main concentration of stars is in a 7′ × 3.5′ NW–SE area on the NW side of the complex. On the NE side is the thin, sharply-outlined E–W dark feature called the "Black Pillar." Many cone-shaped dark projections protrude from the periphery of the nebula inward, their apices pointing toward the complex center: this is the effect of radiation pressure and stellar winds from the hot O-type cluster stars, and of the expansion of the heated nebula-gas into its surroundings, the projections being denser pockets of interstellar dust that provide more resistance to radiation pressure, stellar winds, and expanding ionized gas. The "eagle" or "star queen" features that look so beautiful in photographs are difficult to discern, but lie just SE of the open cluster's main concentration.

IC 4756 Open Cluster 80★   Tr Type II3r
ϕ 52′, m4.6v, Br★ 8.67v   18^{h}39.0^m +05° 27′
Finder Chart 60-4   ★★★
8/10″Scopes–50x: IC 4756 is an exceptionally large, scattered cluster of eighty 7.5 to 11th magnitude stars broadcast over a degree of sky. It is a fine sight at low power, or in giant binoculars and richest-field telescopes. The fainter members are enclosed by a trapezoid of 5th to 7th magnitude stars. The cluster has no central concentration, but several small clumps and pairs can be seen.

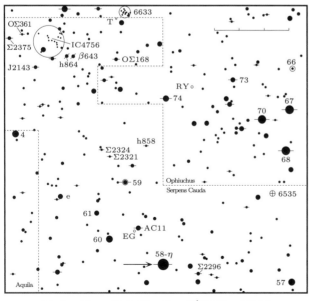

Finder Chart 60-4. 58–η Ser: 18^{h}21.3^m −02° 54′

Chapter 61

Sextans, the Sextant

61.1 Overview

Sextans was created by the Polish astronomer Hevelius to commemorate the large observatory sextant he used in Danzig from 1658 to 1679 to measure star positions. It is a small, faint constellation located on the celestial equator between Leo and Hydra. Sextans' faint stars are difficult to pick out but may easily be found under clear, dark skies by looking due south of Regulus (Alpha Leonis) and NE of Alphard (Alpha Hydrae): Alpha Sextantis is due south of Regulus, and Gamma Sextantis is 3° due east of Alphard. Sextans is in a galaxy-rich region of the heavens and therefore, despite its rather small area, contains a large number of galaxies, the best of which is the strikingly elongated NGC 3115, the "Spindle Galaxy."

Sextans: SEX-tans	
Genitive: Sextantis, SEX-tan-tis	
Abbreviation: Sex	
Culmination: 9 pm–April 8, midnight–Feb. 22	
Area: 314 square degrees	
Showpieces: NGC 3115	
Binocular Objects: NGC 3115	

61.2 Interesting Stars

Σ1441 Sextantis Double Star   **Spec. K5**
m6.4, 9.9; Sep. 2.6″; P.A. 168°   **10ʰ31.0ᵐ −07° 38′**
Constellation Chart 61-2   ★★★★
4/6″ Scopes–150x: Struve 1441 is a close, attractive pair of orange and yellow stars.

35 Sextantis Double Star   **Spec. K0**
m6.3, 7.4; Sep. 6.8″; P.A. 240°   **10ʰ43.3ᵐ +04° 45′**
Finder Chart 61-5   ★★★★
4/6″ Scopes–100x: 35 Sextantis, a fine pair of orange and yellowish-orange stars, is easily split in small telescopes.

61.3 Deep-Sky Objects

NGC 2967 H275² Galaxy Type SAB:(s)bc II
φ 2.6′ × 2.6′, m11.6v, SB13.6   **09ʰ42.1ᵐ +00° 20′**
Finder Chart 61-3, Figure 61-1   ★★★
8/10″ Scopes–100x: NGC 2967, located 3.5′ south of a 10th magnitude star, is a moderately faint galaxy

with a circular 1.5′ diameter halo that gradually brightens toward its center.

16/18″ Scopes–150x: With averted vision, NGC 2967 can be seen to have a 2′ diameter, fairly bright halo with diffuse edges and a well concentrated core containing a very faint nucleus.

NGC 2974 H61¹ Galaxy Type SA:(s)0°
φ 3.0′ × 1.7′, m10.9v, SB12.5   **09ʰ42.6ᵐ −03° 42′**
Finder Chart 61-4, Figure 61-2   ★★★
8/10″ Scopes–100x: NGC 2974 is a fairly faint, diffuse object with a 1′ × 0.5′ NE–SW halo containing a

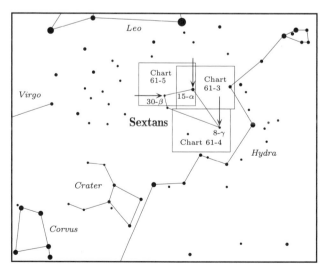

Master Finder Chart 61-1. Sextans Chart Areas
Guide stars indicated by arrows.

379

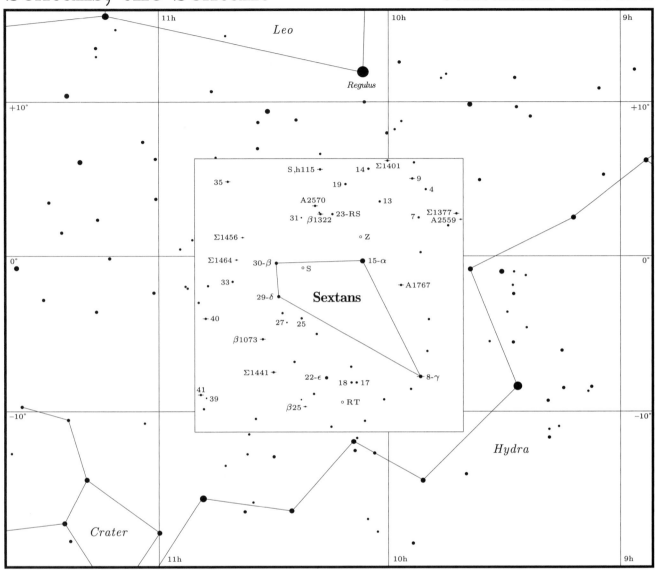

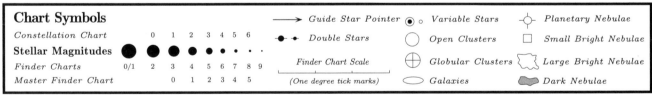

Table 61-1: Selected Variable Stars in Sextans

Name	HD No.	Type	Max.	Min.	Period (Days)	F*	Spec. Type	R.A. (2000)	Dec.	Finder Chart No.	Notes
RT Sex	88517	SRb	8.0	8.5	96		M6	$10^h12.3^m$	$-10° 19'$	61-4	
S Sex	91637	M	8.2	13.5	261	0.50	M3e-M5e	34.9	$-00\ 20$	61-5	

F* = The fraction of period taken up by the star's rise from min. to max. brightness, or the period spent in eclipse.

Table 61-2: Selected Double Stars in Sextans

Name	ADS No.	Pair	M1	M2	Sep.″	P.A.°	Spec	R.A. (2000) Dec		Finder Chart No.	Notes
A2559	7493		7.9	12.8	3.9	256	K2	09ʰ42.3ᵐ	+02° 19′	61-3	
Σ1377	7500		7.4	10.6	3.9	136	F8	43.5	+02 38	61-3	
8–γ Sex	7555	AB	5.6	6.1	0.6	*56	A2	52.5	−08 06	61-4	
(h4256)	7555	AC		12.0	35.8	32.5					
9 Sex			7.0	9.2	52.5	290	K5 K0	54.1	+04 57	61-3	
A1767	7596		6.7	10.3	1.8	19	G5	57.7	−01 57	61-3	
Σ1401	7604		7.8	10.8	23.9	21	F5	10ʰ00.2ᵐ	+06 15	61-3	
β 25	7738		8.2	8.8	1.8	153	G5	21.8	−09 46	61-4	
S, h115			6.6	9.1	58.6	353	F2	23.2	+05 42	61-5	
β 1322	7755	AB	6.3	12.6	10.2	312	K0	24.2	+02 22	61-5	
(h2530)	7755	AC		6.6	212.2	64	K0				
A2570	7769		7.6	7.6	0.4	313	A0	26.0	+02 56	61-5	
Σ1441	7808	AB	6.4	9.9	2.6	168	K5	31.0	−07 38	61-2	Orange and yellow
β 1073	7822		6.9	11.4	3.4	47	K0	32.5	−06 04	61-2	
Σ1456	7862		8.2	9.9	13.5	46	F5	38.3	+01 15	61-5	
Σ1464	7885	AB	8.2	10.9	5.4	302	F0	41.6	−00 16	61-5	
	7885	AC		10.0	59.2	222					
35 Sex	7902	AB	6.3	7.4	6.8	240	K0	43.3	+04 45	61-5	Orange and pale orange
40 Sex	7936		7.0	7.8	2.2	10	A2	49.3	−04 01	61-2	
41 Sex	7942		5.8	11.5	27.3	303	A2	50.3	−08 54	61-2	

Footnotes: *= Year 2000, a = Near apogee, c = Closing, w = Widening. Finder Chart No: All stars listed in the tables are plotted in the large Constellation Chart, but when a star appears in a Finder Chart, this number is listed. Notes: When colors are subtle, the suffix *-ish* is used, e.g. *bluish*.

faint stellar nucleus. A 10th magnitude star is at the SW tip of the halo.

16/18″ Scopes–150x: The fairly bright 1.5′ × 0.75′ NE–SW halo contains a prominent stellar nucleus. Except for the nucleus, the halo's surface brightness is uniform.

NGC 2980 H528³ Galaxy Type SB:(s:)c II
φ 1.6′ × 0.9′, m13.0v, SB 13.2   09ʰ43.2ᵐ −09° 37′

NGC 2978 Galaxy Type (R′:)SAB:(rs:)bc II
φ 1.1′ × 0.9′, m12.7v, SB 12.5   09ʰ43.3ᵐ −09° 45′
Finder Chart 61-4   ★/★

16/18″ Scopes–150x: NGC 2980 is situated between 12.5 magnitude stars, 2.5′ to its NW and SE. Its very faint 1′ × 0.5′ NNW–SSE halo contains a faint stellar nucleus. 8′ to its south is the galaxy NGC 2978, which has a very faint, circular 30″ halo that slightly brightens toward its center. A magnitude 12.5 star is 1.25′ SSE of NGC 2978 and a magnitude 13 star 1.25′ to its NE.

NGC 2990 H624² Galaxy Type Sc: II
φ 1.0′ × 0.5′, m12.7v, SB 11.8   09ʰ46.3ᵐ +05° 43′
Finder Chart 61-3   ★★★

16/18″ Scopes–150x: NGC 2990, located in a sparse star field, has a fairly faint, circular 1′ diameter halo around a broad, weakly concentrated core. A 13th magnitude star lies 1.5′ NE of the galaxy's center, and a more distant star is to its west.

NGC 3018 Galaxy Type SB(s)b? pec
φ 1.2′ × 0.9′, m13.3v, SB 13.3   09ʰ49.7ᵐ +00° 37′

NGC 3023 Galaxy Type SAB(s)bc II
φ 2.9′ × 1.5′, m12.2v, SB 13.6   09ʰ49.9ᵐ +00° 37′
Finder Chart 61-3   ★/★

16/18″ Scopes–150x: NGC 3018 is a mere 45″ SE of one ninth magnitude star and 5.5′ east of another. These two stars make the very low surface brightness object that much more difficult to see. The galaxy has a very faint 45″ × 20″ NNE–SSW halo. A 14th magnitude star is 30″ to its SE and two slightly brighter stars 1.25′ and 2′ SE. 2.5″ east of NGC 3018 is its companion galaxy NGC 3023, which has a

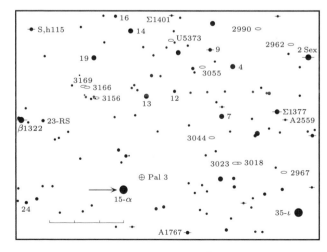

Finder Chart 61-3. 15–α Sex: 10ʰ07.9ᵐ −00° 22′

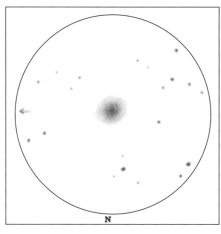
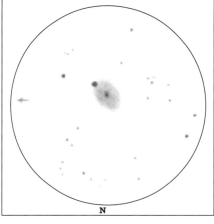
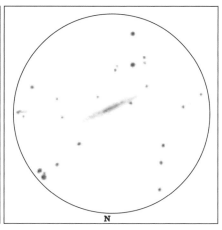

Figure 61-1. NGC 2967
17.5″, f4.5–275x, by G. R. Kepple

Figure 61-2. NGC 2974
18.5″, f5–275x, by Glen W. Sanner

Figure 61-3. NGC 3044
17.5″, f4.5–275x, by G. R. Kepple

faint, diffuse 2′ × 1′ E–W halo containing a slightly brighter core. With averted vision a very faint star or knot can be glimpsed on the SE edge of the galaxy's halo. 1.5′ to the east of NGC 3023 is a magnitude 13.5 star.

NGC 3044 H254³ Galaxy Type Scd: sp II-III?
ϕ 4.3′ × 0.8′, m11.9v, SB 13.1   09ʰ53.7ᵐ +01° 35′
Finder Chart 61-3, Figure 61-3   ★★★

8/10″ Scopes–100x: NGC 3044, centered 3.25′ NNW of a 10th magnitude star, is an edge-on galaxy with a fairly faint, much elongated 3′ × 0.5′ ESE–WNW halo that contains some brightening along its major axis.

Figure 61-4. *NGC 3115, the Spindle Galaxy, may be a transitional type between a flattened elliptical system and a lenticular S0 disk galaxy. Image courtesy of Tim Hunter and James McGaha.*

16/18″ Scopes–150x: NGC 3044 has a thin 4.5′ × 0.75′ ESE–WNW halo elongated to tapered ends. The core is highly extended and contains a few bright spots along its major axis. A 13th magnitude star lies north of the halo's WNW tip 2.5′ from the galaxy's center while a threshold star nearly touches the northern edge of the halo's ESE tip.

NGC 3055 H4⁶ Galaxy Type SAB(s)c II
ϕ 2.0′ × 1.1′, m12.1v, SB 12.8   09ʰ55.3ᵐ +04° 16′
Finder Chart 61-3, Figure 61-5   ★★★

8/10″ Scopes–100x: NGC 3055, located 6′ SSE of a 10.5 magnitude star, is a small, circular, nebulous object of low surface brightness.

16/18″ Scopes–150x: NGC 3055 shows a fairly faint 1.5′ × 1′ NE–SW halo that contains a slight central brightening. The surface brightness drops more sharply toward the eastern edge of the halo than toward the west. A 13th magnitude star lies beyond the SW tip of the halo 2.5′ SW of the galaxy's center, and a magnitude 12.5 star lies 2′ east.

NGC 3115 H163¹ Galaxy Type S0– sp
ϕ 8.1′ × 2.8′, m8.9v, SB 12.1   10ʰ05.2ᵐ −07° 43′
Finder Chart 61-4, Figure 61-4   ★★★★
The Spindle Galaxy

8/10″ Scopes–100x: This bright lens-shaped galaxy is at the western corner of the triangle it forms with magnitude 9.5 stars 7′ to its east and 8′ to its SE. Its dim nebulous envelope is elongated 4′ × 1′ NE–SW to tapered ends and contains a bright, extended core. An 11.5 magnitude star lies 3.25′ south of the galaxy's center.

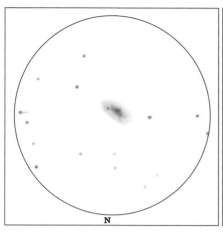

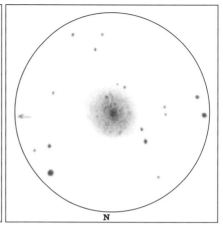

Figure 61-5. NGC 3055	Figure 61-6. NGC 3166 Group	Figure 61-7. NGC 3423
18.5″, f5–275x, by Glen W. Sanner	*17.5″, f4.5–200x, by G. R. Kepple*	*17.5″, f4.5–275x, by G. R. Kepple*

16/18″Scopes–150x: NGC 3115 is a splendid sight in large telescopes. Its smooth, well concentrated 6′ × 1.5′ NE–SW halo elongates to sharply tapered ends and contains a bulging central hub. The bright core is somewhat rectangular in profile. Embedded in it is a stellar nucleus. A 14th magnitude star lies 1.25′ south of the galaxy's center.

NGC 3156 H255³ Galaxy Type S0:
φ 1.8′ × 1.1′, m12.3v, SB12.9   10ʰ12.7ᵐ +03° 08′
Finder Chart 61-5   ★★★

12/14″Scopes–125x: NGC 3156 lies 2′ NW of the westernmost member of a 6′ wide triangle of bright stars. The galaxy has a faint, diffuse 1′ diameter halo that is slightly elongated NE–SW and contains a faint stellar nucleus.

NGC 3166 H3¹ Galaxy Type SAB(rs)0/a
φ 4.6′ × 2.6′, m10.4v, SB12.9   10ʰ13.8ᵐ +03° 26′
Finder Chart 61-5, Figure 61-6   ★★★

8/10″Scopes–100x: NGC 3166 appears nearly identical to its interacting companion NGC 3169 located 8′ to its ENE. It has a bright stellar nucleus embedded in a 2′ × 1.5′ E–W halo that fades smoothly toward its edges.

16/18″Scopes–150x: The fairly bright but diffuse halo is a 4′ × 2.5′ E–W oval containing a tiny core with a bright stellar nucleus. 11th magnitude stars lie 3′ NW, 3.25′ SW, and 5′ SSW of the galaxy's center. 5′ to the SW of NGC 3166 is its companion NGC 3165, a faint, diffuse 1.25′ × 0.5′ N–S oval containing a slight central brightening.

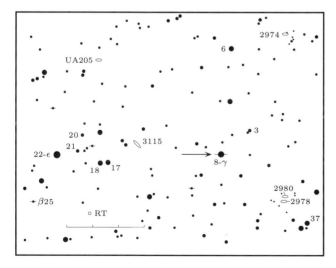

Finder Chart 61-4. 8–γ Sex: 09ʰ52.5ᵐ −08° 06′

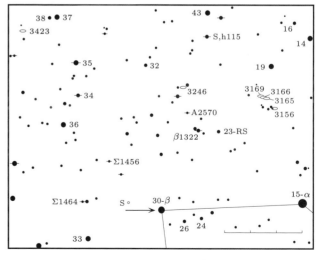

Finder Chart 61-5. 30–β Sex: 10ʰ30.3ᵐ −00° 38′

NGC 3169 H4¹ Galaxy Type SA(s)a pec
φ **5.0′ × 2.8′, m10.2v, SB 12.9**   10ʰ14.2ᵐ +03° 28′
Finder Chart 61-5, Figure 61-6   ★★★

8/10″ Scopes–100x: NGC 3169 is nearly a twin of NGC
    3166 located 8′ to its WSW, but appears slightly
    larger. Its 2.5′ × 2′ NE–SW halo contains a small
    core. An 11th magnitude star lies 1.5′ east of the
    galaxy's center.

16/18″ Scopes–150x: NGC 3169 has a fairly bright
    3′ × 2.5′ NE–SW halo that contains a small oval core
    with a very faint stellar nucleus.

NGC 3246 Galaxy Type SABdm
φ **2.1′ × 1.3′, m12.7v, SB 13.6**   10ʰ26.7ᵐ +03° 52′
Finder Chart 61-5   ★★

16/18″ Scopes–150x: NGC 3246 lies at the NNE vertex
    of the 3′ wide, nearly equilateral, triangle it forms

with a 12th magnitude star to its SW and a
magnitude 12.5 star to its south. Its diffuse halo is
very faint and elongated 1.5′ × 1′ E–W.

NGC 3423 H6⁴ Galaxy Type SA(s)cd II-III
φ **3.9′ × 3.3′, m11.1v, SB 13.8**   10ʰ51.2ᵐ +05° 50′
Finder Chart 61-5, Figure 61-7   ★★★

8/10″ Scopes–100x: NGC 3423 is 2.5′ SW of an 11.5
    magnitude star and 5.5′ SE of a double which
    consists of a 9th magnitude primary with a faint
    companion to its NE. It has a 3.5′ × 2′ NNE–SSW
    halo containing a slightly brighter center.

16/18″ Scopes–150x: In a 17.5″ telescope, the halo
    appears mottled and elongated 4′ × 3′ NNE–SSW,
    and contains a faint irregularly concentrated core.
    A 13th magnitude star touches the halo's NE edge.

Chapter 62

Ursa Major, the Great Bear

62.1 Overview

Ursa Major, the Great Bear, is the third largest constellation in the heavens, covering 1,280 square degrees. Seven of the brightest stars, conveniently labeled Alpha (α) through Eta (η) from west to east by Bayer, form the famous Big Dipper, the best known of all star patterns. The Big Dipper is in fact only the hindquarters and tail of the full constellation figure of the Great Bear as envisioned by later Greek astronomers. However, earlier Greek astronomers had known the seven stars of the Dipper alone as the Bear. In fact the early Greek astronomers had called this asterism both a Bear and a Wagon. Homer used both names for the constellation in the *Iliad* and the *Odyssey*, which probably were first written down around 750 B.C. In classical mythology the celestial Bear was Callisto, daughter of King Lyceon of Arabia, who had been one of Zeus' many mortal lovers and whom he had transformed into a bear to disguise her from his justifiably jealous wife Hera. As a Wagon, the constellation represented the four-wheeled chariot of the high-tempered sorceress Medea: its draught animals were a team of winged Dragons, enconstellated as Draco, which indeed does lie in the sky in front of the Big Dipper. The Greeks had gotten the idea of the Big Dipper as a Wagon, or four-wheeled chariot, from the Babylonians, who had seen it as the vehicle of their weather-god Enlil. Even the Wagon + Winged-Dragon constellation pair went back to Mesopotamia; for a series of Mesopotamian seals dating from around 2300 B.C. show Enlil in his celestial Wagon cracking a whip over the back of a winged dragon.

The conspicuous pattern of the Big Dipper is not entirely merely a chance alignment of stars. The five central stars of the Dipper – from Beta to Zeta Ursae – are the brightest members of the Ursa Major Moving Group, which is centered some 70 light years away and is therefore the nearest open cluster (though to call it a cluster is to stretch the word a bit!). Among the Group's other naked-eye members are 37, 78, and 80 Ursae Majoris and 21 Leo Minoris. Alpha (α) Coronae Borealis is a possible outlying Group member, though it might be better thought of as in the so-called Ursa Major Stream of A-type stars, of which the Moving Group is the core.

> **Ursa Major:** ER-sa MAY-jer
> **Genitive:** Ursae Majoris, ER-see May-JOR-is
> **Abbreviation:** UMa
> **Culmination:** 9 pm–Apr. 25, midnight–Mar. 11
> **Area:** 1,280 square degrees
> **Showpieces:** 79–ζ and 80 UMa (Mizar and Alcor), M81 (NGC 3031), M82 (NGC 3034), M101 (NGC 5457), M108 (NGC 3556)
> **Binocular Objects:** Σ1193, Σ1831, 13–o UMa, 65 UMa,79–β and 80 UMa (Mizar and Alcor), M40 (Wnc 4) M81 (NGC 3031), M82 (NGC 3034), M101 (NGC 5457), M108 (NGC 3556), NGC 2841, NGC 2976, NGC 3184

The Ursa Major Stream shares the Ursa Major Moving Group's motion through our Galaxy and includes such prominent members as Sirius, Delta (δ) and Zeta (ζ) Leonis, Beta Eridani, and Delta Aquarii. The Ursa Major Moving Group covers a $25° \times 10°$ area of the sky and has true dimensions of 32×12 light years. It obviously is very scattered and poor as open clusters go: the total luminosity of all its stars equals the brightness of just 310 suns, an absolute magnitude of a mere -1.4. The total mass of the Group is around 80 suns.

Ursa Major lies well away from the Milky Way's obscuring gas and dust, and therefore, like most off-Milky Way constellations, is rich in galaxies. In fact it is exceptionally abundant in galaxies. The reason for this is that Ursa Major is at the northern end of what might be called a "milky way" of galaxies that extends south and east from Ursa Major through Leo, Canes Venatici, and Coma Berenices to Virgo. In this direction we are looking into the very heart of the Coma-Virgo Supercluster, on the edge of which our own Local Galaxy Group is located. Our Supercluster is rotating on an axis (just like our Galaxy and our Solar System) and therefore is flattened (again just like our Galaxy and Solar System). Hence, a particularly dense, but long and thin, band of galaxies extends from the region of the Big Dipper SSE through Coma Berenices and western Virgo

Ursa Major, the Great Bear

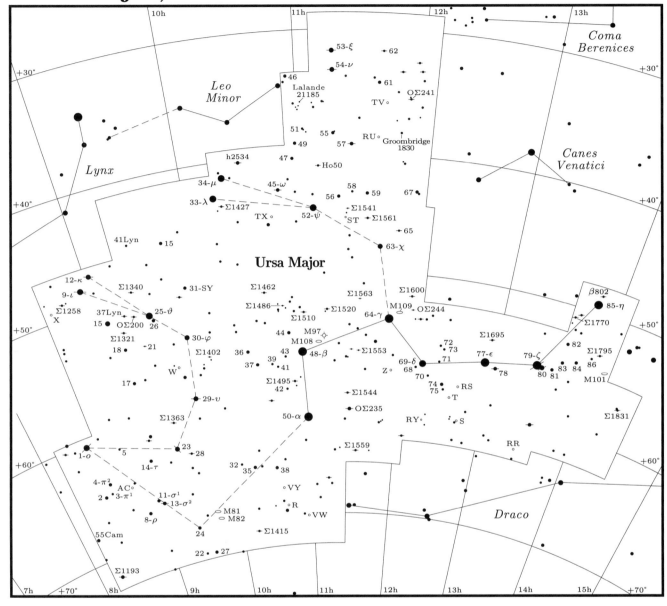

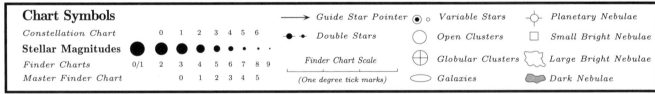

Chart Symbols												
Constellation Chart			0	1	2	3	4	5	6		→ Guide Star Pointer	◉ ○ Variable Stars
Stellar Magnitudes											●—● Double Stars	○ Open Clusters
Finder Charts		0/1	2	3	4	5	6	7	8	9		⊕ Globular Clusters
Master Finder Chart				0	1	2	3	4	5		Finder Chart Scale	⬭ Galaxies

Guide Star Pointer
Double Stars
Finder Chart Scale
(One degree tick marks)

Variable Stars
Open Clusters
Globular Clusters
Galaxies

⬡ Planetary Nebulae
□ Small Bright Nebulae
Large Bright Nebulae
Dark Nebulae

Table 62-1: Selected Variable Stars in Ursa Major

Name	HD No.	Type	Max.	Min.	Period (Days)	F*	Spec. Type	R.A. (2000)	Dec.	Finder Chart No.	Notes
W UMa	83950	EW	7.9	8.63	0.33		F8	$09^h43.8^m$	$+55°57'$	62-4	
R UMa	92763	M	6.7	13.4	301	0.39	M3-M9	$10^h44.6^m$	$+68\ 47$	62-5	
VY UMa	92839	Lb	5.89	6.5			C5	45.1	$+67\ 25$	62-5	
TX UMa	93033	EA	7.06	8.76	3.03	0.13	B8+F2	45.3	$+45\ 34$	62-9	
VW UMa	94902	SR	6.85	7.71	125		M2	59.0	$+69\ 59$	62-5	
ST UMa	99592	SRb	7.7	9.5	81		M4	$11^h27.8^m$	$+45\ 11$	62-9	
Z UMa	103681	SRb	7.9	10.8	196	0.05	M5	56.5	$+57\ 52$	62-10	
RY UMa	107397	SRb	6.68	8.5	311		M2-M3	$12^h20.5^m$	$+61\ 19$	62-1	
T UMa	109729	M	6.6	13.4	256	0.41	M4-M7	36.4	$+59\ 29$	62-1	
S UMa	110813	M	7.0	12.4	226	0.47	S0-S5	43.9	$+61\ 06$	62-13	

F* = The fraction of period taken up by the star's rise from min. to max. brightness, or the period spent in eclipse.

Table 62-2: Selected Double Stars in Ursa Major

Name	ADS No.	Pair	M1	M2	Sep."	P.A.°	Spec	R.A. (2000)	Dec.	Finder Chart No.	Notes
Σ1193	6724	AB	6.1	9.1	43.1	87	K5	$08^h20.7^m$	$+72°24'$	62-1	Pale orange and blue
Σ1258	6945		7.5	7.8	9.9	331	F0	43.4	$+48\ 52$	62-3	
9–ι UMa	7114	AB	3.1	10.8	4.5	16	A5	59.2	$+48\ 02$	62-3	
13–σ²UMa	7203	AB	4.8	8.2	w3.9	*355	F8	$09^h10.4^m$	$+67\ 08$	62-5	Yellowish and blue stars
	7203	AC		9.3	204.6	148					
Σ1321	7251	AB	7.6	7.7	c17.2	*93	K2 K2	14.4	$+52\ 41$	62-3	Gold or orange pair
Σ1340	7324	AB	7.1	8.9	6.2	319	B9	22.5	$+49\ 33$	62-3	Whitish and blue stars
OΣ200	7348		6.5	8.1	1.4	335	G0	24.9	$+51\ 34$	62-3	Yellow and dull orange
21 UMa	7354	AB	7.8	8.8	5.7	311	A2	25.6	$+54\ 01$	62-3	Yellowish and bluish
23 UMa	7402	AB	3.7	8.9	22.7	270	F0	31.5	$+63\ 04$	62-4	Pale yellowish and bluish
Σ1363	7432		7.2	10.9	10.7	354	F0	35.2	$+60\ 54$	62-4	
28 UMa			6.3	11.5	6.3	27	F2	45.9	$+63\ 39$	62-4	
29–υ UMa	7534		3.8	11.4	11.3	295	F0	51.0	$+59\ 02$	62-4	
Σ1402			8.1	9.6	27.2	102	K5 G0	$10^h04.9^m$	$+55\ 29$	62-7	Orangish and blue
Σ1415	7705	AB	6.7	7.3	16.7	167	A3 A3	17.9	$+71\ 03$	62-5	Pale blue pair
Σ1427	7737		7.6	8.1	9.4	214	F5	22.0	$+43\ 54$	62-6	
Σ1462	7894	AB	7.4	9.3	8.3	173	A3	42.9	$+50\ 48$	62-7	Yellowish and blue
Σ1486			8.2	9.5	30.0	102	K5	55.0	$+52\ 07$	62-7	Orange and blue
Σ1495	8001		7.2	9.5	34.4	38	K2	59.8	$+58\ 54$	62-8	Orangish and blue
Σ1510	8065		7.7	9.0	3.9	330	F5	$11^h08.0^m$	$+52\ 49$	62-10	Pale yellowish and blue
Ho50	8093		6.4	9.4	3.1	32	K0	13.7	$+41\ 05$	62-1	
Σ1520	8108		6.6	7.9	12.7	344	F2	16.1	$+52\ 46$	62-10	Yellowish and pale blue
53–ξ UMa	8119		4.3	4.8	1.8	*273	G0	18.2	$+31\ 32$	62-11	Close yellow pair
54–ν UMa	8123		3.5	9.9	7.2	147	K0	18.5	$+33\ 06$	62-11	
Σ1541	8168		7.9	10.3	7.7	29	F8	27.7	$+46\ 18$	62-9	Yellow and bluish stars
57 UMa	8175	AB	5.3	8.3	5.4	359	A2	29.1	$+39\ 20$	62-1	Blue-white and blue
Σ1544	8191		7.2	8.2	12.4	90	A5	31.3	$+59\ 42$	62-8	
OΣ235	8197		5.8	7.1	w0.6	*341	F5	32.3	$+62\ 05$	62-8	72.9 year binary
Σ1553	8236		7.9	8.4	6.0	167	G5	36.6	$+56\ 08$	62-10	Subtle yellowish pair
Σ1561	8250		6.3	8.4	9.4	252	G0	38.7	$+45\ 07$	62-9	
Σ1559	8249		6.8	7.8	2.1	322	A2	38.8	$+64\ 21$	62-8	
Σ1563	8253		8.1	10.3	13.7	158	G0	39.5	$+52\ 11$	62-10	Fine yellow and blue pair
65 UMa	8347	ABxC	6.7	8.3	3.7	38	A0	55.1	$+46\ 29$	62-12	White and yellow
	8347	ABxD		6.5	63.1	114					White
OΣ241	8355	AB	6.8	8.7	1.7	139	F2	56.3	$+35\ 27$	62-11	
OΣ244	8416		8.1	10.1	3.2	321	F5	$12^h05.6^m$	$+52\ 53$	62-10	In field with Σ1600
Σ1600	8414		7.4	8.4	7.7	93	F5	05.6	$+51\ 56$	62-10	White and bluish
Σ1695	8710		6.0	7.9	3.7	283	A2	56.3	$+54\ 06$	62-1	Yellowish and pale blue
79–ζ UMa	8891	AB	2.4	3.9	14.4	150	A2 A2	$13^h23.9^m$	$+54\ 56$	62-14	Mizar: white pair
80 UMa	8891	AC		4.0	708.7	71	A5				Alcor
Σ1770	8979		6.8	8.3	1.8	121	K5	37.7	$+50\ 43$	62-14	Deep and pale yellow
β 802	9030		7.5	10.7	3.6	223	F0	48.6	$+48\ 21$	62-1	
Σ1795	9077		6.8	10.0	7.6	3	A2	58.9	$+53\ 06$	62-14	White and bluish stars
Σ1831	9197	AB	7.1	9.8	6.2	139	F0	$14^h16.2^m$	$+56\ 43$	62-14	AB: Yellowish and bluish
	9197	AC		6.6	107.7	222	F8				C: Yellow

Footnotes: *= Year 2000, a = Near apogee, c = Closing, w = Widening. Finder Chart No: All stars listed in the tables are plotted in the large Constellation Chart, but when a star appears in a Finder Chart, this number is listed. Notes: When colors are subtle, the suffix *-ish* is used, e.g. *bluish*.

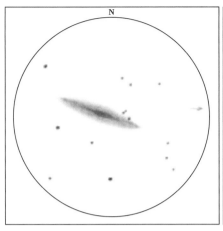

Figure 62-1. NGC 2654
17.5″, ƒ4.5–300x, by G. R. Kepple

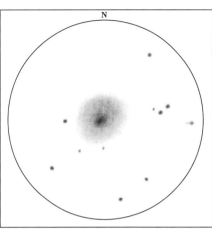

Figure 62-2. NGC 2681
17.5″, ƒ4.5–300x, by G. R. Kepple

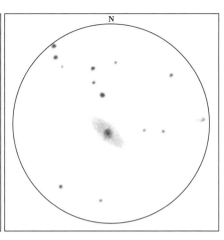

Figure 62-3. NGC 2685
17.5″, ƒ4.5–275x, by G. R. Kepple

to the vicinity of Spica. The Supercluster is divided into smaller clusters of various sizes. Our Local Galaxy Group is one of the small clusters in the Coma-Virgo Supercluster. Other small Coma-Virgo clusters in our vicinity include groups around the M81 + M82 galaxy pair in northern Ursa Major and around M101 at the tail-tip of Ursa Major.

62.2 Interesting Stars

Lalande 21185 Red Dwarf   Spec. dM2
m7.49 $11^h03.2^m$ +35° 58′
Constellation Chart 62-1   ★★
     Lalande 21185, located just 8.1 light years away, is the fourth nearest star to the Solar System after the Alpha Centauri triple, Barnard's Star in Ophiuchus, and Wolf

359 in Leo. It has the 8th largest annual proper motion known (4.78″ per year in P.A.187°). The star is a dM2 red dwarf with an absolute magnitude of +10.5, corresponding to a luminosity just 0.0048 that of the Sun. Faint as it is, Lalande 21165 has an unseen companion.

Xi (ξ) = 53 Ursae Majoris Double Star   Spec. G0
m4.3,4.8; Sep.1.8″; P.A.273° $11^h18.2^m$ +31° 32′
Finder Chart 62-11   ★★★★
4/6″ Scopes–75x: Xi Ursa Majoris is a close binary of
     golden stars which orbit each other in a period of
     60 years. The components were at their closest,
     only 1.6″ apart, in 1992; but at their widest reach
     a separation of just 3″. Xi Ursa Majoris was
     discovered by William Herschel in 1780 and was
     the very first visual binary to have its orbit
     calculated (by Savary in 1828).

Groombridge 1830 Runaway Star   Spec. G8
Apparent Mag. 6.45, Abs. Mag. +6.7 $11^h52.9^m$ +37° 43′
Finder Chart 62-11   ★★
     Groombridge 1830 has the third fastest proper motion known (7.04″ per year) after Barnard's Star (10.29″) and Kapteyn's Star (8.70″). Some 100,000 years from now the star will have moved all the way from Ursa Major to the constellation Lupus. Because it is 28 light years away, as compared to the 6 light years of Barnard's Star, the large apparent motion of Groombridge 1830 must be due to an intrinsically high space velocity rather than to nearness. The star is one of the so-called "high velocity" Population II objects which are part of our Galaxy's halo and therefore are as old as the globular clusters. Arcturus in Boötes is the brightest high velocity Population II star.

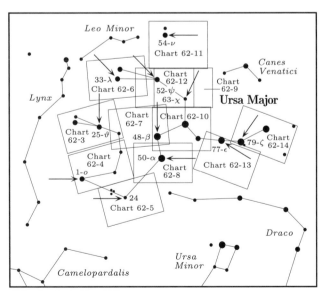

Master Chart 62-2. Ursa Major Chart Areas
Guide stars indicated by arrows.

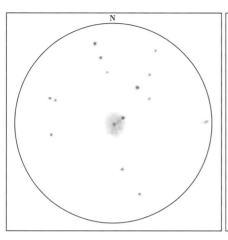

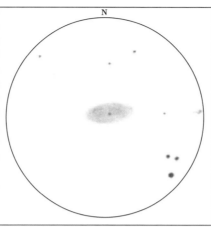

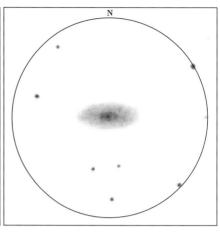

Figure 62-4. NGC 2701
18.5″, f5–275x, by Glen W. Sanner

Figure 62-5. NGC 2742
17.5″, f4.5–300x, by G. R. Kepple

Figure 62-6. NGC 2768
17.5″, f4.5–300x, by G. R. Kepple

Zeta (ζ) = 79 Ursae Majoris Double Star Spec.   A2, A2
m2.3,4.0; Sep.14.4″; P.A.150°   13ʰ23.9ᵐ +54° 56′
Finder Chart 62-14   ★★★★★
Mizar

4/6″Scopes–75x: At the bend of the Dipper's handle is the striking naked-eye duo of Mizar and Alcor, nearly as well-known as the Dipper itself. The two stars are physically related, for they are both members of the Ursa Major Moving Group, but if they are actually gravitationally bound their orbital period must be hundreds of thousands of years long. They are a splendid binocular pair. Low power in a small telescope will separate the pair to opposite ends of the field of view and split Mizar's 4th magnitude companion, which is 14″ away to the SSE: it is five times farther from its primary than Pluto is from the Sun and must take a millennium to orbit it. Alcor and both Mizar A and B are spectroscopic binaries, so the system in fact has a total of six members. An 8th magnitude field star lies between Mizar and Alcor. The Mizar/Alcor multiple is about 70 light years from us, so the absolute magnitudes of Mizar A and B and of Alcor are respectively +0.7, +2.2, and +2.3, luminosities of 44, 11 and 10 suns.

Mizar has been honored by several scientific firsts: it was the first double star to be found by telescope (by Riccioli in 1662), the first star to be photographed (by Bond in 1857), and the first spectroscopic binary detected (by Pickering in 1889).

62.3 Deep-Sky Objects

NGC 2639 H204[1] Galaxy Type (R)SA(r)a:?
φ 1.8′×1.4′, m11.7v, SB12.5   08ʰ43.6ᵐ +50° 12′
Finder Chart 62-3   ★★★
8/10″Scopes–100x: NGC 2639 is at the western vertex

of the triangle it forms with a 10th magnitude star 4.5′ to its east and an 11th magnitude star 5′ to its NE. The galaxy has a fairly bright lenticular halo elongated 1.5′×0.75′ NW–SE containing a bright core with a stellar nucleus.

16/18″Scopes–150x: This galaxy displays a bright, mottled core with several spots knotted within it. The 1.75′×1′ NW–SE halo elongates to tapered ends. A 13th magnitude star is 2.5′ SE.

NGC 2654 Galaxy Type SBab: sp II-III
φ 3.8′×0.7′, m11.8v, SB12.7   08ʰ49.2ᵐ +60° 13′
Finder Chart 62-4, Figure 62-1   ★★★
8/10″Scopes–100x: This edge-on galaxy lies 5′ south of an 11th magnitude star. It is a fairly faint, thin 2.5′×0.5′ ENE–WSW steak containing a slight brightening at its center.

16/18″Scopes–150x: NGC 2654 has a fairly bright, highly elongated 3′×0.75′ ENE–WSW halo. The core is also very much extended ENE–WSW and

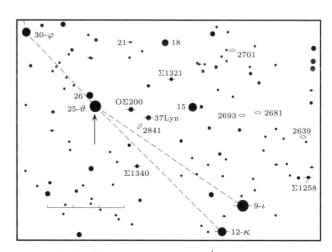

Finder Chart 62-3. 9–ι UMa: 08ʰ59.2ᵐ +48° 02′

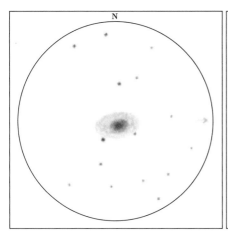

Figure 62-7. NGC 2787
13″, f5.6–1675x, by Steve Coe

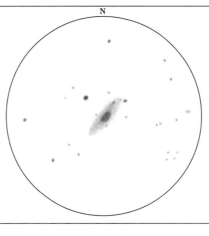

Figure 62-8. NGC 2841
13″, f4.5–115x, by Tom Polakis

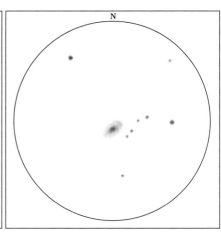

Figure 62-9. NGC 2950
12.5″, f5–300x, by G. R. Kepple

contains a bright stellar nucleus. A few bright spots are visible along the major axis of the core on each side of the nucleus. A close NW–SE double is at the edge of the halo 30″ NW of the galaxy's center, and another faint star lies on the halo's edge 45″ west of the galaxy's center.

NGC 2681 H242[1] Galaxy Type (R′)SAB(rs)0/a
φ **3.5′×3.5′, m10.3v, SB12.9**   **08ʰ53.5ᵐ +51° 19′**
Finder Chart 62-3, Figure 62-2   ★★★
8/10″Scopes–100x: NGC 2681 has a fairly bright 2′ diameter halo containing a small but conspicuous core. A wide NW–SE pair of 12th magnitude stars lies 2′ west of the core's center.
16/18″Scopes–150x: This galaxy has a very small core, sharply concentrated to a stellar nucleus, surrounded by a much fainter, circular 2.5′ diameter halo with diffuse edges. 200x shows a bright spot on each side

of the nucleus, the brighter one to its east. A 13th magnitude star lies 1.5′ east of the galaxy's center, and the increase in aperture reveals that the 12th magnitude pair to the galaxy's west has a 13.5 magnitude companion to the east of the southern component.

NGC 2685 Galaxy Type (R)SB0+ pec
φ **4.3′×2.3′, m11.3v, SB13.6**   **08ʰ55.6ᵐ +58° 44′**
Finder Chart 62-4, Figure 62-3   Helix Galaxy   ★★★
8/10″Scopes–100x: NGC 2685, located 2.5′ south of an 11th magnitude star, is a cigar-shaped galaxy with a fairly faint halo elongated 1.5′×0.5′ NE–SW.
16/18″Scopes–150x: NGC 2685 has a moderately bright 3′×2′ NE–SW halo containing an oval core with a small nucleus. A 12th magnitude star lies 3.5′ SE.

NGC 2693 H823[2] Galaxy Type E3:
φ **1.8′×1.4′, m11.9v, SB12.7**   **08ʰ57.0ᵐ +51° 21′**
Finder Chart 62-3   ★★★
8/10″Scopes–100x: NGC 2693 is a faint, circular 1′ diameter glow containing a slight central brightening with a very faint stellar nucleus intermittently visible. Galaxy NGC 2681 is 32′ WNW.
16/18″Scopes–150x: A very small, sharply concentrated nucleus is embedded in a diffuse, much fainter 1.5′ diameter halo slightly elongated NW–SE. A 14th magnitude star lies 1′ west.

NGC 2701 H66[4] Galaxy Type SAB(rs)c: II–III
φ **1.8′×1.2′, m12.3v, SB13.0**   **08ʰ59.1ᵐ +53° 46′**
Finder Chart 62-3, Figure 62-4   ★★
8/10″Scopes–100x: NGC 2701 is a faint, circular 1′ diameter glow of uniform brightness. A 12th magnitude star lies on its WNW edge.

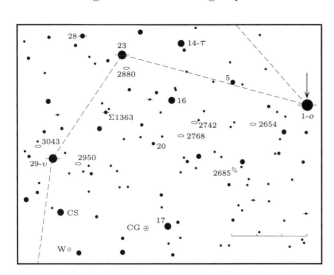

Finder Chart 62-4. 1-o UMa: 08ʰ30.3ᵐ +60° 43′

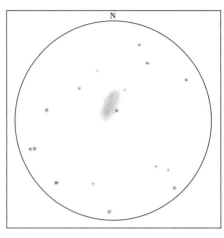

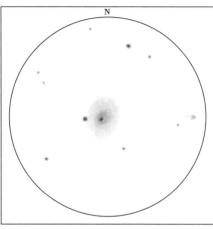

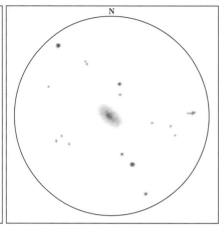

Figure 62-10. NGC 2976
13″, f4.5–165x, by Tom Polakis

Figure 62-11. NGC 2985
12.5″, f5–300x, by G. R. Kepple

Figure 62-12. NGC 2998
12.5″, f5–275x, by G. R. Kepple

16/18″ Scopes–150x: In larger apertures the fairly faint halo appears slightly elongated 1.5′×1.25′ NNE–SSW and contains a poorly concentrated but slightly mottled core. The 12th magnitude star can be seen to be superimposed upon the halo within its WNW edge. A second 12th magnitude star is 2′ NNW of the galaxy.

NGC 2742 H249[1] Galaxy Type
ϕ 3.0′ × 1.6′, m11.4v, SB 13.0   09^{h}07.6^m +60° 29′
Finder Chart 62-4, Figure 62-5   ★★★
8/10″ Scopes–100x: NGC 2742, located 4.5′ SE of a 9th magnitude star, is a fairly faint galaxy elongated 2′×1.5′ E–W and slightly brighter at its center. Centered 3′ to its SW is a conspicuous 1′×0.5′ N–S triangle of one 11.5 and two 13th magnitude stars, the 11.5 magnitude star at the triangle's south corner.
16/18″ Scopes–150x: This galaxy has a fairly bright evenly illuminated 3′×1.75′ E–W halo containing a poorly concentrated, slightly mottled core. With averted vision a threshold stellar nucleus may be glimpsed.

NGC 2768 H250[1] Galaxy Type E6:
ϕ 6.6′ × 3.2′, m9.9v, SB 13.0   09^{h}11.6^m +60° 02′
Finder Chart 62-4, Figure 62-6   ★★★★
8/10″ Scopes–100x: NGC 2768, located in a scattered group of bright stars, has a bright 3′×1.5′ E–W halo containing a much brighter center.
12/14″ Scopes–125x: This nice, bright galaxy has a 4′×1.75′ halo with an extended core that sharply concentrates to a bright stellar nucleus. An 11th magnitude star is 3.75′ NW of the galaxy, and a magnitude 12.5 star is 2.5′ ENE.

NGC 2787 H216[1] Galaxy Type SB(r)0+
ϕ 3.5′ × 2.4′, m10.8v, SB 12.9   09^{h}19.3^m +69° 12′
Finder Chart 62-5, Figure 62-7   ★★★
8/10″ Scopes–100x: NGC 2787 is 14′ NW of a wide, conspicuous ESE–WNW pair of 10th magnitude stars. The galaxy has a bright, circular 1.5′ diameter halo that contains a brighter center. A 13th magnitude star lies on the SSE edge.
12/14″ Scopes–125x: NGC 2787 has a large, broadly concentrated core embedded in an irregular oval halo elongated 2.5′×1.5′ NW–SE which fades smoothly to the edges. The 13th magnitude star lies just inside the halo's SSE edge 50″ from the galaxy's center.

NGC 2841 H205[1] Galaxy Type SA(r)b: I
ϕ 6.8′ × 3.3′, m9.2v, SB 12.4   09^{h}22.0^m +50° 58′
Finder Chart 62-3, Figure 62-8   ★★★★
8/10″ Scopes–100x: This fine galaxy is centered 4.5′ SW of an 8th magnitude star and 22′ SE of the double star 37 Lyncis (6.1, 10.2; 5.7″; 133°). It has a large, bright, much elongated 6′×2′ NNW–SSE halo that contains an abruptly brighter core extended along its major axis. A 12th magnitude star is superimposed upon the halo's NNW tip 1.75′ from the galaxy's center.
12/14″ Scopes–125x: NGC 2841 shows a bright 7′×3′ NNW–SSE halo that contains a large elongated core within which is embedded a bright nucleus. The halo fades sharply toward its NE long side – the consequence of a dust lane on that side of the galaxy. The halo seems to extend beyond a 10th magnitude star near its NNW tip. The 12th magnitude star can be seen to be distinctly within the NNW tip.

NGC 2880 H260¹ Galaxy Type SB0
ϕ 2.4′ × 1.4′, m11.5v, SB 12.9   09ʰ29.6ᵐ +62° 30′
Finder Chart 62-4   ★★★
8/10″ Scopes–100x: NGC 2880, located 34′ SSW of 23
   Ursae Majoris (m3.7), has a fairly bright circular 1′
   diameter halo surrounding a small bright core. An
   11th magnitude star lies 2′ to the galaxy's ENE,
   and four 13th to 14th magnitude stars are located
   nearby to its NW.

NGC 2950 H68⁴ Galaxy Type (R)SB(r)0°
ϕ 3.3′ × 2.4′, m10.9v, SB 13.0   09ʰ42.6ᵐ +58° 51′
Finder Chart 62-4, Figure 62-9   ★★★
8/10″ Scopes–100x: NGC 2950 displays a brilliant stellar
   nucleus embedded in a small bright core surrounded
   by a faint 1.25′ diameter halo.
16/18″ Scopes–150x: In larger aperture telescopes the
   halo of NGC 2950 appears elongated 1.5′ × 1′ NNW–
   SSE, but otherwise the galaxy looks much the same.
   An 11th magnitude star is 2.5′ west. Along the
   western edge of the halo is a N–S arc, concave to
   the SW, of four magnitude 13.5–14 stars.

NGC 2976 H285¹ Galaxy Type SAc pec IV
ϕ 5.0′ × 2.8′, m10.2v, SB 12.9   09ʰ47.3ᵐ +67° 55′
Finder Chart 62-5, Figure 62-10   ★★★★
8/10″ Scopes–100x: NGC 2976, a member of the Messier
   81 Galaxy Group, has a uniformly faint 3′ × 2′
   NNW–SSE halo. A magnitude 12.5 star is 1′ SW,
   and a 14th magnitude star 2.5′ NW, of the galaxy's
   center.
12/14″ Scopes–125x: The diffuse 4′ × 2.5′ NNW–SSE
   halo contains a broad, poorly concentrated core. At
   175x the central area is unevenly bright with a few
   inconspicuous knots.

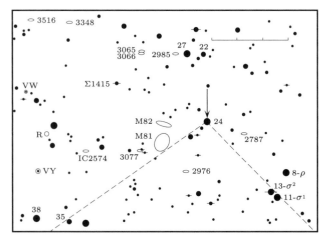

Finder Chart 62-5. 24 UMa: 09ʰ34.5ᵐ +69° 50′

NGC 2985 H78¹ Galaxy Type (R′)SA(rs)ab I
ϕ 3.9′ × 3.0′, m10.4v, SB 13.0   09ʰ50.4ᵐ +72° 17′
Finder Chart 62-5, Figure 62-11   ★★★★
8/10″ Scopes–100x: NGC 2985, located 10′ north of a
   10th magnitude star, has a conspicuous stellar
   nucleus embedded in a fairly bright 2′ diameter
   halo. One 12.5 magnitude star touches the halo's
   east edge and another lies 2.75′ to its NNW.
16/18″ Scopes–150x: This galaxy has a bright, circular
   2.5′ diameter halo slightly elongated N–S and containing a mottled core with a bright nonstellar
   nucleus. Galaxy NGC 3027 is 25′ east.

NGC 2998 H717² Galaxy Type SAB(rs)c I-II
ϕ 2.4′ × 1.2′, m12.5v, SB 13.5   09ʰ48.7ᵐ +44° 05′
Finder Chart 62-6, Figure 62-12   ★★
16/18″ Scopes–150x: NGC 2998 is 3′ NNE of a 9.5
   magnitude star and 2′ SSE of a 12th magnitude
   star, each star a very wide double with a 13th
   magnitude star closer to the halo. The galaxy has
   a faint, uniform 1.5′ × 0.75′ NE–SW glow. 250x
   enhances the brightness of the core area and brings
   out its mottled texture. NGC 2998 has four
   extremely faint companions that require averted
   vision: NGC 3002 is 7′ to the SE, NGC 3005 is only
   6.5′ NE, NGC 3006 is located 9′ SE, and NGC 3008
   is 10′ east.

NGC 3031 Messier 81 Galaxy Type SA(s)ab I-II
ϕ 24.0′ × 13.0′, m6.9v, SB 13.0   09ʰ55.6ᵐ +69° 04′
Finder Chart 62-5, Figure 62-13   ★★★★★
Holmberg IX

   Messier 81 and Messier 82 were discovered by Bode
in 1774, and Messier added them to his catalog in February
1781. These two galaxies are the brightest in a small
cluster of galaxies called the Messier 81 Galaxy Group.
The distance to the center of the cluster is about 10 million
light years: it is the second nearest galaxy group to our
Local Group, the Sculptor Galaxy Group being only about
8 million light years away. The M81 Group includes, in
addition to its two Messier members, NGCs 2976 and
3077 in Ursa Major, NGCs 2366 and 2403 in Camelopar-
dalis, and NGC 4236 in Draco. The absolute magnitudes
of M81 and M82 are −20.8 and −19.3, respectively,
luminosities of 17 billion and 4.4 billion suns. The true
diameter of M81 is at least 70,000 light years and that of
M82 35,000 light years.
4/6″ Scopes–75x: Messier 81 and Messier 82 are a
   striking 38′ wide N–S galaxy pair. The different
   shape of the halos of the two objects is evident even
   in 10×50 binoculars: M81 is an oval, M82 more of
   a streak. In small telescopes the two galaxies fit in
   the same low power field. M81 displays a diffuse oval
   halo containing a bright central hub. The halo is

Figure 62-13. *Messier 81 (NGC 3031) is a fine, bright oval galaxy that in larger telescopes reveals a spiral pattern. At low power Messier 81 forms a very nice pair with Messier 82 (NGC 3034) lying over half a degree to the north. Image courtesy of Martin C. Germano.*

brighter on the galaxy's southern side. To the SSW of the galaxy is a bright N–S pair of stars.

8/10″ Scopes–100x: Messier 81 is a fine, bright 15′ × 7′ NNW–SSE oval that gradually brightens to a prominent nonstellar nucleus. With averted vision very faint spiral arms may be glimpsed: two streaks are visible in the NNW spiral arm. Two 11th magnitude stars are superimposed upon the halo south of the galaxy's core, and a third 11th magnitude star is 5′ WNW of the core near the halo's edge.

16/18″ Scopes–150x: Spectacular! Messier 81 spans the entire field of view. Its halo is a huge 20′ × 10′ oval, its periphery being of rather low surface brightness

extending further outward using averted vision. The central core is a blazing 3′ × 2′ oval containing a bright 30″ diameter nucleus. With averted vision broad, diffuse, indistinct spiral arms can be glimpsed. To the SSE of the core, separated from it by a dark gap, is a thin spiral feature. The spiral arm NNW of the core is wider and much shorter. Two attractive double stars are SSW of the galaxy: ADS 7565 is an E–W pair of magnitude 10.9 stars 9″ apart, and ADS 7566 is a very close ESE–WNW double of magnitude 9.5 components only 2.1″ apart.

Figure 62-14. *Messier 82 (NGC 3034) is a magnificent cigar-shaped galaxy. The halo has an irregularly bright mottled texture, and the core is studded with a maze of short dark streaks. Image courtesy Chris Schur.*

NGC 3034 Messier 82 Galaxy Type I0
ϕ **12.0′ × 5.6′, m8.4v, SB 12.8**   **09ʰ55.8ᵐ +69° 41′**
Finder Chart 62-5, Figure 62-14   ★★★★★
4/6″ Scopes–75x: Messier 82, located only 38′ north of Messier 81, is an edge-on galaxy fainter but much more detailed than its companion. It has a mottled, highly elongated 8′ × 2′ ENE–WSW halo. The central core seems offset toward the halo's SE side. A 10th magnitude star lies just south of the halo's WSW tip.

8/10″ Scopes–100x: Messier 82 has a bright, mottled, irregularly illuminated 9′ × 2′ ENE–WSW halo. A dark lane perpendicular to the major axis bisects the halo into two nearly equal parts. The eastern part is more mottled but fades much more quickly out along the major axis. Both eastern and western parts are spotted with dark areas.

16/18″ Scopes–150x: This magnificent cigar-shaped galaxy has a 10′ × 3′ halo elongated in position angle 60° and containing a 5′ core extended along its major axis. Because of its high surface brightness, the halo has a well-defined outline. The core is very irregular in profile and severed in two almost equally long parts by a diagonal dark band. The western part of the core is brighter and is studded with short dark streaks jutting out at different angles. The eastern half of the core has the largest unbroken area. Several bright knots are strung along the major axis, a couple nearly stellar at their sharpest points of concentration.

NGC 3043 H835² Galaxy Type Sb: sp
ϕ **1.7′ × 0.5′, m12.6v, SB 12.3**   **09ʰ56.2ᵐ +59° 18′**
Finder Chart 62-4   ★★
12/14″ Scopes–125x: NGC 3043, located 8′ south of a 9.5 magnitude star, is a faint 1.25′ × 0.5′ E–W glow surrounding a small, inconspicuous core.

NGC 3065 H333² Galaxy Type SA(r)0°
ϕ **1.8′ × 1.7′, m12.5v, SB 13.6**   **10ʰ01.9ᵐ +72° 10′**

NGC 3066 H334² Galaxy Type SAB(s)bc pec
ϕ **1.1′ × 1.1′, m12.9v, SB 13.0**   **10ʰ02.2ᵐ +72° 07′**
Finder Chart 62-5   ★★/★
12/14″ Scopes–125x: NGC 3065 and NGC 3066, located about 15′ south of a magnitude 8.5 star, are two faint, tiny patches 1′ in diameter and 3′ apart. NGC 3065, the northernmost object, is noticeably brighter

Figure 62-15. *NGC 3079 is a bright edge-on galaxy, its core offset to the east. Image courtesy of Dean Salman.*

Figure 62-16. *NGC 3184 is a face-on, low surface brightness galaxy. Nevertheless, large telescopes show some spiral structure in it. Image courtesy of Martin C. Germano.*

and contains a stellar nucleus. A 13th magnitude star lies 1.5' to its NW. NGC 3066, by contrast, contains only a broad, poorly concentrated core.

NGC 3077 H286¹ Galaxy Type I0 pec
φ 5.5' × 4.1', m9.8v, SB 13.1   10ʰ03.3ᵐ +68° 44'
Finder Chart 62-5, Figure 62-19   ★★★★
8/10″Scopes–100x: NGC 3077, located 4' SE of an 8th magnitude star, is a minor member of the M81 Galaxy Group. Its absolute magnitude is only −17.9, a luminosity of just 1.2 billion suns, and its true diameter not much more than 16,000 light years. NGC 3077 has an evenly concentrated 2' diameter halo containing a broad and only slightly brighter core.
16/18″Scopes–150x: NGC 3077 has a moderately concentrated 30″ diameter core with an occasional twinkle where a nucleus should be. In averted vision the halo appears 4' across, slightly elongated NE–SW, and very diffuse around its edges.

NGC 3073 H853³ Galaxy Type SAB0
φ 1.2' × 1.1', m13.4v, SB 13.6   10ʰ00.9ᵐ +55° 37'
NGC 3079 H47⁵ Galaxy Type SB(s)c II
φ 8.0' × 1.5', m10.9v, SB 13.4   10ʰ02.0ᵐ +55° 41'
Finder Chart 62-7, Figure 62-15   ★/★★★★
8/10″Scopes–100x: NGC 3079 is just north of the NW side of a 6' long E–W triangle formed by one 8th and two 9th magnitude stars. It is a bright thin 6' × 1.5' NNW–SSE streak containing a bright oval

core. A 13th magnitude star is superimposed upon the NNW tip.
16/18″Scopes–150x: NGC 3079 is a bright luminous 7' × 2' NNW–SSE streak containing a long unevenly bright core offset toward the streak's eastern edge. A few dark and light patches are strewn along the core. At this aperture the 13th magnitude star can be seen to be superimposed upon the halo well within its NNW tip, and 14th magnitude stars can be glimpsed outside the west side of the halo 45″ NNW and 1.5' SSW of the galaxy's center. 10' WSW of NGC 3079 is NGC 3073, merely a faint, circular 1.5' diameter patch of haze.

NGC 3184 H168¹ Galaxy Type SAB(rs)cb II-III
φ 7.8' × 7.2', m9.8v, SB 14.0   10ʰ18.3ᵐ +41° 25'
Finder Chart 62-6, Figure 62-16   ★★★
8/10″Scopes–100x: NGC 3184, located in a rather rich star field for an off-Milky Way region, has a faint, 4' diameter halo of uniform surface brightness. An 11th magnitude star touches the halo's north edge.
12/14″Scopes–125x: In medium-size telescopes NGC 3184 shows a fairly bright 5' diameter halo containing a bright center. A hint of spiral structure might be glimpsed in the halo.
20/22″Scopes–175x: The 6' diameter halo is of a low surface brightness but displays two very faint spiral arms curling counterclockwise around a small, faint central hub. Several small knots and tiny concentrations are visible within the arms. The 11th

Figure 62-17. *NGC 3198 has a mottled interior halo containing a bright core surrounded by a faint, highly elongated outer halo. Image courtesy of Bill Logan.*

Figure 62-18. *NGC 3319 has a thin, extended core embedded in a low surface brightness halo. Image courtesy of Adam Block NOAO/AURA/NSF.*

magnitude star to the north of the galaxy's center is clearly inside rather than merely on the halo's edge.

NGC 3198 H199[1] Galaxy Type SB(rs)c II
ϕ **9.2′ × 3.5′, m10.3v, SB 13.9** $10^h19.9^m$ +45° 33′
Finder Chart 62-6, Figure 62-17   ★★★★
8/10″ Scopes–100x: NGC 3198, located 3.5′ SSW of a
   10.5 magnitude star, has a fairly faint 6′ × 2′ NE–
   SW halo that gradually brightens in toward its
   center.
16/18″ Scopes–150x: In larger aperture telescopes NGC
   3198 shows a fairly bright and mottled 8′ × 3′ NE–
   SW halo containing a broadly concentrated core.
   The tips of the halo are blunt rather than tapered

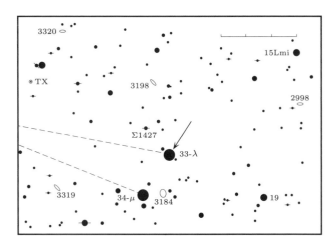

like other edge-on galaxies. The SE long side of the halo is more diffuse than the NW. Two 13th magnitude stars are 2′ and 3′ south of the galaxy's center.

NGC 3259 H870[2] Galaxy Type SAB(rs)bc: III
ϕ **2.1′ × 1.1′, m12.1v, SB 12.8** $10^h32.6^m$ +65° 03′
Finder Chart 62-8   ★★★
8/10″ Scopes–100x: NGC 3259, located 10′ west of a 9th
   magnitude star, is a faint, circular 1′ diameter glow
   containing a conspicuous nonstellar nucleus. At low
   power the galaxy has the appearance of a planetary
   nebula.

NGC 3310 H60[4] Galaxy Type SAB(r)bc II
ϕ **3.5′ × 3.2′, m10.8v, SB 13.3** $10^h38.7^m$ +53° 30′
Finder Chart 62-7, Figure 62-20   ★★★
8/10″ Scopes–100x: NGC 3310 lies 10′ SSW of a beautiful reddish-orange magnitude 5.5 star. The galaxy
   is fairly bright, slightly elongated 2′ × 1.75′ ENE–
   WSW, and uniformly illuminated. An 11th magnitude star lies 3′ north of the galaxy's center.
16/18″ Scopes–150x: The core is broadly concentrated
   but does not have much surrounding halo or a visible
   nucleus. The galaxy's overall size is 2.5′ × 2′ ENE–
   WSW.

NGC 3319 H700[1] Galaxy Type SB(rs)cd II-III
ϕ **6.9′ × 4.0′, m11.1v, SB 14.5** $10^h39.2^m$ +41° 41′
Finder Chart 62-6, Figure 62-18   ★★★
8/10″ Scopes–100x: NGC 3319, located 19′ NW of an
   8th magnitude star, is a very faint, diffuse 4′ × 1′

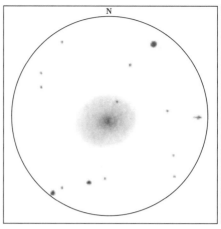

Figure 62-19. NGC 3077
13″, f5.6–165x, by Steve Coe

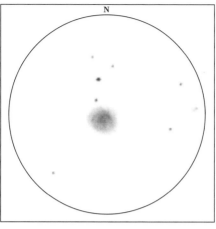

Figure 62-20. NGC 3310
18.5″, f5–300x, by Glen W. Sanner

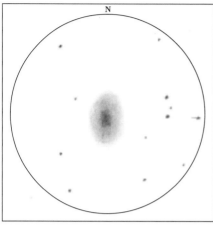

Figure 62-21. NGC 3359
17.5″, f4.5–250x, by G. R. Kepple

NE–SW streak.

16/18″ Scopes–150x: NGC 3319 has a faint 5.5′ × 2′ NE–SW halo containing a thin, faint core. A few slightly brighter patches can be seen along the galaxy's major axis. From a 13th magnitude star 1.5′ NNW of the galaxy's center a jagged chain of 12th and 13th magnitude stars zigzags northward.

NGC 3320 H745[2] Galaxy Type Scd: III
ϕ **2.0′ × 0.9′, m12.3v, SB12.8**   **10^{h}39.6^m +47° 24′**
Finder Chart 62-6   ★★

12/14″ Scopes–125x: NGC 3320, located 2′ south of a 12th magnitude star, is a moderately faint 1.5′ × 0.5′ NNE–SSW spindle containing a small, extended core. A 13.5 magnitude star touches the spindle's SSW tip.

NGC 3348 H80[1] Galaxy Type E0
ϕ **2.0′ × 2.0′, m11.2v, SB12.5**   **10^{h}47.2^m +72° 50′**
Finder Chart 62-5   ★★★

8/10″ Scopes–100x: NGC 3348, located 1.5′ ESE of a 10.5 magnitude star, has a perfectly round 1′ diameter halo that contains a bright tiny oval core.

16/18″ Scopes–150x: With a larger aperture telescope the halo can be traced out to a diameter of 1.5′. At low power (or in smaller telescopes) a 13th magnitude star superimposed upon the halo just east of the core gives the core the appearance of being extended.

NGC 3353 H842[3] Galaxy Type Sb? pec
ϕ **1.4′ × 1.0′, m12.8v, SB13.0**   **10^{h}45.4^m +55° 58′**
Finder Chart 62-7   ★★

12/14″ Scopes–125x: NGC 3353 is a fairly faint galaxy with a small, circular 1.25′ diameter halo containing a nonstellar nucleus. A 13.5 magnitude star lies 1.5′ south.

NGC 3359 H52[5] Galaxy Type SB(rs)c II
ϕ **7.3′ × 4.4′, m10.6v, SB14.2**   **10^{h}46.6^m +63° 13′**
Finder Chart 62-8, Figure 62-21   ★★★

8/10″ Scopes–100x: NGC 3359 has a large conspicuous oval core surrounded by a faint, featureless glow elongated 3′ × 2′ N–S.

16/18″ Scopes–150x: This low surface brightness galaxy has a 6′ × 3′ N–S halo with very faint, diffuse edges. The core is highly extended, moderately well concentrated, and mottled, but does not contain a stellar nucleus. The galaxy lies between and slightly north of the line joining two wide N–S pairs of 14th magnitude stars, one 3′ west and the other 3.5′ ESE of the galaxy's center.

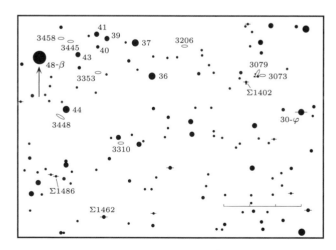

Finder Chart 62-7. 48–β UMa: 11^{h}01.8^m +56° 23′

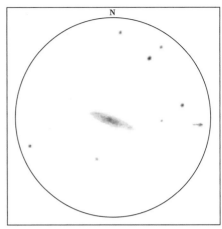

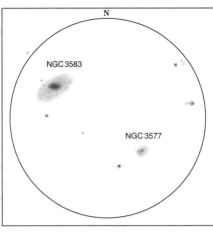

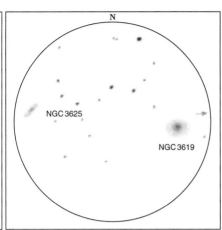

Figure 62-22. NGC 3448
17.5″, f4.5–300x, by G. R. Kepple

Figure 62-23. NGC 3577 and NGC 3583
18.5″, f5–250x, by Glen W. Sanner

Figure 62-24. NGC 3619 and NGC 3625
17.5″, f4.5–250x, by G. R. Kepple

NGC 3415 H718² Galaxy Type SA0+:
φ 1.9′ × 1.1′, m12.7v, SB 13.3   10ʰ51.7ᵐ +43° 43′
Finder Chart 62-9   ★★
12/14″Scopes–125x: NGC 3415 is 1′ north of the northern member of a triangle of 12.5 magnitude stars. The galaxy has a faint, small 1′×0.5′ N–S halo containing a conspicuous stellar nucleus.

NGC 3445 H267¹ Galaxy Type SAB(s)m III-IV
φ 1.6′ × 1.5′, m12.6v, SB 13.4   10ʰ54.6ᵐ +56° 59′
Finder Chart 62-7   ★★
8/10″Scopes–100x: NGC 3445, located 2′ SW of a yellowish 9th magnitude star, has a faint circular 1.25′ halo.
16/18″Scopes–150x: In larger telescopes NGC 3445 shows a faint, diffuse halo that is slightly elongated 1.5′ × 1.25′ ESE–WNW and slightly brighter toward its center. Galaxy NGC 3440 lies 10′ NW.

NGC 3448 H233¹ Galaxy Type I0
φ 4.9′ × 1.4′, m12.1v, SB 14.0   10ʰ54.7ᵐ +54° 19′
Finder Chart 62-7, Figure 62-22   ★★★
8/10″Scopes–100x: NGC 3448, located 17′ SE of 44 Ursae Majoris (m5.1), is a moderately faint 2.5′ × 0.5′ ENE–WSW streak containing a round, poorly concentrated core.
16/18″Scopes–150x: NGC 3448 has a fairly bright lenticular halo that elongates 3.5′ × 1′ ENE–WSW to tapered ends. The bulged core is irregularly bright with a mottled texture. A dark lane is suspected along the southern edge of the halo. Three faint 13.5 to 14th magnitude stars lie ESE, NNW, and WNW of the galaxy within 3′ of its center.

NGC 3458 H268¹ Galaxy Type SAB:
φ 1.4′ × 0.8′, m12.2v, SB 12.2   10ʰ56.0ᵐ +57° 07′
Finder Chart 62-7   ★★
12/14″Scopes–125x: NGC 3458, located 3′ north of a 10th magnitude star, has a fairly bright stellar nucleus embedded in a faint 1′ × 0.75′ N–S halo.

NGC 3478 H705³ Galaxy Type SB(rs)bc I-II
φ 2.4′ × 1.2′, m12.9v, SB 13.9   10ʰ59.5ᵐ +46° 07′
Finder Chart 62-9   ★★
12/14″Scopes–125x: NGC 3478, located 4′ north of a 2′ wide NE–SW pair of 11th magnitude stars, is a faint even glow elongated 2′ × 1.25′ NW–SE. 175x reveals a threshold stellar nucleus.

NGC 3516 H336² Galaxy Type (R)SB(s)0°:
φ 2.1′ × 1.8′, m11.7v, SB 13.0   11ʰ06.8ᵐ +72° 34′
Finder Chart 62-5   ★★★
12/14″Scopes–125x: NGC 3516, located just south of a widely spaced E–W pair of 10th magnitude stars, has a large prominent circular core embedded in a faint 1.5′ × 1′ NE–SW halo. A 13.5 magnitude star lies 1.25′ SE of the galaxy's center.

NGC 3549 H220¹ Galaxy Type SA(s)c: II-III
φ 3.0′ × 0.9′, m12.1v, SB 13.1   11ʰ10.9ᵐ +53° 23′
Finder Chart 62-10   ★★★
12/14″Scopes–125x: NGC 3549 has a faint, diffuse much elongated 2.5′ × 0.75′ NE–SW halo with blunt ends and a slightly brighter central streak. A magnitude 13.5 star 1.5′ east of the galaxy's center begins a chain of similarly faint stars that extends to the SSW.

Figure 62-25. *Messier 108 (NGC 3556) has a large, mottled halo of mixed bright patches and dark streaks. Image courtesy of Jim Burnell.*

Figure 62-26. *Messier 97 (NGC 3587), the Owl Nebula, requires medium aperture for its two internal dark ovals to be seen. Image courtesy Chris Schur.*

NGC 3556 Messier 108 Galaxy Type SB(s)cd III-IV
ϕ **8.1′ × 2.1′, m10.0v, SB 13.0   11^{h}11.5^{m} +55° 40′**
Finder Chart 62-10, Figure 62-25   ★★★★

Messier 108 was discovered by Mechain sometime in 1781 or 1782. This fine edge-on galaxy lies 48′ NW of the Owl Nebula, Messier 97.

4/6″ Scopes–75x: Messier 108 is easily spotted as a faint but conspicuous 7.0′ × 1.5′ E–W streak. The halo is brighter at its center, which is surrounded by vague dark and light streaks. An 8th magnitude star lies 8′ west of the galaxy's center.

8/10″ Scopes–100x: M108 has a low surface brightness 8′ × 2′ E–W halo that contains an extended central core. The halo is mottled with dark areas along its entire length, the most conspicuous dark patch located just west of the galaxy's center. A 12th magnitude star is just south of the halo's west tip.

16/18″ Scopes–150x: In large telescopes the halo of M108 appears as a fairly bright, very detailed 8′ × 2′ bar oriented in position angle 80°. The west end of the halo is tapered, with a slight twist to the SSW; the east end is rounded and curves a little to the NNE. The main body of the halo is a matrix of bright and dark streaks. At the halo's center is a tiny mottled bar with a 13th magnitude star superimposed upon the halo just to the bar's west. A few more foreground stars or galactic knots are on the halo's east and SE edges.

NGC 3577 H723^3 Galaxy Type SB(r)a
ϕ **1.5′ × 1.5′, m13.4v, SB 14.1   11^{h}13.8^{m} +48° 16′**

NGC 3583 H728^2 Galaxy Type SB(s)b II
ϕ **2.5′ × 1.8′, m11.1v, SB 12.6   11^{h}14.2^{m} +48° 19′**
Finder Chart 62-9, Figure 62-23   ★/★★★

12/14″ Scopes–125x: NGC 3583 is a fairly faint 2′ × 1.25′ NW–SE glow containing a mottled, moderately concentrated core elongated E–W. A 13th magnitude star lies 1.5′ SSE of the galaxy's center. 5′ SW of NGC 3583 is its companion galaxy, NGC 3577, which has a very faint 45″ diameter halo containing a faint stellar nucleus. A 12th magnitude star lies 1.25′ to this smaller galaxy's SE.

NGC 3587 Messier 97 Planetary Nebula Type 3a
ϕ **194″, m9.9v, CS 16.01v   11^{h}14.8^{m} +55° 01′**
Finder Chart 62-10, Figure 62-26   ★★★★
Owl Nebula

Messier 97, the famous Owl Nebula, was discovered by Mechain in 1781, and Messier added it to his catalogue that same year. The planetary's disk is about the same diameter as Jupiter's disk, but medium aperture telescopes are necessary to glimpse the two internal ovals which suggest owl eyes.

4/6″ Scopes–75x: The Owl Nebula, 2.5′ SSW of an 11th magnitude star, is a large, faint, circular disk with a bluish tint and diffuse edges.

12/14″ Scopes–125x: Under dark, transparent skies the two indistinct dark patches which constitute the

Owl's eyes can be glimpsed NW and SE of the 3′ diameter disk's center. The nebula is brighter with an O-III filter, but the eyes seem easier at higher power without filters.

16/18″Scopes–200x: The 3.5′ diameter grayish halo is brighter along its northern and southern periphery and seems slightly elongated N–S. The core area is slightly brighter, though the very difficult central star reveals itself only by an occasional twinkle. The core is flanked by the two bean-shaped darker ellipses which form the Owl's "eyes:" the NW eye is larger but the SE eye is more distinct. The planetary is practically ringed by faint stars located from 3′ to 4′ from its edges, the nearest a magnitude 12.5 object 2.5′ to the NNE.

NGC 3610 H270[1] Galaxy Type E5:
φ 3.2′ × 3.2′, m10.8v, SB13.2   11^{h}18.4^m +58° 47′
Finder Chart 62-8   ★★★

8/10″Scopes–100x: NGC 3610 lies south of a degree long NW–SE string of 8th magnitude stars. The galaxy displays a prominent stellar nucleus embedded in a fairly bright 1.75′ × 1.25′ NW–SE halo.

12/14″Scopes–125x: NGC 3610 has a bright 2′ × 1.5′ NW–SE oval halo that brightens abruptly to an oval core containing a brilliant stellar nucleus. A 13.5 magnitude star lies 3′ SSE.

NGC 3613 H271[1] Galaxy Type E6
φ 3.4′ × 1.9′, m10.9v, SB12.8   11^{h}18.6^m +58° 00′
Finder Chart 62-8   ★★★

8/10″Scopes–100x: NGC 3613, located west of a large box-shaped asterism of 10th and 11th magnitude stars, is a moderately faint 2′ × 0.75′ E–W glow

containing a bright center with a stellar nucleus.

12/14″Scopes–125x: NGC 3613 appears fairly faint and elongated 2.5′ × 1.25′ E–W. Its surface brightness increases smoothly inward to a bright oval core with a nonstellar nucleus. Galaxy NGC 3619 is located 16′ SE.

NGC 3614 H729[2] Galaxy Type SAB(r)c I- II
φ 4.2′ × 2.6′, m11.6v, SB14.0   11^{h}18.3^m +45° 45′
Finder Chart 62-9   ★★

12/14″Scopes–125x: NGC 3614 appears faint and diffuse, its 2.5′ × 1.5′ ESE–WNW halo very little brighter in its center. 175x reveals a faint stellar nucleus and a threshold star at the halo's edge 1′ SW of the galaxy's center.

NGC 3619 H244[1] Galaxy Type (R)SA(s)0+:
φ 3.7′ × 2.8′, m11.5v, SB13.9   11^{h}19.4^m +57° 46′

NGC 3625 H885[2] Galaxy Type SAB(s)b:
φ 1.9′ × 0.5′, m13.1v, SB12.9   11^{h}20.5^m +57° 47′
Finder Chart 62-8, Figure 62-24   ★★/★

12/14″Scopes–125x: NGC 3619 has a faint, diffuse 2′ × 1.5′ NE–SW halo containing a faint core. With averted vision a faint stellar nucleus may be glimpsed. 9.5′ east of NGC 3619 is its companion galaxy NGC 3625, a faint, diffuse 1′ × 0.5′ NNW–SSE glow. A 12th magnitude star lies 5.5′ NNE of NGC 3619. A zigzagging chain of 13th magnitude stars starting midway between this star and NGC 3619 leads eastward toward NGC 3625.

NGC 3631 H226[1] Galaxy Type SA(s)c I-II
φ 5.5′ × 4.6′, m10.4v, SB13.8   11^{h}21.0^m +53° 10′
Finder Chart 62-10, Figure 62-27   ★★★

12/14″Scopes–125x: NGC 3631 displays a well concentrated core with a prominent stellar nucleus embedded in a circular 3′ diameter halo. The halo's brightness fades rapidly to diffuse edges.

16/18″Scopes–150x: This galaxy is a fine sight in larger instruments. Its bright 4′ diameter halo is mottled with hints of spiral structure. The well-defined 30″ diameter core contains a bright stellar nucleus. 13th magnitude stars lie 3.5′ NE and 3.5′ WNW of the galaxy's core.

NGC 3642 H245[1] Galaxy Type SA(r)bc: I
φ 5.7′ × 4.6′, m11.2v, SB14.6   11^{h}22.3^m +59° 05′
Finder Chart 62-8, Figure 62-28   ★★★

8/10″Scopes–100x: NGC 3642 is a faint diffuse glow surrounding a faint stellar nucleus. With averted vision the halo seems to be about 3′ across.

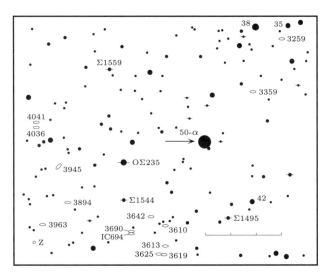

Finder Chart 62-8. 50–α UMa: 11^{h}03.7^m +61° 45′

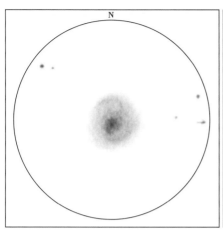

Figure 62-27. NGC 3631
17.5″, f4.5–300x, by G. R. Kepple

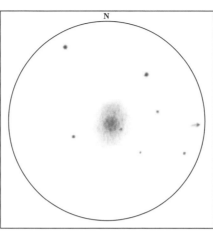

Figure 62-28. NGC 3642
17.5″, f4.5–300x, by G. R. Kepple

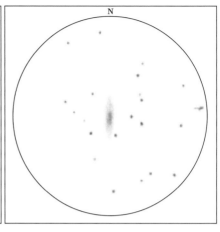

Figure 62-29. NGC 3675
13″, f4.5–165x, by Tom Polakis

16/18″Scopes–150x: In larger telescopes the halo becomes rather large, but remains faint and diffuse. It is elongated 4′ × 3′ N–S and poorly concentrates to a broad, irregularly bright 2′ diameter in which are mingled several knots and stellar beads. Two threshold stars are superimposed upon the halo 1.5′ ESE and 1.75′ WNW of the galaxy's center. A 13th magnitude star is outside the halo 3.5′ NNE of the center.

NGC 3665 H219[1] Galaxy Type SA(s)0°
ϕ **3.5′ × 3.1′, m10.8v, SB13.3**   **11^{h}24.7^m +38° 46′**
Finder Chart 62-11   ★★★

8/10″Scopes–100x: NGC 3665 has a fairly bright 1.5′ × 1′ NNE–SSW halo that smoothly brightens in to a prominent circular core. A 25″ wide NNW–SSE pair of 11th magnitude stars lies 12′ south of the galaxy.

16/18″Scopes–150x: The 2′ × 1.5′ NNE–SSW halo concentrates to a bright core with a stellar nucleus. A very faint star lies just outside the halo's northern edge.

NGC 3675 H194[1] Galaxy Type SA(s)b II
ϕ **6.2′ × 3.2′, m10.2v, SB13.3**   **11^{h}26.1^m +43° 35′**
Finder Chart 62-9, Figure 62-29   ★★★★

8/10″Scopes–100x: NGC 3675 has a stellar nucleus embedded in a smooth, fairly bright 4′ × 1.5′ N–S oval halo. A 12th magnitude star touches the west side of the halo's southern tip, and a magnitude 12.5 star lies further away on the opposite side of the same tip.

16/18″Scopes–150x: This galaxy has a fine bright 5′ × 2′ N–S halo with rounded tips. The bright, highly extended core is offset to the west of the halo's major axis and has a mottled texture with a few knots. With averted vision a dark dust lane can be seen running along the eastern side of the halo.

NGC 3683 H246[1] Galaxy Type SB(s)c? III-IV
ϕ **1.9′ × 0.7′, m12.4v, SB12.6**   **11^{h}27.5^m +56° 53′**
Finder Chart 62-10   ★★★

12/14″Scopes–125x: This edge-on galaxy is a faint 1.5′ × 0.5′ NW–SE streak that is slightly brighter along its major axis.

16/18″Scopes–150x: Although faint, NGC 3683 presents a well defined 2′ × 0.75′ halo that is elongated to tapered ends. The core is highly extended along the major axis of the halo and has a series of faint beads on each side of a stellar nucleus.

NGC 3687 H770[2] Galaxy Type (R′)SAB(r)bc? I-II
ϕ **1.6′ × 1.6′, m12.0v, SB12.9**   **11^{h}28.0^m +29° 31′**
Finder Chart 62-11   ★★

12/14″Scopes–125x: NGC 3687, located 6′ NE of a 10th magnitude star, is a faint, round 1.5′ diameter glow that slightly brightens to a poorly defined core with a stellar nucleus.

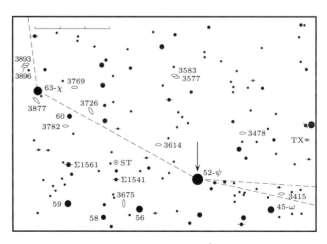

Finder Chart 62-9. 52–ψ UMa: 11^{h}09.7^m +44° 30′

NGC 3690 H247¹ Galaxy Type IBm pec
ϕ **2.5′ × 2.1′, m11.5v, SB13.1   11ʰ28.5ᵐ +58° 33′**

IC 694 Galaxy Type SBm?
ϕ **1.2′ × 1.0′, m11.3v, SB11.3   11ʰ28.5ᵐ +58° 33′**
Finder Chart 62-8   ★★★/★★★

12/14″ Scopes–125x: NGC 3690 and IC694, located 3′
   north of a 10th magnitude star, are a pair of nearly
   merged interacting galaxies that appear as one
   object. The combined halo is a fairly bright 2′ × 1.25′
   E–W oval containing a bright bar-like core. The
   nuclei of the two galaxies are at opposite ends of
   the mottled core area: the eastern nucleus is a small
   knot but the western nucleus is merely stellar.

NGC 3718 H221¹ Galaxy Type SB(s)a pec
ϕ **10.0′ × 4.7′, m10.8v, SB14.8   11ʰ32.6ᵐ +53° 04′**

NGC 3729 H222¹ Galaxy Type SB(r)a pec
ϕ **3.1′ × 2.2′, m11.4v, SB13.4   11ʰ33.8ᵐ +53° 08′**
Finder Chart 62-10, Figure 62-30   ★★★/★★★

12/14″ Scopes–125x: NGC 3718 and NGC 3729 are a
   12′ wide E–W pair of interacting galaxies. The
   western component, NGC 3718, has a uniformly
   faint halo elongated 4′ × 2.5′ NNW–SSE: its core,
   however, is elongated NNE–SSW. The core contains a very faint stellar nucleus. 2.5′ SSW of the
   nucleus, near the halo's edge, is a wide E–W pair
   of 11th magnitude stars. The eastern galaxy, NGC
   3729, is only half the size of its companion. Its
   2′ × 1.25′ N–S halo contains a broad, weakly concentrated core. A faint star is nestled against its
   SSW edge.

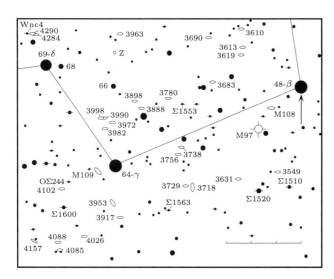

Finder Chart 62-10. 48–β UMa: 11ʰ01.8ᵐ +56° 23′

NGC 3726 H730² Galaxy Type SAB(r)c I-II
ϕ **5.6′ × 3.8′, m10.4v, SB13.6   11ʰ33.3ᵐ +47° 02′**
Finder Chart 62-9, Figure 62-31   ★★★★

8/10″ Scopes–100x: NGC 3726 has a fairly bright 5′ × 3′
   N–S halo with an 11th magnitude star on its
   northern edge. The core is small, somewhat elongated N–S, and has a granular texture.

12/14″ Scopes–125x: The large, diffuse 5.5′ × 3.5′ N–S
   halo has, except for a faint stellar nucleus, uniform
   surface brightness.

20/22″ Scopes–175x: Outstanding! NGC 3726 has a
   fairly bright N–S oval halo that contains a subtle
   clockwise spiral structure. The northern arm is short
   and indistinct. The southern arm has some knots
   and numerous tiny H-II regions and therefore is
   more prominent. At the galaxy's center is a small
   core with a faint bar aligned with the halo's N–S
   major axis.

NGC 3738 H783² Galaxy Type Im III-IV
ϕ **3.2′ × 2.8′, m11.7v, SB14.0   11ʰ35.8ᵐ +54° 31′**
Finder Chart 62-10   ★★★

8/10″ Scopes–100x: NGC 3738, located 30′ NNW of a
   6th magnitude star, has a fairly bright 1.25′ × 0.75′
   NW–SE halo that contains a slightly brighter
   center. A 10th magnitude star lies 2.5′ NE, and an
   11th magnitude star is 4′ ENE of the galaxy's
   center.

16/18″ Scopes–150x: NGC 3738 has a smooth 1.5′ × 0.75′
   NW–SE bar-shaped envelope with rounded ends.
   The NE long side of the envelope is arced, but the
   SW long side is more sharply-bordered. The gal-
   axy's core is highly extended but weakly concen-
   trated. A slightly brighter galactic knot or a super-
   imposed star is on the galaxy's NW edge. Galaxy
   NGC 3756 lies 16′ SE.

NGC 3756 H784² Galaxy Type SAB(rs)bc II
ϕ **4.6′ × 2.3′, m11.5v, SB13.9   11ʰ36.8ᵐ +54° 18′**
Finder Chart 62-10   ★★★

8/10″ Scopes–100x: NGC 3756, located 4′ south of a 10th
   magnitude star, is a faint, smooth 3′ × 1.5′ N–S glow
   without central brightening.

16/18″ Scopes–150x: NGC 3756 is a low surface brightness galaxy with diffuse edges and a faint stellar
   nucleus embedded in a poorly concentrated, somewhat mottled core. Galaxy NGC 3738 lies 16′ NW.

NGC 3769 H731² Galaxy Type SB(r)b: II-III
ϕ **3.0′ × 0.9′, m11.8v, SB12.7   11ʰ37.7ᵐ +47° 54′**
Finder Chart 62-9   ★★★

8/10″ Scopes–100x: NGC 3769, located in a star field
   barren even by off-Milky Way standards, is a faint
   1.5′ × 0.5′ NNW–SSE streak with a thin unconcentrated core along its major axis.

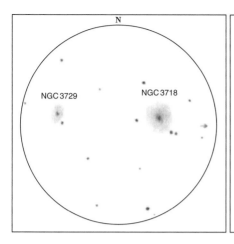

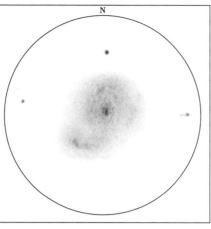

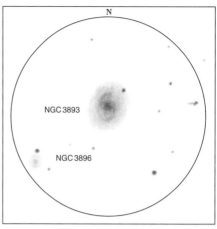

Figure 62-30. NGC 3718 and NGC 3729
13″, f5.6–165x, by Steve Coe

Figure 62-31. NGC 3726
20″, f4.5–175x, by Richard W. Jakiel

Figure 62-32. NGC 3893 and NGC 3896
20″, f4.5–175x, by Richard W. Jakiel

16/18″ Scopes–150x: With larger aperture, NGC 3769 appears more lens-shaped. Its 2′ × 0.75′ NNW–SSE halo has a faint mottled texture and contains a faint core that runs nearly half the length of its major axis. A magnitude 13.5 star is 2′ NE of the galaxy's center.

NGC 3782 H732[2] Galaxy Type SAB(s)cd: IV-V
φ 1.3′ × 0.7′, m12.4v, SB 12.1   11^{h}39.3^m +46° 31′
Finder Chart 62-9   ★★
12/14″ Scopes–125x: NGC 3782 has a diffuse 1′ diameter halo that contains a poorly concentrated core. Its faint patch lies near three 11th to 12th magnitude stars, the nearest of which actually touches the galaxy's SSW edge.

NGC 3780 H227[1] Galaxy Type SA(s)c: II-III
φ 2.8′ × 2.3′, m11.5v, SB 13.3   11^{h}39.4^m +56° 16′
Finder Chart 62-10   ★★★
8/10″ Scopes–100x: NGC 3780 has a faint, diffuse 2.5′ × 2′ NNE–SSW oval halo. 25′ to the galaxy's WSW is the fine double Σ1553, which consists of comparably bright magnitude 7.9 and 8.4 components separated by a comfortable 6″.
16/18″ Scopes–150x: NGC 3780 has a faint 3′ × 2.5′ NNE–SSW halo that contains a faint core with a knot on its east side. A 13th magnitude star lies 2′ ENE.

NGC 3813 H94[1] Galaxy Type SA(rs)b: III
φ 1.9′ × 1.1′, m11.7v, SB 12.3   11^{h}41.3^m +36° 33′
Finder Chart 62-11   ★★★
12/14″ Scopes–125x: NGC 3813 appears fairly bright and much elongated 2.5′ × 0.75′ E–W. A thin, moderately well concentrated core runs for 1′ along the galaxy's major axis. 14th magnitude stars lie near

each tip of the halo, the star near the eastern tip being the closer.

NGC 3877 H201[1] Galaxy Type SA(s)c: II-III
φ 5.1′ × 1.1′, m11.0v, SB 12.7   11^{h}46.1^m +47° 30′
Finder Chart 62-12, Figure 62-33   ★★★★
8/10″ Scopes–100x: NGC 3877 is within an attractive star field that includes the bright magnitude 3.7 Chi (χ) Ursae Majoris 17′ to its north. The galaxy has a moderately faint, highly elongated 4′ × 1′ NE–SW halo containing a well concentrated central condensation.

Figure 62-33. *Edge-on galaxy NGC 3877, located south of the bright star Chi (χ) Ursae Majoris, has a mottled halo around a faint stellar nucleus. Image courtesy Tim Hunter and James McGaha.*

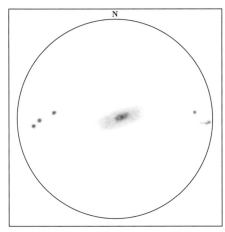

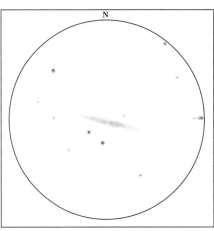

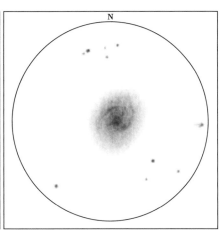

Figure 62-34. NGC 3898
17.5″, f4.5–300x, by G. R. Kepple

Figure 62-35. NGC 3917
18.5″, f5–275x, by Glen W. Sanner

Figure 62-36. NGC 3938
17.5″, f4.5–275x, by G. R. Kepple

16/18″Scopes–150x: In large telescopes NGC 3877 has a mottled 5′×1.25′ envelope elongated in position angle 35°. The central portion contains a faint stellar nucleus surrounded by several nearly stellar beads. The envelope's NE tip nearly extends to the midpoint of the southern side of a 6′ equilateral triangle of 11th to 12th magnitude stars.

NGC 3888 H785² Galaxy Type SAB(rs)c II
φ 1.6′×1.3′, m12.1v, SB12.8   11ʰ47.6ᵐ +55° 58′
Finder Chart 62-10   ★★★

12/14″Scopes–125x: NGC 3888 appears brighter than expected. Its well concentrated football-shaped halo is elongated 1.75′×1′ ESE–WNW and contains a slightly brighter oval core with a indistinct nucleus. Five fairly bright stars NE and NW of the galaxy lie along two parallel rows.

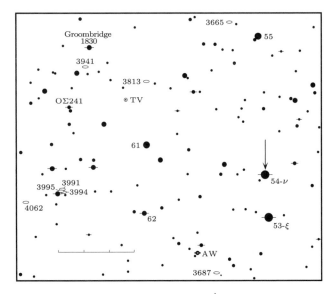

Finder Chart 62-11. 54–ν UMa: 11ʰ18.5ᵐ +33° 06′

NGC 3893 H738² Galaxy Type SAB(rs)c: I
φ 4.2′×2.3′, m10.5v, SB12.8   11ʰ48.6ᵐ +48° 43′

NGC 3896 H739² Galaxy Type SB0/a: pec
φ 1.6′×0.9′, m12.9v, SB13.1   11ʰ48.9ᵐ +48° 41′
Finder Chart 62-12, Figure 62-32   ★★★/★★

8/10″Scopes–100x: NGC 3893, located 3′ NE of a 10th magnitude star, is a fairly bright 2.25′×1.5′ NNW–SSE oval containing a round, prominent core. A 12.5 magnitude star touches the galaxy's NW edge.

16/18″Scopes–150x: NGC 3893 displays a mottled, unevenly bright halo elongated 3′×2′ in position angle 165°. The core is bright and spotted but lacks a distinct nucleus. With averted vision vague spiral arms can be seen springing from the core's east and west edges and arcing in a clockwise direction out beyond the core's north and south points. The SW part of the halo is more distinct. 4′ SE of NGC 3893 is its companion galaxy NGC 3986, a faint, circular 1′ diameter glow with a 13th magnitude star touching its northern edge.

NGC 3898 H228¹ Galaxy Type SA(s)ab I-II
φ 3.3′×1.9′, m10.7v, SB12.5   11ʰ49.2ᵐ +56° 05′
Finder Chart 62-10, Figure 62-34   ★★★

8/10″Scopes–100x: NGC 3898, located within the Dipper's bowl north of the magnitude 2.4 Gamma (γ) = 64 Ursae Majoris, is the brighter and larger of a galaxy-pair with NGC 3888, lying 16′ to its SW. NGC 3898 displays a bright stellar nucleus embedded in a well concentrated core surrounded by a much fainter 2.5′×1.25′ ESE–WNW halo.

16/18″Scopes–150x: The halo is rather faint around its periphery, but with averted vision may be traced to 3.5′×1.5′ ESE–WNW. The brightness rises suddenly to a fairly large, circular core containing a bright nucleus. A 1.25′ long NW–SE arc, concave to the SW, of three 13th and 14th magnitude stars, lies 3.5′ ENE of the galaxy.

NGC 3917 H824² Galaxy Type SAcd: III-IV
ϕ 4.7′ × 1.0′, m11.8v, SB 13.3   11ʰ50.8ᵐ +51° 50′
Finder Chart 62-10, Figure 62-35   ★★★
12/14″ Scopes–125x: NGC 3917 is a faint, flat 4′ × 0.75′ ENE–WSW streak that is slightly brighter along its major axis. Two 13.5 magnitude stars lie off the galaxy's southern long side, 1.25′ SE and 1.5′ south of its center.

NGC 3938 H203¹ Galaxy Type SA(s)c I
ϕ 4.9′ × 4.7′, m10.4v, SB 13.6   11ʰ52.8ᵐ +44° 07′
Finder Chart 62-12, Figure 62-36   ★★★
8/10″ Scopes–100x: NGC 3938 has a rather faint, diffuse 3.5′ × 2.5′ N–S halo that contains a small and inconspicuous core.
16/18″ Scopes–150x: NGC 3938 remains only moderately bright in larger telescopes. Its large 4′ × 3′ N–S halo has indistinct edges. Toward the interior the halo brightens slightly to a circular, somewhat mottled core that contains a faint stellar nucleus. With averted vision and 175x a vague counterclockwise spiral structure may just be glimpsed. A 13th magnitude star is on the halo's SW edge 2′ from the galaxy's center.

NGC 3941 H173¹ Galaxy Type SB(s)0°
ϕ 3.7′ × 2.6′, m10.3v, SB 12.6   11ʰ52.9ᵐ +36° 59′
Finder Chart 62-11   ★★★★
8/10″ Scopes–100x: This galaxy has a fairly bright 2′ × 0.75′ N–S oval halo containing a bright center.
16/18″ Scopes–150x: NGC 3941 has a conspicuous oval core with a stellar nucleus surrounded by a well concentrated 3′ × 1.5′ N–S halo. A 13th magnitude star lies 1.5′ east.

NGC 3945 H251¹ Galaxy Type (R)SB(rs)0+
ϕ 5.9′ × 3.7′, m10.8v, SB 14.0   11ʰ53.2ᵐ +60° 41′
Finder Chart 62-8   ★★★
8/10″ Scopes–100x: NGC 3945 exhibits a conspicuous core with a stellar nucleus, but the halo fades rapidly outward to extremely diffuse edges: its diameter might be around 2′. A 12th magnitude star near the halo's SW edge appears about as bright as the nucleus.
16/18″ Scopes–150x: With larger aperture the very faint outer regions appear elongated 3′ × 2′ E–W. The

Figure 62-37. *NGC 3953 is a bright galaxy containing a prominent core with a stellar nucleus. Image courtesy of Bill Logan.*

core is broad and well concentrated; but the nucleus does not stand out as much as in smaller telescopes. In addition to the 12th magnitude star, two 13th magnitude stars can be seen on the halo's south edge and 1.75′ NW of the galaxy's center.

NGC 3949 H202¹ Galaxy Type SA(s)bc: III-IV
ϕ 2.6′ × 1.6′, m11.1v, SB 12.5   11ʰ53.7ᵐ +47° 52′
Finder Chart 62-12   ★★★
12/14″ Scopes–125x: NGC 3949 is a moderately faint 2′ × 1.25′ NW–SE oval containing a stellar nucleus. The core is not very well concentrated, but averted vision reveals that it has a mottled texture and faint patches. 13th magnitude stars are 3.5′ SW and 4′ NW.

NGC 3953 H45⁵ Galaxy Type SB(r)bc I-II
ϕ 6.0′ × 3.2′, m10.1v, SB 13.1   11ʰ53.8ᵐ +52° 20′
Finder Chart 62-10, Figure 62-37   ★★★★
8/10″ Scopes–100x: This bright galaxy is just west of a N–S string of widely and rather evenly spaced 10th and 11th magnitude stars. A N–S pair of 10.5 magnitude stars due north of the galaxy forms a thin isosceles triangle with the northernmost star in the string. The galaxy's 5′ × 2.5′ N–S halo contains a bright circular core with a stellar nucleus.
16/18″ Scopes–150x: NGC 3953 is a fine object for this aperture range. Its 6′ × 3′ NNE–SSW halo contains a broadly concentrated central region displaying mottled texture in and around the bright oval core. A 14th magnitude star touches the halo's western

flank 1′ NE of the galaxy's center, and a 12.5 magnitude star lies 3′ to the galaxy's ENE.

NGC 3963 H67⁴ Galaxy Type SAB(rs)bc I-II
φ 2.7′ × 2.5′, m11.9v, SB 13.8   11ʰ55.0ᵐ +58° 30′
Finder Chart 62-10   ★★
12/14″Scopes–125x: NGC 3963 has a faint 2′ × 1.5′ NW–SE halo containing a very slightly brighter central region mottled with a mixture of dark areas and indistinct bright knots. Along the halo's southern edge is a row of three faint stars, the two western-most touching the halo's edge. 8′ SSW of NGC 3963 is galaxy NGC 3958, a faint 1′ × 0.5′ NNE–SSW oval containing a stellar nucleus.

NGC 3982 H62⁴ Galaxy Type SAB(r)b: III
φ 2.2′ × 2.0′, m11.0v, SB 12.4   11ʰ56.5ᵐ +55° 08′
Finder Chart 62-10   ★★★
12/14″Scopes–125x: NGC 3982, located 3.5′ NNE of two 12th magnitude stars, is a fairly bright galaxy with a prominent 30″ core embedded in a 1.75′ diameter, slightly elongated N–S, halo. 175x reveals a mottled central area containing a faint nonstellar nucleus.

NGC 3985 H707³ Galaxy Type SB(s)m:
φ 1.0′ × 0.6′, m12.6v, SB 11.9   11ʰ56.7ᵐ +48° 20′
Finder Chart 62-12   ★★
12/14″Scopes–125x: NGC 3985 is a moderately faint, diffuse glow slightly elongated 45″ × 30″ ENE–WSW and containing a tiny dim core. A 14th magnitude star lies 2.5′ SE.

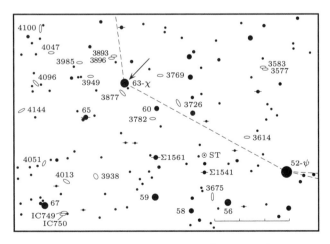

Finder Chart 62-12. 63–χ UMa: 11ʰ46.0ᵐ +47° 47′

NGC 3990 H791² Galaxy Type S0: sp
φ 1.4′ × 0.8′, m12.6v, SB 12.5   11ʰ57.6ᵐ +55° 28′

NGC 3998 H229¹ Galaxy Type SAB(r)b: III
φ 3.0′ × 2.6′, m10.6v, SB 12.7   11ʰ57.9ᵐ +55° 27′
Finder Chart 62-10, Figure 62-39   ★★/★★★
12/14″Scopes–125x: NGC 3990 and NGC 3998 are a 3′ wide E–W galaxy pair. NGC 3998, the eastern component, is by far the larger and the brighter of the two: its prominent stellar nucleus is embedded in the faint 2′ × 1.5′ NW–SE oval halo. NGC 3990, the western galaxy, also has a bright nucleus but its faint halo is extended only 45″ × 25″ NE–SW. A 9th magnitude star lies 5.5′ NW, and a 10th magnitude star is 4.5′ SSW, of NGC 3998.

NGC 3991 Galaxy Type Im pec sp
φ 1.3′ × 0.3′, m13.1v, SB 11.9   11ʰ57.5ᵐ +32° 20′

NGC 3994 Galaxy Type SA(r)c pec?
φ 1.0′ × 0.6′, m12.7v, SB 12.0   11ʰ57.6ᵐ +32° 17′

NGC 3995 Galaxy Type SAm pec III-IV
φ 2.6′ × 0.9′, m12.4v, SB 13.2   11ʰ57.7ᵐ +32° 18′
Finder Chart 62-11, Figure 62-40   ★★/★★/★★
16/18″Scopes–150x: NGC 3991, NGC 3994, and NGC 3995 are a trio of interacting galaxies WNW of a bright 6th magnitude field star. NGC 3995, located 5′ from the star, is the brightest of the three galaxies and has a much-elongated 2′ × 0.5′ NE–SW spindle-shaped halo containing a somewhat mottled core extended along its major axis. NGC 3991, located 3.75′ NW of NGC 3995, is also quite elongated: its 1′ × 0.25′ NE–SW halo contains an extended bright core with a stellar nucleus. The southernmost galaxy of the three, NGC 3994, is 2′ SW of NGC 3995 and has a small, faint 1′ × 0.5′ N–S oval halo that contains a stellar nucleus.

NGC 3992 Messier 109 Galaxy Type SB(rs)bc I
φ 7.6′ × 4.3′, m9.8v, SB 13.5   11ʰ57.6ᵐ +53° 23′
Finder Chart 62-10, Figure 62-38   ★★★★★
Although viewed by Messier, M109 was not added to his catalogue until the twentieth century. It was discovered by Mechain sometime in 1781 or 1782. M109 is around 46 million light years distant. Its absolute magnitude is about −20.9, a luminosity of 19 billion suns, and its true diameter is in excess of 100,000 light years.
8/10″Scopes–100x: Messier 109 lies within a NE pointing isosceles triangle of five unequally bright stars. The northern side of the triangle consists of one 11th and three 12.5 magnitude stars. The brightest member of the triangle, a 10th magnitude object, is at its SW corner 5′ from the galaxy's core. M109

has a faint, diffuse 6′×3.5′ ENE–WSW halo that contains a small bright core.

16/18″Scopes–150x: The fairly low surface brightness halo is elongated 7.5′×5′ ENE–WSW, its SW tip pointing toward a 10th magnitude star 5′ distant. The inner halo is mottled and surrounds an irregularly bright oval core. An ENE–WSW string of one 11th and three 12.5 magnitude stars passes through the northern part of the galaxy's halo: two of the magnitude 12.5 stars lie near the halo's tips and the third is superimposed upon the halo 1′ north of the galaxy's core.

NGC 4013 Galaxy Type Sb III
ϕ 4.7′×1.0′, m11.2v, SB12.8 11^{h}58.5^m +43° 57′
Finder Chart 62-12, Figure 62-41   ★★★
12/14″Scopes–125x: NGC 4013 has a moderately faint, thin halo elongated 4′×0.5′ ENE–WSW. With averted vision and 200x a dark dust lane might be glimpsed. A magnitude 12.5 star is superimposed upon the halo just NE of the galaxy's center and at low power might be mistaken for the nucleus: however, the real nucleus, if potentially visible, is drowned out in the glare of the star.

IC 749 Galaxy Type SAB(rs) cd III
ϕ 2.3′×1.9′, m12.4v, SB13.8   11^{h}58.6^m +42° 44′

IC 750 Galaxy Type Sab: sp
ϕ 2.8′×1.4′, m11.9v, SB13.3   11^{h}58.9^m +42° 43′
Finder Chart 62-12, Figure 62-42   ★★/★★★
8/10″Scopes–100x: IC 749 and IC 750 are a 3′ wide NW–SE galaxy pair near a magnitude 8.5 field star. The eastern system, IC 750, is located 5.5′ ENE of the star: it is the larger and brighter of the two galaxies, and has a thin 1.5′×0.5′ NE–SW halo that is elongated to tapered ends and contains a small, bright oval core. IC 749, located 3′ NE of the magnitude 8.5 star, is a very faint, round featureless glow. A 9th magnitude star lies 4′ SSE of IC750.

16/18″Scopes–150x: IC750 has a fairly bright 2′×0.75′ halo that contains a brighter granular center. The increase in aperture does little to improve IC749: it remains a diffuse haze with a slight brightening at its center.

NGC 4026 H223[1] Galaxy Type S0
ϕ 4.6′×1.2′, m10.8v, SB12.5   11^{h}59.4^m +50° 58′
Finder Chart 62-10, Figure 62-43   ★★★★
8/10″Scopes–100x: NGC 4026, located 7′ SSW of a 9th

Figure 62-38. *Messier 109 (NGC3992) displays a bright core surrounded by a large, faint, diffuse halo. Image courtesy of Jim Burnell.*

magnitude star, is a bright 3.5′×0.75′ N–S streak containing an oval core.

16/18″Scopes–150x: This galaxy displays a sharply concentrated core containing a bright nonstellar nucleus. The surrounding envelope appears to be a 3′×0.75′ N–S spindle, but close inspection reveals that its very faint extensions reach a length of 4′.

NGC 4036 H253[1] Galaxy Type S0
ϕ 3.8′×1.9′, m10.7v, SB12.7   12^{h}01.4^m +61° 54′
Finder Chart 62-8   ★★★★
8/10″Scopes–100x: NGC 4036 lies within a keystone of 10th magnitude stars that is located 0.5′ NE of a row of three 6th to 7th magnitude stars. The galaxy has a bright 2.5′×1′ E–W halo that contains an oval core with a stellar nucleus.

16/18″Scopes–150x: This fine spindle-shaped galaxy has a bright 3.5′×1.25′ E–W halo containing a well concentrated core with a bright stellar nucleus. Averted vision reveals the thin dark dust lane that runs just south of the core.

NGC 4041 H252[1] Galaxy Type SA(rs)bc: II-III
ϕ 2.6′×2.6′, m11.3v, SB13.2   12^{h}02.2^m +62° 08′
Finder Chart 62-8, Figure 62-44   ★★★
8/10″Scopes–100x: NGC 4041, located in a field of faint stars, has a bright, circular 1.5′ diameter halo containing a broad central brightening.

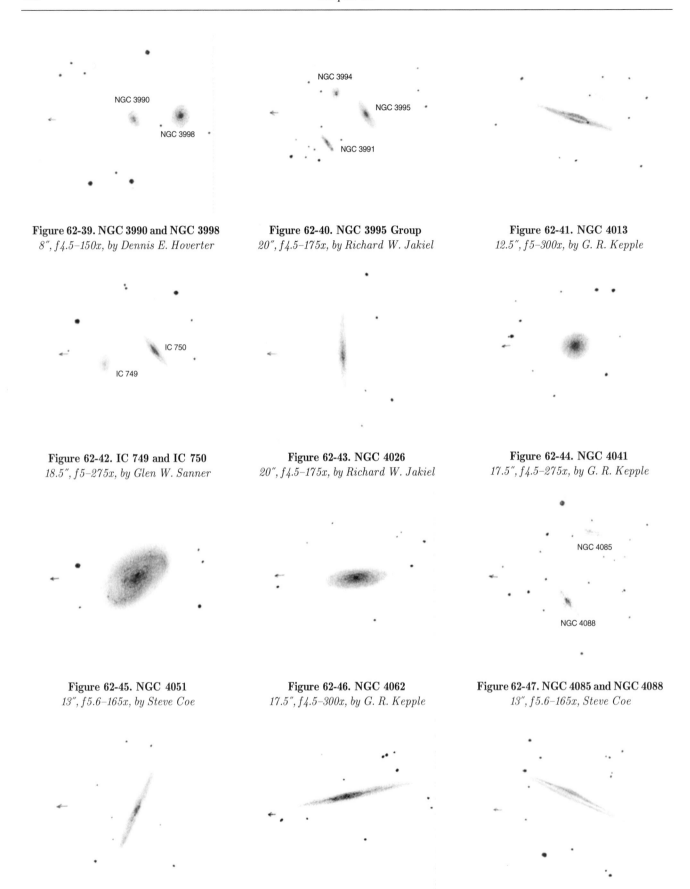

Figure 62-39. NGC 3990 and NGC 3998
8″, f4.5–150x, by Dennis E. Hoverter

Figure 62-40. NGC 3995 Group
20″, f4.5–175x, by Richard W. Jakiel

Figure 62-41. NGC 4013
12.5″, f5–300x, by G. R. Kepple

Figure 62-42. IC 749 and IC 750
18.5″, f5–275x, by Glen W. Sanner

Figure 62-43. NGC 4026
20″, f4.5–175x, by Richard W. Jakiel

Figure 62-44. NGC 4041
17.5″, f4.5–275x, by G. R. Kepple

Figure 62-45. NGC 4051
13″, f5.6–165x, by Steve Coe

Figure 62-46. NGC 4062
17.5″, f4.5–300x, by G. R. Kepple

Figure 62-47. NGC 4085 and NGC 4088
13″, f5.6–165x, Steve Coe

Figure 62-48. NGC 4100
20″, f4.5–175x, by Richard W. Jakiel

Figure 62-49. NGC 4144
20″, f4.5–175x, by Richard W. Jakiel

Figure 62-50. NGC 4157
20″, f4.5–175x, by Richard W. Jakiel

16/18″Scopes–150x: The 2′ diameter halo is bright but diffuse at the edges with a slight brightening to a large core and a very faint stellar nucleus.

NGC 4047 H741[2] Galaxy Type (R)SA(rs)b: II
ϕ **1.1′×0.9′, m12.2v, SB12.0** $12^h02.2^m$ **+48° 38′**
Finder Chart 62-12   ★★
12/14″Scopes–125x: NGC 4047 is a faint circular glow about 1.5′ in diameter and containing a fairly prominent core.

NGC 4051 H56[4] Galaxy Type SAB(rs)bc II
ϕ **5.5′×4.6′, m10.2v, SB13.5** $12^h03.2^m$ **+44° 32′**
Finder Chart 62-12, Figure 62-45   ★★★★
8/10″Scopes–100x: NGC 4051, located 2.5′ east of an 11th magnitude star, displays a bright stellar nucleus embedded in a small core surrounded by an evenly illuminated 3′×2′ NW–SE halo.
16/18″Scopes–150x: In larger telescopes NGC 4051 has a 4.5′×3′ NW–SE halo that contains a mottled central region with a sharp stellar nucleus. Faint spiral arms can be glimpsed in the outer halo. The SW side of the halo is brighter.

NGC 4062 H174[1] Galaxy Type SA(s)c II-III
ϕ **4.4′×1.9′, m11.1v, SB13.3** $12^h04.1^m$ **+31° 54′**
Finder Chart 62-11, Figure 62-46   ★★★★
8/10″Scopes–100x: NGC 4062 has a moderately bright 2.5′×0.75′ E–W halo containing a slightly brighter central region.
16/18″Scopes–150x: This galaxy has a highly extended 4′×1.25′ oval halo elongated toward position angle 100°. The central area is granular and grows slightly brighter to an inconspicuous nonstellar nucleus. A 14th magnitude star lies on the halo's east tip.

NGC 4085 H224[1] Galaxy Type SAB(s)c:? III-IV
ϕ **2.5′×0.8′, m12.4v, SB13.0** $12^h05.4^m$ **+50° 21′**
Finder Chart 62-10, Figure 62-47   ★★★
8/10″Scopes–100x: NGC 4085 is the fainter and smaller of a galaxy-pair formed with NGC 4088 lying 11′ to the north. It has a moderately faint, thin 2′×0.5′ E–W halo containing a slight brightening along its major axis. The galaxy forms a triangle with two 8th magnitude stars 3′ to its SE and 3.5′ to its SW.
16/18″Scopes–150x: NGC 4085 is a 2.5′×0.5′ spindle elongated toward position angle 80°. Several bright spots are distributed along the major axis of the spindle, the brightest spot near the galaxy's center. A 12th magnitude star lies 3.5′ WNW.

Figure 62-51. *Edge-on galaxy NGC 4096 displays a bright core with a stellar nucleus surrounded by an evenly illuminated halo. Image courtesy of Bill Logan.*

NGC 4088 H206[1] Galaxy Type SAB(rs)bc II-III
ϕ **5.4′×2.1′, m10.6v, SB13.0** $12^h05.6^m$ **+50° 33′**
Finder Chart 62-10, Figure 62-47   ★★★★
8/10″Scopes–100x: NGC 4088 is the larger and brighter member of a galaxy-pair with NGC 4085 lying 11′ to its south. The galaxy has a fairly bright 5′×2′ NE–SW halo containing a slightly brighter center.
16/18″Scopes–150x: The central area is fairly bright and cigar-shaped 4′×2′ NE–SW. The outer portion is much fainter with tapered ends reaching to 6′×2.5′.
20/22″Scopes–175x: In large telescopes NGC 4088 shows a central bar that contains a small, nearly stellar nucleus and is encircled by thick spiral arms. Several bright knots or H-II regions are just visible with careful study. The central region is mottled with small light and dark patches.

NGC 4096 H207[1] Galaxy Type SAB(rs)c II-III
ϕ **6.6′×1.6′, m10.8v, SB13.3** $12^h06.0^m$ **+47° 29′**
Finder Chart 62-12, Figure 62-51   ★★★★
8/10″Scopes–100x: NGC 4096 is a bright 5′×1.5′ NNE–SSW streak containing a slightly brighter center with a faint stellar nucleus. An 11th magnitude star 4′ NW of the galaxy's center has a 13th magnitude companion 28″ to its east.
16/18″Scopes–150x: This galaxy contains a large conspicuous oval core with a bright nucleus embedded in an evenly illuminated, highly elongated, 6′×1.5′ NNE–SSW halo.

Figure 62-52. *Messier 40 is the wide pair of 9th magnitude stars toward the upper left corner. Galaxies NGC 4284 and NGC 4290 are at right above the bright star 70 Ursae Majoris. Image courtesy of Bill Logan.*

NGC 4100 H717[3] Galaxy Type (R′)SA(rs)bc I-II
ϕ **5.1′ × 1.8′, m11.2v, SB 13.4**   12^{h}06.2^m +49° 35′
Finder Chart 62-12, Figure 62-48   ★★★★
8/10″ Scopes–100x: NGC 4100 is a faint, thin, uniformly illuminated sliver extending 4′ × 1′ NNW–SSE to tapered ends.
16/18″ Scopes–150x: This fine galaxy shows a bright 5′ × 1.5′ NNW–SSE streak mottled with light and dark areas. Its central area is bulged and within it is a small oval core. A 12.5 magnitude star lies 7′ NNW.

NGC 4102 H225[1] Galaxy Type SAB(s)b? II
ϕ **2.9′ × 1.8′, m11.2v, SB 12.8**   12^{h}06.4^m +52° 43′
Finder Chart 62-10   ★★★
8/10″ Scopes–100x: NGC 4102 is a moderately bright galaxy with a 1.5′ × 0.75′ NE–SW halo containing a tiny core with a stellar nucleus. A magnitude 11.5 star touches the halo's west edge, and a 12th magnitude stars lies 1.5′ ENE of the galaxy's center.
16/18″ Scopes–150x: This galaxy has a well concentrated 2′ × 1′ NE–SW halo containing a small oval core with a stellar nucleus. 175x reveals a dark patch south of the core and a knot 25″ NE of the galaxy's center.

NGC 4144 H747[2] Galaxy Type SAB(s)cd? sp III
ϕ **6.3′ × 1.6′, m11.6v, SB 14.0**   12^{h}10.0^m +46° 27′
Finder Chart 62-12, Figure 62-49   ★★★★
8/10″ Scopes–100x: NGC 4144 is a faint, uniformly illuminated 3.5′ × 0.75′ ESE–WNW streak.
16/18″ Scopes–150x: In larger telescopes NGC 4144 has a moderately faint envelope much-elongated 5′ × 0.75′ in position angle 105°. The core, which extends nearly half the length of the halo's major axis, is thin and splotchy but considerably brighter than the halo. A 13th magnitude star lies just north of the galaxy's WNW tip. 2.5′ SE of the galaxy's center is a thin isosceles triangle of 13th magnitude stars that points NE at the galaxy's ESE tip.

NGC 4157 H208[1] Galaxy Type SAB(s)b? sp II
ϕ **7.1′ × 1.2′, m11.3v, SB 13.5**   12^{h}11.1^m +50° 29′
Finder Chart 62-10, Figure 62-50   ★★★★
8/10″ Scopes–100x: NGC 4157, centered 5′ SSE of an 8th magnitude star, is a silvery shaft of light highly elongated 4′ × 0.75′ ENE–WSW and containing a bright extended core. A 10th magnitude star touching the galaxy's WSW tip is at the north corner of a 2′ × 1.5′ triangle with magnitude 11.5 and 12.5 stars.
16/18″ Scopes–150x: In larger telescopes, NGC 4157 is a thin needle of light measuring 6′ × 0.75′ ENE–WSW. The center has a pronounced bulge, the ends of which taper out along the envelope. The bulge's core is off center to the SE side because of a dust lane that extends for nearly half the length of the envelope's major axis runs along its NW flank. At 175x inconspicuous light and dark areas are just visible along the dust lane's length.

NGC 4284 H798[3] Galaxy Type Sbc
ϕ **2.7′ × 1.2′, m13.5v, SB 14.6**   12^{h}20.2^m +58° 06′

NGC 4290 H805[2] Galaxy Type SAB(s)b? sp II
ϕ **2.3′ × 1.8′, m11.8v, SB 13.2**   12^{h}20.8^m +58° 06′

Messier 40 Winnecke 4 Double Star
m9.0, 9.3; Sep. 50″, P.A.85°   12^{h}22.4^m +58° 05′
Finder Chart 62-10, Figure 62-52   ★/★★★/★★★
12/14″ Scopes–125x: Messier 40, located 20′ NE of magnitude 5.5 star 70 Ursae Majoris, is merely a wide 50″ pair of 9th magnitude stars. Hevelius in the 17th century thought he saw a nebulous glow around these stars. Messier, when he checked them out, saw no nebula but included the stars in his catalogue anyway. 12′ west of M40 is the galaxy NGC 4290, a faint 2′ × 1′ NE–SW oval containing a faint stellar nucleus. 4.5′ west of NGC 4290 is another galaxy, NGC 4284, a very faint, circular 30″ diameter patch. NGC 4284 is at the NW corner of the 1.5′ wide equilateral triangle it forms with magnitude 12.5 and 13 stars.

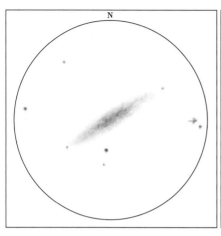

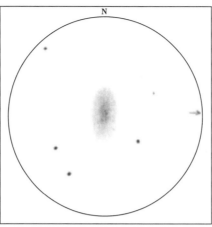

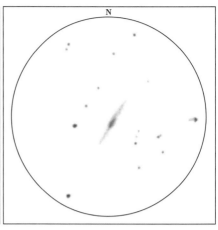

Figure 62-53. NGC 4605
17.5″, f4.5–300x, by G. R. Kepple

Figure 62-54. GC 5204
12.5″, f5–250x, by G. R. Kepple

Figure 62-55. NGC 5422
12.5″, f5–250x, by G. R. Kepple

NGC 4605 H254[1] Galaxy Type SB(s) pec III-IV
φ 6.4′×2.3′, m10.3v, SB13.1   12ʰ40.0ᵐ +61° 37′
Finder Chart 62-13, Figure 62-53   ★★★★

8/10″Scopes–100x: NGC 4605 is a fine, bright edge-on
    galaxy elongated 4.5′×1.5′ NW–SE and containing
    a long, thin core.
16/18″Scopes–150x: This bright luminous streak
    extends 5.5′×2′ in position angle 125°. The 3′ long,
    thin core is mottled but lacks a central nucleus.

NGC 4814 H243[1] Galaxy Type SA(s)b I-II
φ 3.2′×2.3′, m12.0v, SB14.0   12ʰ55.4ᵐ +58° 21′
Finder Chart 62-13   ★★

12/14″Scopes–125x: NGC 4814 is a poorly concentrated,
    oval object elongated 2′×1′ NW–SE and containing
    a faint core with a faint stellar nucleus. A 20″ wide
    N–S pair of 9th and 10th magnitude stars is 11′
    south.

NGC 5204 H63[4] Galaxy Type SA(s)m IV-V
φ 4.9′×3.1′, m11.3v, SB14.1   13ʰ29.6ᵐ +58° 25′
Finder Chart 62-13, Figure 62-54   ★★★

8/10″Scopes–100x: NGC 5204 has a faint 3.5′×2′ N–S
    halo with no central brightening.
16/18″Scopes–150x: This galaxy has a moderately faint
    4′×2.5′ N–S halo with a slight central brightening.
    A 13th magnitude star lies 1.5′ SW of the halo's edge.

NGC 5308 H255[1] Galaxy Type S0
φ 2.6′×0.4′, m11.4v, SB11.3   13ʰ47.0ᵐ +60° 58′
Finder Chart 62-13   ★★★

8/10″Scopes–100x: NGC 5308, located 5′ north of a 9th
    magnitude star, has a fairly bright 2′×0.5′ ENE–

WSW halo around a poorly concentrated center.
16/18″Scopes–150x: NGC 5308 has a bright much-
    elongated 2.25′×0.5′ ENE–WSW spindle-shaped
    halo containing a small oval core. A 13.5 magnitude
    star is 1.5′ east, and a 12th magnitude star lies 3′
    north.

NGC 5322 H256[1] Galaxy Type E3-4
φ 6.1′×4.1′, m10.2v, SB13.6   13ʰ49.3ᵐ +60° 12′
Finder Chart 62-13   ★★★

8/10″Scopes–100x: NGC 5322 has a bright, circular 1.5′
    diameter halo with diffuse edges and a stellar
    nucleus.
16/18″Scopes–150x: With averted vision, the halo
    appears to be 2.5′ in diameter and slightly elongated
    E–W. The central region broadly concentrates to a
    nonstellar nucleus. A 14th magnitude star is super-
    imposed upon the halo just south of the core, and
    a second 14th magnitude star is on the halo's east
    edge.

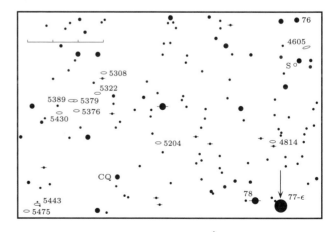

Finder Chart 62-13. 77–ε UMa: 12ʰ54.0ᵐ +55° 58′

NGC 5376 H238[1] Galaxy Type SAB(r)b? II
ϕ 1.6′×1.0′, m12.1v, SB12.5   13^{h}55.3^m +59° 30′
Finder Chart 62-13   ★★
12/14″Scopes-125x: NGC 5376, located 11′ west of a
    9th magnitude star, is a faint, diffuse 2′×1.5′ ENE–
    WSW glow containing a broad, slightly brighter
    core with a faint stellar nucleus. Galaxy NGC 5389
    lies 15′ NE.

NGC 5379 H239[1] Galaxy Type S0
ϕ 2.0′×0.8′, m12.9v, SB13.2   13^{h}55.6^m +59° 45′

NGC 5389 H240[1] Galaxy Type SAB(r)0/a:?
ϕ 4.6′×1.2′, m12.0v, SB13.7   13^{h}56.1^m +59° 44′
Finder Chart 62-13   ★★/★★
12/14″Scopes-125x: NGC 5389, centered 4′ SW of a 9th
    magnitude star, shows a prominent stellar nucleus
    surrounded by a faint 3′×0.75′ N–S halo. 4′ west
    of NGC 5389 is its companion galaxy NGC 5379,
    fainter and smaller, though its 1.5′×0.5′ NE–SW
    halo contains a much brighter center. A wide NW–
    SE pair of 11th magnitude stars is 5′ NNW of the
    galaxy-pair.

NGC 5422 H230[1] Galaxy Type S0
ϕ 3.0′×0.5′, m11.8v, SB12.1   14^{h}00.7^m +55° 10′
Finder Chart 62-14, Figure 62-55   ★★★
12/14″Scopes-125x: NGC 5422, located 50′ NNW of
    Messier 101, is a faint but not difficult 2.5′×0.5′
    NNW–SSE streak containing a circular core well
    concentrated to a stellar nucleus. This galaxy is at
    the WNW corner of the triangle it forms with a
    10th magnitude star 2.5′ to its east and an 11th
    magnitude star 5.5′ to its SE.

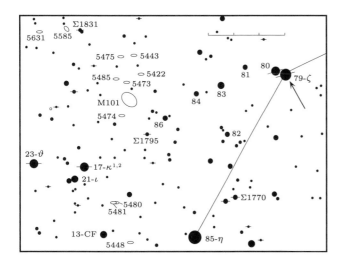

Finder Chart 62-14. 79-ζ UMa: 13^{h}23.9^m +54° 56′

NGC 5430 H827[2] Galaxy Type SB(s)b II
ϕ 2.1′×1.5′, m11.9v, SB13.0   14^{h}00.8^m +59° 20′
Finder Chart 62-13   ★★★
12/14″Scopes-125x: NGC 5430 has a fairly faint 2′×1′
    N–S halo containing a broad circular core. A faint
    star is superimposed upon the halo near the core's
    SSE edge.

NGC 5443 H799[2] Galaxy Type S0
ϕ 2.8′×1.2′, m12.3v, SB13.4   14^{h}02.2^m +55° 49′
Finder Chart 62-14   ★★★
12/14″Scopes-125x: NGC 5443 is at the SE corner of
    the triangle it forms with two 9th magnitude stars.
    The galaxy has an irregularly faint 2′×0.75′ NE–
    SW halo considerably brighter at its center. Faint
    stars are near both ends of the halo. Messier 101 is
    90′ south.

NGC 5448 H691[2] Galaxy Type (R)SAB(r)a
ϕ 3.9′×1.9′, m11.0v, SB13.1   14^{h}02.8^m +49° 10′
Finder Chart 62-14   ★★★
12/14″Scopes-125x: NGC 5448 is a faint, smooth
    2′×0.5′ ESE–WNW streak with a long, poorly
    concentrated core. A 13th magnitude star lies 4.25′
    south.

NGC 5457 Messier 101 Galaxy Type SAB(rs)cd I
ϕ 26.0′×26.0′, m7.9v, SB14.8   14^{h}03.2^m +54° 21′
Finder Chart 62-14, Figure 62-56   ★★★★★
                    Pinwheel Galaxy
    Messier 101 was discovered by Mechain in 1781, and
Messier added it to his catalogue later that year. It is the
largest and brightest member of a small galaxy cluster
of Sc and Sd spirals and dwarf irregulars, located about
25 million light years away. Among the other members
of the M101 Galaxy Group are NGCs 5585, 5574, and
5204. M101 has an absolute magnitude of −21.5, a whole
magnitude brighter than our own Milky Way Galaxy.
Its luminosity is 33 billion suns, and its true diameter is
in excess of 190,000 light years.
8/10″Scopes-75x: Beautiful! Although moderately
    faint, Messier 101 is a huge galaxy displaying faint,
    splotchy spiral arms curving clockwise around a
    bright core. A 12.5 magnitude star is superimposed
    upon the halo 1.25′ north of the core; and a 13th
    magnitude star is superimposed on the halo in its
    NW sector. Two stars are near the halo's southern
    edge.
16/18″Scopes-150x: Larger telescopes show M101 to be
    a magnificent 20′×15′ NNE–SSW spiral galaxy with
    conspicuous arms of mottled texture. Several bright

Figure 62-56. *Messier 101 (NGC5457) is a beautiful object in medium and large telescopes. Under good skies a mottled halo containing a fine spiral arm structure and several H-II regions can be seen. Image courtesy Chris Schur.*

H-II regions stand out in the arms. The UHC and Deep-Sky filters increase the contrast significantly. Three isolated bright patches can be seen 8′ SW, 4.5′ ESE, and 6′ ENE of the galaxy's center, the SW patch just south of a 13th magnitude foreground star. The most prominent spiral arm springs from the SE side of the galaxy's 2′ diameter core and arcs first east and then north out of the central region: a bright knot is embedded in this arm NE of the nucleus. A fainter arm begins at the west side of the core and arcs south and SE: it contains bright knots SW and SE of the nucleus. A vague dark patch is south of the core: photos show this to be a large interarm gap. With careful scrutiny many H-II regions can be glimpsed in the galaxy's halo. Many faint foreground stars are also superimposed upon the halo.

NGC 5473 H231[1] Galaxy Type SAB(s)0:
ϕ **2.2′ × 1.7′, m11.4v, SB12.7**   14^{h}04.7^m +54° 54′
Finder Chart 62-14   ★★★
8/10″Scopes–100x: NGC 5473, located half a degree NNE of Messier 101, appears fairly bright and less than 1′ in diameter. It has a large core but very little surrounding halo. A 13th magnitude star lies on the galaxy's NE edge.

16/18″Scopes–150x: NGC 5473 has a diffuse, circular 1.5′ diameter halo that contains a broad, well defined core with a stellar nucleus.

NGC 5474 H214[1] Galaxy Type SA(s)cd pec IV-V
ϕ **6.0′ × 4.9′, m10.8v, SB14.3**   14^{h}05.0^m +53° 40′
Finder Chart 62-14   ★★
8/10″Scopes–100x: NGC 5474, located 40′ SSE of Messier 101, is a faint, diffuse 3′ diameter object with a 13th magnitude star on its NE edge.
16/18″Scopes–150x: Even in larger telescopes NGC 5474 remains poorly concentrated, with a diffuse periphery and only a slightly brighter center. With averted vision the halo can be seen out to a diameter of 3.5′.

NGC 5480 H692[2] Galaxy Type SA(s)c: III
ϕ **1.6′ × 0.9′, m12.1v, SB12.3**   14^{h}06.4^m +50° 43′
NGC 5481 H693[2] Galaxy Type E+
ϕ **1.8′ × 1.3′, m12.2v, SB13.0**   14^{h}06.7^m +50° 43′
Finder Chart 62-14   ★★/★★
12/14″Scopes–125x: NGC 5480 and NGC 5481, located on the Boötes/Ursa Major frontier, are a 3′ wide E–W galaxy pair. The western system, NGC 5480,

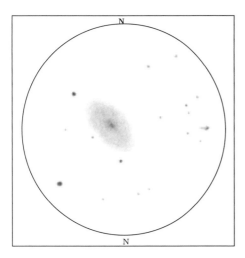

Figure 62-57. NGC 5585
12.5″, f5–250x, by G. R. Kepple

has a faint 1.5′×1′ N–S halo containing a stellar nucleus. The eastern galaxy, NGC 5481, is actually within Boötes. It has a brighter stellar nucleus than its companion, but its 1.25′ diameter halo appears more circular and only about as bright.

NGC 5485 H232[1] Galaxy Type SA0 pec
φ 2.7′×2.1′, m11.4v, SB13.1   14h07.2m +55° 00′
Finder Chart 62-14   ★★★
12/14″Scopes–125x: NGC 5485, located 8′ NNE of a pair of 12th magnitude stars, has a fairly bright,

circular 1.5′ diameter halo that contains a broad, prominent core with a very faint stellar nucleus. At 175x the core appears faintly mottled and the halo seems slightly elongated N–S. A 13th magnitude star is 2′ SSE of the galaxy's center. 3.5′ NW of NGC 5485 is one of its companion galaxies, NGC 5484, merely a very faint spot. 6.25′ NNE is a second companion, NGC 5486, a faint 1′ diameter glow containing a faint stellar nucleus.

NGC 5585 H235[1] Galaxy Type SAB(s)d IV-V
φ 5.6′×3.7′, m10.7v, SB13.9   14h19.8m +56° 44′
Finder Chart 62-14, Figure 62-57   ★★★
12/14″Scopes–125x: NGC 5585, a member of the M101 Galaxy Group, is located 5′ NW of a 9th magnitude star. Its halo is a moderately faint 3.5′×2.5′ NNE–SSW oval that contains a slightly brighter center. A 13th magnitude star is 2′ south, a 12th magnitude star 3.5′ NE, and a 14th magnitude star 2′ east, of the galaxy's center.

NGC 5631 H236[1] Galaxy Type SA(s)0°
φ 1.8′×1.8′, m11.5v, SB12.6   14h26.6m +56° 35′
Finder Chart 62-14   ★★★
12/14″Scopes–125x: NGC 5631 has a moderately faint, circular 1′ diameter halo that contains a bright nonstellar nucleus. The surrounding field is devoid of bright stars.

Chapter 63

Ursa Minor, the Little Bear

63.1 Overview

Ursa Minor, the Little Bear, popularly known as the Little Dipper, is most famous for Polaris, the North Star, which lies near the north celestial pole and therefore seems stationary as, during the course of a night, the other far northern stars move in arcs centered upon it. Ursa Minor is a rather faint constellation: of the seven stars in the Little Dipper only two are of the 2nd magnitude and one of the 3rd. Most people unfamiliar with astronomy, though aware that the pointers at the front of the bowl of the Big Dipper are directed toward Polaris, cannot trace the Little Dipper. The problem is that the Little Dipper does not really resemble the Big Dipper but looks instead like a ladle.

The Little Bear was an afterthought in Greek astronomy. In Hesiod's *Works and Days* and Homer's *Iliad* and *Odyssey*, all of which were probably written before 700 B.C., the celestial Bear is mentioned in a manner that suggests only one existed at the time. Indeed the late 3rd century B.C. poet Callimachus attributes the invention of Ursa Minor to the semilegendary Thales, who lived around 600 B.C. The geographer Strabo of the 1st century B.C. credits Ursa Minor to Phoenician mariners who wanted to navigate by a star group nearer the true pole than the Great Bear. Aratos, in his *Phainomena* of about 270 B.C., states that the Little Bear was also known as Cynosura, the "Dog's Tail," but he does not say why. R.H. Allen in *Star Names* plausibly speculated that Thales, or whoever created Ursa Minor, did so with stars that had marked the wings of the Winged Dragon, Draco.

Because the stars of Ursa Minor range rather evenly from magnitude 2.0 (Polaris and Beta) to magnitude 4.9 (Eta), and because the constellation is always above the horizon at more-or-less the same elevation, it is a convenient measure for any given night's sky transparency. If the magnitude 4.2–4.3 stars in the Handle of the Little Dipper (Delta, Epsilon, and Zeta) are not visible, then the sky is too thick even for basic constellation identification. If the magnitude 4.9 Eta in the Little Dipper's bowl is not visible, then conditions are

Ursa Minor: ER-sa My-ner
Genitive: Ursae Minoris, ER-see MY-nor-is
Abbreviation: UMi
Culmination: 9 pm–June 27, midnight–May 13
Area: 256 square degrees
Showpiece: 1–α UMi (Polaris)
Binocular Objects: h2682, 5 UMi, 7–β UMi, H V 86, π¹ UMi, OΣΣ143, Ku 1, 22–ε UMI

too poor for serious deep-sky work with binoculars or a telescope. If Eta is visible at a suburban location, atmospheric transparency is excellent. From a dark sky country site magnitude 5.2 Theta and magnitude 5.5 19 Ursae Minoris are easily visible even on average nights.

Ursa Minor is a rather small (256 square degree) off-Milky Way constellation that offers little to the observer, most of that being faint galaxies.

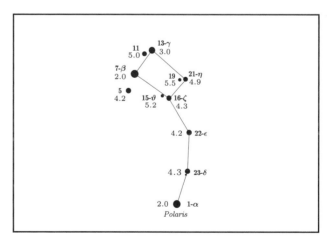

Chart 63-1. Ursa Minor Stellar Magnitudes
The stars of Ursa Minor may be used to judge sky transparency. For serious deep-sky observing, the constellation's 5th magnitude stars should be visible.

Ursa Minor, the Little Bear Constellation Chart 63-2

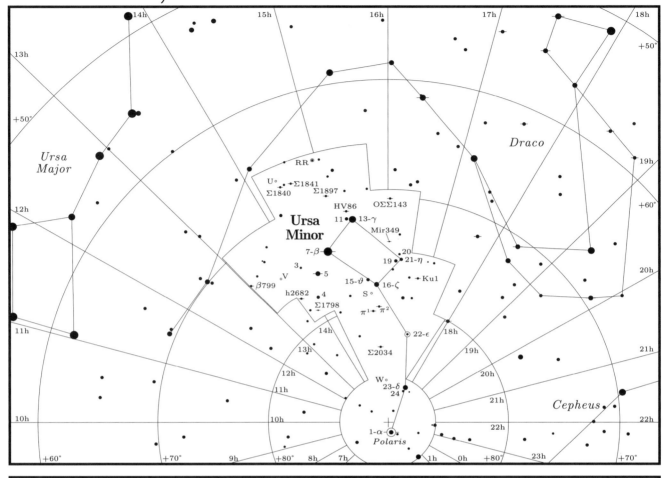

Chart Symbols

Constellation Chart

Stellar Magnitudes   0   1   2   3   4   5   6

Finder Charts   0/1   2   3   4   5   6   7   8   9

Master Finder Chart   0   1   2   3   4   5

→ Guide Star Pointer

●—• Double Stars

Finder Chart Scale

(One degree tick marks)

⊙ ○ Variable Stars

○ Open Clusters

⊕ Globular Clusters

⬭ Galaxies

⊹ Planetary Nebulae

▢ Small Bright Nebulae

⬭ Large Bright Nebulae

▨ Dark Nebulae

Table 63-1: Selected Variable Stars in Ursa Minor

Name	HD No.	Type	Max.	Min.	Period (Days)	F*	Spec. Type	R.A. (2000) Dec.		Finder Chart No.	Notes
1–α UMi	8890	Cδ	1.92	2.07	3.96	0.05	F7	02ʰ31.8ᵐ	+89° 16′	63-2	Polaris
V UMi	119227	SRb	8.8	9.9	72		M5	13ʰ38.7ᵐ	+74 19	63-2	
U UMi	125556	M	7.4	12.7	326	0.50	M6-M8	14ʰ17.3ᵐ	+66 48	63-2	
S UMi	139492	M	7.7	12.9	326	0.50	M7-M9	15ʰ29.6ᵐ	+78 38	63-4	
W UMi	150265	EA	8.7	9.7	1.70	0.23	A3	16ʰ08.5ᵐ	+86 12	63-2	

F* = The fraction of period taken up by the star's rise from min. to max. brightness, or the period spent in eclipse.

Table 63-2: Selected Double Stars in Ursa Minor

Name	ADS No.	Pair	M1	M2	Sep."	P.A.°	Spec	R.A. (2000)	Dec.	Finder Chart No.	Notes
1–α UMi	1477	AB	2.0	8.2	18.4	218	F8	02^{h}31.8^m	+89° 16′	63-2	
β 799	8772	AB	6.5	8.5	1.2	260	A5	13^{h}04.8^m	+73 02	63-2	
h2682	8997	AB	6.7	9.7	26.3	279	A5	40.7	+76 51	63-2	White and blue
	8997	AC		9.0	45.9	316					
Σ1798	9069		8.1	9.9	7.5	12	F2	55.0	+78 24	63-4	
Σ1840	9231		6.8	9.5	27.4	222	A0	14^{h}19.9^m	+67 47	63-2	
Σ1841			7.1	10.7	36.4	265	A2	27.5	+67 48	63-2	
5 UMi	9286	AB	4.3	13.3	21.7	124	K2	27.5	+75 42	63-4	
	9286	AC		9.8	58.8	131					
7–β UMi			2.1	11.3	209.1	342	K5	50.7	+74 09	63-4	Kochab
Σ1897			7.7	10.2	24.7	324	K5	53.6	+69 46	63-5	
HV 86		AB	7.3	11.0	55.6	132	F8	15^{h}17.3^m	+71 13	63-5	
		AC		10.6	89.5	114					
π^1 UMi	9696	AB	6.6	7.3	31.1	80	G5	29.2	+80 27	63-4	Yellow and white
	9696	AC		11.0	135.4	104					
π^2 UMi	9769		7.4	8.2	0.6	*21	F2	39.6	+79 59	63-4	
Σ 2034	9853		7.6	8.1	1.4	115	A3	48.7	+83 37	63-2	
Mir 349			8.0	11.0	7.0	312	K0	16^{h}00.3^m	+73 56	63-5	
OΣΣ 143			6.7	9.3	46.7	84	A0	04.8	+70 16	63-5	
Ku 1	10214	AB	6.1	9.4	2.9	188	F2	43.1	+77 31	63-4	
	10214	AC		9.8	115.0	14					
22–ε UMi	10242		4.2	11.0	76.9	3	G5	46.0	+82 02	63-4	

Footnotes: *= Year 2000, a = Near apogee, c = Closing, w = Widening. Finder Chart No: All stars listed in the tables are plotted in the large Constellation Chart, but when a star appears in a Finder Chart, this number is listed. Notes: When colors are subtle, the suffix *-ish* is used, e.g. *bluish*.

63.2 Interesting Stars

Alpha (α) = 1 Ursae Minoris Double Star Spec. F8
m2.0, 8.2; Sep. 18.4″; P.A. 218°   02^{h}31.8^m +89° 16′
Constellation Chart 63-2   Polaris   ★★★★

Alpha Ursae Minoris, known as the North Star, the Pole Star, or Polaris, is without a doubt the most famous star in the sky, not because of its brightness but due to its unique position near the north celestial pole. It is actually almost a degree away from the true pole, but this distance will diminish until the year 2102 A.D. This change in location is a consequence of *precession*, the slow change in the orientation of the Earth's axis (due to gravitational effects of the Sun and Moon) which makes the north celestial pole trace a 47° diameter circle on the celestial sphere every 25,800 years. (The phenomenon of precession is similar to the wobbling of a top as its spin slows.) Hence, during different epochs different stars have been (and will be) the Pole Star. When the Pyramids were built some 4,600 years ago, the star Thuban (Alpha Draconis) marked the pole. 12,000 years ago Vega was the Pole Star.

Polaris is a lovely double with a yellowish primary and a small, pale white companion 18″ distant. The secondary was first seen by Sir William Herschel in 1780. The two stars have an orbital period many thousands of years in length. The primary is both a spectroscopic binary and a Population II Cepheid vari-

able (though its range is too slight to be followed visually). The star is an F8 Ib supergiant with an absolute magnitude of −5.1, a luminosity of about 9,000 suns. The visual secondary is an F3 V object with an absolute magnitude of +1.2, which corresponds to a luminosity of 28 suns. The Polaris system is 820 light years distant.

Just south of Polaris is a binocular asterism called the Engagement Ring: a 35′ diameter circlet of 7th and 8th magnitude stars, with Polaris representing the diamond.

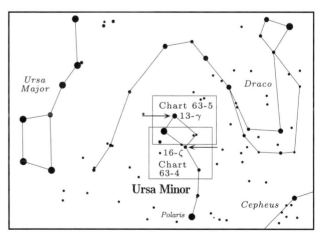

Master Finder Chart 63-3. Ursa Minor Chart Areas
Guide stars indicated by arrows.

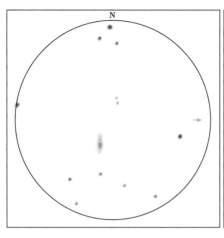

Figure 63-1. NGC 5323
18.5″, f5–250x, by Glen W. Sanner

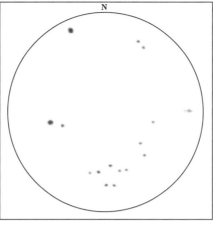

Figure 63-2. NGC 5385
17.5″, f4.5–250x, by G. R. Kepple

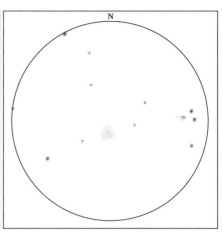

Figure 63-3. NGC 5412
18.5″, f5–250x, by Glen W. Sanner

h2682　Triple Star　　　　　　　　　Spec. A5
AB: m6.7, 9.7; Sep. 26.3″; P.A. 279°　13ʰ40.7ᵐ +76° 51′
Constellation Chart 63-2, Finder Chart 63-4　　★★★★
4/6″ Scopes–50x: Herschel 2682 has a white primary
with two blue companions. The field contains a
triangle of pale blue stars, a chain of fairly bright
stars, and a yellow 6.5 magnitude star to the SW.

Pi–1 (π¹) Ursae Minoris　Double Star　Spec. G5
AB: m6.6, 7.3; Sep. 31.1″; P.A. 80°　15ʰ29.2ᵐ +80° 27′
Finder Chart 63-4　　　　　　　　　　　★★★★
4/6″ Scopes–50x: Pi Ursae Minoris is a binary with a
150 year period. The primary is yellow and the
companion white. The star field around the double
includes a chain of fairly bright stars, a circle, and
a three-star arc.

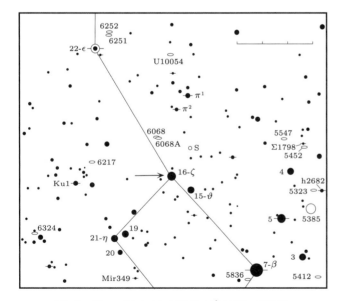

Finder Chart 63-4. 16–ζ UMi. 15ʰ44.1ᵐ +77° 48′

63.3 Deep-Sky Objects

NGC 5323　H899² Galaxy Type Sab
ϕ 1.4′ × 0.4′, m13.5v, SB 12.7　　　13ʰ45.5ᵐ +76° 51′
Finder Chart 63-4, Figure 63-1　　　　　　　★
16/18″ Scopes–150x: NGC 5323, located 15′ east of a
7th magnitude star, is a very faint 1′ × 0.25′ NNW–
SSE streak. 300x reveals what looks like a faint
double nucleus, but the second object is probably
just a superimposed field star. A magnitude 13.5
star 2′ from the galaxy's center beyond its SSE tip
is part of a checkmark-shaped asterism. 10′ NNW
of the galaxy is a 1′ wide equilateral triangle of one
11th and two 13th magnitude stars.

NGC 5385　Open Cluster 12★
[ϕ 10′]　　　　　　　　　　　13ʰ52.4ᵐ +76° 11′
Finder Chart 63-4, Figure 63-2　　　　　　★★★
16/18″ Scopes–150x: NGC 5385, a "nonexistent" open
cluster (according to the *RNGC*), appears as a loose
gathering of ten 10th to 11th magnitude stars
spread over an area elongated 10′ × 5′ NW–SE and
centered 15′ WSW of an 8th magnitude field star.

NGC 5452　H947³ Galaxy Type SAB(s)d
ϕ 2.1′ × 1.7′, m13.3v, SB 14.5　　　13ʰ54.5ᵐ +78° 13′
Finder Chart 63-4, Figure 63-4　　　　　　　★
16/18″ Scopes–150x: NGC 5452, located 10′ south of a
double star Struve 1798 (8.1, 9.9; 7.5″; 12°), is a
very faint, circular 1.5′ diameter patch without
central brightening. A 12.5 magnitude star is 2′
NNW of the galaxy's center. NW and SE of the
galaxy are random sprinklings of 12th and 13th
magnitude stars.

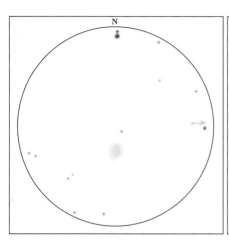

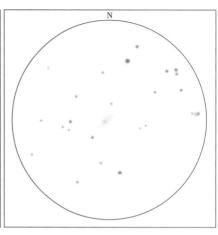

Figure 63-4. NGC 5452
18.5″, f5–250x, by Glen W. Sanner

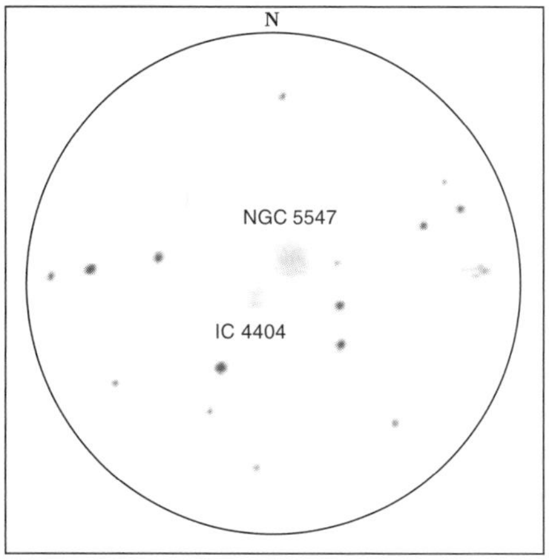

Figure 63-5. NGC 5547
18.5″, f5–250x, by Glen W. Sanner

Figure 63-6. UGC 10054
17.5 f4.5–275x, by G. R. Kepple

NGC 5412 Galaxy Type S0–:
ϕ **1.2′ × 1.0′, m13.4v, SB 13.5**   **13ʰ57.4ᵐ +73° 36′**
Finder Chart 63-4, Figure 63-3   ★
16/18″Scopes–150x: NGC 5412 is a very faint, circular
1′ diameter glow without central brightening. It is
flanked by 13th magnitude stars located 3′ to its
ESE and its WNW. 7′ ESE is a 10th magnitude
star; and 9′ west is a wide NNE–SSW pair of 10th
magnitude stars.

NGC 5547 H948³ Galaxy Type?
ϕ **0.9′ × 0.4′, m13.5v, SB 12.2**   **14ʰ09.8ᵐ +78° 36′**
Finder Chart 63-4, Figure 63-5   ★★
16/18″Scopes–150x: NGC 5547 is a very faint, circular
30″ diameter nebulous patch located in a pleasing
star field. In every direction from the galaxy but
north are conspicuous, though rather wide, pairs of
comparably bright stars. 2′ SSE of NGC 5547 is its
companion IC 4404, an extremely faint smudge less
than half the primary galaxy's size.

NGC 5819 H311³? Galaxy Type SAB(rs)bc
ϕ **0.9′ × 0.9′, m13.5v, SB 13.1**   **14ʰ54.0ᵐ +73° 08′**
Finder Chart 63-5, Figure 63-7   ★★
16/18″Scopes–150x: NGC 5819, located 16′ ENE of an
8th magnitude star and flanked by 12th magnitude
stars, is just visible with averted vision as a very
faint 30″ diameter haze containing a slight central
brightening. The *Revised NGC*'s "nonexistent"
open cluster NGC 5808 may be the sprinkling of
stars around this galaxy. We did not see any stellar
grouping at the NGC 2000 position for NGC 5808,
13ʰ52.5ᵐ +76° 11′, a spot just SSW of NGC 5819.

UGC 10054 Galaxy Type SBdm IV-V
ϕ **2.9′ × 1.3′, m13.1v, SB 14.4**   **15ʰ44.0ᵐ +81° 50′**
Finder Chart 63-4, Figure 63-6   ★
16/18″Scopes–150x: UGC 10054, centered 3′ SSE of a
9.5 magnitude star, has a faint 1.5′ × 1′ NNW–SSE
halo without any central brightening. Magnitude
13.5 stars are 1′ SE and 1.25′ NNW of the galaxy's
halo. 2′ to the galaxy's east is a tiny 30″ wide
equilateral triangle of 13th and 14th magnitude
stars.

Figure 63-7. *NGC 5819 is the small, very faint haze left of center.
The surrounding stars may be the* RNGC's *"nonexistent" open
cluster NGC 5808. Martin C. Germano made this 35 minute
exposure on 2415 film with an 8″, f5 Newtonian.*

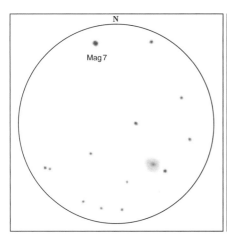

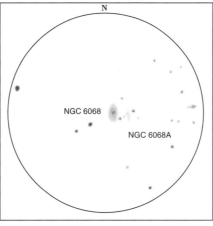

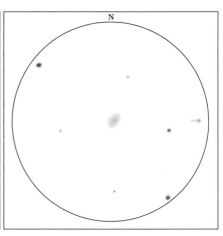

Figure 63-8. NGC 6048
17.5″, f4.5–300x, by G. R. Kepple

Figure 63-9. NGC 6068-68A
18.5″, f5–300x, by Glen W. Sanner

Figure 63-10. NGC 6094
18.5″, f5–300x, by Glen W. Sanner

NGC 6011 H313³ Galaxy Type Sb I-II
φ 1.6′ × 0.7′, m13.5v, SB 13.5   15ʰ46.6ᵐ +72° 09′
Finder Chart 63-5   ★

12/14″ Scopes–125x: NGC 6011 is on the eastern corner of the triangle it forms with two 12th magnitude stars. The galaxy is a very faint 30″ diameter glow without central brightening.

16/18″ Scopes–150x: NGC 6011 shows a faint core embedded in a diffuse haze elongated 1′ × 0.5′ ESE–WNW. A 14th magnitude star is 30″ east of the galaxy's center.

NGC 6068A Galaxy Type S0? sp
φ 0.9′ × 0.2′, m14.0v, SB 12.0   15ʰ54.8ᵐ +79° 00′

NGC 6068 H973³ Galaxy Type SBbc?
φ 1.0′ × 0.7′, m12.8v, SB 12.3   15ʰ55.4ᵐ +79° 00′
Finder Chart 63-4, Figure 63-9   ★/★★

16/18″ Scopes–150x: NGC 6068 is just east of a 2′ wide

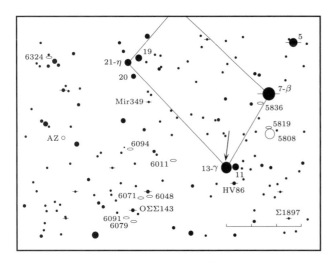

Finder Chart 63-5. 13–γ UMi. 15ʰ20.7ᵐ +71° 50′

equilateral triangle of 12th magnitude stars. Its companion, NGC 6068A, centered 2′ to its west, protrudes into the triangle's NE side. NGC 6068 has a bright core embedded in a faint but obvious halo elongated 1′ × 0.5′ N–S halo. NGC 6068A is much fainter and is elongated in the same direction: its 45″ × 15″ N–S halo contains a thin faint core.

NGC 6048 H873² Galaxy Type E
φ 2.2′ × 1.7′, m12.3v, SB 13.5   15ʰ57.6ᵐ +70° 42′
Finder Chart 63-5, Figure 63-8   ★★

12/14″ Scopes–125x: NGC 6048, located 13′ SSW of a 7th magnitude star, has a circular 1′ diameter halo that surrounds a bright center.

16/18″ Scopes–150x: This galaxy appears fairly faint, is elongated 1.75′ × 1.25′ NW–SE, and contains a bright core with a inconspicuous stellar nucleus. Galaxy NGC 6071 is located 18′ ESE.

NGC 6071 H883³ Galaxy Type SB(s)b
φ 0.9′ × 0.8′, m14.0v, SB 13.5   16ʰ01.1ᵐ +70° 37′
Finder Chart 63-5   ★

12/14″ Scopes–125x: NGC 6071, observable only with averted vision, is an extremely faint, small, round haze of smooth surface brightness.

16/18″ Scopes–150x: NGC 6071 has a very faint, circular 30″ diameter halo with diffuse edges but no central brightening. Galaxy NGC 6048 lies 18′ WNW.

NGC 6079 H884³ Galaxy Type E
φ 1.4′ × 1.0′, m12.7v, SB 13.0   16ʰ04.5ᵐ +69° 40′
Finder Chart 63-5   ★★

16/18″ Scopes–150x: NGC 6079, located half a degree south of a 7th magnitude star, shows a bright core

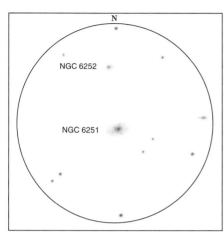

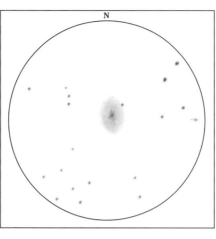

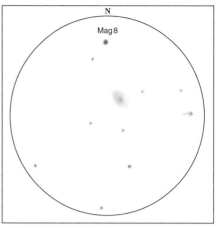

Figure 63-11. NGC 6251 and NGC 6252
18.5″, f5–300x, by Glen W. Sanner

Figure 63-12. NGC 6217
18.5″, f5–300x, by Glen W. Sanner

Figure 63-13. NGC 6324
18.5″, f5–300x, by Glen W. Sanner

surrounded by a faint 1′ diameter halo that is slightly elongated NNW–SSE. A 14th magnitude star is 1.5′ SE. Galaxy IC 1201 lies 7.5′ SE.

NGC 6094 H314³ Galaxy Type S0
φ 1.8′ × 1.4′, m13.2v, SB 14.1   16ʰ06.6ᵐ +72° 30′
Finder Chart 63-5, Figure 63-10   ★
16/18″ Scopes–150x: NGC 6094, located 10′ SW of a 9.5 magnitude star, is a faint, circular 1′ diameter glow that contains a very faint stellar nucleus. A 12th magnitude star lies 5′ to the galaxy's SW.

NGC 6091 Galaxy Type S?
φ 0.4′ × 0.3′, m13.7v   16ʰ07.8ᵐ +69° 55′
Finder Chart 63-5   ★
16/18″ Scopes–150x: NGC 6091, located 23′ SSE of a 7th magnitude star, is a very faint 25″ diameter glow containing a slightly brighter center.

NGC 6252 H975³ Galaxy Type?
φ 0.7′ × 0.4′, m14.2v, SB 12.7   16ʰ32.5ᵐ +82° 36′
NGC 6251 H974³ Galaxy Type E
φ 1.8′ × 1.5′, m12.6v, SB 13.6   16ʰ32.6ᵐ +82° 33′
Finder Chart 63-4, Figure 63-11   ★/★★
12/14″ Scopes–125x: NGC 6251 and NGC 6252 are a close galaxy-pair located 35′ NW of magnitude 4.2 star Epsilon (ε) = 22 Ursae Minoris. The southern component, NGC 6251, is the larger and brighter of the two galaxies, though it has only a faint, circular 1′ diameter halo containing a faint core. NGC 6252, located 2.5′ north of NGC 6251, is a very faint 30″ diameter halo without any central brightening.

16/18″ Scopes–150x: NGC 6251 and NGC 6252 are a pair of oval-shaped galaxies, both slightly elongated roughly E–W. The larger and brighter NGC 6251 has a 1.5′ × 1′ E–W halo that contains a faint stellar nucleus. NGC 6252 has a faint 45″ × 30″ E–W halo containing a very faint stellar nucleus.

NGC 6217 H280¹ Galaxy Type (R)SB(rs)bc II
φ 3.3′ × 3.3′, m11.2v, SB 13.6   16ʰ32.6ᵐ +78° 12′
Finder Chart 63-4, Figure 63-12   ★★★
8/10″ Scopes–100x: NGC 6217 has a faint, diffuse 1.5′ × 1′ NNW–SSE halo that contains a stellar nucleus.
16/18″ Scopes–150x: This galaxy has a fairly bright 2.5′ × 1.5′ NNW–SSE halo containing a small core in which is embedded a stellar nucleus. A very faint star is superimposed upon the halo 20″ SE of the nucleus. A 14th magnitude star is on the halo's NW edge.

NGC 6324 H945³ Galaxy Type S?
φ 0.9′ × 0.5′, m12.8v, SB 11.8   17ʰ05.4ᵐ +75° 25′
Finder Chart 63-5, Figure 63-13   ★★
12/14″ Scopes–125x: NGC 6324 is in a field of bright stars: 15′ to its SW is a 6th magnitude star in a 19′ × 7′ triangle with two 7th magnitude stars. The galaxy may be found 5.5′ south of an 8th magnitude star north of the triangle. It has a very faint, circular 30″ diameter halo containing a slight central brightening.
16/18″ Scopes–150x: NGC 6324 is a faint, diffuse 1′ × 0.5′ ENE–WSW glow containing a small, well concentrated core.

Chapter 64

Virgo, the Virgin

64.1 Overview

In classical mythology the constellation Virgo was associated with a number of important goddesses. Because to her west was Libra the Scales, the next constellation in the Zodiac, she sometimes was identified with Astraea, the goddess of Justice, who held the Scales of Justice in one hand and the Sword of Punishment in the other. But she was also described by classical authors, and shown on the Farnese Globe and Egyptian zodiacs, as holding an Ear of Wheat, the 1st magnitude star Spica: thus Virgo was also, and more properly, identified with Ceres, the goddess of Grains (our word "cereal" derives from the word Ceres), or with Ceres' daughter Persephone. In this fertility aspect Virgo was also identified with the Egyptian Isis and the Syrian Astartre.

Ultimately the association of the stars of the classical constellation Virgo with a fertility goddess goes back to ancient Mesopotamia, where these stars were sacred to, if not actually a representation of, the Babylonian Ishtar and her forerunner, the Sumerian Inanna. The sacred icons of Inanna/Ishtar were the Ear of Grain, the Date-cluster, and the Lion, all three of which were represented in this area of the heavens: the Ear of Grain was of course the classical Spica; the Lion was the celestial Leo; and the Date-cluster was the late Greek Coma Berenices Star Cluster. Thus the connection of this region of the sky with a fertility goddess far anteceded even the earliest Greek cultures: in fact remains found in archeological digs in Inanna/Ishtar's sacred city of Uruk in southern Iraq and dating to the centuries before 3000 B.C. show the goddess with her Grain-ears and Date-clusters.

Virgo is a special constellation astronomically as well as historically. Because it is well away from the obscuring dust of the Milky Way, Virgo would be expected to contain external galaxies. However, it not only contains an abundance of galaxies, it has a superabundance of galaxies, many of them very bright – indeed, eleven of its galaxies have Messier numbers. The reason for this is that toward Virgo is the heart of

Virgo: VER-go
Genitive: Virginis, VER-gin-is
Abbreviation: Vir
Culmination: 9 pm–May 26, midnight–April 11
Area: 1,294 square degrees
Showpieces: 29–γ V, Mir, 51–ϑ Vir, 54 Vir, 84 Vir, Σ1788, 105–ϕ Vir, M49 (NGC 4472), M58 (NGC 4579), M59 (NGC 4621), M60 (NGC 4649), M61 (NGC 4303), M84 (NGC 4374), M86 (NGC 4406), M87 (NGC 4486), M89 (NGC 4552), M90 (NGC 4569), M104 (NGC 4594), NGC 4216, NGC 4526, NGC 4535, NGC 4536, NGC 4666, NGC 4697, NGC 4699, NGC 4762
Binocular Objects: M49 (NGC 4472), M58 (NGC 4579), M59 (NGC 4621), M60 (NGC 4649), M61 (NGC 4303), M84 (NGC 4374), M86 (NGC 4406), M87 (NGC 4486), M89 (NGC 4552), M90 (NGC 4569), M104 (NGC 4594), NGC 4216, NGC 4526, NGC 4535, NGC 4536, NGC 4666, NGC 4697, NGC 4699, NGC 4753, NGC 4762

the Coma-Virgo Supercluster, on the outer fringes of which orbits our small Local Galaxy Group. The center of the Coma-Virgo Supercluster is in southern Coma Berenices and northwestern Virgo between Beta Leonis (Denebola) and Epsilon Virginis (Vindemiatrix); but it is a flattened galaxy aggregation, and the rich wings of its dense core region in Coma and NW Virgo extend SE down through the tail of Hydra to Centaurus and NW through Coma and Canes Venatici to the Big Dipper in Ursa Major. The center of the Supercluster seems to be about 65 million light years distant toward M84 and M86, two of the Supercluster's giant elliptical members. The core of the Supercluster is very dense: in its central $12° \times 10°$ area some 3,000 galaxies can be counted – and these are only the brightest members, because the dwarf ellipticals and irregulars cannot be detected on images taken with ground-based telescopes. Three-fourths of the Supercluster's brightest galaxies are giant spirals sim-

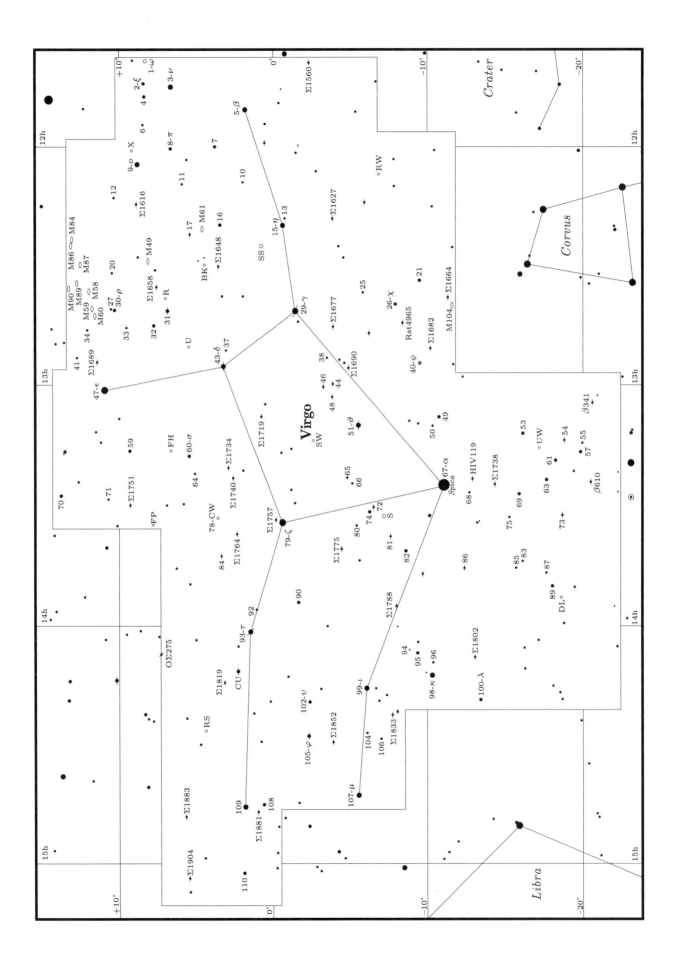

Table 64-1: Selected Variable Stars in Virgo

Name	HD No.	Type	Max.	Min.	Period (Days)	F*	Spec. Type	R.A. (2000)	Dec.	Finder Chart No.	Notes
SS Vir	108105	M	6.0	9.6	354		C5, 3e	$12^h25.3^m$	$+00°48'$	64-5	
BK Vir	108849	SRb	7.28	8.8	150:		M7	30.4	+04 25	64-5	
R Vir	109914	M	6.0	12.1	145	0.50	M4.5	38.5	+06 59	64-6	
U Vir	111691	M	7.5	13.5	206	0.47	M2-M8	51.1	+05 33	64-6	
SW Vir	114961	SRb	6.85	7.88	150:		M7	$13^h14.1^m$	−02 48	64-11	
S Vir	117833	M	6.3	13.2	377	0.45	M7	33.0	−07 12	64-13	
FP Vir	118289	SRb	6.72	7.35	55		gM4	35.9	+08 18	64-10	
DL Vir	120902	EA	7.0	7.5	1.31	0.14	G8+A	52.6	−18 43	64-1	
RS Vir	126753	M	7.0	14.4	352	0.37	M6-M7	$14^h27.3^m$	+04 41	64-16	

F* = The fraction of period taken up by the star's rise from min. to max. brightness, or the period spent in eclipse.

Table 64-2: Selected Double Stars in Virgo

Name	ADS No.	Pair	M1	M2	Sep."	P.A.°	Spec	R.A. (2000)	Dec.	Finder Chart No.	Notes
Σ1560	8247		6.2	10.40	5.2	279	K0	$11^h38.4^m$	$−02°26'$	64-3	
Σ1616	8473	AB	7.6	9.8	23.3	296	G0 K2	$12^h14.5^m$	+08 47	64-4	
	8473	AC		9.7	156.8	293					
Σ1627	8505		6.6	6.9	20.1	196	F0 F0	18.2	−03 57	64-3	Two pale yellow stars
17 Vir	8531		6.6	9.4	20.0	337	F8	22.5	+05 18	64-5	Yellow and orangish
Σ1648	8576		7.6	9.6	8.0	40	K0	30.6	+03 30	64-5	
Σ1658	8601		7.9	9.7	2.5	9	F8	35.1	+07 27	64-6	
Σ1664		AB	8.1	9.3	26.3	237	K0 G5	38.3	−11 31	64-9	
		AC		11.5	62.5	306					
		CD		11.6	32.5	266					
29−γ Vir	8630	AB	3.5	3.5	c1.8	*267	F0 F0	41.7	−01 27	64-5	Bright yellowish binary
Rst 4965			7.8	11.2	7.6	97	K0	45.0	−08 32	46-9	
Σ1677	8657		6.8	8.3	15.9	349	A3	45.3	−03 53	64-5	
Σ1682	8684	AB	6.5	9.3	30.2	301	K0	51.4	−10 20	64-9	
Σ1689	8704		7.1	9.4	29.0	211	M	55.5	+11 30	64-10	Deep yellow and blue
Σ1690	8707		7.0	8.5	5.7	148	A0	56.2	−04 52	64-9	
44 Vir	(Σ1704)		5.8	11.0	20.9	55	A0	59.7	−03 49	64-9	
β 341	8757		6.3	6.4	0.8	312	G0	$13^h03.8^m$	−20 35	64-12	
48 Vir	8759		7.2	7.5	0.8	205	F0	03.9	−03 40	64-9	Equal pale yellow pair
Σ1719	8786		7.6	8.1	7.2	1	F5	07.3	+00 35	64-11	
51−θ Vir	8801	AB	4.4	9.4	7.1	343	A0	09.9	−05 32	64-13	White and pale yellow
(HIII 50)	8801	AC		10.4	69.6	298					
54 Vir	8824		6.8	7.3	5.4	34	A0	13.4	−18 50	64-12	Yellowish-white pair
Σ1734	8864		6.8	7.5	1.0	183	A0	20.7	+02 57	64-11	
HIV 119	8878		7.8	10.8	19.4	310	A2	22.8	−13 11	64-13	
Σ1738	8881		8.5	8.6	3.9	281	F8	23.2	−14 55	64-12	
Σ1740	8883		7.4	7.6	26.5	7.5	G5 G5	23.7	+02 43	64-11	
β 610	8885		6.6	10.6	3.9	18	K0	24.0	−20 55	46-12	
Σ1751	8928		7.1	10.3	5.7	60	K0	30.7	+09 19	64-10	
Σ1757	8949	AB	7.8	8.7	1.6c	*131	K0	34.3	−00 19	64-11	
81 Vir	8972		7.9	7.9	2.8	41	K2	37.6	−07 52	64-13	
Σ1764	8975		7.0	8.7	15.8	31	K0	37.7	+02 23	64-14	
Σ1775	9002		7.1	9.8	27.7	336	K2	43.5	−04 16	46-13	
84 Vir	9000		5.5	7.9	2.9	229	K0	43.1	+03 32	64-14	Orange and pale yellow
Σ1788	9053	AB	6.5	7.7	3.4	86	F8	55.0	−08 04	64-13	Nice pair of yellow suns
93−τ Vir	9085		4.3	9.6	80.0	290	A2	$14^h01.6^m$	+01 33	64-14	
Σ1802	9115		7.6	8.9	5.6	279	G0	08.1	−12 56	64-1	
OΣ275	9127		7.2	10.7	5.0	353	K0	09.2	+07 23	64-14	
Σ1819	9182		7.8	7.9	0.8	*189	F8	15.3	+03 08	64-14	
Σ1833	9237		7.6	7.6	5.7	172	G0	22.6	−07 46	64-15	
105−φ Vir	9273	AB	4.8	9.3	4.8	110	K0	28.2	−02 14	64-15	Unequal yellow and orange
Σ1852	9284		7.1	10.2	25.0	267	F2	30.0	−04 15	64-15	
Σ1881	9383		6.7	9.0	3.5	359	A0	47.1	+00 58	64-16	
Σ1883	9392		7.6	7.6	0.8w	*283	F8	48.9	+05 57	64-16	
Σ1904	9493		7.2	7.2	9.9	347	F0	$15^h04.1^m$	+05 30	64-16	

Footnotes: *= Year 2000, a = Near apogee, c = Closing, w = Widening. Finder Chart No: All stars listed in the tables are plotted in the large Constellation Chart, but when a star appears in a Finder Chart, this number is listed. Notes: When colors are subtle, the suffix *-ish* is used, e.g. *bluish*.

ilar to the Milky Way and the Andromeda Galaxy, M31; but the aggregation also includes a large number of lenticulars and giant ellipticals.

Such superclustering of galaxies – or rather, of small galaxy groups – is the rule rather than the exception in intergalactic space. When we look toward the opposite side of the sky from Coma Berenices and Virgo in the direction of Cetus, Fornax, and Eridanus, we look away from the interior of our own Supercluster out across a comparatively galaxy-poor inter-supercluster gap at the 60 or 70 million light year distant edge of another supercluster which includes most of the brighter galaxies in those constellations. Other, more distant superclusters have been identified, but for the most part their galaxies are inaccessible to amateur telescopes. A few of the members of the Hercules Galaxy Cluster, the Coma Berenices Galaxy Cluster, and the Corona Borealis Galaxy Cluster – all three of which are described under their respective constellations – can be seen in large amateur instruments.

64.2 Interesting Stars

Σ1627 Double Star   **Spec. F0, F0**
m6.6, 6.9; Sep. 20.1″; P.A. 196 $12^h18.2^m -03° 57'$
Finder Chart 64-3   ★★★★
4/6″ Scopes–75x: Struve 1627 is a wide pair of yellow stars easily split with small telescopes.

17 Virginis Double Star   **Spec. F8**
m6.6, 9.4; Sep. 20.0″; P.A. 337° $12^h22.5^m +05° 18'$
Finder Chart 64-5   ★★★★
4/6″ Scopes–75x: 17 Virginis is a nice double for small instruments. Its primary is yellow and its secondary white.

Gamma (γ) = 29 Virginis Double Star   Spec. F0, F0
AB: m3.5, 3.5; Sep. 1.8″; P.A. 267° $12^h18.2^m -03° 57'$
Finder Chart 64-5   ★★★★★
Porrima
8/10″ Scopes–200x: Gamma Virginis is a striking but difficult binary of two equally matched yellowish stars orbiting each other in a 171 year period. The stars are closing and by the year 2010 will be only 0.9″ apart.

Theta (ϑ) = 51 Virginis Triple Star   **Spec. A0**
AB: m4.4, 9.4; Sep. 7.1″; P.A. 343° $13^h09.9^m -05° 32'$
Finder Chart 64-13   ★★★★★
4/6″ Scopes–100x: Theta Virginis has a bright white primary with an easily separated pale yellow companion. The magnitude 10.4 third component lies 69.6″ distant in position angle 298° from the primary.

54 Virginis Double Star   **Spec. A0**
m6.8, 7.3; Sep. 5.4″; P.A. 34° $13^h13.4^m -18° 50'$
Finder Chart 64-12   ★★★★
4/6″ Scopes–100x: 54 Virginis is an attractive pair of yellowish-white stars easily separated in small telescopes.

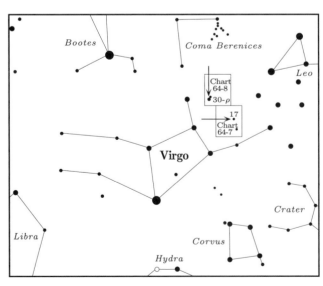

Master Finder Chart 64-2a. Virgo Chart Areas
Guide stars indicated by arrows.

Master Finder Chart 64-2b. Virgo Chart Areas
Guide stars indicated by arrows.

84 Virginis Double Star Spec. K0
m5.5,7.9; Sep.2.9″; P.A.229°   13ʰ43.1ᵐ +03° 32′
Finder Chart 64-14   ★★★★
4/6″ Scopes–150x: 84 Virginis consists of a close pair of strikingly colored orange and pale yellow stars.

Σ1788 Quadruple Star Spec. F8
AB: m6.5,7.7; Sep.3.4″; P.A.86°   13ʰ55.0ᵐ −08° 04′
Finder Chart 64-13   ★★★★
4/6″ Scopes–100x: Struve 1788 has a close pair of beautiful yellow stars accompanied by two distant, much fainter companions. A magnitude 10.3 star 128″ away in PA 293° and a magnitude 10.9 star 157″ distant in PA 215°.

Phi (φ) = 105 Virginis Triple Star Spec. K0
AB: m4.8,9.3; Sep.4.8″; P.A.110°   14ʰ28.2ᵐ −02° 14′
Finder Chart 64-15   ★★★★★
4/6″ Scopes–100x: Phi Virginis is a triple with a deep yellow primary, a close orange secondary, and a wide bluish magnitude 12.4 third component 93″ away in PA 205°.

64.3 Deep-Sky Objects

NGC 3818 H284³ Galaxy Type SAB(s:)0
φ 2.0′ × 1.2′, m11.7, SB12.5   11ʰ42.0ᵐ −06° 09′
Finder Chart 64-3   ★★★
8/10″ Scopes–75x: NGC 3818, located 7′ south of a 9.5 magnitude star and 6.5′ NW of an 11th magnitude star, is a moderately faint galaxy with a circular 1′ diameter halo that contains a stellar nucleus.
16/18″ Scopes–150x: NGC 3818 displays a bright stellar nucleus within an oval core that is surrounded by a diffuse 1.5′ × 1′ ESE–WNW halo. A 13th magnitude star lies 3.5′ east.

NGC 3952 H612³ Galaxy Type IB?m? III
φ 1.7′ × 0.7′, m13.1, SB13.2v   11ʰ53.7ᵐ −04° 00′
Finder Chart 64-3   ★★
12/14″ Scopes–125x: NGC 3952 is at the southern corner of the 12′ × 7′ triangle it forms with 7th and 8th magnitude stars. The galaxy's faint halo is elongated 1.25′ × 0.5′ E–W and contains a slight brightening at its center. A 12.5 magnitude star lies 5.5′ ESE, and a 12th magnitude star 6.75′ WSW, of the galaxy.

NGC 3976 H132² Galaxy Type SAB(s)b I-II
φ 3.3′ × 1.0′, m11.5v, SB12.6   11ʰ56.0ᵐ +06° 45′
Finder Chart 64-4   ★★★
12/14″ Scopes–125x: NGC 3976, centered 7′ SSE of a 9th magnitude star, has a faint 3′ × 1′ NE–SW envelope containing an oval core. 14th magnitude stars lie 4′ SSE and 5.5′ ESE of the galaxy.

NGC 4030 H121¹ Galaxy Type Sc I or I-II
φ 3.8′ × 2.9′, m10.6v, SB13.1   12ʰ00.4ᵐ −01° 06′
Finder Chart 64-5, Figure 64-1   ★★★
12/14″ Scopes–125x: NGC 4030 lies along the east side of the 3.5′ N–S line joining two tenth magnitude stars. The northern of the two stars is nearer the galaxy, lying only 1.5′ NNW of its center. The southern star has an 11.5 magnitude companion 1′ to its SE. The galaxy's halo is faint, diffuse, and elongated 2.5′ × 1.5′ NE–SW. The halo's surface brightness increases inward, at first gradually and then abruptly, to a bright circular core containing an inconspicuous stellar nucleus.

NGC 4045 H276² (R′) SA? (rs)a: pec
φ 2.7′ × 1.8′, m12.0v, SB13.6   12ʰ02.7ᵐ +01° 59′
Finder Chart 64-4   ★★
12/14″ Scopes–125x: NGC 4045, centered 1.75′ NW of a 12th magnitude star, is a faint, diffuse 1′ diameter glow with a stellar nucleus. Only 1.5′ to its south is its companion galaxy NGC 4045A, a faint, stellar spot just 20″ NE of a 13.5 magnitude star.

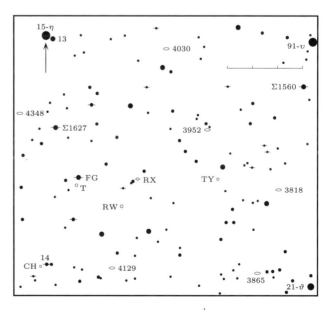

Finder Chart 64-3. 15–η Vir: 12ʰ19.9ᵐ −00° 40′

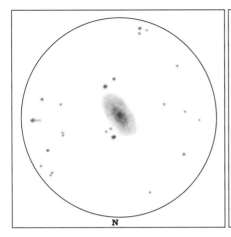

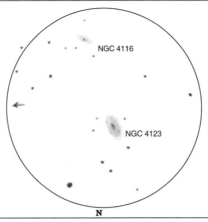

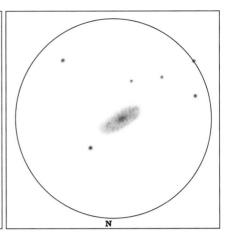

Figure 64-1. NGC 4030
12.5″, f5–250x, by G. R. Kepple

Figure 64-2. NGC 4116 and NGC 4123
13″, f4.5–165x, by Tom Polakis

Figure 64-3. NGC 4124
12.5″, f5–250x, by G. R. Kepple

NGC 4073 H277[2] Galaxy Type E+4/SO–
φ **2.1′×1.6′, m11.4v, SB12.6**   12^{h}04.5^m +01° 54′
Finder Chart 64-4   ★★★
12/14″Scopes–125x: NGC 4073, located 6′ south of a
   close pair of 10th magnitude stars, has a faint
   2′×1.5′ ESE–WNW halo that gradually brightens
   to a stellar nucleus. It is the most prominent
   member in a galaxy group that includes NGC 4063
   only 5′ to its SW, NGC 4077 located 7′ SSE, NGC
   4075 lying 9′ to the NNE, and the more distant
   NGC 4045 located 25′ WNW.

NGC 4116 Galaxy Type SB(rs)dm III-IV
φ **3.5′×2.3′, m12.0v, SB14.1**   12^{h}07.6^m +02° 42′
Finder Chart 64-4, Figure 64-2   ★★
12/14″Scopes–125x: NGC 4116 is the slightly smaller

and fainter of a galaxy pair with NGC 4123 lying
14′ to its NE. It is elongated 1.5′×1.25′ NW–SE
and contains a very faint stellar nucleus. 4′ to the
galaxy's SE is an isosceles triangle of three 13th
magnitude stars, and 8′ SE is an in-line triplet of
magnitude 12.5 stars.

NGC 4123 H4[5] Galaxy Type SB(r)c II-III
φ **4.6′×3.7′, m11.4v, SB14.3**   12^{h}08.2^m +02° 53′
Finder Chart 64-4, Figure 64-2   ★★★
12/14″Scopes–125x: NGC 4123, located 14′ NE of NGC
   4116, has a moderately faint, diffuse 3′×2′ NW–SE
   halo containing a faint nucleus. 12th magnitude stars
   are 2.5′ SSW and 2.75′ SSE, and a 13th magnitude
   star 3.25′ NNE, of the galaxy's center.

NGC 4124 H33[1] Galaxy Type SA(r)0+
φ **4.2′×1.9′, m11.3v, SB13.5**   12^{h}08.2^m +10° 23′
Finder Chart 64-4, Figure 64-3   ★★★
12/14″Scopes–125x: NGC 4124 is a fairly faint 3′×1.25′
   ESE–WNW oval haze surrounding a small oval core
   containing a faint stellar nucleus. A 12th magnitude
   star lies 3′ from the galaxy's center beyond its
   WNW tip. The ESE tip points toward a large "Y"
   of 11th and 12th magnitude stars.

NGC 4129 H548[2] Galaxy Type Scd:
φ **2.3′×0.7′, m12.5v, SB12.9**   12^{h}08.9^m −09° 02′
Finder Chart 64-3   ★★
12/14″Scopes–125x: NGC 4129 is a faint but conspicuous 2′×0.5′ E–W streak of uniform surface brightness. A large arc of three magnitude 12.5 stars is 4′
   west of the galaxy, and a 12th magnitude star is 7′
   SE.

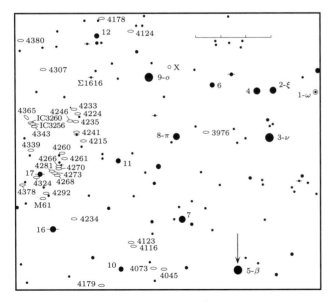

Finder Chart 64-4. 5–β Vir: 11^{h}50.7^m +01° 46′

NGC 4168 H105[2] Galaxy Type E2
φ 2.8′×2.5′, m11.2v, SB13.1   **12ʰ12.3ᵐ +13° 12′**
Finder Chart 64-6   ★★★

12/14″Scopes–125x: NGC 4168 has a bright but tiny core surrounded by a 1.5′ diameter halo which fades to a diffuse periphery. Two companion galaxies are near NGC 4168. Just 3′ to its NNW is NGC 4165, a faint, diffuse object slightly elongated 1′×0.45′ NNW–SSE. 3′ west of NGC 4168 is NGC 4164, a very faint spot with a stellar nucleus.

NGC 4178 IC 3042 Galaxy Type SB(rs)dm II
φ 5.0′×1.6′, m11.4v, SB13.5   **12ʰ12.8ᵐ +10° 52′**
Finder Chart 64-4   ★★★★

8/10″Scopes–100x: NGC 4178, located 7′ NW of a 7.5 magnitude star, is a faint, diffuse galaxy elongated 3′×1′ NNE–SSW and slightly brighter at its center.

16/18″Scopes–150x: NGC 4178 appears fairly bright but diffuse. Its halo is elongated 4′×1.25′ in position angle 30° and contains a very thin 1′ long core. A very faint knot is just visible at the halo's SW tip. A 14.5 magnitude star lies just beyond the SW tip 2.5′ from the galaxy's center, and a 13th magnitude star is 3.25′ SE.

NGC 4179 H9[1] Galaxy Type S0–: sp
φ 3.9′×1.1′, m11.0v, SB12.4   **12ʰ12.9ᵐ +01° 18′**
Finder Chart 64-5, Figure 64-5   ★★★★

8/10″Scopes–100x: NGC 4179, centered 2′ SW of a 10.5 magnitude star, appears fairly bright and quite elongated 2′×0.5′ NW–SE and has a bright extended core.

16/18″Scopes–150x: This fine galaxy is much-elongated 4′×0.5′ NW–SE and contains a bright oval core extended 1′×0.5′. A 14th magnitude star is superimposed upon the core's NW edge. Two more 14th magnitude stars are outside the halo between the core and the bright star to the galaxy's NE. Another faint star lies 1.75′ south of the galaxy's center.

NGC 4193 H163[2] Galaxy Type SAB(s)c:? III
φ 2.1′×1.0′, m12.3v, SB13.0   **12ʰ13.9ᵐ +13° 10′**
Finder Chart 64-6   ★★

12/14″Scopes–125x: NGC 4193 appears moderately faint and elongated 2′×1′ E–W. It has a faint stellar nucleus embedded in a poorly concentrated core. A 13th magnitude star lies 2′ NW of the galaxy's center.

Figure 64-4. *NGC4216, at center, is the largest of three spindle-shaped galaxies lying within a medium-power field of view. Image courtesy of Jim Burnell.*

NGC 4206 IC 3064 H165[2] Galaxy Type SA(s)bc:
φ 5.3′×0.9′, m12.2v, SB13.7   **12ʰ15.3ᵐ +13° 02′**
Finder Chart 64-6, Figure 64-4   ★★★

8/10″Scopes–100x: NGC 4206 is the southern of three spindle-shaped galaxies that can be seen together in the same medium-power field of view, the other two being NGC 4216, located 11′ to the NE, and NGC 4222, across the border in Coma Berenices 23′ distant. NGC 4206 has a faint 3′×0.5′ N–S halo that is slightly brighter along its interior. A 4.5′ long equilateral triangle of faint stars points at the galaxy from the SE. A wide pair of 13th magnitude stars is 3.75′ west of the galaxy's center.

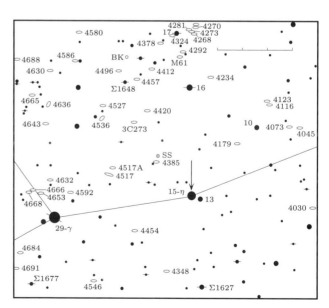

Finder Chart 64-5. 29–γ Vir: 12ʰ41.7ᵐ −01° 27′

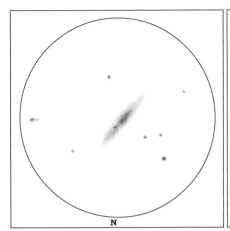

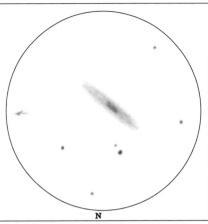

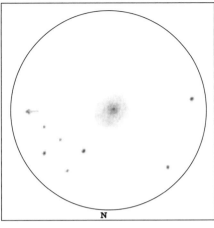

Figure 64-5. NGC 4179
17.5″, f4.5–300x, by G. R. Kepple

Figure 64-6. NGC 4235
17.5″, f4.5–300x, by G. R. Kepple

Figure 64-7. NGC 4267
17.5″, f4.5–275x, by G. R. Kepple

16/18″ Scopes–150x: Larger instruments show a moderately concentrated, much-elongated 4′ × 0.5′ N–S halo with an irregularly brighter streak running along the interior length of its major axis.

NGC 4215 H135² Galaxy Type SA(r)0+: sp
ϕ **1.5′ × 0.6′, m12.1v, SB 11.8   12ʰ15.9ᵐ +06° 24′**
Finder Chart 64-4   ★★★
12/14″ Scopes–125x: NGC 4215, centered 3′ SE of a 12.5 magnitude star, has a moderately faint but well defined 1.75′ × 0.5′ N–S halo elongated to tapered ends. The major axis is well concentrated along the halo's center and contains a bright stellar nucleus.

NGC 4216 H35¹ Galaxy Type SAB(s)b: II
ϕ **7.8′ × 1.6′, m10.0v, SB 12.6   12ʰ15.9ᵐ +13° 09′**
Finder Chart 64-6, Figure 64-4   ★★★★
8/10″ Scopes–100x: NGC 4216 is the finest of three close spindle-shaped galaxies, the other two being NGC 4206 located 11′ SW and NGC 4222 in Coma Berenices 12′ NE. NGC 4216 is a bright 5′ × 0.5′ NNE–SSW streak containing a bright, highly extended core.
16/18″ Scopes–150x: Spectacular! NGC 4216 is a bright, thin spindle elongated 6′ × 1′ NNE–SSW. Its core is very bright and is extended 2′ × 0.5′, the NNE tip of the core more pointed than the SSW. A stellar nucleus stands out well against the core's brilliance. A dark lane can be silhouetted along the core's eastern side. The halo extends further east from the core than west and on its edge due east of the core's center is a 13th magnitude star.

NGC 4224 H136² Galaxy Type SA(s)a: sp
ϕ **1.8′ × 0.8′, m11.8v, SB 12.1   12ʰ16.6ᵐ +07° 28′**
Finder Charts 64-4, 64-7   ★★★
8/10″ Scopes–100x: NGC 4224, located 7′ NNE of an 8th magnitude star, has a fairly bright 1.5′ × 0.75′ ENE–WSW oval halo that gradually brightens toward its center.
16/18″ Scopes–150x: NGC 4224 has a bright 2.5′ × 1′ ENE–WSW halo containing a broad central brightening with a stellar nucleus. A 13th magnitude star is 1.5′ north, and a much fainter star 2′ WSW of the nucleus. Galaxy NGC 4233 lies 13′ NE.

NGC 4233 H496² Galaxy Type S0°
ϕ **2.0′ × 0.9′, m11.9v, SB 12.4   12ʰ17.1ᵐ +07° 37′**
Finder Charts 64-4, 64-7   ★★
8/10″ Scopes–100x: NGC 4233, located 9′ WSW of a 9th magnitude star and 2.75′ NE of a 12.5 magnitude star, has a conspicuous stellar nucleus embedded in a faint, diffuse glow.
16/18″ Scopes–150x: Larger telescopes show NGC 4233 to have an unconcentrated envelope elongated 1.5′ × 0.75′ N–S that contains a small bright core with a stellar nucleus.

NGC 4234 Galaxy Type (R′)SB(s)m IV
ϕ **1.1′ × 1.0′, m12.7v, SB 12.6   12ʰ17.2ᵐ +03° 41′**
Finder Charts 64-5, 64-7   ★★
12/14″ Scopes–125x: NGC 4234 is a fairly faint, diffuse circular glow less than 1′ diameter across and without any central brightening. 13.5 magnitude stars are 4′ to the galaxy's SSE and 4.5′ to its NE.

NGC 4235 IC 3098 Galaxy Type SA(s)a
ϕ 3.6′×0.8′, m11.6v, SB12.6   12^{h}17.2^m +07° 11′
Finder Charts 64-4, 64-7, Figure 64-6   ★★★
8/10″Scopes-100x: NGC 4235, located 14′ SE of an 8th
   magnitude star, is a fairly bright edge-on galaxy
   elongated 3′×0.75′ NE–SW and containing an oval
   core. Three 13th magnitude stars form a 5′ long E–
   W arc concave to the south just north of the galaxy,
   the star at the arc's center 1.75′ north of the
   galaxy's center.
16/18″Scopes-150x: In larger telescopes NGC 4235
   shows a prominent oval core with a faint stellar
   nucleus surrounded by tenuous extensions reaching
   3.5′×0.75′ NE–SW.

NGC 4241 H480^3 Galaxy Type SB(s)0+:
ϕ 2.5′×1.6′, m11.9v, SB13.3   12^{h}17.4^m +06° 41′
Finder Charts 64-4, 64-7   ★★★
12/14″Scopes-125x: NGC 4241, located 5.5′ north of an
   8.5 magnitude star and 2′ NNE of an 11.5 magnitude
   star, has a faint 2.25′×1′ NW–SE halo that elongates to tapered ends. The circular core is poorly
   concentrated but contains a faint stellar nucleus. 1′
   north of the galaxy's center is a tiny isosceles
   triangle of magnitude 13.5 stars.

NGC 4246 H91^3 Galaxy Type SA(s)c II
ϕ 2.2′×1.1′, m12.7v, SB13.5   12^{h}18.0^m +07° 11′
Finder Charts 64-6, 64-7   ★★
12/14″Scopes-125x: NGC 4246, located 12′ east of
   galaxy NGC 4235, is a faint nebulous object elongated 2′×1.25′ E–W and slightly brighter at its
   center. A 14th magnitude star is 2′ ENE of the
   galaxy's center, and a 9th magnitude star is 7′
   south. 5′ to the north of NGC 4246 is its companion
   galaxy NGC 4247, a faint 30″ diameter haze that
   contains a stellar nucleus.

NGC 4260 H138^2 Galaxy Type SB(s)a
ϕ 2.0′×1.1′, m11.8v, SB12.5   12^{h}19.4^m +06° 06′
Finder Charts 64-6, 64-7   ★★★
12/14″Scopes-125x: NGC 4260, located 7′ NW of an
   8th magnitude star, is a fairly bright but diffuse
   1.5′×1′ ENE–WSW oval containing a broad central
   concentration. At 175x a very faint stellar nucleus
   is visible. Only 1.25′ NE of the galaxy's nucleus is
   a 14th magnitude star. 8′ NW of NGC 4260 is galaxy
   IC 3136, a very faint 30″ diameter patch of haze
   slightly elongated NE–SW.

NGC 4261 H139^2 Galaxy Type E2-3
ϕ 3.5′×3.1′, m10.4v, SB12.9   12^{h}19.4^m +05° 49′

NGC 4264 H140^2 Galaxy Type SB(rs)0+
ϕ 0.8′×0.6′, m12.8v, SB11.9   12^{h}19.6^m +05° 51′
Finder Charts 64-6, 64-7   ★★★/★★
8/10″Scopes-100x: NGC 4261 is a bright, circular 1′
   diameter object that is well concentrated to a stellar
   nucleus. A 13th magnitude star lies 2′ NE, and a
   12th magnitude star 3′ south of the galaxy's
   nucleus. Centered 3.5′ ENE of NGC 4261 is its
   companion, NGC 4264, which has a fairly faint,
   diffuse 30″ diameter halo. A 13th magnitude star
   lies 1.5′ NNE of the center of NGC 4264.
16/18″Scopes-150x: Larger telescopes show NGC 4261
   and NGC 4264 as a NE–SW pair of bright galaxies.
   The southwestern system, NGC 4261, is the larger
   and brighter of the two: its 1.5′ diameter halo
   contains a fairly bright core that is well concentrated to a nonstellar nucleus. The NW galaxy,
   NGC 4264, has a large core relative to its 1′ diameter
   halo, and contains a stellar nucleus.

NGC 4266 Galaxy Type SB(s)a? sp
ϕ 1.6′×0.4′, m13.7v, SB13.0   12^{h}19.7^m +05° 32′
Finder Charts 64-6, 64-7   ★
16/18″Scopes-150x: NGC 4266, centered less than 1′
   SE of an 8.5 magnitude star, is a very faint, small,
   diffuse smudge elongated 1′×0.25′ ENE–WSW. The
   galaxy requires averted vision to be seen, and the
   glare of the magnitude 8.5 star does not help
   matters. Galaxy NGC 4270 lies 5′ SSE.

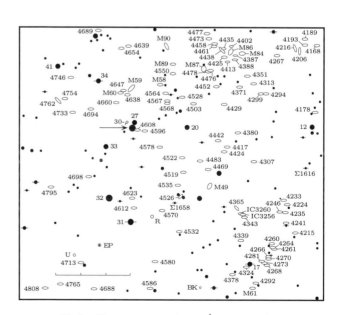

Finder Chart 64-6 30–ρ Vir: 12^{h}41.8^m +10° 14′

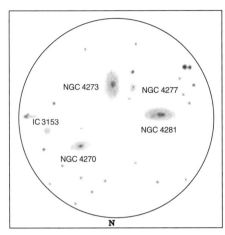

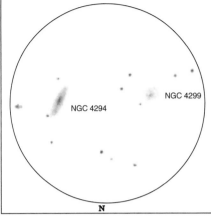

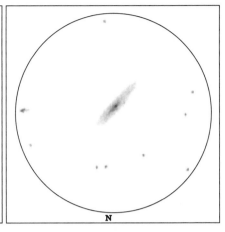

Figure 64-8. NGC 4273-81 Area
17.5″, ƒ4.5–250x, by G. R. Kepple

Figure 64-9. NGC 4294 and NGC 4299
12.5″, ƒ5–250x, by G. R. Kepple

Figure 64-10. NGC 4313
12.5″, ƒ5–250x, by G. R. Kepple

NGC 4267 H166² Galaxy Type SB(s)0–?
φ 3.7′ × 3.7′, m10.9v, SB13.6   12ʰ19.8ᵐ +12° 48′
Finder Chart 64-6, Figure 64-7   ★★★
8/10″Scopes–100x: NGC 4267 has a fairly faint 1′
  diameter halo that contains a stellar nucleus.
16/18″Scopes–150x: The stellar nucleus is conspicuous
  embedded in a faint core surrounded by a diffuse
  2′ diameter halo. A faint star is superimposed upon
  the halo 45″ NE of the nucleus.

NGC 4268 Galaxy Type SB0/a: sp
φ 1.2′ × 0.5′, m12.8v, SB12.1   12ʰ19.8ᵐ +05° 17′
Finder Charts 64-6 and 64-7   ★★
12/14″Scopes–125x: NGC 4268 is on the SSW edge of
  the NGC 4281 galaxy group. It has a conspicuous
  stellar nucleus embedded in a poorly concentrated
  but highly extended core surrounded by a lenticular
  1.25′ × 0.5′ NE–SW halo. A very faint star is less
  than 1′ NW, and a 12th magnitude star lies 3.5′ SSE.

NGC 4270 H568² Galaxy Type S0
φ 1.7′ × 0.7′, m12.2v, SB12.2   12ʰ19.8ᵐ +05° 28′
Finder Charts 64-6 and 64-7, Figure 64-8   ★★
12/14″Scopes–125x: NGC 4270 is in the NGC 4281
  group 5.5′ SSE of an 8.5 magnitude star and
  centered between a 7′ wide E–W pair of magnitude
  13.5 stars. The galaxy has a lenticular 1.25′ × 0.75′
  ESE–WNW halo that contains a broad central
  concentration with a stellar nucleus. Galaxy NGC
  4266 lies 5′ NNW.

NGC 4273 H569² Galaxy Type SB(s)c II-III
φ 2.3′ × 1.1′, m11.9v, SB12.7   12ʰ19.9ᵐ +05° 21′

NGC 4277 H571² Galaxy Type SAB(rs)0/a:
φ 0.8′ × 0.7′, m13.4v, SB12.6   12ʰ20.1ᵐ +05° 21′
Finder Chart 64-7, Figure 64-8   ★★★/★
8/10″Scopes–100x: NGC 4273 is near the center of the
  NGC 4281 galaxy group 7′ SW of the flagship object.
  It is fairly bright, elongated 1.5′ × 1′ N–S, and
  gradually brightens toward its center. It forms a
  right triangle with a 13th magnitude star 2.25′ to
  its SE and with its companion galaxy NGC 4277
  located 2′ to its east. NGC 4277 is a faint, very
  small 25″ diameter patch.
16/18″Scopes–150x: NGC 4273 has a broad, bright core
  without a nucleus. The halo fades smoothly to a
  diffuse periphery with a 1.75′ × 1′ N–S profile. NGC
  4277 is a faint, diffuse glow about 45″ diameter with
  a poorly concentrated core. A 15th magnitude star
  lies 1′ NNW of the center of NGC 4277.

NGC 4281 H573² Galaxy Type S0+: sp
φ 2.5′ × 1.3′, m11.3v, SB12.4   12ʰ20.4ᵐ +05° 23′
Finder Charts 64-4 and 64-7, Figure 64-8   ★★★
8/10″Scopes–100x: NGC 4281 is the brightest member
  of its group and located east of the other members.
  It has a prominent stellar nucleus surrounded by a
  diffuse 1.5′ × 0.5′ E–W halo. 5.5′ south of the galaxy
  is an attractive 13″ wide ESE–WNW double of
  magnitude 12 and 12.5 stars.
16/18″Scopes–150x: This galaxy forms a nice pair with
  NGC 4273 lying 7′ to its SW. NGC 4281 has a broad
  oval core extended 1′ × 0.5′ and containing a conspicuous stellar nucleus. The halo is much fainter
  and diffuse, and reaches to about 2′ × 1′ E–W.

Figure 64-11. *Messier 61 (NGC4303), an impressive sight in large telescopes, has a bright bar-like core and three spiral arms. NGC4303A is at the bottom right of the field and NGC4292 is at the bottom left. Image courtesy of Jim Burnell.*

NGC 4292 Galaxy Type (R)SB(r)0°
ϕ **1.9′×1.3′, m12.2v, SB13.0**   **12ʰ21.3ᵐ +04° 36′**
Finder Charts 64-5, 64-7, Figure 64-11   ★★
16/18″ Scopes–150x: NGC 4292, located 12′ NW of M61 and 1.25′ SSE of a 10.5 magnitude star, has a fairly faint 1.5′×1′ N–S halo containing a faint stellar nucleus. An 8th magnitude star lies 5′ SW.

NGC 4294 H61² Galaxy Type SB(s)cd III
ϕ **2.7′×1.0′, m12.1v, SB13.0**   **12ʰ21.3ᵐ +11° 31′**

NGC 4299 H62² Galaxy Type SAB(s)dm: III-IV
ϕ **1.6′×1.6′, m12.5v, SB13.4**   **12ʰ21.7ᵐ +11° 30′**
Finder Chart 64-6, Figure 64-9   ★★/★★
12/14″ Scopes–125x: NGC 4294 and NGC 4299 are a 5.5′ wide E–W galaxy pair. The western system, NGC 4294, is a faint 1.5′×0.5′ NNW–SSE object containing a poorly concentrated core extended along its major axis. A 14th magnitude star is just west of its NNW tip, and a magnitude 14.5 star lies only 45″ south of its center. The eastern galaxy, NGC 4299, is the smaller and fainter of the two, with a faint, diffuse 1′ diameter halo containing a stellar nucleus. It lies among a sprinkling of very faint stars, the nearest actually touching its south edge.

NGC 4303 Messier 61 Galaxy Type SAB(rs)bc I-II
ϕ **6.0′×5.9′, m9.7v, SB13.4**   **12ʰ21.9ᵐ +04° 28′**

NGC 4303A Galaxy Type SAB(s)cd III
ϕ **1.5′×1.3′, m13.0v, SB13.6**   **12ʰ22.4ᵐ +04° 34′**
Finder Charts 64-5, 64-7, Figure 64-11   ★★★★/★
    NGC 4303 was discovered by Oriani on May 5, 1779, while observing the comet of that year. Messier mistook it for the comet, but by May 11th he had realized his mistake and added it to his catalogue as the 61st entry. M61 is a giant barred-spiral member of the Coma-Virgo Supercluster on the southern fringes of the core of that supercluster. If it is 65 million light years away, its absolute magnitude is −21.8, a luminosity of 44 billion suns, and its true diameter is in excess of 110,000 light years.
4/6″ Scopes–75x: Messier 61 is a bright face-on galaxy with a conspicuous core within a N–S bar. The halo is unevenly bright and slightly elongated 3′×2.75′ NE–SW.
8/10″ Scopes–100x: The 4′×3.5′ NE–SW halo is very bright and mottled, and contains a 30″ diameter core. A dark streak (which photos show to be the wide gap between the eastern spiral arm and the core) extends along the halo's eastern edge.

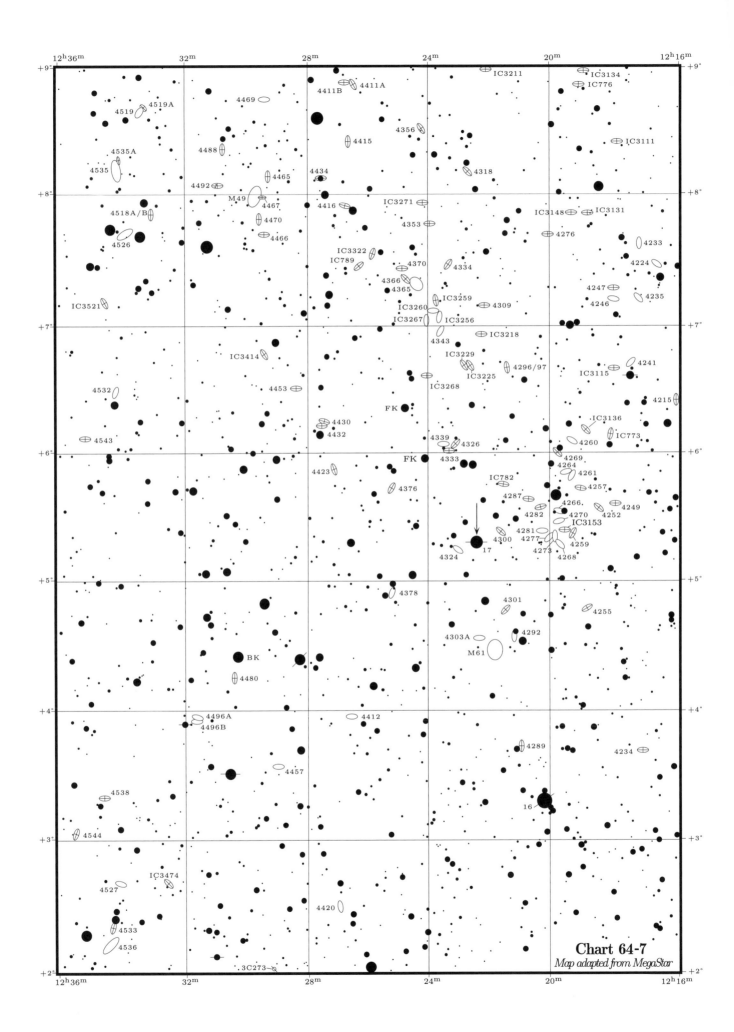

Chart 64-7
Map adapted from MegaStar

Table 64-3: Data for galaxies not reviewed in Chart 64-7

Name	Herschel No.	Type	Size(')	Mag.(v)	SB	P.A.°	R.A. (2000) Dec.
NGC 4215	H135[2]	SA(r)0+:sp	1.5 x 0.6	12.1	11.8	174	12^{h}15.9^m +06° 24′
NGC 4234		(R′)SB(s)m IV	1.1 x 1.0	12.7	12.6		17.2 +03 41
IC 3111		S	0.4 x 0.2	14.0		25	17.8 +08 26
IC 3115		SB(s)cd	1.7 x 1.4	12.1		132	18.0 +06 39
NGC 4247		(R)SAB(s)ab pec?	1.1 x 0.9	13.5	13.3	48	18.0 +07 16
IC 773		SB0+?	0.8 x 0.8	13.5	12.9	0	18.1 +06 08
NGC 4252		Sb? sp	1.1 x 0.3	14.0	12.7	48	18.5 +05 34
IC 3131		S0/a	0.7 x 0.7	13.4	12.5		18.8 +07 51
IC 3134		S	0.7 x 0.3	14.0		164	18.9 +08 58
NGC 4255		SB(r)0°	1.2 x 0.6	12.8	12.3	115	19.0 +04 48
IC 3136		SBc?	0.9 x 0.2	14.2	12.2	32	19.0 +06 11
IC 776		Sdm	1.9 x 1.0	13.8	14.3	98	19.0 +08 51
NGC 4257		Sab: sp	0.9 x 0.2	14.0	12.0	78	19.1 +05 44
IC 3148		SB?	0.9 x 0.9	14.0	13.6		19.3 +07 52
NGC 4259		S0	0.9 x 0.3	13.6	12.0	143	19.4 +05 23
IC 3153		Sc(r)I-II	0.5 x 0.5	13.7			19.6 +05 23
NGC 4276	H166[2]	SB?	1.6 x 1.6	12.4	13.3	3	20.2 +07 42
NGC 4282		S0?	0.7 x 0.5	13.9	12.6	105	20.4 +05 35
NGC 4287		S (edge on)	1.1 x 0.2	13.9	12.1	72	20.8 +05 39
NGC 4289		SA(s)cd: sp	3.9 x 0.3	13.8	13.8	1	21.0 +03 43
NGC 4296	H92[3]	S0	1.5 x 0.9	12.7	11.5	15	21.5 +06 40
NGC 4297	H93[3]	S0	0.5 x 0.2	14.2	12.8	168	21.5 +06 40
NGC 4301		SA(r)0/a: sp	1.2 x 0.4	13.6	12.7	132	21.6 +04 47
NGC 4300	H572[2]	Sa	1.4 x 0.6	12.9	12.6	42	21.7 +05 23
IC 3211		Sb	1.0 x 0.8	14.5	14.1		22.1 +09 00
IC 3218		E?	0.7 x 0.7	14.2	13.3		22.2 +06 55
NGC 4309		SAB(r)0+	1.6 x 0.9	12.7	12.9	85	22.2 +07 09
IC 3225		Sbm:	1.6 x 0.7	14.0	13.9	40	22.6 +06 41
IC 3229		Sbc	1.0 x 0.3	14.4	13.0	47	22.7 +06 41
NGC 4318		E?	0.8 x 0.6	13.3	12.4	65	22.7 +08 12
NGC 4326	H141[2]	SAB(r)ab:	1.6 x 1.0	13.3	13.7	145	23.2 +06 04
NGC 4333	H142[2]	SB(s)ab	0.9 x 0.7	13.6	12.9	171	23.4 +06 02
NGC 4334		SB(s)ab	2.3 x 1.1	13.0	13.8	135	23.4 +07 28
IC 3259		SAB(s)dm?	1.6 x 0.8	13.5	13.6	15	23.8 +07 11
NGC 4353		IBm:	1.1 x 0.7	13.6	13.2	65	24.0 +07 47
IC 3268		Pec	0.6 x 0.6	13.3	12.0	48	24.1 +06 36
IC 3271		SABc°	1.0 x 1.0	13.8	13.7		24.2 +07 57
NGC 4356	H481[3]	Scd:	2.8 x 0.5	13.3	13.5	40	24.3 +08 33
NGC 4370	H144[2]	Sa	1.4 x 0.7	12.6	12.4	83	24.9 +07 27
NGC 4366	H97[3]	E	0.8 x 0.4	14.0	12.6	51	25.0 +07 27
NGC 4376	H530[2]	Im	1.5 x 0.8	13.4	13.4	157	25.3 +04 56
IC 3322		SAB(s)cd: sp	2.2 x 0.5	13.5	13.4	156	25.9 +07 33
IC 789		S0?	1.0 x 0.5	13.9	13.0	140	26.3 +07 27
NGC 4411A		SB(rs)c	2.1 x 2.0	12.7	14.1	30	26.5 +08 53
NGC 4415	H482[3]	S0/a	1.3 x 1.1	12.1	12.3	0	26.6 +08 25
NGC 4416		SB(rs)cd:	1.6 x 1.5	12.4	13.2	108	26.8 +07 56
NGC 4411B		SAB(s)cd	2.9 x 2.9	12.3	14.5		26.8 +08 54
NGC 4423	H145[2]	Sdm:	2.0 x 0.3	13.5	12.8	18	27.1 +05 52
NGC 4430	H146[2]	SB(rs)b:	2.7 x 2.1	12.0	13.7	80	27.4 +06 15
NGC 4434	H497[2]	E	1.3 x 1.3	12.2	12.6		27.5 +08 09
NGC 4432		Sbc	0.9 x 0.6	14.0		6	27.6 +06 14
NGC 4453	H26[2]	S?	0.6 x 0.2	14.8	12.3	153	28.7 +06 30
IC 3414		SABdm?	1.6 x 0.9	13.4	13.7	35	29.4 +06 46
NGC 4466		Sab? sp	1.1 x 0.3	13.5	12.2	101	29.5 +07 42
NGC 4467		E2	0.3 x 0.3	13.8	11.1		29.5 +08 00
NGC 4470	H18[2]	Sa?	1.3 x 0.8	12.1	12.0	0	29.6 +07 49
NGC 4480	H531[2]	SAB(s)c	2.3 x 1.1	12.4	13.3	175	30.4 +04 15
NGC 4488	H484[3]	SB(s)0/a pec:	4.2 x 1.3	12.2	13.9	5	30.9 +08 22
NGC 4492	H499[2]	SA(s)a?	1.9 x 1.9	12.6	13.8	90	31.0 +08 05
IC 3474		Sd sp	2.0 x 0.2	14.2	13.0	36	32.6 +02 40
NGC 4518B			0.9 x 0.3	14.1	12.5	36	33.1 +07 50
NGC 4518A		SB0(r)/a	1.0 x 0.4	13.7	12.6	177	33.2 +07 51
NGC 4519A	H158[2]	SB(r)d II-III	0.6 x 0.2	14.3	11.8	145	33.4 +08 40
NGC 4535A		SAB(s)c I-II	7.1 x 5.0	10.0	13.7	0	34.2 +08 17

See Symbols Under Chart 64-8

Table 64-3: Data for galaxies not reviewed in Chart 64-7 (continued)									
Name	Herschel No.	Type	Size(')	Mag.(v)	SB	P.A°		R.A. (2000) Dec.	
NGC 4535	H500²	SAB(s)c I-II	7.1 x 6.4	10.0	14.0	0	12ʰ34.3ᵐ	+08 12	
NGC 4533		Sab? sp	2.3 x 0.3	13.8	13.2	161	34.4	+02 20	
IC 3521		IBm	1.1 x 0.8	13.2	13.3	27	34.6	+07 09	
NGC 4538		S?	0.5 x 0.2	14.3	12.8	81	34.7	+03 20	
NGC 4543		E3	0.6 x 0.4	13.5	13.0	9	35.4	+06 07	
NGC 4544		SB0/a? sp	2.2 x 0.7	13.0	13.3	161	35.6	+03 02	

16/18″Scopes–150x: Messier 61 is an impressive sight! Two spiral arms are just visible in a 4.5′ × 4′ halo that envelopes a well concentrated but diffuse bar-like core. One spiral arm is attached to the north end of the bar and arcs east and south: a conspicuous dark streak is to the east of the bar between it and this arm. The other spiral arms springs from the south end of the bar and curves west and then north, but fades out at about half the length of the other arm. A bright patch on the NNE edge of the arm near the springing of the other arm is in fact the stub of a third spiral feature. The arms are mottled and unevenly bright. A 14th magnitude star is superimposed upon the halo near its west edge about 1′ from the galaxy's center. A second 14th magnitude star is 2.5′ SW of the center. 10′ to the NE of M61 is NGC 4303A, a faint 1′ diameter glow with a very faint stellar nucleus. A 15th magnitude star lies 45″ WNW of this small galaxy's center, and a 13th magnitude star is 2.5′ to its west. Galaxy NGC 4292 lies 12′ due west of NGC 4303A.

NGC 4307 Galaxy Type Sb II-III
ϕ **3.2′ × 0.7′, m12.0v, SB 12.7**   12ʰ22.1ᵐ +09° 02′
Finder Charts 64-4, 64-6   ★★★
12/14″Scopes–125x: NGC 4307 is a faint, thin, lens-shaped edge-on galaxy elongated 2.5′ × 0.5′ NNE–SSW and containing a slight brightening through its center. Its SSW tip points to the center of a 1.75′ wide triangle of 14th magnitude stars located 2′ from the galaxy's center.

NGC 4313 H63² Galaxy Type SA(rs)ab: sp
ϕ **3.2′ × 0.8′, m11.6v, SB 12.5**   12ʰ22.6ᵐ +04° 48′
Finder Chart 64-6, Figure 64-10   ★★★
12/14″Scopes–125x: NGC 4313 is a fairly faint, thin 3′ × 0.5′ NW–SE streak containing a conspicuous stellar nucleus. A threshold star is on the halo's SE tip. A 13th magnitude star lies 3′ NNE, and a wide pair of 14th magnitude stars is 2′ NNW, of the galaxy's center.

NGC 4324 Galaxy Type SA(r)0+
ϕ **2.1′ × 1.0′, m11.6v, SB 12.3**   12ʰ23.1ᵐ +05° 15′
Finder Charts 64-5, 64-7   ★★★
12/14″Scopes–125x: NGC 4324 is located 9′ ESE of 17 Virginis, a double with a 6.6 magnitude yellow primary and a 9.4 magnitude orangish companion 20″ distant in position angle 337°. The galaxy is a fairly faint, lens-shaped 2.25′ × 1′ NE–SW object that contains a broad oval core with a stellar nucleus.

NGC 4339 H143² Galaxy Type E0
ϕ **2.0′ × 2.0′, m11.3v, SB 12.7**   12ʰ23.6ᵐ +06° 05′
Finder Charts 64-6, 64-7   ★★★
12/14″Scopes–125x: NGC 4339, centered 1.5′ north of an 11th magnitude star, has a fairly bright, round 1.5′ diameter halo that gradually brightens in toward its center but lacks a core or a nucleus.

NGC 4343 H94³ Galaxy Type SA(rs)b: III
ϕ **2.4′ × 0.7′, m12.1v, SB 12.5**   12ʰ23.7ᵐ +06° 57′
Finder Charts 64-6, 64-7   ★★★
12/14″Scopes–125x: NGC 4343 is a moderately faint, diffuse 1.5′ × 0.75′ NW–SE oval of even surface brightness except for a conspicuous stellar nucleus. 13th magnitude stars are 4.5′ east and 6.5′ ENE. Galaxy IC 3256 lies 6′ north.

IC 3256 (NGC 4342) H96³ Galaxy Type S0
ϕ **0.9′ × 0.4′, m12.5v, SB 11.2**   12ʰ23.7ᵐ +07° 03′

IC 3260 Galaxy Type SAB(s)0°
ϕ **1.6′ × 0.5′, m13.2v, SB 12.8**   12ʰ23.9ᵐ +07° 06′
Finder Charts 64-6, 64-7   ★★/★
16/18″Scopes–150x: IC 3256 is the most conspicuous of four IC objects located SSW of NGC 4365 and NNE of NGC 4343. IC 3256, situated 6′ north of NGC 4343, has a very bright stellar nucleus in a distinct but small oval halo elongated 45″ × 20″ NNW–SSE. 5′ NE of IC 3256 is IC 3260, a moderately faint 2′ × 1′ ESE–WNW galaxy containing a slightly

brighter center with a very faint stellar nucleus. IC 3259 and IC 3267, respectively 5′ NNW and 5′ SE of IC 3260, are just visible with averted vision. A curved triplet of 12th magnitude stars lies 8′ NE of IC 3259.

NGC 4348 H625² Galaxy Type Sc: sp II-III
ϕ 2.8′ × 0.6′, m12.5v, SB12.9 $12^h23.9^m$ −03° 27′
Finder Charts 64-3, 64-5   ★★

12/14″ Scopes-125x: NGC 4348 is centered 3′ north of an 11th magnitude star and 1′ east of a 12.5 magnitude star. It is a faint 2′ × 0.5′ NE–SW streak containing an extended, poorly concentrated core with a stellar nucleus. A 12th magnitude star is 7′ NW of the galaxy

NGC 4351 Galaxy Type SB(rs)ab pec:
ϕ 1.7′ × 1.3′, m12.6v, SB13.3 $12^h24.0^m$ +12° 12′
Finder Charts 64-6, 64-8   ★★

12/14″ Scopes-125x: NGC 4351 is a rather faint galaxy elongated 1.0′ × 0.5′ ENE–WSW and containing a broad central brightening. 12.5 magnitude stars lie 4.25′ NNE, 2′ NNW, and 4.25′ ENE of the galaxy's center.

NGC 4365 H30¹ Galaxy Type E3
ϕ 5.6′ × 4.6′, m9.6v, SB12.9 $12^h24.5^m$ +07° 19′
Finder Charts 64-6, 64-7   ★★★★

12/14″ Scopes-125x: NGC 4365 has a fairly bright 3′ × 2′ NE–SW halo, the surface brightness of which increases smoothly to a conspicuous core with a stellar nucleus. A 13th magnitude star lies 3.5′ NW of the galaxy's center. 5′ to the NE of NGC 4365 is its companion, NGC 4366, a small, faint glow containing a weak stellar nucleus. A more distant companion, NGC 4370, located 10′ NE, is a small, faint, diffuse oval.

NGC 4371 H22¹ Galaxy Type SB(r)0+
ϕ 4.6′ × 2.2′, m10.8v, SB13.2 $12^h24.9^m$ +11° 42′
Finder Charts 64-6, 64-8   ★★★★

8/10″ Scopes-100x: NGC 4371 has a fairly bright circular 1.5′ halo that contains a stellar nucleus. A 12th magnitude star is 3′ north of the galaxy's center.
16/18″ Scopes-150x: This galaxy shows a bright stellar nucleus embedded in a circular 2.5′ diameter halo. A threshold star lies on the halo's SE edge, and a 13th magnitude star lies 4′ SE of the galaxy's center.

NGC 4374 Messier 84 Galaxy Type E1
ϕ 5.1′ × 4.1′, m9.1v, SB12.3 $12^h25.1^m$ +12° 53′
Finder Charts 64-6, 64-8, Figure 64-12   ★★★★★

Messier 84 is the beginning of the Markarian Chain of galaxies that runs from M84 first east and then NE to Messier 88 in Coma Berenices. Messier 84 and 86 were both discovered on March 18, 1781 by Charles Messier.

M84 is a giant elliptical member of the Coma-Virgo Supercluster. It and the other giant ellipticals and spirals in this area along the Virgo-Coma Berenices border are at the very core of the Supercluster. If M84 is 65 million light years away, the best recent estimate to the center of the Coma-Virgo Supergalaxy, its absolute magnitude is −22.4, a very impressive luminosity of 76 billion suns, and its true diameter is over – probably well over – 100,000 light years.

4/6″ Scopes-75x: Messier 84 forms a 17′ equilateral triangle with Messier 86 to its ENE and NGC 4388 to its SE. This giant elliptical has a bright, uniform, circular 2′ diameter halo which fades smoothly to a diffuse periphery. M84 is a little brighter but somewhat smaller than its near-twin M86.
8/10″ Scopes-100x: This galaxy has a bright, slightly oval 2.5′ × 2′ NW–SE halo that contains a bright, broadly concentrated core.
12/14″ Scopes-125x: M84 displays a bright 4′ × 3′ NW–SE oval halo that brightens smoothly toward its center and an intense nonstellar nucleus. A 14th magnitude star is on the edge of the halo WSW of the galaxy's center. A wide pair of 15th magnitude stars is 2.5′ NW.

NGC 4378 H123¹ Galaxy Type Sc: sp II-III
ϕ 3.0′ × 2.8′, m11.7v, SB13.8 $12^h25.3^m$ +04° 55′
Finder Charts 64-6, 64-7   ★★★

12/14″ Scopes-125x: NGC 4378 forms a triangle with 9th magnitude stars 4′ to its north and 3.5′ to its SE. Many other stars are sprinkled around the galaxy, including a 12.5 magnitude star 2′ NNW, a 12th magnitude star 2.75′ east, and an 11.5 magnitude star 4.5′ SSW. NGC 4378 has a moderately bright 1.75′ × 1′ NNW–SSE halo that contains a broad, well concentrated core in which is embedded an inconspicuous stellar nucleus.

NGC 4380 Galaxy Type SA(rs)b:?
ϕ 3.2′ × 2.0′, m11.7v, SB13.5 $12^h25.4^m$ +10° 01′
Finder Charts 64-6, 64-8   ★★★

12/14″ Scopes-125x: NGC 4380 is faint but not difficult. Its 2′ × 1′ NNW–SSE halo contains a faint oval core. A 13th magnitude star lies 2.5′ south of the galaxy's center.

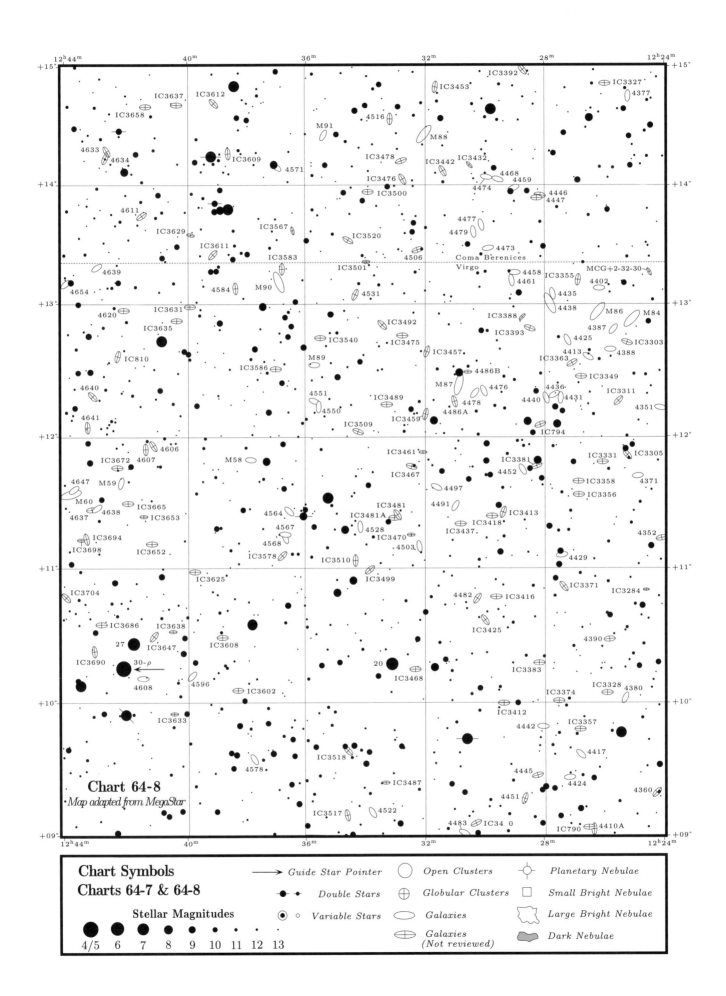

Chart 64-8
· Map adapted from MegaStar

Chart Symbols
Charts 64-7 & 64-8

Stellar Magnitudes

4/5   6   7   8   9   10   11   12   13

→ Guide Star Pointer
●—● Double Stars
◉ ○ Variable Stars

○ Open Clusters
⊕ Globular Clusters
⬭ Galaxies
⊖ Galaxies
(Not reviewed)

⊕ Planetary Nebulae
□ Small Bright Nebulae
⬡ Large Bright Nebulae
▨ Dark Nebulae

Table 64-4: Data for galaxies not reviewed in Chart 64-8

Name	Herschel No.	Type	Size(')	Mag.(v)	SB	P.A.°	R.A. (2000) Dec.
NGC 4352	H64[2]	SA0	2.0 x 1.0	12.6	13.2	102	12ʰ24.1ᵐ +11° 13′
NGC 4360		E	1.4 x 1.1	13. p		145	24.3 +09 17
MCG+2–32–30		SA(r)bc	0.8 x 0.6	14.0	13.1		24.4 +13 14
IC 3284		SBR	0.5 x 0.5	14.3			24.6 +10 49
IC 3303		E+?	1.1 x 0.7	13.8	13.4	73	25.2 +12 43
IC 3305		S?	1.0 x 0.4	14.1	13.0	44	25.2 +11 50
IC 3311		Sdm:	1.9 x 0.3	14.4	13.6	135	25.5 +12 15
NGC 4390	H39[3]	SAB(s)c:	1.6 x 1.3	12.6	13.2	95	25.8 +10 27
IC 3328		E?	0.7 x 0.7	13.7	12.7		25.9 +10 03
IC 3331		S?	0.8 x 0.4	14.3	12.9	53	26.0 +11 48
NGC 4410AB		Sab? Pec	1.3 x 0.8	13.6			26.4 +09 01
IC 790		S0?	0.6 x 0.4	14.5	12.8	96	26.5 +09 01
IC 3349		E?	0.9 x 0.8	13.8	13.3		26.7 +12 27
IC 3355		Im IV-V	1.2 x 0.5	14.9	14.2	172	26.8 +13 11
IC 3356		Im	1.5 x 1.0	14.7	15.0		26.8 +11 34
IC 3357		S	0.4 x 0.1	15.4		160	26.8 +09 45
IC 3358		E?	1.1 x 0.9	13.3	13.1		26.9 +11 39
IC 3363		E?	1.3 x 0.4	14.3	13.5	130	27.0 +12 33
IC 3371		Scd:	1.9 x 0.2	14.0		55	27.3 +10 52
IC 3374		I?	1.0 x 0.5	14.2	13.3		27.5 +09 59
IC 794		E+:	1.4 x 1.0	13.1	13.3	110	28.1 +12 06
IC 3383		E	0.7 x 0.5	14.5		28	28.2 +10 17
NGC 4445		Sab:sp	2.4 x 0.4	12.8	12.6	106	28.3 +09 26
IC 3381		E+:	1.3 x 1.0	13.4	13.6	110	28.3 +11 47
IC 3388		E?	0.6 x 0.3	14.4	12.3	68	28.4 +12 49
NGC 4451		Sbc:	1.4 x 0.9	12.5	12.6	162	28.7 +09 16
IC 3393		S0+:	0.9 x 0.3	13.8	12.3	130	28.7 +12 55
IC 3412		I?	1.0 x 0.4	14.3	13.2	21	29.3 +09 59
IC 3413		E?	1.1 x 0.7	13.7	13.3	160	29.4 +11 26
IC 3416		I?	1.0 x 0.3	14.2	10.2	60	29.6 +10 47
IC 3418		IBm: V	1.4 x 0.9	13.0	13.1	50	29.7 +11 24
IC 3425		S0?	1.9 x 0.8	13.6	13.9	35	29.9 +10 36
IC 3430		I	1.1 x 0.3	14.3	12.9	115	30.2 +09 04
NGC 4482	H40[3]	E	1.7 x 1.0	12.7	13.1	145	30.2 +10 47
NGC 4486B		cE0	0.3 x 0.3	13.3	10.6		30.6 +12 30
IC 3437		E?	0.9 x 0.4	14.3	13.1	73	30.8 +11 20
NGC 4486A		E2	1.0 x 0.9	11.6	11.3	15	31.0 +12 17
IC 3459		Im:	1.1 x 1.0	14.3	14.3	155	31.9 +12 10
IC 3457		E3:	1.0 x 0.7	13.7	13.2	155	31.9 +12 39
IC 3468			1.4 x 1.3	13.6	13.0		32.3 +10 14
IC 3467		Sc	1.1 x 1.0	15.3		72	32.3 +11 47
IC 3470		E?	0.7 x 0.7	13.3	12.4		32.4 +11 15
IC 3475		E:	2.5 x 2.3	13.1	14.9	86	32.7 +12 46
IC 3481		SAB0: pec	0.6 x 0.4	13.3	11.6	41	32.9 +11 24
IC 3481A		E pec:	0.2 x 0.2	13.6	10.0		33.0 +11 24
IC 3487		E6:	0.8 x 0.4	14.0	12.6	79	33.2 +09 24
IC 3489		SA(r)bc	0.7 x 0.6	14.2			33.2 +12 14
IC 3492		S0?	0.3 x 0.3	14.5	11.7		33.2 +12 51
IC 3499		S0/a	1.5 x 0.6	13.3	13.0	125	33.7 +10 59
IC 3510		S?	1.0 x 0.7	13.9	13.3	0	34.3 +11 04
IC 3509		E	0.9 x 0.6	13.9	13.1	66	34.3 +12 04
NGC 4531	H175[2]	SB0+:	3.5 x 2.4	11.4	13.6	155	34.3 +13 05
IC 3517		Sdm:	1.4 x 0.8	14.9	14.9	15	34.5 +09 09
IC 3518		Im:	1.3 x 0.8	14.3		31	34.5 +09 37
IC 3578		Scd:	0.9 x 0.5	14.6	13.5	131	36.6 +11 06
IC 3540		S0?	0.5 x 0.4	13.9	12.0		35.4 +12 45
IC 3583		IBm	2.3 x 1.4	12.8	13.9	0	36.7 +13 15
IC 3586		dS0:	0.7 x 0.6	13.6	12.5		36.9 +12 32
IC 3602		E	0.9 x 0.3	14.3	12.7	135	38.1 +10 05
NGC 4584		SAB(s)a?	1.4 x 1.0	12.9	13.1	5	38.3 +13 07

Table 64-4: Data for galaxies not reviewed in Chart 64-8 (continued)

Name	Herschel No.	Type	Size(')	Mag.(v)	SB	P.A°	R.A. (2000)	Dec.
IC 3608		Sb: III-IV	3.2 x 0.4	13.8	13.9	95	12ʰ38.6ᵐ	+10° 29'
IC 3625		L	0.2 x 0.2	14.5			39.6	+10 59
IC 3631		S?	1.0 x 0.7	13.5		90	39.8	+12 59
IC 3633		E	0.5 x 0.4	14.2	12.3	120	40.2	+09 53
IC 3635		Scd?	1.1 x 1.0	14.3	14.3	168	40.2	+12 53
IC 3647		Im:	1.6 x 1.0	14.0	14.4	140	40.9	+10 28
IC 3652		E	1.0 x 1.0	14.1			41.0	+11 11
NGC 4606	H43³	SB(s)a:	2.6 x 1.5	11.8	13.2	33	41.0	+11 55
IC 3653		E?	0.6 x 0.5	13.8	12.3		41.2	+11 24
NGC 4607		SBb? sp	2.9 x 0.7	12.8	13.4	2	41.2	+11 53
IC 3665		Im:	0.9 x 0.6	14.6	13.7	90	41.8	+11 30
NGC 4620		S0	1.8 x 1.7	12.2	13.3	70	42.0	+12 57
IC 3672		E	1.1 x 1.1	13.5	13.6		42.1	+11 45
IC 810		S0?	1.6 x 0.6	13.4	13.2	166	42.1	+12 36
IC 3686		Sc(s)II	1.5 x 0.3	14.6		171	42.6	+10 34
IC 3690		S?	1.2 x 0.3	14.2	12.9	6	42.8	+10 22
NGC 4637		S0?	1.1 x 0.6	14.0	13.4	97	42.9	+11 26
IC 3694		S?	0.8 x 0.5	14.2	13.1	30	43.1	+11 13
NGC 4640		SB?	1.5 x 1.0	13.4	13.7	45	43.0	+12 18
NGC 4641		S0	1.3 x 0.9	13.2	13.3	15	43.2	+12 03
IC 3698		S?	0.6 x 0.6	14.4	13.1		43.3	+11 13
IC 3704		Sbc	1.2 x 0.3	14.0	12.8	43	43.7	+10 47

NGC 4387 H167² Galaxy Type E
φ 1.5′ × 0.9′, m12.1v, SB 12.3   12ʰ25.7ᵐ +12° 49′
Finder Charts 64-6, 64-8, Figure 64-12   ★★★
12/14″Scopes–125x: NGC 4387, at the center of a
    triangle formed by Messier 84, Messier 86, and NGC
    4388, is outclassed by its larger neighbors and often
    ignored. It has a moderately faint 1.75′ × 0.75′ NW–
    SE halo that contains a smooth, broadly concen-
    trated center with a faint nonstellar nucleus. A 13th
    magnitude star is 1.5′ NNW, and a 15th magnitude
    star is just visible 45″ SSE, of the galaxy's center.

NGC 4388 H168² Galaxy Type SA(s)b: sp II-III
φ 5.7′ × 1.6′, m11.0v, SB 13.3   12ʰ25.8ᵐ +12° 40′
Finder Charts 64-6, 64-8, Figure 64-12   ★★★★
4/6″Scopes–75x: NGC 4388 is at the south corner of
    an equilateral triangle with Messier 84 and Messier
    86. It is an edge-on spiral, and therefore its thin
    streak is a striking contrast to the fuzzy circularity
    of its two giant elliptical neighbors. Its faint enve-
    lope is much elongated 3′ × 0.5′ E–W and contains
    an extended, slightly brighter core.
8/10″Scopes–100x: This fine edge-on galaxy is fairly
    bright and elongated 4′ × 0.75′ E–W, and contains
    a bulging central core with a faint stellar nucleus.
    The core is quite extended and displaced south and
    west of the galaxy's center.
16/18″Scopes–150x: In larger telescopes the halo can

be traced out to dimensions of 4.5′ × 1′ E–W, the
eastern wing more elongated than the western and
the edge of its northern long side better-defined
than the edge of its southern flank. The highly
extended E–W core bulges quite emphatically to
the south, its northern side obscured by a thin dark
dust lane. A 14th magnitude star is 1.25′ NE, and
a 12th magnitude star 3′ SSE, of the galaxy's center.

NGC 4402 Galaxy Type Sb
φ 3.5′ × 1.0′, m11.8v, SB 13.0   12ʰ26.1ᵐ +13° 07′
Finder Charts 64-6, 64-8, Figure 64-12   ★★★★
8/10″Scopes–100x: NGC 4402, located 9′ north of
    Messier 86, is a faint, evenly concentrated object
    much elongated 3′ × 0.75′ E–W.
16/18″Scopes–150x: NGC 4402 shows some mottling
    but very little central concentration in a fairly
    bright 3.5′ × 0.75′ E–W halo. At 200x the central
    portion is unevenly bright with some dark patches
    along the major axis. A 13th magnitude star lies
    1.25′ north of the galaxy's center.

NGC 4406 Messier 86 Galaxy Type E3
φ 12.0′ × 9.3′, m8.9v, SB 13.9   12ʰ26.2ᵐ +12° 57′
Finder Charts 64-6, 64-8, Figure 64-12   ★★★★★
    Messier 86 and Messier 84 were both discovered by
Messier on March 18, 1781. This bright pair of galaxies
lies in the direction of the gravitational center of the
Coma-Virgo Supercluster. However, M86 has a blue-

Figure 64-12. *Messier 84 (NGC 4374) and Messier 86 (NGC 4406), the two bright elliptical galaxies at left, form an impressive galaxy triangle with the edge-on spiral NGC 4388 at upper left. NGC 4387 lies at triangle's center forming a 3-bladed propeller . Image courtesy of Tim Hunter and James McGaha.*

shift rather than a red-shift (which means that it is approaching rather than receding from us) and therefore is probably closer to us than M84.

Assuming that it is 50 million light years from us rather than the 65 million light years to the center of the Supercluster, its absolute magnitude is -22.1, a luminosity of 57 billion suns, and its true diameter at least (and probably well over) 175,000 light years. If M84 and M86 were both 65 million light years away, they would be only about 300,000 light years apart – which is very unlikely since giant ellipticals are solitary systems. Supergiant ellipticals, which have absolute magnitudes around -24, are probably the result of the merging of one of more giant ellipticals that got too near each other.

4/6″ Scopes–75x: Messier 86 appears similar to Messier 84 lying 17′ to the west, but is clearly more extended, being elongated 2′×1.5′ NW–SE. Its halo has a broad central brightening.

8/10″ Scopes–100x: The halo of Messier 86 is noticeably larger and more extended than that of Messier 84, measuring 3.5′×3′ NW–SE, but has the same smooth texture and broad central concentration. The diffuse periphery fades smoothly outward until it can be traced only with averted vision.

16/18″ Scopes–150x: In larger telescopes M86 shows a 5′×3′ oval halo that smoothly brightens to a small, sharp core at its center. A very faint galactic knot or foreground star is on the NNE edge. 14th magnitude stars are 2′ NE and 3′ south, and a 13th magnitude star is 4′ SE of the galaxy's center.

NGC 4413 H169² Galaxy Type (R′)SB(rs)ab:
φ 2.2′×1.6′, m12.2v, SB13.5   12ʰ26.5ᵐ +12° 37′
Finder Charts 64-6, 64-8   ★★
12/14″ Scopes–125x: NGC 4413 is 10′ ESE of NGC 4388 and centered 3′ south of a 10.5 magnitude star and 1.25′ south of an 11.5 magnitude star. Its faint 1.75′×1′ NE–SW halo contains a broadly concentrated center with a faint nonstellar nucleus. 2′ south of the galaxy's center is a 50″ wide NW–SE pair of magnitude 12.5 stars, and a similar double is 5′ SE of the galaxy.

NGC 4412 H34² Galaxy Type SB(r)b? pec II
φ 1.5′×1.3′, m12.4v, SB12.9   12ʰ26.6ᵐ +03° 58′
Finder Charts 64-5, 64-7   ★★
12/14″ Scopes–125x: NGC 4412, located 16′ SE of a 7th

magnitude star, is a moderately faint, circular 1′ diameter glow containing a slight central concentration. The galaxy forms a right triangle with a 12th magnitude star 7′ to its NW and an 11th magnitude star 6.5′ to its SW. 13th magnitude stars are 3′ ESE and 2.5′ north of the galaxy.

NGC 4417 H155² Galaxy Type SB: sp
φ 3.2′ × 1.3′, m11.1v, SB 12.5   12ʰ26.8ᵐ +09° 35′
Finder Charts 64-6, 64-8, Figure 64-13   ★★★
8/10″Scopes–100x: NGC 4417, located 19′ SE of an 8th magnitude star, appears fairly bright, is elongated 1.5′ × 0.5′ NE–SW, and contains a stellar nucleus. Galaxy NGC 4424 lies 11′ SSE.

16/18″Scopes–150x: This galaxy has a highly elongated 2′ × 0.75′ NE–SW halo that contains a central bulge. The bulge is bright but small, and has a granular texture and a stellar nucleus. A 13th magnitude star lies 1.5′ west of the center of the galaxy.

NGC 4420 H23² Galaxy Type SB(r)bc: III-IV
φ 2.0′ × 0.9′, m12.1v, SB 12.6   12ʰ27.0ᵐ +02° 30′
Finder Charts 64-5, 64-7   ★★★
12/14″Scopes–125x: NGC 4420 forms a triangle with 9th magnitude stars 5′ to its SW and 10′ to its north. It has a sharply concentrated nonstellar nucleus embedded in a faint 1.75′ × 0.75′ N–S halo.

NGC 4424 Galaxy Type SB(s)a:
φ 3.3′ × 1.8′, m11.7v, SB 13.4   12ʰ27.2ᵐ +09° 25′
Finder Charts 64-6, 64-8, Figure 64-13   ★★★
8/10″Scopes–100x: NGC 4424, located 11′ SSE of NGC 4417, has a faint, diffuse evenly illuminated 1.5′ × 0.5′ E–W halo. An 11.5 magnitude star lies 2.5′ NNW of the galaxy's center, and a 12.5 magnitude star is 2.5′ NNE, about 1.25′ east of the other star.

16/18″Scopes–150x: NGC 4424 appears slightly larger but fainter than its companion NGC 4417. It has a fairly faint, diffuse 2′ × 0.75′ E–W halo elongated to rounded ends. The core is poorly concentrated and extended 30″ × 15″. The eastern extension is larger.

NGC 4425 H170² Galaxy Type SB0+: sp
φ 2.7′ × 0.8′, m11.8v, SB 12.5   12ʰ27.2ᵐ +12° 44′
Finder Charts 64-6, 64-8, Figure 64-12   ★★★
8/10″Scopes–100x: NGC 4425, located 19′ SE of Messier 86, is a well-defined, thin 1.25′ × 0.5′ NNE–SSW lens containing a bright, thin center. The galaxy lies 4.5′ WSW of a 10th magnitude star.

16/18″Scopes–150x: This galaxy lies SE of a 3.5′ long arc of 13th and 14th magnitude stars, the arc's

center star just 1.25′ west of the galaxy's center. NGC 4425 is a bright 1.75′ × 0.75′ lens oriented towards position angle 25° and containing a highly extended core with a very faint stellar nucleus. A 12.5 magnitude star lies 4.5′ east.

NGC 4429 H65² Galaxy Type SA(r)0+
φ 5.6′ × 2.6′, m10.0v, SB 12.8   12ʰ27.4ᵐ +11° 07′
Finder Charts 64-6, 64-8   ★★★★
8/10″Scopes–100x: NGC 4429 is between an 8′ wide N–S pair of 9th magnitude stars, centered just 2′ SSW of the northern of the two stars. Its small bright core is embedded in a 2.5′ × 1′ E–W nebulous haze.

16/18″Scopes–150x: NGC 4429 has a 3.5′ × 1.5′ E–W oval halo containing a conspicuous 1′ × 0.5′ E–W core with a nonstellar nucleus. A 13th magnitude star 3.75′ ESE of the galaxy's center forms an isosceles triangle with two magnitude 14.5 stars near the halo's ESE tip.

NGC 4428 Galaxy Type Sb: pec II?
φ 1.7′ × 0.8′, m12.6v, SB 12.8   12ʰ27.5ᵐ −08° 10′

NGC 4433 Galaxy Type SB?(s:)b I-II
φ 2.3′ × 1.1′, m12.7v, SB 13.6   12ʰ27.6ᵐ −08° 17′
Finder Chart 64-9   ★★/★★
12/14″Scopes–125x: NGC 4428 and NGC 4433 are a 7′ wide N–S pair of galaxies 25′ north of a 7th magnitude star. The northern galaxy, NGC 4428, has a poorly concentrated 2′ × 1′ E–W halo that contains a very faint stellar nucleus. The southern system, NGC 4433, is a little longer, reaching 2.5′ × 1′ N–S, and has a faint oval core that extends for a little more than half the length of the major axis. A magnitude 13.5 star lies on the northern tip of NGC 4433, and a 13th magnitude star is west of its southern tip.

NGC 4431 H171² Galaxy Type SA(r)0
φ 1.7′ × 1.0′, m12.9v, SB 13.3   12ʰ27.5ᵐ +12° 18′

NGC 4436 H172² Galaxy Type S0
φ 1.6′ × 0.8′, m13.0v, SB 13.1   12ʰ27.7ᵐ +12° 19′

NGC 4440 H173² Galaxy Type SB(rs)a
φ 1.6′ × 1.5′, m11.7v, SB 12.5   12ʰ27.9ᵐ +12° 18′
Finder Chart 64-8   ★★/★/★★★
12/14″Scopes–125x: The galaxy-trio NGC 4431, NGC 4436, and NGC 4440, is on the NNW edge of an 18′ × 14′ pentagon of 8th and 9th magnitude stars. NGC 4440, the brightest of the three, has a fairly bright, circular 1′ diameter halo that contains a small bright ESE–WNW core. 2′ WNW of NGC 4440 is

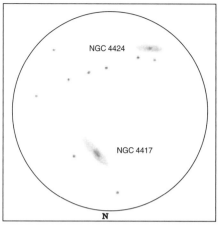

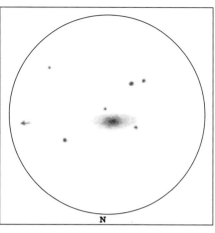

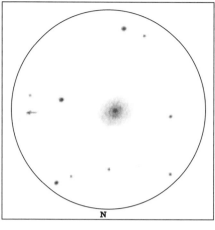

Figure 64-13. NGC 4417 and NGC 4424
20″, f5–175x, by Richard W. Jakiel

Figure 64-14. NGC 4442
12.5″, f5–250x, by G. R. Kepple

Figure 64-15. NGC 4457
17.5″, f4.5–250x, by G. R. Kepple

NGC 4436, a faint 30″ diameter unconcentrated haze slightly elongated ESE–WNW. A 12th magnitude star is 1′ NW of its core. 6.5′ west of NGC 4440 is NGC 4431, about the same size as the brighter galaxy and with a brighter center, but slightly elongated N–S. One 13th magnitude star is 1.25′ east, and another 2′ north, of the core of NGC 4431.

NGC 4435 H28(1)[1] Galaxy Type SB(s)0°
ϕ 3.2′ × 2.0′, m10.8v, SB 12.7   12^{h}27.7^m +13° 05′

NGC 4438 H28(2)[1] Galaxy Type SA(s)0/a pec:
ϕ 8.9′ × 3.6′, m10.2v, SB 13.8   12^{h}27.8^m +13° 01′
Finder Charts 64-6, 64-8, Figure 64-12   ★★★/★★★
8/10″ Scopes–100x: NGC 4435 and NGC 4438, located 20′ ENE of Messier 86, are a 4.25′ wide NNW–SSE pair of bright galaxies. The northern system, NGC 4435, has a conspicuous stellar nucleus in a smooth 1.25′ × 0.75′ NNE–SSW halo. The southern galaxy of the pair, NGC 4438, is much larger, its halo extending 3′ × 1.5′ NNE–SSW, and has a broad central concentration containing a stellar nucleus.
12/14″ Scopes–125x: In medium-aperture telescopes NGC 4435 has a 1.5′ × 1′ halo and NGC 4438 (with averted vision) a 4′ × 2′ halo. Both contain a distinct stellar nucleus but only NGC 4438 has a faint core. A 14th magnitude star lies west of NGC 4435's southern tip 50″ from the galaxy's center.

NGC 4442 H156[2] Galaxy Type SB(s)0°
ϕ 4.6′ × 1.9′, m10.4v, SB 12.6   12^{h}28.1^m +09° 48′
Finder Charts 64-6, 64-8, Figure 64-14   ★★★
8/10″ Scopes–100x: NGC 4442 has a fairly bright oval core containing a stellar nucleus and surrounded by a much fainter 2′ × 1′ E–W halo.

12/14″ Scopes–125x: The halo is diffuse in its outer portions, but averted vision traces it to 3′ × 1.25′ E–W. The halo's surface brightness rises smoothly to a bright 30″ × 15″ oval core containing a stellar nucleus. A row of 13th and 14th magnitude stars runs past the western edge with one of its stars 1′ SSW of center. A 14th magnitude star lies at the eastern tip 1.5′ from center.

NGC 4452 H23[1] Galaxy Type S0?
ϕ 2.7′ × 0.7′, m12.0v, SB 12.5   12^{h}28.7^m +11° 45′
Finder Charts 64-6, 64-8   ★★★
12/14″ Scopes–125x: NGC 4452, positioned 3′ east of a 9th magnitude star, is a mottled, fairly bright 1.5′ × 0.25′ NE–SW spindle containing an extended core. 7.25′ to its WNW is its companion galaxy IC 3381, a very faint object lying 2.25′ south of a 7.5 magnitude star.

NGC 4454 H180[2] Galaxy Type (R′)SAB(r)0/a
ϕ 2.3′ × 2.0′, m11.9v, SB 13.4   12^{h}28.8^m −01° 56′
Finder Chart 64-5   ★★★
12/14″ Scopes–125x: NGC 4454 is at the eastern corner of the triangle it forms with 10th magnitude stars 5′ to its WSW and 4′ to its NNW. It has a moderately faint, smoothly illuminated halo containing a faint stellar nucleus. A 14th magnitude star lies on the halo's edge 1′ south of the galaxy's center, and another faint star is 3.25′ west.

NGC 4457 H35[2] Galaxy Type (R)SAB(s)0/a II
ϕ 3.1′ × 2.6′, m10.9v, SB 13.0   12^{h}29.0^m +03° 34′
Finder Charts 64-5, 64-7, Figure 64-15   ★★★
8/10″ Scopes–100x: NGC 4457, located 2.5′ ENE of a

Figure 64-16. *Messier 49 (NGC4472) is a large, bright elliptical galaxy with a brilliant nucleus. Image courtesy of Jim Burnell.*

12th magnitude star, has a bright core with a stellar nucleus surrounded by a 1.5′×1′ ENE–WSW halo. A 13th magnitude star lies 2.5′ WSW of the galaxy's center, and two 12th magnitude stars are 5′ to the galaxy's NW and 4′ to its south.

16/18″Scopes–150x: In larger telescopes the halo of NGC 4457, though faint and diffuse, extends to a diameter of 3′. It contains a sharply concentrated central area with a stellar nucleus.

NGC 4458 H121² Galaxy Type E0-1
ϕ 1.5′×1.5′, m12.1v, SB12.8   12^h29.0^m +13° 15′

NGC 4461 H122² Galaxy Type SB(s)0+:
ϕ 3.7′×1.4′, m11.2v, SB12.8   12^h29.0^m +13° 11′
Finder Charts 64-6, 64-8   ★★★/★★★
12/14″Scopes–125x: NGC 4458 and NGC 4461 are an attractive 3.75′ wide NNE–SSW galaxy-pair. The southern system, NGC 4461, has a moderately bright 2′×0.5′ N–S halo with a diffuse periphery and a central region that grows smoothly brighter to a small circular core containing a stellar nucleus. A threshold star lies just west of its northern tip. NGC 4458, the northern galaxy, is the smaller and fainter of the pair, its 1′×0.75′ N–S halo containing a well concentrated core with a stellar nucleus.

3C 273 QSO (Quasi-stellar object) "Quasar"
m12.8p, Redshift (z) 0.158   12^h29.1^m +02° 03′
Finder Charts 64-5, 64-7   ★★
3C273, located 3.5° NE of magnitude 3.9 Eta (η) =

15 Virginis, is the brightest example of a quasar ("quasi-stellar object" = QSO). Quasars are thought to be the most luminous objects in the universe. They are strong radio sources and show enormous red shifts in their spectra. This implies that they lie at distances far beyond the most remote galaxies, and therefore are the most distant and some of the oldest objects astronomers have detected. However there may be other causes for their extreme red shifts that astronomers do not yet understand. Research by Halton Arp suggests that quasars are not as distant as their red shifts imply but are associated with galaxies that have active nuclei, possibly powered by black holes. At this time quasars remain an enigma.

16/18″Scopes–150x: QSO 3C273, located 1.5° west of galaxy NGC 4536, may be found 5.5′ NW of a 10th magnitude star. Look for a 3′ wide E–W double of magnitude 12.8 and 13 components: the quasar is the brighter bluish starlike object to the double's east.

NGC 4469 H157² Galaxy Type SB(s)0/a? sp
ϕ 2.9′×1.0′, m11.2v, SB12.2   12^h29.5^m +08° 45′
Finder Charts 64-6 and 64-7   ★★★
8/10″Scopes–100x: NGC 4469 is a faint 2′×1′ E–W oval with a circular core.

16/18″Scopes–150x: The halo is faint but fairly well-defined and elongated 3′×1′ E–W with sharply tapered ends. The mottled, unevenly illuminated central area contains an irregularly-shaped core. A 13th magnitude star is 2′ ESE, and a threshold star 1.5′ NE, of the galaxy's center.

NGC 4472 Messier 49 Galaxy Type E2
ϕ 8.1′×7.1′, m8.4v, SB12.7   12^h29.8^m +08° 00′
Finder Charts 64-6, 64-7, Figure 64-16   ★★★★★
   Charles Messier discovered the galaxy he catalogued as M49 on February 19, 1771. This giant elliptical is one of the largest and most luminous members of the Coma-Virgo Supercluster. Assuming a distance to it of 65 million light years, its absolute magnitude is −23.1, a brilliance of 145 billion suns, and its true diameter is over 153,000 light years.

4/6″Scopes–75x: This fine elliptical galaxy rivals the more famous Messier 87. It has a very bright, circular 3.5′ diameter halo that contains an intense nucleus. A 12.5 magnitude star is superimposed upon the halo on the core's east edge.

8/10″Scopes–100x: Messier 49 displays a bright core embedded in a 4′ diameter halo which fades smoothly to a diffuse periphery.

16/18″Scopes–150x: In larger telescopes M49 is a splendid object with a bright 5′×4′ NNW-SSE oval halo containing a well defined 1′ diameter core with a brilliant nucleus. The 12.5 magnitude star on the east edge of the core looks like a supernova.

NGC 4476 H123[2] Galaxy Type SA(r)0:
ϕ **1.7′×1.1′, m12.2v, SB12.7**   **12ʰ30.0ᵐ +12° 21′**

NGC 4478 H124[2] Galaxy Type E2
ϕ **1.7′×1.4′, m11.4v, SB12.2**   **12ʰ30.3ᵐ +12° 20′**
Finder Charts 64-6, 64-8   ★★/★★★
12/14″Scopes–125x: NGC 4476 and NGC 4478 are a 4.5′ pair of small galaxies near the large and bright M87. NGC 4478, the brighter of the two, is 8′ SW of M87, and has a well concentrated 1′ diameter halo that contains a small bright core with an inconspicuous stellar nucleus. NGC 4476, located 12′ WSW of M87, is much fainter than its companion but clearly elongated 1′×0.5′ NNE–SSW. In its center it suddenly brightens to a small core in which is embedded a stellar nucleus.

NGC 4483 Galaxy Type SB(s)0+:
ϕ **1.5′×0.9′, m12.2v, SB12.4**   **12ʰ30.7ᵐ +09° 01′**
Finder Charts 64-6, 64-8   ★★★
12/14″Scopes–125x: NGC 4483 is a fairly faint 1′×0.5′ NE–SW haze containing a well concentrated core with a faint stellar nucleus. A 10th magnitude star lies 6.5′ west, and a 12th magnitude is 8′ NNW.

NGC 4486 Messier 87 Galaxy Type E+0-1
ϕ **7.1′×7.1′, m8.6v, SB12.7**   **12ʰ30.8ᵐ +12° 24′**
Finder Charts 64-6, 64-8, Figure 64-17   ★★★★★
    Messier 87, a giant elliptical galaxy, is the strong radio source known as Virgo A or 3C 274. Photos taken by large observatory telescopes reveal a jet of matter being ejected toward the NE from the galaxy's bright nucleus. Messier discovered this object in 1781.
    M87 is one of the frontline members of the Coma-Virgo Supercluster and probably very near the supercluster's dynamical center (the point around which other supercluster members – including our own Local Galaxy Group – are orbiting). If the distance to the center of the Supercluster is 65 million light years, M87 has an absolute magnitude of −22.9, which corresponds to a true luminosity of 129 billion suns, and is over 135,000 light years in diameter.
4/6″Scopes–75x: M87, centered 6′ south of an 8th magnitude star, is a fine bright standout in the NW Virgo sea of "faint fuzzies." It has a smooth, broad central region that fades outward, imperceptibly

Figure 64-17. *Messier 87 (NGC4486) is a massive giant elliptical galaxy with explosive activity occurring in its nucleus. Image courtesy of Jim Burnell.*

blending into the background sky.
12/14″Scopes–125x: Messier 87 is a bright luminous 4′ ball with a central area that grows smoothly brighter to a brilliant 45″ diameter core without a stellar nucleus. The field lacks any bright stars. A 14th magnitude star is 3′ to the galaxy's NE.

NGC 4487 H776[2] Galaxy Type SB(s)cd II-III
ϕ **4.1′×2.7′, m10.9v, SB13.4**   **12ʰ31.1ᵐ −08° 03′**
Finder Chart 64-9, Figure 64-18   ★★
8/10″Scopes–100x: NGC 4487 is a faint, unconcentrated 3′×2′ E–W glow without central brightening. One magnitude 12.5 star touches the galaxy's northern edge, and another is beyond its eastern tip 2.5′ ESE of its center.
12/14″Scopes–125x: NGC 4487 has a faint 4′×2′ ENE–WSW halo containing a broad, poorly concentrated central area without a stellar nucleus.

NGC 4491 H41[3] Galaxy Type SB(s)a:
ϕ **1.6′×0.9′, m12.6v, SB12.8**   **12ʰ31.0ᵐ +11° 29′**
Finder Chart 64-8   ★★
12/14″Scopes–125x: NGC 4491 is a faint, unconcentrated 1′ diameter glow slightly elongated NW–SE and surrounding a very faint stellar nucleus. A 13th magnitude star lies 2′ NE of the galaxy's nucleus. 12′ NE of NGC 4491 is the somewhat more conspicuous NGC 4497.

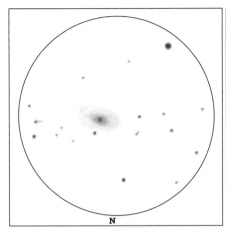

Figure 64-18. NGC 4487
12.5″, f5–250x, by G. R. Kepple

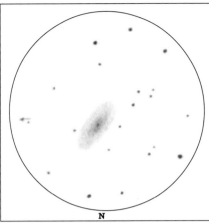

Figure 64-19. NGC 4504
12.5″, f5–275x, by G. R. Kepple

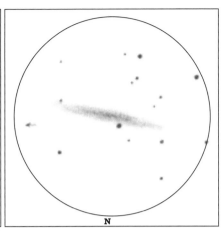

Figure 64-20. NGC 4517
17.5″, f4.5–275x, by G. R. Kepple

NGC 4496A   H36² Galaxy Type SB(rs)m II–IV
ϕ **4.0′ × 3.2′, m11.4v, SB 14.0**   **12ʰ31.7ᵐ +03° 57′**

NGC 4496B   Galaxy Type IB(s)m:
ϕ **1.0′ × 1.0′, m13.5v, SB 13.3**   **12ʰ31.7ᵐ +03° 56′**
Finder Chart 64-7   ★★/★
16/18″ Scopes–150x: NGC 4496A requires good observing conditions to be seen even as only a faint circular
3′ diameter halo containing a faint core. NGC 4496B
is barely visible as a small oval haze, elongated
about 45″ × 20″ WNW–ESE, on its SE edge. A 13th
magnitude star lies just beyond the ESE tip of NGC
4496B, and a slightly brighter star is 1′ to that
galaxy's south.

NGC 4497   H42³ Galaxy Type SAB(s)0+:
ϕ **2.0′ × 1.1′, m12.5v, SB 13.2**   **12ʰ31.5ᵐ +11° 37′**
Finder Chart 64-8   ★★
12/14″ Scopes–125x: NGC 4497 has a moderately faint
1.25′ × 0.75′ ENE–WSW oval halo containing a
highly extended core with a faint stellar nucleus.
12th magnitude stars lie 2.5′ and 5.5′ east of the
galaxy's center.

NGC 4503   H66² Galaxy Type SB0:
ϕ **3.5′ × 1.8′, m11.1v, SB 12.9**   **12ʰ32.1ᵐ +11° 11′**
Finder Charts 64-6, 64-8   ★★★
8/10″ Scopes–100x: NGC 4503, centered 2.75′ NNE of
an 11th magnitude star, is a fairly bright 1.25′ × 0.5′
N–S spindle containing a small, round core.
16/18″ Scopes–150x: NGC 4503 has a bright 1.75′ × 0.75′
N–S halo containing a small, circular core with a
stellar nucleus. Some mottling can be seen around
the core. A threshold star is superimposed upon the
halo 1′ NNE of the galaxy's center. A 12th magni-

tude star with a 14th magnitude companion 18″ to
its WNW is 2.75′ ESE of the galaxy's center.

NGC 4504   H771² Galaxy Type SB(s)cd II–III
ϕ **5.0′ × 3.0′, m11.2v, SB 14.0**   **12ʰ32.3ᵐ −07° 34′**
Finder Chart 64-9, Figure 64-19   ★★★
12/14″ Scopes–125x: NGC 4504 is a faint 3′ × 1.5′ NW–
SE glow containing a broad central concentration
without any visible nucleus. A 14.5 magnitude star
lies 1.25′ ENE, and a 14th magnitude star is 2′ ESE,
of the galaxy's center.

NGC 4517   H5⁴ Galaxy Type Scd sp
ϕ **9.9′ × 1.4′, m10.4v, SB 13.1**   **12ʰ32.8ᵐ +00° 07′**
Finder Chart 64-5, Figure 64-20   ★★★★
8/10″ Scopes–100x: NGC 4517, centered just SW of a
10th magnitude star, is a faint, diffuse 6′ × 1′ E–W
streak. An 11th magnitude star lies north of the
galaxy's eastern tip, and a 10th magnitude star is
7′ to its SSE.
16/18″ Scopes–150x: NGC 4517 is a large, soft, highly
elongated 8′ × 1.75′ ENE–WSW glow around an
irregularly illuminated, patchy center. Its tips are
diffuse but noticeably tapered. A 10th magnitude
star 1.5′ NE of the galaxy's center and a 14th
magnitude star 3′ to its WSW both lie on the edge
of the halo.

NGC 4517A   Galaxy Type SB(s)dm III–IV
ϕ **4.3′ × 2.8′, m12.5v, SB 15.0**   **12ʰ32.5ᵐ +00° 24′**
Finder Chart 64-5   ★★
16/18″ Scopes–150x: NGC 4517A, located 17′ NNW of
NGC 4517 and centered 3.75′ SE of a 10th magnitude
star, is a faint, diffuse, unconcentrated glow without
central brightening. A 14th magnitude star is 45″

south, and a 14.5 magnitude star 2′ ENE, of the galaxy's center.

NGC 4519 H158² Galaxy Type SB(rs)d II-III
ϕ **3.5′ × 2.3′, m11.8v, SB13.9**   12ʰ33.5ᵐ +08° 39′
Finder Charts 64-6, 64-7   ★★
12/14″Scopes–125x: NGC 4519 has a faint 1.5′ × 1′ E–W oval halo containing little central brightening except for a small, very faint core. A sprinkling of faint stars lies to the galaxy's NW, the closest star just 2.5′ NE of its center.

NGC 4522 Galaxy Type SB(s)cd: sp
ϕ **3.8′ × 1.0′, m12.3v, SB13.6**   12ʰ33.7ᵐ +09° 10′
Finder Charts 64-6, 64-8   ★★
12/14″Scopes–125x: NGC 4522 has a low surface brightness 3′ × 0.75′ NNE–SSW halo containing a faint 1′ × 0.5′ core. 12th magnitude stars are 7′ ENE and 8′ SE of the galaxy, and a magnitude 14.5 star lies 2.5′ SE of its center.

NGC 4526 H31¹ Galaxy Type SAB(s)0°:
ϕ **7.1′ × 2.9′, m9.7v, SB12.8**   12ʰ34.0ᵐ +07° 42′
Finder Charts 64-6, 64-7   ★★★
8/10″Scopes–100x: NGC 4526 is a conspicuous galaxy easily located between an E–W pair of two 7th magnitude stars. The rather faint outer halo extends 3′ × 1′ ESE–WNW, but the galaxy's inner third is concentrated to a tiny core. One magnitude 12.5 star is halfway between the galaxy and the 7th magnitude star to its west, and another is 2′ to the south of its center.
16/18″Scopes–150x: The halo of NGC 4526, although very tenuous, can be glimpsed out to dimensions of 5′ × 1.25′ ESE–WNW, its eastern wing longer than its western. The halo's brightness rises smoothly to its center, where a faint stellar nucleus can be glimpsed. With averted vision a narrow dark dust lane might be seen.

NGC 4527 H37² Galaxy Type SAB(s)bc II
ϕ **6.0′ × 2.1′, m10.5v, SB13.1**   12ʰ34.1ᵐ +02° 39′
Finder Charts 64-5, 64-7, Figure 64-22   ★★★★
8/10″Scopes–100x: NGC 4527 is 12′ north of a wide N–S pair of 8th and 9th magnitude stars. The galaxy shows a bright 4′ × 1′ ENE–WSW halo containing an oval core.
16/18″Scopes–150x: NGC 4527 is a fine, bright galaxy elongated 5′ × 1.5′ ENE–WSW and containing a mottled 1′ × 0.5′ core with a stellar nucleus. It is flanked by a 13th magnitude star 2′ to its east and

Figure 64-21. *NGC 4535 is a face-on loose-armed spiral galaxy in a field peppered with foreground stars. NGC 4535A is the elongated smudge at bottom center. Image courtesy of Andreas Roerig.*

a 12.5 magnitude star 4′ to its west. A wide pair of 14th magnitude stars is 2′ to the galaxy's south.

NGC 4528 H67² Galaxy Type S0°:
ϕ **1.5′ × 1.0′, m12.1v, SB12.4**   12ʰ34.1ᵐ +11° 19′
Finder Charts 64-6, 64-8   ★★★
12/14″Scopes–125x: NGC 4528, centered 7.5′ west of an 8th magnitude star, is a fairly bright 1.25′ × 0.75′ N–S oval containing a nuclear bulge. The core is unconcentrated but surrounds a faint stellar nucleus. 11th magnitude stars lie 4′ to the galaxy's NE and 4.5′ to its SE.

NGC 4532 H147² Galaxy Type IBm III-IV
ϕ **3.2′ × 1.1′, m11.9v, SB13.1**   12ʰ34.3ᵐ +06° 28′
Finder Charts 64-6, 64-7   ★★★
12/14″Scopes–125x: NGC 4532, centered 5.5′ north of an 8th magnitude star, appears fairly faint, elongated 2′ × 1′ NNW–SSE, and slightly brighter at its center. A 13th magnitude star lies 30″ east, and a 12.5 magnitude star 3′ SSW, of the galaxy's center.

NGC 4535 H500² Galaxy Type SAB(s)c I-II
ϕ **7.1′ × 6.4′, m10.0v, SB14.0**   12ʰ34.3ᵐ +08° 12′
Finder Charts 64-6, 64-7, Figure 64-21   ★★★★
8/10″Scopes–100x: NGC 4535, lying in a field peppered with faint foreground stars, is a faint, diffuse patch elongated 5′ × 3.5′ N–S.
16/18″Scopes–150x: NGC 4535 is a fine face-on galaxy showing an unevenly bright, mottled halo elongated

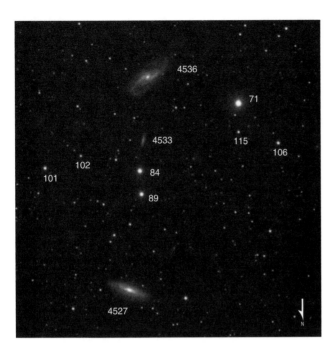

Figure 64-22. *NGC 4527 and NGC 4536 form a nice pair for small and medium size telescopes. Image courtesy of Jim Burnell.*

6′ × 4′ N–S. The 1′ diameter core is unconcentrated and contains a very faint stellar nucleus. Many faint foreground stars are scattered around the galaxy's periphery, and a few are superimposed upon the halo, the most conspicuous a 13th magnitude star 1′ north of the galaxy's center. A second 13th magnitude star lies inside the halo's south edge 2′ from the galaxy's center. Three wide doubles are just outside the NW, SW, and ESE edges of the halo.

NGC 4536 H2⁵ Galaxy Type SAB(rs)bc I-II
φ 6.4′ × 2.6′, m10.6v, SB13.5   12ʰ34.5ᵐ +02° 11′
Finder Charts 64-5, 64-7, Figure 64-22   ★★★★
8/10″Scopes–100x: NGC 4536 forms an equilateral triangle with a 7th magnitude star 10′ to its ENE and an 8th magnitude star 10′ to its north. It has a faint, diffuse 6′ × 2′ NW–SE halo.
16/18″Scopes–150x: This galaxy shows a fairly bright broad bar elongated E–W around which faint spiral arms arc counterclockwise, their extensions giving NGC 4536 an overall size of 6.5′ × 2.5′ NW–SE. A 13.5 magnitude star touches the east edge of the halo. The immediate field is lightly sprinkled with faint stars.

NGC 4546 H160¹ Galaxy Type SB?0:
φ 3.2′ × 1.4′, m10.3v, SB11.8   12ʰ35.5ᵐ −03° 48′
Finder Charts 64-5, 64-9, Figure 64-28   ★★★
8/10″Scopes–100x: NGC 4546, centered 2′ NW of an

11.5 magnitude star, has a bright stellar nucleus embedded in a well concentrated circular core surrounded by a much fainter 1.5′ × 0.5′ E–W halo.
16/18″Scopes–150x: NGC 4546 has a nebulous 3′ × 1′ ENE–WSW halo containing a 30″ × 20″ core and a stellar nucleus. A 13.5 magnitude star lies 2′ NW of the galaxy's center on the opposite side of the halo from the 11.5 magnitude star.

NGC 4550 H36¹ Galaxy Type SB0° : sp
φ 3.3′ × 1.0′, m11.7v, SB12.8   12ʰ35.5ᵐ +12° 13′

NGC 4551 H37¹ Galaxy Type E:
φ 1.7′ × 1.5′, m12.0v, SB12.9   12ʰ35.6ᵐ +12° 16′
Finder Charts 64-6, 64-8, Figure 64-29   ★★★/★★★
12/14″Scopes–125x: NGC 4550 and NGC 4551 are a 3.5′ wide NE–SW pair of similarly bright galaxies. The southwestern system, NGC 4550, measuring 2′ × 0.75′ N–S, is larger than the northwestern galaxy, NGC 4551, which is 1.25′ × 0.75′ ENE–WSW; but each has a small, faint core containing a stellar nucleus. The two galaxies from a parallelogram with a 12th magnitude star 3′ SE of NGC 4550 and a 12.5 magnitude star 2.25′ NW of 4551.

NGC 4552 Messier 89 Galaxy Type E
φ 3.4′ × 3.4′, m9.8v, SB12.3   12ʰ35.7ᵐ +12° 33′
Finder Charts 64-6, 64-8, Figure 64-30   ★★★
Messier 89 was discovered by Charles Messier on March 18, 1781. It is another of the giant ellipticals in the core of the Coma-Virgo Supercluster. Assuming that it is 65 million light years distant, its absolute magnitude is −21.7, a luminosity of 40 billion suns, and its true diameter over 64,000 light years.
4/6″Scopes–75x: Small instruments show a bright, well concentrated 1′ diameter circle of haze WSW of a faint star.
12/14″Scopes–125x: M89 has a bright nucleus embedded within a well concentrated center that fades out to a diffuse periphery. The diameter, as is true of all elliptical galaxies, is ambiguous but no less than 2′. On the south edge is a NNE–SSW pair of magnitude 14.5 stars. A 13th magnitude star is 1.75′ ENE of the galaxy's nucleus.

NGC 4564 H68² Galaxy Type E
φ 2.6′ × 1.7′, m11.1v, SB12.6   12ʰ36.4ᵐ +11° 26′
Finder Charts 64-6, 64-8, Figure 64-23   ★★★
12/14″Scopes–125x: NGC 4564, located 7.5′ NE of an 8th magnitude star, is a fairly bright but diffuse 2′ × 1′ NE–SW oval that suddenly brightens in its center to a stellar nucleus. The galaxy is flanked by 12th magnitude stars 3′ to its NW and 4′ to its SE.

Figure 64-23. *NGC4567-68, at top, are the Siamese Twins. NGC4564, at bottom, is a bright, diffuse oval. Image courtesy of Dean Salman.*

Figure 64-24. *Messier 90 (NGC4569) has a large, bright core within tightly coiled spiral arms. IC3583 is a small companion galaxy. Image courtesy of Jim Burnell.*

NGC 4567 H8⁴ Galaxy Type SA(rs)bc III
ϕ **2.7′× 2.3′, m11.3v, SB13.1   12ʰ36.5ᵐ +11° 15′**

NGC 4568 H9⁴ Galaxy Type SA(rs)bc III
ϕ **4.7′× 2.2′, m10.8v, SB13.2   12ʰ36.6ᵐ +11° 14′**
Finder Charts 64-6, 64-8, Figure 64-23   ★★★/★★★
The Siamese Twins

12/14″Scopes-125x: NGC 4567 and NGC 4568 are a pair of interacting galaxies that appear to be joined at their eastern tips. The northernmost system, NGC 4567, is the brighter of the two, and its fairly bright 2′ × 1′ ENE–WSW oval halo contains a stellar nucleus. NGC 4568 is somewhat fainter than its companion, and its diffuse 2.5′ × 1′ NNE–SSW halo contains only a gradually brighter center. 3.5′ to the east of NGC 4567 is a 1.5′ wide NW–SE pair of 11.5 and 12th magnitude stars.

NGC 4569 Messier 90 Galaxy Type SAB(rs)ab I-II
ϕ **10.5′× 4.4′, m9.5v, SB13.6   12ʰ36.8ᵐ +13° 10′**
Finder Charts 64-6, 64-8, Figure 64-24   ★★★★★

Messier 90 was discovered by Messier on March 18, 1781, the same night he also discovered M84, M85, M86, M87, M88, and M89. M90 is one of the giant spiral members of the Coma-Virgo Supercluster core, and one of the several Coma-Virgo galaxies which show a blue shift. Apparently its orbital motion around the gravita-

tional center of the Supercluster is giving it sufficient velocity in our direction to overcome the general cosmological red shift. The blue shift implies that M90 is somewhat nearer than the 65 million light year distant Supercluster center. If it is 50 million light years away, its absolute magnitude is −21.4, a luminosity of 30 billion suns, and its true diameter at least 150,000 light years.

4/6″Scopes-75x: Messier 90 is a bright, luminous 5′ × 2′ NNE–SSW oval. Its surface brightness is uneven, concentrations being visible in the outer envelope NNE and SSW of the galaxy's center.

8/10″Scopes-100x: This fine, bright galaxy shows a large 3′ × 1′ oval core embedded in a fainter but well defined 6′ × 2′ halo. The western long side of the halo is noticeably flattened compared to the eastern long side.

16/18″Scopes-150x: In larger telescopes Messier 90 is a fine, detailed object. The outer halo is very faint but well defined, its western long side noticeably bulged. Within the halo are faint spiral arms attached to the ends of a highly extended, mottled core and tightly coiled around it counterclockwise. A magnitude 13.5 star lies beyond the galaxy's northern tip 3.5′ from its center. 6′ north of M90 is the galaxy IC 3583, a very faint haze elongated N–S and located within, and near the shortest side, of a triangle of 12th magnitude stars.

Figure 64-25. *Messier 58 (NGC4579) has a bright core with a stellar nucleus surrounded by a diffuse halo. Image courtesy of Jim Burnell.*

NGC 4570 H32[1] Galaxy Type S0
φ **4.3′ × 1.3′, m10.9v, SB12.6**   12ʰ36.9ᵐ +07° 15′
Finder Chart 64-6   ★★★★
12/14″Scopes–125x: NGC 4570 has a bright lens-shaped halo much-elongated 2.5′ × 0.75′ NNW–SSE and containing a sharply concentrated core with a nonstellar nucleus. A 13th magnitude star lies 3′ west, and a 14th magnitude star is 5′ NNW, of the galaxy. But the immediate field is otherwise barren.

NGC 4578 H15[2] Galaxy Type SA(r)0° :
φ **3.2′ × 2.6′, m11.5v, SB13.7**   12ʰ37.5ᵐ +09° 33′
Finder Charts 64-6, 64-8   ★★★
8/10″Scopes–100x: NGC 4578, centered 4.5′ east of an 11.5 magnitude star, is a moderately faint, diffuse patch about 1′ in diameter and containing a stellar nucleus. A 12th magnitude star lies 4.5′ NE of the galaxy's center.
16/18″Scopes–150x: NGC 4578 displays a small, bright core with a stellar nucleus surrounded by a hazy oval halo elongated 2′ × 1.5′ NE–SW.

NGC 4579 Messier 58 Galaxy Type SAB(rs)b II
φ **5.5′ × 4.6′, m9.7v, SB13.0**   12ʰ37.7ᵐ +11° 49′
Finder Charts 64-6, 64-8, Figure 64-25   ★★★★
Charles Messier discovered M58 on April 15, 1779. It is a giant barred spiral member of the core of the Coma-Virgo Supercluster. If it is near the roughly 65 million light year-distant center of the Supercluster core, its absolute magnitude is −21.8, a luminosity of 4 billion suns, and its true diameter is over 100,000 light years.

8/10″Scopes–100x: M58 has a bright stellar nucleus embedded in a broad, well concentrated inner region elongated 2.5′ × 1.5′. The much fainter outer envelope measures 4.5′ × 3.5′ NE–SW.
16/18″Scopes–150x: With averted vision the faint, diffuse halo of M58 can be seen covering about a 5′ × 4′ NE–SW area. The 3′ × 1.75′ inner halo is bright and mottled and contains a 1.5′ × 0.5′ core. The core brightens inward to a 30″ nucleus with a sharp stellar center.

NGC 4580 H124[1] Galaxy Type SAB(rs)a pec
φ **2.4′ × 1.7′, m11.8v, SB13.2**   12ʰ37.8ᵐ +05° 22′
Finder Charts 64-5, 64-6   ★★★
12/14″Scopes–125x: NGC 4580, centered 3.5′ WNW of an 11.5 magnitude star, has a fairly faint 1.5′ × 1.25′ ENE–WSW halo with is a slight central brightening. 12.5 magnitude stars are 5′ NE and 6′ NNE of the galaxy.

NGC 4586 H125[1] Galaxy Type SA(s)a: sp
φ **3.6′ × 1.1′, m11.7v, SB13.0**   12ʰ38.5ᵐ +04° 19′
Finder Charts 64-5, 64-6   ★★★
8/10″Scopes–100x: NGC 4586, located 8′ ENE of a 7th magnitude star, is a faint 2′ × 0.5′ ESE–WNW streak containing a slightly brighter center.
16/18″Scopes–150x: NGC 4586 has a fairly faint 3′ × 0.75′ ESE–WNW halo containing a faint oval core. Two 13.5 magnitude stars are 50″ WSW and 1.25′ south, and two 13th magnitude stars are 2′ and 2.75′ NE, of the galaxy's center.

NGC 4592 H31[2] Galaxy Type Scd: sp III:
φ **4.7′ × 1.4′, m11.7v, SB13.6**   12ʰ39.3ᵐ −00° 32′
Finder Chart 64-5, Figure 64-31   ★★
12/14″Scopes–125x: NGC 4592 is a degree NNW of the fine double star Gamma (γ) = 29 Virginis and 17′ NNE of a 7th magnitude star. It has a dim 3′ × 1′ E–W halo with a poorly concentrated center. Two pairs of 13th magnitude stars separated by 45″ and 30″ are respectively 2.5′ ENE and 2′ NNW of the galaxy's center.

NGC 4593 H183[2] Galaxy Type (R′)SB(rs)a
φ **3.9′ × 3.3′, m10.9v, SB13.5**   12ʰ39.7ᵐ −05° 21′
Finder Chart 64-9, Figure 64-32   ★★★
8/10″Scopes–100x: NGC 4593 is located in a rather well-populated star field for an off-Milky Way region, circumscribed by an 8′ × 6′ circlet of five stars. The brightest star at 11th magnitude is 5′ SE of the galaxy, and the other stars are magnitude 12

and 13. The galaxy is a faint NE–SW glow containing a stellar nucleus.

16/18″ Scopes–150x: NGC 4593 has a stellar nucleus embedded in a moderately concentrated bar extended 1.75′ × 0.5′. The outer halo is elongated 3′ × 1.75′ NE–SW.

NGC 4594 Messier 104 Galaxy Type SA: asp
φ 7.1′ × 4.4′, m8.0v, SB 11.6 12ʰ40.0ᵐ −11° 37′
Finder Chart 64-9, Figure 64-26   ★★★★★
Sombrero Galaxy

Mechain discovered Messier 104 in May, 1781. William Herschel was probably the first observer to notice the galaxy's beautiful dark dust lane. M104 is well away from the core of the Coma-Virgo Supercluster, which is to the north in the M87 region, but undoubtedly is a Coma-Virgo member. Indeed, it is one of the brightest and most massive galaxies in the Coma-Virgo Supercluster. Assuming it to be 65 million light years distant (if anything, an underestimate), M104 has an absolute magnitude of −23.5, a remarkable luminosity of 210 billion suns and about 16 times the brightness of our own very respectable Milky Way Galaxy. The true diameter of M104 is over 135,000 light years. Much of the luminosity of the galaxy comes from its unusually large central bulge.

4/6″ Scopes–75x: M104, centered 4′ ENE of a 10th magnitude star, is a fine, bright object even in small instruments. It is a large ellipse with pointed ends directed toward the east and west. The dark dust lane, which bisects the galaxy into two unequal sections, passes just south of its center and may be seen with direct vision under good skies.

8/10″ Scopes–100x: In telescopes of this aperture, Messier 104 is an attractive object displaying the most prominent dark lanes in any galaxy except Centaurus A. The lane cuts the 6′ × 2′ E–W halo in two unequal parts, the northern part being the larger.

16/18″ Scopes–150x: Magnificent! The halo spans 8′ × 3′ E–W and is severed into unequal N–S segments by the conspicuous dark dust lane, which runs the galaxy's length just south of the prominent bulge's center. The larger segment on the north is the top of the "sombrero." A 13th magnitude star is 1.5′ north of the galaxy's center. Low power accentuates the relative bright-star-richness of the field around M104. 20′ to the WNW of the galaxy is a loose gathering of brighter field stars including the multiple Σ1664, which has components of magnitudes 8.1, 9.3, 11.5, and 11.6.

Figure 64-26. *Messier 104 (NGC 4594), the Sombrero Galaxy, is named after the prominent dark lane which forms the brim of the hat. Image courtesy of Martin C. Germano.*

NGC 4596 H24¹ Galaxy Type SB(r)0+
φ 4.6′ × 4.1′, m10.4v, SB 13.4   12ʰ39.9ᵐ +10° 11′
Finder Charts 64-6 and 64-8   ★★★

8/10″ Scopes–100x: NGC 4596 is 26′ west of the 5th magnitude star Rho (ϱ) = 30 Virginis and 19′ from the galaxy NGC 4608, which is closer to Rho. NGC 4596 is the slightly brighter of the two galaxies and is elongated 2′ × 1′ ENE–WSW with a brighter center. A magnitude 11.5 star is 1′ SSE, and a magnitude 10.5 star is 3′ SE, of the galaxy's center.

16/18″ Scopes–150x: NGC 4596 has a faint, diffuse 2.75′ × 2.5′ halo slightly elongated N–S and containing a mottled bar-like ENE–WSW central region. At this aperture the magnitude 11.5 star 1′ SSE of the galaxy's center can be seen within the periphery of the halo.

NGC 4597 H636² Galaxy Type SB(rs)m III
φ 4.1′ × 1.6′, m12.1v, SB 14.0   12ʰ40.2ᵐ −05° 48′
Finder Chart 64-9   ★★

12/14″ Scopes–125x: NGC 4597 is a very faint 4′ × 1.5′ NE–SW patch without a central concentration. Two 14th magnitude stars are on the halo's SW tip, and a slightly brighter star lies at the NW tip. 13th magnitude stars are 2.5′ NNW and 3.5′ NNW of the galaxy's center.

NGC 4602 H184² Galaxy Type SAB:(s:)c II
φ **3.0′ × 1.1′, m11.5v, SB12.7**   12^{h}40.6^m −05° 08′
Finder Chart 64-9, Figure 64-33   ★★★
12/14″ Scopes–125x: NGC 4602 has a moderately faint
   3′ × 1′ E–W halo containing a broad, mottled central
   core. A 14th magnitude star touches the halo's
   eastern tip, and a 12.5 magnitude star is 6′ to the
   galaxy's ENE.

NGC 4608 H69² Galaxy Type SB(r)0°
φ **3.0′ × 3.0′, m11.0v, SB13.2**   12^{h}41.2^m +10° 29′
Finder Charts 64-6, 64-8   ★★★
8/10″ Scopes–100x: NGC 4608 is near two bright stars:
   magnitude 4.9 Rho (ρ) = 30 Virginis is 8′ to its NE,
   and 5.5 magnitude 27 Virginis is 14′ to its NNW.
   The galaxy has a fairly bright 1.5′ diameter halo
   containing a well concentrated center.
16/18″ Scopes–150x: NGC 4608, which forms a galaxy-
   pair with NGC 4596 located 19′ to its west, has a
   faint, amorphously circular, outer halo roughly 3′
   in diameter surrounding a brighter, more elongated,
   1.5′ × 0.5′ NNE–SSW inner halo. The galaxy's
   bright core rises to a sharp stellar nucleus. The
   vague outer halo reaches toward, but does not quite
   touch, a 14th magnitude star 2′ east of the galaxy's
   center. A 13th magnitude star with a magnitude
   13.5 companion 30″ to its north is 1.75′ west of the
   galaxy's center.

NGC 4612 H20² Galaxy Type (R)SAB0°
φ **1.6′ × 1.3′, m10.9v, SB11.5**   12^{h}41.5^m +07° 19′
Finder Chart 64-6   ★★★
12/14″ Scopes–125x: NGC 4612 is centered just 1′ west
   of a 10.5 magnitude star at the south end of a 9′
   long row of nearly equally bright stars. The star at
   the north end of the row has a 12th magnitude
   companion 20″ to its ENE. The galaxy has a
   moderately faint 1.5′ diameter halo that is well
   concentrated toward its center with a stellar
   nucleus.

NGC 4621 Messier 59 Galaxy Type E5
φ **4.6′ × 3.6′, m9.6v, SB12.5**   12^{h}42.0^m +11° 39′
Finder Charts 64-6, 64-8, Figure 64-27a   ★★★★
   Messier 59 was discovered on April 11, 1779, by J.
   G. Koehler in Dresden while observing the comet of
   1779. Messier saw it four days later, also while observing
   the comet. M59 is a compact, massive giant elliptical
   member of the core of the Coma-Virgo Supercluster.
   Assuming a distance of 65 million light years, it has an
   absolute magnitude of −21.9, a luminosity of 44 billion
   suns, and a true diameter of over 90,000 light years.

4/6″ Scopes–75x: Messier 59, located 25′ WNW of
   Messier 60, is a fairly bright 2′ × 1′ NNW–SSE oval
   with a bright center that fades smoothly to a diffuse
   periphery.
8/10″ Scopes–100x: Messier 59 forms a triangle with an
   11.5 magnitude star 2′ to its north and a 12th
   magnitude star 3′ to its NNE. The halo is a bright
   2.5′ × 1.5′ NNW–SSE ellipse that smoothly brightens to its more circular core.
16/18″ Scopes–150x: In larger telescopes the halo of M59
   appears very bright, elongated 3′ × 2′ NNW–SSE,
   and brightens smoothly to a brilliant center with a
   stellar nucleus. A 14th magnitude star lies near the
   SW edge of the halo, 1′ from the galaxy's nucleus.

NGC 4623 H149² Galaxy Type SB0+: sp
φ **2.0′ × 0.7′, m12.2v, SB12.5**   12^{h}42.2^m +07° 41′
Finder Chart 64-6   ★★
12/14″ Scopes–125x: NGC 4623 is considerably faint
   with a 2′ × 1′ N–S halo containing a small, circular
   core. A 14th magnitude star lies 1.25′ ENE, and an
   11th magnitude star 3.5′ NNW, of the galaxy's
   center.

NGC 4630 H532² Galaxy Type IB(s)m?
φ **1.6′ × 1.2′, m12.7v, SB13.2**   12^{h}42.5^m +03° 58′
Finder Chart 64-5   ★★
12/14″ Scopes–125x: NGC 4630 is a faint unconcentrated 1.5′ × 1′ N–S oval. An 11.5 magnitude star 3′
   NNE of the galaxy has a 13th magnitude companion
   15″ to its north. A pair of 11th and 13th magnitude
   stars is 8′ NW of the galaxy.

NGC 4632 H14¹ Galaxy Type SAB?(r:)bc II
φ **2.9′ × 1.1′, m11.7v, SB12.8**   12^{h}42.5^m −00° 05′
Finder Chart 64-5, Figure 64-34   ★★★
12/14″ Scopes–125x: NGC 4632 has a fairly well concentrated oval core surrounded by a faint 2.5′ × 1′ ENE–
   WSW halo. The galaxy lies inside the northern edge
   of a 7.5′ × 3.5′ triangle of 12th magnitude stars. A
   15″ wide pair of 13.5 and 14th magnitude stars is
   3′ SE of the galaxy.

NGC 4636 H38² Galaxy Type E0-1
φ **7.1′ × 5.2′, m9.5v, SB13.3**   12^{h}42.8^m +02° 41′
Finder Chart 64-5, Figure 64-35   ★★★
8/10″ Scopes–100x: NGC 4636, located 9′ WNW of an
   8th magnitude star, has a bright core embedded in
   a faint, diffuse 1.5′ diameter halo.
16/18″ Scopes–150x: NGC 4636 has a faint halo discern-

Figure 64-27a. *Messier 59 (NGC 4621) is a noticeable elongated ES5 type elliptical galaxy. Three very faint companions are labeled in this figure. Messier 60 lies 23′ ESE. Image courtesy of Jim Burnell.*

Figure 64-27b. *Messier 60 (NGC 4649) is an elliptical galaxy with a brad, well concentrated center. The barred spiral SABc galaxy NGC 4647 forms a close pair with it. Image courtesy of Martin C. Germano.*

ible with averted vision to 4.5′ × 3.5′ NNW–SSE. The core is bright and contains a stellar nucleus. The immediate field is rich with faint stars, the two brightest are 12th magnitude star 3.5′ NNW of the galaxy's center and a 12.5 magnitude star 3.25′ to its SSE.

NGC 4638 H70[2] Galaxy Type S0
ϕ **2.9′ × 2.0′, m11.2v, SB12.9**   **12^h42.8^m +11° 26′**
Finder Charts 64-6, 64-8   ★★★
12/14″ Scopes–125x: NGC 4638 is at the southern corner of a large triangle with Messier 59 lying 15′ to the NW and Messier 60 lying 12′ to the NE. The galaxy has a bright lens-shaped halo elongated 1′ × 0.5′ NW–SE and contains an extended core with a nonstellar nucleus. At its ESE edge is the very faint 14th magnitude companion galaxy NGC 4637. Two magnitude 12.5 stars 3′ south form an isosceles triangle with NGC 4638, and an 11th magnitude star is 5′ to its NNW.

NGC 4639 H125[2] Galaxy Type SAB(rs)bc II-III
ϕ **2.9′ × 2.0′, m11.5v, SB13.3**   **12^h42.9^m +13° 15′**
Finder Charts 64-6, 64-8   ★★★
12/14″ Scopes–125x: NGC 4639 has a fairly bright 1.5′ × 1′ NNW–SSE halo containing a stellar nucleus. A 13th magnitude star lies 1′ SE, and a 14.5 magnitude star 1.5′ west, of the galaxy's center. An 11.5 magnitude star is 9′ to the galaxy's NE.

NGC 4643 H10[1] Galaxy Type (R′)SB(rs)0°
ϕ **3.0′ × 3.0′, m10.8v, SB13.0**   **12^h43.3^m +01° 59′**
Finder Chart 64-5   ★★★
8/10″ Scopes–100x: NGC 4643, centered 2.5′ SE of an 11th magnitude star, contains a bright core with a stellar nucleus in a faint 1.5′ × 1′ NW–SE halo.
16/18″ Scopes–150x: NGC 4643 shows a more tapered profile when viewed in larger telescopes. The halo reaches 2′ × 1′ NW–SE, and the central area is broad and circular and brightens to a stellar nucleus.

NGC 4647 H44³ Galaxy Type SAB(rs)c III-IV
φ 2.7′× 2.2′, m11.3v, SB13.1   12ʰ43.5ᵐ +11° 35′

NGC 4649 Messier 60 Galaxy Type E2
φ 7.1′× 6.1′, m8.8v, SB12.8   12ʰ43.7ᵐ +11° 33′
Finder Charts 64-6, 64-8, Figure 64-27b   ★★★/★★★★
   Messier 59 and 60 were both discovered by Koehler
on April 11, 1779 while he was observing the comet of
1779. M60 is another of the giant elliptical galaxies in
the core of the Coma-Virgo Supercluster. If it is 65 million
light years away, its absolute magnitude is −22.7, a
luminosity of 100 billion suns, and its true diameter is
over 135,000 light years.
4/6″Scopes-75x: Messier 60 is the brighter and larger
   of a galaxy-pair with NGC 4647 centered 2.5′ to its
   NW. Messier 60 has a bright, smooth circular 2′
   diameter halo: the galaxy appears about twice as
   large as its companion giant elliptical system Messier 59, located 22′ to the WNW. NGC 4647, considerably fainter than M59, has a 1′ diameter
   uniformly low surface brightness halo. The halos of
   the two galaxies nearly touch.
8/10″Scopes-100x: Messier 60 has a bright, diffuse 2.5′
   diameter halo containing a broad central region.
   NGC 4647 is an unconcentrated 1.5′ diameter glow
   with a slight central brightening. With averted
   vision the halos of the two galaxies appear to touch.
16/18″Scopes-150x: Messier 60 has a bright opalescent
   halo that fades smoothly to a periphery elongated
   3′× 2.5′ NW–SE toward its companion galaxy. The
   center is broad and well concentrated. NGC 4647
   has a dim 2′ diameter halo containing a weakly
   concentrated core. The halos of the two galaxies
   appear to touch, forming a figure "8."

NGC 4653 H662³ Galaxy Type SA(s)cd II
φ 2.3′× 2.1′, m12.2v, SB13.8   12ʰ43.9ᵐ −00° 34′
Finder Chart 64-5   ★★
12/14″Scopes-125x: NGC 4653, centered 2.5′ NW of an
   11th magnitude star, is a 1.5′ diameter uniformly
   faint glow. A magnitude 12.5 star lies between the
   11th magnitude star and the galaxy's halo. A 13th
   magnitude star is on the halo's edge 1.5′ NW of
   the galaxy's center. NGC 4653 is part of a galaxy
   group with NGC 4642 lying 9′ SW, NGC 4666, the
   brightest of the group, lying 19′ ENE, and NGC
   4668 located 24′ east.

NGC 4654 H126² Galaxy Type SAB(rs)cd II
φ 4.9′× 2.7′, m10.5v, SB13.2   12ʰ44.0ᵐ +13° 08′
Finder Charts 64-6, 64-8   ★★★★
8/10″Scopes-100x: NGC 4654 is located south of several
   fairly bright stars: a 10th magnitude star is 3.5′ to

its WNW, 12th magnitude stars are 2′ and 3.5′ to
its north, and an 11th magnitude star is 5.75′ NE.
The galaxy has a fairly bright, circular 3′ diameter
halo with a slight brightening in its center.
16/18″Scopes-150x: NGC 4654 is a bright, mottled
   object with a few knots visible extending NW from
   its 1.5′× 0.75′ poorly concentrated core. The envelope fades to a diffuse periphery measuring 4′× 2.5′
   NW–SE.

NGC 4658 H558² Galaxy Type SB(rs)ab
φ 1.3′× 0.8′, m12.5v, SB12.4   12ʰ44.6ᵐ −10° 05′
Finder Chart 64-9   ★★
12/14″Scopes-125x: NGC 4658 is a faint galaxy centered 2.5′east of an 8.5 magnitude star. Its 1.5′× 0.5′
   N–S halo contains a weakly concentrated core. A
   13th magnitude star lies near the halo's northern
   tip. Two 12.5 magnitude stars are 2.5′ SSE and 4.5′
   north of the galaxy's center.

NGC 4660 H71² Galaxy Type E:
φ 2.4′× 2.1′, m11.2v, SB12.8   12ʰ44.5ᵐ +11° 11′
Finder Chart 64-6   ★★★
8/10″Scopes-100x: NGC 4660, located in a barren star
   field, is a tiny, bright 45″× 30″ E–W oval.
16/18″Scopes-150x: In larger telescopes the halo of
   NGC 4660 increases to 2′× 1′ E–W and shows a
   bright, elongated central region that contains a
   sharply concentrated stellar nucleus.

NGC 4665 H142¹ Galaxy Type SB(s)0/a
φ 4.1′× 4.1′, m10.5v, SB13.4   12ʰ45.1ᵐ +03° 03′
Finder Chart 64-5   ★★★
8/10″Scopes-100x: NGC 4665 is between a 10th magnitude star 1.75′ to its SW an 11.5 magnitude star
   3.5′ NE. The galaxy has a fairly faint, circular 1.5′
   diameter halo containing a stellar nucleus.
16/18″Scopes-150x: NGC 4665 has an extended
   1.5′× 0.75′ inner halo that brightens to a stellar
   nucleus. The vague outer halo can be traced, with
   averted vision, out to an indefinite 3′ diameter. A
   threshold star is superimposed upon the halo 45″
   NNW of the galaxy's center. A magnitude 14.5 star
   is 1.25′ WNW of the center.

NGC 4666 H15¹ Galaxy Type Sbc II
φ 4.1′× 1.3′, m10.7v, SB12.4   12ʰ45.1ᵐ −00° 28′
Finder Chart 64-5, Figure 64-36   ★★★★
8/10″Scopes-100x: NGC 4666 is a bright 4′× 0.5′ NW–
   SE streak containing a bright center with a stellar
   nucleus.

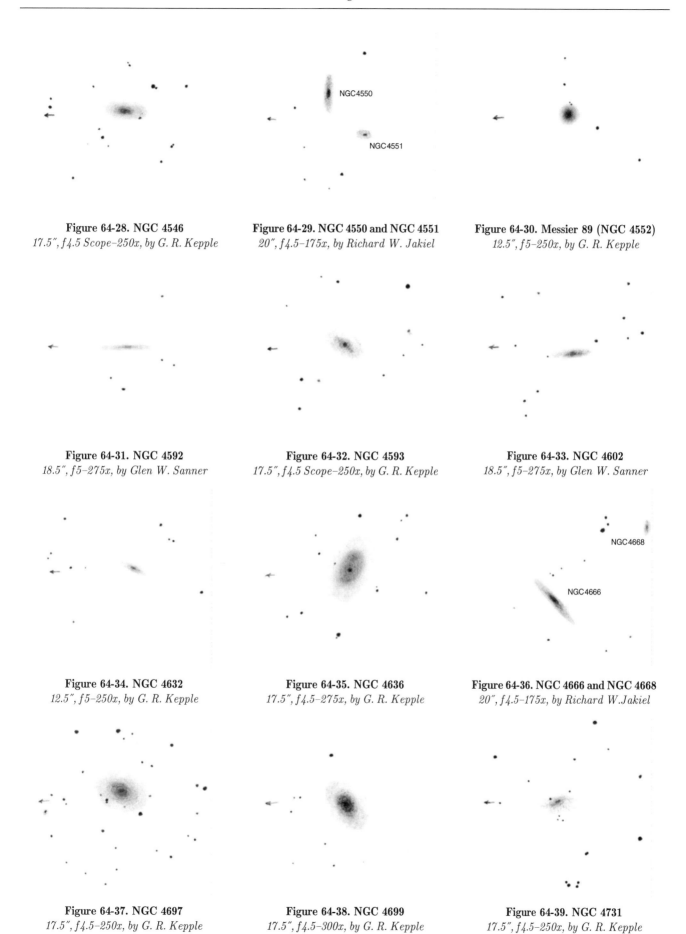

Figure 64-28. NGC 4546
17.5″, f4.5 Scope–250x, by G. R. Kepple

Figure 64-29. NGC 4550 and NGC 4551
20″, f4.5–175x, by Richard W. Jakiel

Figure 64-30. Messier 89 (NGC 4552)
12.5″, f5–250x, by G. R. Kepple

Figure 64-31. NGC 4592
18.5″, f5–275x, by Glen W. Sanner

Figure 64-32. NGC 4593
17.5″, f4.5 Scope–250x, by G. R. Kepple

Figure 64-33. NGC 4602
18.5″, f5–275x, by Glen W. Sanner

Figure 64-34. NGC 4632
12.5″, f5–250x, by G. R. Kepple

Figure 64-35. NGC 4636
17.5″, f4.5–275x, by G. R. Kepple

Figure 64-36. NGC 4666 and NGC 4668
20″, f4.5–175x, by Richard W.Jakiel

Figure 64-37. NGC 4697
17.5″, f4.5–250x, by G. R. Kepple

Figure 64-38. NGC 4699
17.5″, f4.5–300x, by G. R. Kepple

Figure 64-39. NGC 4731
17.5″, f4.5–250x, by G. R. Kepple

16/18″Scopes–150x: In larger telescopes NGC 4666 shows a much-elongated 4′ × 0.75′ NE–SW halo that is mottled and streaked and contains a thin, fairly conspicuous 1′ long core with a stellar nucleus. With averted vision two distinct dark dust lanes may be glimpsed. A 14th magnitude star is 2.25′ north of the galaxy's center, and 5.5′ SE is a short N–S arc, concave to the west, of (from the north) magnitude 11.5, 13, and 12.5 stars. The much smaller and fainter galaxy NGC 4668 lies 7.5′ SE of NGC 4666 and 3′ east of the stellar arc.

NGC 4668 H663³ Galaxy Type I:B(s)m III
ϕ 1.1′ × 0.6′, m13.1v, SB 12.5   12ʰ45.5ᵐ −00° 32′
Finder Chart 64-5, Figure 64-36   ★★

16/18″Scopes–150x: NGC 4668, a faint, small companion of NGC 4666, located 7.5′ to the larger galaxy's SE, is 3′ east of a conspicuous N–S arc of three stars. The galaxy is quite dim and diffuse, lacks any central brightening, and measures 1′ × 0.5′ N–S. A 13th magnitude star lies 2′ ESE of the galaxy's center.

NGC 4684 H181² Galaxy Type S0: sp
ϕ 2.6′ × 1.0′, m11.4v, SB 12.3   12ʰ47.3ᵐ −02° 43′
Finder Chart 64-5   ★★★

12/14″Scopes–125x: NGC 4684, located 8′ SE of an 11th magnitude star, has a 1.5′ × 0.5′ NNE–SSW halo with rounded ends that is fairly well concentrated to a slight central brightening. A 13.5 magnitude star touches the halo's NNE tip, and a very faint star lies 45″ SSE of the galaxy's center.

NGC 4688 H543³ Galaxy Type SB(s)cd III
ϕ 4.0′ × 4.0′, m11.9v, SB 14.8   12ʰ47.8ᵐ +04° 20′
Finder Charts 64-5, 64-6   ★★

12/14″Scopes–125x: NGC 4688, centered 4′ ENE of an 11.5 magnitude star, is a very faint, diffuse glow containing a faint stellar nucleus. The diameter of the galaxy's halo is indefinite, but with averted vision seems to reach 1.5′. A very faint 14th magnitude star lies 35″ NW of the galaxy's center.

NGC 4691 H182² Galaxy Type (R′)SB(rs)0+ pec
ϕ 2.6′ × 2.1′, m11.1v, SB 12.8   12ʰ48.2ᵐ −03° 20′
Finder Charts 64-5, 64-11   ★★★

8/10″Scopes–100x: NGC 4691 has a fairly bright, smoothly illuminated 2′ × 1.5′ E–W oval halo.

16/18″Scopes–150x: This galaxy has a faint, highly extended 1′ × 0.25′ oval core embedded in a 3′ × 2′ E–W halo. A threshold star touches the halo's west edge.

NGC 4694 H72² Galaxy Type SB0 pec
ϕ 3.5′ × 1.7′, m11.4v, SB 13.2   12ʰ48.2ᵐ +10° 59′
Finder Chart 64-6   ★★

12/14″Scopes–125x: NGC 4694 has a faint 2′ × 1′ NNW–SSE halo surrounding a small, poorly concentrated core. At 175x a very faint stellar nucleus can be glimpsed in the core. A 14.5 magnitude star lies 1.25′ west of the galaxy's center.

NGC 4697 H39¹ Galaxy Type SA?0
ϕ 4.4′ × 2.4′, m9.2v, SB 11.6   12ʰ48.6ᵐ −05° 48′
Finder Chart 64-9, Figure 64-37   ★★★

8/10″Scopes–100x: NGC 4697 is a fairly bright galaxy with a 2′ × 1′ ENE–WSW halo that gradually brightens to a stellar nucleus. It lies in a fairly rich star field. A magnitude 12.5 star lies 1.25′ NW, and a 12th magnitude star is 2.5′ NE, of the galaxy's center.

16/18″Scopes–150x: The halo is bright, elongated 3′ × 1.5′ ENE–WSW, and contains a moderately concentrated 45″ × 30″ core with a stellar nucleus.

NGC 4698 H8¹ Galaxy Type SA(s)ab II
ϕ 3.2′ × 1.7′, m10.6v, SB 12.2   12ʰ48.4ᵐ +08° 29′
Finder Chart 64-6   ★★★

8/10″Scopes–100x: NGC 4698 is 6.5′ ESE of a 7.5 magnitude star, and between a 5′ wide N–S pair of magnitude 10.5 stars. It has a fairly bright 2′ × 1′ N–S oval halo containing a brighter center.

16/18″Scopes–150x: NGC 4698 displays a sharply concentrated nonstellar nucleus embedded in a bright core which in turn is surrounded by a faint 3′ × 1.5′ NNW–SSE halo. The halo's NNW tip nearly touches the magnitude 10.5 star to the galaxy's north.

NGC 4699 H129¹ Galaxy Type Sab:
ϕ 4.4′ × 3.2′, m9.5v, SB 12.2   12ʰ49.0ᵐ −08° 40′
Finder Chart 64-9, Figure 64-38   ★★★★

8/10″Scopes–100x: NGC 4699 is a bright galaxy with a 3′ × 2′ NE–SW oval halo surrounding a broad well concentrated core that contains a stellar nucleus.

16/18″Scopes–150x: NGC 4699 has a bright, mottled 1.5′ × 1′ NE–SW oval core which intensifies sharply to a stellar nucleus. By contrast the 3.5′ × 2.5′ NE–SW outer halo is rather faint and smoothly illuminated. The abrupt border between the brightness zones is so distinct that the galaxy rather resembles a fried egg. A 13th magnitude star is just outside the halo's edge 2.25′ SSW of the galaxy's center.

NGC 4700 H524³ Galaxy Type SB?(s?)m: sp III
φ 2.8′×0.6′, m11.9v, SB12.3   12ʰ49.1ᵐ−11° 25′
Finder Chart 64-9   ★★★
12/14″Scopes–125x: NGC 4700 has a fairly faint, but uniformly illuminated, 1.5′×0.5′ NE–SW halo containing a very faint stellar nucleus. A 13th magnitude star is 2′ west of the galaxy's center.

NGC 4701 H578² Galaxy Type SA(s)cd
φ 3.3′×2.8′, m12.4v, SB14.6   12ʰ49.2ᵐ +03° 23′
Finder Chart 64-11   ★★
12/14″Scopes–125x: NGC 4701 is between two 6th magnitude stars: 35 Virginis 20′ to its NE and 37 Virginis 38′ to its SE. The halo is a very faint, low uniform surface brightness glow elongated 1.5′×1′ NE–SW. One 12th magnitude star lies 3′ to the galaxy's WNW, and another a little further away to its SSW.

NGC 4713 H140¹ Galaxy Type SAB(rs)d III
φ 2.9′×1.8′, m11.7v, SB13.4   12ʰ50.0ᵐ +50° 19′
Finder Charts 64-6, 64-11   ★★
12/14″Scopes–125x: NGC 4713, located 10′ NE of a 7th magnitude star, is a faint, diffuse object with a 1.5′×1′ ENE–WSW halo but no central brightening except for a very faint stellar nucleus. A 13th magnitude star lies 2.5′ SE, and a 12th magnitude star 3.5′ SSE, of the galaxy's center.

NGC 4731 H41¹ Galaxy Type SB(s)d pec III
φ 5.4′×2.7′, m11.5v, SB14.2   12ʰ51.0ᵐ −06° 24′
Finder Chart 64-9, Figure 64-39   ★★
12/14″Scopes–125x: This galaxy is a nebulous 5′×1.25′ E–W haze behind a sprinkling of faint foreground stars. A very faint NW–SE central bar can be seen with averted vision. 13th magnitude stars lie beyond the halo's east and west tips. A faint star is superimposed upon the galaxy's halo just SW of its center. 2.5′ NE of the galaxy's center is a 45″ equilateral triangle of magnitude 14 to 14.5 stars.

NGC 4733 H73² Galaxy Type E+:
φ 2.0′×1.8′, m11.8v, SB13.1   12ʰ51.1ᵐ +10° 55′
Finder Chart 64-6   ★★
12/14″Scopes–125x: NGC 4733 is a faint galaxy with a 1.5′×1.25′ E–W halo that contains a broad, poorly concentrated core that covers 75% of the halo. A 13.5 magnitude star lies 1′ west of the galaxy's center. A 12th magnitude star lies 8′ ESE.

NGC 4742 H133¹ Galaxy Type SA?(r:)0° sp
φ 2.3′×1.2′, m11.3v, SB12.3   12ʰ51.8ᵐ −10° 27′
Finder Chart 64-9   ★★★
12/14″Scopes–125x: NGC 4742 is 9′ SE of Σ 1682, a beautiful double of an orange magnitude 6.4 primary with a blue magnitude 9.3 secondary 30″ from it in position angle 301°. The galaxy has a bright 1′×0.5′ ENE–WSW halo containing a well concentrated core with a bright stellar nucleus. 1.5′ to the NW of its center is a magnitude 11.5 star. NGC 4742 is part of a group with NGC 4760, NGC 4781, and other galaxies to its east.

NGC 4746 Galaxy Type Sb: sp
φ 2.0′×0.4′, m12.6v, SB12.2   12ʰ51.9ᵐ +12° 05′
Finder Charts 64-6, 64-10   ★★
12/14″Scopes–125x: NGC 4746 is contained within a 5′ equilateral triangle of magnitude 11 to 13.5 stars. Its halo measures about 1.5′×0.5′ ESE–WNW but is diffuse, very faint, and without any central brightening.

NGC 4753 H16¹ Galaxy Type I0: pec
φ 4.1′×2.3′, m9.9v, SB12.2   12ʰ52.4ᵐ −01° 12′
Finder Chart 64-11, Figure 64-40   ★★★★
8/10″Scopes–100x: NGC 4753 has a 2.5′×1.5′ E–W halo containing a conspicuous circular core with a bright stellar nucleus. A magnitude 13.5 star is 2.5′ WSW, and a 13th magnitude star is 4′ west, of the galaxy's center. 3.5′ to the NNE is a 45″ wide NE–SW pair of 12th and 13th magnitude stars.

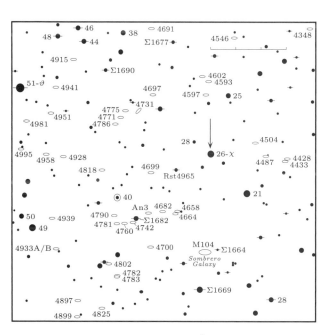

Finder Chart 64-9. 26–χ Vir: 12ʰ39.2ᵐ −08° 00′

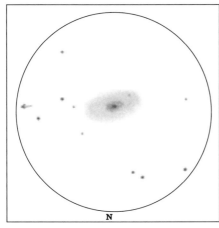

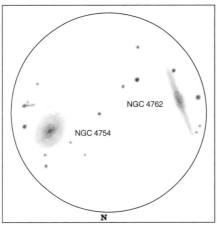

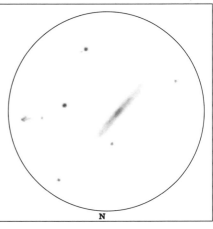

Figure 64-40. NGC 4753
17.5″, f4.5–250x, by G. R. Kepple

Figure 64-41. NGC 4754 and NGC 4762
16″, f4.5–150x, by Tom Osypowski

Figure 64-42. NGC 4771
17.5″, f4.5–300x, by G. R. Kepple

16/18″Scopes–150x: NGC 4753 has a 4′ × 2′ E–W envelope with a dusty or granular texture. Within it is a 1.5′ diameter core that contains a nonstellar nucleus.

NGC 4754 H25[1] Galaxy Type SB(r)0:
ϕ 4.6′ × 2.6′, m10.6v, SB 13.1   12^{h}52.3^m +11° 19′
Finder Charts 64-6, 64-10, Figure 64-41   ★★★★

8/10″Scopes–100x: NGC 4754 and NGC 4762 located 11′ to its SSE are a pair of galaxies with dramatically different shapes. Both are comparably bright, but NGC 4762 is a thin spindle and NGC 4754 is a diffuse 2′ × 1′ NNE–SSW oval with a stellar nucleus. A chain of alternating brighter and fainter stars snakes approximately E–W south of both galaxies.

16/18″Scopes–150x: NGC 4754 has a well-concentrated, circular 1′ diameter core that contains a stellar nucleus. An 11th magnitude star is 3.25′ SW of, and about as bright as, the nucleus. The galaxy's very faint halo measures 3′ × 2′ NNE–SSW. The immediate area has a light sprinkling of 13th and 14th magnitude stars.

NGC 4760 Galaxy Type (R′?)SA0
ϕ 1.9′ × 1.7′, m11.4v, SB 12.5   12^{h}53.1^m −10° 30′
Finder Chart 64-9   ★★★

12/14″Scopes–125x: NGC 4760 is situated between NGC 4742 and NGC 4781 in a group with several other galaxies. It also lies between an 8th magnitude star to its SW and a 9th magnitude star to its NNE, two members in a string of three stars leading to NGC 4757, a small faint galaxy 12′ NNW. NGC 4760 has a fairly faint 1.5′ × 1′ N–S halo containing a weakly concentrated core.

NGC 4762 H75[2] Galaxy Type SB(r)0′? sp
ϕ 9.1′ × 2.2′, m10.3v, SB 13.4   12^{h}52.9^m +11° 14′
Finder Charts 64-6 and 64-10, Figure 64-41   ★★★★

8/10″Scopes–100x: This bright, elegant 4′ × 0.5′ NNE–SSW spindle is in a nice setting of bright field stars with NGC 4754 just 11′ NW. A magnitude 10.5 star lies 3′ east, an 11th magnitude star is 2.5′ south, and a magnitude 9.5 star is 4′ SW, of the core of the spindle.

16/18″Scopes–150x: Spectacular! NGC 4762 is a thin iridescent 8′ × 0.5′ NNE–SSW needle. Its slight central bulge contains a bright circular core with a stellar nucleus. With averted vision a very faint dust lane may be glimpsed.

NGC 4765 H544[3] Galaxy Type S0/a? III-IV
ϕ 1.4′ × 1.0′, m13.0v, SB 13.2   12^{h}53.2^m +04° 28′
Finder Chart 64-11   ★★★

12/14″Scopes–125x: NGC 4765, centered 7′ NE of a 10.5 magnitude star, appears moderately faint, elongated 1.5′ × 1′ ENE–WSW, and gradually brighter toward a small, fairly well concentrated extended core. A 14th magnitude star lies 2′ NW of the galaxy's core. 11.5 magnitude stars are 5.5′ NNE and 5.5′ SSW.

NGC 4771 H535[2] Galaxy Type Sc: II-III:
ϕ 3.7′ × 0.8′, m12.3v, SB 13.3   12^{h}53.4^m +01° 16′
Finder Charts 64-9, 64-11, Figure 64-42   ★★★

12/14″Scopes–125x: NGC 4771, located 2.5′ ENE of a 10th magnitude star, appears fairly faint, elongated 2.5′ × 0.5′ NW–SE, and is slightly brighter through its center. A 13th magnitude star lies 1.5′ north, and a 12.5 magnitude star 3.5′ SSW, of the galaxy's center.

NGC 4772 H24² Galaxy Type (R′?)SAB(rs)0/a pec
φ 2.7′ × 1.3′, m11.0v, SB 12.3   12ʰ53.5ᵐ +02° 10′
Finder Chart 64-11   ★★★
12/14″ Scopes–125x: NGC 4772 has a moderately faint
1.75′ × 1.25′ NNW–SSE oval halo that brightens
smoothly to a well concentrated nonstellar nucleus.
A threshold star lies on the edge of the halo 50″ SW
of the galaxy's center.

NGC 4775 H186² Galaxy Type SAB(rs)cd II-III
φ 2.0′ × 1.0′, m11.1v, SB 12.4   12ʰ53.8ᵐ −06° 37′
Finder Chart 64-9   ★★
12/14″ Scopes–125x: NGC 4775 is a faint unconcentrated haze with a diffuse periphery about 1.75′ in
diameter. A deep-sky filter brings out the very faint
stellar nucleus. Magnitude 13.5 stars are 1.25′ SW
and 2.75′ ENE of the galaxy's nucleus, but otherwise the surrounding star field is sparse.

NGC 4781 H134² Galaxy Type SB(s)cd III
φ 2.9′ × 1.3′, m11.1v, SB 12.4   12ʰ54.4ᵐ −10° 32′
Finder Chart 64-9, Figure 64-43   ★★★
8/10″ Scopes–100x: NGC 4781, located 8′ SW of an 8th
magnitude star, has a fairly faint, smoothly illuminated 2′ × 1′ E–W halo. A curved row of 12th
magnitude stars concave to the south begins at the
west edge of the galaxy's halo and arcs to the WSW.
16/18″ Scopes–150x: In larger telescopes NGC 4781
appears fairly bright, elongated 3′ × 1′ ESE–WNW,
and mottled through its poorly concentrated central
region. 5.5′ to its SE is its companion galaxy NGC
4784, which has a faint stellar nucleus embedded
in a very faint 1′ × 0.25′ ESE–WNW halo. Several
other galaxies are in the vicinity of NGC 4781: NGC
4760 is 17′ to its west, NGCs 4766 and 4757 are
respectively 20′ and 25′ to its NW, and NGC 4790
is 18′ to its NNE.

NGC 4786 H187² Galaxy Type SAB0°
φ 1.1′ × 0.9′, m11.7v, SB 11.6   12ʰ54.5ᵐ −06° 52′
Finder Chart 64-9   ★★★
12/14″ Scopes–125x: NGC 4786 is faint but not difficult.
Its 1′ × 0.25′ NNW–SSE halo contains a stellar
nucleus. A 13th magnitude star lies 2.5′ north, and
a 12th magnitude star 4.5′ south, of the galaxy's
center.

NGC 4790 H560² Galaxy Type SB(rs)dm pec III
φ 1.4′ × 0.8′, m12.1v, SB 12.0   12ʰ54.9ᵐ −10° 15′
Finder Chart 64-9   ★★
12/14″ Scopes–125x: NGC 4790 is 10′ north of an 8th

magnitude star and centered 4.5′ SSE of a 10th
magnitude star. It has a faint unconcentrated 2′ × 1′
E–W halo. 13th magnitude stars are 2.5′ SSW and
5.5′ SSE of the galaxy's center.

NGC 4795 H21² Galaxy Type (R′)SB(r)a Pec:
φ 1.9′ × 1.7′, m12.1v, SB 13.2   12ʰ55.0ᵐ +08° 04′
Finder Charts 64-6, 64-10   ★★
12/14″ Scopes–125x: NGC 4795, centered 4′ south of an
11.5 magnitude star, is a faint, circular 1.5′ diameter
glow of even concentration. Its companion galaxy
NGC 4796 is a nearly stellar spot 25″ ENE of its
center. Another companion galaxy, NGC 4791,
located 5′ west of NGC 4795, is a faint uniform 20″
diameter glow slightly elongated E–W.

NGC 4808 H141¹ Galaxy Type SA(s)cd: III
φ 2.4′ × 0.9′, m11.7v, SB 12.4   12ʰ55.8ᵐ +04° 18′
Finder Chart 64-11   ★★★
12/14″ Scopes–125x: NGC 4808, located one degree
north of the 2nd magnitude star Delta (δ) = 43
Virginis, has a fairly faint 2′ × 0.75′ NW–SE halo.
13th magnitude stars are 1.75′ north and WNW of
the galaxy's center.

NGC 4818 H549² Galaxy Type SB(r:)a pec
φ 3.4′ × 1.4′, m11.1v, SB 12.7   12ʰ56.8ᵐ −08° 31′
Finder Chart 64-9, Figure 64-44   ★★★
8/10″ Scopes–100x: NGC 4818 is located 5′ east of a 9th
magnitude star to the south of which is a 20″ wide
double of magnitude 10 and 11 stars. The galaxy is
merely a 2′ × 0.75′ N–S glow. A 13th magnitude star

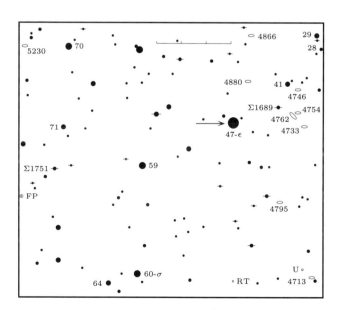

Finder Chart 64-10. 47–ε Vir: 13ʰ02.2ᵐ +10° 58′

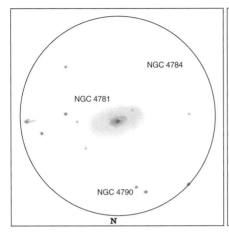

N

Figure 64-43. NGC 4781 Area
17.5″, f4.5–200x, by G. R. Kepple

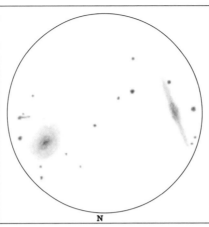

N

Figure 64-44. NGC 4818
17.5″, f4.5–200x, by G. R. Kepple

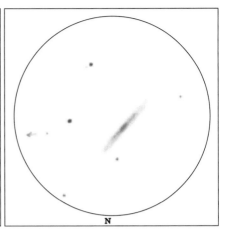

N

Figure 64-45. NGC 4845
17.5″, f4.5–300x, by G. R. Kepple

is on its southern tip 2′ from its center, and a magnitude 13.5 star is 1.5′ east of the galaxy's center.

16/18″ Scopes–150x: NGC 4818 possesses a fairly bright 3′ × 1′ NNE–SSW halo which brightens a little more into its center.

NGC 4845 H536² Galaxy Type Sab of Sb II-III
φ 4.8′ × 1.2′, m11.2v, SB 12.9   12ʰ58.0ᵐ +01° 35′
Finder Chart 64-11, Figure 64-45   ★★★★

8/10″ Scopes–100x: NGC 4845 is a faint but fairly conspicuous galaxy 12′ NE of a 7th magnitude star. Its 2′ × 1′ ENE–WSW halo is slightly brighter toward its center. A 10th magnitude star is 2′ NE, an 11.5 magnitude star 1.5′ SSE, and a 12th magnitude star 2.75′ SW of the galaxy's center.

16/18″ Scopes–150x: At this aperture, NGC 4845 displays a bright 4′ × 1′ halo with a mottled texture and weak core. A faint equatorial dust lane is traceable with averted vision along the halo's southern flank for a quarter of its length.

NGC 4856 H68¹ Galaxy Type SB?(s)0
φ 3.1′ × 0.9′, m10.5v, SB 11.5   12ʰ59.3ᵐ −15° 02′
Finder Chart 64-12   ★★★★

8/10″ Scopes–100x: NGC 4856, located 7′ NW of a 10th magnitude star, has a moderately bright 3′ × 1′ NE–SW halo containing a prominent core with a stellar nucleus. A 13th magnitude star is 20″ SE of the galaxy's center. NGC 4877 lies 22′ SE.

16/18″ Scopes–150x: NGC 4856 has a bright 4′ × 0.75′ NE–SW halo containing a 30″ diameter core. The NE extension of the halo seems slightly brighter than the SW.

NGC 4866 H162¹ Galaxy Type SA(r)0+: sp
φ 5.5′ × 1.2′, m11.2v, SB 13.1   12ʰ59.5ᵐ +14° 10′
Finder Chart 64-10, Figure 64-46   ★★★★

8/10″ Scopes–100x: This fine, bright edge-on galaxy has a 5.5′ × 1′ E–W lens-shaped halo surrounding an extended core containing a stellar nucleus. A 13th magnitude star is on the halo's edge 45″ WNW of the galaxy's center.

16/18″ Scopes–150x: NGC 4866 presents a large 6.5′ × 1′ halo containing a faint bar which protrudes from either side of a bright nucleus. The core extends for a quarter of the halo's length along its major axis.

NGC 4877 H299² Galaxy Type SAB:(rs)ab II-III
φ 1.9′ × 0.9′, m12.4v, SB 12.8   13ʰ00.4ᵐ −15° 17′
Finder Chart 64-12   ★★

12/14″ Scopes–125x: NGC 4877, centered 3′ SE of a 9th magnitude star, is a faint companion of NGC 4856, which is located 22′ to its NW. It is a faint, diffuse 1.5′ × 0.75′ N–S glow containing a faint stellar nucleus.

NGC 4880 H83³ Galaxy Type SA(r)0+:
φ 3.4′ × 2.8′, m11.4v, SB 13.7   13ʰ00.2ᵐ +12° 29′
Finder Charts 64-10   ★★★

8/10″ Scopes–100x: NGC 4880 is a very faint, diffuse 2′ × 1′ N–S glow containing a slight brightening at its center. The field is sprinkled with faint stars.

16/18″ Scopes–150x: The faint halo reaches 3′ × 1.5′ N–S and contains a slight central brightening. 14th magnitude stars are 1.75′ NNW and 2′ SSE of the galaxy's center. A small triangle of 13th magnitude stars lies 6′ SE.

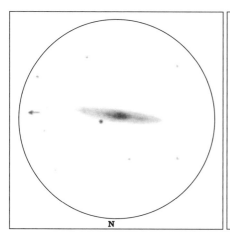

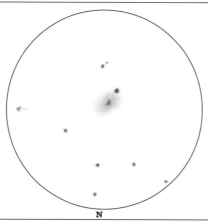

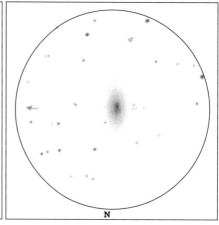

Figure 64-46. NGC 4866
17.5″, ƒ4.5–300x, by G. R. Kepple

Figure 64-47. NGC 4900
20″, ƒ4.5–175x, by Richard W. Jakiel

Figure 64-48. NGC 4939
17.5″, ƒ4.5–300x, by G. R. Kepple

NGC 4900 H143[1] Galaxy Type SB(rs)c III-IV
ϕ 2.3′ × 2.3′, m11.4v, SB13.0   13^{h}00.6^m +02° 30′
Finder Chart 64-11, Figure 64-47   ★★★
8/10″Scopes–100x: NGC 4900 is a fairly bright, round
   uniformly illuminated object 1.5′ in diameter. A
   10th magnitude star touches its SE edge.
16/18″Scopes–150x: Larger telescopes show NGC 4900
   as a 2′ diameter halo with a mottled texture, several
   knots and stellar spots, and a stellar nucleus. The
   10th magnitude star SE of the galaxy's center is
   clearly within the periphery of the halo.

NGC 4897 Galaxy Type SA:(r)bc II-III
ϕ 2.3′ × 2.2′, m11.8v, SB13.4   13^{h}00.8^m −13° 27′
Finder Chart 64-12   ★★
12/14″Scopes–100x: NGC 4897, located 6.5′ SE of a
   10.5 magnitude star and 5.5′ SSW of an 11.5
   magnitude star, is a very faint, circular 2.5′ diameter
   glow containing an inconspicuous core with a stellar
   nucleus. A 12.5 magnitude star lies 2.5′ NW of the
   galaxy's center.

NGC 4899 H300[2] Galaxy Type SB(s)cd: II-III
ϕ 1.9′ × 1.2′, m11.9v, SB12.6   13^{h}00.9^m −13° 57′
Finder Chart 64-12   ★★
8/10″Scopes–100x: NGC 4899 is located 8′ SE of a 7.5
   magnitude star. Its halo is a uniformly faint
   1.5′ × 0.75′ N–S glow.
16/18″Scopes–150x: The fairly faint 2′ × 1′ NNE–SSW
   oval halo of NGC 4899 contains a broad, slight
   central brightening. Magnitude 13 and 14.5 stars
   lie respectively 2′ NE and 1.25′ NE of the galaxy's
   center.

NGC 4902 H69[1] Galaxy Type SB(rs)bc I-II
ϕ 2.5′ × 2.2′, m10.9v, SB12.6   13^{h}01.0^m −14° 31′
Finder Chart 64-12   ★★★
12/14″Scopes–125x: NGC 4902 forms an equilateral
   triangle with two double stars located 2′ to its NW
   and 2′ to its WSW. Each double consists of 10th
   and 12.5 magnitude components separated by 45″;
   however, in the northern star-pair the secondary is
   at position angle 330°, and in the southern pair the
   secondary is in position angle 165°. NGC 4902 is a
   fairly bright galaxy with a diffuse, smoothly illuminated, round 2′ diameter halo.

NGC 4904 H517[3] Galaxy Type SB(s)dm III
ϕ 2.2′ × 1.4′, m12.0v, SB13.0   13^{h}01.0^m −00° 02′
Finder Chart 64-11   ★★
8/10″Scopes–100x: This galaxy, centered 2′ SSE of a

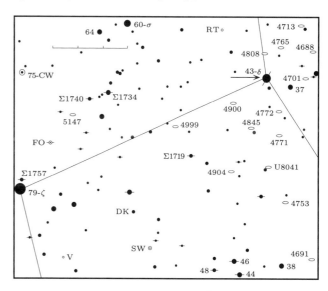

Finder Chart 64-11. 43–δ Vir: 12^{h}55.6^m +03° 24′

magnitude 11.5 star, has a fairly dim, circular 1′ diameter halo with a slightly brighter center. A magnitude 11 star lies 6.5′ NNW of the galaxy.

16/18″Scopes–150x: NGC 4904 shows an extended, poorly concentrated core embedded in a faint 1.5′ × 1′ NNE–SSW halo.

NGC 4915 H47[4] Galaxy Type SAB?0° :
ϕ 1.7′ × 1.4′, m12.1v, SB 12.9   13^{h}01.5^m −04° 33′
Finder Chart 64-9   ★★★

8/10″Scopes–100x: NGC 4915, located 6.5′ SW of a 10.5 magnitude star, is a fairly bright, but small galaxy with a round 30″ diameter halo that contains a brighter center.

16/18″Scopes–150x: NGC 4915 has a fairly bright circular 1′ diameter halo containing a prominent stellar nucleus. 6′ ENE of NGC 4915 is its companion galaxy NGC 4918, a very faint 20″ diameter haze.

NGC 4928 H190[2] Galaxy Type SB:(s)c II-III
ϕ 1.2′ × 0.9′, m12.5v, SB 12.4   13^{h}03.0^m −08° 05′
Finder Chart 64-9   ★★

16/18″Scopes–150x: NGC 4928 has a faint, circular 1′ diameter halo that surrounds a slight central brightening. An 11th magnitude star is 4.5′ east of the halo's northern tip, and a conspicuous pair of 10th and 12th magnitude stars stands out in the field 9.5′ NW of the galaxy.

NGC 4933B H191[2] Galaxy Type S0 pec
ϕ 1.3′ × 0.9′, m11.7v, SB 11.7   13^{h}03.9^m −11° 30′

NGC 4933A Galaxy Type E/S0 pec
ϕ 0.7′ × 0.5′, m12.6v, SB 11.3   13^{h}03.9^m −11° 30′
Finder Chart 64-9   ★★/★★

16/18″Scopes–150x: NGC 4933A and NGC 4933B are a close pair of interacting galaxies 7′ NE of a 9th magnitude star. NGC 4933B has a faint 1.25′ diameter halo that contains a faint stellar nucleus. Centered 45″ to its SW is the smaller NGC 4933A, which has a stellar nucleus embedded in a halo about half the size of the NGC 4933B halo.

NGC 4939 H561[2] Galaxy Type SAB(rs)c I-II
ϕ 4.3′ × 2.4′, m11.3v, SB 13.6   13^{h}04.2^m −10° 20′
Finder Chart 64-9, Figure 64-48   ★★★

8/10″Scopes–100x: This faint galaxy is one degree WNW of the magnitude 5.2 star 49 Virginis. Its faint 2.5′ × 2′ N–S oval halo contains a very faint stellar nucleus.

16/18″Scopes–150x: NGC 4939 has a fairly faint 3′ × 2′

N–S halo that brightens slightly to a faint core containing a nonstellar nucleus.

NGC 4941 H40[1] Galaxy Type (R)SA(rs)a
ϕ 3.7′ × 2.3′, m11.1v, SB 13.2   13^{h}04.2^m −05° 33′
Finder Chart 64-9   ★★★

8/10″Scopes–100x: NGC 4941, centered 2.5′ north of an 11th magnitude star, shows a fairly faint 2′ × 1′ N–S halo that contains a slight central brightening.

16/18″Scopes–150x: NGC 4941 has a fairly faint, low uniform surface brightness, 2.5′ × 1.5′ NNE–SSW halo surrounding a faint 20″ core that contains a faint stellar nucleus.

NGC 4951 H188[2] Galaxy Type SA(s)d III
ϕ 3.2′ × 1.2′, m11.9v, SB 13.2   13^{h}05.1^m −06° 30′
Finder Chart 64-9   ★★

8/10″Scopes–100x: NGC 4951 is a very faint 2.5′ × 0.75′ E–W streak.

16/18″Scopes–150x: Even in larger instruments the galaxy's halo remains fairly faint and diffuse. It is elongated 2.5′ × 1′ E–W and surrounds a faint 30″ diameter core. A threshold star is 1′ west of the galaxy's center. 12th magnitude stars are 4′ NNE, 6′ NE, and 7′ SW of the galaxy.

NGC 4958 H130[1] Galaxy Type S0° : sp
ϕ 3.6′ × 1.4′, m10.7v, SB 12.3   13^{h}05.8^m −08° 01′
Finder Chart 64-9   ★★★★

8/10″Scopes–100x: NGC 4958 is a fairly bright lenticular galaxy much-elongated 1.5′ × 0.5′ NNE–SSW and containing a conspicuous core with a stellar nucleus.

16/18″Scopes–150x: This galaxy is bright, elongated 2′ × 0.75′ NNE–SSW, and contains a bright core with a stellar nucleus. A 13th magnitude star lies 1.5′ WSW of the galaxy's nucleus.

NGC 4981 H189[2] Galaxy Type SAB(r)c II
ϕ 2.7′ × 1.8′, m11.3v, SB 12.9   13^{h}08.8^m −06° 47′
Finder Chart 64-9   ★★★

8/10″Scopes–100x: NGC 4981 is centered 1.75′ NNW of a 10th magnitude star that touches the edge of its fairly faint 1.5′ × 0.75′ NNW–SSE oval halo.

16/18″Scopes–150x: NGC 4981 has a moderately faint 3′ × 2′ halo that contains a small core with a very faint stellar nucleus. At this aperture the 10th magnitude star 1.75′ NNW of the nucleus can be seen distinctly within the periphery of the galaxy's halo.

NGC 4984 H301² Galaxy Type (R)SB(rs)0+
ϕ 3.2′×2.2′, m11.3v, SB13.3   13ʰ09.0ᵐ −15° 31′
Finder Chart 64-12 ★★★
8/10″Scopes-100x: NGC 4984 appears fairly faint. Its circular 1′ diameter halo surrounds a stellar nucleus. The field is well adorned with faint stars, especially to the galaxy's east and NE. An 11th magnitude star lies 2′ ENE of the galaxy's center.
16/18″Scopes-150x: The 1.5′ diameter halo appears moderately faint but contains an abruptly brighter 30″ diameter core with a stellar nucleus. A 13th magnitude star touches the halo's west edge.

NGC 4995 H42² Galaxy Type SAB(r)ab
ϕ 2.5′×1.8′, m11.1v, SB12.6   13ʰ09.7ᵐ −07° 50′
Finder Chart 64-13 ★★★
8/10″Scopes-100x: NGC 4995, centered 3′ SSE of an 8th magnitude star, is a fairly faint, round, diffuse 1′ diameter object that gradually brightens into its center.
16/18″Scopes-150x: With increased aperture this galaxy's faint stellar nucleus becomes visible and its halo increases in size to 2′×1.5′ E–W. The halo appears fairly bright and has a diffuse periphery. A threshold star lies 1.25′ east of center.

NGC 4999 H537² Galaxy Type SB(r)bc II
ϕ 2.1′×1.8′, m11.8v, SB13.1   13ʰ09.6ᵐ +01° 40′
Finder Chart 64-11 ★★★
8/10″Scopes-100x: NGC 4999, located 19′ WSW of an 8th magnitude star, has a faint, diffuse 1.5′ diameter halo surrounding a slightly brighter center.
16/18″Scopes-150x: NGC 4999 has a fairly faint, circular 2′ diameter halo that contains a very small, faint core. A 13th magnitude star 1.25′ east of the galaxy's center nearly touches the halo's edge.

NGC 5017 H669³ Galaxy Type SA?0
ϕ 2.0′×1.2′, m12.6v, SB13.4   13ʰ12.9ᵐ −16° 46′
Finder Chart 64-12 ★★
12/14″Scopes-100x: NGC 5017 is between a 10th magnitude star 8′ to its east and a wide pair of 11th magnitude stars 6′ to its WNW. The galaxy has a faint, round 1′ diameter halo with a well concentrated center in which is embedded a bright stellar nucleus.

NGC 5018 H746² Galaxy Type SB:(s:)0°
ϕ 2.8′×2.2′, m10.7v, SB12.5   13ʰ13.0ᵐ −19° 31′
Finder Chart 64-12 ★★★
8/10″Scopes-100x: NGC 5018, located 30′ NW of the

magnitude 5.6 star 55 Virginis, is bright, elongated 1.5′×0.75′ E–W, and strongly brightens to a tiny core with a stellar nucleus.
16/18″Scopes-150x: NGC 5018 has a bright 2′×1′ E–W halo that grows smoothly brighter to a small conspicuous core containing a stellar nucleus. A 13.5 magnitude star lies 2′ NNE of the galaxy's center. 7′ to its ESE is its companion galaxy NGC 5022, a very faint 2′×0.25′ NNE–SSW streak.

NGC 5035 Galaxy Type SAB(rs)0+
ϕ 1.3′×1.2′, m12.8v, SB13.1   13ʰ14.8ᵐ −16° 30′
Finder Chart 64-12, Figure 64-49 ★★
16/18″Scopes-150x: NGC 5035 is between a 3.75′ wide NNE–SSW pair of 9th magnitude stars. The galaxy has a bright stellar nucleus embedded in a faint 1′×0.45′ NNW–SSE halo. 10′ to its NE is galaxy NGC 5044, and 6′ to its SSE is galaxy NGC 5037.

NGC 5037 H510² Galaxy Type (R)Sa
ϕ 2.2′×1.0′, m12.2v, SB12.9   13ʰ15.0ᵐ −16° 35′
Finder Chart 64-12, Figure 64-49 ★★
8/10″Scopes-100x: NGC 5037 is located 13′ SSW of NGC 5044, in a group of faint galaxies. Its faint halo is elongated 1.25′×0.25′ NE–SW and contains a faint stellar nucleus. A 13th magnitude star is at the halo's NE tip.
16/18″Scopes-150x: NGC 5037 has a moderately faint much-elongated 2′×0.5′ NE–SW halo with faint stars at each tip. The star at the NE tip is conspicuous, but the one at the SW tip is at the threshold of vision. The galaxy's stellar nucleus is embedded in a small, circular core.

NGC 5044 H511² Galaxy Type E0/S0
ϕ 3.0′×3.0′, m10.8v, SB13.1   13ʰ15.4ᵐ −16° 23′
Finder Chart 64-12, Figure 64-49 ★★★
8/10″Scopes-100x: NGC 5044 is the brightest in a group of galaxies that includes NGC 5037 located 13′ to its SSW, NGC 5047 lying 10′ to its SE, and 5049 lying 8.5′ east. It has a fairly bright round 1.5′ diameter halo that contains a faint stellar nucleus.
16/18″Scopes-150x: This galaxy has a bright 1′ diameter core that contains a stellar nucleus and is surrounded by a 3′ diameter halo which fades smoothly to a diffuse periphery.

NGC 5046 Galaxy Type E2:
ϕ 0.8′×0.7′, m12.9v, SB12.1   13ʰ15.8ᵐ −16° 20′
Finder Chart 64-12 ★★
16/18″Scopes-150x: NGC 5046, located south of a 9th

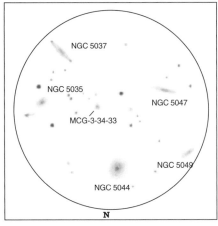

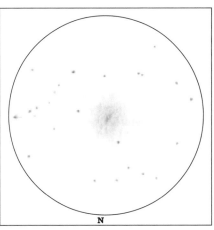

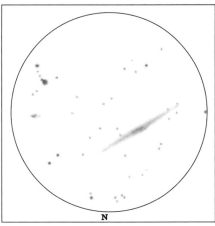

Figure 64-49. NGC 5044 Group
17.5″, f4.5–175x, by G. R. Kepple

Figure 64-50. NGC 5068
18.5″, f5–300x, by Glen W. Sanner

Figure 64-51. NGC 5170
17.5″, f4.5–200x, by G. R. Kepple

magnitude star, is a faint, circular 30″ diameter glow slightly elongated NNE–SSW and surrounding a stellar nucleus. A 12th magnitude star lies 2′ south of the galaxy's center.

NGC 5047 H670[3] Galaxy Type S0+: sp
ϕ **2.5′ × 0.5′, m12.7v, SB 12.8**   **13^{h}15.8^m −16° 31′**
Finder Chart 64-12, Figure 64-49   ★★

16/18″ Scopes–150x: NGC 5047, located 10′ SE of the considerably brighter NGC 5044 in the latter's galaxy group, appears rather faint, elongated 2′ × 0.5′ ENE–WSW, and slightly brighter toward its stellar nucleus. A 14th magnitude star is 45″ east, and a 13th magnitude star 1′ SSE, of the galaxy's center.

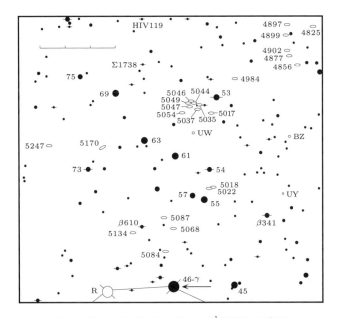

Finder Chart 64-12. 46–γ Hya: 13^{h}18.9^m −23° 10′

NGC 5049 H512[2] Galaxy Type S0: sp
ϕ **1.7′ × 0.8′, m13.0v, SB 13.2**   **13^{h}16.0^m −16° 24′**
Finder Chart 64-12, Figure 64-49   ★★

16/18″ Scopes–150x: NGC 5049, located 8.5′ east of NGC 5044, has a stellar nucleus embedded in a small, well concentrated core surrounded by a faint halo extended to 1.5′ × 0.5′ NW–SE. A magnitude 11.5 star lies 3.5′ ENE, and a 12th magnitude star 4.5′ NW, of the galaxy.

NGC 5054 H513[2] Galaxy Type SA(rs)bc pec I-II
ϕ **4.8′ × 2.8′, m10.9v, SB 13.6**   **13^{h}17.0^m −16° 38′**
Finder Chart 64-12   ★★★

8/10″ Scopes–100x: NGC 5054, located on the east edge of the NGC 5044 galaxy group, is a faint, diffuse 2.5′ × 2′ NW–SE glow. A 12.5 magnitude star lies near the halo's NE edge.

16/18″ Scopes–150x: NGC 5054 appears fairly faint and elongated 3′ × 2′ NW–SE, and has a broadly concentrated, mottled center containing a faint stellar nucleus.

NGC 5068 H312[2] Galaxy Type SB(rs)cd II-III
ϕ **7.1′ × 6.6′, m9.6v, SB 13.6**   **13^{h}18.9^m −21° 02′**
Finder Chart 64-12, Figure 64-50   ★★★

8/10″ Scopes–100x: NGC 5068, a faint face-on galaxy, is a diffuse 4′ diameter low surface brightness glow that is slightly brighter in its center.

16/18″ Scopes–150x: NGC 5068 is a member of the 22 million light year distant Centaurus Galaxy Group with M83 in Hydra and NGC 5128 in Centaurus. Its absolute magnitude is −19.6, a luminosity of 5.7 billion suns, and its true diameter is at least 45,000 light years. In larger instruments NGC 5068 shows a fairly faint halo that is slightly elongated 5′ × 4′ NNW–SSE and contains a faint but distinctly extended 1.5′ × 0.75′ NNW–SSE core. Two magnitude 13.5 stars are superimposed upon the halo 1.5′ NNE and 2.25′ WSW of the galaxy's center.

NGC 5076   Galaxy Type SB(rs)0+
ϕ 1.4′ × 0.8′, m13.2v, SB13.2   13^{h}19.4^m −12° 45′
Finder Chart 64-13   ★★
8/10″ Scopes–100x: NGC 5076 is the southernmost in a close galaxy-trio with NGC 5077 and NGC 5079. It appears faint and diffuse, is elongated 1′ × 0.5′ NNE–SSW, and contains a faint stellar nucleus. A wide pair of 13.5 magnitude stars lies 2′ SW of the galaxy's center.

NGC 5077   H193[2]   Galaxy Type E3
ϕ 1.9′ × 1.6′, m11.3v, SB12.4   13^{h}19.5^m −12° 39′
Finder Chart 64-13   ★★★
8/10″ Scopes–100x: NGC 5077, located 8′ east of a 7th magnitude star, is the brightest in a galaxy group that includes NGC 5072 located 9′ to the NW, NGC 5076 lying 5′ south, NGC 5079 located 3′ SE, and NGC 5088 lying 13′ ENE. NGC 5077 is fairly faint, but its small circular 1′ diameter halo surrounds a prominent stellar nucleus.
16/18″ Scopes–150x: NGC 5077 has a moderately bright 1.5′ × 1′ N–S oval halo that contains a small bright core with a stellar nucleus. A 13.5 magnitude star lies 1′ SE of the galaxy's center, and a 12.5 magnitude star is 4.5′ NW.

NGC 5079   H118[3]   Galaxy Type SB(rs)b II-III
ϕ 1.4′ × 0.9′, m13.0v, SB13.1   13^{h}19.6^m −12° 42′
Finder Chart 64-13   ★★
16/18″ Scopes–150x: NGC 5079 is the easternmost member of a close galaxy-trio with NGC 5077 and NGC 5076. It is a faint, diffuse object with a diameter of less than 1′. A 12.5 magnitude star is 6′ to the galaxy's SE.

NGC 5084   H313[2]   Galaxy Type S0° : pec sp
ϕ 4.8′ × 1.3′, m12.0v, SB13.9   13^{h}20.3^m −21° 50′
Finder Chart 64-12   ★★★
8/10″ Scopes–100x: NGC 5084, located 12′ WSW of an 8th magnitude star, has a small bright core with a stellar nucleus surrounded by faint extensions reaching 2′ × 0.5′ E–W.
16/18″ Scopes–150x: NGC 5084 has a bright 45″ × 0.25′ core containing a nonstellar nucleus. The surrounding envelope is elongated 3′ × 0.75′ ENE–WSW and

has a slight central bulge. A 12.5 magnitude star lies 2.5′ ENE of the galaxy's center.

NGC 5088   Galaxy Type SB:(s)cd: II-III
ϕ 2.8′ × 0.9′, m12.4v, SB13.2   13^{h}20.3^m −12° 34′
Finder Chart 64-13   ★★
12/14″ Scopes–125x: NGC 5088 is 13′ ENE of the triangle of galaxies formed by NGC 5076, NGC 5077, and NGC 5079. It has a faint 1′ × 0.5′ N–S halo containing a faint, nearly stellar nucleus. A 12.5 magnitude star lies 3′ ENE of the galaxy's center.

NGC 5087   H724[3]   Galaxy Type S0°
ϕ 3.0′ × 2.1′, m11.0v, SB12.8   13^{h}20.4^m −20° 37′
Finder Chart 64-12   ★★★
8/10″ Scopes–100x: This galaxy is fairly bright, elongated 1.25′ × 0.75′ N–S, and contains a stellar nucleus. A group of five 9th to 10th magnitude stars is about 7′ east of the galaxy.
16/18″ Scopes–150x: NGC 5087 has a large but faint oval core that contains a stellar nucleus and is surrounded by a much fainter 1.5′ × 1′ N–S halo.

NGC 5134   H314[2]   Galaxy Type SB?(rs)a pec
ϕ 2.8′ × 1.5′, m11.2v, SB12.6   13^{h}25.3^m −21° 08′
Finder Chart 64-12   ★★★
12/14″ Scopes–125x: NGC 5134 has a bright stellar nucleus embedded in a faint 2.5′ × 1.25′ NNW–SSE oval halo. 11′ to its west is the galaxy IC 4237, a small diffuse glow at least a magnitude fainter than NGC 5134. Double star β 610 (6.6, 10.6; 3.9″; 18°) is in the same field to the galaxy's NW.

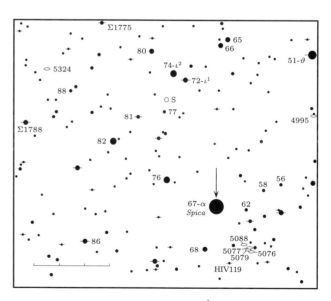

Finder Chart 64-13. 67–α Vir: 13^{h}25.2^m −11° 10′

NGC 5147 H25² Galaxy Type SB:(s)c II
φ **1.6'× 1.5', m11.8v, SB12.6   13ʰ26.3ᵐ +02° 06'**
Finder Chart 64-11   ★★★
8/10" Scopes–100x: NGC 5147 is a fairly conspicuous
     but diffuse, round 1' diameter glow with a stellar
     nucleus. It resembles a planetary nebula disk
16/18" Scopes–150x: NGC 5147 has a bright stellar
     nucleus surrounded by a circular 1.5' diameter halo
     with a mottled texture.

NGC 5170 H22⁵ Galaxy Type Sbc: sp
φ **7.8'× 1.1', m11.3v, SB13.5   13ʰ29.8ᵐ −17° 57'**
Finder Chart 64-12, Figure 64-51   ★★★
8/10" Scopes–100x: NGC 5170 is 9' NE of a 9th magni-
     tude star with a 10.5 magnitude companion 1.75'
     to its SSW. The galaxy is a faint narrow 3.5'× 0.5'
     NW–SE streak that contains a slight brightening
     along the center of its major axis.
16/18" Scopes–150x: NGC 5170 is a fairly faint but
     visually striking shaft of light highly elongated
     7'× 0.5' NW–SE. 200x reveals several spots along
     the center line and a faint stellar nucleus in a thin
     1.5' core. 12.5 magnitude stars are 5.5' and 7.5' ESE
     of the galaxy's center.

NGC 5230 H87³ Galaxy Type SA(s)c I-II
φ **1.9'× 1.7', m12.1v, SB13.2   13ʰ35.5ᵐ +13° 40'**
Finder Chart 64-10   ★★★
8/10" Scopes–100x: This face-on galaxy appears faint,
     small, and round, and contains a slightly brighter
     center.

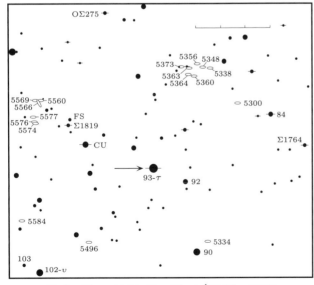

Finder Chart 64-14. 93–τ Vir: 14ʰ01.6ᵐ +01° 33'

16/18" Scopes–150x: NGC 5230 has a fairly faint, cir-
     cular 1.5' diameter halo which envelopes a moder-
     ately concentrated, mottled core. A 12.5 magnitude
     star lies 3.5' NW of the galaxy's center. NGC 5222
     is 9.5' NW of NGC 5230.

NGC 5247 H297² Galaxy Type SA(s)c I
φ **5.2'× 3.2', m10.1v, SB13.0   13ʰ38.1ᵐ −17° 53'**
Finder Chart 64-12   ★★★★
8/10" Scopes–100x: NGC 5247 is a fairly conspicuous
     circular glow 7' SW of a 9th magnitude star. The
     2.5'× 2' N–S halo contains a faint core.
16/18? Scopes–150x: The faint, diffuse halo of NGC
     5247 is elongated 5'× 4' N–S and contains a small
     30" diameter core. 200x and averted vision reveals
     vague counterclockwise spiral structure. The west-
     ern arm curves northward while the eastern arm
     curves southward.

NGC 5300 H533² Galaxy Type SAB(r)c II
φ **3.5'× 2.1', m11.4v, SB13.4   13ʰ48.3ᵐ +03° 57'**
Finder Chart 64-14   ★★
8/10" Scopes–100x: NGC 5300, located 8" SW of a wide
     pair of 8th and 9th magnitude stars, is dim and
     diffuse and elongated 2'× 1' NNW–SSE.
16/18" Scopes–150x: NGC 5300 is very faint, elongated
     3'× 2' NNW–SSE, and slightly brighter at its center.
     A 13th magnitude star lies near the halo's SSE edge
     1.75' from the galaxy's center.

NGC 5324 H307² Galaxy Type SA:(s)c I-II
φ **2.1'× 1.8', m11.7v, SB13.0   13ʰ52.1ᵐ −06° 03'**
Finder Chart 64-13   ★★★
8/10" Scopes–100x: NGC 5324 is a faint and diffuse glow
     about 1.5' in diameter. One 12th magnitude star
     lies 3' SE, and a wide pair of 12th magnitude stars
     is visible 4' NW, of the galaxy's center.
16/18" Scopes–150x: This galaxy has a fairly faint,
     circular 2' diameter halo around a slightly brighter,
     irregularly concentrated central area. A very faint
     star or bright spot in the halo is just east of the
     galaxy's center. A 13th magnitude star is 1.5' SSE
     of the center.

NGC 5334 H665³ Galaxy Type SB(rs)cd II
φ **4.1'× 3.2', m11.3v, SB13.9   13ʰ52.9ᵐ −01° 07'**
Finder Chart 64-14   ★★
8/10" Scopes–100x: NGC 5334, located 35' NW of the
     magnitude 5.1 star 90 Virginis and centered 3.5'
     north of a 12th magnitude star, is a faint 2' diameter
     glow.
16/18" Scopes–150x: NGC 5334 has a faint 4'× 3' NNE–

SSW halo that envelopes a broad weakly concentrated central region.

NGC 5363 H6[1] Galaxy Type I0?
φ 5.0′× 3.2′, m10.1v, SB12.9   13ʰ56.1ᵐ +05° 15′
Finder Chart 64-14, Figure 64-52   ★★★★
8/10″Scopes-100x: This bright galaxy lies 4′ SW of
ADS9060, a close 1″ wide ESE–WNW double of
magnitude 8.4 and 8.9 stars: even at 250x, ADS
9060 does not fully split but is seen as two disks in
contact. NGC 5363 has a stellar nucleus embedded
in a bright core enveloped by a 2.5′× 2′ NW–SE
oval halo.
16/18″Scopes-150x: NGC 5363 is quite bright, elongated 3′× 2′ NW–SE, and contains a well concentrated core with a stellar nucleus. It is surrounded
by faint companions: NGC 5364 and NGC 5360 are
respectively 15′ and 20′ to its south, and NGC 5356,
NGC 5348, and NGC 5338 are progressively more
distant to its west.

NGC 5364 H534[2] Galaxy Type SA(rs)bc pec I
φ 6.6′× 5.1′, m10.5v, SB14.2   13ʰ56.2ᵐ +05° 01′
Finder Chart 64-14, Figure 64-52   ★★★
12/14″Scopes-125x: NGC 5364, located 15′ south of
NGC 5363, has a moderately faint, diffuse 5′× 3.5′
NNE–SSW halo surrounding an irregularly-illumi-
nated granular 1.5′× 1′ oval core. Two 14th magnitude stars are superimposed upon the halo 1.5′
WNW and 1.75′ NNW of the galaxy's center. A
12th magnitude star is beyond one of the 14th
magnitude stars 3.5′ NNW of the center. 8′ WSW
of NGC 5364 is NGC 5360, a faint 1′× 0.25′ ENE–
WSW streak with a 14th magnitude star at its
WSW tip.

NGC 5426 H309[2] Galaxy Type SAB(rs)bc pec II:
φ 2.3′× 1.4′, m12.1v, SB13.2   14ʰ03.4ᵐ −06° 04′

NGC 5427 H310[2] Galaxy Type SA(s)c pec I:
φ 2.6′× 1.8′, m11.4v, SB12.9   14ʰ03.4ᵐ −06° 02′
Finder Chart 64-15, Figure 64-54   ★★★/★★★
12/14″Scopes-125x: NGC 5426 and NGC 5427 are a
pair of interacting galaxies separated by about 2′
N–S. The northern system, NGC 5427, is the larger
and brighter of the two: its 2′ diameter halo is
slightly elongated NE–SW and contains a bright
core with a stellar nucleus. NGC 5426, the southern
component, has a moderately faint 1.5′× 1.25′ N–S
halo that envelopes a prominent extended core with
a faint stellar nucleus. A 13th magnitude star is
superimposed upon the halo of NGC 5426 just 45″
NNE from its nucleus.

Figure 64-52. *NGC 5363, at bottom, and NGC 5364, at top, appear dramatically different in the eyepiece. NGC 5360 lies to the left of NGC 5364, and PGC 49602 is visible at right. Image courtesy of Andreas Roerig.*

NGC 5468 H286[3] Galaxy Type SA(s)cd II-III
φ 2.6′× 2.2′, m12.5v, SB14.3   14ʰ06.6ᵐ −05° 27′
Finder Chart 64-15   ★★
12/14″Scopes-125x: NGC 5468, centered 4.5′ NNW of
an 8th magnitude star, is a faint, unevenly concentrated glow about 2.5′ across. 5′ to its east, located
within a triangle of 13th and 14th magnitude stars,
is its companion galaxy NGC 5472, a very faint,
diffuse smudge elongated 1′× 0.25′ NE–SW.

NGC 5493 H46[4] Galaxy Type S0 pec: sp:
φ 1.5′× 1.5′, m11.4v, SB12.1   14ʰ11.5ᵐ −05° 03′
Finder Chart 64-15   ★★★
12/14″Scopes-125x: NGC 5493, located 16′ NW of a
9th magnitude star, has a bright 1.5′× 1′ ESE–
WNW oval halo in which is embedded a small,
bright extended core. A 12th magnitude star lies 7′
to the galaxy's west, and a 13th magnitude star is
4′ to its east.

NGC 5496 Galaxy Type SB?(s:)cd: II-III
φ 4.1′× 0.8′, m12.1v, SB13.3   14ʰ11.6ᵐ −01° 09′
Finder Charts 64-14, 64-15   ★★
12/14″Scopes-125x: NGC 5496, located in a barren star
field, is a very faint, uniformly illuminated 4′× 0.5′
N–S streak. 175x shows a thin, slightly brighter core
extending nearly one fourth of the halo's length. A
13.5 magnitude star is on the eastern edge of the
halo 1′ north of the galaxy's center.

Figure 64-53. *The large and bright NGC 5566 displays a bright core in a highly extended halo. Its close companion NGC 5569 is visible only as a very faint smudge. NGC 5560 is a bright streak. Image courtesy of Jim Burnell.*

NGC 5534 Galaxy Type (R:)SA:(s:)a: pec
φ 1.6′× 1.4′, m12.3v, SB 13.1   14ʰ17.7ᵐ −07° 25′
Finder Chart 64-15   ★★
12/14″Scopes–125x: NGC 5534 is within a row of five
  10th to 11.5 magnitude stars 9′ NW of a 6.5
  magnitude star. It has a faint 1.5′×0.5′ E–W halo
  on which is embedded a faint stellar nucleus.

NGC 5560 H579² Galaxy Type SB(s)b pec
φ 3.7′× 0.8′, m12.4v, SB 13.4   14ʰ20.1ᵐ +04° 00′
Finder Chart 64-14, Figure 64-53   ★★★
12/14″Scopes–100x: NGC 5560, centered 5′ east of a
  9th magnitude star, is in a fine galaxy-trio with
  NGC 5566 located 5′ to its SE and NGC 5569 lying
  7′ east. It has a thin, bright, well concentrated 1′
  long core embedded in a highly elongated 3′×0.75′
  ESE–WNW halo. A 13th magnitude star is 45″
  north of the galaxy's center.

NGC 5566 H144¹ Galaxy Type SB(r)ab II-III
φ 5.7′× 2.1′, m10.6v, SB 13.1   14ʰ20.3ᵐ +03° 56′
NGC 5569 Galaxy Type SAB(rs)cd:
φ 1.8′× 1.5′, m13.2v, SB 14.1   14ʰ20.5ᵐ +03° 59′
Finder Chart 64-14, Figure 64-53   ★★★★/★★
8/10″Scopes–100x: NGC 5566 is the brightest and
  largest galaxy of a fine trio with NGC 5560 and
  NGC 5569. It has a faint, smooth 4′×1.5′ NNE–

SSW halo enveloping a bright core with a stellar
nucleus. The core is flanked by a 12th magnitude
star 1.75′ to its east and a 13th magnitude star 1.25′
to its WSW.
16/18″Scopes–150x: NGC 5566 has a bright 50″×30″
NNE–SSW oval core embedded with a faint NNW–
SSE bar that is surrounded by a much fainter
5′×1.5′ NNE–SSW halo. NGC 5569, a companion
galaxy of NGC 5566 located just beyond its NNE
tip, is a very faint circular glow about 1′ in diameter
and containing a poorly concentrated center.

NGC 5574 H145¹ Galaxy Type SB0? sp
φ 1.1′× 0.8′, m12.4v, SB 12.1   14ʰ20.9ᵐ +03° 14′

NGC 5576 H146¹ Galaxy Type E3
φ 3.0′× 2.4′, m11.0v, SB 13.0   14ʰ21.2ᵐ +03° 16′

NGC 5577 Galaxy Type SBA(rs)bc: III
φ 2.9′× 0.8′, m12.2v, SB 13.0   14ʰ21.2ᵐ +03° 26′
Finder Chart 64-14, Figure 64-55   ★★/★★★/★★
12/14″Scopes–125x: NGC 5576 is the brightest and
  largest of a trio of galaxies that includes NGC 5577,
  located 10′ to its NNE, and NGC 5574, just 3′ to
  its SW. It has a bright 2′×1.5′ E–W halo that
  contains a circular 30″ diameter core with a stellar
  nucleus. A 13th magnitude star nearly touches the
  halo's periphery 1.25′ NW of the galaxy's center.
  The small satellite of NGC 5576, NGC 5574, has a
  moderately faint ENE–WSW halo containing a very
  faint stellar nucleus. NGC 5577 is the faintest
  member of the galaxy trio but has the most visually
  interesting form: it is a highly elongated, diffuse
  3′×1′ NE–SW streak that is slightly brighter along
  the center of its major axis. NGC 5577 is flanked
  by a 14th magnitude star 30″ NW, and a 14.5
  magnitude star 1′ ENE, of its center.

NGC 5584 Galaxy Type SA(s)c II
φ 3.2′× 2.6′, m11.4v, SB 13.5   14ʰ22.4ᵐ −00° 23′
Finder Charts 64-14, 64-15   ★★
12/14″Scopes–125x: NGC 5584 is 15′ NNW of a 7th
  magnitude star within a group of fainter stars: a
  magnitude 10.5 star lies 3.5′ to its NE; a 12th
  magnitude star lies 2′ to its NNE, and two very
  faint stars are 2.75′ NNW and 2′ SE. The galaxy
  has a faint, diffuse 3′×2′ NW–SE oval halo around
  a broad, slight central brightening.

NGC 5634 H70¹ Globular Cluster Class IV
φ 4.9′, m9.4v   14ʰ29.6ᵐ −05° 59′
Finder Chart 64-15, Figure 64-56   ★★★
8/10″Scopes–150x: NGC 5634, the only globular cluster

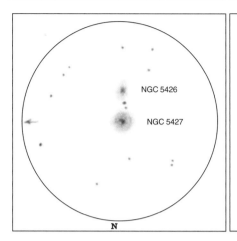

Figure 64-54. NGC 5426 and NGC 5427
13", f4.5–115x, by Tom Polakis

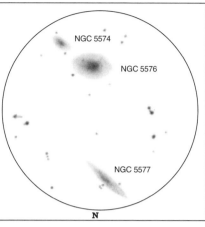

Figure 64-55. NGC 5576 Group
18.5", f5–250x, by Glen W. Sanner

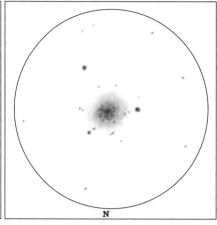

Figure 64-56. NGC 5634
17.5", f4.5–225x, by G. R. Kepple

in Virgo, is located within a triangle composed of a magnitude 8.5 star 1.25′ ESE of the globular, a magnitude 10.5 star 3.5′ to its SSW, and a 12th magnitude star 1.75′ to its NNW. The cluster has a fairly faint, unresolved, 2′ diameter halo around a weakly concentrated center.

16/18″ Scopes–200x: In larger telescopes this globular cluster appears fairly bright, but its granular 2.5′ diameter halo remains unresolved, even around its periphery. It is broadly concentrated with a small, slightly brighter core.

NGC 5638 H581² Galaxy Type E1
φ 2.3′ × 2.1′, m11.2v, SB12.8   14ʰ29.7ᵐ +03° 14′
Finder Chart 64-16   ★★★

8/10″ Scopes–100x: This galaxy has a moderately faint 1.5′ diameter halo surrounding a broad central brightening.

16/18″ Scopes–150x: NGC 5638 has a stellar nucleus embedded in a fairly bright but small core surrounded by a diffuse 2′ diameter halo. 2′ north of NGC 5638 is its companion galaxy NGC 5636, a very faint 1′ × 0.75′ NE–SW oval containing a very faint stellar nucleus.

NGC 5645 H150² Galaxy Type SB(s)d III
φ 2.9′ × 1.6′, m12.5v, SB14.0   14ʰ30.7ᵐ +07° 17′
Finder Chart 64-16   ★★

12/14″ Scopes–125x: NGC 5645, located 6′ west of a 9th magnitude star, has a moderately faint, diffuse 2′ × 1.5′ E–W halo surrounding a poor broadly concentrated core. 13th magnitude stars are 2′ NW and 2.75′ SE, and a 12th magnitude star is 3.5′ NNE, of the galaxy's center.

NGC 5668 H574² Galaxy Type SA(s)d II-III
φ 3.2′ × 2.8′, m11.5v, SB13.8   14ʰ33.4ᵐ +04° 27′
Finder Chart 64-16   ★★

8/10″ Scopes–100x: NGC 5668, located 5.5′ SW of a wide pair of 9th magnitude stars, has a faint, diffuse 1.75′ diameter halo of uniform surface brightness.

16/18″ Scopes–150x: Even in larger telescopes NGC 5668 looks only weakly concentrated. Its broad, mottled core is just slightly brighter than its outer halo, which with averted vision appears to be about 2.5′ in diameter. A faint star is superimposed 45″ NE of the galaxy's center.

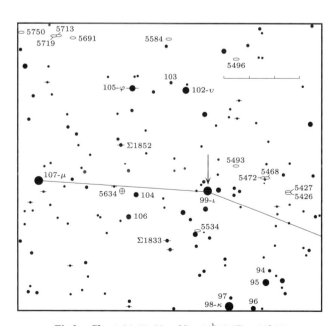

Finder Chart 64-15. 99–ι Vir: 14ʰ16.0ᵐ −06° 00′

Figure 64-57. *NGC5746 is a beautiful needle with a patchy texture and a dust lane along its eastern flank. Image courtesy of Josef Pöpsel and Stefan Benneweis.*

NGC 5690 H582² Galaxy Type SB:(rs:)bc II?
ϕ **3.3′ × 1.0′, m11.8v, SB12.9   14ʰ37.7ᵐ +02° 17′**
Finder Chart 64-16   ★★

12/14″Scopes–125x: NGC 5690 is centered only 3.5′ ENE of a magnitude 6.5 star and its faint glow is almost overwhelmed by the glare: the star should be positioned outside of the field of view. The galaxy has a faint, much-elongated 2.5′ × 0.75′ diameter NW–SE halo enveloping a slightly brighter, very thin, 1′ × 0.25′ core. A 14th magnitude star is superimposed upon the halo near the galaxy's SE tip.

NGC 5691 H681² Galaxy Type SB?(s)m? III?
ϕ **1.7′ × 1.5′, m12.3v, SB13.1   14ʰ37.9ᵐ −00° 24′**
Finder Chart 64-16   ★★

12/14″Scopes–125x: NGC 5691 lies in an attractive star field. Its faint 1.5′ × 1.25′ ESE–WNW halo is slightly brighter in its center and contains a stellar nucleus. A 13th magnitude star lies 4′ NNE of the galaxy's center.

NGC 5701 H575² Galaxy Type (R)SB(rs)0/a
ϕ **4.1′ × 4.1′, m10.9v, SB13.8   14ʰ39.2ᵐ +05° 22′**
Finder Chart 64-16   ★★★

8/10″Scopes–100x: NGC 5701 is flanked by two 11th magnitude stars, and its moderately faint 1.75′ × 1.5′ N–S halo contains a conspicuous core.

16/18″Scopes–150x: NGC 5701 has a stellar nucleus embedded in a bright 30″ diameter core surrounded by a diffuse 2′ × 1.5′ N–S halo. 4′ NE of the galaxy is an arc formed by one 11th magnitude and two fainter stars. A second 11th magnitude star lies 3.5′ west of the galaxy.

NGC 5713 H182¹ Galaxy Type Sb? pec
ϕ **3.0′ × 2.3′, m11.2v, SB13.1   14ʰ40.2ᵐ −00° 17′**

NGC 5719 H682² Galaxy Type Sa pec sp
ϕ **2.9′ × 1.1′, m12.2v, SB13.3   14ʰ40.9ᵐ −00° 19′**
Finder Charts 64-15, 64-16   ★★★/★★

12/14″Scopes–125x: NGC 5713 has a fairly bright 2′ × 1.75′ E–W halo surrounding a poorly concentrated, irregularly bright E–W core containing a very faint stellar nucleus. A magnitude 12.5 star lies 3.5 ENE of the galaxy's center. NGC 5719, located 11.5′ east of NGC 5713 and centered 2′ south of an 11th magnitude star, is a faint, much-elongated 2′ × 0.5′ E–W streak containing a thin, poorly concentrated core.

NGC 5740 H538² Galaxy Type SA(rs)c II
ϕ **2.9′ × 1.7′, m11.9v, SB13.4   14ʰ44.4ᵐ +01° 41′**
Finder Chart 64-16   ★★★

12/14″Scopes–125x: NGC 5740 forms a large triangle with the galaxy NGC 5714 located 19′ to its NNE and the magnitude 3.7 star 109 Virginis 29′ to its NE. Its moderately faint 2.5′ × 1.5′ NNW–SSE oval halo contains a small but conspicuous core. Magnitude 13.5 stars are 1.5′ WNW and 1.75′ SSW of the galaxy's center.

NGC 5746 H126¹ Galaxy Type SA?b sp
ϕ **6.8′ × 1.0′, m10.3v, SB12.3   14ʰ44.9ᵐ +01° 57′**
Finder Chart 64-16, Figure 64-57   ★★★★★

8/10″Scopes–100x: NGC 5746 is located 20′ WNW of the magnitude 3.7 star 109 Virginis and is centered 5′ SSE of a 7th magnitude star. It is a bright edge-on galaxy with a conspicuous central bulge. The core is 2′ long, but with averted vision the thin halo may be traced out to a length of 6′.

16/18″Scopes–150x: NGC 5746 is a beautifully detailed nearly N–S needle of light. The bright 2.5′ long core has a patchy texture, and some knots of light are strung along its northern wing. Beyond the ends of the central bulge the halo, increasingly fainter and more diffuse the farther it extends from the galaxy's center, tapers to thin tips, reaching a

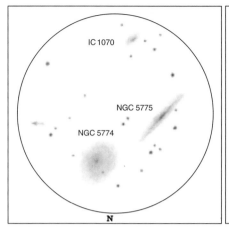

Figure 64-58. NGC 5774 and NGC 5775
17.5″, f4.5–250x, by G. R. Kepple

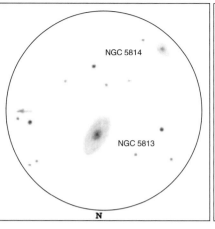

Figure 64-59. NGC 5813 and NGC 5814
18.5″, f5–300x, by Glen W. Sanner

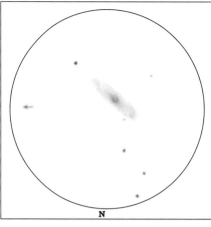

Figure 64-60. NGC 5838
20″, f4.5–175x, by Richard W. Jakiel

full length of 7′. With averted vision a thin dark dust lane may be glimpsed running along the bulge's and the inner halo's eastern long axis. A 14th magnitude star is superimposed upon the halo 2′ south of the galaxy's center.

NGC 5750 H183[1] Galaxy Type SAB(r)0+
ϕ **2.7′ × 1.6′, m11.6v, SB13.1**   **14^{h}46.2^m −00° 13′**
Finder Charts 64-15, 64-16   ★★★
12/14″Scopes–125x: NGC 5750 has a moderately faint 2′ × 1.5′ ENE–WSW halo that slightly brightens toward its center and a fairly conspicuous stellar nucleus. A 13.5 magnitude star lies 1′ north of the nucleus.

NGC 5774 Galaxy Type SAB(rs)d
ϕ **3.1′ × 2.6′, m12.1v, SB14.3**   **14^{h}53.7^m +03° 35′**

NGC 5775 H554[3] Galaxy Type SBc? sp
ϕ **3.8′ × 0.9′, m11.4v, SB12.6**   **14^{h}54.0^m +03° 33′**
Finder Chart 64-16, Figure 64-58   ★★/★★★
8/10″Scopes–100x: NGC 5775 appears fairly faint, elongated 3′ × 1′ NW–SE, and slightly brighter along its center. 4.5′ to its NW is its companion galaxy NGC 5774, a very faint 1′ diameter glow.
16/18″Scopes–150x: NGC 5775 has a thin 2′ long core with faint extensions from its tips toward the NNW and SSE that brings the galaxy's total length to 4′. 13th magnitude stars are 1′ NE and 2′ SSE of the galaxy's center. Its companion galaxy, NGC 5774, is much fainter but rather large, its dim, smoothly faint halo a slightly elongated 1.5′ × 1.25′ E–W oval glow. A 13th magnitude star lies 1.5′ NE of the center of NGC 5774. From the SE tip of NGC

5775 a string of faint stars leads 4′ SSW to IC 1070, visible only with averted vision as an extremely faint 30″ × 15″ NW–SE smudge.

NGC 5806 H539[2] Galaxy Type SAB(rs)b: II-III
ϕ **2.7′ × 1.4′, m11.7v, SB13.0**   **15^{h}00.0^m +01° 54′**
Finder Chart 64-16   ★★★
12/14″Scopes–125x: NGC 5806 is the easternmost member of the NGC 5856 group, a cluster of galaxies scattered over a degree of sky mostly south of the 4th magnitude star 110 Virginis. It appears fairly faint, and its 2′ × 1′ N–S halo contains a moderately concentrated core in which is embedded a faint stellar nucleus. A 13th magnitude star lies 3.25′ SE of the galaxy's center.

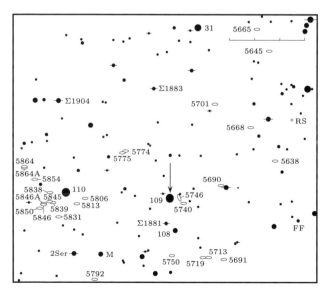

Finder Chart 64-16. 109 Vir: 14^{h}46.2^m +01° 54′

Figure 64-61. *NGC 5846-46A (at left) and NGC 5850 lie in the heart of the NGC 5846 galaxy group. Image courtesy of Chris Schur.*

NGC 5813 H127¹ Galaxy Type SA:0
φ **3.4′ × 2.8′, m10.5v, SB12.8**   15ʰ01.2ᵐ +01° 42′
Finder Chart 64-16, Figure 64-59   ★★★
8/10″Scopes–100x: NGC 5813, a member of the NGC
   5846 group, is half a degree SW of the magnitude
   4.4 star 110 Virginis and within a 5′ × 4′ triangle of
   12th magnitude stars. It is a bright galaxy with a
   1.5′ × 1′ NW–SE halo that contains a small bright
   core.
16/18″Scopes–150x: NGC 5813 shows a well concentrated 2′ × 1.5′ NW–SE halo containing a sharp
   nonstellar nucleus. 5′ to the SE of NGC 5813 is its
   companion galaxy, NGC 5814, which has a faint
   stellar nucleus surrounded by a very faint tiny
   NE–SW halo.

NGC 5831 H540² Galaxy Type E1/SAB0:
φ **2.0′ × 1.8′, m11.5v, SB12.7**   15ʰ04.1ᵐ +01° 13′
Finder Chart 64-16   ★★★
12/14″Scopes–125x: NGC 5831, located 50′ SSE of the

magnitude 4.4 star 110 Virginis, is the southernmost
galaxy of the NGC 5846 group and somewhat
isolated from the other members. It is a fairly bright
but soft round 1′ diameter glow enveloping an
inconspicuous stellar nucleus. A 13th magnitude
star is 1.5′ NNE of the galaxy's center.

NGC 5838 H542² Galaxy Type SAB(s:)0°
φ **3.5′ × 1.6′, m10.9v, SB12.7**   15ʰ05.4ᵐ +02° 06′
Finder Chart 64-16, Figure 64-60   ★★★
8/10″Scopes–100x: NGC 5838, a member of the NGC
   5846 group, is 38′ east of the magnitude 4.4 star
   110 Virginis and centered 5′ NNE of a 9th magnitude star. It is a fairly bright galaxy elongated
   1.5′ × 0.75′ NE–SW and containing a stellar nucleus.
16/18″Scopes–150x: NGC 5838 displays a bright circular 1′ diameter core within a 3′ × 1′ NE–SW halo.
   A 13th magnitude star lies just beyond the halo's
   SW tip, and a slightly brighter star is 2.5′ NNE of
   the galaxy's center.

NGC 5839 H541² Galaxy Type SAB(rs:)0°
ϕ 1.2′×1.2′, m12.7v, SB12.9   15ʰ05.5ᵐ +01° 38′

NGC 5845 H511³ Galaxy Type SAB?0:
ϕ 0.6′×0.4′, m12.5v, SB10.8   15ʰ06.0ᵐ +01° 38′

NGC 5846 H128¹ Galaxy Type E1
ϕ 3.0′×3.0′, m10.0v, SB12.3   15ʰ06.4ᵐ +01° 36′

NGC 5846A Galaxy Type cE1
ϕ 0.5′×0.3′, m12.8v, SB10.6   15ʰ06.5ᵐ +01° 36′
Finder Chart 64-16, Figure 64-61   ★★/★★/★★★/★★

8/10″Scopes–100x: NGC 5846 is the brightest member of its small galaxy group centered nearly a degree SE of the magnitude 4.4 star 110 Virginis. It has a bright, round 1.25′ diameter halo that contains a prominent core. A 12.5 magnitude star lies 2.5′ west of the galaxy's center.

16/18″Scopes–150x: In larger telescopes NGC 5846 appears well concentrated, its 1.5′ diameter halo smoothly brightening to a stellar nucleus. Embedded within the halo 45″ south of its center is the companion of NGC 5846, NGC 4846A, a faint, nearly stellar spot. 7.5′ WNW of NGC 5846 is NGC 5845, visible as a diffuse 45″×30″ NW–SE halo containing a fairly faint core. A 13th magnitude star is 2.5′ east of the center of NGC 5845. Only 15′ west of NGC 5846 is yet another galaxy of the cluster, NGC 5839, a faint 1′ diameter glow around a faint stellar nucleus.

NGC 5850 H543² Galaxy Type SB(r)b II-III
ϕ 4.6′×4.1′, m10.8v, SB13.8   15ʰ07.1ᵐ +01° 33′
Finder Chart 64-16, Figure 64-61   ★★★

12/14″Scopes–125x: NGC 5850, located 10′ SE of NGC

5846 in the latter's galaxy cluster, has a stellar nucleus embedded in a bright, circular core surrounded by a much fainter, diffuse 2.5′ diameter halo. A threshold star lies on the ESE edge of the halo. Two 11th magnitude stars, located 2′ NNW and 2.5′ NNE of the galaxy's center, alternate with two 13th magnitude stars to form a short zigzagging E–W star chain.

NGC 5854 H544³ Galaxy Type SB(s)0+
ϕ 2.2′×0.6′, m11.9v, SB12.0   15ʰ07.8ᵐ +02° 34′
Finder Chart 64-16   ★★★

12/14″Scopes–125x: NGC 5854 lies within the NE edge of the NGC 5846 group and 15′ NE of a 7th magnitude star. It has a moderately bright 2′×0.5′ NE–SW halo that contains a small, fairly conspicuous core. A 13th magnitude star lies 2′ ESE of the galaxy's center.

NGC 5864 H585² Galaxy Type SB(s)0°? sp
ϕ 2.4′×0.9′, m11.8v, SB12.5   15ʰ09.6ᵐ +03° 03′
Finder Chart 64-16   ★★★

12/14″Scopes–125x: NGC 5864, located at the NE edge of the NGC 5846 galaxy group, is that cluster's most isolated member. It is a fairly conspicuous 2′×0.5′ ENE–WSW streak that is slightly brighter along the center of its major axis. 14th magnitude stars are 30″ ESE and 1.25′ SSW of the galaxy's center. A magnitude 10.5 star 7.5′ to the galaxy's north is at the NNE vertex of a thin 2.5′×1′ triangle with 12th and 13th magnitude stars.

Chapter 65

Vulpecula, the Little Fox

65.1 Overview

Vulpecula, the Little Fox, was introduced by Johannes Hevelius in the late 17th century under the name Vulpecula cum Ansere, the Little Fox with the Goose. It occupies a part of the Milky Way between Cygnus on the north and Sagitta and Delphinus on the south which does not contain any bright stars and therefore was not within any of the ancient constellations. Its long thin area extends from the Great Rift on the west across the eastern branch of the Summer Milky Way, which here is not remarkably bright in background glow but outstanding for its profusion of magnitude 7 to 10 stars. The Vulpecula star fields are splendid to sweep in low power binoculars. Vulpecula has a rather large number of open clusters for such a small Milky Way constellation, the most impressive aesthetically being NGC 6940 and, for binoculars and small telescopes, Collinder 399, the "Coathanger." The constellation also contains a small assortment of rather ordinary bright nebulae, double and triple stars, and even, at its far eastern end, galaxies. However, the most famous object in Vulpecula is the Dumbbell Nebula, M27, one of the largest and brightest of the planetary nebulae and visually impressive in any observing instrument, from 7x binoculars to 20″ telescopes.

65.2 Interesting Stars

Σ2445 Triple Star   **Spec. B3**
AB: m7.2, 8.9; Sep. 12.6″; P.A. 263° $19^h04.6^m$ +23° 20′
Finder Chart 65-3   ★★★★
4/6″Scopes–100x: Struve 2445 is an easily split triple, its two closest components appearing white and blue. It stands out well from the moderately rich Milky Way star field surrounding it. Almost a degree to its SE is the 10″ wide double Σ2457.

Vulpecula: Vul-PECK-you-la
Genitive: Vulpeculae, Vul-PECK-you-lee
Abbreviation: Vul
Culmination: 9 pm–Sept. 8, midnight–July 25
Area: 268 square degrees
Showpieces: M27 (NGC 6853)
Binocular Objects: Cr399, Stock 1, M27 (NGC 6853), NGC 6823, NGC 6830, NGC 6885, NGC 6940

Σ2455 Triple Star   **Spec. F0**
AB: m7.4, 8.5; Sep. 6.6″; P.A. 40° $19^h06.9^m$ +22° 10′
Finder Chart 65-3   ★★★★
4/6″Scopes–100x: Struve 2455 is an attractive pair of white and bluish stars. Struve 2457 is in the same low power field half a degree NNE.

Σ2457 Double Star   **Spec. F0**
AB: m7.5, 9.0; Sep. 10.3″; P.A. 201° $19^h07.1^m$ +22° 35′
Finder Chart 65-3   ★★★★
4/6″Scopes–100x: Struve 2457, located half a degree NNE of Struve 2455, consists of a pair of white and bluish stars.

Σ2540 Triple Star   **Spec. A3**
AB: m7.3, 8.8; Sep. 5.1″; P.A. 147° $19^h33.3^m$ +20° 25′
Finder Chart 65-3   ★★★★
4/6″Scopes–100x: Struve 2540 is a relatively tight double of unequally bright white and bluish stars. A 12.4 magnitude companion lies 147″ distant in position angle 221°.

Σ2653 Double Star   **Spec. A0**
m6.9, 9.7; Sep. 2.6″; P.A. 270° $20^h13.7^m$ +24° 14′
Finder Chart 65-4   ★★★★
4/6″Scopes–175x: Struve 2653 is a very close, un-

Vulpecula, the Little Fox

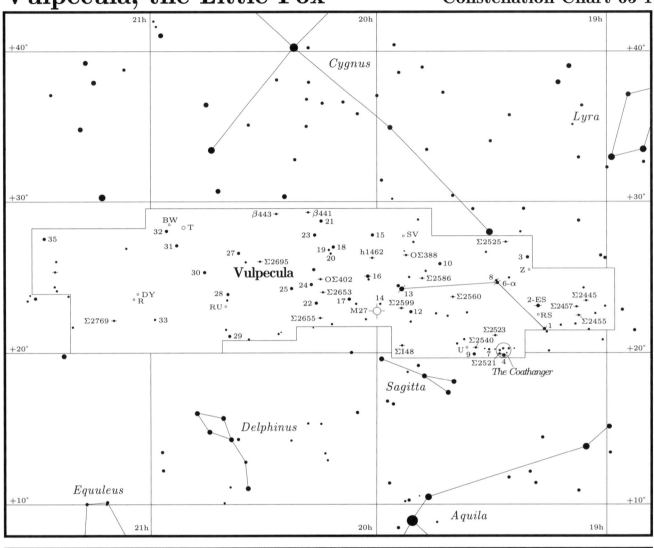

Chart Symbols

Constellation Chart   0   1   2   3   4   5   6

Stellar Magnitudes

Finder Charts   0/1   2   3   4   5   6   7   8   9

Master Finder Chart   0   1   2   3   4   5

→ Guide Star Pointer

•–•–• Double Stars

Finder Chart Scale

(One degree tick marks)

◉ ○ Variable Stars

○ Open Clusters

⊕ Globular Clusters

⬭ Galaxies

⌖ Planetary Nebulae

□ Small Bright Nebulae

⬭ Large Bright Nebulae

▨ Dark Nebulae

Table 65-1: Selected Variable Stars in Vulpecula

Name	HD No.	Type	Max.	Min.	Period (Days)	F*	Spec. Type	R.A. (2000) Dec.		Finder Chart No.	Notes
RS Vul	180939	EA	6.9	7.6	4.47	0.14	B5+A2	19^{h}17.7^m	+22° 26′	65-3	
Z Vul	181987	EA	7.38	9.20	2.45	0.18	B4+A2-3	21.7	+25 34	65-3	
U Vul	185059	Cδ	6.78	7.51	7.99	0.33	F8–G2	36.6	+20 20	65-3	
SV Vul	187921	Cδ	6.73	7.76	45.03	0.19	F7–K0	51.5	+27 28	65-3	
RU Vul	196792	M	8.1	12.2	156	0.47	M3	20^{h}38.9^m	+23 15	65-1	
T Vul	198726	Cδ	5.44	6.06	4.43	0.31	F5–G0	51.5	+28 15	65-5	
R Vul	200687	M	7.0	14.3	136	0.49	M3–M7	21^{h}04.4^m	+23 49	65-5	

F* = The fraction of period taken up by the star's rise from min. to max. brightness, or the period spent in eclipse.

Table 65-2: Selected Double Stars in Vulpecula

Name	ADS No.	Pair	M1	M2	Sep.′	P.A.°	Spec	R.A. (2000) Dec.	Finder Chart No.	Notes
Σ2445	12010	AB	7.2	8.9	12.6	263	B3	19h04.6m +23°20′	65-3	White and blue pair
	12010	AC		8.9	142.7	106				
Σ2455	12050	AB	7.4	8.5	6.6	40	F0	06.9 +22 10	65-3	White and bluish stars
	12050	AC		11.9	93.5	22				
Σ2457	12053		7.5	9.0	10.3	201	F0	07.1 +22 35	65-3	White and bluish
2–ES Vul	12287	AB	5.4	9.2	1.8	127	B0	17.7 +23 02	65-3	White and yellowish
	12237	AC		11.0	50.8	120				
4 Vul	12425	AB	5.2	9.9	18.9	100	K0	25.5 +19 48	65-3	In Cr399
	12425	AC		11.6	52.6	204				
Σ2521	12445	AB	5.9	10.7	26.7	35	K5	26.5 +19 53	65-3	In Cr399
	12445	AC		9.9	10.4	323				
	12445	AD		9.9	70.4	323				
Σ2525	12447		8.1	8.4	*2.1	291	F8	26.6 +27 19	65-3	
Σ2523	12451	AB	8.4	8.5	6.4	148	B8	26.9 +21 10	65-3	Equal white pair
6–α and 8 Vul	12594	AB	4.4	5.8	413.7	28	M K0	28.7 +24 40	65-3	
Σ2540	12594	AB	7.3	8.8	5.1	147	A3	33.3 +20 25	65-3	White and bluish
Σ2560	12778	AB	6.6	8.9	15.3	295	B3	40.7 +23 43	65-3	
Σ2586	12964	AB	7.5	10.4	3.7	227	B9	48.6 +24 58	65-3	White and bluish, C: bluish
OΣ388	13050	AB	8.2	8.2	3.9	139	A0	52.4 +25 52	65-3	Close white pair
	13050	ABxC		8.9	28.4	134				C: bluish
Σ148			7.2	7.5	42.2	147	A0 A0	53.4 +20 20	65-3	
13 Vul			4.6	7.8	0.8	243	A0	53.5 +24 05	65-4	
Σ2599	13076		8.2	9.9	3.9	51	B8	53.7 +23 00	65-4	
h1462			7.7	9.5	33.3	24	K2	20h00.1m +25 57	65-4	
16 Vul	13277		5.8	6.2	0.8	115	F0	02.2 +24 56	65-4	Close yellow suns
Σ2653	13543		6.9	9.7	2.6	270	A0	13.7 +24 14	65-4	Yellowish-white pair
Σ2655	13553	AB	7.9	7.9	6.2	3	A0	14.1 +22 13	65-4	All white triple
	13553	AC		9.6	60.0	154				
OΣ402	13566		8.0	11.5	15.4	35	B9	14.5 +24 51	65-4	
β441	13648		6.2	10.7	5.9	66	K0	17.5 +29 09	65-4	Orangish and blue
		AC		9.9	51.8	227				
β443	13807	AB	7.2	11.2	14.0	138	A5	24.1 +29 00	65-4	
	13807	AC		11.7	35.2	89				
Σ2695	13964		6.5	8.3	0.6	87	A2	32.0 +25 48	65-4	
Σ2769	14710		6.9	7.7	17.9	300	A0 A0	21h10.5m +22 27	65-5	

Footnotes: *= Year 2000, a = Near apogee, c = Closing, w = Widening. Finder Chart No: All stars listed in the tables are plotted in the large Constellation Chart, but when a star appears in a Finder Chart, this number is listed. Notes: When colors are subtle, the suffix *-ish* is used, e.g. *bluish*.

equally bright pair of yellowish-white stars that requires moderate power to separate.

β 441 Double Star   Spec. K0
m6.2, 10.7; Sep. 5.9″; P.A. 66°   **20h17.5m +29° 09′**
Finder Chart 65-4   ★★★★
4/6″ Scopes–100x: Burnham 441 is a color contrast double of golden yellow and blue stars.

65.3 Deep-Sky Objects

NGC 6793 H81[8] Open Cluster 15★ Tr Type III 2p
φ 6′, m –   **19h23.2m +22° 11′**
Finder Chart 65-3   ★★★
8/10″ Scopes–75x: NGC 6793, located in a rich star field east of an 8th magnitude star, is an inconspicuous cluster of four dozen 10th magnitude and fainter stars scattered over a 30′ area. A 1′ triangle of 10th and 11th magnitude stars stands out near the cluster's center, the star at the northern corner has an 11.5 magnitude companion 8″ away in position angle 45°. A small quadrilateral of faint stars lies 2′ SSW of this triangle.

Collinder 399 Open Cluster 40★ Tr Type III 3m
φ 60′, m3.6v, Br★ 5.19v   **19h25.4m +20° 11′**
Finder Chart 65-3, Figure 65-1   ★★★★
The Coathanger or Brocchi's Cluster

4/6″ Scopes–50x: Brocchi's Cluster is a large coarse cluster of three dozen stars spread over a degree of sky. It is well known as the "Coathanger," because of the conspicuous pattern formed by its ten brightest members, magnitude 5 to 7 stars: the "hanger" itself is a nearly straight 1.25° long E–W line of six stars, and the "hook" is a trapezoid south of the central two stars of the line. One of the bright stars has an orangish tint that contrasts nicely with the

Figure 65-1. *Collinder 399 is a large, coarse open cluster, its ten brightest stars forming the conspicuous low-power "Coathanger" asterism. Chris Schur made this eight minute exposure on Fuji 100 film with an 8″, f1.8 Schmidt camera.*

Figure 65-2. *NGC 6800 is a faint, loose, irregular open cluster in a rich Milky Way star field. Lee C. Coombs made this 10 minute exposure on 103a-O film with a 10″, f5 Newtonian reflector at prime focus.*

bluish tone of its companions. 4 Vulpeculae, the southernmost star in the hook, is an easy triple with magnitude 5.2, 9.9, and 11.6 components. To its NE in the hook is Σ 2521, a fine quadruple of magnitude 5.9, 10.7, and two 9.9 stars.

NGC 6800 H21⁸ Open Cluster 20★ Tr Type IV1p
ϕ 5′, m −, Br★ 10.0p $19^h27.2^m$ +25° 08′
Finder Chart 65-3, Figure 65-2   ★★★
8/10″ Scopes–100x: NGC 6800 is a faint cluster in a field of bright stars 35′ NW of the yellow magnitude 4.4 Alpha (α) = 6 Vulpeculae. It consists of two dozen

12th and 13th magnitude stars loosely scattered over a 17′ × 12′ E–W area. The stars in the central portion of the cluster fall around an irregular 10′ × 8′ N–S loop which is practically empty inside. Clumps of slightly fainter stars are on the NE and SE edges of the loop. A 6th magnitude star lies 23′ SW, and a 7th magnitude star is 18′ SE, of the cluster.

NGC 6802 H14⁶ Open Cluster 50★ Tr Type I1m
ϕ 3.2′, m8.8v, Br★ 12.93v $19^h30.6^m$ +20° 16′
Finder Chart 65-3, Figure 65-3   ★★★
8/10″ Scopes–100x: NGC 6802 lies at the east end of the "Coathanger" within a keystone of four 9th to 11th magnitude stars. The two stars at the northern corners of the keystone have widely separated companions. The cluster appears as a faint oval patch of haze in which seven stars are resolved.
16/18″ Scopes–150x: Larger instruments reveal forty 13th magnitude and fainter stars in a 5′ × 2.5′ N–S area. Two 12.5 magnitude stars stand out, one east of the cluster's center, the other on its NNE edge.

Stock 1 Open Cluster 40★ Tr Type III2m
ϕ 60′, m5.3:v, Br★ 7.0:v $19^h35.8^m$ +25° 13′
Finder Chart 65-3   ★★★
4/6″ Scopes–50x: Stock 1 is a huge cluster of forty 7th to 11th magnitude stars spanning a degree of sky. It is nice in binoculars but becomes less conspicuous with any magnification. The brighter stars lie along

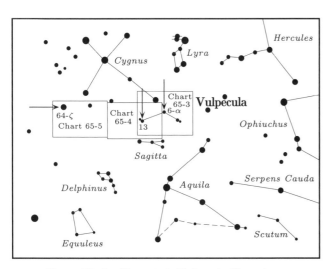

Master Finder Chart 65-2. Vulpecula Chart Areas
Guide stars indicated by arrows.

Figure 65-3. *NGC 6802 is a faint, but fairly rich open cluster lying at the east end of the "Coathanger." Image courtesy of Martin C. Germano.*

Figure 65-4. *NGC 6823 is a small cluster of faint stars immersed in the faint haze of emission nebulae NGC 6820. Image courtesy of Dean Salman.*

its south and SE edges. The cluster is split into two sections: the western section is larger and contains about thirty stars; and the eastern section has only ten stars, but includes the double Σ 2548, an attractive 9″ wide ESE–WNW pair of 9th and 10th magnitude stars.

NGC 6813 Emission Nebula
ϕ 3′, Photo Br 3-5, Color 3-4   **19^{h}40.4^m +27° 18′**
Finder Chart 65-3   ★★
12/14″ Scopes–125x: NGC 6813, centered 2.5′ SE of a
  9th magnitude star, is a faint 2′ diameter haze
  surrounding a pair of white and bluish 12th magnitude stars. Both UHC and O-III filters enhance
  the contrast between the nebula and its sky background.

NGC 6815 Open Cluster
[ϕ 20′]   **19^{h}40.9^m +26° 51′**
Finder Chart 65-3, Figure 65-13   ★★★
12/14″ Scopes–75x: NGC 6815, centered 10′ SE of a 7th
  magnitude star, is a large, inconspicuous cluster of
  forty 10th to 13th magnitude stars irregularly
  scattered over a 20′ area. The surrounding Milky
  Way star field contains four 7th and ten 8th
  magnitude stars within half a degree of the cluster
  to its north and NNE.

NGC 6820 Emission Nebula
ϕ 40′ × 30′, Photo Br 3-5, Color 3-4 19^{h}43.1^m +23° 17′

NGC 6823 H18^7 Open Cluster 30★ Tr Type I3mn
ϕ 12′, m7.1v, Br★ 8.81v   **19^{h}43.1^m +23° 18′**
Finder Chart 65-3, Figure 65-4   ★/★★★
12/14″ Scopes–125x: NGC 6823 is a rich cluster of
  three dozen faint stars irregularly concentrated in
  a 6′ area. The center contains a knot of six 9th and
  10th magnitude stars; but the other cluster members are mostly 13th magnitude and fainter, with
  only two 12th magnitude stars among them. The

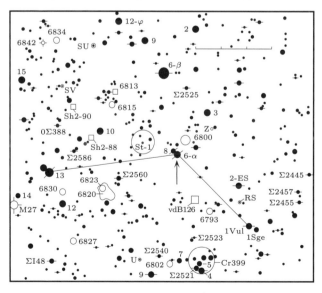

Finder Chart 65-3. 6–α Vul: 19^{h}28.7^m +24° 40′

Figure 65-5. *Emission nebula Sharpless 2-88 is a faint arc-shaped glow in a field of bright stars. Image courtesy of Dean Salman.*

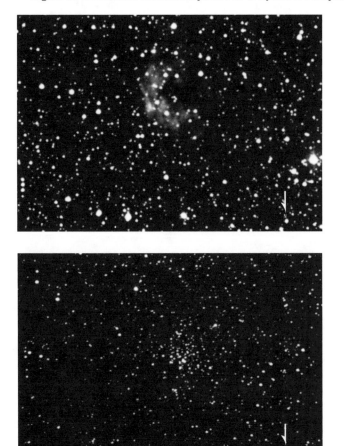

Figure 65-6. *(Above) NGC 6830 is an irregular open cluster of 30 faint stars. Image courtesy of Martin C. Germano.*

Figure 65-7. *(Left center) Sharpless 2-90 is a very faint crescent-shaped nebulosity. Martin C. Germano made this 80 minute exposure on hypered 2415 film with a 14.5″, f5 Newtonian.*

Figure 65-8. *(Bottom left) NGC 6834, with nearly twice as many members, appears much richer and more compressed than NGC 6830. Lee C. Coombs made this 10 minute exposure on 103a-0 film with a 10″, f5 Newtonian at prime focus.*

periphery of the cluster consists of star pairs and short star-rows interspersed with starless gaps. Many of the stars are tinted orange, blue, and yellow. The cluster is immersed in the faint haze of emission nebula NGC 6820, which requires an O-III or UHC filter. The most conspicuous nebulosity lies SW of the cluster center.

Sharpless 2-88 Emission Nebula
ϕ 18′ × 6′, Photo Br 3-5, Color 3-4 19^{h}46.0^m +25° 20′
Finder Charts 65-3, 65-4, Figure 65-5   ★★

12/14″ Scopes–75x: Sharpless 2-88, centered 35′ SW of magnitude 5.5 star 10 Vulpeculae, is a large, faint nebulosity which requires clear, dark skies and an O-III filter to be seen to best advantage. The nebula is a 15′ × 5′ NNE–SSW arc. Its eastern edge is rather clearly defined but its western side fades away gradually into the background Milky Way glow. The surrounding star field is rich with faint stars and well-populated with bright stars. A 6′ knot of bright stars is 8′ SE of the nebula's SE edge.

Sharpless 2-90 Emission Nebula
ϕ 8′ × 3′, Photo Br 2-5, Color 3-4   19^{h}49.3^m +26° 52′
Finder Chart 65-4, Figure 65-7   ★★

16/18″ Scopes–150x: Sharpless 2-90, located 15′ SSW of a 6th magnitude star, is a very faint crescent-shaped nebulosity concave to the east. Its faint haze can be seen without filters; indeed the nebula's glow has such a low contrast with its sky background that it disappears when a filter is added to the eyepiece. A curved E–W string of 11th and 12th magnitude stars, concave to the south, lies some distance NNW of the nebula, and a conspicuous knot of faint stars is 10′ to its NE.

NGC 6830 H9^7 Open Cluster 20★ Tr Type II2p
ϕ 12′, m7.9v, Br★ 9.88v   19^{h}51.0^m +23° 04′
Finder Chart 65-4, Figure 65-6   ★★★

8/10″ Scopes–100x: NGC 6830, located 26′ north of the magnitude 4.9 star 12 Vulpeculae, stands out fairly well as a rich patch of faint stars. Thirty 12th to 13th magnitude members are irregularly scattered over a 6′ area flanked by 9th magnitude stars 8′ WSW and 7′ east of the cluster.

16/18″ Scopes–150x: NGC 6830 has fifty 12th to 15th magnitude members fairly evenly distributed over a 6′ area. The cluster's 12th magnitude lucida is just east of its center. The majority of the group's brighter stars are spread to the lucida's north. A V-shaped asterism points north, and a 1′ wide trapezoid is on the east edge. A jagged chain of faint stars extends west and then curves north.

Figure 65-9. *Even in large telescopes planetary nebula NGC 6842 appears only as a faint, diffuse disk. Martin C. Germano made this 55 minute exposure on 2415 film with a 14.5″, f5 Newtonian reflector.*

Many of the cluster's stars are in wide pairs or small clumps. The cluster periphery is quite irregular because four extensions extend out into it from the cluster center.

NGC 6834 H16^8 Open Cluster 50★ Tr Type II2m
ϕ 5′, m7.8v, Br★ 9.65v   19^{h}52.2^m +29° 25′
Finder Chart 65-4, Figure 65-8   ★★★

8/10″ Scopes–100x: NGC 6834 is a faint but rich rectangular group of fifty 10th to 15th magnitude stars concentrated in a 7′ area. An 8th magnitude star near the southern edge of the cluster is at the center of an E–W row with five 10th magnitude stars. The cluster's densest part is just west of the 8th magnitude star. At 175x the profusion of faint

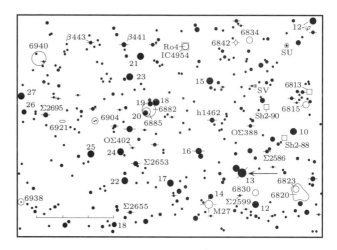

Finder Chart 65-4. 13 Vul: 19^{h}53.5^m +24° 05′

Figure 65-10. *Messier 27 (NGC 6853), the Dumbbell Nebula, has a magnificent hourglass-shaped disk that takes high magnification well. Nearly all powers give the 3-dimensional illusion that the planetary is suspended in front of the starry background. Image courtesy of Jim Burnell.*

outliers that can be seen spreading northward gives the cluster a somewhat triangular rather than a rectangular profile. On the group's northern edge is a small E–W oval star void.

NGC 6842 PK65+0.1 Planetary Nebula Type 3b
φ 50″, m13.1v, CS16.2v   19ʰ55.0ᵐ +29° 17′
Finder Chart 65-4, Figure 65-9   ★★
16/18″Scopes–200x: With an O-III filter NGC 6842 appears as a faint, diffuse 50″ diameter glow without a visible central star. The central area is slightly darker. A jagged NNW–SSE star chain runs past the east edge of the planetary.

NGC 6853 Messier 27 Planetary Nebula Type 3+2
φ 348″, m7.3v, CS13.8   19ʰ59.6ᵐ +22° 43′
Finder Chart 65-4, Figure 65-10   ★★★★★
Dumbbell Nebula
4/6″Scopes–100x: The Dumbbell Nebula, located 22′ south of the magnitude 5.7 star 14 Vulpeculae, is the finest planetary nebula in the sky, visible as a large, bright disk pinched in on its east and west sides. The brighter portions appear as wedges fanning to the north and south from the planetary's

center. A 9th magnitude star lies on the nebula's west edge.
8/10″Scopes–100x: Messier 27 is a magnificent object! The disk looks more like the core of a partially eaten apple than a dumbbell. The two bright triangular lobes that give rise to its name extend north and south to an overall length of 6′. The central star, just visible at the center of the pinch, is surrounded by a slightly darker area. Half a dozen stars are superimposed upon the nebula, the most conspicuous in the center of the northern lobe. The planetary's fainter outer glow, easily visible on good observing nights, fills in the pinched area and brings the nebula's full dimensions to 7′ × 6′ E–W.
16/18″Scopes–150x: Stunning! This hourglass-shaped object is by far the most impressive of all the planetary nebulae. At low and medium power a 3-dimensional illusion makes the disk appear to be suspended in front of the stars that are scattered around it. The brighter dumbbell portion is formed by two triangular lobes extending NNE–SSW, and is full of bright and dark patches, the two most conspicuous knots lying near the edges of the SSW lobe. The pinched area is embedded in a fainter, but quite conspicuous, outer halo that extends to 8′ × 6′

Figure 65-11. *IC 4954-55 is a very faint glow embedded in open cluster Roslund 4. Image courtesy of Martin C. Germano.*

Figure 65-12. *NGC 6882-85 is an irregular cluster centered NW of 20 Vulpeculae. Image courtesy of Lee C. Coombs.*

E–W. O-III and UHC filters add so much contrast to the object that the pinch nearly disappears. The nebula takes high power well, and on a good night you can magnify it to fill the entire field of view. 200x will reveal a dozen stars, in addition to the central star, superimposed upon the disk. These threshold stars are brightest without filters.

IC 4954-55   Reflection Nebula
ϕ –, Photo Br 2-5, Color 1-4 $20^h04.8^m$ +29° 15′

Roslund 4   Open Cluster 30★   Tr Type IV2pn
ϕ 5′, m10.0v, Br★ 11.58v $20^h04.9^m$ +29° 13′
Finder Chart 65-4, Figure 65-11   ★/★★★
12/14″ Scopes–100x: Without filters IC 4954-55 appears as a very faint, circular glow. Because it is a reflection nebula it does not respond as well to the O-III or the UHC filters as it does to the deep-sky filter, in which it appears as a fairly conspicuous 2′ diameter haze in the SW portion of Roslund 4, a small open cluster of three 10th and two dozen 11th to 13th magnitude stars in two loose, irregular NNW–SSE concentrations. A hint of additional nebulosity can be seen in the SSW portion of the cluster. 4′ NE of Roslund 4 is a conspicuous propeller-shaped asterism of four stars, three evenly-spaced 11th magnitude stars marking the propeller tips equidistant from a 12th magnitude star at the propeller hub.

NGC 6882   H22⁸   Open Cluster   Tr Type II2p
ϕ 18′, m8.1:v, Br★ 9.87v $20^h11.7^m$ +26° 33′

NGC 6885   H20⁸   Open Cluster 30★   Tr Type III2p
ϕ 7′, m5.7p, Br★ 6.0p $20^h12.0^m$ +26° 29′
Finder Chart 65-4, Figure 65-12   ★★★/★★
8/10″ Scopes–100x: NGC 6882 and NGC 6885 are not readily distinguishable as separate entities. NGC 6882 has some fifty 9th to 13th magnitude stars in an 18′ area. The distribution is highly irregular, but the majority of its members fall along a broad E–W stream across the northern portion of the cluster. The magnitude 5.9 star 20 Vulpeculae stands out near the group's SE edge. The brighter NGC 6882 stars are in its sparse southern section, where a starless gap separates two wide pairs of 9th magnitude stars, each of which forms a triangle with an 11th magnitude star. NGC 6885 is plotted as centered on 20 Vulpeculae, but no concentration of stars can be seen around 20 Vulpeculae in the eyepiece or on Martin C. Germano's photograph (Figure 65-12).

NGC 6904   Open Cluster [30★]
[ϕ 10′] $20^h21.8^m$ +25° 45′
Finder Chart 65-4, Figure 65-14   ★★★
12/14″ Scopes–125x: NGC 6904, although classified as "nonexistent" in the *RNGC*, is a conspicuous open cluster scattered around a 3′ wide ESE–WNW pair of 9th magnitude stars. These two stars are

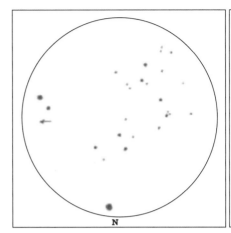

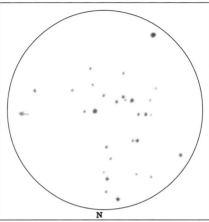

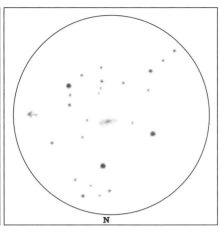

Figure 65-13. NGC 6815
12.5″, f5–75x, by G. R. Kepple

Figure 65-14. NGC 6904
12.5″, f5–150x, by G. R. Kepple

Figure 65-15. NGC 6921
18.5″, f5–300x, by Glen W. Sanner

part of the "bowl" in a dipper-shaped asterism, the "handle" of which extends northward. The area within the bowl is empty of stars, but a dozen cluster members are widely scattered to the bowl's south. The cluster contains some thirty stars in a 10′ × 6′ N–S area. Two of the stars are 9th magnitude, five 11th magnitude, and the rest fainter. A 10th magnitude field star is conspicuously isolated SSE of the dipper bowl.

Figure 65-16. *NGC 6940 is a beautiful cluster of 125 stars spanning half a degree. Image courtesy Martin C. Germano.*

NGC 6921 Galaxy Type SA(r)0/a:
φ 1.0′ × 0.2′, m13.4v, SB 11.5   20ʰ28.5ᵐ +25° 43′
Finder Chart 65-4, Figure 65-15   ★
16/18″ Scopes–150x: NGC 6921 is centered within a 6′ × 4′ SW-pointing isosceles triangle of three 11th magnitude stars. A string of 12.5 to 13th magnitude stars runs to the ESE from the triangle's SW vertex. The galaxy has a faint 1′ × 0.25′ NE–SW halo, within which averted vision reveals a very faint stellar nucleus. The surrounding star field, because it is on the fringes of the Milky Way, is well populated. 13th magnitude stars are beyond each of the halo's tips 2′ from the galaxy's center.

NGC 6940 H8⁷ Open Cluster 60★ Tr Type III2r
φ 31′, m6.3v, Br★ 9.31v   20ʰ34.6ᵐ +28° 18′
Finder Chart 65-4, Figure 65-16   ★★★
4/6″ Scopes–50x: NGC 6940 is a rich, uniformly concentrated cluster containing 75 stars in a 25′ area. An 8th magnitude and three 9.5 magnitude stars form a 9′ × 6′ trapezium on the southern edge, and a single 8th magnitude star marks the cluster's NE edge. The remaining stars are nearly all 11th to 12th magnitude objects, the richest concentration of which is centered 6′ north of the trapezium.
8/10″ Scopes–100x: This rich beautiful open cluster contains 125 stars in a 30′ area. The cluster is moderately compressed at its center, but the majority of its members are irregularly bunched into knots, pairs, short rows, and chains. Two of the longer star chains run E–W through the cluster's center, and a third is visible to their east. Several starless voids are scattered among the star chains and star knots. The reddish-orange variable FG

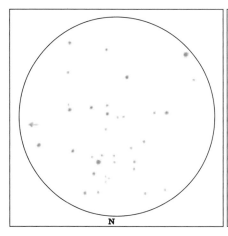

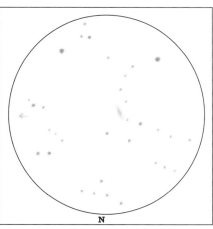

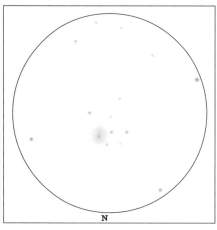

Figure 65-17. NGC 6938
12.5″, f5–300x, by G. R. Kepple

Figure 65-18. NGC 7052
17.5″, f4.5–300x, by G. R. Kepple

Figure 65-19. NGC 7080
18.5″, f5–300x, by Glen W. Sanner

Vulpeculae lies near the cluster center. The cluster lucida, located at the western corner of a trapezoid it forms with three more of the group's brighter stars near its SW edge, is the double Σ 2698, in which an 8th magnitude primary is paired with a 9th magnitude secondary in position angle 302°. The cluster has a fairly distinct periphery except to the north where its outermost stars blend into the surrounding Milky Way field.

NGC 6938 H17[8] Open Cluster [35★]
[ϕ 12′]   **20ʰ34.8ᵐ +22° 15′**
Finder Chart 65-4, Figure 65-17   ★★★
12/14″Scopes–125x: NGC 6938 is another of the open clusters which the *Revised NGC* mistakenly classified as "nonexistent." It is in fact a conspicuous scattering of three dozen magnitude 11 to 13 stars spread over a 12′ area. Eighteen of its members are concentrated around a 9th magnitude star in the northern part of the cluster, and nine form an E–W string to the south. A few field stars, probably not true cluster members, are sprinkled in the space between the E–W string and a 9th magnitude star 12′ to the SE.

PK72–17.1 Planetary Nebula Type 2
ϕ 831″, m>12.2p, CS17.1v   **21ʰ16.8ᵐ +24° 10′**
Finder Chart 65-5   ★★
12/14″Scopes–100x: This huge planetary nebula has a very faint, uniformly illuminated 13′ diameter disk. It may be glimpsed without filters, but a UHC or an O-III filter helps considerably. There is a vague impression that the center may be slightly darker.

NGC 7052 H145[3] Galaxy Type E
ϕ 2.5′×1.5′, m12.4v, SB13.7   **21ʰ18.6ᵐ +26° 27′**
Finder Chart 65-5, Figure 65-18   ★
16/18″Scopes–150x: NGC 7052 is centered 1.5′ west of an 11.5 magnitude star at the northern corner of a 6′×4′ right triangle of three magnitude 11.5 stars. A chain of 13th magnitude stars runs through the center of the triangle and to its east. The star at the NE corner of the triangle of magnitude 11.5 objects lies on the chain. The galaxy has a faint 1.5′×0.75′ ENE–WSW oval halo that contains a faint nonstellar nucleus. A 14th magnitude star touches the halo's edge 40″ east of the galaxy's center. Two wide star pairs are conspicuous 4′ west and 5′ WNW of the galaxy.

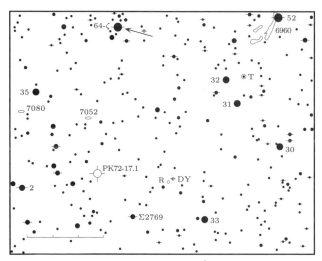

Finder Chart 65-5. 64–ζ Vul: 21ʰ12.9ᵐ +30° 14′

NGC 7080 Galaxy Type SB(r)b I-II
φ 1.6′ × 1.6′, m12.3v, SB 13.2   21^{h}30.0^m +26° 43′
Finder Chart 65-5, Figure 65-19   ★
16/18″ Scopes–150x: NGC 7080, located 7′ NW of a 9th
    magnitude star, is a faint amorphous glow nestled
    against the west side of a 1.5′ wide rhombus of 13th
and 14th magnitude stars. Another faint star lies
2′ SSW of the galaxy's center. At 300x NGC 7080
appears as a circular 1′ diameter halo surrounding
a very faint, nonstellar nucleus. Magnitude 10.5
stars are 4.5′ WNW and 5′ NNE of the galaxy.

Bibliography

Books

Cragin, M., Lucyk, J., Rappaport, B., *The Deep Sky Field Guide to The Uranometria 2000.0*, Willmann-Bell, Inc., 1993.

Eicher, D.J., *Deep-Sky Observing With Small Telescopes*, Enslow, 1989.

Eicher, D.J., *The Universe from Your Backyard*, Cambridge University Press, 1988.

Hirshfeld, A., Sinnott, R.W., *Sky Catalogue 2000.0 Vol. 1, Stars to Magnitude 8.0*, Sky Publishing Corp, 1982.

Hirshfeld, A., Sinnott, R.W., *Sky Catalogue 2000.0 Vol. 2, Double Stars, Variable Stars and Nonstellar Objects, Sky,* Publishing Corp, 1985.

Hynes, S.J., *Planetary Nebulae: A Practical Guide and Handbook for Amateur Astronomers*, Willmann-Bell, Inc., 1991.

Jones, K.G., *Messier's Nebulae and Star Clusters*, 2nd Edition, Published by Cambridge University Press, 1991.

Lovi, G., Tirion, W., *Men Monsters and the Modern Universe*, Willmann-Bell, Inc., 1989.

Luginbuhl and Skiff, *Observing Handbook and Catalog of Deep-Sky Objects,* Published by Cambridge University Press, 1990.

Sinnott, R.W. Ed., *NGC 2000.0: The Complete New General Catalog and Index Catalouges of Nebulae and Star Clusters by J.L.E. Dreyer,* Published by Sky Publishing Corp, 1988.

Staal, J.D.W., *The New Patterns in the Sky,* The McDonald and Woodward Publishing Co., 1988.

Tirion, W., *Bright Star Atlas 2000.0*, Published by Willmann-Bell, Inc., 2006.

Tirion, W., *Sky Atlas 2000.0,* Sky Publishing Corp, 1981.

Tirion, W., Rappaport, B., Lovi, G., *Uranometria 2000.0* Vol. 1, The Northern Sky to {6° Willmann-Bell, Inc., 1987.

Tirion, W., Rappaport, B., Lovi, G., *Uranometria 2000.0* Vol. 2, The Southern Sky to +6° Willmann-Bell, Inc., 1988.

Vickers, J.C., *Deep Space CCD Atlas: North,* Published by John C. Vickeres dba: Graphic Traffic Co., 1994.

Vickers, J.C., Wassilieff, A., *Deep Space CCD Atlas: South,* Published by John C. Vickers dba: Graphic Traffic Co., 1994.

Monographs

Webb Society Observing Section Reports, The Webb Society

Kepple, G.R., *Astro Cards*

Periodicals

Webb Society Quarterly Journal, The Webb Society

The Observer's Guide, Vol. 1 thru 32, by G.R. Kepple and G.W. Sanner

The Deep-Sky Observer, The Webb Society

Computer Databases and Software

Digitized Sky Survey, Space Telescope Science Institute

MegaStar, ELB Software, by Emil Bonanno

Voyager II, Carina Software

Sky Gallery with the Hubble Guide Star Catalog, Carina Software

Index

489

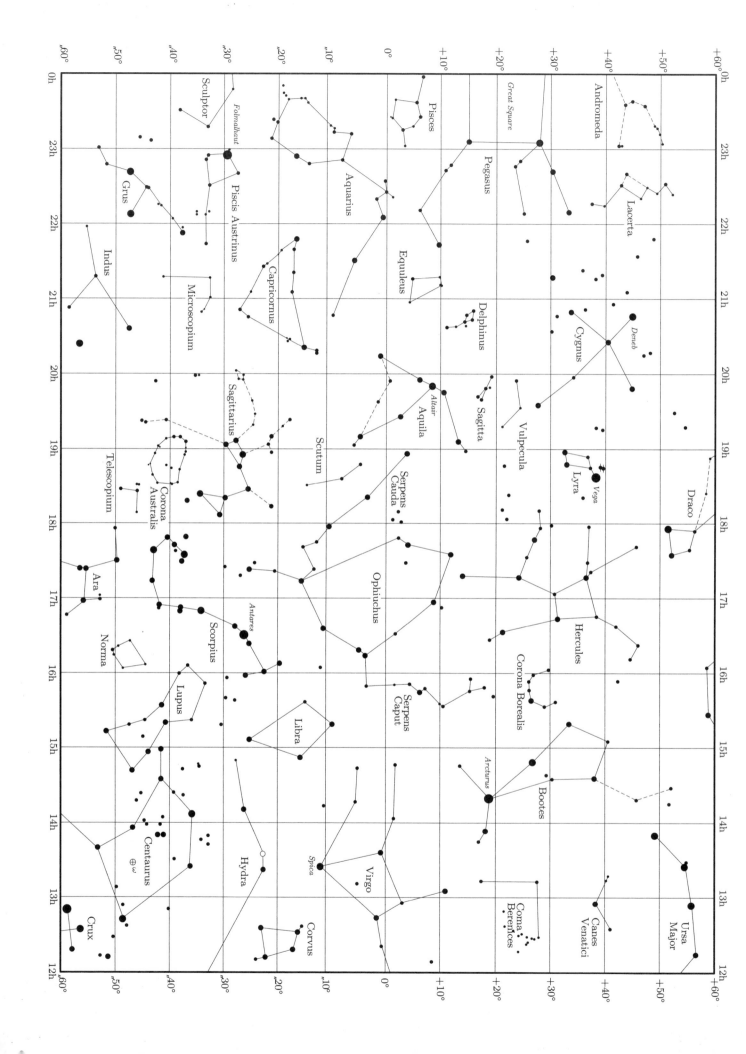